Psychology: The Science of Experience

with contributions by E. Scott Geller and Chris S. Dula
Ut Prosim

Fifth Custom Edition for Virginia Tech

Taken from:
Psychology: The Science of Behavior, Seventh Edition
by Neil R. Carlson, Harold Miller, C. Donald Heth,
John W. Donahoe, and G. Neil Martin

Psychology: Core Concepts, Seventh Edition
by Philip G. Zimbardo, Robert L. Johnson, and Vivian McCann

Psychological Science: Modeling Scientific Literacy
by Mark Krause and Daniel Corts

Cover Art: Courtesy of PhotoDisc/Getty Images and Joanne Dean Geller.

Taken from:

Psychology: The Science of Behavior, Seventh Edition
by Neil R. Carlson, Harold Miller, C. Donald Heth, John W. Donahoe, and G. Neil Martin
Copyright © 2010, 2007, 1997, 1993, 1990, 1987, 1984 by Pearson Education, Inc.
Published by Allyn & Bacon
Boston, Massachusetts 02116

Psychology: Core Concepts, Seventh Edition
by Philip G. Zimbardo, Robert L. Johnson, and Vivian McCann
Copyright © 2014, 2012, 2009 by Pearson Education, Inc.
New York, New York 10013

Psychological Science: Modeling Scientific Literacy
by Mark Krause and Daniel Corts
Copyright © 2012 by Pearson Education, Inc.

Pearson Learning Solutions, 330 Hudson Street, New York, New York 10013
A Pearson Education Company
www.pearsoned.com

Printed in the United States of America

1 2 3 4 5 6 7 8 9 10 V382 18 17 16 15

0002000010271971130

SL/KC

ISBN 10: 1-323-16943-1
ISBN 13: 978-1-323-16943-8

Detailed Contents

CHAPTER 10 MOTIVATION AND EMOTION 287

The Science of Psychology

Taken from *Psychology: The Science of Behavior*, Seventh Edition by Neil R. Carlson, Harold Miller, C. Donald Heth, John W. Donahoe, and G. Neil Martin.

Prologue

The Brain's Future

The moment she entered the classroom, I (Don Heth) knew Laura had something she wanted to say. She sat down, looked at me, and said: "This book is freaking us out!"

I had to stifle a smile. "Oh?" I said, with as much innocence as I could muster.

"It isn't so much the part in the book that talks about replacing some of our nervous system with electronics . . . we realize that might be possible. But this guy says that we'll soon be able to replace all of it. And get this: He talks about actually having sex with a computer! Is this guy for real?"

"Well, that's your job to decide," was my rather unhelpful response. You see, Laura and three of her classmates had been assigned to read a book by one of America's foremost authorities on technology, Raymond Kurzweil. He had entitled it *The Age of Spiritual Machines: When Computers Exceed Human Intelligence,* and in it he had engaged in some heady speculation about the future of technology. We're all familiar with devices that amplify our senses, such as hearing aids and night vision goggles. As computers get more sophisticated, Karzweil wrote, they will be capable of performing all the functions of our natural nervous system and humans will be able to "enhance" their brains with sophisticated implants. As our knowledge of the brain increases, we will, says Kurzweil in his most shocking prediction, be able to download our consciousness into a computer.

Laura's four years of studying psychology had given her a pretty good grounding in the biology of the brain. Now, she had to consider what it would mean to simulate this biology inside a computer program. She and her team had to review Kurzweil's book in a special way: As part of my class assignment, they were to work with our campus radio station and produce a thirty-minute radio documentary that would examine the plausibility of Kurzweil's predictions. And, it would be broadcasted.

In the weeks after our classroom exchange, I noticed that Laura's team was getting more and more involved in the project. I learned later that they had been spending long nights at each other's homes, working out a script and considering the interviews they had conducted with philosophers, psychologists, and computer scientists. One professor even complained to me that these students were spending too much time on *my* assignment and not enough on *hers.* Then, halfway through the term, the team asked me if they could produce a sixty-minute program.

"This assignment has forced us to think about the meaning of everything we've learned about psychology," they said. "We can do something really special if we have the additional time." Thinking I had created some kind of monster, I said yes.

On the day the assignment was due, I stopped by the station and picked up the CD with the team's program. The station manager had reviewed it and had written a note on the CD. "Yikes!" was all it said. ■

Here are two facts about the world you live in:

- There is a man whose otherwise normal life is disturbed at night, when he suddenly leaps from his bed and prowls around his bedroom growling like a lion, his fingers curled into claws. In the morning he remembers nothing of these episodes.

- When atoms are placed in a strong magnetic field, the axes around which their electrons spin become aligned with that magnetic field. If a radio pulse is directed at the atoms, they will wobble like spinning tops and then return to their alignment. It takes different amounts of time for atoms of different elements to realign.

When you started college, you undoubtedly expected to learn facts like these and to understand how they relate to other facts. As you'll soon learn, both of these facts are of interest to psychologists.

Or consider this: If you asked your fellow students the question "What does it mean to study psychology?" you likely would receive several different answers. In fact, if you asked this question of several psychologists, you would still receive more than one answer. Psychologists are probably the most diverse group of people in our society to share the same title. Psychologists engage in research, teaching, counseling, and psychotherapy; they advise industry and governmental agencies about personnel matters, the design of products, advertising and marketing, and legislation; they devise and administer tests of personality, achievement, and ability. Psychologists study a wide variety of phenomena, including physiological processes within the nervous system, genetics, environmental events, personality characteristics, mental abilities, and social interactions. And yet psychology is a new discipline; the first person who ever called himself a "psychologist" was still alive in 1920, and professors he trained lived into the 1960s and 1970s.

Psychology is exciting partly because it is so diverse and many areas are changing so rapidly. But these aspects of the field may sometimes be confusing to you, a student faced with understanding this large and complex discipline. So this first chapter will give you an overview of what it means to be a psychologist. The sections that follow will describe the nature of psychology, its goals, and its history.

The research interests of psychologists vary widely. One researcher might be interested in the origins of aggression; another might be interested in childhood memory. Psychologists seek answers to innumerable research questions through the study of behavior.

What Is Psychology?

In this book we will study the science of **psychology**—a science with a specific focus on behavior. The primary emphasis is on discovering and explaining the causes of behavior. Of course, the book will describe the applications of these discoveries to such subjects as the treatment of mental disorders and the improvement of society—but the focus will be on the way psychologists discover the facts that make these applications possible. This is an important guide to understanding psychology as a science. As you read this book, you should concentrate on how this process of discovery works.

To help you, we should make a key distinction. The word *psychology* comes from two Greek words, *psukhe,* meaning "breath" or "soul," and *logos,* meaning "word" or "reason." The modern meaning of *psycho-* is "mind" and the modern meaning of *-logy* is "science"; thus, the word *psychology* literally means "the science of the mind." But this is a little bit misleading. As the title of this book indicates, psychology is

psychology The scientific study of the causes of behavior; also, the application of the findings of psychological research to the solution of problems.

not the science of the mind, but the science of *behavior*. The distinction can be traced to the way psychologists have thought about the mind. Early in the development of psychology, people conceived of the mind as an independent, free-floating spirit. Later, they described it as a characteristic of a functioning brain whose ultimate role was to control behavior. Thus, the focus turned from the mind, which cannot be directly observed, to behavior, which can. And because the brain is the organ that controls behavior, psychology very soon incorporated the study of the brain. (It is this recognition, by the way, that relates the two facts cited at the start of this chapter. You will see how this is so in later chapters.)

Why Behavior Is Studied

The ultimate goal of research in psychology is to understand human behavior: to explain why people do what they do. But how do we, as psychologists, provide an "explanation" of behavior? First, we must describe it. We must become familiar with the things that people (or other animals) do. We must learn how to categorize and measure behavior so that we can be sure that other psychologists in different places are observing the same phenomena. Next, we must discover the causes of the behavior we observe—the events responsible for a behavior's occurrence. If we can discover the events that caused the behavior, we have "explained" it. Events that cause other events (including behavior) to occur are called **causal events.**

As you will see through this book, different kinds of psychologists are interested in different kinds of behavior and in different levels of explanation. For example, one psychologist might be interested in how vision is coordinated with movement; another might be interested in courtship. But even when they are interested in the same behavior, psychologists may study different categories of causal events— what has been referred to as different "levels of explanation." Some look inside the organism in a literal sense, seeking physiological causes such as the activity of nerve cells or the secretions of glands. Others look inside the organism in a metaphorical sense, explaining behavior in terms of hypothetical mental states such as anger, fear, curiosity, or love. Still others look only for events in the environment (including things that other people do) that cause behavior to occur. The word *levels* does not mean that one approach is superior or is more fundamental than another. Rather, a level of analysis refers to a common choice of causes to study and methods of research to use. The use of different levels of explanation is one reason why psychology is such a diverse discipline.

What is the purpose of this quest for explanations? Intellectual curiosity is one answer. An essential part of human nature seems to be a need to understand what makes things work—and what could be more interesting than trying to understand our fellow human beings? But psychological research is more than an idle endeavor of curious scientists; it holds the promise of showing us how to solve our most important and pressing problems.

One reason for studying behavior is that it is one of the roots of many of the world's problems: poverty, crime, overpopulation, drug addiction, bigotry, pollution, oppression, terrorism, and war. If global warming adversely affects our planet, or if forests and lakes die because of acid rain, it will be because of our behavior. Many health-related problems—such as cardiovascular disease, some forms of cancer, and a large number of stress-related illnesses—are caused (or at least aggravated) by individuals' behavior. For example, heavy smoking, obesity, lack of exercise, poor diet, unsanitary personal habits, and stressful lifestyles are responsible for illnesses found around the world. But there are more positive reasons for studying behavior, too. There are strong relationships between behavior and health, and knowing what these are can improve your well-being. Knowing how people remember, make decisions, and evaluate outcomes can help in your business and commerce dealings. Knowing that your personal relationships with friends, relatives, and partners depend on behaviors and the way you each perceive them can help you understand yourself and others better. Knowing how learning occurs can help you study for that big test. We hope that while reading this book and learning what psychologists have discovered about human behavior, you will think about the contribution psychology could make to you and your society.

Fields of Psychology

Psychologists sometimes identify themselves in terms of their activities. Some of us are scientists, trying to discover the causes of behavior. Some of us are practitioners of *applied psychology,* applying what our scientific colleagues have learned to the solution of problems in the world outside the laboratory. And, of course, some psychologists perform both roles. The Bureau of Labor Statistics estimated that psychologists held about 106,000 jobs in 2006, with about 30,000 more employed as professors at colleges and universities across the United States (Bureau of Labor Statistics, 2006).

Areas of Psychological Research Most research psychologists work in colleges or universities or are employed by private or governmental research laboratories. Research psychologists differ from one another in two principal ways: in the *types of behavior* they investigate and in the *causal events* they analyze. That is, they describe different types of behavior, and they explain them in terms of different types of causes. For example, two psychologists might both be interested in memory, but they might attempt to explain memory in terms of different causal events—one may focus on physiological events, whereas the other may focus on environmental events.

---

causal event   An event that causes another event to occur.

Physiological psychology examines the physiological basis of behavior. The organism's physiology, especially its nervous system, is considered to be the appropriate level of explanation. Physiological psychologists study almost all behavioral phenomena that can be observed in nonhuman animals, including learning, memory, sensory processes, emotional behavior, motivation, sexual behavior, and sleep. The phenomenon in nonhuman animals is considered a model that can help us understand the causal events in human behavior.

Comparative psychology is the study of the behavior of members of a variety of species in an attempt to explain behavior in terms of evolutionary adaptation to the environment. Comparative psychologists study behavioral phenomena similar to those studied by physiological psychologists. They are likely to study inherited behavioral patterns, such as courting and mating, predation and aggression, defensive behavior, and parental behavior.

Behavior genetics is the branch of psychology that studies the role of genetics in behavior. The genes we inherit from our parents include a blueprint for the construction of a human brain. Each blueprint is a little different, which means that no two brains are exactly alike. Therefore, no two people will act exactly alike, even in identical situations. Behavior geneticists study the role of genetics in behavior by examining similarities in physical and behavioral characteristics of blood relatives, whose genes are more similar than those of unrelated individuals. They also perform breeding experiments with laboratory animals to see what aspects of behavior can be transmitted to an animal's offspring. Using new techniques of molecular genetics, behavior geneticists can even alter parts of the gene during these experiments to determine how differences in the genetic code relate to behavioral differences among animals.

Cognitive psychology is the study of mental processes and complex behaviors such as perception, attention, learning and memory, verbal behavior, concept formation, and problem solving. To cognitive psychologists, the events that cause behavior consist of functions of the human brain that occur in response to environmental events. Cognitive researchers' explanations involve characteristics of inferred mental processes, such as imagery, attention, and mechanisms of language. Most cognitive psychologists do not study physiological mechanisms, but recently some have begun collaborating with neurologists and other professionals involved in brain scanning. The study of the biology of cognition has been greatly aided by the development of brain-scanning methods that permit us to measure the activity and structure of various parts of the human brain.

Cognitive neuroscience is closely allied with both cognitive psychology and physiological psychology. Researchers in this branch of psychology are generally interested in the same phenomena studied by cognitive psychologists, but they attempt to discover the particular brain mechanisms responsible for cognitive processes. One of the principal research techniques in cognitive neuroscience is to study the behavior

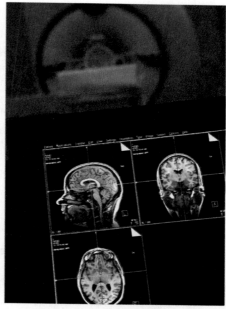

Methods that allow psychologists to scan the brain to show its structure and activity have greatly improved our understanding of the biology of cognition.

of people whose brains have been damaged by natural causes such as diseases, strokes, or tumors.

Developmental psychology is the study of the changes in behavioral, perceptual, cognitive, social, and emotional capacities of organisms as a function of age and experience. Some developmental psychologists study phenomena of adolescence or adulthood—in particular, the effects of aging. The causal events they study are as comprehensive as all of psychology: physiological processes, cognitive processes, and social influences.

Social psychology is the study of the effects people have on one another's behavior. Social psychologists explore phenomena such as perception (of oneself as well as of others); cause-and-effect relations in human interactions; attitudes

---

physiological psychology The branch of psychology that studies the physiological basis of behavior.

comparative psychology The branch of psychology that studies the behavior of members of a variety of species in an attempt to explain behavior in terms of evolutionary adaptation to the environment.

behavior genetics The branch of psychology that studies the role of genetics in behavior.

cognitive psychology The branch of psychology that studies mental processes and complex behaviors such as perception, attention, learning and memory, verbal behavior, concept formation, and problem solving.

cognitive neuroscience The branch of psychology that attempts to understand cognitive psychological functions by studying the brain mechanisms that are responsible for them.

developmental psychology The branch of psychology that studies the changes in behavioral, perceptual, cognitive, social, and emotional capacities of organisms as a function of age and experience.

social psychology The branch of psychology devoted to the study of the effects people have on one another's behavior.

[TABLE 1·1] Some Applied Areas of Psychology

Type of Psychologist	Area of Application	Typical Employment Setting
Clinical neuropsychologists	Identification and treatment of the behavioral consequences of nervous system disorders and injuries	Hospitals, in association with specialists who treat diseases of the nervous system
Clinical psychologists	Identification, assessment, and treatment of mental disorders	Private practice and hospitals
Community psychologists	Welfare of individuals in the social system, especially those who are disadvantaged	Community organizations
Consumer psychologists	Motivation, perception, learning, and purchasing behavior of individuals in the marketplace	Corporations and advertising agencies
Engineering psychologists and ergonomists	Perceptual and cognitive factors in the use of machinery	Corporations and engineering agencies
Forensic psychologists	Behavior as it relates to the legal and justice system	Private law firms and public agencies in the justice system
Health psychologists	Behavior that affects health and lifestyle	Hospitals, government agencies, and corporations
Organizational psychologists	Behavior in industrial work processes	Corporations and government agencies
School psychologists	Behavioral issues of students in the school setting	Educational agencies and institutions

and opinions; interpersonal relationships; group dynamics; and emotional behavior, including aggression and sexual behavior.

Personality psychology is the study of individual differences in temperament and patterns of behavior. Personality psychologists look for causal events in a person's history, both genetic and environmental. Some personality psychologists are closely allied with social psychologists; others work on problems related to adjustment to society and hence study problems of interest to applied psychologists.

Evolutionary psychology seeks to explain cognitive, social, and personality aspects of psychology by looking at their adaptive significance during the evolution of modern species. Clearly, the discoveries of comparative psychologists and behavioral geneticists are of interest to evolutionary psychologists. However, evolutionary psychologists use the theory of evolution by means of natural selection as a guiding principle. The task of the evolutionary psychologist is to trace the

development of such differences and to explore how their adaptive advantages might explain the behavior of modern humans.

Cross-cultural psychology is the study of the impact of culture on behavior. Because the ancestors of people of different racial and ethnic groups lived in different environments that presented different problems and opportunities, different cultures developed different strategies for adapting to their environments. Today, these strategies show themselves in laws, customs, myths, religious beliefs, and ethical principles. The importance of cross-cultural research and the interaction between biological and cultural factors on people's behavior are explored throughout this book.

Clinical psychology is the study and treatment of mental disorders and problems of adjustment. Most clinical psychologists are practitioners who try to help people solve their problems, whatever the causes. The rest are scientists who look for a wide variety of causal events, including genetic and physiological factors as well as environmental factors such as parental upbringing, interactions with siblings, and other social stimuli. They also do research to evaluate and improve methods of psychotherapy.

Although discovering the causes of behavior is important, not all psychologists are involved in research. In fact, most psychologists work outside the laboratory, applying the findings of research psychologists to problems related to people's behavior. Their fields of application are still closely related to the research specialties we've just described, but

personality psychology   The branch of psychology that attempts to categorize and understand the causes of individual differences in temperament and patterns of behavior.

evolutionary psychology   The branch of psychology that explains behavior in terms of adaptive advantages that specific behaviors provided during the evolution of a species. Evolutionary psychologists use natural selection as a guiding principle.

cross-cultural psychology   The branch of psychology that studies the impact of culture on behavior.

clinical psychology   The branch of psychology devoted to the investigation and treatment of abnormal behavior and mental disorders.

their employment situations may be quite different. TABLE 1•1 lists some of these applied areas.

How Is Psychology Used?
Sometimes applications of psychology arise because other disciplines require the special knowledge about behavior that psychologists may provide. Here are two recent examples: one in the field of law enforcement and the other in rehabilitative medicine.

Law Enforcement. If you're familiar with any of the currently popular television shows on criminal investigation agencies, you know that technology plays a large role in police detective work. Eyewitnesses who have seen a crime perpetrator can be very helpful if they can produce a useful description of the person. In the past, police officers relied on sketch artists to help an eyewitness develop a picture that could be circulated to the wider public. However, since artists vary in their skills, it is more common nowadays to use computerized systems that compose a face from a set of isolated features. An eyewitness is given a menu of different depictions of noses, eyebrows, hairlines, and so on, and from the examples selected, a composite face is constructed (see FIGURE 1•1).

Are these constructions accurate? Gary Wells and Lisa Hasel (2007) from Iowa State University argue that they are not. Although it is difficult to come up with any single estimate of accuracy, Wells and Hasel point to many cases both in the laboratory and in real life where composite drawings have led to mistaken identifications. Why would this be? It's not just a case of poor memory on the part of eyewitnesses, because the errors occur even when well-known faces are constructed. Wells and Hasel argue that it is a consequence of the way the brain perceives and remembers faces. A number of research studies show that we remember faces as complete units rather than as isolated features. The use of composite drawing technology, then, works against the way we naturally remember a face we've seen. Wells and Hasel suggest that identification technology might become more accurate by taking into account the psychology of facial memory.

Rehabilitative Medicine. Although modern medicine has increased the survival rate of soldiers wounded in battlefields like those of Iraq and Afghanistan, it is often at the cost of the amputation of an arm or a leg. Technology can produce natural-looking prostheses, but these artificial limbs are capable of, at best, only gross and hard-to-control movement. The main impediment is that modern prostheses do not provide the sensory feedback that comes with moving a natural arm or leg.

Prompted by concern for these returning amputees, the United States Department of Defense has initiated a large project that brings together specialists in engineering with scientists who understand how the brain controls movement (Krause, 2007). The goal is to produce an artificial arm with the full function of a natural one by the year 2009. Using the knowledge of physiological psychology concerning how sensory and motor nerves work, the researchers of this project have begun efforts to "rewire" nerves from other parts of the body (such as the chest) to feel the position of an artificial arm and to control it. If this project succeeds, the knowledge of physiological psychologists and neuroscientists will have

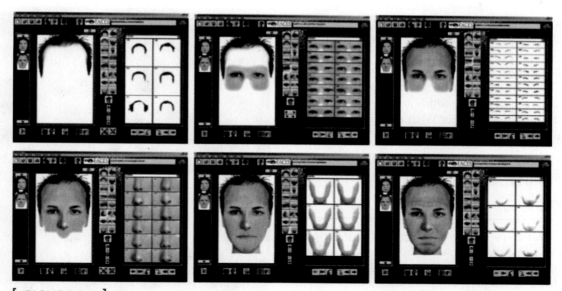

[**FIGURE 1•1**] An example of reconstructing the memory for a face using a computerized composite system (Faces 3.0 by IQBiometrics). In this case, the eyewitness chooses a hairline at the start and then fills in the rest of the face by choosing individual features.

(From Wells, G. L. & Hasel, L. E. [2007]. Facial composite production by eyewitnesses. *Current directions in psychological science, 16*, 6–10.)

A participant tests an artificial arm controlled by direct neural impulses.

been put to use to replace, through technology, a part of a person's nervous system. (It was, by the way, this possibility that was discussed in Ray Kurzweil's book that led to my student Laura's reaction. Perhaps his future scenario is a lot closer than we might think.)

QUESTIONS TO CONSIDER

1. Before you read this section, how would you have answered the questions "What is psychology?" and "What do psychologists do?" Would your answer be different now?
2. What problems would you like psychologists to work on?
3. If you were a psychologist, which field do you think you would be most interested in? What questions might you want to answer?

The Growth of Psychology as a Science

As mentioned earlier, psychology is a young science; it started in the late 1800s in Germany. However, humans have certainly been curious about psychological issues for much longer than that. To understand how psychology as a science came into being, we can trace its roots back through philosophy and the natural sciences, because these disciplines provided the methods

---

animism   The belief that all animals and all moving objects possess spirits controlling their movements and thoughts.

we now use to study human behavior; through the needs of society at the time, psychology became an independent science. These roots took many centuries to develop. Let's examine them and see how they set the stage in the late nineteenth century for the emergence of psychology as a science.

Philosophical Roots of Psychology

Perhaps the most notable part of our mental experience is that each of us is conscious of our own existence. Furthermore, we are aware of this consciousness and tend to relate it to our own behavior. That is, although we may sometimes find ourselves engaged in things we had not planned to do, we generally have the impression that our conscious mind controls our behavior. We consider alternatives, make plans, and then act. We get our bodies moving; we engage in behavior.

It is ironic that, although consciousness is a private experience, we give it such importance in our public lives. Even though we can experience only our own consciousness directly, we assume that our fellow human beings also are conscious; and, to at least some extent, we attribute consciousness to other animals as well. To the degree that our behavior is similar to that of others, we tend to assume that our mental states, too, resemble one another. Much earlier in the history of our species, it was common to attribute a life-giving *animus,* or spirit, to anything that seemed to move or grow independently. Because our ancestors believed that the movements of their own bodies were controlled by their minds or spirits, they inferred that the sun, moon, wind, and tides were similarly animated. This primitive philosophy is called **animism** (from the Latin *animare,* "to

Animism attempts to explain natural phenomena by supernatural means. This painting, from the tomb of Ramses VI, depicts the ancient Egyptian belief that the sun was a god, borne across the heavens on a special boat, to be swallowed each evening by Nut, the goddess of the sky.

René Descartes (1596–1650)

philosophy but also of a biological tradition that led to modern physiological psychology. He advocated a rationalistic approach—the sober, impersonal investigation of natural phenomena by means of sensory experience and human reasoning. He assumed that the world was a purely mechanical entity that, having once been set in motion by God, ran its course without divine interference. To understand the world, people had only to understand how it was constructed. This stance challenged the established authority of the Roman Catholic Church, which believed that the purpose of philosophy was to reconcile human experiences with the truth of God's revelations.

To Descartes, animals were creatures of the natural world only; accordingly, their behavior was controlled by natural causes and could be understood by the methods of science. His view of the human body was much the same: It was a machine affected by natural causes that produced natural effects. For example, the application of a hot object to a finger would cause an almost immediate withdrawal of the arm from the source of stimulation. Reactions like this did not require participation of the mind; they occurred automatically. Descartes called these actions **reflexes** (from the Latin *reflectere*, "to bend back upon itself"). Energy coming from the outside source would be reflected back through the nervous system to the muscles, which would contract (see **FIGURE 1•2**). The term *reflex* is still in use today, though of course we now explain the phenomenon differently.

quicken, enliven, endow with breath or soul"). Even gravity was explained in animistic terms: Rocks fell to the ground because the spirits within them wanted to be reunited with the earth.

Obviously, our interest in animism is historical. Scientific understanding of our natural world requires that we reject such notions as the idea that rocks fall because they "want to." Rather, we refer to the existence of natural forces inherent in physical matter, even if these forces are not completely understood.

Psychology as a science must be based on the assumption that behavior is strictly subject to physical laws, just like any other natural phenomenon. This assumption allows us to discover these laws objectively, using the scientific method. The rules of scientific research impose discipline on humans, whose natural inclinations might lead them to incorrect conclusions. It seemed natural for our ancestors to believe that rocks had spirits. In contrast, the idea that feelings, emotions, imagination, and other private experiences are the products of physical laws of nature did not come easily; it was developed by thinkers and scholars through many centuries.

The ancient Greeks were the first to develop rational speculation about nature and to systematize this speculation using laws of logic and mathematics. But although the history of Western philosophy properly begins with them, we will begin here with René Descartes (1596–1650), a seventeenth-century French philosopher and mathematician. Descartes has been called the father not only of modern

[**FIGURE 1•2**] Descartes's diagram of a withdrawal reflex. The energy from the fire would be transmitted physically to the brain, where it would release a type of fluid that would inflate the muscles and cause movement

(Stock Montage, Inc.)

---

reflex An automatic response to a stimulus, such as the blink reflex to the sudden unexpected approach of an object toward the eyes.

What set humans apart from the rest of the world, according to Descartes, was their possession of a mind. The mind was not part of the natural world, and therefore it obeyed different laws. Thus, Descartes was a proponent of **dualism,** the belief that all reality can be divided into two distinct entities: mind and matter. He distinguished between "extended things," or physical bodies, and "thinking things," or minds. Physical bodies, he believed, do not think; so minds could not be made of ordinary matter. Although Descartes was not the first to propose dualism, his thinking differed from that of his predecessors in one important way: He suggested that a causal link existed between the mind and its physical housing.

Although later philosophers pointed out that this theoretical link actually contradicted the belief in dualism, the proposal of causal interaction between mind and matter was absolutely vital to the development of a psychological science. Descartes reasoned that the mind controlled the movements of the body and that the body, through its sense organs, supplied the mind with information about what was happening in the environment. He hypothesized that this interaction between mind and body took place in the pineal body, a small organ situated on top of the brain stem, buried beneath the large cerebral hemispheres of the brain. When the mind decided to perform an action, it tilted the pineal body in a particular direction, causing fluid to flow from the brain into the proper set of nerves. This flow of fluid caused the appropriate muscles to inflate and move.

How did Descartes come up with this mechanical concept of the body's movements? Western Europe in the seventeenth century was the scene of great advances in the sciences. It was not just the practical application of science that impressed Europeans; it was the beauty, imagination, and fun of it as well. Craftsmen constructed many elaborate mechanical toys and devices during this period. The young René Descartes was greatly impressed by the moving statues in the French royal gardens at Saint-Germain-en-Laye (Jaynes, 1970). These devices served as models for Descartes as he theorized about how the body worked. He conceived of the muscles as balloons. They became inflated when a fluid passed through the nerves that connected them to the brain and spinal cord, just as water flowed through pipes to activate the statues. This inflation was the basis of the muscular contraction that causes us to move.

Descartes's explanation was one of the first to use a technological device as a model of the nervous system. In science, a **model** is a relatively simple system that works on known principles and is able to do at least some of the things that a more complex system can do. For example, after scientists discovered that elements of the nervous system communicate by means of electrical impulses, researchers developed models of the brain initially based on telephone switchboards and later on computers. Abstract models, which are completely mathematical in their properties, also have been developed.

It was an English philosopher, John Locke (1632–1704), who took Descartes's analysis one step farther. Locke did not exempt the mind from the laws of the material universe. In place of Descartes's **rationalism** (pursuit of truth through reason), Locke advocated **empiricism**—the pursuit of truth through observation and experience. Locke rejected the belief, prevalent in the seventeenth century, that ideas were innately present in an infant's mind. Instead, he proposed that all knowledge must come through experience; it is empirically derived. (In Greek, *empeiria* means "experience.") His model of the mind was the *tabula rasa* or "cleaned slate"—the ancient method of writing on waxed tablets that were scraped clean before use. Locke proposed that at birth infants' minds were empty and ready to accept the writings of experience.

Locke believed that knowledge developed through linkages of primary sensations: simple ideas combined to form complex ones. Amending this notion somewhat, the Irish bishop, philosopher, and mathematician George Berkeley (1685–1753) suggested that our knowledge of events in the world also required inferences based on the accumulation of past experiences. For example, our visual perception of depth involves several elementary sensations, such as observing the relative movements of objects as we move our heads and the convergence of our eyes (turning inward toward each other or away) as we focus on near or distant objects. Although our knowledge of visual depth seems to be immediate and direct, it is actually a secondary, complex response constructed from a number of simple elements. Our perceptions of the world can also involve integrating the activity of different sense organs, such as when we see, hear, feel, and smell the same object.

As philosophers, Locke and Berkeley were speculating on the origins of knowledge and dealing with the concept of learning. (In fact, modern psychologists are still concerned with the issues that Berkeley raised.) But although they rejected Descartes's version of the mind, they still were trying to fit a nonquantifiable variable—reason—into the equation.

With the work of the Scottish philosopher James Mill (1773–1836), speculation about the mind completed an intellectual swing from animism (physical matter animated by spirits) to *materialism*—mind composed entirely of matter. **Materialism** is the belief that reality can be known only through an understanding of the physical world, of which the mind is a part. Mill did not invent materialism, but he developed it into a complete system for looking at human nature. He worked on the assumption that humans were fundamentally the same as other animals. Like other species, humans were thoroughly physical in their makeup and were completely subject to the physical laws of the universe. Essentially, Mill agreed with Descartes's approach to understanding the human body, but rejected the concept of an immaterial mind. Mind, to Mill, was as passive as the body. It responded to the environment in precisely the same way. The mind, no less than the body, was a machine.

---

dualism The philosophical belief that reality consists of mind and matter.

model In science, a relatively simple system that works on known principles and is able to do at least some of the things that a more complex system can do.

rationalism The philosophical view that all knowledge is obtained through reason.

empiricism The philosophical view that all knowledge is obtained through observation and experience.

materialism A philosophical belief that reality can be known only through an understanding of the physical world, of which the mind is a part.

focus On

How Scientific Is Psychology, Really?

Researchers who study psychology have tried hard to earn and demonstrate its scientific reputation. There are no such problems with chemistry, physics, and biology: Their history is testament to their status as a science. A new study, however, suggests that psychology is gaining on its scientific elders.

Simonton (2004) compared the scientific status of psychology with that of physics, chemistry, sociology and biology. He identified a number of characteristics that typified a general science:

- the number of theories and laws mentioned in introductory textbooks (the higher the ratio of theory to law, the "softer"—i.e., less scientific—the discipline)

- publication rate (the more frequent, the more scientific the discipline)

- the appearance of graphs in journal papers (the "harder" the discipline, the greater the number of graphs)

- the impact made by young researchers (the more scientific the discipline, the greater the agreement that a researcher's contribution is significant)

- how peers evaluated 60 of their colleagues in their own disciplines, and how often single papers are cited (referred to in research papers).

Simonton also looked at secondary measures of scientific standing: "lecture disfluency" (the number of pause words such as "uh," "er" and "um": these are more common in less formal, structured, and factual disciplines); the extent to which references in journal articles were recent; age at receipt of the Nobel prize; and perceived difficulty of the discipline. Simonton combined these measures to provide a composite measure of scientific status.

Based on the first set of indicators, Simonton found that the natural sciences were judged to be more "scientific" than the social sciences. Psychology fell right on the mean—at the junction between natural and social sciences (see **FIGURE 1·3**). However, psychology's score was much closer to biology than to sociology—the biggest gap in scores was found between psychology and sociology, suggesting that the discipline is closer to its natural science cousins than its social science acquaintances. A gap also separated chemistry and biology, suggesting that the sciences might be grouped according to three clusters: the physical sciences (chemistry and physics), life sciences (biology and psychology) and social science (sociology).

Simonton concludes with an interesting observation. He argues that psychology's position in this hierarchy does not really reflect its scientific approach but its subject matter: Because the subject matter of psychology can be viewed as not directly controllable or manipulable, it can be perceived, despite its adoption of the scientific method, erroneously as neither scientific fish nor fowl.

[**FIGURE 1·3**]   According to Simonton's study, psychology's scientific status was more similar to that of biology than another discipline traditionally associated with it, such as sociology.

(From D. K. Simonton (2004). Psychology's status as a scientific discipline: Its empirical placement within an implicit hierarchy of the sciences. *Review of General Psychology, 8,* p. 65 [Fig. 2].)

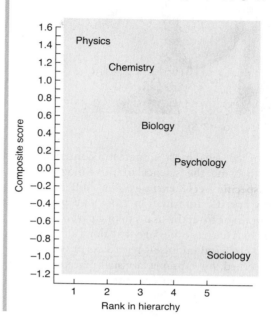

Biological Roots of Psychology

René Descartes and his model of muscular physiology were the beginning of the biological roots of psychology. Descartes's concept was based on an actual working model (the moving statue) whose movements seemed similar to those of human beings. However, Descartes relied on simple similarity as "proof" of his theory; he did not have the means to offer a scientific proof. But technological development soon made experimentation and manipulation possible in the biological realm as well. For example, Descartes's hydraulic model of muscular movement was shown to be incorrect by Luigi Galvani (1737–1798), an Italian physiologist who discovered that he could make muscles contract by applying an electrical current either directly to them or to the nerves attached to them. The muscles themselves contained the energy needed to contract; they did not have to be inflated by pressurized fluid. Indeed, an English physician, Francis Glisson (1597–1677), made the same assertion even more pointedly when he demonstrated, by having a man flex his arm in a barrel of water, that his muscles did not increase in volume as Descartes's theory would have predicted.

The work of the German physiologist Johannes Müller (1801–1858) clearly shows the way emerging biological knowledge shaped the evolution of psychology. Müller was a forceful advocate of applying experimental procedures to the study of physiology. He recommended that biologists should do more than observe and classify; they should remove or isolate animals' organs, test their responses to chemicals, and manipulate other conditions to see how the

Johannes Müller (1801–1858)

organism worked. His most important contribution to what would become the science of psychology was his **doctrine of specific nerve energies,** that different nerve fibers convey specific information from one part of the body to the brain or from the brain to one part of the body. Müller noted that the basic message sent along all nerves was the same—an electrical impulse—regardless of whether the message concerned, for example, a visual perception or an auditory sensation. What, then, accounts for the brain's ability to distinguish different kinds of sensory information? Why do we see what our eyes perceive, hear what our ears detect, and so on? After all, the optic nerves and the auditory nerves both send the same kind of message to the brain.

Müller's answer was that the messages are sent over different channels. Because the optic nerves are attached to the eyes, the brain interprets impulses received from these nerves as visual sensations. You have probably noticed that rubbing your eyes causes sensations of flashes of light. When you rub your eyes, the pressure against them stimulates visual receptors located inside them. As a result of this stimulation, messages are sent through the optic nerves to the brain. The brain interprets these messages as sensations of light.

Müller's doctrine had important implications. If the brain recognizes the nature of a particular sensory input by means of the particular nerve that brings the message, then perhaps the brain is similarly specialized, with different parts having different functions. In other words, if different nerves convey messages about different kinds of information, then those regions of the brain that receive these messages must have different functions.

Pierre Flourens (1774–1867), a French physiologist, provided experimental evidence for the implications of Müller's doctrine of specific nerve energies. Flourens operated on animals, removing various parts of the nervous system. He found

that the resulting effects depended on which parts were removed. He observed what the animal could no longer do and concluded that the missing capacity must have been the function of the part removed. For example, if an animal could not move its leg after part of its brain was removed, then that region must normally control leg movements. This method of removal of part of the brain, called **experimental ablation** (from the Latin *ablatus,* "carried away"), was soon adopted by neurologists, and it is still used by scientists on animals today. Through experimental ablation, Flourens claimed to have discovered the regions of the brain that control heart rate and breathing, purposeful movements, and visual and auditory reflexes.

Paul Broca (1824–1880) applied Müller's logic, although not his method, to humans. In 1861 Broca, a French surgeon, performed an autopsy on the brain of a man who had had a stroke several years previously. The stroke (damage to the brain caused in this case by a blood clot) had robbed the man of the ability to speak. Broca discovered that the stroke had damaged part of the cerebral cortex on the left side of the man's brain. He suggested that this region of the brain is a center for speech.

Although subsequent research has found that speech is not controlled by a single "center" in the brain, the area that Broca identified (now known as *Broca's area*) is indeed necessary for speech production. The comparison of postmortem anatomical findings with patients' behavioral and intellectual deficits has become an important means of studying the functions of the brain.

In 1870 the German physiologists Gustav Fritsch and Eduard Hitzig introduced the use of electrical stimulation as a tool for mapping the functions of the brain. The results of this method complemented those produced by the experimental destruction of nervous tissue and provided some answers that experimental ablation could not. For example, Fritsch and Hitzig discovered that applying a small electrical shock to different parts of the cerebral cortex caused movements of different parts of the body. In fact, the body appeared to be "mapped" on the surface of the brain (see FIGURE 1•4). Decades later, when

[FIGURE 1•4] Cortical motor map. Stimulation of various parts of the motor cortex causes contraction of muscles in various parts of the body.

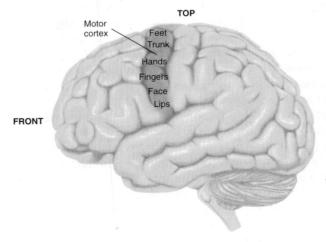

doctrine of specific nerve energies   Johannes Müller's observation that different nerve fibers convey specific information from one part of the body to the brain or from the brain to one part of the body.

experimental ablation   The removal or destruction of a portion of the brain of an experimental animal for the purpose of studying the functions of that region.

techniques of human brain surgery had advanced to the point where painless surgery could be performed on conscious patients, the Canadian neurosurgeon Wilder Penfield would be able to show that highly specific sensory experiences and even memories could be mapped in a similar way.

The work of the German physicist and physiologist Hermann von Helmholtz (1821–1894) did much to demonstrate that mental phenomena could be explained by physiological means. This extremely productive scientist made contributions to both physics and physiology. He actively disassociated himself from natural philosophy, from which many assumptions about the nature of the mind had been derived. Müller, under whom Helmholtz had conducted his first research, believed that human organs were endowed with a vital immaterial force that coordinated physiological behavior, a force that was not subject to experimental investigation. Helmholtz would allow no such assumptions about unproved (and unprovable) phenomena. He advocated a purely scientific approach that would base conclusions on objective investigation and precise measurement.

Before Helmholtz's work, the transmission of impulses through nerves was thought to be as fast as the speed of electricity in wires; under this assumption, transmission would be virtually instantaneous, considering the small distances that impulses have to travel within the human body. Helmholtz successfully measured the speed of the nerve impulse and found that it was only about 90 feet per second, which is considerably slower than the speed of electricity in wires. This finding suggested to later researchers that the nerve impulse is more complex than a simple electrical current passing through a wire, which is indeed true.

Helmholtz next sought to measure the speed of a person's reaction to a physical stimulus. Here, however, he encountered a difficulty that no amount of careful measurement could solve: He discovered that there was too much variability from person to person to formulate the kind of scientific laws that were common in physics. This variability interested scientists who followed him and who tried to explain individual differences in behavior. Because both the velocity of nerve impulses and individuals' reactions to stimuli could be measured, researchers theorized that mental events themselves could be the subject of scientific investigation. Perhaps, if the proper techniques could be developed, it would be possible to investigate what went on within the human brain. Thus, Helmholtz's research was very important in setting the stage for the science of psychology.

In Germany, a contemporary of Helmholtz's, Ernst Weber (1795–1878), began work that led to the development of a method for measuring the magnitude of human sensations. Weber, an anatomist and physiologist, found that people's ability to distinguish between two similar stimuli—such as the brightness of two lights, the heaviness of two objects, or the loudness of two tones—followed orderly laws. This regularity suggested to Weber and his followers that perceptual phenomena could be studied as scientifically as physics or biology. In Chapter 4 we will consider the study of the relation between the physical characteristics of a stimulus and the perceptions produced, a field called **psychophysics.**

Hermann von Helmholtz (1821–1894)

Applications in Education and Therapy

Descartes believed that the mind had *free will*—the ability to make decisions for which it was morally responsible. This viewpoint fit very well with Descartes's Catholic faith, which taught that the individual's soul had to choose between good and evil. But it stood in opposition to a very different, even older, conception—that individual decisions were determined by outside forces, such as the Greek concept of *fate,* the Buddhist concept of *karma,* and the human desires mentioned in the poetic musings of the Persian mathematician Omar Khayyám.

As scientific knowledge expanded, scientists studying the physical world became increasingly precise in predicting phenomena from their antecedent causes. Philosophers began to recognize that a commitment to empiricism and materialism might also imply a commitment to **determinism**—the doctrine that behavior is the result of prior events. Most psychologists assume some form of determinism, in part because of the philosophical and biological developments we've discussed. A third source of this assumption can be found in the political efforts that took place in the nineteenth century to reform society and improve individual well-being. These reformers believed that societal ills could be traced to root causes. They sought to strengthen the factors that caused beneficial effects and eliminate the ones that caused illnesses, ignorance, or unhappiness. This program makes sense only if such cause-and-effect relationships exist in human society.

Producing Change through Education. The period from Descartes's life to that of Helmholtz saw immense changes in Western politics and culture. The American and French revolutions (partly inspired by Locke's writings) ushered in a

---

psychophysics A branch of psychology that measures the quantitative relation between physical stimuli and perceptual experience.

determinism In psychology, the doctrine that behavior is the result of prior events.

new conception of government as an institution to improve the life of its citizens. Education was recognized as an important means of improvement, suggesting a role for the public in an area where such issues had previously been addressed by individuals, churches, or charities. At the same time, medical advances arising from the knowledge of biology promised cures for many diseases, including diseases of the mind.

The notion of change, of betterment, was to become an important topic of study in the 1800s. Educators and physicians began to consider the factors that cause change—whether it be in either a young pupil or a patient. Much of this speculation began with the following incident that, had it occurred in our own times, would have made the headlines of many a supermarket tabloid.

[**CASE STUDY**] In January of 1800, a boy about 12 years old was found living alone in the forests around Aveyron, France. Captured by the authorities, the boy seemed completely divorced from human contact and unable to speak or understand language. His description seemed to match reports from a neighboring district of a boy living alone in the fields; if so, he had been living without human support for two or three years, getting what food he could by raiding village vegetable patches. He was wearing a tattered shirt when found, but refused all attempts by the villagers to clothe him. He seemed mainly interested in food and a place to sleep. He seemed not to care about human company or any kind of social interaction. One of his caretakers showed him a mirror; the boy tried several times to reach through the mirror to grab the object he saw reflected there (Shattuck, 1980).

The village commissioner, who had been active in the French Revolution, must have found something unique about him, for he arranged to house the boy in an orphanage and recommended that the authorities in Paris be contacted. Eventually, the boy was brought to Paris, where he quickly became the object of observation and debate among French scholars. Some assumed that he had grown up in the wild and saw him as an untainted example of the natural state of humanity. Others claimed that he suffered from a mental disorder. When the argument died down, the poor boy was confined to a Parisian institute for the deaf. He was to live there, or in the company of one of its caretakers, until his death in 1828.

The "Wild Boy of Aveyron" is one of the most famous case studies in the history of psychology. Although it was clear that he was not deaf, the Parisian institute seemed to be the only place where he could be housed. There, his case was taken up by a young physician, Jean-Marc Gaspard Itard (1774–1838), who had just been hired by the institute a few months before. Itard worked with the boy (whom he named

"Victor") for about five years. Those who had studied Victor before merely observed his reactions and recorded his deficiencies of language and habits. Itard sought to discover what Victor could learn. He devised a number of procedures to teach the boy words and recorded his progress. His reports charted the successes and failures of different methods. Itard proceeded, in other words, on the assumption "that what the boy *was* hinged on what he could *become*" (Benzaquén, 2006, p. 167). His description was couched in terms of Victor's development in response to this intervention.

Unfortunately, Victor's deficits in language improved only slightly under Itard's teaching. But Itard's efforts had profound consequences beyond his single pupil. Itard had approached the problem of educating Victor much as a doctor would approach a patient: by identifying the problem and devising a procedure to cure it. Itard stressed the identification of factors that could bring about change and inspired a new approach in Europe in the education of individuals with cognitive disabilities. More broadly, educators began to discuss whether *all* children should be educated by methods suited to their individual needs.

Child education had become an important issue in the United States at about this time. Most states had adopted a system known as the "American Common School" by the late-1800s. Reformers centralized school administration, organized classes according to age, and sought the best curriculum for a given age. Educators, such as Booker T. Washington (1856–1915), and philosophers, such as John Dewey (1859–1952), advocated reforms based on the needs and faculties of children. Dewey, in particular, argued that education must match the way children's abilities developed. He argued that children learned activities that were organized around goals; instruction should match this natural way of learning. A staunch empiricist and a passionate defender of the American idea of democracy, Dewey felt that one aim of education should be to establish habits that integrate the child into the community. His views helped shape the movement in the United States known as Progressive Education.

The Law of Effect. It fell to one of Dewey's professional colleagues to suggest how such habits might be learned. Edward Thorndike (1874–1949) originally studied the behavior of animals, looking at responses that might indicate intelligence. Thorndike noticed that some events, usually those that one would expect to be pleasant, seemed to "stamp in" a response that had just occurred, thereby making it more likely to occur again. Noxious events seemed to "stamp out" the response, or make it less likely to occur. (Nowadays, we call these processes *reinforcement* and *punishment*.) Thorndike defined the **law of effect** as follows:

> Any act which in a given situation produces satisfaction becomes associated with that situation, so that when the situation recurs the act is more likely than before to recur also. Conversely, any act which in a given situation produces discomfort becomes disassociated from that situation, so that when the situation recurs the act is less likely than before to recur. (Thorndike, 1905, p. 203)

---

law of effect   Edward Thorndike's statement that stimuli that occur as a consequence of a response can increase or decrease the likelihood of an organism's making that response again.

The law of effect seemed to provide a universal principle by which habits might be learned: Goals produced satisfaction and caused the action to recur more frequently. Larger activities could be built up from these activities; therefore, an ideal curriculum would be based on identifying the discrete units that make up the task to be learned. Extensive tests—some of which Thorndike himself developed and sold to school boards across the nation—would measure how well these units had been acquired (Kremer, 1976).

If this sounds to you like a step backward from Itard's progressive ideas of individual diagnosis and treatment, you're probably correct. Thorndike's emphasis on "stamping in" responses implied that learning was automatic and inevitable. To be sure, Thorndike did acknowledge the role of instinct and individual differences in behavior. But, he was so fond of his Law of Effect that he had the words *stimulus* and *response* carved above the door of his laboratory, so that students would be reminded of how he connected them.

An alternative view of children's learning was, meanwhile, being developed in Italy by Maria Montessori (1870–1952). At a time when teaching was virtually the only profession open to women, Montessori decided to enter medical school and become a doctor, an accomplishment that must have taken extraordinary perseverance. For example, it was considered improper for a woman student to see a naked body in the presence of males, so Montessori was banished from the classroom during dissections; she had to do them herself, alone, at night, surrounded by cadavers. Despite such hardships and harassments, Montessori became the first woman in Italy to earn a medical degree (Kremer, 1976).

Ironically, it is as a teacher that she is best known today. Appointed to administer an institution for children with de-velopmental disabilities, Montessori discovered Itard's work with Victor. She applied Itard's approach to individualized instruction with considerable success. Reflecting on these results, Montessori wondered whether children without such disabilities would also benefit from this approach. She received a chance to test these theories when she was asked to organize a school for poor preschool children near Rome. Montessori added some innovations of her own and developed a system now known as the *Montessori Method*. This method was based on her belief that children matured through stages: They were sensitive to different kinds of instruction at specific age ranges. Education was best when it provided exercises that matched the competency of the child at that stage. And, in contrast to Thorndike's emphasis on rewards as the basis for learning, Montessori felt that extrinsic rewards actually interfered with a child's natural incentive to learn. Montessori also believed that movement was closely related to thought, and encouraged her pupils to move around in the classroom.

Montessori attracted considerable attention in Europe, but her work had little effect on American educational practices. Montessori herself may have been part of the problem: She was a bit of an autocrat and insisted that only she could train teachers in her methods. But it's also the case that Thorndike's philosophy of learning fit better with developing trends in psychology. We'll examine these in the next section. As a consequence, it's likely that the school system you experienced from elementary grade to high school was shaped more by Thorndike than by Montessori (Lillard, 2005).

Regardless of her lack of success in North America, Montessori may have had an influence on a very important figure in psychology, Jean Piaget (1896–1980). Piaget was born in the French-speaking region of Switzerland and studied biology as a young man. In the early years of his life in Switzerland, he taught children at a school that used a modified Montessori approach. Like Montessori, he was struck by the way a child's competency to understand depended on his or her age. It wasn't just that a younger child made errors that an older child would not; what impressed Piaget was that younger children made the same *kinds* of errors. Piaget's immense influence on developmental psychology resulted from his ability to explain these systematic errors by a theory of cognitive development. Piaget's work will be described in Chapter 6.

Producing Change through Psychotherapy Before Itard took responsibility for the care of Victor, the boy had been examined by Phillippe Pinel (1745–1826). Also a physician, Pinel influenced how psychology thought about change, but in a different direction: He is now widely regarded as the father of psychiatry, the medical specialty that treats mental disorders.

Prior to Pinel's time, the care of people with mental illness was largely considered a responsibility of their family. Their treatment, typically by family members who feared or loathed their illness, could be abominable. Visitors to such households often told of how relatives would lock "the insane" in filthy cages, or chain them in pigsties. These reports eventually prompted activist governments to look for solutions,

Maria Montessori (1870–1952)

and to build asylums where persons with mental illness could be centrally cared for. Pinel was hired by the Revolutionary government of France to administer one such facility, the Salpêtrière hospital in Paris.

Pinel introduced some limited humanitarian reforms to the Salpêtrière, but his main influence was to propose that an asylum could, with proper practices, become a therapeutic institution. He and his followers tried new approaches to restore the cognitive abilities of an inmate. Mostly, these approaches were social interventions, such as long conversations with a therapist or poetry readings. They were based on the belief that mental illness had a social cause and could be cured by similar factors.

For a number of reasons, the number of asylums grew rapidly during the 1800s, along with the number of people committed to them (Shorter, 1997). It could be argued that many of these people did not truly have a mental illness, but were placed there for other reasons. Among this suspect category were the women of one ward of the Salpêtrière who were admitted with a collection of symptoms such as memory loss, intermittent paralysis, and insensitivity to painful stimuli. These women were considered to be suffering from a nervous disorder which had been given the label *hysteria*. Beginning in 1862, a neurologist by the name of Jean-Martin Charcot (1825–1893) developed a clinical practice based on observations from the ward. Neurology as a medical specialty deals with the treatment of diseases of the nervous system and is closely allied with psychiatry. Charcot proposed that hysteria was closely related to the condition produced by hypnosis and treated his patients by hypnotizing them. Although "hysteria" is no longer recognized as a disorder (its symptoms are now ascribed to other mental illnesses), Charcot's linking of hypnosis to the treatment of a mental illness was to have important consequences. We'll explore hypnosis in Chapter 8.

QUESTIONS TO CONSIDER

1. Explaining things, whether scientifically or through myths and legends, seems to be a human need. Can you think of an occasion in your recent experience where either you or someone talking to you used an animistic explanation? Do you think these are more common in everyday speech than the scientific explanations we have discussed?

2. Which of the philosophers, scientists, educators, or therapists described in this section appeal to you the most? Would you like to know more about any of them and their times? What questions would you like to ask these people if it were possible to meet them?

3. Thorndike exerted immense influence on the development of schools in America during the early 1900s. Do you see any vestiges of his beliefs about habits and the law of effect in your own schooling experience?

focus On

What Are the Roots of Psychology Within Chinese Culture?

Even though much of psychology's historical milestones took place in the western hemisphere, scholars of the eastern hemisphere have also reflected on human behavior, its causes, and its normal development.

China possesses one of the oldest civilizations on earth, so it is not surprising that there is much speculation on psychological matters in its history. Like Western psychology, many aspects of Chinese understanding of human nature derived from philosophical systems; however, in the case of China, these were primarily concerned with moral philosophy rather than the philosophy of knowledge.

One of the earliest classical texts in Chinese philosophy, the *I Ching*, is traditionally ascribed to teachings and practices from about 2800 BCE. Although it is usually regarded by Westerners as a system for telling the future, the Swiss psychologist Carl Jung (1875–1961) argued that it reflects a profoundly different world view than that of Western science. In contrast to the Western preoccupation with causal factors, the *I Ching* seeks to link the individual to the random, chance factors present at the time the prediction was made (Jung, 1967). If so, then much of Chinese philosophical speculation on human nature can be seen as a way of reconciling humans to the potential conflict and chaos around them. There have been three distinct systems that have influenced Chinese intellectual development, each associated with an Asian philosophy: Confucianism, Taoism, and Buddhism.

Confucius (551–479 BCE) developed guidelines for human relationships according to a hierarchical social structure: the authoritarian patriarchal family. The key to order and harmony in the midst of conflict and change, said Confucius, was in learning, throughout a lifetime, the habits by which one adapted oneself to the family. He believed that all people were born naturally identical, but that, through education, they reached their proper station in life. The habits they learned adjusted both individuals and societies to a utopian ideal. Confucius's psychology, therefore, identified certain traits as characteristics of the fully developed human being: "As a philosophy of life, we have generally associated with Confucianism the quiet virtues of patience, pacifism, compromise, the golden mean, reverence for ancestors, the aged, and the learned" (Jing & Fu, 2001, p. 408).

Taoism can be traced to the writings of two philosophers, Lao Tzu (298–212 BCE) and Chuang Tzu (369–286 BCE). Similar to the way many Greek philosophers described the world, Taoism taught that underneath the natural world of chaos there was a unifying principle of reconciliation: the *Tao*. Through the practice of meditation and suppression of violent emotions one could order one's life according to the Tao.

The third system originated with the Nepali teacher Siddhartha Gautama (ca. 566–486 BCE). As his followers believe, while meditating on the nature of suffering,

The Buddha's teaching emphasized proper living and respect for sentient beings as the desired conduct of human behavior.

Gautama achieved enlightenment, becoming a being known as the Buddha. The Buddha described his achievement as a recognition of four "noble truths": (1) that suffering is universal; (2) that it arises from desire; (3) that eliminating desire can eliminate suffering; and (4) that meditation and wisdom can eliminate desire. The Buddha's teachings reached China in several distinctive forms (e.g., Tibetan Buddhism can be markedly different from Zen Buddhism), but like Confucianism and Taoism, it stressed a particular mode of conduct, called the Eightfold Path: right understanding, thought, speech, action, livelihood, effort, mindfulness, and concentration (Lawson, Graham, & Baker, 2007). The Buddha taught that proper living and the respect for all sentient beings would achieve a permanent state of emptiness and a release from the cycle of suffering present in the world.

These three systems were moral philosophies. Unlike most Western philosophies that influenced psychology, Confucianism, Taoism, and Buddhism were based on an ideal goal to be achieved: For Confucianism, it was a harmonious society; for Taoism, reconciliation of contradiction; and for Buddhism, emptiness. Conduct, whether it was in action or in thought, was considered in terms of its purpose—to achieve those goals. Western psychology, by and large, considered questions of morality to be secondary to questions of origin and causation. Purpose was a result of other factors, such as the Law of Effect. Nevertheless, it is interesting to note that, by the late 1800s and early 1900s, Western psychology, through the work of Montessori and Thorndike, had begun to recognize the significance of education and habit formation in the development of the individual. When it became known in China, John Dewey's work was quite popular. Higgins and Zheng (2002) have also suggested that the Confucian system of examinations to determine one's place in the Chinese civil service sector may have been the origin of the mass testing movement in the United States.

Major Trends in the Development of Psychology

Psychology as a science, as distinct from philosophy and biology, began in Germany in the late nineteenth century with Wilhelm Wundt (1832–1920). Wundt was the first person to call himself a psychologist. He shared the conviction of other German scientists that all aspects of nature, including the human mind, could be studied scientifically. His book *Principles of Physiological Psychology* was the first textbook of psychology; and Wundt is generally considered to have started, in 1879, the first laboratory devoted to the study of psychological phenomena.

You may have already noted the high preponderance of German scholars in our survey of early influences on psychology. The fact that Germany was the birthplace of psychology had as much to do with social, political, and economic influences as with the abilities of the nation's scientists and scholars. The German university system was well established, and professors were highly respected members of society. The academic tradition in Germany emphasized a scientific approach to a large number of subject areas, such as history, phonetics, archaeology, aesthetics, and literature. Thus, in contrast to French and British scholars, who adopted the more traditional, philosophical approach to the study of the human mind, German scholars were open to the possibility that the human mind could be studied scientifically. German science also emphasized the importance of classification. We will see the significance of this to psychology shortly. Experimental physiology, one of the most important roots of experimental psychology, was well established in Germany. It was in this climate that Müller, Helmholtz, and Wundt conducted their research.

Wilhelm Wundt (1832–1920)

Structuralism

Wundt defined psychology as the "science of immediate experience." This approach was labeled **structuralism** by one of his students. Its subject matter was the *structure* of the mind, a structure built from the elements of consciousness, such as ideas and sensations. The raw material of structuralism was supplied by trained observers who described their own experiences. The observers were taught to engage in **introspection** (literally, "looking within"); they observed stimuli and described their experiences. Wundt and his associates made inferences about the nature of mental processes by seeing how changes in the stimuli caused changes in trained observers' verbal reports.

Like George Berkeley, Wundt was particularly interested in the way basic sensory information gave rise to complex perceptions. His trained observers attempted to ignore complex perceptions and to report only the elementary data. For example, the sensation of seeing a patch of red is immediate and elementary, whereas the perception of an apple is complex.

Wundt was an ambitious and prolific scientist who wrote many books and trained many other scientists in his laboratory. Many of these brought the new conception of psychology to North America, where it created quite a sensation. For example, in 1889, one of Wundt's protégés, James Mark Baldwin (1861–1934), was appointed professor of psychology at the University of Toronto. His employment was quite controversial: Students and prominent faculty members petitioned against his appointment, a newspaper denounced his psychological training in an editorial, and the matter almost caused a political scandal (Hoff, 1992). Baldwin survived this controversy, however, and later joined the faculty of Princeton University. There he helped start a journal, *Psychological Review,* that today is one of the premier journals in psychology. Other psychologists trained by Wundt, such as Edward Bradford Titchener, also became leaders of American psychology. However, Wundt's method did not survive the test of time; structuralism died out in the early twentieth century. The major problem with his approach was the difficulty of reporting the raw data of sensation, unmodified by experience. Also, the emphasis of psychological investigation shifted from the study of the mind to the study of behavior. More recently, psychologists have resumed the study of the human mind, but better methods are now available for

studying it. Although structuralism has been supplanted, Wundt's contribution must be acknowledged. He established psychology as an experimental science, independent of philosophy. He trained many psychologists, a number of whom established their own laboratories and continued to advance the new discipline.

Functionalism

The next major trend in psychology was known as **functionalism.** This approach was in large part a reaction against the structuralism of Wundt. Structuralists were interested in what they called the *components* of consciousness (ideas and sensations); functionalists focused on the *processes* of conscious activity (perceiving and learning). Functionalism grew from the new perspective on nature supplied by Charles Darwin (1809–1882) and his followers. Proponents stressed the biological significance (the purpose, or *function*) of natural processes, including behavior. The emphasis was on overt, observable behavior, not on private mental events.

Darwin's theory, which said that evolution occurred in response to the natural selection of inheritable traits, was important to psychology because it suggested that scientists could best explain behavior, like other biological characteristics, by understanding its role in the adaptation of an organism to its environment. Thus, behavior has a biological context. Darwin assembled evidence that behavior could be inherited. In *The Expression of the Emotions in Man and Animals,* published in 1872, he proposed that the facial gestures animals make in expressing emotions were descended from movements that previously had other functions. New areas of exploration were opened for psychologists by the ideas that an evolutionary continuity existed among various animal species and that behaviors, like parts of the body, had evolutionary histories. Darwin's cousin, Francis Galton, was one of these pioneers. He was one of the first to measure human traits objectively. The public's interest in measuring human abilities was so strong that Galton was able to set up a booth at an international exhibition in the 1880s and charge people for the privilege of being tested. (See FIGURE 1•5.)

The most important psychologist to embrace functionalism was the American scholar William James (1842–1910). As James said, "My thinking is first, last, and always for the sake of my doing." That is, thinking was not an end in itself; its function was to produce useful behavior. Although James did not produce any important experimental research during his tenure as professor of philosophy (later, professor of psychology) at Harvard University, his teaching and writing influenced those who followed him. His theory of emotion is one of the most famous and durable psychological theories. It is still quoted in modern textbooks. Psychologists still find it worthwhile to read James's writings; he supplied ideas for experiments that continue to sound fresh and new today.

---

structuralism   The system of experimental psychology that began with Wilhelm Wundt; it emphasized introspective analysis of sensation and perception.

introspection   Literally, "looking within" in an attempt to describe memories, perceptions, cognitive processes, or motivations.

functionalism   An approach to understanding species' behaviors and other processes in terms of their biological significance; this approach stresses the usefulness of such processes with respect to survival and reproductive success.

[**FIGURE 1·5**] Galton advertised his project to collect data on human abilities. Interest was so keen that he even charged people for their participation.

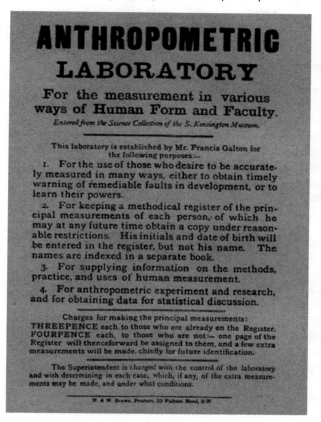

ANTHROPOMETRIC LABORATORY

For the measurement in various ways of Human Form and Faculty.

Entered from the Science Collection of the S. Kensington Museum.

This laboratory is established by Mr. Francis Galton for the following purposes:—

1. For the use of those who desire to be accurately measured in many ways, either to obtain timely warning of remediable faults in development, or to learn their powers.

2. For keeping a methodical register of the principal measurements of each person, of which he may at any future time obtain a copy under reasonable restrictions. His initials and date of birth will be entered in the register, but not his name. The names are indexed in a separate book.

3. For supplying information on the methods, practice, and uses of human measurement.

4. For anthropometric experiment and research, and for obtaining data for statistical discussion.

Charges for making the principal measurements:
THREEPENCE each, to those who are already on the Register.
FOURPENCE each, to those who are not:— one page of the Register will thenceforward be assigned to them, and a few extra measurements will be made, chiefly for future identification.

The Superintendent is charged with the control of the laboratory and with determining in each case, which, if any, of the extra measurements may be made, and under what conditions.

H & W. Brown, Printers, 20 Fulham Road, S.W.

Unlike structuralism, functionalism was not supplanted. Functionalist textbooks were widely used in departments of psychology during their early years, and the tenets of functionalism strongly influenced the development of psychological explanations. One functionalist, James Angell (1869–1949), described its basic principles:

1. Functional psychology is the study of mental operations, not of mental structures. (For example, the mind remembers; it does not contain a memory.) It is not enough to compile a catalogue of what the mind does; we must try to understand what the mind accomplishes by this doing.

2. Mental processes must be studied not as isolated and independent events but as part of the biological activity of the organism. These processes are aspects of the organism's adaptation to the environment and are a product of its evolutionary history. For example, the fact that we are conscious implies that consciousness has adaptive value for our species.

3. Functional psychology studies the relation between the environment and the response of the organism to the environment. There is no meaningful distinction between mind and body; they are part of the same entity.

Consider these points when you read the section on behaviorism.

Freud's Psychodynamic Theory

While psychology was developing as a fledgling science, Sigmund Freud (1856–1939) was formulating a theory of human behavior that would greatly affect psychology and radically influence intellectuals of all kinds. Freud began his career as a neurologist, so his work was firmly rooted in biology. He soon became interested in behavioral and emotional problems and even attended one of Charcot's demonstrations on hypnosis at the Salpêtrière hospital. Freud was impressed with Charcot's demonstration of how a psychological event like hypnosis could cause a presumably neurological disorder like hysteria.

We discuss him here only to mark his place in the history of psychology. His theory of the mind included structures, but his structuralism was quite different from Wundt's. Freud devised his concepts of ego, superego, id, and other mental structures through talking with his patients, not through laboratory experiments. His hypothetical mental operations included many that were unconscious and hence not available to introspection. And unlike Wundt, Freud emphasized function; his mental structures served biological drives and instincts and reflected our animal nature.

Psychology in Transition

Psychology as a science was to take a radical turn in the early decades of the twentieth century. Before we consider this change, it might help you to see how the different intellectual contributions of the structuralists and the functionalists had shaped the way psychology was practiced at universities in North America.

The controversy over James Mark Baldwin's appointment at Toronto quickly died down, helped in part when Baldwin's rival for the job was appointed to a similar position. Baldwin was given a rather handsome budget of $1,550 for equipment, which he promptly used to create one of the first psychological laboratories in North America

James Mark Baldwin (1861–1934)

Mary Whiton Calkins (1867–1930)

(Baldwin, 1892). Like the laboratories of Wundt in Germany and James at Harvard University, the Toronto facility was designed for the experimental investigation of the mind, with attention to the control of noise and light. Baldwin went immediately to work in his new environment, even publishing a paper on handedness based on observations of his infant daughter.

The new emphasis on experimentation and observation was becoming prominent in the classroom as well. Mary Whiton Calkins (1867–1930), for example, wrote a lengthy description of the psychology course she taught to seniors at Wellesley College (Calkins, 1892). Her students studied the anatomy of the brain and received laboratory exercises in the dissection of lamb brains, the measurement of sensation, and the comparison of associations to simple words. Calkins reported that the experiments on taste "were so unpopular that I should never repeat them in a general class of students who are not specializing in the subject." This leads the modern reader to wonder just what it was that she asked her students to taste.

Through the efforts of both researchers and instructors, psychology became part of university curricula throughout the United States. Professors of psychology joined academic societies and became recognized as members of an emerging scientific discipline. Wundt had founded the science of psy-

chology on the assumption that it should describe the contents of the mind. By the beginning of the twentieth century, however, psychologists like James and Baldwin had returned to the problem that vexed Descartes: How do we understand the actions that the mind supposedly determines?

Behaviorism

The next major trend that we will consider, behaviorism, likewise reflected this concern with action. Behaviorists went farther than James or Baldwin, however, by rejecting the special nature of mental events and by denying that unobservable and unverifiable mental events were properly the subject matter of psychology. Behaviorists believe that because psychology is the study of observable behavior, mental events, which cannot be observed, are outside the realm of psychology. **Behaviorism** is thus the study of the relation between people's environments and their behavior, without appeal to hypothetical events occurring within their heads.

We have already examined one of the first behaviorists—Edward Thorndike, who formulated the law of effect. The law of effect is certainly in the functionalist tradition. It asserts that the consequences of a behavior act back upon the organism, affecting the likelihood that the behavior will occur again. This process is very similar to the principle of natural selection that is the basis of Darwin's theory of evolution. Just as organisms that successfully adapt to their environments are more likely to survive and breed, so behaviors that cause useful outcomes become more likely to recur.

Thorndike insisted that the subject matter of psychology was behavior. But his explanations contained mentalistic terms. For example, in his law of effect he spoke of "satisfaction," which is certainly not a phenomenon that can be directly observed. Later behaviorists recognized this contradiction and replaced terms such as *satisfaction* and *discomfort* with more objective concepts that reflected only the behavior.

Another major figure in the development of the behavioristic trend was not a psychologist at all but a physiologist: Ivan Pavlov (1849–1936), a Russian who studied the physiology of digestion (for which he later received a Nobel Prize). In

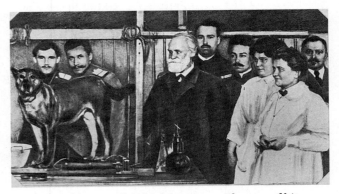

Ivan Pavlov (1849–1936) in his laboratory with some of his collaborators. His research revealed valuable information about the principles of learning.

---

behaviorism A movement in psychology that asserts that the only proper subject matter for scientific study in psychology is observable behavior.

John B. Watson (1878–1958)

the course of studying the stimuli that produce salivation, Pavlov discovered that hungry dogs would salivate at the sight of the attendant who brought in their dishes of food. Although first labeling this phenomenon a "psychic reflex," Pavlov soon traced it to the experience the dog had received. Pavlov found that a dog would salivate at a completely arbitrary stimulus, such as the sound of a bell, if the stimulus was quickly followed by the delivery of a bit of food into the animal's mouth.

Pavlov's discovery had profound significance for psychology. He showed that through experience, an animal could learn to make a response to a stimulus that had never caused this response before. This ability might explain how organisms learn cause-and-effect relations in the environment. In contrast, Thorndike's law of effect suggested an explanation for the adaptability of an individual's behavior to its particular environment. So, from Thorndike's and Pavlov's studies, two important behavioral principles had been discovered.

Behaviorism as a formal school of psychology began with the publication of a book by John B. Watson (1878–1958), *Psychology from the Standpoint of a Behaviorist.* Watson, a professor of psychology at Johns Hopkins University, was a popular teacher and writer and a very convincing advocate of the behavioral perspective. Even after leaving Johns Hopkins for a highly successful career in advertising, he continued to lecture and write magazine articles about psychology.

According to Watson, psychology was a natural science whose domain was restricted to observable events: the behavior of organisms. Watson believed that the elements of consciousness studied by the structuralists were too subjective to lend themselves to scientific investigation. He defined psychology as the objective study of stimuli and the behavior they produced. He reduced even thinking to a form of behavior—"talking to ourselves":

> Now what can we observe? We can observe behavior—*what the organism does or says.* And let us point out at once: that saying is doing—that is, behaving. Speaking overtly or to ourselves (thinking) is just as objective a type of behavior as baseball. (Watson, 1930, p. 6)

Behaviorism is still very much in evidence today in psychology. Its renowned advocates have included B. F. Skinner (1904–1990), one of the most influential psychologists of the twentieth century. But psychologists, including modern behaviorists, have moved away from the strict behaviorism of Watson; mental processes such as imagery and attention are again considered to be proper subject matter for scientific investigation.

In this sense, modern psychologists have moved more toward a view expressed by Margaret Floy Washburn (1871–1939) early in the debate over behavior. Although Washburn (1922) advocated her own version of structuralism, she suggested to behaviorists that they regard introspection itself as a form of behavior that could help them understand the inaccessible processes of mental life. Today, as Washburn would have wished, Watson's emphasis on objectivity in psychological research remains. Even those modern psychologists who most vehemently protest against what they see as the narrowness of behaviorism use the same principles of objectivity to guide their research. As research scientists, they must uphold the principles of objectivity that evolved from empiricism to functionalism to behaviorism. A psychologist who studies private mental events realizes that these events can be studied only indirectly, by means of behavior—verbal reports of inner experiences. Unlike Wundt, present-day psychologists realize that these reports are not pure reflections of these mental events; like other behaviors, these responses can be affected by many factors. Consequently, they strive to maintain an objective stance to ensure that their research findings will be valid and capable of being verified.

Margaret Floy Washburn (1871–1939)

Humanistic Psychology

For many years philosophers and other intellectuals have been concerned with what they see as the special attributes of humanity—free will, spontaneity, creativity, and consciousness. As the science of psychology developed, these phenomena received less attention than others, because researchers could not agree on objective ways to study them. Humanistic psychology developed during the 1950s and 1960s as a reaction against both behaviorism and the psychodynamic approach of Freud. Although psychodynamic theory certainly dealt with mental phenomena that could not be objectively measured, it viewed people as products of their environment and of innate, unconscious forces. Humanistic psychologists insist that human nature goes beyond environmental influences, and they argue that psychologists should study conscious processes, not unconscious drives. In addition, they note that psychoanalytical theory seems preoccupied with disturbed people, ignoring positive phenomena such as happiness, satisfaction, love, and kindness.

Humanistic psychology is an approach to the study of human behavior that emphasizes human experience, choice and creativity, self-realization, and positive growth. Humanistic psychologists emphasize the positive sides of human nature and the potential we all share for personal growth. In general, humanistic psychologists do not believe that we will understand human consciousness and behavior through scientific research. Thus, the humanistic approach has not had a significant influence on psychology as a science. Its greatest impact has been on the development of methods of psychotherapy that are based on a positive and optimistic view of human potential.

Reaction against Behaviorism: The Emphasis on Cognition

Proponents of behaviorism restricted the subject matter of psychology to observable behavior. And, despite their differences from the structuralists, they also tended to analyze behavior by dividing it into smaller elements. Even as behaviorism became the dominant trend in psychology, a contrasting school of thought began to emphasize how unobservable factors influence larger patterns of human consciousness.

This movement began when a German psychologist, Max Wertheimer (1880–1943), bought a toy that presented a series of pictures in rapid succession. Each picture was slightly different from the preceding one, resulting in the impression of continuous motion—like a movie. Wertheimer and his colleagues suggested that psychological processes provided the continuity. They therefore attempted to discover the *organization* of cognitive processes, not their elements. They called their approach **Gestalt psychology.** *Gestalt* is a German word that roughly translates into "unified form." Gestalt psychologists insisted that perceptions resulted from patterns of interactions among many elements, in the same way we recognize a song by the relations between the notes rather than by the individual notes themselves.

Although the Gestalt school of psychology no longer exists, its insistence that the elements of an experience are organized into larger units was very influential. These organizational processes are not directly observable, yet they still determine behavior. Since the 1960s, many psychologists likewise have begun to reject the restrictions of behaviorism and have turned to the study of consciousness, feelings, imagery, and other private events.

Much of *cognitive psychology* (described in the first section of this chapter) analyzes mental activities in terms of **information processing.** According to this approach information received through the senses is "processed" by various systems of neurons in the brain. Some systems store the information in the form of memory; other systems control behavior. Some systems operate automatically and unconsciously, whereas others are conscious and require effort. Because the information processing approach was first devised to describe the operations of complex physical systems such as computers, the modern model of the human brain is, for most cognitive psychologists, the computer. As you will learn in Chapter 5, however, another model—the artificial neural network—is beginning to replace the computer.

Although cognitive psychologists now study mental structures and operations, they have not gone back to the introspective methods that structuralists such as Wundt employed. They use objective research methods, just as behaviorists do. For example, several modern psychologists have studied the phenomenon of imagery. If you close your eyes and imagine what the open pages of this book look like, you are viewing a mental image of what you have previously seen. This image exists only within your brain, and it can be experienced by you and no one else. We have no way of knowing whether your images are like ours any more than we know whether the color red looks the same to you as it does to us. The experience of imagery cannot be shared in a scientific sense.

But behaviors that are based on images can indeed be measured. For example, one researcher (Kosslyn, 1973, 1975) asked a group of people to memorize several drawings. Then he asked the participants to imagine one of the drawings, focusing their attention on a particular feature of the image. Next, he asked a question about a detail of the image that was either "near" the point they were focusing on or "far" from it. For example, if they were picturing a boat, he might ask them to imagine that they were looking at its stern (back). Then he might ask whether the boat had a rudder at the stern, or whether a rope was fastened to its bow (front).

---

humanistic psychology An approach to the study of human behavior that emphasizes human experience, choice and creativity, self-realization, and positive growth.

Gestalt psychology A movement in psychology that emphasized that cognitive processes could be understood by studying their organization, not their elements.

information processing A model used by cognitive psychologists to explain the workings of the brain; according to this model, information received through the senses is processed by systems of neurons in the brain.

[FIGURE 1•6] A drawing used in the imagery study by Kosslyn.

(From Kosslyn, S. M. [1973]. *Perception and Psychophysics, 14,* 90–94. Reprinted with permission.of Psychonomic Society.)

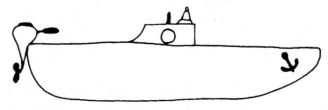

Donald Hebb (1904–1985)

Kosslyn found that people could very quickly answer a question about a feature of the boat that was near the place they were focusing on, but that they took longer to answer a question about a part that was farther away. It was as if they had to scan their mental image to get from one place to the other. (See FIGURE 1•6.)

Because we cannot observe what is happening within a person's head, the concept of imagery remains hypothetical. However, this hypothetical concept very nicely explains and organizes some concrete results—namely, the time it takes for a person to give an answer. Although the explanation for the results of this experiment is phrased in terms of private events (mental images), the behavioral data (how long it takes to answer the questions) are empirical and objective.

Reaction against Behaviorism: The Emphasis on Neurobiology

Although the first scientific roots of psychology were in biology and physiology, the biological approach to behavior has become so prevalent since the early 1990s that it can properly be called a revolution. During the early and mid-twentieth century, the dominance of behaviorism led to a de-emphasis of biological factors in the study of behavior. At the time scientists had no way of studying what went on in the brain, but that did not prevent people from spinning elaborate theories of how the brain controlled behavior. Behaviorists rejected such speculation. They acknowledged that the brain controlled behavior but argued that because we could not see what was happening inside the brain, we should refrain from inventing physiological explanations that could not be verified.

One of the few dissenters from the prevailing behaviorist view of the time was a Canadian psychologist, Donald Hebb (1904–1985). Hebb had graduated from Dalhousie University with aspirations of being a novelist. After a brief stint teaching in Quebec, he was admitted as a part-time student at McGill University. Hebb was inspired by the physiological approach to psychology then taught at McGill by a professor who had worked with Pavlov. Challenging the behaviorists, Hebb argued that behavioral and mental phenomena could be related directly to brain activity. In his most influential work, he suggested several simple principles by which the nervous system organized itself into special "circuits" that could represent mental activity (Hebb, 1949).

Cognitive psychologists had inherited from early behaviorists a suspicion of the value of biology in explaining behavior. Thus, the cognitive revolution did not lead to a renewed interest in biology. But the extraordinary advances in neurobiology in the late twentieth century revolutionized psychology and vindicated Hebb's viewpoint (Klein, 1999). And many of Hebb's students and associates were at the forefront of subsequent developments in psychology (Adair, Paivio, & Ritchie, 1996).

Neurobiologists (biologists who study the nervous system) and scientists and engineers in allied fields have developed ways to study the brain that were unthinkable just a few decades ago. We can study fine details of nerve cells, discover their interconnections, analyze the chemicals they use to communicate with one another, produce drugs that block the action of these chemicals or mimic their effects, see the internal structure of a living human brain, and measure the activity of different parts of the brain—regions as small as a few cubic millimeters—while people are watching visual displays, listening to words, or performing various kinds of cognitive tasks. In addition, it seems as though every day we learn of new genes that play roles in particular behaviors, and drugs that are designed to duplicate or block the effects of these genes.

QUESTIONS TO CONSIDER

1. Although the science of psychology began in Germany, it soon migrated to the United States, where it flourished. Can you think of any characteristics of American society that might explain why psychology developed faster here than elsewhere in the world?

2. As you have learned, psychologists study a wide variety of behaviors. Do you think that there are any behaviors that psychologists cannot explain (or should not try to explain)?

Epilogue

The Brain's Future

For Laura and her group, reading Kurzweil's book accomplished what I had hoped. Kurzweil attempted to construct a utopian vision of the future based on the scientific assumptions that have shaped contemporary psychology: historical themes such as materialism, empiricism, and determinism. It's a challenging notion to push the working assumptions of a science into a prescription for the future. Laura and her partners in this project had to consider whether our current knowledge from the science of behavior is up to the task.

Ironically, fifty years before Kurzweil, the behaviorist B.F. Skinner had likewise written a utopian book (a novel, in this case) in which he proposed that psychology could revolutionize human society (Skinner, 1948). Kurzweil's work extends Skinner's by introducing the concept of replicating our nervous system with machinery, but the issue is the same and goes all the way back to Descartes: How far can we generalize our knowledge? If you want to hear the answer that Laura's group reached, you can hear their program at http//www.cjsr.ualberta.ca/news/news.php?s=p400

CHAPTER SUMMARY

What Is Psychology?

Psychology is the science of behavior, and psychologists study a large variety of behaviors in humans and other animals. They attempt to explain these behaviors by studying the events that cause them. Different psychologists are interested in different behaviors and in different categories of causes.

This section identified 11 different approaches to understanding the causes of behavior. Physiological psychologists study the role of the brain in behavior. Comparative psychologists study the evolution of behavior by comparing the behavioral capacities of various species of animals. Behavior geneticists study the role of genetics in behavior. Cognitive psychologists study complex human behaviors such as perception, memory, and attention. Cognitive neuroscientists study the brain mechanisms responsible for cognition. Developmental psychologists study the development of behavior throughout the life span. Social psychologists study the effects people have on one another's

behavior. Personality psychologists study individual differences in temperament and patterns of behavior. Evolutionary psychologists study the influence of natural selection on behavior. Cross-cultural psychologists study the impact of culture on behavior. Clinical psychologists study the causes and treatment of mental disorders and problems of adjustment.

In addition to thinking of psychology as a scientific discipline, we can also consider it as a profession, in which psychologists apply their knowledge of behavior to the solution of certain kinds of problems. Two recent applications discussed here were the problem of constructing facial drawings from eyewitness reports and the design of artificial limbs for amputees.

The Growth of Psychology as a Science

By the mid-nineteenth century, philosophy had embraced two concepts that would lead to the objective investigation of the human mind: the principles of materialism and empiricism. Materialism maintained that the mind was made of matter. Thus, all natural phenomena, including human behavior, could be explained in terms of physical entities: the interaction of matter and energy. Empiricism emphasized that all knowledge was acquired by means of sensory experience; no knowledge was innate. By directing attention to the tangible, sensory components of human activity, these concepts laid the foundation for a scientific approach in psychology. At this time, the divisions between science and philosophy were still blurred. Subsequent developments in the natural sciences, especially in biology and physiology, provided the necessary ingredients that, united with the critical, analytical components of philosophy, formed the scientific discipline of psychology. These ingredients were experimentation and verification.

Materialism implies the doctrine of determinism, which is opposed to the concept of free will. Determinism makes possible the prediction that an outcome will follow some cause.

Education and psychiatry became matters of public concern during the early 1800s. Both fields emphasized the causal factors that can produce change. Progressive education stressed the natural development of the child and sought methods of teaching that would match the way children normally learned. Thorndike proposed the law of effect as a principle of this learning, while Montessori argued that different methods were appropriate to different ages of a child. Psychiatry saw mental illness as possibly having social causes and explored therapies that relied either relied on either normal human discourse or specialized techniques such as hypnosis.

Major Trends in the Development of Psychology

Psychology has come a long way in a relatively short time. The first laboratory of experimental psychology was established in 1879, less than one and a half centuries ago. Wilhelm

Wundt established psychology as a discipline that was independent of philosophy. Wundt's approach was based on the premise that, through introspection, the mind's contents could be described. Even though Wundt's structuralism did not last, interest in psychology continued to grow. The discipline took on added breadth and scope with the emergence of functionalism, which stressed the adaptive value of biological phenomena. Functionalism gave rise to the objectivity of behaviorism, and scientific objectivity still dominates the way we do research.

The cognitive revolution began because some psychologists believed that a strict emphasis on observable behavior missed the complexity of human cognition and behavior—an opinion that modern behaviorists contest. The biological revolution in psychology is manifested in the increased interest of psychologists in all fields—not just physiological psychology—in the role of biological factors in behavior.

succeed with **PEARSON mypsychlab**

Visit MyPsychLab for practice quizzes, flashcards, and dozens of videos and animated tutorials, including the following items you can find in the "Multimedia Library":

Even the Rat was White: Robert Guthrie
Women and the Field of Psychology:
   Florence Denmark

Psychologists at Work
The Pseudoscience of Astrology

KEY TERMS

animism, *p. 8*
behavior genetics, *p. 5*
behaviorism, *p. 20*
causal event, *p. 4*

clinical psychology, *p. 6*
cognitive neuroscience, *p. 5*
cognitive psychology, *p. 5*
comparative psychology, *p. 5*

cross-cultural psychology, *p. 6*
determinism, *p. 13*
developmental
   psychology, *p. 5*
doctrine of specific
   nerve energies, *p. 12*
dualism, *p. 10*
empiricism, *p. 10*
evolutionary psychology, *p. 6*
experimental ablation, *p. 12*
functionalism, *p. 18*
Gestalt psychology, *p. 22*
humanistic psychology, *p. 22*
information processing, *p. 22*

introspection, *p. 18*
law of effect, *p. 14*
materialism, *p. 10*
model, *p. 10*
personality psychology, *p. 6*
physiological psychology, *p. 5*
psychology, *p. 3*
psychophysics, *p. 13*
rationalism, *p. 10*
reflex, *p. 9*
social psychology, *p. 5*
structuralism, *p. 18*

SUGGESTIONS FOR FURTHER READING

Kurzweil, R. (1999). *The age of spiritual machines: When computers exceed human intelligence.* New York: Viking Penguin.

Lawson, R.B., Graham, J.E., & Baker, K.M. (2007). *A history of psychology: Globalization, ideas, and applications.* Upper Saddle River: NJ: Pearson Prentice Hall.

Reese, R.J. (2005). *America's public schools: From the common school to "No Child Left Behind."* Baltimore, MD: Johns Hopkins University Press.

Shorter, E. (1997). *A history of psychiatry.* New York: John Wiley & Sons.

The book by Lawson, Graham, and Baker is an excellent history of psychology. Particularly notable is its inclusiveness: There are special chapters on the role of women in the history of psychology, the contribution of black Americans, and the development of psychology outside Europe and America. Reese's book is not centrally concerned with psychology, but you may find it of interest to know why your elementary, junior high, and high schools were organized the way they were. Shorter's work is a history of the medical profession of psychiatry. It skips around, but provides some interesting anecdotes on major figures.

CHAPTER 2

The Ways a
Means of
Psychology

Taken from *Psychology: The Science of Behavior*, Seventh Edition, by Neil R. Carlson, Harold Miller,
C. Donald Heth, John W. Donahoe, and G. Neil Martin.

Prologue

Justine's Experiment

Justine's parents operate a small company that employs five people. The employees assemble custom equipment for oil exploration companies. The summer after her first year of college, Justine decided to put her skills to work by trying to increase the company's productivity. She reasoned that if the employees could complete more pieces of equipment per day, the company would be more profitable for her parents and the workers themselves would benefit through their profit-sharing plan.

One evening Justine stayed at the assembly laboratory to work on one of the devices herself. After a couple of hours, her neck was strained and her arms and hands tingled from maintaining a bent position over the bench at which she was working. Justine convinced her parents to invest in height-adjustable chairs to replace the existing stationary seats. When the new chairs arrived, she adjusted them so that each employee seemed to be at a comfortable position. Justine held a meeting with the employees and told them that she thought the new chairs would reduce discomfort and therefore permit them to be more productive. She said that she would keep track of how many units they finished over the next several days and would let them know if the chairs had helped. At the end of the week, the employees eagerly asked Justine how they had done. Justine proudly announced that they had completed 20% more of the testing units than they had during the same amount of time before the chairs arrived. The workers congratulated her for her insight and help.

Over the next week Justine continued to check in with the employees and to collect data. She then got together with her friend Lawrence, who had recently taken a statistics course. Lawrence helped her conduct a formal statistical test to compare the production figures for the seven workdays before Justine introduced the new chairs and the seven workdays afterward. They found that productivity had increased significantly more than would be expected by chance. Her intervention had worked, or so it appeared. Justine stopped her daily visits with the employees.

A few weeks later, though, Justine happened to look at the employees' production figures and was

Is it a change in the type of chair that can improve productivity, or the prospect of any change?

disappointed to find that productivity had fallen to the same level as before the new chairs arrived. Justine decided to start over with the old chairs, monitor the employees' output, and then reintroduce the adjustable chairs to see what would happen. After a week with the old chairs, productivity inexplicably increased 20% again. Justine was understandably perplexed. Increased productivity with the old chairs? Justine gave up on her project. What had happened? Justine was sure that she had diligently applied the scientific method and that her intervention should have had clear-cut results. ▪

The goal of psychology as a science is the explanation of behavior. As scientists, the vast majority of psychologists believe that behavior, like other natural phenomena, can be studied objectively. The scientific method permits us to discover the nature and causes of behavior. This chapter will show you how the scientific method is used in psychological research. What you learn here will help you understand the research described in the rest of the book. But even more than that, what you learn here can be applied to everyday life. Knowing how a psychologist can be misled by the results of improperly conducted research can help us all avoid being misled by more casual observations. We'll see, for example, that Justine made a common, but fundamental, mistake by failing to take into account that her actions as an experimenter could be a causal factor in the behavior of her parents' employees. Understanding the scientific method can also help us, as consumers of information, distinguish worthwhile from flawed research reported in the mass media.

The Scientific Method in Psychology

To explain behavior we must use a method that is both precise enough to be clearly understood by others and general enough to apply to a wide variety of situations. We hope to be able to make general statements about the events that cause phenomena to occur.

Scientists use an agreed-upon approach to discovery and explanation—the scientific method. The **scientific method** consists of a set of rules that dictate the general

procedure for collecting and analyzing data that a scientist must follow in his or her research. These rules are not arbitrary; as we will see, they are based on logic and common sense. The rules were originally devised by philosophers who were attempting to determine how we could understand reality. By nature, we are all intuitive psychologists, trying to understand why others do what they do—so it is important to realize how easily we can be fooled about the actual causes of behavior. Thus, everyone, not just professional psychologists, should know the basic steps of the scientific method.

The scientific method employs a set of rules that apply to a form of research that identifies cause-and-effect relations; this form is called an **experiment,** and it consists of five steps. Some new terms introduced here without definition will be described in detail later in this chapter.

1. *Identify the problem and formulate hypothetical cause-and-effect relations among variables.* This step involves identifying variables (particular behaviors and particular environmental and physiological events) and describing the relations among them in general terms. For example, your own history of late-night studying might have convinced you of the helpful effects of caffeine on fatigue. But does caffeine help when you're about to take a test? You form the hypothesis: *Coffee consumption improves recall of learned information.* The hypothesis states that something about the first affects the second.

2. *Design the experiment.* Experiments involve the manipulation of independent variables and the observation of dependent variables. For example, if we wanted to test the hypothesis about the relation between caffeine and test performance, we might arrange an experiment in which volunteers agreed to consume a controlled amount of caffeine before being tested on some previously learned material. Each variable must be *operationally defined;* and the independent variable (caffeine consumption) must be controlled so that only it, and no other variable, is responsible for any changes in the dependent variable (recall of learned information).

3. *Perform the experiment.* The researcher must organize the material needed to perform the experiment, train the people who will perform the research, recruit volunteers whose behavior will be observed, and randomly assign each of these volunteers to an experimental group or a control group. The experiment is performed and the observations are recorded.

4. *Evaluate the hypothesis by examining the data from the study.* Do the results support the hypothesis, or do they suggest that it is wrong? This step often involves special mathematical procedures used to determine whether an observed effect is *statistically significant*. These procedures will be discussed in the Understanding Research Results section later in this chapter.

5. *Communicate the results.* Once the experimenters have learned something about the causes of a behavior,

---

scientific method   A set of rules that governs the collection and analysis of data gained through observational studies or experiments.

experiment   A study in which the researcher changes the value of an independent variable and observes whether this manipulation affects the value of a dependent variable. Only experiments can confirm the existence of cause-and-effect relations among variables.

they must tell others about their findings. In most cases psychologists write an article that includes a description of the experiment's procedure and results and a discussion of their significance. They send the article to one of the many journals that publish results of psychological research. Journal editors and expert reviewers determine which research is methodologically sound and important enough to publish. In addition, researchers often present their findings at conferences or professional conventions. As a result, other psychologists can incorporate the findings into their own thinking and hypothesizing.

Following these steps decreases the chances that we will be misled by our observations or form incorrect conclusions in our research. We as humans have a tendency to accept some types of evidence even though the rules of logic indicate that we should not. This tendency sometimes serves us well in our daily lives, but it can lead us to make the wrong conclusions when we try to understand the true causes of natural phenomena, including our own behavior.

Types of Research

Psychologists conduct three major types of scientific research. These classes of research are common across many of the sciences. The first type includes **naturalistic observation** (observation of people or animals in their natural environment) and **clinical observation**—(observation of people or animals while they are undergoing treatment or diagnosis for a psychological condition). These methods are the least formal and are constrained by the fewest rules. Naturalistic observations provide the foundations of the biological and social sciences. For example, Charles Darwin's observation and classification of animals, plants, and fossils during his voyage around the world provided him with the raw material for his theory of evolution. Maria Montessori formed many of her ideas about child development by watching children in a classroom. And Paul Broca suggested that language was located in a specific region of the brain after treating a man who had lost his ability to speak. As these examples illustrate, a researcher might perceive new facts following careful observation.

The second type, **correlational studies,** are observational in nature, but they involve more formal measurement—of environmental events, of individuals' physical and social characteristics, and of their behavior. Researchers examine the relations of these measurements in an attempt to explain the observed behaviors. At the conclusion of a correlational study, a researcher might conclude that some of the phenomena measured are related in a particular way.

Finally, experiments go beyond mere measurement. A psychologist performing an experiment makes things happen and observes the results. As you will see, following a properly designed experiment, a researcher can positively identify the causal relations among events.

Researchers communicate their results to other scientists through professional journals or conferences.

Identifying the Problem: Getting an Idea for Research

Like most professions, science is a very competitive enterprise. Most scientists want to be recognized for their work. They want to discover and explain interesting phenomena and to have other scientists acknowledge their importance. They may hope that the fruits of their research will affect the public at large. They certainly need to be hardworking and dedicated—perhaps even obstinate and relentless.

naturalistic observation　Observation of the behavior of people or other animals in their natural environments.

clinical observation　Observation of the behavior of people or animals while they are undergoing diagnosis or treatment.

correlational study　The examination of relations between two or more measurements of behavior or other characteristics of people or other animals.

Often, science that achieves some breakthrough result is the cumulative work of many scientists who are part of a larger collective (and often international) endeavor. It often occurs in institutional settings such as universities, where scientists, students, and technicians all are involved in the effort. Such projects require financial support. Psychological research in the United States has historically been supported by major federal agencies such as the National Science Foundation and the National Institute of Mental Health. Before providing funding, these agencies rigorously review the merits of a proposed research program and its potential for long-term scientific value. They provide an independent evaluation of the worth of a scientific idea.

In this environment of competition and rigorous evaluation, a research program must be based on *good ideas*. Where do the ideas come from?

A theory connecting cell phone use with increased chance of a traffic accident would need to identify the causal factors responsible.

Hypotheses   A hypothesis is the starting point of any study. It is an idea, phrased as a general statement, that a scientist wishes to test through research. In the original Greek, *hypothesis* means "suggestion," and the word still conveys the same meaning. When scientists form a hypothesis, they are suggesting that a relation exists among various phenomena. Thus, a **hypothesis** is a tentative statement about a cause-and-effect relation between two or more events.

Theories   A **theory** is a set of statements that describes and explains known facts, proposes relations among variables, and makes new predictions. For example, a public safety advocate might notice an increase in traffic accidents and propose the theory that this is the result of increased cell phone use by drivers. In a sense, then, a theory is an elaborate form of hypothesis. A scientific theory operates within the scientific method to organize a system of facts and related hypotheses to explain some larger aspect of nature. A good theory fuels the creation of new hypotheses. A good theory is one that generates *testable hypotheses*—hypotheses that can potentially be supported or proved wrong by scientific research. Some theories are so general or so abstract that they do not produce testable hypotheses and hence cannot be subjected to scientific rigor. For example, if someone tells you they have a theory that UFO sightings have increased in America because people are disenchanted with organized religions, you could justifiably object that her proposed cause was not useful: She hasn't told you what *disenchantment* is or how you could tell if someone had it. Because she hasn't told you what it is, you cannot change "disenchantment" or perform an experiment in-

volving it. So, the theory doesn't provide a hypothesis that is testable.

The ability to test a hypothesis is one of the most important aspects of science. Natural phenomena can have many potential causes. If there is no way to choose among them, then we cannot build a consistent explanation of why the phenomenon occurs. So, a theory that does not generate testable hypotheses—either because it uses factors that cannot be observed or manipulated or because it is hopelessly vague as to what those factors are—cannot be a part of science.

Testability is particularly important to psychology, because it is often the case that psychological explanations rely on causal factors that are not directly observable. In the pages of this book that follow, there will be many instances where psychologists have found it useful to refer to such things as "memory," "attention," and "personality trait." We can't observe these directly, but we can, through a good theory, make predictions about how these factors will influence behavior.

Theories can generate testable hypotheses and still be difficult to work with. The earlier example of cell phone use and traffic accidents is a case in point, since the proposed cause—using a cell phone—contains many possible factors: Using a phone takes one of your hands off the wheel; it makes you think of situations other than driving; it blocks out other sounds, and so on. A theory that is vague is usually a poor one. In the next section, we'll see how to approach this problem.

Many, but not all, research endeavors in psychology are directed toward making some particular theory stronger. They try show that the evidence is consistent with the hypothesis, or they explore the relationship between concepts within the theory. Sometimes research stimulates us to think about old problems in new ways by showing how findings that did not appear to be related to each other can be explained by a single concept. There is even a scientific journal, *Psychological Review*, devoted to articles of this type.

---

hypothesis   A statement, usually designed to be tested by an experiment, that tentatively expresses a cause-and-effect relationship between two or more events.

theory   A set of statements designed to explain a set of phenomena; more encompassing than a hypothesis.

An important feature of naturalistic observation is that the observer remains in the background.

Naturalistic and Clinical Observations as Sources of Hypotheses and Theories

Psychology is about behavior. To understand human behavior, or the behavior of other animals, we first have to know something about that behavior. Much of what we know about behavior comes from ordinary experience: from observing other people, listening to their stories, watching films, reading novels. In effect, we perform observations throughout our lives. But systematic observations permit trained observers to discover subtly different categories of behavior and to develop hypotheses about their causes.

Psychologists who are also naturalists apply observational procedures to questions of behavior. The important feature of naturalistic observations is that the observer remains in the background, trying not to interfere with the people (or animals) being observed. For example, suppose we are interested in studying the social behavior of preschoolers. We want to know under what conditions children share their toys or fight over them, how children react to newcomers to the group, and so on. The best way to begin to get some ideas is to watch groups of children. We would unobtrusively start taking notes, classifying behaviors into categories and seeing what events provoked them—and what the effects of these behaviors might be. These naturalistic observations would teach us how to categorize and measure the children's behavior and would help us develop hypotheses that could be tested in experiments or in correlational studies.

Clinical observations are different. In the course of diagnosis or treatment, clinical psychologists can often observe important patterns of behavior. They can then report the results of their observations in detailed descriptions known as **case studies.** As with naturalistic observations, these clinical observations could form the basis of hypotheses about the causes of behavior. Unlike a naturalist, however, a clinical psychologist most likely does *not* remain in the background, because the object of therapy is to change the patient's behavior and to solve problems. Indeed, the psychologist is ethically constrained to engage in activities designed to benefit the patient; he or she cannot arbitrarily withhold some treatment or apply another just for the sake of new observations. So, like the naturalist, a clinician is bound by certain rules that limit the kinds of observations that can be made: The clinician cannot interfere with the treatment regime prescribed for the patient.

In some cases, psychologists *do* interfere with a situation in a natural or clinical setting. They may, for example, ask questions at job sites or on the street—places that we might regard as naturalistic settings. In one common procedure, a **survey study,** researchers may ask people specially designed and controlled questions, perhaps about their beliefs, opinions, or attitudes. Survey studies are designed to elicit a special kind of behavior—answers to the questions. The observations, then, are usually descriptions of the classes of responses to these questions. Many people may participate in a survey study, but they all are given the same, *standardized,* questions. As these questions become more specific and precise, they allow the same formal measurement of relations that underlies correlational studies.

A clinical psychologist, too, may manipulate the treatment given to a patient, with the desire of producing a more beneficial response. The psychologist may report the result in the manner of a case study, but such manipulation would make the process an experiment, not an observational study.

Much can be learned through careful observation of animals in their natural environment. The results of such observations often suggest hypotheses to be tested by subsequent studies.

case study   A detailed description of an individual's behavior during the course of clinical treatment or diagnosis.

survey study   A study of people's responses to standardized questions.

[FIGURE 2·1] Basic design of the driving and cell phone distraction experiment

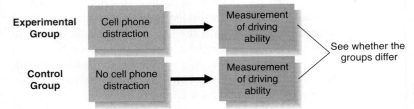

Designing an Experiment

Although naturalistic observations enable a psychologist to classify behaviors into categories and to offer hypothetical explanations for these behaviors, only an experiment can determine whether these explanations are correct. Let us see how to design an experiment. We will examine experimental variables and their operational definition and control.

Variables   The hypothesis proposed earlier—"Cell phone distraction while driving increases the likelihood of a traffic accident"—describes a relation between distraction and the likelihood of a driving mistake. Scientists refer to these two components as **variables**: things that can vary in value. Thus, temperature is a variable, and so is happiness. Virtually anything that can differ in amount, degree, or presence versus absence is a variable.

Scientists either *manipulate* or *measure* the values of variables. **Manipulation** literally means "handling" (from *manus*, "hand"). Because of abuses in the history of human research (described later), the term *manipulation* is sometimes incorrectly understood to mean something that researchers do to participants. Psychologists use the word, however, to describe setting the values of a variable in order to examine that variable's effect on another variable. In the cell phone experiment, one value of the distraction variable might be "a cell phone call every minute" and another might be "complete absence of cell phone calls." Measuring variables means exactly what you think it does. Just as we measure the variable of temperature with a thermometer, so psychologists devise instruments to measure psychological variables. The results of experimental manipulations and measurements of variables help us evaluate hypotheses.

To test the cell phone distraction hypothesis with an experiment, we would assemble two groups of volunteers to serve as participants. We would ask them to perform some activity that measures driving ability. We could, for example, have them use a video game that simulates driving. We would present participants in the **experimental group** with a certain level of distraction, such as a high rate of cell phone calls. We would not give participants in the **control group** such an experience, and they therefore would have no distraction. We would then measure the ability of participants in both groups to avoid driving errors; from these results, we could then determine whether the outcomes in the two groups differed. Provided that we had randomly assigned the volunteers to make sure that our two groups were alike at the start of the experiment, we could attribute any differences in driving ability to the experimental manipulation of distraction. (See FIGURE 2·1.)

Our imaginary experiment examines the effect of one variable on another. The variable that we manipulate (distraction from a cell phone) is called the **independent variable.** The variable that we measure (likelihood of driver error) is the **dependent variable.** An easy way to keep the names of these variables straight is to remember that a hypothesis describes how the value of a dependent variable *depends* on the value of an independent variable. Our hypothesis proposes that a high frequency of cell phone distraction causes a high likelihood of driving errors. (See FIGURE 2·2.)

Scientists want to understand the causes of behavior in more than one specific situation. Thus, the variables that hypotheses deal with are expressed in general terms. Independent and dependent variables are *categories* into which various behaviors are classified. For example, we would probably classify hitting, kicking, and throwing objects at someone within the category of "interpersonal aggression." Pre-

variable   Anything capable of assuming any of several values.

manipulation   Setting the values of an independent variable in an experiment to see whether the value of another variable is affected.

experimental group   The group of participants in an experiment that is exposed to a particular value of the independent variable, which has been manipulated by the researcher.

control group   A comparison group used in an experiment, the members of which are exposed to the naturally occurring or zero value of the independent variable.

independent variable   The variable that is manipulated in an experiment as a means of determining cause-and-effect relations.

dependent variable   The variable measured in an experiment and hypothesized to be affected by the independent variable.

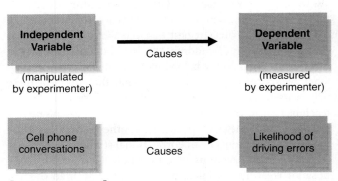

[FIGURE 2·2] Independent and dependent variables

sumably, these forms of aggression would have very similar causes. A psychologist must know enough about a particular type of behavior to be able to classify it correctly.

Even though one of the first steps in psychological research involves naming and classifying behaviors, however, we must be careful to avoid committing the nominal fallacy. The **nominal fallacy** is the erroneous belief that we have explained an event merely by naming it. (*Nomen* means "name.") Classifying a behavior does not explain it; classifying only prepares us to examine and discover events that cause a behavior.

For example, suppose that we see a man frown and shout at other people without provocation, criticize their work when it is really acceptable, and generally act unpleasantly toward everyone around him. Someone says, "Wow, he's really angry today!" Does this statement explain his behavior? No; it only *describes* the behavior. Instead of saying he is angry, we might better say that his behavior is hostile and aggressive. This statement does not claim to explain why he is acting the way he is. To say that he is angry suggests that an internal state is responsible for his behavior—that anger is causing his behavior. But all we have observed is his behavior, not his internal state. Even if he is experiencing feelings of anger, these feelings are not a full account of his behavior. What we really need to know is *what events made him act the way he did.* Perhaps he has a painful toothache. Perhaps he just learned that he failed to get a job he wanted. Perhaps he just read a book that promoted assertiveness. Events like these are causes of both behavior and feelings. Unless the underlying events are discovered and examined, we have not explained the behavior in a scientifically meaningful way.

Yet identifying causes is not as simple as merely identifying preceding events. Many internal and external events may precede any behavior. Some of these events are causal, but some almost certainly will be completely unrelated to the observed behavior. For example, you get off your commuter train because your stop is announced, not because someone coughs or someone else turns the page of a newspaper, even though all of these events may happen just before you stand up and leave the train. The task of a psychologist is to determine which of the many events that occurred before a particular behavior caused that behavior to happen.

The cell phone example, up to now, has this problem. There are many things that happen when you answer a call. Similarly, driving ability is a complex behavior with many components. A good theory would provide more detail about both independent and dependent variables. Let's look at a possible candidate.

Driving is clearly dependent on our ability to recognize the changing conditions ahead of us on the road. Later in this book, in Chapter 8, we'll examine a psychological condition

nominal fallacy The false belief that we have explained the causes of a phenomenon by identifying and naming it; for example, believing that we have explained lazy behavior by attributing it to "laziness."

[FIGURE 2·3] An example of our ability to detect a change in a traffic scene. Study this picture for about 3 seconds. Then turn to Figure 2.4.

called *change blindness* which, as the name implies, is an insensitivity to a changed scene. For example, look at **FIGURE 2·3**, which depicts a traffic scene. Now look at **FIGURE 2·4**, which depicts the same scene—but with one detail missing. Can you tell what it is?

Most likely, you would have had trouble spotting the difference. Because the two figures were on separate pages, there's a visual interruption as you looked from one to the other. Psychologists who study change blindness feel that this interruption interferes with our ability to compare two scenes (Rensink, 2002). We could possibly generalize this to any interruption, including an auditory one. So, perhaps cell phone conversations cause accidents because they increase change blindness.

Notice that we've expanded our theory about traffic accidents considerably. Our explanation for the distracting effects of a call says that they are similar to a more general phenomenon. We can therefore understand a practical problem like preventing accidents by studying a psychological process that occurs in other situations too. Our theory about cell phones and traffic accidents suggests that factors that increase our resistance to distractions will decrease change blindness.

Operational Definitions Hypotheses are phrased in general terms, but when we design an experiment (step 2 of the scientific method) we need to decide what *particular* variables we will manipulate and measure. For example, remember our hypothesis about caffeine and test-taking? Caffeine seems to improve alertness and reaction time (e.g., Smith, 2005). Perhaps it can improve our resistance to distractions and thereby increase our ability to detect changes like those between Figures 2.3 and 2.4. Our hypothesis, then, is that caffeine consumption will decrease change blindness. To test this particular hypothesis, we must carefully describe how much caffeine we will administer to participants in our experiment and under what conditions. Similarly, we must also describe how we will measure change blindness.

[FIGURE 2·4] How does this photograph differ from the previous one?

This translation of generalities into specific operations is called an **operational definition:** the definition of independent variables and dependent variables in terms of the operations a researcher performs in order to set their values or to measure them. In our proposed experiment, a rudimentary operational definition of the independent and dependent variables and the setting in which they were studied might be the following:

> *Setting:* Participants in the experiment are comfortably seated in front of a computer screen. Participants receive 20 change detection tests. Each test consists of a sequence in which an image like Figure 2.3 is shown for three seconds, followed by a blank white screen for a half-second, and then followed by a changed version of the first figure for three seconds. Changed versions are computer-modified versions of the first image, with one randomly selected component erased, as in Figure 2.4. The original and the changed versions alternate back and forth in this way until the participant presses a button to indicate that he or she has detected the change.

> *Independent variable:* Two hours before the test, each participant is given a standard-sized coffee cup containing a hot decaffeinated coffee drink. For participants in the experimental group, this drink contains 0.2 grams of caffeine; for participants in the control group, the drink is not altered.

> *Dependent variable:* On each test, change detection is measured by the time elapsed between the first appearance of the original image and the participant's pressing the response button. All participants were asked to be reasonably confident they had detected the object before pressing the button.

---

operational definition   Definition of a variable in terms of the operations the researcher performs to measure or manipulate it.

validity   The degree to which the operational definition of a variable accurately reflects the variable it is designed to measure or manipulate.

confounding of variables   Inadvertent simultaneous manipulation of more than one variable. The results of an experiment in which variables are confounded permit no valid conclusions about cause and effect.

Any general concept can be operationalized in many different ways. By selecting one particular operational definition, the researcher may or may not succeed in manipulating the independent variable or in measuring the dependent variable. For example, there are many sources of caffeine (coffee, soft drinks, condiments, and so on) and several ways of administering it (e.g., through a fluid, an injection, taken after a meal, taken four hours after a meal, and so on). Which operational definition is correct? Which set of results should we believe? To answer these questions, we need to address the issue of *validity.*

The **validity** of operational definitions has to do with how appropriate they are for testing the researcher's hypothesis—how accurately they represent the variables whose values have been manipulated or measured. Obviously, only experiments that use valid operational definitions of their variables can yield meaningful results. Let's consider this operational definition of detection: the length of the time interval between initial presentation of the original image and the pressing of the response button. How can we know that the participant has actually seen the change? Even with the best of intentions, a person in an experiment like this might be reacting to his or her own imagination rather than actual visual perception. As one possible check, we could ask each participant to point to the location of the change and to describe it. Using only those times that were associated with correct points would increase the validity of our measure.

Control of Independent Variables

We have seen that a scientist performs an experiment by manipulating the value of the independent variable and then observing whether this change affects the dependent variable. If an effect is seen, the scientist can conclude that there is a cause-and-effect relation between the variables. That is, changes in the value of the independent variable cause changes in the value of the dependent variable.

When conducting an experiment, the researcher must manipulate the value of the independent variable—and *only* the independent variable. For example, if we want to determine whether background environmental noise has an effect on people's reading speed, we must choose our source of noise carefully. If we used the sound track from a television show to supply the noise and found that it slowed people's reading speed, we could not conclude that the effect was caused purely by "noise." We might have selected an interesting show, thus distracting the participants' attention from the material they were reading because of the content of the TV program rather than because of "noise." If we want to do this experiment properly, we should use noise that is neutral and not a source of interest by itself—for instance, noise like the *sssh* sound that is heard when a radio is tuned between stations.

If we used a TV program sound track as our manipulation of noise, we would inadvertently cause **confounding of variables**—we would introduce the effects of another variable besides noise on reading speed. One of the meanings of the word *confound* is "to fail to distinguish." If a researcher inadvertently introduces one or more extra, unwanted, independent variables that vary along with the intended independent variable, he or she will not be able to distinguish the effects of any one of them on the dependent variable. That is, the effects of the variables will be confounded. In our example, the noise of the TV program would be mixed with the content of the program in the experimental condition, whereas in the control condition there would be neither noise nor content. You can see that any effect of the manipulation on reading could be due to either noise or content or even to their combination. It would be impossible to reach any conclusion about the experimental hypothesis.

It is often difficult to be sure that independent variables are not confounded. Sometimes even experienced researchers overlook a possible problem, as is illustrated in the following case.

[CASE STUDY] A visitor to a zoology department of a well-known university described research he had conducted in a remote area of South America. He was interested in determining whether a particular species of bird could recognize a large bird that normally preys on it. He had constructed a set of cardboard models that bore varying degrees of resemblance to the predator: They ranged from a perfect representation, to two models of noncarnivorous birds, to a neutral stimulus (such as a triangle). The researcher restrained each bird he was testing and suddenly presented it with each of the test stimuli, in decreasing order of similarity to the predator—that is, from predator to harmless birds to triangle. He observed a relation between the amount of alarm that the birds showed and the similarity that the model bore to the predator. The most predator-like model produced the greatest response. (See **FIGURE 2·5**.)

It was pointed out—to the embarrassment of the speaker—that the study contained a fatal flaw that made it impossible to conclude whether a relation existed between the independent variable (similarity of the model to the predator) and the dependent variable (amount of alarm).

It's a fairly subtle but important problem. Can you figure it out? Reread the previous paragraph, consult Figure 2.5, and think about the problem before you read on.

Now, the answer: When testing the birds' responses to the models, the investigator presented each model at a different time *but always in the same order*. Very likely, even if the birds had been shown the *same* model again and again, they would have exhibited less and less of a response. We very commonly observe this phenomenon, called *habituation*, when a stimulus is presented repeatedly. The last presentation produces a much smaller response than the first. Consequently, we do not know whether the decrease in signs of alarm occurred because the stimuli looked less and less like the predator or simply because the birds became habituated to the stimuli.

Could the zoologist have carried out his experiment in a way that would have permitted him to infer a causal relation? Yes, and perhaps the solution has occurred to you already: The researcher should have presented the stimuli in different orders to different birds. Some birds would see the predator first, others would see the triangle first, and so on. Then he could have calculated the average amount of alarm that the birds showed to each of the stimuli, without contaminating the results by habituation. This type of procedure is called **counterbalancing**. To *counterbalance* means to "weigh evenly," and counterbalancing would have been accomplished if the investigator had made sure that each of the models was presented equally often (to different participant birds, of course) as the first, second, third, or fourth stimulus. The effects of habituation would thus be spread equally among all the stimuli. (See **FIGURE 2·6**.)

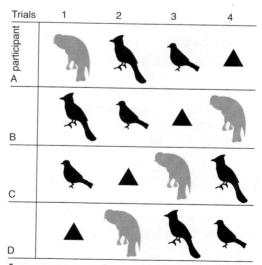

[**FIGURE 2·6**] Counterbalancing in the predator experiment. The predator experiment could be improved by changing the order of presentation of the models.

Stimuli arranged in order of similarity to predator

[**FIGURE 2·5**] A schematic representation of the flawed predator experiment.

counterbalancing Systematic variation of conditions in an experiment, such as the order of presentation of stimuli, so that different participants encounter the conditions in different orders; prevents confounding of independent variables with time-dependent processes such as habituation or fatigue.

*f*ocus O*n*

Response Bias in Different Cultures

Response bias—responding to a questionnaire in a way that is not genuine or honest but in some other irrelevant way—is an important concept in research methods because it can skew results and tell researchers something that is not very meaningful. A Dutch study of six European countries has found examples of response bias that is specific to certain cultures.

Van Herk, Poortinga, & Verhallen (2005) from The Netherlands used existing data from a multinational marketing questionnaire survey to examine response bias in participants from Greece, Italy, Spain, France, Germany, and the United Kingdom. They found that contrary to participants from northwestern European countries, those from Mediterranean countries showed an abnormally high tendency to agree with answers (acquiescence), and a greater likelihood to choose extreme response categories (e.g., selecting 1 or 5 on a five-point scale). Greek participants, in particular, significantly exhibited these response biases. Participants from Spain and Italy scored higher on these two biases than did participants from the United Kingdom, France, and Germany. The British were the least acquiescent.

The authors suggest that such differences might reflect the different types of cultures in these countries: collectivistic vs. individualistic—whether they value the skills necessary to work together or the effort of people working as individuals. The more individualistic the societies were, the less acquiescent they seemed.

Performing an Experiment

After designing a study with due regard for the dangers of confounds, we must decide how best to conduct it. We are now at step 3 of the scientific method: Perform the experiment. We must decide who will participate, what instructions to give, and what equipment and materials to use. We must ensure that the data collected will be accurate; otherwise, all effort will be in vain.

Reliability of Measurements A procedure described by an operational definition that produces consistent results under consistent conditions is said to have high **reliability.** For example, measurements of people's height and weight are extremely reliable. Measurements of their academic aptitude (by means of standard commercial tests) also are reliable, but somewhat less so.

Suppose that we operationally define detection of changed image as the time it takes before the participant blinks. Eye-blink measurements can be made reliably and accurately, but it is problematic to consider this as a valid or true measure of image detection, because there are many reasons for a participant to blink other than having detected the hidden image. Achieving reliability is usually much easier than achieving validity. Reliability is mostly a result of care and diligence on the part of researchers in the planning and execution of their studies.

Let's look at an example of a factor that can decrease the reliability of an operationally defined variable. Suppose that in our study on the effects of change detection, we select the images to be presented to each participant by randomly drawing 20 images from a large collection of digital photographs. However, some of the images were poorly scanned, so they are out of focus when projected. You can easily appreciate how this extraneous factor would affect our measurement of detection and would add to the differences we observe among the participants.

Careful researchers can identify and control most of the extraneous factors that might affect the reliability of their measurements. Conditions throughout the experiment should always be as consistent as possible. For example, the same instructions should be given to each person who participates in the experiment, all equipment should be in good working order, and all assistants hired by the researcher should be well trained in performing their tasks. Noise and other sources of distraction should be kept to a minimum.

The subjectivity of the experimenters who are taking a measurement is another factor that affects reliability. Our definition of inducing an expectation is *objective*; that is, even a non-expert could follow our procedure and obtain the same results. But researchers often attempt to study variables whose measurement is *subjective*; that is, it requires judgment and expertise. For example, suppose that a psychologist wants to count the number of friendly interactions that a child has with other children in a group. This measurement requires that someone watch the child and note each time a friendly interaction occurs. But it is difficult to be absolutely specific about what constitutes a friendly interaction and what does not. What if the child looks at another child and their gazes meet? One observer may say that the look conveyed interest in what the other child was doing and so should be scored as a friendly interaction. Another observer may disagree.

The solution in this case: First, to make the measurement as objective as possible, try to specify as precisely as possible the criteria to be used for defining an interaction as "friendly." Next, two or more people should watch the child's behavior and score it independently; that is, neither person should be aware of the other person's ratings. If the two observers' ratings agree, we can say that the scoring system has high **interrater reliability.** If they disagree, interrater reliability is low, and there is no point in continuing the study. Instead, the rating system should be refined, and the raters should be trained to apply it consistently. Any investigator who performs a study in which measuring the dependent

---

response bias   Responding to a questionnaire in a way that is not genuine or honest but in some other irrelevant way.

reliability   The repeatability of a measurement; the likelihood that if the measurement were made again, it would yield the same value.

interrater reliability   The degree to which two or more independent observers agree in their ratings of an organism's behavior.

variables requires some degree of skill and judgment must do what is necessary to produce high interrater reliability.

Selecting the Participants

Suppose a professor wants to determine which of two teaching methods works best. She teaches two courses in introductory psychology, one that meets at 8:00 A.M. and another that meets at 4:00 P.M. She considers using one teaching method for the morning class and the other for the afternoon class. She speculates that at the end of the term, the final examination scores will be higher for her morning class. If her surmise proves correct, will she be able to conclude that the morning teaching method is superior to the method used in the afternoon? No; a good researcher would understand that the method considered here would produce a significant interpretation problem. There likely would be differences between the two groups of participants other than the teaching method they experienced. People who sign up for a class that meets at 8:00 A.M. are likely, for many reasons, to differ in some ways from those who sign up for a 4:00 P.M. class. Some people prefer to get up early; others prefer to sleep late. Perhaps the school schedules athletic practices in the late afternoon, which means that athletes will not be able to enroll in the 4:00 P.M. class. Therefore, the professor would not be able to conclude that any observed differences in final examination scores were caused solely by the differences in the teaching methods. Personal characteristics of the participant groups would be confounded with the two teaching methods.

The most common way to avoid confounding participant characteristics with the manipulated values of an independent variable is **random assignment.** Random assignment means that each participant has an equal chance of being assigned to any of the conditions or groups of the experiment. Typically, random assignment is made by computer or by consulting a list of random numbers. We can expect people to have different abilities, personality traits, and other characteristics that may affect the outcome of the experiment. But if people are randomly assigned to the experimental conditions, these differences should be equally distributed across the groups. Randomly assigning students to two sections of a course meeting at the same time of day would help solve the problem faced by the professor who wants to study different teaching methods.

Even after researchers have designed an experiment and randomly assigned participants to the groups, they must remain alert to the problem of confounding participant characteristics with their independent variable manipulations. Some problems will not emerge until the investigation is actually performed. Suppose that we wish to learn whether anger decreases a person's ability to concentrate. As we'll see in the next part of this chapter, any experiment to test this would require careful consideration of the ethics of making someone angry and would be approved only

if the benefits of the results were clear. Assuming that the experiment was approved, one of the researchers might begin by acting very rudely toward the participants in the experimental group, which presumably makes them angry, but treating the participants in the control group politely. After the rude or polite treatment, the participants watch a video that shows a constantly changing display of patterns of letters. Participants are instructed to press a button whenever a particular letter appears. This vigilance test is designed to reveal how carefully participants are paying attention to the letters.

The design of this experiment seems sound. Assuming that the participants in the experimental group are really angry and that our letter identification test is a good dependent measure of concentration, we should be able to draw conclusions about the effects of anger on concentration. However, the experiment, as performed under real conditions, may not work out the way we expect. Suppose that some of our "angry" participants simply walk away. All researchers must assure participants that their participation is voluntary and that they are free to leave at any time; some angry participants may well exercise this right and withdraw from the experiment. If they do, we will now be comparing the behavior of two groups of participants that have a different mix of personal characteristics—one group composed of people who are willing to submit to the researcher's rude behavior (because the objectors have withdrawn) and another group of randomly selected people, some of whom would have left had they been subjected to the rude treatment. Now the experimental group and the control group are no longer equivalent. (See **FIGURE 2•7.**)

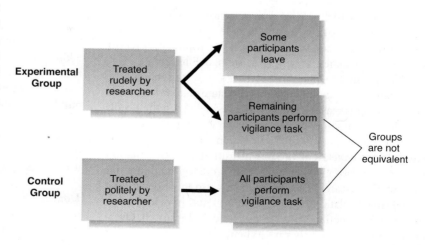

[FIGURE 2•7] A possible problem with the anger and concentration experiment: unequal loss of participants with specific characteristics from the comparison group.

random assignment Procedure in which each participant has an equally likely chance of being assigned to any of the conditions or groups of an experiment.

Expectancy Effects Research participants are not passive beings whose behavior is controlled solely by the independent variables manipulated by the researcher. This is a basic concept in the sciences: Observation can change that which you observe. This is what is known as the *Hawthorne effect.* Back in the 1930s, the managers of the Hawthorne plant of the Western Electric company wondered whether increasing the level of lighting in the plant would increase productivity. It did, but the managers found that the increase in productivity was short-lived. They went on to do some more investigating and found that productivity actually went up when they subsequently lowered the level of lighting. The commonly accepted explanation of these findings is based on the fact that the workers knew that an experiment was being conducted and that they were being monitored. That knowledge may have made them work harder regardless of whether lighting levels were increased or decreased. The workers may even have been pleased—and motivated—by the fact that management was obviously trying to improve their work environment, and may have tried to return the favor. Of course, the effect did not last indefinitely, and eventually production returned to normal. Adair (1984) provides a detailed analysis of these original studies and the methods that have evolved in field experiments to counter the Hawthorne effect.

One way to think about the Hawthorne effect is that the participants were trying to help the researchers confirm their expectation that changes in lighting would improve productivity. There is compelling evidence that this type of cooperation with researchers can occur even in very sophisticated laboratory research: If research participants figure out the researcher's hypothesis, they will sometimes behave as if the hypothesis is true, even if it is not. For example, one issue in the design of virtual reality displays is that they can sometimes make people seasick. Many designers now test their equipment for this possibility. But, if people are given a motion-sickness questionnaire before they test the display, they report more motion sickness (Young, Adelstein, & Ellis, 2007).

The possibility that a researcher's expectations can be guessed by a participant is a dangerous state of affairs for good science. For this reason, researchers routinely keep the details of their hypotheses to themselves when dealing with participants, at least until after the independent variable is manipulated and the dependent variable measured. But the situation is more troublesome when participants manage to figure out not only the researcher's hypothesis but also the independent variable manipulations on their own. You may have heard that deception is sometimes used in psychological research. Overall, deception is relatively rare. When it is used, however, the sole reason is to disguise the nature of an independent variable manipulation (and perhaps the dependent measure). If researchers mislead participants about the reason for the ex-

perimental events, the intention is to prevent the participants from acting as if the hypothesis were true when it might in fact not be. When deception is used, researchers take great pains to disclose the truth to participants at the earliest possible moment and to reestablish a trusting relationship. Interestingly, people who actually have participated in deception experiments are generally quite accepting of the rationale for the use of this technique (Sharpe, Adair, & Roese, 1992). Let's turn now to other techniques that have been developed to reduce the likelihood that research participants will become aware of the investigator's expectations.

Single-Blind Experiments. Suppose that we want to study the effects of a stimulant drug on a person's ability to perform a task that requires good motor control. We will administer the drug to one group of participants and leave another group untreated. (Of course, the experiment will have to be supervised by a physician, who will prescribe the drug.) We will count how many times each participant can thread a needle in a 10-minute period (our operational definition of fine manual dexterity). We will then see whether taking the drug had any effect on the number of needle threadings.

But there is a problem in our design. Can you see what it is? For us to conclude that a cause-and-effect relation exists, the treatment of the two groups must be identical except for the single variable that is being manipulated. In this case the mere administration of a drug may have effects on behavior, independent of its pharmacological effects. The behavior of participants who know that they have just taken a stimulant drug is very likely to be affected by this knowledge as well as by the drug circulating in their bloodstreams.

To solve this problem we would give pills to the members of both groups. People in one group would receive the stimulant; those in the other group would receive an identical-looking pill that contained no active drug—a **placebo** pill. Participants would not be told which type of pill they were taking, but they would know that they had a 50–50 chance of receiving either the stimulant or the inactive substance. By using this improved experimental procedure, called a **single-blind study,** where the participants are kept unaware of their assignment to a particular experimental group, we could infer that any observed differences in needle-threading ability of the two groups were produced solely by the pharmacological effects of the stimulant drug.

Double-Blind Experiments. Now let us look at an example in which it is important to keep both the researchers and the participants in the dark. Suppose we believe that if patients with mental disorders take a particular drug, they will be more willing to engage in conversation. This would be an important outcome, because enhanced communicativeness could facilitate their therapy. So we give the real drug to some patients and administer a placebo to others. We talk with all the patients afterwards and rate the quality of the conversation. But "quality of conversation" is a difficult dependent variable to measure, and the rating is therefore likely to be

---

placebo An ineffectual treatment used as the control substance in a single-blind or double-blind experiment.

single-blind study An experiment in which the researcher knows the value of the independent variable but participants do not.

subjective. The fact that we, the researchers, know who received the drug and who received the placebo leaves open the possibility that we may, unintentionally, give higher conversation quality ratings to those who took the drug.

The solution to this problem is simple. Just as the participants should not know whether they are receiving a drug or a placebo, neither should the researchers. That is, we should use a **double-blind study.** Either another person should administer the pills, or the researchers should be given a set of identical-looking pills in coded containers so that both researchers and participants are unaware of the nature of the contents. Now the researchers' ratings of conversation quality cannot be affected by any preconceived ideas they may have. Keep in mind that someone who has no direct contact with the participants is keeping track of who gets which pills so that the effect of the independent variable manipulation can be tested.

The double-blind procedure can be used in other experiments also. Suppose that the experiment just described attempted to evaluate the effects of a new form of psychotherapy, not a drug, on the willingness of a participant to talk. If the same person does both the psychotherapy and the rating, that person might tend to see the results in the light most favorable to his or her own expectations. In this case, then, one person should perform the psychotherapy and another person should evaluate the quality of conversation with the participants. The evaluator will not know whether a particular participant has just received the new psychotherapy or is a member of the control group that received the old standard therapy.

Performing a Correlational Study

To be sure that a cause-and-effect relation exists between variables, we must perform an experiment in which we manipulate an independent variable and measure its effects on a dependent variable. But there are some variables—especially variables intrinsic to an individual—that a psychologist cannot manipulate. For example, a person's gender, genetic history, income, social class, family environment, and personality are obviously not under the researcher's control. Because these variables cannot be manipulated, they cannot be investigated by means of an experiment. Nevertheless, such variables are important and interesting, because they often affect people's behavior. A different method must therefore be used to study them: a correlational study.

The design and conduct of a correlational study is relatively simple: For each member of a group of people we measure two or more variables as they are found to exist, and we determine whether the variables are related by using a statistical procedure called *correlation*. Correlational studies often investigate the effects of personality variables on behavior. For example, we may ask whether shyness is related to daydreaming. Our hypothesis is that shy people tend to daydream more than less shy people. We decide how to assess a person's shyness and the amount of daydreaming he or she engages in each day, and we then measure these two

variables for a random group of people. Some people will be very shy and some not shy at all. Some people will daydream a lot and others will hardly daydream at all. If we find that relatively shy people tend to daydream more (or less) than relatively less shy people, we can conclude that the variables are related.

Suppose that we do, in fact, find that shy people spend more time daydreaming. Such a finding tells us that the variables are related—we say they are *correlated*—but it does not permit us to make any conclusions about cause and effect. Shyness may have caused the daydreaming, or daydreaming may have caused the shyness, or perhaps some other variable that we did not measure caused both shyness and an increase in daydreaming. In other words, *correlations do not necessarily indicate cause-and-effect relations.* (See FIGURE 2•8.) An experiment is necessary to prove a cause-and-effect relation.

A good illustration of this principle is provided by a correlational study that attempted to determine whether membership in the Boy Scouts would affect a man's subsequent participation in community affairs (Chapin, 1938). The investigator compared a group of men who had once been Boy Scouts with a group of men who had not. He found that the men who had been Boy Scouts tended to join more community affairs groups later in life.

The investigator concluded that the experience of being a Boy Scout increased a person's tendency to join community organizations. However, this conclusion was not warranted. All we can say is that people who join the Boy Scouts in their youth tend to join community organizations later in life. It could be that people who, for one reason or another, are "joiners" tend to join the Boy Scouts when they are young and community organizations when they are older. To determine cause and effect, we would have to perform an experiment. For example, we would make some boys join the Boy Scouts and prevent others from doing so, and then see how many organizations they voluntarily joined later in life. But because we cannot interfere in people's lives in such a way, we can never be certain that being a Boy Scout increases a person's tendency to join community organizations later.

The news media often report the results of correlational studies as if they implied causal relations. For example, one newspaper routinely points out the high incomes earned by its subscribers, implying that by subscribing you can cause your own income to rise. But correlation does not prove causation. It could be that having a high income causes you to buy the newspaper (perhaps for the specific news of your profession). You might think of this logic when you receive that seductive recruiting brochure from some business school showing that its graduates earn 40% more than those of other schools.

[**FIGURE 2·8**] An example of a correlation. Correlations do not necessarily indicate cause-and-effect relations: Daydreaming could cause shyness, or shyness could cause daydreaming.

Daydreaming keeps a person from making many contacts with other people; experiences in fantasies are more successful and gratifying than those in real life.

He does not know how to respond in the company of other people.

Person has poor social skills; finds contacts with other people uncomfortable.

He turns to daydreaming because he receives no gratification from social contacts.

Can anything be done to reduce some of the uncertainty inherent in correlational studies? The answer is yes. When attempting to study the effects of a variable that cannot be altered (such as gender, age, socioeconomic status, or personality characteristics), we can use a procedure called **matching.** Rather than selecting participants randomly, we *match* the participants in each of the groups on all of the relevant variables except the one being studied. For instance, if we want to study the effects of shyness on daydreaming, we might select two groups of participants: one group composed of people who score very high on the shyness test and another group composed of people who score very low. We could then place further restrictions so that the effects of other variables are minimized. We could make sure that average age, intelligence, income, and personality characteristics (other than shyness) of people in the two groups are the same. If we find that the shy group is, on average, younger than the non-shy group, we will replace some of the people in the shy group with older shy people until the average age is the same.

If, after following this matching procedure, we find that shyness is still related to daydreaming, we can be more confident that the differences between the two variables are not caused by a third variable. The limitation of the matching procedure is that we may not know all the variables that should be held constant. If, unbeknownst to us, the two groups are not matched on an important variable, the results will be misleading. In any case, even the matching procedure does not permit us to decide which variable is the cause and which is the effect; we still do not know whether shyness causes daydreaming or daydreaming causes shyness.

The strengths and limitations of correlational studies will become evident in subsequent chapters in this book. For example, almost all studies that attempt to discover the environmental factors that influence personality character-

To study possible causes of daydreaming when we cannot manipulate variables, we could use a matching procedure.

---

matching Systematically selecting participants in groups in an experiment or (more often) a correlational study to ensure that the mean values of important participant variables of the groups are similar.

istics or the relation between these characteristics and people's behavior are correlational.

Reporting and Generalizing a Study

Scientists in all disciplines report the details of their research methods in professional publications known as *journals,* using sufficient detail that other investigators can repeat, or *replicate,* the research. The **replication** process is one of the great strengths of science; it ensures that erroneous results and incorrect conclusions are weeded out. When scientists publish a study, they know that if the findings are important enough, others will try to replicate their work to be sure that the results were not just a statistical fluke—or the result of errors in the design or execution of the original study. Statistical anomalies and incompetently conducted research usually will be uncovered through unsuccessful attempts to replicate. The insistence on replicability of research results also helps inhibit fraud in science, because the unreliability of falsified findings is likely to be discovered.

When we carry out an experiment or a correlational study, we probably assume that our participants are representative of the larger population. In fact, a representative group of participants is usually referred to as a **sample** of the larger population. For example, if we study the behavior of a group of five-year-old children, we want to make conclusions about five-year-olds in general. We want to be able to **generalize,** or extend, our specific results to the population as a whole—to conclude that the results tell us something about human nature in general, not simply about our particular participants.

Many researchers recruit their participants from introductory courses in psychology. The results of studies that use these students as participants can be best generalized to other groups of students who are similarly recruited. But in the strictest sense, the results cannot be generalized to students in other courses, to adults in general, or even to all students enrolled in introductory psychology—after all, students who volunteer to serve as participants may be different from those who do not. Even if we used truly random samples of all age groups of adults in our area, we could not generalize the results to people who live in other geographical regions. If our ability to generalize is really so limited, is it worthwhile to do psychological research?

The answer is that we are not so strictly limited. Most psychologists assume that a relation among variables that is observed in one group of humans also will be found in other groups, as long as the sample of participants is not especially unusual. For example, we may expect data obtained from prisoners to have less generality than data obtained from university students. One feature of the scientific method we have discussed before helps achieve generalizability: replication. When results are replicated with different samples of people, we gain confidence in their generalizability.

focus On

Cross-Cultural Research

Cross-cultural psychologists (see Chapter 1) are interested in studying the similarities and differences in behavior between cultures. (As an aside, *comparative psychologists,* also discussed in Chapter 1, study the similarities and differences across species.) The term *culture* traditionally referred to a group of people who live together in a common environment, who share customs and religious beliefs and practices, and who often resemble one another genetically. However, definitions of culture now vary widely. For example, "American culture" includes people of diverse ethnic and religious backgrounds, political beliefs, sexual orientation, and economic statuses, while "Fore people" includes a small, fairly homogeneous group of people living in the highlands of Papua New Guinea. Within a broadly defined culture, we can identify subcultures based on ethnicity, age, political beliefs, and other characteristics by which people define themselves. Keep in mind that "culture" is not synonymous with country or continent. Many cultures can exist within a single geographic zone.

Cross-cultural research lets psychologists test the generality of the results of a study performed with members of a particular culture. If similar studies performed with members of different cultures produce similar results, we can be more confident that we have discovered a general principle that applies broadly to members of our species. On the other hand, if the studies yield different results in different cultures, we need to carry out further research. The cross-cultural approach also lends itself to questions of immense political and economic importance. For example, think of the many issues that arise when people migrate from one culture to another (Berry, 2001).

Cultures differ with respect to two major classes of variables: biological and ecological. Biological variables include such factors as diet, genetics, and endemic diseases. Ecological variables include such factors as geography, climate, political systems, population density, religion, cultural myths, and education.

Identifying the cultural variables responsible for behavioral differences is a difficult process, for culture can be viewed as affecting behavior in different ways (Lonner & Adamopoulos, 1997). In cross-cultural research, culture is considered to be a *treatment variable*—analyzed as if it were an independent variable (Berry et al., 2002). But cultures,

---

replication Repetition of an experiment or observational study in an effort to see whether previous results will be obtained; ensures that incorrect conclusions are weeded out.

sample A selection of elements representative of a larger population—for example, a group of participants selected to participate in an experiment.

generalize To extend the results obtained from a sample to the population from which the sample was taken.

The term *culture* can refer to a large and diverse population, or to a small homogeneous group, such as the Fore people living Papua New Guinea.

like people, differ in many ways, and people are born into their cultures, not assigned to them by psychologists performing experiments. Thus, cross-cultural comparisons are subject to the same limitations we discussed when we examined correlational studies—we cannot attribute causality to a cultural factor until we have ruled these other variables out. For example, a hunting and gathering culture living in a marginal environment may show a higher level of altruism than a technological culture like ours. Does the poverty of their environment make them more attentive to each other? Or is it that the scarcity of resources brings people physically closer than in other cultures, making sharing easier to do?

Psychologists who do cross-cultural research have investigated social behaviors, personality differences, approaches to problem solving, intellectual abilities, perceptual abilities, and aesthetics. (Segall et al., 1999, provide an engaging overview.) Behind research endeavors in psychology is a guiding aim: to discover a psychological universal. According to Norenzayan & Heine (2005), psychological universals are "core mental attributes shared by humans everywhere." That is, they are conclusions from psychological research that can be generalized across groups—ways of reasoning, thinking, making decisions, interpreting why people behave in the way that they do, recognizing emotions and so on. All of these are examples of core mental attributes. A strong case for a psychological universal can be made if a phenomenon exists in a large variety of different cultures.

Cross-cultural psychologists have argued that some behaviors may be universal. They cite the recognition of basic emotions as one example. A variety of behaviors, however, is not seen, or is seen to a lesser extent, across cultures and nations. TABLE 2·1 summarizes those that have been found to vary across cultures.

One way of demonstrating a psychological universal is to examine a behavior in three or more cultures, two of which are very different, with a third falling between them. A better way, however, may be to examine a variety of cultures. This is what Daly and Wilson (1988) did,

for example, when they examined sex differences in the international rates of homicide (they found that men were more likely to kill men than women were to kill women). Debate then ensues as to why this universal should exist (and that debate is often heated, as most in psychology are). A related approach is to examine the degree to which a psychological phenomenon is present—personality type is a good example of this. The dominant approach in personality views us as differing along five major personality dimensions. Cross-cultural research has highlighted not only the universality of these five dimensions but also the differences or "variation" that exist between cultures within each dimension—some cultures may express more or less of a personality type such as extraversion or conscientiousness, for example.

[TABLE 2·1] Behaviors That Have Been Reported to Vary across Cultures, or That May Be Less Evident in Certain Cultures. (Unfamiliar terms are defined in the chapters referred to in parentheses.)

Memory for and categorization of focal colors
Spatial reasoning (see Chapter 7)
Some types of category-based inductive reasoning
Some perceptual illusions
Some ways of approaching reasoning
Aspects of numerical reasoning
Risk preferences in decision-making
Self-concept
Similarity-attraction effect
Approach-avoidance motivation
The fundamental attribution error
Predilection for aggression
Feelings of control
High subjective well-being and positive affect
Communication style
Prevalence of major depression
Prevalence of eating disorders
Mental illness
Noun bias in language learning
Moral reasoning
Prevalence of different attachment style
Disruptive behavior in adolescence
Personality types
Response bias (see Chapter 2)
Recognition of emotion

Source: Adapted from Norenzayan & Heine (2005).

QUESTIONS TO CONSIDER

1. Global warming is an obvious problem, with the key issue being the contribution of human activity to the problem. But is the evidence for this correlational or experimental? To the extent that some evidence is correlational, at what point do you think world leaders would be willing to accept correlational evidence as conclusive?

2. How might you apply the five steps of the scientific method to a question of your own—for example, the question of whether occasionally taking time out from studying for stretching and a little exercise affects your grades?

3. What is the relation between theories and hypotheses?

4. Suppose that you were interested in studying the effects of sleep deprivation on learning ability. Which of these two variables would be the independent variable and which would be the dependent variable? How might you operationally define these variables?

5. What is the difference between description and explanation in psychology?

6. In what ways might an operational definition be reliable yet not valid? Valid yet not reliable?

Ethics

The objective study of behavior means that people and animals are the focus of psychological research. Psychologists must therefore apply the methods of science while retaining the sensitivity that is necessary to study living beings. Now that we have examined the details of the scientific method, it is important to understand how psychologists maintain this balance.

Most psychological research takes place in universities or within institutions that receive support from government agencies. Consequently, researchers do not work in the isolated environment of their own laboratory or research group. They receive the advice of their peers on how to conduct their research ethically and they are accountable for their actions. This is true of research for both human and animal behavior. In this section we'll look at the principles that guide ethical research practices.

Research with Human Participants

Great care is needed in the treatment of human participants, because we can hurt people in very subtle ways. Title 42 of the United States Code requires that every institution receiving research support funds have an institutional review board (IRB) that will review the ethics of human research and ensure that researchers comply with ethical principles and guidelines. But in addition to this regulatory requirement, psychological researchers also subscribe to the Ethical Principles of Psychologists and Code of Conduct (American Psychological Association, 2002) or follow it as a matter of state legislation. As a code of conduct, these principles focus the attention of researchers on fundamental values and issues, because they and similar codes (e.g., Canadian Psychological Association, 2000) have developed from common social and cultural roots (see Adair, 2001; Hadjistavropoulos et al., 2002). Codes of research ethics make these shared values explicit.

Codes of human research ethics echo our widely accepted values about everyday interpersonal relations. In their everyday lives, most people believe that (1) it is wrong to hurt others needlessly; (2) it is good to help others; (3) it is usually wrong to make others do things contrary to their wishes and best interests; (4) it is usually wrong to lie to others; (5) we should respect others' privacy; (6) under most circumstances we should not break our promises to keep others' secrets; and (7) we should afford special protection to those who are relatively powerless or especially vulnerable to harm.

How are these interpersonal values translated to research relationships between researchers and participants? Codes of research ethics tell us that (1) we should minimize harm to participants, whether physical or mental; (2) we should maximize the benefits of research to participants in particular and society in general; (3) participants should be fully informed about the nature of the research in which they are invited to participate, including risks and benefits, and their **informed consent** to participate must be voluntary; (4) deception in research is generally unacceptable, although it may be tolerated under limited circumstances; (5) we should not intrude into the private lives of participants without their permission; (6) with certain exceptions, we should promise **confidentiality**—we should guarantee participants that information they provide will be kept anonymous or confidential unless they agree to make it public; and (7) vulnerable populations (e.g., children, prisoners, seriously ill patients, persons with compromised cognitive abilities) should be treated with special care. A university's IRB will have very strict guidelines about how these values must be translated into research procedures. For example, because children are members of a vulnerable population, a parent or guardian must also consent to participation in research.

[**CASE STUDY**] In the late 1930s, a young psychologist at the University of Iowa, Wendell Johnson, was beginning to develop a new explanation for the speech problem known as stuttering. In contrast to the prevailing theory, which held it to be a result of brain physiology, Johnson felt that stuttering originated when children were overcorrected for minor lapses of correct speech.

---

informed consent A person's agreement to participate in an experiment after he or she has received information about the nature of the research and any possible risks and benefits.

confidentiality Privacy of participants and nondisclosure of their participation in a research project.

To test this theory, Johnson and his graduate student devised a study in which children residing at a nearby orphanage were divided into different groups and given different types of feedback regarding their speech. Six children, judged to not be stutterers, were assigned to a group in which each hesitancy in speaking was pointed out to them by the experimenter over a four- to five-month period. The objective was to see if speech fluency could be adversely affected by this type of feedback (Reynolds, 2003).

Decades later, this study contrasts sharply with the research ethics we use today. The children and their caretakers (the teachers at the orphanage) were given false information to conceal the purpose of the study, and it's unclear how much the administrators knew about the intent of the project. Notice that the hypothesis envisioned that the treatment would produce speech impairments. Yet Johnson and his student apparently did not develop a preplanned debriefing or a prearranged means to ameliorate the possible harm that might ensue (Schwartz, 2006).

When contacted sixty years later and informed of the details, the people who had been subjected to this treatment reacted with dismay and outrage (Dyer, 2001). Some reported an adult life of shyness, speech deficits, and social difficulties and, when they heard the news, attributed these problems to the consequences of the study. They sued. In August, 2007, the state of Iowa agreed to pay $925,000 to three of the surviving subjects and the estates of three others for the distress the study had caused them.

It's clearly difficult to compare an ethical decision made seventy years ago to one we would make today. However, it's helpful to consider why the former participants of this study felt so betrayed. Basically, their complaints were related to many of the principles we've just discussed: They were subjected to procedures that they, at least, felt were harmful (Principle 1); they had not given informed consent (Principle 3); they were deceived (Principle 4); and they felt that their status as wards of the state had made them vulnerable (Principle 7) (Luna, 2007). Their distress underlines the need for a code of ethics that addresses these possible results of research.

Johnson's colleagues considered him a kindly, altruistic man who would not knowingly subject children to a harmful procedure (Yairi, 2006). The lesson we can take from this episode is that such good intentions are not enough. Difficulties sometimes arise when researchers try to translate everyday values to research. Research procedures that represent good science are sometimes in conflict with respect for participants' dignity. You will read about an experiment conducted by the psychologist Philip Zimbardo, in which he attempted to study the way prison guards treated inmates under their supervision. He asked participants to play the role of either a guard or a prisoner. Although this project had considerable scientific merit and important implications for real situations (such as the incidents of abuse at Abu Ghraib prison in Iraq), Zimbardo decided to stop the project in its early stage after he realized that the role of a "prisoner" resulted in increased risk to a participant's self-esteem and dignity. The interesting problem that researchers set for themselves is how to resolve these conflicts—to accomplish the best possible research while simultaneously ensuring that participants are treated properly. Sometimes researchers speak as though the values of scientific inquiry themselves are contrary to the value of respecting people. This is not the case. Effective research procedures, not the values of scientific inquiry, are sometimes in conflict with good treatment of participants. The goal is to identify and use research procedures that are both as ethical and as scientifically valid as possible.

You may have noticed that the list of research ethics values derived from interpersonal values includes exceptions to the general rules (as is the case for the interpersonal values themselves). For example, sometimes telling participants the full truth about the nature of the research will invalidate the research results (see Principle 4). In this type of situation, the researcher may decide that concealing the hypothesis from participants, or actively deceiving them about the nature of the hypothesis, would be good science.

Yet there is a conflict with the interpersonal value of not telling lies. The result of ethical decision making and ethics review by IRBs is sometimes to identify an acceptable balance. The researcher may be permitted to use concealment or minor deception, but only if there is no foreseeable harm to participants and if the researcher can re-establish trust with participants by immediately disclosing the truth to them on completion of the experiment, a process called **debriefing.**

Research with Animals

Although most psychologists study the behavior of humans, some study the behavior of other animals. Any time another species of animal is used for research purposes, the research itself should be humane and worthwhile. Humane treatment is a matter of procedure. We know how to maintain laboratory animals in good health and in comfortable, sanitary conditions. For experiments that involve surgery, we know how to administer anesthetics and analgesics so that animals do not suffer. Most industrially developed societies have very strict regulations about the care of animals and require approval of the procedures that will be used in animal experiments. American psychologists who use animals in their research adhere to ethical guidelines developed by the American Psychological Association (2007) and regulations of various federal agencies such as the National Institutes of Health and the U.S. Department of Agriculture. Under these guidelines projects involving animals, including teaching and research projects but excepting some purely observational studies, are reviewed by a committee that must include a veterinarian and a member of the public community not affiliated with the institution where the research is carried out (Public Health Service, 2002). These committee members

---

debriefing Full disclosure to research participants of the nature and purpose of a research project after its completion.

Should animals be used in psychological research? Most psychologists and other researchers strongly believe that animal research, conducted humanely, is necessary and ethically justified.

rigorously review the experimental procedures and have the authority to prevent or halt a project that does not adhere to ethical principles. The guidelines provide very specific instructions about how animals are to be housed, how they are to be fed, and how sources of stress are to be minimized.

Whether the use of animals in research is justified is a question that must be asked every time a study is proposed. One factor to consider is the nature of the controls placed on research activity as compared to the controls on some other uses of animals. For example, we know that, sadly, some pet owners cause much more suffering among animals than scientific research does. As Miller (1983) notes, pet owners are not required to receive permission from boards of experts that include veterinarians; nor are they subject to periodic inspections to ensure that their homes are clean and sanitary, that their pets have enough space to exercise properly, and that their diets are appropriate.

The core reality is that virtually all animals on this planet, especially our own species, are beset by medical, mental, and behavioral problems, many of which can be solved only through research involving nonhuman animals. Research with laboratory animals has produced important discoveries about the possible causes or potential treatments of neurological and mental disorders, including Parkinson's disease, schizophrenia, bipolar disorder, anxiety disorders, obsessive-compulsive disorders, anorexia nervosa, obesity, and drug addictions. Although much progress has been made, these problems are still with us and cause much human suffering.

But, as a result of discoveries you will read about in Chapter 3, we now have the ability to describe the inner workings of the human brain in healthy and alert people and to even produce motion pictures of the brain at work. This research has the promise of providing answers to the problems that have been mentioned, but only if we can understand the basic principles of neurology and behavior. Often, this understanding can only be gained by research that involves animals. Some people (e.g., the Alternatives Research and Development Foundation of Jenkinton, Pennsylvania)

have suggested that instead of using laboratory animals in our research, we could use tissue cultures or computer simulations. Unfortunately, tissue cultures or computer simulations are not necessarily interchangeable substitutes for living organisms. We have no way to study behavioral problems such as addictions in tissue cultures, nor can we program a computer to simulate the workings of an animal's nervous system. If we could, we would already have all the answers.

QUESTIONS TO CONSIDER

1. In your opinion, should principles of ethical research be absolute, or should they be flexible? Suppose that a researcher proposed to perform an experiment whose results could have important and beneficial consequences for society, perhaps a real reduction in violent crime. However, the proposed study would violate ethical guidelines, because it would involve deception and a significant degree of psychological pain for the participants. Should the researcher be given permission to perform the experiment? Should an exception be made because of the potential benefits to society?

2. Is there a difference between using animals for research and exploiting animals for other purposes? Why might people differ in the way they answer this?

3. Think of an experiment you would like to conduct. What ethical issues do you think would arise from it and how would you address these?

Understanding Research Results

Our study is finished. We have a collection of data—numbers representing the measurements of behavior we have made. Now what do we do? How do we know what we found? Was our hypothesis supported? To answer these questions, we must analyze the data we have collected. We will use some statistical methods to do so.

Descriptive Statistics: What Are the Results?

In the examples of experimental research that we have considered so far, the behavior of participants assigned to groups (conditions) was observed and measured. Once a study is finished, we need some way to compare these measurements. We use **descriptive statistics,** mathematical procedures that permit us to summarize sets of numbers. Using these procedures, we will calculate measures that summarize the performance of the participants in each group. Then we can compare these measures to see whether the groups of participants behaved differently (step 4 of the scientific method). We can also use these measures to describe the results of the experiment to others (step 5 of the scientific method). You are already familiar with

descriptive statistics   Mathematical procedures for organizing collections of data.

some descriptive statistics. For example, you know how to calculate the average of a set of numbers; an average is a common *measure of central tendency.* You may be less familiar with *measures of variability,* which tell us how groups of numbers differ from one another, and with measures of *relations,* which tell us how closely related two sets of numbers are.

Measures of Central Tendency

When we say that the average weight of an adult male in North America is 173 pounds or that the average salary of a female university graduate was $40,750 in 2004, we are using a **measure of central tendency,** a statistic that represents many observations. There are several different measures of central tendency, but the most common is the average, also called the **mean.** We calculate the mean of a set of observations by adding the individual values and dividing by the number of observations. The mean is the most frequently used measure of central tendency in reports of psychological experiments.

Although the mean is usually selected to measure central tendency, it is not the most precise measure, especially if a set of numbers contains a few extremely high or low values. Under these conditions, the most representative measure of central tendency is the **median,** the midpoint of values. Using the median avoids the distortion produced by exceptionally large number values.

Measures of Variability

Many experiments produce two sets of numbers, one consisting of the experimental group's scores and one consisting of the control group's scores. If the mean scores of these two groups differ, the researcher can conclude that the independent variable had an effect. However, the researcher must decide whether the difference between the two groups is large. To make this decision, the researcher calculates a **measure of variability**—a statistic that describes the degree to which scores in a set of numbers differ from one another. The psychologist then uses this measure as a basis for comparing the means of the two groups.

Two sets of numbers can have the same mean or median and still be very different in their overall character. For example, the mean and the median of both sets of numbers listed in **TABLE 2·2** are the same, but the sets of numbers are clearly different. The variability of the scores in Sample B is greater.

One way of stating the difference between the two sets of numbers in Table 2.2 is to say that the numbers in Sample A

measure of central tendency A statistical measure used to characterize the value of items in a sample of numbers.

mean A measure of central tendency; the sum of a group of values divided by their number; the arithmetical average.

median A measure of central tendency; the midpoint of a group of values arranged numerically.

measure of variability A statistic that describes the degree to which scores in a set of numbers differ from one another.

range The difference between the highest score and the lowest score of a sample.

standard deviation A statistic that expresses the variability of a measurement; square root of the average of the squared deviations from the mean.

[**TABLE 2·2**] Two Sets of Numbers Having the Same Mean and Median but Different Ranges

Sample A		Sample B	
8		0	
9		5	
10	Median	10	Median
11		15	
12		20	
Total:	50	Total:	50
Mean:	50/5 =10	Mean:	50/5 = 10
Range:	12 – 8 = 4	Range:	20 – 0 = 20

range from 8 to 12 and the numbers in Sample B range from 0 to 20. The **range** of a set of numbers is simply the largest number minus the smallest. Thus, the range of Sample A is 4 and the range of Sample B is 20.

The range is not used very often to describe the results of psychological experiments, however, because another measure of variability, the **standard deviation,** has more useful mathematical properties. As **TABLE 2·3** shows, to calculate the standard deviation of a set of numbers, you first calculate the mean

[**TABLE 2·3**] Calculation of the Variance and Standard Deviation of Two Sets of Numbers Having the Same Mean

SAMPLE A			
	Score	Difference between Score and Mean	Difference Squared
	8	10 – 8 = 2	4
	9	10 – 9 = 1	1
	10	10 – 10 = 0	0
	11	11 – 10 = 1	1
	12	12 – 10 = 2	4
Total:	50	Total:	10
Mean:	50/5 = 10	Mean (variance):	10/5 = 2
		Square root (standard deviation):	$\sqrt{2}$ = 1.41
SAMPLE B			
	Score	Difference between Score and Mean	Difference Squared
	0	10 – 0 = 10	100
	5	10 – 5 = 5	25
	10	10 – 10 = 0	0
	15	15 – 10 = 5	25
	20	20 – 10 = 10	100
Total:	50	Total:	250
Mean:	50/5 = 10	Mean (variance):	250/5 = 50
		Square root (standard deviation):	$\sqrt{50}$ = 7.07

and then find the difference between each number and the mean. These different scores are squared (that is, multiplied by themselves) and then summed. The mean calculated from this total is called the *variance*; the standard deviation is the square root of the variance. The more different the numbers are from one another, the larger the standard deviation will be.

Measurement of Relations

In correlational studies, the investigator measures the degree to which two variables are related. For example, suppose that we have developed a new aptitude test and hope to persuade a college administrator to use the test when evaluating applicants. We need to show a relation between scores on our test and measures of success (such as grades) in the college's program. Assume that the college uses a letter grading system in which A designates the top grade and F designates a failure. To analyze our test quantitatively, we need to convert these labels into numerical scores; we use the convention that an A is 4, an F is 0, and the letters in between have corresponding values.

We give the test to 10 students entering the college and later obtain their average grades. We will have two scores for each person, as shown in TABLE 2·4. We can examine the relation between these variables by plotting the scores on a graph. For example, student R. J. received a test score of 14 and earned an average grade of 3.0. We can represent this student's score as a point on the graph shown in FIGURE 2·9. The horizontal axis represents the test score, and the vertical axis represents the average grade. We put a point on the graph that corresponds to R. J.'s score on both of these measures.

We do this for each of the remaining students and then look at the graph, called a **scatterplot**, to determine whether the two variables are related. When we examine the scatterplot (refer to Figure 2.9), we see that the points tend to be located along a diagonal line that runs from the lower left to the upper right, indicating that a rather strong relation exists between students' test scores and their average grades. High scores are associated with good grades, low scores with poor grades.

Although scatterplots are useful, we need a more convenient way to communicate the results to others, so we calculate the **correlation coefficient,** a number that expresses the strength

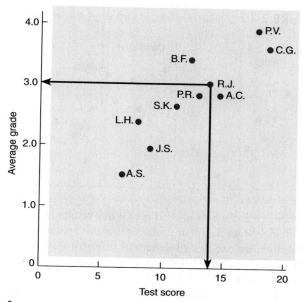

[**FIGURE 2·9**] A scatterplot of the test scores and average grades of 10 students. An example of graphing one data point (student R. J.) is shown by the colored lines.

of a relation. Calculating this statistic for the two sets of scores gives a correlation of +0.9 between the two variables.

The size of a correlation coefficient can vary from 0 (no relation) to plus or minus 1.0 (a perfect relation). A perfect relation means that if we know the value of a person's score on one measure, then we can predict exactly what his or her score will be on the other. Thus, a correlation of +0.9 is very close to perfect; our hypothetical aptitude test is an excellent predictor of how well a student will do at the college. A *positive correlation* indicates that high values on one measure are associated with high values on the other and that low values on one are associated with low values on the other.

Correlations can be negative as well as positive. A *negative correlation* indicates that high values on one measure are associated with low values on the other, and vice versa. An example of a negative correlation is the relation between people's mathematical ability and the amount of time it takes them to solve a series of math problems. People with the highest level of ability will take the least time to solve the problems. For purposes of prediction, a negative correlation is just as good as a positive one. Examples of scatterplots illustrating high and low correlations, both positive and negative, are shown in FIGURE 2·10.

Inferential Statistics: Distinguishing Chance from Significance

When we perform an experiment, we'd like to say that our results are not due to some rare fluke or chance accident. We

[**TABLE 2·4**] **Test Score and Average Grades of Ten Students**

Student	Test Score	Average Grade[a]
A. C.	15	2.8
B. F.	12	3.2
C. G.	19	3.5
L. H.	8	2.2
R. J.	14	3.0
S. K.	11	2.6
P. R.	13	2.8
A. S.	7	1.5
J. S.	9	1.9
P. V.	18	3.8

[a]0 = F; 4 = A

scatterplot   A graph of items that have two values; one value is plotted against the horizontal axis and the other against the vertical axis.

correlation coefficient   A measurement of the degree to which two variables are related.

[FIGURE 2·10] Scatterplots of variables having several different levels of correlation.

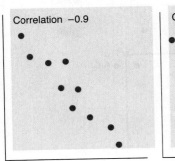

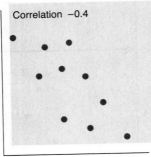

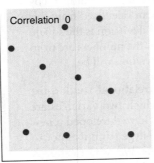

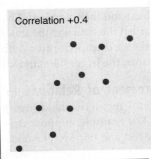

must, then, measure how likely it is that our results might be due to chance. If we find it improbable that our results are accidental, then we can describe them as possessing **statistical significance**—as being probably not due to chance. As we saw, descriptive statistics enable us to summarize our data. **Inferential statistics** enable us to calculate the probability that our results are due to chance and thereby tell us whether the results are statistically significant.

The concept of statistical significance is not easy to grasp, so I want to make sure you understand the purpose of this discussion. Recall our experiment designed to test the hypothesis that caffeine increases the rate of detection of a change in the image of a traffic scene. We give some of the participants in our experiment a measured dose of caffeine. Next, we show presentations of the original image and its changed version to participants in both groups and record how long it takes them to detect the changed image. To see whether caffeine has improved detection of the change, we calculate the mean response time for both groups. If the means are different, we can conclude that visual expectation *does* affect people's ability to recognize a change.

But how different is different? Suppose that we tested two groups of people, both treated exactly the same way. Would the mean scores of the two groups be precisely the same? Of course not. *By chance,* they would be at least slightly different. Suppose that we find that the mean score for the group that was given caffeine is lower than the mean score for the control group. How much lower would it have to be before we could rightfully conclude that the difference between the groups was significant?

Assessment of Differences between Samples

The obvious way to determine whether two group means differ significantly is to look at the size of the difference. If it is large, then we can be fairly confident that the independent variable had a significant effect. If it is small, then the difference may well

be due to chance. What we need are guidelines to help us determine when a difference is large enough to be statistically significant.

The following example, based on a real classroom demonstration and results, will explain how these guidelines are constructed. A few years ago, a simple correlational study was performed to test the following hypothesis: In North America people whose first names end in vowels will, on average, be shorter than people whose first names end in consonants. (The rationale for this hypothesis will be revealed later.)

First, each student in a psychology class received a blank card and was asked to print his or her first name on the card together with his or her height. There were 76 students in the class, and the mean height for all students was 67.2 inches. Next, the participants were divided into two groups: those whose first names ended in vowels and those whose first names ended in consonants. **TABLE 2·5** contains a listing of these two groups. You can see that the means for the two groups differed by 4.1 inches.

A difference of 4.1 inches seems large, but how can we be sure that it is not due to chance? What we really need to know is how large a difference there would be if the means had been calculated from two groups that were randomly selected. For comparison, the class was divided into two random groups by shuffling the cards with the students' names on them and dealing them out into two piles, "A" and "B." Then, the mean height of the people whose names were in each of the piles was calculated. Subtracting the "B" group mean from the "A" group showed that the difference between the means was –0.7 inch. (See **TABLE 2·6.**)

The cards were then divided into two random piles five more times, and each time the means were calculated and the "B" mean was subtracted from the "A" mean. The differences for these five random divisions ranged from −0.3 to 0.7 inch. (See **TABLE 2·7.**) It began to look as if a mean difference of 4.1 inches was bigger than would be expected to occur by chance.

Next, the cards were divided into two random piles 1000 times. (A computer performed this chore.) *Not once in 1000 times was the difference between the means greater than 3.0 inches.* The researcher concluded that if the class was divided randomly into two groups, the chance that the means of their heights would differ by 4.1 inches was much

---

statistical significance   The likelihood that an observed relation or difference between two variables really exists rather than being due to chance factors.

inferential statistics   Mathematical and logical procedures for determining whether relations or differences between samples are statistically significant.

[TABLE 2·5] Height (in Inches) of Selected Samples of Students

Name Ends in Consonant		Name Ends in Vowel
65	61	67
67	68	68
71	70	62
72	65	63
73	73	62
65	60	64
74	70	60
74	72	63
67	63	61
69	67	69
68	73	63
75	66	65
72	71	69
71	72	71
65	64	69
66	69	65
70	73	70
72	75	63
72	72	63
71	66	64
62	71	65
62	68	63
80	70	66
	75	62
Total:	3257	72
Mean:	3257/47 = 69.3	65
		66
		65
		65
		Total: 1890
		Mean: 1890/29 = 65.2
		Difference between means: 69.3 − 65.2 = 4.1

[TABLE 2·6] Height (in Inches) of Students Assigned Randomly to Two Groups

Group A		Group B	
65	71	63	62
72	63	62	63
72	74	70	65
70	72	70	75
61	71	65	71
69	65	64	80
66	71	75	71
70	67	63	68
66	72	70	71
65	66	75	73
66	72	67	62
65	73	65	72
64	63	68	65
72	69	63	72
63	62	69	66
65	60	67	73
62	70	68	65
67	68	60	73
69		61	
64		74	
Total: 2561		Total: 2586	
Mean: 67.4		Mean: 68.1	
	Difference: −0.7		

that the difference between the means fell between −0.2 and +0.2 inch.

The method used to determine the statistical significance of these findings involves the same principles that researchers use to determine whether the results observed in an experiment represent a real difference or are merely due to chance. In this example two possibilities were considered: (1) that the difference between the means was due to chance, and (2) that the difference between the means occurred because the last letter of a person's first name is related to his or her height. Because a difference of 4.1 inches would be expected less than one time in a thousand, the researcher rejected alternative 1

[TABLE 2·7] Mean Heights (in Inches) of Five Random Divisions of Students into Two Groups

Group A	Group B	Difference
67.6	67.9	−0.3
68.1	67.4	0.7
67.8	67.6	0.2
67.9	67.5	0.4
68.0	67.4	0.6

less than one time in a thousand, or 0.1%. Thus, it is safe to say that when the students were divided into two groups according to the last letters of their first names, they were being divided in a way that was somehow related to their height. The division was *not* equivalent to random selection; a person's height *really is* related to the last letter of his or her first name.

FIGURE 2·11 presents a frequency distribution of the differences between the means of the two groups for 1000 random divisions of the class. The height of a point on the graph represents the number of times (the frequency) that the difference between the means fell into that particular range. Notice that the most frequent case includes a difference of 0—according to the graph, there were 170 times

and concluded that alternative 2 was correct. The results supported the original hypothesis.

Ordinarily, psychologists who conduct experiments or correlational studies like this one do not use their computers to divide their participants' scores randomly 1000 times. Instead, they calculate the mean and standard deviation for each group and consult a table that statisticians have already prepared for them. The table is based on special mathematical properties of the mean and standard deviation, and describes what is called a *normal distribution;* the shape of a normal distribution is similar to the frequency distribution depicted in Figure 2.11. Using a normal distribution as a guide, psychologists can tell how likely it is that their results could have been obtained by chance. For example, the table would tell us how likely it is that the last letter of a person's first name is *not really* related to his or her height. If the likelihood of a chance result is low enough, psychologists will conclude that their research results are statistically significant. Most psychologists consider a 5% probability of chance to be statistically significant but are much more comfortable with 1% or less. Please note that statistical tests help us decide whether results are representative of the larger population, but not whether they are *important.* In general usage the word *significant* does mean "important," but *statistical* significance simply means that the results appear not to be caused by chance.

Oh yes, why would anyone ever guess (hypothesize) that the last letter of a person's first name would be related to his or her height? The answer is that in English, feminine names are more likely than masculine names to end in a vowel (Paula, Tara, Marie, etc.). Because women tend to be shorter than men, one could expect that among a group of English-speaking students, a group of students whose first names ended in vowels would be shorter, on average, than those whose first names ended in consonants.

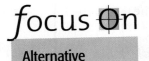

Alternative Methods

You might be asking: Are there other ways of using the scientific method? **Qualitative research** is an alternative research method that does not use numerically measured variables. Although this sounds like a classification defined by an absence, in reality qualitative researchers add a number of new dimensions to applications of the scientific method. We'll examine a few of them here.

Qualitative psychologists examine diaries, poems, people's conversations and interactions with others, and other forms of personal expression. Their research settings can be naturalistic observation, clinical case studies, structured interviews, or even cultural ceremonies in which the researcher participates. Often, the emphasis is on gaining insight into the subjective meaning of experiences and behaviors. The data used in qualitative research can be quite varied. In a study of how people remember and reason about the spatial aspects of their neighborhoods, Hart (1979) accompanied children to their favorite haunts and asked them to draw maps or build models in a sandbox of how they would get there. Studying the same general problem of spatial knowledge, Hutchins (1995) copied the organizational charts of the U.S. Navy and transcribed the dialog between different members of the bridge staff. Gladwin (1970) studied the navigational knowledge of indigenous peoples by accompanying Oceanic sailors in their canoes across the South Pacific and describing their traditional star constellations. Clearly, a single research area (spatial cognition) can be studied in quite varied (and exotic) ways. (See FIGURE 2•12.)

---

qualitative research   An alternative research strategy stressing the observation of variables that are not numerically measurable.

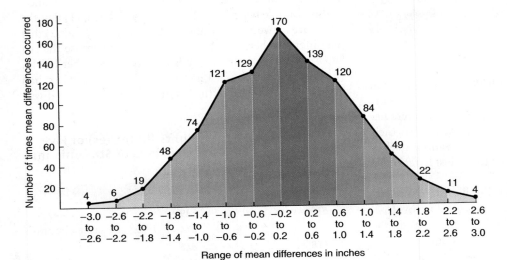

[**FIGURE 2•11**] A frequency distribution. This distribution illustrates the number of occurrences of various ranges of mean differences in height. The group of 76 people was divided randomly into two sets of numbers 1000 times.

[**FIGURE 2·12**] Some examples of qualitative data. *Upper panel:* A sketch map drawn by a nine-year-old girl of her play area, including imaginary features. From Hart, R. (1979). *Children's experience of place.* New York: Irvington. *Middle panel:* A schematic diagram of the star sightings on a typical course navigated by a Puluwat Atoll islander. From Gladwin, T. (1970). *East is a bird bird: Navigation and logic on Puluwat Atoll.* Cambridge, MA: Harvard University Press. *Lower panel:* A transcript of three bridge personnel organizing the steps of navigating a large naval ship. From Hutchins, E. (1995). *Cognition in the wild.* Cambridge, MA: MIT Press.

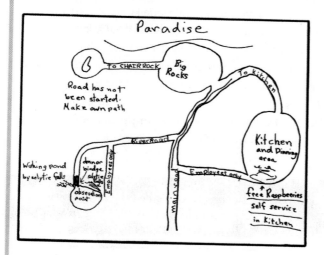

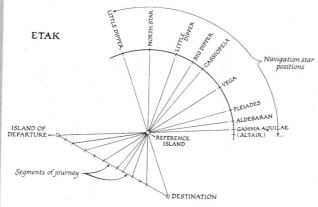

SW: John?

Recorder: Yo!

SW: Is the Dive Tower right on our beam?

Recorder: Say again?

SW: Dive Tower. Isn't it just about on our beam?

Recorder: Yeah, just about. (2 seconds) Ok, Shades?

PW: What?

Recorder: Steve's gonna be shooting the Dive Tower first, so let him say, uh, let him say the bearing first.

PW: You want Point Loma last, then?

Recorder: Yeah, that's fine.

However, you shouldn't form the impression that qualitative research is somehow exempt from the rigor that the scientific method demands. Qualitative research can, and often does, follow the five-step progression outlined earlier (although the notion of an "experiment" is usually quite different). It is also the case that qualitative data can be translated into numerical forms and analyzed with statistical techniques (Trochim, 2005). Guba and Lincoln (1981) have suggested that qualitative research results should be credible, transferable, dependable, and confirmable. *Credible* means that the data are believable from the standpoint of the participant. *Transferability* means that another person has sufficient information to generalize the results to another setting. *Dependable* means that the researcher has described all the conditions under which the results will be consistently obtained. Finally, *confirmability* means that persons other than the researcher can check the accuracy of the results. Meeting these criteria can be a considerable challenge for the qualitative researcher.

Single-subject designs are alternatives to the use of conventional statistical techniques. In a single-subject design, the researcher observes the effect of some manipulation on an individual participant or subject. The method is most often employed by behavior analysts, who are interested in the way behavior changes because of its consequences. Usually, single-subject designs employ a sequence: Behavior is measured as it occurs in some original state; this is known as the *behavioral baseline.* Then, some change is introduced, such as modifying the consequences of the behavior being observed; the researcher looks to see if the behavior has changed as well. Finally, the change is reversed in some manner, so that the baseline state is presumably reestablished. If the behavior returns to its baseline level, the researcher can be confident that a cause-and-effect relationship exists between the manipulation and the behavior.

Single-subject researchers concentrate on investigations that have one, or at most a few, participants. They believe that if the evidence of a cause-and-effect relationship in one case is strong enough, it will generalize to other cases. Furthermore, they believe that proper scientific procedures will eliminate chance factors and hence make statistical procedures superfluous. When a clinical psychologist is treating someone with a psychological problem, this is often enough: After all, the goal of therapy is to heal. A pioneer of the single-subject approach, the behaviorist B. F. Skinner, once observed: "When you have the responsibility of making absolutely sure that a given organism will engage in a given sort of behavior at a given time, you quickly grow impatient with principles, hypotheses, theorems, and statistical proof at the .05 level of significance. No one goes to the circus to see the average dog jump through a hoop significantly oftener than untrained dogs raised under the same circumstances . . ." (Skinner, 1956, p. 228).

single-subject design An alternative research strategy that examines the effects of a manipulation on an individual participant or subject.

QUESTIONS TO CONSIDER

1. Can you think of some real-life variables that you would expect to be positively and negatively correlated?
2. What does it mean to say that a study produced statistically significant results? Why might the results of a study be statistically significant but nevertheless unimportant?
3. What behaviors do you think could be studied cross-culturally and what do you predict you would find?

Epilogue

Bias and Sensitivity in Justine's Experiment

Our discussion of the ways and means of psychology gives us some insight into Justine's project described in the opening vignette. Though it cost her a sore neck and back, Justine's naturalistic observation generated her hypothesis about a possible cause. With Lawrence's help, her introduction of new chairs was a test of that hypothesis.

Justine was facing two issues common to any test of a hypothesis: Was her procedure *sensitive* and was it free of *bias*? Now that you understand the concepts of psychological research, we can explore these two issues further.

A procedure that tests a hypothesis is sensitive to the extent that it can detect whether the hypothesis is true. The fact that a hypothesis is correct could be obscured by the many chance factors that operate during an experiment. As we've seen, single-subject methods of research try to increase sensitivity by strict controls that eliminate random factors. Statistical approaches accomplish this by increasing the number of participants in a study so that random factors cancel each other out. Justine's experiment was clearly sensitive, since she was able to obtain a significant result.

Bias is a more subtle matter. Bias is the combination of factors that tend to produce positive research findings when they are not, in fact, true (Ioannidis, 2005). Irrespective of the sensitivity of a test, bias can make a non-effect look real or, in the case of reverse bias, make a real effect look false.

We have discussed several possible sources of bias. Assignment of participants to an experimental condition could be a source of bias: If Justine had given new employees the new chairs and compared their productivity to older employees, her experiment clearly would be susceptible to bias. As it was, Justine would have to be careful that the week in which she introduced the chairs didn't overlap with some other factor that could increase productivity (such as a week with a payday in it). Justine's eagerness to report a solution to her parents (akin to "publishing" an article) could also be a source of bias. The competitive nature of science similarly tends to induce a bias to prematurely publish research findings.

The lesson from Justine's story, of course, is that her very attempt to test her hypothesis was a source of bias—her own expectations and the desire of her parents' employees to match those expectations. By now, you understand this as the Hawthorne effect—a special case of expectancy effects. But there's a general point to be made here as well. Aside from naturalistic studies and some kinds of correlational research, psychological investigation is itself a form of intervention. When we, as psychologists, study behavior, we conceivably alter it. Questions of ethics have been an important part of our discussion of the ways and means of psychology. We must always consider that our procedures have consequences. Doing so makes us better psychologists and better neighbors to our fellow humans.

CHAPTER SUMMARY

The Scientific Method in Psychology

The scientific method allows us to determine the causes of phenomena. There are three basic forms of scientific research: naturalistic or clinical observations, correlational studies, and experiments. Only experiments permit us to be certain that a cause-and-effect relation exists. An experiment tests the truth of a hypothesis—a tentative statement about a relation between an independent variable and a dependent variable.

To perform an experiment, a scientist manipulates the values of the independent variable and measures changes in the dependent variable. Because a hypothesis is stated in general terms, the scientist must specify the particular operations that he or she will perform to manipulate the independent variable and to measure the dependent variable. That is, the researcher must provide operational definitions, which may require some ingenuity and hard work. Operational definitions are a necessary part of the procedure of testing a hypothesis; they also can eliminate confusion by giving concrete form to the hypothesis, making its meaning absolutely clear to other scientists.

Validity is the degree to which an operational definition succeeds in producing a particular value of an independent variable or in measuring the value of a dependent variable. Reliability has to do with the consistency and precision of an operational definition. Researchers achieve high reliability by carefully controlling the conditions of their studies and by ensuring that procedures are followed correctly.

When designing an experiment, researchers must be sure to control extraneous variables that may confound their results. Confounding of participant variables can be caused by improper assignment of participants to groups or by treatments that cause some participants to leave the experiment. Another problem involves participants' expectations. If knowledge of the experimental condition could alter the participants' behavior, one solution is to conduct the experiment with a single-blind procedure. Concealment or deception is sometimes a solution as well. If knowledge about the participants' condition might also alter the researcher's assessment of the participants' behavior, a double-blind procedure can be used.

Correlational studies involve assessing relations among variables that the researcher cannot readily manipulate. The investigator attempts to hold these variables constant by matching members in each of the groups on all relevant variables except for the one being studied. But even a well-designed correlational study cannot determine which variable is the cause and which is the effect.

Researchers are almost never interested only in the particular participants they study; they want to be able to generalize their results to a larger population. The confidence that researchers can have in their generalizations depends on both the nature of the variables being studied and the composition of the sample group of participants. Replicability also supports generalization.

Ethics

Because psychologists study living organisms, they must follow ethical principles in the treatment of these organisms. Federal law requires review by an institutional review board before any human research is undertaken in institutions receiving funding from agencies of the United States. Ethical principles for research are similar to those that guide people in their everyday lives and include minimizing harm to participants, ensuring informed consent, respecting confidentiality, and avoiding deception in most circumstances.

Research that involves the use of laboratory animals also is guided by ethical principles. It is incumbent on all scientists using these animals to see that they are housed comfortably and treated humanely, and laws have been enacted to ensure that they are. Research with animals has produced many benefits to humankind and promises to continue to do so.

Understanding Research Results

Psychologists need ways to communicate their results to others accurately and concisely. They typically employ three kinds of descriptive statistics: measures of central tendency, variability, and relations. The most common examples of these measures are the mean, the median, the standard deviation, and the correlation coefficient.

Psychologists perform experiments by observing the performance of two or more groups of participants who have been exposed to different conditions, each representing different values of the independent variable. Next, they calculate the group means and standard deviations of the values of the dependent variable that were measured. Finally, they determine the statistical significance of the results. If the probability of obtaining these results by chance is sufficiently low, the psychologists will reject the possibility that the independent variable had *no effect* and will decide in favor of the alternative—that the independent variable really did have an effect on the dependent variable.

succeed with mypsychlab

Visit MyPsychLab for practice quizzes, flashcards, and dozens of videos and animated tutorials, including the following items you can find in the "Multimedia Library":

Before Informed Consent: Robert Guthrie
Research Methods

Correlations Do Not Show Causation
Diversity in Psychological Inquiry

Distinguishing Independent and
   Dependent Variables
Doing Simple Statistics

KEY TERMS

case study *p. 31*
clinical observation *p. 29*
confidentiality *p. 43*
confounding of variables *p. 34*
control group *p. 32*
correlation coefficient *p. 47*
correlational study *p. 29*
counterbalancing *p. 35*
debriefing *p. 44*
dependent variable *p. 32*
descriptive statistics *p. 45*
double-blind study *p. 39*
experiment *p. 28*
experimental group *p. 32*
generalize *p. 41*
hypothesis *p. 30*
independent variable *p. 32*
inferential statistics *p. 48*
informed consent *p. 43*
interrater reliability *p. 36*
manipulation *p. 32*
matching *p. 40*
mean *p. 46*
measure of central tendency *p. 46*

measure of variability *p. 46*
median *p. 46*
naturalistic observation *p. 29*
nominal fallacy *p. 33*
operational definition *p. 34*
placebo *p. 38*
qualitative research *p. 50*
random assignment *p. 37*
range *p. 46*
reliability *p. 36*
replication *p. 41*
response bias *p. 36*
sample *p. 41*
scatterplot *p. 47*
scientific method *p. 28*
single-blind study *p. 38*
single-subject design *p. 51*
standard deviation *p. 46*
statistical significance *p. 48*
survey study *p. 31*
theory *p. 30*
validity *p. 34*
variable *p. 32*

SUGGESTIONS FOR FURTHER READING

Ethical Issues in Psychological Testing

Blum, D. (1994). *The monkey wars.* Oxford: Oxford University Press.

Gale, A. (1995). Ethical issues in psychological research. In A. M. Coleman (Ed.), *Psychological research methods and statistics.* London: Longman.

Wilhelm, K. (2006). Do animals have feelings? *Scientific American Mind, 17*(1), 24–29.

Blum's book is a well-written, generally well-balanced account of the use of animals (primarily primates) in science research. Gale's succinct chapter is a good introduction to ethics and psychological research. Wilhelm gives a provocative look at the question of emotions in other animals.

Research Methods: General Reading

Abelson, R. P. (1995). *Statistics as principled argument.* Hillsdale, NJ: Lawrence Erlbaum Associates.

Christensen, L. B. (2003). *Experimental methodology* (9th ed.). Boston: Allyn and Bacon.

Sternberg, R. J. (2006). *Reviewing scientific works in psychology.* Washington, D.C.: American Psychological Association.

Several standard textbooks discuss the scientific method in psychological research. The Christensen book covers ethical and practical issues as well as theoretical ones. Abelson's book explores the logic behind statistical tests. Sternberg's book is actually a manual written for researchers who review other researchers' work. It's a good look at how research reports are evaluated for publication.

Alternative Research Methods

Haworth, J. (1996). *Psychological research: Innovative methods and statistics.* London: Routledge.

Hayes, N. (1997). *Doing qualitative analysis in psychology.* Hove, UK: Psychology Press.

Haworth's text covers unusual (or "innovative") approaches to studying psychology; there is not much on quantitative analysis but a great deal on surveys and the approaches taken by sub-areas of psychology (such as the single-case study in psychology and hypnotic techniques in clinical/consciousness research). The chapters in Hayes's book, written by experts in the field, introduce qualitative psychology in a readable and sometimes critical way.

Biology of Behavior

Taken from *Psychology: The Science of Behavior*, Seventh Edition, by Neil R. Carlson, Harold Miller, C. Donald Heth, John W. Donahoe, and G. Neil Martin.

Prologue

The Left Is Gone

Miss S. was a 60-year-old woman who had a history of high blood pressure, which was not responding well to the medication she was taking. One evening she was sitting in her reclining chair reading the newspaper when the phone rang. She got out of her chair and walked to the phone. As she did, she began to feel giddy and stopped to hold on to the kitchen table. She had no memory of what happened after that.

The next morning a neighbor, who usually stopped by to have coffee with Miss S., found her lying on the floor, mumbling incoherently. The neighbor called an ambulance, which took Miss S. to a hospital.

Two days after her admission, the neurological resident in charge of her case told a group of us that she had had a stroke in the back part of the right side of the brain. He attached a CT scan to an illuminated viewer mounted on the wall and showed us a white spot caused by the accumulation of blood in a particular region of her brain. (You can look at the scan yourself; it is shown in Figure 3.15.)

We then went to see Miss S. in her hospital room. Miss S. was awake but seemed a little confused. The resident greeted her and asked how she was feeling. "Fine, I guess," she said. "I still don't know why I'm here."

"Can you see the other people in the room?"

"Why, sure."

"How many are there?"

She turned her head to the right and began counting. She stopped when she had counted the people at the foot of her bed. "Seven," she reported. "What about us?" asked a voice from the left of her bed. "What?" she said, looking at the people she had already counted. "Here, to your left. No, toward your left!" the voice repeated. Slowly, rather reluctantly, she began turning her head to the left. The voice kept insisting, and finally, she saw who was talking. "Oh," she said, "I guess there are more of you."

The resident approached the left side of her bed and touched her left arm. "What is this?" he asked. "Where?" she said. "Here," he answered, holding up her arm and moving it gently in front of her face.

"Oh, that's an arm."

"An arm? Whose arm?"

"I don't know." She paused. "I guess it must be yours."

"No, it's yours. Look, it's a part of you." He traced with his fingers from her arm to her shoulder.

"Well, if you say so," she said, sounding unconvinced.

When we returned to the residents' lounge, the chief of neurology said that we had seen a classic example of unilateral (one-sided) neglect, caused by damage to a particular part of the brain. "I've seen many cases like this," he explained. "People can still perceive sensations from the left side of their bodies, but they just don't pay attention to them. A woman will put makeup on only the right side of her face, and a man will shave only half of his beard. When these patients put on a shirt or a coat, they will use their left hand to slip it over their right arm and shoulder, but then they'll just forget about their left arm and let the garment hang from one shoulder. They also don't look at things located toward the left—or even at the left halves of things. Once I saw a man who had just finished eating breakfast. He was sitting in his bed, with a tray in front of him. There was half a pancake on his plate. 'Are you all done?' I asked. 'Sure,' he said. I turned the plate around so that the uneaten part was on his right. He gave a startled look and said, 'Where the hell did that come from?'" ■

The human brain is the most complex object that we know. As far as our species is concerned, it is the most important piece of living tissue in the world. It is also the only object capable of studying itself. Our perceptions, our thoughts, our memories, and our emotions are all products of our brains. If a surgeon transplants a heart, a liver, or a kidney—or even all three organs—we do not ask ourselves whether the identity of the recipient has been changed. But if a brain transplant were feasible (it isn't), we would undoubtedly say that the donor of the brain was getting a new body rather than the reverse.

The Brain and Its Components

The brain is the largest part of the nervous system. It contains approximately 100 billion neural cells and about as many helper cells, which take care of important support and housekeeping functions. For many decades, neuroscientists have known that the brain contains many different types of neural cells. These cells differ in shape, size, and the kinds of chemicals they produce, and they perform different functions.

To understand how the brain works, we need to understand how individual neural cells work and how they communicate with one another. Let's look first at the basic structure of the nervous system and at the nature and functions of the cells that compose it.

Basic Structure of the Nervous System

The brain has three major functions: controlling behavior, processing and retaining the information we receive from the environment, and regulating the body's physiological processes. How does it accomplish these tasks?

[TABLE 3•1] The Major Divisions of the Nervous System

Central Nervous System (CNS)	Peripheral Nervous System (PNS)
Brain	Nerves
Spinal cord	

The brain cannot act alone. It needs to receive information from the body's sense organs, and it must be connected with the muscles and glands of the body if it is to affect behavior and physiological processes. The nervous system consists of two divisions. The brain and the spinal cord make up the **central nervous system.** The **spinal cord** is a long, thin structure attached to the base of the brain and running the length of the spinal column. The central nervous system communicates with the rest of the body through the **peripheral nervous system,** which consists of **nerves**—bundles of fibers that transmit information to and from the central nervous system. Sensory information (information about what is happening in the environment or within the body) is conveyed from sensory organs to the brain and spinal cord. Information from the head and neck region (for example, from the eyes, ears, nose, and tongue) reaches the brain through the **cranial nerves.** Sensory information from the rest of the body reaches the spinal cord (and ultimately the brain) through the **spinal nerves.** The cranial nerves and spinal nerves also carry information away from the central nervous system. The brain controls muscles, glands, and internal organs by sending messages to these structures through these nerves. (See **TABLE 3•1.**)

FIGURE 3•1 shows an overview of the nervous system. The man's back has been opened, and the back part of the vertebral column has been removed so that we can see the spinal cord and the nerves attached to it. The skull has been opened, and a large opening has been cut in the meninges, the membranes that cover the central nervous system, so that we can see the surface of the brain.

The human brain consists of three major parts: the *brain stem,* the *cerebellum,* and the *cerebral hemispheres.* **FIGURE 3•2** shows a view of the left side of the brain. The lower portions of the cerebellum and brain stem extend beneath the left cerebral hemisphere; the upper portions are normally hidden.

***

central nervous system (CNS) The brain and the spinal cord.

spinal cord A long, thin collection of neural cells attached to the base of the brain and running the length of the spinal column.

peripheral nervous system (PNS) The cranial and spinal nerves; that part of the nervous system peripheral to the brain and spinal cord.

nerve A bundle of nerve fibers that transmit information between the central nervous system and the body's sense organs, muscles, and glands.

cranial nerve A bundle of nerve fibers attached to the base of the brain; conveys sensory information from the face and head and carries messages to muscles and glands.

spinal nerve A bundle of nerve fibers attached to the spinal cord; conveys sensory information from the body and carries messages to muscles and glands.

[**FIGURE 3·1**] The central nervous system (brain and spinal cord) and the peripheral nervous system (cranial nerves and spinal nerves).

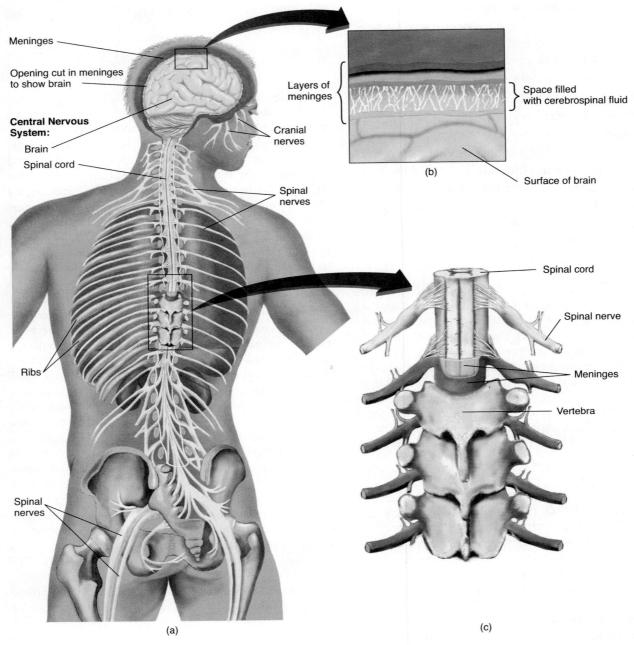

Meninges

Opening cut in meninges to show brain

Central Nervous System:

Brain

Spinal cord

Ribs

Spinal nerves

Layers of meninges

Space filled with cerebrospinal fluid

Surface of brain

(b)

Cranial nerves

Spinal nerves

Spinal cord

Spinal nerve

Meninges

Vertebra

(a)

(c)

We also see the *thalamus,* a part of the brain described later in this chapter.

If the human brain is cut away from the spinal cord and removed from the skull, it looks as if it has a handle or stem.

The **brain stem** is one of the most primitive regions of the brain, and its functions are correspondingly basic—primarily control of physiological functions and automatic behaviors. The brains of some animals, such as amphibians, consist primarily of a brain stem and a simple cerebellum.

The **cerebellum,** attached to the back of the brain stem, looks like a miniature version of the cerebral hemispheres. The primary function of the cerebellum is to control and coordinate movements; especially rapid, skilled movements. The pair of **cerebral hemispheres** (the two halves of the *cerebrum*) form the largest part of the human brain. The cerebral hemispheres

brain stem   The "stem" of the brain, including the medulla, pons, and midbrain.

cerebellum (*sair a bell um*)   A pair of hemispheres resembling the cerebral hemispheres but much smaller and lying beneath and in back of them; controls posture and movements, especially rapid ones.

cerebral hemisphere   The largest part of the brain; covered by the cerebral cortex and containing parts of the brain that evolved most recently.

[FIGURE 3•2] A view of the left side of the brain, showing its three major parts: brain stem, cerebellum, and cerebral hemisphere. The thalamus is attached to the anterior end of the brain stem.

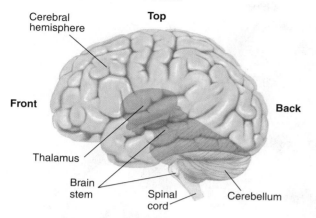

[FIGURE 3•3] A photograph of a slice of a human brain showing fissures and gyri and the layer of cerebral cortex that follows these convolutions.

(Harvard Medical School/Betty G. Martindale.)

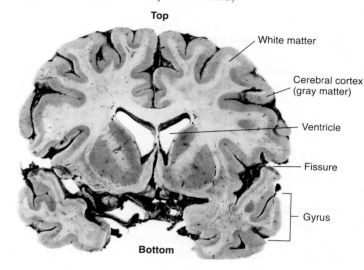

contain the parts of the brain that evolved most recently—and thus are involved in perceptions, memories, and behaviors of particular interest to psychologists. (See Figure 3.2.)

Because the central nervous system is vital to survival, it is exceptionally well protected. The brain is encased in the skull, and the spinal cord runs through the middle of the spinal column—through a stack of hollow bones known as **vertebrae.** [See Figure 3.1(c).] Both the brain and the spinal cord are enclosed by a three-layered set of membranes called the **meninges.** (*Meninges* is the plural of *meninx*, the Greek word for "membrane." You have probably heard of a disease called *meningitis*, which is an inflammation of the meninges.) The brain and spinal cord do not come into direct contact with the bones of the skull and vertebrae. Instead, they float in a clear liquid called **cerebrospinal fluid (CSF).** This fluid fills the space between two of the meninges and provides a cushion surrounding the brain and spinal cord, protecting them from being bruised by the bones that encase them. CSF is produced in the **cerebral ventricles,** hollow, fluid-filled chambers located within the brain. [See Figure 3.1(b).]

The brain is protected from chemical assault as well as physical shock. The cells of the body receive water and nutrients from the capillaries, the smallest of the blood vessels. In most of the body, the walls of the capillaries have small openings that let chemicals freely pass from the blood into the surrounding tissue. The brain is an exception: Its capillaries do not have these openings, so fewer substances can pass from the blood to the brain. This impediment to the exchange of chemicals is called the **blood–brain barrier.** Its major function is to make it less likely that toxic chemicals found in what we eat or drink can find their way into the brain, where they might do damage to neurons. Of course, many poisons can affect the brain, so this barrier is not foolproof.

The surface of the cerebral hemispheres is covered by the **cerebral cortex.** (The word *cortex* means "bark" or "rind.") The cerebral cortex consists of a thin layer of tissue approximately 3 millimeters thick. It is often referred to as **gray matter** because of its appearance. It contains billions of neural cells. (The

structure and functions of neural cells are described in the next section.) It is in the cerebral cortex that perceptions take place, memories are stored, and plans are formulated and executed. The neural cells in the cerebral cortex are connected to other parts of the brain by bundles of nerve fibers called **white matter,** so named because of the shiny white appearance of the substance that coats and insulates these fibers. **FIGURE 3•3** shows a slice of the brain. As you can see, the gray matter and white matter look distinctly different.

The human cerebral cortex is very wrinkled; it is full of bulges separated by grooves. The bulges are called *gyri* (singular: gyrus), and the large grooves are called *fissures*. Fissures and gyri expand the amount of surface area of the cortex and greatly increase the number of neural cells it can contain. Animals with the largest and most complex brains, including

---

vertebra (plural, vertebrae)   One of the bones that encases the spinal cord and constitutes the vertebral column.

meninges (*men in jees*)   The three-layered set of membranes that enclose the brain and spinal cord.

cerebrospinal fluid (CSF)   The liquid in which the brain and spinal cord float; provides a shock-absorbing cushion.

cerebral ventricle   One of the hollow spaces within the brain, filled with cerebrospinal fluid.

blood–brain barrier   A barrier between the blood and the brain produced by the cells in the walls of the brain's capillaries; prevents some substances from passing from the blood into the brain.

cerebral cortex   The outer layer of the cerebral hemispheres of the brain, approximately 3 mm thick.

gray matter   The portions of the central nervous system that are abundant in cell bodies of neurons rather than axons. The color appears gray relative to white matter.

white matter   The portions of the central nervous system that are abundant in axons rather than cell bodies of neurons. The color derives from the presence of the axons' myelin sheaths.

humans and the larger primates, have the most wrinkled brains and thus the largest cerebral cortexes.

As we saw, the peripheral nervous system consists of the cranial and spinal nerves that connect the central nervous system with sense organs, muscles, internal organs, and glands. Nerves are bundles of many thousands of individual fibers, all wrapped in a tough, protective membrane. Under a microscope, nerves look something like telephone cables, with their bundles of wires. Like the individual wires in a telephone cable, nerve fibers transmit messages through the nerve, from a sense organ to the brain or from the brain to a muscle or gland. (See **FIGURE 3•4**.)

Cells of the Nervous System

Neurons, or neural cells, are the elements of the nervous system that bring sensory information to the brain, store memories, reach decisions, and control the activity of the muscles. Neurons can receive information from other neurons (or from cells in sense organs), process this information, and communicate the processed information to other neurons (or to cells in muscles, glands, or internal organs). Thus, neurons contain structures specialized for receiving, processing, and transmitting information. These structures are shown in **FIGURE 3•5**.

Neurons are assisted in their tasks by another kind of cell: the **glia.** Glia (or *glial cells*) get their name from the Greek word for *glue*. At one time, scientists thought that glia simply

---

neuron A neural cell; consists of a cell body with dendrites and an axon whose branches end in terminal buttons that synapse with muscle fibers, gland cells, or other neurons.

glia (*glee ah*) Cells of the central nervous system that provide support for neurons and supply them with some essential chemicals.

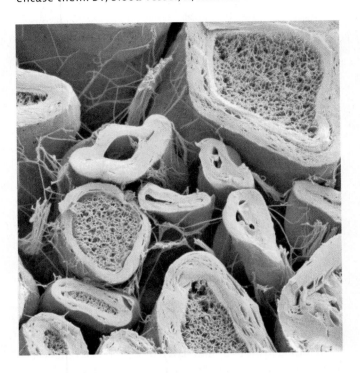

[FIGURE 3•4] A scanning-electron micrograph of the cut end of a nerve, showing bundles of nerve fibers (also known as axons) and sheaths of connective tissue that encase them. BV, blood vessel; A, individual axons.

held neurons in place. They do that, but they also do much more. During development of the brain, some types of glial cells form long fibers that guide developing neurons from their place of origin to their final resting place. Other types of glia manufacture chemicals that neurons need to perform

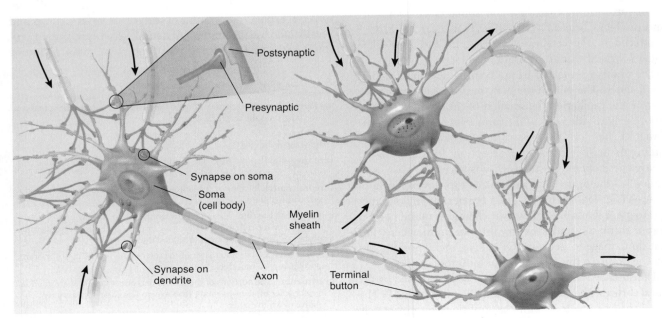

[FIGURE 3•5] The basic parts of a neuron and its connections with other neurons (synapses). The inset depicts the structure of a synapse.

their tasks and absorb chemicals that might impair neurons' functioning. Others form protective insulating sheaths around nerve fibers. Still others serve as the brain's immune system, protecting it from invading microorganisms.

Dendrites, treelike growths attached to the body of a neural cell, function principally to receive messages from other neurons. (*Dendron* means "tree.") They transmit the information they receive down their "trunks" to the cell body. The **soma,** or cell body, is the largest part of the neuron and contains the mechanisms that control the metabolism and maintenance of the cell. In most neurons, the soma also receives messages from other neurons. The nerve fiber, or **axon,** carries messages away from the soma toward the cells with which the neuron communicates. These messages, called *action potentials,* consist of brief changes in the electrical charge of the axon.

Axons end in **terminal buttons,** which are located at the ends of the "twigs" that branch off their ends. Terminal buttons secrete a chemical called a **neurotransmitter** whenever an action potential is sent down the axon (that is, whenever the axon *fires*). The neurotransmitter affects the activity of the other cells with which the neuron communicates. Thus, the message is *chemically* conveyed from one neuron to another. Most drugs that affect the nervous system and hence alter a person's behavior do so by affecting the chemical transmission of messages between cells.

Many axons, especially long ones, are insulated with a substance called *myelin.* The white matter located beneath the cerebral cortex gets its color from the **myelin sheaths** around the axons that travel through these areas. Myelin, part protein and part fat, is produced by glial cells that wrap parts of themselves around segments of the axon, leaving small bare patches of the axon between them. (Refer to Figure 3.5.) The principal function of myelin is to insulate axons from one another and thus to prevent the scrambling of messages. Myelin also increases the speed of the action potential.

To appreciate how important the myelin sheath is, consider the symptoms of a neurological disease: *multiple sclerosis* (MS). In this disorder, a person's immune system begins to attack parts of his or her central nervous system. Multiple sclerosis is so named because an autopsy of the brain and spinal cord will show numerous patches of hardened, damaged tissue. (*Skleros* is Greek for "hard.") The immune system of a person with multiple sclerosis attacks a protein in the myelin sheath of axons in the central nervous system, stripping it away. Although most of the axons survive this assault, they can no longer function normally, and so—depending on where the damage occurs—people who have multiple sclerosis experience a variety of neurological symptoms.

FIGURE 3•6 is a photograph made with a scanning electron microscope. It shows the actual appearance of a neuron and some terminal buttons that form synapses with it. The terminal buttons were broken off from their axons when the tissue was being prepared, but by comparing this photograph with Figure 3.5, you can begin to imagine some of the complexity of the nervous system.

[FIGURE 3•6] A scanning-electron micrograph of a neuron.

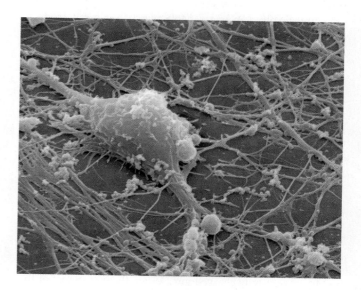

The Excitable Axon: The Action Potential

The message carried by the axon—the **action potential**—an electrical current, but it does not travel down the axon the way electricity travels through a wire. Electricity travels through a wire at hundreds of millions of feet per second. As you learned in Chapter 1, Hermann von Helmholtz discovered that the axon transmits information at a much slower rate—about 90 feet per second.

The membrane of an axon is electrically charged. When the axon is resting (that is, when no action potential is occurring), the inside is charged at −70 millivolts (thousandths of a volt) with respect to the outside. An action potential is an abrupt, short-lived reversal in the electrical charge of an axon. This temporary reversal begins at the end of the axon that attaches to the soma and is transmitted to the end that divides into small branches capped with terminal buttons. For convenience, an action potential is usually referred to as the *firing* of an axon.

The electrical charge of an axon at rest—the **resting potential**—occurs because of an unequal distribution of

---

dendrite A treelike part of a neuron on which other neurons form synapses.

soma A cell body; the largest part of a neuron

axon A long, thin part of a neuron attached to the soma; divides into a few or many branches, ending in terminal buttons.

terminal button The rounded swelling at the end of the axon of a neuron; releases a neurotransmitter.

neurotransmitter A chemical released by the terminal buttons that causes the postsynaptic neuron to be excited or inhibited.

myelin sheath The insulating material that encases most large axons.

action potential A brief electrochemical event that is carried by an axon from the soma of the neuron to its terminal buttons; causes the release of a neurotransmitter.

resting potential The membrane potential of a neuron when it is not producing an action potential.

positively and negatively charged particles inside the axon and in the fluid that surrounds it. These particles, called **ions,** are produced when various substances—including ordinary table salt—are dissolved in water. Molecules of table salt (sodium chloride) break down into positively charged sodium ions (Na^+) and negatively charged chloride ions (Cl^-). (In case you were wondering, sodium is abbreviated as Na because its original Latin name was *natrium.*) Normally, ions cannot penetrate the membrane that surrounds all cells. However, the membrane of axons contains special submicroscopic proteins that serve as **ion channels** or **ion transporters.** Ion channels can open or close; when they are open, a particular ion can enter or leave the axon. As we will see, the membrane of the axon contains two types of ion channels: sodium channels and potassium channels. Ion transporters work like pumps. They use the energy resources of the cell to transport particular ions into or out of the axon. (See **FIGURE 3·7.**)

When the axon is resting, the outside of the membrane is positively charged, and the inside is negatively charged, because the fluid inside the axon contains more negatively charged ions and fewer positively charged ions. When the membrane of the axon is resting, its ion channels are closed, so ions cannot move in or out of the axon. An action potential is caused when the end of the axon attached to the soma becomes excited, which opens sodium ion channels located there (you will learn about excitation later). The opening of these ion channels permits positively charged sodium ions (Na^+) to enter; this reverses the membrane potential at that location. This reversal causes nearby ion channels to open, which produces another reversal at *that* point. The process continues all the way to the terminal buttons at the ends of the branches at the other end of the axon.

Note that an action potential is a *brief* reversal of the membrane's electrical charge. As soon as the charge reverses, the sodium ion channels close, and potassium ion channels open for a short time, letting positively charged potassium ions (K^+) flow out of the axon. This outflow of positive ions restores the normal electrical charge. Thus, an action potential resembles the "wave" that sports fans often make in a stadium during a game. People in one part of the stadium stand up, raise their arms over their heads, and sit down again. People seated next to them see that a wave is starting, so they do the same—and the wave travels around the stadium. Everyone remains at the same place, but

---

ion   A positively or negatively charged particle; produced when many substances dissolve in water.

ion channel   A special protein molecule located in the membrane of a cell; controls the entry or exit of particular ions.

ion transporter   A special protein molecule located in the membrane of a cell; actively transports ions into or out of the cell.

all-or-none law   The principle that once an action potential is triggered in an axon, it is propagated, without becoming smaller, to the end of the axon.

sensory neuron   A neuron that detects changes in the external or internal environment and sends information about these changes to the central nervous system.

motor neuron   A neuron whose terminal buttons form synapses with muscle fibers. When an action potential travels down its axon, the associated muscle fibers will twitch.

[**FIGURE 3·7**] Ion channels and ion transporters. These structures regulate the numbers of ions found inside and outside the axon. An unequal distribution of positively and negatively charged ions is responsible for the axon's electrical charge.

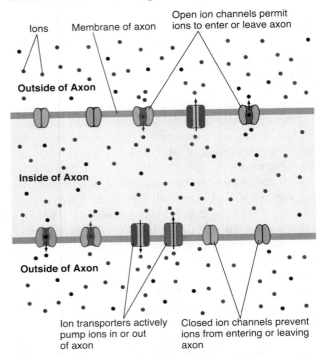

the effect is that of something circling in the stands around the playing field. Similarly, electricity does not really travel down the length of an axon. Instead, the entry of positive ions in one location reverses the charge at that point and causes ion channels in the adjacent region to open, and so on. (See **FIGURE 3·8.**)

You may be wondering what happens to the sodium ions that enter the axon and the potassium ions that leave it. This is where the ion transporters come in. As diagrammed in Figure 3.8, after an action potential has moved along the axon, the ion transporters pump sodium ions out of the axon and pump potassium ions back in, restoring the normal balance.

An action potential is an all-or-none event—either it happens or it does not. Action potentials in a given axon are all the same size; there are no large or small action potentials. This fact has been stated as the **all-or-none law.** But if action potentials cannot vary in size, how can axons convey quantitative information? For example, how can **sensory neurons**—neurons that receive information from sensory organs such as the eyes—tell other neurons in the brain about the strength of a stimulus? And how can **motor neurons**—neurons whose axons form synapses with a muscle—tell the muscle how forcefully to contract? The answer is simple: A single action potential is not the basic element of information; rather, quantitative information is represented by an axon's rate of firing. Strong stimuli (such as bright lights) trigger a high rate of firing in axons of sensory neurons that receive visual information. Similarly, a high rate of firing in the axons of motor neurons causes strong muscular contractions.

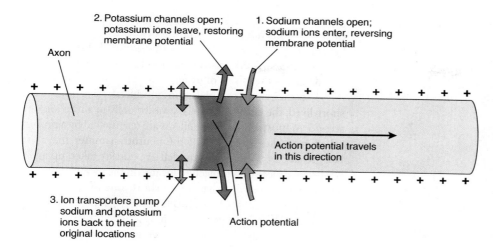

2. Potassium channels open; potassium ions leave, restoring membrane potential

1. Sodium channels open; sodium ions enter, reversing membrane potential

Axon

Action potential travels in this direction

3. Ion transporters pump sodium and potassium ions back to their original locations

Action potential

[FIGURE 3·8] Movement of sodium and potassium ions during the action potential. Sodium ions (Na⁺) are represented by red arrows; potassium ions (K⁺), by green arrows.

Communication with Other Cells: Synapses

Neurons communicate with other cells through **synapses,** by means of a process known as *synaptic transmission.* A synapse is the junction of a terminal button of one neuron and the membrane of another cell—another neuron or a cell in a muscle, a gland, or an internal organ. Let us first consider synapses between one neuron and another. The terminal button belongs to the **presynaptic neuron**—the neuron "before the synapse" that sends the message. As we saw, when terminal buttons become active, they release a chemical called a neurotransmitter. The neuron that receives the message (that detects the neurotransmitter) is called the **postsynaptic neuron**—the neuron "after the synapse." (Refer to detail, Figure 3.5.) A neuron receives messages from many terminal buttons, and in turn, its terminal buttons form synapses with many other neurons. The drawing in Figure 3.5 is much simplified; thousands of terminal buttons can form synapses with a single neuron.

Two major types of synapses exist: *excitatory synapses* and *inhibitory synapses.* Excitatory synapses do just what their name implies—when the axon fires, the terminal buttons release a neurotransmitter that excites the postsynaptic neurons with which they form synapses. The effect of this excitation is to increase the rate of firing of the axons of the postsynaptic neurons. Inhibitory synapses do just the opposite—when they are activated, they lower the rate at which these axons fire.

The rate at which a particular axon fires is determined by the activity of all the synapses on the dendrites and soma of the cell. If the excitatory synapses are more active, the axon will fire at a high rate. If the inhibitory synapses are more active, it will fire at a low rate or perhaps not at all. (See FIGURE 3·9.)

How do molecules of a neurotransmitter exert their excitatory or inhibitory effect on the postsynaptic neuron? Terminal buttons contain large numbers of **synaptic vesicles**—little bubbles of membrane that are filled with molecules of the neurotransmitter. (*Vesicle* is Latin for "little bladder.") When an action potential reaches a terminal button, it causes

several of the vesicles to fuse with the inside of the presynaptic membrane, burst open, and spill their contents into the **synaptic cleft,** the fluid-filled space between the terminal button and the membrane of the postsynaptic neuron. (Note that the terminal button and the presynaptic membrane do not touch each other.) The molecules of the neurotransmitter then cause reactions in the postsynaptic neuron that either excite or inhibit it. These reactions are triggered by special submicroscopic protein molecules embedded in the postsynaptic membrane called **neurotransmitter receptors.** (See FIGURE 3·10.)

A molecule of a neurotransmitter binds with its receptor in the same way that a particular key fits in a particular lock. After their release from a terminal button, molecules of a neurotransmitter diffuse across the synaptic cleft, bind with the receptors, and activate them. Once they are activated, the receptors produce excitatory or inhibitory effects on the postsynaptic neuron. They do so by opening ion channels. Most ion channels found at excitatory synapses permit sodium ions to enter the postsynaptic membrane; most of those found at inhibitory synapses permit potassium ions to leave. [See FIGURE 3·10(a).]

As mentioned earlier, multiple sclerosis is caused by an autoimmune disorder that attacks a protein in the myelin

---

synapse The junction between the terminal button of one neuron and the membrane of a muscle fiber, a gland, or another neuron.

presynaptic neuron A neuron whose terminal buttons form synapses with and excite or inhibit another neuron.

postsynaptic neuron A neuron with which the terminal buttons of another neuron form synapses and that is excited or inhibited by that neuron.

synaptic vesicle (*vess i kul*) A small, hollow, beadlike structure found in terminal buttons; contains molecules of a neurotransmitter.

synaptic cleft A fluid-filled gap between the presynaptic and postsynaptic membranes; the terminal button releases a neurotransmitter into this space.

neurotransmitter receptor A special protein molecule located in the membrane of the postsynaptic neuron that responds to molecules of the neurotransmitter.

[FIGURE 3•9] Interaction between the effects of excitatory and inhibitory synapses. Excitatory and inhibitory effects combine to determine the rate of firing of the neuron.

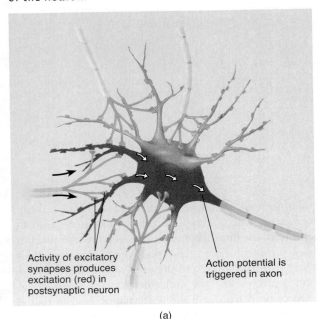

Activity of excitatory synapses produces excitation (red) in postsynaptic neuron

Action potential is triggered in axon

(a)

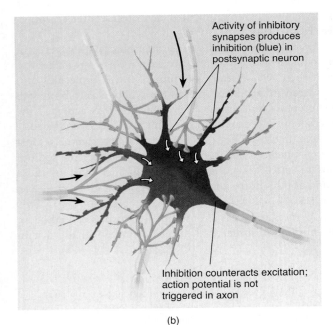

Activity of inhibitory synapses produces inhibition (blue) in postsynaptic neuron

Inhibition counteracts excitation; action potential is not triggered in axon

(b)

sheaths of axons in the central nervous system. Another autoimmune disorder attacks a different protein—the neurotransmitter receptor that is found in the membrane of muscle fibers. Almost as fast as new receptors are produced, the immune system destroys them. The result of this attack is pro-

gressive *myasthenia gravis,* or "grave muscle weakness." Myasthenia gravis is not a very common disorder, but most experts believe that many mild cases go undiagnosed. We will have more to say about this disorder later in this chapter, in a section that describes the effects of drugs on synaptic transmission.

The excitation or inhibition produced by a synapse is short-lived; the effects soon pass away, usually in a fraction of a second. At most synapses, the effects are terminated by a process called **reuptake.** Molecules of the neurotransmitter that have been released into the synaptic cleft are quickly taken up again by special transporter molecules located in the terminal button, so the neurotransmitter has only a short time to stimulate the postsynaptic receptors. [See **FIGURE 3•10(b).**] The rate at which the terminal button takes back the neurotransmitter determines how prolonged the effects of the chemical on the postsynaptic neuron will be. The faster the neurotransmitter is taken back, the shorter its effects will be on the postsynaptic neuron.

QUESTIONS TO CONSIDER

1. The brain is the seat of our perceptions, thoughts, memories, and feelings. Why, then, do we so often refer to our hearts as the location of our feelings and emotions? For example, why do you think we say, "He acted with his heart, not with his head"?
2. The blood–brain barrier keeps many chemicals in the blood out of the brain. In a few places in the brain, this barrier does not exist, including the part of the brain stem that contains the neural circuits that trigger vomiting. Can you think of an explanation for the lack of a blood–brain barrier in this region?

Drugs and Behavior

Long ago, people discovered that the sap, fruit, leaves, bark, or roots of various plants could alter their perceptions and behavior, could be used to relieve pain or treat diseases, or could be used as poisons to kill animals for food. They also discovered that some substances affected people's moods in ways that they wanted to experience again and again.

Why do plants produce chemicals that have specific effects on the cells of our nervous system? They do so because the chemicals are toxic to animals—primarily insects—that eat them. Of course, some chemicals produced by plants have beneficial effects in humans and have consequently been extracted or synthesized in the laboratory for use as therapeutic drugs. The therapeutic use of drugs is of obvious benefit to society, and the abuse of addictive drugs is responsible for much misery and unhappiness. But drugs are also important tools to help scientists discover how the brain works. For example, we know that certain drugs relieve anxiety, and others reduce the symptoms of schizophrenia. Discovering how these drugs affect the brain can help our understanding of the causes of these disorders and can provide information we need to develop even better forms of treatments.

---

reuptake The process by which a terminal button retrieves the molecules of a neurotransmitter that it has just released; terminates the effect of the neurotransmitter on the receptors of the postsynaptic neuron.

[FIGURE 3•10] The release and reuptake of a neurotransmitter from a terminal button. The drawing depicts the inset portion of Figure 3.5. The arrival of an action potential at the terminal button causes several synaptic vesicles to fuse with the membrane and spill their cargo of neurotransmitter molecules into the synaptic cleft. (a) Details of the attachment of a molecule of the neurotransmitter to a postsynaptic receptor. An ion channel opens, permitting the movement of ions through the membrane that either excites or inhibits the postsynaptic neuron. For purposes of clarity, the drawing is schematic; molecules of neurotransmitter are actually much larger than individual ions. (b) Details of reuptake. Neurotransmitter transporters pump molecules of the neurotransmitter from the synaptic cleft back into the terminal button, thus ending the excitatory or inhibitory effects.

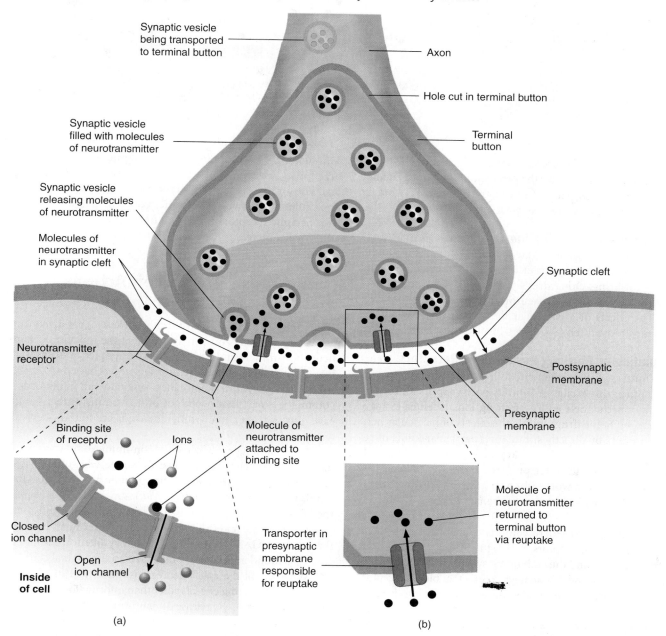

Effects of Drugs on Synaptic Transmission

Drugs that affect our thoughts, perceptions, emotions, and behavior do so by affecting the activity of neurons in the brain. As we saw, communication between neurons involves the release of neurotransmitters, which bind with receptors and either excite or inhibit the activity of the postsynaptic cell. Drugs can affect this process in many ways. They can stimulate or inhibit the release of neurotransmitters, mimic the effects of neurotransmitters on postsynaptic receptors, block these effects, or interfere with the reuptake of a neurotransmitter once it is released.

[FIGURE 3•11] A summary of the ways in which drugs can affect the synaptic transmission.

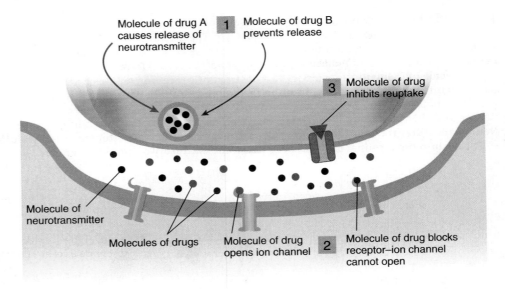

Through these mechanisms (and others too complicated to describe here), a drug can alter the perceptions, thoughts, and behaviors controlled by particular neurotransmitters. Let's briefly examine some of these mechanisms.

Stimulating or Inhibiting the Release of Neurotransmitters

Some drugs stimulate certain terminal buttons to release their neurotransmitter continuously, even when the axon is not firing. Other drugs prevent certain terminal buttons from releasing their neurotransmitter when the axon fires. The effects of a particular drug are usually specific to one neurotransmitter. (See step 1 in FIGURE 3•11.)

Stimulating or Blocking Postsynaptic Receptors

Neurotransmitters produce their effects by stimulating postsynaptic receptors; this excites or inhibits postsynaptic neurons by opening ion channels and permitting ions to enter or leave the neurons. Some drugs mimic the effects of particular neurotransmitters by directly stimulating particular kinds of receptors. If we use the lock-and-key analogy to describe the effects of a neurotransmitter on a receptor, then a drug that stimulates receptors works like a master key, turning the receptors on even when the neurotransmitter is not present. (See step 2 in Figure 3.11.)

Some drugs bind with receptors and do not stimulate them. This action blocks receptors, making them inaccessible to the neurotransmitter and thus inhibiting synaptic transmission. To continue the lock-and-key analogy, a drug that blocks receptors plugs up the lock so that the key will no longer fit into it.

Inhibiting Reuptake

As we saw, the effects of most neurotransmitters are kept brief by the process of reuptake. Molecules of the neurotransmitter are released by a terminal button,

stimulate the receptors in the postsynaptic membrane for a fraction of a second, and are then taken back into the terminal button. Some drugs inhibit the process of reuptake so that molecules of the neurotransmitter continue to stimulate the postsynaptic receptors for a long time. Therefore, inhibition of reuptake increases the effect of the neurotransmitter. (See step 3 in Figure 3.11.)

Neurotransmitters, Their Actions, and Drugs That Affect Them

Now that we've seen the most important ways that drugs can affect synaptic transmission, let's look at the most important neurotransmitters and consider some examples of drugs that interact with them. Because neurotransmitters have two general effects on postsynaptic membranes—excitatory or inhibitory—you might expect that two kinds of neurotransmitters would exist, but in reality, many different kinds are found—several dozen, at least.

In the brain, most synaptic communication is accomplished by two neurotransmitters: **glutamate**, which has excitatory effects, and **GABA**, which has inhibitory effects. (GABA stands for *gamma-amino butyric acid*.) Almost every neuron in the brain receives excitatory input from terminal buttons that secrete glutamate and inhibitory input from terminal buttons that secrete GABA. (Another inhibitory neurotransmitter, *glycine*, is found in the lower brain stem and the spinal cord.)

What do all the other neurotransmitters do? In general, they have modulating effects rather than information-transmitting effects. That is, the release of neurotransmitters other than glutamate and GABA tends to activate or inhibit entire circuits of neurons that are involved in particular brain functions. These effects include facilitation of learning, control of wakefulness and vigilance, suppression of impulsive behaviors, and suppression or enhancement of anxiety. Thus, because particular drugs can selectively affect neurons that secrete particular neurotransmitters, these drugs can have specific effects on behavior.

---

glutamate The most important excitatory neurotransmitter in the brain and spinal cord.

GABA The most important inhibitory neurotransmitter in the brain.

Given the importance of glutamate and GABA, let's look at these two neurotransmitters first.

Glutamate

As previously mentioned, glutamate is the most important excitatory neurotransmitter in the brain. It is also the major excitatory neurotransmitter in the spinal cord. With the exception of neurons that detect painful stimuli, all sensory organs transmit information to the brain through axons whose terminals release glutamate.

One type of glutamate receptor (the *NMDA receptor*) plays a critical role in the effects of environmental stimulation on the developing brain and is also responsible for many of the changes in synaptic connections that are responsible for learning. This receptor is partially deactivated by alcohol, which accounts for the fact that binge drinkers often have no memory of what happened while they were drunk.

GABA

Some drugs depress behavior, causing relaxation, sedation, or even loss of consciousness. Most of these drugs act on a particular type of GABA receptor (the $GABA_A$ receptor), increasing its sensitivity to the neurotransmitter. **Barbiturates** act this way. In low doses, barbiturates have a calming effect. In progressively higher doses, they produce difficulty in walking and talking, unconsciousness, coma, and death. A dose of a barbiturate sufficient to cause relaxation is not much lower than a fatal dose; thus, these drugs do not have much of a safety factor. Physicians rarely prescribe barbiturates.

By far the most commonly used depressant drug is ethyl alcohol, the active ingredient in alcoholic beverages. This drug also acts on the $GABA_A$ receptor. The effects of alcohol and barbiturates are additive: A moderate dose of alcohol plus a moderate dose of barbiturates can be fatal.

Many **antianxiety drugs** are members of a family known as the **benzodiazepines,** which include the well-known tranquilizer Valium (diazepam). These drugs, too, act on $GABA_A$ receptors on neurons in various parts of the brain, including a region that is involved in fear and anxiety. Benzodiazepines are much safer than barbiturates—a lethal dose is more than a hundred times higher than a therapeutic dose. They are sometimes used to treat people who are afflicted by periodic attacks of severe anxiety. In addition, some benzodiazepines serve as sleep medications.

Acetylcholine

Acetylcholine (ACh) is the primary neurotransmitter secreted by the axons of motor neurons, and it is also released by several groups of neurons in the brain. Because all muscular movement is accomplished by the release of acetylcholine, you will not be surprised to learn that the immune systems of people with myasthenia gravis (described in the previous section) attack acetylcholine receptors.

The axons and terminal buttons of acetylcholinergic neurons are distributed widely throughout the brain. Three systems have received the most attention from neuroscientists. One system activates the brain mechanisms responsible for rapid eye movement (REM) sleep—the phase of sleep during which most dreaming occurs. Another system is involved in activating neurons in the cerebral cortex and facilitating learning, especially

The venom of the black widow spider causes the release of acetylcholine, which can cause numbness, muscle pain and cramps, sweating, salivation, and difficulty breathing. Fortunately, a single bite is very rarely fatal for a healthy adult.

perceptual learning. A third system controls the functions of another part of the brain involved in learning: the hippocampus. (You will see this structure later in this chapter.)

Two drugs, botulinum toxin and the venom of the black widow spider, affect the release of acetylcholine. **Botulinum toxin,** produced by a bacterium that can grow in improperly canned food, prevents the release of ACh. The drug is an extremely potent poison. Very dilute solutions (they had better be!) of this drug, usually referred to as botox, can be injected into people's facial muscles to stop muscular contractions that are causing wrinkles. **Black widow spider venom** has the opposite effect: It stimulates the release of ACh. Although the effects of black widow spider venom can also be fatal to infants or frail, elderly people, the venom is much less toxic than botulinum toxin. The following case describes the effects of the botulinum toxin in humans.

[CASE STUDY] One day, just before dinner, Mr. F. opened a jar of asparagus that his family had canned. He noted right away that it smelled funny. Because his family had grown the asparagus in their own garden, he was reluctant to throw it away. However, he decided that he wouldn't take any chances. He dipped a spoon into the liquid in the jar and touched it to his tongue. It didn't taste right, so he didn't swallow it. Instead, he stuck his tongue out and rinsed it

---

barbiturate A drug that causes sedation; one of several derivatives of barbituric acid.

antianxiety drug A "tranquilizer," which reduces anxiety.

benzodiazepine (*ben zoe dy* **azz** *a peen*) A class of drug having anxiolytic ("tranquilizing") effects, such as diazepam (Valium).

acetylcholine (ACh) (*a see tul* **koh** *leen*) A neurotransmitter found in the brain, spinal cord, and parts of the peripheral nervous system; responsible for muscular contraction.

botulinum toxin (*bot you* **lin** *um*) A drug that prevents the release of acetylcholine by terminal buttons.

black widow spider venom A drug that stimulates the release of acetylcholine by terminal buttons.

under a stream of water from the faucet at the kitchen sink. He dumped the asparagus into the garbage disposal.

About an hour later, as the family was finishing dinner, Mr. F. discovered that he was seeing double. Alarmed, he asked his wife to drive him to the hospital. When he arrived at the emergency room, he was seen by one of the neurological residents, who asked him, "Mr. F., you haven't eaten some home-canned foods recently, have you?"

Learning that he had indeed let some liquid from a suspect jar of asparagus touch his tongue, the resident ordered a vial of botulinum antitoxin from the pharmacy. Meanwhile, he took a blood sample from Mr. F.'s vein and sent it to the lab for some testing in mice. He then administered the antitoxin, but already he could see that it was too late: Mr. F. was showing obvious signs of muscular weakness and was having difficulty breathing. He was immediately sent to the intensive care unit, where he was put on a respirator. Although he became completely paralyzed, the life-support system did what its name indicates, and eventually his acetylcholinergic terminal buttons repaired themselves, and he regained control of his muscles. (By the way, the first symptom of his poisoning was double vision because the delicate balance among the muscles that move the eyes is upset by any interference with acetylcholinergic transmission.)

The results of the testing procedure for the presence of botulinum toxin in Mr. F.'s blood were fascinating. Plasma extracted from the blood was injected into several mice, half of which had been pretreated with botulinum antitoxin. The pretreated mice survived; the others all died. Just think: Mr. F. had touched a few drops of the contaminated liquid on his tongue and then rinsed it off immediately, but enough of the toxin entered his bloodstream so that a small amount of his blood plasma could kill a mouse.

Although the effects of most neurotransmitters on the postsynaptic membrane are terminated by reuptake, acetylcholine is an exception. After being released by the terminal button, ACh is deactivated by an enzyme that is present in the postsynaptic membrane. This enzyme, AChE (acetylcholinesterase), can be inactivated by various drugs. One of them, **neostigmine,** can help people with myasthenia gravis. The drug lets the patients regain some strength, because the acetylcholine that is released in their muscles has a more prolonged effect on the few acetylcholine receptors that remain. (Fortunately, neostigmine cannot cross the blood–brain barrier, so it does not affect the AChE found in the central nervous system.)

The best-known drug that affects acetylcholine receptors is **nicotine,** found in the leaves of the tobacco plant, *Nicotiniana tabacum.* Nicotine is a highly addictive drug; as evidence, consider the fact that after undergoing surgery for lung cancer, approximately 50 percent of patients continue to smoke (Hyman & Malenka, 2001). The addictive nature of nicotine indicates that acetylcholine plays a role in the reinforcement (reward) mechanisms of the brain.

Another drug, **curare,** blocks acetylcholine receptors. Because these are the receptors on muscles, curare, like botulinum toxin, causes paralysis. However, the effects of curare are much faster. The drug is extracted from several species of plants found in South America, where it was discovered long ago by people who used it to coat the tips of arrows and darts. Within minutes of being struck by one of these points, an animal collapses, ceases breathing, and dies. Nowadays, curare (or any of various drugs with the same site of action) is used to paralyze patients who are to undergo surgery so that their muscles will relax completely and not contract when they are cut with a scalpel. An anesthetic also must be used, because a person who receives only curare will remain perfectly conscious and sensitive to pain, even though paralyzed. And, of course, a respirator must supply air to the lungs during the procedure.

Monoamines Dopamine, norepinephrine, and serotonin are three chemicals that belong to a family of compounds called **monoamines.** Because the molecular structures of these substances are similar, some drugs affect the activity of all of them to some degree. The monoamines are produced by several systems of neurons in the brain. Most of these systems consist of a relatively small number of cell bodies located in the brain stem, whose axons branch repeatedly and give rise to an enormous number of terminal buttons distributed throughout many regions of the brain. Monoaminergic neurons thus serve to modulate the function of widespread regions of the brain, increasing or decreasing the activities of particular brain functions.

This native of Peru is inserting a curare-tipped dart into his blowgun. Curare kills animals by blocking acetylcholine receptors, which paralyzes muscles and causes suffocation.

---

neostigmine (*nee o stig meen*)   A drug that enhances the effects of acetylcholine by blocking the enzyme that destroys it.

nicotine   A drug that binds with and stimulates acetylcholine receptors, mimicking the effects of this neurotransmitter.

curare (*kew rahr ee*)   A drug that binds with and blocks acetylcholine receptors, preventing the neurotransmitter to exert its effects.

monoamine (*mahn o a meen*)   A category of neurotransmitters that includes dopamine, norepinephrine, and serotonin.

Dopamine (DA) has been implicated in several important functions, including movement, attention, learning, and the reinforcing effects of drugs that people tend to abuse. A progressive degenerative disease that destroys one set of DA neurons causes **Parkinson's disease,** a movement disorder characterized by tremors, rigidity of the limbs, poor balance, and difficulty in initiating movements. People with Parkinson's disease are given a drug called L-DOPA. Once this chemical reaches the brain, it is taken up by the DA neurons that still survive and is converted to dopamine. As a result, these neurons release more dopamine, which alleviates the patients' symptoms.

Dopamine has also been implicated as a neurotransmitter that might be involved in schizophrenia, a serious mental disorder, whose symptoms include hallucinations, delusions, and disruption of normal, logical thought processes. Drugs such as Thorazine (chlorpromazine) and Clozaril (clozapine) relieve the symptoms of this disorder, apparently by blocking particular types of dopamine receptors.

Several drugs inhibit the reuptake of dopamine, thus serving to prolong and strengthen its effects. The best known of these drugs are amphetamine and cocaine. The fact that people abuse these drugs indicates that dopamine plays an important role in reinforcement. (Nicotine exerts its reinforcing effect by indirectly increasing the activity of terminal buttons that release dopamine.)

Almost every region of the brain receives input from neurons that secrete the second monoamine, **norepinephrine (NE).** Release of NE (also known as *noradrenaline*) appears to cause an increase in vigilance—attentiveness to events in the environment.

The third monoamine neurotransmitter, **serotonin,** has complex behavioral effects. Serotonin plays a role in the regulation of mood; in the control of eating, sleep, and arousal; and in the regulation of pain. A deficiency in the release of serotonin in the cerebral cortex is associated with alcoholism and antisocial behavior. Like NE neurons, serotonin-secreting neurons are involved in the control of REM sleep. Drugs such as Prozac (fluoxetine), which inhibit the reuptake of serotonin and thus strengthen and prolong its effects, are used to treat depression, anxiety disorder, and obsessive–compulsive disorder. A drug that causes the release of serotonin (fenfluramine) was used as an appetite suppressant in the 1990s, but adverse side effects took this drug off the market.

Several hallucinogenic drugs appear to produce their effects by interacting with serotonergic transmission. For example, **LSD** (lysergic acid diethylamide) produces distortions of visual perceptions that some people find awesome and fascinating but that simply frighten other people. This drug, which is effective in extremely small doses, stimulates one category of serotonin receptor.

Peptides As we saw earlier, terminal buttons excite or inhibit postsynaptic neurons by releasing neurotransmitters. These chemicals travel a very short distance and affect receptors located on a small patch of the postsynaptic membrane. Some neurons release chemicals that get into the general circulation of the brain and stimulate receptors on many thousands of neurons, some located a considerable distance away. These chemicals are called **neuromodulators,** because they modulate the activity of the neurons they affect. We can think of neuromodulators as the brain's own drugs. As these chemicals diffuse through the brain, they can activate or inhibit circuits of neurons that control a variety of functions; thus, they can modulate particular categories of behavior.

Most neuromodulators are peptides. (The most important exception to this rule is described in the next subsection.) **Peptides** are molecules that consist of two or more amino acids attached together by special chemical links called peptide bonds. One of the best-known families of peptides is the **endogenous opioids.** Endogenous means "produced from within"; *opioid* means "like opium." Several years ago, it became clear that opiates—drugs such as opium, morphine, and heroin—reduce pain because they have direct effects on the brain. (Please note that the term *opioid* refers to endogenous chemicals, and *opiate* refers to drugs.) The endogenous opioids stimulate special opioid receptors located on neurons in several parts of the brain. Their behavioral effects include decreased sensitivity to pain and a tendency to persist in ongoing behavior. Opioids are released while an animal is engaging in important species-typical behaviors, such as mating or fighting. The behavioral effects of opioids ensure that a mating animal or an animal fighting to defend itself is less likely to be deterred by pain; thus, conception is more likely to occur, and a defense is more likely to be successful.

People abuse opiates not because opiates reduce pain, but because they cause the release of dopamine in the brain, which has a reinforcing effect on behavior. It is this reinforcing effect that normally encourages an animal performing a useful and important behavior to continue in that behavior. Unfortunately, the reinforcing effect is not specific to useful and important behaviors and can lead to addiction.

---

dopamine (DA) A monoamine neurotransmitter involved in control of brain mechanisms of movement and reinforcement.

Parkinson's disease A neurological disorder characterized by tremors, rigidity of the limbs, poor balance, and difficulty in initiating movements; caused by degeneration of a system of dopamine-secreting neurons.

norepinephrine (NE) (*nor epp i neff rin*) A monoamine neurotransmitter involved in alertness and vigilance and control of REM sleep.

serotonin (*sair a toe nin*) A monoamine neurotransmitter involved in the regulation of mood; in the control of eating, sleep, and arousal; and in the regulation of pain.

LSD Lysergic acid diethylamide; a hallucinogenic drug that blocks a category of serotonin receptors.

neuromodulator A substance secreted in the brain that modulates the activity of neurons that contain the appropriate receptors.

peptide A category of neurotransmitters and neuromodulators that consist of two or more amino acids, linked by peptide bonds.

endogenous opioid (*ope ee oyd*) A neuromodulator whose action is mimicked by a natural or synthetic opiate, such as opium, morphine, or heroin.

To help drug addicts, pharmacologists have developed drugs that block opioid receptors. One of them, **naloxone,** is used clinically to reverse opiate intoxication. This drug has saved the lives of many drug abusers brought to the emergency room in heroin-induced comas. An injection of naloxone blocks the effects of the heroin, and the person quickly revives.

Various peptide neuromodulators other than the opioids play important roles in behaviors important to survival, such as control of eating and metabolism, drinking, mineral balance, mating, parental care, and social bonding. Some reduce anxiety; others increase it. Some promote eating; others curb the appetite.

Cannabinoids You have undoubtedly heard of Cannabis sativa, the plant that produces hemp and marijuana. You probably also know that the plant produces a resin that has physiological effects on the brain. The principal active ingredient in this resin is THC (tetrahydrocannibinol), which affects perception and behavior by activating receptors located on neurons in the brain. THC mimics the effects of **endogenous cannabinoids**—chemicals produced and released by neurons in the brain.

THC produces analgesia and sedation, stimulates appetite, reduces nausea caused by drugs used to treat cancer, relieves asthma attacks, decreases pressure within the eyes in patients with glaucoma, and reduces the symptoms of certain motor disorders. Conversely, THC interferes with concentration and memory, alters visual and auditory perception, and distorts perception of the passage of time (Iversen, 2003). Devane and colleagues (1992) discovered the first—and most important—endogenous cannabinoid, a lipid-like (fatlike) substance, which they named **anandamide,** from the Sanskrit word *ananda,* or "bliss."

Cannabinoid receptors are found on terminal buttons of neurons that secrete glutamate, GABA, acetylcholine, dopamine, norepinephrine, and serotonin. (That is, almost all of the neurotransmitters mentioned in this chapter.) Thus, the secretion of anandamide—or the smoking of marijuana—alters the release of these neurotransmitters, and this has widespread effects in the brain. Recent research indicates that the endogenous cannabinoids modulate the synaptic changes that appear to be responsible for learning, which accounts for the fact that THC disrupts short-term memory (Fegley et al., 2004).

The effects of the endogenous cannabinoids, produced and released in the brain, are mimicked by THC, the active ingredient of Cannabis sativa, the marijuana plant.

TABLE 3·2 lists the neurotransmitters discussed in this section, summarizes their effects, and lists some drugs that interact with them.

QUESTIONS TO CONSIDER

1. As we saw, opioids are useful neuromodulators because they encourage an animal to continue fighting or mating. Can you think of other behaviors that might be influenced by neuromodulators? Can you think of mental or behavioral problems that might be caused if too much or too little of these neuromodulators were secreted?

2. Suppose that a woman is taking a drug for anxiety. Suppose further that she is planning to go out for drinks with friends. Her husband advises her to enjoy an evening with her friends but not to have any drinks. Why is this a good suggestion?

3. If you were in charge of the research department of a pharmaceutical company, what new behaviorally active drugs would you seek? Analgesics? Antianxiety drugs? Antiaggression drugs? Memory-improving drugs? Should behaviorally active drugs be taken only by people who clearly have afflictions such as schizophrenia, depression, or obsessive–compulsive disorder? Or should we try to find drugs that help people who want to improve their intellectual performance or social adjustment or simply to feel happier?

---

naloxone (*na lox own*) A drug that binds with and blocks opioid receptors, preventing opiate drugs or endogenous opioids from exerting their effects.

endogenous cannabinoid (*can ob in oid*) A neuromodulator whose action is mimicked by THC and other drugs present in marijuana.

anandamide (*a nan da mide*) The most important endogenous cannabinoid.

[TABLE 3·2] The Major Neurotransmitters, Their Primary Effects, and Drugs That Interact with Them

Neurotransmitter	Primary Effects	Drugs That Interact with Neurotransmitter	Effects of Drugs
Glutamate	Primary excitatory neurotransmitter in brain	Alcohol	Desensitization of NMDA receptor
GABA	Primary inhibitory neurotransmitter in brain	Barbiturates Benzodiazepines ("tranquilizers") Alcohol	Desensitization of GABAA receptor
Acetylcholine (ACh)	Excites muscular contraction, activates cerebral cortex, controls REM sleep, controls hippocampus	Botulinum toxin Black widow spider venom Neostigmine Nicotine	Blocks release of ACh Stimulates release of ACh Blocks AChE, enhances effects of ACh Stimulates ACh receptors
Monoamines			
Dopamine (DA)	Facilitates movement, attention, learning, reinforcement	L-DOPA Amphetamine, cocaine Antipsychotic drugs	Increase synthesis of dopamine Inhibit reuptake of dopamine Block dopamine receptors
Norepinephrine (NE)	Increases vigilance, controls REM sleep		
Serotonin	Regulates mood, controls eating, sleep, arousal, regulation of pain, suppresses risky behaviors	Fluoxetine (Prozac) LSD	Inhibits reuptake of serotonin Stimulates certain serotonin receptors
Endogenous opioids	Reduce pain, reinforce ongoing behavior	Opiates (heroin, morphine, etc.) Naloxone	Stimulate opioid receptors Block opioid receptors
Anandamide	Analgesia, nausea reduction, decreased pressure in eyes, interference with short-term memory	THC	Stimulates cannabinoid receptors

Study of the Brain

Recent advances in science and technology have given us the means to study—and perhaps some day understand—the brain. We now have at our disposal a range of research methods that would have been impossible to imagine just a few decades ago. We have ways to identify neurons that contain particular chemicals. We have ways to use special microscopes to observe particular ions entering living neurons when the appropriate ion channels open. We have ways to inactivate individual genes or to insert new genes into laboratory animals to see what happens to the animals' physiology and behavior. We have ways to view details of the structure of a living human brain and to study the activity of various brain regions while the person is performing various perceptual or behavioral tasks. Just listing and briefly describing these methods would take up an entire chapter. This section describes only the most important research methods, which will introduce you to the research performed by physiological psychologists.

Experimental Ablation

The earliest research method of physiological psychology involved the study of brain damage. As Chapter 1 described, Pierre Flourens developed the method of experimental ablation in studies with laboratory animals, and Paul Broca applied this method when he studied a man whose brain damage had destroyed his language abilities.

To study the effect of experimental brain disruption on animal behavior, the investigator produces a **brain lesion,** an injury to a particular part of the brain, and then studies the effects of the lesion on the animal's behavior. Of course, researchers do not deliberately damage the brains of humans to study their functions. Instead, like Paul Broca, we study the behavior of people whose brains have been damaged by a stroke, by disease, or by head injury. If particular behaviors are disrupted, we can conclude that the damaged part of the brain must somehow be involved in those behaviors.

brain lesion   Damage to a particular region of the brain.

To produce a brain lesion in laboratory animals, the researcher must follow the ethical rules described in Chapter 2. The researcher first anaesthetizes an animal, prepares it for surgery, and drills a hole in its skull. In most cases, the region under investigation is located deep within the brain. To reach this region, the investigator uses a special device called a **stereotaxic apparatus** to insert a fine wire (called an electrode) or a thin metal tube (called a cannula) into a particular location in the brain. The term "stereotaxic" refers to the ability to manipulate an object in three-dimensional space. (See FIGURE 3•12.)

Once the correct region is located, its function can be altered. Experimenters can produce *electrolytic lesions* by passing an electrical current through the electrode, which produces heat that destroys a small portion of the brain around the tip of the electrode. Alternatively, they may establish *excitotoxic lesions* by injecting a chemical through the cannula that overstimulates neurons in the region around the tip of the cannula, which kills the neurons. After a few days, the animal recovers from the operation, and the researcher can assess its behavior. Later, the investigator can remove the animal's brain from the skull, slice it, and examine it under a microscope to determine the true extent of the lesion. (See FIGURE 3•13.)

Obviously, researchers studying the behavior of a person with brain damage cannot remove the brain and examine it

---

stereotaxic apparatus A device used to insert an electrode into a particular part of the brain for the purpose of recording electrical activity, stimulating the brain electrically, or producing localized damage.

CT scanner A device that uses a special x-ray machine and a computer to produce images of the brain that appear as slices taken parallel to the top of the skull.

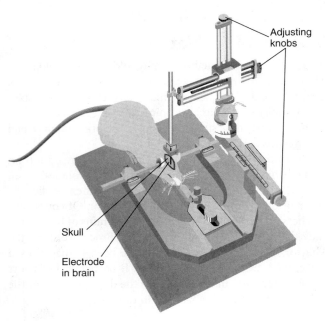

[**FIGURE 3•12**] A stereotaxic apparatus, used to insert a wire or a cannula into a specific portion of an animal's brain.

[**FIGURE 3•13**] A brain lesion made with the aid of a stereotaxic apparatus. The photograph shows a thin slice of a mouse brain, stained with a dye that shows the location of cell bodies.

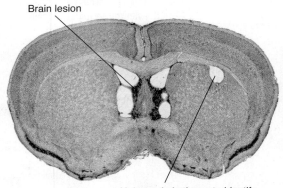

Brain lesion

Hole made in tissue to identify left and right sides of brain

(unless the person happens to die and the family consents to an autopsy for this purpose). This means that researchers seldom have the opportunity to examine the brains of patients they have studied. Fortunately, the development of brain scanners permits us to determine the location and extent of damage to a living brain.

Visualizing the Structure of the Brain

Brain-scanning techniques were originally developed to permit physicians to determine the causes of patients' neurological symptoms by locating regions of brain damage, visualizing brain tumors, or revealing abnormalities in brain structure caused by faulty development. Once researchers gained the ability to see the three-dimensional structure of the brain, they could correlate brain damage or abnormalities in brain development with the observations they had made of the behavior and abilities of patients they had studied.

The first machine to reveal the three-dimensional structure of the brain was the **CT scanner** (see FIGURE 3•14). (CT stands for *computed tomography*. *Tomos*, meaning "cut," describes the CT scanner's ability to produce a picture that looks like a slice of the brain. The device is often called a CAT *scanner*—the A is for *axial*—but the neurologists we've talked with use the term "CT." They probably think that CAT sounds a little too cute.) The scanner sends a narrow beam of x-rays through a person's head. The beam is moved around the head, and a computer calculates the amount of radiation that passes through it at various points along each angle. The result is a two-dimensional image of a "slice" of the person's head, parallel to the top of the skull.

FIGURE 3•15 shows three CT scans of the brain of a patient with an injury—Miss S., whose case is described in this chapter's Prologue. The scans are arranged from the bottom of the brain (scan 1) to the top (scan 3). You can easily see the damaged area, a white spot, in the lower left corner of scan 2.

[**FIGURE 3•14**] A patient whose brain is being scanned by a computed tomography (CT) scanner.

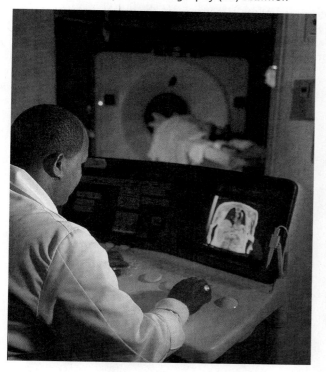

[**FIGURE 3•16**] An MRI scan of a human brain.

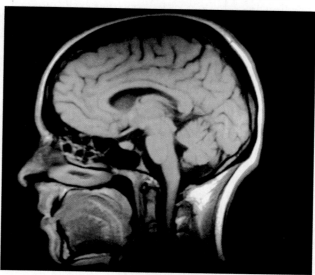

produce images of the brain with higher resolution than those produced by CT scanners (see **FIGURE 3•16**). However, CT scanners are still in use because they are less expensive and do not contain magnets; the magnetism exerted by an MRI scanner can interact with objects such as pacemakers or metal clips that have been placed in a patient's body.

Measuring the Brain's Activity

Because the brain's physiology involves both electrical and chemical processes, measuring techniques have been developed for each. **Microelectrodes** are extremely thin wires able to detect the electrical currents of individual neurons. With suitable amplification, microelectrodes can be used to measure the minute electrical changes of individual action potentials. Arrays of dozens of ultrathin wires can even enable a researcher to record simultaneously the activity of dozens of neurons. Other electrical recording techniques involve larger electrodes placed outside the skull. These electrodes can measure the electrical activity of large groups of neurons. For example, the **electroencephalogram (EEG)** is a recording of the brain's activity, recorded through metal disks and traced on a long sheet of paper or stored in a computer. (See **FIGURE 3•17**.) The EEG can be used to diagnose seizure disorders (epilepsy) and to monitor the various stages of sleep (described in Chapter 8).

In another method, known as **magnetoencephalography (MEG)**, a recording device detects the minute magnetic fields

A more recent brain-imaging technique is known as **magnetic resonance imaging (MRI)**. MRI scans are produced by placing a person's head within a strong magnetic field. This field causes the molecules within its influence to become oriented with the lines of magnetic force. A radio signal is then generated around the person, which has the effect of tilting these aligned atoms, just as you might nudge a spinning top and cause it to wobble. The scanner measures the time it takes the molecules to stop wobbling and recover to their aligned state. Because different molecules take different times to recover, an image can be constructed that distinguishes between different materials within the head, such as gray matter, white matter, and cerebrospinal fluid. MRI scanners can

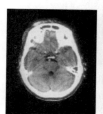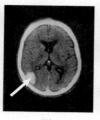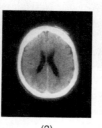

(1)   (2)   (3)

[**FIGURE 3•15**] CT scans from a patient with a brain lesion caused by a damaged area (the white spot in the lower left corner of scan 2). Because left and right are traditionally reversed on CT scans, the damaged area is actually in the right hemisphere.

(Courtesy of Dr. J. McA. Jones, Good Samaritan Hospital, Portland, Oregon. Photos provided by Neil Carlson.)

magnetic resonance imaging (MRI) A technique with a device that uses the interaction between radio waves and a strong magnetic field to produce images of slices of the interior of the body.

microelectrode A thin electrode made of wire or glass that can measure the electrical activity of a single neuron.

electroencephalogram (EEG) An electrical brain potential recorded by placing electrodes on the scalp.

magnetoencephalography (MEG) A method of brain study that measures the changes in magnetic fields that accompany action potentials in the cerebral cortex.

[FIGURE 3•17] A record from an EEG machine. The pens trace changes in the electrical activity of the brain, recorded by electrodes placed on a person's scalp.

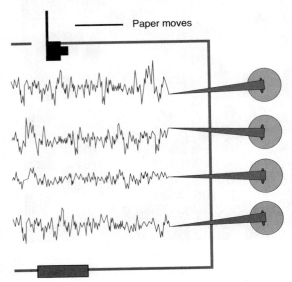

[FIGURE 3•18] Magnetoencephalography. The apparatus measures magnetic fields produced by the electrical activity of neurons on the cerebral cortex. A region of increased activity is shown in the inset in the lower right, superimposed on an image of the brain derived from an MRI scan.

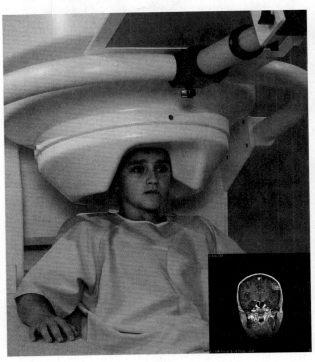

that are produced by the electrical activity of neurons in the cerebral cortex. These devices can be used clinically—for example, to find brain abnormalities that produce seizures so that they can be removed surgically. MEG can also be used in experiments to measure regional brain activity that accompanies the performance of various behaviors or cognitive tasks. (See FIGURE 3•18.)

The activity of specific brain regions can be measured by two special scanning methods: *PET scanning* and *functional MRI scanning*. **Positron emission tomography (PET)** takes advantage of the fact that when radioactive molecules decay, they emit subatomic particles called positrons. The first step in PET is to give a person an injection of a radioactive chemical that accumulates in the brain. (The chemical eventually breaks down and leaves the cells. The dose given to humans is harmless.) The person's head is placed in the PET scanner, which detects the positrons. The computer determines which regions of the brain have taken up the radioactive chemical, and it produces a picture of a slice of the brain, showing which regions contain the highest concentrations of the chemical. Researchers can use a wide variety of chemicals. For example, they can use a chemical that accumulates in metabolically active cells, in which case. the PET scan reveals the brain regions that are most active. They can also use chemicals that bind with particular receptors (for example, serotonin receptors) and determine which brain regions contain these receptors.

FIGURE 3•19 shows yet another use of PET. The scans were taken before and after dopamine-secreting neurons were surgically implanted into the brain of a person with Parkinson's disease. The scan shows an increase in the amount of dopamine in a region of the brain that controls movements, revealed by the presence of a radioactive chemical that becomes incorporated into molecules of dopamine.

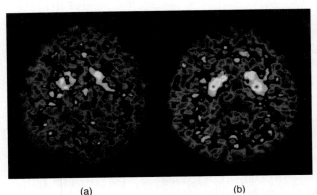

(a)   (b)

[FIGURE 3•19] PET scans of a patient with Parkinson's disease showing accumulation of radioactive l-DOPA in a brain region involved in movement that receives input from terminal buttons that secrete dopamine. (a) Preoperative scan. (b) Scan taken 13 months after receiving a transplant of dopamine-secreting cells. The increased uptake of l-DOPA indicates that the transplant was secreting dopamine.

(Adapted from Widner, H., et al. (1992). Bilateral fetal mesencephalic grafting in two patients with parkinsonism induced by 1-methyl-4-phenyl-1,2,3,6-tetrahydropyridine (MPTP). *New England Journal of Medicine, 327,* 1556–1563. Scans reprinted with permission.)

---

positron emission tomography (PET)   The use of a device that reveals the localization of a radioactive tracer in a living brain.

[FIGURE 3·20] Functional MRI scans of human brains. Localized increases in neural activity of males (left) and females (right) while they were judging whether pairs of written words rhymed.

(From Shaywitz, B. A., et al. (1995). Sex differences in the functional organization of the brain for language. *Nature, 373,* 607–609. By permission.)

Anterior

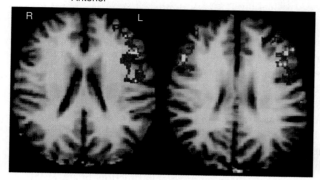

Posterior

The most recent development in brain imaging is **functional MRI (fMRI).** Biomedical engineers have devised modifications to existing MRI scanners that measure the rate of metabolism in regions of the brain by detecting levels of oxygen in the brain's blood vessels. Functional MRI scans have a higher resolution than PET scans, they can be acquired much more rapidly, and they do not require the production of radioactive chemicals with very short half-lives, which is expensive. Thus, *f*MRI has become the preferred method of measuring the activity of the human brain. (See **FIGURE 3·20.**)

Stimulating the Brain's Activity

So far, this section has discussed studying the brain by observing the effects of damage to parts of it, visualizing the brain's structure, and measuring the brain's activity. Another research method artificially activates neurons in particular parts of the brain to see what effects this stimulation has on behavior. For example, weak electrical stimulation of one part of a laboratory animal's brain, just sufficient to trigger action potentials in axons in that region, has a reinforcing (rewarding) effect on the animal's behavior. If the animal has the opportunity to press a lever that delivers a brief pulse of electricity through electrodes that have been surgically implanted in its brain, it will do so—up to thousands of times an hour. (See **FIGURE 3·21.**) The implication is that the brain has a system of neurons involved in reinforcement; this hypothesis is confirmed by recording studies in both humans and laboratory animals, which indicate that the neurons activated by this stimulation also are activated by events that reinforce behavior, such as the administration of food, water, or addictive drugs. One fMRI study of heterosexual male college students even found that the sight of a photograph of a beautiful woman activates this region (Aharon et al., 2001).

As we saw in the previous subsection, neural activity induces magnetic fields that can be detected by means of magnetoencephalography. Similarly, magnetic fields can be used to stimulate neurons by inducing electrical currents in brain tissue. **Transcranial magnetic stimulation (TMS)** uses a coil of wires, usually arranged in the shape of the numeral 8, to stimulate neurons in the human cerebral cortex. The stimulating coil is placed on top of the skull so that the crossing point in the middle of the 8 is located immediately above the region to be stimulated. Pulses of electricity send magnetic fields that activate neurons in the cortex. Because the processing of information in the cerebral cortex involves intricate patterns of activity in particular circuits of neurons, the stimulation disrupts normal activity in that region of the brain. For example, stimulation of a particular region of the cerebral cortex will disrupt a person's ability to detect movements in visual stimuli. These findings confirm the results of recording and lesion studies with laboratory animals and studies of people with brain damage, which indicate that this region is involved in perception of visual

functional MRI (fMRI) A modification of the MRI procedure that permits the measurement of regional metabolism in the brain.

transcranial magnetic stimulation (TMS) Direct stimulation of the cerebral cortex induced by magnetic fields generated outside the skull.

[FIGURE 3·21] An example of an electrical stimulation experiment. When the rat presses the switch, it receives a brief pulse of electricity to its brain through electrodes.

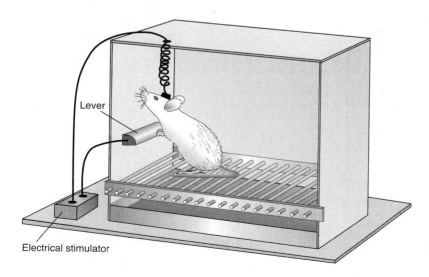

Lever

Electrical stimulator

[**FIGURE 3·22**] Transcranial magnetic stimulation. The coil applies electromagnetic stimulation to the brain, which interferes with the region of the cerebral cortex below the crossing point of the figure 8 of the coil.

(Photo by George Ruhe/*The New York Times*.)

movement. In addition, TMS has been used to treat the symptoms of mental disorders such as depression.

FIGURE 3·22 shows an electromagnetic coil used in transcranial magnetic stimulation and its placement on a person's head.

Altering Genetics

Neuroscientists can now manipulate genetic mechanisms that control the development of the nervous system. For example, a **targeted mutation** (a genetic "knockout") can be produced in mice. This procedure inactivates a gene—for example, the gene responsible for producing a particular neurotransmitter or a particular receptor. The effects of the knockout on the animals' behavior suggest what the normal role of the neurotransmitter might be. For example, a targeted mutation that prevents production of a particular peptide causes a hereditary sleep disorder known as narcolepsy, which, we now know, is caused by degeneration of the neurons that secrete this peptide (Chemelli et al., 1999).

Researchers also can insert genes into animals' DNA, which can alter the development of the brain or the functioning of particular types of neurons after the animals are born. For example, Tang and colleagues (1999) found that a genetic modification that increased the production of a particular type of receptor increased the animals' learning ability in a particular task. Along with the findings of other experiments, these results suggest that these receptors are involved in producing changes in synapses that are responsible for memory formation.

---

targeted mutation   A mutated gene (also called a "knockout gene") produced in the laboratory and inserted into the chromosomes of mice; abolishes the normal effects of the gene.

neural plasticity   The production of changes in the structure and functions of the nervous system, induced by environmental events.

focus ⊕n

The Ever-Changing Brain: Neural Plasticity and Neurogenesis

Once people achieve adulthood, the organs of their bodies change very little. Muscles can grow larger or smaller, the amount of fat tissue can increase or (less often) decrease, and, of course, aging can cause pathological changes—but the structure and functions of the organs remain basically the same. The brain is the exception to this rule. The human brain reaches 95 percent its adult weight by the age of five, but significant changes in brain development continue for many years. For example, the volume of the cerebral cortex—especially that of the frontal and parietal lobes—decreases during adolescence (Gogtay et al., 2004; Toga et al., 2006). Most investigators believe that during this period, excess numbers of synapses are pruned, enhancing the efficiency of the functions of these regions of the brain. A *decrease* in tissue volume produces an *increase* in function. In any event, behavioral studies clearly indicate that people show a gain in self-control and a decreased tendency to engage in risky behavior after adolescence, which may be at least partly caused by increased effectiveness of inhibitory functions of the prefrontal cortex (Kelley, Schochet, & Landry, 2004).

Even after adolescence, experience can induce significant changes in the structure and functions of the brain. Some of the developmental changes in the brain are programmed in the genes, but the environment plays an important role in shaping our brains—not just during childhood and adolescence, but throughout our lives.

Experience, Learning, and Neural Plasticity

Research clearly indicates that experience can affect the structure and functions of the brain—a phenomenon known as **neural plasticity.** *Plasticity* (from the Greek *plastikos*) refers to the ability to be shaped or molded, and, indeed, the environment can shape the development of the brain or mold its structure and the connections of its neurons. In the 1960s, Rosenzweig and his colleagues began a research program designed to determine whether the environment could shape brain development (Rosenzweig & Bennett, 1996). The researchers divided litters of rats and placed the animals into two kinds of environments: enriched and impoverished. The enriched environment contained such things as running wheels, ladders, slides, and toys that the rats could explore and manipulate. The researchers changed these objects every day to maximize the animals' experiences and to ensure that they would learn as much as possible. In contrast, the impoverished environments were plain cages in a dimly illuminated, quiet room.

Rosenzweig and his colleagues found many differences in the brains of the animals raised in the two environments. The brains of rats raised in the enriched environment had a thicker cerebral cortex, a better blood supply, more protein content, and more acetylcholine (a neurotransmitter that plays an important role in learning, as you'll remember from earlier in this chapter). Subsequent studies have found changes on a microscopic level as well. Greenough and Volkmar (1973) found that the neurons of rats raised in the enriched environment had larger and more complex dendritic trees. Turner and Greenough (1985) found that synapses in their cerebral cortexes were larger and that more synapses were found on each of their neurons.

Evidence indicates that neural rewiring can even be accomplished in the adult brain. For example, after a person's arm is amputated, the region of the cerebral cortex that previously analyzed sensory information from the missing limb soon begins analyzing information from adjacent regions of the body, such as the stump of the arm, the trunk, or the face. The person becomes more sensitive to touch in these regions after the changes in the cortex take place (Elbert et al., 1994; Kew et al., 1994; Yang et al., 1994). London taxi drivers provide another example of brain plasticity. They spend years learning the maze-like layout of the city streets, and only after passing a demanding exam are they licensed to operate. The drivers' navigational ability must be a result of changes in the neural circuitry of their brain that occurred during their years of training. With MRI technology, Maguire and colleagues (2000) found that these taxi drivers' brains were physically different from those of other Londoners: A portion of the hippocampus, a part of the brain known to be involved in learning, was enlarged. Furthermore, the longer an individual taxi driver had spent in this occupation, the larger was the volume of this region.

The most common form of neural plasticity occurs almost every moment of every day. As we will see in Chapter 7, learning involves changes in the brain. (That shouldn't come as a surprise—where else could learning take place?) For example, learning to recognize the face of a person we just met induces changes in synaptic connections in a specialized region of the cerebral cortex. In recent years, researchers have learned much about the nature of these changes and the biochemical events responsible for them.

Neurogenesis: Birth of New Neurons in an Adult Brain

Most cells of the body turn over. That is, they live for a limited amount of time, die, and are replaced by new cells that are produced by stem cells residing nearby. Thus, our organs continuously rebuild themselves. For example, our skin cells live for about three weeks, die, and slough off the surface of our body. They are replaced by new skin cells that are produced by the division of stem cells located deep within the skin. For many years, neurobiologists have regarded the brain as the most important exception to this general rule. Their conclusion was this: The developing brain produces massive numbers of neurons before birth, continues to produce them at a slower rate postnatally, and eventually (within a few years of birth), the development of new neurons totally stops. After that point, the brain has as many neurons as it will ever have. Because neurons

can never be replaced, their number declines throughout life. As we will see, recent evidence contradicts this conclusion. In fact, the adult brain *can* produce new neurons.

Before examining this evidence, let's take a brief look at the basics of human brain development. Early in development, the brain consists of a hollow tube (the *neural tube*) that later develops into the ventricles. This tube is surrounded by the **ventricular zone,** which consists of a layer of *founder cells*—a special type of **stem cell.** During the first phase of development, founder cells divide, making new ones and increasing the size of the ventricular zone. This phase is referred to as *symmetrical division,* because the division of each founder cell produces two identical cells. Then, seven weeks after conception, founder cells receive a chemical signal to begin a period of *asymmetrical division.* During this phase, founder cells divide asymmetrically, producing another founder cell, which remains in place, and a neuron, which travels outward into the developing brain.

The period of asymmetrical division lasts about three months. The end of this stage of development occurs when the founder cells receive a chemical signal that causes them to die—a phenomenon known as **apoptosis** (literally, a "falling away"). All cells contain killer genes, but only certain cells—including the brain's founder cells—contain receptors that detect the chemical death signal and activate these genes.

But that is not the end of the matter. For many years, researchers have believed that **neurogenesis** (production of new neurons) ceases early in life and cannot take place in the fully developed brain. However, more-recent studies have shown this belief to be incorrect: The adult brain contains some stem cells that can divide asymmetrically and produce neurons. Researchers detect the presence of newly produced cells in the brains of laboratory animals by administering a small amount of a radioactive form of one of the molecules that cells use to produce the DNA, which is needed for neurogenesis. The next day, the animals' brains are removed and examined with methods described in earlier in this chapter.

Neurogenesis takes place in at least two regions of the ventricular zone in the mammalian brain (Doetsch and Hen, 2005). Stem cells in the *subventricular zone* produce neurons that migrate into the olfactory bulbs, stalklike protrusions of the brain that receive information from the odor receptors in the nose. Stem cells in the *subgranular*

---

ventricular zone A layer of cells that line the inside of the neural tube; contains founder cells that divide and give rise to cells of the central nervous system.

stem cell An undifferentiated cell that can divide and produce any one of a variety of differentiated cells.

apoptosis (*ay po toe sis*) Death of a cell caused by a chemical signal that activates a genetic mechanism inside the cell.

neurogenesis The process responsible for the production of a new neuron.

[FIGURE 3•23] Effects of learning on neurogenesis. Sections through a part of the hippocampus of rats that received training on a learning task or were exposed to a control condition that did not lead to learning. Arrows indicate newly formed cells.

(From Leuner, B., et al. (2004) Learning enhances the survival of new neurons beyond the time when the hippocampus is required for memory. *Journal of Neuroscience, 24,* 7477–7481. Copyright © 2004 by the Society of Neuroscience.)

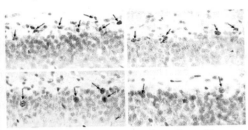

1 day after training

60 days after training

Training task   Control condition

zone produce neurons that migrate into the hippocampus, a brain region that plays a critical role in the formation of new memories. Some preliminary but inconclusive evidence suggests that neurogenesis may take place in other parts of the brain, including the cerebral cortex (Gould, 2007). Evidence from functional imaging studies suggests that neurogenesis takes place not only in the brains of laboratory animals but also in the human brain (Pereira et al., 2007).

New neurons quickly grow dendrites and axons, and establish functional synaptic connections with existing neurons that surround them (Ramirez-Amaya et al., 2006; Toni et al., 2007). Furthermore, environmental events can influence this process: Exposure to new odors increases the numbers of new neurons in the olfactory bulbs of rats, and training on a learning task enhances neurogenesis in the hippocampus. (See **FIGURE 3•23**.)

Recent evidence suggests a link among stress, depression, and neurogenesis. Depression or exposure to stress suppresses neurogenesis in the hippocampus, and drugs or other treatments (even exercise) that reduce stress and depression reinstate neurogenesis Paizanis, Hamon, and Lanfumey, 2007). Unfortunately, no evidence exists that neurogenesis can repair the effects of brain damage, such as that caused by head injury or strokes.

QUESTIONS TO CONSIDER

1. Suppose you had an *f*MRI scanner and many volunteers. You could present various types of stimuli while scans were being taken, and you could have the volunteers perform various types of mental tasks and behaviors that did not involve their moving around. What kinds of experiments would you perform?

2. Although the basic program that controls brain development is contained in our genes, environmental factors also can influence this process. Why do you think the process of development is not completely automatic and programmed? What is the evolutionary benefit of letting the environment influence it? Would humans be better off if development were simply automatic, or does such flexibility have some potential benefits?

Control of Behavior and the Body's Physiological Functions

As you read earlier, the brain has three major functions: controlling behavior, processing and retaining information about the environment, and regulating the physiological functions of the body. The first two roles look outward toward the environment, and the third looks inward. The outward-looking roles include several functions: perceiving events in the environment, learning about them, making plans, and acting. The inward-looking role requires the brain to measure and regulate internal characteristics such as body temperature, blood pressure, and nutrient levels. The outward-looking roles are, of course, of particular interest to psychology. This section examines how the brain performs all three kinds of functions, beginning with the portions of the brain that control behavior and process information.

The cells of the brain are organized in modules—clusters of neurons that communicate with one another. Modules are connected to other modules, receiving information from some of them, processing this information, and sending the results to others. Particular modules have particular functions, just as the transistors, resistors, and capacitors in a computer chip do. The task of psychologists interested in understanding the brain is to identify the modules, discover their functions, trace their interconnections, and understand the ways in which the activities of these complex assemblies give rise to our perceptions, memories, feelings, and actions. Despite the progress we have made so far, the end of this task is not even remotely in sight.

Organization of the Cerebral Cortex

If we want to understand the brain functions most important to the study of behavior—perceiving, learning, planning, and moving—we should start with the cerebral cortex. Because we will be discussing the various regions of the cerebral cortex, it will be good to start with the names used for them. The cerebral cortex contains a large groove, or fissure, called the **central fissure.** The central fissure provides an important dividing line between the anterior (front) part of the cerebral cortex and the posterior (back) regions. (See **FIGURE 3•24**.)

As Figure 3.24 shows, the cerebral cortex is divided into four areas, or *lobes,* named for the bones of the skull that

---

central fissure   The fissure that separates the frontal lobe from the parietal lobe.

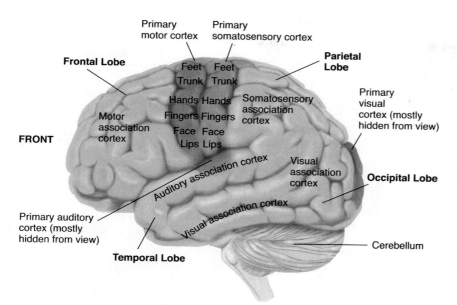

[**FIGURE 3·24**] A side view of the human brain showing the location of the four lobes of the cerebral cortex, the primary sensory and motor areas, and the regions of association cortex.

cover them: the **frontal lobe** ("front"), the **parietal lobe** ("wall"), the **temporal lobe** ("temple"), and the **occipital lobe** (*ob*, "against," *caput*, "head"). Of course, the brain contains two of each lobe, one in each hemisphere, on each side of the brain. The discussions that follow look in detail at the functions of each of these lobes.

Regions of Primary Sensory and Motor Cortex

We become aware of events in our environment by means of the five major senses: vision, audition, olfaction (smell), gustation (taste), and the somatosenses (the "body" senses: touch, pain, and temperature). Three areas of the cerebral cortex receive information from the sensory organs: the **primary visual cortex,** the **primary auditory cortex,** and the **primary somatosensory cortex.** In addition, the base of the somatosensory cortex receives gustatory information, and a portion of the frontal lobe, not visible from the side, receives olfactory information.

The three regions of primary sensory cortex in each hemisphere receive information from the opposite side of the body. Thus, the primary somatosensory cortex of the left hemisphere learns what the right hand is holding, the left primary visual cortex learns what is happening to the person's right, and so on. The connections between the sensory organs and the cerebral cortex are said to be **contralateral** (*contra*, "opposite"; *lateral*, "side"). However, the two most primitive forms of sensory information, smell and taste, are transmitted to the **ipsilateral** hemisphere. That is, the right side of the tongue and the right nostril send information to the right side of the brain.

The region of the cerebral cortex most directly involved in the control of movement is the **primary motor cortex** within the frontal lobe, located just in front of the primary somatosensory cortex. Neurons in different parts of the primary motor cortex are connected to muscles in different parts of the body. The connections, like those of the sensory regions of the cerebral cortex, are contralateral; the left

primary motor cortex controls the right side of the body and vice versa. Thus, for example, if a neurosurgeon electrically stimulates the "hand" region of the left primary motor cortex, the patient's right hand will move. (Refer to Figure 3.24.) I like to think of the strip of primary motor cortex as the keyboard of a piano, with each key controlling a different movement. We will see shortly who the "player" of this piano is.

Association Cortex

The regions of primary sensory and motor cortex occupy only a small part of the cerebral cortex. The rest of the cerebral cortex accomplishes what is done between sensation and action: perceiving, learning and remembering, planning, and moving. These processes take place in the association areas of the cerebral cortex.

---

frontal lobe The front portion of the cerebral cortex, including the prefrontal cortex and the motor cortex; damage impairs movement, planning, and flexibility in behavioral strategies.

parietal lobe (*pa rye i tul*) The region of the cerebral cortex behind the frontal lobe and above the temporal lobe; contains the somatosensory cortex; is involved in spatial perception and memory.

temporal lobe (*tem por ul*) The portion of the cerebral cortex below the frontal and parietal lobes; contains the auditory cortex.

occipital lobe (*ok sip i tul*) The rearmost portion of the cerebral cortex; contains the primary visual cortex.

primary visual cortex The region of the cerebral cortex that receives information directly from the visual system; located in the occipital lobes.

primary auditory cortex The region of the cerebral cortex that receives information directly from the auditory system; located in the temporal lobes.

primary somatosensory cortex The region of the cerebral cortex that receives information directly from the somatosensory system (touch, pressure, vibration, pain, and temperature); located in the front part of the parietal lobes.

contralateral Residing in the side of the body opposite the reference point.

ipsilateral Residing in the same side of the body as the reference point.

primary motor cortex The region of the cerebral cortex that directly controls the movements of the body; located in the posterior part of the frontal lobes.

[**FIGURE 3•25**] The relation between the association cortex and the regions of primary sensory and motor cortex. Arrows refer to the flow of information.

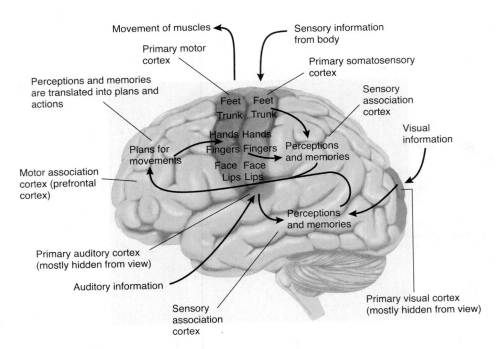

The anterior region is involved in movement-related activities, such as planning and executing behaviors. The posterior part is involved in perceiving and learning.

Each primary sensory area of the cerebral cortex sends information to adjacent regions, called the **sensory association cortex.** Circuits of neurons in the sensory association cortex analyze the information received from the primary sensory cortex; perception takes place there, and memories are stored there. Most regions of the sensory association cortex receive information from more than one sensory system, which makes it possible to integrate information from more than one sensory system. For example, we can learn the connection between the sight of a particular face and the sound of a particular voice. (Refer again to Figure 3.24.)

Just as regions of the sensory association cortex of the posterior part of the brain are involved in perceiving and remembering, so the frontal association cortex is involved in the planning and execution of movements. The anterior part of the frontal lobe—known as the **prefrontal cortex**—contains the **motor association cortex.** The motor association cortex controls the primary motor cortex; thus, it directly controls behavior. If the primary motor cortex is the keyboard of the piano, then the motor association cortex is the piano player.

Obviously, we behave in response to events happening in the world around us. Therefore, the sensory association cortex

of the posterior part of the brain sends information about the environment—and information about what we have learned from past experience—to the motor association cortex (prefrontal cortex), which translates the information into plans and actions. (See **FIGURE 3•25.**)

The Thalamus If you stripped away the cerebral cortex and the white matter that lies under it, you would find the **thalamus,** located in the heart of the cerebral hemispheres. (*Thalamos* is Greek for "inner chamber.") The thalamus is divided into two parts, one in each cerebral hemisphere. Each part looks rather like a football, with the long axis oriented from front to back. **FIGURE 3•26** shows the two halves of the thalamus, along with several other brain structures that are described later in this chapter.

The thalamus performs two basic functions. The first—and most primitive—is similar to that of the cerebral cortex. Parts of the thalamus receive sensory information, integrate this information, and assist other brain regions in the control of movements. However, the second role of the thalamus—that of a relay station for the cortex—is even more important. As the cerebral hemispheres evolved, the cerebral cortex grew in size, and its significance for behavioral functions increased. The thalamus has taken on the function of receiving sensory information from the sensory organs, performing some simple analyses and passing the results on to the primary sensory cortex. Thus, all sensory information (except for olfaction, which is the most primitive of all sensory systems) is sent to the thalamus before it reaches the cerebral cortex.

Lateralization of Function

Although the two cerebral hemispheres cooperate with each other, they do not perform identical functions. Some functions are *lateralized*—performed by neural circuits located

---

sensory association cortex Those regions of cerebral cortex that receive information from the primary sensory areas.

prefrontal cortex The anterior part of the frontal lobe; contains the motor association cortex.

motor association cortex Those regions of the cerebral cortex that control the primary motor cortex; involved in planning and executing behaviors.

thalamus A region of the brain near the center of the cerebral hemispheres. All sensory information except that of olfaction is sent to the thalamus and then relayed to the cerebral cortex.

[**FIGURE 3·26**] The location of the basal ganglia, thalamus, and hypothalamus, ghosted into a semi-transparent brain.

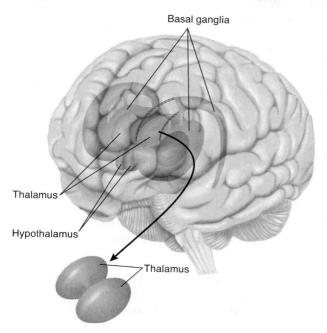

cerebral hemispheres. The corpus callosum connects corresponding parts of the left and right hemispheres: the left and right temporal lobes, the left and right parietal lobes, and so on. Because of the corpus callosum, each region of the association cortex knows what is happening in the corresponding region of the opposite side of the brain. **FIGURE 3·27** shows a photograph of a brain, viewed from above, that has been partially dissected. We see bundles of axons that pass through the corpus callosum, connecting groups of neurons in corresponding regions of the left and right hemispheres.

If the corpus callosum connects the two hemispheres and permits them to interchange information, what happens if the corpus callosum is cut? Neurosurgeons sometimes deliberately cut the corpus callosum (in a procedure called the *split-brain operation*) to treat a particular form of epilepsy. As a result, the two hemispheres process information independently and sometimes even attempt to engage in competing behaviors. You'll learn more about the interesting effects of this operation on perceptions and consciousness in Chapter 8.

corpus callosum (*core pus ka low sum*)   A large bundle of axons ("white matter") that connects the cortex of the two cerebral hemispheres.

primarily on one side of the brain. In general, the left hemisphere participates in the analysis of information—the extraction of the elements that make up the whole of an experience. This ability makes the left hemisphere particularly good at recognizing serial events—events whose elements occur one after another. The left hemisphere also is involved in controlling serial behaviors. The serial functions performed by the left hemisphere include verbal activities, such as talking, understanding the speech of other people, reading, and writing. In general, damage to the various regions of the left hemisphere disrupts these abilities. (In a few people, the functions of the left and right hemispheres are reversed.) We'll look at language and the brain in more detail in Chapter 8.

In contrast, the right hemisphere is specialized for synthesis; it is particularly good at putting isolated elements together to perceive things as a whole. For example, our ability to draw sketches (especially of three-dimensional objects), read maps, and construct complex objects out of smaller elements depends heavily on circuits of neurons located in the right hemisphere. The right hemisphere is also especially involved in understanding the meaning of metaphorical statements such as "People who live in glass houses shouldn't throw stones" or the moral of stories such as the one about the race between the tortoise and the hare. Damage to the right hemisphere disrupts these abilities.

We are not aware of the fact that each hemisphere perceives the world differently. Although the two cerebral hemispheres perform somewhat different functions, our perceptions and our memories are unified. This unity is accomplished by the **corpus callosum**, a large band of axons that connects the two

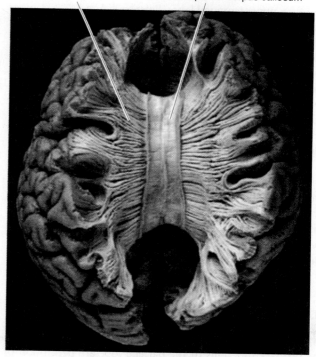

[**FIGURE 3·27**] A photograph of a brain, viewed from above, that has been partially dissected, showing bundles of axons that pass through the corpus callosum.

(Photo from Williams, T.H., Gluhbegovic, N., and Jew, J. Y. *The Human Brain: Dissections of the Real Brain*, 1980. New York: Harper & Row.)

Vision

The primary business of the occipital lobe—and of the lower part of the temporal lobe—is seeing. Total damage to the primary visual cortex, located in the inner surface of the posterior occipital lobe, produces blindness. Because the visual field is "mapped" onto the surface of the primary visual cortex, a small lesion in the primary visual cortex produces a "hole" in a specific part of the field of vision.

The visual association cortex is located in the rest of the occipital lobe and in the lower portion of the temporal lobe. (Refer to Figure 3.24.) Damage to the visual association cortex will not cause blindness, but visual acuity may be very good; people with such damage may be able to see small objects and may even be able to read. However, they will not be able to *recognize* objects by sight. For example, when looking at a drawing of a clock, these individuals may say that they see a circle, two short lines forming an angle in the center of the circle, and some dots spaced along the inside of the circle; but they will not be able to recognize what the picture shows. We'll deal with this phenomenon further in Chapter 5.

Audition

The temporal lobe contains both the primary auditory cortex and the auditory association cortex. The primary auditory cortex is hidden from view on the inner surface of the upper temporal lobe. The auditory association cortex is located on the lateral surface of the upper temporal lobe. (Refer to Figure 3.24.) Damage to the primary auditory cortex leads to hearing losses, whereas damage to the auditory association cortex produces more-complex deficits. Damage to the left auditory association cortex causes language deficits. People with such damage are no longer able to comprehend speech, presumably because they have lost the circuits of neurons that decode speech sounds. However, the deficit is more severe than that. They also lose the ability to produce meaningful speech; their speech becomes a jumble of words.

Damage to the right auditory association cortex does not seriously affect speech perception or production, but it does affect people's ability to recognize nonspeech sounds, including patterns of tones and rhythms. The damage also can impair the ability to perceive the location of sounds in the environment. The right hemisphere is very important in the perception of space, and the contribution of the right temporal lobe to this function is to participate in perceiving the placement of sounds.

Somatosensation and Spatial Perception

The primary functions of the parietal lobe are perception of our own body and the location of objects in the world around us. (Refer to Figure 3.24.) Damage to parts of the parietal lobe that receive information from the visual system disrupts people's ability to perceive and remember the location of items in their environment. Damage to parts of the left parietal lobe can

[FIGURE 3·28] Attempts to copy a drawing of a house by patients with damage to the right parietal lobes.

(Reproduced From Gainotti, G., & Tiacci, C. (1970). *Neuropsychologia, 8,* 289–303 with permission from Elsevier.)

Model for patients to copy

Drawings by patients with right-hemisphere damage

disrupt the ability to read or write without causing serious impairment in the ability to talk and understand the speech of other people. Damage to part of the right parietal lobe can interfere with people's ability to perceive designs and three-dimensional shapes. A person with such damage can analyze a picture into its parts but has trouble integrating these parts into a consistent whole. Thus, he or she has difficulty drawing a coherent picture. (See FIGURE 3·28.)

The right parietal lobe also plays a role in people's ability to pay attention to stimuli located toward the opposite (left) side of the body. As we saw in the Prologue to this chapter, Miss S. displayed a symptom called unilateral neglect. A CT scan of her brain (shown in Figure 3.15) reveals that her stroke damaged part of the association cortex of the right parietal lobe. You will learn more about this phenomenon in the Epilogue of this chapter.

Most neuropsychologists believe that the left parietal lobe plays an important role in our ability to keep track of the location of the moving parts of our own body, whereas the right parietal lobe helps us keep track of the space around us. People with right parietal lobe damage usually have difficulty with spatial tasks such as reading maps. People with left parietal lobe damage usually have difficulty identifying parts of their own bodies by name. For example, when asked to point to their elbows, they may actually point to their shoulders.

Planning and Moving

As we have seen, a considerable amount of the brain is devoted to gathering and storing sensory information. Similarly, much of the brain is involved in the control of movement.

The Frontal Lobes The frontal lobes occupy the largest portion of the cerebral cortex. Although the principal function of the frontal lobes is control of movement, they also are involved in planning strategies for action, evaluating them, and changing them if necessary. They also contain a region involved in the control of speech. (Refer to Figure 3.24.)

Damage to the primary motor cortex produces a very specific effect: paralysis of the side of the body opposite to the brain damage. If a portion of the region is damaged, then only the corresponding parts of the body will be paralyzed. However, damage to the prefrontal cortex (refer to Figure 3.25) produces more-complex behavioral deficits.

People with damage to the prefrontal cortex show perseveration—they have difficulty adopting new strategies. One of the reasons for this tendency appears to be that these people have difficulty in evaluating the success of what they are doing. If given a task to solve, they may solve it readily; but if the problem is changed, they will fail to abandon the strategy and learn a new one. They have little insight into their own problems and are uncritical of their performance on various tasks.

In terms of daily living, the most important consequences of damage to the prefrontal cortex are probably lack of foresight and difficulty making plans. A person with damage to the prefrontal cortex might perform fairly well on a test of intelligence but be unable to hold a job. Presumably, planning is related to the general motor functions of the frontal lobes. Just as we can use the posterior regions of the brain to imagine something we have perceived, so we can use the frontal region to imagine something we might do. Perhaps we test various possible actions by imagining ourselves doing them and guessing what the consequences of these actions might be. When people's prefrontal cortex is damaged, they often do or say things that have unfavorable consequences because they have lost the ability to plan their actions.

The Cerebellum The cerebellum ("little cerebrum") plays an important role in the control of movement. (Refer to Figure 3.24.) The cerebellum receives sensory information, especially about the position of body parts, so it knows what the parts of the body are doing. It also receives information from the cortex of the frontal lobes, so it knows what movements the frontal lobes intend to accomplish. The cerebellum is basically a computer that compares the location of body parts with the intended movements and assists the frontal lobes in executing these movements—especially rapid, skilled ones. Without the cerebellum, the frontal lobes would produce jerky, uncoordinated, inaccurate movements—which is exactly what happens when a person's cerebellum is damaged. Besides helping the frontal lobes accomplish their tasks, the cerebellum monitors information regarding posture and balance; it keeps us from falling down when we stand or walk, and it produces eye movements that compensate for changes in the position of the head. The following case describes the effects of damage to the cerebellum.

[CASE STUDY] Dr. S., a professor of neurology at the medical school, stood on the stage of the auditorium. A set of MRI scans appeared on the screen. "As you can see, Mr. P.'s cerebellum shows substantial degeneration."

Dr. S. left the stage and returned, pushing Mr. P. onstage in a wheelchair.

"Mr. P., how are you feeling today?"

"I'm fine," he replied. "Well, I'd feel better if I could have walked out of here myself."

"Of course."

Dr. S. talked with Mr. P. for a few minutes. We could see that his mental condition was lucid and that he had no obvious speech or memory problems.

"Okay, Mr. P., I'd like you to make some movements." He faced Mr. P. and said, "Please stretch your hands out and hold them like this." Dr. S. suddenly raised his arms from his sides and held them out straight in front of him, palms down, fingers pointing forward.

Mr. P. looked as if he were considering what to do. Suddenly, his arms straightened out and lifted from the armrests of the wheelchair. Instead of stopping when they were pointed straight ahead of him, they continued upward. Mr. P. grunted and his arms began flailing around—up, down, left, and right—until he finally managed to hold them outstretched in front of him. He was panting with the effort to hold them there.

"Thank you, Mr. P. Please put your arms down again. Now try this." Dr. S. very slowly raised his arms from his side until they were straight out in front of them. Mr. P. did the same, and this time there was no overshoot.

After a few more demonstrations Dr. S. thanked Mr. P. and wheeled him offstage. When he returned, he reviewed what we had seen.

"When Mr. P. tried to raise his arms quickly in front of him, his primary motor cortex sent messages to the appropriate muscles, and his arms straightened out and began to rise. Normally, the cerebellum is informed about the movement and, through its connections back to the motor cortex, brings the arms to rest in the intended position. Mr. P. could get the movement started just fine, but the damage to his cerebellum eliminated the help this structure gives to rapid movements, and he couldn't stop his arms in time. When he tried to move slowly, he could see and feel his arms moving, and used this feedback to control their movement. Your cerebellum isn't nearly as important in the control of simple, slow movements. For that you need your basal ganglia, but that's another story."

Recently researchers have discovered that the cerebellum may also play a role in people's cognitive abilities. For a long time neurologists have known that cerebellar damage can interfere with people's ability to speak, but the deficit seemed to involve control of the speech muscles rather than the cognitive abilities involved in language. In the 1990s, however, researchers making PET scans of the brains of people working on various types of cognitive tasks discovered that parts of their cerebellums became active—even when the people were not moving. Many neuroscientists now believe that as we learn more about the cerebellum, we will discover that its functions are not limited to motor tasks (Fordon, 2007; Olivieri et al., 2007). By the way, the cerebellum contains about as many neurons as the cerebrum does.

The Basal Ganglia The **basal ganglia** are a collection of groups of neurons located in the depths of the cerebral hemispheres, adjacent to the thalamus. (Refer to Figure 3.26.) The basal ganglia are involved in the control of slow movements and movements that involve the large muscles of the body. For example, Parkinson's disease is caused by degeneration of dopamine-secreting neurons in the midbrain whose axons travel to parts of the basal ganglia. The release of dopamine in the basal ganglia helps facilitate movements. The symptoms of Parkinson's disease are weakness, tremors, rigidity of the limbs, poor balance, and difficulty in initiating movements.

The basal ganglia also play an important role in learning—especially in learning how to perform particular actions. As we will see in the next subsection, the hippocampus is involved in learning things we can talk about, such as episodes in our lives, and in learning to get from place to place in our environment. In contrast, the basal ganglia are necessary for us to learn skilled behaviors, many of which we do not have to think about when we perform them. For example, learning the skills we need to ride a bicycle requires the participation of the basal ganglia, but being able to remember when we learned to ride and who taught us requires the participation of the hippocampus.

Episodic and Spatial Memory: Role of the Hippocampus

The **limbic system**, a set of structures located in the cerebral hemispheres, plays an important role in learning and memory and in the expression of emotion. The limbic system consists of several regions of the **limbic cortex**—the cerebral cortex located around the edge of the cerebral hemispheres where they join with the brain stem. (*Limbus* means "border"; hence the term "limbic system.") Besides the limbic cortex, the most important components of the limbic system are the *hippocampus* and the *amygdala*. The hippocampus and the amygdala get their names from their shapes; *hippocampus* means "sea horse" and *amygdala* means "almond."

FIGURE 3•29 shows a view of the right hemisphere of the brain, rotated slightly and seen from the left. We can see the limbic cortex, located on the inner surface of the right cerebral hemisphere. The left hippocampus and amygdala, located in the

[**FIGURE 3•29**] The principal structures of the limbic system.

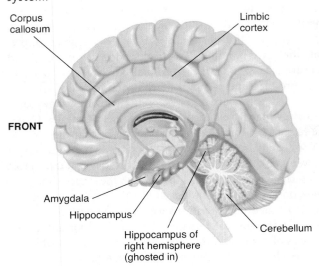

Corpus callosum · Limbic cortex · FRONT · Amygdala · Hippocampus · Hippocampus of right hemisphere (ghosted in) · Cerebellum

middle of the temporal lobe, are shown projecting out into the place where the missing left hemisphere would be. We can also see the right hippocampus and amygdala, "ghosted in." We also see a structure that does not belong to the limbic system—the corpus callosum. As mentioned earlier, the corpus callosum consists of a band of nerve fibers that enables the left and right cerebral hemispheres to communicate with each other.

We already encountered the **hippocampus** earlier in this chapter, where we saw evidence that when London taxi drivers successfully learn to navigate around the city, part of their hippocampus increases in size. The hippocampus is also involved in episodic memory—that is, in our ability to learn and remember experiences from our daily lives. As we will see in Chapter 7, when the hippocampus is destroyed, people can still remember events that occurred before their brains were damaged, but they lose the ability to learn anything new. For them, "yesterday" is always the time before their brain damage occurred. Everything after that slips away, just as the memory of a dream often slips away soon after a person awakens. In addition, although these people can find their way around places that were familiar to them before the damage occurred, they are unable to learn to navigate new neighborhoods—or even the interiors of buildings that are new to them.

Emotions: Role of the Amygdala

Damage to the **amygdala**, located in the middle of the temporal lobe, just in front of the hippocampus, affects emotional behavior—especially negative emotions, such as those caused by painful, threatening, or stressful events. In addition, the amygdala controls physiological reactions that help provide energy for short-term activities such as fighting or fleeing. If an animal's amygdala is destroyed, it no longer reacts to prevent events that normally produce stress and anxiety. We might think that an animal would be better off if it did not become "stressed out" by unpleasant or threatening situations, but research has shown

---

basal ganglia A group of nuclei in the brain interconnected with the cerebral cortex, thalamus, and brain stem; involved in control of slow movements and movements of large muscles.

limbic system A set of interconnected structures of the brain important in emotional and species-typical behavior; includes the amygdala, hippocampus, and limbic cortex.

limbic cortex The cerebral cortex located around the edges of the cerebral hemispheres where they join with the brain stem; part of the limbic system.

hippocampus A part of the limbic system of the brain, located in the temporal lobe; plays important roles in episodic memory and spatial memory.

amygdala (*a mig da la*) A part of the limbic system of the brain located deep in the temporal lobe; damage causes changes in emotional and aggressive behavior.

that animals with damaged amygdalas do not survive in the wild. These animals fail to compete successfully for food and other resources, and they often act in ways that provoke attacks by other animals. Similarly, people with damage to the amygdala must live in institutions where they can be cared for so that they will not harm themselves or others.

Control of Internal Functions and Automatic Behavior

The brain stem and the hypothalamus are involved in homeostasis and control of species-typical behaviors. **Homeostasis** (from the root words *homoios,* "similar," and *stasis,* "standstill") refers to maintenance of a proper balance of physiological variables such as temperature, concentration of fluids, and the amount of nutrients stored within the body. **Species-typical behaviors** are the more or less automatic behaviors exhibited by most members of a species that are important to survival, such as eating, drinking, fighting, courting, mating, and caring for offspring.

The Brain Stem The *brain stem* contains three structures: the medulla, the pons, and the midbrain. FIGURE 3•30 shows a view of the left side of the brain. The cerebral hemispheres are semitransparent so that the details of the brain stem can be seen. We also see the hypothalamus and the pituitary gland (discussed later), which are attached to the front of the brain stem.

The brain stem contains circuits of neurons that control functions vital to the survival of the individual in particular and the species in general. For example, circuits of neurons in the **medulla**—the part of the brain stem adjacent to the spinal cord—control heart rate, blood pressure, rate of respiration, and—especially in simpler animals—crawling or swimming motions. Circuits of neurons in the **pons,** the part of the brain stem just above the medulla, are involved in control of sleep and wakefulness. Circuits of neurons in the **midbrain,** the part of the brain stem just above the pons, control movements used in fighting and sexual behavior and decrease sensitivity to pain while a person is engaged in these activities.

The Hypothalamus *Hypo-* means "less than" or "beneath"; as its name suggests, the **hypothalamus** is located below the thalamus, at the base of the brain. (Refer to Figure 3.29.) The hypothalamus is a small region, consisting of less than 1 cubic centimeter of tissue (smaller than a grape), but its relative importance far exceeds its size.

The hypothalamus, like the brain stem, participates in homeostasis and species-typical behaviors. It receives sensory information, including information from receptors inside the organs of the body; thus, it is informed about changes in the body's physiological status. It also contains specialized sensors that monitor various characteristics of the blood that flows through the brain, such as temperature, nutrient content, and amount of dissolved salts. Neural circuits within the hypothalamus control both eating and drinking.

The hypothalamus controls the **pituitary gland,** an endocrine gland attached by a stalk to the base of the hypothalamus. (Refer to Figure 3.30.) Hormones are chemicals produced by endocrine glands (from the Greek *endo-,* "within," and *krinein,* "to secrete"). Hormones also are secreted by fat tissue and by special cells in the walls of the stomach and intestines.) **Endocrine glands** secrete hormones into the blood, which carries them to all parts of the body. **Hormones** are chemicals

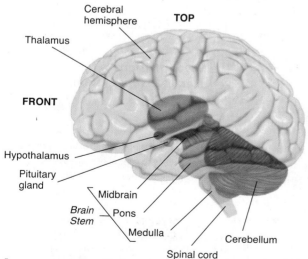

[**FIGURE 3•30**] The divisions of the brain stem: the medulla, the pons, and the midbrain. The thalamus, hypothalamus, and pituitary gland are attached to the anterior end of the brain stem.

---

homeostasis (*home ee oh **stay** sis*) The process by which important physiological characteristics (such as body temperature and blood pressure) are regulated so that they remain at their optimal levels.

species-typical behavior A behavior seen in all or most members of a species, such as nest building, special food-getting behaviors, or reproductive behaviors.

medulla (*me **doo** la*) The part of the brain stem closest to the spinal cord; controls vital functions such as heart rate and blood pressure.

pons The part of the brain stem just anterior to the medulla; involved in control of sleep.

midbrain The part of the brain stem just anterior to the pons; involved in control of fighting and sexual behavior and in decreased sensitivity to pain during these behaviors.

hypothalamus A region of the brain located just above the pituitary gland; controls the autonomic nervous system and many behaviors related to regulation and survival, such as eating, drinking, fighting, shivering, and sweating.

pituitary gland An endocrine gland attached to the hypothalamus at the base of the brain.

endocrine gland A gland that secretes a hormone.

hormone A chemical substance secreted by an endocrine gland that has physiological effects on target cells in other organs.

[FIGURE 3•31] The location and primary functions of the principal endocrine glands.

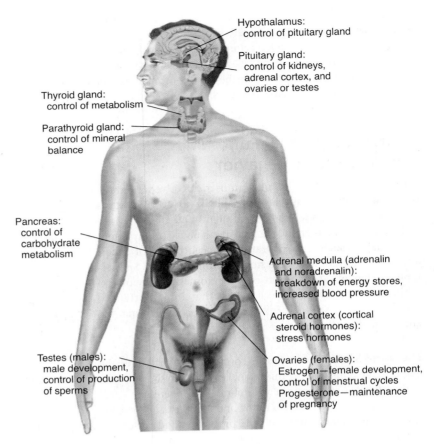

Hypothalamus: control of pituitary gland

Pituitary gland: control of kidneys, adrenal cortex, and ovaries or testes

Thyroid gland: control of metabolism

Parathyroid gland: control of mineral balance

Pancreas: control of carbohydrate metabolism

Adrenal medulla (adrenalin and noradrenalin): breakdown of energy stores, increased blood pressure

Adrenal cortex (cortical steroid hormones): stress hormones

Testes (males): male development, control of production of sperms

Ovaries (females): Estrogen—female development, control of menstrual cycles Progesterone—maintenance of pregnancy

similar to neurotransmitters or neuromodulators, except that they act over much longer distances. Like neurotransmitters and neuromodulators, hormones produce their effects by stimulating receptors. These receptors are located on (or in) particular cells, which are known as **target cells.** When hormones bind with their receptors, they produce physiological reactions in these cells. Almost every cell of the body contains hormone receptors of one kind or another. This includes neurons, which means that hormones can affect behavior by altering the activity of particular groups of neurons in the brain. For example, sex hormones have important effects on behavior, which is discussed in later chapters.

The pituitary gland has been called the "master gland," because the hormones it secretes act on target cells located in other endocrine glands; thus, the pituitary gland controls the activity of other endocrine glands. Because the hypothalamus controls the pituitary gland, the hypothalamus controls the endocrine system. The more important endocrine glands and the functions they regulate are shown in **FIGURE 3•31.**

The hypothalamus also controls much of the activity of

target cell   A cell whose physiological processes are affected by a particular hormone; contains special receptors that respond to the presence of the hormone.

autonomic nervous system (ANS)   The portion of the peripheral nervous system that controls the functions of the glands and internal organs.

somatic nervous system   The portion of the peripheral nervous system that transmits information from sense organs to the central nervous system and from the central nervous system to the muscles.

the **autonomic nervous system (ANS),** a division of the peripheral nervous system that consists of nerves that control the functions of the glands and internal organs. The other division of the peripheral nervous system—the one that transmits information from sense organs to the central nervous system and from the central nervous system to the muscles, is called the **somatic nervous system.** Through the nerves of the autonomic ("self-governing") nervous system, the hypothalamus controls activities such as sweating, shedding tears, sali-

[TABLE 3•3] The Major Divisions of the Peripheral Nervous System

Division	Function
Somatic nervous system	
Sensory nerves	Transmission of information from sense organs to central nervous system
Motor nerves	Control of skeletal muscles
Autonomic nervous system	
Sympathetic branch	Support of activities that require the expenditure of energy (increased blood flow to muscles, increased supply of nutrients of muscles)
Parasympathetic branch	Support of quiet activities that help restore energy supplies (increased blood flow to digestive system, secretion of digestive enzymes)

vating, secreting digestive juices, changing the size of blood vessels (which alters blood pressure), and the secretions of some endocrine glands. The autonomic nervous system has two branches. The **sympathetic branch** directs activities that involve the expenditure of energy. For example, activity of the sympathetic branch can increase the flow of blood to the muscles when we are about to fight someone or run away from a dangerous situation. In contrast, the **parasympathetic branch** controls quiet activities such as digestion of food. For example, activity of the parasympathetic branch stimulates the secretion of digestive enzymes and increases the flow of blood to the digestive system. (See TABLE 3·3 and FIGURE 3·32.)

Researchers can monitor the activity of the autonomic nervous system and its relation to psychological phenomena such as emotion. For example, when people become angry, their heart rate and blood pressure increase. The lie detector works (or, more accurately, is said to work) by recording emotional responses controlled by the autonomic nervous system.

The homeostatic functions of the hypothalamus can involve either internal physiological changes or behavior. For example, the hypothalamus is involved in the control of body temperature. It can directly lower a person's body temperature by causing sweating to occur, or it can raise it by causing shivering to occur. If these measures are inadequate, the hypothalamus can send messages to the cerebral cortex that will cause the person to engage in a learned behavior, such as turning on an air conditioner or turning up the thermostat. Damage to the hypothalamus can cause impaired regulation of body temperature, changes in food or water intake, sterility, and stunting of growth.

---

sympathetic branch   The portion of the autonomic nervous system that activates functions that accompany arousal and expenditure of energy.

parasympathetic branch   The portion of the autonomic nervous system that activates functions that occur during a relaxed state.

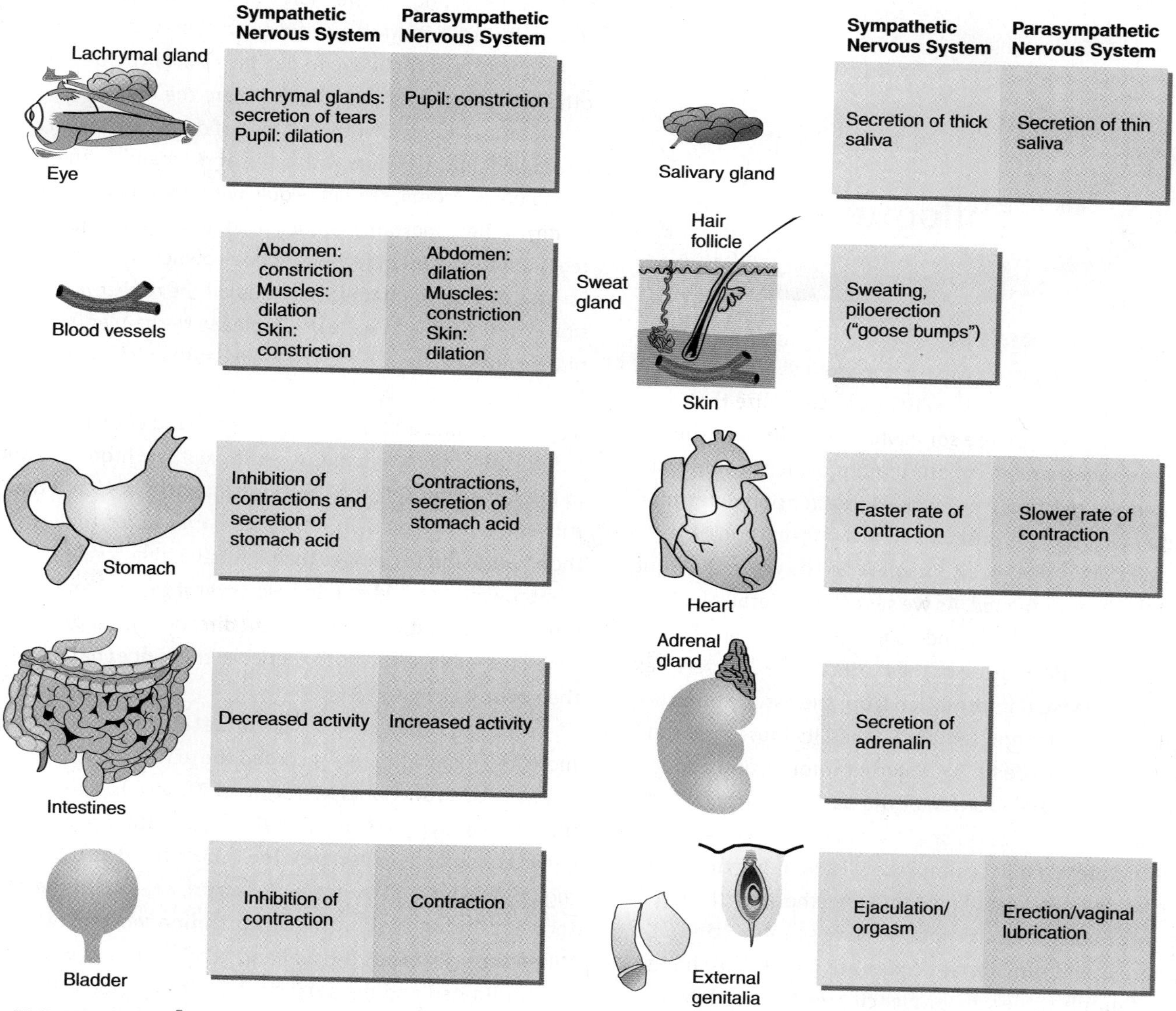

[**FIGURE 3·32**] The organs controlled by the autonomic nervous system. The reciprocal actions of the sympathetic and parasympathetic branches are noted next to each organ.

QUESTIONS TO CONSIDER

1. If you were to have a stroke (and let's hope you don't), in which region of the cerebral cortex and in which hemisphere would you prefer the brain damage to be located? Why?

2. Damage to the corpus callosum produces different behavioral deficits depending on whether the anterior or the posterior corpus callosum is affected. Why do you think this is so?

3. Explain why a brain lesion that impairs a person's ability to speak often also affects movements of the right side of the body.

4. The cerebellum is one of the largest parts of the brain and contains billions of neurons. What does this fact suggest about the complexity of the task of coordinating movements of the body?

5. Tranquilizers reduce negative emotional reactions. In what part (or parts) of the brain do you think these drugs might act? Why?

Epilogue

Unilateral Neglect

When we see people like Miss S., the woman with unilateral neglect described in the Prologue, we realize that perception and attention are somewhat independent. The perceptual mechanisms of our brain provide the information, and the mechanisms involved in attention determine whether we become conscious of this information.

Unilateral ("one-sided") neglect occurs when the right parietal lobe is damaged. As we saw, the parietal lobe is concerned with the body and its position. But that is not all. The association cortex of the parietal lobe also receives auditory and visual information from the association cortex of the occipital and temporal lobes. Its most important function seems to be to put together information about the movements and location of the parts of the body with the locations of objects in space around us.

If unilateral neglect simply consisted of blindness in the left side of the visual field and anesthesia of the left side of the body, it would not be nearly so interesting. But individuals with unilateral neglect are neither half blind nor half numb. Under the proper circumstances, they *can* see things located to their left, and they *can* tell when someone touches the left side of their bodies. But normally, they ignore such stimuli and act as if the left side of the world and of their bodies did not exist.

Volpe, LeDoux, and Gazzaniga (1979) presented pairs of visual stimuli to people with unilateral neglect—one stimulus in the left visual field and one stimulus in the right. Invariably, the people reported seeing only the right-hand stimulus. But when the investigators asked the people to say whether the two stimuli were identical, they answered correctly *even though they said that they were unaware of the left-hand stimulus.*

If you think about the story that the chief of neurology told about the man who ate only the right half of a pancake, you will realize that people with unilateral neglect *must* be able to perceive more than the right visual field. Remember that people with unilateral neglect fail to notice not only things to their left but also the *left halves* of things. But to distinguish between the left and right halves of an object, you first have to perceive the entire object—otherwise, how would you know where the middle was?

Although neglect of the left side of one's own body can be studied only in people with brain abnormalities, an interesting phenomenon seen in people with undamaged brains confirms the importance of the parietal lobe (and another region of the brain) in feelings of body ownership. Ehrsson, Spence, and Passingham (2004) studied the *rubber-hand illusion.* Normal subjects were positioned with their left hand hidden out of sight. They saw a lifelike rubber left hand in front of them. The experimenters stroked both the subject's hidden left hand and the visible rubber hand with a small paintbrush. If the two hands were stroked synchronously and in the same direction, the subjects began to experience the rubber hand as their own. If they were then asked to use their right hand to point to their left hand, they tended to point toward the rubber hand. However, if the real and artificial hands were stroked in different directions or at different times, the subjects did *not* experience the rubber hand as their own. (See FIGURE 3•33.)

While the subjects were participating in the experiment, the experimenters recorded the activity of their brains with a functional MRI scanner. The scans showed increased activity in the parietal lobe, and then, as the subjects began to experience the rubber hand as belonging to their body, in the *premotor cortex,* a region of the motor association cortex involved in planning movements. When the stroking of the real and artificial hands was uncoordinated and the subjects did not experience the rubber hand as their own, the premotor cortex did not

[**FIGURE 3·33**] The rubber-hand illusion. If the subject's hidden left hand and the visible rubber hand are stroked synchronously in the same direction, the subject will come to experience the artificial hand as his or her own. If the hands are stroked asynchronously or in different directions, this illusion will not occur.

(Adapted from Botwinick, M. (2004). Probing the Neural Basis of Body Ownership. *Science, 305,* 782–783.)

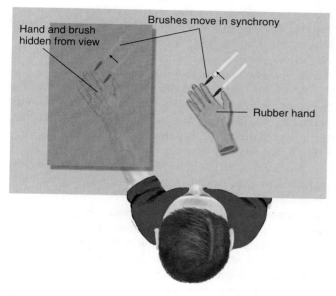

become activated. The experimenters concluded that the parietal cortex analyzed the sight and the feeling of brush strokes. When the parietal cortex detected that they were congruent, this information was transmitted to the premotor cortex, which gave rise to the feeling of ownership of the rubber hand.

CHAPTER SUMMARY

The Brain and Its Components

The brain has three major functions: controlling behavior, processing and storing information about the environment, and regulating the body's physiological processes.

The central nervous system consists of the spinal cord and the three major divisions of the brain: the brain stem, the cerebellum, and the cerebral hemispheres. The central nervous system floats in a pool of cerebrospinal fluid, contained by the meninges, which protects it from physical shock. The blood–brain barrier protects the brain from toxic substances in the blood. The cerebral cortex, which covers the cerebral hemispheres, is wrinkled by fissures and gyri. The brain communi-cates with the rest of the body through the peripheral nervous system, which includes the spinal nerves and cranial nerves.

The basic element of the nervous system is the neuron, with its dendrites, soma, axon, and terminal buttons. Neurons are assisted in their tasks by glia, which provide physical support, aid in the development of the nervous system, provide neurons with chemicals they need, remove unwanted chemicals, provide myelin sheaths for axons, and protect neurons from infections.

One neuron communicates with another (or with cells of muscles, glands, or internal organs) through synapses. A synapse is the junction of the terminal button of the presynaptic neuron with the membrane of the postsynaptic cell. Synaptic communication is chemical; when an action potential travels down an axon (when the axon "fires"), it causes a neurotransmitter to be released by the terminal buttons. An action potential consists of a brief change in the electrical charge of the axon, produced by the brief entry of positively charged sodium ions into the axon followed by a brief exit of positively charged potassium ions. Ions enter the axon through ion channels, and ion transporters eventually restore the proper concentrations of ions inside and outside the cell.

Molecules of the neurotransmitter released by terminal buttons bind with neurotransmitter receptors in the postsynaptic membrane and either excite or inhibit the firing of the postsynaptic cell. The combined effects of excitatory and inhibitory synapses acting on a particular neuron determine the rate of firing of that neuron.

Drugs and Behavior

Drugs can facilitate or interfere with synaptic activity. Facilitating drugs include those that cause the release of a neurotransmitter (such as the venom of the black widow spider); drugs that directly stimulate postsynaptic receptors, thus duplicating the effects of the neurotransmitter itself (such as nicotine); and drugs that inhibit the reuptake of a neurotransmitter (such as amphetamine and cocaine). Drugs that interfere with synaptic activity include those that inhibit the release of a neurotransmitter (such as botulinum toxin) and those that block receptors (such as curare).

In the brain, most synaptic communication is accomplished by two neurotransmitters: glutamate, which has excitatory effects, and GABA, which has inhibitory effects. Acetylcholine (ACh) controls muscular movements and is involved in control of REM sleep, activation of the cerebral cortex, and modulation of a brain structure involved in memory. Nicotine stimulates ACh receptors, and curare blocks them (and causes paralysis). Neostigmine, which is used to treat myasthenia gravis, suppresses the destruction of ACh by an enzyme. The monoamines also modulate important brain functions. Dopamine (DA) facilitates movements and plays a role in reinforcing behaviors. L-DOPA, which stimulates production of DA, is used to treat Parkinson's disease; and cocaine produces reinforcing effects on behavior by blocking the reuptake of dopamine. Drugs that block dopamine receptors are used to treat the symptoms of schizophrenia. The release of norepineph-rine (NE) increases vigilance. The release of serotonin helps suppress aggressive behavior and risk-taking behavior, and drugs that inhibit the reuptake of serotonin are used to treat anxiety disorders, depression, and obsessive–compulsive disorder.

Most peptides serve as neuromodulators, which resemble neurotransmitters but travel farther and are dispersed more widely within the brain, where they can modulate the activity of many neurons. The best-known neuromodulators are the endogenous opioids, which are released when an animal is engaged in important behavior. Anandamide, the most important of the endogenous cannabinoids, helps regulate the release of many neurotransmitters. THC, the active ingredient in marijuana, acts on cannabinoid receptors and mimics the effects of anandamide. Cannabinoids have some beneficial effects but also impair short-term memory.

Study of the Brain

The study of the brain, with all its complexity, requires a variety of research methods. Some methods alter the brains of laboratory animals. These methods may include selective destruction of parts of the brain, recording of the brain's electrical or chemical activity, electrical or chemical stimulation of specific brain regions, or modification of the parts of the genetic code that affect neural processes. Electroencephalography and magnetoencephalography reveal the electrical events in the human brain. Other methods, including CT scans, PET imaging, and structural and functional MRI scans, provide images of the structure and activity of the human brain.

The brain changes most rapidly during fetal, childhood, and adolescent development, but neural plasticity—changes in the wiring of the brain induced by environmental events—occurs even in adulthood. Furthermore, new neurons are produced throughout life in the olfactory bulb and the hippocampus, and possibly in the cerebral cortex as well. Neurogenesis is increased by environmental stimulation and decreased by stress.

Control of Behavior and the Body's Physiological Functions

Anatomically, the cerebral cortex is divided into four lobes: frontal, parietal, occipital, and temporal. Functionally, the cerebral cortex is organized into the primary sensory cortex (with its visual, auditory, and somatosensory regions); the primary motor cortex; and the association cortex. The association cortex consists of sensory regions that are responsible for perceiving and learning and the motor regions that are responsible for planning and acting. Within the cerebral hemispheres, the thalamus relays sensory information to the cerebral cortex.

Some brain functions are lateralized; that is, the right and left hemispheres are involved with somewhat different functions. The left hemisphere is mostly concerned with the details of perception, such as the series of sounds that constitute speech or the symbols that constitute writing. The right hemisphere is mostly concerned with global events. The two hemispheres share information through the corpus callosum, a large bundle of axons.

The three lobes behind the central fissure are generally concerned with perceiving, learning, and remembering: visual information in the occipital and lower temporal lobes, auditory information in the upper temporal lobe, and somatosensory information in the parietal lobe. The parietal lobes are also concerned with perception of space and knowledge about the body, and the frontal lobes are also concerned with motor functions and planning strategies for action. The cerebellum and basal ganglia assist the frontal lobes with the details of executing movements.

The limbic system includes the limbic cortex as well as the hippocampus and the amygdala, both located within the temporal lobe. The hippocampus is involved in learning and memory, and the amygdala is involved in emotions and emotional behaviors.

The brain stem, which consists of the medulla, the pons, and the midbrain, contains neural circuits that control vital physiological functions and produce species-typical automatic movements such as those used in locomotion, fighting, and sexual behavior. The hypothalamus receives sensory information from sense receptors elsewhere in the body and also contains its own specialized receptors, such as those used to monitor body temperature. It controls the pituitary gland, which in turn controls most of the endocrine glands of the body; it also controls the internal organs through the autonomic nervous system. Hormones, secreted by endocrine glands, are chemicals that act on hormone receptors in target cells and produce physiological reactions in these cells. The hypothalamus can control homeostatic processes directly and automatically through its control of the pituitary gland and the autonomic nervous system, or it can cause neural circuits in the cerebral cortex to execute more complex, learned behavior.

succeed with PEARSON mypsychlab

Visit MyPsychLab for practice quizzes, flashcards, and dozens of videos and animated tutorials, including the following items you can find in the "Multimedia Library":

 MKM and Brain Scans

 Structure of Neuron
The Action Potential
Healthy vs. Unhealthy Behaviors
and Brain Functioning

 Split-Brain Experiments
Hemispheric Experiment

KEY TERMS

acetylcholine *p. 67*

action potential *p. 61*

all-or-none law *p. 62*

amygdala *p. 74*

anandamide *p. 70*

antianxiety drug *p. 67*

apoptosis *p. 77*

autonomic nervous system (ANS) *p. 86*

axon *p. 61*

barbiturate *p. 67*

basal ganglia *p. 84*

benzodiazepine *p. 67*

black widow spider venom *p. 67*

blood–brain barrier *p. 59*

botulinum toxin *p. 67*

brain lesion *p. 71*

brain stem *p. 58*

central fissure *p. 78*

central nervous system (CNS) *p. 57*

cerebellum *p. 58*

cerebral cortex *p. 59*

cerebral hemisphere *p. 58*

cerebral ventricle *p. 59*

cerebrospinal fluid (CSF) *p. 59*

contralateral *p. 79*

corpus callosum *p. 81*

cranial nerve *p. 57*

CT scanner *p. 72*

curare *p. 68*

dendrite *p. 61*

dopamine (DA) *p. 69*

electroencephalogram (EEG) *p. 73*

endocrine gland *p. 85*

endogenous cannabinoid *p. 70*

endogenous opioid *p. 69*

frontal lobe *p. 79*

functional MRI (*f*MRI) *p. 75*

GABA *p. 66*

glia *p. 60*

glutamate *p. 66*

gray matter *p.59*

hippocampus *p. 84*

homeostasis *p. 85*

hormone *p. 85*

hypothalamus *p. 85*

ion channel *p. 62*

ion *p. 62*

ipsilateral *p. 79*

limbic cortex *p. 84*

limbic system *p. 84*

LSD *p. 69*

magnetic resonance imaging (MRI) *p. 73*

magnetoencephalography (MEG) *p. 73*

medulla *p. 85*

meninges *p. 59*

microelectrode *p. 73*

midbrain *p. 55*

monoamine *p. 68*

motor association cortex *p. 80*

motor neuron *p. 62*

myelin sheath *p. 61*

naloxone *p. 70*

neostigmine *p. 68*

nerve *p. 57*

neural plasticity *p. 76*

neurogenesis *p. 77*

neuromodulator *p. 69*

neuron *p. 60*

neurotransmitter *p. 61*

neurotransmitter receptor *p. 63*

nicotine *p. 68*

norepinephrine (NE) *p. 69*

occipital lobe *p. 79*

parasympathetic branch *p. 87*

parietal lobe *p. 79*

Parkinson's disease *p. 69*

peptide *p. 69*

peripheral nervous system (PNS) *p. 57*

pituitary gland *p. 85*

pons *p. 85*

positron emission tomography (PET) *p. 74*

postsynaptic neuron *p. 63*

prefrontal cortex *p. 80*

presynaptic neuron *p. 63*

primary auditory cortex *p. 79*

primary motor cortex *p. 79*

primary somatosensory cortex *p. 79*

primary visual cortex *p. 79*

resting potential *p. 61*

reuptake *p. 64*

sensory association cortex *p. 80*

sensory neuron *p. 62*

serotonin *p. 69*

soma *p. 61*

somatic nervous system *p. 86*

species-typical behavior *p. 85*

spinal cord *p. 57*

spinal nerve *p. 57*

stem cell *p. 77*

stereotaxic apparatus *p. 72*

sympathetic branch *p. 87*

synapse *p. 63*

synaptic cleft *p. 63*

synaptic vesicle *p. 63*

target cell *p. 86*

targeted mutation *p. 76*

temporal lobe *p. 79*

terminal button *p. 61*

thalamus *p. 80*

transcranial magnetic stimulation (TMS) *p. 75*

ventricular zone *p. 77*

vertebra *p. 59*

white matter *p. 59*

SUGGESTIONS FOR FURTHER READING

Grilly, D. M. (2006). *Drugs and Human Behavior* (5th ed.). Boston: Allyn and Bacon.

Meyer, J. S., and Quenzer, L. F. (2005). *Psychopharmacology: Drugs, the Brain, and Behavior.* Sunderland, MA: Sinauer Associates.

If you are interested in learning more about the effects of drugs that are often abused, you may want to read these books, both of which contain much helpful information about the effects of popular drugs and their use and abuse in society.

Carlson, N. R. (2008). *Foundations of Physiological Psychology* (7th ed.). Boston: Allyn and Bacon.

My introductory textbook of physiological psychology discusses the topics presented in this chapter in more detail.

CHAPTER

4

Sensation

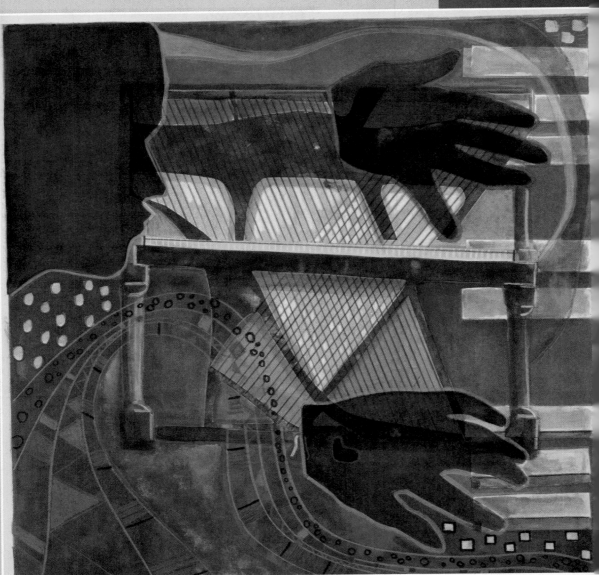

Taken from *Psychology: The Science of Behavior*, Seventh Edition, by Neil R. Carlson, Harold Miller,
C. Donald Heth, John W. Donahoe, and G. Neil Martin.

Prologue

All in Her Head?

Melissa, a junior at the state university, had volunteered to be a subject in an experiment at the dental school. She had been told that she might feel a little pain but that everything was under medical supervision, and no harm would come to her. She didn't particularly like the idea of pain, but she would be well paid; she saw in the experience an opportunity to live up to her own self-image as being as brave as anyone.

She entered the reception room, where she signed consent forms saying that she agreed to participate in the experiment and knew that a physician would be giving her a drug and that her reaction to pain would be measured. The experimenter greeted her, led her to a room, and asked her to be seated in a dental chair. He inserted a needle attached to a plastic tube into a vein in her right arm so that he could inject drugs.

"First," he said, "we want to find out how sensitive you are to pain." He showed her a device that looked something like an electric toothbrush with a metal probe on the end. "This device will stimulate nerves in the pulp of your tooth. Do you have some fillings?" She nodded. "Have you ever bitten on some aluminum foil?" She winced and nodded again. "Good, then you will know what to expect." He adjusted a dial on the stimulator, touched the tip of it to a tooth, and pressed the button. No response. He turned the dial and stimulated the tooth again. Still no response. He turned the dial again, and this time, the stimulation made her gasp and wince. He recorded the voltage setting in his notebook.

"Okay, now we know how sensitive this tooth is to pain. Now I'm going to give you a drug we are testing. It should decrease the pain quite a bit." He injected the drug and, after a short while, said, "Let's try the tooth again." The drug apparently worked; he had to increase the voltage considerably before she felt any pain.

"Now," he said, "I want to give you some more of the drug to see if we can make you feel even less pain." He gave another injection and, after a little wait, tested her again. But the drug had not further decreased her pain sensitivity; instead, it had *increased* it; she was now as sensitive as she had been before the first injection.

After the experiment was over, the experimenter walked with Melissa into a lounge. "I want to tell you about the experiment you were in, but I'd like to ask you not to talk about it with other people who might also serve as subjects." She nodded her head in agreement.

"Actually, you did not receive a painkiller. The first injection was pure salt water."

"It was? But I thought it made me less sensitive to pain."

"It did. When an innocuous substance such as an injection of salt water or a sugar pill has an effect like that, we call it a placebo effect."

"You mean that it was all in my mind? That I only *thought* that the shock hurt less?"

"No. Well, that is, it was necessary for you to think that you had received a painkiller. But the effect was a physiological one. We know that, because the second injection contained a drug that counteracts the effects of opiates."

"Opiates? You mean like morphine or heroin?"

"Yes." He saw her start to protest, shook his head, and said, "No, I'm sure you don't take drugs. But your brain makes them. For reasons we still do not understand, your believing that you had received a painkiller caused some cells in your brain to release a chemical that acts the way opiates do. The chemical acts on other neurons in your brain and decreases your sensitivity to pain. When I gave you the second injection—the drug that counteracts opiates—your sensitivity to pain came back."

"But then, did my mind or my brain make the placebo effect happen?"

"Well, think about it. Your mind and your brain are not really separate. Experiences can change the way your brain functions, and these changes can alter your experiences. Mind and brain have to be studied together, not separately." ■

Behavior does not exist in a vacuum, nor do our thoughts and emotions. Our actions are provoked, informed, and guided by events that occur in our environment, and we think about—and have feelings about—what is happening there. Our senses are the means by which we experience the world; everything we learn about the world comes from information detected by sense organs and transmitted to our brains by sensory nerves. Without sensory input, a human brain would be utterly useless; it would learn nothing, think no thoughts, have no experiences, and control no behaviors.

Vision, to most people, is the most important sense modality. Through it we recognize family and friends, see their facial expressions and gestures, learn to read, perceive objects that are beyond our reach, and find our way around our environment. It provides us with information about the size, shape, color, and movement of objects nearby and at a distance. Through vision, we receive some of our most powerful aesthetic experiences, in the form of art and other beautiful images—experiences rivaled only by the hearing of music that we appreciate.

The other senses also contribute to the richness of experience. Because of the role that speech plays in human culture, audition is extremely important for social behavior. With vision, it provides information about distant events, as does the sense of smell, which can tell us about sources of aromatic molecules far upwind. The other senses deal with events occurring immediately nearby, for instance, the taste of our favorite foods or the touch of a loved one. The body senses are closely tied to our own movements. When we feel an object, the experience is active, not passive; we move our hands over it to determine its shape, texture, and temperature. And information from specialized organs in the inner ear and from receptors in the muscles and joints is actually produced by our own movements. This information helps us to maintain our balance as we engage in our everyday activities.

Sensory Processing

Experience is traditionally divided into two classes: sensation and perception. Most psychologists define **sensation** as the detection of simple properties of stimuli, such as brightness, color, warmth, and sweetness. **Perception** is the recognition of objects (both animate and inanimate), their locations, their movements, and their backgrounds. According to these definitions, seeing the color red is a *sensation,* but recognizing a red apple is a *perception.* Similarly, seeing a movement is a sensation, but recognizing the trajectory of a baseball coming toward us—which informs us where we should go to catch it—is a perception. This classification is a convenient way of organizing a set of complex topics, but neither behavioral nor physiological research has established a clear boundary between sensations and perceptions.

Chapter 5 explores research on visual perception. This chapter describes our sensory mechanisms: the visual, auditory, gustatory, olfactory, and somatosensory systems. According to tradition, we have five senses, but we have several more. For example, the somatosensory system includes separate components that are able to detect touch, warmth, coolness, vibration, physical damage (pain), head tilt, head movement, limb movement, muscular contraction, and various events occurring within our bodies. Whether we choose to call each of these components "senses" depends on whether we want to overturn a tradition.

Transduction

Your brain, floating in cerebrospinal fluid, swaddled in its protective sheath of meninges, and sheltered in a thick skull, is isolated from the world around you. The only sense receptors that the brain possesses detect local conditions, such as the temperature and salt concentration of its blood supply.

---

sensation   The detection of the elementary properties of a stimulus.

perception   The detection of the more-complex properties of a stimulus, including its location and nature; involves learning.

These receptors cannot inform the brain about what is going on elsewhere. That information must be gathered by the sense organs that lie outside the brain.

Sense organs detect stimuli such as light, sound, taste, odor, or touch. Information about these stimuli is transmitted to the brain through neural impulses—action potentials carried by the axons in sensory nerves. The task of the sense organs is to transmit signals to the brain that are coded in such a way as to represent certain features of events that have occurred in the environment. The task of the brain is to analyze this information and decide what has occurred.

Transduction (literally, "leading across") is the process by which the sense organs convert energy from environmental events into neural activity. Each sense organ responds to a particular form of energy given off by an environmental stimulus and translates that energy into neural firing to which the brain can respond. The means of transduction are as diverse as the kinds of stimuli we can detect. For example, electromagnetic energy in the form of light is detected by special chemicals found in cells in our retinas, and mechanical energy in the form of pressure waves is detected by hair cells in our inner ears. In most senses, specialized sensory neurons called **receptor cells** release chemical neurotransmitters that stimulate other neurons, thus altering the rate of firing of their axons. In the somatosenses ("body senses"), dendrites of neurons respond directly to physical stimuli without the intervention of specialized receptor cells. However, some of these neurons do have specialized endings that enable them to respond to particular kinds of sensory information. TABLE 4•1 summarizes the types of transduction accomplished by our sense organs.

Sensory Coding

As we saw in Chapter 3, nerves are bundles of axons, each of which can do no more than transmit action potentials. These action potentials are fixed in size and duration; they cannot be altered. Thus, different stimuli cannot be translated into different types of action potentials, yet we can detect an enormous number of different stimuli with each of our sense organs. For example, we are capable of discriminating among tens of thousands of different colors. We can recognize up to

10,000 odors. We can also identify touches to different parts of the body; and we can further distinguish the degree of pressure involved and the sharpness or bluntness, softness or hardness, and temperature of the object touching us. But how, then, if action potentials cannot be altered, do the sense organs tell the brain that, for instance, a red apple or a yellow lemon is present—or that the right hand is holding a small, cold object or a large, warm one? The information from the sense organs must somehow be coded in the activity of axons carrying information from the sense organs to the brain.

A code is a system of signals representing information. Spoken English, written Spanish, traffic lights, key presses on a cell phone, and the electrical zeros and ones in the memory of a computer are all examples of codes. As long as we know the rules of a code, we can convert a message from one medium to another without losing any information, as when we convert from the sound of spoken English to a meaningful message. Although we do not know the precise rules by which the sensory systems transmit information to the brain, we do know that the rules take two general forms: *anatomical coding* and *temporal coding*.

Anatomical Coding Since the early 1800s, when Johannes Müller formulated his doctrine of specific nerve energies (discussed in Chapter 1), we have known that the brain learns what is happening through the activity of specific sets of neurons. Sensory organs located in different places in the body send their information to the brain through different nerves. Because the brain has no direct information about the physical energy impinging on a given sense organ, it uses **anatomical coding** to interpret the location and type of sensory stimulus according to which incoming nerve fibers are active. For example, if you rub your eyes, you will mechanically stimulate the light-sensitive receptors they contain. This stimulation produces action

---

transduction   The conversion of physical stimuli into changes in the activity of receptor cells of sensory organs.

receptor cell   A neuron that directly responds to a physical stimulus, such a light, vibrations, or aromatic molecules.

anatomical coding   A means by which the nervous system represents information; different features are coded by the activity of different neurons.

[TABLE 4•1]   The Types of Transduction Accomplished by the Sense Organs

Location of Sense Organ	Environmental Stimuli	Energy Transduced
Eye	Light	Radiant energy
Ear	Sound	Mechanical energy
Tongue	Taste	Recognition of molecular shape
Nose	Odor	Recognition of molecular shape
Skin	Touch	Mechanical energy
	Temperature	Thermal energy
	Vibration	Mechanical energy
	Pain	Chemical reaction
Internal organs; muscle	Stretch	Mechanical energy
Vestibular system	Tilt and rotation of head	Mechanical energy

potentials in the axons of the nerves that connect the eyes with the brain (the optic nerves). The visual system of the brain has no way of knowing that the light-sensitive receptors of the eyes have been activated by a nonvisual stimulus. As a result, the brain acts as if the neural activity in the optic nerves were produced by light—so you "see" stars and other flashes. Experiments performed during surgery have shown that artificial stimulation of the nerves that convey taste produces the perception of taste, electrical stimulation of the auditory nerve produces the perception of a buzzing noise, and so forth.

Anatomical coding enables the brain to distinguish not only among the sensory modalities, but also among stimuli of the same sensory modality. Sensory coding for the body surface is anatomical. The primary somatosensory cortex contains a neural "map" of the skin. Receptors in the skin in different parts of the body send information to different parts of the primary somatosensory cortex; thus, we can easily discriminate between a touch on the arm and a touch on the knee. Similarly, the primary visual cortex maintains a map of the visual field.

Temporal Coding
Temporal coding is the coding of sensory information in terms of time. The simplest form of temporal code is rate. By firing at a faster or slower rate according to the intensity of a stimulus, an axon can communicate quantitative information to the brain. For example, a soft touch to the skin can be encoded by a low rate of firing, and a more-forceful touch, by a high rate. Thus, signals produced by a particular set of neurons (an anatomical code) tell where the body is being touched; the rate at which these neurons fire (a temporal code) tells how intense that touch is. It is commonly assumed that all sensory systems use rate of firing to encode the intensity of stimulation.

Psychophysics

As you learned in Chapter 1, nineteenth-century Europe was the birthplace of **psychophysics**, the systematic study of the relation between the physical characteristics of stimuli and the psychological responses (or perceptions) they produce (thus the "physics of the mind"). To study perceptual phenomena, scientists had to find reliable ways to measure people's responses to stimuli. We will examine two of these methods—the just-noticeable difference and the procedures of signal detection.

The Principle of the Just-Noticeable Difference
Ernst Weber (1795–1878), a German anatomist and physiologist,

---

temporal coding A means by which the nervous system represents information; different features are coded by the pattern of activity of neurons.

psychophysics A branch of psychology that measures the quantitative relation between physical stimuli and perceptual experience.

just-noticeable difference (jnd) The smallest difference between two similar stimuli that can be distinguished. Also called *difference threshold*.

Weber fraction The ratio between a just-noticeable difference and the magnitude of a stimulus; reasonably constant over the middle range of most stimulus intensities.

---

investigated the ability of humans to discriminate between various stimuli. He measured the **just-noticeable difference (jnd)**—the smallest change in the magnitude of a stimulus that a person can detect. He discovered a principle that held true for many sensory systems: The jnd is directly related to the magnitude of the existing stimulus. For example, when he presented participants with two metal objects and asked them to say whether the objects differed in weight, the participants reported that the two weights felt the same unless they differed by a ratio of at least 1 in 40. That is, a person could just barely distinguish a 40-gram weight from a 41-gram weight, an 80-gram weight from an 82-gram weight, or a 400-gram weight from a 410-gram weight. Psychologically, the difference between a 40-gram weight and a 41-gram weight is equivalent to the difference between an 80-gram weight and an 82-gram weight: one jnd. Different sensory systems had different ratios. For example, the ratio for detecting differences in the brightness of white light is approximately 1 in 60. These ratios are called **Weber fractions.**

Gustav Fechner (1801–1887), another German physiologist, used Weber's concept of the just-noticeable difference to measure people's perceptual experience. That is, he measured the absolute magnitude of perceptual experience in jnds.

For example, suppose we want to measure the strength of a person's experience of light of a particular intensity. We seat the participant in a darkened room facing two disks of frosted glass, each having a light bulb behind it; the brightness of the light bulbs is adjustable. One of the disks serves as the sample stimulus; the other, as the comparison stimulus. We start with the sample and comparison stimuli turned off completely and increase the brightness of the comparison stimulus until our participant can just detect a difference. (See FIGURE 4•1.) That level of brightness is one jnd. Then we set the sample stimulus to the same intensity (one jnd) and again increase the brightness of the comparison stimulus until our participant can just tell them apart. The new level of the comparison stimulus is two

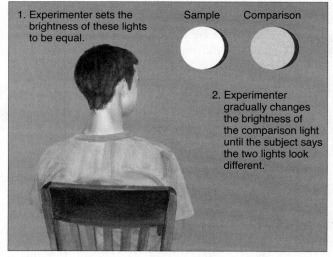

1. Experimenter sets the brightness of these lights to be equal.

Sample   Comparison

2. Experimenter gradually changes the brightness of the comparison light until the subject says the two lights look different.

[**FIGURE 4•1**] The method for determining a just-noticeable difference (jnd).

[FIGURE 4•2] A hypothetical range of perceived brightness (in jnds) as a function of intensity.

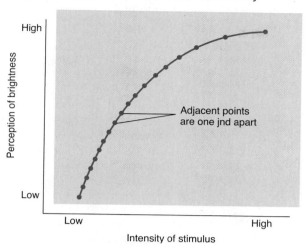

jnds. We continue making these measurements until the comparison stimulus is as bright as we can make it or until it becomes uncomfortably bright for the participant. Finally, we construct a graph indicating the perceived brightness (in jnds) in relation to the physical intensity of the stimulus. The graph, which relates the strength of a perceptual experience to physical intensity, might look something like FIGURE 4•2.

How should you interpret a graph such as Figure 4.2? First, note the two scales. The values along the X axis are measures of physical intensity—something measured with respect to the objective world. The values along the Y axis are very different. Each one is a jnd—a measure of the extent that the subjective experience is increasing. So, in other words, Figure 4.2 provides a mapping between the physical and the psychological worlds—it depicts a psychophysical function.

Second, notice that if you trace the distance between dots on the X axis, the distances become larger as you move to the right on the graph. This is a consequence of what Weber found; namely, that the amount of physical energy necessary to produce a jnd increases with the magnitude of the stimulus.

Finally, note the shape of the curve. It rises steeply at first, but then it begins to level off. This kind of curve is characteristic of the mathematical function known as a logarithm. Fechner's great contribution to psychology was to show that the ratio between the physical intensity of a stimulus and its perceived intensity followed a logarithmic function.

Signal-detection Theory Psychophysical methods rely heavily on the concept of a **threshold,** the thin line between not perceiving and perceiving. The just-noticeable difference can also be called a **difference threshold,** the *minimum* detectable difference between two stimuli. An **absolute threshold** is the *minimum* intensity of a stimulus that can be detected—that is, discriminated from no stimulus at all. Thus, the first comparison in the experiment described above—that used two frosted disks and two lamps—measured an absolute threshold. The subsequent comparisons measured difference thresholds.

Even early psychophysicists realized that a threshold is not an absolutely fixed value. When a researcher flashes a very dim light, a participant may report seeing it on some trials but not on others. By convention, the absolute threshold is the point at which a participant detects the stimulus 50 percent of the time; the difference threshold, the point at which the difference is detected 50 percent of the time. This conventional definition is necessary because of the inherent variability of activity in the nervous system. Even when neurons are not being stimulated, they are never absolutely inactive; they continue to fire even when at rest. If a very weak stimulus occurs when neurons in the visual system happen to be less active, the brain is likely to detect it. But if the neurons are already quite active, the effects of the stimulus are likely to be lost in the "noise."

An alternative method of measuring a person's sensitivity to changes in physical stimuli takes account of random changes in the nervous system. According to **signal-detection theory** (Green & Swets, 1974), every stimulus event requires discrimination between a signal (the stimulus) and noise (the combination of background stimuli and the random activity of the nervous system).

Signal-detection theory takes into account our willingness to report detecting a signal. For example, suppose you are participating in an experiment. You are seated in a quiet room, facing a small warning light. The researcher tells you that when the light flashes, you may hear a faint tone one second later. Your task is to say yes or no after each flash of the warning light, according to whether you hear the tone. At first the task is easy: Some flashes are followed by an easily heard tone; others are followed by silence. You are confident about your yes and no decisions. But as the experiment progresses, the tone gets fainter and fainter, until it is so soft that you have doubts about how you should respond. The light flashes. What should you say? Did you really hear a tone, or were you only imagining it?

At this point, your *response bias*—your tendency to say yes or no when you are not sure whether you detected the stimulus—can have an effect. According to the terminology of signal-detection theory, *hits* are saying "yes" when the stimulus is presented; *misses* are saying "no" when it is presented; *correct negatives* are saying "no" when the stimulus is not presented; and *false alarms* are saying "yes" when the stimulus is not presented. Hits and correct negatives are correct responses; misses and false alarms are incorrect responses. (See FIGURE 4•3.) Suppose you want to be very sure that you are correct when you say yes, because you would feel foolish saying you heard something that is not there. Your response bias will be to err in favor of avoiding false alarms, even at the risk of making misses. Someone else's

---

threshold The point at which a stimulus, or a change in the value of a stimulus, can just be detected.

difference threshold An alternate name for *just-noticeable difference (jnd)*.

absolute threshold The minimum value of a stimulus that can be detected.

signal-detection theory A mathematical theory of the detection of stimuli, which involves discriminating a signal from the noise in which it is embedded and which takes into account subjects' willingness to report detecting the signal.

[**FIGURE 4·3**] Four possibilities in judging the presence or absence of a stimulus.

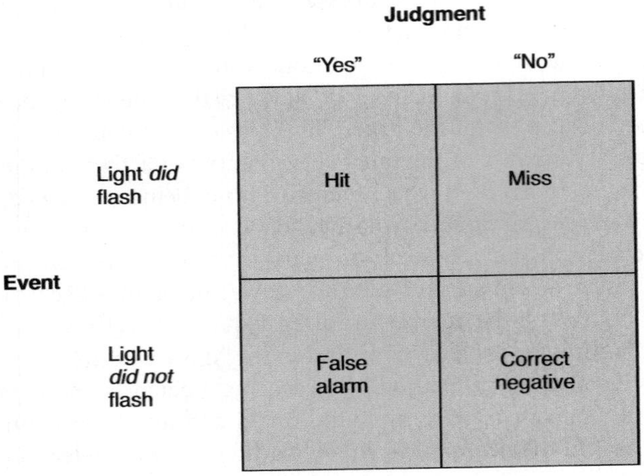

Judgment

	"Yes"	"No"
Light *did* flash	Hit	Miss
Light *did not* flash	False alarm	Correct negative

Event

[**FIGURE 4·4**] A receiver-operating-characteristic (ROC) curve. The percentage of hits and false alarms in judging the presence of a stimulus under several payoff conditions.

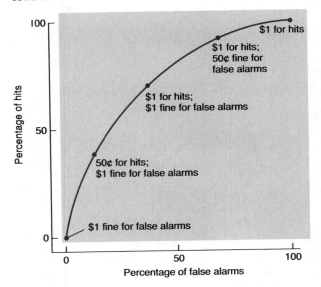

response bias might be to err in favor of detecting all the stimuli, even at the risk of making false alarms.

A person's response bias can seriously affect the threshold of detection. A person with a response bias to avoid false alarms will appear to have a higher threshold than will someone who does not want to let a tone go by without saying yes. To avoid this problem, signal-detection researchers have developed a method of assessing people's sensitivity, regardless of their initial response bias. They deliberately manipulate the response biases and observe the results of these manipulations on participants' judgments.

Suppose you were a participant and the researcher promised you a dollar every time you made a hit, with no penalty for false alarms. You would undoubtedly tend to say yes on every trial, even if you were not sure you had heard the tone; after all, you'd have nothing to lose and everything to gain. In contrast, suppose the researcher announced that she would fine you a dollar every time you made a false alarm and would give you nothing for making hits. You would undoubtedly say no every time, because you would have everything to lose and nothing to gain: You would be extremely conservative in your judgments.

Now consider your response bias under intermediate conditions. If you receive a dollar for every hit but also are fined 50 cents for every miss, you will say yes whenever you are reasonably sure you hear the tone. If you receive 50 cents for every hit but are fined a dollar for each false alarm, you will be more conservative. But if you are sure you heard the tone, you will say yes to earn 50 cents. (Note, however, that there are other, less expensive ways to change people's response biases, which is fortunate for researchers on limited budgets.) FIGURE 4·4 graphs your performance over this range of payoff conditions.

The graph in Figure 4.4 is a **receiver-operating-characteristic curve (ROC curve),** named for its original use in research at the Bell Laboratories to measure the intelligibility of speech

transmitted through a telephone system. The curve shows performance when the sound is difficult to detect. If the sound were louder, so that you rarely doubted you heard it, you would make almost every possible hit and very few false alarms. The few misses you made would be under the low-payoff condition, when you wanted to be absolutely certain you heard the tone. The few false alarms would occur when guessing did not matter because the penalty for being wrong was low or nonexistent. In FIGURE 4·5, the ROC curve (the magenta line) reflecting this new condition is shown together with the original curve (the

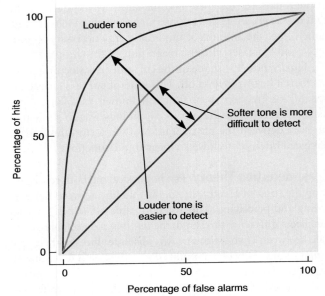

[**FIGURE 4·5**] Two ROC curves, obtained by presenting a more-discriminable stimulus (black curve) and a less-discriminable stimulus (blue curve).

---

receiver-operating-characteristic curve (ROC curve) A graph of hits and false alarms of subjects under different motivational conditions; indicates people's ability to detect a particular stimulus.

blue line). The difference between the two curves demonstrates that the louder tone is easier to detect. Detectability is measured by the relative distances of the curves from a 45-degree line.

The signal-detection method is the best way to determine a person's sensitivity to the occurrence of a particular stimulus. Note that the concept of threshold is not used. Instead, a stimulus is considered more or less detectable. The person decides whether a stimulus occurred, and the consequences of making hits or false alarms can bias this decision. Signal-detection theory emphasizes that perceptual experience involves factors other than the activity of the sensory systems, factors such as motivation and prior experience.

QUESTIONS TO CONSIDER

1. Which sensory modalities would you least want to lose? Why?
2. If you could design a new sensory modality, what kind of information would it detect? What advantages would this new ability provide? Or do you think that our sense organs already detect all the useful information that is available? Why or why not?

Vision

The visual system performs a remarkable job. We take for granted the fact that in a quick glance, we can recognize what there is to see: people, objects, and landscapes, in depth and in full color. Researchers who have tried to program computers to recognize visual scenes realize just how complex this task is. This section begins our tour of the visual system. We will consider the eye and its functions in this chapter, and we'll explore visual perception in Chapter 5. But first, let's start with the stimulus: light.

Light

The eye is sensitive to light. But what is light? Light consists of radiant energy similar to radio waves. Radiant energy oscillates as it is transmitted from its source. For example, the antenna that broadcasts the programs of your favorite FM station

transmits radio waves that oscillate at 88.5 MHz (megahertz, or a million times per second). Because electromagnetic energy travels at 186,000 miles per second, the waves transmitted by the FM radio antenna are approximately 11 feet apart. (One 88.5 millionth of 186,000 miles equals 11.09 feet.) Thus, the **wavelength** of the signal from the station—the distance between the waves of radiant energy—is 11 feet.

The wavelength of visible light is much shorter, ranging from 380 through 760 nanometers (a nanometer, nm, is one billionth of a meter). When viewed by the human eye, different wavelengths of visible light have different colors: for instance, 380-nm light looks violet and 760-nm light looks red.

All other radiant energy is invisible to our eyes. Ultraviolet radiation, x-rays, and gamma rays have shorter wavelengths than visible light has, whereas infrared radiation, radar, radio and television waves, and AC circuits have longer wavelengths. The entire range of wavelengths is known as the electromagnetic spectrum. The part our eyes can detect—the part we see as light—is referred to as the visible spectrum. (See **FIGURE 4·6**.)

The definition of the visible spectrum is based on the human visual system. Other species of animals would undoubtedly define the visible spectrum differently. For example, bees can see ultraviolet radiation that is invisible to us. Some plants have taken advantage of this fact and produce flowers that contain pigments that reflect ultraviolet radiation, presenting patterns that attract bees to them. Some snakes (notably, pit vipers such as the rattlesnake) have special organs that detect infrared radiation. This ability enables them to find their prey in the dark by detecting the heat emitted by small mammals in the form of infrared radiation.

The Eye and Its Functions

The eyes are important and delicate sense organs—and they are well protected. Each eye is housed in a bony socket and can be covered by the eyelid to keep out dust and dirt. The eyelids are edged by eyelashes, which help keep foreign matter from falling into the open eye. The eyebrows prevent sweat on the forehead from dripping into the eyes. Reflex mechanisms provide additional protection: The sudden approach of an

wavelength The distance between adjacent waves of radiant energy; in vision most closely associated with the perceptual dimension of hue.

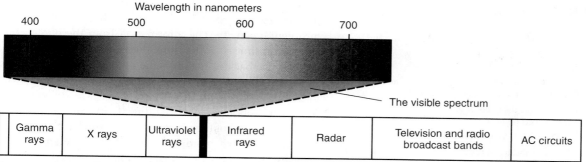

Wavelength in nanometers

| 400 | 500 | 600 | 700 |

The visible spectrum

| Gamma rays | X rays | Ultraviolet rays | Infrared rays | Radar | Television and radio broadcast bands | AC circuits |

[FIGURE 4·6] The electromagnetic spectrum.

[**FIGURE 4·7**] A cross section of the human eye.

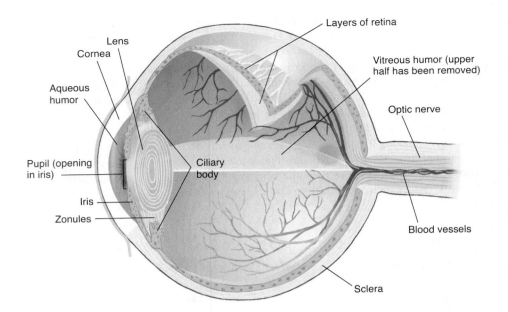

object toward the face or a touch on the surface of the eye causes automatic eyelid closure and withdrawal of the head.

FIGURE 4·7 shows a cross section of a human eye. The transparent **cornea** forms a bulge at the front of the eye and admits light. A tough white membrane called the **sclera** (from the Greek skleros, "hard") coats the rest of the eye. The **iris** consists of two bands of muscles that control the amount of light admitted into the eye. The brain controls these muscles and thus regulates the size of the pupil, which is the circular opening formed by the iris. The pupil constricts in bright light and dilates in dim light. The space immediately behind the cornea is filled with aqueous humor, which simply means "watery fluid." This fluid is constantly produced by tissue behind the cornea that filters the fluid from the blood. In place of blood vessels, the aqueous humor nourishes the cornea and other portions of the front of the eye; this fluid must circulate and be renewed. (If aqueous humor is produced too quickly or if the passage that returns it to the blood becomes blocked, the pressure within the eye can increase and cause damage to vision—a disorder known as glaucoma.) Because of its transparency, the cornea must be nourished in this unusual manner. Our vision would be less clear if the cornea had blood vessels within it.

---

cornea The transparent tissue covering the front of the eye.

sclera The tough outer layer of the eye; the "white" of the eye.

iris The pigmented muscle of the eye that controls the size of the pupil.

lens The transparent organ situated behind the iris of the eye; helps focus an image on the retina.

retina The tissue at the back inside surface of the eye that contains the photoreceptors and associated neurons.

accommodation Changes in the thickness of the lens of the eye that focus images of near or distant objects on the retina.

photoreceptor A receptive cell for vision in the retina; a rod or a cone.

optic disk A circular structure located at the exit point from the retina of the axons of the ganglion cells that form the optic nerve.

The curvature of the cornea and of the **lens,** which lies immediately behind the iris, causes images to be focused on the **retina,** located on inner surface of the back of the eye. Although this image is upside down and reversed from left to right, the brain compensates for this alteration and appropriately interprets the information. A special set of muscles, the *ciliary muscles,* can alter its shape so that images of either nearby or distant objects can be focused on the retina. This change in the shape of the lens to adjust for distance is called **accommodation.**

Normally, the length of the eye from front to back is such that the image of the visual scene is sharply focused on the retina. However, for some people, the eye is too long or too short, so the image on the retina is out of focus. These people may need extra lenses (in the form of eyeglasses or contact lenses) to bring the image into focus. In some cases, people elect to undergo surgical reshaping of the cornea by means of a laser. People whose eyes are too long are said to be *nearsighted;* they need a concave lens to correct the focus. People whose eyes are too short are said to be *farsighted;* they need a convex lens. As people get older, the lenses of their eyes become less flexible, and it becomes difficult for them to focus on objects close to them. They may need to wear reading glasses with convex lenses or, if they already wear glasses, switch to bifocals. (See FIGURE 4·8.)

The retina performs the sensory functions of the eye. Embedded in the retina are more than 130 million **photoreceptors**—specialized neurons that transduce light into neural activity. The information from the photoreceptors is transmitted to neurons that send axons toward one point at the back of the eye—the **optic disk.** All axons leave the eye at this point and join the optic nerve, which connects to the brain. (See FIGURE 4·9, and refer again to Figure 4.7.) Because no photoreceptors lie directly in front of the optic disk, this portion of the retina is blind. If you have not yet discovered your own blind spots, you might want to try the demonstration shown in FIGURE 4·10.

[FIGURE 4·8] Lenses used to correct nearsightedness and farsightedness.

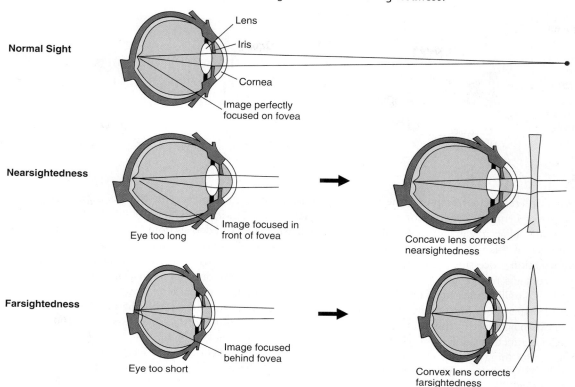

Before the seventeenth century, scientists thought that the lens sensed the presence of light. Johannes Kepler (1571–1630), the astronomer who discovered the elliptical shape of the planets' orbits around the sun, is credited with suggesting that the retina, not the lens, contained the receptive tissue of the eye. It remained for Christoph Scheiner (another German astronomer) to demonstrate in 1625 that the lens is simply a focusing device. (Perhaps astronomers had a special interest in vision and gave some thought to it during the long nights spent watching the sky.) Scheiner obtained an

ox's eye from a slaughterhouse. After carefully peeling the sclera away from the back of the eye, he was able to see an upside-down image of the world through the thin, translucent membrane that remained. As an astronomer, he was familiar with the fact that convex glass lenses could cast images, so he recognized the function of the lens of the eye.

FIGURE 4·11 shows a schematic cross-section of the retina. The retina has three principal layers. Light passes successively through the *ganglion cell layer* (front), the *bipolar cell layer* (middle), and the *photoreceptor layer* (back). Early anatomists were surprised to find the photoreceptors in the deepest layer of the retina. As you might expect, the cells that are located above the photoreceptors are transparent.

Photoreceptors respond to light and pass signals by means of a neurotransmitter to the **bipolar cells,** the neurons with which they form synapses. Bipolar cells transmit this information to the **ganglion cells,** neurons whose axons travel across the retina to form the optic nerve. Thus, visual information passes through a three-cell chain to the brain: photoreceptor → bipolar cell → ganglion cell → brain.

A single photoreceptor responds only to light that reaches its immediate vicinity, but a ganglion cell can receive

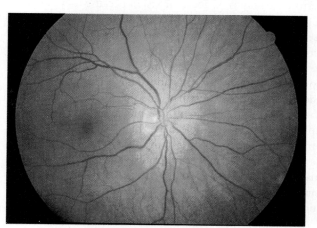

[FIGURE 4·9] A view of the back of the eye. The photograph shows the retina, the optic disk, and blood vessels. (Courtesy of Douglas G. Mollerstuen, New England Medical Center.)

bipolar cell A neuron in the retina that receives information from photoreceptors and passes it on to the ganglion cells, from which axons proceed through the optic nerves to the brain.

ganglion cell A neuron in the retina that receives information from photoreceptors by means of bipolar cells, and from which axons proceed through the optic nerves to the brain.

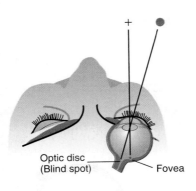

[**FIGURE 4·10**] A test for the blind spot. With the left eye closed, look at the + with your right eye, and move the page back and forth, toward and away from yourself. At about 20 centimeters, the colored circle disappears from your vision because its image falls on your blind spot.

Optic disc (Blind spot)

Fovea

information from many different photoreceptors. The retina also contains other types of neurons that interconnect both adjacent photoreceptors and adjacent ganglion cells. (Refer to Figure 4.11.) The existence of this neural circuitry indicates that some kinds of information processing occur in the retina.

The human retina contains two general types of photoreceptors: approximately 125 million rods and 6 million cones, so called because of their shapes. **Rods** function mainly in dim light; they are very sensitive to light but are insensitive to differences between colors. **Cones** function when the level of illumination is bright enough to see things clearly. They are also responsible for color vision. The **fovea**, a small pit in the back of the retina approximately 1 millimeter in diameter, contains only cones. (Refer to Figure 4.8.) In most cases, a cone sends signals to only one ganglion cell via the bipolar cell to which it is

connected. As a consequence, the fovea is responsible for our highest acuity. (*Acuity* refers to the ability of the eye to detect fine details. The word derives from the Latin *acus,* "needle." We sometimes say of someone with good visual acuity that he or she has "sharp eyes.") When we focus on a specific point in our visual field, we move our eyes so that the image of that point falls directly on the cone-packed fovea.

Farther away from the fovea, the number of cones decreases and the number of rods increases. Up to 100 rods may send signals to a single ganglion cell. A ganglion cell that receives information from so many rods is sensitive to very low levels of light. Rods are therefore responsible for our sensitivity to very dim light, but the visual information they convey lacks the same sharpness produced by cones.

Transduction of Light by Photoreceptors

Although light-sensitive sense organs have evolved independently in a wide variety of animals—from insects to fish to mammals—the chemistry is essentially the same in all species: A molecule derived from vitamin A is the central ingredient in the transduction of the energy of light into neural activity. (Carrots are said to be good for vision because they contain a substance that the body easily converts to vitamin A.) In the absence of light, this molecule is attached to another molecule, a protein. The two molecules together form a **photopigment.** The photoreceptors of the human eye contain four kinds of photopigments (one for rods and three for cones), but their basic mechanism is the same. When a photon (a particle of light) strikes a photopigment, the photopigment splits apart into its two constituent molecules. This event starts the process of transduction. The splitting of the photopigment causes a series of chemical reactions that stimulate the photoreceptor and cause it to send a signal to the bipolar cell with which it forms a synapse. The bipolar cell sends a signal to the ganglion cell, which then sends a signal to the brain. (See **FIGURE 4·12.**)

An intact photopigment has a characteristic color. **Rhodopsin,** the photopigment of rods, is pink (rhodon means "rose" in Greek). However, once photopigments are split apart by the action of light, they lose their color—they become bleached. Franz Boll discovered this phenomenon in 1876 when he removed an eye from an animal and pointed it toward

Photoreceptor Layer　**Bipolar Cell Layer**　**Ganglion Cell Layer**

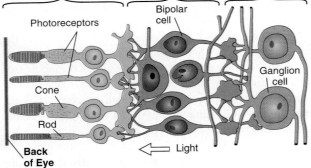

Photoreceptors

Bipolar cell

Cone

Ganglion cell

Rod

Back of Eye

Light

[**FIGURE 4·11**] The cells of the retina.

(Redrawn by permission of the Royal Society and the authors from Dowling, J. E., & Boycott, B. B. (1966). *Proceedings of the Royal Society (London), Series B, 166,* 80–111.)

rod A photoreceptor that is very sensitive to light but cannot detect changes in hue.

cone A photoreceptor that is responsible for acute daytime vision and for color perception.

fovea A small pit near the center of the retina containing densely packed cones; responsible for the most acute and detailed vision.

photopigment A complex molecule found in photoreceptors; when struck by light, it splits apart and stimulates the membrane of the photoreceptor in which it resides.

rhodopsin The photopigment contained by rods.

[**FIGURE 4•12**] Transduction of light into neural activity. A photon strikes a photoreceptor and causes the photopigment to split apart. This event initiates the transmission of information to the brain.

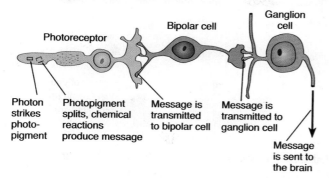

a window that opened onto a brightly lit scene. He then examined the retina under dim light and found that the image of the scene was still there. The retina was pink where little light had fallen and pale where the image had been bright. Boll's discovery led others to suspect that a chemical reaction was responsible for the transduction of light into neural activity.

After light has caused a molecule of photopigment to split and become bleached, energy from the photoreceptor's metabolism causes the two molecules to recombine. The photopigment is then ready to be bleached by light again. Each photoreceptor contains many thousands of molecules of photopigment. The number of intact, unbleached molecules of photopigment in a given cell depends on the relative rates at which they are being split by light and being put back together by the cell's energy. The brighter the light, the more bleached photopigment there is, causing decreased sensitivity to light.

Adaptation to Light and Dark

Think for a moment about how difficult it can be to find a seat in a darkened movie theater. If you have just come in from bright sunlight, your eyes do not respond well to the low level of illumination. However, after a few minutes you can see rather well—your eyes have adapted to the dark. This phenomenon is called **dark adaptation.**

As already stated, the detection of light requires that photons split molecules of rhodopsin or one of the other photopigments. When high levels of illumination strike the retina, the rate of regeneration of rhodopsin falls behind the rate of the bleaching process. With only a small percentage of the rhodopsin molecules intact, the rods are not very sensitive to light. If you enter a dark room after being in a brightly lit room or in sunlight, there are too few intact rhodopsin molecules for your eyes to respond immediately to dim light. The probability that a photon will strike an intact molecule of rhodopsin is very low. However, after a while the regeneration of rhodopsin overcomes the bleaching effects of the light energy. The rods become full of unbleached rhodopsin, and a photon passing through a rod is likely to find a target. The eye has become dark adapted.

Eye Movements

Although our field of vision is rather wide, visual acuity falls off rapidly just a small distance away from the fixation point. For example, if you focus on the first word in a line of this book, you will not be able to read the last word on that line. When we want to see what is to be found in the scene in front of us, we simply move our eyes and scan the scene, examining the important parts of it with our foveal vision.

The eyes make three types of movements: saccadic movements, vergence movements, and pursuit movements. When you scan the scene in front of you, your gaze travels from point to point as you examine important or interesting features. As you do so, your eyes make jerky **saccadic movements**—you shift your gaze abruptly from one point to another. (See FIGURE 4•13.) For example, when you read a line in this book, your eyes stop several times, moving very quickly

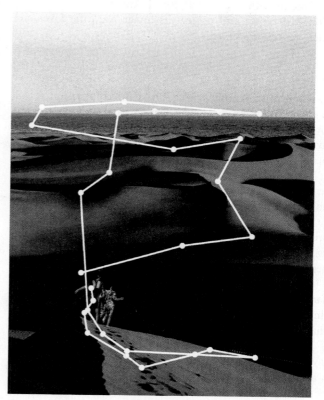

[**FIGURE 4•13**] Saccadic eye movements. The gaze shifts from point to point as we examine a scene. The white line traces a series of saccadic movements that might be made by someone looking at the scene shown in the photo.

(From Nature Publishing Group. (2004). *Nature Neuroscience, 7,* cover image. Reprinted with permission.)

***

dark adaptation   The process by which the eye becomes capable of distinguishing dimly illuminated objects after going from a bright region to a dark one.

saccadic movement   The rapid movement of the eyes that is used in scanning a visual scene, as opposed to the smooth pursuit movements used to follow a moving object.

between each stop. You cannot consciously control the speed of movement between stops; during each saccade, or jump, the eyes move as fast as they can.

When making **vergence movements,** both eyes remain fixed on the same target—or, more precisely, such movements keep the image of the target object focused on corresponding parts of the two retinas. If you hold up a finger in front of your face, look at it, and then bring your finger closer to your face, your eyes will make vergence movements toward your nose. If you then look at an object on the other side of the room, your eyes will rotate outward, and you will see two separate blurry images of your finger. As you will learn in Chapter 5, vergence eye movements assist the perception of distance.

Much of the time, the visual scene in front of us contains moving objects: other people, objects blown by the wind, automobiles, airplanes, animals. When we concentrate on one of these objects, we fix our gaze on it and smoothly track its movements with our eyes. These tracking movements, which follow the object and project its image onto the fovea, are called **pursuit movements.**

Color Vision

Among mammals, only primates have full color vision. A bull does not charge a red cape; he charges what he sees as an annoying gray object being waved at him. Many birds and fishes have excellent color vision; a brightly colored lure may really appeal to fish as much as to the angler who buys it.

Light (as we humans define it) consists of radiant energy having wavelengths between 380 and 760 nm. Light of different wavelengths gives rise to the perception of different colors. How are we able to tell the differences? Experiments have shown that three types of cones are found in the human eye, each containing a different type of photopigment. Each type of photopigment is most sensitive to light of a particular wavelength. That is, light of a particular wavelength most readily causes a particular photopigment to split. Thus, different types of cones are stimulated by different wavelengths of light. This information is what enables us to perceive colors.

Wavelength is related to color, but the terms are not synonymous. For example, the spectral colors (the colors we see in a rainbow, which contains the entire spectrum of visible radiant energy) do not include all the colors that we can see, such as brown, pink, and the metallic colors silver and gold. The fact that not all colors are found in the spectrum means

---

vergence movement   The cooperative movement of the eyes, which ensures that the image of an object falls on identical portions of both retinas.

pursuit movement   The movement that the eyes make to maintain an image upon the fovea.

hue   A perceptual dimension of color, most closely related to the wavelength of a pure light. The effect of a particular hue is caused by the mixture of lights of various wavelengths.

brightness   A perceptual dimension of color, most closely related to the intensity or degree of radiant energy emitted by a visual stimulus.

saturation   A perceptual dimension of color, most closely associated with purity of a color.

[**TABLE 4·2**] Physical and Perceptual Dimensions of Color

Perceptual Dimension	Physical Dimension	Physical Characteristics
Hue	Wavelength	Length of oscillation of light radiation
Brightness	Intensity	Amount of energy of light radiation
Saturation	Purity	Intensity of dominant wavelength relative to total light energy

that differences in wavelength alone do not account for the differences in the colors we can perceive.

The Dimensions of Color   Most colors can be described in terms of three physical dimensions: wavelength, intensity, and purity. Three perceptual dimensions corresponding to these physical dimensions—hue, brightness, and saturation—describe what we see. (See TABLE 4·2.) The **hue** of most colors is determined by wavelength; for example, light having a wavelength of 540 nm is perceived as green. A color's **brightness** is determined by the intensity, or amount of energy, of the light that is present, all other factors being equal. A color of *maximum* brightness dazzles us; a color of *minimum* brightness is simply black. The third perceptual dimension of color, **saturation,** is roughly equivalent to purity. A fully saturated color consists of light of only one wavelength—for example, pure red or pure blue. Desaturated colors look pastel or washed out. FIGURE 4·14 illustrates how a color with a particular dominant wavelength (hue) can vary in brightness and saturation.

Additive Color Mixing   Vision can be considered a synthetic sensory modality. That is, vision synthesizes (puts together) rather than analyzes (takes apart). When two wavelengths of light are present, we see an intermediate color rather than the two components. (In contrast, the auditory system can be considered analytical. If a high note and a low

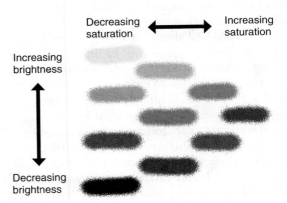

[**FIGURE 4·14**] Hue, brightness, and saturation. The colors shown have the same dominant wavelength (hue) but different saturation and brightness.

[FIGURE 4•15] Additive color mixing. White light can be split into a spectrum of colors with a prism and recombined through another prism.

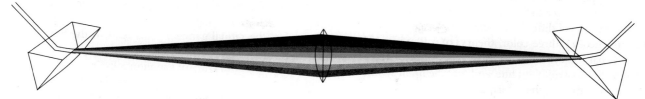

note are played together on a piano, we hear both notes instead of a single, intermediate tone.) The addition of two or more lights of different wavelengths is called **additive color mixing.** If we pass a beam of white light through a prism, we break it into the spectrum of the different wavelengths it contains. If we recombine these colors by passing them through another prism (as Sir Isaac Newton did in 1666), we obtain white light again. (See **FIGURE 4•15.**)

Do not confuse additive color mixing with pigment mixing—what we do when we mix paints. An object has a particular color because it contains pigments that absorb some wavelengths of light (converting them into heat) and reflect other wavelengths. For example, the chlorophyll found in the leaves of plants absorbs less green light than light of other wavelengths. When a leaf is illuminated by white light, it reflects a high proportion of green light and appears green to us.

When we mix paints, we are subtracting colors, not adding them. Mixing two paints yields a darker result. (See **FIGURE 4•16.**) For example, adding blue paint to yellow paint yields green paint, which certainly looks darker than yellow. But mixing two beams of light of different wavelengths always yields a lighter color. For example, when red and green light are shone together on a piece of white paper, we see yellow. In fact, we cannot tell a pure yellow light from a synthesized one made of the proper intensities of red and green light. To our eyes, both yellows appear identical.

To reconstitute white light, we do not even have to recombine all the wavelengths in the spectrum. If we shine a

blue light, a green light, and a red light together on a sheet of white paper and properly adjust their intensities, the place where all three beams overlap will look perfectly white (refer to Figure 4.16). A color television or a computer screen uses this principle. When white appears on the screen, it actually consists of tiny dots of red, blue, and green light.

The spectral colors, contained in a rainbow, do not include all the colors we can see. Thus, differences in wavelength do not account for all the differences in the colors we can perceive.

---

additive color mixing The perception of two or more lights of different wavelengths seen together as light of an intermediate wavelength.

[FIGURE 4•16] Additive color mixing and paint mixing. When blue, red, and green light of the proper intensity are all shone together, the result is white light. When red, blue, and yellow paints are mixed together, the result is a dark gray.

Color Coding in the Retina In 1802 Thomas Young (1773–1829), a British physicist and physician, noted that any color that the human eye can see can be synthesized by mixing almost any set of three colors of different wavelengths. Young proposed a **trichromatic theory** ("three-color" theory) of color vision. He hypothesized that the eye contains three types of color receptors, each sensitive to a different hue, and that the brain synthesizes colors by combining the information received from each type of receptor. He suggested that these receptors were sensitive to three of the colors that people perceive as "pure": blue, green, and red. (His theory ignored the fact that people also perceive yellow as a pure color; more about this fact later.) Young's suggestion was incorporated later in the nineteenth century into a more elaborate theory of color vision developed by Hermann von Helmholtz.

Experiments in recent years have shown that the cones in the human eye do contain three types of photopigments, each of which preferentially absorbs light of a particular wavelength: 420, 530, and 560 nm. Although these wavelengths actually correspond to blue-violet, green, and yellow-green, most investigators refer to these receptors as blue, green, and red cones. To simplify the discussion here, let's pretend that the three cones respond to these three pure hues. The retina contains about twice as many red cones as green cones. There are far fewer blue cones.

The eye uses the principle of the color television screen, but in reverse: Instead of displaying colors, it senses them. If a spot of white light shines on the retina, it stimulates all three types of cones equally, and we perceive white light. If a spot of pure blue, green, or red light shines on the retina, it stimulates only one of the three classes of cones, and a pure color is perceived. If a spot of yellow light shines on the retina, it stimulates red and green cones equally well but has little effect on blue cones. (You can look back at Figure 4.6 and see that yellow is located between red and green.) Stimulation of red and green cones, then, is the signal that yellow light has been received.

Other investigators after Young and Helmholtz devised theories that took into account the fact that people also perceive yellow as a pure hue. Late in the nineteenth century, Ewald Hering (1834–1918), a German physiologist, noted that the four primary hues appeared to belong to pairs of opposing colors: red/green and yellow/blue. We can imagine a bluish green or a yellowish green, or a bluish red or a yellowish red. However, it is more difficult to imagine a greenish red or a yellowish blue. Hering originally suggested that we cannot imagine these blends because there are two types of photoreceptors, one kind responding to green and red and the

other kind responding to yellow and blue. (We'll look at the reasoning behind his statement shortly.)

Hering's hypothesis about the nature of photoreceptors was wrong, but he accurately described the characteristics of the information the retinal ganglion cells send to the brain. Two types of ganglion cells encode color vision: red/green cells and yellow/blue cells. Both types of ganglion cells fire at a steady rate when they are not stimulated. If a spot of red light shines on the retina, excitation of the red cones causes the red/green ganglion cells to begin to fire at a high rate. Conversely, if a spot of green light shines on the retina, excitation of the green cones causes the red/green ganglion cells to begin to fire at a slow rate. Thus, the brain learns about the presence of red or green light by the increased or decreased rate of firing of axons attached to red/green ganglion cells. Similarly, yellow/blue ganglion cells are excited by yellow light and inhibited by blue light. Because red and green light, and yellow and blue light, have opposite effects on the rate of axon firing, this temporal coding scheme is called an **opponent process.**

The retina contains red/green and yellow/blue ganglion cells because of the nature of the connections between the cones, bipolar cells, and ganglion cells. The brain detects various colors by comparing the rates of firing of the axons in the optic nerve that signal red or green and yellow or blue. Now you can see why we cannot perceive (and therefore cannot imagine) a reddish green or a bluish yellow: An axon that signals red or green (or yellow or blue) can either increase or decrease its rate of firing. It cannot do both at the same time. A reddish green would have to be signaled by a ganglion cell firing slowly and rapidly at the same time, which is obviously impossible.

Negative Afterimages FIGURE 4•17 demonstrates an interesting property of the visual system: the formation of a **negative afterimage.** Stare at the cross in the center of the colorful but odd-looking image on the left for approximately 30 seconds. (Doing so will focus the image on the same retinal location in each eye.) Then quickly look at the cross in the center of the white rectangle on the right. You will have a fleeting experience of seeing the more familiar red and green colors of a radish—colors that are complementary, or opposite, to the ones on the left. Items that are complementary go together to make up a whole. In color vision, complementary colors are those that make white (or shades of gray) when added together.

The most important cause of negative afterimages is the adaptation in the rate of firing of retinal ganglion cells that occurs during prolonged exposure to the original stimulus. When ganglion cells are excited or inhibited for a prolonged period of time, they later show a rebound effect, firing faster or slower than normal. For example, the green of the radish in Figure 4.17 inhibits some red/green ganglion cells. When this region of the retina is then stimulated by the neutral-colored light reflected off the white rectangle, the red/green ganglion cells—no longer inhibited by the green light—fire faster than normal. Thus, we see a red afterimage of the radish.

---

trichromatic theory The theory that color vision is accomplished by three types of photodetectors, each of which is maximally sensitive to a different wavelength of light.

opponent process The representation of colors by the rate of firing of two types of neurons: red/green and yellow/blue.

negative afterimage The image seen after a portion of the retina is exposed to an intense visual stimulus; a negative afterimage consists of colors complementary to those of the physical stimulus.

[**FIGURE 4•17**] A negative afterimage. Stare for approximately 30 seconds at the cross in the center of the left figure; then quickly transfer your gaze to the cross in the center of the right figure. You will see colors that are complementary to the originals.

Defects in Color Vision Approximately one in twenty males has some form of defective or anomalous color vision. These defects are sometimes called color blindness, but this term should probably be reserved for the very few people who cannot see any color at all. Males are affected more than females because many of the genes for producing photopigments are located on the X chromosome. Females have two X chromosomes, but males have only one; so in males, a defective gene on that chromosome will always be expressed.

There are many different types of defective color vision. Two of the three we'll consider involve the red/green system. People with these defects confuse red and green. Their primary color sensations are yellow and blue; red and green both appear yellowish. **FIGURE 4•18** shows one of the figures from a commonly used test for defective color vision. A person who confuses red and green will not be able to see the number 5 in this image.

The most common defect in color vision, called **protanopia** (literally, "first-color defect"), appears to result from a lack of the photopigment for red cones. The fact that people with protanopia have relatively normal sharpness of vision suggests that they have red cones but that these cones are filled with green photopigment (Boynton, 1979). If red cones were missing, almost half of the cones would be gone from the retina, and vision would be less acute. To a person with protanopia, red looks much darker than green. The second form of red/green defect, called **deuteranopia** ("second-color defect"), appears to result from the opposite kind of substitution: Green cones are filled with red photopigment.

This third form of color defect, called **tritanopia** ("third-color defect"), involves the yellow/blue system and is much rarer: It affects fewer than 1 in 10,000 people. People with tritanopia see the world in greens and reds; to them, a clear blue sky is a bright green, and yellow appears pink. The faulty gene that causes tritanopia is not carried on a sex chromosome; therefore, it is equally common in males and females. This defect appears to involve the loss of blue cones. There are far fewer of these than of red and green cones to begin with, and investigators have not yet determined whether the blue cones of people with tritanopia are missing or are filled with one of the other photopigments. And yes, in case you were wondering, a person with both protanopia or deuteranopia along with tritanopia will have no color vision at all, and will see the world in shades of gray.

QUESTION TO CONSIDER

Birds, certain species of fish, and some primate species have full, three-cone color vision. Why is color vision useful? What are its specific benefits for humans?

Audition

Vision involves the perception of objects in three dimensions, at various distances, and with a multitude of colors and textures. These complex stimuli may occur at a single point in time or over an extended period. They also may involve either an unchanging or a rapidly changing scene. In contrast to vision, the other senses either analyze much simpler stimuli (such as an

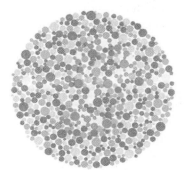

[**FIGURE 4•18**] A figure commonly used to test for defective color vision. People with red/green color blindness will fail to see the 5. (Courtesy of American Optical Corporation.)

protanopia A form of hereditary anomalous color vision; caused by defective "red" cones in the retina.

deuteranopia A form of hereditary anomalous color vision; caused by defective "green" cones in the retina.

tritanopia A form of hereditary anomalous color vision; caused by a lack of "blue" cones in the retina.

[**FIGURE 4•19**] Sound waves. Changes in air pressure from sound waves move the eardrum in and out. Air molecules are closer together in regions of higher pressure and farther apart in regions of lower pressure.

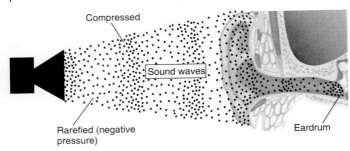

Compressed

Sound waves

Rarefied (negative pressure)

Eardrum

odor or a taste) or require time and stimulus change for the development of a complex perception. For example, to perceive a solid object in three dimensions by means of touch, we must manipulate it—turn it over in our hands or move our hands over its surface. The stimulus must change over time for a full-fledged perception of form to emerge. The same is true for audition: We hear nothing meaningful in an instant.

Sound

Sound consists of rhythmical pressure changes in air. As an object vibrates, it causes the air around it to move. The vibration creates waves of pressure, positive and negative, as molecules of air alternately undergo compression and rarefaction (thinning out). As a positive-pressure wave arrives at your ear, it bends your eardrum in. The following wave of negative pressure causes your eardrum to bend out. (See **FIGURE 4•19**.)

Sound waves are measured in frequency units of cycles per second or **hertz (Hz)**. The human ear perceives vibrations

---

hertz (Hz) The primary measure of the frequency of vibration of sound waves; cycles per second.

timbre (*tamm ber*) A perceptual dimension of sound that corresponds to its complexity.

ossicle (*ahss i kul*) One of the three bones of the middle ear (the *hammer, anvil,* and *stirrup*) that transmit acoustical vibrations from the eardrum to the membrane behind the oval window of the cochlea.

cochlea (*cock lee uh* or *coke lee uh*) A snail-shaped chamber set in bone in the inner ear, where audition takes place.

oval window An opening in the bone surrounding the cochlea. The stirrup presses against a membrane behind the oval window and transmits sound vibrations into the fluid within the cochlea.

between approximately 30 and 20,000 Hz. Sound waves can vary in intensity (amplitude) and frequency. These variations produce corresponding changes in our perception of a sound's loudness and of its pitch (highness or lowness). Consider a loudspeaker, a device that contains a paper cone moved back and forth by a coil of wire located in a magnetic field. Alternations in the electrical current transmitted from an amplifier to this coil cause the coil (and the paper cone) to move back and forth. If the vibrations become more intense (that is, if the cone moves in and out over a greater distance), the loudness of the sound increases. (See **FIGURE 4•20**.) If the cone begins vibrating more rapidly, the pitch of the sound rises. A third perceptual dimension, **timbre,** corresponds to the complexity of the sound. We'll examine all three dimensions of sound waves in more detail later in the chapter.

The Ear and Its Functions

When people refer to the ear, they usually mean what anatomists call the *pinna*—the flesh-covered cartilage attached to the side of the head. (*Pinna* means "wing" in Latin.) But the pinna performs only a small role in audition. It helps funnel sound waves through the ear canal toward the middle and inner ear, where the business of hearing gets done. (See **FIGURE 4•21**.)

The eardrum (or, more properly, the tympanic membrane) is a thin, flexible membrane that vibrates back and forth in response to sound waves and passes these vibrations on to the receptor cells in the inner ear. The eardrum is attached to the first of a set of three middle-ear bones called the **ossicles** (literally, "little bones"). The three ossicles are known informally as the hammer, the anvil, and the stirrup, because of their shapes. The technical terms are malleus, incus, and stapes, respectively. These bones act together, in lever fashion, to transmit the vibrations of the eardrum to the fluid-filled structure of the inner ear.

The bony structure that contains the auditory receptor cells is called the **cochlea.** *Kokhlos* is the Greek word for "snail," which accurately describes its shape; refer to Figure 4.21. The cochlea is filled with a liquid. A bony chamber (the vestibule) is attached to the cochlea and contains two openings, the oval window and the round window. The last of the three ossicles (the stirrup) presses against a membrane behind the **oval window,** thus

[**FIGURE 4•20**] The physical and perceptual dimensions of sound waves.

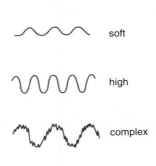

Physical Dimension	Perceptual Dimension				
Amplitude (intensity)	Loudness		loud		soft
Frequency	Pitch		low		high
Complexity	Timbre		simple		complex

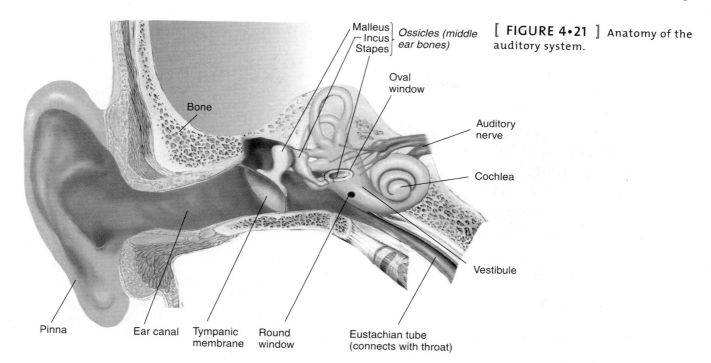

[**FIGURE 4·21**] Anatomy of the auditory system.

Labels: Malleus, Incus, Stapes } Ossicles (middle ear bones); Oval window; Auditory nerve; Cochlea; Vestibule; Eustachian tube (connects with throat); Round window; Tympanic membrane; Ear canal; Pinna; Bone

transmitting sound waves into the liquid inside the cochlea. The cochlea is divided into three chambers by two membranes. One of them, the **basilar membrane,** contains the auditory receptor cells. As the footplate of the stirrup presses back and forth against the membrane behind the oval window, pressure changes in the fluid above the basilar membrane cause the basilar membrane to vibrate. Because the basilar membrane varies in its width and flexibility along its length, different frequencies of sound cause different parts of the basilar membrane to vibrate.

High-frequency sounds cause the end near the oval window to vibrate, medium-frequency sounds cause the middle to vibrate, and low-frequency sounds cause the tip to vibrate. (See **FIGURE 4·22**.)

For the basilar membrane to vibrate freely, the fluid in the lower chamber of the cochlea must have somewhere to

basilar membrane (*bazz i ler*)   A membrane that divides the cochlea of the inner ear into two compartments. The receptive organ for audition resides here.

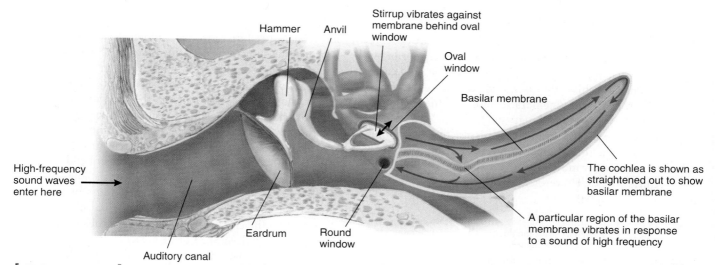

Labels: Hammer; Anvil; Stirrup vibrates against membrane behind oval window; Oval window; Basilar membrane; The cochlea is shown as straightened out to show basilar membrane; A particular region of the basilar membrane vibrates in response to a sound of high frequency; High-frequency sound waves enter here; Eardrum; Round window; Auditory canal

[**FIGURE 4·22**] Responses to sound waves. When the stirrup pushes against the membrane behind the oval window, the membrane behind the round window bulges outward. Different high-frequency and medium-frequency sound vibrations cause flexing of different portions of the basilar membrane. In contrast, low-frequency sound vibrations cause the tip of the basilar membrane to flex in synchrony with the vibrations.

[FIGURE 4·23] The transduction of sound vibrations in the auditory system.

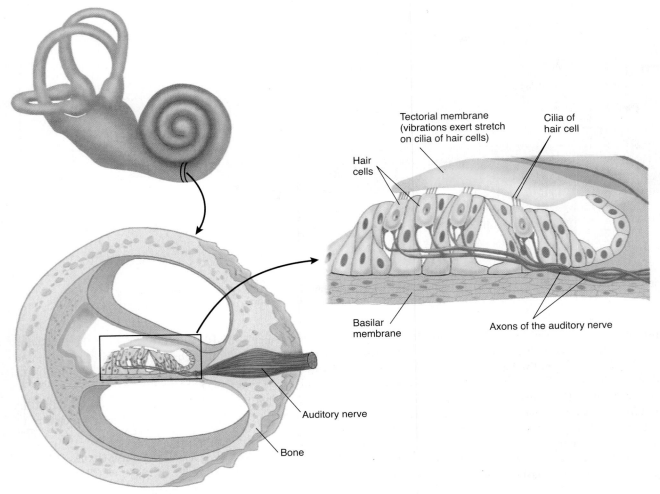

Tectorial membrane
(vibrations exert stretch
on cilia of hair cells)

Cilia of
hair cell

Hair
cells

Basilar
membrane

Axons of the auditory nerve

Auditory nerve

Bone

Slice through the Cochlea

go—because unlike gases, liquids cannot be compressed. Free space is provided by the **round window.** When the basilar membrane flexes down, the displacement of the fluid causes the membrane behind the round window to bulge out. In turn, when the basilar membrane flexes up, the membrane behind the round window bulges in.

Some people have a middle-ear disease that causes bone to grow over the round window. Because their basilar membrane cannot easily move back and forth, these people have a severe hearing loss. However, their hearing can be restored by a surgical procedure called *fenestration* ("window making"), in which the surgeon drills a tiny hole in the bone where the round window should be.

Sounds are detected by special neurons known as auditory hair cells, located on the basilar membrane. **Auditory hair cells** transduce mechanical energy caused by the movement of the basilar membrane into neural activity. These cells possess hairlike protrusions called **cilia** ("eyelashes"). The ends of the cilia are embedded in the **tectorial membrane,** a fairly rigid shelf that hangs over the basilar membrane like a balcony. When sound waves cause the basilar membrane to vibrate, the cilia are stretched. This pull on the cilia of the auditory hair cells is translated into neural activity. (See **FIGURE 4·23.**)

When a mechanical force is exerted on the cilia of a cell, ion channels in the membrane of the cilia open, permitting positive ions to enter. The resulting change in the membrane potential of the cilia causes the hair cell to release a neurotransmitter that causes a message to be sent through the auditory nerve to the brain.

round window An opening in the bone surrounding the cochlea. Movements of the membrane behind this opening permit vibrations to be transmitted through the oval window into the cochlea.

auditory hair cell The sensory neuron of the auditory system; located on the basilar membrane.

cilium (plural: cilia) A hairlike appendage of a cell; involved in movement or in transducing sensory information. Cilia are found on receptors in the auditory and vestibular system.

tectorial membrane A membrane located above the basilar membrane; serves as a shelf against which the cilia of the auditory hair cells move.

Detecting and Localizing Sounds in the Environment

Sounds can differ in pitch, loudness, and timbre. They also come from particular locations in the auditory environment. How does the ear distinguish these characteristics? The ear's ability to distinguish sounds by their timbre depends on its ability to distinguish pitch and loudness. So let's examine these two characteristics first.

Pitch and Loudness Scientists originally thought that the sensory neurons of the auditory system represented pitch (frequency) by firing in synchrony with the vibrations of the basilar membrane. However, they subsequently learned that axons cannot fire rapidly enough to represent the high frequencies that we can hear by means of a simple temporal code (or, as auditory scientists put it, a rate code. A good, young ear can hear frequencies of more than 20,000 Hz, but axons cannot fire more than 1,000 times per second. Therefore, high-frequency sounds, at least, must be encoded in some other way.

As we saw, high-frequency and medium-frequency sounds cause different parts of the basilar membrane to vibrate. Thus, sounds of different frequencies stimulate different groups of auditory hair cells located along the basilar membrane. At least for high-frequency and medium-frequency sounds, therefore, the brain is informed of the pitch by the activity of different sets of axons in the auditory nerve that represent different groups of hair cells. (You will recognize this as an anatomical code—which auditory scientists refer to as a *place code*.) When medium-frequency sound waves reach the ear, auditory hair cells located in the middle of the basilar membrane are activated. In contrast, high-frequency sounds activate auditory hair cells located at the base of the basilar membrane near the oval window. (Refer to Figure 4.23.)

Experiments have found that damage to specific sets of hair cells along the basilar membrane causes loss of the ability to perceive specific frequencies. Perhaps the most convincing evidence that the basilar membrane uses a place code to detect pitch comes from the effectiveness of cochlear implants. **Cochlear implants** are devices that are used to restore hearing in people with deafness caused by damage to the hair cells. The external part of a cochlear implant consists of a microphone and a miniaturized electronic signal processor. The internal part contains a very thin, flexible array of electrodes, which the surgeon carefully inserts into the cochlea in such a way that it follows the snaillike curl and ends up resting along the entire length of the basilar membrane. Each electrode in the array stimulates a different part of the basilar membrane. Information from the signal processor is passed to the electrodes by means of flat coils of wire, implanted under the skin. (See FIGURE 4•24.)

The primary purpose of a cochlear implant is to restore a person's ability to understand speech. Because most of the important acoustical information in speech is contained in frequencies that are too high to be accurately represented by a rate code, the multichannel electrode was developed in an attempt to duplicate the place coding of pitch on the basilar

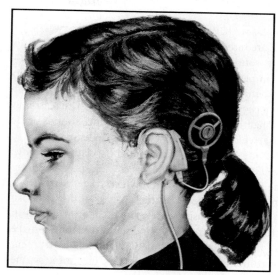

[**FIGURE 4•24**] A child with a cochlear implant. The microphone and processor are worn over the ear, and the headpiece contains a coil that transmits signals to the implant.

membrane (Copeland & Pillsbury, 2004). When different regions of the basilar membrane are stimulated, the person perceives sounds with different pitches. The signal processor in the external device analyzes the sounds detected by the microphone and sends separate signals to the appropriate portions of the basilar membrane. This device can work well; many people with cochlear implants can understand speech well enough to use a telephone.

Although high-frequency and medium-frequency sounds are detected because they cause different sets of hair cells to respond, low-frequency sounds are detected by a different method. Kiang (1965) recorded the electrical activity of single axons in the auditory nerve and found many that responded best to sounds of particular frequencies. Presumably, these axons originated in neurons stimulated by hair cells located on different regions of the basilar membrane. However, Kiang did not find any axons that responded uniquely to particular frequencies below 200 Hz—and yet tones lower than 200 Hz are easily perceived. How, then, are the lower frequencies encoded?

The answer is this: Frequencies lower than 200 Hz cause the tip of the basilar membrane to vibrate in synchrony with the sound waves. Neurons that are stimulated by hair cells located there are able to fire in synchrony with these vibrations, thus firing at the same frequency as the sound. The brain "counts" these vibrations (so to speak) and thus detects low-frequency sounds. This process is obviously an example of temporal (rate) coding.

What about loudness (intensity, or amplitude)? The axons of the auditory nerve appear to inform the brain of the loudness of a stimulus by altering their rate of firing—another example

---

cochlear implant An electronic device surgically implanted in the inner ear that can enable a deaf person to hear.

of temporal coding. More-intense vibrations stimulate the auditory hair cells more intensely. This stimulation causes them to release more transmitter substance, which results in a higher rate of firing by the axons in the auditory nerve.

Timbre So far we have been considering pure sine waves, but such sounds are rarely heard outside the laboratory. Instead, we usually hear sounds with a rich mixture of frequencies—sounds of complex timbre. For example, consider the sound of a clarinet playing a particular note. If we hear it, we can easily say that it is a clarinet and not a flute or a violin. The reason we can do so is that these three instruments produce sounds of different timbre, which our auditory system can distinguish.

FIGURE 4·25 shows the waveform from a clarinet playing a steady note (*top*). The shape of the waveform repeats itself regularly at the **fundamental frequency,** which corresponds to the perceived pitch of the note. A Fourier analysis of the waveform shows that it actually consists of a series of sine waves that includes the fundamental frequency and many **overtones,** integer multiples of the fundamental frequency. Different instruments produce overtones with different intensities. Electronic synthesizers simulate the sounds of real instruments by producing a series of overtones of the proper intensities, mixing them, and passing them through a loudspeaker.

When the basilar membrane is stimulated by the sound of a clarinet, different portions respond to each of the overtones. This response produces a unique anatomically coded pattern of activity in the auditory nerve, which is subsequently identified by circuits in the auditory association cortex.

Perception of Environmental Sounds Actually, the recognition of complex sounds is not quite as simple as I implied in the previous subsection. Figure 4.25 shows the analysis of a sustained sound of a clarinet. But most sounds (including those produced by a clarinet) are dynamic; that is, their beginnings, middles, and ends are different from each other. The beginning of a note played on a clarinet (the attack) contains frequencies that appear and disappear in a few milliseconds. At the end of the note (the decay), some harmonics disappear before others. If we are to recognize different sounds, the auditory cortex must analyze a complex sequence of multiple frequencies that appear, change in amplitude, and disappear. And when you consider the fact that we can listen to an orchestra and identify several instruments that are playing simultaneously, you can appreciate the complexity of the analysis performed by the auditory system. We will revisit this process later in this chapter.

The task of the auditory system in identifying particular sound sources is one of *pattern recognition*. The auditory system must recognize that particular patterns of constantly changing activity received from the hair cells on the basilar membrane belong to different sound sources, and few patterns

fundamental frequency The lowest, and usually most intense, frequency of a complex sound; most often perceived as the sound's basic pitch.

overtone A component of a complex tone; one of a series of tones whose frequency is a multiple of the fundamental frequency.

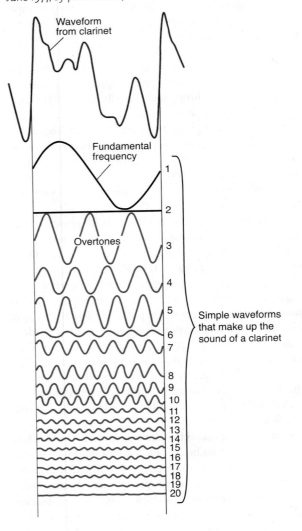

[**FIGURE 4·25**] Analysis of timbre. The shape of a sound wave from a clarinet is shown at the top. The waveforms under it show the frequencies into which it can be analyzed.

(Copyright © 1977 by CBS Magazines. Reprinted from *Stereo Review,* June 1977, by permission.)

are simple mixtures of fixed frequencies. Consider the complexity of sounds that occur in the environment: cars honking, birds chirping, people coughing, doors slamming, and so on.

A functional imaging study by Lewis et al. (2004) presented subjects with recordings of environmental sounds—sounds made by various tools, animals, dropped objects, and poured or dripping liquids. They also presented these sounds recorded backward, which preserved their complexity but made it impossible for them to be recognized. All sounds activated the auditory cortex, but only recognized sounds activated a region of the left hemisphere centered on the posterior temporal lobe—a region also activated by the recognition of objects by seeing them or hearing verbal descriptions of them.

[CASE STUDY] Patient I. R., a right-handed woman in her early forties, sustained damage to regions of the cortex of her left hemisphere, including portions of the auditory association cortex. Ten years later, Peretz and her colleagues studied the effects of her brain damage on her musical ability (Peretz, Gagnon, and Bouchard, 1998; Peretz et al., 2001). Although Patient I. R. had normal hearing, could understand speech and converse normally, and could recognize environmental sounds, she showed a nearly complete *amusia*—loss of the ability to perceive or produce melodic or rhythmic aspects of music. She had been raised in a musical environment: Both her grandmother and brother were professional musicians. After her surgery, she lost the ability to recognize melodies that she had been familiar with previously, including simple pieces such as "Happy Birthday." She was no longer able to sing.

Remarkably, despite her inability to recognize melodic and rhythmic aspects of music, she insisted that she still enjoyed listening to music. Peretz and her colleagues discovered that I. R. was still able to recognize emotional aspects of music. Although she could not recognize pieces that the experimenters played for her, she recognized whether the music sounded happy or sad. She could also recognize happiness, sadness, fear, anger, surprise, and disgust in a person's tone of voice. However, she was totally insensitive to dissonant music, the sound of which irritates normal listeners. Even four-month-old babies prefer consonant music to dissonant music, which shows that recognition of dissonance develops very early in life (Zentner and Kagan, 1998). This case tells us that the brain mechanisms that recognize emotion in music or people's voices are different from those that recognize the melodic and rhythmic aspects of music.

Locating the Source of a Sound

When we hear an unexpected sound, we usually turn our heads quickly to face its source. Even newborn infants can make this response with reasonably good accuracy. Once our faces are oriented toward the source of the sound, we can detect changes in its location by as little as 1 degree. To locate the source, we make use of two qualities of sound: relative loudness and difference in arrival time.

Relative loudness is the most effective means of perceiving the location of high-frequency sounds. Acoustic energy, in the form of vibrations, does not actually pass through solid objects. Low-frequency sounds can easily make a large solid object, such as a wall, vibrate, setting the air on the other side in motion and producing a new sound across the barrier. But large solid objects cannot vibrate rapidly, so they effectively damp out high-frequency sounds. They cast a "sound shadow," just as opaque objects cast a shadow in the sunlight. The human head is one such object, and it damps out high-frequency sounds so that they appear much louder to the ear nearer the source of the sound. Thus, if a source on your right produces a high-frequency sound, your right ear will receive more-intense stimulation than your left ear will. The brain uses this difference to calculate the location of the source of the sound. (See FIGURE 4•26.)

[FIGURE 4•26] Localizing the source of high-frequency sounds. The head casts a "sound shadow" for high-frequency sound vibrations. The brain uses the difference in loudness to detect the location of the source of the sound.

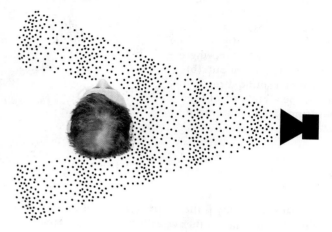

The second method involves detecting differences in the arrival time of sound pressure waves at each eardrum. This method works best for frequencies below approximately 3000 Hz. A 1000-Hz tone produces pressure waves approximately 1 foot apart. Because the distance between a person's eardrums is somewhat less than half that, a source of 1000-Hz sound located to one side of the head will cause one eardrum to be pushed in while the other eardrum is pulled out. In contrast, if the source of the sound is directly in front of the listener, both eardrums will move in synchrony. (See FIGURE 4•27.)

Researchers have found that when the source of a sound is located to the side of the head, as in Figure 4.27(a), axons in the right and left auditory nerves will fire at different times. The brain detects this disparity and so perceives the location of the sound at one side or the other. The brain can detect differences in firing times of a fraction of a millisecond. The easiest auditory stimuli to locate are those that produce brief clicks, which cause brief bursts of neural activity. Apparently, it is easiest for the brain to compare the arrival times of single bursts of sound.

focus On

The Deaf Community

From 0.1 to 0.2 percent of children in the Western world are born deaf. Deafness profoundly affects a person's ability to communicate with others. Imagine trying to join a group of people whose voices you cannot hear. But now imagine that the other people are also deaf. It is only in the company of people who have normal hearing that deafness hinders a person's ability to communicate (Erting et al., 1989; Sachs, 1989; Schein, 1989).

Deaf people aren't just people who have a particular sensory loss. They share a common culture. What unites

[**FIGURE 4·27**] Localizing the source of medium-frequency and high-frequency sounds through differences in arrival time. (a) Source of a 1000-Hz tone to the right. The pressure waves on each eardrum are out of phase; one eardrum is pushed in, whereas the other is pushed out. (b) Source of a sound directly in front. The vibrations of the eardrums are synchronized.

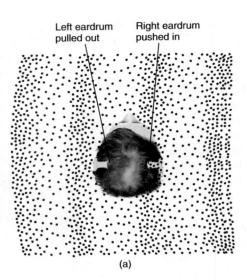

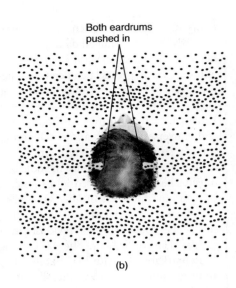

(a)

(b)

the Deaf community is the ability of its members to communicate with one another visually through sign language. In this way the Deaf community provides a remedy for what would seem the disadvantage of deafness: the inability to communicate readily with others.

Not all deaf people are members of the Deaf community. People who are postlingually deaf—people who become deaf later in life after they have learned oral and written language—are unlikely to learn sign language and join the Deaf community. (In this context, *lingual,* from the word for "tongue," refers to the acquisition of spoken language.) In addition, some prelingually deaf people—people who are born deaf or who become deaf during infancy—never learn sign language, primarily because they are "mainstreamed" in community schools or attend a school for the deaf that teaches oral communication.

There is no single, universal sign language. Deaf people from North America cannot communicate with deaf people from Great Britain. (They can write to each other, of course, but written English bears no relation to the sign language used in North America or Great Britain.) However, deaf people in France and North America can understand each other reasonably well, because American Sign Language (ASL) is partly based on the sign language that was used in France in the early nineteenth century.

Several attempts have been made (invariably by people who are not deaf) to "improve" sign languages. Deaf people resent such attempts, just as you might resent it if a foreigner tried to improve the English language by cleaning up its inconsistencies. Most people cherish their native languages, and deaf people are particularly proud of theirs.

The education of deaf persons poses special problems. Deafness follows the so-called 90 percent rule. That is, 90 percent of deaf children have parents who can hear, 90 percent of deaf people marry other deaf people, and 90 percent of deaf parents have children who can hear. Most parents of deaf children, not being themselves deaf, know nothing about the Deaf community. Thus, they are unable to

transmit to their children the most important characteristic of this community: a sign language. The current practice of "mainstreaming" children who have disabilities—that is, placing them in neighborhood schools with the rest of the population—means that most deaf children's teachers have no experience educating deaf students. Most of their teachers have never even met a deaf child before. Thus, deaf youngsters may not learn a sign language until late childhood or adolescence, when they finally meet other deaf people. Some never learn it.

Some schools for deaf students use the oralist approach to education. Children are taught to communicate orally with the rest of the population by reading lips and speaking. Both tasks are extremely difficult. Try watching a news broadcast with the sound turned off to see how much you can understand. Ask a friend to mouth, "bear, bar, pear," and see if you can detect the difference. Of course, you could get better with years of practice, but even a very skilled lip-reader must do a lot of guessing and anticipating. And you would be starting out knowing English as a

Communication by means of American Sign Language is as rapid, efficient, and rich in nuance and detail as communication by means of any spoken language.

native language, so you would know what words to look out for and anticipate. A congenitally deaf child taught with the oralist approach starts out with no knowledge of language at all, which makes the process doubly difficult. Also, learning to lipread and to speak (without the opportunity to hear yourself) takes so much time that not much of the school day is left for other academic subjects.

Most people in the Deaf community who communicate with one another by means of signing have negative reactions to oral communication. The difficult task of deciphering lip movements makes them feel tense. They also realize that their pronunciation is imperfect and that their voices sound strange to others. They feel at a disadvantage with respect to hearing people in a spoken conversation. In contrast, they feel relaxed and at ease when communicating with other deaf people by signing. A young man wrote about his experience when he entered Gallaudet University, an institution for deaf students in Washington, D.C., that uses sign language:

> As I made my way through many educational and enjoyable semesters, learning a "new" way of communicating, I was enthralled. I was able to understand a person 100 percent of the time without having to lipread or depend on notes. It is a special feeling to relax and listen when in the past you have had to pay so much attention to the person you were speaking with that you could never really relax. (Mentkowski, 1983, p. 1)

Like other people who closely identify with their cultures, members of the Deaf community feel pride in their common heritage and become defensive when they perceive threats to it. Some deaf people say that if they were given the opportunity to hear, they would refuse it. Some deaf parents have expressed happiness when they learned that their children were born deaf: They no longer needed to fear that their children would not be included in their own Deaf culture.

The cochlear implant, a technological development described earlier in this chapter, is perceived by many members of the Deaf community as a serious threat to their culture. Cochlear implants are most useful for two groups: people who became deaf in adulthood and very young children. Cochlear implants in postlingually deaf adults pose no threat to the Deaf community, because postlingually deaf persons never were members of Deaf culture. Putting a cochlear implant in a young child, however, means that the child's early education will take the oralist approach. In addition, many deaf people resent the implication that deafness is something that needs to be repaired. They see themselves as different but not at all defective.

QUESTIONS TO CONSIDER

1. A naturalist once noted that when a male bird stakes out his territory, he sings with a very sharp, staccato song that says, in effect, "Here I am, and stay away!" In contrast, if a predator appears in the vicinity, many birds will emit alarm calls that consist of steady whistles that start and end slowly. Knowing what you do about the two means of localizing sounds, why do you think these two types of calls have different characteristics?

2. If you had a child who was born deaf, would you send him or her to a school that taught sign language or to a school that emphasized speaking and lip-reading? Why? Now imagine that you are deaf (or, if you are deaf, that you are hearing). Does your answer change? Why or why not?

The Chemical Senses

We have two senses specialized for detecting chemicals in our environment: taste and smell. Together, they are referred to as the **chemosenses.**

Gustation

Taste, or **gustation,** is the simplest of the sensory modalities. Taste is not the same as flavor; the flavor of a food includes its odor and texture as well as its taste. You have probably noticed that the flavors of foods are diminished when you have a head cold. This loss of flavor occurs not because your taste buds are inoperative but because mucus congestion makes it difficult for odor-laden air to reach your receptors for the sense of smell. Without their characteristic odors to serve as cues, onions taste much like apples (although apples do not make your eyes water).

Taste Receptors and the Sensory Pathway Taste reception begins with the tongue. The tongue has a corrugated appearance marked by creases and bumps. The bumps are called **papillae** (from the Latin, meaning "nipple"). Each

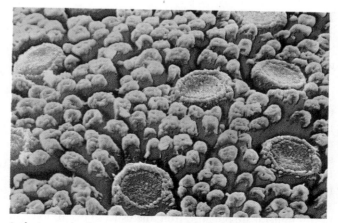

A photograph of taste buds taken with a scanning electron microscope.

---

chemosense One of the two sense modalities (gustation and olfaction) that detect the presence of particular molecules present in the environment.

gustation The sense of taste.

papilla A small bump on the tongue that contains a group of taste buds.

[FIGURE 4•28] The tongue. (a) Papillae on the surface of the tongue. (b) A taste bud.

Cross-section of a papilla

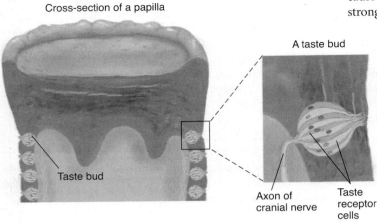

Taste bud

A taste bud

Axon of cranial nerve

Taste receptor cells

(a)   (b)

papilla contains numerous taste buds (in some cases as many as 200). A **taste bud** is a small organ containing receptor cells shaped like the segments of an orange. The cells have hairlike projections called microvilli that protrude through the pore of the taste bud into the saliva that coats the tongue and fills the trenches of the papillae. (See **FIGURE 4•28.**) Molecules of chemicals dissolved in the saliva stimulate the receptor cells by interacting with specialized receptor molecules on the microvilli. The receptor cells form synapses with dendrites of neurons that send axons to the brain through three different cranial nerves. Taste receptor cells have a life span of only ten days. They quickly wear out, being directly exposed to a rather hostile environment. As they degenerate, they are replaced by newly developed cells; the dendrite of the bipolar neuron is passed on to the new cell (Beidler, 1970).

The Five Qualities of Taste Gustation is clearly related to eating; this sense modality helps us to determine the nature of things we put in our mouths. The five qualities of taste are bitterness, sourness, sweetness, saltiness, and umami. You are familiar with the first four qualities, and we will consider the fifth one shortly. The gustatory system of most vertebrates responds to all five taste qualities. (An exception is the cat family; lions, tigers, leopards, and house cats do not detect sweetness—but then, none of the food they normally eat is sweet.) Clearly, sweetness receptors are food detectors. Most sweet-tasting foods, such as fruits and some vegetables, are safe to eat (Ramirez, 1990). Saltiness receptors detect the presence of sodium chloride. In some environments, inadequate amounts of this mineral are obtained from the usual source of food, so sodium chloride detectors help the animal to detect its

presence. If the body's store of sodium falls too low, the body cannot retain water. Blood volume will decrease, which can cause heart failure. Not surprisingly, loss of sodium stimulates a strong craving for the salty taste of sodium chloride.

Researchers now recognize the existence of a fifth taste quality: *umami.* **Umami,** a Japanese word that means "good taste," refers to the taste of monosodium glutamate (MSG), a substance that is often used as a flavor enhancer in Asian cuisine (Kurihara, 1987; Scott & Plata-Salaman, 1991). The umami receptor detects the presence of glutamate, an amino acid found in proteins. Presumably, the umami receptor provides the ability to taste proteins, an important nutrient.

Most species of animals will readily ingest substances that taste sweet or somewhat salty. Similarly, they are attracted to foods that are rich in amino acids, which explains the use of MSG as a flavor enhancer. However, they will tend to avoid substances that taste sour or bitter. Because of bacterial activity, many foods become acidic when they spoil. The acidity tastes sour and causes an avoidance reaction. (Of course, we have learned to make highly preferred mixtures of sweet and sour, such as lemonade.) Bitterness is almost universally avoided and cannot easily be improved by adding some sweetness. Many plants produce poisonous alkaloids, which protect them from being eaten by animals. Alkaloids taste bitter; thus, the bitterness receptor undoubtedly serves to warn animals away from these chemicals.

Olfaction

The sense of smell—**olfaction**—is one of the most puzzling sensory modalities and is unlike the other sensory modalities in two important ways. First, people have difficulty using words to describe odors. Second, odors have a powerful ability to evoke memories and feelings, even many years after an event (Chu & Downes, 2000). At some time in their lives, most people encounter an odor that they recognize as belonging to their childhood, even though they cannot identify it specifically. The phenomenon may occur because the olfactory system sends information to the limbic system, a part of the brain that plays a role in both emotions and memories.

Olfaction, like audition, seems to be an analytical sensory modality. That is, when we sniff air that contains a mixture of familiar odors, we usually can identify the individual components. The molecules do not blend together and produce a single odor the way lights of different wavelengths produce a single color. For example, when visiting a carnival, we can distinguish the odors of popcorn, cotton candy, crushed grass, and diesel oil in a single sniff.

Although many other mammals, such as dogs, have more sensitive olfactory systems than humans do, we should not underrate our own. The olfactory system is second only to the visual system in the number of sensory receptor cells, with an estimated 10 million cells. We can smell some substances at lower concentrations than the most-sensitive laboratory instruments can detect. For years we have written that one reason

---

taste bud   A small organ on the tongue that contains a group of gustatory receptor cells.

umami (*oo mah mee*)   The taste sensation produced by glutamate; identifies the presence of amino acids in foods.

olfaction   The sense of smell.

for the difference in sensitivity between our olfactory system and those of other mammals is that other mammals put their noses where odors are the strongest—just above the ground. For example, a dog following an odor trail sniffs along the ground, where the odors of a passing animal may have clung. Even a bloodhound's nose would not be very useful if it were located five or six feet above the ground, as ours is. It was gratifying to learn that a scientific study established the fact that when people sniff the ground like dogs do, their olfactory systems work much better. Porter et al. (2006) prepared a scent trail—a string moistened with essential oil of chocolate and laid down in a grassy field. The subjects were blindfolded and wore earmuffs, kneepads, and gloves, which prevented them from using anything other than their noses to follow the scent trail. They did quite well, and adopted the same zigzag strategy used by dogs. (See **FIGURE 4·29**.) As the authors wrote, these findings ". . . suggest that the poor reputation of human olfaction may reflect, in part, behavioral demands rather than ultimate abilities" (Porter et al., 2006, p. 27).

Anatomy of the Olfactory System

FIGURE 4·30 shows the anatomy of the olfactory system. The receptor cells lie in the **olfactory mucosa,** patches of mucous membrane on the roof of the nasal sinuses, just under the base of the brain. The receptor cells have cilia that are embedded in the olfactory mucosa. They also have axons that pass through small holes in the bone above the olfactory mucosa and form synapses with neurons in the olfactory bulbs. The **olfactory bulbs** are stalklike structures located at the base of the brain. They contain neural circuits that perform the first analysis of olfactory information.

The interaction between odor molecule and receptor cell is similar to the interaction between neurotransmitter and postsynaptic receptor on a neuron. That is, when a molecule of an odorous substance fits a receptor molecule located on the cilia of a receptor cell, the cell becomes excited. This excitation is passed on to the brain by the axon of the receptor cell.

[**FIGURE 4·29**] Scent-tracking behavior by a dog and a human. The path followed during the scent tracking is shown in red.

(From Porter, J., Craven, B., Khan, R. M., Chang, S.-J., Kang, I Judkewitz, B., Volpe, J., Settles, G., & Sobel, N. (2007). Mechanisms of scent-tracking in humans. *Nature Neuroscience, 10,* 27–29.)

Unlike information from all other sensory modalities, olfactory information is not sent to the thalamus and then relayed to a specialized region of the cerebral cortex. Instead, olfactory information is sent directly to several regions of the limbic system—in particular, to the amygdala and to the limbic cortex of the frontal lobe.

---

olfactory mucosa (*mew koh za*) The mucous membrane lining the top of the nasal sinuses; contains the cilia of the olfactory receptors.

olfactory bulb One of the stalklike structures located at the base of the brain that contain neural circuits that perform the first analysis of olfactory information.

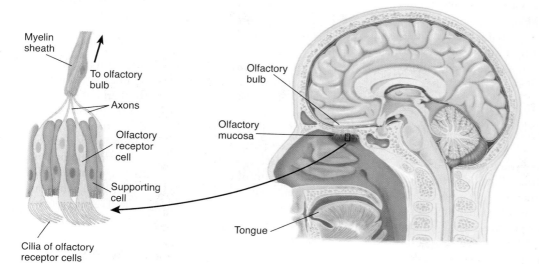

[**FIGURE 4·30**] The olfactory system.

Myelin sheath

To olfactory bulb

Axons

Olfactory receptor cell

Supporting cell

Cilia of olfactory receptor cells

Olfactory bulb

Olfactory mucosa

Tongue

The Dimensions of Odor We know that there are five qualities of taste, and a color can be specified in terms of hue, brightness, and saturation. Research in molecular biology has found that the olfactory system contains several hundred different receptor molecules, located in the membrane of the cilia of the receptor cells (Buck & Axel, 1991). These receptor molecules detect different categories of odors. Humans have 339 different types of olfactory receptors, and mice have 913 (Malnic, Godfrey, & Buck, 2004; Godfrey, Malnic, & Buck, 2004).

Humans can recognize up to 10,000 different odorants, and other animals can probably recognize even more of them (Shepherd, 1994). Even with 339 different olfactory receptors, that leaves many odors unaccounted for. And every year, chemists synthesize new chemicals, many with odors unlike those that anyone has previously detected. How can we use a relatively small number of receptors to detect so many different odorants?

The answer is that a particular odorant binds to more than one receptor. Thus, because a given glomerulus receives information from only one type of receptor, different odorants produce different *patterns* of activity in different glomeruli. Recognizing a particular odor, then, is a matter of recognizing a particular pattern of activity in the glomeruli. The task of chemical recognition is transformed into a task of spatial recognition.

FIGURE 4·31 illustrates this process (Malnic et al., 1999). The left side of the figure shows the shapes of eight hypothetical odorants. The right side shows four hypothetical odorant-receptor molecules. If a portion of the odorant molecule fits the binding site of the receptor molecule, it will activate it and stimulate the olfactory neuron. As you can see, each odorant molecule fits the binding site of at least one of the receptors and in most cases fits more than one of them. Notice also that the *pattern* of receptors activated by each of the eight odorants is different, which means that if we know which pattern of receptors is activated, we know which odorant is present. Of course, even though a particular odorant might bind with several different types of receptor molecules, it might not bind equally well with each of them. For example, it might bind very well with one receptor molecule, moderately well with another, weakly with another, and so on. (See Figure 4.31.) Presumably, the brain recognizes particular odors by recognizing different patterns of activation that it receives from the olfactory bulbs.

[**FIGURE 4·31**] A hypothetical explanation of coding of olfactory information. Different odorant molecules attach to different combinations of receptor molecules. (Activated receptor molecules are shown in blue.) Unique patterns of activation represent particular odorants.

(Adapted from Malnic, B., Hirono, J, Sato, T., & Buck, L. B. (1999). Combinatorial receptor codes for odors. *Cell, 96,* 713–723.)

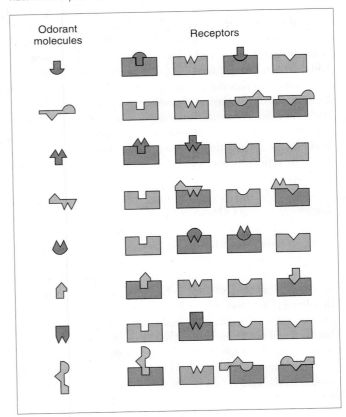

ƒocus On

Sensory-Specific Satiety

Have you ever found that after eating all you wanted of a really good meal you found that you could still manage to eat some dessert? (Who hasn't?) This phenomenon is an example of sensory-specific satiety (SSS), the decrease in the pleasantness and consumption of a specific food—but not a food with a different taste or texture—after eating it to satiety. This phenomenon explains why we tend to eat more of a meal if it is composed of a variety of different foods than just a single dish. SSS has survival value; if we become bored with eating one food, we are more likely to be motivated to taste some other foods, thus eating a greater variety of nutrients.

Rolls et al. (1981) found that if people eat a food to satiety, they will eat much more of an unexpected second course if it consists of a different food than if it consists of the same food. The subjects' ratings of the pleasantness of the food correlated well with the amount they ate. In another study, participants ate either a four-course meal of sausages, bread and butter, chocolate dessert, and bananas or ate only one of these foods to satiety. The subjects ate 60 percent more when foods were presented together than when they were presented separately (Rolls et al., 1981b). Even shape influences the amount of food eaten. If subjects are given three courses of pasta of different shapes, they eat more than when they are given three courses of the same pasta (Rolls et al., 1982).

SSS is also seen in the sense of smell. In an experiment in which participants were asked to rate the pleasantness of the odors of banana, tangerines, fish paste, chicken, and rose water before and after consuming bananas and chicken to satiety. Ratings of the pleasantness of chicken and banana odors (but not odors of other foods) significantly declined after satiety (Rolls & Rolls, 1997).

A functional imaging study by O'Doherty et al. (2000) suggests that a brain region, the orbitofrontal cortex (OFC), is involved in sensory-specific satiety. The investigators measured the response of the OFC to the odor of bananas before and after people had eaten all the bananas they wanted. The investigators found that the activation in the OFC was smaller when people sniffed the odor after they were satiated. No such decrease was observed when people sniffed the odor of vanilla, which indicates that the change was specific to the odor of the food eaten to satiety.

In another functional-imaging study, volunteers ate chocolate to satiety while their brains were scanned (Small et al., 2001). The subjects first ate a chunk of chocolate, rated it for pleasantness, and were then asked if they would like another. If they said yes, they were given another piece and again asked to rate its pleasantness. This continued until the participants indicated that they had eaten enough chocolate. The researchers found that when participants ate chocolate that they found pleasant, there was increased activity in several brain regions, including the *insula* (a region of the cerebral cortex hidden deep in the fissure that separates the frontal and parietal lobes) and a part of the OFC called the caudomedial OFC. When participants were sated, activity blood flow increased in several different brain regions, including a different part of the OFC (the caudolateral OFC) but *not* the insula.

Small and her colleagues suggest that the brain activity elicited by chocolate before and after satiation reflects two different systems, which mediate two aspects of behavior: approach and avoidance. That is, activation of the insula and caudomedial OFC reflect motivation to approach a desirable stimulus, and activation of the caudolateral OFC reflects motivation to avoid an undesirable stimulus. Activation of the insula is correlated with self-reports of cocaine craving among people who abuse this drug (Wang et al., 1999), and damage to the insula decreases the smoker's craving for cigarettes and makes it easy for them to quit smoking (Naqvi et al., 2007).

QUESTIONS TO CONSIDER

1. Bees and birds can taste sweet substances, but cats and alligators cannot. Obviously, the ability to taste particular substances is related to the range of foods a species eats. If, through the process of evolution, a species develops a greater range of foods, what do you think comes first, the food or the receptor? Would a species start eating something having a new taste (say, something sweet) and later develop new taste receptors by which to detect the taste, or would the taste receptors evolve first and then provide the animal with a new taste when it came across the food? Why?

2. As we saw, odors have a peculiar ability to evoke memories—a phenomenon vividly described by Marcel Proust in his novel *Remembrance of Things Past* and named the *Proust effect* in his honor. Have you ever encountered an odor that you knew was familiar, but you couldn't say exactly why? What explanations can you think of? Might this phenomenon have something to do with the fact that the sense of olfaction appeared very early during the evolutionary development of the human brain?

The Somatosenses

The body senses, or **somatosenses,** include our abilities to respond to touch, vibration, pain, warmth, coolness, limb position, muscle length and stretch, tilt of the head, and changes in the speed of head rotation. As we will see, each of these stimuli is detected by a different type of receptor.

Many experiences require simultaneous stimulation of several different sensory modalities. For example, taste and odor alone do not determine the flavor of spicy food; mild (or sometimes not-so-mild) stimulation of pain detectors in the mouth and throat gives hot food its special characteristic. Sensations such as tickle and itch are apparently mixtures of varying amounts of touch and pain. Similarly, our perception of the texture and three-dimensional shape of an object that we touch involves our senses of pressure, muscle and joint sensitivity, and motor control simultaneously (to manipulate the object). If we handle an object and find that it moves smoothly in our hands, we may conclude that it is slippery. If, after handling this object, our fingers subsequently slide across each other without much resistance, we perceive a feeling of oiliness. In contrast, if we perceive vibrations when we move our fingers over an object, we may consider it rough. And so on. If you close your eyes as you manipulate soft and hard, warm and cold, and smooth and rough objects, you can make yourself aware that the separate sensations interact and give rise to a complex perception.

The following discussion of the somatosenses groups them into three major categories: the skin senses, the internal senses, and the vestibular senses.

The Skin Senses

The entire surface of the human body is *innervated* (supplied with nerves) by the dendrites of neurons that transmit somatosensory information to the brain. Cranial nerves convey information from the face and the rest of the front portion of the head (including the teeth and the inside of the mouth and

---

somatosense Bodily sensations; sensitivity to such stimuli as touch, pain, and temperature.

[**FIGURE 4•32**] Sensory receptors. (a) In hairy skin. (b) In hairless skin.

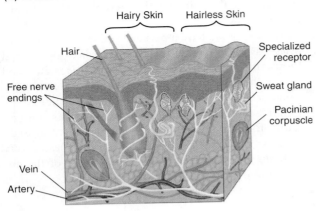

throat); spinal nerves convey information from the rest of the body's surface. All somatosensory information is detected by the dendrites of neurons; the system uses no separate receptor cells. However, some of these dendrites have specialized endings that modify the way they transduce energy into neural activity.

FIGURE 4•32 shows the sensory receptors found in hairy skin and in smooth, hairless skin (such as the skin on the palms of the hands or soles of the feet). The most common type of skin sensory receptor is the **free nerve ending,** which resembles the fine roots of a plant. Free nerve endings infiltrate the middle layers of both smooth and hairy skin and surround the hair follicles in hairy skin. If you bend a single hair on your forearm, you will see how sensitive the free nerve endings are.

The largest of the specialized skin receptors, called the **Pacinian corpuscle,** is actually visible to the naked eye. Pacinian corpuscles are very sensitive to touch. When they are moved, their axons fire a brief burst of impulses. Among the possible functions of Pacinian corpuscles is providing information about vibration.

Other specialized receptors detect different sensory qualities, including pressure, warmth, coolness, and pain.

Touch and Pressure Psychologists speak of touch and pressure as two separate sensations. They define touch as the sensation of very light contact of an object with the skin, and pressure as the sensation produced by more forceful contact. Sensations of pressure occur only when the skin is actually moving (being pushed in), which means that the pressure detectors respond only while they are being bent. If you rest your forearm on a table and place a small weight on your skin, you will feel the pressure at first, but eventually you will feel nothing

at all, if you keep your arm still. You fail to feel the pressure not because your brain "ignores" incoming stimulation but because the sensory endings no longer send impulses to your brain. Studies that have measured very slow, very minute movements of a weight sinking down into the skin have shown that sensory transmission ceases when the movements stop. With the addition of another weight on top of the first one, movement and sensory transmission begin again (Nafe & Wagoner, 1941). Of course, a person will feel a very heavy weight indefinitely, but the sensation of pain rather than pressure.

The ability to localize precisely the part of the body being touched varies widely across the surface of the body. The most sensitive regions are the lips and the fingertips. The most common measure of tactile discrimination (the ability to tell touches apart) is the **two-point discrimination threshold.** To determine this measure, a researcher touches a person with one or both legs of a caliper and asks the person to say whether the sensation is coming from one or two points. (See **FIGURE 4•33.**) The farther apart the legs of the caliper are before the person reports feeling two separate sensations, the lower the sensitivity of that region of skin. For example, we can detect two very closely spaced points on our lips, but the spacing must be much larger for us to detect them on our forearm, and very much larger on our back.

[**CASE STUDY**] In the past, neuroscientists believed that in humans tactile information was transmitted to the central nervous system only by large-diameter, rapidly conducting myelinated axons. However, Olausson et al. (2002) discovered a new category of tactile sensation that is transmitted by small-diameter unmyelinated axons. At age 31, patient G. L., a 54-year-old woman, "suffered a permanent and specific loss of large myelinated [sensory axons] after episodes of acute [nerve diseases] that affected her whole body below the nose. A . . . nerve biopsy indicated a complete loss of large-diameter myelinated fibers. . . . Before the present study, she denied having any touch sensibility below the nose, and she lost the ability to perceive tickle [after her nerves were damaged]. She states that her perceptions of temperature, pain and itch are intact" (Olausson et al., 2002, pp. 902–903).

G. L. could detect the stimuli that are normally attributed to small-diameter unmyelinated axons—temperature, pain, and itch—but she could not feel when her skin was

free nerve ending An unencapsulated (naked) dendrite of somatosensory neurons.

Pacinian corpuscle (*pa* **chin** *ee un*) A specialized, encapsulated somatosensory nerve ending, which detects mechanical stimuli, especially vibrations.

two-point discrimination threshold The minimum distance between two small points that can be detected as separate stimuli when pressed against a particular region of the skin.

[**FIGURE 4•33**] The method for determining the two-point discrimination threshold.

being touched with a stationary or vibrating object. However, when the hairy skin on her forearm or the back of her hand was stroked with a soft brush, she reported a faint, pleasant sensation. The investigators concluded that besides conveying information about pain and temperature, small-diameter unmyelinated axons constitute a "system for . . . touch that may underlie emotional, hormonal and affiliative responses to caresslike, skin-to-skin contact between individuals" (Olausson et al., 2002, p. 900). That sounds like a nice system to have, doesn't it?

Temperature

We can detect thermal stimuli over a very wide range of temperatures, from less than 8° C (noxious cold) to more than 52° C. (noxious heat). Investigators have long believed that no single receptor could detect such a range of temperatures, and recent research indicates that this belief was correct. At present, we know of six mammalian thermoreceptors (Voets et al., 2004). One of these receptors, which is sensitive to ranges of temperatures close to body temperature, is found in the anterior hypothalamus (Güler et al., 2002), the region of the brain that is responsible for measuring and maintaining body temperature.

Some of the thermal receptors respond to particular chemicals as well as to changes in temperature. For example, one of them is stimulated by menthol, a compound found in the leaves of many members of the mint family. As you undoubtedly know, peppermint tastes cool in the mouth, and menthol is added to some cigarettes to make the smoke feel cooler (and perhaps to try to delude smokers into thinking that the smoke is less harsh and damaging to the lungs). Menthol provides a cooling sensation because it binds with and stimulates this receptor and produces neural activity that the brain interprets as coolness. As we will see in the next subsection, chemicals can produce the sensation of heat also.

Pain

Pain reception, like temperature reception, is accomplished by the networks of free nerve endings in the skin. There appear to be at least three types of pain receptors (usually referred to as nociceptors, or "detectors of noxious stimuli"). High-threshold mechanoreceptors are free nerve endings that respond to intense pressure, which might be caused by something striking, stretching, or pinching the skin. A second type of free nerve ending appears to respond to extremes of heat, to acids, and to the presence of capsaicin, the active ingredient in chile peppers (Kress & Zeilhofer, 1999). (Note that we say that chile peppers make food taste "hot.") Caterina et al. (2000) found that mice with a targeted mutation against this receptor showed less sensitivity to painful high-temperature stimuli and would drink water to which capsaicin had been added. Ghilardi et al. (2005) found that a drug that blocks this type of receptor reduced pain in patients with bone cancer, which is apparently caused by the production of acid by the tumors.

Another type of nociceptor contains receptors that are sensitive to *ATP*, a chemical that serves as an energy source in all cells of the body (Burnstock & Wood, 1996). ATP is released when the blood supply to a region of the body is disrupted or when a muscle is damaged. It is also released by rapidly growing tumors. Thus, these nociceptors may be at least partly responsible for the pain caused by angina, migraine, damage to muscles, and some kinds of cancer.

Pain is a complex perception involving not only intense sensory stimulation but also emotion. That is, a given sensory input to the brain might be interpreted as pain in one situation and as pleasure in another. For example, when people are sexually aroused, they become less sensitive to many forms of pain and may even find such intense stimulation pleasurable. Opiates such as morphine produce *analgesia* (a reduction in pain) by stimulating opioid receptors on neurons in the brain; these neurons block the transmission of pain information. In contrast, some tranquilizers (e.g., diazepam [Valium]) depress neural systems that are responsible for the emotional reaction to pain but do not diminish the intensity of the pain. Thus, people who have received a drug such as Valium will report that they feel the pain but that it does not bother them as much.

Pain—or the fear of pain—is one of the most effective motivators of human behavior. It also serves us well in the normal course of living. As unpleasant as pain is, we would have difficulty surviving without it. People without any sensitivity to pain, caused by a genetic deficit that prevents them from detecting noxious stimuli, have failed to recognize that they have sprained an ankle or broken a bone, and have died of an undetected inflamed appendix.

A particularly interesting form of pain sensation occurs after a limb has been amputated: Up to 70 percent of amputees report that they feel as though their missing limbs still exist and that they often hurt. This phenomenon is referred to as the **phantom limb** (Melzack, 1992; Ramachandran & Hirstein, 1998). People who have phantom limbs report that the limbs feel very real; that if they try to reach something with their missing limb, it feels as though the limb responds. Sometimes they perceive the limb as protruding, and they may feel compelled to avoid knocking the limb against a door frame or sleeping with the limb between them and the mattress. People have reported all sorts of sensations in phantom limbs, including pain, pressure, warmth, cold, wetness, itching, sweatiness, and prickliness.

Melzack suggests that the phantom-limb perception is inherent in the organization of the parietal cortex. As we saw in Chapter 3, the parietal cortex is involved in our perception of our own bodies. Indeed, people who have sensory neglect, caused by lesions of the right parietal lobe, have been seen to push their own legs out of bed, believing that they actually belong to someone else. Melzack reports that some people who were born with limbs missing nevertheless experience the phantom limb. This suggests that our brains are genetically programmed to provide sensations from all four limbs—even if one or more limbs are absent.

---

phantom limb Sensations that appear to originate in a limb that has been amputated.

The Internal Senses

Sensory receptors located in our internal organs, bones and joints, and muscles convey painful, neutral, and, in some cases, pleasurable sensory information. For example, the internal senses convey the pain of arthritis, the physical location of our limbs in three dimensions, the pangs of hunger, and the pleasure of a warm drink descending to our stomach.

Muscles contain special sensory receptors. One class of receptors, located at the junction between muscles and the tendons that connect them to the bones, provides information about the amount of force the muscle is exerting. These receptors protect the body by inhibiting muscular contractions when they become too forceful. During competition, weight lifters may receive injections of a local anesthetic near the tendons of some muscles to eliminate this protective mechanism. This enables the athletes to lift even heavier weights. Unfortunately, tendons may snap or bones may break under the increased force.

Another stretch-detection system consists of spindle-shaped receptors distributed throughout the muscle. These receptors, appropriately called **muscle spindles**, inform the brain about changes in muscle length. Although we are not conscious of the specific information provided by the muscle spindles, the brain uses the information, together with information from joint receptors, to keep track of the locations of parts of our body and to control muscular contractions.

The Vestibular Senses

What we call our "sense of balance" involves several senses, not merely one. For example, if you stand on one foot and then close your eyes, you immediately realize how important vision is to balance. The **vestibular apparatus** of the inner ear provides additional sensory input that helps us remain upright.

The three liquid-filled **semicircular canals**—located in the inner ear and oriented at right angles to one another—detect changes in the rotation of the head. (See FIGURE 4•34.) Rotation of the head causes motion of the liquid, which stimulates the receptor cells located in the canals.

Another set of inner ear organs, the **vestibular sacs**, contains crystals of calcium carbonate that are embedded in a gelatin-like substance attached to receptive hair cells. In one sac, the receptive tissue is on the wall; in the other, it is on the floor. When the head tilts, the weight of the calcium carbonate crystals shifts, producing different forces on the cilia of the hair cells. These forces change the activity of the hair cells, and the information is transmitted to the brain.

---

muscle spindle   A muscle fiber that functions as a stretch receptor; arranged parallel to the muscle fibers responsible for contraction of the muscle, it detects muscle length.

vestibular apparatus   The receptive organs of the inner ear that contribute to balance and perception of head movement.

semicircular canal   One of a set of organs in the inner ear that responds to rotational movements of the head.

vestibular sac   One of two sets of receptor organs in each inner ear that detect changes in the tilt of the head.

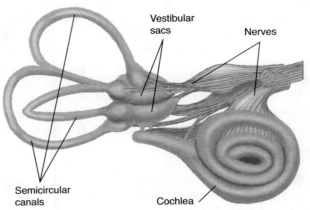

[**FIGURE 4•34**]   The three semicircular canals and two vestibular sacs located in the inner ear.

The vestibular sacs help us maintain an upright head position. They also participate in a reflex that enables us to see clearly even when the head is being jarred. When we walk, our eyes are jostled back and forth. The jarring of the head stimulates the vestibular sacs to cause reflex movements of the eyes that partially compensate for the head movement. People who lack this reflex because of localized brain damage must stop walking to see things clearly—for example, to read a street sign.

QUESTION TO CONSIDER

Why does repetitive vestibular stimulation (like that provided by a boat ride on rough water) sometimes cause nausea and vomiting? What useful functions might this response serve?

Natural Analgesia

The brain contains neural circuitry through which certain types of stimuli can produce analgesia, primarily through the release of the endogenous opioids (the opiate-like chemicals produced in the brain). What functions does this system perform? Most researchers believe that it prevents pain from disrupting behavior in situations in which pain is unavoidable and in which the damaging effects of the painful stimuli are less important than the goals of the behavior. For example, males fighting for access to females during mating season will fail to pass on their genes if pain elicits withdrawal responses that interfere with fighting. Indeed, these conditions (fighting or mating) *do* diminish pain.

Komisaruk and Larsson (1971) found that genital stimulation produced analgesia. They gently probed the cervix of female rats with a glass rod and found that the procedure diminished the animals' sensitivity to pain. It also increased the activity of neurons in the periaqueductal gray matter and decreased the pain response in the thalamus (Komisaruk & Steinman, 1987). The phenomenon also occurs in humans; Whipple and Komisaruk (1988) found that self-administered vaginal stimulation reduces women's sensitivity to painful stimuli but not to neutral tactile stimuli. Presumably, copulation also triggers analgesic mechanisms. The adaptive significance of this phenomenon is clear: Painful stimuli that are encountered during sexual intercourse are less likely to cause the behavior to be interrupted; thus, the chances of pregnancy are increased. (As you will recall, passing on one's genes is the ultimate criterion of the adaptive significance of a trait.)

Pain can also be reduced, at least in some people, by administering a pharmacologically inert placebo. When some people take a medication that they believe will reduce pain, it triggers the release of endogenous opioids and actually does reduce pain sensations. This effect is eliminated if the people are given an injection of naloxone, a drug that blocks opiate receptors (Benedetti, Arduino, & Amanzio, 1999). Thus, for some people, a placebo is not pharmacologically inert—it has a physiological effect. The experimenter in the chapter prologue used this drug when he blocked the analgesic effect of Melissa's own endogenous opiates. The placebo effect may be mediated through connections of the frontal cortex with a region of the midbrain that controls the transmission of pain information to the brain. A PET imaging study by Zubieta et al. (2005) confirmed that analgesia produced by a placebo caused the release of endogenous opiates in the brain.

A functional imaging study by Wager et al. (2004) supports this suggestion. They administered painful stimuli (heat or electrical shocks) to people's skin with or without the application of an "analgesic" skin cream that was actually an unmedicated placebo. They observed a placebo effect—reports of less-intense pain and decreased activity in the primary pain-reactive regions of the brain. They also observed increased activity of the prefrontal cortex and the midbrain. Presumably, the expectation of decreased sensitivity to pain activated the prefrontal cortex, and connections of this region with the midbrain activated endogenous mechanisms of analgesia.

Another procedure, hypnosis, can also reduce pain—or at least, people's reaction to pain. Rainville et al. (1997) produced pain sensations in human subjects by having them put their arms in ice water. Under one condition, the researchers used hypnosis to diminish the unpleasantness of the pain. The hypnosis worked; the subjects said that the pain was less unpleasant, even though it was still as intense. Functional imaging showed that the painful stimulus activated both the primary somatosensory cortex and the *anterior cingulate cortex,* a region of the limbic cortex in the frontal lobe. When the subjects were hypnotized and found the pain less unpleasant, the activity of the anterior cingulate cortex decreased—but the activity of the primary somatosensory cortex remained high. It appeared that the pain signal was still strong, but that it produced less of an unpleasant emotional reaction. Several functional imaging studies have shown that under certain conditions, stimuli associated with pain can activate the anterior cingulate cortex even when no actual painful stimulus is applied.

In a functional imaging study of romantically involved couples, Singer et al. (2004) found a painful electrical shock delivered to the back of women's hands activated both the somatosensory cortex and the anterior cingulate cortex. When the women saw their partners receive a painful shock but did not receive one themselves, the anterior cingulate cortex became active, but the somatosensory cortex did not. Thus, the emotional component of pain—in this case, a vicarious experience of pain, provoked by empathy with the feelings of a loved one—caused responses in the brain similar to the ones caused by actual pain. Just as we saw in the study by Rainville et al. (1997), the somatosensory cortex is activated only by an actual noxious stimulus. These studies indicate that different brain mechanisms are involved in perception of pain and the unpleasant feeling that pain normally provokes.

CHAPTER SUMMARY

Sensory Processing

We experience the world through our senses. Our knowledge of the world stems from the accumulation of sensory experience and subsequent learning. All sensory experiences are the result of energy from events that is transduced into activity of receptor cells, which are specialized neurons. Transduction causes changes in the activity of axons of sensory nerves, and these changes in activity inform the sensory mechanisms of the brain about the environmental event. The information received from the receptor cells is transmitted to the brain by means of two coding schemes: anatomical coding and temporal coding.

To study the nature of subjective experience scientifically, we must be able to measure it. In nineteenth-century Germany, Weber devised the concept of the just-noticeable difference (jnd), and Fechner used the jnd to measure perceived intensity of stimuli. Signal-detection theory gave rise to methods that enabled psychologists to assess people's sensitivity to stimuli despite individual differences in response bias. The methods of psychophysics apply to all sensory modalities, including sight, hearing, taste, smell, and touch.

Vision

Imagine yourself watching an ice-skating competition on television with a friend. The cornea and lens of each eye cast an image of the screens on your retinas, which contain photoreceptors: rods and cones. In bright illumination, only your cones gather visual information; your rods work only when the light is very dim. The energy from the light that reaches the cones in your retinas is transduced into neural activity when photons strike molecules of photopigment, splitting them into their two constituents. This event causes the cones to send information through the bipolar cells to the ganglion cells. The axons of the ganglion cells form the optic nerves and have synapses with neurons in the brain.

Vision requires the behavior of looking, which consists of moving our eyes and head. The eyes have a repertoire of movements that function for visual perception. Experiments using stabilized images show that small, involuntary movements keep an image moving across the photoreceptors, thus preventing them from adapting to a constant stimulus. (As you will see later in this chapter, other sensory systems also respond better to changing stimuli than to constant ones.) As the skaters glide across the ice, your eyes follow them with pursuit movements. Now your friend says something, so you turn your head toward him. Your eyes make rapid saccadic movements so that you can look directly at your friend's face. These vergence movements orient the eyes so that each eye is fixed on the same point. Because your friend is closer to you than the television screen, you must also accommodate for the change in distance, adjusting the focus of the lenses of your eyes.

When an image of the visual scene is cast on the retina, each part of the image has a different color, which can be specified in terms of its hue (corresponding to the dominant wavelength), brightness (intensity), and saturation (purity). Information about color is encoded trichromatically by your cones; the red, green, and blue cones respond in proportion to the amount of the appropriate wavelength contained in the light striking them. This information is transformed into an opponent-process coding, signaled by the firing rates of red/green and yellow/blue ganglion cells, and is transmitted to the brain. If you stare for a while at a colored image and then look at a light-colored blank wall, you will see a negative afterimage. If you are a male, the chances are about 1 in 20 that you will have some defect in red/green color vision. If this is the case, your red or green cones contain the wrong photopigment. Male or female, chances are very slim that you will have a blue/yellow defect caused by the absence of functioning blue cones.

Audition

The human auditory system is sophisticated enough to differentiate among a vast array of sounds. Audition translates the physical dimensions of sound—amplitude, frequency, and complexity—into the perceptual dimensions of loudness, pitch, and timbre for sounds ranging from 30 to 20,000 Hz. Sound-pressure waves put the process in motion by setting up vibrations in the eardrum, which are passed on to the ossicles. Vibrations of the stirrup against the membrane behind the oval window create pressure changes in the fluid within the cochlea that cause the basilar membrane to vibrate. This causes the auditory hair cells on the basilar membrane to move relative to the tectorial membrane. The resulting pull on the cilia of the hair cells stimulates them to secrete a neurotransmitter that excites auditory neurons and stimulates axons in the auditory nerve, which brings this information to the brain.

Two different methods of detection enable the brain to recognize the pitch of a sound. Different high-frequency and medium-frequency sounds are perceived when different parts of the basilar membrane vibrate in response to these frequencies. Low-frequency vibrations are detected when the tip of the basilar membrane vibrates in synchrony with the sound, which causes some axons in the auditory nerve to fire at that frequency.

Locating the source of a sound depends on two systems. The ear locates low-frequency sounds by differences in the arrival time of the sound waves in each ear. It locates high-frequency sounds by differences in intensity that result from the "sound shadow" cast by your head.

The auditory system analyzes sounds with complex timbre into their constituent frequencies, each of which causes a particular part of the basilar membrane to vibrate. All of these functions proceed automatically, so the brain can hear the sound of a clarinet or any other combination of fundamental frequency and harmonics. The sources of complex sounds are recognized by a region in the posterior temporal lobe that is also involved in recognizing objects by sight.

The Deaf community consists of deaf people who communicate visually by means of a sign language. The social isolation that a deaf person may feel among oral communicators disappears in the company of other people who can sign. Communication by sign languages can be as accurate and efficient as spoken communication.

The Chemical Senses

Both gustation and olfaction are accomplished by cells whose receptors respond selectively to various kinds of molecules. Taste buds have at least five kinds of receptors, which respond to molecules that we perceive as sweet, salty, sour, bitter, or umami. To most organisms, sweet, umami, and moderately salty substances taste pleasant, whereas sour or bitter substances taste unpleasant. Sweet, umami, and salty receptors permit us to detect nutritious foods and sodium chloride. Sour and bitter receptors help us avoid substances that might be poisonous.

Olfaction is a remarkable sense modality. Olfactory information combines with information about taste to provide us with the flavor of a food present in our mouths. We can distinguish countless different odors and can recognize smells from childhood, even if we cannot remember when or where we first encountered them. Although we recognize similarities between different odors, most seem unique. Unlike visual stimuli such as colors, odors do not easily blend. The detection of different odors appears to be accomplished by a little more than 300 different receptor molecules located in the membrane of the cilia of the olfactory receptor cells. The brain recognizes particular odors by analyzing the pattern of neural activity produced by activation of these receptors.

The Somatosenses

The somatosenses gather several different kinds of information from different parts of the body. The skin senses of temperature, touch and pressure, vibration, and pain inform us about the nature of objects that come in contact with our skin. The sensitive Pacinian corpuscles in the skin detect vibration. A special set of receptors detects the pleasurable feeling of a caress. The skin's temperature receptors convey the sense of warmth or coolness, responding chiefly to changes in temperature but also, in some cases, to chemicals such as menthol or capsaicin. Also in the skin, free nerve endings give rise to sensations of pain. The internal senses convey sensations such as hunger pangs or the pain of a kidney stone. Sensory receptors in our muscles and joints inform the brain of the movement and location of our arms and legs. The vestibular senses help us keep our balance and produce eye movements that compensate for head movements.

succeed with mypsychlab

Visit MyPsychLab for practice quizzes, flashcards, and dozens of videos and animated tutorials, including the following items you can find in the "Multimedia Library":

Ear Ringing
Noise and the Brain
Brain Pain

Normal Vision, Nearsightedness
Light and the Optic Nerve

Weber's Law

SUGGESTIONS FOR FURTHER READING

General

Coren, S., Ward, L. M., & Enns, J. T. (2003). *Sensation and perception* (6th ed.). New York: Wiley.

Vision

Bruce, V., Green, P. R., & Georgeson, M. A. (2003). *Visual perception: Physiology, psychology and ecology* (4th ed.). New York: Psychology Press.

Gregory, R. L. (1997). *Eye and brain: The psychology of seeing* (5th ed.). Princeton, N.J.: Princeton University Press.

Audition

Yost, W. A. (2000). *Fundamentals of hearing: An introduction* (4th ed.). San Diego, CA: Academic Press.

Chemical Senses

Doty, R. L. (2003). *Handbook of olfaction and gustation* (2nd ed.). New York: Dekker.

Martin, G. N. (2004). A neuroanatomy of flavour. *Petits Propos Culinaires, 76,* 58–79.

Smith, D. V., & Margolskee, R. F. (2001). Making sense of taste. *Scientific American, 284(3),* 26–33.

Sensory-Specific Satiety

Naqvi, N. H., Rudrauf, D., Damasio, H., & Bechara, A. (2007). Damage to the insula disrupts addiction to cigarette smoking. *Science, 315,* 531–534.

O'Doherty, J., Rolls, E. T., Francis, S., Bowtell, R., McGlone, E., Kobal, G., Renner, B., & Ahne, G. (2000). Sensory-specific satiety-related olfactory activation of the human orbitofrontal cortex. *Neuroreport, 11,* 399–403.

Rolls, B. J., Rolls, E. T., Rowe, E. A., & Sweeney, K. (1981a). Sensory specific satiety in man. *Physiology and Behavior, 27,* 137–142.

Rolls, B. J., Rowe, E. A., & Rolls, E. T. (1982). How flavour and appearance affect human feeding. *Proceedings on the Nutrition Society, 41,* 109–117.

Rolls, B. J., Rowe, E. A., Rolls, E. T., Kingston, B., Megson, A., & Gunary, R. (1981b). Variety in a meal enhances food intake in man. *Physiology and Behavior, 26,* 215–221.

Rolls, E. T., & Rolls, J. H. (1997). Olfactory sensory-specific satiety in humans. *Physiology and Behavior, 61,* 461–473.

Small, D. M., Zatorre, R. J., Dagher, A., Evans, A. C., & Jones-Gotman, M. (2001). Changes in brain activity related to eating chocolate: From pleasure to aversion. *Brain, 124,* 1720–1733.

Wang, G. J., Volkow, N. D., Fowler, J. S., Cervany, P., Hitzemann, R. J., Pappas, N. R., Wong, C. T., & Felder, C. (1999). Regional brain metabolic activation during craving elicited by recall of previous drug experiences. *Life Sciences, 64,* 775–784.

CHAPTER 5

Perception

Taken from *Psychology: The Science of Behavior*, Seventh Edition, by Neil R. Carlson, Harold Miller,
C. Donald Heth, John W. Donahoe, and G. Neil Martin.

Prologue

The Case of Mrs. R.

Mrs. R.'s recent stroke had not impaired her ability to talk or to move about, but it had affected her vision. Mrs. R. went to see Dr. L., a young neuropsychologist.

"How are you, Mrs. R.?" asked Dr. L.

"I'm fine. I can do just about everything that I did before I had my stroke."

"Good. How is your vision?"

"Well, I'm afraid that's still a problem."

"What seems to give you the most trouble?"

"I just don't seem to be able to recognize things. When I'm working in my kitchen, I know what everything is as long as no one moves anything. A few times my husband tried to help me by putting things away, and I couldn't see them any more." She laughed. "Well, I could see them, but I just couldn't say what they were."

Dr. L. took some objects out of a paper bag and placed them on the table in front of Mrs. R.

"Can you tell me what these are?" he asked. "And," he added, "please don't touch them."

Mrs. R. stared intently at the objects. "No, I can't rightly say what they are."

Dr. L. pointed to one of them, a wristwatch. "Tell me what you see here," he said.

Mrs. R. looked thoughtful, turning her head one way and then the other. "Well, I see something round, and it has two things attached to it, one on the top and one on the bottom." She continued to stare at it. "There are some things inside the circle, I think, but I can't make out what they are."

"Pick it up."

She did so, made a wry face, and said, "Oh. It's a wristwatch." At Dr. L.'s request, she picked up the rest of the objects, one by one, and identified each of them correctly.

"Do you have trouble recognizing people, too?" asked Dr. L.

"Oh, yes!" she sighed. "While I was still in the hospital, my husband and my son both came in to see me, and I couldn't tell who was who until my husband said something—then I could tell which direction his voice was coming from. Now I've trained myself to recognize my husband. I can usually see his glasses and his bald head, but I have to work at it. And I've been fooled a few times."

"What does a face look like to you?" asked Dr. L.

"Well, I know that it's a face, because I can usually see the eyes, and it's on top of a body. I can see a body pretty well, by how it moves." She paused a moment. "Oh, yes, I forgot, sometimes I can recognize a person by how he moves. You know, you can often recognize friends by the way they walk, even when they're far away.

I can still do that. That's funny, isn't it? I can't see people's faces very well, but I can recognize the way they walk."

Dr. L. made some movements with his hands. "Can you tell what I'm doing?" he asked.

"Yes, you're mixing something—like some cake batter."

He mimed the gestures of turning a key, writing, and dealing out playing cards, and Mrs. R. recognized them without any difficulty.

"Do you have any trouble reading?" he asked.

"Well, a little, but I don't do too badly."

Dr. L. handed her a magazine, and she began to read the article aloud—somewhat hesitantly, but accurately. "Why is it," she asked, "that I can see the words all right but have so much trouble with things and with people's faces?" ∎

The primary function of the sense organs, as we saw in Chapter 4, is to provide information to guide behavior. But the sensory mechanisms cannot achieve this function by themselves. Consider vision, for example, in light of the opening case. The brain receives fragments of information from approximately 1 million axons in each of the optic nerves. It combines and organizes these fragments into the perception of a scene—objects having different forms, colors, and textures, residing at different locations in three-dimensional space. Even when our bodies or our eyes move, exposing the photoreceptors to entirely new patterns of visual information, our perception of the scene before us does not change. The brain keeps track of the body's movements and those of the eyes and compensates for the constantly changing patterns of neural firing that these movements cause. **Perception,** as indicated in Chapter 4, is the process of responding to the information that the sense organs provide and gives unity and coherence to sensory input. Perception implies meaningfulness—that we understand what the sensory systems are conveying and respond in a knowing way to it.

Perception is a rapid, automatic, largely unconscious process; it is not a deliberate, effortful activity in which we puzzle out the meaning of what we see. We do not first see an object and then perceive it; we simply perceive the object. Although occasionally what we see is ambiguous, requiring us to reflect on what it might be or gather further evidence to decide what it is, doing so is more problem solving than perceiving. If we look at a scene carefully, we can describe the elements of the objects that are present, but we do so because we perceive the objects and the background of which they are a part. For example, if you look at a tall, cylindrical object

on a countertop, you immediately perceive a glass and subsequently perceive the smudges near its top, the lettering on its side, and the few sips of beverage remaining at its bottom. Also note that our awareness of the process of visual perception comes only after it is complete; we are presented with a finished product, not the details of the process.

The distinction between sensation and perception is not easy to make; in some respects, the distinction is arbitrary. Probably because of the importance we give to vision and because of the richness of the information provided by our visual system, psychologists make a more-explicit distinction between visual sensation and perception than they do for the other sensory systems. Hence, this chapter on perception will focus primarily on the visual system, while recognizing that the other perceptual systems could be analyzed similarly. You will recall that, in its consideration of vision, Chapter 4 focused largely on the eye. Accordingly, in this chapter, we turn first to the brain's processing of information transmitted from the eyes.

Brain Mechanisms of Visual Perception

Although the eyes contain the photoreceptors that detect areas of different brightness and color in the visual field, perception takes place hierarchically in the brain. The optic nerves send visual information to the thalamus, which relays the information to the primary visual cortex, located in the occipital lobe at the back of the brain. In turn, neurons in the primary visual cortex send visual information to the visual association cortex—the brain regions where visual perception takes place. (See **FIGURE 5·1.**)

The Primary Visual Cortex

Our knowledge of the earliest stages of visual analysis has come from investigations of the activity of individual neurons in the thalamus and the primary visual cortex. For example, in their pioneering studies, Nobel Prize laureates David Hubel and Torsten Wiesel inserted microelectrodes—extremely small wires with microscopically sharp points—into various regions of the visual systems of cats and monkeys to detect the action potentials produced by individual neurons (Hubel & Wiesel, 1977, 1979, 2004). The signals picked up by the microelectrodes are electronically amplified and sent to a recording device for later analysis.

After positioning a microelectrode close to a neuron, Hubel and Wiesel presented various stimuli on a large screen in front of the open-eyed but anesthetized animal. The anesthesia makes the animal unconscious but does not prevent neurons in the visual system from responding. The researchers moved a

---

perception The brain's use of information provided by sensory systems to produce a response.

[**FIGURE 5•1**] The visual system of the brain. Arrows represent the flow of visual information. Sensory information from the eye is transmitted through the optic nerve to the thalamus, and from there it is relayed to the primary visual cortex. The results of the analysis performed there are sent to the visual association cortex of the occipital lobe (first level) and then on to that of the temporal lobe and parietal lobe (second level). At each stage, additional analysis takes place.

(From Carlson, N. R. (2004). *Physiology of Behavior,* 8/e. Published by Allyn and Bacon, Boston, MA. Copyright © 2004 by Pearson Education. Reprinted by permission of the publisher.)

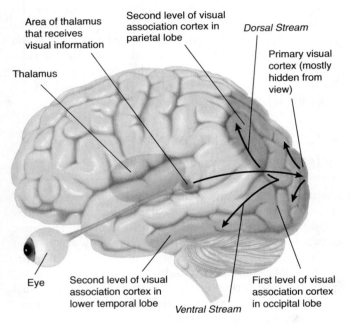

stimulus around on the screen until they located the point where it had the largest effect on the electrical activity of the neuron. Next, they presented stimuli of various shapes to learn which ones produced the greatest response from the neuron.

From their experiments, Hubel and Wiesel concluded that the geography of the visual field is retained in the primary visual cortex. That is, the surface of the retina is "mapped" on the surface of the primary visual cortex. However, this map on the brain is distorted, with the largest amount of area given to the center of the visual field, where our vision is most precise. The map is actually like a mosaic—a picture made of individual tiles or pieces of glass. Each "tile" or, in neural terms, **module,** consists of a block of tissue approximately 0.5 × 0.7 millimeters in size and containing approximately 150,000 neurons. All of the neurons within a module receive information from the same small region of the retina. The primary visual cortex contains approximately 2,500 of these modules.

module   An area of tissue in the primary visual cortex whose neurons receive their input from the same small region in the retina.

receptive field   That portion of the visual field in which the presentation of visual stimuli will produce an alteration in the firing rate of a particular neuron.

Because each module in the primary visual cortex receives information from a small region of one retina, that means it receives information from a small region of the visual field—the scene that is currently projected onto the retina. Hubel and Wiesel found that neural circuits within each module analyzed various characteristics of their own particular part of the visual field—that is, of their **receptive field.** For example, some circuits detected the presence of lines passing through the field and signaled the orientation of these lines (that is, the angle they made with respect to the horizon). Other circuits detected the width of these lines. Others detected the movement of the lines and the direction of these movements. Still others detected the lines' colors.

FIGURE 5•2 shows a recording of the responses of an orientation-sensitive neuron in the primary visual cortex. This neuron is located in a cluster of neurons that receives information from a small portion of the visual field. (That is, the neuron has a small receptive field.) The neuron responds maximally when a line oriented at 50 degrees to the vertical is placed in this location—especially when the line is moving through the receptive field. This response is highly specific to orientation; the neuron responds very little when a line having a 70-degree or 30-degree orientation is passed through the receptive field. Other neurons in this cluster share the same receptive field but respond to lines of different orientations. Thus, the orientation of lines that pass through this receptive field is signaled by an increased rate of firing of particular neurons in the cluster.

The Visual Association Cortex

Although the primary visual cortex is necessary for visual perception, the perception of objects and of the totality of the visual scene does not take place there. If you closed one eye and looked at the scene in front of you through a drinking straw, you would see about the amount of information received by an individual module of the primary visual cortex. Thus, for us to perceive objects and entire visual scenes, the information from these individual modules must be combined. That combination takes place in the visual association cortex.

Two Streams of Visual Analysis   Visual information analyzed by the primary visual cortex is further analyzed in the visual association cortex. So far, investigators have identified more than two dozen distinct regions and subregions of the visual cortex of the rhesus monkey. These regions are arranged hierarchically, beginning with the primary visual cortex (Grill-Spector & Malach, 2004). Circuits of neurons analyze particular aspects of visual information and send the results of their analysis to other circuits, which perform further analysis. At each step in the process, successively more-complex features are analyzed. Remarkably, within a matter of milliseconds, the process leads to the perception of the scene and the objects in it. The higher levels of the perceptual process also interact with memories. The viewer recognizes familiar objects and learns to recognize new, unfamiliar ones.

[FIGURE 5•2] Responses of a single cortical neuron to lines of particular orientations that are passed through its receptive field.

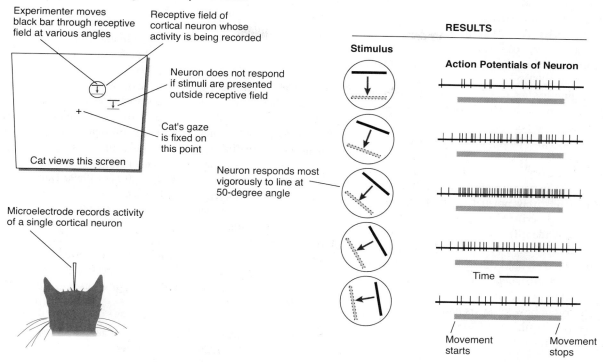

Neurons in the primary visual cortex send axons to the region of the visual association cortex that surrounds the striate cortex. At this point, the visual association cortex divides into two pathways: the **ventral stream** and the **dorsal stream** (Ungerleider & Mishkin, 1982; Tong & Pearson, 2007). Figure 5.1 shows that the ventral stream continues forward and ends in the inferior temporal cortex. The dorsal stream ascends into the posterior parietal cortex. The ventral stream functions in the recognition of *what* an object is, that is, what *form* it has, as well as what *color* it has. For the dorsal stream, it is *where* an object is located and whether it is *moving*. (See **FIGURE 5•3**.)

ventral stream The flow of information from the primary visual cortex to the visual association area in the lower temporal lobe; used to form the perception of an object's shape, color, and orientation (the "what" system).

dorsal stream The flow of information from the primary visual cortex to the visual association area in the parietal lobe; used to form the perception of an object's location in three-dimensional space (the "where" system).

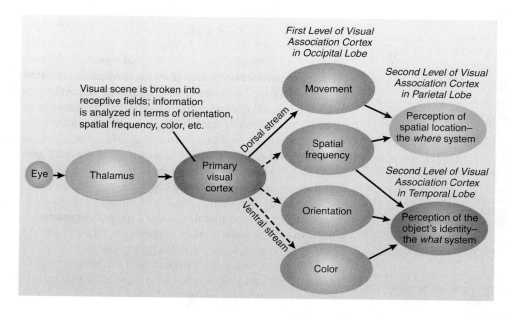

[FIGURE 5•3] A schematic diagram of the types of analyses performed on visual information in the primary visual cortex and the various regions of the visual association cortex.

The Ventral Stream: Perception of Form Studies with laboratory animals have found that the recognition of visual patterns and identification of particular objects takes place in the inferior temporal cortex, located at the end of the ventral stream. It is here that analyses of form and color are put together, and perceptions of three-dimensional objects emerge (Riesenhuber & Poggio, 2002).

Functional-imaging studies and the study of people with damage to the visual association cortex confirm the conclusions of animal studies. Brain damage can cause a category of deficits known as **visual agnosia.** *Agnosia* ("failure to know") refers to an inability to perceive or identify a stimulus that exists within a specific sensory modality. The inability occurs even though the person can perceive the details of the stimulus and otherwise retain relatively normal intellectual capacity. Mrs. R., whose case was described in the Prologue, had visual agnosia. She could not identify common objects by sight, even though she had relatively normal visual acuity. When she was permitted to hold an object that she could not recognize visually, she could immediately recognize it by touch and say what it was. Clearly she had not lost her memory of the object or simply forgotten how to say its name.

Prosopagnosia (prah-suh-pagg-NOSE-yuh) is the inability to recognize familiar faces (*prosopon* is Greek for "face"). That is, patients with this disorder can recognize that they are looking at a face and can recognize its gender, approximate age, and ethnicity, but they cannot say whose face it is—even if it belongs to a relative or close friend. They see eyes, ears, a nose, a mouth, but they cannot recognize the particular configuration of these features that identifies a specific individual's face. They still remember who these people are and will usually recognize them when they hear their voice. Perhaps the best-known case of prosopagnosia was reported by the neurologist Oliver Sacks (2006).

[**CASE STUDY**] The patient, Dr P., was a renowned music teacher, who attended a neurological examination with his wife. On rising to leave, Dr P. looked around for his hat. He put out his hand and placed it on his wife's head, then attempted to lift it to his head, as if it were a hat! Had she spoken he would have instantly recognized her. As another patient said, "I have trouble recognizing people from just faces alone. I look at their hair color, listen to their voices . . . I use clothing, voice, and hair. I try to associate something with a person one way or another . . . what they wear, how their hair is worn" (Buxhaum, Glosser, & Coslett, 1999, p. 43).

Studies with brain-damaged people and functional imaging studies indicate that face-recognizing circuits are found in the **fusiform** (FYOO-zih-form) **face area (FFA),** a region of the ventral stream located at the base of the brain.

Several kinds of evidence suggest that face-recognition circuits develop as a result of experience in seeing people's faces. For example, brain lesions that produce prosopagnosia can also impair the ability of a farmer to recognize his cows or the ability of a driver to recognize her own car except by reading its license plate (Bornstein, Stroka, & Munitz, 1969; Damasio, Damasio, & Van Hoesen, 1982). In other words, the failure of recognition is not confined to faces. Two recent functional imaging studies (Gauthier et al., 2000; Xu, 2005) found that when bird or car experts viewed pictures of birds or cars, the FFA was activated. This did not occur when nonexperts viewed the same pictures. Thus, Tarr and Gauthier (2000) suggested that the FFA be relabeled as the *flexible* fusiform area, given its participation in the visual recognition of diverse objects.

To test whether activation of the FFA is specific to face recognition and not to the recognition of familiar objects in general, Rhodes et al. (2004) showed faces and pictures of Lepidoptera (moths and butterflies) to experts in the latter. By using *f*MRI, they found greater activation in the FFA in response to faces than to Lepidoptera, supporting the claim that the FFA is differentially involved in face perception. People with autistic disorder fail to develop normal social relations. In severe cases, they give no indication even that other people exist. Grelotti, Gauthier, and Schultz (2002) found that people with autistic disorder showed a deficit in the ability to recognize faces and that looking at faces failed to activate the FFA. The authors speculated that other brain abnormalities associated with autistic disorder may result in a lack of interest in other people and consequently in the failure to acquire face recognition during childhood, as normally would occur.

Functional-imaging studies have revealed several additional regions of the ventral stream that are differentially responsive to particular categories of visual stimuli. For example, the **extrastriate body area (EBA)** is specifically activated by photographs, silhouettes, or stick figures of human bodies or body parts and not by control stimuli such as photographs or drawings of tools, scrambled silhouettes, or scrambled stick drawings of bodies (Downing et al., 2001). Urgesi, Berlucchi, and Aglioti (2004) found that when the EBA was temporarily inactivated by transcranial magnetic stimulation (see Chapter 3), people lost the ability to recognize photographs of body parts but not parts of faces or motorcycles. A separate region of the ventral stream, the **parahippocampal place area (PPA),** is activated by visual scenes (that is, collections of several objects) and backgrounds. Steeves et al. (2004) reported the case of a woman with bilateral damage to the ventral stream that resulted in profound visual agnosia for objects. Functional imaging showed that her PPA was undamaged. She was still able to recognize both natural and

---

visual agnosia   The inability of a person who is not blind to recognize the identity or use of an object by means of vision; usually caused by damage to the brain.

prosopagnosia   A form of visual agnosia characterized by difficulty in the recognition of people's faces; may be accompanied by difficulty in recognizing other complex objects; caused by damage to the visual association cortex.

fusiform face area (FFA)   A region of the ventral stream in the human brain containing face-recognizing circuits.

extrastriate body area (EBA)   A region of the ventral stream in the human brain that is activated by images of bodies or body parts but not faces.

parahippocampal place area   A region of the ventral stream in the human brain that is activated by visual scenes and backgrounds.

human-made scenes, such as beaches, forests, deserts, cities, markets, and rooms. However, she was unable to recognize the specific objects that belonged to these scenes.

Ventral Stream: Perception of Color

Laboratory research has shown that individual neurons in a region of the ventral stream respond to particular colors, which suggests that this region is involved in combining the information from red/green and yellow/blue signals that originate in retinal ganglion cells (see Chapter 4). Heywood, Gaffan, and Cowey (1995) found that damage to this region disrupted the ability of monkeys to distinguish different colors. The animals could still distinguish between different shades of gray, so the deficit was not caused by a more general impairment of visual perception.

Lesions of a particular region of the human ventral stream can also cause loss of color vision without disrupting visual acuity. The patients describe their vision as resembling a black-and-white film (Damasio et al. 1980; Heywood & Kentridge, 2003). The condition is known as **cerebral achromatopsia** (ey-krow-muh-TOP-see-uh; the word means "vision without color"). If the brain damage occurs on only one side of the brain, people will lose their color vision in only half of the visual field (see **FIGURE 5•4**). If the damage is bilateral, they lose all color vision and cannot even imagine colors or remember the colors of objects they saw before their brain damage occurred.

A functional MRI study by Hadjikhani et al. (1998) found a color-sensitive region in the human ventral stream. Indeed lesions that cause achromatopsia must damage either this region or other brain regions that provide input to it.

The Dorsal Stream: Perception of Spatial Location

The parietal lobe (see Chapter 3) receives visual, auditory, somatosensory, and vestibular information and is involved in spatial and somatosensory perception. Damage to the parietal lobe disrupts performance on a variety of tasks that require (a) perceiving and remembering the location of objects, and (b) controlling the movement of the eyes and the limbs. As Figure 5.1 shows, the end of the dorsal stream is located in the posterior parietal cortex.

Studies with monkeys and functional-imaging studies with humans indicate that neurons in the dorsal stream are involved in visual attention and control of eye movements, the visual control of reaching and pointing, as well as the visual control of grasping and other hand movements, and the perception of depth (Snyder, Batista, & Anderson, 2000; Culham & Kanwisher, 2001; Astafiev et al., 2003; Tsao et al., 2003; Frey et al., 2005).

Goodale and his colleagues (Goodale & Milner, 1992; Goodale et al., 1994; Goodale & Westwood, 2004) suggested that the primary function of the dorsal stream of the visual cortex is to guide actions rather than simply to perceive spatial locations. As Ungerleider and Mishkin (1982) originally put it, the ventral and dorsal streams of the visual association cortex tell us "what" the object is and "where" it is located, respectively. Instead, Goodale and his colleagues recommend the combination of "what" and "how," that is, how to perform the action. For example, a woman with bilateral lesions of the posterior parietal cortex had no difficulty recognizing line drawings (indicating that her ventral stream was intact), but picking up objects was difficult for her (Jakobson et al., 1991). She could easily perceive differences in the size of wooden blocks placed in front of her. But she could not adjust the distance between her thumb and forefinger to the size of a block in order to pick it up. In contrast, a patient with profound visual agnosia caused by damage to the ventral stream *could not* distinguish between wooden blocks of different sizes but *could* adjust the distance between her thumb and forefinger when she picked them up. Moreover, she made this adjustment before she actually touched the blocks (Milner et al., 1991; Goodale et al., 1994). This suggests that visual information in the dorsal stream was sufficient to enable the adjustment. Functional imaging of the same patient (James et al., 2003) showed normal activity in the dorsal stream while she was picking up objects.

The suggestion by Goodale and his colleagues that the function of the dorsal stream is captured better by the notion of *how* rather than *where* should not imply an absence of the capacity to recognize spatial location. After all, if the primary role of the dorsal stream is to direct movements toward objects, it *must* be involved in locating them. In addition, it must possess information about their size and shape, or it could not control the distance between thumb and forefinger when objects are grasped and picked up.

Dorsal Stream: Perception of Movement

We need to know not only what things are but also where they are and where they are going. Without the ability to perceive the velocity (that is, the direction and speed) of objects, we could

[**FIGURE 5•4**] A photograph illustrating the way the world would look to a person who had achromatopsia in the right visual field, caused by damage on the left side of the brain to the region of the visual association cortex shown in Figure 5.1.

(Photo courtesy of Neil Carlson.)

cerebral achromatopsia The inability to discriminate colors; caused by damage to the visual association cortex.

not predict where they will be. We would be unable to catch them or avoid letting them catch us.

Brain research with laboratory animals has identified a region of the visual association cortex that contains neurons that respond differentially to movement. The region is located in the extrastriate cortex. Damage to this region severely disrupts a monkey's ability to perceive moving stimuli (Siegel & Andersen, 1986). Bilateral damage to a similar region in humans produces a similar loss, known as **akinetopsia** (ay-kinn-eh-TOP-see-yuh). For example, Zihl et al. (1991) reported the case of a woman with such damage.

[**CASE STUDY**] Patient L. M. had an almost total loss of movement perception. She was unable to cross a street without traffic lights, because she could not judge the speed at which cars were moving. Although she could perceive movements, she found moving objects very unpleasant to look at. For example, while talking with another person, she avoided looking at the person's mouth because she found its movements very disturbing. When the investigators asked her to try to detect movements of a visual target in the laboratory, she said, "First, the target is completely at rest. Then it suddenly jumps upwards and downwards" (Zihl et al., 1991, p. 2244). She was able to see that the target was changing its position, but she did not perceive it in motion between those positions. (Carlson, 2007, p. 201)

Walsh et al. (1998) used transcranial magnetic stimulation temporarily to inactivate the same region in normal human participants. The investigators found that, during the stimulation, participants were able to recognize different-shaped objects displayed on a computer screen but were unable to detect which of the objects was moving. When the stimulation was absent, they had no trouble detecting the motion.

Form from Motion Perception of movement can even help us to perceive three-dimensional forms—a phenomenon known as *form from motion* (as well as *biological motion*). Johansson (1973) demonstrated just how much information we can derive from movement. He dressed actors in black and attached small lights to several points on their bodies, such as their wrists, elbows, shoulders, hips, knees, and feet. He made movies of the actors in the darkened room while they were performing various behaviors, such as walking, running, jumping, limping, doing pushups, and dancing with a partner who was also equipped with lights. Even though observers who watched the films could see only a pattern of moving lights against a dark background, they could readily perceive the pattern as belonging to a moving human and could identify the behavior the actor was performing. Subsequent studies (for example, Kozlowksi & Cutting, 1977) showed that people could even tell, with reasonable accuracy, the sex of the actor wearing the lights. The cues appeared to

be supplied by the relative amounts of movement of the shoulders and hips as the actor walked.

A functional imaging study by Grossman et al. (2000) found that when people viewed a video that showed form from motion, a bilateral brain region [specifically, the ventral bank of the posterior end of the superior temporal sulcus (SULL-kuss)] became active. However, more activity was observed in the right hemisphere, whether the video images were presented to the left or the right visual field. Grossman and Blake (2001) found that this same region was activated even when people just *imagined* that they were watching points of light representing form from motion.

Perception of form might seem like something that only shows up in a laboratory, but it does occur under natural circumstances. For example, people with visual agnosia often can still perceive *actions* (such as someone pretending to stir food items in a bowl or to deal out some playing cards from a deck), even though they are unable to recognize the objects by sight. Thus, they may be able to recognize friends by the way they walk, even though they cannot recognize their faces. The following case study is illustrative.

[**CASE STUDY**] Lê et al. (2002) reported the case of patient S. B., a 30-year-old man whose ventral stream was extensively damaged bilaterally by encephalitis (inflammation of the brain) when he was three years old. As a result, he was unable to recognize objects, faces, textures, or colors. However, he could perceive movement and could even catch a ball that was thrown to him. Furthermore, he could recognize other people's arm and hand movements that mimed common activities such as cutting something with a knife or brushing one's teeth, and he could recognize people he knew by their gait. (Carlson, 2007, p. 202)

Such clinical findings suggest that form from motion involves brain mechanisms different from those involved in the perception of objects. Recall that Mrs. R. in the Prologue could recognize forms from motion (those of Dr. L. when he mimed turning a key, writing, and dealing playing cards) and had no difficulty perceiving spatial location and movement. On this basis, it seems reasonable to conclude that her profound visual agnosia, including prosopagnosia, was attributable to ventral stream deficits.

QUESTIONS TO CONSIDER

1. If you partially damaged your primary visual cortex, what would your symptoms be? Your visual association cortex partially? How would this affect your normal functioning?

2. If you had one of the perceptual deficits described in this section, what coping strategies might you adopt? Suppose that you could not identify people by sight, or recognize your automobile. Or suppose that you could not recognize common objects but could read. How could you arrange things so that you would function at a high level of independence?

---

akinetopsia Loss of the ability to perceive movement due to damage in the visual association cortex.

3. Suppose that you had complete achromatopsia. What would you miss seeing? What practical difficulties would you face, and how would you cope with them?

Visual Perception of Objects

At this point we turn from a consideration of brain mechanisms in visual perception to consider the relation between visual perception and the physical characteristics of the environments in which perception takes place. As previously mentioned, when we look at the world, we do not first see patches of colors, the frequency of vertical lines, or shades of brightness per se. We see things—cars, streets, people, desks, books, trees, dogs, chairs, walls, flowers, clouds, cell phones—with immediacy. We see where each thing is located, how large it is, and whether it is moving. We recognize familiar things; we also recognize when we see something we have never seen before. This section considers factors that contribute to the immediacy of perception, to knowing right away what something is and where it is located.

Figure and Ground

We classify most of what we see as either object or background. Objects are things having particular shapes and particular locations in space. (In this context, people can be considered as objects.) Backgrounds are perceived as less well formed and serve mostly to help us judge the location of objects we see in front of them. Psychologists use the terms **figure** and **ground** to label an object and its background, respectively. Whether you perceive an item as a figure or as a part of the ground is not an intrinsic property of the item. Rather, it depends on your behavior as observer. If you are watching some birds fly overhead, they are figures, and the

[**FIGURE 5•6**] The object on the left is defined by its boundaries. When the boundaries disappear, as in the camouflage on the right, it is not readily perceived.

blue sky and clouds behind the birds are the ground. If, instead, you are watching the clouds move, then the birds become the ground. If you are looking at a picture hanging on a wall, it is a figure. If you are looking at a person standing between you and the wall, the picture is part of the ground. Sometimes we receive ambiguous cues and have difficulty telling what is figure and what is ground. For example, do you see the bust of Voltaire in **FIGURE 5•5**?

In a study of Chinese and American participants, Chua, Boland, and Nisbett (2005) asked them to look at scenes containing objects that appeared against complex backgrounds. The researchers monitored the participants' eye movements and found that Americans tended to focus more quickly on the objects, whereas the Chinese participants' eye movements were concentrated on the background. It was the authors' conclusion that the difference may reflect Americans' relatively greater cultural emphasis on individuality and that of the Chinese on collectivity and thus the context.

One of the most important aspects of the perception of an object's form is the existence of a boundary. If a sharp and distinct change in brightness, color, or texture is seen, we may perceive an edge. If this edge forms a continuous boundary, we probably will perceive the space enclosed by the boundary as a figure rather than a ground. Otherwise, we may be slower to detect the figure. (See **FIGURE 5•6**.)

[**FIGURE 5•5**] "The Slave Market with Disappearing Bust of Voltaire." A painting by Salvadore Dali in which figure and ground can be reversed. You can see either two housewomen in their characteristic dress or a bust of the 18th-century abolitionist philosopher.

---

figure A visual stimulus that is perceived as an object.

ground A visual stimulus that is perceived as a background against which objects are seen.

[FIGURE 5•7] Object perception and boundaries. We immediately perceive even an unfamiliar figure when it is closed.

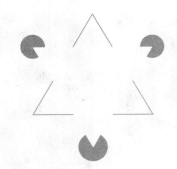

Gestalt Laws of Perceptual Organization

Although most figures are defined by a boundary, the presence of a boundary is not necessary for the perception of an object. **FIGURE 5•7** demonstrates illusory contours—lines that do not exist on the page. In this figure, the three pie-shaped objects (resembling Pacman) and the three pairs of line segments intersecting at 45-degree angles produce the visual illusion of two triangles, one on top of the other. Note that the illusory triangle that looks as if it is superimposed on three green circles even appears to be brighter than the background.

Early in the twentieth century, a group of German psychologists developed a theory of perception based on our readiness to perceive whole scenes and not their elements per se (see Hothersall, 2004). As Chapter 1 discussed, they called their movement *Gestalt psychology,* and they maintained that in perception, the whole is more than the sum of its parts. That is, because of the innate characteristics of the visual system of the brain, we are prepared to see a scene and not just its elements. What we perceive is a holistic pattern, a form, a Gestalt that reflects more the arrangement or organization of the elements.

Gestalt psychologists proposed several principles or laws that describe our ability to distinguish a figure from its ground and also tell why we are more likely to perceive certain figures than others. In this way, the laws may be thought of as describing common perceptual biases or preferences. They include:

1. The Gestalt **law of proximity** states that elements that are closest together will be perceived as belonging together (see **FIGURE 5•8(a)**).

2. The Gestalt **law of symmetry** refers to our tendency to perceive symmetrical elements as belonging together in a pattern, regardless of their distance from each other. For example, gazing at a tiled floor or tiled wall containing tiles of different color arranged in an alternating pattern may prompt the perception of a particular color zigzagging across the floor or wall.

3. The Gestalt **law of similarity** states that elements that have a similar appearance will be perceived as part of the same object (see **FIGURE 5•8(b)**).

4. The Gestalt **law of continuity** or good continuation refers to the relative simplicity of prediction. Which of the two sets of gray dots best describes the continuation of the line of black dots in **FIGURE 5•8(c)**? Most people choose the gray dots that continue the curve down and to the right. It seems simpler to perceive the line as following a smooth course than as suddenly making a sharp bend.

5. The Gestalt **law of closure** states that our visual system often "closes" the outline of an incomplete figure. For example, **FIGURE 5•8(d)** looks as if it might be a triangle, but if you place a pencil on the page so that it covers both of the gaps, the figure is undeniably a triangle.

6. The Gestalt **law of common fate** states that elements that move in the same direction will be perceived as belonging together and forming a figure. In the forest, an animal is camouflaged if its surface is covered with the same elements found in the background—spots of brown, tan, and green; its boundary is obscured. As long as the animal remains stationary, no perceptual basis appears for organizing the elements that belong to it alone, and it remains well hidden. However, once it moves, the elements on its surface will move together, and the animal's size and shape will quickly be visible. (Note the similarity between this example and the phenomenon of form from motion.)

Models of Pattern Perception

Stimulus objects, large and small, can come together simultaneously or in a sequence and be perceived as a pattern. Cognitive psychologists interested in the cognitive processes responsible for perception attempt to identify and analyze the steps that take place between the time a person's eye is exposed to objects and the time when a pattern is perceived (Peterson, 2005). They collect behavioral data and try to make inferences about the nature of these intervening processes. Let's look at some of the models cognitive psychologists have proposed.

---

law of proximity A Gestalt law of perceptual organization; elements located closest to one another are perceived as belonging to the same figure.

law of symmetry A Gestalt law of perceptual organization; symmetrical objects are perceived as belonging together even if a distance separates them.

law of similarity A Gestalt law of perceptual organization; similar elements are perceived as belonging to the same figure.

law of continuity A Gestalt law of perceptual organization; given two or more possible interpretations of the elements that form the outline of a figure, the brain will adopt the simplest interpretation.

law of closure A Gestalt law of perceptual organization; elements missing from the outline of a figure are "filled in" by the visual system.

law of common fate A Gestalt law of perceptual organization; elements that move together give rise to the perception of a particular figure.

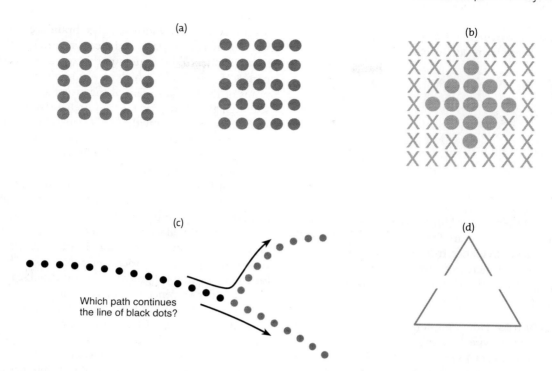

Which path continues
the line of black dots?

[FIGURE 5•8] (a) *The Gestalt law of proximity.* Different spacing of the dots produces five vertical or five horizontal lines. (b) *The Gestalt law of similarity.* Similar elements are perceived as belonging to the same form. (c) *The Gestalt law of good continuation.* It is easier to perceive a smooth continuation than an abrupt shift. (d) *The Gestalt law of closure.* We tend to supply missing information in order to close a figure and separate it from its background. Lay a pencil across the two gaps and see how much stronger the perception of a complete triangle becomes.

Templates and Prototypes Our ability to recognize the shape of an object might be explained by special memories known as templates. A **template** is a device used to produce a series of objects that resemble each other. For example, a cookie cutter is a template used to cut out identical shapes from a flat sheet of dough. According to the template model, visual perception reverses the process. When a particular pattern of visual stimuli is encountered, the visual system searches its store of templates and compares each of them with the pattern. If it finds a match, the pattern is recognized as familiar. Templates stored in memory could be used to identify patterns of stimuli as letters or numbers, or as more sophisticated objects such as cats or dogs.

The template model of pattern recognition has the virtue of simplicity. However, most cognitive psychologists dismiss it as infeasible—the visual system would have to store an impossibly large number of templates. A more feasible model of pattern perception suggests that the visual system compares patterns of stimuli with prototypes rather than templates. A **prototype** (Greek for "original model") is an idealized pattern; it resembles a template but is used in a much more flexible way. The visual system does not require an exact match between the present pattern and a specific template but instead accepts a degree of disparity. Think of how many different people you can recognize by sight, how

We can recognize particular objects as well as general categories of objects.

template A hypothetical pattern that is stored in the nervous system and is used to perceive objects or shapes by a process of comparison.

prototype A hypothetical idealized pattern that resides in the nervous system and is used to perceive objects or shapes by a process of comparison; recognition can occur even when an exact match cannot be found.

[**FIGURE 5·9**] Distinctive features. We easily recognize all of these items as the letter *N*.

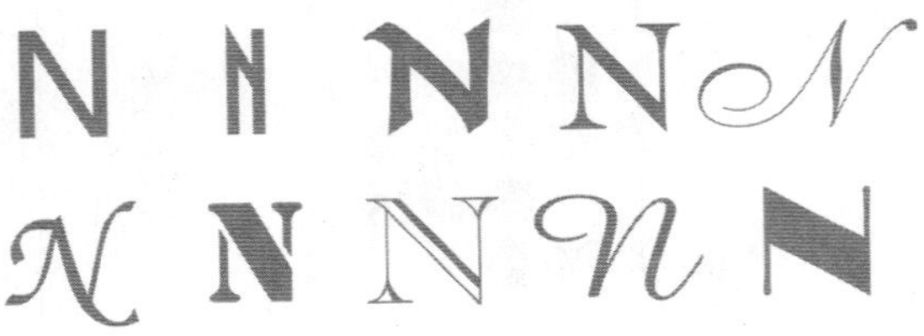

many different buildings in your town or city you can identify, how many of the pieces of furniture in your house and in your friends' houses you are familiar with—the list will be very long indeed. Evidence from studies of nonhuman primates suggests that increased familiarity with categories of objects may lead to the development of more specific prototypes (Humphrey, 2003).

Distinctive Features How complete does the information in a template or prototype have to be for pattern recognition to occur? Does it have to exist as an image, or can it exist in some shorthand way? Some cognitive psychologists have suggested another approach to object perception in terms of **distinctive features**—the essential physical features that specify a particular category of objects. For example, FIGURE 5·9 contains several examples of the capital letter N. Although the examples vary in size and style, you have no trouble recognizing them.

A classic experiment by Neisser supports the hypothesis that object perception involves distinctive features. FIGURE 5·10 shows one of the tasks Neisser used that involved two vertical arrays of letters. Scan through them until you find the letter Z, which occurs once in each array.

Chances are good that you found the Z much faster in the left column than in the right column, just as the participants in Neisser's study did. Perhaps you guessed why: The letters in the left column have few distinctive features in common with those found in the letter Z, so the Z stands out from the others. In contrast, the letters in the right column have many features in common with the target letter, and thus the Z is camouflaged, so to speak.

An ambitious theory of feature-based object perception was proposed by Biederman (1987, 1995). Critical to the theory is a fixed set of "primitives," or feature detectors for specific three-dimensional geometrical shapes—called *geons*—that reside in the brain. A sample of geons appears in FIGURE 5·11, together with familiar objects that represent combinations of geons. The perception of an object occurs as the brain analyzes its visual image using geons. Biederman argued that it is possible to decode all visual information, even the most complex—for example, a face—in terms

of geons. The theory also specifies brain areas where geon detection may take place, and recent research with monkeys has implicated the inferotemporal cortex (Kayeart, Biederman, & Vogels, 2005), which as you might recall, is the terminus of the lateral stream of the visual association cortex. Although the theory makes comprehensive claims, as you might expect, it is not without detractors (see Pinker, 1997).

Some phenomena cannot easily be explained by the distinctive-features model. According to the model, perception consists of analysis and synthesis: The visual system first identifies the features of a pattern and then combines them to determine what the pattern is. We might expect, then, that more complex patterns have more distinctive features and would take longer to perceive. In reality, the addition of more features, especially in the form of contextual cues, often speeds the process of perception. The tendency for certain stimuli to "pop out" during visual search of a display provides evidence that perception does not necessarily involve a strict search for features. For example, Enns and Rensink (1991) found that the orientation (downward to the right or upward to the left) of wire-frame objects like those in panel (a) in FIGURE 5·12 was quickly detected in a visual search. If the vertices of the object were not connected, however, as in panel (b), orientation was much more difficult to detect. In another study. Pilon and Friedman (1998) found that misaligned vertices, as at the bottom right of panel (c), were difficult to detect when vertices were not

GDOROC	IVEMXW
COQUCD	XVIWME
DUCOQG	VEMIXW
GRUDQO	WEXMVI
OCDURQ	XIMVWE
DUCGRO	IVMWEX
ODUCQG	VWEMXI
CQOGRD	IMEWXV
DUZORQ	EXMZWI
UCGROD	IEMWVX
QCUDOG	EIVXWM
RQGUDO	WXEMIV
DRGOQC	MIWVXE
OQGDRU	IMEVXW
UGCODQ	IEMWVX
ODRUCQ	IMWVEX
UDQRGC	XWMVEI
ORGCUD	IWEVXM
QOGRUC	VMIWEX

[**FIGURE 5·10**] A letter-search task. Look for the letter *Z* hidden in each vertical array.

___
distinctive features Physical characteristics of an object that help distinguish it from other objects.

[FIGURE 5•11] Geons for perception. (a) Several different geons. (b) The combination of two or three geons (indicated by the numbers) into common three-dimensional objects.

(Adapted from Biederman, I. In *An Invitation to Cognitive Science. Vol 2: Visual Cognition and Action*, edited by D. N. Osherson, S. M. Kosslyn, and J. Hollerbach. Copyright © 1990 by the Massachusetts Institute of Technology; published by MIT Press, Cambridge, MA.)

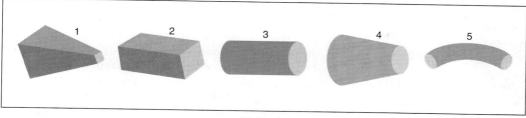

(a) Geons

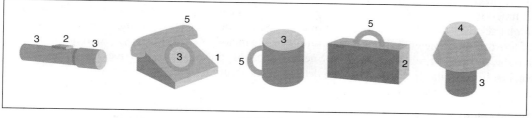

(b) Objects

connected. Presumably, only by connecting the vertices with solid lines, and thus providing additional features, was "pop-out" perception achieved.

It also may be the case that prolonged exposure to particular features simplifies object perception. For example, try to read the paragraph that appears in **FIGURE 5•13**. Most of the words in the paragraph have been scrambled—except for the first and last letters—yet you probably are able to make your way through the paragraph with only a slight slowing of your normal reading speed. Demonstrations such as this suggest that your ability to perceive the meaning of visual stimuli—in this case strings of letters—may eventually rely on only some of the features that are present; for example, the "outer boundaries" of words. Dehaene (2003) has speculated that such ability derives from the exploitative reuse of brain modules that originally served other functions, such as object recognition in the natural world. He used the term "neural recycling" to refer to this possibility.

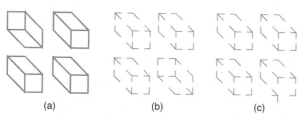

[FIGURE 5•12] Wire-frame figures similar to those used by Enns and Rensink (1991) and Pilon and Friedman (1998). Panel (a) depicts the wire-frame figures with connected vertices; panel (b) depicts figures with unconnected vertices. Pilon and Friedman used figures like those depicted in panel (c), in which the individual vertices in a figure were individually rotated and could be misaligned with the rest of the figure.

(Redrawn from Enns and Rensink (1991) and Pilon and Friedman (1998). Copyright © 1998. Canadian Psychological Association. Reprinted with permission.)

Aoccdrnig to rseerach at Cmabrigde Uinervtisy, it deosn't mttaer in waht oredr the ltteers in a wrod are, the olny iprmoatnt thing is taht the frist and lsat ltteer be at the rghit pclae. The rset can be a tatol mses and you can sitll raed it wouthit a porbelm. This is bcuseae the huamn mnid deos not raed ervey lteter by istlef, but the wrod as a wlohe. Amzanig huh?

PS: Hwo'd you lkie to run tihs by yuor sepll ckehcer?

[FIGURE 5•13] A paragraph in which the letters in each word have been scrambled except for the first and last letters.

("Are Reading and Writing Innate Skills?" www.brainconnection.com/content/198_1. Reprinted by permission of Scientific Learning Corporation.)

focus On

Does the Brain Work Like a Computer?

When we try to understand something extremely complicated (such as the functioning of the human brain), we tend to think in terms of things that are familiar to us. Although cognitive psychology as a discipline dates back to the early twentieth century, most of its philosophy and methodology have developed since the mid-1960s (Gardner, 1987). During this time, the best-known physical device that performs functions similar to those of the human brain has been the computer. The computer continues to provide much of the inspiration for the models of human brain function proposed by cognitive psychologists. As you look back over the chapter thus far, note the frequent use of terms compatible with the computer: information, pathway, connection, system, process, pattern, storage, etc. Just how similar is a computer to the human brain?

Using Computers to Model Cognitive Processes

Computers can be programmed to store any kind of information that can be coded in numbers or words, can solve any logical problems that can be explicitly described, and can compute any mathematical equations that can be written. Therefore—in principle, at least—they can be programmed to do the things we do: perceive, remember, make logical deductions, solve problems. Consequently, psychologists, linguists, and computer scientists have constructed computer-inspired models of memory, visual pattern perception, speech comprehension, reading, and the control of movement, for example (see Baars & Gage, 2007).

The creation of computer programs that simulate human cognitive processes belongs to a branch of cognitive science known as **artificial intelligence (AI).** For instance, to construct a program that simulates human perception and classification of certain types of patterns, AI researchers begin with a computational model. In addition to specifying what the task of pattern perception requires, the model generates a computer program. If the program fails to recognize the patterns when they are presented, then the researchers know that something is wrong with the model or with the way it has been implemented in the program. They may revise the model until the program finally works, or they decide to try a new model.

Critics of artificial intelligence have pointed out that although it is entirely possible to write a program that performs a task the human brain performs—and to show that the brain produces exactly the same results—the brain may perform the task in an entirely different way. Given the way computers work and what we know about the structure of the human brain, some critics argue that the computer program is guaranteed to work differently (see, e.g., Dreyfus & Dreyfus, 2000).

Serial and Parallel Processing

A computer works one step at a time. In other words, a computer is a *serial processor*. Each step takes time, even if it is measured in thousandths or millionths of a second. A complicated program will contain more steps and will take more time to execute. For example, for visual processing, a computer must first analyze the scene that is transmitted through an input device, such as a digital camera. The program must then convert information about the brightness of each point in the scene into a number and store the numbers in a memory location. Then it examines each memory location, one at a time, and does calculations that determine the locations of lines, edges, textures, and shapes. Finally, it tries to determine what these details represent.

Humans do some things extremely quickly that it takes computers much longer to do. If the brain were to operate in serial fashion like a computer, it could never keep up with a computer, because neurons cannot fire more than a thousand times per second (Rumelhart, McClelland, & the PDP Research Group, 1986). Obviously, when we perceive visual images, our brain is not processing information step by step. Instead, the brain appears to be a *parallel processor,* in which many different neural modules (collections of circuits of neurons) work simultaneously at different tasks. The brain breaks a complex task into many smaller ones, and separate modules work on each of them. Because the brain consists of many billions of neurons, it can afford to devote different modules to different tasks. That is, it can use *parallel distributed processing* with many things happening at the same time, thus finishing the task in an instant. Parallel distributed processing has contributed to the success of computer programs that have defeated world chess champions (Saletan, 2007) and checker-playing programs guaranteed not to lose (Chang, 2007).

Artificial Neural Network Models

In recent decades, psychologists have begun to devise models of cognitive processes that are based, more or less, on the way the brain seems basically to be constructed. These models are called **artificial neural networks.** Donald Hebb (1949) developed the concept of a neural network long before the age of modern computers. Now cognitive psychologists and neuroscientists have pursued the implications of Hebb's ideas to considerable lengths.

Investigators developing artificial neural networks construct a network of simple units that have properties like those of neurons (see Faucett, 1994). The units are connected to one another through junctions similar to synapses. Like synapses, these junctions can have either excitatory or inhibitory effects. When a unit is activated, it

---

artificial intelligence (AI)   A field of cognitive science in which researchers design computer programs to simulate human cognitive abilities; this endeavor may help cognitive psychologists understand the mechanisms that underlie these abilities.

artificial neural networks   A model of the nervous system based on interconnected networks of units that have some of the properties of neurons.

[**FIGURE 5·14**] A simple neural network used as a model of brain function. The circles are units having properties similar to those of neurons. The connections (arrows) can be excitatory or inhibitory, depending on the particular network.

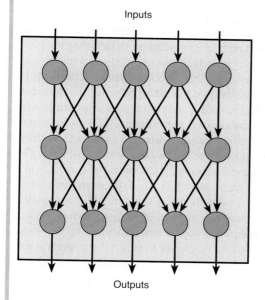

Inputs

Outputs

So what is the answer to the question posed at the beginning of this section: Does the brain work like a computer? The answer seems to be that it does, but not like the most familiar kind of computer—the serial processor—that cognitive psychologists first used as a basis for constructing models of brain function. Instead, the brain seems to be organized as a parallel processor using a massive array of neural networks.

[**FIGURE 5·15**] Simple elements that are difficult to recognize without a context.

[**FIGURE 5·16**] An example of top-down processing. The context facilitates our recognition of the items shown in Figure 5.20.

(Adapted from Palmer, S. E. in *Explorations in Cognition*, edited by Donald A. Norman and David E. Rumelhart. Copyright © 1975 by W. H. Freeman and Company. Used with permission.)

sends a message to the units with which it communicates, and so on. Some of the units of a network have input lines that can receive signals from the "outside," which could represent a sensory organ or the information received from another network. Other units have output lines, which could communicate with other networks or produce actions. (See **FIGURE 5·14**.) The specific connections between units can be either strengthened or weakened by the extent to which the response matches the desired outcome in some way. In this sense, artificial neural networks not only mimic the structural connections between neurons in the brain but also simulate brain plasticity.

Artificial neural networks can be taught to "recognize" particular stimuli. A stimulus is presented, and the network's output is monitored. If the response is incorrect, the network receives a signal indicating the correct response. This signal causes the strength of some of the connections to be changed (a process known as "backward propagation"), just as learning is thought to alter the strength of synapses in the brain. After several repetitions, the network learns to make correct responses. Artificial neural networks can learn to recognize not only particular patterns but also variations on that pattern. Some networks also appear to learn general rules about the occurrence of features within a pattern (Berkeley et al., 1995). In a specific application to the acquisition of reading, selectively disabling some of the network's connections produced errors similar to dyslexia (Hinton & Shallice, 1991). Other applications to developmental disorders have been reported (see, e.g., Munakata, Casey, & Diamond, 2004; Elman, J. L., 2005).

Bottom-Up and Top-Down Processing: The Roles of Features and Context

We often perceive objects under conditions that are less than optimal; the object is in a shadow, camouflaged against a similar background, or obscured by fog. Nevertheless, we usually manage to recognize it correctly. We are often helped by the context in which we see the object. For example, look at the four objects in **FIGURE 5·15**. Can you tell what larger object they belong to? Now look at **FIGURE 5·16**, where, with the aid of a context, they are easily recognized.

An early study by Palmer (1975) made the same point by using more general forms of context. He first showed his participants familiar scenes, such as a kitchen. (See **FIGURE 5·17**.) Next, he showed drawings of individual objects and asked participants to identify them. The drawings were shown very rapidly, making them difficult to identify. Sometimes the participants were shown an object that was appropriate to the kitchen scene, such as a loaf of bread. Other times, they were shown a similarly shaped but non-kitchen object, such as a mailbox. Palmer found that when the objects fit the context provided by the scene, the participants correctly identified about 84 percent of them. When they did not, performance decreased to about 50 percent. In the no-context control condition, under which participants did not first see a scene, performance was intermediate. Thus, compared with the no-context control condition, an appropriate context facilitated recognition, and an inappropriate context interfered with it.

The Palmer study suggests the parallel operation of two processes—one that uses information directly available from the stimulus (the drawing of a loaf of bread) and the other that

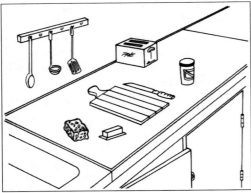

Contextual scene

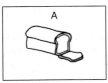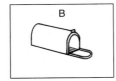

A   B

Target object (presented very briefly)

[FIGURE 5•17] Stimuli from the experiment by Palmer (1975). After looking at the contextual scene, the participants were shown one of the stimuli below it very briefly.

(From Palmer, S. E. (1975). *Memory and cognition, 3*, 519–526. Reprinted by permission of the Psychonomic Society, Inc.)

uses information from memory (objects that a typical kitchen would contain). Cognitive psychologists often refer to first process as *bottom-up processing* and the second as *top-down processing*. In **bottom-up processing** (also called *data-driven* or *stimulus-driven processing*), the process starts with the features—the bits and pieces—of the stimulus, beginning with the image that falls on the retina. This information is processed hierarchically by successively higher levels of the visual system until the highest levels (the "top" of the system) are reached, and the object is perceived. **Top-down processing** (also called *knowledge-driven processing*), involves the use of contextual information supplied from memory—the "big picture." The application of this model to Palmer's study, for example, suggests that information from memory about kitchen-specific features was sent from the "top" of the system down through lower levels. Then, when the participant saw a drawing of a loaf of bread, information about its features came up more readily through the successive levels of the bottom-up system, and recognition was faster and more accurate. In other words, information from the top (typical kitchen contents) primed the processing of information from the bottom (the loaf of bread).

The relative contribution of top-down and bottom-up processing to visual search was the focus of a series of experiments reported by Wolfe et al. (2003). In the design of their studies, the

researchers sought to minimize top-down information to isolate the bottom-up process. In one study designed to vary the extent of top-down information available to participants, the researchers presented stimuli containing red or green lines that were arranged either vertically or horizontally. On each trial, the participant judged whether the stimulus met the description provided by the experimenter (the target). Feedback (right or wrong) followed each trial. In addition to recording the participant's answer, the researchers also recorded reaction time.

To separate top-down processing from bottom-up processing, Wolfe et al. varied the extent to which the dimensions of color or orientation defined the target. For example, in one condition that maximized the influence of top-down information, any stimulus that contained the color red was the target; the orientation of the bars was irrelevant. For example, in **FIGURE 5•18**, the stimulus on the left would be correct, and the stimulus on the right, incorrect. Thus, for example, a participant could use the simple top-down rule of "always pick red when it appears" and be assured of success. Conversely, to reduce the influence of top-down information, the experimenters introduced a condition in which the target was never consistently red, green, horizontal, or vertical. Instead it was any stimulus in which one of the bars that appeared was discrepant from all the other bars in color or orientation. Thus in Figure 5.18 both of the stimuli would be correct. Now no simple top-down rule in terms of color or orientation applied. The researchers argued that this allowed bottom-up influences a larger role in the participants' judgments. Consequently, average reaction time was slowest in that condition. It was fastest in the condition with full top-down information.

Perceptual ("What") and Action ("Where") Systems: A Possible Synthesis

Our examination of the visual perception of objects has brought us to a puzzle. It is clear that the features of objects play some role in our ability to recognize them, but it is less

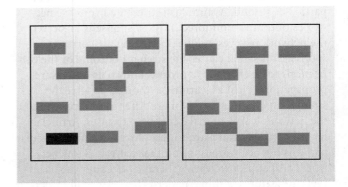

[FIGURE 5•18] Two sample stimuli from the Wolfe et al. study (2003) that varied the relative influence of bottom-up and top-down information.

(Adapted from Wolfe, J. M., Butcher, S. J., Lee, C., & Hyle, M. (2003). Changing your mind: On the contributions of top-down and bottom-up guidance in visual search for feature singletons. *Journal of Experimental Psychology: Human Perception and Performance, 29*, 483–502.)

bottom-up processing Perception based on successive analyses of the details of the stimuli that are present.

top-down processing Perception based on information provided by the context in which a particular stimulus is encountered.

[FIGURE 5•19] Examples of combined top-down/ bottom-up processing. The effect of context enables us to perceive the letters despite the missing or ambiguous features. Note in the top example that a given letter may be perceived in more than one way, depending on the letters surrounding it.

(Adapted from McClelland, J. L., Rumelhart, D. E., & Hinton, G. E. in *Parallel Distributed Processing. Vol. I: Foundations*, edited by D. E. Rumelhart, J. L. McClelland, and the PDP Research Group. Copyright © 1986 by the Massachusetts Institute of Technology; published by the MIT Press Cambridge, MA.)

clear that feature-analysis theories can fully explain that ability. Top-down factors such as context exert powerful influences, but we still must ask how that influence is exerted.

In most cases, visual perception seems to consist of a combination of top-down and bottom-up processing. FIGURE 5•19 shows several examples of objects that can be recognized only by a combination of both forms of processing. Our knowledge of the configurations of letters in words (top-down processing) provides us with the contexts that permit us to organize (and expedite) the flow of featural information from the bottom up. Concluding that the perception of objects requires the interaction of both types of processing still leaves unanswered the question of what that interaction is composed of. How do bottom-up and top-down processing come together to produce object recognition?

This puzzle is likely to remain unsolved for some time, but findings from cognitive neuroscience are providing some provocative clues. For example, Goodale and Milner (2005) described extensive observations of a Scottish woman named "Dee."

[CASE STUDY] While living in Italy, Dee had carbon monoxide poisoning that left her unable to identify objects visually. Once she returned to Scotland and was examined there, it became clear that her visual deficits were not global

but specific in a peculiar way. She had normal acuity and could readily discriminate colors and surface textures. For example, she could tell that a kitchen bowl was made of red plastic. However, she would not be able to identify the object as a bowl. She was unable to identify the boundaries of objects—the edges, curves, and corners by which the object was differentiated from another object or from its background. Nonetheless, she was still able to reach for specific objects appropriately. For example, Dee would be unable to tell whether the slot on a mailbox was oriented horizontally or vertically, but if you gave her an envelope and asked her to deposit it in the slot, her movements would be just right. Moreover, if asked to draw an object she was familiar with, she could do so reasonably well but not if drawing with her eyes closed, because she could not recognize the object she had drawn.

Goodale and Milner (2005) suggest a strong dissociation between what they describe as "vision for perception" (the "what" system) and "vision for action" (the "where" system). These two categories of vision are consistent with the ventral and dorsal streams in the visual association cortex that were introduced earlier in the chapter. The what system provides us with information about objects and their meanings and involves pathways that lead to the temporal lobe—the ventral stream. The where system provides us with information necessary for acting on objects with guided movement and involves pathways that lead to the parietal lobe—the dorsal stream.

Dee's brain damage apparently affected her perception of objects—her what system—but left intact her ability to respond to the location and orientation of objects—her where system. The dorsal stream provides information necessary for guiding our actions toward objects but does not provide us with the ability to recognize or name them. Dee's condition is reminiscent of that of Mrs. R., who, in the Prologue, could not identify an object as a watch. When asked to pick it up, she did so readily, and having done so, could now say what it was. Goodale and Milner argue that visual perception involves the interplay between these two systems. The dorsal stream responds to the location and orientation of objects and coordinates the actions we take with respect to them. The ventral stream gives us information about what the objects are so that we know, for example, that it will take less effort to turn this page than it will to turn the cover of this book.

QUESTIONS TO CONSIDER

1. Find examples of figure and ground in your immediate visual environment. Try changing your focus of attention to make items previously seen as figures become part of the ground and vice versa. Provide examples from your own experience of each of the Gestalt laws of perceptual organization.

2. Approximately how many unique objects do you think you can recognize at this point in your life? How many more do you think you will learn to recognize during the years ahead of you? What problem(s) does this potential for unlimited acquisition pose for a theory of object perception?

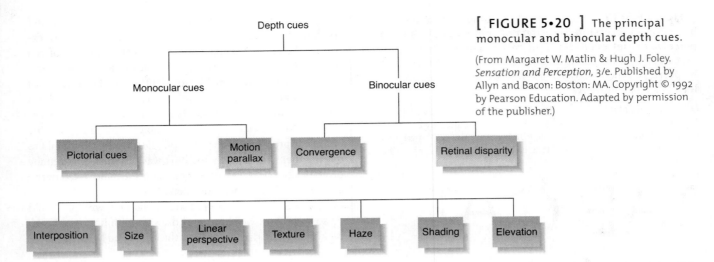

[**FIGURE 5·20**] The principal monocular and binocular depth cues.

(From Margaret W. Matlin & Hugh J. Foley. Sensation and Perception, 3/e. Published by Allyn and Bacon: Boston: MA. Copyright © 1992 by Pearson Education. Adapted by permission of the publisher.)

3. What do you do when you try to assemble the pieces of a complex picture puzzle? Relate this experience to the concepts of templates, prototypes, and distinctive features.

4. Suppose that Goodale and Milner are correct about a visual system that is specialized for movements such as reaching. Are you aware of orienting your hand when you reach for, say, a computer mouse that is at an odd angle on a tabletop? What might this say about the role of consciousness in guided movement?

Visual Perception of Space and Motion

We not only are able to perceive the objects in our environment (what) but also can judge quite accurately their relative location in space and their movements, as well as our movements relative to them (where). In this section, we take up the perception of depth and movement.

Depth Perception

Depth perception requires that we perceive the distance between us and objects in the environment as well as their distance from one another. This is an impressive feat, given that the three-dimensional quality of depth perception must be derived from the two-dimensional images that fall on the retina in each eye. We accomplish this feat by means of two kinds of visual cues: binocular ("two-eye") and monocular ("one-eye"). Binocular cues arise from the fact that the visual

---

binocular cue   A cue for the perception of depth that requires the use of both eyes.

monocular cue   A cue for the perception of depth that requires the use of only one eye.

convergence   In depth perception, the result of conjugate eye movements whereby the fixation point for each eye is identical; feedback from these movements provides information about the distance of visual objects from the viewer.

retinal disparity   The fact that objects located at different distances from the observer will fall on different locations on the two retinas; provides a binocular cue for depth perception.

---

fields of the two eyes overlap. Only animals that have eyes on the front of the head (such as primates, cats, and some avian species) have **binocular cues** as well as **monocular cues** available to them. Animals that have eyes on the sides of their heads (such as rabbits and fish) are strictly dependent on monocular cues. In a comparative study of animal taxa, Heesey (2008) concluded that binocularity may have evolved in mammals as a means of detecting camouflaged prey at night, particularly in arboreal environments.

Among the monocular cues, one involves movement and thus must be experienced in the natural environment or in a motion picture. The others are available in a drawing or a photograph and were originally identified by visual artists and only later studied by psychologists. FIGURE 5·20 provides a classification of the principal distance cues. Let's look more closely at each.

Binocular Cues   An important cue for distance is supplied by **convergence**. Recall from Chapter 4 that the eyes make conjugate movements so that both look at (converge on) the same point of the visual scene. If an object is very close to your face, your eyes are turned inward. If it is farther away, they turn straight ahead. Thus, the eyes can be used like range finders. The brain controls the extraocular muscles that move each eye and presumably can compute the angle between them and, from that, the distance between the object and the eyes. Convergence is most important for perceiving the distance of objects located close to us—especially those we can reach with our hands. (See **FIGURE 5·21**.)

Another important cue for the perception of distance is provided by **retinal disparity**. (Disparity means "unlikeness" or "dissimilarity.") Hold up a finger of one hand at arm's length, and then hold up a finger of the other hand midway between your nose and the distant finger. If you look at one of the fingers, you will see a double image of the other one. (Try it; you may be surprised.) Because of the physical distance between the eyes, whenever they are pointed in a particular direction, the images of objects at different distances will fall on different portions of the retina in each eye. The disparity between the images of an object on the two retinas

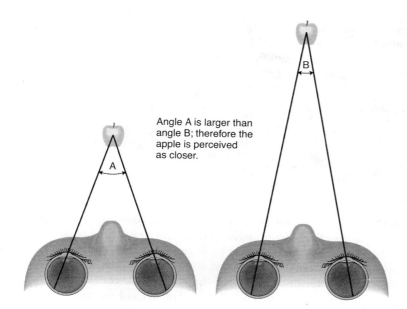

Angle A is larger than angle B; therefore the apple is perceived as closer.

[FIGURE 5•21] Convergence. When the eyes converge on a nearby object, the angle between them is greater than when they converge on a distant object. The brain uses this information in perceiving the distance of an object.

is an important source of information about their distance from you. Hubel (1995) described a class of cells in the primary visual cortex of monkeys—*binocular cells*—that fire in response to the slightly disparate images from each eye.

Research on retinal disparity has sometimes used a *stereoscope*, a device that shows two slightly different pictures, one to each eye. The pictures are taken by a camera equipped with two lenses, located a few inches apart, just as our eyes are. When you look through a stereoscope, you see a three-dimensional image. In an ingenious experiment, Julesz (1965, 2006) demonstrated that retinal disparity is essential for the perception of depth. With a computer, he produced two displays of randomly positioned dots. If some of the dots in one of the displays were displaced slightly to the right or the left of where they were found in the other display, the two displays produced the perception of a three-dimensional scene when viewed together through a stereoscope.

FIGURE 5•22 shows a pair of these random-dot stereograms. If you look at them very carefully, you will see that some of the dots near the center in the right stereogram have been moved slightly to the left in the left stereogram. Some people can look at these figures without using a stereoscope and see depth. If you want to try this, hold the book at arm's length and stare at

the space between the figures, at the same time pretending you are looking "through" the book at something behind it. If you keep looking, you may be able to make the two images fuse into one, located right in the middle. Eventually, you may see a small square in the center of the image, raised above the background. The process can be eased by using special viewers that separate the images. The growing popularity of 3-D movies testifies to the entertainment potential of retinal disparity.

Monocular Cues Among the most important monocular cues is **interposition** ("placed between"). If one object is placed between you and another object so that the closer object partially obscures your view of the more distant one, you can immediately perceive which object is closer to you. Obviously, interposition works best when you are familiar with the objects and know what their shapes should look like. In FIGURE 5•23, panel (a) can be seen either as two rectangles located one in front of the other—panel (b)—or as a rectangle nestled against an L-shaped object—panel (c). Because we tend to perceive an ambiguous drawing on the basis of shapes that are already familiar, we are more likely to perceive Figure 5.23 (a) as two rectangles, one partly hiding the other.

Another important monocular cue is provided by the **relative size** of an object. For example, if an automobile casts a very small image on our retinas, we will perceive it as being far away. We already know how large cars are, so our visual system automatically computes the approximate distance based on the size of the retinal image.

FIGURE 5•24 shows two columns, one closer than the other. The scene demonstrates **linear perspective:** the tendency

[FIGURE 5•22] A pair of random-dot stereograms.

(From Julesz, B. (1965). Texture and visual perception. *Scientific American, 12,* 38–48.)

interposition A monocular cue for depth perception; an object that partially blocks another object is perceived as closer.

relative size A monocular cue for depth perception based on the retinal size of an object.

linear perspective A monocular cue for depth perception; the arrangement of lines drawn in two dimensions such that parallel lines receding from the viewer are seen to converge at a point on the horizon.

[FIGURE 5•23] Interposition. The two objects shown in panel (a) could be two identical rectangles, one in front of the other, as shown in (b), or a rectangle and an L-shaped object, as shown in (c). When the objects are familiar. We tend to see them in their simplest form—in this case, a rectangle. As a result, the shape slightly to the right is perceived as being partly hidden and thus farther away from us.

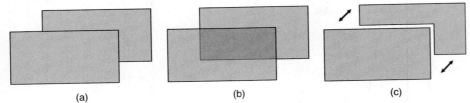

(a) (b) (c)

for parallel lines that recede from us eventually to converge at a single point. Thus, objects accompanied by greater convergence are perceived as farther away.

A **texture gradient** provides another cue for the distance of objects. A coarser texture appears to be closer, and a finer texture looks more distant. (See FIGURE 5•25.) The earth's atmosphere, which always contains a certain amount of **haze,** also can supply cues about the relative distance of objects or parts of the landscape. Parts of the landscape that are farther away become less distinct because of haze in the air. (See FIGURE 5•26.)

The patterns of light and shadow in a scene—its **shading**—can provide us with cues about distance, although the cues that shading provides may not tell us much about the absolute distances of objects. FIGURE 5•27 illustrates this phenomenon. Some of the circles look convex, as if they bulge out toward you (bumps); others look concave, as if they are hollowed out (dimples). You may perceive this figure as a collection of dimples surrounded by bumps. Try turning the page upside down. The only difference is the direction of the shading, but your perception of the bumps and dimples changes. The visual system appears to interpret the scene as if it were illuminated from above. Thus, the top of a convex object will be in light and the bottom will be in shadow and vice versa for a concave object. Using a "pop-out" image comparable to Figure 5.27, Sun and Perona (1998) found that dimples tended to pop out faster when the perceived direction of lighting was slightly more from the top left. The next

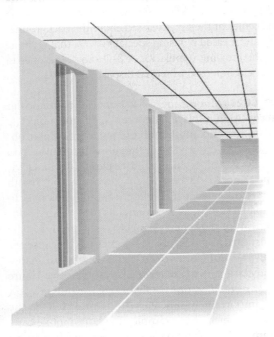

[FIGURE 5•24] Linear perspective. The use of straight lines that converge to a single point gives the appearance of distance and makes the two inset columns look similar in size.

texture gradient A monocular cue for depth perception; the relative fineness of detail present in the surfaces of objects or the ground or floor.

haze A monocular cue for depth perception; objects that are less distinct in their outlines and texture are perceived as farther from the viewer.

shading A monocular cue for depth perception; the apparent light source determines whether the surface of an object is perceived as concave or convex.

[FIGURE 5•25] Textures. Variations in texture can produce the perception of distance. The stones diminish in size toward the top of the photo; we therefore perceive the top of the photo as being farther away from us.

[**FIGURE 5•26**] Cues from atmospheric haze. Variation in detail, owing to haze, produces the perception of distance.

(Photo © Mark Keller/SuperStock)

[**FIGURE 5•28**] Depth cues supplied by elevation. The objects nearest the horizontal line appear farthest away from us.

(From Margaret W. Matlin & Hugh J. Foley. *Sensation and Perception,* 3/e. Published by Allyn and Bacon, Boston, MA. Copyright © 1992 by Pearson Education. Adapted by permission of the publisher.)

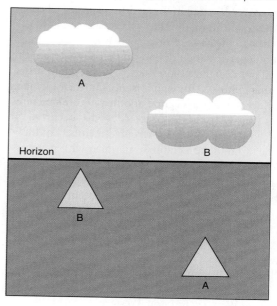

time you visit an art gallery, check the shadows in portraits and see if the artists have followed this convention.

Horizon proximity provides another cue for distance. When we are able to see the horizon, we perceive objects near it as being distant and those above or below it as being nearer to us. For example, cloud B and triangle B in **FIGURE 5•28** appear farther away than cloud A and triangle A even though the triangles are the same size, as are the clouds.

Another important source of distance information is **motion parallax** (*parallax* comes from a Greek word meaning "change"). Try the following demonstration: Focus on an object a few feet in front of you. Then move your head from side

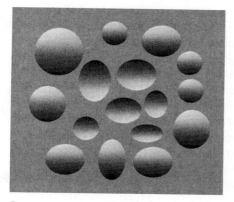

[**FIGURE 5•27**] Depth cues supplied by shading. A viewer tends to interpret this configuration as a group of bumps surrounding a group of dimples.

(From Sun, J. & Perona, P. (1998). *Nature Neuroscience, 1.* Reprinted by permission from Macmillan Publishers, Ltd.)

to side while continuing to focus. The rest of the scene will move back and forth with the motion of your head. However, the part of the scene that is closer to you than the object you are focusing on will move faster across the field of vision than the part of the scene that is farther away from the object. This perceived difference in objects' relative rate of motion is the cue for distance. In the natural world, it may be particularly useful for predators' perception of the distance to their prey.

focus On

How Does Culture Affect Visual Perception?

As we saw in Chapter 3, the development of the nervous system is shaped by interplay between heredity and environment. The development of visual perception certainly involves learning. From birth onward, we explore our environment with our eyes. The patterns of light and dark, color, and movement produce changes in the visual system of the brain.

Consider geographical variables. If our physical environment lacks certain features, we may fail to recognize them if we encounter them later in life. For example, we might expect that people living in a treeless environment without pronounced vertical features would perceive the world differently

horizon proximity A monocular cue for depth perception; objects closer to the horizon appear farther away that objects more distant from the horizon.

motion parallax A monocular cue for depth perception; as we pass by a scene, objects closer to us appear to move farther than those more distant.

from inhabitants of dense forests who are surrounded by vertical features but very seldom encounter vast, open fields.

The variance in cultural codes found in pictorial representations may also affect perceptual development. For example, visual artists have learned to use the monocular depth cues (except motion parallax) in paintings, but not all these cues are represented in the traditional art of all cultures. For example, in many cultures, visual art lacks linear perspective. Will the absence of particular monocular cues in the art of a particular culture mean that people from this culture will not recognize those cues when they view art from another culture? Although it is quite rare for members of one culture to fail to recognize another culture's pictures as pictures (Russell et al., 1997), consider what occurred when Deregowski et al. (1972) presented members of the Me'en tribe of Ethiopia, a culture unfamiliar with pictures, with a series of pictures from a children's coloring book. They responded by smelling the pictures, listening to the pages while flexing them, and giving close attention to the texture of the pages. According to Berry et al. (1992), Asians who are unfamiliar with art that uses linear perspective are more likely to judge the shapes that appear in Figure 5.24 as other than rectangles.)

Segall, Campbell, and Herskovits (1966) presented the Müller-Lyer illusion (and several others) to groups of participants from Western and non-Western cultures. (See **FIGURE 5•29.**) Most investigators believe that the Müller-Lyer illusion is a result of experience with the angles formed by the intersection of walls, ceilings, and floors (Redding and Hawley, 1993). The angled lines can be seen as examples of linear perspective. (See **FIGURE 5•30.**) Segall and his colleagues did find that people from "carpentered" cultures were more susceptible to this illusion.

The effects on visual perception of a culture's language have received close attention in psychological research. In

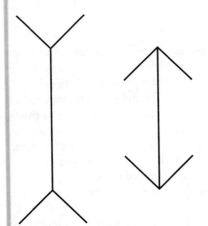

[**FIGURE 5•29**] The Müller-Lyer illusion. The two vertical lines are actually equal in length, but the one on the left appears to be longer.

---

linguistic relativity hypothesis The hypothesis that the language a person speaks influences his or her thoughts and perceptions.

[**FIGURE 5•30**] The impact of culture on the Müller-Lyer illusion. People from "non-carpentered" cultures that lack rectangular corners are less likely to be susceptible to this illusion. Although the two vertical lines are actually the same height, the line on the right looks shorter.

(Photos courtesy of Neil Carlson)

the mid-nineteenth century, the British statesman William Gladstone noted that the writings of the ancient Greeks did not contain words for brown or blue. Is it possible the ancient Greeks did not perceive these colors? At about the same time, a German ophthalmologist, H. Magnus (1880) investigated this hypothesis by gathering both linguistic and perceptual data. He sent questionnaires and color chips to colleagues living in the Americas and asked them to test the abilities of the native people to distinguish among various colors. Magnus was surprised to discover very few cultural differences in people's ability to perceive the colors. Linguistic differences did not appear to reflect perceptual differences.

The issue emerged again in the mid-twentieth century as the **linguistic relativity hypothesis,** sometimes called the Whorfian hypothesis. Briefly stated, the hypothesis asserts that the language used by the members of a particular culture strongly influences the thoughts and perceptions that characterize the culture. Supporters of linguistic relativity suggested that color names are cultural conventions—that members of a given culture could have divided the countless combinations of hue, saturation, and brightness that we call colors into any number of different categories. Each category was assigned a name, and when members of that culture looked out at the world, they perceived each of the colors they saw as belonging to one of these categories.

Two anthropologists, Berlin and Kay, tested this hypothesis (Berlin & Kay, 1969; Kay, 1975). They studied a wide range of languages and found 11 primary color terms: in English, they are black, white, red, yellow, green, blue, brown, purple, pink, orange, and gray. The authors referred to these as focal colors. Not all languages used all 11 terms (as English does). Some languages used only two terms: black and white. If a language contained words for three primary colors, they were for black, white, and red. If it contained words for six primary colors, they were for black, white, red, yellow, green, and blue. The fact that all cultures had words for focal colors suggests that the physiology of the visual system—and not arbitrary cultural conventions—is responsible for the selection of color names.

Other evidence supports this conclusion. In their study of infants' color perception, Bornstein (1975) and Bornstein, Kessen, and Weiskopf (1976) found evidence for color categories identical to those of adults, and Zemack and Teller (2007) reported that infants' color preferences remain stable. Eleanor Heider (1971) reported that both children and adults found it easier to remember a color chip of a focal color (such as red or blue) than one of a nonfocal color (such as turquoise or peach). In her study of a specific culture—the Dani culture of New Guinea—Rosch (formerly Heider) found that the language of the Dani people has only two basic color terms: *mili* ("black") and *mola* ("white"). Rosch assembled two sets of color chips, one containing focal colors and the other containing nonfocal colors. She taught her participants arbitrary names that she made up for the colors. Even though the participants had no words in their language for any of the colors, the group learning names for focal colors learned the names faster and remembered them better (Heider, 1972; Rosch, 1973).

Although Rosch's experiments have been interpreted as evidence against linguistic relativity, Roberson et al. (2000) claimed evidence supporting it. They compared British adults with adult speakers of Berinmo, a language spoken by a stone-age cultural group that lives in Papua, New Guinea. Berinmo speakers have five basic color terms, including *nol,* which describes shades of green, blue, and purple, and *wor,* which covers yellow, orange, brown, and khaki. Unlike British adults, then, Berinmo speakers do not distinguish green and blue as colors with separate names, nor do they discriminate among the different colors denoted by the word "wor."

Roberson and her colleagues showed participants from both linguistic groups three cards, each with a color on it, and asked them to pick the color that was different from the other two. For English speakers, when shown two shades of green and a shade of blue, the choice was obvious: the shade of blue was different. For the Berinmo speakers, however, the distinction between two greens and a blue was arbitrary; all three were nol colors. They chose the blue only about half the time. However, when shown cards with a yellow, a khaki, and a green shade, the tables were turned. For the Berinmo speakers, the choice was between two wor cards and a nol. For the English speakers, the distinction looked arbitrary. Roberson and her colleagues found that each group of speakers could distinguish colors across its own linguistic category boundaries, but was only at a chance level when making decisions relevant in the other group's language.

What may we conclude from the research summarized here? Obviously perceptual "primitives" exist; that is, perceptual universals that cross cultural boundaries—color, brightness, form, and quantity, for example. But within these universal categories, cultural differences may very well shape diverse subcategories, as the work of Roberson et al. suggests. Among the elements of culture, language may be a particularly powerful producer of perceptual diversity.

Constancies of Visual Perception

Although Gestalt psychologists argued that similarities in human brains assure perceptual regularities—the Gestalt laws of perception—learning also plays a role in perception. Repeated exposure to a particular set of objects may allow us eventually to classify them accurately despite dramatic differences in the sensory information they produce. If you close the book you are reading and turn it around in front of you, the light reflected from the book will create quite different retinal images. Now imagine that another person is holding the same book while standing several feet from you and turns it around in much the same way. The retinal images will be much smaller. In both cases, however, you will recognize the size and shape of the book easily. Such experience-based invariance in our recognition of objects is referred to as **perceptual constancy** and comes in several types—*form* (or shape) *constancy, size constancy, color constancy,* and *brightness constancy.* Even though the viewing conditions may vary considerably, we learn that certain characteristics of objects remain the same.

Motion Perception

Detection of movement is one of the most primitive perceptual abilities. It is exhibited even by animals whose visual systems do not obtain detailed images of the environment. In animals that must avoid obstacles and elude predators, accurate estimation of motion is essential. Pigeons are a good example, as they are prey to fast-moving predators able to catch them in flight. Sun and Frost (1998) found that the pigeon's visual system contains three distinct classes of neurons that

---

perceptual constancy The experience-based ability to recognize an object and certain of its characteristics—its form, size, color, and brightness—as invariant despite the shifting retinal images it produces.

separately carry information about looming objects. The information provided by these neurons provides a sort of "early warning" system of an impending collision, as well as an accurate estimate of the time to collision. Of course, the human visual system can detect more than the mere presence of movement. We can detect what is moving in our environment and the direction in which it is moving.

Chapter 4 made the point that all sensory systems show adaptation and aftereffects. Motion is no exception. Perhaps you have stood on a foot bridge and stared at the water in the stream below you as it ran under the bridge. If you shifted your gaze and looked down at the bridge instead, it may have appeared to move in the direction opposite that of the water. Tootell et al. (1995) presented research participants with a display showing a series of concentric rings moving outward like the ripples in a pond. When the rings suddenly stopped moving, the participants had the impression of the opposite movement—that the rings were moving inward. During this time, the researchers produced *f*MRI images of the participants' brains. The scans showed increased activity in the dorsal stream of the visual association cortex, which lasted as long as the illusion of movement did. Thus, the neural circuits that give rise to this illusion appear to be located in the same region that responds to actual moving stimuli.

Compensation for Eye Movements Objects in the visual field move, but if a person moves his or her eyes, head, or whole body, the image on the retina will move, even if everything within the person's visual field remains stable. (Recall the demonstration of motion parallax, see page 147.) Often, of course, both kinds of movements will occur at the same time. This presents a problem for the visual system: to determine which images of motion are produced by movements of objects in the environment and which are produced by movements of the person's own eyes, head, and body.

To illustrate this problem, think about how this page of the book is projected onto your retinas as you read it. If we could make a digital recording of one of your retinas, we would see that the image of the page projected there is in constant movement as your eyes make several saccades along a line and then snap back to the beginning of the next line. Conversely, if you look at a single point on the page (say, a period at the end of sentence) and then move the page around while following the same point with your eyes, you perceive the book as moving, even though the image on your retina remains fairly stable. (Try it.) Then think about the images on your retinas while you are driving in busy traffic, constantly moving your eyes around to keep track of your own location and that of other cars moving in different directions at different speeds. At every instant, the visual system is distinguishing movements that originate with you (eyes and head) from those of objects external to you.

Haarmeier et al. (1997) reported the case of a German patient with bilateral damage to the visual association cortex who could not compensate for image movement caused by head and eye movements. When the patient moved his eyes, it looked to him as if the world were moving in the opposite direction. Without the ability to compensate for head and eye movements, any movement of the image on the retina was perceived as movement of objects in the environment.

Perception of Movement When It Is Absent If you sit in a darkened room and watch two small lights that are alternately turned on and off at a certain rate, your perception will be of a single light moving back and forth. You will not see the light turn off at one position and then turn on at the second position. If the distance and timing are just right, the light will appear to stay on at all times, quickly moving between the positions. This demonstration is known as the **phi phenomenon** and was originally studied by the Gestalt psychologists referred to earlier in the chapter. Theater marquees, "moving" neon signs, and computer animations make use of it. This characteristic of the visual system accounts for the fact that we perceive the images in motion pictures and on television as continuous rather than discrete. The images actually jump from place to place, but we perceive smooth movement.

QUESTIONS TO CONSIDER

1. Why do you suppose that artists sometime hold their thumbs up in front of them while looking at the scenes they are painting?
2. Why does the full moon appear to be larger when it appears just above the horizon than when it appears overhead?

A Fundamental Conundrum

As in previous chapters, the case studies cited in Chapter 5 give us pause: What is going on in the patient's perception? What is missing, specifically? And what has happened to the brain to produce such unusual symptoms? The case of Mrs. R is illustrative. Somehow a cerebral stroke had altered her brain so that she, who was a perfectly intelligent woman otherwise, could no longer perform what children could easily perform and what she had long

---

phi phenomenon The perception of movement caused by the turning on and off of two or more lights, one at a time, in sequence; often used on theater marquees; responsible for the apparent movement of images in movies and television.

performed almost automatically—naming familiar objects. She often could name their characteristic features, but somehow she couldn't tie those features together sufficiently to produce the right name. Only when additional information was provided—through gesture or movement or by direct contact, for example—did things finally click.

The case of Mrs. R. and the related case of Dee remind us that, even though once-familiar stimuli are present, the appropriate, knowledgeable response to them may not be forthcoming. Something about the disruption of cerebrovascular functioning in Mrs. R. and the too-long exposure to carbon monoxide in Dee had changed their brains sufficiently to render them visually agnostic.

In analyzing perception, psychologists sometimes make a distinction between *distal* and *proximal* stimuli (see Gibson, 1960). A distal stimulus is, as the term implies, at a distance—out there. It is the source of the energy, emitted or reflected, that strikes the sensory receptors. A proximal stimulus is close by, immediate—the image on the retina for example. In the case of Mrs. R and Dee, the distal stimuli used by the cognitive neuroscientists who examined them—the items used in formal or informal testing—were similar to those the two women had encountered many times before their brain injury. The new strangeness of their responses to those items—their inability to name them accurately—was due not to the changes in the distal stimuli but to changes in the processing of the proximal stimuli.

The differences in the brains of Mrs. R. and Dee before and after brain injury may account for the dramatic change in their ability to name familiar objects accurately. Their cases bring to light a larger issue: that all of us are dependent on the proximal stimuli that are available to us. None of us has direct access to the distal stimuli. We are, as Plato famously put it, captives of our senses. We only perceive what is proximal.

What this implies is that the "world out there"—the world of other people and of nonhuman objects, the world that includes the parts of our own bodies that perceive—are constructions. Theirs is a provisional reality. We could never perceive them directly, but only the proximal stimuli they are presumed to induce.

A fundamental conundrum exists here: what it means to perceive reality. Our study of perception may make us more humble about offering such claims. It may also allow us to better appreciate the delicious insights of the American poet, Wallace Stevens, who, on gazing out at the ocean in the dusk at Key West, saw a woman walking along the beach, singing. He wondered about the origin of her song—was she singing what she heard from the waves, or was it something else? With formidable insight into the constructedness of human perception, Wallace went on:

> It was her voice that made
> The sky acutest at its vanishing.
> She measured to the hour its solitude.
> She was the single artificer of the world
> In which she sang, And when she sang, the sea,
> Whatever self it had, became the self
> That was her song, for she was the maker. Then we,
> As we beheld her striding there alone,
> Knew that there never was a world for her
> Except the one she sang, and singing, made.

—[From "The Idea of Order at Key West" (Stevens, 1972)]

CHAPTER SUMMARY

Brain Mechanisms of Visual Perception

Visual information proceeds from the retina to the thalamus and then to the primary visual cortex. This brain area is organized into modules, each of which receives information from a small region of the retina. Neural circuits within each module analyze specific information from their part of the visual field, including the orientation and thickness of lines, movements, and color.

The visual cortex consists of the primary visual cortex and the visual association cortex. Studies with laboratory animals, functional-imaging studies with humans, and the study of patients with damage to specific regions of the visual association cortex indicate that the visual association cortex consists of two streams. The ventral stream, which ends in the inferior temporal cortex, is involved with the visual perception of objects and color. Damage to this region can cause cerebral achromatopsia (inability to perceive colors) or various forms of visual agnosia, including prosopagnosia (inability to recognize faces). The development of neural circuits in the fusiform face area may be a result of extensive experience in looking at faces. Specific regions of the ventral stream are also devoted to the perception of bodies or body parts or of scenes and backgrounds. The dorsal stream, which ends in the parietal cortex, is involved in perception of space and in visually guided control of reaching, grasping, and manipulating. Regions of the dorsal stream are also involved in the perception of motion.

Visual Perception of Objects

Perception of objects requires, first, recognition of figure and ground. The Gestalt laws of proximity, symmetry, continuity, closure, and common fate describe some of the ways we distinguish figure from ground, even when the outlines of the figures are not explicitly bounded by lines.

Psychologists have advanced hypotheses about the mechanism of pattern perception, or the visual recognition of particular shapes. The first hypothesis suggests that our brain contains templates of all the shapes we can perceive. We compare a particular pattern of visual input with these templates until we find a fit. But can the brain hold infinitely many shapes? Another hypothesis suggests that our brain contains prototypes, which are more flexible than simple templates. According to a different hypothesis, prototypes are collections of distinctive features (such as the two parallel lines and the connecting diagonal of the letter N). One such view posits the brain's possession of a set of feature detectors known as geons. Further hypotheses are based on the artificial neural network model and assert that the ability of neural networks to learn to recognize patterns of input is the best explanation of pattern perception.

Cognitive psychologists originally based their information-processing models of the human brain on the computer as a serial processor. However, the fact that a computer program can simulate a brain function does not mean that the brain and the computer perform the function in the same way; they do not. The brain consists of billions of interconnected neurons that operate comparatively slowly. However, by doing many things simultaneously, the brain can perform complex operations quickly. It acts as a parallel processor. Thus, more recent attempts to devise models of mental functions—especially pattern perception—have used artificial neural networks that operate in parallel fashion. This approach uses assemblies of units having properties similar to those of neurons.

Perception involves both bottom-up and top-down processing. Our perceptions are influenced not only by the details of the particular stimuli we see (bottom-up), but also by prior knowledge of their relations to each other and by our expectations (top-down). Evidence from cognitive neuroscience suggests that our perceptions arise from a system that is specialized for object identification—the "what" system—that involves the ventral stream. A second system—the "where" system—involves the dorsal stream and may function independently to guide our actions in three-dimensional space.

Visual Perception of Space and Motion

Our visual system accomplishes a remarkable feat: It manages to accurately perceive objects, even in the face of movement and changes in levels of illumination. Because the size and shape of a retinal image—a two-dimensional image—vary with the location of an object relative to the eye, accurate form perception requires depth perception—perception of the locations of objects in three-dimensional space. Depth perception comes from binocular cues (from convergence and retinal disparity) and monocular cues (from interposition, size, linear perspective, texture, haze, shading, visual horizon, and head and body movements).

A person's culture may affect his or her perceptions, but probably not in a fundamental way. The linguistic relativity hypothesis, which suggested that language could strongly affect the way we perceive the world, has received limited empirical support. It is also possible that experience with some environmental features, such as particular geographical features or buildings composed of straight lines and right angles, may influence the way people perceive the visual world.

As a consequence of repeated exposure to the same classes of objects under what may be very different conditions, we learn to recognize them as unchanged, despite the diverse retinal images they produce. These perceptual constancies may be specific to the form, size, color, and brightness of objects.

Because our bodies may well be moving while we are visually following some activity in the outside world, the visual system has to make further compensations. It keeps track of the commands to the eye muscles and compensates for the direction in which the eyes are pointing. Movement is perceived when objects move relative to one another. In particular, a smaller object is likely to be perceived as moving across a larger one. Movement is also perceived when our eyes follow a moving object, even though its image remains on the same part of the retina.

The phi phenomenon is our tendency to see a sequence of discrete images as a continuously moving object. Because of the phi phenomenon, we perceive television shows and movies as real motion, not as a series of disconnected images.

succeed with mypsychlab

Visit MyPsychLab for practice quizzes, flashcards, and dozens of videos and animated tutorials, including the following items you can find in the "Multimedia Library":

Receptive Fields
Top-Down Processing
Five Well-Known Illusions

Distinguishing Figure-Ground Relationships
Gestalt Laws of Perception
Perceptual Set

KEY TERMS

SUGGESTIONS FOR FURTHER READING

Bruce, V., & Young, A. W. (1998). *In the eye of the beholder: The science of face perception.* Oxford: Oxford University Press.

A comprehensive look at the psychology and physiology of face perception, with reference to works of art featured in an exhibit at the Scottish National Portrait Gallery.

Dowling, J. E. (2004). *The great brain debate: Nature or nurture?* Washington, DC: Joseph Henry Press.

A foremost expert on the visual system examines the development of visual perception in the context of the larger issue of gene–environment interaction.

Goldstein, E. B. (2004). *Blackwell handbook of sensation and perception.* Oxford: Blackwell.

A collection of authoritative overviews of sensory systems and perceptual processes in vision, audition, olfaction, gustation, and the cutaneous senses.

Goodale, M., & Milner, D. (2004). *Sight unseen: An exploration of conscious and unconscious vision.* Oxford, UK: Oxford University Press.

Drawing from clinical observations of a patient with visual agnosia, this provocative book introduces the concept of two visual systems: one for the perception of objects and the other for the control of movement.

Hoffman, D. D. (1998). *Visual intelligence: How we create what we see.* New York: Norton.

This is an authoritative work on visual perception as representation, that is, on how the visual system creates models of the visual world.

Hubel, D. H., & Wiesel, T. (2004). *Brain and visual perception: The story of a 25-year collaboration.* New York: Oxford University Press.

One half of the Nobel-prize–winning team provides a marvelous summary of their work and its implications.

Pinker, S. (1997). *How the mind works.* New York: Norton.

If you only read one book about cognitive neuroscience, you'll do no better than this comprehensive, well-told introduction.

Sacks, O. (1998). *The island of the colorblind.* New York: Vintage.

The noted neurologist and superb storyteller weaves a fascinating tale of research findings in Micronesia and their larger, darwinian implications. Part of the book is devoted to his observations of an isolated population of individuals with achromatopsia.

Life-Span Developme

Taken from *Psychology: The Science of Behavior*, Seventh Edition, by Neil R. Carlson, Harold Miller, C. Donald He
John W. Donahoe, and G. Neil Martin.

Prologue

A Rescue Mission

On December 25, 1989, furious at the way he had ruled their country, Romanian revolutionaries executed Nicolae Ceaușescu and his wife, Elena. In the subsequent months, the outside world learned that, among the horrors of their regime, the Ceaușescus had perpetrated a terrible ordeal on the nation's young children. Anxious to increase the country's birth rate and, at the same time pay off the national debt with food exports, Ceaușescu had restricted access to birth control while confiscating farm harvests. Thousands of families had no choice but to consign their infant children to state-run orphanages.

Collectively, these orphanages were warehouses for children. Many were unheated, with poor sanitation, few trained staff, and few resources. Westerners who visited the orphanages after the coup found many children left naked and forgotten in crowded wards. By almost any comparison, the children of these orphanages had suffered extreme neglect and deprivation of adult company.

Anxious to help, many couples from other countries sought to adopt these children. Thousands of orphans found foster homes in foreign countries, with parents who had made the special effort to rescue them and to provide a nurturing environment. Although complaints about bureaucratic corruption forced the Romanian government to suspend international adoptions in 2001, for a time it seemed that, at least in the case of those adopted children, adoption had allowed some to escape the ravages of the orphanage system.

Elinor Ames, a Canadian psychologist who spearheaded an effort to rescue some of the orphans, soon found that there were troubling aftermaths (Fisher et al., 1997). When Ames and her colleagues interviewed the parents who had adopted these children, she found that even though the children were still young, they showed significant difficulties in adjusting to their new lives. The parents reported eating problems (usually voracious appetites), medical problems, and frequent bouts of repetitive and robotic movements. Compared to Canadian children, the Romanian orphans also showed more problems related to siblings and peers. They seemed unable to adapt to new social situations and to adjust their behavior to life outside an institution. At the time, these children were about 2 to 3 years of age.

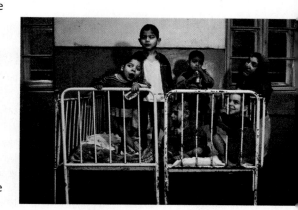

To Ames and her colleagues in 1997, the future of these children looked deeply uncertain. How extensive was the psychological damage caused by the neglect these children received early in life? How broad were the effects? The children's bodies responded quickly to improvements in their environments. Could psychological damage be likewise repaired by the efforts of the foster parents who had adopted them? What does the future hold for these children? ■

In this chapter, we discuss the physical, intellectual, and social changes we go through as we age, and some problems associated with abnormal development, similar to those described in the chapter prologue. We examine each of the major developmental periods of a person's life—prenatal development, infancy and childhood, adolescence, adulthood, and old age—and look at the psychological processes that change over these periods. TABLE 6•1 shows highlights of common physical and psychological changes people experience throughout the phases of the life span.

Developmental psychologists study both the similarities and the differences among people as they develop and change. Because they study change, developmental psychologists use special strategies of research. In a **cross-sectional study,** individuals of different ages are simultaneously compared with respect to some test or observation. For example, a developmental psychologist might present mathematical problems to groups of 5-, 7-, and 9-year-olds to measure the children's grasp of the concept of negative numbers. In contrast, a **longitudinal study** compares observations for the same individuals at different times of their lives. A longitudinal study of children's grasp of negative numbers might test a group of children when they were 5 years of age, and then repeat the test on the same children at 7 and then at 9.

Cross-sectional studies are usually more convenient to carry out, and they avoid the problems associated with repeatedly testing or observing the same individuals. However, they contain an important problem in interpretation. We examine this problem in connection with a concrete issue later in this chapter. Meanwhile, let's begin our consideration of life-span development by exploring the prenatal period.

Prenatal Development

The **prenatal period** extends over the approximately 9 months between conception and birth. The length of a normal pregnancy is 266 days, or 38 weeks. During this time, development depends on two factors whose effects characterize themes of this chapter. First, the genetic contribution from egg and sperm determines the genotype of the new individual. A child develops from this single source of genetic "instructions."

Although all cells of an individual (with the exception of reproductive cells) have the same genetic contents, they obviously differ—blood cells are not the same as neurons. Some factor must direct the mechanisms of replication so that cells that are genetically identical will develop along different paths. The biological mechanisms that determine development do this by suppressing and enhancing the chemical basis by which cells replicate. One example of how this process has worked is apparent from just looking around you: Although men and women have obvious differences, it is the case that the sexes are otherwise pretty similar. Yet, as we saw earlier (see Figure 3.8), women have two copies of the X chromosome, whereas men have only one. Because the X chromosome is larger and has many more genes than the Y, it would be expected that women would produce more of the proteins controlled by X chromosome genes, yet, this does not occur. Through a process known as X-chromosome inactivation, one of the X chromosomes is "silenced" shortly after

cross-sectional study A study of development in which individuals of different ages are compared at the same time.

longitudinal study A study of development in which observations of the same individuals are compared at different times of their lives.

prenatal period The approximately 9 months between conception and birth. This period is divided into three developmental stages: the zygotic, the embryonic, and the fetal.

[TABLE 6•1] Phases of the Life Span

Phase	Approximate Age	Highlights
1. Prenatal period	Conception through birth	Rapid physical development of both nervous system and body
2. Infancy	Birth to 2 years	Motor development; attachment to primary caregiver
3. Childhood	2 years to 12 years	Increasing ability to think logically and reason abstractly; refinement of motor skills; peer influences
4. Adolescence	13 years to about 20 years	Thinking and reasoning becomes more adultlike; identity search; continued peer influences
5. Adulthood	20 years to 65 years	Love, committed relationship; career; stability and then decrease in physical abilities
6. Old age	65 years and older to death	Reflection on life's work and accomplishments; physical health deteriorates; preparation for death; death

fertilization so that most of its genes do not produce the proteins they normally would. This means that, although a woman receives an X chromosome from her mother and another from her father, only one of these is active. (Which one is largely a matter of chance.) Furthermore, each cell passes along the inactivation to the next generation of cells, so that all cells in an adult woman reflect the silencing that occurred early in life. Interestingly, a woman's germ cells reactivate the silenced chromosome, so that a woman can pass along, say, her father's X chromosome—even if it was silenced in her.

Inactivation occurs because the proteins that surround the DNA molecule undergo complex chemical changes that condense the protein structure and make the DNA contained within it nonfunctional (Brockdorff & Turner, 2007). These changes persist through cell divisions, condensing the same part of the chromosome in later cells and passing along the inactivation. In this way, a molecular change early in the life of a woman affects all the cells that develop thereafter, although the DNA code itself has not changed.

X-chromosome inactivation is one example of an **epigenetic modification,** a modification of cell inheritance that is not due to alterations of the DNA sequence itself. Epigenetic changes include the way the DNA molecule is folded within other proteins, chemical changes in the structure of the DNA molecule itself, and complex modifications in the way DNA information is mapped into protein synthesis (Allis, Jenuwein, & Reinberg, 2007). Epigenetic modifications form a second factor of early development and illustrate the important point that the cell's chemical environment moderates the expression of its genetic code.

Stages of Prenatal Development

The union of the ovum (egg) and sperm, or conception, is the starting point for prenatal development. During the **zygotic stage,** which lasts about 2 weeks, the zygote, or the single new cell that is formed at conception, replicates many times, and the internal organs begin to form. By the end of the first week, the zygote consists of about 100 cells. Many of the cells are arranged in two layers: one layer for the skin, hair, nervous system, and sensory organs, and the other for the digestive and respiratory systems and glands. Near the end of this stage, a third layer of cells appears that will eventually develop into muscles and the circulatory and excretory systems.

The **embryonic stage** of prenatal development, the second stage, begins at about 2 weeks and ends about 8 weeks after conception. During this stage, development occurs at an incredibly rapid pace. By a month after conception, a heart has begun to beat, a brain and spinal cord have started to function, and most of the major body structures are beginning to form. By the end of this stage, the major features that define the human body— arms, hands, fingers, legs, toes, shoulders, head, and eyes—are discernible. Behaviorally, the embryo can react reflexively to stimulation. For example, if the mouth is stimulated, the embryo moves its upper body and neck. Because so many changes depend on a delicate chemical balance, the embryo at this stage

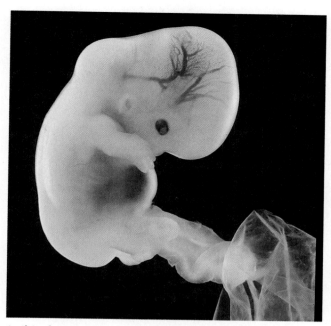

As this photograph of a six-week-old fetus illustrates, most of the major features that define the human body are present near the end of the embryonic stage of development (which starts at about two weeks and ends about eight weeks after conception).

is most susceptible to external chemical influences, including alcohol and other drugs, or toxins produced by diseases such as rubella (German measles). These substances are **teratogens** (from the Greek *teras*, meaning "monster"). The term *teratogen* refers to any substance, agent, or event that can cause mental or physical birth defects.

The beginning of sexual development occurs during the embryonic stage. The 23rd chromosome pair determines the sex of the embryo. The female partner always contributes an X chromosome to this pair at conception, whereas the male partner contributes either an X or a Y chromosome. If the male partner contributes a Y chromosome, the embryo will become a male (XY); if it is an X, the embryo will become a female (XX). Early in prenatal development, the embryo develops a pair of gonads that will become either ovaries or testes. (The word *gonad* comes from the Greek *gonos*, "procreation.") If a Y chromosome is present, a gene located on it causes the production of a chemical signal that makes the gonads develop into testes. Otherwise, the gonads become ovaries.

---

epigenetics Mechanisms through which cells inherit modifications that are not due to DNA sequences.

zygotic stage The first stage of prenatal development, during which the zygote divides many times and the internal organs begin to form.

embryonic stage The second stage of prenatal development, beginning 2 weeks and ending about 8 weeks after conception, during which the heart begins to beat, the brain starts to function, and most of the major body structures begin to form.

teratogens Substances, agents, and events that can cause birth defects.

[**FIGURE 6·1**] Differentiation and development of the sex organs.

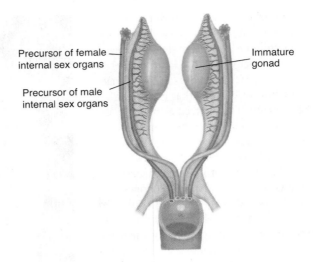

Precursor of female internal sex organs

Precursor of male internal sex organs

Immature gonad

Early in Fetal Development

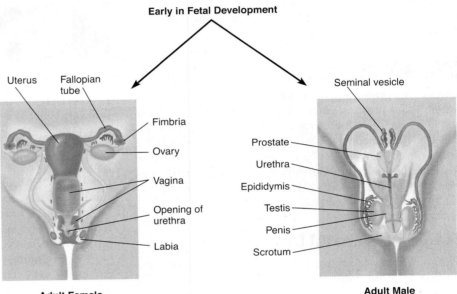

Adult Female

Uterus

Fallopian tube

Fimbria

Ovary

Vagina

Opening of urethra

Labia

Adult Male

Seminal vesicle

Prostate

Urethra

Epididymis

Testis

Penis

Scrotum

The presence or absence of testes determines the development of the other sex organs. If testes are present, they begin to secrete a class of sex hormones known as **androgens** (*andros* means "man"; *gennan* means "to produce"). The most important androgen is testosterone. Androgens bring about the development of the male internal sex organs, the penis, and the scrotum. These hormones are therefore absolutely necessary for the normal development of a male's sex organs. The development of female sex organs (uterus, vagina, and labia) occurs on its own; it does not need to be stimulated by a hormone. (See **FIGURE 6·1**.)

The **fetal stage** is the final period of prenatal development and lasts about 7 months. It officially begins with the appearance of bone cells and ends with birth. At the end of the second month of pregnancy, the fetus is about 1.5 inches long and weighs about 1 ounce. By the end of the third month, the development of major organs is completed, and the bones and muscles are beginning to develop. The fetus is now 3 inches long and weighs about 3 ounces. The fetus may show some movement, especially kicking.

By the end of the fourth month, the fetus is about 6 inches long and weighs about 6 ounces. It is also now sleeping and waking regularly. Fetal movements also become strong enough to be felt by the mother, and the heartbeat is loud enough to be heard through a stethoscope. Sound and light sensitivity will emerge within a few weeks. During the sixth month, the fetus grows to more than a foot long and weighs about 1.5 pounds. The seventh month is a critical month: If the fetus is born at this point, it has a fair chance of surviving. However, fetuses mature at different rates; some 7-month-old fetuses may be mature enough to survive premature birth, whereas others may not.

---

androgens   The primary class of sex hormones in males. The most important androgen is testosterone.

fetal stage   The third and final stage of prenatal development, which lasts for about 7 months, beginning with the appearance of bone tissue and ending with birth.

During the last 2 months of prenatal development, the fetus gains weight at the rate of about half a pound per week. On average the fetus is about 20 inches long and weighs about 7 pounds at the end of this period. The fetus is ready to be born.

Threats to Normal Prenatal Development

Probably the single most important factor in the fetus's development is the mother's diet: The food she eats and the vitamins and minerals she ingests are the fetus's only source of nutrition. If the mother is extremely malnourished, the fetus's nervous system develops abnormally, and intellectual deficits may result.

Not only malnutrition but also teratogens, as mentioned earlier, can cause birth defects. Psychologists who study birth defects are very interested in how drugs affect the fetus. Certain antibiotics, especially when taken in large quantities over long periods, can produce fetal defects. For example, tetracycline, a common antibiotic, can cause irregularities that develop later in the bones and in the coloration of the teeth. Cocaine use by mothers during pregnancy produces dramatic effects. If a pregnant woman uses cocaine, an increased risk of premature birth, low birth weight, and a smaller-than-normal head circumference occurs. One study showed that growth deficits attributable to prenatal cocaine exposure were still remarkable in children at age 7 (Covington et al., 2002). Research evidence also suggests that prenatal exposure to cocaine interferes with neural development, and that long-term consequences may ensue in the areas of arousal and attention (Bard, Coles, Plaatzman, & Lynch, 2000; Potter, et al., 2000; Singer et al., 2002; Mayes, et al., 2003). Further, some babies are born addicted and show withdrawal symptoms such as hyperactivity, irritability, tremors, and vomiting (Zuckerman & Brown, 1993).

A pregnant woman's cigarette smoking is another behavior that can affect the fetus. The carbon monoxide contained in cigarette smoke reduces the supply of oxygen to the fetus. Reduced oxygen levels are particularly harmful to the fetus during the last half of pregnancy, when the fetus is developing most rapidly and its need for oxygen is greatest. The main physical effects of mothers' smoking are increased rates of miscarriages, low-birth-weight babies, premature births, and births by cesarean section (Floyd et al., 1993; Kirchengast & Hartmann, 2003). Research suggests that prenatal exposure to cigarette smoking may produce lowered arousal levels in newborns (Franco et al., 2000), and there are indications of relatively uncommon but statistically related birth defects, such as cleft palate (e.g., Chung et al., 2000). Maternal smoking is associated with deficits in the ability of a newborn baby's brain to process speech sounds (Key et al., 2007) and may be related to behavior problems in adolescence (Weissman et al., 1999).

The damaging effects of alcohol use during pregnancy have been most widely studied (Steinhausen & Spohr, 1998;

Kelly, Day, & Streissguth, 2000; Streissguth, 2001; Henderson, Kesmodel, & Gray, 2007). These effects can include both pre- and postnatal growth deficits, deformations of the eyes and mouth, low brain mass, other brain and central nervous system abnormalities, and heart deformation—the problems collectively known as fetal alcohol syndrome, or FAS (Niccols, 2007). Even if children with FAS are reared in healthy environments with regular, nutritious meals, their physical and intellectual development still falls short of that of normal children. The effects of alcohol on the fetus depend on its age and the amount that the mother consumes. Conflicting advice is found on this issue (Nathanson, Jayesinghe, & Roycroft, 2007; O'Brien, 2007). In the face of uncertainty, the best advice should be clear: Don't drink during pregnancy.

Tragically, some teratogens are much more difficult to avoid. Among these are the chemicals that occur in our environment because of industrial or agricultural pollution. For example, many pesticides use a class of chemicals based on phosphorus. Sánchez-Peña et al. (2004) found that Mexican agricultural workers exposed to such organophosphorus pesticides had a much larger risk of damage to the chromosome structure of their sperm cells than did those without such exposure. Of course, pesticides are just one of the many contaminants that we may be exposed to; lead, mercury, and polychlorinated biphenyls (PCBs) are other environmental teratogens. Their prevalence in our environment has led some researchers to seek "anti-teratogens" that could reduce these risks (e.g., Guna Sherlin and Verma, 2001).

QUESTIONS TO CONSIDER

1. Each of us experiences similar prenatal developmental stages and processes, so why do differences among people start to emerge from this very early period?
2. What would be the significance of showing that a fetus can learn?
3. Suppose that you are a psychologist working in a pediatric clinic. A woman, pregnant with her first child, asks you for advice on what she can do to care for her unborn child. Based on what you now know about prenatal development, what advice would you give her?

Physical and Perceptual Development in Infancy and Childhood

The terms "infant" and "toddler" apply to babies up to the age of 2 years. A newborn human infant is helpless and absolutely dependent on adult care. Recent research has shown, however, that newborns do not passively await the ministrations of their caregivers (Gartstein, Crawford, & Robertson, 2008). They quickly develop skills that shape the behavior of the adults with whom they interact. This section looks at motor

[FIGURE 6•2] Milestones in a child's motor development.

(Adapted from Shirley, M. M. (1933). *The first two years: Vol. 2. Intellectual development.* Minneapolis: University of Minnesota Press.)

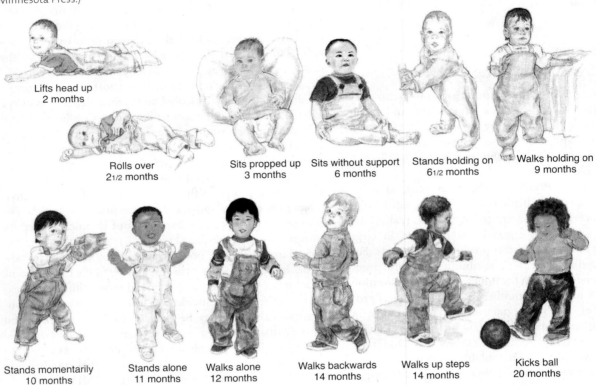

Lifts head up
2 months

Rolls over
2½ months

Sits propped up
3 months

Sits without support
6 months

Stands holding on
6½ months

Walks holding on
9 months

Stands momentarily
10 months

Stands alone
11 months

Walks alone
12 months

Walks backwards
14 months

Walks up steps
14 months

Kicks ball
20 months

development and perceptual development in infancy and early childhood; in the next section we examine some influential theories of cognitive development.

Motor Development

Normal motor development follows a distinct pattern, which appears to be dictated by maturation of the muscles and the nervous system. The term **maturation** refers to any relatively stable change in thought, behavior, or physical growth that is due to the aging process and not to experience. Although individual children progress at different rates, their development follows the same basic maturational pattern. (See **FIGURE 6•2**.)

At birth, the infant's most important movements are reflexes—automatic movements in response to specific stimuli. The most important reflexes are the rooting, sucking, and swallowing responses. If a baby's cheek is lightly touched, the baby will turn its head toward the direction of the touch (the rooting response). If the object makes contact with the baby's lips, the baby will open its mouth and begin sucking. When milk or any other liquid enters the mouth, the baby will automatically make swallowing movements. Obviously, these reflexes are important for the baby's survival. As we see later

in this chapter, these behaviors are important for an infant's social development as well.

Development of motor skills requires two ingredients: maturation of the child's nervous system and practice. Development of the nervous system is not complete at birth; considerable growth occurs during the first several months, and the amount of this growth seems to be associated with IQ in later childhood (Gale et al., 2004). Important changes in brain structure occur throughout the life span as a result of experience (Kolb & Whishaw, 1998; Kolb, Gibb, & Robinson, 2003).

Particular kinds of movements must await the development of the necessary neuromuscular systems, but motor development is not merely a matter of using these systems once they develop. Instead, physical development of the nervous system depends to a large extent on the ways the baby moves while interacting with the environment. In turn, more complex movements depend on further development of the nervous system, creating an interplay between motor and neural development. Thus, different steps in motor development are both an effect of previous development and a cause of further development (Thelen & Corbetta, 2002).

Perceptual Development

We have known for a long time that fetal experience with sensory stimuli can prepare the way for the newborn's experience.

---

maturation Any relatively stable change in thought, behavior, or physical growth that is due to the aging process and not to experience.

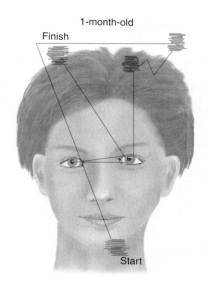

1-month-old

Finish

Start

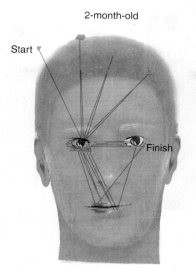

2-month-old

Start

Finish

[FIGURE 6•3] The scanning sequence used by infants viewing faces.

(From Salapatek, P. (1975). Pattern perception in early infancy. In *Infant Perception: From Sensation to Cognition, Vol 1: Basic Visual Processes*, edited by L. B. Cohen and P. Salapatek. New York: Academic Press. Copyright © 1975. Reprinted with permission from Elsevier.)

Kisilevsky et al. (2003) found that playing a recording of the mother's voice outside her abdomen increased the heart rate of her fetus, whereas playing a stranger's voice did not. At the time of birth, a child's senses are already functioning, at least to a certain extent (e.g., Maurer & Maurer, 1988). We know that the newborn's auditory system can detect sounds, because the baby will show a startle reaction when presented with a sudden loud noise. Similarly, a bright light will elicit eye closing and squinting. A cold object or a pinch will produce crying, so the sense of touch must be present. If held firmly and tilted backward, a baby will stiffen and flail his or her arms and legs, indicating that babies have a sense of balance. We also know that newborn infants have a sense of taste, because they indicate their taste preferences by facial expression and by choosing to swallow or not to swallow different liquids. Infants have an early-developing ability to distinguish odors, an ability that can be seen as an element of mother–infant bonding. For example, infants at 2 weeks can distinguish their own mother from other lactating women by breast odor (Porter, et al., 1992). We also know that infants very early on can recognize and prefer their mother's voice (e.g., DeCasper & Fifer, 1980; Purhonen et al., 2005). Research shows that preference and discrimination likely develop before birth as a result of the fetus's in utero exposure to the mother's voice (Kisilevsky et al., 2003).

Observations such as these establish the sensory abilities of infants, but when do infants develop the capacity to interpret sensory signals? Is perception present at birth? Developmental psychologists have looked at many perceptual systems to answer this question. We consider two systems: the perception of forms and the perception of distance.

Form Perception

Form Perception Researchers study the visual perceptual abilities of infants by observing their eye movements with an eye-tracking device while showing them visual stimuli. A harmless spot of infrared light, invisible to humans, is directed onto the baby's eyes. A special television camera, sensitive to infrared light, records the spot and superimposes it on an image of the display that the baby is looking at. The technique is precise enough to enable experimenters to tell which parts of a stimulus the baby is scanning. For example, Salapatek (1975) reported that a 1-month-old infant tends not to look at the inside of a figure. Instead, the baby's gaze seems to be "trapped" by the edges. Babies have low visual acuity at this age, so the results are largely a result of their looking at areas of high contrast. By the age of 2 months, the baby scans across the border to investigate the interior of a figure. FIGURE 6•3 shows a reconstruction of the paths followed by the eye scans of infants of these ages. (The babies were looking at real faces, not the drawings shown in the figure.)

The work by Salapatek and his colleagues suggests that at the age of 1 or 2 months, babies do not perceive complete shapes; their scanning strategy is limited to fixations on a few parts of the object at which they are looking. By 3 months, however, babies show clear signs of pattern recognition. For example, by this age, they prefer to look at stimuli that resemble the human face (Rosser, 1994), and by 4 or 5 months, they can discriminate between even very similar faces (Fagan & Singer, 1979; Bornstein & Arterberry, 2003).

Distance Perception The ability to perceive three-dimensional space comes at an early age. Gibson and Walk (1960) placed 6-month-old babies on what they called a visual cliff. On one side of this apparatus is a platform containing a checkerboard pattern. The platform adjoins a glass shelf mounted 3 or 4 feet over a floor that also is covered by the checkerboard pattern. Most babies who could crawl would not venture out onto the glass shelf. The infants acted as if they were afraid of falling; that is, they could perceive the distance between themselves and the floor.

Remember from Chapter 5 that several different types of cues in the environment contribute to depth perception. One cue arises from retinal disparity. As explained in Chapter 5, under normal circumstances, points on objects that are different distances from the viewer fall on slightly different points

A visual cliff. The child does not cross the glass bridge.

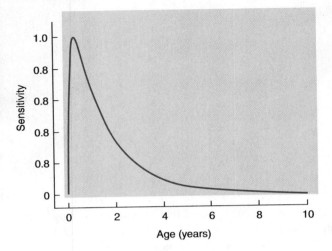

[FIGURE 6•4]   Sensitivity of stereopsis development to disruption in retinal disparity.

(Adapted from Fawcett, S. L., Wang, Y-Z., and Birch, E. E. (2005). The critical period for susceptibility of human stereopsis. *Investigative Ophthalmology & Visual Science, 46,* 521–525.)

of the two retinas. The perception of depth occurs when the two images are fused through visual processing. This form of depth perception, stereopsis ("solid vision"), depends on neurons that can respond to identical objects that stimulate different parts of the two eyes' retina (Parker, 2007). We are not born with neurons that do this. Rather, regions of the brain's visual system develop the connections that create neurons with this capacity. These connections will not develop unless animals have experience viewing objects with both eyes and consistent disparity during a period early in life.

The dependence of stereopsis on proper retinal disparity has important implications for the development of normal vision. If an infant's eyes are crossed, the same objects have inconsistent disparity, and the brain does not learn the relation between disparity and distance. Crossed vision can be corrected through surgery or through special glasses, but an infant requires disparity at a particular age to experience depth perception through stereopsis. Fawcett, Wang, & Birch (2005) examined children who had experienced crossed vision in infancy to see when loss of disparity most affects stereopsis. There are different reasons why crossed vision occurs, but overall, it has its worst influence at 3.5 months after birth, although its influence can affect stereopsis even at 4 years of age. (See FIGURE 6•4.)

Critical and Sensitive Periods in Perceptual Development Psychologists use the term **critical period** to denote a specific time during which certain experiences must occur if an individual is to develop normally. Many perceptual, behavioral, and cognitive abilities are subject to critical periods. For example, as we saw in the opening prologue and as we shall see later in this chapter, if infants are not exposed to a stimulating environment and do not have the opportunity to interact with caregivers during the first 2 years of their lives, their cognitive development will be impaired.

Other abilities may show a weaker dependence on experience: The ability in question may develop in response to experience that occurs any time within a broad range, but the effect may be stronger during some periods than during others. This weaker form of dependency is often referred to as a **sensitive period.** Acquisition of a second language seems to be such a case. A person can learn a second language throughout life; but, a second language is learned more easily in childhood than later.

Critical periods and sensitive periods demonstrate that human development is more than an unfolding of a genetically determined program. It consists of a continuous interaction between physical maturation and environmental stimulation.

QUESTIONS TO CONSIDER

1. Suppose you are expecting your first child. How might you design your child's room (or nursery) to facilitate motor and perceptual development? What kinds of toys would you include in the room? What sorts of experiences might you wish to have with your child to promote normal motor and sensory development?

2. If it could be shown that a child is genetically predisposed to prefer some visual stimuli over others, what stimuli would they be?

Cognitive Development in Infancy and Childhood

As children grow, their nervous systems mature, and they undergo new experiences. Perceptual and motor skills develop in complexity and competency. Children learn to recognize people

---

critical period A specific time in development during which certain experiences must occur for normal development to take place.

sensitive period A period during which certain experiences have a greater effect on development than they would have if they had occurred at another time.

and their voices, begin to talk and respond to the speech of others, and learn how to solve problems. Infants as young as 12 months are even able to form memories of specific events (see Bauer, 2002). In short, their cognitive capacities develop.

This section begins by highlighting the importance of a responsive environment to cognitive development; then we turn to Piaget's theory, Vygotsky's theory, the information-processing model, and the controversial question of television's impact on cognitive development.

The Importance of a Responsive Environment

Cognitive development is the process by which infants get to know things about themselves and their world. One of the first steps in a baby's cognitive development is for the baby to learn that events in the environment can be dependent on its own behavior. It appears that the type of setting that is most effective in promoting cognitive development is an environment in which the infant's behavior has tangible effects.

In an experimental test of this hypothesis, Watson and Ramey (1972) presented three groups of infants with a mobile 10 minutes per day for 14 days. A pillow containing a pressure-sensitive switch was placed under each baby's head, and the mobile was suspended above the baby's face. For one group, the mobile automatically rotated whenever the infant moved its head and activated the switch. For another group, the mobile remained stationary. For a third group, the mobile intermittently moved on its own (but not in response to infant head movements). So the first group of infants had experience controlling the mobile's movements, whereas the other two groups experienced no association between their own actions and the mobile's movement.

The babies were tested again. This time, the mobile was connected to the pillow switch for infants in all three of the experimental groups. Infants who had learned the contingency

Watson and Ramey's experiment using mobiles demonstrated the importance of a responsive environment in promoting cognitive development.

between head turning and mobile movement again turned their heads when they saw the mobile. They seemed to have learned that they could control its movements. In contrast, when the babies in the second and third groups were given the opportunity to make the mobile move by turning their heads, they did not learn to do so. It was as if they had learned from their prior experience that they could not affect whether the mobile would move. Research using similar methods found that infants were visibly pleased when they controlled the onset of a Sesame Street music video (Lewis, Alessandri, & Sullivan, 1990). Losing this type of contingent control, conversely, produces facial expressions of anger (Lewis et al., 1990; Sullivan & Lewis, 2003). The babies in the mobile study showed the importance of a responsive environment. In contrast, J.F. spent the first 3 years of her life in a Romanian orphanage and, in all that time, had only once been outside for fresh air and sunshine. The following case illustrates J.F.'s story.

[CASE STUDY] When J.F.'s prospective foster parents first saw her, sores and dirt covered her skin, and her fingernails were so long they curled around to the other side. One of her legs was so disfigured by injections of tranquilizing drugs that it would later need surgery to help her walk. Although 3 years of age, she looked less than half that age. The Canadian woman who was visiting felt so touched by the child's plight that she dropped her plans to adopt a younger child, and adopted J.F. instead.

J.F.'s new mother and father tried hard to provide the care that the child had been denied for the first 3 years of her life, but J.F. seemed incapable of accepting the attachment between a child and her parents. As described by Faulder (2006), J.F.'s emotional maturity was like that of an 18-month-old. Her mother described her as always in "spin cycle"—unable to focus on any behavior, even on play. The problems of adjustment that Elinor Ames had observed in her sample had, in J.F.'s case, led to a downward spiral.

By the time she was 10, J.F.'s behavior had turned her household into a "living hell." She had been diagnosed with the conditions of autism, attention deficit, and hyperactivity. Other suspected conditions included attachment disorder and Tourette's syndrome. One day, overwhelmed by the chaos of J.F.'s behavior, her mother phoned the social agency screaming for help. Up to this point, a stable home life and the love of two parents had not been enough. J.F. would spend the next 6 years living in a group home in another town.

Findings from research on infant control of stimuli in their environments are consistent with a great deal of other evidence about adults. For each of us, the abilities to extend ourself and to affect objects and other people are important aspects of personal and social functioning. Le Mare, Audet, & Kurytnik (2007) studied the frequency with which the foster parents of Romanian adoptees used social-support agencies and found that the parents requested help more often than those of nonadopted children. The group differences were especially pronounced when the adopted children were between 10 and 11 years of age, when the parents sought assistance for behavioral and academic problems.

Nelson (2007) suggested that at key times, the brain's development requires the stimulation that normal childhood provides; without this stimulation, regions of the brain lack directions for further development. Cognitive and social development might be characterized as a sequence. If earlier periods in the sequence are disrupted, then development is delayed. This notion of sequence, with distinct and ordered stages, was suggested by early observers of child development, such as Baldwin and Montessori (see Chapter 1). Nowadays, it is most closely associated with the theories of Jean Piaget.

The Work of Jean Piaget

Jean Piaget (1896–1980), was a Swiss researcher who viewed cognitive development as a maturational process. Piaget considered himself a philosopher concerned with the development of knowledge rather than a developmental psychologist. Piaget's work began with observations he made on his own children. He noticed that they tended to engage in behaviors that were distinctive to their age and to make related mistakes in problem solving. Other children of similar ages tended to engage in similar behaviors and to make the same kinds of mistakes. He concluded that these similarities are the result of a sequence of development that all normal children follow. Completion of each period, with its corresponding abilities, is the prerequisite for entering the next period.

An important component of Piaget's theory is the notion of an **operation.** In the field of both logic and mathematics, an operation is a transformation of an object or thing. For example, multiplication by 2 transforms 6 into 12. Similarly, saying "Rhonda is my sister" transforms your conception of "Rhonda" into another conception, that of "my sister." For Piaget, an important logical characteristic of an operation is that it is invertible; that is, it can be reversed. By inverting the operation of multiplication into division, we can transform 12 back to 6. According to Piaget, an important aspect of cognitive development is whether a child possesses the ability to use operations of different types.

As children develop, Piaget suggested, they acquire mental representations or frameworks that are used for understanding and dealing with the world and for thinking about and solving problems. As Chapter 7 explained, a mental framework that organizes and synthesizes information

According to Piaget, children develop schemas, such as schemas for grasping objects or putting them into their mouths, that become the basis for understanding current and future experiences.

about a person, place, or thing is known as a schema. Piaget proposed that schemas are first defined in terms of objects and actions but that later they become the basis of the concrete and abstract concepts that constitute adult knowledge. For example, a baby girl is said to have a "grasping schema" when she is able to grasp a rattle in her hand. Once she has learned how to grasp a rattle, she can then apply the same schema to other objects. Later, she can incorporate the "grasping schema" with others to accomplish the behavior of picking an object up. At this point, she will possess a "picking up schema."

Let's consider schemas further. Infants acquire schemas by interacting with their environment. According to Piaget, two processes help a child adapt to his or her environment: assimilation and accommodation. **Assimilation** is the process by which new information is incorporated into existing schemas. For example, suppose that a young boy has schemas for what adults are like and for what children are like. Adults are tall and drive cars. Children are short and ride bikes. When this child meets new children and adults, they will usually fit, or be assimilated, into his existing schemas and will be properly categorized. But our child will be challenged when he meets his mother's older sister Marge, who is no taller than the average 12-year-old and rides a bike. The child will need to account for the fact that Aunt Marge is nevertheless identifiably an adult. The process by which existing schemas are changed by new experiences is called **accommodation.** Our children's schemas for children and adults will have to change to include the possibility that some short people are adults rather than children. As you continue in this chapter, keep in mind that assimilation and accommodation apply not just to categorization of people and objects, but to methods of doing things and even to abstract concepts as well.

---

operation In Piaget's theory, a logical or mathematical rule that transforms an object or concept into something else.

assimilation In Piaget's theory, the process by which new information about the world is incorporated into existing schemas.

accommodation The process of altering the thickness of the lens to focus images of near or distant objects on the retina. In Piaget's theory of cognitive development, the process by which existing schemas are modified or changed by new experiences.

[**TABLE 6•2**] The Four Periods of Piaget's Theory of Cognitive Development

Period	Approximate Age	Major Features
Sensorimeter	Birth to 2 years	Grasp of object permanence; deferred imitation; rudimentary symbolic thinking
Preoperational	2 to 6 or 7 years	Increased ability to think symbolically and logically; egocentrism; cannot yet master conservation problems
Concrete operational	6 or 7 years to 11 years	Mastery of conservation problems; understanding of categorization; cannot think abstractly
Formal operational	11 years upward	Ability to think abstractly and hypothetically

Piaget's Four Periods of Cognitive Development Although development is a continuous process, Piaget argued that at key points in an individual's life, the two processes of assimilation and accommodation fail to adjust adequately to the child's knowledge of the world. At these points, by a process that Piaget labeled **equilibration,** the individual's schemas are radically reorganized. According to Piaget, these key points in a child's life divide cognitive development into four periods: sensorimotor, preoperational, concrete operational, and formal operational. (See **TABLE 6•2.**) What a child learns in one period enables him or her to progress to the next period. Crucially, it matters whether the schemas of an earlier period can be reorganized in a way that will permit operations to occur in the next. The periods in Piaget's theory are more than just intervals of time; they are necessary stages in a progression from primitive sensory knowledge to abstract reasoning.

The Sensorimotor Period The **sensorimotor period,** which lasts for approximately the first 2 years of life, is the first stage in Piaget's theory of cognitive development. It is marked by an orderly progression of increasingly complex cognitive development ranging from reflexes to symbolic thinking. During this period, cognition is closely tied to external stimulation, including that produced by physical objects and people (see Muller & Carpendale, 2000).

At around 3 months, infants become able to follow moving objects with their eyes. If an infant's doll disappears behind a barrier, the infant will continue to stare at the place where the doll has disappeared but will not search for it.

At around 5 months, infants can grasp and hold objects and gain experience with manipulating and observing them. They also can anticipate the future position of a moving object. If a doll is made to pass behind a screen, infants will turn their eyes toward the far side of the screen, seeming to anticipate the doll's reappearance on the other side.

An important development in the sensorimotor period is the child's grasp of **object permanence:** the realization that objects do not cease to exist when they are out of sight. Until about 6 months of age, children appear to lose all interest in an object that disappears from sight—the saying "out of sight, out of mind" seems particularly appropriate. In addition, cognition is inseparable from action or behavior: Thinking is doing.

During the last half of the first year, infants develop much more complex concepts concerning the nature of physical objects. They grasp objects, turn them over, and investigate their properties. By looking at an object from various angles, they learn that the object can change its visual shape and still be the same object. In addition, if an object is hidden, infants will actively search for it; their object concept now contains the rule of object permanence. For infants at this stage of development, a hidden object still exists. Out of sight is no longer out of mind. In the game of peekaboo, babies laugh because they know that after momentarily disappearing, you will suddenly reappear and say, "Peekaboo!"

By early in the second year, awareness of object permanence is well enough developed that infants will search for an object in the last place they saw it hidden. However, at this stage, infants can keep track of changes only in a hiding place they can see. For example, if an adult picks up an object, puts it under a cloth, drops the object while his or her hand is hidden, closes the hand again, and removes the hand from the cloth, infants will look for the object in the adult's hand. When they do not find the object there, they look puzzled or upset and do not search for the object under the cloth. (See **FIGURE 6•5.**)

The Preoperational Period. Piaget's second period of cognitive development, the **preoperational period,** lasts from approximately age 2 to age 7 and involves the ability to think logically as well as symbolically. This period is characterized by rapid development of language ability and of the ability to represent things symbolically. The child arranges toys in new ways to represent other objects (for example, a row of blocks can represent a train), begins to classify and categorize objects, and starts learning to count and to manipulate numbers. During the preoperational period, schemas are reorganized around words. Words are symbols that have no physical

---

equilibration A process activated when a child's abilities to assimilate and accommodate fail to adjust.

sensorimotor period The first period in Piaget's theory of cognitive development, lasting from birth to 2 years, and marked by an orderly progression of increasingly complex cognitive development from reflexes to object permanence to deferred imitation and rudimentary symbolic thinking.

object permanence In Piaget's theory, the idea that objects do not cease existing when they are out of sight.

preoperational period The second period in Piaget's theory of cognitive development, lasting from 2 years of age to 7, and representing a transitional period between symbolic and logical thought. During this stage, children become increasingly capable of speaking meaningful sentences.

[**FIGURE 6·5**] Object permanence. An infant will not realize that the object has been left under the cloth.

(Adapted from Bower, T. G. R. (1972). *Development in infancy* (2nd ed.). Copyright © 1982 by W. H. Freeman and Company. Used with permission.)

Object is in researcher's hand.

Researcher closes hand...

...puts hand under cloth...

...removes hand, leaving object under the cloth.

Infant looks in researcher's hand.

Obviously upset, infant quits.

resemblance to the concept they represent; Piaget referred to such abstract symbols as signs. Signs are social conventions. They are understood by all members of a culture. A child who is able to use words to think about reality has made an important step in cognitive development.

Egocentrism, a child's belief that others see the world in precisely the way he or she does, is another important characteristic of the preoperational period. A preoperational child sees the world only from his or her own point of view. For example, a preoperational child playing hide-and-seek may run to a corner, turn his back to you, and "hide" by covering his eyes. Although in plain sight of you, he believes that because he cannot see you, you must not be able to see him.

A third important characteristic of the preoperational period—and the reason for its name—is that the child's schemas do not permit invertible operations. For example, if pennies piled into a neat stack on a table are picked up and spread out all over the tabletop, they have been transformed

from a column into a different array. A child in the preoperational period cannot conceptualize that this operation can be reversed. Instead, he or she believes something about the pennies has radically changed and will describe the pennies as being different in some way.

Piaget's work demonstrated this belief quite clearly and, in doing so, showed that a child's representation of the world is strikingly different from that of an adult. For example, most adults realize that the volume of water remains constant when the water is poured from a short, wide container into a taller, narrower container, even though its level is now higher. However, early in the preoperational period, children will fail to recognize this fact; they will say that the taller container contains more water. (See **FIGURE 6·6**.) The ability to realize that an object retains volume, mass, length, or number when it undergoes various transformations is referred to as a grasp of **conservation;** the transformed object conserves its original properties. **FIGURE 6·7** depicts three additional tests of children's understanding of conservation.

The Period of Concrete Operations. Piaget's third stage of cognitive development, the **period of concrete operations,** spans approximately ages 7 to 11 and involves children's developing understanding of the conservation principle and other concepts, such as categorization. The end of this period marks the transition from childhood to adolescence. The period of concrete operations is characterized by the emergence of the

---

egocentrism Self-centeredness; Piaget proposed that preoperational children can see the world only from their own perspectives.

conservation The fact that specific properties of objects (for example, volume, mass, length, or number) remain the same despite apparent changes in the shape or arrangement of those objects.

period of concrete operations The third period in Piaget's theory of cognitive development, lasting from age 7 to 11, during which children come to understand the conservation principle and other concepts, such as categorization.

[**FIGURE 6·6**] Conservation. In the preoperational period, a child does not grasp the fact that the volume of a liquid remains the same even if the liquid is poured into a different-shaped container.

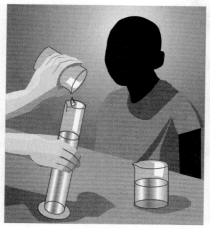

ability to perform logical analysis, by an increased ability to empathize with the feelings and attitudes of others, and by an understanding of more complex cause-and-effect relations.

The child becomes much more skilled at the use of symbolic thought. For example, even before the period of concrete operations, children can arrange a series of objects in order of size and can compare any two objects and say which is larger. However, if they are shown that stick A is larger than stick B and that stick B is larger than stick C, they cannot infer that stick A is larger than stick C. Children become capable of making such inferences during the early part of this period. At this stage, however, although they can reason with respect to concrete objects, such as sticks that they have seen, they cannot do so with hypothetical objects. For example, they cannot solve the following problem: "Judy is taller than Frank, and Frank is taller than

Carl. Who is taller, Judy or Carl?" The ability to solve such problems awaits the next period of cognitive development.

The Period of Formal Operations. During the **period of formal operations,** which begins at about age 11, children first become capable of abstract reasoning. They can now think and reason about hypothetical objects and events. They also begin to understand that under different conditions, their behavior can have different consequences. Formal operational thinking is not "culture free"; that is, it is influenced by cultural variables,

---

period of formal operations The fourth period in Piaget's theory of cognitive development, from age 11 onward, during which individuals first become capable of more formal kinds of abstract thinking and hypothetical reasoning.

Conservation of Mass

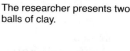

The researcher presents two balls of clay.

The researcher rolls one ball into a "sausage" and asks the child whether they still contain the same amount of clay.

[**FIGURE 6·7**] Various tests of conservation.

(Adapted from *Of Children: An Introduction to Child Development,* 4th ed., by Guy R. Lefrancois, Belmont, CA: Wadsworth Publishing Company.)

Conservation of Length

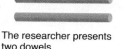

The researcher presents two dowels.

The researcher moves one dowel to the right and asks the child whether they are still the same length.

Conservation of Number

The researcher presents two rows of poker chips.

The researcher moves one row of chips apart and asks the child whether each row still contains the same number.

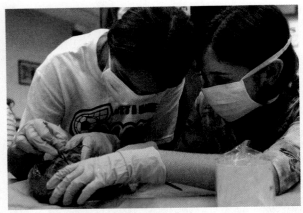

Formal operational thinking is influenced by cultural variables, especially formal schooling.

especially formal schooling (Piaget, 1972; Rogoff & Chavajay, 1995). Without exposure to the principles of scientific thinking, such as those taught in middle school and high school science classes, people do not develop formal operational thinking.

According to Piaget, not all people pass through all four stages and reach the formal operational period, even as physically mature adults. In some cases, adults show formal operational thought only in their areas of expertise. Thus, a mechanic may be able to think abstractly while repairing an engine but not while solving math or physics problems. A physicist may be able to reason abstractly when solving physics problems but not while reading poetry. However, once an individual does reach the formal operational level of thinking, he or she will always (except in the case of damage to the brain from injury or disease) perform intellectually at that level.

Evaluation of Piaget's Contribution Piaget's theory has had an enormously positive impact, stimulating interest and research in developmental psychology and educational psychology (e.g., Brainerd, 2003; Voyat, 1998). Not all of Piaget's conclusions have been universally accepted, however. One criticism leveled at Piaget is that he did not always define his terms operationally. Consequently, it is difficult for others to interpret the significance of his generalizations. Many of his studies lack the proper controls discussed in Chapter 2. Thus, much of his work was not experimental, which means that cause-and-effect relations among variables cannot be identified with certainty.

Research evidence suggests that a child's ability to understand conservation of various physical attributes occurs earlier than Piaget supposed. For example, Gelman (1972) found that when the appropriate task is used, even 3-year-old children are able to demonstrate a grasp of conservation of number. Also, some children are able to anticipate conservation (for example, by predicting what will happen if a liquid is poured into a differently shaped glass) even if they fail the actual test (Caroff, 2002). Piaget also appears to have underestimated the ability of young children to understand another person's point of view. In other words, children are less egocentric at early ages than Piaget thought (Flavell, 1992). Children as young as 2 years old make inferences about other people's knowledge that require

understanding what the others could or could not have seen happen (O'Neill, 1996).

Although Piaget's method of observation led him to underestimate some important abilities, his meticulous observations of child behavior have been extremely important in the field of child development and have had a great influence on educational practice.

Vygotsky's Sociocultural Theory of Cognitive Development

Another important contributor to our understanding of cognitive development was the Russian psychologist Lev Vygotsky (1896–1934). Although Vygotsky's work was conducted during the 1920s and early 1930s, his writings continue to influence present-day conceptualizations of cognitive development during childhood (Kozulin & Falik, 1995).

Vygotsky agreed with Piaget that experience with the physical world is an important factor, but he disagreed that this is the whole story. He argued that the culture in which a child lives also plays a significant role in the child's cognitive development (Vygotsky, 1934/1987). Vygotsky argued that children do not learn to think about the physical world in a vacuum. The cultural context—what they hear others say about the world and how they see others interact with physical aspects of the world—matters (Behrend, Rosengren, & Perlmutter, 1992; Thomas, 1996). Thus, parents, teachers, friends, and many others help children acquire ideas about how the world works. We would expect, then, that the development of children raised in nonstimulating environments devoid of interesting interactions with other people, with books, and, yes, with television would lag behind that of children raised in more stimulating environments.

Vygotsky further believed that children's use of speech also influences their cognitive development. Children up to about age 7 often talk to themselves. When drawing in a coloring book, a child may say, "I'll color her arms and face green and her pants black." Piaget would focus on such talk as reflecting egocentrism. Vygotsky's focus would be different. He would say that the child's talk reflects a cognitive developmental process—the child is developing a mental plan that will serve as a guide to subsequent behavior. According to Vygotsky, language is the basis for cognitive development, including the abilities to remember, to solve problems, to make decisions, and to formulate plans.

After about age 7, children stop vocalizing their thoughts and instead carry on what Vygotsky labeled inner speech. Inner speech represents the internalization of words and the mental manipulation of them as symbols for objects in the environment. As children interact with their parents, teachers, and peers, they learn new words to represent new objects. Given Vygotsky's linking of language with thought, this increased facility with language would imply better cognitive skill as well.

These two themes of Vygotsky's theory—the interconnection between thought and language, and the importance of society and culture—led him to propose a developmental distinction important to educational psychologists. The skills and problem-solving abilities that a child can show on his or her own indicate the level of development that the child has mastered. Vygotsky called this the **actual developmental level.** For Piaget, this level would represent the limit of the child's cognitive skill. However, Vygotsky argued that a patient parent or a skilled mentor could assist a child to achieve a potentially higher level. Perhaps you've had the experience of studying for the Scholastic Aptitude Test and being stumped by a particular kind of problem. That would, loosely, define your actual developmental level. But now suppose a teacher shows you a method for solving the problem that not only makes perfect sense to you but also helps you to solve similar problems. That increased capacity for problem solving resulting from guided help, Vygotsky called the **zone of proximal development.** And indeed, as the "expertise" of the people they interact with increases, so do the children's cognitive skills. For example, Rogoff and her colleagues (e.g., Rogoff, 1990) have shown that children become better problem solvers if they practice solving problems with their parents or with more experienced children than if they practice the problems alone or with children of similar cognitive ability.

Applying Information-Processing Models to Cognitive Development

As our knowledge about human memory has expanded since the time of Piaget and Vygotsky, developmental psychologists have examined how an information-processing perspective on human sensation, perception, and memory might fit within an account of human development. One approach is to consider how processes of memory might change during development, and what effects these changes might have. Another approach has looked not at the processes of cognition per se, but rather at the knowledge base that children have at different ages. Presumably, if we knew how a child understood the world, we would be able to know how he or she would encode, store, and retrieve the semantic information required to adjust to it.

Changes in Cognitive Processes
Can infants remember? Piaget's observations on the concept of object permanence seemed to indicate that infants younger than 6 months do not encode objects; therefore, they cannot remember them. Rovee-Collier and her colleagues, however, challenged this conclusion by using a variation of the mobile task described at the start of this section (e.g., Rovee-Collier, 1999). Infants from 2 to 6 months of age were shown a mobile that they could move by means of a ribbon attached to one of their legs. After varying amounts of time, they would be shown the mobile again, but with the ribbon disconnected. If the infant kicked at a rate higher than normal, Rovee-Collier would conclude that the infant recognized the mobile on the second presentation. Infants 6 to 18 months of age were tested in a similar way by using a mechanical switch to operate a toy train.

Rovee-Collier's results suggest not only that memory is present in infants, but also that the retention span increases

[**FIGURE 6·8**] Retention of memory of the sight of an infant mobile or a toy train by infants 2 to 18 months of age. Blue circles depict data from infants tested with a mobile that they could move by leg motions. Orange circles depict data from infants trained with the toy train. Six-month-old infants were tested with both the mobile and the train.

(From Rovee-Collier, C. (1999). The development of infant memory. *Current Directions in Psychological Science, 8,* 80–85. Copyright © 1978 American Psychological Society.)

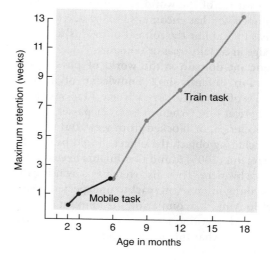

systematically over the 2- to 18-month period of life (Rovee-Collier, 1999). FIGURE 6·8 shows data from both the mobile and train test situations; the maximal delay over which the infants show retention is plotted against their age. By using a similar procedure, Rovee-Collier and her colleagues have shown that retrieval cues increase retrieval in infants—and that infants apparently demonstrate an implicit/explicit differentiation similar to that discussed in Chapter 7.

Case (1998) claimed that cognitive development is a matter of a child's becoming more efficient in using memory and other cognitive processes. The heart of Case's model is a hypothetical information-processing construct similar to short-term or working memory, whose chief function is the processing of information from the external world. According to Case, as the brain matures, so does its capacity to process greater amounts of information by using memory. The result is the acquisition of central conceptual structures—networks of schemas that allow children to understand the relations among the objects and events represented by the schemas. As increasingly complex central conceptual structures are formed, children advance to higher levels of cognitive development, as represented in Piaget's stages.

---

actual developmental level In Vygotsky's theory, the stage of cognitive development reached by a child, as demonstrated by the child's ability to solve problems on his or her own.

zone of proximal development In Vygotsky's theory, the increased potential for problem-solving and conceptual abilities that exists for a child if expert mentoring and guidance are available.

Changes in Cognitive Content The increased complexity of children's knowledge as they develop has figured prominently in development theories. Contemporary research based on information-processing models of memory has clarified the importance of the specific knowledge an individual can use to encode information, store it, or retrieve it. We have seen, for example, that elaborative rehearsal is more effective in maintaining information than is simple repetition. As Case suggests, increased cognitive ability is facilitated by a richer knowledge of the world surrounding the child. This simple proposition has encouraged many developmental psychologists to examine the content of infants' and children's knowledge in certain areas or domains.

One important domain is the world of physics and mechanical action. Infants show knowledge of at least some of the laws of physics at an early age. One very simple law is an optical one: When one object passes behind another, it is occluded, or blocked from view, but if a gap exists in the occluding object, the object should be visible. Luo and Baillargeon (2005) found that infants develop this knowledge piece by piece. They discovered this by using the fact that even young infants will react to unexpected events by prolonged looking. By comparing the amount of time infants spend looking at one scene as opposed to another, it's possible to infer what infants consider to be "normal" and what is "unexpected."

To understand Luo and Baillargeon's experiment, think of an old-fashioned theater stage with a main curtain across the front and side curtains on the left and right. If someone were to wave at you, walk behind the left side curtain, and later emerge at the edge of the right side curtain, you would find nothing unusual about that sequence. But if the central curtain were raised and you saw someone enter one side and exit the other without seeing that person cross the open stage, you'd be pretty surprised, right? It would appear that this person had teleported from behind the left curtain to the right curtain. When Luo and Baillargeon (2005) used a bit of stage magic to accomplish this apparent act of teleportation, infants of this age spent a lot of time looking at the scene.

This knowledge about occlusion is only partially present in infants. Luo and Baillargeon performed another test, similar to what the stage would be like if the central curtain were only half raised. Now, you would expect to see legs as someone walked across the stage. Infants 2 and a half months of age, however, are not surprised if they don't see this partial occlusion (although infants of 3 months are). Rather, the younger infants are surprised if they do see the partial occlusion. They seem to treat a partial gap as if it were no gap at all. Apparently, knowledge about optical occlusion develops incrementally, as infants acquire an understanding about the solidity and continuity of occluding objects.

Theory of Mind Another important domain, especially as the infant or child encounters social settings, is knowledge about others' beliefs or state of mind. For example, suppose you notice that your professor keeps a whiteboard marker in a drawer of the classroom podium. One day, you come to the classroom early, before your professor, and see someone from the class before yours reach into the drawer, pick up the marker, and leave with it. You would still expect your professor to look for the marker in the drawer. You recognize that your knowledge about the marker can be different from your professor's. You have developed expectations about how experiences relate to beliefs, something that developmental psychologists describe as **theory of mind.**

Four-year-olds seem capable of correctly inferring how events can shape the state of mind or beliefs of another. But 3-year-olds do not: They use their own beliefs to predict the beliefs and actions of others. Developmental psychologists have observed this difference in a procedure sometimes called the "Sally-Anne" test (e.g., Baron-Cohen, Leslie, & Frith, 1985). A child is shown two dolls—Sally and Anne. The Sally doll is shown placing a marble in a basket within a doll house and then shown leaving the house. While she is away, the Anne doll takes the marble and places it in a box. The Sally doll returns to the house, and the child is asked: "Where will Sally look for her marble?" A 3-year-old girl watching this little drama would think that, because she knows where the marble is, another, such as Sally, would know that too. She has, in other words, not differentiated her own beliefs from another's. By the following year, however, she will have developed a type of "naive psychology" by which she will recognize that other people's behaviors follow patterns based on their own beliefs (Kail, 2001; Slaughter & Repacholi, 2003).

Wellman, Cross, and Watson (2001) examined the results of 178 separate studies on theory of mind. Their analysis showed that the results of the studies were consistent and robust. Children improved on false-belief tasks from age 3 to 5. The understanding of belief and false belief was also found to be culture free (at least, not specific to the cultures included in the analysis). Whether European, North American, East Asian, Australian, or African, children acquired understanding of others' beliefs at around the same time. Some forms of tasks do improve performance when compared with others, however. Two reasons could explain this: either these forms are a more sensitive measure of theory of mind, or they are easy for unrelated reasons; unfortunately, the analysis doesn't suggest which is correct. When studies across the developmental trajectory are analyzed, a significant and discernible improvement occurs with age, for easy and difficult tasks.

The term "naive psychology" is not meant to imply anything negative. When a child develops a theory of mind, he or she acquires a sophisticated tool for predicting the actions of others. Think of your own ability to understand a friend's nuanced reaction to a forgotten birthday greeting, and you'll recognize the significance of this developmental change. It's been suggested that the lack of a theory of mind may underlie some severe developmental disorders, such as autism (Baron-Cohen, Leslie, & Frith, 1985).

---

theory of mind Expectations concerning how experience affects mental states, especially those of another.

focus On

Cognitive Development and Television Viewing

Cognitive development is influenced by many factors. These factors vary enormously, but almost all children in industrialized societies, even those in the poorest households, are exposed for several hours a day to a near-universal factor—television. Although certainly other modern media resemble television's visual experience, such as video games and the Internet, it has been argued that television is especially important to the development of children because it is present in almost every home, occupies a large part of a child's time, and is accessible to children across a wide span of their lives (Huston & Wright, 1998). It is important to understand the impact of this technological presence on a child's cognitive development.

How much of a child's time is dominated by the medium? Estimates vary according to the method used. A study of Australian 5-year-old children that asked parents to fill out diaries of what their children did reported a median of 114 minutes per day spent watching television—more than any other activity aside from sleeping (Tey et al., 2007). Boys tend to view more television than do girls; and, across all ages, children with low IQs from low-income families watch more television than do other children (Huston, Watkins, & Kunkel, 1989; Huston et al., 1990). According to Anderson and Collins (1988), while watching television, children often are engaged in other activities: They eat, play with toys, draw or color pictures, read, play games, sleep, talk with others, or do their homework. They often enter and leave the room while the television is on.

Two issues concern us here—the content of television programs and the general effects of the medium itself. Let us consider content first. One of the best examples of good television is demonstrated by Sesame Street, a program that was devised to teach school-readiness skills such as counting, letter recognition, and vocabulary. Research indicates that the program has succeeded in its goals; children who watch Sesame Street have better vocabularies, have better attitudes toward school, adapt better to the classroom, and have more positive attitudes toward children of other races (Fisch & Truglio, 2001). Rice et al. (1990), studied a large sample of 3- to 5-year-old children from a wide range of socioeconomic backgrounds and found that children of all backgrounds profited from watching Sesame Street—the advantages were not restricted to middle-class children. Conversely, many television programs are full of violence, and watching them may well promote aggressiveness and impatience with nonviolent resolution of disagreements in the children who watch such shows (Huesmann, et al., 2003; Murray, 2008).

The second issue that people have raised about children and television regards the nature of the medium itself. Many people who have written about the potential effects

Does television viewing promote or retard cognitive development in children?

of television as a medium on children's cognitive development have concluded that the medium is generally harmful. Winn (2002) metaphorically described television and related computer technologies as the "plug-in drug" and others have argued that it dominates a child's attention to the exclusion of other developmental opportunities. Studies that actually observe children who are watching television find no such effects. Children are rarely "glued" to the television set. They look away from it between 100 and 200 times each hour (Anderson & Field, 1983). They rarely look at the screen for much more than 1 minute at a stretch. Their viewing behavior is related to program content: They tend to pay attention when they hear other children's voices, interesting sound effects, or peculiar voices, and when they see movement on the screen. They tend not to pay attention when they hear men's voices or see no signs of activity on the screen (Anderson & Lorch, 1983). If they hear certain kinds of sounds, children turn their attention away from the alternative activity and look at the screen to see whether something interesting is happening. The child is an active viewer, using the sights and sounds of the program to choose when to pay attention (Bickham, Wright, & Huston, 2001).

However, as a visual medium, television could be considered as a competitor to other behaviors that require visual attention, such as reading. Indeed, one criticism of television—that it retards children's reading achievement—has received some support. Measurements of children's reading skills before and after television became available suggested that television viewing decreased the reading skills of young children (Corteen & Williams, 1986). However, the effects were slight and were not seen in older children. Perhaps, then, television viewing does interfere with reading achievement in young children. As our parents told us when we were young, trying to read with the television on in the background is not conducive to comprehension and learning (Armstrong & Chung, 2000).

However, the possibility exists that television programs could do more to stimulate children's cognitive development. We have focused on the potential harm that may be done by watching television, not on the potential good that could be achieved through this medium. Educational programs and other shows that take into account children's developmental needs would seem to be especially conducive to the stimulation of children's imagination, creativity, language skills, and prosocial behavior. This, of course, is a hypothesis, and like the hypothesis of negative effects, would need to be empirically tested.

QUESTIONS TO CONSIDER

1. In a Question to Consider earlier in this chapter, we asked you to design a home environment that would facilitate your child's motor and perceptual development. How might you also construct that environment to facilitate your child's cognitive development? What types of toys would you give your child, and what kinds of personal interactions would you want to have with him or her?

2. Suppose that you want to develop a test for determining which of Piaget's periods of cognitive development a child is in. What kinds of activities would you include in such a test, and how would the child's behavior with respect to those activities indicate the child's stage of development?

Social Development in Infancy and Childhood

The first adults with whom infants interact are usually their parents. As many studies have shown, a close relationship called attachment is extremely important for infants' social development. **Attachment** is a social and emotional bond between infant and caregiver. It involves both the warm feelings that the parent and child have for each other and the comfort and support they provide for each other, which become especially important during times of fear or stress. This interaction must work both ways, with each participant fulfilling certain needs of the other. According to theorist John Bowlby (1907–1990), the innate capacity for the development of attachment is a part of the native endowment of many organisms (Bowlby, 1969, 1988). Bowlby and Mary Ainsworth have developed an approach that has succeeded in identifying many of the variables that influence attachment in humans (Ainsworth & Bowlby, 1991). We are going to look at what Bowlby, Ainsworth, and other researchers have learned about human attachment.

Be mindful that cultural variables strongly influence the development of attachment. Interactions between in-

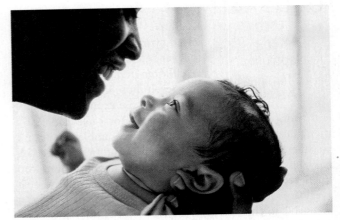

Attachment is the cornerstone of an infant's social development, and it has important implications for the parent's social behavior as well.

fant and parent produce different sorts of attachment behaviors that vary from culture to culture. For example, in an extensive comparison of cross-cultural attachment patterns, Harwood (Harwood, Miller, & Irizarry, 1995; Miller & Harwood, 2002) found that white American mothers want their children to be self-sustaining individuals and so emphasize independence, self-reliance, and self-confidence in their interactions with their children. In contrast, Puerto Rican mothers want their children to be polite and law-abiding, and thus stress the importance of respect, courtesy, interdependence, and tact in interacting with their children.

Behaviors of the Infant That Foster Attachment

What factors cause attachment to occur? Evidence suggests that human infants are innately able to produce special behaviors that shape and even control the behavior of their caregivers. As Bowlby (1969) noted, the most important of these behaviors are sucking, cuddling, looking, smiling, and crying.

Sucking A baby must be able to suck to obtain milk, but not all sucking is related to nourishment. Piaget (1952) noted that infants often suck on objects even when they are not hungry. Nonnutritive sucking appears to be an innate behavioral tendency in infants that serves to inhibit a baby's distress. In modern societies, most mothers cover their breasts between feedings or feed with a bottle, so a baby's nonnutritive sucking must involve inanimate objects or the baby's own thumb.

Cuddling Infants of all species of primates have special reflexes that encourage front-to-front contact with their mothers. For example, a baby monkey clings to its mother shortly after birth. This clinging leaves the mother free to use her hands

---

attachment A social and emotional bond between infant and caregiver that spans both time and space.

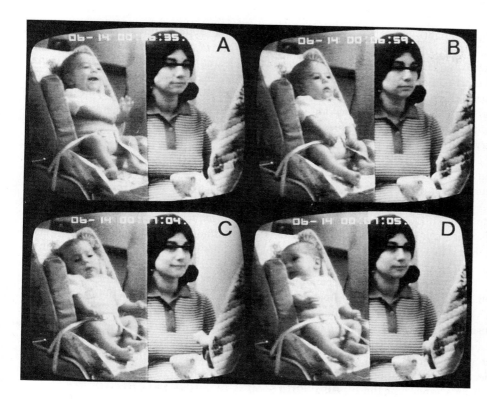

[**FIGURE 6•9**] Reaction of an infant to its mother's expressionless face. Although each panel shows mother and infant side by side, they actually faced each other. The infant greets the mother with a smile and, getting no response, eventually turns away from her.

(From Tronick, E., Als, H., Adamson, L., Wise, S., & Brazelton, T. B. The infant's response to entrapment between contradictory messages in face-to-face interaction. *Journal of the American Academy of Child Psychiatry*, 1978, 17, 1–13. Copyright © 1978 American Academy of Child Psychiatry.)

and feet. Human infants are carried by their parents and do not hold on by themselves. However, infants do adjust their posture to mold themselves to the contours of the parent's body. This cuddling response plays an important role in reinforcing the behavior of the caregiver.

Psychologist Harry Harlow (1905–1981) conducted a series of experiments on infant monkeys and showed that clinging to a soft, cuddly form appears to be an innate response (Harlow, 1974). Harlow and his colleagues isolated baby monkeys from their mothers immediately after birth and raised them alone in cages containing two mechanical surrogate mothers. One surrogate mother was made of bare wire mesh but contained a bottle that provided milk. The other surrogate was padded and covered with terry cloth but provided no nourishment.

The babies preferred to cling to the cuddly surrogate and went to the wire model only to eat. If they were frightened, they would rush to the cloth-covered model for comfort. These results suggest that close physical contact with a cuddly object is a biological need for a baby monkey, just as food and drink are. A baby monkey clings to and cuddles with its mother because the contact is innately reinforcing, not simply because she provides food.

Looking In human infants, looking serves as a signal to parents: Even very young infants seek eye-to-eye contact with their parents. If a parent does not respond when eye contact is made, the baby usually shows signs of distress. Tronick and colleagues (1978) observed face-to-face interactions between mothers and their infants. When the mothers approached their babies, they typically smiled and began talking in a gentle, high-pitched voice. In return, infants smiled and stretched their arms and legs. The mothers poked and gently jiggled their babies, making faces at them. The babies responded with facial expressions, wiggles, and noises of their own.

To determine whether the interaction was really two-sided, the researchers had each mother approach her baby while keeping her face expressionless or masklike. At first, the infant made the usual greetings, but when the mother did not respond, the infant turned away. (See **FIGURE 6•9**.) From time to time, the infant would look at her again, giving a brief smile, but again would turn away when the mother continued to stare without changing her expression. These interactions were recorded on videotape and were scored by raters who did not know the purpose of the experiment, so the results were not biased by the researchers' expectations.

Smiling and Imitation By the time an infant is 5 weeks old, visual stimuli begin to dominate as elicitors for smiling. A face (especially a moving one) is a more reliable elicitor of a baby's smile than a voice is; even a moving mask will cause an infant to smile. At approximately 3 months of age, specific faces—those of people to whom the infant has become attached—will elicit smiles. Furthermore, newborns and infants will often repeat the facial movements of another, suggesting the presence of an early mechanism for imitation (Lepage & Théoret, 2007). The significance of these observations should be obvious. An infant's smile is very rewarding. Almost every parent reports that parenting becomes a real joy when the baby starts to smile as the parent approaches—the infant is now a "person."

Crying For almost any adult, the sound of an infant's crying is intensely distressing or irritating. For a baby, the event that most effectively terminates crying is being picked up and cuddled, although unless the baby is fed and made more comfortable, he or she will soon begin crying again. Because picking up the baby stops the crying, the parent learns through negative reinforcement to pick up the infant when he or she cries. Thus, crying serves as a useful means for a cold, hungry, colicky, or wet child to obtain assistance.

Individual differences in how caregivers perceive distress in an infant's crying is an important quality that determines adult reactions and is influenced by context and expectations. Wood and Gustafson (2001), for example, found that adults responded more quickly to infant cries that they personally interpreted as communicating distress; they somewhat inhibited their response to the same cries if they believed the infant needed sleep.

Although an infant's behavioral repertoire is limited, it is apparent that a complex process is at work. At a very early age, perhaps through innate mechanisms, infants perform behaviors that their adult caregivers find reinforcing. The baby, in other words, is partially teaching the parent. From the baby's perspective, what is the object of this? Evolutionary psychologists would respond that the baby is teaching the parent to behave in ways that enhance the baby's chances to survive and eventually reproduce.

The Nature and Quality of Attachment

For an infant, the world can be a frightening place. The presence of a primary caregiver provides a baby with considerable reassurance when he or she first becomes able to explore the environment. Although the unfamiliar environment produces fear, the caregiver provides a secure base that the infant can leave from time to time to see what the world is like. Let's look at two categories of behavior that develop as infants explore their world: first, stranger anxiety and separation anxiety; and second, reactions to strange situations.

---

stranger anxiety The wariness and fearful responses, such as crying and clinging to their caregivers, that infants exhibit in the presence of strangers.

separation anxiety A set of fearful responses, such as crying, arousal, and clinging to the caregiver, that an infant exhibits when its caregiver attempts to leave the infant.

Strange Situation A test of attachment in which an infant is exposed to different stimuli that may cause distress.

secure attachment A kind of attachment in which infants use their mothers as a base for exploring a new environment. In the Strange Situation test, securely attached infants will venture out from their mothers to explore, but will return periodically.

resistant attachment A kind of attachment in which infants show mixed reactions to their mothers. In the Strange Situation test, when mothers return after being absent, such infants may approach their mothers but at the same time may continue to cry or even push their mothers away.

avoidant attachment As observed in the Strange Situation test, a kind of attachment in which infants avoid or ignore their mothers and often do not cuddle when held.

Stranger Anxiety and Separation Anxiety Attachment partially reveals itself in two specific forms of infant behavior: stranger anxiety and separation anxiety. **Stranger anxiety,** which usually appears in infants between the ages of 6 and 12 months, consists of wariness and sometimes fearful responses, such as crying and clinging to their caregivers, that infants exhibit in the presence of strangers. **Separation anxiety** is a set of fearful responses, such as crying, arousal, and clinging to the caregiver, that an infant exhibits when the caregiver attempts to leave the infant. Separation anxiety first appears in infants when they are about 6 months old and generally peaks at about 15 months—a finding consistent across many cultures (Kagan, Kearsley, & Zelazo, 1978). Like stranger anxiety, separation anxiety can occur under different conditions with different degrees of intensity. For example, if an infant is used to being left in a certain environment, say a day-care center, he or she may show little or no separation anxiety (Maccoby, 1980). The same holds true for situations in which the infant is left with a sibling or other familiar person (Bowlby, 1969). However, if the same infant is left in an unfamiliar setting with unfamiliar people, he or she is likely to show separation anxiety (Bowlby, 1982). Familiarity, then, at least for infants, breeds attachment.

Ainsworth's Strange Situation Ainsworth and her colleagues (Ainsworth, et al., 1978) developed a test of attachment based on unfamiliar situations called the **Strange Situation.** The Strange Situation consists of a series of eight episodes, during which a baby is exposed to various events that might cause some distress related to attachment and security. In different episodes of increasing stress, the researcher introduces the infant and its parent to an unfamiliar playroom and then leaves, the parent leaves and later is reunited with the infant, or a stranger enters the playroom with or without the parent present. The Strange Situation is based on the idea that if the attachment process has been successful, an infant should use his or her mother as a secure base from which to explore an unfamiliar environment. The episodes permit the observation of separation anxiety, stranger anxiety, and the baby's reactions to comforting by both the parent and the stranger.

The use of the Strange Situation led Ainsworth and her colleagues to identify three patterns of attachment; a fourth was identified later by Main and Solomon (1990).

- **Secure attachment** is the ideal pattern: The infants show a distinct preference for their caregiver over the stranger. Infants may cry when their caregiver leaves, but they stop crying and seek contact when she returns. The majority of babies form a secure attachment. Babies may also form three types of insecure attachments.

- Babies with **resistant attachment** show tension in their relations with their caregiver. Infants stay close to their caregiver before the caregiver leaves but show both approach and avoidance behaviors when the caregiver returns. Infants continue to cry for a while after their caregivers return and may even push them away.

- Infants with **avoidant attachment** generally do not cry when they are left alone, and they tend to react to strangers much as they react to their caregivers. When their caregiver returns, these infants are likely to avoid or ignore her. They tend not to cling and cuddle when they are picked up.

- Babies with **disoriented attachment** have the least quality of attachment and appear to be the most troubled. They react to their caregiver in confused and contradictory ways. They may stop crying when held, but they may show no emotion on their faces, turn their heads away from their caregiver, or become rigid. A common way of describing the emotional tone of such infants is that they appear dazed.

Although infants' personalities certainly affect the nature of their interactions with their caregivers and hence the nature of their attachment, mothers' behavior appears to be the most important factor in establishing a secure or insecure attachment (Ainsworth, et al., 1978; Pederson & Moran, 1996; Pederson, et al., 1998). Mothers of securely attached infants tend to be those who respond promptly to their crying and who are adept at handling them and responding to their needs. The babies apparently learn that their mothers can be trusted to react sensitively and appropriately. Mothers who do not modulate their responses according to their infants' own behavior—who appear insensitive to their infants' changing needs—are most likely to foster avoidant attachment. Mothers who are impatient with their infants and who seem more interested in their own activities than in interacting with their offspring tend to foster resistant attachment. Some evidence indicates that mothers who interfere with their infants' behaviors, but without sensitivity to their infants' needs, are likely to foster disoriented attachment (Carlson, 1998). Of course, mothers are not the only people who can form close attachments with infants; so do fathers (see Parke, 2000) and other adults who interact with them.

In our culture, secure attachment would seem to be more adaptive in terms of getting along with both peers and adults than would insecure attachment. It has become clear that attachment plays an influential role in social relationships, including those that we form in adolescence and adulthood, such as romantic love (Feeney & Noller, 1991). Among women, insecure attachment in infancy seems to be correlated with clinical depression and difficulties in coping with stress in adult life (Barnas, Pollina, & Cummings, 1991).

Effects of Child Day Care
This recognition of the importance of attachment inevitably leads to the question of whether child day care has deleterious effects on a child's development. In recent decades, many families have entrusted their infants to day care because both parents work. In 2004, for example, 53% of mothers of children younger than 1 year were employed outside the home (United States Department of Labor, 2005). Thus, because so many infants spend many of their waking hours away from their families, the question of the effects of day care is not simply academic.

Without question, the quality of care provided in a day-care setting is critical (Zaslow, 1991). High-quality day care

Notwithstanding the importance of attachment, high quality day care can benefit social development.

either produces no impairment of attachment or actually benefits social development (Field, 1994; Broberg, et al., 1997; National Institute of Child Health and Human Development, 1997), although it is difficult to generalize this conclusion across the full range of day-care programs available, because this latter issue is measured by correlational methods (NICHD Early Child Care Research Network, 2003). Nevertheless, high-quality day care is expensive, and not enough subsidized spaces are available for all of the families that need them. Worldwide, the day care available to low-income families is generally of lower quality than that available to middle- or upper-income families. Regrettably, the infants who receive the poorest day care tend to be members of unstable households, often headed by single mothers. Thus, they are at risk of receiving a double dose of less-than-optimal care.

Approaches to Child Rearing

Our consideration of social development has emphasized the way the child and the parents affect each other. A family, in other words, is a type of system in which the members have interacting roles. The parents provide the support for the child's attachment. However, the child also controls much of the parent's behavior through reactions that are intrinsically reinforcing. It is a developmental partnership.

As Vygotsky recognized, the child–parent partnership works best when the parent provides scaffolding for the child's development. **Scaffolding** is the matching of the mentor's efforts to the child's developmental level. For example, when teaching a child the motor skills of riding a bicycle, a mother might run alongside the child, taking her hands off the bicycle during straight segments, but helping her child do the steering. As she becomes more confident in her child's

---

disoriented attachment As observed in the Strange Situation test, a kind of attachment in which infants behave in confused and contradictory ways toward their mothers.

scaffolding The matching of a mentor's efforts to a child's developmental level.

ability to steer, she can reduce this help. When well practiced, scaffolding is generally the most effective form of parent–child instruction or mentoring (Meadows, 1996).

Social adjustment is a type of skill, and it is interesting to consider what types of child-rearing practices best support its development. The notion of scaffolding would imply that certain approaches to parenting will work best in the child–parent partnership. What might those approaches be?

Parents seem to adopt one of four approaches when raising their children: authoritarian, permissive, authoritative, or indifferent (Baumrind, 1983, 1991). Authoritarian parents establish firm rules and expect them to be obeyed without question. Disobedience is met with punishment. Permissive parents adopt the opposite strategy: They impose few rules and do little to influence their children's behavior. Authoritative parents also establish rules and enforce them, but not merely through punishment. Instead, they seek to explain the relation between the rules and punishment. Authoritative parents also allow exceptions to the rules. They set rules, not as absolute or inflexible laws, but rather as general behavioral guidelines. Indifferent parents exhibit a lack of interest in their children's behavior, to the point of possible neglect.

Not surprisingly, authoritarian parents tend to have children who are more unhappy and distrustful than are children of permissive or authoritative parents. You might imagine that children of permissive parents would be the most likely to be self-reliant and curious. Not so. They appear to be the least so, probably because they never received parental encouragement and guidance for developing these sorts of behaviors. Rather, they are left on their own without the benefit of learning directly from an adult's experience and without the guidance needed to learn self-control. Authoritative parents bring up their children in an environment in which individuality and personal responsibility are encouraged, and so they tend to rear children who are self-controlled, independent, and socially competent. Psychologically, then, one important element in raising happy and independent children is an open line of communication between parent and child. As you might expect, children of indifferent parents tend to be the least competent (Baumrind, 1991).

Cultural differences also seem to play a role in child rearing, as Vygotsky suggested. Children living in the United States but from Mexican families with mothers who had received limited schooling, U.S. children whose mothers' had extensive schooling, and children of Mexican families with mothers who had extensive schooling were studied to see the degree of social cooperation that would be seen when three children from each group were given a task to complete together (Mejia-Arauz et al., 2007). The task was to follow instructions for origami.

Children from Mexican families with mothers who had received limited schooling not strongly influenced by U.S. or European influences were more likely to work on the task together than were the other groups. The U.S. children were more likely to work individually or in pairs; they were also more likely to chat more when interacting than to interact nonverbally (which was the common form of interaction in the Mexican children). The results seem to confirm studies showing that certain cultures (even children from those cultures)—such as those in Mexico—are more likely to show evidence of collaboration on a shared task.

Interactions with Peers

Although the attachment between an infant and his or her primary caregiver is the most important social interaction in early life, a child's social development also involves other people. A normal infant develops attachments with other adults, and with older siblings, if there are any. But interaction with peers—children of a similar age—is especially significant to social development. This is not attachment in the sense that we have discussed so far, because attachment depends on a caregiving relationship. At this stage, infants and children don't provide care for each other. Nevertheless, the relationships are important.

Harlow and his colleagues (e.g., Harlow, 1974) showed that social contact with peers is essential to an infant monkey's social development. An infant monkey that is raised with only a cuddly surrogate mother can still develop into a reasonably normal adult if it has peers to play with. However, an isolated monkey that does not interact with other juveniles before puberty shows severe deficits. When a previously isolated adolescent monkey is introduced to a colony of normally reared age mates, it will retreat with terror and huddle in a corner in a desperate attempt to hide.

QUESTIONS TO CONSIDER

1. We know that attachment occurs in humans and other primates. Do you think it occurs in other species, especially other mammalian species, as well? What kind of evidence would you need to collect to say that it does? Could you develop a test like Harlow's for researching attachment in other species? Develop your answer with a specific species in mind; for example, cats or dogs.
2. If there were a predisposition to certain attachment styles, when do you think it would first appear?

Development of Gender Roles

Physical development as a male or a female is only one aspect of sexual development (Bostwick & Martin, 2007). The social side of sexual development is also important. **Gender identity** is a person's private sense of being male or female and consists primarily of the person's acceptance of membership in a particular group of people: males or females. **Gender roles** are cultural expectations about the ways in which men and

---

gender identity A person's private sense of being male or female.

gender role Cultural expectations about the ways in which a male or a female should think and behave.

Many people acquire their gender identities and gender roles as a result of the gender stereotypes they learn as children.

women should think and behave. Closely related to them are **gender stereotypes**—beliefs about differences between the behaviors, abilities, and personality traits of males and females. Society's gender stereotypes have an important influence on the behavior of its members. Many people unconsciously develop their gender identity and gender roles based on gender stereotypes they learned as children. This section considers the part gender stereotypes play in influencing the nature and development of gender roles.

Berk (2005) noted that by age 3, many children perceive themselves as being a boy or a girl. At that same age, boys and girls (though girls more than boys) have a fairly good grasp

of gender roles and stereotypes (e.g., O'Brien et al., 2000). Later, in the process of learning what it means to be boys or girls, children associate some attitudes, abilities, and behaviors with one gender or the other (e.g., Jacklin & Maccoby, 1983). For example, Meelissen and Drent (2008) found that, in a sample of Dutch elementary school children, most boys felt that boys, in general, know more about computers than girls. About a third of the girls felt the same.

Where do children learn gender stereotypes? Although a child's peer group and teachers are important, parents play an especially important role in the development of gender stereotypes (Deaux, 1999). Parents tend to encourage and reward their sons for playing with "masculine" toys such as cars and trucks and objects such as baseballs and footballs (Fagot and Hagan, 1991) and encourage baby boys to generate gross motor activity, whereas they are more soothing and calming with baby girls (Smith and Lloyd, 1978). Parents also tend to encourage and reward their daughters for engaging in "feminine" activities that promote dependence, warmth and sensitivity, such as playing house or hosting a make-believe tea party (Dunn, Bretherton, & Munn, 1987; Lytton and Romney, 1991). Parents who do not encourage or reward these kinds of stereotypical activity tend to have children whose attitudes and behavior reflect fewer sex stereotypes (Weisner & Wilson-Mitchell, 1990).

In supposedly "masculine" academic subjects, girls are perceived as performing less well than boys. Many reasons have been suggested for the discrepancy, but one of the most frequently cited is socialization: that is, parents and teachers are more likely to engage boys in science and scientific explanations than they are girls.

In an ingenious experiment to test this hypothesis, Crowley et al. (2001) sought the permission of parents visiting a Californian children's museum to film and record their interactions with their children as they made their way around the exhibitions. Data were collected from 298 interactions between mothers and fathers and their daughters and sons on 26 days over a 30-month period. Conversations were rated according to whether they involved explanations, descriptions of, or directions for exhibitions.

The researchers found that parents were more likely to explain exhibits to their sons than to their daughters. If the behavior of parents helps shape the behavior of their children, the researchers suggest that this disparity could have a significant effect on the child's interest in and knowledge of science.

The Nature of Gender Differences

The origin and nature of gender differences has long been and is likely to continue to be a controversial topic in psychology (Shibley Hyde & Plant, 1995; Eagly & Wood, 1999; Wood & Eagly, 2002). Consider the following case of D.R., which illustrates how complex the issue is.

---

gender stereotypes Beliefs about differences in the behaviors, abilities, and personality traits of males and females.

[CASE STUDY] D.R. was born as the elder of two identical twin boys. When he was 8 months of age, he underwent what was to have been routine circumcision to correct a urinary problem. Tragically, the surgery went horribly wrong, and D.R.'s penis was physically destroyed. D.R. would not be able to live as a normal boy.

In their efforts to come to grips with this accident, D.R.'s parents sought medical and psychological advice on how best to raise their son. They accepted the rather controversial advice that D.R.'s sex should be reassigned by removing his testes and raising him as a girl. This program of surgical and psychological therapy had been performed on intersex individuals (those both with sexual characteristics that are not phenotypically male or female), but its use on a unambiguous boy was experimental.

For 14 years, D.R.'s parents tried to raise him as a girl. The physicians and therapists who had developed this protocol could compare D.R.'s development with that of his twin brother. Many of their reports during this time were interpreted to show that D.R.'s upbringing had successfully acculturated him to be, psychologically, a girl.

The reality, apparently, was quite different. As a child, D.R. was not told of what had been done to him, but he remembers never feeling comfortable as a girl. He was teased in school and reacted strongly with physical aggression. Although he would wear feminine clothing to please his mother, he never felt comfortable in it. When asked by his therapists to envision his future, he would imagine himself as an adult male. He prided himself on being able to dominate his twin brother and would adopt the role of the protector. Throughout his childhood, he preferred to urinate standing up.

D.R.'s childhood and early adolescence were marked by his steadfast resistance to acting the gender role of a girl. Faced with his obvious unhappiness with his life, his parents told him the truth when he was 14. The news actually came as a relief to D.R., because he had been dreading the demands that puberty would bring; he decided immediately that he wanted to revert to the sex of his birth. In the subsequent years, he became popular, as a young man, with peers of both sexes. Within 10 years, D.R. would marry and become a stepfather with three children.

Part of the controversy over gender differences stems from the way differences between males and females are measured and the apparent magnitude of those differences, and part of it stems from the sociopolitical implications of the differences (for example, sexism). Berk (2005) reviewed the research on gender differences and concluded that the most reliable differences are the following: On average, girls show earlier verbal development, more effective expression and interpretation of emotional cues, and a higher tendency to comply with adults and peers. Boys show stronger spatial abilities, more aggression, and greater tendency toward risk taking. Boys also are more likely to show developmental problems such as language disorders, behavior problems, or physical impairments.

These differences are unlikely to be wholly biologically determined. Socialization undoubtedly has a strong influence.

Gender differences for many psychological characteristics are small. For example, after reviewing scores obtained from the Wechsler Intelligence Scales and the California Achievement Tests between 1949 and 1985, Feingold (1993). concluded that cognitive gender differences were small or nonexistent in preadolescent children and small in adolescents. Deaux (1985) reported that, on average, only 5% of the variability in individual differences among children can be attributed to gender; the other 95% is due to individual genetic and environmental factors. Therefore, gender, by itself, is not a very good predictor of a person's talents, personality, or behavior.

Children readily learn gender stereotypes and adopt the roles that society deems appropriate for their gender. Two causes—biology and culture—may be responsible.

Biological Causes A likely site of biologically determined gender differences is the brain. Studies using laboratory animals have shown that the exposure of a developing brain to male sex hormones has long-term effects. The hormones alter the development of the brain and produce changes in the animals' behavior, even in adulthood (Carlson, 2005; Bostwick & Martin, 2007). In addition, the human brain shows some structural gender differences. These, too, are probably caused by exposure to different patterns of hormones during development (Kolb & Stewart, 1995), although the precise effects of these differences on the behavior of males and females are not well understood at present. As well, investigations using ƒMRI techniques show

Women minus men

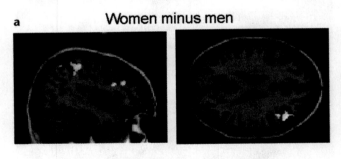

Men minus women

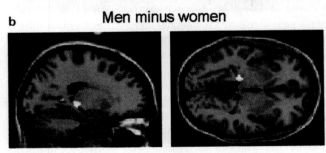

Men and women show different patterns of brain activity during navigation of a virtual maze. Women show greater activity than men in right hemispheric structures (bright areas in top photos) and men show greater activity than women in the left hippocampus (bright areas in bottom photos).

(Grön, G., Wunderlich, A. P., Spitzer, M., Tomczak, R., & Riepe, M. W. (2000). Brain activation during human navigation: Gender different neural networks as substrate of performance. *Nature Neuroscience, 3,* 404–408.)

neural activation differences between men and women during navigation in a virtual maze; men show greater activation of the left hippocampus, and women show greater involvement of right hemispheric structures (Grön et al., 2000).

Gender differences in two types of cognitive ability—verbal ability and spatial ability—may be at least partly caused by differences in the brain. Girls tend to learn to speak and to read sooner than boys, and boys tend to be better at tasks requiring spatial perception. Kimura (1999) suggested possible reasons for these sex differences. When the human brain was evolving into its present form, our ancestors were hunter–gatherers, and men and women probably had different roles. Women, because of restrictions on their movements imposed by childbearing, were more likely to work near the home, performing fine manual skills with small objects. Men were more likely to range farther from home, engaging in activities that involved coordination of body movements with respect to distant objects, such as throwing rocks or spears or launching darts toward animals. In addition, men had to be able to keep track of where they were so they could return home after following animals for long distances.

According to Ecuyer-Dab and Robert (2004), however, this dichotomy suggests that rather than showing a superior spatial advantage by men over women, it shows how context can affect the way in which each sex expresses its specific spatial skills: spatial cognition in men would be used to navigate the environment for a mate and food, whereas women's spatial cognition developed to deal with the immediate environment because they were more concerned with the survival of their offspring in the home. They, therefore, had no need to develop the navigational spatial skills that men did. In short, men developed and evolved large-scale navigation mechanisms, and women evolved small-scale ones. Ecuyer-Dab and Robert cited evidence from recent studies to support the hypothesis. Women, for example, were more likely than men to use landmarks when giving map directions. Men were more likely to provide more detail on direction and distance; although women are capable of doing this, they simply do not use these references as their primary source of information.

If the evolutionary reasoning is correct, it is possible to see why, on average, men's spatial abilities would be expressed differently from those of women. But why would females learn to speak and read sooner than males? Many researchers believe that our ancestors used hand gestures long before verbal communication developed. Kimura suggests that fine motor control and speech production are closely related—that the neural circuits that control the muscles we use for speech may be closely related to those we use to move our hands. Presumably, then, women would be better at both.

Buss (1995) argued that other differences in the adaptive challenges that men and women have faced in the course of evolution also have led to gender differences. Chief among these adaptive challenges are issues tied to reproduction. For women, such challenges include identifying and attracting a mate who is willing to invest his resources (time, energy, property, food, and so on) in her and her children. For men, they include identifying and attracting a fertile mate who is willing to copulate with him. Buss argued that over the course of evolution, men and women have come to differ because the challenges posed by reproduction and child rearing require different strategies for their successful resolution.

Kimura's and Buss's accounts are based on evolutionary arguments that can be tested only indirectly. However, they provide a good example of the biological approach—in particular, the functional, evolutionary approach—to an understanding of human behavior.

Cultural Causes   Although evolutionary forces may have laid the groundwork for gender differences in brain mechanisms associated with verbal ability and spatial ability, practice at and training in tasks involving these abilities can improve people's performance at them (Hoyenga & Hoyenga, 1993). Most psychologists believe that socialization plays the most significant role in the establishment of gender role differences. First adults and then peers teach, by direct instruction and by example, what is expected of boys and girls. These expectations are deeply ingrained in our culture and unconsciously affect our perceptions and our behavior.

The effect of gender on an adult's perception of infants is clear and has been confirmed in many studies. What about differences in the behaviors adults direct toward boys and girls? The strongest difference in the way parents socialize their sons and daughters appears to lie in their encouragement of gender-typed play and their choice of "gender-appropriate" toys. Many parents encourage their boys to play with trucks, blocks, and other toys that can be manipulated; they encourage their girls to play with dolls. However, a cross-cultural review of 172 studies conducted in North America, Australia, and Western Europe concluded that parents do not consistently treat their sons and daughters differently in any other important ways (Lytton & Romney, 1991).

Although parents do encourage "gender-appropriate" play, evidence suggests that biological factors may play an initial role in children's preferences. Although fathers are less likely to give dolls to 1-year-old boys than to 1-year-old girls, the boys who do receive the dolls are less likely to play with them (Snow, Jacklin, & Maccoby, 1983). Perhaps, as Lytton and Romney (1991) suggest, adults' expectations and encouragement build on children's innate tendencies, producing an amplifying effect. Then, because boys' toys provide more opportunity for developing motor skills, spatial skills, and inventiveness, and girls' toys provide more opportunity for nurturance and social exchange, some important differences in gender roles may become established.

Once children begin to play with other children outside the home, peers have a significant influence on the development of their gender roles. Stern and Karraker (1989) found that the behavior of 2- to 6-year-old children toward a baby was influenced by the children's knowledge of the baby's gender even more than was the behavior of adults. By the time children are 3 years old, they reinforce gender-typed play by praising, imitating, or joining in the behavior. In contrast, they criticize gender-inappropriate behavior (Langlois & Downs, 1980).

Of course, the research cited in this section describes tendencies of parents and children to act in a particular way. Some parents make a conscious attempt to encourage their children's interest in both "masculine" and "feminine" activities, with the hope that doing so will help keep all opportunities for achievement and self-expression open to them, regardless of their gender.

QUESTIONS TO CONSIDER

1. Can you imagine an alternative course of human evolution in which gender roles would have developed along different lines? What events in the course of human evolution could have happened (but did not, of course) that would have changed the nature of gender roles as we know them today?

2. Imagine that you were born the opposite gender—that instead of being a male, you are a female, or vice versa. In what significant ways would your life be different? For example, in what important ways would your social, emotional, and intellectual experiences be different? (Be careful not to base your answer on stereotypes you have of the other gender.)

Moral Development

The word *morality* comes from a Latin word that means "custom." Moral behavior is behavior that conforms to a generally acknowledged set of rules. With very few exceptions, by the time a person reaches adulthood, the person has accepted his or her culture's rules about personal and social behavior. These rules vary in different cultures and may take the form of codified laws or of informally accepted taboos (Chasdi, 1994). Moral reasoning is the way these rules are used cognitively. Consequently, a close relation exists between moral reasoning and cognitive development. Let us begin our look at moral development by considering the way a child acquires a concept of morality. The pioneer in this field, as in cognitive development, was Jean Piaget.

Piaget's Theory of Moral Development

According to Piaget, the first stage of moral development (ages 5 to 10 years) is **moral realism,** which is characterized by egocentrism, or self-centeredness, and blind adherence to rules. Egocentric children can evaluate events only in terms of their personal consequences. The behavior of children at this stage is not guided by the effects it might have on someone

---

moral realism   The first stage of Piaget's model of moral development, which includes egocentrism and blind adherence to rules.

morality of cooperation   The second stage of Piaget's model of moral development, which involves the recognition of rules as social conventions.

else, because young children are not capable of imagining themselves in the other person's place. Thus, in Piaget's view, young children do not consider whether an act is right or wrong but only whether it is likely to have good or bad consequences for them personally. Punishment is a bad consequence, and the fear of punishment is the only real moral force at this age. A young child also believes that rules come from parents (or other authority figures, such as older children or God) and that rules cannot be changed.

As children mature, however, two changes occur. First, older children judge an act by the intentions of the actor as well as by the consequences of the act—unlike young children, who consider only an act's objective outcomes, not the subjective intent that lay behind the act. For example, Piaget told children two stories, one about John, who accidentally broke 15 cups, and another about Henry, who broke 1 cup while trying to do something that was forbidden to him. When young children were asked which of the two boys was the naughtiest, they said that John was, because he broke 15 cups. They did not take into account the fact that the act was entirely accidental, as more mature individuals would.

Second, as children mature cognitively, they become less egocentric. Their lack of egocentrism makes them more capable of empathy. Children who are no longer egocentric (older than age 7) can imagine how another person feels. This shift away from egocentrism means that children's behavior may be guided not merely by the effects their actions have on the children themselves but also by the effects they have on others. At around 10 years of age, children enter Piaget's second stage of moral development, **morality of cooperation.** During this stage, rules become more flexible; the child is more empathic but also understands that many rules (such as those that govern games) are social conventions that may be altered by mutual consent.

Kohlberg's Theory of Moral Development

Piaget's description of moral development was considerably elaborated on by the psychologist Lawrence Kohlberg (1927–1987). Kohlberg studied boys between 10 and 17 years of age over the course of several years. He presented the children with stories involving moral dilemmas. For example, one story described a man named Heinz whose wife was dying of a cancer that could be treated only by a medication discovered by a druggist living in the same town. The man could not afford the price demanded by the druggist, so the distraught man broke into the druggist's store and stole enough of the drug to save his wife's life. The boys were asked what Heinz should have done and why he should have done it. On the basis of his research, Kohlberg decided that moral development progressed through three levels, which he divided into seven stages. (See **TABLE 6•3**.)

[TABLE 6•3] Levels and Stages of Kohlberg's Theory of Moral Development

Level and Stage	Highlights
Preconventional Level	
Stage 1: Morality of punishment and obedience	Avoidance of punishment
Stage 2: Morality of naive instrumental hedonism	Egocentric perspective; weighing of potential risks and benefits
Conventional Level	
Stage 3: Morality of maintaining good relations	Morality based on approval from others
Stage 4: Morality of maintaining social order	Morality defined by rules and laws
Postconventional Level	
Stage 5: Morality of social contracts	Recognition that societal rules are for the common good, although individual rights sometimes outweigh laws
Stage 6: Morality of universal ethical principles	Perception of societal laws and rules as based on ethical values
Stage 7: Morality of cosmic orientation	Adoption of values that transcend societal norms

Although Kohlberg's theory is a stage theory like Piaget's, it is less tied to a specific age. Moral development involves a sequence, so that early stages are more characteristic of children, and later stages tend to characterize adults. However, what is important is the progression of stages rather than any particular age at which a stage might appear. Kohlberg's first two stages belong to the **preconventional level,** during which morality is externally defined. During stage 1, morality of punishment and obedience, children blindly obey authority and avoid punishment. When asked to decide what Heinz should do, children at this stage base their decisions on fears about Heinz's being punished for letting his wife die or for committing a crime. During stage 2, morality of naive instrumental hedonism, children make moral choices egocentrically, guided by the pleasantness or unpleasantness of the consequences of a behavior. Heinz's dilemma is reduced to a weighing of the probable risks and benefits of stealing the drug.

The next two stages belong to the **conventional level,** which includes an understanding that the social system has an interest in people's behavior. During stage 3, morality of maintaining good relations, children want to be regarded by people who know them as good, well-behaved children. Moral decisions are based on perceived social pressure; so either Heinz should steal the drug because people would otherwise regard him as heartless, or he should not steal it because they would regard him as a criminal. During stage 4, morality of maintaining social order, laws and moral rules are perceived as in-

struments for maintaining social order and, as such, must be obeyed. Thus, both protecting a life and respecting people's property are seen as rules that help maintain social order.

Kohlberg also described a final level of moral development—the **postconventional level,** during which people realize that moral rules reflect important underlying principles that apply to all situations and societies. During stage 5, morality of social contracts, people recognize that rules are social contracts, that not all authority figures are infallible, and that individual rights can sometimes take precedence over laws. During stage 6, morality of universal ethical principles, people perceive rules and laws as being justified by abstract ethical values, such as the value of human life and the value of dignity. In stage 7, the morality of cosmic orientation, people adopt values that transcend societal norms as they grapple with issues such as "why be moral at all?" This stage represents the zenith of moral development. As Kohlberg noted, only a very few people—perhaps the prophets of major religions—ever reach stage 7. Kohlberg believed that not all people reach the postconventional level of moral development.

Evaluation of Piaget's and Kohlberg's Theories of Moral Development

Piaget's and Kohlberg's theories have greatly influenced research on moral development, but they also have come under some criticism. For example, Piaget's research indicated that children in the first stage (moral realism) respond to the magnitude of a transgression rather than to the intent behind it; even adults respond to the magnitude of a transgression, and rightly so. The theft of a few postage stamps by an office worker is not treated in the same way as the embezzlement of hundreds of thousands of dollars.

Kohlberg's conclusions also have been challenged. For example, Carpendale (2000) points out that it is not uncommon for people to perform at less than their highest level of achieved moral reasoning, although Kohlberg believed that people would use lower levels only if extreme conditions undermined their higher moral sense. Many researchers agree with Rest (1979), who concluded that Kohlberg's "stages" are not coherent entities but do describe a progression in the ability of children to engage in more and more complex moral reasoning.

---

preconventional level Kohlberg's first level of moral development, which bases moral behavior on external sanctions such as authority and punishment.

conventional level Kohlberg's second level of moral development, in which people realize that a society has instituted moral rules to maintain order and to serve the best interests of members of the society.

postconventional level Kohlberg's third and final level of moral development, in which people come to understand that moral rules include principles that apply across all situations and societies.

QUESTION TO CONSIDER

Laticia's parents are going away for the weekend and ask her to go with them. Laticia, who is 15 years old, says that she can't go because she has a special soccer practice on Saturday. Disappointed, her parents accept her answer; they agree to let her stay home, because they know how important soccer is to her. Later, after they return, they learn that Laticia lied to them about the practice. When they confront her, she tells them that she knows that she lied to them but that she did it so as not to hurt their feelings—she really did not want to go away with them for the weekend. Laticia's parents say that they understand her dilemma, but that they feel they must punish her anyway for breaking an important family rule. How do you suppose that Piaget and Kohlberg would explain Laticia's level of morality? How would they explain her parents' level of morality?

Adolescence

After childhood comes adolescence, the threshold to adulthood. (In Latin, *adolescere* means "to grow up.") The transition between childhood and adulthood is as much social as it is biological. In some societies, people are considered to be adults as soon as they are sexually mature, at which time they may assume adult rights and responsibilities, including marriage. In most industrialized societies, in which formal education often continues into the late teens and early 20s, adulthood officially comes several years later. The end of adolescence is difficult to judge, because the line between adolescence and young adulthood is fuzzy: no distinct physical changes mark this transition. In this section, we explore the physical, social, and cognitive changes that mark the adolescent years.

Physical Development

Puberty (from the Latin *puber*, meaning "adult"), the period during which people's reproductive systems mature, marks the beginning of the transition from childhood to adulthood. Many physical changes occur during this stage: People reach their ultimate height, develop increased muscle size and body hair, and become capable of reproduction.

Sexual Maturation The internal sex organs and genitalia do not change much for several years after birth, but they begin to develop again at puberty. When boys and girls reach about 11 to 14 years of age, their testes or ovaries secrete hormones that begin the process of sexual maturation. This activity of the gonads is initiated by the hypothalamus, the part of the brain to which the pituitary gland is attached. The hypothalamus instructs the pituitary gland to secrete hormones, which in turn stimulate the gonads to secrete sex hormones. These sex hormones act on

various organs of the body and initiate the changes that accompany sexual maturation.

The sex hormones secreted by the gonads cause growth and maturation of the external genitalia and of the gonads themselves. In addition, these hormones cause the maturation of ova and the production of sperm. All of these structures are considered primary sex characteristics, because they are essential to the ability to reproduce. The sex hormones also stimulate the development of secondary sex characteristics, the physical changes that distinguish males from females. Before puberty, boys and girls look much the same—except, perhaps, for their hairstyles and clothing. At puberty, adolescent males' testes begin to secrete testosterone; this hormone causes their muscles to develop, their facial hair to grow, and their voices to deepen. Females' ovaries secrete estradiol, the most important estrogen, or female sex hormone. Estradiol causes women's breasts to grow and their pelvises to widen, and it produces changes in the layer of fat beneath the skin and in the texture of the skin itself.

Development of the adult secondary sex characteristics takes several years, and not all characteristics develop at the same time. The process begins in girls at around age 11. The first visible change is the accumulation of fatty tissue around the nipples, followed shortly by the growth of pubic hair. The spurt of growth in height commences, and the uterus and vagina begin to enlarge. The first menstrual period, menarche, begins at around age 12 on average—at about the time a girl's rate of growth in height begins to decline. In boys, sexual maturation begins slightly later. The first visible event is the growth of the testes and scrotum, followed by the appearance of pubic hair. A few months later, the penis begins to grow, and the spurt of growth in height starts. The larynx grows larger, which causes the voice to become lower. Sexual maturity in males occurs at around age 15. The growth of facial hair usually occurs later; often a full beard does not grow until the late teens or early 20s.

Behavioral Effects of Puberty The changes that accompany sexual maturation have a profound effect on young people's behavior and self-concept. They become more sensitive about their appearance. Many girls worry about their weight and the size of their breasts and hips. Many boys worry about their height, the size of their genitals, their muscular development, and the growth of their beards. In addition, most adolescents display a particular form of egocentrism that develops early in the transition into the stage of formal operations: self-consciousness. Some developmental psychologists believe that self-consciousness results from teenagers' difficulty in distinguishing their own self-perceptions from the views other people have of them, although the evidence for this is not conclusive (Vartanian, 2000).

Because the onset of puberty occurs at different times in different individuals, young adolescents can find themselves more or less mature than some of their friends, and this difference can have important social consequences. An early study by Jones and Bayley (1950) found that early-maturing boys tended also to become more socially mature and were most likely to be

---

puberty The period during which people's reproductive systems mature, marking the beginning of the transition from childhood to adulthood.

perceived as leaders by their peers. Late-maturing boys tended to become hostile and withdrawn and often engaged in negative attention-getting behavior. Later studies have generally confirmed these findings (Peterson, 1985; Brooks-Gunn, 1988). The effect of age of maturity in girls is less clear. Some studies indicate that early-maturing girls may benefit from higher status and prestige; but they also are more likely to engage in norm-breaking behaviors such as stealing, cheating on exams, staying out late, and using alcohol (Brooks-Gunn, 1989). Brooks-Gunn suggested that the primary cause of the norm-breaking behaviors is the fact that early-maturing girls are more likely to become friends with older girls.

Cognitive Development

The techniques described in Chapter 3, such as functional magnetic resonance imaging (fMRI), have enabled researchers to how the brain develops as individuals become adolescents. Giedd et al. (1999) compared the development of the brains of people as they aged from age 4 to 20 years, at 2-year intervals, by using magnetic resonance imaging. They found that white matter increased steadily over time, but the development of gray matter was slightly more irregular. Recall from Chapter 3 that gray matter is made up of blood vessels and neurons, whereas white matter is made up of nerve fibers. The development of gray matter peaked just before adolescence and occurred in specific regions of the brain. Frontal and parietal lobe development peaked at 12 and 16 years, respectively, but occipital lobe development continued to 20 years. Although the initial sample was large ($N = 145$), the number of individuals who underwent more than three scans was only 33, which suggests caution in interpreting the results; nevertheless, the results do suggest that development in some form continues past adolescence to adulthood. How is this brain development reflected in behavior? As Piaget saw it, adolescents' cognitive changes were based on the logical power of abstract reasoning. In late childhood, said Piaget, a child entered the stage of formal operations. Adolescence, then, should be characterized as a sort of Sherlock Holmesian phase in which adolescents apply deductive skills to problems. Certainly evidence exists that this period of development is marked by increased facility with the tools of formal reasoning (Morris & Sloutsky, 2002). However, formal logic does not necessarily dominate adult thinking, let alone that of adolescents. We use heuristics, biases, and mental models in place of, or as supplements to, formal logic. The prevalence of these strategies for reasoning has led some investigators (e.g., Klaczynski, 2004) to suggest that two reasoning systems exist: an analytic processing system and an experiential processing system. The **analytic processing system** is the basis of deliberate, abstract, and higher-order reasoning. It provides the capacity to remove a problem from its context and to apply logical rules to solve it. The **experiential processing system,** conversely, is rapid, mostly unconscious, and heuristic. It provides the memories for particular solutions to problems and forms the basis for the biases and stereotypes that we may apply to problems.

Adolescence may be the time at which we not only develop our analytic abilities but also become good at knowing when they must be used. The two systems give us a large number of reasoning tools, which work in some cases but not in all. Thus, cognitive development during adolescence is marked by choice: The individual shows increased capacity to select consciously the mode of reasoning appropriate to the context (Keating, 2004).

Social Development

During adolescence, a person's behavior and social roles change dramatically. As a child, a person is dependent on parents, teachers, and other adults. As an adolescent, he or she is expected to assume more responsibility. Relations with peers also suddenly change; teenagers begin to have romantic attachments. Adolescence is not simply a continuation of childhood, then; it marks a real transition from the dependency of childhood to the relative independence of adulthood. Adolescence is also a period during which many young people seek out new experiences and engage in reckless behavior—behavior that involves psychological, physical, and legal risks for them as well as for others, such as driving too fast, having unprotected sex, or using illegal drugs. These behaviors often reflect the great challenges teenagers face as they search for an identity, focus on self-perceptions, cope with their emerging sexuality, and adjust to new relationships with peers and parents.

Forming an Identity Erik Erikson, a psychoanalyst who studied with Anna Freud, Sigmund Freud's daughter, developed a theory of psychosocial development that divides human development into eight stages. Erikson proposed that people encounter a series of crises or conflicts in their social relations with other people and that the way these conflicts are resolved

The transition between childhood and adulthood is as much social as it is biological.

---

analytic processing system   The basis of deliberate, abstract, and higher-order reasoning.

experiential processing system   The basis of rapid, mostly unconscious, and heuristic reasoning.

[**TABLE 6•4**] Erikson's Eight Stages of Psychosocial Development

PERIOD	STAGE	OUTCOME	
		Positive Resolution	**Negative Resolution**
Childhood	1. Crisis of trust vs. mistrust 2. Crisis of autonomy vs. self-doubt 3. Crisis of initiative vs. guilt 4. Crisis of competence vs. inferiority	Trust, security, confidence, independence, curiosity, competence, industry	Insecurity, doubt, guilt, low self-esteem, sense of failure
Adolescence	5. Crisis of identity vs. role confusion	Strong sense of self-identity	Weak sense of self
Adulthood	6. Crisis of intimacy vs. isolation 7. Crisis of generativity vs. stagnation 8. Crisis of integrity vs. despair	Capacity to develop deep and meaningful relationships and care for others; consideration for future generations; personal sense of worth and satisfaction	Isolation, unhappiness, selfishness, stagnancy, sense of failure and regret

determines the nature of development. According to Erikson, the resolution of these conflicts is development. If a given conflict is resolved positively, the outcome is happy; if it is not resolved or is resolved negatively, the outcome is unhealthy and impairs development. Because the nature of people's social relations changes throughout life, their psychosocial development does not end when they become adults. TABLE 6•4 lists Erikson's eight stages of development, the nature of the crisis that defines each stage, and the possible consequences.

Erikson argued that the primary crisis faced by adolescents is identity versus role confusion. If young people are able to develop plans for accomplishing career and personal goals and to decide which social groups they belong to, they have formed a personal identity. Failure to form an identity leaves a teenager confused about his or her role in life. You have probably heard the term "identity crisis," as in "She's having an identity crisis." Erikson coined this phrase.

Erikson's concept of the identity crisis has been researched extensively by Marcia (1980, 1994; Bradley & Marcia, 1998), who asserted that developing an identity consists of two components, crisis and commitment. Marcia defines a crisis as a period during which an adolescent struggles intellectually to resolve issues related to personal values and goals. For example, a teenager who questions his or her parents' religious and moral values is experiencing a crisis. Commitment is a decision based on consideration of alternative values and goals that leads to a specific course of action. For instance, a teenager who decides to go to a different religious institution than his or her parents is said to make a commitment. In this case, the teenager also is said to identify with the beliefs of that institution.

Marcia hypothesized that adolescents experience different degrees and combinations of crisis and commitment. Some teenagers never experience crises, and others do but may never resolve them. Marcia developed four main possibilities, which he called identity statuses. (See FIGURE 6•10.) As shown in the figure, in Marcia's model, adolescents who experience a crisis, consider alternative solutions to it, and are committed to a course of action based on personal values are said to be identity achievers. Identity achievers are self-confident and have a

high level of moral development (Dellas & Jernigan, 1990). Adolescents who experience a crisis but do not resolve it and therefore cannot become committed are said to be in moratorium. Teenagers who are in moratorium will express doubts about an identity but are still seeking information regarding it. Adolescents who have not experienced a crisis but who are nonetheless committed to a course of action are said to be in foreclosure. Teenagers in foreclosure are typically adolescents who identify strongly with people such as their parents and never consider alternatives to those identities. They can be dogmatic in their views and may feel threatened by others who challenge their identities (Frank, Pirsch, & Wright, 1990). Adolescents who do not experience a crisis and who do not become committed are said to experience identity diffusion. Because they have not considered alternative courses of action and made a decision, teenagers who are identity diffused, especially over a long period, tend to be immature and impulsive and to have a sense of hopelessness about the future (Archer & Waterman, 1990). Erikson would probably have considered these people identity confused.

Marcia's research has shown that adolescents move in and out of the different statuses as they experience new situ-

[**FIGURE 6•10**] Marcia's four identity statuses. Different combinations of crises and commitment yield four different identity statuses.

ations and crises. A teenager does not necessarily move progressively from one status to another. For example, after thinking about whether to major in business or engineering, a college student may decide on engineering because she thinks that she will like the work and earn good money. In terms of this decision, she is an identity achiever. However, after taking several engineering courses, she may decide that she really doesn't like engineering after all. Now she must decide whether to keep her major or to change it. She is now no longer committed; she is in moratorium.

Marcia's research is interesting for two reasons. First, it shows that most adolescents do indeed experience crises in their search for an identity—although "crisis" may be too strong a word for it, as many teens resolve its challenges without stress. Second, it shows that a teenager's psychological reaction to a crisis depends on the time at which he or she is dealing with it. That four possible avenues can be involved in achieving an identity testifies to the complexity of "finding oneself."

Identity and Self-Perception The search for a personal identity brings with it changes in self-concept and self-esteem (Berk, 2005). During childhood, children tend to perceive themselves in terms of both physical traits, such as "I am a boy and have brown hair and blue eyes," and individual personality characteristics, such as "I am honest" or "I am smart" (Damon & Hart, 1992). During adolescence, teenagers become more focused on their social relationships and tend to perceive themselves more in terms of their interactions with others. They may use phrases such as "I am outgoing" or "I am trustworthy" to describe themselves. In late adolescence, teenagers begin to perceive themselves more in terms of the values that they hold. They may now describe themselves in terms of their political, social, or philosophical views, as in "I am a conservative" or "I am an environmentalist." As a teenager strives to develop an identity, earlier self-perceptions, including those held during childhood, are incorporated into his or her emerging self-concept. Newer self-perceptions do not merely replace older ones. Instead, the newer ones augment the older ones.

Sexuality Sexuality was always a part of life (after all, our species has managed to propagate during all periods of history), but since the latter part of the 20th century, it has become much more open and evident than it was previously—and this is notably the case among adolescents. With so many examples of adult sexual behaviors given them, it is not surprising that adolescents adopt sexuality as part of their identity. According to the Centers for Disease Control and Prevention, 30% of female teens between the ages of 15 and 17 have had sexual intercourse; 31% of male teens of this age also reported having experienced sex (Abma, et al., 2004).

Of course, a possible consequence of sexuality is that adolescents may find themselves becoming parents. Statistics from a 2005 survey found that, among sexually active 9th through 12th grade students, 44% of female and 30% of male students reported that a condom was not used during their last sexual intercourse (Centers for Disease Control and Prevention, 2006). Preliminary data for 2006 in the United States showed that the birth rate among women 15 to 19 years of age was 41.9 births per 1,000 women (Hamilton, Martin, & Ventura, 2007).

Relations with Parents As adolescents begin to define their new roles and to assert them, they almost inevitably come into conflict with their parents. However, research indicates that most of the differences between people of different generations are in style rather than in substance. Adolescents and their parents tend to have similar values and personal ideals (Zentner & Renaud, 2007). Unless serious problems occur, family conflicts tend to be provoked by relatively minor issues, such as messy rooms, loud music, clothes, curfews, and household chores. These problems tend to begin around the time of puberty; if puberty occurs particularly early or late, so does the conflict (Paikoff & Brooks-Gunn, 1991).

QUESTIONS TO CONSIDER

1. What important behavioral effects did you experience as a result of your own sexual maturation? In what ways did your social and emotional lives change? How does your experience compare with those of your friends who underwent puberty before or after you did?
2. It is often said (by adults) that adolescents act as if they are incapable of properly judging risk. Do you think this is true? Could this be related to the different types of identity resolutions discussed by Marcia?

Adulthood and Old Age

It is much easier to outline child or adolescent development than adult development; children and adolescents change faster, and the changes are closely related to age. Adult development is much more variable. Physical changes in adults are more gradual. Mental and emotional changes during adulthood are more closely related to individual experience than to age. In the social realm, some people achieve success and satisfaction with their careers; others hate their jobs. Some marry and have happy family lives; others never adjust to the roles of spouse and parent. No single description of adult development will fit everyone.

Physical Development

As we grow older, we can count on one set of changes—physical alterations. Our physical abilities peak at around age 30 and decline gradually thereafter. By maintaining a well-balanced diet, exercising regularly, and not smoking, drinking, or using drugs, we can, in large measure, help our bodies maintain some of their physical vigor even into old age. This is not to say that good diet and exercise habits can make a

Loss of physical ability during adulthood can be minimized by following a program of regular exercise.

70-year-old look and feel like a 25-year-old, but if we don't eat well and exercise regularly, we will have less physical energy and poorer muscle tone than if we do. Apparently, staying in shape as a younger adult pays off in later life. Older people who were physically fit as younger adults are generally in better health and feel better about themselves than do those who weren't (Perlmutter & Hall, 1995).

Unfortunately, though, even prudent diets and exercising cannot reverse the physical changes that accompany aging. People in their later 40s, 50s, and 60s often experience decreases in visual acuity and in depth perception, hearing, sensitivity to odors and flavors, reaction time, agility, physical mobility, and physical strength.

Muscular strength peaks during the late 20s or early 30s and then declines slowly thereafter as muscle tissue gradually deteriorates. By age 70, strength has declined by approximately 30% in both men and women (Young, Stokes, & Crowe, 1984). However, age has much less of an effect on endurance than on strength. Both laboratory tests and athletic records reveal that older people who remain physically fit show remarkably little decline in the ability to exercise for extended periods (Spirduso & MacRae, 1990).

Although it is easy to measure a decline in the sensory systems (such as vision or hearing), older people often show very little functional change in these systems. Most people learn to make adjustments for their sensory losses, using additional cues to help them decode sensory information. For example, people with hearing loss can learn to attend more carefully to other people's gestures and lip movements; they also can profitably use their experience to infer what is said.

Functional changes with age are also minimal in highly developed skills. For example, Salthouse (1984, 1988) found that experienced older typists continued to perform as well as younger ones, despite the fact that they performed less well on standard laboratory tests of sensory and motor skills,

including the types of skills that might be expected to be important in typing. The continuous practice these typists received enabled them to develop strategies to compensate for their physical decline.

Cognitive Development

Psychologists have studied the effects of education and experience on intellectual abilities and have questioned whether intelligence inevitably declines with age. Most of us can conceive of a future when we can no longer run as fast as we do now or perform well in a strenuous sport, but we do not like to think of being outperformed intellectually by younger people. Research indicates that people can get old without losing their intellectual skills.

Cognitive Development and Brain Disease
Before we consider the normal effects of aging in a healthy individual, we should look at some changes that can be caused by disease. As people become older, they have a greater risk of developing dementia (literally "an undoing of the mind")—a class of diseases characterized by the progressive loss of cortical tissue and a corresponding loss of mental functions. The most prevalent form of dementia is **Alzheimer's disease.** About 2–3% of Americans between the age of 71 and 79 show diagnostic evidence of Alzheimer's disease; the prevalence rate increases rapidly with age, such that 30% of people 90 years of age or older show the disease (Plassman et al., 2007). Three relatively distinct subgroups of Alzheimer's patients are found (Fisher, Rourke, & Bieliauskas, 1999). The disease may manifest itself through (1) global deficits, or it may be most evident in functions identified with (2) the left hemisphere (deficits in word knowledge) or (3) the right hemisphere (deficits in the ability to copy geometric forms). In general, though, Alzheimer's disease is characterized by progressive loss of memory and other mental functions (Ashford, Schmitt, & Kumar, 1996). At first, the person may have difficulty remembering appointments and may sometimes fail to come up with words or people's names. As time passes, the individual shows increasing confusion and increasing difficulty with tasks such as balancing a checkbook. In the early stages of the disease, memory deficit involves recent events; but as the disease progresses, even old memories are affected. If the person ventures outside alone during the advanced stages of the disease, he or she is likely to become lost. Eventually the person becomes bedridden, becomes completely helpless, and finally dies (Terry & Davies, 1980; Khachaturian & Blass, 1992).

Geneticists have discovered an association between defects on chromosomes 14, 19, and 21 and at least one kind of Alzheimer's disease, which seems to involve reduced levels of the neurotransmitter acetylcholine (Gottfries, 1985; Selkoe, 1989; Cruts & Van Broeckhoven, 1996; Schellenberg, 1997; Poduslo & Yin, 2001). Alzheimer's disease produces severe degeneration of the hippocampus and cerebral cortex, especially the association cortex of the frontal and temporal lobes.

Alzheimer's disease A fatal degenerative disease in which neurons of the brain progressively die, causing loss of memory and deterioration of other cognitive processes.

[FIGURE 6•11] Alzheimer's disease. A computer-enhanced photograph of a slice through the brain of a person who died of Alzheimer's disease (left) and a normal brain (right). Note that the grooves (sulci and fissures) are especially wide in the Alzheimer's brain, indicating degeneration of the brain.

(Photo © Alfred Pasieka/Photo Researchers, Inc.)

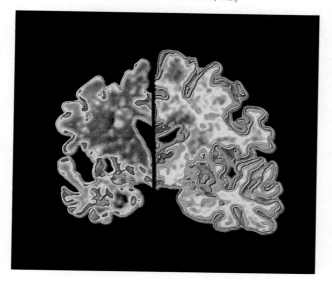

FIGURE 6•11 shows a computer-enhanced photograph of a slice through a normal brain (right) and the brain of a patient who died of Alzheimer's disease (left). You can see that much of the tissue of the Alzheimer's brain has been lost; the grooves in the brain (sulci and fissures) are much wider.

Cognitive Development and Normal Aging

Aging affects different intellectual abilities to different degrees. Schaie (1990), describing the results of the Seattle Longitudinal Study of Aging, reported that on average, people's scores on five tests of intellectual abilities showed an increase until their late 30s or early 40s, then a period of stability until their mid-50s or early

60s, followed by a gradual decline. **FIGURE 6•12** shows the participants who maintained stable levels of performance on each of the tests over a 7-year period. As you can see, the performance of most of the participants—even the oldest—remained stable, although some reductions appeared. Subsequent results from the Seattle Longitudinal Study of Aging (Schaie, 1996) suggest that these declines are due to the way different intellectual abilities change with age. Some abilities, such as the ability to perform rapid numerical or perceptual tasks, decline markedly as age increases. Verbal ability, as measured by vocabulary, shows little change. Other abilities, such as verbal memory, show a moderate decline at advanced age.

Related research by Kirasic (1991) has shown that, at least for performance on spatial tasks, deficits in short-term memory may coincide with aging. For example, Kirasic and Bernicki (1990) showed young and older adults 66 slides of a walk through a real neighborhood. Sometimes the slides were in the correct order; at other times, they were mixed up. All participants were then asked to make distance estimates between some of the scenes shown in the slides. Both younger and older participants performed equally well in estimating distances for the slides presented in logical order. But older participants performed less well than younger participants when the slides were scrambled. Kirasic and Bernicki concluded that information from the slides presented in normal order was encoded into short-term memory similarly for both sets of participants. However, the scrambled presentation of slides taxed available resources in the older participants' short-term memory, resulting in performance decline.

If memory shows wear with age, one might reasonably suspect that intelligence, too, would show a similar decline. This was once thought to be true, based on results from cross-sectional studies (studies that compare different age groups on the same task). However, we now know that intelligence does not decline until late adulthood, largely thanks to the work of Schaie and Strother (1968), who compared results from a cross-sectional approach with results from a longitudinal approach. For example, look at **FIGURE 6•13**, which

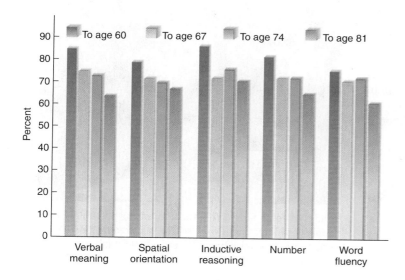

[FIGURE 6•12] Results from the Seattle Longitudinal Study of Aging. Percentage of participants of various age groups who maintained stable levels of performance on each of five tests of intellectual ability over a seven-year period.

(From Schaie, K. W. In *Handbook of the Psychology of Aging*, 3rd ed., edited by J. E. Birren and K. W. Schaie. San Diego: Academic Press, 1990. Reprinted with permission from Elsevier.)

[**FIGURE 6•13**] A comparison of cross-sectional and longitudinal data concerning changes in verbal ability with age. In contrast to the cross-sectional data, the longitudinal data show that verbal ability increased gradually to about age 55 and then decreased gradually.

(Based on Schaie, K. W., & Strother, C. R. (1968). A cross-sequential study of age changes in cognitive behavior. *Psychological Bulletin, 70,* 675. Reprinted with permission from K. Warner Schaie.)

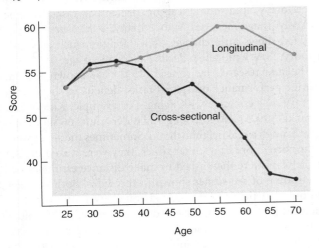

shows performance on a verbal abilities subsection of an intelligence test plotted as a function of age. (Here, verbal abilities means the ability to understand ideas represented by words.) The cross-sectional data indicate that intelligence scores decrease—and rather precipitately so—after age 50. But the longitudinal data paint a different picture: Scores increase until about age 55, then decline gradually.

Why would different methods produce these different patterns of results? Cross-sectional studies do not take into account possible cohort effects—the fact that the people being tested were reared in different time periods. Thus, one explanation for these disparate results is that the older people tested had not had the same educational and career opportunities as their younger counterparts might have had. The longitudinal method takes this possibility into consideration by testing the same people at regular intervals spanning many years. In doing so, it gives a more accurate picture of the relation between age and intelligence.

Many investigators believe that intelligence can be divided into two broad categories. In general, older people in good health do well on tests of crystallized intelligence—of the mental abilities that depend on knowledge and experience. Vocabulary, the ability to see similarities between objects and situations, and general information all are aspects of crystallized intelligence. Conversely, fluid intelligence—the capacity for abstract reasoning—appears to decline with age (Baltes & Schaie, 1974; Horn, 1982). The abilities to solve puzzles, to memorize a series of arbitrary items such as unrelated words or letters, to classify figures into categories, and to change problem-solving strategies easily and flexibly are aspects of fluid intelligence.

The facts that older people excel in crystallized intelligence and that younger people excel in fluid intelligence are reflected in the kinds of intellectual endeavors for which the two age groups seem to be best suited. For example, great mathematicians usually make their most important contributions during their 20s or early 30s; apparently the ability to break out of the traditional ways of thinking and to conceive new strategies is crucial in such achievements. In contrast, great contributions to literature and philosophy, in which success depends heavily on knowledge and experience, tend to be made by older people. Evidence exists, too, that mental activity pursued in the first two decades of life can increase cognitive functioning later. Fritsch et al. (2007) looked at a number of cognitive abilities of a sample of older adults in their mid-70s and statistically related their performance to IQ tests and school activities when these people were in their teen years. They found that participation in high school activities requiring intellectual skills was associated with higher verbal fluency as an older adult. IQ as an adolescent also was positively associated with increased episodic memory, speed of information processing, and general cognitive skill when the person had participated in intellectual activities in high school.

Social Development

Recall from Table 6.4 that Erikson believed that the adult years consist of three psychosocial stages during which the conflicts are intimacy versus isolation, in which people succeed or fail in loving others; generativity versus stagnation, in which people either withdraw inwardly and focus on their problems or reach out to help others; and integrity versus despair, in which people review their life with either a sense of satisfaction or despair.

Adult development occurs against the backdrop of what many developmental psychologists consider to be the two most important aspects of life: love and work. For most of us, falling in love is more than just a compelling feeling of wanting

Studies of aging must take into account the possibility that people of different ages were reared in different time periods and may have had different educational experiences.

to be with someone. It often brings with it major responsibilities, such as marriage and children. Work, too, is more than just a way to pass time. It involves setting and achieving goals related to income, status among peers, and accomplishments outside the family. For most adults, overall satisfaction with life reflects the degree to which they have been successful in marriage, raising a family, and achieving goals. With this in mind, let's look briefly at how love and work ebb and flow over the course of adult development.

Marriage and Family Most young people envision themselves falling in love and getting married. Fifty-one percent of women and 66% of men agreed with the statement "It is better to get married than to go through life being single" (Martinez, et al., 2006). Whether men and women actually encounter that life or not, statistics indicate that the path can take many turns. The most comprehensive description of marriage and family patterns is the National Survey of Family Growth, which completed a large survey in 2002 . Among women 15 to 44 years of age, 46% were currently married. Cohabitation with a male, however, was a common pattern reported by 43% of women—either before marriage, or as an arrangement for women who had never married. Of women in the 15- to 44-year age group surveyed, 48% had, in their lifetime, one husband or cohabiting male partner; 27% had never married or cohabited (Chandra et al., 2005). For men, 42% were in currently in a marriage; 49% had cohabited with a woman. In contrast to women, only 37% had a marriage or cohabiting relationship with a single woman during their lifetime (Martinez, et al., 2006).

Romantic relationships, whether they lead to marriage or cohabitation, need not involve a member of the opposite sex. Roisman et al. (2008) looked at the quality of the relationship between engaged, married, gay male, and lesbian couples. They found that positive views of their relationship were expressed similarly by married woman, married men, gay males, and lesbians. Relative to those in longer-term relationships, dating heterosexual couples and engaged women have more positive evaluations of their relationships. When individuals interacted with each other, committed couples—either opposite sex or same sex—were judged as having a higher quality of interaction than were heterosexual dating couples. In other words, same-sex partnerships were indistinguishable from opposite-sex relationships in terms of perceived and actual quality.

What produces a positive relationship? Of course, romantic partners wrestle with that issue all the time. One intriguing hint may be found in the early experience we might have had with the romantic partners we would have observed in our childhood—our caregivers. Earlier, we discussed how different caregiver behaviors could result in secure or insecure attachment personalities. Simpson et al. (2007) examined how attachment issues—assessed in adulthood—could affect the kind of care one would want to receive from a romantic partner. They assessed the attachment state of men and women who were dating and classified them as exhibiting either secure or insecure attachment attitudes toward

For most adults, satisfaction with life reflects the degree to which they have been successful in marriage, raising a family, and achieving goals.

their childhood caregivers. They then looked to see how, as a couple, each partner would react to different kinds of support given by the other when they were discussing relationship problems. A person with secure attachment responded best when his or her romantic partner offered emotional support; in contrast, someone with insecure attachment seemed to prefer practical advice.

Partners certainly test their relationship if it involves raising children. Both men and women in the National Survey of Family Growth said, "The rewards of being a parent are worth it, despite the cost and work it takes," with fewer than 5% disagreeing. A majority of both men and women said that they would be upset if they failed to have children, and a majority of women (but not of men) agreed that gay or lesbian adults should have the right to adopt children (Martinez, et al., 2006).

A strong majority of the National Survey of Family Growth believed "It is more important for a man to spend a lot of time with his family than to be a success at his career" (Martinez, et al., 2006). Of course, the care of young children is a difficult responsibility, but as children grow older and become more self-sufficient, the day-to-day burdens of raising a family taper off, and spouses are able to spend more time with each other. However, adolescents pose new problems for their parents: Teenage offspring may question parental authority, and their burgeoning social agendas may put a wrinkle in their parents' personal and social calendars. For many parents, rearing adolescents, particularly during the years just before young people leave home, represents the low point of marital happiness (Cavanaugh, 1990).

Generally speaking, once a family's youngest child has left home, marital happiness increases—and it continues to do so through the remainder of the couple's life together. It once was thought that the "empty nest" posed problems for the middle-aged couple, particularly for the mother, who in earlier generations was thought to define her role mainly around her children. Although parents may miss daily contact with their children, they also feel happy (not to mention relieved) that a major responsibility of life—raising self-reliant children who become responsible members of society—has been completed successfully. Just as important, the parents now have time for each other and freedom to pursue their own interests. Empty-nest couples report an increase in marital happiness. If they maintain frequent contact with their children, they also report increased satisfaction with life (White & Edwards, 1990).

Work The task of raising a family must be balanced against the demands of work outside the home. Events that occur in the workplace often affect the quality of home life. A promotion and a raise can mean that the family can now do things that they could not before—they can now pursue a new hobby or travel together. Working long hours to get that raise can decrease the amount of time that a couple can spend together with their children.

With the dramatic increase in the number of women who work outside the home since the early 1970s, many psychologists have focused their research efforts on understanding dual-earner marriages—those in which both parents work in full- or part-time jobs. In 2006, 52% of married-couple families had two wage earners (Bureau of Labor Statistics, May 9, 2007), making this an important area of future study.

Death Death is the final event of life. It is both a biological and a social event—family and friends are affected in many ways by the death of a loved one. Although a death may claim a life at any time, most people die when they are old. One question that developmental psychologists have asked about death and dying among the elderly is, "How do old people view the inevitability of their own deaths?"

At one time or another, most of us contemplate our own deaths. Some of us may contemplate death more than others, but the thought of death crosses everyone's mind at least occasionally. As you might expect, elderly people contemplate their deaths more often than do younger people. For the most part, they fear death less than their younger counterparts do (Kalish, 1976). Why? No one knows for sure, but a tentative explanation may be that older people have had more time to review the past and to plan for the future in the knowledge that death is close at hand. Thus, they are able to prepare themselves psychologically (and financially) for death.

Contemplating and preparing for death, though, is not like knowing that you are actually dying. The changes in attitudes that terminally ill people experience have been studied by Elisabeth Kübler-Ross (1969, 1981). After interviewing hundreds of dying people, Kübler-Ross concluded that people undergo five distinct phases in psychologically coping with death. The first stage is denial. When terminally ill people learn of their condition, they generally try to deny it. Anger comes next—people go through a period of resenting the certainty of death. In the third stage, bargaining, people attempt to negotiate their fate with God or others, pleading that their lives be spared. But even while bargaining, they actually realize that

they are going to die. This leads to depression, the fourth stage, which is characterized by a sense of hopelessness and loss. The fifth and final stage, acceptance, is marked by a more peaceful resignation to reality.

Kübler-Ross's work points up the psychological factors involved in dying and provides an interesting model of how the dying come to grips with their fate. Her conclusions, though, have not escaped criticism. Her research was not scientific—her method for interviewing people was not systematic, and her results are largely anecdotal. Moreover, of the five stages, only denial appears to be universal. Apparently, not all terminally ill people have the same psychological responses to the fact that they are dying.

Despite its flaws, however, Kübler-Ross's work is important because it has enhanced awareness, both scientific and public, of the experiences undergone by people who are terminally ill. The scientific response, as you might guess, has been to do medical research in the hope of prolonging the lives of people with cancer and other terminal illnesses. The public response has emphasized attempts to provide support for dying individuals and their families, often through hospice services (Aiken, 2001). In past centuries, hospices were places where strangers and pilgrims could find rest and shelter. Today, hospice programs provide invaluable medical and psychological support for dying persons and their families.

QUESTION TO CONSIDER

Imagine that you are the director of a new community mental health program for adults. The focus of this program is on prevention—on minimizing the negative effects of the aging process on adults who participate in the program. Your first task is to design a comprehensive plan to maximize adults' physical, social, emotional, and intellectual capacities. What activities would you include in such a plan? Why?

Epilogue

It may have occurred to you that the two case histories of this chapter, those of J. F. and D. R., provide different perspectives on the topic of development. D. R.'s biological constitution dominated his rearing conditions. As much as can be determined, his family genuinely tried to raise him as a girl. Nevertheless, D.R. did not think of himself as a girl, and, when given the choice, decided to live his life as a man. Nature seems to have trumped over nurture.

J. F.'s genetic history isn't known, and it is possible that the trouble she experienced with her foster family originated with a congenital disorder. However, her case is not that different from those of a large number of Romanian orphans, and the great common factor to all of them is the neglect they suffered during their early institutionalization. Nurture (or rather, lack of it) seems to have predominated in her case.

How can we make sense of these two disparate outcomes? The concept of critical periods may provide a clue. Charles A. Nelson of Harvard Medical School, who has studied the effect of institutional neglect on brain development (e.g., Nelson, 2007), suggests that early cognitive and social growth depends on genetic and environmental influences in two ways: experience-expectant mechanisms and experience-dependent ones. The first responds to the kind of environment that should be common to all of us as members of our species. It includes nutrition, shelter, and parental care. Our genetic mechanisms rely on these features, because they have been reliably part of our evolutionary history. When they fail to occur, as they did for the children caught in the Ceaușescu regime, then the normal sequences of development lack the necessary foundations. It would be like expecting an automobile to operate on the surface of the moon—its design is based on assumptions that don't apply in the other environment.

Experience-dependent mechanisms provide the fine tuning of development. If the expectancies of the environment are met, then these mechanisms respond to the normal variation of rearing conditions. D. R.'s basic psychological needs were met by a concerned and loving family from birth—the surgical accident notwithstanding—and he does not seem to have exhibited the attachment deficits from which many of the Romanian orphans suffer. If his past had not been disclosed to him, he might well have been able to live as an adult female. His genetic background had still prepared him for life as a male, and it seems likely that he would have not fit a conventional gender role in those circumstances. It seems clear that he would have had a much happier childhood if his nurturing had matched his nature.

Liane Faulder, the reporter who described J. F.'s story, called it "one of the most emotionally difficult stories I have witnessed in my career." Anyone who reads her account (Faulder, 2006) would have to concur. Even as an adult, J. F. exhibits an emotional detachment that she herself finds hard to comprehend. Nevertheless, it is gratifying to end this story by saying that, when she was 18 and could make the decision as an adult, J. F. returned to live with her foster parents, who never stopped giving her the love she was denied as a baby.

J.F. at age 18 with her foster parents.

CHAPTER SUMMARY

Prenatal Development

The three stages of prenatal development span the time between conception and birth. In just 9 months, the zygote grows from a single cell, void of human resemblance, into an embryo and then a fully developed fetus. Gender is determined by the sex chromosomes. Male sex organs are produced by the action of a gene on the Y chromosome that causes the gonads to develop into testes. The testes secrete androgens, which stimulate the development of male sex organs. If testes are not present, the fetus develops as a female. The most important factor in normal fetal development is the mother's nutrition. Normal fetal development can be disrupted by the presence of teratogens, which can cause intellectual deficits and physical deformities. One well-studied teratogen is alcohol, which, when consumed by a pregnant woman, may lead to fetal alcohol syndrome.

Physical and Perceptual Development in Infancy and Childhood

A newborn infant's first movements are actually reflexes that are crucial to its survival. For example, the rooting, sucking, and swallowing reflexes are important in finding and consuming food. More sophisticated motor skills develop and are refined through natural maturation and practice.

A newborn's senses appear to be at least partially functional at birth. However, normal development of perceptual abilities, like that of motor abilities, depends on experience. Genetically, an infant has the potential to develop motor and sensory abilities that coincide with the maturation of its nervous system, but for this potential to be realized, the infant's environment must give the infant opportunities to test and practice these skills. If an infant is deprived of the opportunity to practice them during a critical or sensitive period, these skills may fail to develop fully, which will affect his or her performance as an adult.

Cognitive Development in Infancy and Childhood

The first step in a child's cognitive development is learning that many events are contingent on his or her own behavior. This understanding occurs gradually and is controlled by the development of the nervous system and by increasingly complex interactions with the environment.

Piaget hypothesized that a child's cognitive development is divided into four periods. The periods are determined by the joint influences of the child's experiences with the physical and social environment and the maturation of the child's nervous system. An infant's earliest cognitive abilities are closely tied to the external stimuli in the immediate environment; objects exist for the infant only when they are present. Gradually, infants learn that objects exist even when hidden. The development of a grasp of object permanence leads to the ability to represent things symbolically, which is a prerequisite for the use of language. Next to develop is the ability to perform logical transformations on concepts. A key aspect of these transformations is that that they are reversible. Piaget designated these transformations as concrete operations and thought that their appearance was accompanied by the recognition that some properties were preserved across physical transformations. Around the age of 11, a child develops more adult-like cognitive abilities—abilities that may allow the child to solve difficult problems by means of abstract reasoning, or formal operations.

Critics point out that in some cases, Piaget's tests of cognitive development underestimated children's abilities. For example, if tested appropriately, it is evident that children understand the conservation of various properties earlier than Piaget thought, and that their egocentrism is less pronounced than his tests indicated. Nevertheless, his conclusions continue to have a profound impact on the field of child development.

Vygotsky's writings and the research they have stimulated have showed that the sociocultural context in which children grow up has a significant impact on their cognitive development. In particular, language appears to influence how children learn to think, solve problems, formulate plans, make decisions, and contemplate ideas.

Information-processing accounts of cognitive development have been developed more recently. These accounts describe how cognitive development proceeds according to the brain's information-processing capacity. Capacity expands because of three factors: brain maturation, practice using schemas, and the integration of schemas for different objects and events. Such models essentially reinterpret Piaget's theory in the language of information processing.

Social Development in Infancy and Childhood

Because babies are totally dependent on their parents, the development of attachment between parent and infant is crucial to the infant's survival. A baby has the innate ability to shape and reinforce the behavior of the parent. To a large extent, the baby is the parent's teacher. In turn, parents reinforce the baby's behavior, which facilitates the development of a durable attachment between them. Some of the behaviors that babies possess innately are sucking, cuddling, looking, smiling, and crying. These behaviors promote parental responses and are instrumental in satisfying physiological needs.

Normally, infants show both stranger anxiety and separation anxiety. They also tend to be afraid of novel stimuli, but the presence of their caregiver provides a secure base from which they can explore new environments. Ainsworth's Strange Situation allows a researcher to determine the nature of the attachment between infant and caregiver. By using this test, several investigators have identified some of the variables—some involving infants and some involving mothers—that influence secure or insecure attachment. Fathers, as well as mothers, can form close attachments with infants.

Development also involves the acquisition of social skills. Interaction with peers is probably the most important factor in social development among children and adolescents. However, a caregiver's style of parenting also can have strong effects on the social development of children and adolescents, especially when the caregiver engages in scaffolding. Authoritative parents, compared with authoritarian, permissive, and indifferent parents, tend to rear more competent, self-reliant, and independent children.

Development of Gender Roles

Children's gender roles tend to conform to their society's gender stereotypes. Very few real differences exist between the sexes, and those that do are relatively small. Female children tend to show earlier verbal development, are better at expressing emotion and interpreting emotional cues, and show more compliance with adults and peers. Male children tend to have better spatial abilities, are more aggressive, and tend to take more risks.

Some of these differences may have biological roots. Kimura suggested that the different tasks performed by our ancestors shaped brain development and favored men with better spatial skills and women with better fine motor skills. Buss argued that challenges related to reproduction and child rearing have caused gender differences in how these challenges are solved. Socialization undoubtedly plays a significant part in gender role differences.

Research has shown that both parents and peers tend to encourage children to behave in "gender-appropriate" ways—especially with regard to play activities and toys. However, scientific studies have revealed few other reliable differences in the ways parents treat young boys and girls.

Moral Development

Piaget suggested that moral development consists of two principal stages: moral realism, characterized by egocentrism and blind adherence to rules, and morality of cooperation, characterized by empathy and a realization that behavior is judged by the effects it has on others. Kohlberg suggested that moral development consists of three levels, each further divided into stages. During the preconventional level, morality is based on the personal consequences of an act. During the conventional level, morality is based on the need to be well regarded and on sharing a common interest in social order. During the postconventional level, which is achieved by only a few people, morality becomes an abstract, philosophical virtue.

Critics of Piaget and Kohlberg point out that the stages of moral development are not necessarily fixed and that individuals will often perform at a level lower than what they are capable of. However, it is recognized that as children mature, they become progressively able to reason about more complex moral situations.

Adolescence

Adolescence is the transitional stage between childhood and adulthood. Puberty is initiated by the hypothalamus, which causes the pituitary gland to secrete hormones that stimulate maturation of the reproductive system as well as secondary sex characteristics.

Puberty marks a significant transition, both physically and socially. Early maturity appears to be socially beneficial to boys, because early maturers are more likely to be perceived as leaders. The effects of early maturity in girls are mixed; although their advanced physical development may help them acquire some prestige, early-maturing girls are more likely to engage in norm-breaking behavior.

Conflict may underlie cognitive development in adolescence. Just before adolescence, children develop the tools of logical reasoning. However, adult reasoning uses a variety of reasoning strategies, of which logic is just one. Adolescence may be a period of growth in our capacity to choose among these strategies.

A focal point in adolescent development is the formation of an identity. Both Erikson and Marcia argue that adolescents face an identity crisis, the outcome of which determines the nature and level of identity that teenagers will form. Marcia argues that forming an identity has two primary components—the crisis itself and the commitment or decision that a young person makes regarding a course of action after considering possible alternatives. The extent to which a teenager experiences a crisis and the way in which he or she resolves it lead to identity achievement, moratorium, foreclosure, or identity diffusion. An adolescent's identity is bound to his or her perceptions of self which, during this time of life, will often be based on social relationships.

Sexuality becomes important in adolescence, and many people engage in sexual intercourse in their teens. Although adolescence brings conflicts between parents and children, these conflicts tend to be centered on relatively minor issues. Most adolescents hold the same values and attitudes concerning important issues as their parents do.

Adulthood and Old Age

Up to the time of young adulthood, human development can reasonably be described as a series of stages: a regular sequence of changes that occur in most members of our species. However, development in adulthood is much more variable, and few generalizations apply. Aging brings with it a gradual deterioration in people's sensory capacities as well as changes in physical appearance that many people regard as unattractive.

Older people are more likely than young people to develop dementia because of illnesses such as Alzheimer's disease. Rather than undergoing sudden intellectual deterioration, older people are more likely to exhibit gradual changes, especially in abilities that require flexibility and the learning of new behaviors. Intellectual abilities that depend heavily on crystallized intelligence—an accumulated body of knowledge—are much less likely to decline than are those based on fluid intelligence—the capacity for abstract reasoning.

Adult social development occurs within the context of love, marriage, family, and work. Marriages appear to be most unhappy just before the children leave home—possibly because of the emotional and time demands that adolescents place on their parents. Many families have parents who both work, which helps ease the financial burdens of raising a family and meeting long-term financial obligations.

Older people have less fear of death than do younger people, perhaps because they have had more time to contemplate and prepare for it. In interviews with terminally ill people, Kübler-Ross found that many people seem to go through a five-stage process in facing the reality that they are going to die. Although her research has been found to have some methodological flaws, it has drawn both scientific and public attention to the plight of terminally ill individuals and the necessity of properly caring for them.

succeed with mypsychlab

Visit MyPsychLab for practice quizzes, flashcards, and dozens of videos and animated tutorials, including the following items you can find in the "Multimedia Library":

 Fetal Development Attachment in Infants

 Cross-Sectional and Longitudinal Research Designs Key Issues in Developmental Psychology

 Attachment Classifications in the Strange Situation Teratogens and Their Effects

KEY TERMS

accommodation *p. 164*

actual developmental level *p. 179*

Alzheimer's disease *p. 186*

analytic processing system *p. 183*

androgens *p. 158*

assimilation *p. 164*

attachment *p. 172*

avoidant attachment *p. 174*

conservation *p. 166*

conventional level *p. 181*

critical period *p. 162*

cross-sectional study *p. 156*

disoriented attachment *p. 175*

egocentrism *p. 166*

embryonic stage *p. 157*

epigenetics *p. 157*

equilibration *p. 165*

experiential processing system *p. 183*

fetal stage *p. 158*

gender identity *p. 176*

gender role *p. 176*

gender stereotypes *p. 177*

longitudinal study *p. 156*

maturation *p. 160*

moral realism *p. 180*

morality of cooperation *p. 180*

object permanence *p. 165*

operation *p. 164*

period of concrete operations *p. 166*

period of formal operations *p. 167*

postconventional level *p. 181*

preconventional level *p. 181*

prenatal period *p. 156*

preoperational period *p. 165*

puberty *p. 182*

resistant attachment *p. 174*

scaffolding *p. 175*

secure attachment *p. 174*

sensitive period *p. 162*

sensorimotor period *p. 165*

separation anxiety *p. 174*

Strange Situation *p. 174*

stranger anxiety *p. 174*

teratogens *p. 157*

theory of mind *p. 170*

zone of proximal development *p. 169*

zygotic stage *p. 157*

SUGGESTIONS FOR FURTHER READING

Berk, L. E. (2005). *Infants, children, and adolescents* (5th ed.). Boston: Allyn & Bacon.

This text presents an excellent overview of research and theory in the fields of infant, childhood, and adolescent development.

Lemme, B. H. (2006). *Development in adulthood* (4th ed.). Boston: Allyn & Bacon.

A well-written and thorough introduction to the major issues involved in the study of adult development.

Hoyenga, K. B., & Hoyenga, K. T. (1993). *Gender-related differences: Origins and outcomes*. Boston: Allyn & Bacon.

This book examines gender differences from evolutionary, physiological, and cultural perspectives.

Harwood, R. L., Miller, J. G., & Irizarry, N. L. (1997). *Culture and attachment: Perceptions of the child in context*. New York: Guilford Press.

As its title implies, this book considers cultural variables that influence the development of attachment between infants and their caregivers, including socioeconomic status, perceptions of different attachment behaviors, and perceptions of children themselves.

Colapinto, J. (2000). *As nature made him: The boy who was raised as a girl*. Toronto, ON: HarperCollins.

Colapinto's book is an excellent description of the case of D.R., described in the text. D.R. did reveal his full identity for the sake of Colapinto's book in an effort to make his story known and to change medical thinking about the value of sexual reassignment after genital trauma. You can find full details about his story in this account. Sadly, D.R.'s life became increasingly unhappy; he died in 2004.

Memory

Taken from *Psychology: The Science of Behavior*, Seventh Edition, by Neil R. Carlson, Harold Miller, C. Donald Heth, John W. Donahoe, and G. Neil Martin.

Prologue

The Salem Witch Trials

In 1680, Juan, a slave to a New England farmer, testified in a court deposition that, about a month before, he had seen two black cats while eating dinner. Juan thought this strange because the farm housed only one cat. What made it stranger was that, only the week before, his horses had startled and had run away from him. But also—and here Juan's testimony was to take a turn down a deadly path—he remembered seeing his neighbor, Bridget Oliver, sitting in his barn that same afternoon with an egg in her hand. Juan remembered seeing her clearly, but unaccountably, she was nowhere to be found a few seconds later.

Juan's testimony about events a month old must have been threatening for Bridget to hear. For this was the town of Salem, Massachusetts, and Bridget was on trial for witchcraft. Manifestations of a sinister invisible world were considered plausibly real, and testimony like Juan's was regarded as hard evidence of a capital crime. Fortunately for Bridget, her jurors weren't persuaded this time, and she was acquitted of witchcraft, but the suspicions of witchcraft lingered. A few years later, they would lead to her death.

In 1692, in a nearby village, a group of young girls began showing mysterious ailments while remembering strange visitations. For reasons that are debated to this day, their stories touched off an unprecedented level of community hysteria and fear. Gossip about Bridget's earlier brush with charges of witchcraft must have reached these girls, for they soon began to name her as one of the apparitions that afflicted them. Bridget by this time had remarried after the death of her husband and was known as Bridget Bishop. Her remarriage (it was her third) and a penchant for clothing that was a bit too colorful by Puritan standards probably accelerated the gossip around her. Whatever the cause, her neighbors began to remember other odd instances and to relate them to the grand jury. One recalled that, fourteen years ago, he had encountered Bridget on the way to his father's mill, and, shortly thereafter, the wheel of his cart had fallen off. Another, relying on an eight-year-old memory, said that he had exchanged words with Bridget, and right thereafter, had seen a black pig that had vanished when he approached it. Two

Bridget Bishops's tombstone. Bridget was accused of witchcraft and subsequently killed.

workmen claimed that, seven years ago, they had seen some unusual dolls in a house that Bridget had lived in.

Bridget was hauled once again into court to defend herself against charges of witchcraft. This time she had no hope. To her plea that she didn't even know what a witch was, her interrogator snarled, "How do you know then that you are not a witch?" One has to admire the cool contempt in her answer to this verbal trap: "I do not know what you say." But such courage was no match for the hysteria around her.

Bridget Bishop was put on trial for witchcraft on June 2, 1692. Within eight days, she would be tried, convicted, and executed. ■

Bridget Bishop was the first of the so-called "Salem witches" to be tried and executed. Although the legal charge against her related to a supposed spectral assault on the young girls of Salem Village, the issue turned on whether evidence existed that Bridget had practiced witchcraft before (Norton, 2003). Much of the testimony that convicted her concerned supposedly supernatural occurrences recollected many years later (remarkably, records of this testimony still exist; see Boyer & Nissenbaum, 1972). Bridget was condemned, in part, because the people of her time believed that a narrative recollection was a reliable mirror of the experience. To be sure, people could lie, and they could forget; but a memory that was honestly real to the recaller was considered plausibly real itself. (The only substantive debate about the veracity of the evidence was whether Satan was manipulating real events to make the innocent look guilty.) Yet notice the small twists of coincidences in the stories told against Bridget: If that argument had occurred after the pig sighting, would it have been so damning? If another cat had strayed into Juan's farm without his remembering it, would his dinnertime vision have seemed so mysterious? Notions of devilment aside, Bridget's life rested on the assumption that her accusers could accurately reconstruct a sequence of events months or years in the past. This is a remarkable belief, yet, in everyday matters, it's an assumption we make all the time.

Overview of Memory

Learning is the tendency for behavior to change as a result of experience; learning reflects the brain's plasticity. Our ability to learn allows us to engage in an enormous variety of behaviors in response to different situations. But a lapse of time may occur between the act of learning and a change in behavior caused by that learning. For example, you may observe that a new restaurant has opened, and then, some days later, decide you want to eat out. Choosing the new restaurant is possible because you have retained information about it.

This chapter concerns **memory**—the cognitive processes of encoding, storing, and retrieving information. **Encoding** is the active process of putting stimulus information into a form that can be used by our memory system. **Storage** is the process of maintaining information in memory. **Retrieval** includes the active processes of locating and using information stored in memory. Our choosing the restaurant, then, is a joint result of encoding the location, type of food, and other attributes of the restaurant, storing this information, and retrieving it when you are later looking for a place to eat.

One of the first things to note about memory is that you are aware of these processes in different ways. Noticing the restaurant, judging its compatibility to your tastes, marking its location—all are activities that can be described; we are highly conscious of them. (Consciousness will be the topic of Chapter 8.) In contrast, most of the time, the storage of the information is not so directly available. You don't actively think of every restaurant you've seen every moment of the day; neither do we consciously think about every person we've met, every song we've heard, and every place we've been in such a continuous way. The information is latent and unactivated. Retrieval is a bit of a blend. Quickly now, what is the last line to the carol "Silent Night"? Normally, you have to start thinking about earlier parts of the song before you can retrieve its ending. Retrieving the information is a progressive reactivation.

In 1949, Donald Hebb used this active/latent distinction to suggest that the brain remembered information in two different ways—a view known as *dual trace theory* (Hebb, 1949). Information that was active was in this state because neurons were firing continuously. Hebb thought this activity was due to feedback circuits of neurons. Repeated firing, in turn, strengthened the synaptic efficiency of the circuit, leading to structural changes in the neurons involved. This structural change would persist after the activity had ceased. The brain therefore retained traces of an experience either in an active state or in the latent structural state. The gist of Hebb's theory has been strikingly supported by the finding of long-term potentiation.

Back in the 1960s, Richard Atkinson and Richard Shiffrin suggested a way of thinking about memory that psychologists have found useful. They proposed that memory takes at least three forms: sensory memory, short-term memory, and long-term memory (Atkinson & Shiffrin, 1968). The first two roughly correspond to memory systems that retain active traces, whereas the last retains latent traces. **Sensory memory** is memory in which representations of the physical features of a stimulus are stored for a very brief time—perhaps for a second or less. This form of memory is difficult to

---

memory The cognitive processes of encoding, storing, and retrieving information.

encoding The process by which sensory information is converted into a form that can be used by the brain's memory system.

storage The process of maintaining information in memory.

retrieval The active processes of locating and using stored information.

sensory memory Memory in which representations of the physical features of a stimulus are stored for very brief durations.

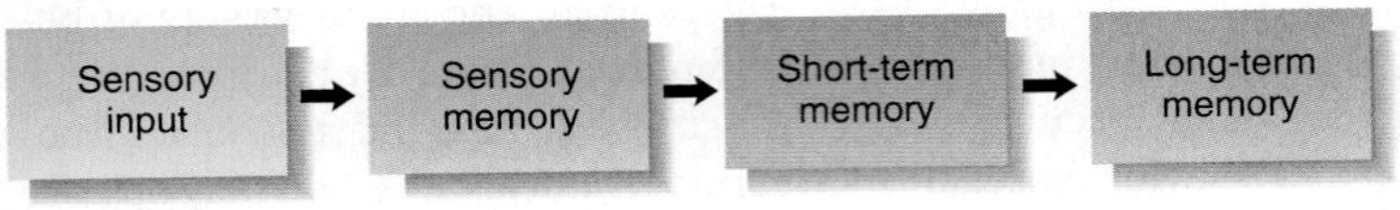

[**FIGURE 7•1**] A simplified model of information flow in human memory.

distinguish from the act of perception. The information contained in sensory memory represents the original stimulus fairly accurately and contains all or most of the information that has just been perceived. For example, sensory memory contains a brief image of a sight we have just seen or a fleeting echo of a sound we have just heard. The function of sensory memory appears to be to hold information long enough for it to become part of the next form of memory, short-term memory.

Short-term memory is an immediate memory for stimuli that have just been perceived. As we will soon see, its capacity is limited in terms of the number of items it can store and its duration. If you go to the movies and the cashier tells you "Your movie is playing in theater six," you obviously need to remember it long enough to find the entrance. We can remember information like this by keeping it active, such as repeating it once or twice. However, if you let the information become inactive (say, you stop to talk with friends and buy some popcorn), you may not be able to remember it later. Information soon leaves short-term memory, and unless it is stored in long-term memory, it will be lost forever.

To demonstrate the fact that short-term memory can hold only a limited amount of information for a limited time, read the following numbers to yourself just once, and then close your eyes and recite them back.

1 4 9 2 3 0 7

You probably had no trouble remembering them. Now, try the following set of numbers, and go through them only once before you close your eyes.

7 2 5 2 3 9 1 6 5 8 4

Very few people can repeat 11 numbers; in fact, you may not have even bothered to try once you saw how many numbers there were. Even if you practice, you will probably not be able to recite more than seven to nine independent pieces of information that you have seen only once. Thus, short-term memory has definite limits (Marois & Ivanoff, 2005).

If you wanted to, you could recite the 11 numbers again and again until you had memorized them. You could rehearse the information in short-term memory until it was eventually part of **long-term memory**—memory in which information is represented on a permanent or near-permanent basis. Unlike short-term memory, long-term memory has no known limits; and, as its name suggests, it is relatively durable. For example, Standing (1973) showed people 10,000 color slides and found that they could recognize most of them weeks later, even though they had seen them just once. Presumably, long-term memory involves physical changes that take place in the brain. If we stop thinking about something we have just perceived (that is, something contained in short-term memory), we may not remember the information later. However, information in long-term memory need not be continuously rehearsed. We can stop thinking about it until we need the information at a future time.

The implication that information flows from one type of memory to another has been termed the "modal model" of memory because it seems so widely assumed. (See FIGURE 7•1.) However, some cognitive psychologists argue that it is unnecessary to assume that distinctive types of memory exist (Crowder, 1993). Instead, they suggest that there is really only one memory, but several phases in the way information is continuously processed. A loose analogy might be in the way cars could be manufactured in the global economy. One car-maker might manufacture the frame in Japan, ship it to a factory in Canada to add the engine, and then finish the assembly at a factory in the United States. The different factories would have their own methods of operation, and the transfer of cars from one to another is a significant part of the story. The alternative method is to assemble the entire car in different stages within the same factory. The emphasis in the second method is on the way the car body changes as it moves through the process. The next few sections will follow the general outline of Figure 7.1, but you will see that psychologists have discovered that memory is more complex than this model would have us believe (Healy & McNamara, 1996).

Sensory Memory

Information we have just perceived remains in sensory memory just long enough to be transferred to short-term memory. We become aware of sensory memory only when information is presented so briefly that we can perceive its aftereffects. For example, a thunderstorm at night provides us with an opportunity to become aware of visual sensory memory. When a bright flash of lightning reveals a scene, we see things before we recognize them. That is, we see something first, then study the image it leaves behind. Although we probably have a sensory memory for each sense modality, research efforts so far have focused on the two most important forms: *iconic* (visual) and *echoic* (auditory) memory.

---

short-term memory An immediate memory for stimuli that have just been perceived. It is limited in terms of both capacity (7±2 chunks of information) and duration (less than 20 seconds).

long-term memory Memory in which information is represented on a permanent or near-permanent basis.

Images to which we are briefly exposed, such as a bolt of lightning, linger momentarily in iconic memory.

Iconic Memory

Visual sensory memory, called **iconic memory** (*icon* means "image"), is a form of sensory memory that briefly holds a visual representation of a scene that has just been perceived. Because the representation is so closely tied to the perception, this form of memory is sometimes called "visible persistence." To study this form of memory, Sperling (1960) presented visual stimuli to people on a screen for extremely brief durations. Sperling flashed a set of letters (three rows of letters) on the screen for 50 milliseconds. (See FIGURE 7·2.) He then asked the participants to recall as many letters as they could, a method known as the *whole-report procedure*. On average, participants could remember only four or five letters. They insisted that for a brief time they could see more; however, the image of the letters faded too fast for people to identify them all.

To determine whether the capacity of iconic memory accounted for this limitation, Sperling used a partial-report procedure. He sounded tones when presenting the stimuli, and he asked people to name the letters in only one of the three horizontal rows: Depending on whether a high, middle, or low tone was sounded, they were to report the letters in the top, middle,

[**FIGURE 7·2**] The critical features of Sperling's iconic memory study.

(Adapted from Sperling, G. (1960). The information available in brief visual presentations. *Psychological Monographs*, 74, 1–29.)

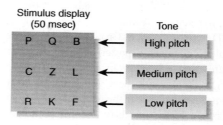

or bottom line. When the participants were warned beforehand to which line they should attend, they had no difficulty naming all three letters correctly. But then Sperling sounded the tone *after* he flashed the letters on the screen. The participants had to select the line from the mental image they still had: *They could use only information from memory.* With brief delays, they recalled the requested line of letters with high accuracy. For example, after seeing all nine letters flashed on the screen, they would hear the high tone, direct their attention to the top line of letters in their iconic memory, and "read them off" much as one might read the headlines in a newspaper. The participants' high level of performance indicated that there was little difference between having the letters physically present in front of them and having them present as a memory. However, Sperling also varied the delay between flashing the nine letters on the screen and sounding the high, medium, or low tone. If the delay was longer than one second, people could report only around 50 % of the letters. Apparently, during the delay, the information had faded before all of it could be transferred to longer lasting memory. This result indicated that the image of the visual stimulus fades quickly from iconic memory. It also explains why participants who were asked to report all nine letters failed to report more than four or five. They had to scan their iconic memory, identify each letter, and name it verbally. This process took time, and during this time the image of the letters was fading and the information becoming unreliable (Dixon, et al., 1997). Although their iconic memory originally contained all nine letters, participants had time to recognize and report only four or five before the mental image disappeared.

Echoic Memory

Auditory sensory memory, called **echoic memory,** is a form of sensory memory for sounds that have just been perceived. It is necessary for comprehending many sounds, particularly those that constitute speech. When we hear a word pronounced, we hear individual sounds, one at a time. We cannot identify the word until we have heard all the sounds, so acoustical information must be stored temporarily until all the sounds have been received. For example, if someone says "harbor," we may think of an anchorage for ships; but if someone says "harvest," we will think of something entirely different. The first syllable we hear—*har*—has no meaning by itself in English, so we do

---

iconic memory A form of sensory memory that holds a brief visual image of a scene that has just been perceived; also known as visible persistence.

echoic memory A form of sensory memory for sounds that have just been perceived.

not identify it as a word. However, once the last syllable is uttered, we can put the two syllables together and recognize the word. At this point, the word enters short-term memory. Echoic memory holds a representation of the initial sounds until the entire word has been heard. Although early use of partial-report procedures suggested that echoic memory lasts less than 4 seconds (Darwin, Turvey, & Crowder, 1972), more recent evidence employing repeated patterns of random, or "white," noise indicates that echoic memory can last up to 20 seconds (Kaernbach, 2004). Indeed, if you consider your ability to recognize a friend's voice over the telephone, there's a sense in which we retain sound patterns for much longer (Winkler & Cowan, 2005). This everyday phenomenon presents a problem for the simplified model that we've been discussing. To understand why, we need to consider the next stages in that model: short-term and long-term memory.

QUESTIONS TO CONSIDER

1. It is easy to understand how we can rehearse verbal information in short-term memory—we simply say the information to ourselves again and again. But much of the information we learn is not verbal. Can we rehearse nonverbal information in short-term memory? How do we do so?

2. Suppose that your iconic memory malfunctioned—that instead of holding information only briefly, your iconic memory retained information for longer periods of time. What complications or problems might follow from such a malfunction? Would there be any advantages to this sort of malfunction?

Short-Term or Working Memory

Short-term memory has a limited capacity, and most of the information that enters it is subsequently forgotten. What, then, is its function? Before we try to answer this question, let us examine its nature a little more closely.

Encoding of Information in the Short-Term: Interaction with Long-Term Memory

So far, the story I have been telling about memory has been simple: Information in sensory memory enters short-term memory, where it may be rehearsed for a while. The rehearsal process keeps the information in short-term memory long enough for it to be transferred into long-term memory. After that, a person can stop thinking about the information; it can be recalled later, when it is needed (refer to Figure 7.1).

However, this simple story is incomplete. First of all, information does not simply "enter short-term memory." For example, read the letters below. Put them into your short-term memory, and keep them there for a few seconds while you look away from the book.

P X L M R

How did you keep the information in short-term memory? You would probably say that you repeated the letters to yourself. You may even have whispered or moved your lips. You are able to say the names of these letters because many years ago you learned them. But that knowledge is stored in long-term memory. Thus, when you see some letters, you retrieve information about their names from long-term memory, and then you hear yourself rehearse those names (out loud or silently, "within your head"). The five letters you looked at contain only visual information; their names came from your long-term memory, which means that the information put into short-term memory actually came from long-term memory.

To convince yourself that you used information stored in long-term memory to remember the five letters, study the symbols below, look away from the book, and try to keep them in short-term memory for a while.

ζ ∩ ∂ ∋ ℘

Could you do it? You have never learned the names of these symbols, so you have no way of rehearsing them in short-term memory. Perhaps, then, **FIGURE 7.3** more accurately

[**FIGURE 7.3**] Relations between iconic memory, short-term memory, and long-term memory. Letters are read, transformed into their acoustic equivalents, and rehearsed as "sounds" in the head. Information can enter short-term memory from both iconic memory and long-term memory. Visual information enters short-term memory from iconic memory, but what is already known about that information (such as names of letters) is moved from long-term memory to short-term memory.

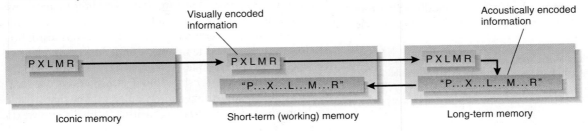

represents the successive stages of the memory process than does the diagram you saw in Figure 7.1.

You can see now that short-term memory is more than a simple way station between perception and long-term memory. Information can enter short-term memory from two directions: from sensory memory or from long-term memory. In Figure 7.3 this feature is represented by arrows pointing to short-term memory from both iconic memory and long-term memory. Perhaps another example will clarify the process further. When we are asked to multiply 7 by 19, information about the request enters our short-term memory from our sensory memory. Actually performing the task, though, requires that we retrieve some information from long-term memory. What does *multiply* mean? What is *7*, and what is *19*? At the moment of the request, such information is not being furnished through our senses; it is available only from long-term memory. Note, however, most versions of the model of Figure 7.1 assume that information is not recalled directly from long-term memory. Instead, it is first moved into short-term memory and then recalled. So, short-term memory contains information when we are trying to encode that information and when we are trying to retrieve it.

The fact that short-term memory contains both new information and information retrieved from long-term memory, and also seems more than a passive recording of information, has led some psychologists, such as Alan Baddeley, to prefer the decidedly more active term **working memory** (Baddeley, 1993). Working memory does seem to work on what we have just perceived. In fact, working memory represents a sort of behavior that takes place within our heads. It represents our ability to remember what we have just perceived and to think about it in terms of what we already know (Haberlandt, 1994). We use this form of memory to remember what a person says at the beginning of a sentence until we finally hear the end. We use it to remember whether any cars are coming up the street after we look left and then right. We use it to think about what we already know and to come to conclusions on the basis of this knowledge. These behaviors are similar to what were described as short-term memory, and from now on this chapter will use the terms *short-term memory* and *working memory* interchangeably. Some psychologists, however, prefer to distinguish the two forms of memory on the basis of the functions they serve (Kail & Hall, 2001).

---

working memory   Memory for new information and information retrieved from long-term memory; used in this text as another name for short-term memory.

primacy effect   The tendency to remember initial information. In the memorization of a list of words, the primacy effect is evidenced by better recall of the words early in the list.

recency effect   The tendency to recall later information. In the memorization of a list of words, the recency effect is evidenced by better recall of the last words in the list.

Primacy and Recency Effects

Imagine yourself as a participant in a memory study. You are asked to listen to the researcher as she slowly reads words, one at a time, off a long list. As soon as she finishes reading the list, she asks you to write down each word that you can remember. (This task is called a free-recall task.) Which words in the list do you think you are most likely to remember? If you are like most people in free-recall tasks of this type, you will tend to remember the words at the beginning and the end of the list and forget the words in between. The tendency to remember the words at the beginning of the list is called the **primacy effect;** the tendency to remember words at the end of the list is called the **recency effect.**

What causes these effects? Research that has addressed this question points to two factors (Atkinson & Shiffrin, 1968). The primacy effect appears to be due to the fact that words earlier in a list have the opportunity to be rehearsed more than do words in the other parts of a list. This makes good sense—the first words are rehearsed more because, at the experiment's outset, these are the only words available to rehearse. The rehearsal permits them to be stored in long-term memory. As more and more words on the list are presented, short-term memory becomes more and more full, so words that come later have more competition for rehearsal time. Because the first words on the list are rehearsed the most, they are remembered better.

What about the recency effect? Atkinson and Shiffrin (1968) point out one possible explanation: Because the words at the end of the list were the last to be heard, they are still available in short-term memory. Thus, when you are asked to write the words on the list, the last several words are still available in short-term memory, even though they did not undergo as much rehearsal as words at the beginning of the list.

The Limits of Working Memory

How long does information remain in working memory? The answer to this question was provided in classic studies conducted by John Brown (1958) and Lloyd and Margaret Peterson (1959). The Petersons presented participants with a stimulus composed of three consonants, such as *JRG.* Not surprisingly, with rehearsal, people easily recalled the consonants 30 seconds later. The Petersons then made the task a bit more challenging: They prevented the participants in their study from rehearsing by assigning a distracter task. After they presented the participants with *JRG,* they asked them to count backward by 3s from a three-digit number they gave them immediately after they had presented the set of consonants. For example, they might present people with *JRG,* then say, "397." The participants would count out loud, "397 . . . 394 . . . 391 . . . 388 . . . 385," and so on until the researchers signaled them to recall the consonants. The accuracy of participants' recall was determined by the length of the interval between presentation of the consonants and the signal for recall. (See FIGURE 7•4.) When rehearsal was disrupted by backward counting—which prevented participants from rehearsing information in short-term memory—the consonants

[**FIGURE 7·4**] Limits of recall from working memory. Shown here is the percentage correct in the recall of the stimulus as a function of the duration of the distracter task used in the study by Peterson and Peterson.

(Adapted from Peterson, L. M., & Peterson, M. J. (1959). Short-term retention of individual verbal items. *Journal of Experimental Psychology, 58,* 193–198.)

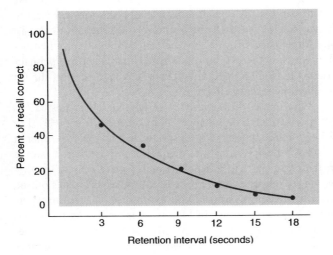

remained accessible in memory for only a few seconds. After a 15- to 18-second delay between the presentation of the consonants and the recall signal, recall dropped to near zero. So, for now at least, we can conclude that stimuli remain in working memory for less than 20 seconds *unless they are rehearsed.*

As a matter of fact, working memory may be even more limited. Muter (1980) pointed out that in the procedure used by Brown and the Petersons, the counting task always appeared after the letters. Consequently, participants in their experiments would be expecting a distraction. What would happen if a distraction were *unexpected*? This would be like hearing a phone number you wanted to remember and then having the doorbell ring right afterward. Muter examined this question by using the Peterson procedure, but with the counting task appearing only on a small proportion of trials, making it unexpected. He found that an unexpected distractor seriously disrupted working memory: most people found it hard to recall three letters after only 2 seconds.

And what is the capacity of working memory? A while ago, you were asked to try to repeat 11 numbers, which you were almost certainly unable to do. Miller (1956), in an article entitled "The Magical Number Seven, Plus or Minus Two," demonstrated that people could retain, on average, about seven pieces of information in their short-term memories: seven numbers, seven letters, seven unrelated words, or seven tones of a particular pitch. But if we can remember and think about only seven pieces of information at a time, how can we manage to write novels, design buildings, or even carry on simple conversations? The answer comes in a particular form of encoding of information that Miller called **chunking.** In chunking, information is simplified by rules, which make the information easily remembered once the rules are learned.

A simple demonstration illustrates this phenomenon. Read the 10 numbers printed below and see whether you have any trouble remembering them.

1 3 5 7 9 2 4 6 8 0

These numbers are easy to retain in short-term memory because we can remember a rule to chunk the numbers instead of 10 independent numbers. In this case, the rule concerns odd (1, 3, 5, 7, and 9) and even (2, 4, 6, 8, and 0) numbers. The actual limit of short-term memory, then, is seven chunks, not necessarily seven individual items. Thus, the total amount of information we can store in short-term memory depends on the particular rules we use to organize it.

In life outside the laboratory (and away from the textbook), we are seldom required to remember a series of numbers. The rules that organize our short term memories are much more complex than those that describe odd and even numbers, but the principles of chunking apply to more realistic learning situations. For example, say the group of words below, look away from the page, and try to recite the words from memory.

along got the was door crept locked slowly he until passage the he to which

No doubt you found the task hopeless; there was just too much information to store in short-term memory. Now try the following group of words:

He slowly crept along the passage until he got to the door, which was locked.

This time you were probably much more successful. Once the same 15 words are arranged in a sequence that makes sense, they are not difficult to store in short-term memory.

Unless we actively rehearse the material we are studying, we are unlikely to remember it for very long: It is relegated to short-term memory, in which information is stored for relatively short periods of time.

---

chunking A process by which information is simplified by rules, which make it easily remembered once the rules are learned. For example, the string of letters NBCCBSNPR is easier to remember if a person learns the rule that organizes them into smaller "chunks": NBC, CBS, and NPR.

The capacity of short-term memory for verbal material is not measured in letters, syllables, or words. Instead, the limit depends on how much *meaning* the information has. The first set of words above merely contains 15 different words. Because few people can immediately recite back more than five to nine independent items, we are not surprised to find that we cannot store 15 jumbled words in short-term memory. However, when the items are related, we can store many more of them. We do not have to string 15 words together in a meaningless fashion. Instead, we can let the image of a man creeping down a passage toward a locked door organize the new information. Thus, we can read or hear a sentence, understand what it means, and remember that meaning.

This aspect of short-term memory suggests a way of making working memory more efficient in everyday use. If information can be organized into a more meaningful sequence, there is less to be remembered. McNamara and Scott (2001) taught people to chain unrelated words together as they listened to them. The chaining technique was simple: People were to imagine a story involving these words. This technique sharply improved short-term memory. Later in this chapter, we discuss similar strategies to improve long-term memory.

Varieties of Working Memory

So far, you have seen short-term or working memory referred to in the singular, but evidence suggests that working memory can contain a variety of sensory information: visual, auditory, somatosensory, gustatory, and olfactory. It also can contain information about movements that we have just made (motor memories), and it may provide the means by which we rehearse movements that we are thinking about making. Is all this information contained in a single system, or do we have several independent working memories?

Baddeley (1993, 2000) has suggested that working memory consists of several components, all coordinated by a "central executive" function. One component maintains verbal information; another retains memories of visual stimuli. A third component might serve to store more general information, including memory for nonspeech sounds (such as the sound of your friend's voice over the telephone), touch, odors, or other types of information.

Phonological Working Memory Although we receive information from different senses, much of it can be encoded verbally. For example, we can see or smell a rose and think the word *rose*; we can feel the prick of a thorn and think the word *sharp*; and so on. Thus, seeing a rose, smelling a rose, and feeling a thorn can all result in words running through our working memory. How is verbal information stored in working memory?

Evidence suggests that the short-term storage of words, whether originally presented visually or acoustically, occurs in **phonological short-term memory**—short-term or working memory for verbal information. The Greek word *phōne* means both "sound" and "voice"; as the name implies, phonological coding could involve either the auditory system of the brain or the system that controls speech. As we shall see, it involves both.

In an experiment Conrad (1964) showed how quickly visually presented information becomes encoded acoustically. He briefly showed people lists of six letters (each list was shown within 4.5 seconds) and then asked them to write the letters. The errors these people made were almost always acoustical rather than visual. For instance, they sometimes wrote *B* when they had seen *V* (these letters sound similar), but they rarely wrote *F* when they had seen *T* (these letters look similar). Keep in mind that Conrad presented the letters visually. The results suggested that people read the letters, encoded them acoustically ("heard them in their minds"), and remembered them by rehearsing the letters as sounds. During this process, they might easily mistake a *V* for a *B*.

The fact that the errors seem to be acoustical may reflect a form of acoustical coding in working memory. That is, phonological memory may be produced by activity in the auditory system—say, circuits of neurons in the auditory association cortex. People often talk to themselves. Sometimes, it's aloud; sometimes, they whisper or simply move their lips. At other times, no movements can be detected, but people still report that they are thinking about saying something. They are engaging in **subvocal articulation,** an unvoiced speech utterance. Even though no actual speech movement may occur, it is still possible that activity occurs in the neural circuits in the brain that normally control speech. When we close our eyes and imagine seeing something, the mental image is undoubtedly caused by the activity of neurons in the visual association cortex. Similarly, when we imagine saying something, the "voice in our head" is probably controlled by the activity of neurons in the motor association cortex. Research suggests that even deaf children perform acoustical encoding in terms of the movements they would make to pronounce letters (Conrad, 1970). People may therefore use both acoustic and articulatory codes: They may simultaneously hear a word and feel themselves saying it in their heads. Phonological codes stored in long-term memory also may help to strengthen the rehearsed information (Roodenrys et al., 2002).

The best neurological evidence for the existence of phonological short-term memory comes from a disorder called **conduction aphasia,** which is usually caused by damage to a region of the left parietal lobe. Conduction aphasia appears as a profound deficit in phonological working memory. People who have conduction aphasia can talk and can comprehend what others are saying, but they are very poor at repeating precisely what they hear. When they attempt to repeat words that other people say, they often get the meaning correct but use different words. For example, if asked to repeat the sentence, "The cement truck ran over the bicycle," a person who has conduction aphasia may reply, "The concrete mixer got into an accident with a bike."

phonological short-term memory Short-term memory for verbal information.

subvocal articulation An unvoiced speech utterance.

conduction aphasia An inability to remember words that are heard, although they usually can be understood and responded to appropriately. This disability is caused by damage to Wernicke's and Broca's areas.

[FIGURE 7·5] A diagram showing how conduction aphasia is caused.

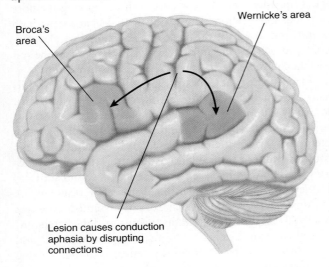

[FIGURE 7·5] A diagram showing how conduction aphasia is caused.

Broca's area

Wernicke's area

Lesion causes conduction aphasia by disrupting connections

Most investigators believe that conduction aphasia is caused by brain damage that disrupts the connections between two regions of the cerebral cortex that play important roles in people's language ability. These two regions are *Wernicke's area,* which is concerned with the perception of speech, and *Broca's area,* which is concerned with the production of speech. As we've seen, phonological working memory appears to involve both articulatory and acoustical coding. Because the brain damage that produces conduction aphasia disconnects regions of the brain involved in speech perception and production, perhaps the damage disrupts acoustical short-term memory by making such subvocal verbal rehearsal difficult or impossible. (See **FIGURE 7·5**.)

Visual Working Memory Verbal information can be received by means of the auditory system or the visual system—that is, we can hear words or read them. As we saw in the previous section, both forms of input produce acoustic and articulatory codes in phonological working memory, but much of the information we receive from the visual system is nonverbal. We recognize objects, perceive their locations, and find our way around the environment. We can look at objects, close our eyes, and then sketch or describe them. We can do the same with things we saw in the past. Thus, we apparently possess a working memory that contains visual information, either obtained from the immediate environment by means of the sense organs or retrieved from long-term memory.

Much of what we see is familiar; we have seen the particular items—or similar items—before. Thus, our visual working memory does not have to encode all the details, the way a photograph copies all the details in the scene gathered by the lens of a camera. For example, our short-term memory of the sight of a dog does not have to store every visual feature we saw, such as four legs, whiskers, ears, a tail. Instead, we already have mental images of dogs in our long-term memory. When we see a dog, we can

select a prototype that fits the bill, filling in a few features to represent the particular dog we just saw.

DeGroot (1965) performed an experiment that provides a nice example of the power of encoding visual information in working memory. He showed chessboards to expert players and to novices. If the positions of the pieces represented an actual game in progress, with legal moves, the experts could glance at the board for a few seconds and then look away and report the position of each piece; the novices could not. However, if the same number of pieces had been placed haphazardly on the board, the experts recognized immediately that their positions made no sense, and they could not remember their positions any better than a nonexpert could. Thus, the experts' short-term memories for the positions of a large number of chess pieces depended on organizational rules stored in long-term memory as a result of years of playing chess. Novices could not remember the location of the pieces in either situation, because they lacked long-term memories for patterns of chess pieces on a board and could not acquire the information as efficiently (Reingold, et al., 2001).

Humans have a remarkable ability to manipulate visual information in working memory. Shepard and Metzler (1971) presented people with pairs of drawings that could be perceived as three-dimensional constructions made of cubes. The participants' task was to see whether the shape on the right was identical to the shape on the left; some were and some were not. Even when the shapes were identical, the one on the right was sometimes drawn as if it had been rotated. For example, in **FIGURE 7·6**, the shape on the right in panel

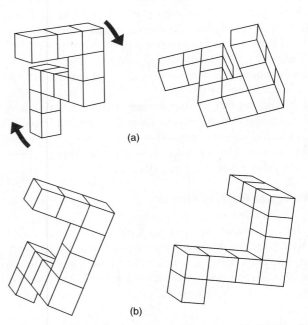

[**FIGURE 7·6**] The mental rotation task. (a) The shape on the right is identical to the one on the left but rotated 80 degrees clockwise. (b) The two shapes are different.

(Adapted from Shepard, R. N., & Metzler, J. Mental rotation of three-dimensional objects. *Science,* 1971, 171, 701–703. Reprinted with permission from AAAS. Copyright © 1971 by the AAAS.)

Expert chess players can remember the position of many pieces during a game because their experience allows efficient encoding.

(a) is identical but has been rotated clockwise 80 degrees; but in panel (b), the two shapes are different.

Shepard and Metzler found that people were very accurate in judging whether the pairs of shapes were the same or different. However, they took longer to decide when the right-hand shape was rotated. They reported that they formed an image of one of the drawings in their heads and rotated it until it was aligned the same way as the other one. (Mental manipulation of shapes is an important component of the ability to design and construct tools, buildings, bridges, and other useful objects.) If the participants' rotated images coincided with the other drawings, they recognized them as having the same shape. If they did not, they recognized them as being different (Shepard & Metzler, 1971).

Loss of Information from Short-Term Memory

The essence of short-term memory is its transience; hence, its name. Information enters from sensory memory and from long-term memory; is rehearsed, thought about, and modified; and then leaves. Some of the information controls ongoing behavior, and some of it causes changes in long-term memory, but ultimately it is lost from short-term memory. What causes it to leave?

As mentioned earlier, psychologists have described working memory as a kind of behavior that we use to maintain information over the short term. This way of thinking about working memory provides a useful framework to explain how we lose information, if we assume that information has a tendency to be degraded or to decay with time. Rehearsal activity of phonological short-term memory, such as subvocal articulation, prevents decay. Nairne (2002) has suggested a metaphor of how this might work. Working memory, Nairne says, is like a juggler trying to maintain several plates or balls in the air. As long as the juggler works actively at catching and throwing the plates, they don't fall and hit the ground (decay). With increased skill or more effort, the juggler can keep even more plates in the

air, but any distraction or other competing behavior will reduce the number of plates that can be juggled.

If you accept this metaphor, then consider this: Anything that makes the plates easier to handle should decrease the risk that they will be dropped. With respect to words, shorter words are easier to articulate and therefore should be easier to rehearse. Psychologists have shown that shorter words are remembered better under conditions of short-term memory (e.g., Tehan, Hendry, & Kocinski, 2001)—a finding that supports the rehearsal-and-decay explanation.

However, as Nairne himself points out, "decay" is a nonspecific term and risks falling prey to the nominal fallacy discussed in Chapter 2. Why should information decay? Perhaps more active processes work to degrade the information or to make it more difficult to recall. Later in this chapter, after we have surveyed long-term memory, we discuss one such possibility.

QUESTIONS TO CONSIDER

1. Suppose that someone has sustained a brain injury that prohibits her from putting information into, and getting information out of, long-term memory. Would this injury affect only her long-term memory, or would her short-term memory be affected, too? Can you think of an experiment that you could perform that would answer this question? What would this person's life be like?

2. Take a few moments to imagine the shortest route you can take to get from your home to your favorite restaurant. In terms of how your short-term memory operates, explain how you are able to accomplish this bit of mental imagery.

Learning and Encoding in Long-Term Memory

As we have seen, information that enters short-term memory may or may not be available later. It depends on the number of "chunks" of information and how much time has elapsed. But once information has successfully made its way into long-term memory, it remains relatively stable (Burt, Kemp, & Conway, 2001). Of course, we do forget things, but nevertheless, our brains have the remarkable ability to store vast amounts of information and numerous experiences from our past.

What kinds of information can be stored in long-term memory? To answer this question, let us consider the kinds of things we can learn. We can learn to recognize things: objects, sounds, odors, textures, and tastes. Thus, we can remember perceptions received by all of our sensory systems, which means that we have visual memories, auditory memories, olfactory memories, somatosensory memories, and gustatory memories. Perceptual memories also can contain information about the order in which events occurred, so we can remember the plot of a movie we saw or hear the melody of a song in our heads.

We can also learn from experience. We can learn to make new responses—as when we learn to operate a new machine,

The performance of complex behaviors likely involves connections between sensory and motor association areas of the cortex.

ride a bicycle, or say a new word—or we can learn to make old responses in new situations. Perceptual memories presumably involve alterations in circuits of neurons in the sensory association cortex of the brain—visual memories in the visual cortex, auditory memories in the auditory cortex, and so on. Memories that involve combinations of perceptual information presumably involve the establishment of connections between different regions of the association cortex. Motor memories (memories for particular behaviors) presumably involve alterations in circuits of neurons in the motor association cortex of the frontal lobes. Thus, learning to perform particular behaviors in particular situations likely involves the establishment of connections between the appropriate regions of the sensory and motor cortexes.

Memory involves both active and passive processes. Sometimes we use deliberate strategies to remember something (to encode the information into long-term memory), as when we rehearse the lines of a poem or memorize famous dates for a history course. At other times, we simply observe and remember without any apparent effort, as when we tell a friend about an interesting experience we had. Memories can be formed even without our being aware of having learned something. What factors determine whether we can eventually remember information and experiences? Let's look at some hypotheses that have been proposed.

The Consolidation Hypothesis

Hebb's dual-trace theory was based on the distinction between active processing of information and latent retention due to structural changes in the brain. One way to think about the traditional view of memory is that sensory memory and short-term memory represent information in its active state. That is, these two memory systems do not represent places in the brain *per se,* but instead are the result of brain processes that keep the information active (Crowder, 1993). Once this activity subsides, the information can be retained only through longer-lasting structural changes.

The change of information from a state of short-term activation into structural changes in the brain has been called

consolidation. These structural changes make the information stronger, easier to recall, and more resistant to forgetting. Consolidated information is long-term memory. Rehearsal itself is not consolidation; it is viewed as one of the mechanisms that allow consolidation to occur. In addition, consolidation may occur without awareness and could be a lengthy process.

Some of the best evidence in favor of the consolidation hypothesis comes from events that disrupt brain functioning. From the earliest times, people have observed that a blow to the head can affect memory. A blow to the head disrupts the balance in ions surrounding brain cells. The neurons' ion pumps increase as a result, causing large metabolic changes (Iverson, 2005). In such "closed-head injury" incidents, individuals' working memory seems to be strongly impaired (McAllister, et al., 2004). For example, Dutch amateur boxers were given standard tests for memory ability before and after a boxing match and compared with nonboxers who simply exercised; the memory scores for the boxers showed significant impairments (Matser, et al., 2000). In very severe cases, the injury produces a prolonged lack of memory for events, a condition called **retrograde amnesia** (*retro-* means "backward": in this case, backward in time). Consolidation theorists assume that this occurs because the brain centers for consolidation have been damaged. Significantly, retrograde amnesia shows a distinctive pattern: recent memories are affected more strongly than older ones (Brown, 2002). This is the pattern that consolidation theory would predict: recent memories have had less time to be consolidated and therefore are weaker, more difficult to retrieve, and more prone to forgetting.

The Levels-of-Processing Approach

The modal model discussed at the start of this chapter makes several assertions about the learning process. For one, the model asserts that all information gets into long-term memory only after passing through short-term memory. Also, it asserts that the most important factor determining whether a particular piece of information reaches long-term memory is the amount of time it spends in short-term memory.

Craik and Lockhart (1972) developed a different approach. They pointed out that the act of rehearsal may effectively keep information in short-term memory but does not necessarily result in the establishment of long-term memories. They suggested that people engage in two different types of rehearsal: maintenance rehearsal and elaborative rehearsal. **Maintenance rehearsal** is the rote repetition of verbal information—simply repeating an item over and over. This behavior serves to maintain the information in short-term

---

consolidation   The change of information from a state of short-term activation into structural changes in the brain. These changes are considered permanent and are hence part of long-term memory.

retrograde amnesia   Loss of the ability to retrieve memories of the past, particularly memories of episodic or autobiographical events.

maintenance rehearsal   Rote repetition of information; repeating a given item over and over again.

Taking notes while studying from a text (left) is a more active method of processing information than merely highlighting important passages in the text (right). Note taking involves deep processing, and highlighting involves shallow processing.

In contrast with the traditional model of rehearsal, Craik and Lockhart (1972) proposed a levels-of-processing framework for understanding the way information enters long-term memory. They suggested that memory is a by-product of perceptual analysis. A central processor, analogous to the central processing unit of a computer, can analyze sensory information on several different levels. Craik and Lockhart conceived of the levels as being hierarchically arranged, from shallow (superficial) to deep (complex), providing the kind of information as the earlier sentence did about the old man and the watch. A person can control the level of analysis by *paying attention* to different features of the stimulus. If a person focuses on the superficial sensory characteristics of a stimulus, then these features will be stored in memory. If the person focuses on the meaning of a stimulus and the ways in which it relates to other things the person already knows, then these features will be stored in memory. For example, consider the word written below.

memory but does not necessarily result in lasting changes. In contrast, when people engage in elaborative rehearsal, they think about the information and relate it to what they already know. **Elaborative rehearsal** involves more than new information. It involves deeper processing: forming associations, attending to the meaning of the information, thinking about that information, and so on. Thus, we *elaborate* on new information by recollecting related information already in long-term memory. Here's a practical example: You are more likely to remember information for a test by processing it deeply or meaningfully; simply rehearsing, or "cramming," the material to be tested will not do.

This example suggests that a memory is more effectively established if the item is presented in a rich context—a context that is likely to make us think about the item and imagine an action taking place. Consider the different images conjured up by these two sentences (Craik & Tulving, 1975):

He dropped the watch.

The old man hobbled across the room and picked up the valuable watch.

The second sentence provides much more information. The image that is evoked by the more-complex sentence provides the material for a more complex memory. This complexity makes the memory more distinctive and thus helps us pick it out from all the other memories we have.

tree

You can see that the word is written in black type, that the letters are lowercase, that the bottom of the stem of the letter *t* curves upward to the right, and so on. Craik and Lockhart referred to these characteristics as *surface features* and to the analysis of these features as **shallow processing**. Maintenance rehearsal is an example of processing that is relatively shallow. In contrast, consider the meaning of the word *tree*. You can think about how trees differ from other plants, what varieties of trees you have seen, what kinds of foods and what kinds of wood they provide, and so on. These features refer to a word's meaning and are called *semantic features*. Their analysis is called deep processing. Elaborative rehearsal is an example of deep processing. According to Craik and Lockhart, **deep processing** generally leads to better retention than surface processing does.

Knowledge, Encoding, and Learning You might think that memory would be related to knowledge: As we gain more knowledge over time, our recall of that knowledge ought to improve. However, merely possessing knowledge does not always facilitate recall; even the brightest people have problems with remembering things. What seems to be more important is what happens during the encoding of information. Remember, encoding involves getting material into memory. More than that, how we encode information is likely to affect our ability to remember it later. We have already seen that, to some degree, encoding information involves paying attention to it. We have also seen that if we can

---

elaborative rehearsal   Processing information on a meaningful level, such as forming associations, attending to the meaning of the material, thinking about it, and so on.

shallow processing   Analysis of the superficial characteristics of a stimulus, such as its size or shape.

deep processing   Analysis of the complex characteristics of a stimulus, such as its meaning or its relation to other stimuli.

make material more meaningful during encoding, we may decrease the likelihood of forgetting that information later.

Automatic Versus Effortful Processing. Psychologists and educators have long known that practicing or rehearsing information enhances retrieval. Practicing or rehearsing information, through either shallow or deep processing, is called **effortful processing.** As a student, you know that the more you concentrate on your studies, the more likely it becomes that you will do well on an exam. But your experience also tells you that you have stored information in memory that you never rehearsed in the first place. Somehow, without any effort, information is encoded into your memory. This formation of memories of events and experiences with little or no attention or effort is called **automatic processing.**

Encoding Specificity. When encoding is not automatic, it is effortful, and the most useful effort we can expend is to attempt to make the new material meaningful. We can think of making new or difficult material meaningful as *elaborative encoding;* you encountered this idea earlier as elaborative rehearsal. Two conclusions concern elaborative encoding. First, it seems clear that more rehearsal is better than less.

The second conclusion concerns **encoding specificity,** the principle that *how* we encode information determines our ability to retrieve it later. For example, suppose that someone reads you a list of words that you are to recall later. The list contains the word *beet* along with several terms related to music, such as *melody, tune,* and *jazz.* When asked if the list contained the names of any vegetables, you may report that it did not. Because of the musical context, you may have encoded *beet* as *beat* and never thought of the root vegetable while you were rehearsing the list (Flexser & Tulving, 1978).

Many experiments have made the point that meaningful elaboration during encoding is helpful and probably necessary for the formation of useful memories. Imagine, for example, trying to remember the following passage:

> With hocked gems financing him, our hero bravely defied all scornful laughter that tried to prevent his scheme. "Your eyes deceive," he had said. "An egg, not a table, correctly typifies this unexplored planet." Now three sturdy sisters sought proof, forging along, sometimes through calm vastness, yet more often over turbulent peaks and valleys. Days became weeks as many doubters spread fearful rumors about the edge. At last, from nowhere, welcome winged creatures appeared, signifying momentous success.

How do you think you would have done on this task? Could you have remembered this passage very well? Probably not, for it is phrased rather oddly. However, what if, *before* you read the paragraph, you were told that it had a title: "Columbus Discovers America"? Do you think you might have encoded the story differently and so improved your recall? Dooling and Lachman (1971) found that people who were told the title of a story such as this remembered the information much better, but if they were given

the title *after* they had read and processed the story, their recall was not improved (Bransford & Johnson, 1972). Apparently, the time to make information meaningful is during encoding.

Criticisms of the Levels-of-Processing Approach The concept of processing depth has been useful in guiding research efforts to understand how we learn and remember. However, many psychologists have noted that the distinction between shallow and deep processing has never been rigorously defined. The difference between looking at the shape of the letters of a word and thinking about its meaning is clear, but most instances of encoding cannot be so neatly categorized. The term *depth* seems to be metaphorical. It roughly describes the fact that information is more readily remembered when we think about it in relation to what we already know, but it is not exact and specific enough to satisfy most memory theorists.

Another problem with trying to understand exactly what is meant by a term such as *depth of processing* is that no matter what we may ask a person to do when we present a stimulus (for example, "Count the letters"), we have no way of knowing what else he or she may be doing that may aid recall of that item. In other words, researchers may not be able to control the depth to which a person processes information because they have no way of peering into his or her head and knowing exactly how the information is being manipulated. For each of us, our memory, its processes, and its contents are private. Memory, like all cognitive processes, is not an observable phenomenon.

Some psychologists have criticized the assertion that tasks that encourage people to focus on superficial features of stimuli inevitably lead to poorer memory than do tasks that encourage them to focus on deeper features. For example, after reading something new, people often can remember exactly where the information appeared on a page (Rothkopf, 1971). Despite such exceptions, however, the levels-of-processing approach has succeeded in showing that we deal with information in different ways depending on what we need to use it for. These ways provide a context for the way we later remember it.

Improving Long-Term Memory through Mnemonics

When we can imagine information vividly and concretely, and when it fits into the context of what we already know, it is easy to remember later. Earlier, I described how chaining words together in a meaningful pattern can improve working memory. Vividness and context can improve remembering;

---

effortful processing Practicing or rehearsing information through either shallow or deep processing.

automatic processing Forming memories of events and experiences with little or no attention or effort.

encoding specificity The principle that how we encode information determines our ability to retrieve it later.

[FIGURE 7•7] The method of loci. Items to be remembered are visualized in specific, well-known places.

Cheese

Milk

Eggs

Taco sauce

Lettuce

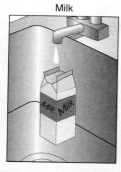

What do I need to get here?

mnemonic systems (from the Greek *mnemon,* meaning "mindful") that take advantage of this fact. **Mnemonic systems**—special techniques or strategies consciously used to improve memory—use information already stored in long-term memory to make memorization an easier task.

Mnemonic systems do not simplify information; they make it more elaborate. More information is stored, not less. However, the additional information makes the material easier to recall. Furthermore, mnemonic systems organize new information into a cohesive whole so that retrieval of part of the information ensures retrieval of the rest of it. These facts suggest that the ease or difficulty with which we learn new information depends not on *how much* we must learn but on *how well it fits with what we already know.* The better it fits, the easier it is to retrieve.

Method of Loci In Greece before the sixth century BCE, few people knew how to write, and those who did had to use cumbersome clay tablets. Consequently, oratory skills and memory for long epic poems (running for several hours) were highly prized, and some people earned their livings by cultivating these abilities. Because people could not carry around several hundred kilograms of clay tablets, they had to

keep important information in their heads. To do so, the Greeks devised the **method of loci,** a mnemonic system in which items to be remembered are mentally associated with specific physical locations. (The word *locus* means "place"; the plural is *loci,* pronounced "low sigh.")

Suppose that you wish to remember a short shopping list without writing it down. Your list consists of five items: cheese, milk, eggs, taco sauce, and lettuce. To use the method of loci technique, you would first think of a familiar place, perhaps your house. Next, you would mentally walk through your house, visually placing different items from your list at locations—*loci*—in the house: a package of cheese hanging from a coat rack, milk dripping from the kitchen faucet, eggs lying in the hallway, a bottle of taco sauce on the kitchen chair, and a head of lettuce on the sofa. (See **FIGURE 7•7.**) Then, in the grocery store, you would mentally retrace your path through the house and note what you had stored at the different loci. Any familiar location will do the trick as long as you can visually and vividly imagine the items to be remembered in the various landmarks.

Peg-Word Method A similar technique is the **peg-word method** (Miller, Galanter, & Pribram, 1960). As with the method of loci, the goal involves visually associating the new with the familiar. In the peg-word method, the familiar material is a set of "mental pegs" that you already have in memory. One way to create pegs is to take the numbers from 1 to 10 and rhyme each number with a peg word; for example, one is a bun, two is a shoe, three is a tree, four is a door, five is a hive, and so on. So for your grocery list you might imagine the package of cheese in a hamburger *bun,* a *shoe* full

---

mnemonic system A special technique or strategy consciously used in an attempt to improve memory.

method of loci (low-sigh) A mnemonic system in which items to be remembered are mentally associated with specific physical locations or landmarks.

peg-word method A mnemonic system in which items to be remembered are associated with a set of mental pegs already in memory, such as key words of a rhyme.

of milk, eggs dangling from a *tree*, taco sauce on a *door*, and the lettuce on top of a bee*hive*. In the grocery store you would review each peg word in order and recall the item associated with it. At first this technique may seem silly, but ample research suggests that it actually works (Marshark, et al., 1987).

Narrative Stories and Songs

Another useful aid to memory is to place information into a **narrative** to link items to be remembered together by a story. Bower and Clark (1969) showed that even inexperienced people can use this method. The investigators asked people to try to learn 12 lists of 10 concrete nouns each. They gave some of the people the following advice:

> A good way to learn the list of items is to make up a story relating the items to one another. Specifically, start with the first item and put it in a setting which will allow other items to be added to it. Then, add the other items to the story in the same order as the items appear. Make each story meaningful to yourself. Then, when you are asked to recall the items, you can simply go through your story and pull out the proper items in their correct order. (Bower & Clark, 1969, p. 181)

Here is a typical narrative, described by one of the participants (list words are italicized): "A *lumberjack darted* out of the forest, *skated* around a *hedge* past a *colony* of *ducks*. He tripped on some *furniture*, tearing his *stocking* while hastening to the *pillow* where his *mistress* lay."

People in the control group were merely asked to learn the lists and were given the same amount of time as the people in the "narrative" group to study them. Both groups could remember any given 10-word list equally well immediately afterward. However, when all of the lists had been learned, recall of all 120 words was far superior in the group that had constructed narrative stories.

Music, like narrative, provides a structure for information. Songs that link melody to a sequence of words could serve the same role as the narrative elements of a story. Many advertisers use music with their messages, apparently believing that placing their slogan in a song will improve its memorability (Yalch, 1991). Some evidence supports this notion. Wallace (1994) asked people to learn the words to a ballad by listening to either a spoken or a sung version. She found that, provided people had a chance to learn the melody of the song, they learned the sung ballad more quickly than the spoken version. Changing the melody after each verse, in contrast, failed to improve learning. Melodies also slow the rate at which you hear information, which can allow you to encode the information better (Kilgour, Jakobson, & Cuddy, 2000).

Obviously, mnemonic systems have their limitations. They are useful for memorizing information that can be reduced to a list of words, but not all information can easily be converted to such a form. For example, if you were preparing to take an examination on the information in this chapter, figuring out how to encode it into lists would probably take you more time than studying and learning it by the more-traditional methods suggested in the study guide.

QUESTION TO CONSIDER

Suppose that a friend comes to you for advice about studying for an upcoming English test. He explains to you that half of the test involves multiple-choice questions over key terms, and the other half involves essay questions about the narrative of several short stories. Based on what you now know about encoding and memory, what suggestions might you offer him regarding how to prepare for the test? (Hints: Is there a difference between how rote information is best encoded and how more elaborate, complex information is best encoded? What role might the idea of levels of processing play in preparation for a test?)

The Organization of Long-Term Memory

As we just saw, memorization is not a simple, passive process. Many investigators believe that long-term memory consists of more than a simple pool of information. Instead, different kinds of information are encoded differently and stored in different ways (Sherry & Schacter, 1987).

Episodic and Semantic Memory

Endel Tulving suggested that there are two kinds of long-term memory: episodic memory and semantic memory (Tulving, 1972). **Episodic memory** provides us with a record of our life experiences. Events stored there are autobiographical; episodic memory consists of memory about specific things

Long-term memory has no known limits. Shakespearean actors, like these actors performing a scene from *The Taming of the Shrew*, may remember their parts long after their performances are over.

---

narrative A mnemonic system in which items to be remembered are linked together by a story.

episodic memory A type of long-term memory that serves as a record of life experiences.

(a)

(b)

Remembering the correct spelling of a word involves semantic memory—memory for academic-type information (a). Remembering important life events, such as an important social event, involves episodic memory—memory for specific events that occurred at a specific time (b).

we have done, seen, heard, felt, tasted, and so on. The memories are tied to particular contexts: this morning's breakfast, your fifteenth birthday party, the first time you went skiing, and so forth. **Semantic memory** consists of conceptual information; it is a long-term store of data, facts, and information, including words and their meanings. Your knowledge of what psychology is, how human sensory systems operate, and how behavior is affected by its consequences is now part of your semantic memory. (If not, you need to review some of the material presented earlier in this book!) In other words, information of the "academic" type is stored as semantic memory. Semantic memories appear to interact with episodic ones. For example, when you go shopping, you undoubtedly remember the kinds of items you usually buy. Suppose you like yogurt for breakfast. Your preference is a fact about yourself that you recall from semantic memory. However, when you're trying to decide whether it's time to buy some more yogurt on this shopping trip, you'd probably try to think of the last time you looked in the refrigerator. Remembering whether you had eaten the last of the yogurt is a decision you would have to make from episodic memory.

The distinction between episodic and semantic memory reflects the fact that we make different uses of things we have learned: We describe things that happened to us (or that we witnessed) or talk about facts we have learned. The following case provides evidence that different brain regions are involved in episodic memory and semantic memory.

[**CASE STUDY**] K. C. was born in 1951. At the age of 30, he had a serious closed head injury in a motorcycle accident [that caused extensive brain damage]. . . . His intelligence

and language are normal; he has no problems with reading or writing; his ability to concentrate and to maintain focused attention are normal; his thought processes are clear; he can play the organ, chess, and various card games; his ability to visually imagine things is intact; and his performance on primary (short-term) memory tasks is normal. He knows many objective facts concerning his own life, such as his date of birth, the address of his home for the first 9 years of his life, the names of the some of the schools he attended, [and] the make and color of the car he once owned. . . . [However], he cannot recollect any personally experienced events. . ., whereas his semantic knowledge acquired before the critical accident is still reasonably intact. His knowledge of mathematics, history, geography, and other "school subjects," as well as his general knowledge of the world is not greatly different from others' at his educational level. (Tulving, 2002, pp. 13–14)

As you can see, K. C.'s episodic memories were destroyed by the brain damage that he sustained, but his semantic memories are relatively intact.

Explicit and Implicit Memory

For many years, most cognitive psychologists studied memory as a conscious operation. Experimenters presented people with lists of words, facts, episodes, or other kinds of stimuli and asked them to recognize or recollect the items later. In many cases, a verbal response was required. In recent decades, however, psychologists have come to appreciate the fact that people also possess an unconscious memory system, which is capable of controlling complex behaviors (Squire, 1992). Psychologists use the terms *explicit memory* and *implicit memory* when making this distinction. **Explicit memory** is memory of which we are aware; we know that we have learned something, and we can talk about what we have learned with others. (For this reason, some psychologists prefer to use the term *declarative memory*.) **Implicit memory** is unconscious;

---

semantic memory   A type of long-term memory that contains data, facts, and other information, including vocabulary.

explicit memory   Memory that can be described verbally and of which a person is therefore aware.

implicit memory   Memory that cannot be described verbally and of which a person is therefore not aware.

we cannot talk directly about its contents. However, the contents of implicit memory can affect our behavior. Some psychologists use the term *procedural memory,* because this system is responsible for remembering "how-to" skills such as bicycle riding; still others use the term *nondeclarative memory.* (See FIGURE 7•8.)

Implicit memory appears to operate automatically. It does not require deliberate attempts on the part of the learner to memorize something. It does not seem to contain facts; instead, it controls behaviors. For example, suppose we learn to ride a bicycle. We do so quite consciously and develop episodic memories about our attempts: who helped us learn, where we rode, how we felt, how many times we fell, and so on. But we also acquire implicit memories: We learn to ride. We learn to make automatic adjustments with our hands and bodies that keep our center of gravity above the wheels. Most of us cannot describe the rules that govern our behavior. For example, what do you think you must do if you start falling to the right while riding a bicycle? Many cyclists would say that they compensate by leaning to the left. But they are wrong; what they really do is turn the handlebars to the right. Leaning to the left would actually make them fall faster, because it would force the bicycle even farther to the right. The point is that although they have learned to *make* the appropriate movements, they cannot necessarily describe in words what these movements are.

The acquisition of specific behaviors and skills (such as driving a car, turning the pages of a book, playing a musical instrument, dancing, throwing and catching a ball, etc.) is probably the most important form of implicit memory. We do not need to be able to describe these activities to perform them. We may not be aware of all the movements involved while we are performing them.

The Biological Basis of Long-Term Memory

Psychologists agree that long-term memory involves more or less permanent changes in the structure of the brain. Much of what we know about the biology of human memory has been derived from studies of people who have memory loss—amnesia—or from studies of animals in which investigators use some of the methods described in Chapter 3 to learn more about the specific brain mechanisms involved in memory. In more recent years, functional imaging studies with humans help us determine which parts of the brain become active when we learn or remember particular kinds of memories.

Human Anterograde Amnesia Damage to particular parts of the brain can permanently impair people's ability to form new long-term memories, a phenomenon known as **anterograde amnesia.** (*Anterograde* means "in a forward direction.") The brain damage can be caused by the effects of long-term alcoholism, severe malnutrition, disease, stroke, head trauma, or surgery (Parkin et al., 1991). In most cases, people with anterograde amnesia can still remember events that occurred before the damage, but they cannot remember what has happened since that time. They do not learn the names of people they subsequently meet, even if they see them daily for years. For these people, yesterday is always some time in the past, before they sustained their brain damage. (Yes, as time goes by, they are surprised to see such an old person looking back at them in the mirror.)

One of the most famous cases of anterograde amnesia is that of patient H. M. (Milner, Corkin, & Teuber, 1968; Milner, 1970; Corkin et al., 1981). H. M.'s case is interesting because his amnesia is both severe and relatively uncontaminated by other serious neuropsychological deficits.

[CASE STUDY] In 1953, when H. M. was 27, a neurosurgeon removed part of the temporal lobe on both sides of his brain. The surgery was performed to alleviate very severe epilepsy, which was not responding to drug treatment. The surgery cured the epilepsy, but it caused anterograde amnesia. (This type of operation is no longer performed.)

Since the operation, H. M. has been unable to learn anything new. He cannot identify by name people he has met since the operation. His family moved to a new house after his operation, and he never learned how to get around in the new neighborhood. (His parents have since died, and he now lives in a nursing home where he can be cared for.) He is capable of remembering a small amount of verbal information as long as he is not distracted; constant rehearsal can maintain information in his short-term memory. However, rehearsal does not appear to have any long-term effects; if he is distracted for a moment, he will completely forget whatever he had been rehearsing. Indeed, because he so quickly forgets what previously happened, he does not easily become bored. He can endlessly reread the same magazine or laugh at the same jokes, finding them fresh and new each time.

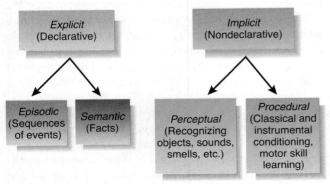

[**FIGURE 7•8**] Major categories of long-term memory.

---

anterograde amnesia A condition in which a person has difficulty forming new long-term memories of events that occur after that time.

H. M. is aware that he has a memory problem. For example, here is his response to an investigator's question.

> Every day is alone in itself, whatever enjoyment I've had, and whatever sorrow I've had. . . . Right now, I'm wondering. Have I done or said anything amiss? You see, at this moment everything looks clear to me, but what happened just before? That's what worries me. It's like waking from a dream; I just don't remember. (Milner, 1970, p. 37)

Since the case of H. M. was reported, many investigators have described similar cases of people who acquired an anterograde amnesia after sustaining damage to the temporal lobes. The critical site of damage appears to be the hippocampus, a structure located deep within the temporal lobe, and regions of the cortex of the medial temporal lobe with which the hippocampus is connected. (Look back at Figure 4.29, which illustrates the shape and location of the hippocampus.)

H. M.'s memory deficit is striking and dramatic. However, when he and other patients with anterograde amnesia are studied more carefully, it becomes apparent that the amnesia does not represent a total failure in learning ability. When the patients are appropriately trained and tested, we find that they are able to acquire new implicit (nondeclarative) memories. For example, Cavaco et al. (2004) tested amnesic patients on a variety of tasks modeled on real-world activities, such as weaving, tracing figures, operating a stick that controlled a video display, and pouring water into small jars. Both amnesic patients and normal subjects did poorly on these tasks at first, but their performance improved through practice. Thus, as you can see, patients with anterograde amnesia are capable of a variety of tasks that require perceptual learning, stimulus–response learning, and motor learning.

The most remarkable thing is that although the patients can learn to perform these tasks, *they do not remember anything about having learned them.* They do not remember the experimenters, the room in which the training took place, the apparatus that was used, or any events that occurred during the training. When we learn to ride a bicycle, we form two different kinds of memories: explicit (episodic) memories—the details of who taught us and where the training took place—and implicit (nondeclarative) memories—the skills required to ride a bicycle successfully. Clearly, the hippocampus is involved in forming new explicit memories, but is not necessary for the formation of new implicit memories.

After H. M.'s family moved, he was unable to learn how to get around in the new neighborhood. Many studies have found that one of the features of anterograde amnesia is the inability to form new spatial memories—to learn to use spatial cues to navigate in a new environment. For example, Luzzi et al. (2000) reported the case of a man with temporal lobe damage who lost his ability to find his way around a new environment. The only way he could find his room was by counting doorways from the end of the hall or by seeing a red napkin that was located on top of his bedside table.

The Roles of the Hippocampus and Basal Ganglia

Just what role does the hippocampus play in the consolidation of episodic memories? Through its connections with the medial temporal cortex, the hippocampus receives information from all association areas of the cerebral cortex and sends information back to them (Gluck & Myers, 1997). Thus, the hippocampal formation is in a position to know—and to influence—what is going on elsewhere in the brain. Most investigators believe that permanent long-term memories of episodes are stored in the cerebral cortex, not in the hippocampus. However, through its connections with the cerebral cortex, the hippocampus plays an essential role in consolidating these memories. The consolidation process takes time, but once it is completed, the hippocampus is no longer needed for retrieval of the memory of these episodes. Thus, people with anterograde amnesia are able to recall episodic memories of events that occurred before their brain damage occurred (Miyashita, 2004; Squire & Bayley, 2007).

If declarative memories are consolidated through the actions of the hippocampus, what brain regions are responsible for nondeclarative memories? Evidence suggests that the basal ganglia play an essential role. Several experiments have shown that people with diseases of the basal ganglia have deficits that can be attributed to difficulty in learning automatic responses. For example, Owen et al. (1992) found that patients with Parkinson's disease were impaired on learning a visually

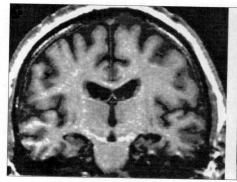 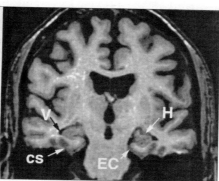

An *f*MRI photo of a brain with a larger-than-average hippocampus as compared to an fMRI of a normal brain.

cued instrumental conditioning task, and Willingham and Koroshetz (1993) found that patients with Huntington's disease failed to learn a sequence of button presses. (Parkinson's disease and Huntington's disease are both degenerative diseases of the basal ganglia.)

A series of experiments using both structural and functional brain imaging provides evidence for the role of the hippocampus in declarative learning and the role of the basal ganglia in nondeclarative learning. Hartley et al. (2003) trained subjects to find their way in a computerized virtual-reality town. Some subjects became acquainted with the town by exploring it, giving them the opportunity to learn where various landmarks (shops, cafés, etc.) were located with respect to each other. Other subjects were trained to follow a specific pathway from one landmark to the next, making a sequence of turns to get from a particular starting point to another. The investigators hypothesized that the first task, which involved spatial learning, would require the participation of the hippocampus, whereas the second task, which involved learning a set of specific responses to a set of specific stimuli, would require the participation of the basal ganglia. The results were as predicted: Functional MRI revealed that the spatial task activated the hippocampus, and the response task activated the caudate nucleus (a component of the basal ganglia).

Iaria et al. (2003) used a similar task that permitted subjects to learn a maze either through distant spatial cues or through a series of turns. About half of the subjects spontaneously used spatial cues, and the other half spontaneously learned to make a sequence of responses at specific locations. Again, *f*MRI showed the hippocampus was activated in people who followed the spatial strategy and the caudate nucleus was activated in those who followed the response strategy. Even more remarkably, a structural MRI study by Bohbot et al. (2007) found that people who tended to follow a spatial strategy had a larger-than-average hippocampus, and people who tended to follow a response strategy had a larger-than-average caudate nucleus. (You may recall from Chapter 3 that the right hippocampus of London taxi drivers, who have learned an extremely complex layout of streets, is larger than average.)

Explicit Memory in Animals Although the words "explicit" and "declarative" cannot apply to nonhuman animals (after all, they cannot talk), the distinction between these two categories of memory systems is also seen in species besides our own. Although we cannot ask laboratory animals to tell us about episodes that occurred earlier in their lives, we can certainly determine whether they can perform spatial tasks similar to the ones just described.

In one common spatial learning task, rats are placed in a large circular tank filled with water mixed with an opaque white powder. This apparatus is known as the "Morris water maze," after the investigator who developed it (Morris et al., 1982). The murky water hides the location of a small platform, situated just beneath the surface of the liquid. The experimenters put the rats into the water and let them swim until they encounter the hidden platform and climb onto it. They release the rats from a new position on each trial, which means that they cannot simply learn to swim in a particular direction. After a few trials, normal rats learn to swim directly to the hidden platform from wherever they were released.

The Morris water maze requires spatial learning; to navigate around the maze, the animals get their bearings from the relative locations of stimuli located outside the maze—furniture, windows, doors, and so on. But the maze can be used for stimulus–response learning, too. If the animals are always released at the same place, they learn to head in a particular direction—say, toward a particular landmark they can see above the wall of the maze (Eichenbaum, Stewart, & Morris, 1990).

If rats with hippocampal lesions are always released from the same place, they learn this nonrelational, stimulus–response task about as well as normal rats do. However, if they are released from a new position on each trial, they swim in what appears to be an aimless fashion until they finally encounter the platform. (See **FIGURE 7•9.**)

One of the most intriguing discoveries about the hippocampal formation was made by O'Keefe and Dostrovsky (1971), who recorded the activity of individual pyramidal cells in the hippocampus as an animal moved around the environment. The experimenters found that some neurons fired at a high rate only when the rat was in a particular location. Different neurons had different *spatial receptive fields;* that is, they responded when the animals were in different locations. A particular neuron might fire twenty times per second when the animal was in a particular location but only a few times per hour when the animal was located elsewhere. For obvious reasons, these neurons were named **place cells.**

When a rat is placed in a symmetrical chamber, where few cues exist to distinguish one part of the apparatus from another, the animal must keep track of its location from objects it sees (or hears) in the environment outside the maze. Changes in these items affect the firing of the rats' place cells as well as their navigational ability. When experimenters move the stimuli as a group, maintaining their relative positions, the animals simply reorient their responses accordingly. However, when the experimenters interchange the stimuli so that they are arranged in a new order, the animals' performance (and the firing of their place cells) is disrupted. (Imagine how disoriented you might be if you entered a familiar room and found that the windows, doors, and furniture were in new positions.)

Evidence indicates that firing of hippocampal place cells appears to reflect the location where an animal "thinks" it is. Skaggs and McNaughton (1998) constructed an apparatus that contained two nearly identical chambers

---

place cell A neuron that becomes active when the animal is in a particular location in the environment; most typically found in the hippocampal formation.

[**FIGURE 7·9**] The Morris water maze. (a) Environmental cues present in the room provide information that permits the animals to orient themselves in space. (b) Variable and fixed start positions. Normally, rats are released from a different position on each trial. If they are released from the same position every time, the rats can learn to find the hidden platform through stimulus-response learning. (c) Performance of normal rats and rats with hippocampal lesions using variable or fixed start positions. Hippocampal lesions impair acquisition of the relational task. (d) Representative samples of the paths followed by normal rats and rats with hippocampal lesions on the relational task (variable start positions).

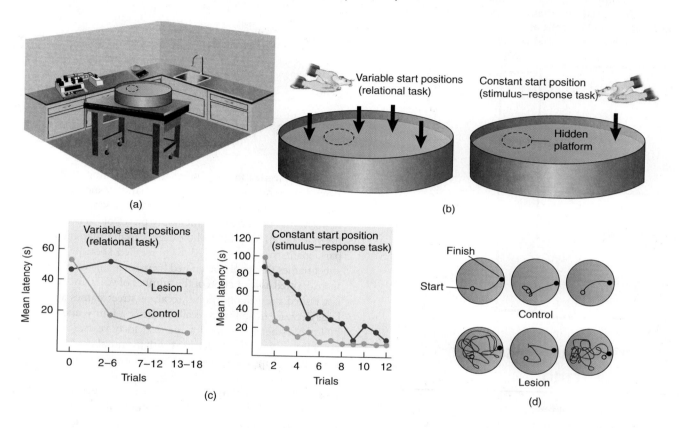

connected by a corridor. Each day, rats were placed in one of the chambers, and a cluster of electrodes in the animals' brains recorded the activity of hippocampal place cells. Each rat was always placed in the same chamber each day. Some of the place cells showed similar patterns of activity in each of the chambers, and some showed different patterns, which suggests that the hippocampus "realized" that there were two different compartments but also "recognized" the similarities between them. Then, on the last day of the experiment, the investigators placed the rats in the other chamber of the apparatus. For example, if a rat was usually placed in the north chamber, it was placed in the south chamber. The firing pattern of the place cells in at least half of the rats indicated that the hippocampus "thought" it was in the usual chamber—the one to the north. However, once the rat left the chamber and entered the corridor, it saw that it had to turn to the left to get to the other chamber and not to the right. The animal apparently realized its mistake, because for the rest of that

session the neurons fired appropriately. They displayed the "north" pattern in the north chamber and the "south" pattern in the south chamber. (See **FIGURE 7·10**.)

QUESTIONS TO CONSIDER

1. What is your earliest memory? How old were you? Why do you think you can't remember events that occurred before that time?

2. When getting directions to a particular location in an unfamiliar city, some people prefer step-by-step directions (turn right at the third traffic light, cross the railroad tracks, turn left at the next stop sign, etc.), whereas others prefer to have a map that they can follow. What are the advantages and disadvantages of each strategy? How would you expect these preferences to be related to the hippocampus and caudate nucleus?

[**FIGURE 7•10**] The apparatus used in the study by Skaggs and McNaughton (1998). Place cells reflect the location where the animal "thinks" it is. Because the rat was normally placed in the north chamber, its hippocampal place cells responded as if it were there when it was placed in the south chamber one day. However, once it stuck its head into the corridor, it saw that the other chamber was located to its right, so it "realized" that it had just been in the south chamber. From then on, the pattern of firing of the hippocampal place cells accurately reflected the chamber in which the animal was located.

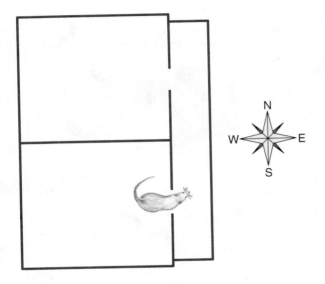

Remembering, Recollecting, and Forgetting

So far, we have looked at research and theorizing on the act of learning and the nature of long-term memory. But what do we know about remembering, the process of retrieving information from long-term memory, and forgetting, the absence of this process?

How Long Does Memory Last?

The question "How long does memory last?" has fascinated psychologists and other researchers for many years. In fact, a German psychologist, Hermann Ebbinghaus, reported the results of the first experiment to determine memory duration back in 1885. Using himself as a participant, Ebbinghaus memorized 13 nonsense syllables such as *dax, wuj, lep,* and *pib*. He then studied how long it took him to relearn the original list after intervals varying from a few minutes up to 31 days. **FIGURE 7•11** shows what he found. Much of what he learned was forgotten very quickly—usually within a day or two. But even after 31 days, he could still recall some of the original information.

Ebbinghaus's research dealt with remembering nonsense syllables. What about remembering aspects of real life? For example, how long might you remember the important experiences of your youth? Schmidt et al. (2000) tried to answer this question by asking former students of an elementary school in

[**FIGURE 7•11**] Ebbinghaus's (1885) forgetting curve.

(Adapted from Ebbinghaus, H. (1885/1913). *Memory: A contribution to experimental psychology.* (Translated by H. A. Ruger & C. E. Bussenius.) New York: Teacher's College, Columbia University.)

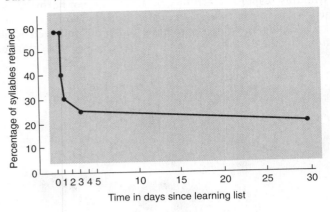

the city of Heerlen in the Netherlands to recall the street names around the school. Dutch cities have many meandering streets, so the participants of this study would have had extensive experience trying to remember the many places of their childhood neighborhood. Schmidt and colleagues found that, on average, participants who had moved away recalled about 60% of the street names that could be named by participants who still lived there. Plotted as a function of the number of years since they had last visited the neighborhood, recall of street names showed a large decrease in ability to recall for the first four years, followed by little further forgetting for the next forty years. (See **FIGURE 7•12**.) Interestingly, recall declined with the number of times participants had moved between different cities, showing that another city's geography could interfere with their memory. We'll return to this possibility in the next section. In general, the rate of forgetting of this kind of information, which also includes knowledge of a second language, people's names, music, and special situations, is greatest in the first few years after it is learned and decreases slowly afterwards (Bahrick, 1984; Kausler, 1994).

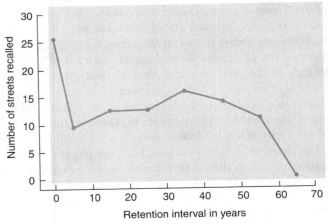

[**FIGURE 7•12**] Observed number of street names recalled by former students of a Dutch elementary school as a function of the years that they were not exposed to the neighborhood.

Researchers have found that there is little decline in recall of information such as names and faces, even after 50 years.

focus On

Cultural Contexts for Remembering

Although it is true that many people "know" the same things—the basic rules of arithmetic, the fact that the sun rises in the east, and so on—it is also true that the way we use our memory, the way we get information out of our memory, and the personal meaning of that information differ considerably from person to person. We should not be surprised to learn, then, that culture provides an important context for remembering.

Some researchers, such as Mistry and Rogoff (1994), argue that "remembering is an activity that is defined . . . in terms of its function in the social and cultural system" (p. 141). According to this view, the act of remembering cannot be separated from its cultural context. In support of this position, let's consider two studies that compared the remembering abilities of Guatemalan Maya and American children.

In the first study (Rogoff & Waddell, 1982), the children were given a test of free recall of lists of material they had learned earlier. The American children performed better—after all, American children learn such lists consistently in school: names, dates, places, events, and so on. Maya children receive no such training. In their agriculturally based culture, this sort of information is of little practical value.

To compare how children from these two cultures would perform on a task that was not biased toward the experiences common to children in either culture, Rogoff and Waddell had the Maya and American children watch a local researcher place 20 small toy objects (cars, animals, and so on) in a model of a country village. After the children viewed the scene for a few minutes, the objects were removed and mixed in with 60 other objects from which the 20 items had been originally selected. After a short delay, each child was asked to reconstruct the scene the way the researcher had constructed it. This time, the Maya children performed as well as the American children. (In fact, they did slightly better.) The cross-cultural differences were eliminated when the American children were not permitted to use well-practiced, culturally based mnemonic strategies. The Maya children did not have defective memories; their culture simply had not prepared them for learning long lists of unrelated items.

Cultural customs also seem to affect remembering. In a second study, Rogoff and Waddell asked American and Maya children to recall a story five minutes after hearing it told in their respective native languages by a local teenager. Although the story was taken from Maya oral history, neither the Maya nor the American children had heard the story before. Interestingly, though, the American children seemed to remember the story better than the Maya children did, as evidenced by their retelling of the story to an adult. For example, consider the responses of two children, one from each culture (as cited in Mistry & Rogoff, 1994).

As retold by the Maya child:

> When the angel came, cha (so I have been told), from Heaven, well, when the angel came, he came to see the flood (The adult listener prompts: What else?) He ate the flesh of the people. . . . (and then?) He didn't return right away, cha. . . . (What else?) That's all. He threw up, cha, he threw up cha, the flesh. "I like the flesh," he said, cha. . . . (What else?) "Now you're going to become a buzzard," they told him, cha. . . . (With further prompts, the retelling continued similarly.) (p. 140)

Here is the same story as retold by an American child:

> There once was a buzzard and he was an angel in heaven and God sent him down to . . . to take all the dead animals and um, and so the buzzard went down and he ate the animals and then he was so full he couldn't get back up to heaven and so he waited another day and then he flew back up to heaven and God said, "You're not an angel anymore," and he goes, "Why?" And . . . and he said that "you ate the raw meat and now you're a buzzard and you'll have and . . . and you'll have to eat the garbage," and . . . and he goes, "I didn't eat anything," and God said, "Open your mouth and let's see," and then he opened his mouth and there was all the raw meat and he goes, "It's true I did eat, I did eat the meat," and God goes, "That's . . . that's why you're the buzzard now," and the . . . and the . . . and . . . and so the buzzard flew down and he, um, then he ate all the trash and everything. (p. 139)

If you were asked to say which of these children retold the story better, clearly you would say the American child did. You would probably express some surprise at the Maya child's *inability to remember* the story any better than he did. What you might not know, though, is that in Maya culture, children do not speak openly to adults. When they cannot avoid speaking to an adult, they must include the word *cha* (so I have been told) in their conversation to show to the adult that they are not behaving disrespectfully by having superior knowledge. Thus, the Maya child may have remembered the story, but the discomfort produced

The culture in which we are raised plays an important role in providing us with learning experiences and memories of those experiences.

by having to retell it to an adult may have interfered with his ability to provide the adult with the story's details. In contrast, the American child, who undoubtedly was used to speaking freely to adults, *appeared* to have a better memory for the story.

Remembering or verbally expressing a memory is not an activity that occurs independent of cultural practices and rules. Culture influences remembering to the extent that it provides the context for what information is learned, the strategies for learning it, and social contingencies for expressing it.

Remembering and Recollecting

Remembering is a process that seems enormously variable. Thinking about examinations you may have taken should help make that point. Sometimes the information you need comes to mind immediately; at other times, it's an effort to remember information you just studied. In these latter cases, what is effortful is the attempt to come up with the thoughts (the internal stimuli) that cause the information to be retrieved.

The retrieval of implicit memories seems automatic: When the appropriate stimulus occurs, it automatically evokes the appropriate response. For example, when I open my car door, I do not have to think about how the latch works; my hand goes to the appropriate place, my fingers arrange themselves in the proper positions, and I make the necessary movements. In some cases, explicit memories, too, are retrieved automatically. Whisper your name to yourself. How did you manage to remember what your name is? How did you retrieve the information needed to move your lips in the proper sequence? Those questions simply cannot be answered by the method of introspection. The information simply pops out at us when the proper question is asked (or, more generally, when the appropriate stimulus is encountered).

Reading provides a particularly compelling example of the automatic nature of memory retrieval. When an experienced reader looks at a familiar word, the name of the word occurs immediately, and so does the meaning. It is difficult to look at a word and not think of its name. FIGURE 7•13 contains a list of words that can be used to demonstrate a phenomenon known as the Stroop effect (MacLeod, 1991; Stroop, 1935). Look at the words and, as quickly as you can, say the names of the colors in which the words are printed; do not read the words themselves.

Most people cannot completely ignore the words and simply name the colors; the tendency to think of the words and pronounce them is difficult to resist. The Stroop effect indicates that even when we try to suppress a well-practiced memory, it tends to be retrieved automatically when the appropriate stimulus occurs.

But what about the fact that some memories seem to be difficult to recall? The experience is often frustrating. We know that the information is "in there someplace," but we just cannot seem to get it out: "Oh, what is his name? I can see his face; he has a moustache, and he's skinny. It seems like his

[FIGURE 7·13] The Stroop effect. Name the color in which each word is printed as quickly as you can; you will find it difficult to ignore what the words say.

blue blue blue **green**
green **yellow** red
yellow yellow blue
red green yellow
yellow green **yellow**
yellow **red yellow**
green blue yellow
red blue green **green**
blue blue **green red**

name starts with a D: Don? No. Dave? Nope. Dennis? No, that's not it either—what is his name?! Now I remember, his name is Doug. Doug Hoisington, a friend of mine in New York." This phenomenon is known as the **tip-of-the-tongue phenomenon** and has fascinated psychologists since the days of William James (1893). It was first studied carefully during the 1960s (Brown & McNeill, 1966), and since then we have learned a good deal about it (A. S. Brown, 1991). It is a common, if not universal, experience; it occurs about once a week and increases with age; it often involves proper names and knowing the first letter of the word; and it is solved during the experience about 50% of the time.

The active search for stimuli that will evoke the appropriate memory, as exemplified in the tip-of-the-tongue phenomenon, has been called recollection (Baddeley, 1982). Recollection may be aided by contextual variables, including physical objects, suggestions, or other verbal stimuli. These contextual variables are called retrieval cues. For example, if you're trying to remember who gave you a particular gift at your last birthday party, you might find it helpful to look at photographs. The pictures of the people and the image of the scene provide retrieval cues for the information you're trying to recall.

Retrieval cues demonstrate that memory may be a response to internal stimuli. When we say we remember some-

---

tip-of-the-tongue phenomenon An occasional problem with retrieval of information that we are sure we know but cannot immediately remember.

retrieval cues Contextual variables, including physical objects, or verbal stimuli, that improve the ability to recall information from memory.

thing, we are describing that response. But are we describing that response accurately?

Marcia Johnson has argued that remembering is based on our ability to discriminate different responses to retrieval cues (Johnson, 2006). Her theory is known as the source-monitoring framework and is based on the premise that remembering requires the ability to discriminate between different internal experiences. Experiences that are due to real episodes in our life must be differentiated from other experiences, based on vividness, plausibility, emotional context, and other factors.

For example, suppose you have an heated discussion with your mother. Later that day, you describe this to your brother when he comes home from work, who takes your mother's side and repeats many of her arguments, adding some of his own. If you try to recall this incident months later, you now have a problem: Which of the arguments were hers and which were your brother's? Both are vivid and both elicit the emotion you felt at the time. Because they're so similar, you might find it hard to distinguish who said what. Indeed, you might even fail to distinguish that you had two separate arguments and "remember" that you were arguing with both your mother and your brother at the same time.

The source-monitoring framework suggests that retrieval cues are supplemented by perceptual and cognitive processes that help us evaluate the accuracy of a memory. In the example we've been discussing, you might rely on logical clues to refine your memory, such as deducing that because your brother worked that day, he couldn't have been present when you argued with your mother. Johnson's approach to memory emphasizes the extent to which the subjective qualities of experience, our knowledge, and the social and motivational context of an episode are all factors that determine our ability to remember. These can be very important: in the Focus On section later in this chapter, we see how errors in source monitoring cause people to "remember" airplane crashes that they could not possibly have seen.

Forgetting and Interference

Although long-term memory appears to last for a long time, you have probably heard the notion that people often forget something they once knew because so much time has elapsed since the memory was last used that the memory has *decayed*. A similar term has been used to describe the loss of items from short-term memory when they are not rehearsed. But the notion that items are forgotten because they decay provides little explanation. Why does time have this effect? One popular alternative explanation for long-term memory failure is *interference*. (It has also been used to describe some aspects of short-term memory failure as well.)

The concept of interference is based on the well-established finding that some memories may interfere with the retrieval of others. An early study by Jenkins and Dallenbach (1924) showed that we are less likely to remember information after an interval of wakefulness than after an

What do these famous lines have in common? "Beam me up, Scotty," "Me Tarzan, you Jane," "Play it again, Sam," "Elementary, my dear Watson"? Their fame, yes. But none of these lines attributable to their characters were actually said. The fact that people quote them may lead you to remember them incorrectly, as the source monitoring framework would suggest.

[**FIGURE 7•14**] Interference in memory retrieval. The graph shows the mean number of nonsense syllables people recalled after sleeping or staying awake for varying intervals of time.

(Adapted from Jenkins, J. G., & Dallenbach, K. M. (1924). Oblivescence during sleep and waking. *American Journal of Psychology, 1924, 35,* 605–612. Copyright © 1924 by the Board of Trustees of the University of Illinois. Used with permission of the University of Illinois.)

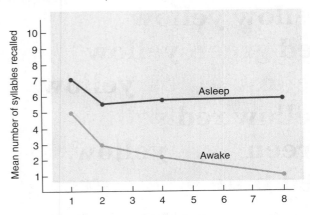

interval of sleep, presumably because of new memories that are formed when we are awake. (See **FIGURE 7•14**.)

Subsequent research soon showed that two types of interference exist in retrieval. Sometimes we experience **retroactive interference**—when we try to retrieve information, other information, which we have learned more recently, interferes. The top part of **FIGURE 7•15** charts how researchers test for the effects of retroactive interference. The experimental group first learns a list of words (we'll call the list "A"). Next, during the retention interval, the experimental group learns a second list of words, "B." Finally, the experimental group is asked to recall the first list of words ("A"). Meanwhile, the control group learns only the words in list "A"—the group is not asked to learn the words in list "B" during the retention interval. However, the control group is asked to recall the words in list "A" immediately after the retention interval. If the experimental group recalls fewer words during the test than does the control group,

retroactive interference is said to have occurred in the people in that group.

To take a real-life example, you may have a hard time recalling the presents you received on your seventh birthday because you have had many birthdays since. If your seventh birthday had been just yesterday, you would likely show perfect recall. When memories that interfere with retrieval are formed *after* the learning that is being tested, we have retroactive interference.

At other times, retrieval is impaired by **proactive interference,** in which our ability to recall new information is reduced because of information we learned previously. The bottom

---

retroactive interference Interference in recall that occurs when recently learned information disrupts our ability to remember older information.

proactive interference Interference in recall that occurs when previously learned information disrupts our ability to remember newer information.

Retroactive Interference

Group	Initial learning	Retention interval	Retention test
Experimental	Learn A	Learn B	Recall A
Control	Learn A		Recall A

Proactive Interference

Group	Initial learning		Retention interval	Retention test
Experimental	Learn A	Learn B		Recall B
Control		Learn B		Recall B

[**FIGURE 7•15**] Retroactive and proactive interference.

part of Figure 7.15 illustrates the experimental procedure used to test for proactive interference. In this procedure, before learning a list (we'll call it list "B" in this procedure) the experimental group learns the words in another list, "A." The control group learns only the words in list "B." Both groups then experience a retention interval before they are asked to recall the words in list "B." If the experimental group recalls fewer words in list "B" during the test than does the control group, proactive interference is said to have occurred.

For example, let's assume that you took French for several years in high school and that you are now taking a Spanish class in college. You find that some of the knowledge and study skills from high school are beneficial, but occasionally you discover that when you try to recall some Spanish, French pops up instead.

As reasonable and intuitive as the concept of interference may be, it has not gone unchallenged. Researchers agree that interference can affect retrieval, but some argue that the kinds of recall tasks people are asked to perform in the laboratory are exceptionally likely to be affected by interference. In real life, such effects may not be so powerful. For example, meaningful prose, such as the kind found in novels, is resistant to interference. Laboratory studies most often use lists of nonsense syllables and unrelated words.

Reconstruction: Remembering as a Creative Process

Much of what we recall from long-term memory is not an accurate representation of what actually happened. Many errors in memory, however, are not mere inaccuracies: They tend to show systematic patterns. Often, our recollection corresponds to what makes sense to us at the time we retrieve it. It becomes, in other words, a plausible account of what *might* have happened or even of what we think *should* have happened. Psychologists have long recognized that the context of remembering is a very important determinant of memory.

The Role of Schemas From the discussion about encoding specificity earlier in the chapter, you'll recall that when a retrieval cue is understood to have a different meaning at the time of remembering than it did at the time of encoding, it loses its effectiveness. The framework that provides the meaning is called a **schema.** Schemas help us encode information in more meaningful ways, but they also can induce systematic errors. For example, thinking of living things as either animals, plants, or fungi might help you classify organisms; however, your schema of "living things" might lead you to overlook the possibility that viruses could be a form of life.

An early experiment by Bartlett (1932) called attention to the way schemas affect memory. The experimenter had people read a story or essay or look at a picture. Then he asked them on several later occasions to retell the prose passage or draw the picture. Each time, the participants "remembered" the original a little differently. If the original story had contained peculiar and unexpected sequences of events, people tended to retell it in a more coherent and sensible fashion, as if their memories had been revised to make the information accord more closely with their own schema for what the story was about. Bartlett concluded that people remember only a few striking details of an experience and that during recall, they reconstruct the missing portions in accordance with their own interpretation of what was likely.

Eyewitness Testimony Elizabeth Loftus (1979) has investigated a different set of variables that affect the recall of details from episodic memory. Her research indicates that the kinds of questions used to elicit information can have a major effect on what people remember. In courts of law, lawyers are not permitted to ask witnesses leading questions—questions phrased so as to suggest what the answer should be. Loftus's research showed that even subtle changes in a question can affect people's recollections. For example, Loftus and Palmer (1974) showed people films of car accidents and asked them to estimate vehicles' speeds when they *contacted, hit, bumped, collided,* or *smashed* each other. As **FIGURE 7·16** shows, the people's estimates of the vehicles' speeds were directly related to the force of the impact suggested by the verb, such as *hit,* that appeared in the question.

In a similar experiment, when people were asked a week after viewing the film whether they saw any broken glass (there was none), people in the *smashed* group were most likely to say yes. Thus, a leading question that encouraged them to remember the vehicles going faster also encouraged them to remember that they saw nonexistent broken glass. The question appears to have modified the memory itself.

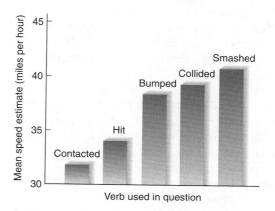

[**FIGURE 7·16**] Leading questions and recall. Shown are the mean estimated speeds of vehicles as recalled by people in the study by Loftus and Palmer (1974).

(Based on data from Loftus, E. F., & Palmer, J. C. (1974). Reconstruction of automobile destruction: An example of the interaction between language and memory. *Journal of Verbal Learning and Verbal Behavior, 13,* 585–589.)

---

schema A mental framework or body of knowledge that organizes and synthesizes information about a person, place, or thing.

The questions asked during a pretrial investigation may affect an eyewitness's later testimony.

Another experiment indicates that how events are reviewed affects this suggestibility. Lane et al. (2001) showed people a videotape of a staged crime, then asked questions that were designed to suggest things that were not part of the video. For example, the witnesses might be asked, "At the beginning of the scene, a young man dressed in jeans, a T-shirt, and gloves entered the house. Did he enter through the door?" In the video, the thief did not wear gloves; the test was to see if witnesses would incorrectly include the gloves in their recall of the scene later on. Before recalling information about the scene, however, they were asked, as witnesses might reasonably be asked to do, to review the videotape mentally. Some were asked to review as much detail as possible; others were asked to review only the highlights. Instructions to focus on details led to an increased tendency to incorporate the suggested, and false, information, such as the presence of gloves. Apparently, after being asked to review details, eyewitnesses rehearse the suggestions and come to view these as true.

Experiments such as these have important implications for eyewitness testimony in courts of law. A judge can prevent a lawyer from asking leading questions during a trial, but he or she cannot undo the effects of leading questions put to the witness during pretrial investigations. Many experiments indicate that learning new information and recalling it later are active processes—we do not simply place an item of information in a mental filing cabinet and pick it up later (Roediger & McDermott, 1995). We organize and integrate information in terms of what we already know about life and have come to expect about particular experiences. Thus, when we recall the memory later, it may contain information that was not part of the original experience. Even more disturbing, our confidence in this new information may be quite high.

At first, this phenomenon may appear to be maladaptive because it means that we cannot always trust our own recollections, no matter how hard we try to be accurate. However, our tendency to reconstruct memories probably reflects the fact that information about an episode can be more efficiently stored by means of a few unique details. The portions of an episode that are common to other experiences, and hence resemble information already stored in long-term memory, need not be retained. If every detail of every experience had to be encoded uniquely in long-term memory, perhaps we would run out of storage space. Unfortunately, this process sometimes leads to instances of faulty remembering, both in the witness stand and in life in general.

Flashbulb Memories   Are some memories immune to this reconstructive process? One possibility is that some episodic memories are acquired under such powerful personal experiences of emotion and surprise that they become especially vivid and long-lasting. Consider your personal memory of when you first heard about the attack on the World Trade Center on September 11, 2001. Can you recall where you were, what you were doing, and who gave you the news? Do you remember your personal feelings? The feelings of those around you? Can you recall what you did next?

Roger Brown and James Kulik provided a name for memories activated by events of extreme surprise and great personal consequence: **flashbulb memories.** Using the assassination of President John F. Kennedy as an example, Brown and Kulik (1977) suggested that surprising, traumatic events could result in the encoding of some (but not all) of the context surrounding the individual at the time. When they asked people in 1977 to recollect their personal situation at the time they heard of Kennedy's 1963 assassination, they discovered that most accounts included the information behind the six questions asked in the last paragraph. Brown and Kulik speculated that flashbulb memories were not only especially vivid but also, possibly, especially long-lasting or even permanent.

However, other evidence suggests that flashbulb memories are not immune to the effects of distortion and modification discussed in the previous section. Schmolck, Buffalo, and Squire (2000) looked at an event that, although it was less consequential than the Kennedy assassination or 9/11, nevertheless produced flashbulb memories in students at the University of California: the 1995 acquittal of O. J. Simpson in his trial for the murder of his wife, Nicole, and her friend Ron Goldman. The investigators asked the students to record their reactions to the event three days after it happened. Then, either 15 months or 32 months later, they asked them to recall the event again. In general, recollection after 15 months was accurate. After 32 months, however, more than 40% of the recollections were seriously distorted. Schmolck, Buffalo, and Squire found that of 50 individuals who could be described as having a flashbulb memory of the verdict, 38% could not remember it as they had originally described it three days after the event. A significant source of error in the years after the event was in people's recall of the source of the news, with many people misreporting that they had heard about the verdict from the media rather than from another person. Rather than saying they couldn't remember, these individuals apparently assumed that because they get much of their news from the media, they must have heard about the Simpson verdict the same way. This assumption was then incorporated into their memory of the event.

---

flashbulb memories   Memories established by events that are highly surprising and personally of consequence.

focus ⊕n

Some Sins of Memory

In the opening vignette of this chapter, we saw how witnesses in the Salem witchcraft trials testified to fantastic episodes of supernatural occurrences. In reading some of these accusations, you might have immediately thought that the witnesses were lying; people could not possibly recall things so counter to actual fact. Or could they?

Daniel Schacter has suggested that memory can exhibit seven deficiencies or "sins." These sins of memory are transience, absent-mindedness, blocking, misattribution, suggestibility, bias, and persistence. The first three are deficiencies of omission: Transience is the weakening of memory over time; absent-mindedness is the failure to register information that needs to be memorized; and blocking is the failure to retrieve information we know we possess. The other four are deficiencies of commission and add wrong information to our memory: Misattribution confuses different sources of memory; suggestibility embellishes memory under the influence of misleading questions or statements from others; bias creates errors because of our own beliefs; and persistence brings to mind information that we would rather forget (Schacter, 2001; Schacter & Dodson, 2002).

Schacter's "seven sins" have particular relevance to the criminal justice system. In many criminal investigations—particularly those in which little or no physical evidence is available—the memory of witnesses becomes especially important. Their ability to remember events and faces can determine the success or failure of the investigation—and of the subsequent prosecution, should a suspect be brought to trial. But memories of eyewitnesses are transient, especially when the events in question are fast-paced, confusing, and frightening. Elizabeth Loftus has explored some of the implications of memory deficiencies in her laboratory, but it is relevant to consider how many of these deficiencies could occur outside the laboratory.

In 1996, inspired in part by Loftus's work, Crombag, Wagenaar, and van Koppen (1996) pushed the notion of an eyewitness to the limit. In 1992, a Boeing 747 had crashed into an Amsterdam apartment building, creating a blazing fire but with, fortunately, fewer casualties than first feared. Crombag, Wagenaar, and van Koppen subsequently circulated a questionnaire to college students and faculty asking whether they had seen the television footage of the moment when the plane hit the building. Although no such footage existed, 55% of the respondents to the questionnaire claimed to have personally seen it. Furthermore, from among this group claiming to have seen the footage, 82% were so confident of what they had seen that they provided details about the crash. A group of law students tested later was even more prone to false memories of the crash: 66% of them claimed to have seen it.

Crashing memories have been found for other high-profile events. For example, Jelicic, et al. (2006) asked undergraduates whether they had seen video of the murder of a prominent Dutch politician, Pim Fortuyn. Again, no such footage existed; yet, 63% of respondents reported seeing it. Asked if they could describe details of what they had seen, 23% provided accounts.

What produces this tendency to confidently recall memories of things that cannot be? Jelicic et al. (2006) found evidence that it was associated with a tendency to fantasize. People reporting memories of the film were more likely to answer *yes* to questions like "In general, I spend at least half of the day fantasizing or daydreaming" and "My fantasies are so vivid that they are like a good film." In another study, Smeets et al. (2006) found that crashing memories depend in part on the way the question is asked. By using the nonexistent Pim Fortuyn assassination film as their example, Smeets et al. found that they received the highest number of false recollections when they asked about the film in an ambiguous way ("Did you see the amateur film about the Fortuyn shooting?") rather than in a highly specific manner ("Did you see the amateur film of the moment Fortuyn was shot by Volkert van der G.?"). When the question was phrased in the first way 63% answered *yes*; 30% answered positively to the second phrasing. So, as in the work by Loftus and her colleagues, language plays an important role in how we evaluate our memories, leading us to commit Schacter's "sin" of suggestibility.

Suggestibility is not the sole cause of a crashing memory, however. Smeets et al. (2006) also asked about the film in a very neutral manner: "Do you remember whether there was a film of the moment Fortuyn was shot by Volkert van der G.?" Twenty-seven percent of their participants could remember there being such a film. Crombag, Wagenaar, and van Koppen (1996) suggested that misattribution (another one of the sins) could play a strong role. Perhaps, because the event was such a prominent one to Dutch citizens, people imagined what the shooting was like and incorporated that image into memory of video that they did see.

If so, this possibility validates another legal principle. Crombag, Wagenaar, and van Koppen point out the principle of many Western legal traditions is to prohibit "hearsay" testimony—testimony about what someone else has remembered. Far from being just a legal nicety, the prohibition against hearsay testimony emphasizes that evidence must have a clear source. Our memory system may not be the best for keeping its sources straight.

QUESTIONS TO CONSIDER

1. Given what you know about memory, was Ebbinghaus right to use nonsense syllables?
2. Recall a particularly important event in your life. Think about the activities that led up to this event and how the event has affected your life since. How much of the information you recall about this event is accurate? How many of the details surrounding this event have you reconstructed? How would you go about finding the answers to these questions?

Epilogue

The Salem Testimony Reconsidered

Reading the transcripts of the Salem Witch Trials is a sobering experience. The charges sound preposterous, the evidence flimsy, and the sentences were harsh. One man, who refused to enter a plea at his trial, was placed under heavy rocks and crushed to death over a two-day period. Before the trials ended, fifteen women and six men had been executed. One quickly gains an appreciation as to what the term "witch-hunt" really means.

Many theories have been advanced to explain the accusations. It's conceivable that some of the young girls who started the witch-hunt had a mental illness; however, it seems unlikely that all were. Perhaps they became frightened at what they had started and couldn't find a way to admit it. From this distance in time, the answer will probably never be fully known.

What is startling, even now, is the credulity of the investigators, judges, and jurors for testimony that was based on fantasy. One incident brings this home: Early in the investigation, the young girls accused a four-year-old child of haunting them. The authorities promptly jailed this unfortunate girl. Undoubtedly confused and terrified, and relying on a child's imagination, she told her inquisitors that she had been given a black snake that sucked her blood. The investigators noted for the record that they then found a small wound, "the size of a flea bite," on the child's finger. Given that she had been housed in the town jail, it probably was, indeed, a flea bite. Asked who had given her the snake, she mentioned her mother. Accused with testimony like that, her mother, Sarah Good, was hanged nine days after Bridget Bishop.

Now that you've learned about the work of Elizabeth Loftus and others, you can better appreciate how much the interrogators contributed to the whole episode. The witnesses must have also received some strong coaching, implicit or not, from their neighbors in the village—each with their own agendas. The opening vignette also hinted that subtle matters of timing may have played a role. A sighting of a mysterious black pig after an argument with a presumed witch makes for a much better schema than some random encounter. Similarly, remembering that he lost some coins right after she gave them to him probably

seemed like a more plausible scenario to one of Bridget's accusers than admitting his own absentmindedness. Finally, one can't help but wonder how many of the encounters with apparitions in the middle of the night were merely dreams confused as reality.

As the research with Dutch street names shows, we are capable of recalling information from our past to a surprising extent. Yet, memory is not a DVD recorder. Memory is the outcome of brain processes that evolved for special functions, and we weren't designed by natural selection to be perfect courtroom witnesses. As Schacter has put it, our memory is prone to seven deadly sins. In all likelihood, that was the real devil at work in Salem.

CHAPTER SUMMARY

Sensory Memory

Memory involves encoding, storage, and retrieval. An early view of memory suggested that it consisted of three forms: sensory, short-term, and long-term. The characteristics of each form differ, which suggests that the three forms differ physiologically as well. Sensory memory is very limited—it provides temporary storage until newly perceived information can be stored in short-term memory. Short-term memory contains a representation of information that has just been perceived, such as an item's name. Although the capacity of short-term memory is limited, we can rehearse the information as long as we choose, thus increasing the likelihood that we will remember it indefinitely (that is, that it will enter long-term memory).

Information in iconic memory is considered to last for only a very short time. The partial-report procedure shows that when a visual stimulus is presented in a brief flash, all of the information is available for about a second. If the viewer is asked to recall one line of information after one second, the information is no longer present in iconic memory. Although echoic memory was originally considered a similar type of memory for auditory stimulation, recent evidence suggests it can last longer.

Short-Term or Working Memory

Information in short-term memory is encoded according to previously learned rules. Information in long-term memory determines the nature of the encoding. Because short-term memory contains information retrieved from long-term memory as well as newly perceived information, many researchers conceive of it as working memory. Working memory is not simply a way station between sensory memory and long-term memory; it is where thinking occurs. When presented with a list of items, we tend to remember the items at the beginning of the list (the primacy effect) and at the end of the list (the recency effect) better than items in the middle of the list. The primacy effect presumably occurs because we have a greater opportunity to rehearse items early in the list and thus store them in long-term memory, and the recency effect because we can retrieve items at the end of the list that are still stored in short-term memory.

Working memory lasts for about 20 seconds and has a capacity of about seven items—give or take two. We often simplify large amounts of information by organizing it into "chunks" of information, which can then be more easily rehearsed and remembered.

Although each sensory system probably has a working memory associated with it, psychologists have devoted most of their attention to two kinds: phonological and visual working memory. The existence of acoustical errors (rather than visual ones) in the task of remembering visually presented letters suggests that information is represented phonologically in short-term memory. Because deaf people (but only those who can talk) also show this effect, the code appears to be articulatory. Phonological working memory is encoded acoustically as well. People who have conduction aphasia show a specific deficit in phonological short-term memory, apparently because their brain damage interrupts direct communication between Wernicke's area and Broca's area.

The processes of working memory act to maintain information over time. Variables that affect rehearsal ability, such as the length of the items being remembered, affect short-term memory. This account, however, raises the question as to what might cause items to decay when they are not rehearsed.

Learning and Encoding in Long-Term Memory

Long-term memory appears to consist of physical changes in the brain—probably within the sensory and motor association cortexes. Consolidation of memories is likely caused by rehearsal of information, which sustains particular neural activities and leads to permanent structural changes in the brain.

Craik and Lockhart's model of memory points out the importance of elaboration in learning. Maintenance rehearsal, or simple rote repetition, is usually less effective than elaborative rehearsal, which involves deeper, more meaningful processing. These theorists assert that long-term memory is a by-product of perceptual analysis. The level of processing can be shallow or deep and is controlled by changes in the amount of attention we pay to information. Having read a description of Craik and Tulving's experiment, you can probably remember the end of the sentence "The old man hobbled across the room and picked up the valuable _____."

Encoding of information to be stored in long-term memory may take place automatically or effortfully. The principle of encoding specificity—how we encode information into memory—determines the ease with which we can later retrieve that information. To produce the most durable and useful memories, information should be encoded in ways that are meaningful. However, critics of the levels-of-processing model point out that shallow processing sometimes produces very durable memories, and the distinction between shallow and deep has proved impossible to define explicitly.

Mnemonic systems are strategies used to enhance memory and usually use information that is already contained in long-term memory as well as visual imagery.

The Organization of Long-Term Memory

Episodic and semantic memory involve different memories: We remember events that happen to us as episodic memories, whereas general facts are remembered as semantic memories. Another distinction—between explicit and implicit memory—has received much attention. We use explicit memory when we remember facts and events that we can consciously describe. Implicit memory, in contrast, is unconscious; it is, for example, the memory system that we use when we acquire specific behaviors and skills.

Much of what we have learned about the biological basis of memory comes from studies involving humans with brain damage and from laboratory studies in which animals undergo surgical procedures that produce amnesia. Anterograde amnesia appears to reflect a deficit of explicit memory but not a major impairment of implicit memory. The deficit in explicit memory appears to be strongly related to normal functioning of the hippocampus; it may be that the hippocampus is involved in the consolidation of long-term explicit memory. Conversely, the basal ganglia may be responsible for implicit memory. The behavior of laboratory animals also demonstrates this distinction between episodic and other kinds of memories.

Remembering, Recollecting, and Forgetting

Remembering sometimes requires the generation of thoughts that are associated with the information and the discrimination of their source. As research of childhood memories shows, the forgetting of information occurs primarily in the first few years after it is learned, and the rate of forgetting decreases slowly thereafter. Once we have learned something and retained it for a few years, chances are that we will remember it for a long time afterward. The process of remembering information is influenced by how cultures teach their members to learn about the world. In addition, a culture's customs governing social interaction may influence what people tell others about what they have learned.

Sometimes retrieval of one memory is made more difficult by the information contained in another memory, a phenomenon known as *interference*. In retroactive interference, information that we have recently learned interferes with our recollection of information learned earlier. In proactive interference, information that we learned a while ago interferes with information we have learned more recently. Although interference has been demonstrated in the laboratory, interference may not operate so obviously in real life. Prose and other forms of everyday language appear to be more resistant to interference than are the nonsense syllables often used in memory experiments.

Recalling a memory of a complex event entails a process of reconstruction that uses old information. As Loftus's research has established, our ability to recall information from episodic memory is influenced by retrieval cues, such as the questions lawyers ask people in courts of law to establish how an event occurred. Sometimes the reconstruction introduces new "facts" that we perceive as memories of what we previously perceived. Reconstructions also affect the recollection of flashbulb memories—especially vivid memories of surprising and consequential events. This reconstructive process undoubtedly makes more efficient use of the resources we have available for storage of long-term memories.

Reconstructions can be so strong that people may even claim to have witnessed impossible events. Schacter has suggested seven "sins of memory." Two of these, suggestibility and misattribution, might be responsible for memories of events that did not happen.

succeed with mypsychlab

Visit MyPsychLab for practice quizzes, flashcards, and dozens of videos and animated tutorials, including the following items you can find in the "Multimedia Library":

The Effects of Sleep and Stress on Memory:
  Jessica Payne
Memory: Elizabeth Loftus

Encoding, Storage, and Retrieval in Memory
Key Processes in Stages of Memory

Serial Position Effect
Experiencing the Stroop Effect

KEY TERMS

SUGGESTIONS FOR FURTHER READING

Luria, A. R. (1968). *The mind of a mnemonist.* New York: Basic Books.

Given the importance of learning and forgetting in almost everyone's life, it is not surprising that many popular books have been written about human memory. This book is the great Russian neurologist's account of a man with an extraordinary memory.

Loftus, E. F., & Ketcham, K. (1994). *The myth of repressed memory: False memories and allegations of sexual abuse.* New York: St. Martin's.

Elizabeth Loftus is an internationally recognized authority on remembering. She has researched and written extensively on the errors people make in recalling events. This book deals with case studies of individuals who purportedly were able to recall significant events that had been "repressed" because of their traumatic nature. As Loftus and Ketcham note, such repressed memories likely never existed in the first place. You might wish to compare what you learn in this book with the actual Salem trial documents; they can be found online at http://jefferson.village.virginia.edu/salem/home.html.

Ormrod, J. E. (2008). *Human learning* (5th ed.). Upper Saddle River, NJ: Pearson.

Schacter, D. L. (2001). *The seven sins of memory.* Boston: Houghton Mifflin.

The Ormrod book is an upper-level undergraduate text that contains a well-written and thoughtful consideration of memory and its processes. The book's discussion of memory is placed in the larger context of learning. The Schacter book is an engaging overview of memory errors.

Consciousn

Taken from *Psychology: The Science of Behavior*, Seventh Edition, by Neil R. Carlson, Harold Miller, C. Donald
John W. Donahoe, and G. Neil Martin.

Prologue

The Persistent Loss of Consciousness

It is not usual to learn of persons who have lost consciousness due to head injury, heart failure, stroke, or disease, and who continue to live but never regain consciousness. Often their condition is referred to as "living in a coma." Despite the sustained efforts of the physicians and nurses who attend them, the condition persists for years. Then one day, all of a sudden, the patient awakens and begins a return to normalcy, or at least to as much normalcy as might be recoverable after so long an absence. In other cases, no awakening and no recovery may occur, but instead, the solemn decision is made by loved ones to remove the life-sustaining devices and allow life to expire.

The cases of Jan Grzebski (gurr-ZEB-skee) and Terri Schiavo (SHY-voe) illustrate these end points. Grzebski was a railroad worker in his native Poland when, in 1988, an accident on the job rendered him comatose and, in the judgment of the physicians who treated him, unlikely to live more than a few years. In June 2007, Grzebski suddenly was no longer comatose. Now 65, recovery from the 19-year lapse in his consciousness meant repeated amazement as he came face to face with the altered circumstances—locally and nationally—in the no-longer-Communist country. He credited his wife, who had provided constant care, with his recovery. In commenting on his experience while comatose, he spoke only of dim recollections of family events to which his wife had taken him and of efforts she and their children made to communicate with him.

Terri Schiavo was an American who became an international celebrity while in a persistent vegetative state (PVS). It followed acute respiratory and cardiac arrest that occurred early in 1990 and was accompanied by extensive brain damage. She was 26. Initially she was in a comatose condition. The diagnosis of PVS came later and included the failure to display voluntary action and to interact and communicate purposefully. After persistent rehabilitative efforts, her husband made the decision, consistent with what he claimed were Terri's wishes, to withdraw life support. Her parents objected on grounds that she remained conscious. What followed was a high-profile, sometimes bitter legal contest for the right to decide Terri's fate—a contest waged in state and federal courts

and eventually involving the U.S. Congress and Supreme Court. The contest unfolded amid highly publicized campaigns by citizens who organized on both sides of the issue. Ultimately the decision sided with the husband's right, and, in 2005, Terri's life ended through dehydration.

In the interest of his wife's recovery, Terri's husband took her to the University of California, San Francisco in late 1990 for an experimental procedure that involved the implantation of a device that produced electrical stimulation of the thalamus. Although the treatment lasted for several months, it was unsuccessful. ■

The cases cited in the Prologue made reference to a comatose state and to a persistent vegetative state. Shadlen and Kiani (2007) drew distinctions between them: "**Coma.** The patient seems to be asleep and cannot be awoken. . . . **Persistent vegetative state (PVS).** This is similar to coma in all respects except that, at times, the patient does not seem to be asleep." They also identified a third condition: "**Minimally conscious state (MCS).** In contrast to PVS, patients show occasional signs of arousal and organized behavior. Nevertheless, for the most part, there is a profound deficit of consciousness" (p. 540). These states are further differentiated from the *locked-in syndrome,* which is distinguished by near-complete paralysis of the voluntary muscles (León-Carrión et al., 2002). Clearly, there are different ways to characterize unconsciousness and, if symmetry holds, perhaps different ways to characterize consciousness as well.

What is consciousness, and why are we conscious? How do we direct our consciousness from one object or event to another, paying attention to some while ignoring others? What about the alternation of consciousness that appears to take place in hypnosis–can another person really take control of our thoughts and actions? Why do we regularly undergo the profound alternation of consciousness called sleep? This chapter first explores what it is to be conscious and to be self-conscious, that is, to have a sense of perceptions, thoughts, memories, and feelings that are one's own. Then it examines the phenomenon of selective attention before looking at the brain mechanisms that have been implicated in consciousness. Finally, the chapter turns to topics typically of interest to students—hypnosis and sleep, including dreams.

---

coma A condition in which an individual seems to be sleeping but cannot be awakened.

persistent vegetative state A condition similar to coma except that the individual intermittently appears to be awake.

minimally conscious state A condition in which the individual shows occasional arousal and organized behavior but otherwise appears to be asleep.

consciousness The awareness of complex private processes such as perception, thinking, and remembering.

Consciousness as a Language-Dependent Phenomenon

It is one thing to be aware of what is happening in the world "out there" beyond one's body as well as within one's body. Such awareness amounts to one's ability to report those happenings verbally or in other ways that people recognize. But it is something else to know why we are aware of our actions, our perceptions, our thoughts, our memories, and our feelings. Is some purpose served by such abilities? Philosophers have puzzled over this question for centuries without finding a convincing answer. Early behaviorists approached the issue by denying that there was anything to explain. For them, the only subject matter for psychological investigation was behavior. They argued that consciousness was not behavior, though aspects of consciousness, such as thinking, might turn out to be very subtle forms of behavior. More recently, investigators have begun to apply the methods of inquiry developed jointly by psychology and neuroscience, and finally we seem to be making some progress. The nature of consciousness is coming into clearer focus. This section of the chapter makes the claim that having consciousness relies on having language and on using it to affect others' actions. Thus, consciousness may have social effects.

The Adaptive Significance of Consciousness

To discover the functions of consciousness, we must not confuse consciousness with complex cognitive processes such as perceiving, thinking, or remembering. **Consciousness** is the awareness of these processes, not the processes themselves. Thus, consciousness is its own process, a process that exists in addition to perception, thinking, remembering, and feeling.

It is difficult to see why a living organism having elaborate behavioral abilities plus consciousness would have any

When do we become aware of our own existence?

advantages over an organism that possessed the same abilities but lacked consciousness. If the behaviors of these two types of organisms were identical in all situations, they should be equally successful. For this reason, it may more fruitful to approach the question of adaptive functionality from a different angle. Consider the possibility that consciousness is a by-product of another characteristic of the human brain that does have useful functions. What might this characteristic be?

Let us reflect on what we know about consciousness. First, although the word consciousness is a noun, it does not refer to a thing. The word "life" is a noun, too, but modern biologists know better than to look for "life." Instead, they study the *characteristics* of living organisms. Similarly, rather than look for consciousness per se, we might study the characteristics of conscious organisms. So, then, what does it mean to be conscious? Consciousness refers to private experience, which therefore cannot be shared directly nor can we directly experience the consciousness of another. We experience our own consciousness and can say publicly what it is like. We conclude that other people are conscious because they are like us and because they can tell us that they, too, are conscious. (In Chapter 6, this will be referred to as having a *theory of mind*.)

Another clue to the functions of consciousness is that we are not conscious of everything about ourselves, nor are we equally conscious of the same thing all the time. That is, consciousness is not a general property of all parts of the brain. This becomes clear in the following case.

[CASE STUDY] Laverne J. had brought her grand-father to see Dr. M., a neuropsychologist. Mr. J. had had a stroke that had left him almost completely blind; all he could see was in a tiny spot at the middle of his visual field. Dr. M. had learned about the situation from Mr. J.'s neurologist and had asked Mr. J. to come to his laboratory so that he could do some tests there as part of his research project.

Dr. M. helped Mr. J. find a chair and sit down. Mr. J., who walked with the aid of a cane, gave it to his granddaughter to hold for him. "May I borrow that?" asked Dr. M. Laverne nodded and handed it to him. "The phenomenon I'm studying is called blindsight," he said. "Let me see if I can show you what it is."

"Mr. J., please look straight ahead. Keep looking that way, and don't move your eyes or turn your head. I know that you can see a little bit straight ahead of you, and I don't want you to use that piece of vision for what I'm going to ask you to do. Fine. Now, I'd like you to reach out with your right hand and point to what I'm holding."

Dr. M. moved and stood to the side of Mr. J. He held out the cane but remained silent. "But I don't see anything—I'm blind!" said Mr. J., obviously exasperated. Dr. M. continued to point the cane toward him.

Mr. J. shrugged his shoulders and pointed, extending his arm in the direction of the cane. He looked startled when his finger encountered the end of the cane.

"Gramps, how did you do that?" asked Laverne, amazed. "I thought you were blind."

"I am!" he said, emphatically. "It was just luck."

"Let's try it just a couple more times," said Dr. M. "Keep looking straight ahead." He changed his position and reversed the cane, so that now the handle was pointing toward Mr. J.

Mr. J. reached out with an open hand and grabbed hold of the cane.

"Good," said Dr. M. "Now put your hand down, please, and try it again." Dr. M. quickly rotated the cane 90 degrees, so that the handle was oriented vertically. As Mr. J.'s arm came up, he turned his wrist so that his hand matched the orientation of the handle, which he grabbed hold of again.

"Good. Thank you, you can put your hand down." Dr. M. turned to Laverne. "I think it's safe to say that there's a lot more to your grandfather's vision than just luck."

The phenomenon Dr. J. was studying was **blindsight,** an odd-seeming word that refers to a clinical condition in which a person with cortical damage is unaware of visible objects ("I'm blind") while otherwise behaving as though they are visible. Mr. J. could reach accurately for objects that he insisted he couldn't see. Someone observing the situation, who didn't know that Mr. J. was blind, naturally would assume he could see them. But Mr. J. remained adamant. All he was aware of was what appeared in the tiny spot at the middle of his visual field, but none of the objects he reached for appeared there. Blindsight is caused by damage to the visual cortex, or to pathways leading into or from it (Weiskrantz, 1986, 1999; Danckert & Rossetti, 2005). Apparently, a part of the visual system can control our ability to react to the presence of objects, directing our eye movements, our limbs, and other behaviors toward or away from them, but not at the level of awareness that would be considered conscious. Linden (2007) has referred to blindsight as evidence of an amphibian (or reptilian) core of consciousness that, despite subsequent evolutionary overlays, continues to reside in the human brain. (However, see Fendrich et al., 1992, and Weiskrantz, 1996, for alternative views that depend on retinal pathways and undamaged cortical regions, respectively.) Conscious awareness comes about with a special effort that can be referred to as concentrating or "paying" attention. Exerting such efforts allows us to report them to ourselves and other people, that is, to be conscious of them.

Consciousness and the Ability to Communicate

It is no coincidence that the principal evidence we have of consciousness in ourselves and other people comes through the use of language. That is, the most likely explanation for consciousness lies in its relation to language. Our ability to

---

blindsight The ability of a person who cannot perceive objects in a part of his or her visual field to reach for them accurately while remaining unaware of seeing them.

communicate (through words, signs, or other symbolic means) provides us with the ability to be aware (conscious) and self-aware (self-consciousness).

How does the ability to communicate symbolically give rise to consciousness? Consider what can be accomplished through verbal communication: we can express our needs, perceptions, thoughts, memories, intentions, and feelings to other people, and they, to us. All of these accomplishments require two general capacities. First, we must be able to translate private events—such as thinking, remembering, and feeling, for example—into language. This means that the brain mechanisms for communicating with others must receive input from the systems of the brain involved in perceiving, thinking, remembering, feeling, and so on (see Gazzaniga, 1987). Second, our words must have an effect on the person who is receiving them. Once the words are decoded in the receiver's brain, they must affect the listener's own perceptions, thoughts, memories, feelings, and—behavior. The last is critical. Otherwise we would be unsure of whether the communication had been received. For example, if we describe a specific event that we witnessed, our listener may be able to imagine that event and remember the description, but it is something in the listener's behavior that gives us confidence that such imagining and remembering actually have occurred. Of course, we can also be our own talkers and listeners. We can make plans in words, think about the consequences of these plans in words, and use words to produce behaviors—all without actually ever saying the words aloud. As we saw in Chapter 7, thinking in words appears to involve *subvocal articulation*. Thus, the brain mechanisms that permit us to understand words and produce speech are the same ones we use to think. Similarly, investigators have noted that when deaf people are thinking to themselves (Sacks, 2000), they often make small movements with their hands, just as those of us who can hear and speak sometimes talk to ourselves under our breath.

Are humans the only organisms with consciousness? Based on other species' communication systems, the answer is probably not. The evolutionary process is incremental: New traits and abilities—including the ability of humans to use language—build on those that that already exist. Most forms of communication among animals other than humans—for example, mating displays and alarm calls—are inborn and automatic and probably do not involve consciousness. However, other animal species may learn forms of communication, just as we learn our own language. Certainly, your dog can learn to communicate with you—to tell you when it wants to eat, go for a walk, or play. This learned ability to report may indicate consciousness, but consciousness with a particular inflection—dog consciousness. Humans' ability to communicate with language seems to surpass by far that of any other species. Thus, we assume our consciousness is much more highly developed. But the underlying brain mechanisms, such as the hippocampal mechanisms implicated in explicit memory we examined in Chapter 7, may be present in species closely related to ours (Morris, 2001). Studies looking at the behavior of animals viewing mirror images suggest that other primate species may possess something like self-awareness (see Boysen and Himes, 1999, for a review; but also see Bekoff, 2002, for a critique).

A daub of red paint on the chimpanzee's face draws a knowing response to its reflection in the mirror. The animal rubs at the paint. Is its response evidence of self-awareness?

Does Conscious Thought Control Behavior?

In the past, psychologists found fault with using consciousness to explain behavior. Many considered it pointless to explain something we could observe (behavior) in terms of something we could not (consciousness). This view has lately been reconsidered, largely because of the techniques of brain research described in Chapter 3. Today psychologists are more willing to address some of the deeper issues that figured in the discipline's early history.

Recent research in cognitive psychology and cognitive neuroscience has addressed the issue of conscious control of behavior and been helpful in distinguishing action from conscious action. Some of the research uses the phenomenon of visual illusions discussed in Chapter 5. For example, consider the two crayons in FIGURE 8•1. Although they are both the same size, the horizontal crayon tends to look shorter—a visual illusion known as the "top-hat illusion" because it is often demonstrated by using judgments about the crown versus the brim of a top hat. Suppose, now, that I ask you to pick up each crayon by grasping the ends. Would you reach for the horizontal crayon with your fingers closer together?

It seems reasonable to suppose that the fingers would move closer together to grasp shorter objects. Goodale and his colleagues have evidence that our actions are little affected by our visual judgments, including those involving illusions. In one experiment, Ganel and Goodale (2003) compared perceptual judgments of object shape with the ability to pick up the object. They showed participants a wooden block on a table and asked them whether the block was wide or narrow. They then replaced the block with another and again asked for a judgment of width. This continued for several trials. It is easy to judge width under these conditions when the blocks all have the same length, but if the blocks vary in length, the task becomes more difficult. Shape, in other words, is holistic, in the sense meant by the Gestaltists discussed in Chapter 5. However, when Ganel and Goodale

[**FIGURE 8·1**] The "top-hat illusion" depicted with naturalistic objects. The two crayons are the same lengths; however, the vertically positioned crayon looks longer.

asked the participants to take hold of a block at its middle, their grasping action was not affected by variation in length. In other words, the distance between their fingers was the same for the blocks they had previously perceived to be of varying widths. According to Ganel and Goodale, our perceptual judgment of objects—what they are, what features they have (such as their width), and so on—may be based on a different visual system from the one we use for actions (such as picking them up).

If our perception differs from our actions, then what might this imply about consciousness and behavior? When you reach for the coffee cup on your desk, is the sequence of actions controlled by your conscious thoughts of picking it up? Certainly, the thought and the action go together, but remember the lesson from Chapter 2: Correlation does not necessarily imply causation. It could be that the conscious thought and the coordinated actions have a common cause elsewhere in the brain, or it may be that actions caused the conscious thought (Wegner, 2003).

Some of the brain-recording techniques discussed in Chapter 4 have been used to test these possibilities. In a set of experiments performed in 1983, Libet and his colleagues (Libet et al., 1983; see also Libet, 2002, 2004) instructed participants to make a simple flick of their wrist while watching a rapidly moving clock hand displayed in front of them. They were to report the location of the clock hand at the moment they became aware of an intention to flick their wrist. Their verbal reports indicated that they experienced the intention

about three-tenths of a second before the actual movement began. The researchers also measured the "readiness potential," the electrical brain activity of the motor cortex. This potential occurred about seven-tenths of a second before the wrist movement began—even earlier than the conscious intention. Remarkably, the brain seemed to be starting the movement before there was awareness of "willing" it.

Considerable controversy exists over what these observations mean. Much of the debate concerns how to interpret the readiness potential. Recall that the readiness potential precedes a person's awareness of the intention to act. Does it reflect the brain's "decision" to initiate a movement? Haggard and Eimer (1999) reasoned that if the readiness potential was the cause of movement, then it should show covariation in time with awareness. That is, the later awareness is reported, the later the readiness potential will occur. On each trial, they asked participants to move either their left or right index finger and to report when they were aware of the intention to move it. The researchers identified those trials on which the report of awareness was "late" (that is, closer in time to the actual movement) to see whether the readiness potential was also late. It was not. However, they also used another measure of brain activity, the "lateralized readiness potential." Remember from Chapter 3 that motor control of the body is contralateral, with the left motor cortex controlling the right side of the body. The lateralized readiness potential measures the difference between the activity in the two motor cortices. This potential did covary with the report of awareness. When awareness was late, the lateralized readiness potential also was late; when awareness was early, the potential appeared earlier.

So the lateralized readiness potential may reflect brain activity that leads to awareness of the initiation of action, but it involves both sides of the brain. This may imply that it results from an even earlier brain event. In other words, the lateralized readiness potential may be only a step in a sequence of brain activity leading up to conscious awareness. To explore this sequence further, Haggard and Clark (2003) contrasted awareness of both voluntary and involuntary movements. It is possible to elicit involuntary muscle twitches by delivering transcranial magnetic stimulation (TMS; another technique described in Chapter 3). The researchers used this technique to produce involuntary movements of the participants' right index finger and compared trials with stimulation with those in which a participant used the finger to press a key voluntarily. As in the Libet et al. experiment, each participant watched a clock hand spinning around a dial and reported where the clock hand was when he or she became aware of either moving the finger or the involuntary movement produced by TMS. On some trials, called "operant" trials, a tone was presented a fourth of a second after movement occurred, and the participant was asked to also report the position of the clock hand at the time the tone sounded. Often on these trials, the participant reported the perception of causing the tone to come on.

An interesting pattern emerged. On the operant trials, the participants reported being aware of moving their finger later than on the trials involving involuntary movements of the finger. They also reported the tone occurring earlier than on the involuntary trials. In other words, they perceived that, on the voluntary trials, awareness of their intentional movement and of the tone occurred closer together, which may have been critical for their perception of having turned the tone on. On involuntary trials, the perception was that the two events were farther apart. Haggard and Clark argued, therefore, that that brain must "bind together" the experience of voluntary movement with its external consequences. This binding process may be essential if we are to recognize specific external events as the consequences of our behaviors (see also Haggard, 2005).

So then, what does it mean to be conscious? As you have just read, consciousness is defined as more than merely being awake. Rather it depends crucially on being able to report on one's perceptions, thoughts, feelings—on the "what" of one's private experience—in ways that others acknowledge as appropriate. In addition, it is important to remember that consciousness is not a single condition but consists of distinguishable states, just as unconsciousness does.

QUESTIONS TO CONSIDER

1. What do you think about the possibility that members of other species may be conscious? What evidence would you look for to answer this question?

2. If our thesis about human consciousness is correct, babies acquire consciousness as they acquire language. How might this conclusion be related to the fact that we cannot remember what happened to us when we were very young?

3. Suppose a person were raised in isolation and never came in contact with (or communicated with) another person. That person would not have language. What would that person's private experience be like?

Selective Attention

We do not become conscious of all the stimuli detected by our sensory organs. For example, if an angler is watching a large trout circling underneath an artificial fly she has deftly cast on the water, she probably will not notice the chirping of birds in the trees behind her or the temperature of the water surrounding her wading gear or the floating twigs drifting by with the current. Her attention is completely devoted to the behavior of the fish, and she is poised to respond with the appropriate movements of her fly rod if the fish takes the fly. The process that controls our focus on specific categories of events in the environment, to the exclusion of others, is called **selective attention.**

---

selective attention The process that controls our awareness of, and readiness to respond to, particular categories of stimuli or stimuli in a particular location to the exclusion of others.

divided attention The process by which we distribute awareness among different stimuli or tasks so that we can respond to them or perform them simultaneously.

But now consider what happens if the fish strikes. The angler's task changes drastically to one of divided attention: She must monitor the tension on the line, control the rod, and watch her footsteps on the slippery rocks underneath as she maneuvers into position to reel in her catch. **Divided attention** is the process by which we allocate our attention to two or more tasks to perform them simultaneously (the term *multitasking* is similar).

Attention may be related to consciousness. Selective attention narrows our awareness to particular experiences, at the same time leaving us unaware of others. Divided attention is basically a different decision process of the brain that determines how our awareness will be allocated between different experiences. Attention may be shifted suddenly and automatically, as when an unexpectedly intense stimulus (such as a loud and novel sound) occurs [Pavlov (1927) referred to it as the *orienting reflex*]. A rapid shift of attention to a novel stimulus may allow the individual to respond to it more effectively than otherwise and may thus be considered adaptive, or the shift may be controlled by others' instructions ("Hey, pay attention to the car on your right!"). We may try to divide our attention, to multitask, as when we use a cell phone while driving—with possibly adverse consequences. For example, Strayer and Drew (2007) reported that driving while talking on a cell phone produces *inattention blindness*, which is discussed in a later section. Attention to visual events, in particular, tends to act like a spotlight, or perhaps more like a zoom lens, that highlights the events within a spatial context (McCormick, Klein, & Johnston, 1998). The brain's attentional mechanisms serve to enhance our responsiveness to certain stimuli, effectively tuning out irrelevant information. As we saw in the case of blindsight, attention may be irrelevant to certain kinds of experiences in which behavior proceeds without awareness.

Attention also plays an important role in memory. By exerting control over the information that reaches short-term memory, it determines what information ultimately becomes stored in explicit long-term memory. But, as Chapter 7 indicated, the storage of information in implicit memory does not require conscious attention. Thus, information is not necessarily lost if we fail to attend to it.

Why, then, does attention exist? Why not process all of the information that our sensory receptors capture? After all, we may miss something important if our attention is directed elsewhere. The answer, according to Broadbent (1958), is that the brain mechanisms responsible for processing sensory information have a limited capacity. Only so much information can be accommodated by these mechanisms at any instant in time. Thus, we need another mechanism that serves as a gatekeeper, controlling the flow of information over time. Broadbent suggested that attention solves this problem by serving as a filter—allowing information of one type (such as the fly on the water in my fishing example) to be processed while deflecting other information (such as the birds chirping in that example). Although the concept of selective attention as a gatekeeper is widely accepted, it remains the subject of ongoing research.

The trading-market floor swirls with visual and auditory messages that vie for the traders' attention.

Auditory Information

The first experiments to investigate selective attention systematically took advantage of the fact that we have two ears. Cherry (1953; see also Hugdahl, 1988) devised a **dichotic** (die-KAH-tick) **listening test** that requires a person to listen to one of two messages presented simultaneously, one to each ear. (Dichotic means "divided into two parts.") He placed headphones on his participants and presented recordings of different spoken messages to each ear. He asked the participants to "**shadow**" the message presented to one ear—continuously to repeat back aloud what that voice was saying. Shadowing ensured that participants would pay attention to only that message.

Cherry was interested in what happened to the information that entered the unattended ear—the unshadowed message. In general, it appeared to be lost. When questioned about

what they had heard in that ear, participants responded that they had heard something, but they could not say what it was. Even if the voice presented to the unattended ear suddenly began talking in a foreign language, the change was not reported.

These results suggest that a sensory channel that is a specific stream of sensory input (in this case, the message presented to one ear) can simply be turned off. Perhaps the neurons in the auditory system that detect sound from the unattended ear are inhibited and cannot respond to sounds presented to that ear as they would ordinarily. (See FIGURE 8·2(a) for a depiction of this possibility.)

The story is not that simple, however. Other evidence shows that selective attention is not simply a matter of turning off a sensory channel. Some information gets through regardless, as long as the ear is healthy. For example, if a person's name is suddenly included in the message presented to the unattended ear, he or she will very likely hear it and remember it later (Moray, 1959, 1970). Or, if the message presented to the unattended ear contains sexually explicit words, participants tend to notice them immediately (Nielsen & Sarason, 1981). The fact that some kinds of information presented to the unattended ear can so readily capture attention indicates that even unattended verbal information undergoes some analysis. If the unattended information is, in fact, "filtered out" at some level, this filtration must not occur until after the sounds are identified as words. (See FIGURE 8·2(b).)

---

dichotic listening test   A task that requires a person to listen to one of two different messages being presented simultaneously, one to each ear, through headphones.

shadowing   The act of continuously repeating verbal material aloud as soon as it is heard.

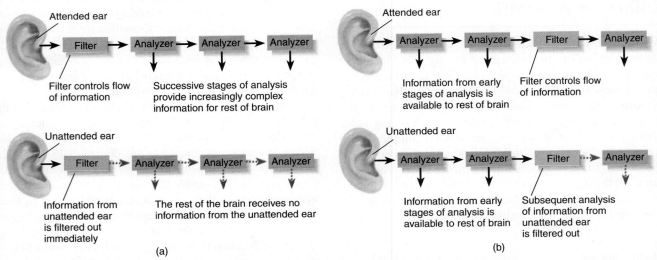

[**FIGURE 8·2**]   Models of selective attention in the dichotic listening task. (a) Filtering of unattended sensory information immediately after it is received by the sensory receptors. This model cannot explain the fact that some information presented to the unattended ear enters consciousness. (b) Filtering of unattended sensory information after some preliminary analysis.

[FIGURE 8•3] Shadowing a message that switches ears. When the message switches, the person must retrieve from memory some words that were heard by the unattended ear.

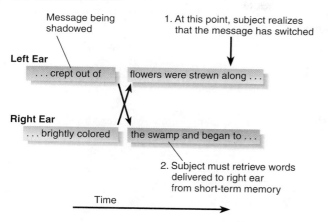

[FIGURE 8•3] Shadowing a message that switches ears. When the message switches, the person must retrieve from memory some words that were heard by the unattended ear.

McKay (1973; see also Johnson & Proctor, 2003) showed that messages presented to the unattended ear can influence verbal processing even when the listener is not conscious of them. In the attended ear, participants heard sentences such as the following:

> They threw stones toward the bank yesterday.

While this sentence was being presented, the word "river" or the word "money" was presented in the unattended ear. Later, participants were asked which of the following sentences they had heard:

> They threw stones toward the side of the river yesterday.
> They threw stones toward the savings and loan association yesterday.

Of course, neither of these sentences had been presented. But as Sachs (1967) showed in a classic study (see Chapter 7), people quickly forget the particular words a sentence contains, although they remember its meaning for much longer. McKay found that the participants' choices between the two sentences were consistent with whether the word "river" or "money" had been presented to the unattended ear. They did not specifically recall hearing the words themselves, but the words had nevertheless affected their perception of the meaning of the word "bank" in the original sentence.

Besides being able to attend to and remember some of the information in the unattended sensory channel, we are able to store information temporarily as it arrives. No doubt you have had the following sort of experience. You are intently reading or thinking about something, when you suddenly become aware that someone nearby has asked you a question. You look up and say, "What?" but then proceed to answer the question before the other person has had a chance to repeat it. First you became aware that you had just been asked a question, but you did not know what it was. However,

a moment later, you remembered what the question was—you heard it again in your mind's ear, so to speak. That information, held in temporary storage, now became accessible to your language system, and you answered the question.

Treisman (1960, 1988) showed that participants can follow a message that is being shadowed even if it switches from one ear to the other. Suppose a participant is shadowing the message presented to the left ear, while the message to the right ear is unshadowed. (See **FIGURE 8•3**.) In the example given in Figure 8.3, the participant says "crept out of the swamp" and not "crept out of flowers." Apparently, the participant's switch from one message to the other occurs when the originally shadowed message begins to make no sense. However, by the time the participant becomes aware that "crept out of flowers" makes no sense, "the swamp" has already been presented to the right ear. Because the participant is able to continue the message without missing any words—"crept out of the swamp"—he or she must be able to retrieve the latter words from memory of the unshadowed message. Thus, even though an unshadowed message cannot be remembered later, it remains long enough to be retrieved, but only if attention is directed to it soon after the words are presented. According to Treisman (1969), the "gatekeeping" role of selective attention is not that of a nonpermeable filter. Rather, nonattended information remains available, if only partially, and can still be retrieved under the right conditions.

Selective attention to auditory messages has practical significance outside the laboratory. For example, sometimes we have to sort out one message from several others. It isn't as simple as hearing one voice in one ear and another voice in the other. For example, we may be trying to converse with one person while we are in a room in which several other people are carrying on their own conversations. Even in the situation shown in **FIGURE 8•4**, we can usually sort out one voice from another—an example of what Cherry (1953) originally termed

[FIGURE 8•4] The cocktail-party phenomenon. We can follow a particular conversation even when other conversations are going on around us.

the "**cocktail-party problem**" (also referred to as the *cocktail-party phenomenon*). In this case we are trying to listen to the person opposite us and to ignore the cross-conversation of the people to our left and right. Our ears receive a jumble of sounds, but we are able to pick out and string together those that form a meaningful message, ignoring the rest. To do this is effortful, and following one person's words in such circumstances is even more difficult when what he or she is saying is not very interesting, that is, not very attention getting. If we overhear a few words of another conversation that seems more interesting, attention likely will stray to that conversation. If it contains our name, such straying is almost unstoppable.

Visual Information

Since the pioneering work on dichotic listening, the study of selective attention has increasingly involved visual stimuli. This research has shown that people can successfully attend either to the location of the information or to the nature of the information (as revealed by its physical features, such as form or color).

Location Sperling's classic studies on sensory memory (see Chapter 7) were probably the first to demonstrate the role of attention in selectively transferring visual information into verbal short-term memory (or, for our purposes here, into consciousness). Later psychologists studied the same phenomenon in more detail. For example, Posner, Snyder, and Davidson (1980; Posner and DiGirolamo, 2000) instructed participants to watch a computer-controlled display screen. A small mark in the center of the screen served as a fixation point for the participants' gaze. A warning stimulus then appeared near the fixation point, followed by the target stimulus—a letter displayed just slightly to the left or the right of the fixation point. The warning stimulus consisted of either a plus sign or an arrow that pointed right or left. The arrows served as cues to the participants to expect the letter to occur either to the right or to the left. The plus sign served as a neutral stimulus devoid of spatial cues. The participants' task was to press a button as soon as they detected the letter.

On 80 percent of the trials, the arrow accurately pointed toward the location in which the letter was presented. However, on the rest of the trials, the arrow pointed away from the location. The warning stimulus clearly had an effect on the participants' response times: When the arrows correctly informed them of the location of the letter, they responded faster; and when they were incorrectly informed, they responded more slowly. (See FIGURE 8•5.)

This study shows that selective attention can affect the detection of visual stimuli: If a stimulus occurs where we expect it, we perceive it more quickly; if it occurs where we do not expect it, we perceive it more slowly. Because the participants' gaze remained fixed on the center of the screen in this study, the allocation of attention to one side of the fixation point or the other occurred independent of any eye movements. The results of the study suggest that selective attention sensitizes the neural circuits for detecting a particular kind of stimulus, making it more readily located. By analogy, suppose

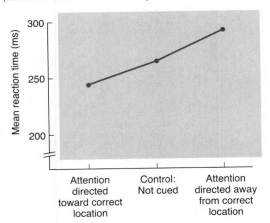

[**FIGURE 8•5**] Location as a cue for selective attention. Mean reaction time in response to a letter displayed on a screen after participants received a cue directing attention toward the location in which the letter appears was less than when no cue or an incorrect cue was received.

(Based on data from Posner, Snyder, and Davidson (1980).)

you misplace your car keys and search for them in several places, to no avail; a roommate notices you searching and mentions having seen them in the kitchen near the toaster. Sure enough, you locate them there right away, even though they had been in the same place during your earlier search.

A possible clue to the way these attentional circuits work comes from an interesting extension of the task used by Posner and his colleagues. Suppose the arrow is completely nonpredictive (that is, it sometimes points to where the letter will be presented but just as often does not). As we know, when the letter is presented right after the arrow is presented, people are usually faster at recognizing the letter when it appears at the location the arrow indicated. That is, even though the arrow is sometimes correct and sometimes wrong, the attentional "spotlight" is directed by the arrow. However, if the interval between the presentation of the arrow and the letter is a little longer (about 100 to 300 milliseconds), then recognition is now slower when the letter appears at the location to which the arrow pointed. Posner and his colleagues have called this surprising effect the **inhibition of return (IOR).** Speaking loosely, once the arrow appears, the attentional spotlight sweeps momentarily over to the location signaled by the arrow. Because no letter appears there, it sweeps back, but then is inhibited from returning immediately to the same spot where it swept originally. It's as if, having shifted to the location indicated by the arrow, the attentional system is now slower to return to it (Posner & Cohen, 1984). Some have argued that IOR biases attention to novel stimuli. Recently, it has been extended to more complex phenomena, such as memory for words (Massen

cocktail-party problem Trying to follow one conversation while other, potentially distracting conversations are going on around us.

inhibition of return (IOR) A reduced tendency to perceive a target when the target's presentation is consistent with a cue, but the target is presented a few hundred milliseconds after the cue.

& Stegt, 2007) and facial cues (Stoyanova, Pratt, & Anderson, 2007). Continuing the earlier analogy, if, given your roommate's mention, you looked for your keys near the toaster but failed to find them there, you would probably be unlikely to search again in the vicinity of the toaster.

Features The second dimension of selective visual attention are the features of the object being attended to (Vecera & Farah, 1994; Desimone & Duncan, 1995). Sometimes, two events happen in close proximity, but we can separate them, watching one while ignoring the other. For example, Neisser and Becklen (1975) showed participants a videotape that presented a situation similar to that confronted by the person who is trying to listen to a specific voice at a cocktail party. The videotape contained two different action sequences presented one on top of the other: a game in which people are passing a basketball around and a hand game in which people try to slap their opponents' hands, which are resting on top of theirs. The participants could easily follow one game and remember what had happened in it; however, they could not attend simultaneously to both games. (See FIGURE 8•6.)

What happens to the information that is not attended to? As we have seen, in the auditory system, information that is of personal relevance, such as someone calling our name, can override attention to something else. Similarly, our name seems to jump out if it appears in print, even if it appears in text that we ignore (Neisser, 1969). In an evolutionary perspective, this readiness to tune rapidly to personally relevant information may have conferred a selective advantage.

Recent evidence suggests that the visual system is prone to **inattention blindness** (Most et al., 2005), a failure to perceive an event when attention is diverted elsewhere. You may have had the experience of shopping in a crowded place, looking for a particular item and, while doing so, failing to notice that a friend was shopping only a few feet away. But suppose you were watching the game mentioned earlier in which participants were asked to count the number of times a basketball was passed between them, and a woman in a gorilla suit walked right through the action, stopping in the middle to pound her chest? (See FIGURE 8•7.) You would definitely notice that, right? Remarkably, half of the research participants who observed this action in a film sequence designed by Simons and Chabris (1999) failed to notice the gorilla. This occurred despite the fact that the unusual event was in the center of the action. Interestingly, the unusual nature of the event seemed to make it more likely to be missed: When the game was interrupted by a woman carrying an umbrella, more of the participants noticed her. In related experiments using picture and words, Finnish researchers Koivisto and Revonsuo (2007) showed that unexpected stimuli (for example, a person in a gorilla suit) semantically unrelated to the current interests of the observer (counting the number of times the basketball is passed) are more likely to remain unseen.

Simons and Rensink (2005) have made the general point that, although our visual experience is rich with information,

[**FIGURE 8•6**] Drawings of the scenes from the videotapes in Neisser and Becklen's study. (a) The hand game. (b) The basketball game. (c) The two games superimposed.

(Reprinted from Neisser, U., & Becklen, R. (1975). *Cognitive Psychology, 1975, 7,* 480–494. Copyright © 1975, with permission from Elsevier.)

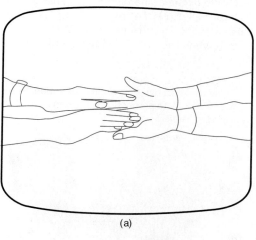

(a)

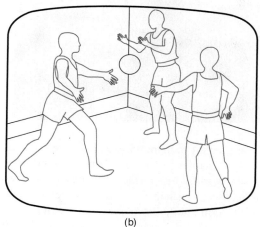

(b)

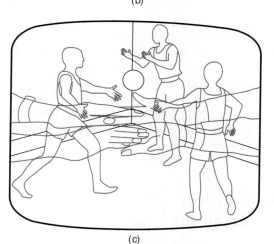

(c)

---

inattention blindness Failure to perceive an event when attention is diverted elsewhere.

[FIGURE 8·7] A frame from the film constructed by Simons and Chabris for their study of inattentional blindness. Observers were asked to watch a basketball passing game being played by two teams and to count the passes between members of each team. As they watched, a woman wearing a gorilla suit walked in from the right, paused in the middle of the game facing the camera, and then walked out to the left. Half of the observers failed to notice this unusual event. To learn more about the "gorilla" study or to view the original video, go to www.viscog.net

(From Simons, D. J., & Chabris, C. F. (1999). Gorillas in our midst: Sustained inattentional blindness for dynamic events. *Perception, 28,* 1059–1074, Figure 3. Reprinted with permission from Pion Limited, London. Figure provided by Daniel Simons.)

our ability to represent it in memory may be limited. We saw such limitations in Chapter 7. Perhaps when we attend selectively to the visual world, consciousness requires that the rest of it remains relatively unchanging. After all, people we're talking to don't spontaneously change hair color or the clothes they're wearing just because we briefly look away from them.

Would we notice it if they did? Surprisingly, the answer seems to be no, at least under some circumstances. If a visual display is artificially changed during an eye movement or other visual distraction, **change blindness** often results: People often fail to notice significant changes in the display (O'Regan, Rensink, & Clark, 1999). In one memorable study, people who were talking to a construction worker failed to notice when the person himself changed during a brief distraction (Simons & Levin, 1998)!

Brain Mechanisms of Selective Attention

As previously noted, a possible explanation for selective attention is that some components of the brain's sensory system are temporarily sensitized, which enhances their ability to detect particular categories of stimuli. For example, if a research participant were watching for changes in stimulus shapes, colors, or movements (that is, if the person's attention were focused on one of these attributes), we might expect to see increased activity in the portions of the visual cortex devoted to the analysis of shapes, colors, or movements.

This result is exactly what Corbetta and colleagues (1991) found. They instructed participants to look at a computerized display containing 30 colored rectangles, which could change in shape, color, or speed of movement. The stimuli were the same during each condition of the experiment. Thus, the only difference between the conditions was the type of stimulus change the participants were instructed to report.

The investigators used a PET scanner to measure brain activity as the participants watched the display. They found that paying attention to shape, color, or speed of movement caused activation of different regions of the visual association cortex. More recent work by Shulman et al. (2003) used *f*MRI to parse selective visual attention into sensory, search, and detection components according to the same brain regions Corbetta et al. had identified.

Luck and colleagues (1993) obtained similar results in a study with monkeys and the activity of single neurons in the visual association cortex. When a visual cue indicated that the monkey should watch for a stimulus to be presented in a particular location within the visual field, neurons that received input from that location began firing more rapidly, even before the stimulus was presented. These neurons thus seemed to be "primed" for detecting a stimulus.

The interrelatedness of visual memory (specifically, iconic memory—see Chapter 7) and visual selective attention was recently reported by Ruff, Kristjánsson, and Driver (2007). They instructed participants to look at a fixation point in the center of a screen, and then to report the number of specific objects that were presented in either the left or right half of a brief display. The objects were circles that were either partially or fully closed. Three circles appeared in each half of the display. Participants pressed a button to signal the number of closed circles. A tone indicated which half of the display the report should come from. The cue was presented either shortly (200 milliseconds) before or after the display appeared. The pre-cue activated selective attention, and the post-cue, iconic memory.

By using *f*MRI, the researchers found similar brain activity after pre-cues and post-cues. The activity occurred in the lateral occipital cortex that was contralateral to the side on which the cued display was presented. That is, if the tone signaled a report of the circles in the right visual field, then activity increased in the left lateral occipital cortex. (Recall from Chapter 4 that, in the visual system, the flow of information from the right visual field is to the left visual cortex, and vice versa.) This occurred regardless of whether the tone functioned as a pre-cue or post-cue. Ruff et al. concluded that similar mechanisms are involved in selective visual attention and iconic memory, respectively.

---

change blindness   Failure to detect a change when vision is interrupted.

QUESTIONS TO CONSIDER

1. Have you ever had an experience in which someone asked you a question when you weren't paying attention, and then, before the question could be repeated, you realized what it was? How long do you think the unattended information lasts before it is eventually lost? Can you think of an experiment that would permit you to find out? If so, briefly describe it.

2. Let's reconsider the cocktail-party problem. Suppose that a person is carrying on a conversation and then happens to overhear a word or two from another conversation that seems much more interesting. Wanting to be polite, the person tries to ignore the other conversation but finds it difficult, hemming and hawing while trying to attend to both conversations. Should we regard this example as a failure of selective attention? Or is it actually useful that we usually don't become so absorbed in one thing that we miss out on potentially interesting information? What is your view, and why?

3. It isn't unusual for students to say they have a hard time studying because they are easily distracted. This implies that paying attention is effortful, that studying effectively can be hard work. If you were trying to make this point, which research findings cited in this section of the chapter would be most useful to you? Why?

Consciousness and the Brain

We know that brain damage can alter human consciousness. For example, Chapter 7 described the phenomenon of anterograde amnesia, caused by damage to the hippocampus. Although people with this defect cannot form new verbal memories, they can learn some kinds of tasks (Sacks, 2007). However, they remain unaware they have learned, even when their behavior indicates they have. The brain damage does not prevent all kinds of learning, but it does prevent awareness of what has been learned.

If human consciousness is related to speech, then it is probably related to the brain mechanisms that control comprehension and production of speech. This hypothesis suggests that for us to be aware of an event, information about it must be transmitted to neural circuits in the brain responsible for language ability. Several reports of cases of human brain damage support this suggestion. Let's consider some examples.

Isolation Aphasia: A Case of Global Unawareness

Geschwind, Quadfasel, and Segarra (1968) described the case of a woman who had severe brain damage as a result of inhaling

---

isolation aphasia   Language disorder in which a person cannot comprehend speech or produce meaningful speech but is able to repeat speech and to learn new sequences of words.

carbon monoxide from a faulty water heater. The damage spared the primary auditory cortex, the speech areas of the brain, and the connections between these areas. However, the damage destroyed large parts of the visual association cortex and isolated the speech mechanisms from other parts of the brain. The syndrome that Geschwind and colleagues reported is referred to as **isolation aphasia** (see Hegde, 2001), a language disturbance in which a person is unable to comprehend speech or to produce meaningful speech but is able to repeat speech and to learn new sequences of words. It is also classified as *mixed transcortical aphasia* (Berthier, 1999).

The woman remained in the hospital until she died nine years later. During this time, she made few movements except with her eyes, which were able to follow moving objects. She gave no evidence of recognizing objects or people in her hospital environment. She did not spontaneously say anything, answer questions, or give any signs that she understood what other people said to her. By all available criteria, she was not conscious of anything that was going on, much like Jan Gzrebski and Terri Schiavo, described in the Prologue. However, the woman could repeat words that were spoken to her. And if someone started a poem she recognized, she would finish it. For example, if someone said, "Roses are red, violets are blue," she would respond, "Sugar is sweet, and so are you." She even learned new poems and songs and sang along with the radio—but never in any knowing or conscious way. Her case suggests that consciousness is not simply a matter of the brain's speech mechanisms. It requires their connectedness to other parts of the brain, including those that serve memory and attention. Of course, it is also possible that the limitations of awareness that were observed could be attributed to more generalized loss rather than to that specific to speech mechanisms. It is important to realize the difficulties that can beset any claim of a specific deficit due to a specific site of brain damage. Alternative ways to account for the deficit will almost always exist.

Visual Agnosia: Loss of Awareness of Visual Perceptions

The case just described was of a woman who appeared to have completely lost her awareness of herself and her environment. In other instances, people with brain damage have become selectively unaware, that is, unaware of particular kinds of information. For example, in blindsight, individuals can point to and grasp objects they cannot see—or rather, that they are not aware of seeing. Margolin, Friedrich, and Carlson (1985) studied a young man with a different kind of disconnection between perception and awareness. His brain had been damaged by an inflammation of the blood vessels, and he consequently had *visual agnosia* (recall the case of Mrs. R. in Chapter 5)—the inability to recognize the identity of an object visually. The man had great difficulty identifying common objects by sight. For example, he could not say what a hammer was by looking at it, but he quickly identified it when he was permitted to pick it up and feel it. He was not blind; he could

[FIGURE 8·8] Hypothetical exchanges of information within the brain of a patient with visual agnosia.

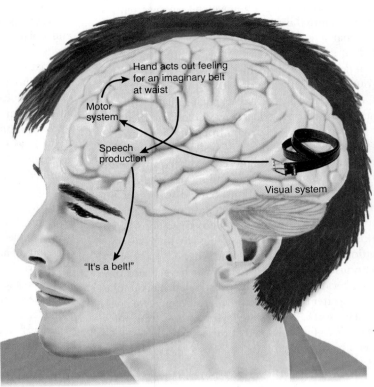

walk around without bumping into things, and he had no trouble making visually guided movements to pick up an object that he wanted to identify. The researchers' simplest conclusion was that his disease had damaged the neural circuits responsible for visual perception.

However, the simplest was not their eventual conclusion. Although the patient had great difficulty visually recognizing objects or pictures of objects, he often made hand movements that appeared to be related to the object he could not identify. For example, when shown a picture of a pistol, he stared at it with a puzzled look, then shook his head and said that he couldn't tell what it was. While continuing to study the picture, he clenched his right hand into a fist and began making movements with his index finger. When asked what he was doing, he looked at his hand, made a few tentative movements with his finger, and then raised his hand in the air and moved it forward each time he moved his finger. He was unmistakably miming the way a person holds and fires a pistol. "Oh!" he said. "It's a gun. No, a pistol." Clearly, he was not aware of what the picture was until he paid attention to what his hand was doing. On another occasion, he looked at a picture of a belt and said it was a pair of pants. Then he was asked him to point to where the legs and other parts of the pants were. When he tried to do so, he became puzzled. His hands went to the place where his belt buckle ordinarily would be (he was wearing hospital pajamas at the time) and moved his hands as if he were feeling one. "No," he said, after noticing the motions

of his hand. "It's not a pair of pants—it's a belt!" **FIGURE 8·8** depicts a possible neural basis for his discovery.

The patient's visual system was not normal, yet it functioned better than could be inferred from his verbal behavior alone. That is, he was aware in a way that his words failed to indicate. The fact that he could mime the use of a pistol or feel an imaginary belt buckle with his hands indicated that his visual system worked well enough to initiate appropriate nonverbal behaviors, although not the appropriate words. Once he selectively attended to what his hands were doing, he could name the object.

Although the patient had lost his ability to read, speech therapists were able to teach him to use finger spelling to read, the form of spelling used by deaf people. He could not say what a particular letter was, but he could learn to make a particular hand movement when he saw the letter. After he had learned the finger-spelling alphabet, he could read slowly and laboriously by making the hand movements for each letter and learning the sequences of movement that corresponded to words.

This case could be interpreted as supporting the conclusion that consciousness is synonymous with a person's ability to talk about his or her perceptions or memories. In this particular situation, disruption of the normal interchange between the visual perceptual system and the verbal system prevented the patient from being directly aware of his own visual perceptions. Instead, it was as if his hands talked to him, telling him what he had just seen. Conversely, it is possible that, although brain damage prevented direct visual recognition of objects, alternative forms of recognition may have been supported by undamaged areas of association cortex (for example, the kinesthetic association cortex; Fiehler et al., 2008). Thus recognition may have occurred without the need for access to speech mechanisms.

The Split-Brain Syndrome

A surgical procedure exists whose effects demonstrate dramatically how various brain functions can be disconnected from one another and from language mechanisms. It is used rarely and as something of a last resort for people who have severe epilepsy that cannot be controlled with drugs. In these people, highly erratic neural activity first engulfs one cerebral hemisphere and is transmitted to the other by the corpus callosum, the large bundle of axons that connects the cortex in one hemisphere with that in the other. This produces a grand mal or generalized epileptic seizure, which can occur many times each day, preventing the individual from leading a normal life. Neurosurgeons discovered that the **split-brain operation**—cutting the corpus callosum to disconnect the two cerebral hemispheres (sometimes referred to as a callosumotomy)—greatly reduces the frequency of the seizures.

Sperry (1966) and Gazzaniga and his associates (Gazzaniga, 1970, 2000; Gazzaniga & LeDoux, 1978) studied split-brain patients extensively. Normally, the left and right cerebral cortices exchange information through the corpus callosum. With one exception (described later), each hemisphere receives

split-brain operation A surgical procedure that severs the corpus callosum, thus abolishing the direct connections between the cortex of the two cerebral hemispheres.

sensory information from the opposite side of the body and controls muscle movements on that side. The corpus callosum permits these activities to be coordinated, so that what originates in one hemisphere may be transmitted to the other. After the two hemispheres are surgically disconnected, they are essentially independent. The sensory mechanisms, perceptions, memories, and motor systems of one hemisphere are essentially isolated from those of the other. The effects of this disconnection are not obvious to a casual observer, for the simple reason that only one hemisphere—in most people, the left—controls speech. The right hemisphere can comprehend speech reasonably well but because Broca's speech area is located in the left hemisphere; the right hemisphere cannot produce speech.

With only the left hemisphere able to talk, a casual observer will not detect the independence of the operations of the right hemisphere. Even the patient's left hemisphere has to learn about the independent existence of the right. One of the first things these patients report after the surgery is that their left hand "seems to have a mind of its own." For example, they may find themselves putting down a book held by the left hand, even though they are reading it with great interest. At other times, they may surprise themselves by making obscene gestures with the left hand. Because the right hemisphere controls the movements of the left hand, the left hemisphere is informed about them only when they occur.

An exception to the cross-hemispheric transmission of sensory information noted earlier is the olfactory system. When a person with the corpus callosum intact sniffs a flower through the left nostril, only the left hemisphere receives the sensation. Thus, if the right nostril of a split-brain patient is blocked, and the left nostril is left open, the patient will accurately identify odors verbally. Conversely, if the odor enters

[**FIGURE 8·9**] Identification of an object by a person with a split brain in response to an olfactory stimulus.

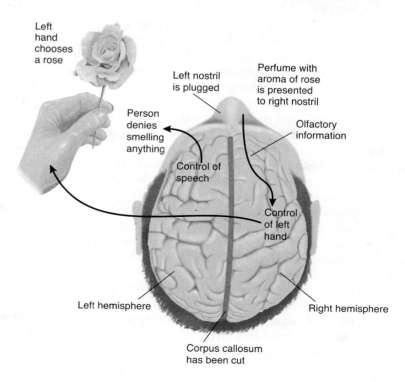

only the right nostril, the patient will say that he or she doesn't smell anything, but the sensory signals were transmitted to the right hemisphere, and the odor is perceived there. This fact can be demonstrated by asking the patient to reach for some objects hidden from view by a partition. If asked to use the left hand only, and with the left nostril blocked, the patient will select the object that corresponds to the odor—a plastic flower for a floral odor, a toy fish for a fishy odor, a small plastic tree for the odor of pine, and so forth. But if the left nostril is blocked, the right hand fails this test, because it is controlled by the left hemisphere, which did not receive the odor signals. (See FIGURE 8•9; Gazzaniga, 1989.)

As we saw in Chapter 3, the left hemisphere, besides giving us the ability to read, write, and speak, is good at other tasks that require verbal abilities, such as mathematics and logic. The right hemisphere excels at visual and spatial perception and skills related to the visual arts. For example, if a split-brain patient tries to use his or her right hand to arrange blocks in a pattern to duplicate a geometrical design provided by a researcher, the hand will fumble with the blocks and fail to arrange them properly. The left hand may then brush the right hand aside and proceed to complete the task. It is as if the right hemisphere becomes impatient with the ineptitude of the left.

*f*ocus On

Embodied Consciousness and the Out-of-Body Experience

Human consciousness is embodied. The ability to report one's perceptions, thoughts, and feelings to others, and to oneself, generally includes the report that such events occur within one's skin, that one is reporting on how it seems from "in here." Psychologists have an interest in understanding the necessary and sufficient conditions for the near-universal experiences of consciousness, including consciousness of self (also called "embodied consciousness").

How is embodied consciousness studied? Ehrrson (2007) attempted this by experimentally inducing out-of-body experiences (OBEs) in their participants. Participants at the Karolinska Institute in Stockholm were healthy adults who wore head-mounted viewing devices that received their input from a pair of video cameras located two meters behind them. The cameras were placed side by side so as to simulate a pair of eyes. The images from the left camera appeared in the left-eye display of the device the participant wore, and the images from the right camera in the right-eye display. The experimenter stood to the right of the seated participant and, while in the participant's view, moved a pair of plastic rods. With the rod in his right hand, the experimenter stroked the participant's chest and, simultaneously with his left hand, moved the rod just below the cameras, as if stroking an invisible chest

in approximately the same location. In their viewers, participants only saw Ehrrson's arm moving, but this occurred as they felt the rod on their own chests.

After two minutes of exposure to chest stroking, the participants completed a questionnaire designed to test the strength of the illusion they reported, namely, that they were actually sitting behind their bodies and looking at them from that altered position. According to Ehrrson, "You really feel that you are sitting in a different place in the room and you're looking at this thing in front of you that looks like yourself and you know it's yourself but it doesn't feel like yourself." (Miller, 2007, p. 1021). In a second experiment, Ehrrson measured the participants' skin-conductance response (SCR), a widely used correlate of emotional arousal. To induce the OBE, he used the plastic rods as he had previously and introduced a control condition in which, instead of applying the rods simultaneously, he alternated their application. In both conditions, he interrupted the use of the plastic rods by suddenly picking up a hammer and swinging it toward the imaginary chest. The emotional reaction was immediate in terms of the participants' movements and the SCR, and was greater in the experimental than the control condition.

Lenggenhager et al. (2007) reported a study conducted at the Swiss Federal Institute of Technology in Lausanne. Their participants stood and wore 3-D video-display devices in which the computer-controlled images originated from a video camera placed 2 meters behind them. Thus they viewed a virtual body that seemed to be located in front of them about the same distance. They subsequently viewed the back of the virtual body being stroked by a highlighter pen at the same time their own backs were stroked (the synchronous condition; see FIGURE 8.10(a)). In another condition (asynchronous), the stroking alternated as in Ehrrson's study. After exposure to stroking, participants were blindfolded, led away from their original position and asked to return to it. They tended to end up at a position ahead of where they had been originally, that is, closer to the virtual body. This finding, together with the participants' responses to a self-attribution questionnaire, suggested that they perceived themselves to be in the virtual body. This illusion was replicated in a second experiment that involved the participant's virtual body, a virtual fake body, and a virtual body-sized rectangular solid (see FIGURES 8.10(b), 8.10(c)). Both the virtual real body and fake body produced the illusion—"It felt as if the virtual condition was my body"—but the virtual object condition did not.

Although the procedures used in the two laboratories produced the illusion of spatial displacement of body consciousness, it fell short of the more widely known phenomenon in which individuals report leaving their bodies and viewing them from a distance. Still, the findings provide the strong suggestion that the feeling of being an embodied self depends on the integration of visuospatial and somatosensory information. A disjunction between the two forms of information may render us susceptible to the experience of being ourselves in other bodies.

[FIGURE 8•10] (a) The participant appears in dark blue pants and views his own virtual body (light blue pants) in front of him. Stroking of the back occurs either synchronously or asynchronously. (b) A virtual fake body (red pants) replaces the virtual own body. (c) A virtual object appears in place of the virtual own body.

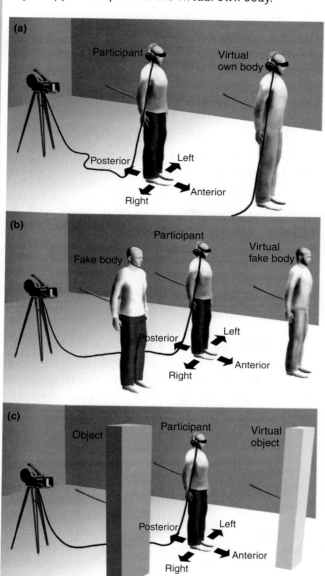

QUESTIONS TO CONSIDER

1. Some split-brain patients have reported that they can use only one hand to hold a book while reading. If they use the other hand, they find themselves putting the book down, even though they want to continue reading. Which hand puts the book down? Why does it do so?

2. When a stimulus is presented to the right hemisphere of a split-brain patient, the person (speaking with his or her left hemisphere) claims to be unaware of it. Because the right hemisphere cannot talk to us, should we conclude that it lacks conscious self-awareness? If you think it is conscious, has the surgery produced two independent consciousnesses where only one previously existed? If so, how different would they be?

Hypnosis

Hypnosis is a specific and unusual form of verbal control that apparently enables one person to control some of another person's (or one's own) behavior, including thinking and perceiving (see Kihlstrom, 2004). Under hypnosis, a person can be induced to bark like a dog, act like a baby, or tolerate being pierced with needles or exposed to icy coldness. Although these examples are sometimes the stuff of entertainment, hypnosis is important to psychology because it provides insights into the nature of consciousness. It also has effective applications in psychotherapy and medicine (Gafner & Benson, 2003; Stewart, 2005).

Although hypnosis may have been in use among religious cults in classical Greece (Spanos & Chaves, 1991), the modern phenomenon of hypnosis, or mesmerism, was introduced by Franz Anton Mesmer (1734–1815), a Viennese physician. He found that when he passed magnets back and forth over people's bodies (in an attempt to restore their "magnetic fluxes" and cure them of disease), they often would convulse and enter a trancelike state during which seemingly miraculous cures could be achieved. As Mesmer discovered later, the patients were not affected directly by the magnetism of the iron rods; they were responding to his undoubtedly persuasive and compelling personality. We now know that convulsions and trancelike states do not necessarily accompany hypnosis, and we also know that hypnosis does not reliably cure physical illnesses. Mesmer's patients' symptoms were alleviated by suggestions he provided during the trance. In some cases, the alleviation was shorter-lived than in others but adequately impressive to allow him a storied career in Vienna and later in Paris (see Wegner, 2003).

Hypnotic Induction and Suggestion

A person undergoing hypnotic induction can be alert, relaxed, tense, lying quietly, or exercising vigorously. There is no need to move an object in front of her or his face while saying, "You are getting sleepy." Numerous techniques can be used to induce hypnosis in a susceptible person (Temes, 2004). The only essential feature seems to be the person's understanding that he or she is to be hypnotized (see Killeen & Nash, 2003).

Not everyone is hypnotizable. Hypnotic susceptibility varies from person to person. Psychologists who study hypnotic phenomena use tests known as hypnotic susceptibility scales to measure individual differences (Hilgard, 1986). Once hypnotized, people are very suggestible. Their behavior will conform to what the hypnotist suggests, even to the extent of appearing to misperceive reality. Generally, hypnotic suggestions are of three types (Kirsch & Lynn, 1998):

- Ideomotor suggestions are those in which the hypnotist suggests that a particular action will occur without awareness of voluntary action, such as raising an arm.

- Challenge suggestions are those for which the hypnotized individual will be unable to perform a normally voluntary action.

- Cognitive suggestions may induce the hypnotized person to report distortions of perceptual or cognitive experiences, such as not feeling pain or not being able to remember something.

One of the most dramatic phenomena of hypnosis is **posthypnotic suggestion,** in which a person is given instructions under hypnosis and follows those instructions after returning to a nonhypnotized state. Typically this requires the use of a cue. For example, a hypnotist might tell a man that he will become unbearably thirsty when he sees the hypnotist look at her watch. She might also admonish him not to remember anything on leaving the hypnotic state, so that **posthypnotic amnesia** is also achieved. After leaving the hypnotic state, the man acts normally and professes ignorance of what he perceived and did during hypnosis, perhaps even apologizing for not having succumbed to hypnosis. The hypnotist later looks at her watch, and the man suddenly rises and leaves the room to get a drink of water.

The most common report of persons undergoing hypnosis is that the actions they perform seem to occur with much less effort than would be the case when out of hypnosis. Sometimes the lack of effort is accompanied by an absence of voluntariness—the arm that rises in response to the hypnotist's suggestion is described as having "a mind of its own" (see Nash, 2001).

Research has indicated that when changes in perception are induced through cognitive suggestions, the changes occur in explicit perception but not in implicit perception. That is, the change is not so much in what the person perceives but in what she or he reports about the perceptions. For example, Miller, Hennessy, and Leibowitz (1973) used the Ponzo illusion to test the effects of hypnotically induced blindness. Although the two parallel horizontal lines in the left portion of FIGURE 8•11 are the same length, the top one looks longer than the bottom one. This effect is produced by the presence of the slanted lines to the left and right of the horizontal ones; if these lines are removed, the horizontal lines appear to be the same length. Through hypnotic suggestion, the researchers made the slanted lines "disappear." Even though the participants reported that they could not see the slanted lines, they still perceived the upper line as longer than the lower one. This result indicates that the visual system continues to process sensory information during hypnotically induced blindness; otherwise, the participants would have perceived the lines as equal in length. The reported blindness appeared to occur not because of altered activity in the visual system but because of altered activity in the verbal system (and in consciousness).

[**FIGURE 8•11**] The Ponzo illusion and hypnotic blindness. The short horizontal lines are actually the same length. Even when a hypnotic suggestion made the slanted lines disappear, the visual system still perceived the illusion.

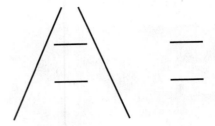

Rainville et al. (1999, 2002) reported studies of hypnotized participants instructed to relax or to reduce the perception of pain produced by the immersion of their hands in hot water. By using EEG and PET measures (see Chapter 3), the researchers found that brain activity and regional cerebral blood flow shifted between the two tasks. Specifically, hypnotically induced relaxation lowered overall cortical activity and made it less likely that activity in the cortical area associated with one sensory modality would suppress activity in an area associated with another modality. With the pain-reduction task, however, activity increased in the cortical and subcortical areas associated with selective attention.

QUESTION TO CONSIDER

Some people prefer explanations that demystify puzzling phenomena such as hypnosis. Others resist such explanations, arguing that an interesting phenomenon is spoiled by an explanation that necessarily places it in the realm of science. How do you respond to each of these viewpoints?

Sleep

Sleep is not a state of unconsciousness—it is a state of *alternate* consciousness. During sleep, we have dreams that can be just as vivid as waking experiences, and yet we forget most of them as soon as they are over. Our amnesia leads us to think that we were unconscious while we were asleep. Two distinct kinds of sleep occur—and thus, two states of consciousness during sleep.

We spend approximately one third of our lives sleeping—or trying to. You might therefore think that the reason we sleep would be clearly understood by scientists who study this phenomenon. And yet, despite the efforts of many talented researchers (see Kleitman, 1939, for an early example), we are still not completely sure why we sleep. Before we discuss proposed functions of sleep, you should understand the stages of sleep.

posthypnotic suggestion A suggestion made by a hypnotist that is carried out some time after the participant has left the hypnotic state and usually according to a specific cue.

posthypnotic amnesia Failure to remember what occurred during hypnosis; induced by suggestions made during hypnosis.

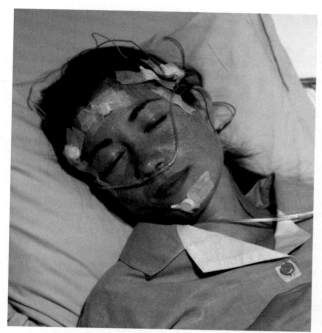

A participant prepared for a night's sleep in a sleep laboratory.

(Photo © Christian Voulgaropoulos/ISM/phtake,Inc.)

The Stages of Sleep

Sleep is not uniform. We can sleep lightly or deeply; we can be restless or still; we can have vivid dreams, or our consciousness can be relatively uninvolved. Researchers have found that sleep occurs in stages that usually follow an orderly, predictable sequence.

The best research on human sleep is conducted in a sleep laboratory, which consists of one or several small bedrooms adjacent to an observation room, where the researcher spends the night (trying to stay awake). The researcher prepares the sleeper for electrophysiological measurements by attaching electrodes to the scalp to monitor the electroencephalogram (EEG) and to the chin to monitor muscle activity, recorded as the **electromyogram (EMG).** Electrodes attached around the eyes monitor eye movements, recorded as the **electro-oculogram (EOG).** In addition, other electrodes and transducing devices can be used to monitor autonomic measures such as heart rate, respiration, and changes in the ability of the skin to conduct electricity.

During wakefulness, the EEG of a normal person shows two basic patterns of activity: *alpha activity* and *beta activity.* **Alpha activity** consists of regular, medium-frequency waves

of 8 to 12 Hz. The brain produces this activity when a person is resting quietly, not particularly aroused or excited, and not engaged in strenuous mental activity (such as problem solving). The other type of waking EEG pattern, **beta activity,** consists of irregular, mostly low-amplitude waves of 13 to 30 Hz. Beta activity reflects the fact that many different neural circuits in the brain are actively processing information. This activity occurs when a person is alert and attentive to events in the environment or is thinking actively. (See FIGURE 8•12.)

By using Figure 8.12 as a guide, let's look at a typical night's sleep of a female college student recorded in the laboratory. (Of course, we would obtain similar results from a male, with one exception, which is noted later.) The experimenter attaches the electrodes, turns the lights off, and closes the door. The participant becomes drowsy and soon enters stage 1 sleep, marked by the presence of some **theta activity** (3.5–7.5 Hz). About 10 minutes later, she enters stage 2 sleep. The EEG during this stage is generally irregular but contains periods of theta activity and *K complexes*—sudden sharp,

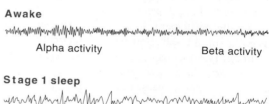

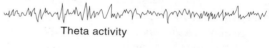

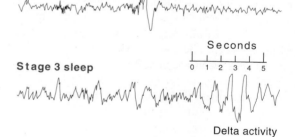

[**FIGURE 8•12**] An EEG recording of the stages of sleep.

(Adapted from Horne, J. A. (1989). *Why We Sleep: The Functions of Sleep in Humans and Other Mammals.* Oxford, England: Oxford University Press, 1989. Copyright © 1988 Oxford University Press. Reprinted by permission of Oxford University Press.)

electromyogram   A record of muscle activity.

electro-oculogram   A record of eye movements.

alpha activity   Rhythmical, medium-frequency electroencephalogram activity, usually indicating a state of quiet relaxation.

beta activity   Irregular, high-frequency electroencephalogram activity, usually indicating a state of alertness or arousal.

theta activity   Electroencephalogram activity of 3.5 to 7.5 Hz; occurs during the transition between sleep and wakefulness.

high-amplitude waveforms. It is not unusual for persons awakened from stage 1 or stage 2 sleep to deny being asleep.

About 15 minutes later, the participant enters stage 3 sleep, signaled by the occurrence of high-amplitude **delta activity** (slower than 3.5 Hz). The distinction between stage 3 and stage 4 is not clear-cut; stage 4 simply contains a greater percentage of delta activity. The sleep of stages 3 and 4 is called **slow-wave sleep.**

About 90 minutes after the beginning of sleep (and about 45 minutes after the onset of stage 4 sleep), we notice an abrupt change in a number of physiological measures recorded from the participant. The EEG suddenly becomes mostly desynchronized, with a sprinkling of theta waves, very similar to the record obtained during stage 1 sleep. We also note that her eyes are rapidly darting back and forth beneath her closed eyelids. We also see that the EMG becomes silent; a profound loss of muscle tonus is present. Physiological studies have shown that, aside from occasional twitching of the hands and feet, a person actually becomes paralyzed during REM sleep. This peculiar stage of sleep is very different from the quiet sleep we saw earlier. It is usually referred to as **REM sleep** (for the rapid eye movements that characterize it).

If we arouse the participant during REM sleep and ask her what was going on, she will almost always report that she had been dreaming. The dreams of REM sleep tend to be narrative in form; a story-like progression of events is noted. If we wake her during slow-wave sleep and ask, "Were you dreaming?" she will most likely say, "No," but she might report the presence of a thought, an image, or some emotion.

During the rest of the night, the participant's sleep alternates between periods of REM and non-REM sleep. Each cycle is approximately 90 minutes long, containing a 20- to 30-minute bout of REM sleep. Thus, an 8-hour sleep will contain four or five periods of REM sleep. **FIGURE 8·13** shows a graph of a typical night's sleep. The vertical axis indicates the EEG activity that is being recorded; thus REM sleep and stage 1 sleep are placed on the same line because similar patterns of EEG activity occur at these times. Note that most slow-wave sleep (stages 3 and 4) occurs during the first half of night.

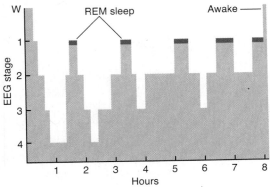

[**FIGURE 8·13**] Typical progression of stages during a night's sleep. The dark blue shading indicates REM sleep.

(From Hartmann, E. (1967). *The Biology of Dreaming*, 1967. Courtesy of Charles C. Thomas, Publisher, Ltd., Springfield, Illinois.)

[**TABLE 8·1**] Principal Characteristics of REM Sleep and Slow-Wave Sleep

REM Sleep	Slow-wave Sleep
Rapid EEG waves	Slow EEG waves
Muscular paralysis	Lack of muscular paralysis
Rapid eye movements	Slow or absent eye movements
Penile erection or vaginal secretion	Lack of genital activity
Story and narrative dreams	Static, rarely narrative dreams; night terrors; sleepwalking

Subsequent bouts of non-REM sleep contain more and more stage 2 sleep, and bouts of REM sleep (indicated by the horizontal bars) become more prolonged. (See Figure 8.13.)

As we saw, during REM sleep, we become paralyzed; most of our spinal and cranial motor neurons are strongly inhibited. (Obviously, the ones that control respiration and eye movements are spared.) At the same time, the brain is very active. Cerebral blood flow and oxygen consumption are accelerated. In addition, during most periods of REM sleep, a male's penis will become at least partially erect, and a female's vaginal secretions will increase. However, these genital changes are reflexive and usually *not* associated with sexual arousal or dreams of a sexual nature. **TABLE 8·1** lists the principal characteristics of REM sleep and the deeper stages of slow-wave sleep.

Functions of Sleep

Sleep is one of the few universal behaviors. All mammals, all birds, and some cold-blooded vertebrates spend part of each day sleeping. Sleep is seen even in species that would seem to be better off without it. For example, the Indus dolphin (*Platanista indi*) lives in the muddy waters of the Indus estuary in Pakistan (Pilleri, 1979). Over the ages, it has become blind, presumably because vision is not useful in the animal's environment. (It has an excellent sonar system, which it uses to navigate and find prey.) The Indus dolphin never stops swimming; doing so would result in injury, because of the dangerous currents and the vast quantities of debris carried by the river during the monsoon season. However, despite the dangers caused by sleeping, sleep has not disappeared. Pilleri (1979) captured two Indus dolphins and studied their habits. He found that they slept a total of seven hours a day, in very brief naps of 4 to 60 seconds each. If sleep did not perform an important function, we might expect that it, like vision, would have been eliminated in this species through the process of natural selection.

delta activity Rhythmical electroencephalogram activity with a frequency of less than 3.5 Hz, indicating deep (slow-wave) sleep.

slow-wave sleep Sleep other than REM sleep, characterized by regular, slow waves on the electroencephalogram.

rapid-eye-movement (REM) sleep A stage of sleep during which dreaming, rapid eye movements, and muscular paralysis occur and the EEG shows beta activity.

Sleep as Repair   The universal nature of sleep suggests that it does something important. But just what? The simplest explanation for sleep is that it serves to repair the wear and tear on our bodies caused by moving and exercising. Perhaps our bodies just get worn out by performing waking activities for 16 hours or so.

It should be easy to discover why we sleep by seeing what happens to a person who goes without sleep. However, sleep-deprivation studies with human subjects have provided little evidence that sleep is needed to keep the body functioning normally. Horne (1978) reviewed more than 50 experiments in which people had been deprived of sleep. He reported that most of them found that sleep deprivation did not interfere with people's ability to perform physical exercise. Thus, the primary role of sleep does not seem to be rest and recuperation of the body. However, people's cognitive abilities are affected, even though they may remain unaware of their deprivation-induced deficits (Van Dongen et al., 2003); some people reported perceptual distortions or even hallucinations and had trouble concentrating on mental tasks. Perhaps sleep provides the opportunity for the *brain* to rest.

During stage 4 sleep, the metabolic activity of the brain decreases to about 75 percent of the waking level (Sakai et al., 1979), which suggests that stage 4 sleep gives the brain a chance to rest. If people are awakened during slow-wave sleep, they act groggy and confused—as if their cerebral cortex has been shut down and has not yet resumed its functioning. These observations suggest that during stage 4 sleep, the brain is, indeed, resting.

An ingenious study by Horne and Minard (1985) found that mental exercise seems to increase the demand for slow-wave sleep. The investigators asked volunteers to show up for an experiment in which they were supposed to take tests designed to assess reading skills. When the people turned up, they were told that the plans had been changed. They were invited for a day out, at the expense of the researchers. (Not surprisingly, they willingly accepted.) They spent the day visiting an art exhibition, a shopping center, a museum, an amusement park, a zoo, and an interesting mansion. After a scenic drive through the countryside, they watched a movie at a local theater. They were driven from place to place and certainly did not become overheated by exercise. After the movie, they returned to the sleep laboratory. They said they were tired, and they readily fell asleep. Their sleep duration was normal, and they awoke feeling refreshed. However, their slow-wave sleep—particularly stage 4 sleep—was increased.

de Bruin, Beersma, and Daan (2002), working in the Netherlands, reported a different outcome when they assigned male participants to two groups. One engaged in what the researchers termed "light mental activity" and watched videos while relaxing for 8 hours. The other group performed complex tasks using a computer, tasks that required their sustained attention, memory, and problem-solving skills for the same length of time. Participants in the latter group could not be roused as readily shortly after falling asleep, but there were no other differences between the groups. de Bruin et al. concluded that slow-wave sleep does not increase with a more demanding workload prior to sleep.

Sleep and Learning   Research with both humans and laboratory animals indicates that sleep does more than allow the brain to rest: It also aids in the consolidation of long-term memories (Marshall and Born, 2007; Rasch & Born, 2008). Slow-wave sleep and REM sleep play different roles in memory consolidation.

As we saw in Chapter 7, two major categories of long-term memory exist: declarative memory (also called explicit memory) and nondeclarative memory (also called implicit memory). Declarative memories include those that people can talk about, such as memories of past episodes in their lives. They also include memories of the relations between stimuli or events, such as the spatial relations between landmarks that permit us to navigate around our environment. Nondeclarative memories include those gained through experience and practice that do not necessarily involve an attempt to "memorize" information, such as learning to drive a car, throw and catch a ball, or recognize a person's face. Research has found that slow-wave sleep and REM sleep play different roles in the consolidation of declarative and nondeclarative memories.

Before we tell you about the results of this research, let's compare the consciousness of a person engaged in each of these stages of sleep. During REM sleep, people normally have a high level of consciousness. If we awaken people during REM sleep, they will be alert and clear-headed and will almost always be able to describe the details of a dream that they were having. However, if we awaken people during slow-wave sleep, they will be groggy and confused, and will usually tell us that nothing was happening. So which stages of sleep do you think aid in the consolidation of declarative and nondeclarative memories?

We would have guessed that REM would be associated with declarative memories, and slow-wave sleep, with nondeclarative memories. However, just the opposite is true. Let's look at evidence from two studies that looked at the effects of a nap on memory consolidation. Mednick, Nakayama, and Stickgold (2003) asked participants to learn a nondeclarative visual discrimination task at 9:00 A.M. The participants' ability to perform the task was tested ten hours later, at 7:00 P.M. Some, but not all, of the participants took a 90-minute nap during the day between training and testing. The investigators recorded the EEGs of the sleeping participants to determine which of them engaged in REM sleep and which of them did not. (Obviously, all of them engaged in slow-wave sleep, because this stage of sleep always comes first in normal people.) The investigators found that the performance of participants who did not take a nap was worse when they were tested at 7:00 P.M. than it had been at the end of training. The participants who engaged only in slow-wave sleep did about the same during testing as they had done at the end of training. However, the participants who engaged in REM sleep performed significantly better. In other words, REM sleep, but not slow-wave sleep, facilitated the consolidation of a nondeclarative memory. (See FIGURE 8·14.)

[**FIGURE 8·14**] Role of REM sleep in learning a nondeclarative visual discrimination task. Only after a 90-min nap that included both slow-wave sleep and REM sleep did the subjects' performance improve.

(Adapted from Mednick, S., Nakayama, K., and Stickgold, R. *Nature Neuroscience,* 2003, 6, 697–698.)

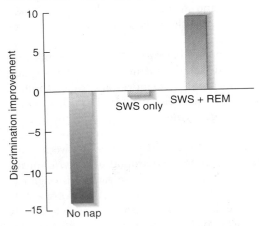

In the second study, Tucker et al. (2006) trained participants on two tasks: a declarative task (learning a list of paired words) and a nondeclarative task (learning to trace a pencil-and-paper design while looking at the paper in a mirror). Afterward, some participants were permitted to take a nap lasting for about one hour. Their EEGs were recorded, and they were awakened before they could engage in REM sleep. The participants' performance on the two tasks was then tested six hours after the original training. The investigators found that a nap consisting of slow-wave sleep increased the participants' performance on the declarative task but had no effect on performance of the nondeclarative task. (See **FIGURE 8·15**.) So these two experiments (and others we have not described) indicate that REM sleep facilitates consolidation of

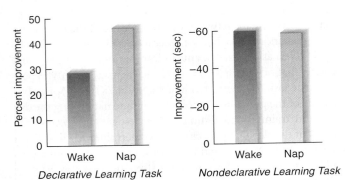

[**FIGURE 8·15**] Role of slow-wave sleep in learning a declarative learning task (list of paired words) and a nondeclarative learning task (mirror tracing). After a nap that included just slow-wave sleep, only subjects who learned the declarative learning task showed improved performance, compared with subjects who stayed awake.

(Adapted from Tucker, M. A., Hirota, Y., Wamsley, E. J., Lau, H., Chaklader, A., and Fishbein, W. *Neurobiology of Learning and Memory,* 2006, 86, 241–247.)

nondeclarative memories, and slow-wave sleep facilitates consolidation of declarative memories.

One last experiment on this topic: In a Belgian research lab, Peigneux et al. (2004) asked participants to learn their way around a computerized virtual-reality town. This task is very similar to what people do when they learn their way around a real town. They must learn the relative locations of landmarks and streets that connect them so that they can find particular locations when the experimenter "placed" them at various starting points. As we saw in Chapter 7, the hippocampus plays an essential role in learning of this kind. Peigneux and his colleagues used functional brain imaging to measure regional brain activity and found that the same regions of the hippocampus were activated during route learning and during slow-wave sleep the following night. These patterns were *not* seen during REM sleep. Thus, although people awakened during slow-wave sleep seldom report that they had been dreaming, the sleeping brain appears to rehearse information that was acquired during the previous day. (Many studies with laboratory animals that directly recorded the activity of individual neurons in the animals' brains have obtained the same results.)

Dreaming

One of the most fascinating aspects of sleep is the fact that we enter a fantasy world several times each night during which we perceive imaginary events and perform imaginary behaviors. Again, why do we do so?

Consciousness during Sleep As noted earlier, a person who is awakened during REM sleep and asked whether anything is happening will almost always report a dream. The typical REM-sleep dream resembles a play or movie—it has a narrative form. Conversely, reports of narrative, story-like dreams are rare among people awakened from slow-wave sleep. In general, cognitive activity during slow-wave sleep appears to be more static. It involves situations rather than narratives, and generally the situations are unpleasant. For example, a person awakened from slow-wave sleep might report a sensation of being crushed or suffocated. It is during slow-wave sleep that young children will experience **night terrors** (a vague but anguished emotion with no clear memory of its cause) and **sleepwalking.**

Almost everyone has four or five bouts of REM sleep each night, with accompanying dreams. Yet if the dreamer does not happen to awaken while the dream is in progress, it is lost. People who claimed not to have had a dream for many years have slept in a sleep laboratory and found that, in fact, they did dream. They were able to remember their dreams when the researcher awakened them during REM sleep. Solms (2000) has argued that the connectedness of REM sleep and dreaming is only apparent. Though they coincide, they are distinct processes, controlled by different mechanisms.

night terrors The experience of anguish without a clear memory of its cause; occurs during slow-wave sleep, usually in childhood.

sleepwalking The experience of walking during sleep without a clear memory of doing so; occurs during slow-wave sleep, usually in childhood.

Functions of Dreams Two major research approaches exist to the study of dreaming: psychological analysis of the contents of dreams, and cognitive neuroscientific research on the nature and functions of REM sleep. The first approach is closely associated with Sigmund Freud's proposal that dreams symbolize unfulfilled desires of which we are unaware. The second approach considers dreams to be the product of the brain's information processing

Dreaming as Wish Fulfillment Beginning in ancient times, dreams were regarded as meaningful. For example, they were used to prophesy the future, to decide whether to go to war, and to determine the guilt or innocence of a person accused of a crime. At the beginning of the twentieth century, Sigmund Freud (1900) proposed what was to become a very influential theory of dreaming. For Freud, dreams arise out of inner conflicts between unconscious desires (primarily sexual ones) and cultural prohibitions against acting on these desires. Although all dreams represent unfulfilled wishes, their contents are disguised and expressed symbolically—the result of what Freud referred to as "dreamwork." The **latent content** of the dream (*latent* is from the Latin word for "hidden") is transformed into the **manifest content** (the actual storyline or narrative) of the dream. Taken at face value, the manifest content may seem incidental, but a knowledgeable psychoanalyst can interpret the unconscious desires that are disguised as symbols in the manifest content of the dream. For example, climbing a set of stairs or shooting a gun might symbolize the desire for sexual intercourse. One problem with Freud's theory is that it is not falsifiable, that is, disprovable. Even if the theory is wrong, a psychoanalyst can always provide a plausible interpretation of a dream that reveals hidden conflicts disguised in obscure symbols.

Dreaming as Story Construction Hobson and Pace-Schott (2002) advanced a model of brain activity during sleep that explains dreaming without relying on unconscious conflicts or wish fulfillment. As we will see later, research with laboratory animals has shown that REM sleep occurs when a circuit of acetylcholine-secreting neurons in the area of the brain stem known as the pons (see Chapter 3) becomes active. This activation in turn stimulates rapid eye movements, activation of the cerebral cortex, and muscular paralysis—all components of REM sleep. (Yes, other species exhibit REM sleep, and they appear to dream, too, which may support the claim of some form of consciousness in those species.) The activation of the visual system

produces both eye movements and images. Several experiments have found that the particular eye movements a person makes during a dream correspond, at least roughly, to the content of a dream. That is, the eye movements are those that a person would be likely to make if the imaginary events were really occurring (Dement, 1974; Dement and Vaughan, 2000). The images evoked by cortical activation often incorporate episodic memories of recent events or other contents of recent thinking. Presumably, the circuits responsible for these memories are more readily activated because of their recency.

Hobson and Pace-Schott (2002) suggest that both slow-wave sleep and REM sleep work together. Memories that are consolidated during slow-wave sleep are reactivated during REM sleep and newly consolidated with other memories. The activation of these brain mechanisms produces fragmentary images that our brains try to render meaningful by piecing them together in at least roughly plausible narratives. This theory is known as the **activation–synthesis theory**, because it proposes that activation of the cortex by the pons causes the brain to create a narrative experience quite apart from the sensory activation that occurs during waking. When we later communicate these experiences to ourselves or to others, we call them dreams. Although this view of dreaming does not attach necessary significance to the content of dreams, some theorists argue that the synthesis provided by the cortex serves an adaptive function, such as the simulation of threatening events (Revonsuo, 2000).

Dreaming as Learning As we saw earlier, sustained sleep deprivation impairs people's ability to perform tasks that require alertness and vigilance, but what happens when only REM sleep is disrupted? Research participants who are sleeping in a laboratory can be selectively deprived of REM sleep. A researcher awakens them whenever the **polygraph** record indicates they have entered REM sleep. The researcher must also awaken control participants just as often at random intervals to identify any effects produced by simply being awakened several times during the night.

If someone is deprived of REM sleep on several consecutive nights and is then allowed to sleep without interruption, the onset of REM sleep becomes more frequent during the uninterrupted sleep. It is as if there is an increased need for REM sleep. The effect is referred to as *REM rebound*: The person engages in more bouts of REM sleep than normal during the next night or two, as if catching up on what was missed.

Several investigators have suggested that REM sleep may play a role in learning, a view consistent with the activation-synthesis theory. Smith and Lapp (1991) observed increased REM sleep in college students during examination periods, which may be a time of increased learning. Walker (2005) focused on procedural (as opposed to semantic) learning and distinguished between acquisition and consolidation of learning. Within the latter, he further distinguished two stages: stabilization and enhancement. Although acquisition and stabilization occur when one is

---

latent content The hidden message of a dream produced by the unconscious.

manifest content The apparent storyline of a dream.

activation-synthesis theory A theory of dreaming that explains dreams as resulting from the incidental synthesis of cortical activity produced by mechanisms in the pons.

polygraph An instrument that records changes in physiological processes such as brain activity, heart rate, and breathing.

awake, enhancement seems to require sleep. Research participants who had acquired stable performance in skilled motor reaching and finger-tapping tasks nonetheless showed improvement after sleep.

Many studies with laboratory animals have shown that chronic deprivation of REM sleep impairs their ability to learn a complex task, although they still manage to learn it. Thus, REM sleep may be essential for learning. If it does play a role in human learning, the effect appears to be subtle—at least in adults (Maquet, 2001). In fact, neurologists (see, for example, Lavie et al., 1984; Gironell et al., 1995) have described patients who showed little or no REM sleep after sustaining damage to the brain stem, but few, if any, serious side effects. After brain injury, one patient completed high school, attended law school, and entered law practice.

Disorders of Sleep

Because we spend about one third of our lives sleeping, sleep disorders can have a significant impact on our quality of life. They can also affect the way we feel while we are awake.

Insomnia   Insomnia is reported to affect approximately 25 percent of the population occasionally and 9 percent regularly (Ancoli-Israel and Roth, 1999). But we need to define *insomnia* carefully. The amount of sleep individuals require varies. A short sleeper may feel fine with 5 hours of sleep; a long sleeper may still feel unrefreshed after 10 hours of sleep. Insomnia must be defined in relation to a person's particular sleep needs.

For many years, the goal of sleep medications was to help people fall asleep. However, if a medication puts people to sleep right away but produces grogginess and difficulty concentrating the next day, it has limited value. Many drugs traditionally used to treat insomnia had just this effect. Fortunately, researchers now recognize that the evaluation of a new sleep medication must include the quality of wakefulness the following day, and "hangover-free" drugs are being developed and marketed (Hajak et al., 1995).

Narcolepsy   Narcolepsy (*narke* means "numbness," and *lepsis* means "seizure") is a neurological disorder characterized by sleep (or some of its components) at inappropriate times. The primary symptom of narcolepsy is the sleep attack—an overwhelming urge to sleep that can happen at any time but occurs most often under monotonous, boring conditions. Sleep generally lasts for 2 to 5 minutes, and the person usually wakes up feeling refreshed.

The most striking symptom of narcolepsy is **cataplexy** (from *kata*, "down," and *plexis*, "stroke"). During a cataplectic attack, a person will suddenly wilt and fall, then lie there, *fully conscious,* for a few seconds to several minutes. What apparently happens is that one of the components of REM sleep—muscular paralysis—occurs at an inappropriate time. Cataplexy is usually precipitated by strong emotional reactions or by sudden physical effort. Laughter, anger, or an

effort to catch a suddenly thrown object can trigger a cataplectic attack. Common triggers include attempting to discipline one's children and making love (an awkward time to become paralyzed!). Wise (2004) notes that patients with narcolepsy often try to avoid thoughts and situations that are likely to evoke strong emotions.

Lin et al. (1999) discovered that a mutation of a specific gene causes narcolepsy in laboratory animals. The product of this gene is a receptor for a recently discovered peptide neurotransmitter called **hypocretin,** so called because the lateral *hypo*thalamus contains the cell bodies of the neurons that se*cret*e this peptide. Hypocretin helps stabilize sleep/waking cycles and suppresses the inappropriate onset of components of REM sleep. In humans, narcolepsy appears to be caused by a hereditary autoimmune disorder (Nishino et al., 2000). Most humans who develop narcolepsy are born with hypocretin-secreting neurons, but during adolescence, the immune system attacks these neurons, and the symptoms of narcolepsy begin.

The symptoms can be treated with stimulant drugs. In the past, patients have been treated with drugs such as amphetamine or methylphenidate (also known as Ritalin), but most people are treated with modafinil, a drug that has a low potential for abuse (Saper, Scammell, and Lu, 2006).

REM Sleep Behavior Disorder   Schenck et al. (1986) reported the existence of an intriguing disorder: REM sleep behavior disorder. As you now know, REM sleep is accompanied by paralysis. Although the neural circuits of the brain that control body movements are extremely active during REM sleep (McCarley and Hobson, 1979), people remain immobile.

That people are paralyzed during REM sleep suggests the possibility that, but for the paralysis, they would act out their dreams. Indeed, they would. The behavior of people who exhibit REM sleep behavior disorder corresponds with the contents of their dreams. Consider the following case:

> [CASE STUDY] I was a halfback playing football, and after the quarterback received the ball from the center, he lateraled it sideways to me and I'm supposed to go around end and cut back over tackle and—this is very vivid—as I cut back over tackle, there is this big 280-pound tackle waiting, so I, according to football rules, was to give him my shoulder and bounce him out of the way . . . when I came to I was standing in front of our dresser and I had [gotten up out of bed and run and] knocked lamps, mirrors and everything off the dresser, hit my head against the wall and my knee against the dresser. (Schenck et al., 1986, p. 294)

---

insomnia   A general category of sleep disorder related to difficulty in falling asleep and remaining asleep.

narcolepsy   A sleep disorder characterized by sleep attack—irresistibly falling asleep at inappropriate times.

cataplexy   A symptom of narcolepsy; although awake, the individual is temporarily paralyzed.

hypocretin   A neurotransmitter secreted by cells in the hypothalamus; helps regulate sleep-wake cycles.

Like narcolepsy, REM sleep behavior disorder appears to be a neurodegenerative disorder (Schenck et al., 1993). It is often associated with better-known neurodegenerative disorders such as Parkinson's disease (Boeve et al., 2007). The symptoms of REM sleep behavior disorder are the opposite of those of cataplexy. Rather than exhibiting paralysis outside REM sleep, patients with REM sleep behavior disorder *fail* to exhibit paralysis *during* REM sleep. As you might expect, the drugs used to treat the symptoms of cataplexy will heighten the symptoms of REM sleep behavior disorder. Instead, its symptoms are usually treated with clonazepam, a tranquilizer (Schenck and Mahowald, 2002).

Problems Associated with Slow-Wave Sleep Some maladaptive behaviors occur during slow-wave sleep, especially during its deepest phase, stage 4. These behaviors include bedwetting (*nocturnal enuresis*) and sleepwalking (*somnambulism*). Both behaviors occur most frequently in children. Often bedwetting can be cured by training methods, such as an electronic circuit ring device that rings a bell when the first few drops of urine are detected in the bed sheet. Sleepwalking usually cures itself as the child gets older. This phenomena does not occur during REM sleep; a sleepwalking person is *not* acting out a dream.

Schenck et al. (1991) reported nineteen cases of people with histories of eating during the night while they were asleep, a condition the authors labeled **sleep-related eating disorder.** Almost half of the patients had become overweight from night eating. Once patients realize that they are eating in their sleep, they often use such stratagems as keeping their food under lock and key or setting alarms that will awaken them when they try to open their refrigerator. Morgenthaler and Silber (2002) reported that sleep-related eating disorder may occur together with *restless legs syndrome,* which is marked by frequent, disruptive involuntary leg movements (Hening et al., 1999) and *obstructive sleep apnea,* that is, the cessation of breathing during sleep due to constriction of the airway.

Several sleep disorders, including *delayed steep phase syndrome (DSPS),* are related to malfunctions of the circadian rhythm (see below; Dagan, 2001). Individuals with DSPS tend to fall asleep very late at night and to have real difficulty rising the next morning. They may well sleep until noon. However, when allowed to sleep without externally imposed restrictions, the length of sleep was normal.

Brain Mechanisms of Sleep

If sleep is a behavior, then some parts of the brain must be responsible for its occurrence. Researchers have discovered

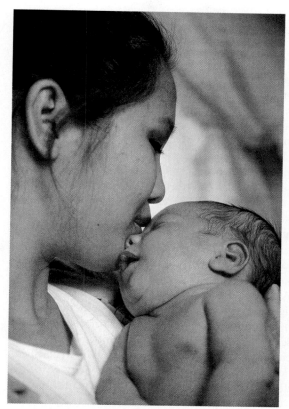

Late-term fetuses and newborn infants spend much time in REM sleep, which has led some investigators to hypothesize that this activity plays a role in brain development.

several brain regions that have special roles in sleep and biological rhythms.

The Circadian Clock Let us first consider biological rhythms. Some rhythms are controlled by an internal "clock" located in the brain. This clock controls **circadian rhythms**—rhythms that oscillate once a day (*circa,* "about"; *dies,* "day").

The clock that controls circadian rhythms is located in a small pair of structures located at the bottom of the hypothalamus: the **suprachiasmatic nuclei (SCN).** The activity of neurons in the SCN oscillates once each day; the neurons are active during the day and inactive at night. Connections between the SCN and other brain regions permit the SCN to control daily cycles of sleep and wakefulness, hormone secretion, body temperature, and many other physiological functions. If people are placed in a windowless room with constant lighting, they will continue to show circadian rhythms, controlled by the oscillations of their SCN. However, because this biological clock is not very accurate (its cycle length is 25 hours), people's circadian rhythms will eventually get out of synchrony with the day/night cycles outside the building. But within a few days after leaving the building, their rhythms will be resynchronized with those of the sun. This resynchronization involves a direct connection between the eyes and

---

sleep-related eating disorder Occurs during sleepwalking as the individual seeks out food and consumes it, usually with no memory of having done so.

circadian rhythm A daily rhythmical change in behaviors or physiological processes.

suprachiasmatic nuclei An area of the hypothalamus that provides a biological clock for circadian rhythms.

the SCN. Each morning, when we see the light of the sun (or turn on the room lights), our biological clock resets and begins ticking off the next day.

Neural Control of Sleep When we are awake and alert, most of the neurons in our brain—especially those of the forebrain—are active, permitting us to pay attention to and process sensory information, to think about what we are perceiving, and to engage in a variety of behaviors during the day. The level of brain activity is largely controlled by several small clusters of neurons in the midbrain and hindbrain whose axons travel forward, branch repeatedly, and form synaptic connections with the billions of neurons in the forebrain. The terminal buttons of these neurons release four neurotransmitters, which were described in Chapter 3: norepinephrine (NE), serotonin (5-HT), acetylcholine (ACh), and dopamine (DA). Another group of neurons, located in the posterior hypothalamus, releases a neurotransmitter called histamine. (Yes, antihistamines can make us drowsy by inhibiting the effects of these neurons. However, today's antihistamines do not cross the blood–brain barrier, so they do not cause drowsiness.) These neurotransmitters activate forebrain neurons in different ways, controlling different aspects of alertness and behavioral arousal. For simplicity, we collectively refer to the neurons that release these neurotransmitters as arousal neurons.

For many years, researchers have known that the activity of our arousal neurons determines whether we are awake or asleep: A high level of activity of these neurons keeps us awake, and a low level puts us to sleep. The question has been: What causes the activity of the arousal neurons to decrease, thus putting us to sleep? An answer to this question was suggested in the early twentieth century by a Viennese neurologist, Constantin von Economo, who observed that patients afflicted by a new type of encephalitis that was sweeping through Europe and North America showed the severe disturbance of sleep and waking (Triarhou, 2006). Most patients slept excessively, waking only to eat and drink. According to von Economo, these patients had brain damage at the junction of the brain stem and forebrain, that is, at a location where the axons of the arousal neurons entering the forebrain would be destroyed. Some patients, however, showed just the opposite symptoms: They slept only a few hours each day. Although they were tired, they had difficulty falling asleep and usually awakened shortly thereafter. Von Economo reported that patients who displayed insomnia had damage to the region of the anterior hypothalamus. We now know that this region, usually referred to as the **preoptic area,** is the one most involved in the control of sleep. The preoptic area contains neurons whose axons form inhibitory synaptic connections with the brain's arousal neurons. When our preoptic neurons (let's call them *sleep neurons*) become active, they suppress the activity of our arousal neurons, and we fall asleep (Saper, Scammell, & Lu, 2005).

What makes us become sleepy and eventually puts us to sleep? (In other words, what activates neurons in the preoptic area?) Two factors influence the preoptic sleep neurons. The first is time of day. As we saw earlier, sleep is affected by our circadian rhythms, which are controlled by the SCN. Unless we are on an unusual schedule (or work late into the night or engage in an enjoyable activity), we get sleepy sometime after dark, go to bed, and fall asleep. The SCN is connected to the preoptic sleep neurons and thus affects our sleep/waking cycles.

The second factor reflects the reason we sleep: to provide an opportunity for the brain to rest (Basheer et al., 2004). One of the products of brain metabolism is a chemical called **adenosine.** The more active cells in our brain are, the more adenosine they produce, and some of this adenosine leaks out into the fluid that surrounds them. One of the effects of adenosine in the brain is to increase the activity of the preoptic sleep neurons. So if we have a long, busy day that keeps our neurons active, the accumulation of adenosine activates the preoptic area, which suppresses the activity of the arousal neurons, and we become sleepy. The busier the day or the longer we stay awake, the more adenosine accumulates, and the sleepier we get. Once we fall asleep, the metabolic rate of our brain decreases, and the level of adenosine decreases. If we get a good night's sleep, adenosine levels are low by the time our SCN signals that it is time to wake. The activity of the preoptic sleep neurons decreases, the activity of the arousal neurons increases, and we wake up. (See **FIGURE 8•16**.)

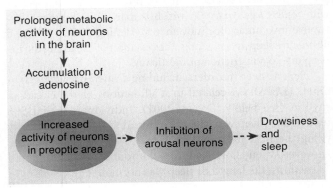

[FIGURE 8•16] The role of adenosine in sleep. Extended neural activity causes adenosine accumulation, which activates neurons in the preoptic areas of the anterior hypothalamus. In turn, this inhibits the arousal neurons in the midbrain and hindbrain, inducing sleep.

---

preoptic area An area of the hypothalamus that contains neurons that inhibit arousal neurons to produce sleep.

adenosine A product of brain metabolism; activates neurons in the preoptic area, inducing sleep.

QUESTIONS TO CONSIDER

1. Some people report they are "in control" of some of their dreams—that they feel as if they decide what comes next and are not simply swept along passively. Have you ever had this experience or that of a "lucid dream," in which you were aware of the fact that you were dreaming? What characteristics of a person might allow her or him to take control of dreams?

2. What does dreaming accomplish? Some researchers believe that the subject matter of a dream has little if any significance—it is the REM sleep itself that is vital. Others believe that the subject matter has consequence. Some researchers believe that if we remember a dream, the dream failed to accomplish all of its functions. Others say that remembering is useful, because it can give us some insights into our problems. What is your position on these two controversies?

3. Until recently (that is, in terms of the evolution of our species), our ancestors tended to go to sleep when the sun set and to wake up when it rose. Once our ancestors learned how to control fire, they undoubtedly stayed up somewhat later, sitting in front of a fire. But it was only with the development of cheap, effective lighting that many members of our species adopted the habit of staying up late and waking several hours after sunrise. Considering that the neural mechanisms of sleep evolved long ago, how might changes in our daily rhythms affect our physical and intellectual abilities?

Epilogue

Nudging to Consciousness

For most of us, there is a daily experience of emerging from one of the stages of the altered consciousness known as sleep and resuming our waking consciousness. Cycles of activity in certain brain areas assure this resumption. Generally it is accomplished in a way that gives us little pause: We are the same person—the same self—that fell asleep several hours earlier. Moreover, the intervening time seems to have passed in the blink of an eye, despite the evidence of the clock and the grogginess and occasional stiffness that may attend awaking. To have it otherwise is the stuff of science fiction, from Washington Irving's tale of Rip Van Winkle to Franz Kafka's Gregor Samsa in "The Metamorphosis."

The Prologue introduced cases of adult patients who spent long years in coma (Jan Grzebski) or in a persistent vegetative state (Terri Shiavo). You will recall that Michael Shiavo arranged for his wife to receive direct electrical stimulation of the thalamus in hopes of her recovery. The procedure was unsuccessful. However, a recent report of a similar procedure with a patient in a minimally conscious state (MCS) was encouraging (Schiff et al., 2007). In this case, the patient had been in MCS for six years after traumatic brain injury. The design of the experiment alternated the periods when deep-brain stimulation was applied with those when it was absent. Recovery of function accompanied stimulation, including his near-immediate resumption of fine motor movements, including speech. But this was more than waking from sleep, as he was unable to sustain his new consciousness when the stimulation was discontinued. Although the neural circuits that brought about his awakening may have been different from those described in the chapter for sleep and waking, his resumption of at least partial function can be considered analogous to the daily experience of waking and resuming one's self. We can only wonder about the extent to which the newly awakened patient recognized his self.

The nudging to altered consciousness reported in the case study was achieved by deliberately altering the patterns of electrical activity in the interior of the patient's brain. By analogy, we might ask about the alterations of brain activity that nudged the human species toward its own form of consciousness at some point during the evolutionary past. What changes instrumented by natural selection "awakened" human consciousness in the first place and ultimately led to humans having a sense of self?

Attempts to answer these questions have surged in recent years and demonstrate the growing nexus between psychology, neuroscience, computer science, and philosophy. Jaynes's (1976) masterwork on the origins of human consciousness posits an ancestral era not so long ago when the voices inside a person's head were not recognizably one's own but those of others whom one held in high esteem. According to Jaynes, a widespread cataclysm brought the necessary historical conditions for the discrimination of one's own voice among the others vying for one's private attention, and human consciousness, as we know it, emerged. Jaynes articulated his theory with rich references to human history as well as to brain structures and clinical disorders.

More recently, Damasio (1994, 1999) has introduced a neurologically inspired theory of human emotion that depends heavily on brain mechanisms for mapping the moment-to-moment state of the body and monitoring changes in that state that are induced by the arrival of sensory messages. Damasio distinguishes between what he terms core consciousness and extended consciousness and illustrates the emergence of the latter from the former with neurological case studies.

Greenfield (2000) and Koch (2004) represent a different approach to the analysis of consciousness that emphasizes neural activity distributed across multiple brain areas rather than relying on localized brain areas as the substrate of consciousness. The principal difference in their views is in what the neurons responsible for consciousness are doing. Greenfield requires the emergence of synchronous firing (that is, large numbers of neurons firing in temporal harmony). For Koch, all that is required is that the stream of consciousness be accompanied by a corresponding cascade of demonstrably different (but not synchronous) patterns of neural activity.

Perhaps it is appropriate to conclude this chapter with a humble expression of thanks—for our consciousness—and a humble acknowledgement that we are still unraveling the mystery of its origin and functions. The autobiographical words of Eiseley (1975), who, desperately ill with the flu, had just taken his last final examination as a college student, are apt:

> On that afternoon without knowing the results of my efforts, I slowly climbed the second-floor steps of my rooming house. As I fumbled for the key to my door I suddenly heard, very far away, as though in another part of the house, the small faint thump of something hitting the floor. That was the last I knew until I awoke upon the landing. Everything had grown dark and I crawled frantically about on my knees, dimly realizing that I had lost all sense of direction. Instinctively, I seemed to know that there was a stairway in back of me down which I might tumble. My location slowly came back through the sense of touch. I threw open the door and tumbled in upon my bed.
>
> . . . what if I had not recovered consciousness upon that upstairs landing? When one faints there is normally a little forthcoming awareness, a final chance to get down before one falls. I had dropped as though a bullet felled me. The thud of my head hitting the floor had sounded so remote I never had time to relate it to myself. I simply ceased to be. There was a body lying in the dusk on the stairs, but whatever motivated that body, consciously dwelt upon its problems, looked after its needs, had vanished.
>
> . . . I was gone so far into the dark that no dream whispered to me, no sound again troubled my ear. Consciously I did not exist. But something was still alert within me . . . Something, some toiling cellular entity of which I was unaware was searching me out, reconstructing me, setting failing ganglions to sputtering, reactivating all manner of wildly spinning compasses. . . . In all my remaining years I have been grateful to those unseen toilers, who, when my will had failed, had recreated what individually they neither knew nor cared about. (pp. 74–78)

CHAPTER SUMMARY

Consciousness as a Language-Dependent Phenomenon

Consciousness, as it is defined here, is related to the activity of language and motor mechanisms of the brain. The private use of language (thinking to oneself) and private nonverbal processes may be considered conscious if we can describe them to ourselves or others. In the same way, our consciousness of external events is demonstrated by our ability to verbalize about our perceptions of them. These perceptions may be different from the actions we take to interact with the external events. Even our awareness of "voluntary" movements may be a by-product of other brain activities that initiate behavior and bind perceived events in ways that produce such awareness. However, it would be misleading to suppose that language necessarily predicates consciousness. Forms of consciousness may well have existed before the emergence of language.

Selective Attention

As we saw in the first section of this chapter, consciousness can be analyzed as a social phenomenon derived through evolution of the brain mechanisms responsible for our ability to communicate with one another (and, in addition, with ourselves). However, because verbal mechanisms can contain only a limited amount of information at one time, we cannot be conscious of all that occurs in the environment. The process of selective attention determines which stimuli will be noticed and which will be ignored. Dichotic listening experiments show that what is received by the unattended ear is lost within a few seconds unless something causes the listener to take heed of it; after those few seconds, what was presented is lost. Studies using visually presented information indicate that attention can focus on location or on shape: We can locate objects in physical space and also say what they are. Possibly because visual stimulation is so complex, distractions can produce inattentional blindness in certain conditions. Brain-imaging studies have found that when people pay attention to particular features of visual stimuli, the activity of particular regions of the brain is enhanced.

Consciousness and the Brain

The suggestion that consciousness is a function of our ability to communicate with one another receives support from some cases of human brain damage. As we saw, people with certain kinds of damage can point to objects they say they cannot see; people with isolation aphasia can perceive speech and talk without apparent awareness; and a patient with a particular form of visual agnosia can make appropriate hand movements when looking at objects that cannot be consciously recognized. Thus, brain damage can disrupt a person's awareness of perceptual mechanisms without disrupting other functions performed by these mechanisms. Although a person whose corpus callosum has been severed can make perceptual judgments with the right hemisphere, he or she cannot talk about them and appears to be unaware of them.

Hypnosis

Mesmer introduced the modern form of hypnosis that features induction and suggestion, including posthypnotic amnesia. Susceptibility to hypnosis varies among individuals. A common experience while in hypnosis is that of reduced effort and the suspension of voluntary control. There are several theories of hypnosis, but research shows that it largely alters what the hypnotized individual reports rather than what that person perceives.

Sleep

Sleep consists of several stages of slow-wave sleep, characterized by increasing amounts of delta activity in the EEG, and REM sleep. REM sleep is characterized by beta activity in the EEG, rapid eye movements, general paralysis (with twitching movements of the hands and feet), and dreaming. Sleep is behavior, not simply an altered state of consciousness. Although evidence suggests that sleep is not necessary for repairing the wear and tear of daily life, sleep may play an important role in providing an opportunity for the brain to rest. Sleep also contributes to memory consolidation. Specifically, research involving memory tasks and the presence or absence of naps showed that slow-wave sleep contributes to the consolidation of declarative (explicit) memories and REM sleep to that of nondeclarative (implicit) memories.

Although narrative dreams occur only during REM sleep, people often are conscious of static situations during slow-wave sleep. Freud suggested that dreams provide the opportunity for unconscious conflicts to express themselves symbolically in dream content. An alternative suggestion—the activation-synthesis theory—is that dreams are the brain's effort to make sense of the pons-initiated activation of the cerebral cortex. The function of REM sleep in adults is uncertain, but it may be involved somehow in learning. Long bouts of REM-sleep deprivation result in the REM rebound in which sleep is dominated by the REM component.

Sleep disorders include difficulty falling asleep and remaining asleep, which is known as *insomnia*, the sudden onset of sleep at inappropriate times known as *narcolepsy* (and related cataplexy), and REM sleep behavior disorder in which REM-specific paralysis no longer occurs. The slow-wave sleep disorders include bedwetting, sleepwalking, and sleep-related eating disorder.

The suprachiasmatic nucleus of the hypothalamus controls circadian (daily) rhythms. This clock is reset when morning light strikes the retina. Clusters of activity neurons in the midbrain and hindbrain control wakefulness. Neurons in the preoptic area of the hypothalamus inhibit the activity neurons and thereby induce sleep. Time of day and the level of adenosine are two factors that control these sleep neurons.

succeed with mypsychlab

Visit MyPsychLab for practice quizzes, flashcards, and dozens of videos and animated tutorials, including the following items you can find in the "Multimedia Library":

Hypnosis
Roberta: Insomnia
Lucid Dreaming

Theories of Dreaming

Hypnosis

KEY TERMS

activation-synthesis theory *p. 249*

adenosine *p. 252*

alpha activity *p. 245*

beta activity *p. 245*

blindsight *p. 230*

cataplexy *p. 250*

change blindness *p. 238*

circadian rhythm *p. 251*

cocktail-party problem *p. 236*

coma *p. 229*

consciousness *p. 229*

delta activity *p. 246*

dichotic-listening test *p. 234*

divided attention *p. 233*

electromyogram *p. 245*

electro-oculogram *p. 245*

hypocretin *p. 250*

inattention blindness *p. 237*

inhibition of return *p. 236*

insomnia *p. 250*

isolation aphasia *p. 239*

latent content *p. 249*

manifest content *p. 249*

minimally conscious state *p. 229*

narcolepsy *p. 250*

night terrors *p. 248*

persistent vegetative state *p. 229*

polygraph *p. 249*

posthypnotic amnesia *p. 244*

posthypnotic suggestion *p. 244*

SUGGESTIONS FOR FURTHER READING

Damasio, A. (2000). *The feeling of what happens: Body and emotion in the making of consciousness.* New York: Harcourt.

A leading neuroscientist looks at the topic of consciousness and offers an unconventional suggestion regarding its origins.

Dennett, D. C. (1992). *Consciousness explained.* Boston: Little, Brown.

This book provides a provocative look at consciousness from a philosophical, psychological, and computational viewpoint.

Gazzaniga, M. S. (2008). *Human: The science behind what makes us unique.* New York: Ecco.

A major figure in cognitive neuroscience shares his view of the brain as an evolutionary product in which language uniquely inflects human sociality.

Jaynes, J. (2000). *The origin of consciousness in the breakdown of the bicameral mind.* Boston: Houghton Mifflin.

Jaynes's book presents the intriguing hypothesis that human consciousness is a recent phenomenon that emerged long after the evolution of the human brain as we know it now. You do not need to agree with Jaynes's thesis to enjoy reading this scholarly book.

Nash, M., & Barnier, A. (Eds.) (2008). *The Oxford handbook of hynosis: Theory, research, and practice.* New York: Oxford University Press.

A scholarly overview of historical and contemporary research in hypnotic phenomena and applications.

Horne, J. (2006). *Sleepfaring: A journey through the science of sleep.* Oxford: Oxford University Press.

Horne's book about sleep is wide-ranging and well-referenced.

Linden, D. (2007). *The accidental mind: How brain evolution has given us love, memory, dreams, and God.* Cambridge, MA: Belknap Press of Harvard University Press.

An entertaining overview of the evolutionary process that produced the unique patchwork that is the human brain.

Hofstadter, D. (2007). *I am a strange loop.* New York: Basic Books.

A highly evocative, autobiographical introduction to the strange-loop theory of consciousness. Alternately humorous and touching, Hofstadter develops the theory by reference to many analogies, including computer analogies and Gödel's impossibility theorem.

Learning: How Do We Learn?

Chris S. Dula, Ph.D.
—East Tennessee State
University
E. Scott Geller, Ph.D.
—Virginia Tech

CHAPTER OUTLINE

"Every act you have ever performed since the day you were born was performed because you wanted something."

—Dale Carnegie

Section 1: Learning About Learning— The Essence

Learning is a factor in almost every human activity. From recognizing family members and understanding concepts to getting what we want and avoiding what we don't want, virtually everything we do is influenced by learning. How can parents get their kids to be well-behaved at home? How can teachers get children to follow instructions and learn in school? How can coaches get the best performance from athletes? Why do we shudder at the smell of a food many years after we ate it and became ill? Why do we have a hard time quitting bad habits and starting good ones? These questions and more are answered in this chapter.

Psychological Literacy—Why Psychology Matters

Generally, when people hear the terms 'behavior modification' or 'behavior change,' they think of something bad. The word 'manipulative' comes to mind. However, manipulate simply means to 'change' and at times we all want to change others' behavior. When someone says "let's go to this restaurant," and you say, "No, let's go to a different one," you're trying to change that person's behavior. Parents attempt to get their children to behave in ways society finds acceptable or desirable. At times we also want to change our own behavior, perhaps to do things more efficiently or effectively, learn new skills, or quit bad habits. It turns out there are evidence-based methods to improve all types of behaviors.

Actually there's no chapter in this book of greater importance, because the principles covered here can be applied to so many life activities. The methods we explain work and can be used either benevolently or malevolently. We hope you'll use the powers you gain from this chapter in a compassionate manner to accomplish noble goals in your own life and in the lives of others. It'll take a while to arrive at the more practical and interesting applications of the principles, so hang in there while we cover the basics.

Foundational Concepts: Getting Started

Learning Objectives At the end of this section, you'll be able to:

9.1.1 Define *learning* and describe elements important to understanding the definition (e.g., intensity, duration, frequency, stimulus, response, impact).

9.1.2 Explain the concept of *habituation*.

9.1.3 Compare/contrast *contingency* with *contiguity*.

Learning is a relatively durable change in behavior or knowledge resulting from experience. *Experience* is any event in which you participated, as either an actor or observer. A *change* can represent a gain or

---

learning A relatively permanent change in behavior or knowledge as a result of experience.

a loss of a behavior. Behaviors are often reactions to a prompt of some kind—like circling an answer to a test item which reflects knowledge gained or running from a threat which represents an adaptation to a bad situation.

A more formal term for a prompt is *stimulus* (plural *stimuli*), which is any detectable sensory input from the environment; something seen, heard, smelled, tasted, or physically felt. Stimuli can be measured in terms of intensity, duration and frequency. *Intensity* is the strength or magnitude of a stimulus on a relevant scale. *Duration* refers to how long a stimulus lasts, which may range from a fraction of a second to hours. *Frequency* is how often a stimulus is presented or occurs. When reactions to a stimulus are measured and recorded, they become data which are essential to science and to developing effective behavior-change techniques.

Any specific occurrence of behavior following a stimulus is a *response*. As with stimuli, responses also vary in intensity, duration, and frequency. *Stimulus impact* refers to the effect a stimulus has on a response. A very intense stimulus will typically produce a greater reaction than one of low intensity. For example, an unexpected loud sound might make you jump, whereas an unexpected quiet sound may produce little response. However, an intense stimulus that occurs frequently or lasts a long time, like workers using a jackhammer for many hours outside your office or classroom, may eventually have little impact on you. *Habituation* is the process by which we 'tune out' and stop responding to irrelevant stimuli.

Learning has a lot to do with making associations between events. *Contingencies* can be thought of as 'if-then' arrangements. For example, *if* Anya is sitting in the sun and it gets too hot (stimulus) *then* she'll move to the shade (response). We make associations based on *contiguity*, which is the perceived relation between events in space and time. Often this linkage is a true 'if-then' contingency, though sometimes it's not, as we'll see later.

Section 2: Classical Conditioning: Reflexive Learning

Classical conditioning is where previously neutral stimuli come to elicit autonomic responses. That probably sounds confusing at the moment, but we'll explain thoroughly. This type of learning happens to everyone, though we may not notice the learning taking place. Yet such learning can stay with us for a lifetime and in some cases, after only one experience. While classical conditioning has always been part of the human experience, we didn't truly understand its function and force until it was studied scientifically. Let's meet the first person to undertake this important work.

---

classical conditioning A process whereby previously neutral stimuli come to elicit autonomic responses.

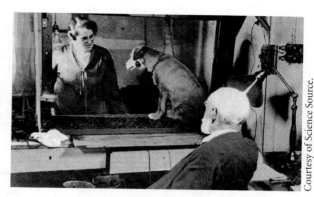

[**FIGURE 9•1**] Pavlov and 'His' dog.

Does the Name 'Pavlov' Ring a Bell?

Learning Objectives At the end of this section, you'll be able to:

9.2.1 Describe Ivan Pavlov's experiments and contributions to the domain of Learning.

Ivan Pavlov (1849–1936; pictured in **FIGURE 9•1**) wasn't a psychologist, but rather a physiologist who studied digestion in dogs (Gentile & Miller, 2009). He started his research in the 1890's and his name has since become well-known in popular culture, and his concepts show up in films, television and music. Pavlov's work was important in helping us understand how animals learn, and by extension, how humans learn.

Pavlov started his investigation in the mouths of dogs. The mouth houses the first stage of digestion, providing lubrication for mastication. In other words, slobbering makes your mouth wet so it's easier to chew and swallow food. Pavlov strapped hungry dogs in harnesses and put food in front of them, at which point they salivated. He measured how quickly and how long they salivated, as well as how much saliva they produced.

Not only did dogs salivate when food was presented, they also learned to salivate to seemingly irrelevant stimuli associated with food. For example, Pavlov's dogs started salivating to the sound of footsteps because footsteps were reliably associated (contiguity) with the presentation of food. Dogs are not born with a footstep-salivation connection, so this connection was learned. This was unexpected and Pavlov realized he was onto something important. He began systematic studies of stimuli that could be made to produce salivation in dogs.

For example, if a bell was rung consistently before food was presented, dogs would eventually salivate to the sound of the bell alone. This led to the expression "Does the name Pavlov ring a bell?" Actually, Pavlov didn't ring a bell but used tones, buzzers, and metronomes (Pavlov, 1902; 1927). Other researchers working with him used bells, so we'll use a bell to illustrate the concepts. You may ask yourself, "Who cares?" We'll get to practical applications, but first, let's appreciate the fundamentals of *classical conditioning*.

Before Conditioning

Food Alone Triggers A Salivation Response

Unconditioned
Stimulus (UCS)

Unconditioned
Response (UCR)

Food is a
stimulus that
naturally
produces a
salivation
response.

Before Conditioning

The Bell Rung Alone Originally Does Not Trigger A Salivation Response

Originally Neutral
Stimulus

No Salivation

The bell alone
does not cause
salivation. So, it
is considered a
neutral stimulus
with regard to
salivation.

During Conditioning

The Bell Is Now Rung Regularly Before Presenting Food (Which Triggers Salivation Response)

Food causes
salivation. But,
we now regularly
ring a bell before
presenting food.
So, the bell now
predicts arrival
of food.

After Conditioning

The Bell Rung Alone Now Triggers A Salivation Response

Conditioned Stimulus
(CS)

Conditioned Response
(CR)

Thus, our dog
learned to salivate
to the bell without
food having to be
presented.

[**FIGURE 9•2**] The Classical conditioning process.

Key Terms: A UCS Causes a UCR, Which Becomes a CR to a CS. Say What?

Learning Objectives At the end of this section, you'll be able to:

9.2.2 Define *classical conditioning*.

9.2.3 List the four types of *unconditioned* and *conditioned stimuli* and *responses*.

9.2.4 Describe and compare/contrast those four types of *stimuli* and *responses*.

Classical conditioning occurs when stimuli in the environment come to pull forth or *elicit* responses from organisms. Generally, responses in classical conditioning are autonomic and happen reflexively. We don't usually think of salivating as behavior, but it is. Breathing, our hearts beating, and hormones being released into the blood are also types of behavior. As autonomic behaviors, they occur reflexively and without awareness. They also occur without prior learning.

We don't think, "Here's food, I should salivate." Salivating to food happens automatically and we're all born with an unlearned and lifelong food-salivation reflex. But as with Pavlov's dogs, we can learn to salivate to things unrelated to food. Note *conditioned* means *learned*, while *unconditioned* is *unlearned*.

An **unconditioned stimulus** (also called UCS) is a stimulus that reflexively triggers an autonomic response. The behavior or response triggered by a UCS is called the **unconditioned response** (or UCR). For Pavlov's dogs, the food was a stimulus that caused a salivation response. Dogs don't *learn* to salivate to

---

unconditioned stimulus A stimulus that automatically or naturally triggers an autonomic (involuntary) response without prior learning.

unconditioned response The autonomic response triggered by an unconditioned stimulus; also unlearned.

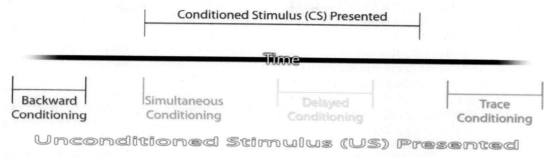

[**FIGURE 9•3**] Four conditioning types defined by timing of the CS and UCS presentation.

food, so here food is the *unconditioned stimulus* (UCS) which automatically causes salivation, which is the *unconditioned response* (UCR). As another example, when light (UCS) hits your eye, your pupil reflexively constricts (UCR).

A **conditioned stimulus** (CS) is initially neutral (a bell doesn't naturally make a dog salivate) in terms of triggering a particular autonomic response. It's called a CS when it comes to elicit a similar response to one triggered by an *unconditioned stimulus* (UCS), because of its association with that UCS. The salivation dogs produced in response to a bell is called a *conditioned response* (CR) because it was learned. A **conditioned response** (CR) is the same type of response originally elicited by the UCS. Once it's triggered by a *conditioned stimulus* (CS), it's called a *conditioned response* (CR). FIGURE 9•2 shows the conditioning process with a bell, including the technical labels applied to the relevant stimuli and responses.

As a practical example, the smell of pizza (UCS) makes your mouth reflexively water (UCR). Then stimuli originally neutral with regard to salivation, like the sight of a restaurant or its logo, become associated with pizza. If seeing or thinking of a restaurant or its logo makes your mouth water, even a little, the restaurant or logo has become a conditioned stimulus (CS) and your salivation is a conditioned response (CR).

You can explore several conditioning approaches in **Beyond the Basics** (FEATURE 9•1). In general, a potential conditioned stimulus (CS) would have to precede presentation of food (UCS), and ideally there would not be much time between the two (contiguity). As the bell predicts food, the dog learns to respond to the sound by salivating prior to food being presented. The more consistently a bell predicts food (an obvious contingency), the more quickly an association will form, but this conditioning can still take quite a few trials to establish. Let's look at phases and effects of this type of learning.

feature 9.1

> **Beyond the Basics: Subtypes of Conditioning**

There are several conditioning subtypes. The sooner an unconditioned stimulus (UCS) is presented after the conditioned stimulus (CS), the stronger the predictive association and conditioned response (CR). Presenting a CS right before the UCS is called *forward conditioning*. It doesn't work as well to present the CS and UCS far apart (no contiguity), simultaneously, or to present the CS *after* the UCS. Ringing a bell ten minutes before giving food, at the same time food is given, or afterwards, doesn't predict food arrival, though these may produce a weak CR.

Presenting the UCS before a CS ends is called *delayed conditioning*. If the UCS starts after the CS (with only a very brief delay), we have *trace conditioning*. Presenting a CS and UCS at the same time is *simultaneous conditioning*; but as noted, doesn't work well because the CS is redundant with the UCS. *Backward conditioning* occurs when the UCS is presented before the CS, but this can inhibit the CR because the CS may now signal an *absence* of the UCS. FIGURE 9•3 displays these types of conditioning, where the timing of the CS presentation appears above the timeline, the timing of the UCS onset appears below the timeline, and conditioning types are defined by the timing of the CS and UCS pairings.

Some Central Concepts of Classical Conditioning

Learning Objectives At the end of this section, you'll be able to:

9.2.5 Discuss the conditioning process in terms of *acquisition* and *extinction*.

9.2.6 Describe how *spontaneous recovery* can be adaptive in relearning previously extinguished responses.

9.2.7 Compare/contrast *stimulus discrimination* and *stimulus generalization*, and give relevant examples from your own life.

---

conditioned stimulus A stimulus which was previously neutral with regard to triggering a particular response, but which acquires the property of causing the same type of response.

conditioned response A response ordinarily produced by an unconditioned stimulus but *after* it comes to be elicited by a conditioned stimulus.

Acquisition, Extinction, & Recovery—It Comes & Goes & Comes Back The initial learning phase is called **acquisition**. This is the period in which our dogs *acquire*, or learn, the response of salivating (CR) to a bell (CS). Once acquired, and as long as food (UCS) is still occasionally given after the bell, the dogs will continue to exhibit the CR and salivate whenever the bell rings. However, if we keep ringing the bell but *completely stop* giving food afterwards, the dogs will eventually stop salivating to the bell—a process called **extinction**. This occurs because the bell no longer predicts food. If a UCS no longer supports the predictive power of the CS, the CR will degrade until it's gone (extinguished). But, an extinguished CR can reappear again, seemingly 'out of the blue.'

Spontaneous recovery occurs when a CR suddenly returns after extinction is complete. In our example, if food (UCS) is no longer presented, salivation to the bell (CR) eventually extinguishes. But after time passes, the CR will spontaneously reappear following a presentation of the CS. This CR will be relatively weak compared to the peak level achieved at the end of the acquisition phase. However, if food is presented during this spontaneous recovery of salivation to the bell, full salivation will occur the next time the bell rings, as if the CS–CR connection was never extinguished. Thus, relearning occurs faster than initial learning, and you can see how this can be adaptive in many situations. If food (UCS) isn't forthcoming after the bell rings (CS) during the spontaneous recovery, then relearning won't occur and salivating to the bell will extinguish quickly and be less likely to spontaneously recur later.

Additional effects are seen in what's called higher-order conditioning, which has implications for how we learn language. This is a more advanced concept and thus is contained in **Beyond the Basics (FEATURE 9•2)**. Now, let's look at factors involved with acquiring a CR to some, but not all, stimuli that resemble a CS.

feature 9.2

Beyond the Basics: Higher-Order Conditioning— Linking Up Links

Not all classical conditioning requires a conditioned stimulus (CS) to be directly connected with an unconditioned stimulus (UCS) for a conditioned response (CR) to be acquired. **Higher-order conditioning** occurs when a well-established CS serves as the UCS in conditioning a new CS. Sound confusing? Bear with us.

If a previously neutral light were turned on just before we receive a substantial electric shock (UCS), the shock would cause an adrenaline response (UCR). If the light (CS) is later turned on, we'd have an adrenaline reaction (CR) to the light. After establishing a light-fear connection (CS-CR), we might then ring a bell before turning on the light, yet not administer the shock when the bell is present. But, an adrenaline reaction (CR) would occur to the bell because of the association with the light (CS), even

though the bell had never been paired directly with a shock (UCS). So the light (as a well-established CS) essentially functions like a shock (UCS) in conditioning a new adrenaline response to the bell (CS).

Let's consider the application of this principle to learning language. Words are initially neutral stimuli because they don't originally mean anything to us as infants. But when babies are cuddled, fed, or cleaned, caregivers typically speak in sweet tones, saying things like "I love you." Cuddling, feeding, and cleaning (UCS) produce pleasant feelings (UCR) and these are paired with words and tones such that similar pleasant feelings are later elicited (CR) when we hear "I love you" from a sweet-sounding voice (CS).

At this point we've not achieved anything but a classically-conditioned association. However, by pairing new neutral stimuli (say nicknames, like Pooky) with a well-established CS (like a sweet-sounding "I love you"), the new stimuli may also come to elicit a CR. Thus, other words not connected with a UCS become associated with "I love you" (CS) and these new words also come to elicit pleasant feelings. So, now hearing "Pooky" may make us feel as nice as the words, "I love you."

However, if told "you're awful" when spanked (UCS) as a child, later in life the word "awful" (CS) may make you feel bad even if voiced without physical punishment. Other words like "jerk," may become connected with the word "awful," and could come to elicit similar negative feelings. Again, if the new words acquire the power of a CR, and were not directly linked to a UCS but only to an already-established CS, higher-order conditioning has occurred.

Generalization & Discrimination—When You Do & Don't Respond

In brief, **stimulus generalization** occurs when a conditioned response (CR) is triggered by a stimulus similar to the original conditioned stimulus (CS). **Stimulus discrimination** occurs when a CR is not exhibited in the presence of other stimuli, because they are sufficiently different from the original CS. As an example, let's say Nikila was bitten by a dog, a German Shepherd, owned by a friend.

---

acquisition In classical and operant conditioning, the period of learning during which a conditioned response is developed.

extinction Where a conditioned response weakens and eventually ceases because it is no longer paired with a conditioned stimulus (classical conditioning) or a reinforcer (operant conditioning).

spontaneous recovery When a previously extinguished learned response returns suddenly in the presence of a conditioned stimulus (classical conditioning) or a discriminative stimulus (operant conditioning).

higher-order conditioning A well-established conditioned stimulus serves as an unconditioned stimulus for conditioning a new response.

stimulus generalization When a learned response occurs to following a stimulus *similar* to, but not identical to, the original conditioned stimulus (classical conditioning) or discriminative stimulus (operant conditioning).

stimulus discrimination When a learned response does *not* occur following a stimulus that is sufficiently *different* from the original conditioned stimulus (classical conditioning) or discriminative stimulus (operant conditioning).

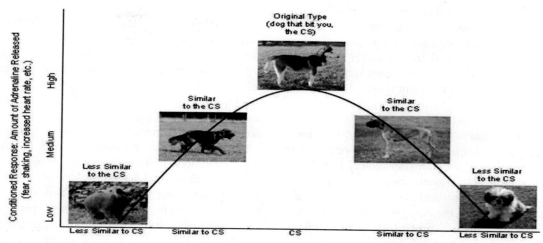

Generalization vs. Discrimination
(Conditioned Responses to Conditioned Stimulus and Similar Stimuli)

[**FIGURE 9•4**] Distinguishing generalization from discrimination.

The painful bite (unconditioned stimulus, UCS) causes a natural release of adrenaline (unconditioned response, UCR) which may be experienced as fear. The dog was originally neutral with regard to adrenaline, but was paired with adrenaline brought about by pain. The next time Nikila sees this dog she'd likely have a conditioned adrenaline release response and feel fear because the dog is now a CS, causing the release of adrenaline (now a CR). If Nikila feels fear when seeing dogs of a similar size, breed or color, we have *stimulus generalization.*

If Nikila later sees a dog not similar to a German Shepherd, say a poodle, and has no fear reaction, we would have *stimulus discrimination.* The more dissimilar the new stimulus is to the original CS, the less intense the CR, until the CR doesn't occur at all. If she experienced fear to all dogs later, this would be extensive stimulus generalization. But, even if this happened, she would likely not feel fear in the presence of cats, which share some features of dogs, but are sufficiently different to enable stimulus discrimination. So, generalization and discrimination are flip sides of the same coin. FIGURE 9•4 depicts a generalization/discrimination curve that might result from a dog bite. Sometimes only one experience (trial) is needed to produce a powerful learning effect.

Taste Aversions & Phobias as One-Trial Learning: I Can't Eat (Or Do) That Again!
Learning Objectives At the end of this section, you'll be able to:

9.2.8   Describe the concepts of *one-trial learning* and *biological preparedness.*

9.2.9   Explain why *conditioned taste aversion* and *phobias* are types of one-trial learning and have survival value.

9.2.10   Analyze the roles of fear, sickness, and pain in one-trial learning.

Learning occurring from one experience is called **one-trial learning.** One-trial learning usually happens as a response to *fear, pain, and sickness* because this prevents us from getting into similar situations later. **Biological preparedness** is our natural tendency to learn some associations quickly, and sometimes permanently, because avoiding dangerous situations has survival value (Alexander, 2003; Cummins & Cummins, 1999; Rachman, 2002). Let's examine how and why getting sick makes for quick and robust learning.

Conditioned Taste Aversion—Leaves a Bad Taste in Your Mouth Have you ever eaten a food and later gotten so sick you never wanted to see or smell that food again, let alone eat it? Many of us have. While it appears the food caused you to get sick, it was actually bacteria that made you ill. Later, we feel queasy when we see or smell that kind of food and we're unlikely to eat it again.

This is called **conditioned taste aversion** and it happens in one trial. The food was originally neutral and possibly experienced as pleasurable. The bacteria which made us sick was the *unconditioned stimulus* (UCS), producing an *unconditioned response* of nausea (UCR). Thus, the food became a *conditioned stimulus* (CS) when it produced a *conditioned response* of nausea (CR). *Biological preparedness* holds that we have this ability so when we encounter dangerous foods in

---

one-trial learning When conditioning occurs after a single experience involving relatively intense fear, pain, or sickness.

biological preparedness A tendency for organisms to learn some kinds of associations very quickly because doing so has survival value.

conditioned taste aversion When getting sick (unconditioned stimulus) is paired with food/drink (conditioned stimulus) leads to feeling nauseous in the presence of the same food/drink later.

the wild, say attractive but poisonous berries, if we survive, we'd never make the same mistake again.

John Garcia (1917–), perhaps the first Hispanic-American to earn a Ph.D. in Psychology, systematically studied the phenomenon of conditioned taste aversion (Thorne & Henley, 2005). In fact, conditioned taste aversion is also known as the 'Garcia Effect'. Garcia and colleagues (1955) showed that rats developed an aversion to sweetened solutions after drinking samples irradiated to the point the rats became sick. Even though rats preferred sweetened liquids, those made sick thereafter avoided the very treat they used to enjoy.

This has implications for human cancer treatment, though it would be a while before the findings were applied widely. In the early days of chemotherapy and radiation, patients got ill as a result of treatment, often experiencing nausea and vomiting (e.g., Bernstein, 1978; Carrell et al., 1986). With good intentions, some medical personnel told patients to eat a favorite meal before such procedures, as they wouldn't want to eat for days after treatments. Then the treatments not only caused nausea, but the nausea became associated with the patients favorite meal, often resulting in a conditioned aversion to a favorite food—an unfortunate and unintended consequence.

Nowadays physicians administer anti-nausea medication before chemotherapy or radiation treatment, so any resulting nausea occurs long after the patient leaves the facility. This prevents nausea from being associated with the clinical environment, and prevents the development of a conditioned aversion to the facility, staff, instruments, or food. Pain or nausea caused by otherwise beneficial treatment helps explain why some people wish to avoid doctors, dentists, physical therapists, and medical settings in general.

Patients often endure anxiousness about medical settings because they have a strong enough motivation to receive beneficial therapy. And, such aversions are eventually extinguished after repeatedly forcing oneself to eat an aversive food without getting sick again, or repeatedly going to medical facilities without any resulting pain or sickness. However, sometimes classically-conditioned anxiety leads to total avoidance of the feared stimulus or situation, eliminating the possibility of extinction.

Phobias—Acquired Classically, Though Unfortunately

Another type of one-trial learning is represented by the acquisition of a phobia. Phobia is a clinical term and isn't just any fear. Many fears are rational, but phobias are irrational by definition. Everyone should be afraid of a gun pointed to their head, but that's not a phobia because it's a rational fear. However, fears of small spaces, airplane flights, or high buildings are irrational because you know you are quite safe, statistically speaking. While these situations produce mild and temporary fear in many people, most people don't avoid them. When a fear meets the criteria for a phobia, the feared stimulus or situation will either be avoided at all costs or endured only with a serious and persisting sense of dread.

Though phobias may develop over time, it can take only one experience with an aversive object or situation to create a phobia (e.g., Coelho & Purkis, 2009). We don't wish to oversimplify the issue as learning history is not the only factor involved (Mineka & Zinbarg, 2006). But generally speaking, after an encounter produces profound pain and/or fear (e.g., assault, vehicle crash, combat, natural disaster), a fear reaction is likely to occur the next time we find ourselves in a situation resembling the one in which we experienced the initial threat.

Of course, if similar situations are dangerous in the future, it's adaptive to avoid them. However, many times future situations are not dangerous, but share similar features to those in which the initial bad encounter occurred. If we're in similar future situations that aren't actually dangerous and endure them without any bad outcomes, the fear will subside and extinguish. But, if our fear is so strong that we avoid or quickly leave similar situations later, even though they're actually safe, the conditioned fear response cannot be extinguished.

Let's say Brandon is standing on the corner where he always waits for the bus and he's hit by a car (UCS). He feels pain and also fear as adrenaline is released (UCR). The car was a previously neutral stimulus in the situation, as was the street corner. When Brandon finally recovers and comes to that corner again (now a CS), he will likely have an automatic release of adrenaline and feel some fear (now a CR). But, if he stays on that street corner long enough and nothing bad happens, the anxiety will start to subside and eventually go away. The more he does this, the more thoroughly the CR will be extinguished. He may then come to the same corner again and again and not feel anxious ever again.

However, the fear may suddenly return one day (spontaneous recovery). And, if Brandon deals with that feeling and stays in the situation, it should subside relatively quickly and stay away longer. However, if he leaves the situation while experiencing the fear, his conditioned fear reaction is likely to recur the next time at the pre-extinguished level. This fear may not occur on all street corners (stimulus discrimination) but it may spread to other similar street corners (stimulus generalization) and ultimately have profound consequences on Brandon's life. It is important to note that phobias are highly treatable with therapies based on the basic learning principles covered in this chapter. Speaking of negative feelings acquired through learning, let's consider the most famous example of emotional conditioning—the case of John Watson and Little Albert.

Does the Name 'Watson' Ring a Bell? Another Psychology Heavyweight

Learning Objectives At the end of this section, you'll be able to:

9.2.11   Define *behaviorism* and explain why Watson thought behavior was the only thing we should study in Psychology.

9.2.12 Describe how Watson used classical conditioning to induce Little Albert to fear rats, and interpret why Albert feared some new items and not others after conditioning.

John B. Watson (1878–1958; see **FIGURE 9•5**) is another prominent name in Psychology. Considered the father of behaviorism, Watson published a revolutionary article in 1913, entitled *Psychology as the Behaviorist Views It*. Essentially, Watson said for Psychology to be taken seriously as a science, it must focus only on observable phenomena, the most obvious and relevant of which is behavior (Watson, 1913).

Behaviorism is the school of psychology focused on the study of behavior, especially its activators (what happens before a behavior) and consequences (what happens after a behavior). Watson's behaviorist view of psychology dramatically conflicted with those of many researchers at the time. Watson went so far as to say all emotions are acquired by classical conditioning. To illustrate his point, Watson conducted research on a child known as Little Albert.

Little 'Albert B.' was brought to Watson's lab several times between the ages of 9 and 13 months (Watson & Rayner, 1920). Albert's mother was employed at a John's Hopkins University facility, where Watson was a faculty member working with graduate student Rosalie Rayner (Beck, Levinson, & Irons, 2009). Watson and Rayner found most babies were easily upset when blankets under them were yanked upon. But, at age 8 months and 26 days, Albert never got upset when his blanket was yanked. Watson and Rayner wrote "His stability was one of the principal reasons for using him as a subject . . . We felt that we could do him relatively little harm by carrying out such experiments . . ." (Watson & Rayner, 1920, pgs. 1–2).

During the first session, they presented Albert with stimuli to demonstrate he didn't naturally fear them. They said Albert was " . . . confronted suddenly and for the first time successively with a white rat, a rabbit, a dog, a monkey, with masks with and without hair, cotton wool, burning newspapers, etc." They noted Albert showed no fear to these objects. Then they performed their conditioned emotion procedure.

Upon putting the rat in front of Albert again, they stood behind him and struck a large steel bar with a hammer (UCS) which startled him and made him cry (UCR). In fact, they did this to him seven times. When they placed the rat in front of Albert during later sessions, he cried immediately and tried to crawl away. The rat had done nothing to cause fear in Albert; the association between the startling noise and the rat produced the new fear. So, Albert acquired a fear (CR), of the rat (CS). Watson (1923) recorded Albert's reactions before and after conditioning in a silent film; perhaps the first video ever in our discipline.

Courtesy of Underwood & Underwood/ Corbis Images.

[**FIGURE 9•5**] John B. Watson.

Albert later showed a similar fear to other furry objects which had not elicited a fear reaction before the procedure. These included the rabbit, the dog, a fur coat, and a Santa-Claus mask. Since these stimuli were not paired with a loud noise (UCS) but are somewhat similar to the rat (CS), Albert's aversive reaction to them illustrates *stimulus generalization*. Watson and Rayner noted that Albert didn't acquire a fear response to the room, the table he was on, nor the sets of blocks present throughout the fear-conditioning sessions. No doubt you recognize these as examples of *stimulus discrimination*. In later sessions when Albert stopped showing a pronounced fear response to the rat or rabbit (an example of *extinction* of the CR), they struck the bar again and reestablished the fear reaction.

FIGURE 9•6 playfully shows the connection between the UCS (a loud noise), the UCR (a fear reaction to the loud noise), and the rat (previously a neutral stimulus that became a CS eliciting the CR of fear). Watson and Rayner never tried to remove the fears they conditioned in Albert. They said, "Unfortunately Albert was taken from the hospital the day the above tests were made. Hence the opportunity of building up an experimental technique by means of which we could remove the conditioned emotional responses was denied us" (Watson & Rayner, 1920, p. 12). They noted things they'd liked to have tried, but it was Mary Cover Jones (1924; 1924a) who later discovered ways to remove phobias.

Section 3: Operant Conditioning: Learning by Consequences

Learning Objectives At the end of this section, you'll be able to:

9.3.1 Define *operant conditioning* and distinguish it from *classical conditioning*.

---

behaviorism The study of overt behavior, especially its antecedents (activators), its intensity, duration, and frequency, and its consequences.

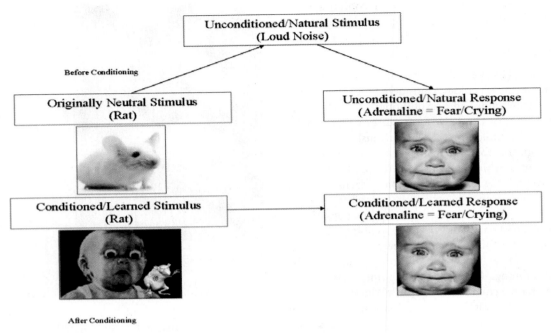

[**FIGURE 9•6**]   Little Albert and 'The' Rat: an emotional experience.

9.3.2   Contrast the role of the autonomic nervous system and the somatic nervous system in *classical* and *operant conditioning*, respectively.

As with much human learning, both *classical conditioning* and *operant conditioning* were involved in Albert's conditioned fear, though we've said nothing about the latter until now. **Operant conditioning** occurs when voluntary behavior is controlled by the consequences produced. Albert not only had internal reflexive fear to the rat, he also tried to crawl away from the aversive stimulus. This crawling was an *operant response*.

While Albert's conditioned fear was an involuntary autonomic nervous-system response, he was operantly conditioned to voluntarily crawl away from the feared stimuli. This is the case with phobias, which are maintained because people are *operantly conditioned* to avoid what they fear, preventing them from remaining in feared (but safe) situations long enough for their *classically conditioned* fear to extinguish. These operantly-conditioned behaviors (e.g., crying, hitting the breaks when a vehicle pulls in front of us) are controlled by the somatic nervous system, so we control their occurrence. Let's delve deeper into the operant learning of voluntary behaviors.

The Law of Effect—Why Do That Again?

Learning Objectives   At the end of this section, you'll be able to:

9.3.3   Describe the *Law of Effect* and give examples of its influence in your life.

Edward Thorndike (1874–1949) worked with children, chickens, and dogs, but he's best known for his experiments with cats. He first tested the **Law of Effect**—the notion that when you do something with results you like, you'll be more likely to repeat that behavior in similar situations. Equally, when you do something yielding results you dislike, you'll be less likely to do the same thing in similar situations. Sounds like common sense, but it used to be 'common sense' that the Sun orbited Earth. Let's see how Thorndike verified the Law of Effect.

Thorndike constructed a puzzle-box (see FIGURE 9•7) with a latched door that could be opened from the inside only " . . . by turning a wooden button that held the door, pulling a loop attached to the bolt, or pressing down a lever" (Thorndike, 1898, p. 818). We'll use a lever for our explanation. He put a hungry cat inside the box where it could see and smell food on the outside. Of course, the cat didn't initially know how to get out of the box, but it wanted to escape and eat. At first it did random things (meowing, pacing, pawing at openings), none of which helped. Eventually, by chance, the cat pressed the lever and opened the door. Thorndike measured how long this took and put the cat back in the box for repeated trials.

The first time Thorndike put a cat back in the box, it did random things again and didn't press the lever immediately. With successive trials, the cats got faster at lever-pressing and

---

operant conditioning   Voluntary behavior comes to be controlled by consequences following its occurrence.

law of effect   Behaviors producing pleasant consequences are likely to be repeated in similar situations and behaviors producing negative consequences are less likely to be repeated.

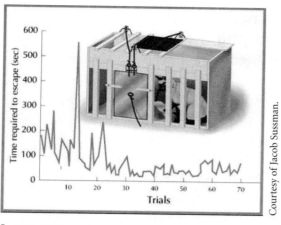

[**FIGURE 9•7**] Thorndike's puzzle box.

escaping the box, demonstrating learning had occurred. Presumably this was due to the *Law of Effect* (Thorndike, 1927), where lever-pressing was repeated in future situations because it yielded a consequence the cat desired, namely getting out and eating.

Thorndike also studied whether cats learned from observation by having first-time cats watch cats that had learned to quickly escape the box. First-timer cats who observed old-timer cats did not benefit from observing other cats escape the box (Thorndike, 1898). They did not experience observational learning, which we discuss later in this chapter. Thorndike also wondered whether cats developed sudden insight by making an immediate escape connection. This didn't happen. Instead the cats learned gradually, getting quicker over time, as shown on the graph in Figure 9•7.

Such learning occurred as a gradual result of behavioral consequences. Many consider this to be 'trial-and-error learning,' as in, "we learn from our mistakes." But, it's more appropriate to consider this 'trial-and-success' learning. The cats didn't learn much from errors. They learned most when they succeeded at escaping. After several random successes, cats made a connection between a lever press and escape. Yes, we humans do learn from our mistakes, as when a coach or teacher points out our error and gives us corrective feedback. But in terms of speed and quality of learning, we usually gain more from focusing on our successful behaviors.

Does the Name 'Skinner' Ring a Bell? Another Big Name in Behaviorism

Learning Objectives At the end of this section, you'll be able to:

9.3.4   Describe the *Skinner Box/Operant Chamber*, and suggest advantages to studying behavior in such a controlled environment.

Before we dive fully into operant conditioning, we should say a few words about Burrhus Frederic (B.F.) Skinner (1904–1990). Skinner was a pioneer in the experimental analysis of behavior and the application of findings to improve human well-being. He took Watson's *Behaviorism* and Thorndike's *Law of Effect* to the next level, with unsurpassed scientific rigor.

Working largely with rats and pigeons, Skinner designed equipment and methods to control and measure behavior more effectively than ever before. For example, he invented the cumulative recorder to measure behavior continuously over time (Skinner, 1938; Skinner & Morse, 1957). He also created an enclosure called an **operant chamber** (Skinner, 1938; see **FIGURE 9•8**), where he could systematically manipulate consequences and record responses precisely. It became popularly known as a 'Skinner Box,' a label he disliked immensely.

Skinner also invented an 'Air Crib' for infants (Skinner, 1945, also see Figure 9.8) and 'pigeon-guided' bombs (Skinner, 1960). Both were thoroughly misconstrued by the public. People reacted negatively to putting a child in a 'box.' However, this was no ordinary box, but rather an enhanced crib. It foreshadowed modern child-care practice with sanitary climate-controlled conditions, and an intercom system we now call a 'baby-monitor'. His daughter (Deborah, pictured in the Air Crib in Figure 9.8) grew up physically and psychologically healthy, despite mean-spirited myths to the contrary. People also disliked the idea of a pigeon inside a bomb, pecking a mechanism to guide the bomb to a target it was trained to recognize from aerial photos. Although this was a successful

---

operant chamber   An enclosure in which an animal's responses can be precisely recorded and specific consequences can be systematically manipulated. Also known as Skinner Box.

[**FIGURE 9•8**]   B.F Skinner, an Operant Chamber, and his daughter's air crib.

and patriotic undertaking, it was abandoned following development of reliable missile-guiding technology.

Skinner even wrote a novel, *Walden Two* (1948) which explained how behavioral science could solve lots of society's large-scale dilemmas. Many people detested the book, where 'behavior control' for the common good was seen not as utopian but dystopian. Interestingly, society controls people's behavior all the time (essentially by rules and laws) that threaten negative consequences for undesirable behavior. In contrast, Skinner proposed in *Walden Two* the use of only positive consequences to manage human behavior and address societal problems. Within Psychology, Skinner is pre-eminent, authoring 180 seminal research publications, and 21 books. Let's consider the basic principles of operant learning first researched by B.F. Skinner.

Discriminative Stimuli (Activators)—How We Know When to Do Something

Learning Objectives At the end of this section, you'll be able to:

9.3.5 Discuss how *discriminative stimuli* (S^D) come to influence some of our behaviors.

How do you know when to engage in a particular behavior? If you carefully analyze your own behavior, you'll notice a **discriminative stimulus** (S^D) signals when to emit a particular behavior in order to obtain a certain outcome or consequence. For example, in class students typically sit, face forward, and take notes. The classroom itself is an S^D that prompts certain behaviors, like sitting to face the instructor. The instructor starting a lecture is an S^D that signals students to become quiet and take notes. After exiting the class, the hallway (a new S^D) indicates students may now talk loudly or make a cell-phone call.

What about behavior at a party? Do people sit down quietly and take notes? A party suggests certain festive behaviors are acceptable. Thus, environmental settings help us discriminate, or differentiate, which behaviors are currently appropriate or effective.

Consider the *A-B-C Model of Behavior*, where *A = Activator*, *B = Behavior*, and, *C = Consequence*. In our lives, we learn which <u>a</u>ctivators (S^D) signal the most useful <u>b</u>ehaviors to yield the best <u>c</u>onsequences in a given setting. For example, a red traffic light (S^D) is an **activator** directing us to stop. If we stop, we have the consequence of avoiding a potential citation and crash. However, activators don't always have their intended impact on behavior. To understand why, let's consider the qualities of effective **reinforcers** and **punishers**.

---

activators A stimulus that offers direction for a particular behavior, sometimes pinpointing the availability of certain consequences.

discriminative stimulus A stimulus that indicates the availability of a reinforcer or punisher following a particular behavior.

reinforcer Consequences that make a behavior more likely to occur in a given situation.

Basic Concepts of Operant Conditioning

Learning Objectives At the end of this section you'll be able to:

9.3.6 Describe *reinforcement* and *punishment*.

9.3.7 Compare/contrast the use of the terms *positive* and *negative* in defining two types of *reinforcement* and two types of *punishment*.

9.3.8 Define *primary reinforcer* and *secondary reinforcer* with real-world examples.

9.3.9 Describe the function of the terms *variable* vs. *fixed* and *ratio* vs. *interval* with regard to *reinforcement schedules*.

9.3.10 Compare/contrast each *reinforcement schedule* with regard to typical *rates of behavior* and *post-reinforcement pause*, and give examples of each type from your life.

9.3.11 List the six *rules of effective punishment* and explain the rationale behind each.

9.3.12 Explain how the *Premack Principle* influences behavior.

Contingency management techniques regulate behavior by controlling its consequences. No matter the method, the impact of a consequence on behavior determines the label we apply. If a consequence causes a behavior to *increase* in intensity, frequency, and/or duration, the procedure was *reinforcement*. If a consequence causes a *decrease* in these properties of behavior, the procedure was *punishment*. It's also important to note different ways to administer reinforcement and punishment.

Reinforcement: Makes You Want to Do It Again Consequences that compel us to perform a specific behavior again in similar situations are called **reinforcers**. With *positive reinforcement* we perform behaviors to *obtain* or *add* pleasant consequences. A **positive reinforcer** is any consequence that *maintains* or *increases* the behavior it follows. Positive reinforcers are always 'rewarding,' but rewards per se may not actually influence behavior. For example, getting a trophy or plaque usually makes us feel good, but it may not cause us to actually do similar behaviors again. By definition, *reinforcers* always increase or sustain the behavior they follow.

---

punisher Consequences that make a behavior less likely to occur in a given situation.

positive reinforcement When the frequency, intensity, and/or duration of a behavior increases because its occurrence results in presentation of a desirable consequence.

Situation	Activator (S^D)	Behavior 1	Behavior 2	Consequence
Beanie was being bullied by Bama who would steal his food. Joanne let Beanie eat alone in the bathroom to protect his food from being eaten by Bama.	A closed door, with Beanie eating food behind it, signals it's time for a behavior. Door-opening was learned by Bama through trial-and-error (or success).	Once door-opening was learned, it soon became easier to do it more quickly and efficiently. Now, the behavior seems to occur automatically. But, we know better!	Once past the door, Bama does another learned behavior. He moves Beanie away from the food and then eats it. Not very nice, but it certainly does work.	Bama is reinforced for door-opening and bullying. Beanie gives up the food if challenged, to avoid conflict. So, both cats have learned situational behavior.

[**FIGURE 9•9**] Thinking outside the Puzzle Box—real world cats.

While we seek desirable consequences, we also try to avoid undesirable consequences (Infante, 1975). If a behavior makes things we dislike go away, we'll be more likely to do that behavior again in similar situations. This process is termed **negative reinforcement**, and the undesired consequence escaped or avoided is a *negative reinforcer*. For example, if you have a headache and take aspirin and your headache goes away, you're more likely to take aspirin the next time you have a headache. With both *positive* and *negative reinforcement*, a specific behavior is maintained or increased because it brings a desired consequence, either getting something we want or avoiding something we don't want.

Let's consider another cat example to explain further. Scott's wife, Joanne, has two cats, Beanie and Bama. Joanne fed Beanie in a bathroom in order to keep Bama (who was older) from eating Beanie's food. However, Bama learned to reach and pull down the door handle to enter the bathroom where Beanie was eating. Bama's problem solving was *positively reinforced* with food, and thus he performed *more* door-opening behavior (see the photo sequence in **FIGURE 9•9**).

What works to reinforce behavior for one person or animal, doesn't necessarily work for another. If you want six-year-old Madison to sit in her seat in kindergarten, you might give her something tangible, like a sticker for every 15 minutes she stays seated. If Madison likes stickers, this technique should work well. If she doesn't like them, it won't work. Madison might sit for new pencils, trinkets, extra play time, or simple attention like, "Thank you for sitting in your seat quietly the last 15 minutes; it's awesome you're big enough to do that!" Thus, a positive reinforcer doesn't have to be a material consequence. It could be a word of encouragement or recognition, or a physical hug or a pat on the back.

Social consequences are powerful reinforcers for most people. We all do things to gain the attention, affection, and/or admiration of people we like or respect. Sometimes behavior is undesirable and the attention is negative. Do you know a student or employee who gets social approval from peers for getting a rise out of the teacher or supervisor? If positive attention is not available, many people prefer negative attention over no attention, especially children.

This is where many parents go wrong with discipline. They sometimes think they're 'punishing' a behavior by scolding, grounding, spanking, or whatever. If a behavior *decreases or stops*, then *punishment* occurred. But, if a behavior is *maintained or increased*, it was *reinforced*. Saying "I *punished* him, but he *keeps on* doing it," is a failure to understand this principle. If a child *keeps on* doing a behavior, the behavior was by definition *reinforced* somehow.

Check out the runner and coach in **FIGURE 9•10**. The coach motivates the behavior he wants with *negative reinforcement*. This runner will likely take off running to avoid the obvious unpleasant consequence. Some coaches use threats and penalities to

---

negative reinforcement When behavior increases in frequency, intensity, and/or duration because its occurrence results in the decrease or elimination of an aversive situation.

[**FIGURE 9•10**] Motivating with threats doesn't get you far.

motivate behavior, like cutting game time or making an athlete do extra work. Athletes who value playing a sport and being on the team will usually comply with such demands. Thus, the common *negative* reinforcement strategy seems to work. But, how long will this runner run? Will he run as fast when the coach isn't watching and holding him accountable? Will he experience natural positive consequences of running if it's always associated with something unpleasant? This is a critical weakness of *negative* reinforcement; it makes people feel threatened and controlled rather than encouraged and self-motivated.

Whether attaining power, attention, or fun, or avoiding pain, annoyance or boredom, it's all about 'selection by consequences' (Skinner, 1981). We do what we do to gain pleasant consequences or to avoid or escape aversive consequences—the *Law of Effect*. Some consequences have reinforcing properties because we require them for survival, and some we learn to value. Here we're referring to two types of reinforcers—primary and secondary.

Primary *vs.* Secondary Reinforcers—Yearning & Learning to Yearn

Primary reinforcers are biologically-based and help us survive or maintain physiological balance (i.e., homeostasis). They have built-in satisfying or gratifying properties, as with food, water, shelter, oxygen, and sex.

Imagine you had no means to satisfy your basic biological needs. For example, if you had no shelter when it's freezing outside, what would you do to get a warm place to stay? If you had no food and were literally starving, what would you do to get food? Probably, whatever it took. Most of us don't work directly for primary reinforcers, but rather for the means to indirectly obtain them. Now we're talking about secondary reinforcers.

Secondary reinforcers acquire power to motivate behavior because of initial or higher-order conditioned associations with primary reinforcers. While secondary reinforcers don't have built-in biologically-satisfying or gratifying properties, they've been linked in some way to primary reinforcers and have become capable of motivating behavior themselves.

The most straightforward example is money. Would you give a $100 bill to a one-year-old baby? We wouldn't! A baby will do with it what's naturally reinforcing and put the bill in its mouth or play with it until it's destroyed. For a baby, money has no naturally-gratifying properties. But, young children learn that money buys things which are naturally gratifying. For example, when a child wants a snack (primary reinforcer) in a store, a parent might say, "We've got food and that costs money we don't have right now." A connection is made: Money (secondary reinforcer) can be exchanged for naturally-reinforcing things (primary reinforcers).

So, tangible secondary reinforcers initially function as stand-ins for primary reinforcers. But over time, secondary reinforcers can appear to be naturally gratifying. For example,

what adult wouldn't feel 'naturally' delighted to win a huge cash prize or a new car? And, some secondary reinforcers are intangible. For example, a job is initially a means to acquire money one needs for other things, but for some people work becomes an end in itself. A typical 'workaholic' doesn't need more money (a tangible secondary reinforcer), but rather works all the time because work has become self-reinforcing. The gratification that comes from additional work is intangible, unlike money.

Secondary reinforcers that can be exchanged for goods or services are *tokens*. Money is essentially a token we exchange for other things we want, though some very rich people acquire money for money's sake, where accruing more than can ever be used has become self-reinforcing. For an in-depth look at the value we ascribe to money, and other tokens reliably used to motivate behavior, check out **Psychological Literacy** (FEATURE 9•3).

feature 9.3

Psychological Literacy: All Economies are 'Token' Economies

Ayllon and Azrin (1968) showed the power of using tokens similar to poker chips to manage patients in psychiatric wards, where behavior was sometimes difficult to control. They merely made receiving tokens contingent upon doing desired behaviors. Staff members gave a specified numbers of tokens to patients when they engaged in designated desirable behaviors, like getting up on time, cleaning an area, maintaining hygiene, following rules, and so on. Tokens could be exchanged for things patients wanted, like cigarettes, candy, sodas, services, and extra privileges.

When undesired behaviors occurred, a specified number of tokens were taken from the patient. As a result, desired behavior increased and undesired behavior decreased substantially. This procedure was highly effective and beneficial for both patients and staff. Tokens are also an excellent means of managing classroom behavior (Iverson, 2001; Nelson, 2010). Further, Geller and colleagues (1977) used the same basic approach to increase constructive behaviors and decrease destructive behaviors among inmates in a maximum security prison.

So, what about money? Is it something with 'real' value? Many would say "yes" without hesitation. But, what could you do with a dollar bill if you couldn't buy something with it? Not much. Paper money and coins were created for convenience and enhanced stability of economies, but values fluctuate over time (e.g., Ahamed, 2011). Printed and minted forms of money are tokens with value because we collectively agree they have value. Stocks are tokens with value because they represent a portion of a company which itself has value.

Stock 'bubbles' happen when people collectively *think* stocks are worth more than they could be in practical terms. When demand exceeds supply, prices rise until

---

primary reinforcer Reinforcers that are biologically-based and necessary for survival (i.e., food, water, shelter, air, sex).

secondary reinforcers Reinforcers that have been reliably associated with primary reinforcers and can be reinforcing consequences.

values are inflated. But, if people suddenly *think* stocks are losing value, they may panic and sell them off in huge numbers, which actually *causes* stocks to lose value, crashing markets as supply now dramatically exceeds demand (Western, 2004). Even gold is only worth what people are willing to pay for it at any given time, either in goods, services or other forms of money.

Today, much of our money is routed and exchanged through electronic systems, such that many of our tokens are essentially 'virtual.' So, now you see all economies are really token economies and the 'value' of our tokens comes from a collective, often implicit, agreement that they are worth some particular amount at some particular time. Thus, contingencies exist whereby we may 'earn' and 'spend' any particular medium of exchange. Tokens are powerful means to motivate behavior, and teaching people these principles should give them a more thorough appreciation of the contingencies and reinforcers in our world. This enables improved people management, leading to a higher frequency of desirable behavior and a lower occurrence of undesirable behavior.

Some behaviors are maintained by primary reinforcers, others by secondary reinforcers, and some by both. Plus, some behaviors become self-reinforcing, where the reinforcement is *intrinsic*. What about desirable behaviors that 'ought' to be self-motivated and self-reinforcing? Should people be reinforced for doing what they 'ought' to be self-motivated to do? Does reinforcing these 'ought-to-do' behaviors decrease self-motivation?

The fact is we're all motivated by consequences. Doing what we 'ought' to do usually brings desirable consequences, such as respect from people we admire, affection or attention, power or influence, money, or avoiding trouble. As employees, we want "a fair day's wage for a fair day's work," though we 'ought' to be self-motivated on the job. Would you work for free? Volunteers help out not just because they're good people, but also because they feel good as a result (*intrinsic reinforcement*).

So, we often do what we 'ought' to do because it brings pleasurable consequences, like a paycheck, or a word of thanks from someone we've helped, or a sense of accomplishment. An extra reward is an *extrinsic* consequence. Do the natural positive reinforcers of an activity become less influential if we reward the behavior with an additional positive consequence? This is a hotly debated and important question. You can learn more about this issue in **Psychological Literacy** (FEATURE 9•4).

Schedules of Reinforcement—What Works & When

How many behaviors do you need to perform in order to obtain a reinforcer? How wide is the window of opportunity to perform a behavior and still get a reinforcer? Answers to such questions require an understanding of **schedules of reinforcement**, which reflect the timing and frequency of

feature 9.4

Psychological Literacy: Reinforcing 'Ought-To-Do' Behaviors

Should we 'reward' people for doing things they ought to want to do? If we could agree on an answer, it would settle debates between those who want to emphasize 'tough love' versus those who want to teach values by the most effective means. Psychological science reveals which approaches are most effective.

Here's a related question of general long-standing interest: Is the natural reinforcement of an activity decreased after the activity is extrinsically rewarded? For example, if you give $25 (extrinsic reward) to an 8-year-old to read a book on a topic of low personal interest, you may unintentionally send an unspoken message that reading is not naturally gratifying. But *if* the child values money, this extrinsic reward may motivate him/her to read the book.

However, most children who read for natural consequences (e.g., reading for fun, learning something new) had parents who read to them regularly as young children (e.g., Evans & Shaw, 2008; Mol, Bus, de Jong & Smeets, 2008; Saracho & Spodek, 2010; Snow, Burns & Griffin, 1998). Attention or praise from a loved parent is also an extrinsic reward (coming from outside the child), which may motivate children to begin reading on their own, thereby getting positive regard from others for their success. Eventually, many learn to obtain intrinsic reinforcement from activities that were initially prompted by extrinsic rewards.

Behaviors we want in our society don't just happen because they're inherently the 'right' or 'good' thing to do; they're acquired because adults who value them support their acquisition and maintenance through a combination of modeling (setting the right example), along with appropriate administration of reinforcement and/or punishment contingencies. Then, children grow up performing 'ought-to-do' behaviors until the behaviors become seemingly natural. As adults, we often fail to realize the importance of extrinsic positive consequences in helping children acquire the socially-desirable behaviors we want to see in them as future citizens.

By teaching all citizens these principles, we could theoretically end many debates which miss the mark. It isn't really a question of whether we *should* reward 'ought-to-do' behaviors; of course we should, if we want our children to learn them and adults to do them. We should focus upon a more important question: What are the best ways to reward 'ought-to-do' behaviors in order to help their occurrence become self-reinforcing?

---

schedule of reinforcement The timing and/or frequency of reinforcer delivery following a behavior.

reinforcer delivery relative to occurrences of a target behavior. Understanding how these schedules influence behavior will assist you in developing the most effective behavior-management program for your pets, your children, your students, your employees, and yourself.

When the ratio of behavior to its reinforcing consequences is one-to-one, which is to say a reinforcer is delivered every time the target response occurs, we have **continuous reinforcement**. Here the organism quickly learns the connection between the target behavior and a reinforcing consequence. Each occurrence of the behavior results in a pleasant consequence. Eating a delicious food is an example of continuous reinforcement. Every bite tastes great, and thus you're likely to take another bite and select that food again in the future. However, if suddenly you were not reinforced for performing a behavior that had been continually reinforced, you'd notice the change quickly and stop performing the behavior.

Unlike continuous reinforcement, **partial** or *intermittent* **reinforcement** occurs when a behavior is not reinforced every time it occurs. Here, learning is slower, but the learned behavior is more resistant to extinction. Extinction is slower because it's more difficult to predict whether a reinforcer will actually follow the target response. The more difficult it is to predict whether a learned behavior will be followed by a reinforcer, the greater the resistance to extinction. In other words, we continue performing a particular behavior until we are certain it will no longer be reinforced.

Reinforcement delivery can be based on the *interval* that must pass before a reinforcer is available following a target behavior. Or, a reinforcer can depend on the occurrence of a certain number of behaviors—the *ratio* of behaviors to reinforcers. Interval or ratio schedules vary according to a *fixed*

(*consistent*) or *variable* (*inconsistent*) amount of time or number of responses, respectively. Hence, we have *fixed-interval*, *variable-interval*, *fixed-ratio* and *variable-ratio* schedules. The timing and predictability of reinforcer delivery influences the acquisition, maintenance, and extinction of a target behavior (e.g., Ferster & Skinner, 1957).

To understand the impact of various reinforcement schedules, we examine *cumulative responses* whereby each occurrence of a target behavior adds increasingly to the total number of behaviors depicted on the vertical (Y) axis of a graph. The time periods within which a behavior is measured are shown on the horizontal (X) axis of the graph, and these can vary from seconds to hours, or days to weeks, months or years.

One more term to cover before we launch into the behavioral effects of schedules is **post-reinforcement pause**. This refers to the amount of time after a reinforcer is received before the organism begins performing the behavior again. The pause varies with the magnitude, value, or impact of the reinforcer, as well as the amount of time or effort spent to obtain the reinforcer. Let's consider the differing types of reinforcement schedules represented FIGURE 9•11.

Fixed-Interval Schedule of Reinforcement A **fixed-interval (FI) schedule** refers to how much time must pass before a reinforcer is available for a target behavior, where the first such behavior occurring within the 'available' time period will be reinforced. *Interval* refers to time and *fixed* means a set amount that doesn't change. Consider a family who just moved into a new home and checks the mailbox throughout the day. Not knowing the mail is typically delivered in late afternoon, they check mid-morning, noon, mid-afternoon, etc. They soon

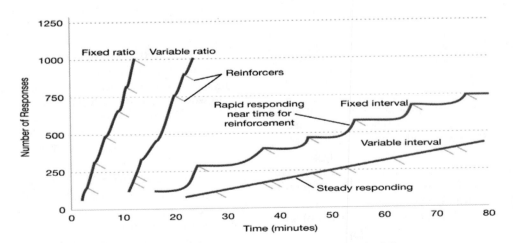

[**FIGURE 9•11**] Behavior as a function of the four reinforcement schedules.

Note: Behavior is measured cumulatively; marks show when a reinforcer was obtained.

partial reinforcement Behavior is reinforced after a certain number of occurrences (ratio) or after a certain amount of time (interval), but not continuously.

continuous reinforcement A 1:1 ratio between an instance of behavior and delivery of related reinforcement.

post-reinforcement pause The amount of time that passes after a behavior isreinforced and before the same behavior recurs.

fixed-interval schedule A learning schedule where a reinforcer is only available after a certain amount of time (interval) has passed, regardless of how often a behavior is performed.

learn when mail arrives and then check for mail only *after* the typical delivery time. Checking for mail before delivery will not be reinforced. Thus, mailbox-checking behavior occurs after the reinforcer (mail) is available. This example is a FI-24hr. reinforcement schedule. 'FI' means 'fixed interval' and '24hr' refers to the available time period during which one could be reinforced for checking for mail, which is typically once a day.

This schedule produces a scalloped response rate when graphed (see Figure 9.11). After a reinforcer is obtained, the behavior stops for a while—a *post-reinforcement pause*. After you get mail, you don't go and check the mailbox again. You wait until the next day, after the time the carrier normally comes. As the fixed interval approaches (late afternoon in our example), mail-checking behavior may occur more often.

Scheduled course exams work the same way. They're fixed to occur on certain days and at certain times one behavior (test-taking) could be reinforced. A relevant behavior in this case is the frequency and duration of studying. Generally, the cumulative amount of studying behavior steadily increases as the exam time approaches, particularly the night before or hours before a test.

Once the exam is taken, reinforcers come in a couple of forms, one immediate and one delayed. The first is a sense of relief. No matter how you think you did, it's done. The second is a grade, which if high may have a reinforcing effect on study behavior. If your grade isn't high, depending on a variety of factors including previous test-taking experiences, the perceived importance of the course, whether you believe the teacher is fair, and so on, you may or may not be motivated to increase your studying for the next test. Regardless, once the exam is taken, you don't immediately go right back to your books and study for that course. You engage in a *post-reinforcement pause* and studying behavior picks up again as the next exam gets closer.

Let's consider extinction and see if we can predict how a behavior is influenced by the reinforcement schedule. If we know when a reinforcer is supposed to be available for a certain behavior and the reinforcer is not delivered when expected, we know immediately the schedule has changed. If the mail doesn't come for several days in a row, you'd probably soon stop checking the box and call the post office to see what's wrong. Sometimes extinction is built into a situation, like a college course. After the final exam, there's a permanent post-reinforcement pause, because you never need to study that particular course material again. So, fixed-interval schedules promote quick extinction when reinforcement is discontinued.

Variable-Interval Schedule of Reinforcement

When time intervals between the availability of a reinforcer are inconsistent, we have a **variable-interval (VI) schedule**. An example is checking email or getting notifications on social networks. You can check all you want, but the *amount* of checking has nothing to do with *when* you'll actually get reinforced. It depends on when someone sends an email or something happens to prompt a notification. The interval between reinforced behaviors is unpredictable. It may be a few seconds, minutes, hours or days. If you get an email every three hours on average, your email checking behavior is reinforced on a VI-3hr. schedule.

Most of us check email periodically to see what, if anything has accumulated. Consult Figure 9.11 again for a graph of the relative rate of behavior influenced by a VI schedule. Generally, rates are low but quite steady and there's little in the way of a post-reinforcement pause following the delivery of a reinforcer. A person who derives a great deal of reinforcement from email or notifications may check quite often. As reinforcement intervals are unpredictable, behavior extinguishes relatively slowly when reinforcers are no longer forthcoming. If your computer stopped receiving emails because of a server malfunction, for example, you'd likely continue checking your email account for quite a while before contacting a technician.

Fixed-Ratio Schedule of Reinforcement

When reinforcement is contingent on the *number* of behaviors performed and the criterion for reinforcement is unchanging, we have a **fixed-ratio schedule** (*FR*). This produces a relatively high and steady rate of behavior with a significant post-reinforcement pause, as shown in Figure 9.11. On a fixed-ratio schedule the performer knows exactly when to expect a reinforcer. If the reinforcer doesn't come after the fixed number of behaviors, the organism will quickly realize the contingency has changed. Thus, extinction occurs quickly.

Vending machines are on a continuous reinforcement schedule, which is a one-to-one ratio or FR-1. Every time you put in the right amount of money and push a button, you get a drink or a snack. If you put in money and push a button a couple of times but nothing comes out, you will soon stop putting in money and pushing buttons. You may do other behaviors, like hitting the 'money return' button or kicking the machine. But, those behaviors aren't reinforced unless you get your money back.

Another common example of a fixed-ratio schedule is piece-work whereby a worker gets paid for every set number of items produced. That type of work is common in the garment and textile industries, and for some electronics products. If one were paid a certain amount for every 25 items assembled, we would have a FR-25 schedule, and the worker on this schedule would likely take a short pause after each increment of 25 items. Note that employees on an exclusive piece-work contingency that only rewards quantity of items are apt to look for shortcuts, or ways to produce the product faster. Thus, quantity might increase at a loss of quality. You get what you pay for.

Variable-Ratio Schedule of Reinforcement

Ever buy scratch tickets in a state lottery system? If so, your behavior was on a

---

variable-interval schedule A reinforcer is available after varying amounts of time (intervals) have passed, regardless of how often a behavior is performed.

fixed-ratio schedule A learning schedule where a behavior must be performed a certain (fixed) number of times before it is reinforced.

[TABLE 9•1] Summarizing the Features of Reinforcement Schedule Types

Schedule Type	Rate of Response	Pause Post-Reinforcement	Rate of Extinction	Example Scenarios
Fixed-Interval: Reinforced after a fixed amount of time passes.	Increases as deadline nears.	Behavior slows after reinforcement.	Fairly quick extinction, depending on activity and reinforcer.	Checking mail; weekly or monthly payday; pre-scheduled tests; using a washer or dryer or any device on a timer.
Variable-Interval: Reinforced after a random amount of time passes.	Relatively slow, but steady.	Behavior continues after reinforcement, but may slow a bit.	Slower than both fixed schedules, but faster than variable-ratio.	Checking for email or notifications at work or social networking sites; pop quizzes; fishing (amount of time with baited hook in water).
Fixed-Ratio: Reinforced after a fixed number of target behaviors occur.	Stable once it begins.	Behavior usually stops after reinforcement, then returns to stable rate.	Extinction is quickest of schedules.	Piece-work in factories; giving a dog a treat every n^{th} time it does a trick; a salesperson receiving a bonus for every x cars sold.
Variable-Ratio: Reinforced after a random number of target behaviors occur.	Highest and most stable rate of all schedules.	Behavior is more or less continuous, as breaks are taken at random.	Extinction is slowest of schedules.	Gambling; video games when tokens are collected; getting high quality food/service at fast-food chains; fishing (number of casts).

variable-ratio (VR) schedule whereby reinforcer delivery is determined by the average number of behaviors performed (i.e., the actual number varies from trial to trial). You don't know *which*, if any, of your ticket-scratching behaviors will result in reinforcement. If you buy enough scratch tickets, or bet on enough games, or play enough hands of cards, or pull enough slot-machine levers, you'll *eventually* win big—so you hope! With regard to lotteries, you've likely heard the truism, "You can't win if you don't play." There's an excitement in fantasizing about a 'big win,' which is an intrinsic reinforcing aspect of gambling. However, statistically, it's virtually certain you're not going to 'win big.' So, why do people gamble?

In addition to being exciting, it's not always an all-or-nothing situation. If you have the money, sooner or later, you'll win *something*. It could be on the very first bet or the thousandth bet, or anywhere in between. In fact, making sure customers win with some regularity is critical to running a successful gambling operation. A small win encourages the recipient to play again.

Let's say there's a small win (between $1 and $100) for every 10 scratch tickets, on average. That would be a 10-to-1 ratio, or VR-10. In other words, it takes 10 ticket purchases on average to win a prize. That's an average. So you might win the very next time you buy a ticket, the 5th time, 27th, or 103rd (you get the idea). If you won $25 on one scratch, you might feel like a winner, but if you bought $50 worth of tickets to get that winning ticket, you actually lost money. Rates of behavior on a VR schedule are high and post-reinforcement pauses are brief and few in number, and not very dependent on reinforcer delivery, as depicted in Figure 9.11.

Summarizing Schedules of Reinforcement TABLE 9•1 summarizes the four reinforcement schedules with examples, notations, behavioral and extinction patterns, and post-reinforcement-pause information. Some behaviors fit more than one schedule, depending on how you look at the situation. For example, fishing is always on a variable schedule. Considering the *amount of time it takes to catch a fish*, we have a variable-interval schedule. But considering the *number of times you cast a hook or lure* into the water, we have a variable-ratio schedule. To understand the impact of any schedule you need to define clearly the target behavior and identify its actual (as opposed to perceived) reinforcer. To understand better the application of reinforcement to improve your own corner of the world, please read about ways to decrease the frequency of unwanted behaviors without using punishment in **Beyond the Basics** (FEATURE 9•5).

We are usually controlled by more than one schedule of reinforcement at a time. In other words, we're on *concurrent schedules of reinforcement*. We're on reinforcement schedules for activities such as going to bed, getting up, eating, interacting with people, working, playing, shopping, studying, checking mail/email, going to movies, watching TV, Internet use, fishing, playing the lottery, and so on. The most powerful schedule at any given time will likely have the greatest influence over our behavior. But, it's good to be thoughtful about choosing behaviors with regard to long-term consequences.

---

variable-ratio schedule A behavior must be performed a certain number of times before it's reinforced; the number of times the behavior needs to occur before reinforcer delivery is not fixed but varies around a given average.

feature 9.5

Let's consider differential reinforcement schedules more complex than the basic schedules already discussed. These schedules increase one behavior while decreasing another.

Differential reinforcement of incompatible behavior (DRIB) avoids the use of punishment to decrease the occurrences of undesired behavior by using positive reinforcement to increase the frequency of desirable behavior incompatible with the unwanted behavior. For example, Scott and his students developed a successful program to reduce bullying behavior in elementary schools by reinforcing interpersonal caring and sharing behaviors incompatible with bullying (McCarty & Geller, 2011; 2012).

Similar to DRIB is *differential reinforcement of other behavior* (DRO). Here any acceptable behavior other than the undesired target behavior is reinforced, thereby reducing the occurrence of the undesirable behavior without using punishment. For example, a teacher could decrease the frequency of disruptive classroom behavior by giving one-to-one or group attention to only the appropriate classroom behavior observed.

Differential reinforcement of high rates of behavior (DRH) aims to increase occurrences of a target behavior within a specific time period. For example, if you wanted telemarketers to make at least 15 phone calls per hour, you could apply a bonus system whereby participants accumulate points toward a prize for every one-hour period in which at least 15 calls are made. However, this contingency doesn't ensure the calls will be successful. As with piecework, when quantity is reinforced, quality may suffer.

Differential reinforcement of lower rates of behavior (DRL) is used to obtain lower rates of a particular behavior without eliminating a behavior completely. Consider an application used by Scott's students to reduce alcohol intoxication among those attending fraternity parties (Fournier et al., 2004). The team knew alcohol consumption at fraternity parties couldn't be stopped completely. But because excessive alcohol use has been found to be consistently related to increased risk for sexual assault, unsafe sexual activity, physical violence, property damage, vehicle crashes, and poor academic/work performance,

they implemented an if-then contingency to lower rates of alcohol consumption at fraternity parties. Using breathalyzers to measure party goers' blood-alcohol concentration (BAC) when leaving fraternity parties, researchers set up the following DRL contingency.

Upon entering an intervention party, attendees were given a flyer announcing they'd be entered in a raffle for a cash prize of $100 if their BAC was below .05 at the time of BAC measurement (near the end of the party). Flyers had attached nomograms (pocket-sized charts, see FIGURE 9•12 below) to help them estimate intoxication levels by accounting for variables such as gender, weight, number of drinks, and time between drinks. Thus, participants had an incentive to keep their BACs at low levels, and a tool to help them monitor their levels.

The overall average BAC at the party and the number of partiers with BAC, above .05 were both significantly lower when this DRL contingency was in place as compared to non-intervention baseline parties. In follow-up interviews, some partiers indicated the lottery helped them drink fewer alcoholic beverages because they had a valid excuse to resist peer pressure to drink more. Essentially they said, "Thanks, but I don't want another drink because I want to win the cash." Imagine if hosts of a party collected a dollar from attendees who want to enter a DRL/BAC .05 lottery. Might this be a practical approach to preventing excessive consumption of alcohol? Behavior change is often a matter of figuring out the most practical if-then contingencys to use in a particular situation.

Without self-discipline, behavior bringing *swift*, *certain*, and *positive* consequences is more likely to occur than behavior followed by *delayed*, *uncertain*, and *positive* consequences. For example, texting or playing on the Internet usually yields immediate pleasant consequences. Studying on the other hand has pleasant consequences if done diligently (good grades), but grades are delayed and take effort that usually isn't pleasant. Thus, without self-discipline to engage in diligent studying for the longer-term consequences of getting good grades and ultimately a good career, we're more likely to text and play on the Internet than we are to study long and hard.

WIN $100 TONIGHT!

Virginia Tech researchers will be giving free BAC (blood alcohol concentration) assessments tonight.

If your BAC is **below .05**, you will be registered in a drawing for $100.

Here are some tips to help you keep a safe Buzz:

• Drink a glass of water between each alcohol-containing drink.
• Snack on food before and while drinking.
• Use the attached chart to estimate a safe number of drinks for your body weight.

MALE   ALCOHOL IMPAIRMENT CHART
APPROXIMATE BLOOD ALCOHOL PERCENTAGE

SUBTRACT 1 DRINK FOR EVERY HOUR OF DRINKING

Drinks	100	120	140	160	180	200	220	240	
0	.00	.00	.00	.00	.00	.00	.00	.00	ONLY SAFE DRIVING LIMIT
1	.04	.03	.03	.02	.02	.02	.02	.02	IMPAIRMENT BEGINS
2	.08	.06	.05	.05	.04	.04	.03	.03	
3	.11	.09	.08	.07	.06	.06	.05	.05	DRIVING SKILLS SIGNIFICANTLY IMPAIRED
4	.15	.12	.11	.09	.08	.08	.07	.06	
5	.19	.16	.13	.12	.11	.09	.09	.08	LEGALLY INTOXICATED
6	.23	.19	.16	.14	.13	.11	.10	.09	
7	.25	.22	.19	.16	.15	.13	.12	.11	CRIMINAL PENALTIES
8	.30	.25	.21	.19	.17	.15	.14	.13	
9	.34	.28	.24	.21	.19	.17	.15	.14	POSSIBLE DEATH @ LOW BODY WEIGHT
10	.38	.31	.27	.23	.21	.19	.17	.16	

Body Weight in Pounds

1 drink = 1.5 oz. 80 proof liquor, 12 oz. beer, 5 oz. table wine

[**FIGURE 9•12**] Fraternity Party Flyer and Attached Nomogram.

Punishment: Makes You NOT Want to It Again Simply put, *punishers* are consequences that make a specific behavior less likely to happen again in a similar situation. **Positive punishment** means a target behavior *decreases* (in intensity, frequency, and/or duration) because it's followed by the *addition* of an unwanted stimulus. Let's say five-year-old Joshua writes on the wall and Dad catches him and spanks him. *If Joshua never writes on the wall again, the behavior was punished because it decreased in frequency of occurrence.*

It was *positive punishment* because the consequence, getting spanked, was *added* to the situation. This isn't to say spanking is a "good" thing. In fact, physical punishment often does more harm than good. Below we offer reasons to use punishment rarely and carefully (Zolotor et al., 2008). Yet, the defining issue in this context is whether a behavior increases or decreases as the result of a consequence, and whether the consequence was added or subtracted from the situation. If behavior decreases because of the addition of an unpleasant consequence, we have positive punishment.

With **negative punishment**, the behavior in question *decreases* because it causes the *loss* of a desired stimulus. Consider Joshua's wall-writing from a different perspective. Dad catches him and takes away a favorite toy for the afternoon. *If Joshua writes on the wall less often, the behavior was punished because it decreased in frequency. Here it was negative punishment* because the consequence was *removal* (*subtraction*) of his favorite toy from the situation.

Punishment is certainly warranted sometimes, like when someone intentionally hurts another person. But, punishment is sometimes motivated more by a wish for retribution than rehabilitation. As a behavior-change technique, punishment usually leaves much to be desired. Negative consequences do have the potential to suppress behavior if the punisher is *swift, certain, and sufficiently severe* (Azrin & Holz, 1966). However, before using "the stick" instead of "the carrot," consider the practical limitations and side-effects of punishment explained in **Psychological Literacy** (FEATURE 9•6).

feature 9.6

Punishment can have at least six undesirable side-effects: *escape/avoidance, negative emotions, promoting aggression, apathy, counter-control, and punishment insensitivity* (Chance, 2008; Skinner, 1953; 1974; Sidman, 1989). With *escape/avoidance,* punished individuals do whatever they can to evade or leave situations where punishment is probable. We also escape or avoid negative consequences by 'tuning out'

the punisher, suppressing behavior only around the punisher (often with a rebound of the target behavior when the punisher leaves), cheating or lying to avoid punishment, and/or avoiding the punisher all together. When raising children, the last thing we want is for them to tune us out, lie or cheat, or avoid us, to keep from being punished.

When punished, we often experience *negative emotions,* including fear, sadness, shame, anger, or envy for those who aren't caught. When a child gets spanked, for example, s/he is likely to get very upset. The spanking may stop the undesired behavior, but it causes other undesired reactions (e.g., crying, screaming), and doesn't promote desired behavior. In fact, when people are experiencing negative emotions, they're unlikely to initiate desired behaviors.

Moreover, parental use of physical punishment models aggression as a means to solve problems. It's been shown that parents who frequently use corporal punishment have children who are physically aggressive and accepting of aggression as a means of solving conflicts (e.g., Oates, 2011; Simons & Wurtele, 2010; Strassberg, 1994; Stauss, 1996). In addition, highly aggressive children tend to have more behavioral and health problems later in life (e.g., Afifi et al., 2006; Bradshaw et al., 2010; Gershoff et al., 2010; Reef et al., 2010; Temcheff et al., 2011).

Alternatively, the person targeted with recurrent punishment may become *apathetic* and simply become resigned to doing only what's required and nothing more. With *counter-control,* a frequently punished person might intentionally sabotage the punisher with passive-aggressive behavior, as depicted in FIGURE 9•13. Finally, with *punishment insensitivity,* a habitually punished person eventually no longer responds. This is reflected in hardened juvenile

[**FIGURE 9•13**] Counter-control enables a sense of freedom from Top-down mandates.

Courtesy of George Vaughn Willis.

---

positive punishment When the frequency, intensity, and/or duration of a behavior decreases because its occurrence results in the presentation of an undesirable consequence.

negative punishment When behavior decreases in frequency, intensity and/or duration because its occurrence results in the removal of a desired stimulus.

or adult offenders whose behavior seems unaffected by repeated or long jail sentences and other punishers.

It's important to realize very young children can't *understand* the logic of stopping undesired behavior to prevent being punished or to get reinforcement for alternative behavior. Some may need an exceedingly light spanking to get their attention and provide a direct negative consequence to unwanted behavior. But this consequence should follow the undesired behavior immediately (no "wait until your Dad/Mom gets home") and be accompanied by stern verbal behavior. As soon as the child is calmed, s/he should be rewarded for engaging in alternative desired behavior. When old enough to understand basic rules, children's behavior can be shaped using non-physical punishment (e.g., verbal reprimand, removal of privileges).

It's usually possible to apply positive reinforcement in some form to promote desired behaviors, rather than simply rely on punishment to curtail undesired behaviors. Of course, this requires profound understanding of the principles of applied behavior analysis. And, that's our pitch: Teach these principles to those you know to help better their lives and our world.

Obviously, no one wants to create more problems than they solve. If you use punishment, you would be wise to employ the following six rules:

1. Use punishment immediately after the behavior in question (*swift*);

2. Always be consistent (*certain*; what is punished one day, should be punished every day);

3. Use an appropriate level of punishment (*sufficient severity*; but not a level greater than is needed and never use excessive severity);

4. Explain all rules and punishment contingencies to those old enough to understand;

5. Reinforce alternative desired behaviors incompatible with the undesired behavior;

6. Use physical punishment rarely and never allow corporal punishment to cause true suffering, marks, bruises, sores, cuts, etc. Abuse is abuse and no justification exists for abuse.

Keep in mind that when adults regularly use corporal punishment with children, they model poor problem-solving skills. Essentially such behavior says, "When I don't know what else to do, I lash out at people physically." Child behavior can be difficult to manage at times, but constructive and effective methods that work well under most circumstances are available. You can get information about such methods by checking out **Why We Care** (FEATURE 9•7).

To help keep straight the positive/negative/reinforcement/punishment paradigm, TABLE 9•2 shows a 2×2 matrix labeling strategies with regard to whether: 1) the target behavior increases or decreases; and 2) whether the consequence is applied or removed from the situation. For this

feature 9.7

Why We Care: Managing 'Difficult Child' Behavior

Most parents want to teach children right from wrong, how to be safe, and how to be socially appropriate. This can be difficult. But, if you really understand operant conditioning, you'll be a more effective parent. Start with the notion that a child's 'bad' behavior is not indicative of a 'bad' child. It's just behavior you'd like to change. Children, especially young ones, don't plan to be 'bad.' They just respond to environmental contingencies. Chaotic environments (e.g., frequent changes in homes, schools, rules or caretakers, situations of neglect or abuse, high parental conflict) contribute to child behavior problems. But, so does the failure to understand and apply basic behavior-management principles.

Consider the case of a child whining or throwing a tantrum in a store. The child is just trying to get a desired consequence like a toy, candy, or parental attention. When a child screams, a parent is annoyed or embarrassed and is tempted to give in to stop the unpleasant behavior. That's usually a mistake because it signals screaming results in obtaining desired consequences. Of course, parents should always make sure whining or screaming is not caused by a genuine need, like an injury or illness, needing to use the bathroom, or legitimate thirst or hunger. But if the child is not in need of assistance, withholding attention from tantrums is recommended, and removing them from situations is a good alternative if a tantrum is socially unacceptable (like in a store). If we give in and reinforce screaming, screaming will likely occur again in similar situations.

While giving in may keep a child quiet for a while, sooner or later parents want to reassert control. So, now the parent doesn't give in. At this point, the child isn't likely to quit screaming. Indeed, s/he is likely to scream louder! This is called an *extinction burst*, a dramatic increase in the intensity, duration, and/or frequency of a previously reinforced behavior during the process of extinction. As tantrum intensity and duration increase it becomes more annoying and draws stares from others. As a result, a parent may give in to the child's request again or lose his/her own temper. Both of those reactions are mistakes.

Giving in reinforces the tantrum at an even more intense level, meaning this is the level such behavior is likely to begin at, or quickly escalate to, next time. A parent who loses his or her temper is almost three times more likely to implement harsh punishment (Regalado et al., 2004) in ways that can have undesirable side-effects as noted in Psychological Literacy (Feature 9.5).If the parent holds to an extinction process, not giving in and not getting upset, the screaming behavior will lessen and eventually cease.

This is difficult and may seem insensitive on the surface, but it's effective in the long run. It's also highly recommended parents add positive reinforcement for any good

[TABLE 9•2] Reinforcement or Punishment? Positive or Negative?

	Stimulus Applied (Positive)	Stimulus Removed (Negative)
Behavior Increases (Reinforcement)	Positive Reinforcement	Negative Reinforcement
Behavior Decreases (Punishment)	Positive Punishment	Negative Punishment

behavior that occurs, as soon as it occurs. Thus, while ignoring tantrum behavior, the psychologically-literate parent looks for, and praises, desirable behavior incompatible with tantrum behavior.

Also, beware of *behavioral substitution*, where a child engages in another undesirable behavior after the first is no longer reinforced. For example, children forced to sleep alone in their own rooms for the first time might start drawing on the wall if screaming fails to bring desired parental attention. In this case, an effective punishment technique may be appropriate, and the most effective non-physical punishment for young children is *time-out*.

Time-out is essentially removing the child from opportunities for reinforcing activities. If the behavior in question decreases, time-out was effective. However, many parents and teachers don't implement time-out properly. Some think time-out is just sending a child to his or her room. But if the room contains pets, games, toys, art supplies, computers, books, and so on, it's unlikely to work as a punisher. So, time-out is most effective when the time-out environment is devoid of reinforcing stimuli or opportunities.

Sulzer-Azaroff and Mayer (1977) listed the following components of an effective time-out procedure: a) remove reinforcers potentially supportive of undesirable behavior; b) avoid time-out when a child's undesired behavior might be a normal reaction to a bad situation (e.g., crying because parents are arguing); c) have the personal control to consistently implement and maintain time-out; d) use time-out procedures consistently; f) keep time-out durations as short as possible (lowest effective level of severity); g) be up-front and clear about rules; h) prompt and reinforce desirable alternative behaviors; and i) use time-out as a last resort, when other more positive interventions have failed or are impractical. Few parents know these guidelines, which are consistent with the *swift*, *certain*, and *sufficiently severe* model, so please share them!

purpose, think of 'positive' and 'negative' in math terms, with 'positive' for adding, and 'negative' for subtracting. The best way to change a target behavior is to analyze any activators, the behavior itself, and its consequences (*A-B-C Model*), and then systematically manage consequences to most effectively impact the target behavior. Additional information on systematic contingency management can be found in **Psychological Literacy** (FEATURE 9•8).

feature 9.8

Psychological Literacy: Systematic Contingency Management

What if everyone understood how to systematically change behavior for the better? Some behaviors desired by governments, societies, businesses, or families are not readily motivated by natural consequences and may need extra extrinsic support. Such behaviors can be improved by using the *Four-Contingency Management Model*.

The *Four-Contingency Management Model* is a process of identifying target behaviors to increase and/or decrease in frequency of occurrence, and then arranging consequences to: 1) increase pleasant consequences for desired behaviors, if natural reinforcers are insufficient to support the behavior; 2) decrease unpleasant consequences for desired behaviors, if they act as barriers to performing the desirable behavior; 3) decrease pleasant consequences for undesired behaviors; and 4) increase aversive consequences for undesired behaviors.

To design a successful contingency-management program, carefully define which behaviors are desired, which are undesired, what reinforcers and punishers might be used. For contingency management to be effective, consequences for target behaviors must be clearly understood and consistently delivered soon after the behavior occurs. Failure to deliver promised consequences following the target behavior sends a mixed message to the person whose behavior is targeted for improvement. Again, this is a concept worthy of teaching everyone, so please spread the word.

The Premack Principle—What Did Grandma Always Say? Grandma said, "If you eat your spinach (or whatever food you didn't like but was good for you), then you may have dessert." This reflects a seemingly common-sense idea: Allow opportunities to do pleasant activities only after less pleasant but desired behavior is performed first. In this case, psychological science supports common sense. David Premack (1925–) found behaviors naturally occurring at high rates could be used to increase behaviors occurring at low rates (Premack, 1959). Thus, this technique is often referred to as the *Premack Principle*.

Though much of his work involved chimpanzees and monkeys, Premack tested this principle with young children (average age = 6.7 years). In his seminal study, a non-preferred activity had to be completed in order to get access to a preferred activity. Preferred activities included playing pinball or eating candy, where the activity each child preferred was established by observing them in a Baseline phase. During Baseline, children rarely did a non-preferred activity if allowed free access to their preferred activity. During the Intervention phase, the non-preferred activity had to be performed in order to gain access to a preferred activity. They usually had to be told how one behavior led to the other, but once the connection was made, the children did the non-preferred activity in order to gain access to the preferred activity (Premack, 1959). This is very practical knowledge for rearing children, but the principle applies to adults as well. It even works with professional engineers (Makin & Hoyle, 1993).

How do we determine what activities people prefer? Careful observation is critical. You may notice a child play a videogame continuously if left to his/her own choices. You may notice "room-cleaning" happens infrequently, if ever. To get the child to increase "room-cleaning" behavior, withhold access to videogames until the room is cleaned. Another child may not like videogames, but may spend a lot of time listening to music, playing with toys, reading comic books, watching TV, or surfing the Internet. Whatever behaviors spontaneously occur at high rates may be used to reinforce behaviors that happen less often.

Students use the Premack Principle when they require themselves to study in a certain amount of time before engaging in a more pleasant activity like watching TV, texting friends, enjoying the Internet, or playing videogames. This is self-management with the Premack Principle. But, enforcing a stipulated contingency is crucial to its effectiveness. If it's not enforced, it won't work well, and that includes self-management.

Shaping—Complex Behaviors Consist of Simple Steps

Learning Objectives At the end of this section, you'll be able to:

9.3.13 Describe the *process of shaping* and give examples from your own life.

9.3.14 Define *differential reinforcement of successive approximations* in *shaping*.

9.3.15 Discuss the influence of *instinctive drift* in conditioning.

We often take complicated behaviors for granted, as if we always knew how to perform them. Most complex behaviors are a product of step-by-step learning, though they become so well-learned as to seem automatic. **Shaping** is a process used by trainers to get animals to do impressive tricks and to get people to do complicated tasks. It's also called **differential reinforcement of successive approximations** as it involves stepwise reinforcement of relevant behaviors as they sequentially approach and build toward a target behavior.

If you want your dog to sit, lay down, roll over and play dead, simply telling him to do it will never work. You must start with the most basic step of the behavioral sequence,

and reinforce it. Once he's performing it successfully, move to the next step and reinforce the first step only occasionally, but frequently reinforce the combination of steps one and two together, such that they must be performed in sequence on command (the S^D), in order to obtain the reinforcer. Each new step is added in the same way, until the whole sequence is performed fluidly. Then performance of the entire sequence is reinforced. With such shaping, your dog can learn some very cool tricks. People learn some neat tricks, too.

Scott was once a teaching assistant for a class of about 400 students at Southern Illinois University. He arrived before the professor and asked the class, "How would you all like to see the professor walk off the stage?" After some laughter, he explained how students could use their body language to shape this behavior. Scott told them to look at the professor very attentively any time he approached the edge. But, if the professor moved back from the position he'd previously reached nearest the edge, he asked the students to show no interest by looking down at their notes.. Thus, the reinforcer was everyone looking at the professor with intent; the punisher was ignoring him.

Within ten minutes the professor was standing at the edge of the stage while lecturing. He was unaware his behavior had been shaped until virtually the entire class looked down when he stepped back to a safer position on the stage. Realizing something was up, he yelled "Geller! What did you do?" "Sir, it wasn't me," Scott replied. Your students just gave us a great demonstration of shaping! Don't you agree?"

Complex behaviors that seem simple after learning, like driving a car, are actually a series of behaviors linked together (e.g., using a safety belt, mirrors, ignition, gears, accelerator, break, etc.). Teaching complex behaviors effectively involves breaking them into a sequence of component parts and then successively teaching each part. As each step is more or less mastered, a complex behavior evolves.

How would you teach 5-year-old Kayla to tie her shoes? Shoe-tying seems simple to adults until we try to tell a child how to do it. To shape this behavior, we'd start by having Kayla find a pair of shoes. When she brings a matching pair, you'd say "Awesome!" or anything positive. That makes the child feel good, thanks to higher-order conditioning. Once Kayla does this reliably, stop reinforcing finding a matching pair, except on occasion (intermittent reinforcement). Move to the next step of having her put the shoes on the correct feet. When Kayla gets this right, say congratulatory things with enthusiasm to reinforce this next successive step of the sequence. Once that's done, reinforce the crossing of the laces, and so forth with each step until the full behavioral sequence is achieved.

What keeps the behavioral sequence going? Once a behavioral sequence is mastered, it often becomes self-reinforcing. Knowing how to drive a car or tie one's shoes leads to natural desirable consequences, like feeling pride, enjoying fruits of the behavior, avoiding criticism, and so on. Or, it may continue to be externally or extrinsically reinforced like when we learn a skill set for work and we continue to get paid for doing it.

Shaping Sequential reinforcement of behaviors that reflect successive steps to the occurrence of a more complex target behavior.

Ever learn how to run a cash register? At first, something so 'simple' can seem daunting, especially if it's your first day on the job and you have a line of customers. But, soon it becomes nearly automatic. Yet, you wouldn't use a cash register at home in your spare time; it wouldn't be self-reinforcing. Sometimes we learn behavioral sequences that are not actually necessary to obtain desired consequences, but we wind up doing them anyway. These represent superstitions or habits, and we explore these topics in **Why We Care** (FEATURE 9•9).

feature 9.9

Why We Care: Understanding Superstitions

We do a lot of things simply out of habit and not because the behaviors are necessary for desirable outcomes. We bet you don't think of yourself as doing unnecessary behaviors often, but we bet you do them. In high school, Scott had a 'lucky shirt' he wore on exam days and when Chris 'finds a penny, he picks it up' knowing his luck really has nothing to do with that action. Let's explore habitual and superstitious behaviors further.

Contiguity plays a big part in our learning. At times, things appear to be related in time and space when they really aren't. Incorrect interpretations of contingencies can result in *superstitious behavior*, which occurs when we learn to do something because we think it contributes to an outcome, when it doesn't.

If an athlete wears a certain pair of socks and the team wins a big game, wearing those socks and the win could *appear* to be related. If more wins occur when wearing these socks, the association gets stronger, and 'lucky socks' emerge. Once such an association is made, it's often hard to break. While such behavior doesn't make logical sense, it can be a powerful connection.

Not to pick on athletes, but in a sample of male and female basketball players between ages 12 and 22, 40% had some sport-related superstitious belief or behavior. These varied by age, gender, degree of religious faith, and amount of athletic involvement, but weren't rare (Buhrmann & Zaugg, 1981). In another study of top-performing football, hockey, and volleyball players, 80.3% engaged in one or more superstitious rituals before a game (Schippers & Van Lange, 2006). The average number of rituals was 2.6 per player, and included such things as eating pancakes before a game, wearing protective gear while travelling to a game, placing a piece of chewed gum on the field, kissing a specific shirt, and feeling a need to see the number '13' at least once before a match.

Actually, many of our routine behaviors or habits are simply products of non-contingent reinforcement. Edwin R. Guthrie (1886–1959) called this *stereotyped behavior*, noting we tend to repeat whatever worked the first time to achieve a goal. In other words, we do some of what we do even when the *way* we do it has little or no bearing on obtaining the consequence. Guthrie and Horton (1946) took a series of photographs of cats in puzzle boxes with an upright lever that required only a simple touch to open the box. Cats initially triggered the lever with a random behavior, using their tail, body, head, or paw. What, whatever cats did on the first few trials to open the box, they tended to do the same from then on, even though a variety of other behaviors would have achieved the same consequence.

What about humans? We wake up in the morning, get out of bed, take a shower, get dressed, eat breakfast, surf the Internet, and head to school or work. Those behaviors produce a successful outcome of being clean, properly dressed, fed, informed, and on time for work. But, aside from waking up and leaving, the order of the other behaviors is just an arbitrary routine. We could wake up or hit the snooze button a few times, eat breakfast or not, have a shower or not, surf the Internet or not, get dressed first or last, before leaving. Thus, we tend to engage in consistent routines even though the particular behavioral sequence is not necessary for the ultimate consequence.

There's nothing wrong with this of course, at least not usually. But, it's interesting to note how often behavioral patterns in which we are entrenched have little, if any, functional logic behind them. They are not necessarily the most effective and/or efficient means to the end, yet we stick to our routines rather than explore alternative response patterns or strategies.

There are limits of learning in animals which are reflected by a concept called **instinctive drift**. This is a tendency for an animal to do instinct-driven behaviors that lessen or prevent the effectiveness of some conditioning procedures. Breland and Breland (1961) used operant-conditioning principles to train many types of animals to perform unusual behaviors. However, they had difficulty training animals to emit behaviors conflicting with natural behaviors. Some animals were unable to learn certain behaviors or learned behavior eventually 'drifted' back to more natural, or *instinctive*, behaviors.

The point is no matter which techniques are used, there are limits to what can be conditioned in various species, including humans. It doesn't matter what reinforcers or punishers are available, no matter how hard you try you can't condition a penguin to fly. You can't condition a person to fly either, but you can help them condition themselves not to be anxious when they travel on an airplane.

Classical & Operant Conditioning: Overlapping Features

Learning Objectives At the end of this section, you'll be able to:

9.3.16 Explain how *classical* and *operant conditioning* can occur simultaneously.

---

instinctive drift The tendency for animals to resist learning behaviors relatively far afield of their natural repertoire, favoring instead the performance of instinct-related behaviors.

Courtesy of George Vaughn Willis.

[FIGURE 9•14] We all Scream (and Drool) for Ice Cream.

Often classical and operant conditioning happens at the same time. For example, **FIGURE 9•14** below shows kids running after an ice-cream truck while salivating. Their reflexive physiological (autonomic) salivation is classically-conditioned to the sound of the music and sight of the truck. At the same time, their voluntary (somatic) running, begging, whining, and/or buying behaviors are operant actions, selected to obtain the desired consequence of ice cream.

Many drivers experience both classical and operant conditioning when they see the blue light of a police car in their rearview mirror. Regardless of their speed, most drivers experience an immediate burst of adrenaline (like 'butterflies' in your stomach) and 'automatically' hit the brakes. The physiological arousal is a classically-conditioned involuntary autonomic nervous system response. And, even though quick braking may feel automatic, it's ultimately under voluntary control within the somatic nervous system.

Cognition Matters—Beyond a Behavior-Based Focus

Learning Objectives At the end of this section, you'll be able to:

9.3.17 Explain how behaviorism incorporated a cognitive perspective.

9.3.18 State the definition of *cognitive map* and give a personal example of cognitive mapping.

Early classical and operant conditioning paradigms focused heavily on stimulus-response (S-R) connections, and they didn't directly tackle cognitive processes. Some staunch behaviorists considered it impossible to study thinking because it couldn't be examined objectively. We now have vastly improved research methods and techniques to help us understand the complexity of cognition. Edward Tolman (1886–1959) deserves much credit for starting behaviorism down the road to incorporating cognitive processes.

Tolman and his colleagues conducted maze studies with rats. Most behaviorists at the time objected to making interpretations about what rats might be 'thinking.' However, Tolman (1948) proposed rats made mental maps of the mazes they ran. Thus, they developed a **cognitive map**, or a mental representation of the environment. Tolman (1949) was quick to note similar cognitive processes of a much more complex

nature occur in humans. For example, try to visualize how to get from your home to a favorite location. You can likely think of many places you might go, many reasons to go, and lots of alternative routes to take. Now that we have thinking in mind, let's think about how we learn from observing others.

Section 4: Observational & Insight Learning: We See, We Do, & Figure It Out, Too

Have you ever watched someone and thought, "I see how that's done!" and then you did what you saw? While this may seem trivial at this point in our understanding of human experience, only a few decades ago observational learning was not fully understood or appreciated. Have you ever had a moment when you suddenly realized the answer to a problem or a dilemma? If so, you experienced insight learning. Let's consider both of these topics.

Observational (Vicarious) Learning— I See How It's Done

Learning Objectives At the end of this section, you'll be able to:

9.4.1 Define *observational learning*.

9.4.2 List the four requirements for observational learning.

9.4.3 Describe the concept of *latent learning* and give a personal example of your own.

9.4.4 Describe Bandura's '*Bobo Doll*' studies and explain how reinforcement plays a role in children imitating others' aggressive behavior.

9.4.5 Define *vicarious reinforcement* and *vicarious punishment* and describe how these influence learning and performance.

Observational learning, also known as *vicarious learning*, occurs when we gain new information from observing others doing particular behaviors. If they are rewarded or penalized for their behavior, our tendency to engage in that behavior is influenced. When we're *less* likely to perform a behavior because we know others were penalized for it, we experience *vicarious punishment*. When we're *more* likely to emit a behavior because we saw others receive a reward for doing so, we experience *vicarious reinforcement*. It's *vicarious* because we're learning from someone else's experience.

There are four main ingredients to learning how to do something by observing others: a) you need to pay attention to the behavior in question, b) you need to remember how the observed behavior is performed, c) you need to have the ability

---

cognitive map A mental representation of environments stored for later use.

observational learning When behavior is learned by watching others' behavior. Also known as vicarious learning.

Courtesy of Sparkstudio/
Fotolia.

Courtesy of Jon Brenneis/Getty Images, Inc.

[**FIGURE 9•15**] Albert Bandura & the 'Bobo Doll'.

to perform the behavior in question, and d) you must be motivated to do the observed behavior (e.g., Bandura, 1977). If you didn't pay attention, you may not understand or remember the behavior. If you can't remember it, you certainly can't do it. If you can remember the behavior, but don't have the ability to do it, you might still be able to instruct others. But even if you paid attention, remembered, and had the ability, observational learning will remain undemonstrated if motivation is not present.

In other words, it will remain latent or hidden. **Latent learning** occurs cognitively and it remains unexpressed when consequences are not available to support the behavior. We learn all sorts of behaviors from watching others at home, school, work, and from various media, from photos in magazines to YouTube. But, we don't always do what we learn by watching others. Do you know how to rob a bank? Of course you do! That doesn't mean you would, which is good.

While the notion of imitative learning had been addressed early on (e.g., Miller & Dollard, 1941; Rotter 1945), Albert Bandura (1925– ; see FIGURE 9•15) was one of the first to systematically study observational learning. Bandura conducted 'Bobo Doll' experiments with preschoolers and showed the dramatic impact modeling has on aggression. A Bobo doll was an inflatable toy, a few feet in height, which when knocked over quickly bounced upright again. The children he studied observed an adult model 'play' roughly with a Bobo doll in very specific aggressive ways. The model hit it, punched it, pinned it to the ground, sat on it, and said things, like "Sock him!" and "Kick him!" Then, the children were invited to play with the Bobo doll, and researchers observed what happened. What did they see?

Preschoolers readily imitated the behavior of the adult models, including specific aggressive acts. Girls exhibited much less aggression than boys, supporting the prevailing notion that girls were naturally less aggressive than boys. However, a critical issue was whether girls were *capable* of aggressive behavior. Perhaps girls learned aggressive behaviors but simply didn't display them. How might such latent learning be verified?

Bandura (1965) assigned preschoolers to three groups, who then watched a televised film of an adult being very aggressive with the Bobo doll. In one condition, the model was reprimanded severely by another adult for the aggressive behavior. In another condition the model was rewarded generously by another adult for the same behavior. In a third condition, the

model was neither rewarded nor penalized for aggressive behavior. The children in each group were subdivided into two other groups: those offered rewards (stickers and juice treats) for imitating the model's aggressive acts and those given no rewards.

Those who weren't given rewards for imitating the aggressive model exhibited significantly fewer aggressive behaviors when they saw the model penalized (vicarious punishment). And, girls behaved less aggressively than boys regardless of the consequences to the model. But what about kids who got rewards for imitating the model's aggression? In Bandura's words, this use of rewards "... completely wiped out the previously observed performance differences, revealing an equivalent amount of [aggressive] learning among children in the model-rewarded, model-punished, and the no-consequences conditions." (1965, p. 589).

So, girls *did* learn aggressive behaviors to the same degree as the boys, and *were* capable of performing them as accurately as the boys. They just hadn't displayed such behavior before because they'd been socialized to be non-aggressive. The reward was all the motivation the girls needed to demonstrate their *latent learning*. Boys having been socialized to display aggression in many life situations didn't need additional motivation to be aggressive.

There are many practical applications of this information. For example, does watching or playing violent videogames make people more likely to exhibit aggression? Can people be taught to avoid socially undesirable behaviors simply by vicarious punishment? These topics are addressed in **Psychological Literacy** (FEATURE 9•10).

feature 9.10

Psychological Literacy: Violent Videogames & Vicarious Punishment

Do violent videogames promote aggressive behavior? This question can be answered with a meta-analysis of the relevant scientific literature. A meta-analysis compares and contrasts results across many relevant studies. This helps identify commonalities among findings and allows for more general, evidence-based conclusions. Regarding aggression and violent videogames, Anderson and Bushman (2001) found 35 articles with 54 independent samples involving a total of 4,262 participants, just over half of which were 18 or older. The authors only included published research with valid experimental designs that statistically controlled for participant age differences.

They concluded their results " ... clearly support the hypothesis that exposure to violent video games poses a public-health threat to children and youths, including college-age individuals" (p. 358). In both experimental and correlational designs, for males and females, and for children and young adults, exposure to violent videogames was linked to increased physiological arousal, aggressive affect and aggressive behavior. Exposure to such games was also linked to lower levels of pro-social behavior or altruism. In fact, these scholars went so far as to say a high

---

latent learning When a behavior is learned but not displayed, often because reinforcing consequences are not available.

level of exposure to violent video games was potentially related to the development of an aggressive personality.

A meta-analysis also examined the effects of vicarious punishment, where participants had observed a model penalized for particular aggressive behaviors (Malouff et al., 2009). This analysis included 21 research reports with a total of 876 participants. They found watching models receive negative consequences for aggressive acts led to significantly lower occurrences of target behaviors among the observers. A key conclusion was ". . . punishment of a model can be powerful enough to reduce the likelihood of the observers exhibiting the behavior" (p. 282). This suggests the occurrence of undesirable behaviors can be decreased with vicarious punishment, thereby avoiding some of the negative side-effects of direct punishment.

Insight Learning—AHA!

Learning Objectives At the end of this section, you'll be able to:

9.4.6 Define *insight learning* and cite an example of its occurrence in your own life.

Sometimes we learn information without necessarily being conscious of it. There it lays dormant until a moment where two or more ideas come together in a new way to yield insight learning. **Insight learning** is the sudden discovery of a solution to a problem, when one connects two or more elements of previously unconnected knowledge.

Wolfgang Köhler (1887–1967) studied insight learning in chimpanzees. Köhler (1924) found chimps could solve unique problems when solutions were not obvious. For example, he placed bananas out of reach outside their cage. Sticks were in the chimps' cage and after what appeared to be much pondering, chimps got the idea the sticks could be fastened together and used to reach the bananas and drag them back into the cage. Joining sticks seemed to happen spontaneously, but Kohler believed the chimps had prior life experiences they suddenly combined to generate a new idea.

Problems designed to be solved with seemingly unrelated objects in the environment are known as *detour problems*. Other investigators have used this method to test the insight abilities of humans. For example, Tagawa (1937) studied whether young children could solve detour problems through observational learning. Using a piece of cake instead of a banana, children from two- to five-years-old solved a detour problem as well as did chimps. But, with advanced cognitive development, children six-years-old and up learned to solve these problems by observing others solve problems, where chimps could not. Thus as we mature, we soon surpass chimps in intellectual abilities and problem-solving skills. In fact, we humans develop some pretty amazing mental abilities, made possible by a dynamic capacity to learn.

With that, we'll leave it to you to study the concepts in this chapter and learn them well enough to obtain exemplary grades on any tests designed to demonstrate your knowledge of the material. We hope you clearly see the applicability of this information to everyday living, for you, your pets, your friends, families, colleagues, society, and the world as a whole. We hope you will apply these principles of learning frequently, correctly, and responsibly.

KEY TERMS

Acquisition *p. 260*
Activator *p. 268*
Behaviorism *p. 265*
Biological preparedness *p. 263*
Classical conditioning *p. 259*
Cognitive map *p. 281*
Conditioned response *p. 260*
Conditioned stimulus *p. 260*
Conditioned taste aversion *p. 263*
Continuous reinforcement *p. 272*
Discriminative stimulus *p. 268*
Extinction *p. 262*
Fixed-interval schedule *p. 272*
Fixed-ratio schedule *p. 273*
Higher-order conditioning *p. 262*
Insight learning *p. 263*
Instinctive drift *p. 280*
Latent learning *p. 282*
Law of Effect *p. 266*
Learning *p. 258*
Negative punishment *p. 276*
Negative reinforcement *p. 269*

Observational learning *p. 281*
One-trial learning *p. 263*
Operant chamber *p. 267*
Operant conditioning *p. 266*
Partial reinforcement *p. 272*
Positive punishment *p. 276*
Positive reinforcement *p. 268*
Post-reinforcement pause *p. 272*
Primary reinforcer *p. 270*
Punisher *p. 268*
Reinforcer *p. 268*
Schedule of reinforcement *p. 271*
Secondary reinforcers *p. 270*
Shaping *p. 279*
Spontaneous recovery *p. 262*
Stimulus discrimination *p. 262*
Stimulus generalization *p. 262*
Unconditioned response *p. 260*
Unconditioned stimulus *p. 260*
Variable-interval schedule *p. 273*
Variable-ratio schedule *p. 274*

ASSESSMENT ITEMS

1. All his life, Terrence's mother lit candles on the table when it was time for dinner. Now, the smell of candles anywhere makes his mouth water due to the process of

   a. classical conditioning.

   b. cognitive restructuring.

   c. operant conditioning.

   d. neural realignment.

Insight learning A sudden realization of a solution to a problem, which makes use of previously unconnected knowledge of two or more elements.

2. An **unconditioned** stimulus is a
   a. stimulus that is always present in the environment.
   b. previously neutral stimulus that elicits a response after learning.
   c. stimulus that produces a response without any prior learning.
   d. new stimulus that is elicited by a related stimulus.

3. You start feeding your cat canned food. The first time you run the electric opener, the cat pays no attention to the noise, but runs over when it smells the food. Soon, the cat comes running whenever it hears the can opener. The **electric can opener noise when it makes the cat come running thereafter**, represents the
   a. unconditioned stimulus.
   b. discriminative stimulus.
   c. unconditioned response.
   d. conditioned response.

4. In the above example, the cat **salivating because of the noise** of the electric can opener, represents the
   a. unconditioned stimulus.
   b. conditioned stimulus.
   c. unconditioned response.
   d. conditioned response.

5. Every time Mary whistled, she gave her dog a food treat. After a while, the dog salivated whenever Mary whistled. Mary then stopped giving her dog the treat after she whistled. **Eventually, Mary's dog no longer salivated to her whistle.** This illustrates what principle?
   a. spontaneous recovery.
   b. latent learning.
   c. acquisition.
   d. extinction.

6. Four-year-old Brad was badly bitten by a German Sheppard dog. Now when Brad sees any kind of dog, he starts shaking and begins crying. Brad's shaking and crying when he sees **any** dog, as opposed to just German Sheppard dogs, illustrates what principle?
   a. stimulus generalization.
   b. stimulus discrimination.
   c. learned helplessness.
   d. counter conditioning.

7. A form of associative learning in which **the consequences of a behavior affect the probability of the behavior recurring** is known as
   a. classical conditioning.
   b. counter-conditioning.
   c. observational conditioning.
   d. operant conditioning.

8. Which of the following is a **secondary** reinforcer?
   a. food. b. sex.
   c. money. d. water.

9. Four-year-old Andre's mom tells him to stop writing on the wall. He does not stop. She **spanks him and he never again writes on the wall**. What is the correct classification of this scenario?
   a. positive reinforcement.
   b. negative reinforcement.
   c. positive punishment.
   d. negative punishment.

10. Tonya taught her dog to play dead. She first gave the dog a treat and a pat for sitting. Later, she required the dog to sit and lay down before giving the treat and pat. Finally, Tonya required her dog to sit, lie down, and roll on its back before giving the treat and pat. This illustrates the principle of
    a. shaping. b. flooding.
    c. simplification. d. treat management.

11. The schedule of reinforcement used in slot machines for gambling that produces **high rates of responding, without post-reinforcement pauses, and is very resistant to extinction**.
    a. fixed ratio. b. variable ratio.
    c. fixed interval. d. variable interval.

12. The circumstances which determine what responses lead to which consequences, is called a(n)
    a. understanding. b. contingency.
    c. fixation situation. d. superstition.

13. Which name is most associated with social learning theory and Bobo dolls?
    a. Skinner.
    b. Maslow.
    c. Pavlov.
    d. Bandura.

14. Which of the following is **NOT** one of the key processes in **observational learning**?
    a. remembering.
    b. social skill.
    c. motivation.
    d. attention.

15. Learning that occurs but is not immediately demonstrated is called _____ learning.
    a. latent.
    b. independent.
    c. cognitive.
    d. insight.

ANSWER KEY

1. a	**2.** c	**3.** b	**4.** d	**5.** d	**6.** a
7. d	**8.** c	**9.** c	**10.** a	**11.** b	**12.** b
13. d	**14.** b	**15.** a			

REFERENCES

Afifi, T. O., Brownridge, D. A., Cox, B. J., & Sareen, J. (2006). Physical punishment, childhood abuse and psychiatric disorders. *Child Abuse & Neglect, 30(10)*, 1093–1103. doi:10.1016/j.chiabu.2006.04.006

Ahamed, L. (2011). Currency wars, then and now. *Foreign Affairs, 90(2)*, 92–103.

Alexander, G. M. (2003). An evolutionary perspective of sex-typed toy preferences: Pink, blue, and the brain. *Archives of Sexual Behavior, 32(1)*, 7–14. doi:10.1023/A:1021833110722

Anderson, C. A., & Bushman, B. J. (2001). Effects of violent video games on aggressive behavior, aggressive cognition, aggressive affect, physiological arousal, and prosocial behavior: A meta-analytic review of the scientific literature. *Psychological Science, 12(5)*, 353–359. doi:10.1111/1467-9280.00366

Ayllon, T., & Azrin, N. (1968). *The token economy: A motivational system for therapy and rehabilitation*. East Norwalk, CT US: Appleton-Century-Crofts.

Azrin, N. H., & Holz, W. C. (1966). Punishment. In W. K. Honig (Ed.), *Operant behavior: Areas of research and application*. New York: Appleton-Century-Crofts.

Bandura, A. (1965). Influence of models' reinforcement contingencies on the acquisition of imitative responses. *Journal of Personality and Social Psychology, 1(6)*, 589–595. doi:10.1037/h0022070

Bandura, A. (1977). *Social learning theory*. Morristown, NJ: General Learning Press.

Beck, H. P., Levinson, S., & Irons, G. (2009). Finding Little Albert: A journey to John B. Watson's infant laboratory. *American Psychologist, 64(7)*, 605–614. doi:10.1037/a0017234

Bernstein, I. L. (1978). Learned taste aversions in children receiving chemotherapy. *Science, 200(4347)*, 1302–1303. doi:10.1126/science.663613

Bradshaw, C. P., Schaeffer, C. M., Petras, H., & Ialongo, N. (2010). Predicting negative life outcomes from early aggressive–disruptive behavior trajectories: Gender differences in maladaptation across life domains. *Journal of Youth and Adolescence, 39(8)*, 953–966. doi:10.1007/s10964-009-9442-8

Breland, K., & Breland, M. (1961). The misbehavior of organisms. *American Psychologist, 16(11)*, 681–684. doi:10.1037/h0040090

Buhrmann, H. G., & Zaugg, M. K. (1981). Superstitions among basketball players: An investigation of various forms of superstitious beliefs and behavior among competitive basketballers at the junior high school to university level. *Journal of Sport Behavior, 4(4)*, 163–174.

Carrell, L. E., Cannon, D. S., Best, M. R., & Stone, M. J. (1986). Nausea and radiation-induced taste aversions in cancer patients. *Appetite, 7(3)*, 203–208.

Chance, P. (2008). *Learning and behavior (6th ed.)*. Belmont, CA: Wadsworth Publishing Company.

Coelho, C., & Purkis, H. (2009). The origins of specific phobias: Influential theories and current perspectives. *Review Of General Psychology, 13(4)*, 335–348. doi:10.1037/a0017759

Cummins, D., & Cummins, R. (1999). Biological preparedness and evolutionary explanation. *Cognition, 73(3)*, B37-B53. doi:10.1016/S0010-0277(99)00062-1

Evans, M., & Shaw, D. (2008). Home grown for reading: Parental contributions to young children's emergent literacy and word recognition. *Canadian Psychology, 49(2)*, 89–95. doi:10.1037/0708-5591.49.2.89

Ferster, C. B., & Skinner, B. F. (1957). *Schedules of reinforcement*. East Norwalk, CT US: Appleton-Century-Crofts.

Fournier, A. K., Ehrhart, I. J., Glindemann, K. E., & Geller, E. S. (2004). Intervening to decrease alcohol abuse at university parties: Differential reinforcement of intoxication level. *Behavior Modification, 28(2)*, 167–181. doi:10.1177/0145445503259406

Garcia, J. J., Kimeldorf, D. J., & Koelling, R. A. (1955). Conditioned aversion to saccharin resulting from exposure to gamma radiation. *Science, 122*, 157–158. doi:10.1126/science.122.3179.1089

Geller, E. S., Johnson, D. F., Hamlin, P. H., & Kennedy, T. D. (1977). Behavior modification in a prison: Issues, problems, and compromises. *Criminal Justice and Behavior, 4*, 11–43.

Gentile, B. F., & Miller, B. O. (2009). *Foundations of psychological thought: A history of psychology*. Thousand Oaks, CA US: Sage Publications, Inc.

Gershoff, E. T., Grogan-Kaylor, A., Lansford, J. E., Chang, L., Zelli, A., Deater-Deckard, K., & Dodge, K. A. (2010). Parent discipline practices in an International sample: Associations with child behaviors and moderation by perceived normativeness. *Child Development, 81(2)*, 487–502. doi:10.1111/j.1467-8624.2009.01409.x

Guthrie, E. R., & Horton, G. P. (1946). *Cats in a puzzle box*. Oxford England: Rinehart.

Infante, D. A. (1975). Differential functions of desirable and undesirable consequences in predicting attitude and attitude change toward proposals. *Speech Monographs, 42(2)*, 115–134. doi:10.1080/03637757509375886

Iverson, M. K. (2011). Evaluation of a token economy's effectiveness in a self-contained classroom in a psychiatric rehabilitation facility with secondary students diagnosed with emotional and behavioral disabilities. *Dissertation Abstracts International Section A, 71*, Retrieved from EBSCOhost.

Jones, M. C. (1924). The elimination of children's fears. *Journal of Experimental Psychology, 7(5)*, 382–390. doi:10.1037/h0072283

Jones, M. C. (1924a). A laboratory study of fear: The case of Peter. *Pedagogical Seminary, 31(4)*, 308–316.

Kohler, W. W. (1924). *The mentality of apes*. Oxford England: Harcourt, Brace.

Malouff, J., Thorsteinsson, E., Schutte, N., & Rooke, S. (2009). Effects of vicarious punishment: A meta-analysis. *Journal of General Psychology, 136(3)*, 271–285. doi:10.3200/GENP.136.3.271-286

Makin, P. J., & Hoyle, D. J. (1993). The Premack Principle: Professional engineers. *Leadership & Organization Development Journal, 14(1)*, 16–21. doi:10.1108/01437739310023872

Miller, N. & Dollard, J. (1941). *Social learning and imitation*. New Haven, Connecticut: Yale University Press.

Mineka, S., & Zinbarg, R. (2006). A contemporary learning theory perspective on the etiology of anxiety disorders: It's not what you thought it was. *American Psychologist, 61(1)*, 10–26. doi:10.1037/0003-066X.61.1.10

Mol, S. E., Bus, A. G., de Jong, M. T., & Smeets, D. H. (2008). Added value of dialogic parent-child book readings: A meta-analysis. *Early Education and Development, 19(1)*, 7–26.

Nelson, K. G. (2010). Exploration of classroom participation in the presence of a token economy. *Journal of Instructional Psychology, 37(1)*, 49–56. Retrieved from EBSCO*host*.

Oates, K. (2011). Physical punishment of children: Can we continue to accept the status quo? *Journal of Paediatrics & Child Health, 47(8)*, 505–507. doi:10.1111/j.1440-1754.2011.02144.x

Pavlov, I.P. (1902). *The work of the digestive glands*. (W.H. Thompson, Trans.). London, Eng: Charles Griffen & Co.

Pavlov, I. P. (1927). *Conditioned reflexes: An investigation of the physiological activity of the cerebral cortex*. (G.V. Anrep, Trans, Ed). London: Oxford University Press.

Premack, D. (1959). Toward empirical behavior laws: I. Positive reinforcement. *Psychological Review, 66(4)*, 219–233. doi:10.1037/h0040891

Rachman, S. J. (2002). Fears born and bred: Non-associative fear acquisition? *Behaviour Research and Therapy, 40*, 121–126.

Reef, J., Diamantopoulou, S., van Meurs, I., Verhulst, F., & van der Ende, J. (2010). Predicting adult emotional and behavioral problems from externalizing problem trajectories in a 24-year longitudinal study. *European Child & Adolescent Psychiatry, 19(7)*, 577–585. doi:10.1007/s00787-010-0088-6

Regalado, M., Sareen, H., Inkelas, M., Wissow, L. S., & Halfon, N. (2004). Parents' discipline of young children: Results from the National Survey of Early Childhood Health. *Pediatrics*, 1131952–1958.

Rotter, J.B. (1945). *Social learning and clinical psychology*. Upper Saddle River, New Jersey: Prentice-Hall.

Saracho, O. N., & Spodek, B. (2010). Parents and children engaging in storybook reading. *Early Child Development and Care, 180(10)*, 1379–1389. doi:10.1080/03004430903135605

Schippers, M. C., & Van Lange, P. M. (2006). The psychological benefits of superstitious rituals in top sport: A study among top sportspersons. *Journal of Applied Social Psychology, 36(10)*, 2532–2553. doi:10.1111/j.0021-9029.2006.00116.x

Sidman, M. (1989). *Coercion and its fallout*. Boston, MA: Authors Cooperative.

Simons, D. A., & Wurtele, S. K. (2010). Relationships between parents' use of corporal punishment and their children's endorsement of spanking and hitting other children. *Child Abuse & Neglect, 34(9)*, 639–646. doi:10.1016/j.chiabu.2010.01.012

Skinner, B. F. (1938). *The behavior of organisms: An experimental analysis*. New York: Appleton-Century.

Skinner, B. F. (1945). Baby in a box: The mechanical baby-tender. *The Ladies Home Journal, 62*, 30–31, 135–136, 138.

Skinner, B. F. (1948). *Walden two*. New York: Macmillan, Inc.

Skinner, B. F. (1953). *Science and human behavior*. New York: Free Press.

Skinner, B.F. (1960) Pigeons in a pelican. *American Psychologist 15*, 28–37.

Skinner, B. F. (1981). Selection by consequences. *Science, 213(4507)*, 501–504. doi:10.1126/science.7244649

Skinner, B. F., & Morse, W. H. (1957). Concurrent activity under fixed-interval reinforcement. *Journal of Comparative Physiology and Psychology, 50*, 279–281.

Snow, C. E., Burns, M. S., & Griffin, P. (1998). *Preventing reading difficulties in young children*. Washington, DC: National Academy Press.

Strassberg, Z., Dodge, K. A., Pettit, G. S., & Bates, J. E. (1994). Spanking in the home and children's subsequent aggression toward kindergarten peers. *Development and Psychopathology, 6(3)*, 445–461. doi:10.1017/S0954579400006040

Straus, M. A. (1996). Spanking and the making of a violent society. *Pediatrics, 98(4)*, 837.

Sulzer-Azaroff, B., & Mayer, G. R. (1977). *Applying behavior-analysis procedures with children and youth*. New York : Holt, Rinehart and Winston.

Tagawa, S. S. (1937). The imitation of the detour problem solved with the stick. *Transactions of the Institute of Child Studies, 17*, 121–137.

Temcheff, C. E., Serbin, L. A., Martin-Storey, A., Stack, D. M., Ledingham, J., & Schwartzman, A. E. (2011). Predicting adult physical health outcomes from childhood aggression, social withdrawal and likeability: A 30-year prospective, longitudinal study. *International Journal of Behavioral Medicine, 18(1)*, 5–12. doi:10.1007/s12529-010-9082-0

Thorndike E. (1898). Some experiments on animal intelligence. *Science, 7*, 818–824. doi: 10.1126/science.7.181.818.

Thorndike, E.L. (1927). The law of effect. *The American Journal of Psychology, 39(1)*, 212–222.

Thorne, M.B., & Henley, T.B. (2005). *Connections in the history and systems of psychology (3rd ed.)*. Houghton Mifflin Company: Boston, New York.

Tolman, E. C. (1948). Cognitive maps in rats and men. *Psychological Review, 55(4)*, 189–208. doi:10.1037/h0061626

Tolman, E. C. (1949). The psychology of social learning. *Journal of Social Issues. Supplement Series, 3*, 20.

Watson, J. B. (1913). Psychology as the behaviorist views it. *Psychological Review 20(2)*, 158–177.

Watson, J. B. (Writer/Director). (1923). *Experimental investigation of babies* [motion picture]. (Distributed by C. H. Stoelting Co., 424 N. Homan Ave, Chicago, IL).

Watson, J. B., & Rayner, R. (1920). Conditioned emotional reactions. *Journal of Experimental Psychology, 3*, 1–14.

Western, D. (2004). *Booms, bubbles and bust in the U.S. Stock Market*. Florence, KY: Routledge.

Zolotor, A. J., Theodore, A. D., Chang, J., Berkoff, M. C., & Runyan, D. K. (2008). Speak softly—and forget the stick: Corporal punishment and child physical abuse. *American Journal of Preventive Medicine, 35(4)*, 364–369. doi:10.1016/j.amepre.2008.06.031

CHAPTER

10

Motivation and Emotion

Courtesy of Steve Lipofsky/Corbis Images.

Taken from *Psychology: Core Concepts*, Seventh Edition, by Philip G. Zimbardo, Robert L. Johnson, and Vivian McCann.

10.1 What Motivates Us?
Why People Work: McClelland's Theory • The Unexpected Effects of Rewards on Motivation

CORE CONCEPTS Motives are internal dispositions to act in certain ways, although they can be influenced by multiple factors, both internal and external.

PSYCHOLOGY MATTERS
Using Psychology to Learn Psychology
When you study, try to get into a state of *flow*.

10.2 How Are Our Motivational Priorities Determined?
Instinct Theory • Drive Theory • Freud's Psychodynamic Theory • Maslow's Hierarchy of Needs • Putting It All Together: A New Hierarchy of Needs

CORE CONCEPTS A new theory combining Maslow's hierarchy with evolutionary psychology solves some long-standing problems by suggesting that functional, proximal, and developmental factors set our motivational priorities.

PSYCHOLOGY MATTERS
Determining What Motivates Others
If it's not extrinsic, motivation may well come from feelings of personal inadequacy.

10.3 Where Do Hunger and Sex Fit into the Motivational Hierarchy?
Hunger: A Homeostatic Drive and a Psychological Motive • The Problem of Will Power and Chocolate Cookies • Sexual Motivation: An Urge You Can Live Without • Sex, Hunger, and the Hierarchy of Needs

CORE CONCEPTS Although dissimilar in many respects, hunger and sex both have evolutionary origins, and each has an essential place in the motivational hierarchy.

PSYCHOLOGY MATTERS
The What and Why of Sexual Orientation
It is still a puzzle, but it's not a choice.

10.4 How Do Our Emotions Motivate Us?
What Emotions Are Made Of • What Emotions Do for Us • Counting the Emotions • Cultural Universals in Emotional Expression

CORE CONCEPTS Emotions are a special class of motives that help us attend to and respond to important (usually external) situations and communicate our intentions to others.

PSYCHOLOGY MATTERS
Gender Differences in Emotion Depend on Biology and Culture
Culture and socialization account for many of the differences—but not for everything.

10.5 What Processes Control Our Emotions?
The Neuroscience of Emotion • Arousal, Performance, and the Inverted U • Theories of Emotion: Resolving Some Old Issues • How Much Conscious Control Do We Have Over Our Emotions?

CORE CONCEPTS Research has clarified the processes underlying both our conscious and unconscious emotional lives, shedding light on some old controversies.

PSYCHOLOGY MATTERS
Detecting Deception
Nonverbal cues are the best signs of deceit.

Chapter Problem
Motivation is largely an internal and subjective process: How can we determine what motivates people like Lance Armstrong to work so hard at becoming the best in the world at what they do?

Critical Thinking Applied
Do Lie Detectors Really Detect Lies?

What motivates Lance Armstrong? The world's best-known cyclist, Lance has seven times won his sport's premiere event, the Tour de France, a gruelling three-week bicycle race covering more than 2,000 miles. His mother Linda declared that he was always a competitive child—and one that often tested the boundaries, as well as her patience.

Did his competitive spirit originate in his tumultuous family life? When Lance was a baby, his father moved out, and his parents divorced. About three years later, his mother remarried a man named Armstrong, who adopted the boy and gave him his name. But it was always his mother who was the dominant figure in Lance's early years in Plano, Texas ("Lance Armstrong," 2010).

Despite having little money, his mother managed to buy Lance his first bicycle when he was seven. He loved the bike, but it was the Plano city swim team that gave him, at age 12, his first competitive athletic experiences. (Lance rode his bike 10 miles to swim practice in the morning and then cycled on to school. After school in the afternoon, he rode back to swim some more—after which he pedalled home.) At the peak of his swimming career, the young Armstrong won fourth at the state tournament in the 1500-meter freestyle.

Armstrong's focus shifted when, at age 13, he entered the Iron Kids Triathlon, an event that combined swimming with biking and running. He won easily. Three years later, he turned professional and soon triumphed in several national triathlon championships. Eventually Armstrong's achievements attracted the attention of scientists at the Cooper Institute for Aerobic Research, who found that his oxygen consumption during exercise was the highest they had ever recorded. Clearly, he was a specimen ideally suited for sustained aerobic exercise. So, was it Lance's natural athletic ability, plus a string of early successes, that kept him training and eventually pushed him onto the world stage?

In 1992, he decided to narrow his focus exclusively to bicycle racing. A spot on the U.S. Olympic team quickly led to a sponsorship by Motorola on the professional cycling tour. A string of increasingly prestigious victories followed—until the bad news came in 1996. At the age of 25, Armstrong, who was experiencing unexplained fatigue and pain while riding, received a diagnosis of advanced testicular cancer. Worse, tests showed that the disease had spread to his lungs and brain.

After consultations with doctors, he chose an aggressive regimen of surgery and chemotherapy, even though the doctors estimated his chances of survival at less than 40 percent. Two years later, when they said that somehow, he had beaten the odds, Lance was already training for a comeback.

And come back he did. In 1999, he won the first of his seven Tour de France titles. And in 2002, *Sports Illustrated* magazine named him Sportsman of the Year.

Shortly after he fell ill, he launched the Lance Armstrong Foundation, devoted to fighting cancer through national awareness programs and funding initiatives for new treatments. But what role did the disease play in his motivation to excel? His website quotes him as saying, "Cancer was the best thing that ever happened to me" ("Lance's Bio," 2010).

PROBLEM: Motivation is largely an internal and subjective process: How can we determine what motivates people like Lance Armstrong to work so hard at becoming the best in the world at what they do?

Throughout this chapter, we will use Lance Armstrong's case to illustrate the basic concepts involved in motivation and emotion. We begin by defining what we mean by motivation, followed by consideration of what motivates people to work—or, like Lance Armstrong, to log hours of gruelling training for the Tour de France. Is it for some external (*extrinsic*) reward, or is it done for personal (*intrinsic*) satisfaction?

10.1 Key Question: What Motivates Us?

In everyday conversation, we use many terms that refer to motivation: *drive, instinct, energy, purpose, goal, intensity, perseverance, desire, want,* and *need.* You will note that all these terms refer to internal psychological "forces" that presumably make us do what we do. But the fact that we cannot observe these internal forces is what makes the psychology of motivation so challenging.

Questions about motivation seldom arise when people behave predictably: getting up in the morning, answering the phone, stopping for red lights, or greeting their friends. On the other hand, we *do* wonder what motivates people whose behavior falls outside the bounds of the ordinary, such as those who seem obsessed with food or sex, those who gamble away their life savings, those who rob banks—and those celebrities who behave indiscreetly.

Yet another part of the problem of motivation involves motivating people. If you are also an employer, you probably want to motivate your employees to work hard. If you are a coach, you want to motivate your players to train hard so the team can win. But let's bring it closer to home: As a student, you probably also want to learn how to motivate yourself to study a bit more.

So, how do we go about understanding and controlling motivation? Let's begin with the basics, by defining what we mean by *motivation.*

More broadly, the concept of **motivation** refers to all the processes involved in (a) *sensing a need or desire,* and then

CORE CONCEPT 10.1

Motives are internal dispositions to act in certain ways, although they can be influenced by multiple factors, both internal and external.

---

motivation Refers to all the processes involved in initiating, directing, and maintaining physical and psychological activities.

(b) *activating and guiding the organism* by selecting, directing, and sustaining the mental and physical activity aimed at meeting the need or desire; and finally, when the need is met, (c) *reducing the sensation of need*. Take thirst, for example: On a warm day, you may sense a biological need for fluids that causes you to feel thirsty. That feeling of thirst then focuses your behavior on getting something to drink. When you have drunk your fill, the uncomfortable sensation of thirst diminishes, and the motive fades into the background.

Sometimes, of course, students drink beer not to quench their thirst, but because their friends are drinking or because TV ads have primed them to associate beer drinking with fun. In this case, the need is said to be purely *psychological*, not a *biological* need. In fact, many of our motives involve a complex combination of biological and psychological needs, especially those involving our social interactions, emotions, and goals. Take, for example, the complex processes that underlie our motivation for work.

Why People Work: McClelland's Theory

Most people work to make money, of course. Psychologists refer to money and other incentives as *extrinsic motivators*, because they come from outside the person. In general, **extrinsic motivation** involves external stimuli that goad an organism to action. For students, grades are one of the most powerful extrinsic motivators. Other examples of extrinsic motivators include food, drink, praise, awards, and sex.

People can also have *intrinsic motives* for working—motives that arise from within the person. You are intrinsically motivated when you enjoy meeting a new challenge on the job. More generally, **intrinsic motivation** involves engaging in an activity—work or play—for its own sake, regardless of an external reward or threat. You just do it because it meets a psychological need. In short, an intrinsically motivated activity is its own reward.

So, how could we assess a person's motivation for work? Psychologist David McClelland (1958) suspected that the stories people would tell to describe a series of ambiguous pictures could reveal their motives—using the *Thematic Apperception Test (TAT)*, developed by Henry Murray (1938). You can see one such picture in FIGURE 10•1, but before you read the caption, imagine what might be happening with the boy and the violin. Initially, McClelland rated the stories for what they described as the **need for achievement (n Ach)**, defined as the desire to attain a difficult, but desired, goal.

Now read the caption for FIGURE 10•1 if you haven't already done so: It gives examples of how a high–*n Ach* individual and a low–*n Ach* individual might interpret the same picture. With these examples in mind, you can judge whether your own story is low or high in *n Ach*.

Indeed, McClelland found that certain characteristics distinguish people with a high need for achievement, as measured by the stories they told about ambiguous pictures. They not only work harder and become more successful at their work than those lower in achievement motivation, but they

[**FIGURE 10•1**] **Alternative Interpretations of an Ambiguous Picture** Story Showing High *n Ach*: The boy has just finished his violin lesson. He's happy at his progress and is beginning to believe that all his sacrifices have been worthwhile. To become a concert violinist, he will have to give up much of his social life and practice for many hours each day. Although he knows he could make more money by going into his father's business, he is more interested in being a great violinist and giving people joy with his music. He renews his personal commitment to do all it takes to make it.

Story Showing Low *n Ach*: The boy is holding his brother's violin and wishing he could play it. But he knows it isn't worth the time, energy, and money for lessons. He feels sorry for his brother, who has given up all the fun things in life to practice, practice, practice. It would be great to wake up one day and be a top-notch musician, but it doesn't happen that way. The reality is boring practice, no fun, and the likelihood that he'll become just another guy playing a musical instrument in a small-town band.

also show more persistence on difficult tasks (McClelland, 1987b; Schultz & Schultz, 2006). In school, those with high *n Ach* tend to get better grades (Raynor, 1970), perhaps because they also tend to have higher IQ scores (Harris, 2004). In their career paths, they take more competitive jobs (McClelland, 1965), assume more leadership roles, and earn more rapid promotions (Andrews, 1967). If they go into business, they are more successful than those with low *n Ach* (McClelland, 1987a, 1993).

[**CONNECTION**] Money can also be a *secondary reinforcer*, because it can be associated with things that satisfy more basic needs.

---

extrinsic motivation The desire to engage in an activity to achieve an external consequence, such as a reward.

intrinsic motivation The desire to engage in an activity for its own sake rather than for some external consequence, such as a reward.

need for achievement (*n Ach*) In McClelland's theory, a mental state that produces a psychological motive to excel or to reach some goal.

I/O Psychology: Putting Achievement Motivation in Perspective

Worker motivation is the domain of industrial/organizational (I/O) psychologists, who know that not everyone has a high need for achievement, nor does every job offer intrinsic challenges. At least two other motives propel us to work (McClelland, 1985). For some of us, work meets a *need for affiliation,* while for others work satisfies a *need for power.* (The need for power should not necessarily be construed as negative but rather in the more positive sense of wanting to plan projects and manage people to get a job done.) Given these three needs for work—achievement, affiliation, and power—it becomes the manager's task to structure jobs so that workers simultaneously meet their own needs as well as the manager's goal for productivity. (Managers, themselves, are usually motivated both by the needs for achievement and power.)

There are, of course, other reasons why we work beyond achievement, affiliation, and power needs. As we have said, work is a way to make a living. It is also a means to a desired lifestyle. But most of all, work is wrapped up in a person's identity: I am a teacher, a surgeon, a farmer, a park ranger, and so on. We focus on achievement, affiliation, and power here because those are the motives that have received the most attention so far by psychologists.

Should you find yourself in a management position, here are some need-specific pointers that come out of the research on motivating employees:

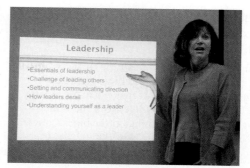

According to McClelland, people have different patterns of motivation for work. Some are motivated by affiliation, some by power, and some by the need for achievement (*n Ach*). A good leader knows how to capitalize on each of these.

- Give those high in *n Ach* tasks that challenge them, but with achievable goals. Even though high–*n Ach* employees are not primarily motivated by extrinsic rewards, you can use bonuses, praise, and recognition effectively with them as feedback for good performance.

- A cooperative, rather than competitive, environment is best for those high in the need for *affiliation.* Find opportunities for such employees to work with others in teams rather than at socially isolated workstations.

- For those high in *power,* give them the opportunity to manage projects or work teams. You can encourage power-oriented workers to become leaders who help their subordinates satisfy their own needs. Again—although power motivation can be purely self-serving—don't fall into the trap of thinking that the need for power is necessarily bad.

Satisfying people's needs should make them happier with their jobs and more motivated to work. I/O psychologists call this *job satisfaction.* But does job satisfaction actually lead to better employee performance? Studies show that higher job satisfaction indeed correlates with lower absenteeism, lower employee turnover, and increased productivity—all of which are reflected in increased profits for any business (Schultz & Schultz, 2006).

It is also worth noting that the need for achievement is not limited to work. It can also boost performance in art, science, literature—and in athletics. Let's explore two instructive cases in point.

Misty Hyman (top) and Naoko Takahashi (bottom) have very different perspectives on their athletic achievements—perspectives that reflect their cultural differences.

A Cross-Cultural View of Achievement When she won the Olympic gold medal in the women's 200-meter butterfly, American swimmer Misty Hyman said:

> I think I just stayed focused. It was time to show the world what I could do. I am just glad I was able to do it. I knew I could beat Suzy O'Neil, deep down in my heart I believed it, and I know this whole week the doubts kept creeping in, they were with me on the blocks, but I just said, "No, this is my night" (Neal, 2000).

Contrast that with Naoko Takahashi's explanation of why she won the women's marathon:

> Here is the best coach in the world, the best manager in the world, and all of the people who support me—all of these things were getting together and became a gold medal. So I think I didn't get it alone, not only by myself (Yamamoto, 2000).

As you can see from these distinctively different quotes, the American's perspective on achievement motivation reflects a distinctively Western bias. Americans tend to see achievement as the result of individual talent, determination, intelligence, or attitude. Much of the world, however, sees achievement differently—in a broader context, as a combination of personal, social, and emotional factors (Markus et al., 2006).

This observation fits with Harry Triandis's (1990) distinction between cultures that emphasize *individualism* or *collectivism*. Western cultures, including the United States, Canada, Britain, and Western Europe, emphasize **individualism.** People growing up in these cultures learn to place a premium on individual performance. By contrast, says Triandis, the cultures of Latin America, Asia, Africa, and the Middle East often emphasize **collectivism,** which values group loyalty and subordination of self to the group. Even in the collectivist cultures of Japan, Hong Kong, and South Korea, where high values are placed on doing well in school and business, the overarching goal is not achieving individual honors but bringing honor to the family, team, or other group.

Without a cross-cultural perspective, it would be easy for Americans to jump to the erroneous conclusion that motivation for individual achievement is a "natural" part of the human makeup. But Triandis's insight suggests that *n Ach* has a strong cultural component. In collectivist cultures, the social context is considered just as important for achievement as are talent, intelligence, or other personal characteristics in individualistic cultures.

The Unexpected Effects of Rewards on Motivation

We have suggested that extrinsic rewards are among the many reasons people work. But what do you suppose would happen if people were given extrinsic rewards (praise, money, or other incentives) for leisure activities—rewards for doing things that they find *intrinsically* enjoyable? Would the reward make the activity more—or less—enjoyable? Would a reward affect motivation?

Overjustification To find out, Mark Lepper and his colleagues (1973) performed a classic experiment using two groups of schoolchildren who enjoyed drawing pictures. One group agreed to draw pictures for a reward certificate, while a control group made drawings without any expectation of reward. Both groups made their drawings enthusiastically. Some days later, however, when given the opportunity to draw pictures again, without a reward, the previously rewarded children were much less enthusiastic about drawing than those who had not been rewarded. In fact, the group that had received no rewards were actually *more* interested in drawing than they had been the first time!

Lepper's group concluded that external reinforcement had squelched the internal motivation in the reward group, an effect they called **overjustification.** As a result of overjustification, they reasoned, the children's motivation had changed from intrinsic to extrinsic. Consequently, the children were less interested in making pictures in the absence of reward. It appears that a reward can sometimes take the fun out of doing something for the sheer pleasure of it.

When Do Rewards Work? But do rewards *always* have this overjustification effect? If they did, how could we explain the fact that many professionals both love their work and get paid for it? Subsequent experiments have made it clear that rewards can interfere with intrinsic motivation, but only under certain conditions (Covington, 2000; Eisenberger & Cameron, 1996).

Overjustification occurs when extrinsic rewards for doing something enjoyable take the intrinsic fun out of the activity. It is likely that this person would not enjoy video games as much if he were paid for playing.

---

individualism The view, common in the Euro-American world, that places a high value on individual achievement and distinction.

collectivism The view, common in Asia, Africa, Latin America, and the Middle East, that values group loyalty and pride over individual distinction.

overjustification The process by which extrinsic (external) rewards can sometimes displace internal motivation, as when a child receives money for playing video games.

Specifically, the overjustification effect occurs when a reward is given *without regard for quality of performance.* This explains what happened to the children who were given certificates for their drawings. The same thing can happen in the business world, when employees are given year-end bonuses regardless of the quality of their work or in the classroom when all students get As.

The lesson is this: Rewards can be used effectively to motivate people—but only if the rewards are given for a job well done, contingent on quality of performance, not as a bribe. In general, rewards can have three major effects on motivation, depending on the conditions:

- Rewards can be an effective way of motivating people *to do things they would not otherwise want to do*—such as mowing the lawn or taking out the garbage.

- Rewards can actually add to intrinsic motivation, *if given for good performance:* We saw this clearly in the case of Lance Armstrong.

- And, as we have also seen, rewards can *interfere* with intrinsic motivation, *if given without regard for the quality of the work*—as Lepper's study showed.

So, if a child doesn't like to practice the piano, wash the dishes, or do homework, no amount of reward is going to change her attitude. On the other hand, if she enjoys piano practice, you can feel free to give praise or a special treat for a job well done. Such rewards can make a motivated person even more motivated. Similarly, if you have disinterested employees, don't bother trying to motivate them with pay raises (unless, of course, the reason they're unmotivated is that you are paying them poorly). But when it is deserved, impromptu praise, an unexpected award, or some other small recognition may make good employees perform even better. The danger of rewards seems to occur only when the rewards are extrinsic and are given without regard to the level of performance.

So, how do you think professors should reward students in order to encourage their best work?

psychology matters

Stress Reduction and Relaxation Techniques

The world's greatest achievements in music, art, science, business, and countless other pursuits usually arise from intrinsically motivated people pursuing ideas or goals in which they are deeply interested. People achieve this state of mind when absorbed by some problem or activity that makes them lose track of time and become oblivious to events around them. Psychologist Mihaly Csikszentmihalyi (1990, 1998) calls this special state of mind **flow**. And although some people turn to drugs or alcohol to experience an artificial flow feeling, meaningful work produces

far more satisfying and sustained flow experiences. Athletes, such as Lance Armstrong, could probably not endure their intense daily training regimens without entering the flow state.

What is the link with studying and learning? If you find yourself lacking in motivation to learn the material for a particular class, the extrinsic promise of eventual good grades may not be enough to prod you to study effectively tonight. You may, however, be able to trick yourself into developing intrinsic motivation and flow by posing this question: What do people who are specialists in this field find interesting? Among other things, the experts are fascinated by an unsolved mystery, a theoretical dispute, or the possibility of an exciting practical application. A psychologist, for example, might wonder: What motivates violent behavior? Or, how can we increase people's motivation to achieve? Once you find such an issue, try to discover what solutions have been proposed. In this way, you will share the mindset of those who are leaders in the field. And—who knows?—perhaps you will become fascinated too.

CHECK YOUR UNDERSTANDING

✓ Study and Review at MyPsychLab

1. **Recall:** Give four reasons why psychologists find the concept of *motivation* useful.

2. **Application:** Give an example of an *extrinsic* motivator that might induce a child to do her homework.

3. **Recall:** McClelland theorized that some workers are motivated by *n Ach,* while others are motivated by needs for

   a. money and praise.
   b. affiliation and power.
   c. sex and aggression.
   d. intrinsic reinforcement.

4. **Understanding the Core Concept:** Motivation takes many forms, but all involve inferred mental processes that select and direct our

   a. cognitions.   b. behaviors.
   c. sensations.   d. emotions.

Answers: 1. The concept of motivation (1) connects observable behavior to internal states, (2) accounts for variability in behavior, (3) explains perseverance despite adversity, and (4) relates biology to behavior. **2.** Any incentive, such as money, extra TV time, or a favorite food. (Threat of punishment could also be an intrinsic motivator, but probably wouldn't work as well.) **3.** b **4.** b

---

flow In Csikszentmihalyi's theory, an intense focus on an activity accompanied by increased creativity and near-ecstatic feelings Flow involves intrinsic motivation.

10.2 Key Question: How Are Our Motivational Priorities Determined?

Until recently, psychology had no comprehensive explanation or theory that successfully accounted for the whole range of motivation. Hunger seemed so different from the need for achievement. Fears often have roots hidden from consciousness. Most biological drives feel unpleasant, but sexual arousal is pleasurable. The result was that some psychologists concentrated on the most basic survival motives, such as hunger and thirst, while other psychologists tried to explain sex, affiliation, creativity, and a variety of other motives. No one, however, managed to put together a motivational "theory of everything" that could encompass all our motives and, at the same time, be consistent with real-world observations.

But now, a new contender has emerged that, many psychologists say, may be able to do it all.

CORE CONCEPT 10.2

A new theory combining Maslow's hierarchy with evolutionary psychology solves some long-standing problems by suggesting that functional, proximal, and developmental factors set our motivational priorities.

About a half-century ago, Abraham Maslow proposed one of the most influential ideas ever to come out of psychology: that different motives have different priorities, based on a *hierarchy of needs*. For example, a threat to one's life usually trumps thirst. But thirst takes priority over the needs for affiliation or respect. But what about the artist who, in the *flow* state, disregards the need for food or warmth, sometimes for days at a time? And what about those "instincts" that drive animal migrations and, perhaps, some human behaviors, such as nursing in newborn infants? Let's see how a new hierarchy of needs incorporates these concepts.

Instinct Theory

Since the early days of William James, psychologists have realized that all creatures, humans included, possess an inborn set of behaviors that promotes survival. According to **instinct theory,** these built-in behaviors account reasonably well for the regular cycles of animal activity, found in essentially the same form across a species. We see these cycles in bird migrations, in the mating rituals of antelope, and in the return of salmon to the streams in which they were hatched only to spawn and die after a journey of more than 1,000 miles.

Although such so-called "instinctive" behavior patterns do not depend heavily on learning, experience can modify them. Thus, we see a combination of instinctive behavior and learning when bees communicate the location of food to each other or a mother cat helps her kittens hone their hunting skills. Such examples show that "instincts" involve both a lot of nature (genetically determined) and a little nurture (learning).

Because the term *instinct* seemed to explain so much, it migrated quickly from the scientific vocabulary to the speech of everyday life. Unfortunately, it lost precision in the process. So we now speak casually of "maternal instincts" or of an athlete who "instinctively catches the ball" or of an agent who has an "instinct" for picking new talent. In fact, we use the term in so many ways that its meaning has become almost meaningless—a mere label rather than an explanation for behavior.

As a result, the term *instinct* has long since dropped out of favor among scientists (Deckers, 2001). Ethologists, who study animal behavior in natural habitats, now prefer the term **fixed-action patterns,** more narrowly defined as unlearned behavior patterns that are triggered by identifiable stimuli and that occur throughout a species. Examples of fixed-action patterns include not only the "instinctive" behaviors described earlier but also such diverse behaviors as nest building in birds, suckling responses in newborn mammals, and dominance displays in baboons.

Do instincts—perhaps in their new guise as fixed-action patterns—explain any part of human behavior? The question raises the nature–nurture controversy under a new name. Biology *does* seem to account for some human behaviors, such as nursing, that we see in newborns. But instincts or fixed-action patterns are not very useful in explaining the array of more complex behaviors found in people at work and play. For example, while we might speculate that the motivation of a hard-driving executive could involve some basic "killer" instinct, such an explanation is no better than attributing Lance Armstrong's success to a bicycle-riding instinct.

Drive Theory

The concept of *drive* originated as an alternative to instinct for explaining behavior with a strong biological basis, as in eating, drinking, and mating. Psychologists defined a **biological drive** as the state of energy or tension that moves an organism to meet a biological need (Woodworth, 1918). Thus, thirst drives an animal in need of water to drink. Likewise, a need for food arouses a hunger that drives organisms to eat. So, in **drive theory,**

---

instinct theory The now-outmoded view that certain behaviors are completely determined by innate factors. The instinct theory was flawed because it overlooked the effects of learning and because it employed instincts merely as labels rather than as explanations for behavior.

fixed-action patterns Genetically based behaviors, seen across a species, that can be set off by a specific stimulus. The concept of fixed-action patterns has replaced the older notion of instinct.

biological drive A motive, such as thirst, that is based primarily in biology. A drive is a state of tension that motivates an organism to satisfy a biological *need*.

drive theory Developed as an alternative to instinct theory, drive theory explains motivation as a process in which a biological *need* produces a *drive* that moves an organism to meet the need. For most drives this process returns the organism to a balanced condition, known as *homeostasis*.

a biological **need** produces a drive state that, in turn, channels behavior toward meeting the need. When the need is satisfied, drive level subsides—a process called *drive reduction*. You have experienced drive reduction when you feel satisfied after a big meal or when you get in a warm bath after being chilled.

According to drive theory, what organisms seek is a balanced condition in the body, known as **homeostasis** (Hull, 1943, 1952). So, creatures that have an *un*balanced condition (caused, say, by lack of fluids) are driven to seek a homeostatic balance (by drinking). Similarly, we can understand hunger as an imbalance in the body's energy supply. It is this imbalance that drives, or motivates, a food-deprived animal to eat in order to restore a condition of equilibrium.

Unfortunately for drive theory, the story of motivation has proved not to be that simple. In particular, drive theory faltered when cognitive, social, and cultural forces were at work, as we will see later in our discussion of hunger. Moreover, drive theory cannot explain why, in the absence of any apparent deprivation or obvious needs, organisms sometimes act merely to *increase* stimulation. It is hard to imagine, for example, a basic need or a biological drive that could prompt people to go skiing or jump out of airplanes. Even at an animal level, laboratory rats that are hungry or thirsty and given opportunity to eat or drink in a new maze environment do not initially eat or drink. Rather, they explore the novel setting first: Curiosity trumps hunger and thirst (Zimbardo & Montgomery, 1957).

Cognitive psychologists also pointed out that biological drives could not explain behavior motivated by goals, such as getting a promotion at work or an A in psychology. Nor will

According to drive theory, a need for fluids motivates (drives) us to drink. A homeostatic balance is reached when the need is satisfied.

---

homeostasis The body's tendency to maintain a biologically balanced condition, especially with regard to nutrients, water, and temperature.

need In drive theory, a need is a biological imbalance (such as dehydration) that threatens survival if the need is left unmet. Biological needs are believed to produce drives.

drives explain why laboratory rats will cross an electrified grid merely to reach a novel environment to explore or why Lance Armstrong endured thousands of hours of grueling training to win glory. Psychologists call these *psychological motives*. In contrast to *biological drives*, psychological motives serve no immediate biological need but, rather, are strongly rooted in learning, incentives, threats, or social and cultural pressures. The human need for achievement is another good example of a psychological motive. Obviously, many motivated behaviors, especially in humans, can stem from a combination of biological and cognitive or environmental factors. We will see the practical side of the biological versus psychological distinction later when we dissect hunger, the quintessential example of a combined biological drive and psychological motive.

For these reasons, psychologists have concluded that drive theory holds some—but not all—answers to the riddle of motivation. Still, they have been reluctant to abandon the concept of *drive*, which has come to mean a biologically based motive that plays an important role in survival or reproduction. We now look on drive theory as a useful but incomplete theory of motivation.

Freud's Psychodynamic Theory

Sigmund Freud challenged the view that we know what motivates our own behavior. Instead, Freud proposed, most human motivation stems from the murky depths of the unconscious mind, which he called the *id*. There, he said, lurked two basic desires: *eros*, the erotic desire; and *thanatos*, the aggressive or destructive impulse. Virtually everything we do, said Freud, is based on one of these urges or on the maneuvers that the mind uses to keep these desires in check. To avoid mental problems, we must continually seek acceptable outlets for our sexual and aggressive needs. Freud believed that work, especially creative work, indirectly satisfied the sex drive, while aggressive acts like swearing and shouting or playing aggressive games serve as a psychologically safe outlet for our deeper destructive tendencies.

It is important to realize that Freud developed his ideas in the heyday of instinct theory, so eros and thanatos are often thought of as instincts. But it would oversimplify Freud's theory to think of it as just another instinct theory. He wasn't trying to explain the everyday, biologically based behaviors that we find in eating, drinking, mating, nursing, and sleeping. Rather, he was trying to explain the symptoms we find in mental disorders such as phobias or depression.

The new evolutionary theory of motivation borrows Freud's notion that two main motives underlie all we do. Evolutionary psychologists agree that just two fundamental motives underlie everything we do. But in place of sex and aggression, the new theory posits the Darwinian needs for survival and reproduction.

Modern-day psychologists also agree that Freud had put his finger on another important idea: Much mental activity, including motivation, *does* occur outside of consciousness.

[TABLE 10•1] Theories of Motivation Compared

Theories	Emphasis	Examples
Instinct Theory	Biological processes that motivate behavior patterns specific to a species	bird migration, fish schooling
Drive Theory	Needs produce drives that motivate behavior until drives are reduced	hunger, thirst
Freud's Theory	Motivation arises from unconscious desires; developmental changes in these urges appear as we mature	sex, aggression
Maslow's Theory	Motives result from needs, which occur in a priority order (a needs hierarchy)	esteem needs, self-actualization
Evolutionary Theory	Priority of motives determined by functional, proximal, and developmental factors	Food odor (proximal stimulus) may raise the priority of hunger drive

But, they stand divided on the details of the Freudian unconscious, a thread that will continue in the next chapter (Bornstein, 2001; Westen, 1998).

One more of Freud's ideas was also on target, according to the evolutionary theorists. Among the principal theories of motivation discussed in this chapter, Freud's is the only one that takes a *developmental* approach to motivation. That is, Freud taught that our motives undergo change as we move from childhood to adulthood. With maturity, he said, our sexual and aggressive desires become less conscious. We also develop more and more subtle and sophisticated ways of meeting our needs—particularly desires for sex and aggression—without getting into trouble (see **TABLE 10•1**).

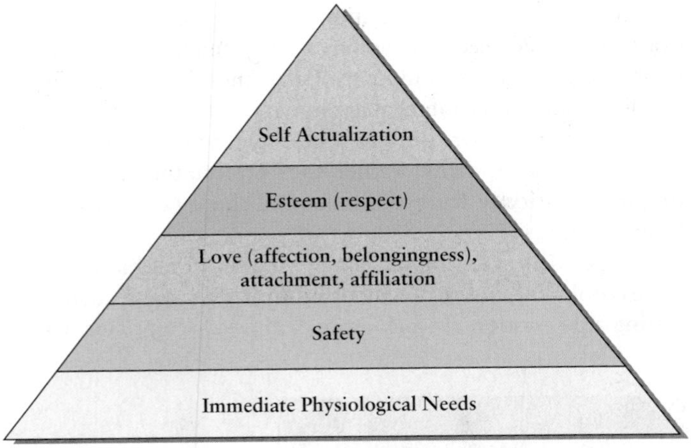

[**FIGURE 10•2**] Maslow's Hierarchy of Needs

Maslow's Hierarchy of Needs

What happens when you must choose between meeting a biological need and fulfilling a desire based on learning—as when you choose between sleeping and staying up all night to study for an exam? Abraham Maslow (1970) said that you usually act on your most pressing needs, which occur in a natural *hierarchy* or priority order, with biological needs taking precedence. Unlike the other theories of motivation we have considered, Maslow's perspective attempts to span the whole gamut of human motivation from biological drives to social motives to creativity (Nicholson, 2007).

Maslow's most memorable innovation, then, was his **hierarchy of needs,** which posited six classes of needs listed in priority order (see **FIGURE 10•2**). The "higher" needs exert their influence on behavior only when the more basic needs are satisfied:

- *Biological needs,* such as hunger and thirst, lie at the base of the hierarchy and must be satisfied before higher needs take over.

- *Safety needs* motivate us to avoid danger, but only when biological needs are reasonably well satisfied. Thus, a hungry animal may risk its physical safety for food until it gets its belly full, at which point the safety needs take over.

- *Love, attachment, and affiliation needs* energize us when we are no longer concerned about the more basic drives such as hunger, thirst, and safety. These "higher" needs make us want to affiliate with others, to love, and to be loved.

- *Esteem needs,* following next in the hierarchy, include the needs to like oneself, to see oneself as competent and effective, and to do what is necessary to earn the respect of oneself and others.

- *Self-actualization,* the "highest" need, but with the lowest priority, motivates us to seek the fullest development of

hierarchy of needs In Maslow's theory, the notion that needs occur in priority order, with the biological needs as the most basic.

our creative human potential. Self-actualizing persons are self-aware, self-accepting, socially responsive, spontaneous, and open to novelty and challenge.

In his original formulation, Maslow put self-actualization at the peak of the needs hierarchy. But late in his life, Maslow suggested yet another highest order need, which he called *self-transcendence*. This he conceptualized as going beyond self-actualization, seeking to further some cause beyond the self (Koltko-Rivera, 2006). Satisfying this need could involve anything from volunteer work to absorption in religion, politics, music, or an intellectual pursuit. What distinguishes self-transcendence from self-actualization is its shift beyond personal pleasure or other egocentric benefits.

[**CONNECTION**] Note the similarity between *self-transcendence* and Erikson's notion of *generativity*, which involves making a contribution to family, work, society, or future generations.

But how does Maslow's theory square with observation? It explains why we may neglect our friends or our career goals in favor of meeting pressing biological needs signaled by pain, thirst, sleepiness, or sexual desire. Yet—in contradiction to Maslow's theory—people may sometimes neglect their basic biological needs in favor of higher ones, as we might see in a father risking his life to rescue his child from a burning building. To Maslow's credit, he recognized these problems. Just as important, he called attention to the role of social motivation in our lives at a time when these motives were being neglected by psychology (Nicholson, 2007). As a result, a great body of work now demonstrates this need we have for relationships with others.

Critics point out that Maslow's theory also fails to explain other important human behaviors: why you might miss a meal when you are absorbed in an interesting book or why sensation seekers would pursue risky interests (such as rock climbing or auto racing) that override their safety needs. The theory also fails to explain the behavior of people who deliberately take their own lives. And it ignores the powerful sex drive.

Cross-cultural psychologists have also criticized Maslow's theory and other "self theories," noting that an emphasis on self-actualization applies primarily to individualistic cultures, which emphasize individual achievement (Gambrel & Cianci, 2003). In contrast, group-oriented (collectivistic) cultures emphasize success of the group rather than *self-actualization* (Shiraev & Levy, 2006). In fairness to Maslow, however, we should note that he recognized that there could be cultural differences in motivation (1943). And even the severest critics will acknowledge that, with all its flaws, Maslow's theory was an important step toward a comprehensive theory of motivation. 📖

📖 **Read** about Maslow's Influence at **MyPsychLab**

Putting It All Together: A New Hierarchy of Needs

In the face of such criticism, can we find something in Maslow's theory worth saving? Douglas Kenrick and his colleagues (2010) point to the idea of a *motivational hierarchy* as Maslow's singular great insight. But, they note, its major difficulty is that our motivational priorities are not rigidly fixed—as Maslow himself realized. Indeed, an individual may change motivational priorities from time to time. Nor do different people necessarily have the same motivational priorities. The solution, said Kenrick's group, is to understand that that we must view the needs hierarchy as fluid—subject to change by three sorts of influences, seen as what they call the *functional, proximal,* and *developmental levels of analysis*.

The **functional level of analysis** looks at the *function* of a motive, which (from an evolutionary perspective) relates to survival and reproductive success. Functional influences arrange our motives in a kind of "default" hierarchy, grounded in the basic needs, such as hunger and thirst. These needs motivate us to seek such things as food drink, warmth, and shelter, without which we could not live. Similarly, sexual motivation arises from the evolutionary mandate to propel one's genes into future generations. This need for sexual gratification and reproduction, then, gives rise to a whole range of social needs, including not only the physical urge for sex but also needs for affiliation, esteem, and parenting. These "higher" reproductive needs, however, generally have lower priority than the survival needs.

Proximal means "nearby"—so the **proximal level of analysis** focuses on immediate events, objects, incentives, and threats that influence motivation. For example, the aroma of freshly baked bread is a proximal stimulus that can suddenly arouse the hunger motive. Or imagine that you are at a theater enjoying a movie when someone yells, "Fire!" Your motivation suddenly shifts from relaxation and enjoyment of the movie to fear and self-preservation. In more formal terms, an important *proximal* stimulus can trigger a temporary modification in your usual motivational hierarchy.

Your stage of life can also affect your motivational profile. Thus, the **developmental level of analysis** shows how the order in which motives appear changes throughout your life span. For example, hunger, thirst, and contact comfort held

---

functional level of analysis Concerns the adaptive function of a motive in terms of the organism's survival and reproduction.

proximal level of analysis Concerns stimuli in the organism's immediate environment, which can change motivational priorities. (In humans, proximal could also refer to things that the individual is thinking about.) need In drive theory, a need is a biological imbalance (such as dehydration) that threatens survival if the need is left unmet. Biological needs are believed to produce drives.

developmental level of analysis Concerns changes in the organism's developmental progress that might change motivational priorities, as when hormones heighten sexual interest in adolescence.

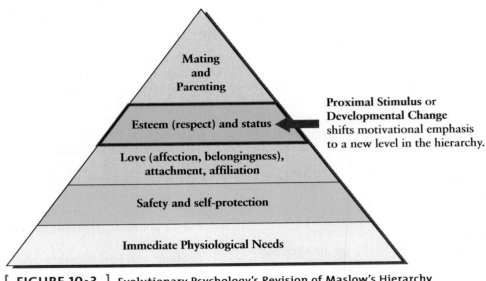

[**FIGURE 10·3**] Evolutionary Psychology's Revision of Maslow's Hierarchy

center stage when you were a baby, but you didn't give a whit about reproduction or about garnering the esteem of your peers. But, when you became a teenager, sexual motives and the need for social approval probably occupied a prominent place in your needs hierarchy, sometimes trumping even the biological hunger and thirst drives. Likewise, proximal cues may affect you differently at different developmental stages. So, you may be most sensitive to different proximal cues—for example to contact comfort when you are young or to a comely peer in your teens.

Less obvious are the evolutionary foundations for artistic creativity, athletic pursuits, stamp collecting, or any of a thousand other human pursuits. And this is where the new theory proposed by Kenrick and his group becomes controversial: They push self-actualization off the pinnacle of Maslow's hierarchy and replace it with needs for mating and parenting (which Maslow had neglected). All the productivity and creativity that Maslow thought of as self-actualization is really just a means to the real ends of reproduction and assuring the survival of one's genetic offspring. As you might expect, critics have raised objections (Ackerman & Bargh, 2010; Kesebir et al., 2010; Lyubomirsky & Boehm, 2010; Peterson & Park, 2010).

What Kenrick's group may have overlooked is the possibility that "higher" motives—including a need to be creative or to satisfy one's curiosity—may have become functionally independent of their evolutionary roots. Certainly, creative persons—famous entertainers, for example—have an advantage in the mating game. Nevertheless, evolution may also have taken a shortcut by wiring our creative urges directly to our pleasure centers. If that is true—and it remains to be explored by researchers—people may pursue their interests just for the pure joy of doing so (Peterson & Park, 2010). This

intrinsic motivation may have become functionally independent of its original biological aims.

Where does all this leave us? A consensus seems to be emerging on a few ideas that may bring some unity to the field of motivation at long last (Schaller et al., 2010). Most psychologists would likely agree that:

- Our motives have a "default" hierarchy or priority order that is essentially the same from person to person—much as Maslow described.

- This default hierarchy of motives must be understood in a functional or evolutionary context, with the most basic motives being related to survival, followed by motives related to reproduction and to survival of offspring.

- An individual's motivational hierarchy is not rigid but can be influenced by proximal stimuli and by the person's developmental level.

As we have noted, there remains some disagreement as to whether the "higher" motives (such as creativity) are always based on the reproductive urge or can instead become independent *intrinsic* motives.

What this new hybrid approach to motivation does for us, then, is to bring together Maslow's hierarchy and evolutionary psychology to make a big tent that can encompass motivation of all sorts—from hunger and thirst to affiliation, status, and creativity. All must be ultimately understood in terms of a hierarchy and in terms of their evolutionary roots. We still don't know precisely how the brain manages to arrange and rearrange the motivational hierarchy, but at last we may have a framework within which the theoretical details can be worked out.

psychology matters

Determining What Motivates Others

Where do you start when you want to know what motivates a person's behavior—perhaps someone who has been self-destructive or hurtful to you? We suggest caution before deciding that the source is some immutable personality trait. Instead, we recommend first looking for any external incentives or threats—extrinsic motivators—that might be at work. Many times, these will tell the whole story.

Beyond that, we suggest you consider social motivation. While Maslow emphasized social motives in his hierarchy of needs, he wasn't the first to suggest their importance in human behavior. Alfred Adler, a contemporary of Sigmund Freud, was arguably the first social psychologist (Ansbacher & Ansbacher, 1956). Adler taught that problem behavior often grows out of feelings of personal inadequacy and perceived social threats. The counterbalancing trend in the healthy personality is a goal or need for cooperation and the desire for acceptance by others. He called this *social interest*. Modern social psychologists combine the notions of social motivation with extrinsic incentives and threats in what they call the "power of the situation."

Applying these notions to Lance Armstrong, it is not a stretch to suspect that his motivation involves a highly competitive desire to win. But whether that is a "neurotic" goal growing out of deep feelings of inferiority, we do not have enough information to know. Should he ever seek psychological help, the therapist would certainly raise that question—to which Armstrong may or may not know the answer. 📖

📖 **Read** about Athletes and Performance Enhancing Drugs at **MyPsychLab**

Adler's ideas are much more complex than we can detail here. Suffice it to say that a person who feels threatened may respond defensively, with annoying behavior or aggression. If you are that person's parent, teacher, employer, or friend, the trick is not to respond in kind. Don't give attention to an attention getter. Don't respond aggressively to an aggressor. Don't try to "get even" with a vengeful person. And don't smother a withdrawn individual with pity. Instead, treat the person with respect—and an understanding of the social motives behind the unwanted behavior.

[**CONNECTION**] For social psychologists, the *power of the situation* better explains human behavior than do personality traits.

CHECK YOUR UNDERSTANDING

✔● **Study** and **Review** at **MyPsychLab**

1. **Recall:** Why has the term *instinct* dropped out of favor with psychologists?

2. **Analysis:** What is the role of *homeostasis* in drive theory?

3. **Recall:** In Freud's theory, our basic motives are
   a. social.
   b. conscious.
   c. unconscious.
   d. established by evolutionary pressures.

4. **Analysis:** Explain why self-actualization is characterized as the "highest" need, but with the lowest priority.

5. **Understanding the Core Concept:** The evolution-based modification of Maslow's hierarchy of needs suggests that our motivational priorities can change, depending primarily on
   a. our developmental level and proximal stimuli.
   b. our stress level and social status.
   c. our intellect and experience.
   d. peer pressure and social status.

Answers: 1. *Instinct* has become an imprecise term that merely labels behavior rather than explaining it. **2.** *Homeostasis* refers to the equilibrium condition to which an organism tends to return after reducing a biological drive. **3.** c **4.** Self-actualization is at the top of the pyramid of Maslow's hierarchy—and in this sense is the "highest" of the needs. However, the needs lower in the hierarchy are more basic and so have higher priority than self-actualization. **5.** a

10.3 Key Question: Where Do Hunger and Sex Fit into the Motivational Hierarchy?

In this section of the chapter, we focus on hunger and sex, two quite different motives that represent the twin forces that evolution has used to shape the human species: the drives to *survive* and *reproduce*. Everyone reading this book inherited the genes of ancestors who managed to do both. Here's the big idea around which this section is organized.

Ultimately, our task is to show how an evolutionary new perspective on motivation manages to bring both of these motives together under one theoretical umbrella.

CORE CONCEPT 10.3

Although dissimilar in many respects, hunger and sex both have evolutionary origins, and each has an essential place in the motivational hierarchy.

Hunger: A Homeostatic Drive *and* a Psychological Motive

You will probably survive if you don't have sex, but you will die if you don't eat. Unlike sex, hunger is one of our personal biological survival mechanisms (Rozin, 1996). When food is available, the hunger drive leads quite naturally to eating. Yet there is more to hunger than biology: It has social and cognitive foundations, too, as we will see in the *multiple-systems approach* to hunger and weight control (see FIGURE 10•4).

The Multiple-Systems Approach to Hunger

Your brain generates hunger by combining biological and psychological information of many kinds, including your body's energy requirements and nutritional state, your food preferences, food cues in your environment, and cultural demands. For example, your readiness to eat a slice of bacon depends on factors such as your blood sugar level, how long it has been since you last ate, whether you like bacon, what time of day it is (breakfast?), whether a friend might be offering you a slice, and whether bacon is an acceptable food in your culture. Assembling all these data, the brain sends signals to neural, hormonal, organ, and muscle systems to start or stop bacon seeking and eating (DeAngelis, 2004b; Flier & Maratos-Flier, 2007). As you may have surmised, the multiple-systems approach is another way of saying that hunger operates at many levels of the motivational hierarchy, meeting many needs that do not necessarily stem from the biological hunger drive.

Biological Factors Affecting Hunger and Eating. In the brain, the stomach, the blood, and fat cells stored all over the body, a host of biological factors work to regulate hunger and eating behavior. Among the most important are these:

- **Brain mechanisms controlling hunger.** The hypothalamus is literally a "nerve center" for hunger, with one region activating feelings of hunger and another dampening hunger. But the hypothalamus does not operate alone. Other regions, particularly in the brain stem, work with the hypothalamus to monitor the status of blood sugar, nutrients in the gut, and fat stores, using a suite of receptors and chemical messengers (Flier, 2006).

- **Set point (homeostatic) mechanisms.** An internal biological "scale" continually assesses the body's fat stores and informs the central nervous system of the result. Whenever deposits stored in specialized fat cells fall below a certain level, or **set point**, signals trigger eating behavior—a homeostatic process. Research suggests that obesity may result when this homeostatic balance gets off kilter. Studies implicate certain chemicals (such as the hormone *ghrelin*) that signal hunger, along with others (such as *leptin*) that

---

set point Refers to the tendency of the body to maintain a certain level of body fat and body weight.

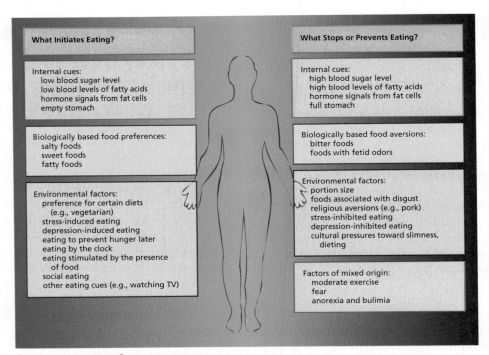

[FIGURE 10•4] Multiple-Systems Model of Hunger and Eating Hunger isn't just a matter of an empty stomach. The multiple-systems model combines all the known influences on hunger and eating.

signal when the set point has been reached. Animals lacking leptin, for example, continue to eat even when not hungry (Grimm, 2007).

- **Sensors in the stomach.** Pressure detectors in the stomach signal fullness or a feeling of emptiness. These messages are sent to the brain, where they combine with information about blood nutrients and the status of the body's fat cells.

- **Reward system preferences.** The brain's reward system gives us preferences for sweet and high-fat foods. These preferences have a biological basis that evolved to steer our ancestors toward calorie-dense foods, enabling them to survive when food supplies were unpredictable. This tendency has been exploited in modern times by the manufacturers of sweet and fatty snack foods.

- **Exercise.** Physical activity also contributes to hunger and satiation. Extreme exercise provokes hunger, but studies show that moderate exercise actually suppresses appetite (Hill & Peters, 1998).

These biological hunger mechanisms operate at the most basic level of the needs hierarchy.

Psychological Factors Affecting Hunger and Eating. In addition to the biological mechanisms that regulate eating, our emotional state can encourage or discourage eating. For example, both humans and animals refrain from eating when they feel threatened. (These are some of the *proximal* factors that we discussed earlier.) Stress and depression can also affect appetite, although the effects are variable: Some people respond by eating more and some by eating less.

Learning plays a role too. Because we also associate certain situations with food, we may feel hungry regardless of our biological needs. This explains why you suddenly want to eat when you notice that the clock says lunchtime. It also explains why you snack while watching TV or dish up a second helping at Thanksgiving dinner.

Culture can have a huge effect too. This can be seen in societies, such as the United States, where media influences and social norms promote a thin body type. On the other hand, in Oceania, where larger figures are often considered more attractive, social norms promote heftier bodies (Newman, 2004).

While the ideal promoted in movies, magazines, and on TV is one of thinness, Americans receive a different message from commercials that encourage eating. That message, combined with an abundance of cheap, tasty junk food results in a growing obesity problem in a population obsessed with weight. Moreover, as the influence of U.S. culture becomes more global, American eating habits have become more universal, with the result that calorie-dense snacks and fast foods are making people fatter all over the world (Hébert, 2005; Popkin, 2007).

Eating Disorders Only rarely does the condition called *anorexia* (persistent lack of appetite) result from a physical disorder, such as shock, nausea, or an allergic reaction. More commonly, the cause has psychological roots—in which case the syndrome is called **anorexia nervosa.** "Nervous anorexia" typically manifests itself in extreme dieting. It can be so extreme, in fact, that the disorder posts the highest mortality rate of any recognized psychological condition (Agras et al., 2004; Park, 2007). In the following discussion, we will revert to common usage by calling the disorder simply *anorexia.*

What qualifies as anorexia? When a person weighs less than 85 percent of her desirable weight and still worries about being fat, anorexia is the likely diagnosis. People with anorexia may also face a problem called *bulimia* or **bulimia nervosa,** characterized by periods of binge eating followed by drastic purging measures, which may include vomiting, fasting, or using laxatives. In many cases, depression and obsessive-compulsive disorder further complicate the clinical picture.

Commonly, a person with anorexia acts as though she is unaware of her condition and continues dieting, ignoring

[**CONNECTION**] People with obsessive-compulsive disorder have persistent and intrusive thoughts and may also feel compelled to act out ritual behaviors.

In the global economy, calorie-dense fast foods have become readily available, changing dietary habits and contributing to a worldwide epidemic of obesity.

---

anorexia nervosa An eating disorder involving persistent loss of appetite that endangers an individual's health and stemming from emotional or psychological reasons rather than from organic causes.

bulimia nervosa An eating disorder characterized by eating binges followed by "purges," induced by vomiting or laxatives; typically initiated as a weight-control measure.

other danger signs that may include cessation of menstruation, osteoporosis, bone fractures, and shrinkage of brain tissue. Over time, bulimic vomiting, done to purge the food she has eaten, results in damage to her esophagus, throat, and teeth caused by stomach acid.

What causes anorexia? A strong hint comes from the finding that most persons with the disorder are young females. Significantly, such eating disorders are most prevalent in Western cultures, particularly among middle- and upper-middle-class young women (Striegel-Moore & Bulik, 2007). Clearly, it is not a hunger disorder caused by lack of resources.

Those with anorexia commonly have histories of good behavior, as well as academic and social success, but they nevertheless starve themselves, hoping to become more acceptably thin and attractive (Keel & Klump, 2003). In an effort to lose imagined "excess" weight, the person with anorexia rigidly suppresses her appetite, feeling rewarded for such self-control when she does lose pounds and inches—but never feeling quite thin enough (see **FIGURE 10•5**).

Work focusing on genetic factors has complicated the assumption that social pressures cause anorexia and bulimia (Novotney, 2009; Striegel-Moore & Bulik, 2007). This makes sense from an evolutionary standpoint, says clinical psychologist Shan Guisinger (2003). She points out the hyperactivity often seen in individuals with anorexia—as opposed to the

lethargy common in most starving persons—suggesting that hyperactivity under conditions of starvation may have been an advantage that motivated the ancestors of modern-day individuals with anorexia to leave famine-impoverished environments.

All in all, it is beginning to appear that anorexia—like hunger itself—is a condition caused by multiple factors that stem from biology, cognition, and social pressures.

Obesity and Weight Control   At the other extreme of weight control, the problem of obesity has grown at an alarming rate since the early 1980s, with the result that 65 percent of Americans are overweight and 30 percent are now classified as obese (DeAngelis, 2004b; Mann et al., 2007). The real problem, of course, is not obesity but the associated health risks for such problems as heart disease, stroke, and diabetes—although experts disagree on just how much of a problem this is among those who are only slightly overweight (Couzin, 2005; Gibbs, 2005). Unfortunately, the fundamental causes of this obesity epidemic are not well understood (Doyle, 2006).

No one in the field of obesity research believes that the condition results from the lack of "will power"—a simplistic and scientifically useless concept, as we will see in the next section (Friedman, 2003). Rather, most experts believe that

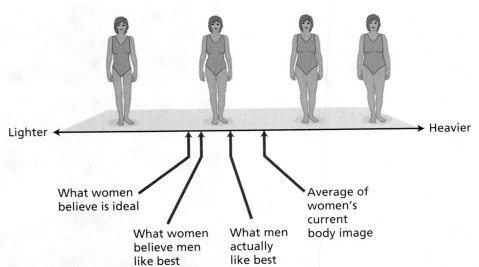

[**FIGURE 10•5**] **Women's Body Images**   April Fallon and Paul Rozin (1985) asked female college students to give their current weight, their ideal weight, and the weight they believed men would consider ideal. The results show that the average woman felt that her current weight was significantly higher than her ideal weight—and higher than the weight she thought men would like. To make matters worse, women also see their bodies as looking larger than they actually are (Thompson, 1986). When men were asked to rate themselves on a similar questionnaire, Fallon and Rozin found no such discrepancies between ideal and actual weights. But, when asked what they saw as the ideal weight for women, they chose a higher weight than women did. No wonder women go on diets more often than men and are more likely to have a major eating disorder (Mintz & Betz, 1986; Striegel-Moore et al., 1993).

obesity results from multiple factors. Prominent among them are poor diet, including super-size portions and an increasing prevalence of food high in fat and sugar. In one laboratory experiment, rats given a diet of sausage, Ho Hos, pound cake, bacon, and cheesecake lost the ability to control their eating and quickly became obese (Johnson & Kenny, 2010).

Genetics also have a role (Bell, 2010; DeAngelis, 2004a; Flier & Maratos-Flier, 2007), but so does activity level. For example, the long-term Nurses' Health Study showed that every two-hour increase in daily TV watching translated into a 23-percent increase in obesity among the nurses in the sample (Hu et al., 2003). Finally, one study suggests not getting enough sleep may trigger eating and a resulting weight gain, perhaps because the body mistakes sleepiness for hunger (Hasler et al., 2004).

From an evolutionary viewpoint, humans are still Stone Age creatures biologically adapted to deal with periods of feast and famine. So we tend to eat more than we need when food is abundant as a hedge against future periods of starvation. Unfortunately, this Stone-Age strategy is not well suited to life in a modern world—where most people in developed countries also have no need to expend energy running down game or digging roots. Nor are we well suited for a world of French fries, deep-dish pizzas, donuts, Snickers, and nachos, which appeal to our deeply ingrained tastes for salty, fatty, and sweet foods—which just happen to be rich in calories (Parker-Pope, 2009; Pinel et al., 2000).

The problem is also not lack of awareness. Americans, especially, seem obsessed by weight and weight loss, as a glance at the magazine headlines on the newsstand will show. At any given time, approximately three out of ten adult Americans say they are on some sort of weight-control diet (Gallup, 2010).

Yet, despite all we know about hunger and weight control, no one has yet discovered a weight-loss scheme that really works for most people. Notwithstanding nationally advertised claims, no diet, surgical procedure, drug, or other weight-loss gimmick has ever produced long-term weight loss for a majority of the people who have tried it. At this point, the best odds for most people lie in cognitive-behavioral therapies (Institute of Medicine, 2002; Rich, 2004). And for those struggling with weight, it is encouraging to know that some potentially effective weight-control chemicals are being tested as you read this, although it may be several years before anything both safe and effective comes to market (Flier & Maratos-Flier, 2007). In the meantime, experts suggest that the best pathway to long-term weight control involves maintaining a well-balanced diet, a program of moderate exercise and, if you want some extra help, cognitive-behavioral therapy.

The Problem of Will Power and Chocolate Cookies

Psychologists don't talk much about "will power," although the term can be heard in everyday conversation, where it usually refers to resisting food, drink, or some other temptation.

In particular, psychologists don't like the archaic assumption of the "will" as a special faculty of the mind—a throwback to 19th-century phrenology. Thus, "will power" is like the term "instinct"—merely a label rather than an explanation. Psychologists also object to the term "will power" because it is often used as a moral judgment, suggesting that a person has a deficiency in character—a "weak will."

Alternatives to Will Power Modern psychologists usually prefer terms such as *self-control* or *impulse control*—terms that carry less baggage and can be related to environmental influences and to known brain mechanisms. For example, we know that controlling one's eating is more difficult during the holiday season, with its abundance of food. Similarly, damage to parts of the limbic system is known to make control of eating more difficult.

Psychologists have also contrived devilish tests to measure impulse control. What have they found? To nobody's surprise, the ability to control one's impulses correlates with all sorts of positive outcomes, including better mental health, more effective coping skills, better relationships, and higher academic achievement. But such findings still leave the big question unanswered: What *is* self-control—or "will power"?

The Biology of Self-Control A team of researchers at Florida State University seems to have placed the ability to resist temptation on a solid scientific footing (Gailliot et al., 2007). What they found is that self-control has a biological basis. And it also has a price.

The Florida group first placed undergraduate psychology students in one of several onerous situations in which they were asked to exercise self-control—such as resisting a tempting plate of warm, freshly baked chocolate cookies or watching a funny video clip without laughing. Then the researchers gave the students a second task, such as a scrambled-word problem or a hand–eye coordination test. A control group also performed the second task, but they were not first asked to stifle their laughter, nor were they exposed to plates of tempting cookies.

Before we go any further, see if you can predict who did better on the second task. Was it those in the experimental group, who had to resist their impulses? Or was it the control group, who had been allowed to indulge themselves?

You were right if you guessed that those who had to face down temptation (resisting the cookies or soberly watching the funny video) were *less* successful on the second task. Apparently self-control is a cognitive resource that, like physical stamina, can become temporarily depleted. And, surprisingly, self-control seems to have a physical presence in the blood, as well as in behavior. The study found that those who had been asked to control their urges had lower blood-sugar levels than those who had not restrained themselves. Because sugar (glucose) is an energy source for the body, the researchers speculate that exerting will power used up some of that energy, making people less efficient on the second task (Baumeister et al., 1998, 2007; Wargo, 2009).

But there is hope for those weak of will! A sugared drink not only brought blood glucose back up to its original level, but it brought the performance of the self-controllers back to the level of the indulgers. Apparently, what we call "will power" is based, at least in part, on the body's ready energy reserves.

So, should you have a cola and a candy bar to boost your "will" before the next psychology test? Probably not such a good idea, says Matthew Gaillot, leader of the Florida study—especially if you are trying to control your weight. Better, he says, to keep your energy level up with a diet that includes longer-lasting proteins or complex carbohydrates (Cynkar, 2007).

And some additional advice from a cognitive perspective: If you want to insure that you are mentally sharp, moderation is a better strategy than denial.

Our cultural lessons and life experiences influence the meaning of sex in our lives.

Sexual Motivation: An Urge You Can Live Without

No one enjoys being hungry or thirsty. But we can't say the same for sex: Unlike hunger or thirst, *arousal* of the sex drive can be pleasurable. And even though sexually aroused individuals may seek to reduce the tension by mating or other sexual activity, the sex drive is not homeostatic—again unlike hunger and thirst. That is, having sex does not return the body to an equilibrium condition. Moreover, sexual motivation can serve diverse goals, including pleasure, reproduction, and social bonding. In other words, sex—like hunger—is linked with diverse motives in the hierarchy.

In one other respect, sexual motivation has a kinship with hunger and thirst: It has its roots in survival. But even in this respect, sex is unique among biological drives because lack of sex poses no threat to the *individual's* survival. We can't live for long without food or water, but some people live their lives without sexual activity (although some would say that that's not really living!). Rather, sexual motivation involves the survival of the species, not the individual.

All the biological drives—sex included—exert such powerful influences on behavior that they have led to numerous social constraints and taboos, such as prohibitions on eating certain meats or drinking alcohol. In the realm of sexuality, we find extensive culture-specific rules and sanctions involving a wide variety of sexual practices. In fact, all societies regulate sexual activity, but the restrictions vary widely. For example, homosexuality has been historically suppressed in the United States and in Arab cultures, but it is widely accepted in many Asian and Pacific Island nations. Rules about marriage among relatives and

exposure of genitals and breasts also vary from culture to culture.

Even the discussion of sex can become mired in taboo, misinformation, and embarrassment. Scientists who study human sexuality have felt intense social and political pressures, which show no signs of abating in the present. The result is that the scientific understanding of sexuality, which we will survey below, has been hard won.

The Scientific Study of Sexuality In the mid-20th century, a titillated public clamored to read the first major scientific study of human sexuality, based on interviews of some 17,000 Americans. In two notorious books—one on men and one on women—Alfred Kinsey and his colleagues (1948, 1953) revealed that certain behaviors (oral sex, for example) previously considered rare and even abnormal were actually quite widespread. While Kinsey's data are now more than 50 years old, his interviews continue to be considered an important source of information about human sexuality, especially since no one else has conducted such in-depth interviews of such a large and varied sample.

In the 1990s, another large survey of American sexuality was described in *The Social Organization of Sexuality: Sexual Practices in the United States* (Laumann et al., 1994) and in a smaller, more readable companion volume called *Sex in America* (see **TABLE 10•2**) (Michael et al., 1994). This project, known as the National Health and Social Life Survey (NHSLS), involved interviews of 3,432 adults, ages 18 to 59. While there were some built-in sources of bias (for example, only English-speaking persons were interviewed), the NHSLS managed to get a remarkable response rate: Of those recruited for the survey, 79 percent agreed to participate. When melded with other surveys taken since Kinsey's time, this study showed, among other things, a marked

[TABLE 10•2] Sexual Preferences and Behaviors of Adult Americans

Frequency of Intercourse	Not at All	A Few Times per Year	A Few Times per Month	Two or More Times per Week		
Percentage of men	14	16	37	34		
Percentage of women	10	18	36	37		
Number of Sexual Partners Since Age 18	**0**	**1**	**2–4**	**5–10**	**10–20**	**21+**
Percentage of men	3	20	21	23	16	17
Percentage of women	3	31	31	20	6	3
Infidelity While Married						
Men				15.1%		
Women				2.7%		
Sexual Orientation	**Males**			**Females**		
Heterosexual	96.9			98.6		
Homosexual	2.0			0.9		
Bisexual	0.8			0.5		

Source: Adapted from Michael, R. T., Gagnon, J. H., Laumann, E. O., & Kolata, G. (1994). Sex *in America: A definitive survey.* New York: Little, Brown. Table based on survey of 3,432 scientifically selected adult respondents. There has not been a major survey of American sexual preferences and behaviors since 1994.

increase in the percentage of youth who are sexually active, along with a declining age at first intercourse (Wells & Twenge, 2005). A smaller but more recent survey, however, shows that the percentage of teens who say they are virgins has increased slightly in the past decade (Doyle, 2007). Estimates of homosexual and bisexual preferences have also risen moderately.

But sexuality is not controlled solely by social pressures. In a study comparing identical twins with fraternal twins, researchers have found that the age at which individuals first have sex is strongly influenced by genetics (Weiss, 2007). Because the same work also showed a genetic influence on the tendency to get in trouble with the law, the scientists speculate that the underlying factor may be a risk-taking tendency.

Masters and Johnson: Gender Similarities and the Physiology of Sex.

Although Kinsey first shocked the nation's sexual sensibilities, it was William Masters and Virginia Johnson (1966, 1970, 1979) who really broke with tradition and taboo by bringing sex into their laboratory. Never before had scientists studied sex by directly observing and recording the responses of people engaging in sexual behavior of various sorts, including masturbation and intercourse. During these observational studies, Masters and Johnson discovered not what people *said* about sex but how people actually *reacted*

physically during sex. In the wake of their daring departure from tradition, the study of human sexual behavior has become much more accepted as a legitimate field of scientific inquiry.

These observations revealed four phases of human sexual responding, which Masters and Johnson collectively called the **sexual response cycle** (see FIGURE 10•6). Here are the distinguishing events of each phase:

- In the *excitement phase,* blood vessel changes in the pelvic region cause the clitoris to swell and the penis to become erect. Blood and other fluids also become congested in the testicles and vagina.

- During the *plateau phase,* a maximal level of arousal is reached. Rapid increases occur in heartbeat, respiration, blood pressure, glandular secretions, and muscle tension.

- Reaching the *orgasm phase,* males and females experience a very intense and pleasurable sense of release from the cumulative sexual tension. Orgasm, characterized by rhythmic genital contractions, culminates in ejaculation of semen in men and clitoral and vaginal sensations in women.

---

sexual response cycle The four-stage sequence of arousal, plateau, orgasm, and resolution, occurring in both men and women.

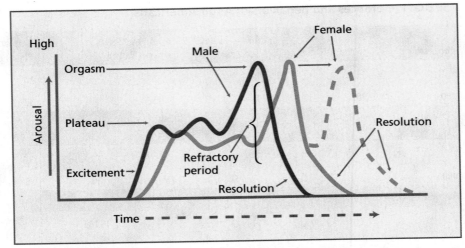

[**FIGURE 10•6**] **The Sexual Response Cycle** Note that the phases of sexual response in males and females have similar patterns. The primary differences are in the time it takes for males and females to reach each phase and in the greater likelihood that females will achieve multiple orgasms.

Source: Gagnon, J. H. (1977). *Human Sexualities.* Glenview, IL: Scott Foresman. Reprinted by permission of J. H. Gagnon.

- During the *resolution phase,* the body gradually returns to its preexcitement state, as fluids dissipate from the sex organs. At the same time, blood pressure and heart rate, which had increased dramatically, drop to their customary levels.

Note also that Masters and Johnson focused on physiological arousal and responses. Accordingly, they paid relatively little attention to psychological aspects of sexuality, such as emotional responses or social pressures on sexual activity. Nevertheless, Masters and Johnson drew several newsworthy conclusions about the biology of sex:

- Men and women have remarkably similar patterns of biological response, regardless of the source of sexual arousal—whether it be intercourse or masturbation.

- Although the phases of the sexual response cycle are similar in the two sexes, women tend to respond more slowly but often remain aroused longer. This makes sense from a biological standpoint because the male is likely to ejaculate before the female loses interest.

- Many women can have multiple orgasms in a short time period, while men rarely do.

- Size of the genitals or other physical sex characteristics (such as vulva, breasts, and penis) is generally unrelated to any aspect of sexual performance (except, perhaps, attitudes about one's sexual capability).

Most important, perhaps, Masters and Johnson used their discoveries about sexual behavior to develop effective behavioral therapies for a variety of sexual disorders, including male erectile disorder (inability to achieve or maintain an erection), premature ejaculation, and female orgasmic disorder.

[CONNECTION] The behavior therapies focus on what people do rather than on what they think or feel. Such treatments are effective for a variety of problems, including not only sexual problems but also phobias and other anxiety disorders.

An Alternative View: Men and Women Differ in Their Sexuality. While Masters and Johnson called our attention to the similarities between men and women in the sexual response cycle, other researchers have focused on the differences. For example, Meredith Chivers and her colleagues (2007) have discovered that heterosexual women are aroused by a broader range of erotic stimuli than are heterosexual men. Moreover, gay men and lesbian women are more particular in their erotic tastes than were their heterosexual counterparts. Other researchers have looked deep in the brain, pinpointing the reward areas associated with orgasm—which can be as strong, for example, as the brain's response to heroin (Portner, 2008).

Ann Peplau (2003) has pointed out four especially important differences between men and women. First, she notes, *men show more interest in sex than do women*—on the average, of course. Men not only think about sex more often, but they are also more likely to attend to visual sexual stimuli. They also generally prefer to have sex more frequently than do women.

Second, *women are more likely than men to view sex in the context of a committed relationship.* That is, says Peplau, women are more likely to "romanticize" sexual desire as a longing for emotional intimacy, while men tend to see sex more as physical pleasure. As a result, women generally (both heterosexual and lesbian women) have a less permissive attitude toward casual sex than do men (including both gay and straight men).

Third, *sex is more likely to be linked with aggression for males than for females.* As you probably know, rape is almost exclusively an act committed by males. But even in milder forms, aggression is more a male than a female characteristic. For example, men are more likely to be domineering or abusive in a sexual relationship. (We should add that, even though these gender differences seem to have a biological basis, nothing in this fact excuses hurtful or forced sexual behavior.)

Fourth, Peplau argues that *women's sexuality has greater "plasticity."* By that she means that women's behaviors and beliefs are more readily shaped by cultural and social factors, as well as by the immediate situation. For example, women's sexual activity over time is far more variable in its frequency than men's. This is especially true when circumstances change, as in a divorce. Cultural factors, such as religion and cultural norms, also influence women's sexuality more than men's. Especially interesting is the fact that higher education is, for both men and women, correlated with more liberal sexual attitudes—but the effect is much stronger for women.

Neuroscientists have also found gender differences in the brain's responses (Portner, 2008). Specifically, during orgasm, many regions associated with emotional control in a woman's brain—unlike a man's—seem to fall silent. That response, suggest researcher Gert Holstege and her colleagues (2003), involves the dampening of anxiety responses that could otherwise inhibit orgasm.

An Evolutionary Perspective on Sexuality

The evolutionary perspective looks for the basis of sexual motivation in the pressures of natural selection. Accordingly, some observers (Buss, 2008) argue that selection pressures have produced different mating strategies and, therefore, different gender roles for men and women. (We are speaking of heterosexuals here, because the evolutionary aspects of homosexuality and bisexuality are unclear at this point.)

Read about Sexual Cues and Sexual Scripts at **MyPsychLab**

[CONNECTION] *Natural selection* is Darwin's term for the environmental conditions that favored the "survival of the fittest".

Biologically speaking, the goal of both sexes is to leave as many offspring as possible. Yet the potential physical costs of mating and parenting differ for males and females (Bjorklund & Shackelford, 1999). As a result, the sexes have evolved different—and sometimes conflicting—mating strategies, say evolutionary psychologists.

Females can produce only a few children over a lifetime, and they make a huge biological investment in pregnancy and a substantial commitment of time and energy in child rearing. Therefore, the best sexual strategy for females involves caution in mate selection. For males, however, the costs and benefits are much different because they cannot become pregnant—nor do they usually spend as much time with children as women do. For males, evolutionary theory says, the biggest payoff results from copulating as often as possible with mates who are in prime breeding condition. As a result, men tend to seek young and physically well-developed partners, while females may seek somewhat older mates who can offer resources, status, and protection for offspring. Not incidentally, these agendas often produce conflict, promiscuity, and sexual jealousy.

Although the evolutionary perspective may seem cold hearted in its view of sexual motivation, it *does* account for many gender differences in mating behaviors, such as the larger number of sexual partners typically reported by men than women (see TABLE 10•2 on page 305). Even so, biology does not prohibit the learning of alternative sex roles and scripts, nor does it explain the social and cultural pressures that cast men and women in different roles (Eagly & Wood, 1999). Moreover, evolutionary psychology does not explain why most people remain with their mates over extended periods of time (Hazan & Diamond, 2000) or why gay and lesbian relationships persist across cultures. A complete understanding of human sexual motivation, therefore, must include both its evolutionary roots and the many variations that occur through learning.

Sex, Hunger, and the Hierarchy of Needs

Maslow said almost nothing about sex. The new evolution-based needs hierarchy, however, corrects this omission. Kenrick's group still gives priority to hunger, thirst, and other survival needs at the base of the hierarchy. Sex and related motives follow at the "higher" levels: attachment, affiliation, belongingness, and parenting. But this doesn't mean that a pizza always wins over the opportunity for sex. As we have seen, the hierarchy is fluid, not rigid. In addition, hunger and sex are both biological drives *and* psychological motives. Because biological drives generally have priority over psychological motives, the attraction of sex can sometimes take precedence over eating—in which case proximal sex overpowers proximal pizza.

psychology matters

Ever since Kinsey's first reports were published, we have known that human **sexual orientation** is a complex issue relating to sexual attraction, along with several other aspects of human relating, including our sexual behavior, desired intimate relationships, affiliation with gay or straight (or other) communities, and how we personally identify our sexual orientation (Herek et al., 2010).

Heterosexuality and homosexuality represent the two major forms of sexual orientation: A *heterosexual orientation* is to the opposite sex; a *homosexual orientation* is to the same sex. Another common variation is *bisexuality,* which refers to sexual interest in both males and females (Diamond, 2008). But to complicate matters, cross-cultural studies reveal considerable variability in sexual orientation. In parts of New Guinea, for example, the culture dictates that homosexual behavior is universal among young males, who then switch to a heterosexual orientation when they marry (Money, 1987). Among American adults, various estimates put the percentage of homosexuality at 1 to 9 percent, more or less, depending on whether homosexuality is defined as (a) feelings of attraction to persons of the same sex, (b) one's primary orientation or, (c) having *ever* engaged in same-sex erotic behavior (Diamond, 2007; Savin-Williams, 2006). As Table 10.2 (page 305) indicates, the incidence of homosexuality among females is about half that of males. Incidentally, homosexual behavior is quite common among animals—particularly bonobos (pigmy chimpanzees), who are genetically close relatives to humans (Driscoll, 2008).

Transsexualism refers to people who view themselves as persons of the sex opposite to their biological sex. Thus, a transsexual person with the phenotype of a male thinks of him/herself as a female. Such persons should not be confused with cross-dressers, who indulge in a sexual fetish known as *transvestism.* (Those who cross-dress for non-sexual reasons are not classified under transvestism.) It is also important to realize that none of these variations predicts sexual orientation. That is, knowing that a person is transsexual or a cross-dresser does not tell us whether he or she is gay, lesbian, bisexual, or straight (Devor, 1993).

Origins of Sexual Orientation

So, what does the available evidence tell us about the factors that determine sexual orientation? We know several things that are *not* involved. Speaking biologically, we know that sexual orientation in adults is *not* related to testosterone levels—although the issue of testosterone or estrogen influences on the fetus is still an open question (McAnulty & Burnette, 2004). From a social perspective, we also know that parenting styles or family configurations do *not* cause children to identify as straight or gay (Golombok & Tasker, 1996). Similarly, researchers have come up empty handed in their attempts to link human sexual orientation to early sexual experiences, such as molestation or other abuse.

Although much of the work has focused on biology, most experts have concluded that a combination of biological, environmental, and social factors are at play. To illustrate this research, let's look at a famous study of male identical twins. Richard Pillard and Michael Bailey (1991) discovered that when one twin is homosexual, the chance of the other being homosexual is about 50 percent. This compares with an incidence of roughly 5 or 6 percent in the general population. The same study also found that the rate drops to 22 percent for fraternal twins and 11 percent for adoptive brothers of homosexuals. A later study of female twin pairs produced essentially the same results (Bower, 1992).

One of the more puzzling findings links sexual orientation in males (but not females) to birth order, specifically how many older brothers one has (Abrams, 2007; Blanchard, 2008; Bogaert, 2005). The more older brothers a boy has, the more likely he is to have a same-sex orientation. This effect occurs whether or not boys are raised with their biological brothers, according to a study of adopted versus biological brothers—a finding that apparently rules out environmental influences after birth (Bogaert, 2006). While

The origins of sexual orientation are unclear, although some evidence points to biological factors. What is clear is that research on sexual orientation often generates controversy.

---

sexual orientation One's erotic attraction toward members of the same sex (a homosexual orientation), the opposite sex (heterosexual orientation), or both sexes (a bisexual orientation).

no one knows what the causative factor is, some scientists believe that some aspect of the prenatal environment tips the balance one way or the other. (Bower, 2006a).

Again, research shows that social and environmental factors must also be taken into account. While few studies examine how adolescents develop a sexual orientation, some scholars theorize that social influences such as peers, the media, schools, and parenting can affect the direction of sexual development. Hyde and Jaffee (2000) reviewed numerous large studies that suggest adolescent girls who become heterosexual often develop their identities and social roles amidst messages that disparage homosexuality and promote heterosexuality.

Turning to the earlier preadolescent period, a longitudinal study of 182 children in fourth to eighth grade looked at the ways some children enter into a period of sexual questioning (Carver et al., 2004). Specifically, the researchers found that girls and boys who, for various reasons, question whether they will marry someone of the other sex and whether they will fulfill typical gender roles come to feel distressed about their competence in peer relationships (although this turmoil seems not to affect how much they are liked and accepted by their peers).

Research in this area remains controversial because of the strong feelings, political issues, and prejudices involved (Herek, 2000). Further, it has attracted scientific criticism because much of it is correlational—rather than experimental—so the data cannot establish cause and effect with certainty. Moreover, some observers object to this whole line of research, saying that gay men and lesbians should not feel pressured to justify their behavior by seeking a "cause" for it (Byne, 1995).

Not a Disorder

We should also note that, until the 1970s, the diagnostic manual of the American Psychiatric Association listed homosexuality as a mental disorder—a classification that has since been removed and repudiated by both psychologistsand psychiatrists (Greenberg, 1997). Then, more recently, the American Psychological Association passed a resolution advising against therapies aimed at changing sexual orientation, on the grounds that they are ineffective, unnecessary, and potentially harmful (Munsey, 2009).

And what does the evidence say about sexual orientation and mental health? The message coming through numerous studies says that mental disorders and relationship problems occur in about the same proportion in heterosexuals and homosexuals (DeAngelis, 2002c; Kurdek, 2005). As we might expect, the only exception involves stress-related problems—e.g., anxiety and depression—associated with discrimination against homosexuals. The research also shows no differences in adjustment or development of children raised by heterosexual or homosexual parents (APA, 2010; Patterson, 2006).

So, where does this leave us in our understanding of sexual orientation? Attitudes toward minority forms of sexual orientation, such as homosexuality, differ sharply among cultures around the world, with Americans among the most divided on issues such as gay marriage. Most experts—but not all—would say that the research strongly supports some biological influence on sexual orientation. Just how biology might influence our behavior in the bedroom, however, remains a major puzzle and a topic for continuing research.

CHECK YOUR UNDERSTANDING

✓●─ **Study** and **Review** at **MyPsychLab**

1. **Recall:** Describe the *multiple systems approach* to understanding hunger.

2. **Analysis:** Explain, from an evolutionary perspective, why obesity is becoming more prevalent in industrialized nations.

3. **Recall:** From a biological perspective, in what respect is sex different from other biological drives, such as hunger and thirst?

4. **Recall:** What are the four major differences between men's and women's sexuality, according to Peplau?

5. **Analysis:** Why do psychologists avoid the term *will power*? What terms do they prefer instead?

6. **Understanding the Core Concept:** For which of the motives discussed in this section would biological factors be *least* important in accounting for the differences between one person and another?

   a. hunger   b. thirst
   c. a *n Ach*   d. sex

Answers: 1. Because hunger has not only biological components but also cognitive, social, and cultural aspects, it must be understood as involving a complex interaction of factors. The multiple systems approach recognizes such factors as blood sugar and fat levels monitored by the hypothalamus, homeostatic feedback from fat cells, pressure and nutrient detectors in the stomach, reward systems in the brain, physical activity, emotional state, food-related stimuli, and social-cultural pressures. **2.** From an evolutionary standpoint, the human body evolved in an environment that required much more physical exertion than is required of most people in industrialized countries. This decrease in activity, along with an abundance of calorie-dense foods, has led to obesity. **3.** Sex is not a homeostatic drive, nor is it essential for the survival of the individual. **4.** Peplau says that (a) men show more interest in sex than do women, (b) women are more likely to view sex in the context of a committed relationship, (c) males are more likely to associate sex with aggression, and (d) women's sexuality has more plasticity than men's. **5.** The term *will power* suggests that it is a separate faculty of the mind, yet there is no evidence of a "will" that cannot be explained in more conventional terms that do not carry the baggage of a defect in character. Psychologists prefer to speak of "self-control" or "impulse control." **6.** c (because all the others involve biological drives)

10.4 Key Question: How Do Our Emotions Motivate Us?

One of the most pervasive misunderstandings about the human mind is the idea that emotion is the opposite of reason. Consider the case of Elliot. Once a model employee, he had let the quality of his work slip to the point that he finally lost his job. If anything, said his supervisors, Elliot had become almost too focused on the details of his work, yet he had trouble setting priorities. He often latched onto a small task, such as sorting a client's paperwork, and spent the whole afternoon on various classification schemes—never quite getting to the real job he had been assigned (Damasio, 1994).

His personal life also fell apart. A divorce was followed by a short marriage and another divorce. Several attempts at starting his own business involved glaringly flawed decisions that finally ate up all his savings.

Yet, surprisingly, in most respects Elliot seemed normal. He had a pleasant personality and an engaging sense of humor. He was obviously smart—well aware of important events, names, and dates. He understood the political and economic affairs of the day. In fact, examinations revealed nothing wrong with his movements, memory, perceptual abilities, language skills, intellect, or ability to learn.

Complaints of headaches led the family doctor to suspect that the changes in Elliot pointed to something wrong in his brain. Tests proved the suspicion correct, revealing a mass the size of a small orange that was pressing on the frontal lobes just above Elliot's eyes.

The tumor was removed, but not before it had damaged the frontal lobes in a pattern remarkably similar to that of the notorious Phineas Gage. But the effects in Elliot were more subtle than in Gage. As a psychologist who examined him said, "We might summarize Elliot's predicament as *to know but not to feel*" (Damasio, 1994, p. 45). His reasoning abilities were intact, but the damage to the circuitry of Elliot's frontal lobes disrupted his ability to use his emotions to establish priorities among the objects, events, and people in his life. In short, Elliot had been emotionally crippled. With a disruption in his ability to connect concepts and emotions, Elliot could not value one course of action over another.

So, what does Elliot's case tell us about the role of emotions in our thinking? What happened to Elliot, Phineas Gage, and others with similar problems makes it clear that emotion is a vital ingredient in thinking and, especially, in decision making (Forgas, 2008; Gray, 2004). In the remainder of this chapter, we will explore some discoveries about how the brain processes emotions and what these discoveries mean about the intimate connection between emotion and reason.

How is emotion linked to motivation? Note that both words share a common root, "*mot-*" from the Latin *motus*, meaning "move." The psychology of emotion has retained this meaning by viewing emotion as a special sort of motivation directed outward. Emotions also increase our arousal, attach the values we call "feelings" to people, objects, and events that we judge important, and produce an approach or avoidance response. Let's look more closely at these components of emotion.

CORE CONCEPT 10.4

Emotions are a special class of motives that help us attend to and respond to important (usually external) situations and communicate our intentions to others.

What Emotions Are Made Of

In brief, every **emotion** has four main components: *physiological arousal, cognitive interpretation, subjective feelings,* and *behavioral expression.* We can illustrate with an example closer to home.

Suppose that you win a cool $50 million in the lottery. Chances are that the news will make you jump and shout, your heart race, and a wave of joy wash over your brain. Congratulations! You have just had an emotion! The *physiological arousal* component involves an alarm broadcast simultaneously throughout the autonomic nervous system and the endocrine system. The result is an extensive visceral response that includes your racing heart.

The second component of emotion, a *cognitive interpretation* of events and feelings, involves a conscious recognition and interpretation of the situation. Undoubtedly, you would interpret the news about your winning lottery ticket as good fortune. The same processes—both conscious and unconscious—can happen with unpleasant experiences too. (Think of a hungry bear chasing you.)

The *subjective feeling* component of your fear may come from several sources. One involves the brain sensing the body's current state of arousal. The other comes from memories of the body's state in similar situations in the past. There, the brain stores a sort of emotional "body-image" that Antonio Damasio (1994, 2003) calls a *somatic marker.* In response to the hungry bear, your brain retrieves a body-image memory of how you felt during past encounters with danger, including a racing heart, a cold sweat, and the feeling of running away.

The recently discovered "mirror neuron" system is yet another source of emotional feelings. These brain circuits activate to make you feel the somatic marker of an emotion when you see someone else's emotional state, as in a sad movie (Miller, 2006c; Niedenthal, 2007). In our hungry bear

[CONNECTION] "Mirror neurons" allow us to understand others' behaviors, emotional states, and intentions.

---

emotion A four-part process that involves physiological arousal, subjective feelings, cognitive interpretation, and behavioral expression. Emotions help organisms deal with important external events.

example, your mirror neurons may reflect the emotions of a companion who sees the bear before you do. Numerous studies support this conjecture, but one of the more interesting ones involved the positive emotions of romantically involved couples. When researchers looked at the simultaneous brain scans of such couples, they found that when one had an unpleasant experience, the other showed essentially the same changes in the emotion-related parts of the brain (Singer et al., 2004).

Finally, the fourth component of emotion produces an *expression of emotion in behavior.* So, when you learned of your lottery winnings, you probably smiled, gave a whoop of joy, and perhaps danced around the room as you babbled the news to your companions. Alternatively, the sight of a hungry bear most likely would activate the "fight-or-flight" response, as well as in emotion-laden facial expressions and vocalizations, such as crying, grimacing, or shouting.

And what functions do these emotional responses serve? Surely emotions must do more than just adding variety or "color" to our mental lives. Let's see.

What Emotions Do for Us

Whether they occur in humans, hyenas, cats, or kangaroos, emotions serve as arousal states that signal important events, such as a threat or the presence of a receptive mate. They also become etched in memory to help the organism recognize such situations quickly when they recur (Dolan, 2002; LeDoux, 1996; Lee, 2009). Thus, Lance Armstrong uses emotion in deciding when to overtake an opponent in a race. And our own ability to connect emotional memories to new situations accounts for emotions as diverse as the fear generated by a hungry bear, the joy produced by a winning lottery ticket, or an A on a term paper.

In general, emotions are either *positive* or *negative,* which leads to a tendency for *approach* or *avoidance* (Davidson et al., 2000). The "approach" emotions, such as delight and joy, are generally positive, and they make a person, object, or situation attractive (as when we find another person desirable). Brain scans suggest that these approach emotions involve the dopamine reward system. In contrast, most of the negative emotions, such as fear and disgust, are associated with rejection or avoidance (as when we fear going to the dentist). These avoidance emotions usually involve the amygdala.

Natural selection has shaped our emotions, which explains why they well up in situations that might affect our survival or reproductive success (Gross, 1998; Izard, 2007). For example, fear undoubtedly helped individuals in your family tree to avoid situations that could have made them a meal instead of an ancestor. Similarly, the emotion we call "love" may commit us to a family, which helps to continue our genetic line. Likewise, sexual jealousy can be seen as an emotion that evolved to deal with the biologically important problem of mate infidelity, which threatens the individual's chances of producing offspring (Buss & Schmitt, 1993). Humor, too, may have evolved to serve a social purpose, as we

Sexual jealousy probably has an evolutionary basis because mate infidelity threatens the individual's chances of producing offspring.

[**CONNECTION**] The amygdala is a part of the limbic system that is particularly involved in fear.

can surmise from the "in-jokes" and rampant laughter among people in tightly knit social groups (Ayan, 2009; Provine, 2004; Winerman, 2006d).

We glimpsed yet another important-but-little-known function of emotions in Elliot's story. You will recall that his tumor interfered not only with his ability to process emotion but also with his judgment. The cases of Elliot and others like him confirm that our emotions help us make decisions, because they attach values to the alternatives (De Martino et al., 2006; Miller, 2006a).

And where do emotions fit in the new evolution-based hierarchy? Obviously, many emotions relate to survival, as does the fear you might feel in our hungry-bear example. Other emotions relate to sexual arousal and reproduction, as in the attraction you feel to potential mate. The survival-related emotions, then, would operate near the bottom of the motivational pyramid, where they generally have a high priority. That leaves the sex- and affiliation-related emotions—attraction and love, for example—on the upper levels of the hierarchy, where they generally have lower priority than the survival-based motives.

Counting the Emotions

How many emotions are there? A long look in the dictionary turns up more than 500 emotional terms (Averill, 1980). Most experts, however, see a more limited number of *basic emotions.* Carroll Izard (2007) argues for six: interest, joy/ happiness, sadness, anger, disgust, and fear. Paul Ekman's list

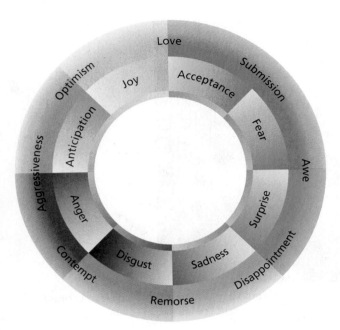

[FIGURE 10•7] The Emotion Wheel Burnout is
Robert Plutchik's emotion wheel arranges eight primary
emotions on the inner ring of a circle of opposite
emotions. Pairs of adjacent emotions can combine to
form more complex emotions noted on the outer ring of
the figure. For example, love is portrayed as a
combination of joy and acceptance. Still other emotions,
such as envy or regret (not shown), emerge from still
other combinations of more basic emotions portrayed
on the wheel.

Source: Plutchik, R. (1980, February) A language for the emotions.
Psychology Today, 13(9), 68–78. Used with permission of *Psychology
Today* © 2008.

contains seven: anger, disgust, fear, happiness, sadness, contempt, and surprise—based on the universally recognized
facial expressions he has studied. And Robert Plutchik
(1980, 1984) has made a case for eight basic emotions that
emerged from a mathematical analysis of people's ratings
of a large number of emotional terms (see **FIGURE 10•7**).
Recent work suggests that Plutchik's list could be expanded
to include pride (Azar, 2006; Tracy & Robins, 2006). Even
though different theorists approach the problem in different ways, their differences are relatively minor. The essential idea that we have a limited number of basic emotions
with a larger number of *secondary emotions* involves blends
of the more basic emotions.

Cultural Universals in Emotional Expression

You can usually tell when a friend is happy or angry by the
look on her face or by her actions. This can be useful in
deciding whether to spend Friday evening with her at the
movies. More generally, communication through emotional

expression aids our social interactions. But does raising the
eyebrows and rounding the mouth convey the same message
in Minneapolis as it does in Madagascar? Much research on
emotional expression has centered on such questions.

According to Paul Ekman (2003), the leading authority
on facial expression of emotions, people speak and understand the same basic "facial language" the world around.
Ekman's group has demonstrated that humans share a built-
in set of emotional expressions that testify to the common
biological heritage of the human species. Smiles, for example,
usually signal happiness, and frowns indicate sadness on the
faces of people in such far-flung places as Argentina, Japan,
Spain, Hungary, Poland, Sumatra, the United States, Vietnam,
the jungles of New Guinea, and the native villages north of the
Arctic Circle (Biehl et al., 1997).

But it may not surprise you to learn that gender can make
a difference in what we read into other people's facial expressions. One study found a bias toward seeing anger in men's faces
and happy expressions in women's faces (Becker et al., 2007).
This finding makes sense from an evolutionary perspective,
because angry men have always been a source of danger, while
a happy woman's face may have signaled safety (Azar, 2007).

You can check your own skill at interpreting facial
expressions by taking the quiz in the *Do It Yourself!* box on the
next page. Ekman and his colleagues (1987) claim that people
everywhere can recognize at least seven basic emotions: sadness, fear, anger, disgust, contempt, happiness, and surprise.
Nevertheless, huge differences exist across cultures in both
the context and intensity of emotional displays—because of
so-called **display rules.** In many Asian cultures, for example,
children are taught to control emotional responses—
especially negative ones—while many American children are
encouraged to express their feelings more openly (Smith
et al., 2006). As a result, people are generally better at judging
emotions of people from their own culture than in members
of another cultural group (Elfenbein & Ambady, 2003).

Regardless of culture, babies express emotions almost at
birth. In fact, a lusty cry is a sign of good health. And from
their first days of life, babies display a small repertoire of
facial expressions that communicate their feelings (Gan-
chrow et al., 1983). Likewise, the ability to read facial expressions develops early (but not so early as emotional expression).
Very young children pay close attention to facial expressions,
and by age 5 they nearly equal adults in their skill at reading
emotions in people's faces (Nelson, 1987). New evidence,
however, suggests that at least one of Ekman's "basic" emotional expressions doesn't come so easily. According to James
Russell, children do not understand the facial expressions
indicating disgust until about age 5, even though they use
words to express disgust (such as "gross" and "yucky") much
earlier (Bower, 2010; Russell & Widen, 2002).

---

display rules The permissible ways of displaying emotions in a particular
society.

do it yourself!

Take the facial emotion identification test to see how well you can identify each of the seven emotions that Ekman claims are culturally universal. Do not read the answers until you have matched each of the following pictures with one of these emotions: disgust, happiness, anger, sadness, surprise, fear, and contempt. Apparently, people everywhere in the world interpret these expressions in the same way. This tells us that certain facial expressions of emotion are probably rooted in our human genetic heritage.

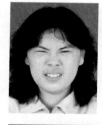 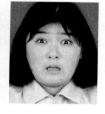

Answers The facial expressions are (top row from left) happiness, surprise, anger; (middle row) disgust, fear; (bottom row) sadness, contempt.

All this work on facial expressions points to a biological underpinning for our abilities to express and interpret a basic set of human emotions. Moreover, as Charles Darwin pointed out more than a century ago, some emotional expressions cross species boundaries. Darwin especially noted the similarity of our own facial expressions of fear and rage to those of chimpanzees and wolves (Darwin, 1998/1862; Ekman, 1984).

But are *all* emotional expressions universal? Cross-cultural psychologists tell us that certain emotional responses carry different meanings in different cultures (Ekman, 1992,

1994; Ellsworth, 1994). These, therefore, must be learned rather than innate. For example, what emotion do you suppose might be conveyed by sticking out the tongue? For Americans, this might indicate disgust or fatigue, while in China it can signify surprise. Similarly, a grin on an American face may indicate joy, while on a Japanese face it may just as easily mean embarrassment. To give one more example, a somber expression and downcast eyes might indicate unhappiness to someone in a Euro-American culture, whereas it could be a sign of respect to many Asians. Clearly, culture influences emotional expression. ◉▸

◉▸ **Simulate** the **Experiment**
Recognizing Facial Expressions of
Emotions at **MyPsychLab**

psychology matters

You may have suspected that some emotional differences between males and females have a biological basis. This would explain, for example, why certain emotional disturbances, such as panic disorder and depression, occur more commonly in women. Biological differences may also explain why men show more anger and display more physiological signs of emotional arousal during interpersonal conflicts than do women (Fischer et al., 2004). Anger, of course, can lead to violence—and men commit most of the world's violent acts.

Some gender differences, however, may depend as much on culture as on biology. For instance, in the United States, males and females may learn quite different lessons about emotional control. Display rules dictate that men and boys show their anger (Fischer, 1993). Indeed, they may be rewarded for displays of anger and aggression. On the other hand, they may also be punished for "weak" emotional displays such as crying, depression, and sadness (Gottman, 1994). At the same time, the pattern of reinforcement and punishment is reversed for females. Women and girls may receive encouragement for emotions that show vulnerability. But they may be punished for displaying emotions that suggest dominance (Fischer et al., 2004).

Despite these differences, neither sex is more emotionally expressive overall. Rather, cultures differ in emotional expression much more than do the sexes (Brannon, 2008; Wallbott et al., 1986). In Israel and Italy, for instance, men more often than women hide their feelings of sadness. The opposite holds true in Britain, Spain, Switzerland, and Germany, where women are more likely than men to hide sadness. In many collectivist cultures, as we have noted, both genders learn display rules to restrain all their emotional expressions. Overall, however, the differences among individuals overshadow the differences of either gender or culture.

CHECK YOUR UNDERSTANDING

✓•─[**Study** and **Review** at **MyPsychLab**

1. **Recall:** What are four main components of emotions?

2. **Recall:** Name an emotion that is not one of the culturally universal emotions identified by Ekman's research.

3. **Analysis:** Give an example that illustrates how *display rules* can modify the universal facial expressions of emotion.

4. **Recall:** What differences in emotional expression of men and women seem to be heavily influenced by culture?

5. **Understanding the Core Concept:** What is the adaptive value of communicating our emotional states?

   a. to help us understand our own needs better
   b. to help us deceive others about our emotional states and get what we want
   c. to help us anticipate each other's responses and so to live more easily in groups
   d. to help us get rid of strong negative emotions, such as fear and anger

Answers: 1. Four main components of emotions: physiological arousal, cognitive interpretation, subjective feelings, and behavioral expression **2.** Pride, optimism, jealousy, envy, anxiety—in fact, any emotion other than Ekman's seven universal emotions: sadness, fear, anger, disgust, contempt, happiness, and surprise **3.** Smiles may indicate happiness in some cultures and embarrassment in others. Other examples are mentioned in the section on display rules. **4.** Cultures often encourage men to show emotions related to anger, aggression, and dominance, while they encourage women to show emotions related to compliance and submission. **5.** c; our emotions convey our intentions to others.

‒ ‒ ‒ ‒ ‒ ‒

10.5 Key Question: What Processes Control Our Emotions?

Suppose that you are touring a haunted house at Halloween when a filmy figure startles you with ghostly "Boo!" Your emotional response is immediate. It may involve an outward reaction such as jumping, gasping, or screaming. At the same time, you respond internally with changes in your body chemistry, the function of your internal organs, and arousal in certain parts of your brain and autonomic nervous system. Moreover, gut-level emotional responses, such as an accelerated heartbeat, can persist long after you realize that you were really in no danger—after you realize that you were frightened merely by someone dressed in a sheet.

This suggests that emotion operates on both the conscious and unconscious levels. And that idea connects to one of the great recent discoveries in psychology: the existence of two emotion pathways in the brain. These dual pathways are the focus of the Core Concept for this section.

In the following pages, we will see how the young neuroscience of emotion has begun to identify the machinery that

CORE CONCEPT 10.5

Research has clarified the processes underlying both our conscious and unconscious emotional lives, shedding light on some old controversies.

produces our emotions. The details have not yet become fully clear, but we do have a broad-brush picture of the emotion pathways in the brain and their connections throughout the body. So in this last section, we will first see how the two emotion pathways work. Then we will see how they have helped resolve some ancient disputes in the field. Finally, at the end of this section, we will turn to a practical application to learn how emotional arousal can affect our performance on an examination or in an athletic contest.

The Neuroscience of Emotion

People who suffer from intense fears of snakes or spiders usually know that their responses are irrational, yet they can't seem to conquer them. But how can a person to hold two such conflicting mindsets? The answer lies in the brain's two distinct emotion processing systems (LeDoux, 1996, 2000).

Emotions in the Unconscious One emotion-processing system—the *fast response system*—operates mainly at an unconscious level, where it quickly screens incoming stimuli and helps us respond quickly to potentially dangerous events, even before they reach consciousness. This system, linked to *implicit memory,* acts as an early-warning defense that produces, for example, a near-instantaneous fright response to an unexpected loud noise (Helmuth, 2003b). It relies primarily on deep-brain circuitry that operates automatically, without requiring deliberate conscious control (see FIGURE 10•8).

[CONNECTION] Implicit memories involve material of which we are unaware—but that can affect behavior.

The unconscious emotion circuits have a built-in sensitivity to certain stimuli, such as snakes and spiders, that posed threats throughout human history. This explains why fears of spiders and snakes are more common than fears of, say, electricity or automobiles, which now cause more deaths than do spiders and snakes but have only recently become dangers. Moreover, this quick-response system can easily learn new fears through classical conditioning.

You can see how this configuration of the fast response system could be adaptive, because it errs on the side of caution. Unfortunately, the fast response system is also a slow-to-forget system, making it hard to extinguish the anxieties and fears that, instead, can blossom into more serious problems known as *phobias.*

[CONNECTION] *Phobias* are one form of anxiety disorder.

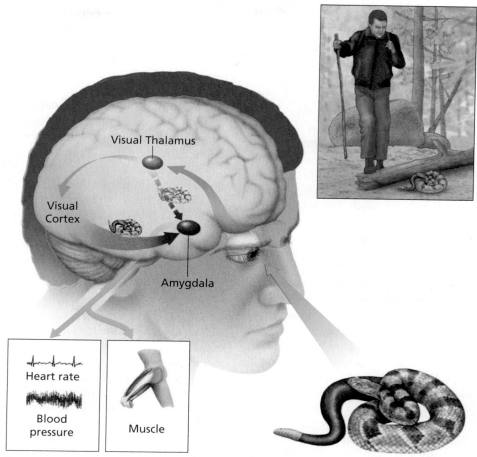

[FIGURE 10•8] Two Emotion-Processing Pathways Two emotion systems are at work when the hiker sees a snake. One is fast and unconscious; the other operates more slowly and consciously. The fast system routes incoming visual information through the visual thalamus to the amygdala (dotted pathway), which quickly initiates fear and avoidance responses—all occurring unconsciously. The slower pathway involves the visual cortex, which makes a more complete appraisal of the stimulus and also sends an emotional message to the amygdala and other lower brain structures. The result of this is a conscious perception of the situation and a conscious feeling of fear.

Conscious Emotional Processing The other emotional system—the one that involves conscious processing—has links to *explicit memory* (LeDoux, 1996; Mather, 2007). Its responses are comparatively slow and considered. This is the system that makes our hiker become cautious in places likely to harbor snakes. Because the conscious system uses different brain circuits from those supporting unconscious emotional processing, your conscious view of events can differ significantly from the emotions roused by your unconscious. Thus, if you have a phobia, you can truly be of "two minds"—feeling fear, despite "knowing" that there is no sensible basis for the feeling.

The Cerebral Cortex's Role in Emotion The cerebral cortex—the outermost layer of brain tissue and our "thinking cap"—plays the starring role in the conscious emotion path-

way, where it both interprets events and associates them with memories and feelings. As we have seen, emotional memories help us make decisions by attaching emotional values to the choices we face. It is this process at work when you ask yourself, "Do I want chocolate or strawberry?" or, "Do I want to save my money or buy a new stereo?"

We must add a caution here: Although emotion is an integral part of decision making, it does not necessarily guarantee the *right* decisions. Moreover, intense emotions can immobilize the organism, rendering measured decision making impossible (Pham, 2007). Extreme or prolonged emotional responses can produce physical illness.

One other cortical quirk deserves mention: The two frontal lobes have complementary roles in controlling our emotions. Just as distinct patches of cortex produce different sensations, positive and negative emotions are associated with opposite hemispheres, an effect called **lateralization of emotion**. The evidence comes from EEG recordings of normal people's emotional reactions along with EEGs of people with damage to the right or left hemisphere (Davidson et al., 2000). In general, the right hemisphere specializes in negative emotions, such as anger and depression, while the left processes more positive, joyful emotions (Kosslyn et al., 2002).

Emotions Where the Cortex Meets the Limbic System Neuroscientists now think they know where emotion and reason meet in the brain—where the conscious emotion-processing pathway meets the limbic system. It's a small patch of brain with a big name: the *ventromedial prefrontal cortex (VMPFC)*. Located on the floor of the brain's frontal lobes, just behind the eyes, the VMPFC has extensive connections with both the amygdala and the hippocampus (Wagar & Thagard, 2006). There, like a recording technician combining inputs for a sound track, the VMPFC mixes external stimulation with the body's "gut" reaction and converts the result into an emotional memory: Was it positive or negative? Did it make your skin creep? Did you feel a lump in your throat? A knot in your stomach? Thanks to your VMPFC, most of your memories probably have such visceral associations attached.

The fast-and-unconscious emotional pathway also connects to the brain's limbic system, as you can see in **FIGURE 10•8**. Situated in the layer above the brain stem, the limbic structures undoubtedly evolved as control systems for behaviors used in attack, defense, and retreat: the "fight-or-flight" response (Caldwell, 1995; LeDoux, 1994, 1996). Evidence for this comes from lesioning (cutting) or electrically stimulating parts of the limbic system, which can produce dramatic changes in emotional responding. Depending on which part of the limbic system is affected, tame animals may become killers, whereas prey and predators may become peaceful companions (Delgado, 1969).

Particularly well documented is the importance of the amygdala in the emotion of fear (LeDoux, 1996; Whalen,

1998; Winkielman et al., 2007). Like a guard dog, the amygdala stands alert for threats (Hamann et al., 2002; Helmuth, 2003a). As you can see in the figure, the amygdala receives messages from the quick-and-unconscious emotion-processing pathway as well as from the longer-and-slower conscious pathway.

The Autonomic Nervous System's Role in Emotion
When you become emotionally aroused, the messages that you "take to heart" (and to your other internal organs) flash to their destinations through the autonomic nervous system (Levenson, 1992). It's the parasympathetic division that usually dominates in pleasant emotions. But when you are startled or when you experience some unpleasant emotion, the sympathetic division goes into action (see **TABLE 10•3**).

[**CONNECTION**] The autonomic nervous system controls the internal organs along with many signs of emotional arousal.

Suppose you are in an emergency. (A speeding car is coming directly at you!). Your brain alerts your body by means of messages carried along the nerves of the sympathetic system. Signals speeding along the sympathetic pathways direct the adrenal glands to release stress hormones. Other signals make your heart race and blood pressure rise. Simultaneously, the sympathetic system directs certain blood vessels to constrict, diverting energy to the voluntary muscles and away from the stomach and intestines. (This causes the feeling of a "knot" in your stomach.)

When the emergency passes, the parasympathetic division takes over, carrying instructions that counteract the emergency orders of a few moments earlier. You may, however, remain aroused for some time after experiencing a

lateralization of emotion The two brain hemispheres process different various emotions. The left hemisphere apparently focuses on positive emotions (for example, happiness), while the right hemisphere deals primarily with negative emotions (such as anger).

[**TABLE 10•3**] Responses Associated with Emotion

Component of Emotion	Type of Response	Example
Physiological arousal	Neural, hormonal, visceral, and muscular changes	Increased heart rate, blushing, becoming pale, sweating, rapid breathing
Subjective feelings	The private experience of one's internal affective state	Feelings of rage, sadness, happiness
Cognitive interpretation	Attaching meaning to the emotional experience by drawing on memory and perceptual processes	Blaming someone, perceiving a threat
Social/behavioral reactions	Expressing emotion through gestures, facial expressions, or other actions	Smiling, crying, screaming for help

strong emotional activation because hormones continue to circulate in the bloodstream. If the emotion-provoking situation is prolonged (as when you work for a boss who hassles you every day), the sustained emergency response can sap your energy and cause both physical and mental problems.

Emotional Chemistry The body produces hundreds of chemicals, but among the most important for our emotions are the neurotransmitters serotonin, epinephrine (adrenalin), and norepinephrine. Serotonin is linked with feelings of depression. Epinephrine is the hormone that accompanies fear. Norepinephrine is more abundant in anger.

[CONNECTION] Drugs that inhibit the reuptake of serotonin are often used to treat depression.

Steroid hormones (the same ones abused by some bodybuilders and other athletes) also exert a powerful influence on our emotions. In addition to their effects on muscles, steroids act on nerve cells, causing them to change their excitability. This is a normal part of the body's response to emergency situations. But when steroid drugs are ingested over extended periods, these potent chemicals have the effect of keeping the body (including the brain) in a continual emergency state. Brain circuits, especially those associated with arousal, threat, stress, and strong emotions, remain in a state of heightened alert. The result can be "roid" rage or, sometimes, depression (Daly et al., 2003; Miller et al., 2002). You will learn much more about the effects of steroid hormones in our discussion of stress in Chapter 13.

Can you learn to control these responses? Yes—at least to some extent. Biofeedback and cognitive-behavioral therapy target just such responses associated with anxiety, fear, and anger. In the final section of this chapter, we will see how programs aimed at developing *emotional intelligence* can help people learn to control their emotional responses before they catapult out of control. In the meantime, let's see how a certain level of emotional arousal helps you achieve your best performance in athletics, on the job, and even during your next psychology exam.

[CONNECTION] Cognitive-behavioral therapy focuses on changing both mental and behavioral responses.

Arousal, Performance, and the Inverted U

Athletes always want to be "up" for a game—but how far up should they be? Cheering sports fans might think that increased arousal will always improve performance—but that is not necessarily true. Too much arousal can make an athlete "choke" and cause performance to falter. The same is true when you take an examination. Up to a point, increasing levels of arousal can motivate you to study and to remember at

exam time what you studied. Unfortunately, only slightly higher levels can cause test anxiety and poor performance.

This complex relationship between arousal and behavior has been studied both in laboratory animals and in humans under all sorts of conditions. For example, in experiments on learning, the curve plotting the performance of hungry rats working to get a food reward first rises and then later declines with increasing arousal. The same pattern holds for humans in a variety of circumstances, including neurosurgeons, truck drivers, and professional entertainers.

Psychologists call this the **inverted U function** (so named because the graph resembles an upside-down letter U, as you can see in FIGURE 10•9). It suggests that either too little or too much arousal can impair performance. Think about it: How much pressure would you want your dentist or surgeon to feel? Which brings us to a second important point.

The optimum amount of arousal varies with the task. As you see in the figure, it takes more arousal to achieve peak performance on simple tasks or tasks in which responses have been thoroughly rehearsed (as in most sports) than it does on complex tasks or those that require much thinking and planning as the situation develops. So it should not surprise you that cheers and high levels of arousal are more likely to boost performance in basketball games than in brain surgery.

Finally, the amount of stimulation needed to produce optimal arousal also varies with the individual. In fact, some people seem to thrive on the thrill of dangerous sports, such as rock climbing and skydiving—activities that would produce immobilizing levels of arousal in most of us. Marvin Zuckerman (2004), who has studied people he calls **sensation seekers,** believes that such individuals have a biological need for high levels of stimulation. Frank Farley also refers to them as Big T (thrill-seeking) personalities, who he believes are prominent in sports, business, science, and art. Einstein was a Big T "mental personality," says Farley (Munsey, 2006). Research suggests that the underlying biology involves the brain's dopamine pathways (Bevins, 2001). You can test your own sensation-seeking tendencies with Zuckerman's scale, found in the *Do It Yourself!* box.

Theories of Emotion: Resolving Some Old Issues

Let's return to our hungry bear: Suppose that you have the unlikely misfortune to encounter a this creature while on your way to class one morning. We will bet that you will experience the emotion of fear. But what internal process actually produces the *feeling* of fear? Does it come from

---

inverted U function A term that describes the relationship between arousal and performance. Both low and high levels of arousal produce lower performance than does a moderate level of arousal.

sensation seekers In Zuckerman's theory, individuals who have a biological need for higher levels of stimulation than do most other people.

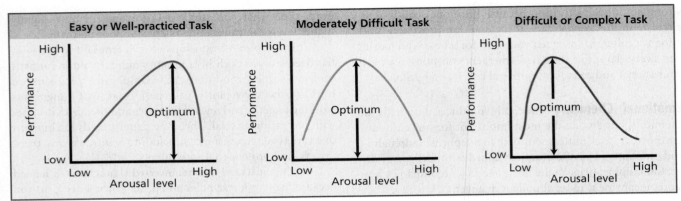

[**FIGURE 10•9**] **The Inverted U** Performance varies with arousal level and task difficulty. For easy or well-practiced tasks, a higher level of arousal increases performance effectiveness. However, for difficult or complex tasks, a lower level or arousal is optimal. A moderate level of arousal is generally best for tasks of moderate difficulty. These inverted U-shaped functions show that performance is poorest at both low and high extremes.

do it yourself!

Are You a Sensation Seeker?

Different people seem to need different levels of emotional arousal. Marvin Zuckerman argues that "sensation seekers" have an unusually high need for stimulation that produces arousal. In addition to the need for thrills, sensation seekers may be impulsive, engage in risky behaviors, prefer new experiences, and be easily bored (Kohn et al., 1979; Malatesta et al., 1981; Zuckerman, 1974).

From your score on the Sensation Seeking Scale below, you can get a rough idea of your own level of sensation seeking. You may also want to give this scale to some of your friends. Do you suppose that most people choose friends who have sensation-seeking tendencies similar to their own? Wide differences in sensation-seeking tendencies may account for strain on close relationships when one person is reluctant to take the risks that the other actively seeks.

The Sensation-Seeking Scale

Choose A or B for each item, depending on which response better describes your preferences. The scoring key appears at the end.

1. **A** I would like a job that requires a lot of traveling.

   B I would prefer a job in one location.

2. **A** I am invigorated by a brisk, cold day.

   B I can't wait to get indoors on a cold day.

3. **A** I get bored seeing the same old faces.

   B I like the comfortable familiarity of everyday friends.

4. **A** I would prefer living in an ideal society in which everyone is safe, secure, and happy.

   B I would have preferred living in the unsettled days of our history.

5. **A** I sometimes like to do things that are a little frightening.

   B A sensible person avoids activities that are dangerous.

6. **A** I would not like to be hypnotized.

   B I would like to have the experience of being hypnotized.

7. **A** The most important goal of life is to live it to the fullest and experience as much as possible.

   B The most important goal of life is to find peace and happiness.

8. **A** I would like to try parachute jumping.

   B I would never want to try jumping out of a plane, with or without a parachute.

9. **A** I enter cold water gradually, giving myself time to get used to it.

   B I like to dive or jump right into the ocean or a cold pool.

10. **A** When I go on a vacation, I prefer the comfort of a good room and bed.

    B When I go on a vacation, I prefer the change of camping out.

11. **A** I prefer people who are emotionally expressive even if they are a bit unstable.

    B I prefer people who are calm and even tempered.

Sensation seekers thrive on stimulation that might terrify others.

12. A A good painting should shock or jolt the senses.

   B A good painting should give one a feeling of peace and security.

13. A People who ride motorcycles must have some kind of unconscious need to hurt themselves.

   B I would like to drive or ride a motorcycle.

Key: Each of the following answers earns one point: 1A, 2A, 3A, 4B, 5A, 6B, 7A, 8A, 9B, 10B, 11A, 12A, 13B. Compare your point total with the following norms for sensation seeking: **0–3:** Very low, **4–5:** Low, **6–9:** Average, **10–11:** High, **12–13:** Very high

Source: Zuckerman, M. (1978, February). The search for high sensation. *Psychology Today, 12,* 38–46. Reprinted by permission of Sussex Publishers, Inc.

the thought, "Uh-oh. I'm in danger"? Or does it come from sensing your racing heart and wrenching gut? And, you may be wondering, why would anyone care where emotions come from?

In response to the last question: Psychologists have long argued over the relationship between emotion, cognition, and physical responses—not only out of intellectual curiosity but also because an understanding of emotion is a key to finding effective treatments for certain emotional problems, such as panic attacks and depression, as well as the everyday problems of anger, envy, and jealousy. Should we try to treat anger, for example, by targeting angry thoughts? Or should we focus on angry behaviors or, perhaps, the visceral responses that accompany rage?

Recent discoveries in neuroscience have helped us resolve some long-disputed issues surrounding the interaction of biology, cognition, and behavior in emotion (Forgas, 2008). Let's look briefly at the controversies and how new insights have begun to resolve them.

Do Our Feelings Come from Physical Responses?

In the early days of psychology, just over a century ago, William James taught that physical sensations underlie our feelings. "We feel sorry because we cry, angry because we strike, afraid because we tremble," James said (1890/1950, p. 1006). As for your response to the bear, James argued that you would not run because you are afraid, but that *you would feel afraid because you run.* While this statement may appear absurd on its face, James was no fool. He knew that emotion was more than just feelings. What he was really saying was something quite sensible—that emotions require a *combination* of cognitions and physical sensations—and that the physical sensations were the feelings. In James' (1884) own words:

> Without the bodily states following on the perception [of the bear], the latter would be purely cognitive in form, pale, colourless, destitute of emotional warmth. We might then see the bear, and judge it best to run, receive the insult and deem it right to strike, but we could not actually *feel* afraid or angry (pp. 189–190).

This view, simultaneously proposed by Danish psychologist Carl Lange, became known as the **James–Lange theory.**

Or Do Our Feelings Come from Cognitions?

Other scientists, notably Walter Cannon and Philip Bard, objected that physical changes in our behavior or our internal organs occur too slowly to account for split-second emotional reactions, such as those we feel in the face of danger. They also objected that our physical responses are not varied enough to account for the whole palate of human emotion. In their view, referred to as the **Cannon–Bard theory,** cognitive appraisal of a situation (the hungry bear again) simultaneously produces both the emotional feeling and the physical response.

Which side was right? It turns out that each had part of the truth. On the one hand, modern neuroscience has confirmed that our physical state can influence our emotions—much as the James–Lange theory argued (LeDoux, 1996). In fact, you may have noted how your own physical state affects your emotions, as when you get edgy feelings after drinking too much coffee or become grumpy when hungry. In a similar fashion, psychoactive drugs, such as alcohol or nicotine or Prozac, influence the physical condition of the brain and hence alter our moods.

Other support for the James–Lange theory comes from the discovery that the brain maintains memories of physical states that are associated with events. These are the "somatic markers" we mentioned earlier (Damasio, 1994; Niedenthal, 2007). When you see the bear leaping toward you, your brain quickly conjures a body-memory of the physical response it had previously in another threatening situation. This *somatic-marker hypothesis,* then, effectively counters Walter Cannon's objection that physical changes in the body occur too slowly to cause our feelings—because the somatic marker of emotion resides in the brain itself.

James–Lange theory The proposal that an emotion-provoking stimulus produces a physical response that, in turn, produces an emotion.

Cannon–Bard theory The counterproposal that an emotional feeling and an internal physiological response occur at the same time: One is not the cause of the other. Both were believed to be the result of cognitive appraisal of the situation.

On the other hand—and in support of the Cannon–Bard view—emotions can also be aroused by external cues detected either by the conscious or the unconscious emotional system. Thus, emotion can result from conscious thought (as when you fret over an exam) or from unconscious memories (as when you feel disgust at the sight of a food that had once made you sick). Incidentally, cognitive psychologists now believe that both depression and phobic reactions can result from conditioned responses of the unconscious emotional system.

When the Situation Gets Complicated: The Two-Factor Theory

As we noted, you can make yourself emotional just by thinking, as any student with "test anxiety" will testify. The more you think about the dire consequences of failing a test, the more the anxiety builds. "Method" actors, like the late Marlon Brando, have long exploited this fact to make themselves feel real emotions on stage. They do so by recalling an incident from their own experience that produced the emotion they want to portray, such as grief, joy, or anger.

Stanley Schachter's (1971) **two-factor theory** adds an interesting twist to the role of cognition in emotion. His theory suggests that the emotions we feel depend on our appraisal of both (a) our internal *physical state* and (b) the *external situation* in which we find ourselves. Strange effects occur when these two factors conflict—as they did in the following classic study of emotion, which enterprising students may want to adopt in order to spice up their romantic lives.

An attractive female researcher positioned herself at the end of a footbridge and interviewed unsuspecting males who had just crossed. On one occasion she selected a safe, sturdy bridge; another time, a wobbly suspension bridge across a deep canyon—deliberately selected to elicit physical arousal. The researcher, pretending to be interested in the effects of scenery on creativity, asked the men to write brief stories about a picture. She also invited them to call her if they wanted more information about the study. As predicted, those men who had just crossed the wobbly bridge (and were, presumably, more physically aroused by the experience) wrote stories containing more sexual imagery than those who used the safer structure. And four times as many of them called the female researcher "to get more information"! Apparently, the men who had crossed the shaky bridge interpreted their increased arousal as emotional attraction to the female interviewer (Dutton & Aron, 1974).

Before you rush out to find the love of your life on a wobbly bridge, we must caution you, numerous attempts to test the two-factor theory have supported the two-factor theory only under certain conditions (Leventhal & Tomarken, 1986; Sinclair et al., 1994). What are the conditions under which we are likely to confound physical arousal with emotion? Normally, external events confirm what our biology tells us, without much need for elaborate interpretation—as when you feel disgust at smelling an unpleasant odor or joy at seeing an

The two-factor theory would predict that decaffeinated-coffee drinkers who accidentally drank coffee with caffeine could mistake the resulting physical arousal for an emotion. Could that be happening here?

During a break at the Western Psychological Association convention near Vancouver, British Columbia, psychologists Susan Horton and Bob Johnson (one of your authors) reenact the Dutton study of attraction on the Capilano Bridge, where the original study was performed.

old friend. But what happens when we experience physical arousal from not-so-obvious sources, such as exercise, heat, or drugs? Misattribution, it seems, is most likely in a complex environment where many stimuli are competing for our attention, as in the bridge study. It is also likely in an environment where we have faulty information about our physical

---

two-factor theory The idea that emotion results from the cognitive appraisal of both physical arousal (Factor #1) and an emotion-provoking stimulus (Factor #2).

emotional intelligence The ability to understand and control emotional responses.

Theories of Emotion

James–Lange Theory: Every emotion corresponds to a distinctive pattern of physiological arousal.

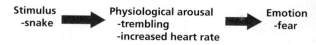

Cannon–Bard Theory: Emotions arise from a cognitive appraisal (interpretation) of the stimulus. (This theory was proposed as an alternative to the James–Lange theory because Cannon and Bard believed that emotions occur too quickly to be the result of physiological arousal, as the James–Lange theory asserted.)

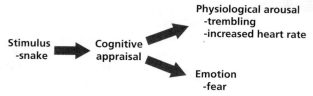

Schacter's Two-Factor Theory: Emotions arise from a cognitive interpretation of the stimulus *and* physiological arousal. Sometimes, however, the person attributes feelings of arousal to one stimulus (the snake), even though the arousal has really been caused by another stimulus—e.g., caffeine or, as in the Capilano Bridge study, having just crossed the swinging bridge. (Dutton & Eron, 1974).

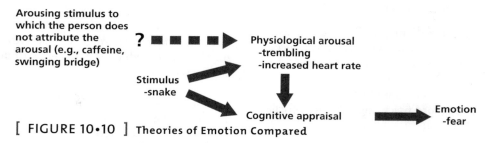

[**FIGURE 10•10**] **Theories of Emotion Compared**

arousal, as when unsuspected caffeine in a soft drink makes us edgy (see FIGURE 10•10).

How Much Conscious Control Do We Have Over Our Emotions?

The ability to deal with emotions is important in many professions. Physicians, nurses, firefighters, and police officers, for example, must be able to comfort others yet maintain a "professional distance" when dealing with disability and death. Likewise, in many social situations, it can be desirable to mask or modify what you are feeling. If you dislike a professor, you might be wise not to show your true emotions. And if you have strong romantic feelings toward someone—more than he or she realizes—it might be safest to reveal the depth of your feelings gradually, lest you frighten the person away with too much too soon. Even in leisure activities like

playing poker or planning your next move in chess, you will be most successful if you keep your real feelings, beliefs, and intentions guarded. All of these examples testify that emotional control has an important role in our ability to interact with other people.

Developing Emotional Intelligence Peter Salovey and John Mayer (1990) have suggested that it takes a certain sort of "smarts" to understand and control one's emotions. They called it **emotional intelligence.** More recently, Salovey and his colleague Daisy Grewal (2005) have emphasized four components of emotional intelligence:

- **Perceiving emotions.** The ability to detect and decipher emotions in oneself and others
- **Using emotions.** The ability to harness one's emotions in the service of thinking and problem solving

An Army squad leader needs emotional intelligence to lead people under stressful conditions.

- **Understanding emotions.** The ability to comprehend the complex relationships among emotions, such as the relationship between grief and anger or how two people can have different emotional reactions to the same event

- **Managing emotions.** The ability to regulate one's own emotions and influence those of others

The Predictive Power of Emotional Intelligence. As Salovey and Grewal suggest, those with high emotional intelligence are not only tuned in to their own emotions and those of others, but they can also manage their negative feelings and curtail inappropriate expression of their impulses. The power of this ability can be seen in Stanford psychologist Walter Mischel's ingenious "marshmallow test."

> Just imagine you're four years old, and someone makes the following proposal: If you'll wait until after he runs an errand, you can have two marshmallows for a treat. If you can't wait until then, you can have only one—but you can have it right now (Goleman, 1995, pp. 80–81).

How did the children in this experiment respond to the temptation of the single marshmallow that sat before them, within reach? Goleman continues:

Some four-year-olds were able to wait what must surely have seemed an endless fifteen to twenty minutes for the experimenter to return. To sustain themselves in their struggle they covered their eyes so they wouldn't have to stare at temptation, or rested their heads in their arms, talked to themselves, sang, played games with their hands and feet, even tried to go to sleep. These plucky preschoolers got the two-marshmallow reward. But others, more impulsive, grabbed the one marshmallow, almost always within seconds of the experimenter's leaving the room on his "errand" (Goleman, 1995, pp. 80–81).

When these same children were tracked down in adolescence, the amazing predictive power of the marshmallow test was revealed. As a group, those who had curbed their impulse to grab the single marshmallow were, as adolescents, better off on all counts. They had become more self-reliant, more effective in interpersonal relationships, better students, and better able to handle frustration and stress. By contrast, the children who had given in to temptation had adolescent lives marked by troubled relationships, shyness, stubbornness, and indecisiveness. They also were much more likely to hold low opinions of themselves, to mistrust others, and to be easily provoked by frustrations. In the academic sphere, they were more likely to be uninterested in school. Daniel Goleman (1995) notes that the marshmallow test also correlated clearly with SAT scores: Those who, as 4-year-olds, were able to delay gratification scored, on the average, 210 points higher than did their counterparts who had grabbed the single marshmallow years earlier.

The usefulness of the marshmallow test, of course, is limited to young children. But other, more sophisticated measures have been developed for use with older children and adults (see FIGURE 10•11). The Mayer-Salovey-Caruso Emotional Intelligence Test (MSCEIT), for example, predicts satisfaction with social relationships among college students, deviant behavior in male adolescents, marital satisfaction, and success on the job (Salovey & Grewal, 2005).

But, cautions John Mayer (1999), emotional intelligence is not a perfect predictor of success, happiness, and good relationships. Nor should we think of it as a replacement for tra-

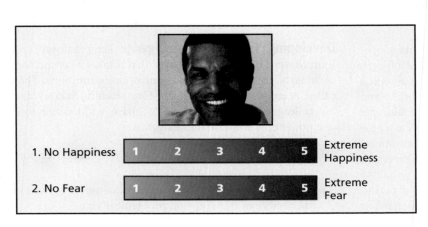

1. No Happiness [1 2 3 4 5] Extreme Happiness
2. No Fear [1 2 3 4 5] Extreme Fear

[FIGURE 10•11] Sample Item from a Test of Emotional Intelligence Shown is an item similar to those found on the Mayer-Salovey-Caruso Emotional Intelligence Test. Respondents are asked to click on the number on each scale that corresponds to the emotional state of the person shown in the photo.

Source: Salovey, P. & Grewel, D. (2005) The science of emotional intelligence. Current Directions in *Psychological Science, 14,* 283. Reprinted by permission of Blackwell Publishing.

ditional IQ scores. Rather, says Mayer, emotional intelligence is merely another variable that can help us refine our understanding of behavior.

The Nature and Nurture of Emotional Intelligence. Is emotional intelligence a characteristic fixed by nature, or is it nurtured by experience? Indeed, studies show that severely maltreated children often have difficulty as adults in forming attachments and interpreting emotional expressions (Pollak, 2008).

But Goleman (1995) believes that learning can also have a positive effect. Based on programs already in place in visionary schools across the country, he has a plan for adding emotional training to the curriculum. The result, he believes, will bring improved relationships, increased self-respect, and even, perhaps, gains in academic achievement. The takeaway message, then, is that while emotions do sometimes slip out of control, we are not simply at their mercy. Emotional understanding and control are skills that can be acquired (Clifton & Myers, 2005).

Not so fast, say Matthew Lieberman and Robert Rosenthal (2001) in an article titled "Why Introverts Can't Always Tell Who Likes Them." Lieberman and Rosenthal suggest that emotional intelligence may be just another name for extraversion, a personality characteristic that has roots in biology as well as learning. Introverts, according to their study, are just not as good at sensing other people's emotions, especially in settings that require multitasking—and, Lieberman and Rosenthal suggest, perhaps they can never learn to be as sensitive as extraverts. The resolution of this issue remains uncertain at the moment.

Critics also point out that emotional control has a dark side. Just as some people get into trouble when they let their emotions—particularly negative emotions—go unchecked, others take emotional control to the opposite extreme. They become so guarded that they never convey affection, humor, or honest displeasure. Studies also show that overcontrolling emotions interferes with memory for emotionally charged events (Carpenter, 2000; Richards & Gross, 2000). Before we launch a program of encouraging emotional control, perhaps we should consider what such training may do to people who already overcontrol their emotions. In fact, research shows that emotionally healthy people know how both to control and to express their emotions—and when it is appropriate to do so (Bonanno et al., 2004).

Read about Keeping Anger Under Control at **MyPsychLab**

Let It Out: A Dangerous Myth Experts agree that the public clings to some dangerous misinformation about venting anger, a process also known as *catharsis*. On television shows, for example, you can see people attacking and humiliating others, as if the public dumping of hostile feelings will somehow eliminate their anger. In fact, "getting it out of your system" is likely to bring only the most fleeting feeling of satisfaction. It's also likely to encourage more angry responses in the future.

While many people believe that "bottling up" emotions risks an uncontrollable emotional outburst, this belief is at odds with the truth. While expressing your anger can sometimes be helpful, merely giving vent to your rage usually just makes you more angry—even if you just punch the wall or throw your coffee mug. Moreover, studies show that such ventilation makes you more apt to react with anger the next time you are provoked (Tavris, 1989, 1995).

Sure, there are examples of angry workers who have "gone postal" on a murderous rampage—but there is no evidence at all to suggest that giving them an opportunity to hit a punching bag or give the boss "a piece of their mind" would have prevented such tragedies. In fact, the evidence suggests just the opposite.

As for your own anger management, a saner and safer strategy is to keep your feelings to yourself, at least until the passion of your anger has subsided and you can be more rational about the nature of your real complaint and what might be done to solve the problem (Tavris, 1989, 1995). Often, all it takes to defuse a tense and angry situation is to communicate the facts and your feelings to the person toward whom you feel anger.

psychology matters

Detecting Deception

How easy is it for people to conceal their emotions while telling a lie? You might think you can spot deception when someone fails to "look you in the eye" or fidgets nervously. If so, you could be setting yourself up to be duped. Most of us are poor lie detectors—or truth detectors, for that matter. One reason is that our social interactions usually occur in familiar situations, with people we know and trust, and where we pay little attention to nonverbal cues.

Experts who study deception find that these nonverbal cues are the best signs of deceit: A person who deliberately tries to hoodwink us may "leak" uncontrolled nonverbal signals of deception. Knowing how to read these cues could help you decide whether a huckster is lying to you, your physician might be holding back some bad news, or a politician is shading the truth. Keep in mind, however, that the studies of deception are based on probabilities, not certainties. None of this has yet reached the level of an exact science.

The real key to effective deception detection, say the experts, is observing a person's behavior over time. Without the chance for repeated observations, you are much less able to judge a person's honesty (Marsh, 1988). Still, we can offer some pointers for situations in which even a little help in deception detection might be better than none at all (Adelson, 2004; DePaulo et al., 2003):

- Some lies involve giving false information, as when a used-car salesperson is telling you that a junker is in good working order. In such cases, the effort to hide the truth requires some cognitive effort. This may result in heightened attention (evident in dilation of the pupils), longer pauses in speech (to choose words carefully), and more constrained movement and gesturing (in an attempt to avoid "giving away" the truth).

- Criminals sometimes confess to crimes for which they know the police have other evidence of guilt. In these cases, criminals may lie to minimize the extent of their involvement in the crime. Analysis of such taped confessions shows that the liar tends to repeat selectively the distorted or falsified details of the story (Dingfelder, 2004c).

- When a lie involves hiding one's true feelings of anger or exuberance—as a good poker player does when holding a straight flush—the liar may become physically and behaviorally more aroused and animated. This becomes evident in postural shifts, speech errors, nervous gestures (such as preening by touching or stroking the hair or face), and shrugging (as if to dismiss the lie).

- The face is easier to control than the body, so a deceiver may work on keeping a "poker face" but forget to restrain bodily clues. A smart deception detective might therefore concentrate on a speaker's body movements: Are they rhythmic? Are they calculated? Do the hands move freely or nervously?

- The eyes sometimes give deceivers away—especially when they're using the common social deception of trying to look happy or amused when they are not. While our attention may more naturally focus on a smile as an indicator of happiness or amusement, the mouth can be manipulated much more easily than the muscles around the eyes. Only in genuine grins do the eye muscles crinkle up the skin on either side of the eyes. You can test your ability to tell a real from a fake smile in the *Do It Yourself!* box.

- Speaking of eyes, the ability to "look you straight in the eye" is, in fact, a reasonably good indicator of truth telling—but only when dealing with people who usually tell the truth. When they do lie, their amateurish efforts to deceive often show up in averted gaze, reduced blinking (indicating concentration of attention elsewhere), and less smiling. You may be fooled by a practiced liar who can look straight at you while telling complete fiction.

- Culture affects the way we distinguish truth from lies. Thus, people are more accurate in detecting liars among people in their own culture. For example, one study found that Jordanians are generally more animated than Americans when talking and that Americans may incorrectly perceive this as "nervousness" and judge the Jordanian to be lying (Bond & Atoum, 2000; Dingfelder, 2004c).

And what about *polygraph* machines—so-called "lie detectors" that are sometimes used by police interrogators and government security agencies? We will take a closer look at these devices in our *Critical Thinking Applied* section on the next page.

do it yourself!

The Eyes Have It

Can you tell if people are sincere when they smile at you? Smiles aren't made just with the mouth, but with the whole face, especially the eyes. A real smile is different from a fake one, primarily around the eyes. Specifically, when we feel genuine joy or mirth, the orbicularis occuli muscles wrinkle up the skin around the eyes.

With this in mind, take a look at these two pictures of smiling faces and see if you can tell which one is the real smile and which one is forced.

CHECK YOUR UNDERSTANDING

✔•─Study and **Review** at **MyPsychLab**

1. **Recall:** During emotional arousal, the _____ nervous system sends messages to the internal organs.

2. **Application:** Give an example of a situation in which a person would be likely to misattribute the source of arousal.

3. **Recall:** The debate between William James and Walter Cannon over the nature of emotion involved the roles played by

   a. biology, cognition, and behavior.
   b. nature and nurture.
   c. learning, memory, and instincts.
   d. arousal and stress.

4. **Recall:** Damasio's *somatic marker hypothesis* gives support for the James–Lange theory of emotion because

    a. it argues that emotions are purely psychological, not biological.

    b. it requires cognitive appraisal of all factors involved in emotion.

    c. it argues that physical responses involved in emotion are represented in the brain.

    d. it requires *no* cognitive appraisal of feelings.

5. **Analysis:** The "marshmallow test" revealed emotional intelligence by measuring a child's

    a. self-control.

    b. ability to manipulate others.

    c. blood sugar level.

    d. interactions with other children under highly stressful conditions.

6. **Application:** Venting your anger on some safe object, such as a punching bag, is likely toaccounting for the differences between one person and another?

    a. help you get rid of your anger.

    b. make you more angry.

    c. have no effect.

    d. extinguish the aggressive impulse in your unconscious (fast) emotional pathway.

7. **Understanding the Core Concept:** Briefly describe the two emotion pathways that neuroscientists have discovered.

Answers 1. autonomic **2.** The "swinging bridge" study is the classic example, but others include unexpected physical changes that might occur when you are getting sick, becoming overheated or dehydrated, or mistakenly drinking a caffeinated beverage instead of one without caffeine. **3.** a **4.** c **5.** a **6.** b **7.** The fast pathway produces a near-immediate response and operates mainly at an unconscious level. The slower pathway involves the cerebral cortex and operates largely at the conscious level.

— — — — — — —

CRITICAL THINKING APPLIED

Do Lie Detectors Really Detect Lies?

The **polygraph** or "lie detector" test is based on the assumption that people will display physical signs of arousal when lying; so most polygraph machines make a record of the suspect's heart rate, breathing rate, perspiration, and blood pressure. Occasionally, voice-print analysis is also employed. Thus, the device really acts as an emotional arousal detector rather than a direct indicator of truth or lies. But does it work? Let's see how a polygraph examination is conducted.

Polygraphers typically employ several tricks of their trade. They may start the interview by persuading the subject that the machine is highly accurate. A common ploy is to ask a series of loaded questions designed to provoke obvious emotional reactions. For example, "Did you ever, in your life, take anything that did not belong to you?" In another favorite technique, the examiner uses a deceptive stimulation procedure, or "stim test," in which the subject draws a card from a "stacked" deck. Then, the examiner pretends to identify the card from the subject's polygraph responses (Kleinmuntz & Szucko, 1984).

When the actual interrogation begins, it will consist of an artistic mix of *relevant questions, irrelevant questions,* and *control questions.* The irrelevant questions ("Are you sitting down right now?") are designed to elicit truthful answers accompanied by a physical response consistent with truth telling. The control questions ("Did you ever lie to your parents?") are designed to elicit an anxious, emotionally aroused response pattern. Then, the examiner can compare the subject's responses to these two types of questions with responses to the relevant questions ("Did you steal the jewels?"). It is assumed that a guilty suspect will give a stronger response to these questions than to the irrelevant and control questions.

What Are the Critical Issues?

If you are unfamiliar with the controversy surrounding "lie detectors," you should inform yourself on the positions taken by both sides (not a bad approach to any issue!). A good way to begin is by typing "polygraph" into your favorite search engine. Your authors have done this and have searched the scientific literature, as well. Here's what we have turned up.

Is There a Possibility of Bias? We think there is, and it comes in two forms—both on the "pro" side of the issue. A formidable polygraph industry has an economic interest in convincing the public that polygraph tests can, indeed, distinguish truth tellers from liars. A second form of bias comes from those obsessed by fear of crime and terrorism and who see humanity in stark black-and-white terms—as consisting of good people and evil people.

Are There Logical Errors Involved? We believe that proponents of the polygraph commit two types of logical error. The first involves pointing to individual cases in which they claim a "lie detector" test either revealed a liar or forced a confession from a reluctant suspect. This is nothing more than "proof by testimonial," as we see all the time in ads for "miracle" weight-loss products or engine-oil additives. The fact is that testimonials are no substitute for a controlled scientific test.

The other main logical error is *oversimplification.* By focusing on apparent successes, they may gloss over the failures—which, in the case of the polygraph, can be quite serious. As we will see, the polygraph failures can lead to a

---

polygraph A device that records or graphs many ("poly") measures of physical arousal, such as heart rate, breathing, perspiration, and blood pressure. A polygraph is often called a "lie detector," even though it is really an arousal detector.Cannon–Bard theory

surprisingly large number of honest people being identified as liars.

What Is the Evidence? Without a doubt, wrongdoers sometimes confess when confronted with polygraph evidence against them. Yet, critics have pointed out several problems with the polygraphic procedure that could easily land innocent people in prison and let the guilty walk free (Aftergood, 2000). For example, polygraph subjects know when they are suspects, so some will give heightened responses to the critical questions even when they are innocent. On the other hand, some people can give deceptive responses because they have learned to control or distort their emotional responses. To do so, they may employ simple physical movements, drugs, or biofeedback training—a procedure in which people are given moment-to-moment information on certain biological responses, such as perspiration or heart rate (Saxe et al., 1985). Either way, a polygraph examiner risks incorrectly identifying innocent people as guilty and failing to spot the liars.

Important statistical issues call the polygraph procedure into further question. Even if the examination were 95 percent accurate, a 5 percent error rate could lead to the misidentification of many innocent people as being guilty. To illustrate, imagine that your company arranges for all 500 of your employees to take a polygraph test to find out who has been stealing office supplies. Imagine also that only about 4 percent (20 out of 500 people) are really stealing, which is not an unreasonable estimate. If the lie detector test is 95 percent accurate, it will correctly spot 19 of these 20 thieves. But the test will also give 5 percent **false positives**, falsely fingering 5 percent of the innocent people. Of the 480 innocent employees, the polygraph will inaccurately implicate 24 as liars. That is, *you could end up with more people falsely accused of lying than people correctly accused of lying.* This was borne out in a field study of suspected criminals who were later either convicted or declared innocent. The polygraph results were no better than a random coin flip (Brett et al., 1986).

An equally serious concern with polygraphy is that there are no generally accepted standards either for administering a polygraph examination or for interpreting its results. Different examiners could conceivably come to different conclusions based on the same polygraph record.

What Conclusions Can We Draw?

For these reasons, the U.S. Congress has outlawed most uses of polygraph tests in job screening and in most areas of the government, except for high-security-risk positions. National Academies of Science (2003) has gone even further in a report saying that the polygraph is too crude to be useful for screening people to identify possible terrorists or other national security risks. Your authors agree.

As far as criminal investigations are concerned, we find a patchwork of laws on the admissibility of polygraph evidence among the states. Few have gone so far as imposing complete bans and 20 more allow such evidence only on agreement of both sides—although, in a few states, polygraph results are still routinely admissible in court (Gruben & Madsen, 2005). So where do you come down on the issue of using the polygraph in criminal cases? Does the fact that a "lie detector" test can sometimes force a confession from a suspect justify its use?

Alternative Approaches to Deception Detection

The reining-in of polygraph testing has spurred the development of alternative means of detecting dishonesty (Capps & Ryan, 2005; Lane, 2006). Much of this work has been devoted to paper-and-pencil instruments that are often called "integrity tests." How well do these instruments work? Not very well, according to reports by the American Psychological Association and by the U.S. government's Office of Technology Assessment. In general, like the polygraph, these instruments seem to be more accurate than mere interviews, but they also suffer from a high false-positive rate.

do it yourself!

Thinking Critically About Polygraphy

A quick Web search, using such terms as *polygraph*, *lie*, and *lie detection*, will reveal hundreds of sites arguing either for or against the use of *polygraph* exams to identify lawbreakers, potential terrorists, or other security risks. Pick a site—either pro or con—and analyze it according to our six criteria for critical thinking:

1. The source is credible—either an expert on the subject or someone who relies on those with expertise.
2. The claim is reasonable—not extreme.
3. The claim is supported by scientifically sound evidence, not testimonials or anecdotes.
4. There is no reasonable suspicion of bias, such as self-interest, emotional bias, or confirmation bias.
5. The claim avoids common logical fallacies, such as selective use of the evidence (e.g., using only the data that support one's position, while ignoring the rest).
6. Does the source use multiple psychological perspectives when appropriate?

Additional resources to help you with this Thinking Critically exercise are available in MyPsychLab. See also "The Truth About Lie Detectors (aka Polygraph Tests)" on the American Psychological Association's website: /www.apa.org/research/action/polygraph.aspx.

---

false positive Mistaken identification of a person as having a particular characteristic. In polygraphy, a false positive is an erroneous identification of a truthful person as being a liar.

More recently, researchers have turned to brain scanning techniques to see if they can catch liars (Ross, 2003). A certain brain wave pattern known as P300 has been linked with a variety of attention-getting cues, such as hearing one's name, but studies show it can also be evoked by fibbing. In addition, fMRI images show that lying activates all the brain areas involved in telling the truth, plus several more (Langleben et al., 2002). This suggests that lying is not something completely separate from the truth but an operation the liar must perform on the truth, says psychiatrist Daniel Langleben, all of which raises the concern that there is too much hype and too little solid evidence behind brain-scan-based lie detection (Gamer, 2009; Stix, 2008). In addition, some neuroscientists worry about the ethics of peering directly into people's brains to "read" the neural traces of their private thoughts (Pearson, 2006).

The potential advantage of these newer brain-scan techniques is that they bypass the anxiety-response pathway used by polygraphy. By registering neural activity, they get much closer to the person's actual thoughts. But how well do these alternative methods work? Not well enough for the police and the courts—yet.

Finally, Paul Ekman—the same one who studies universal facial expressions of emotion—has found that liars often display fleeting "microexpressions" and other nonverbal cues. In one study, Ekman and his colleague Maureen O'Sullivan found that some people are especially good at detecting deception, but they are a small minority. In their tests, most people perform at about the chance level. Still, Ekman and O'Sullivan hope to learn what those most skilled at detecting deception look for and teach that to police officers and other concerned with crime and security issues (Adelson, 2004).

CHAPTER SUMMARY

CHAPTER PROBLEM: Motivation is largely an internal and subjective process: How can we determine what motivates people like Lance Armstrong to work so hard at becoming the best in the world at what they do?

- The subjective nature of motivation has forced psychologists to study the underlying processes indirectly, using a variety of methods, including animal studies, the *TAT*, and brain scans.
- Psychologists have identified many important influences on motivation, including culture, goals, unconscious processes, various biological factors, and social pressures. Rewards, both *intrinsic* and *extrinsic* are also important for world-class athletes like Lance Armstrong.

- One of the biggest questions involves the priorities we give to our motives—an issue that Maslow addressed in his famous *hierarchy of needs*. Recently, evolutionary psychologists have proposed an updated needs hierarchy. Many athletes, performers and artists apparently do much of their work in a state of *flow*—a mental state in which the person focuses on an intrinsically rewarding task to the exclusion of all other needs.
- Understanding motivation also requires understanding a person's emotions—because emotions are a class of motives aroused by persons, objects, and situations in the individual's external world. Emotions serve as the "values" we place on alternatives when we make choices and decisions.

10.1 What Motivates Us?

CORE CONCEPT 10.1

Motives are internal dispositions to act in certain ways, although they can be influenced by multiple factors, both internal and external.

The concept of **motivation** refers to inferred internal processes that select and direct behavior toward a goal. Motivation also helps explain behavior that cannot be explained by the circumstances alone. Psychologists find it useful to distinguish **intrinsic motivation** from **extrinsic motivation**.

David McClelland pioneered the study of the **need for achievement (n Ach)**, a motive important for I/O psychologists concerned about worker motivation and job satisfaction. The need for achievement also correlates with academic success and other accomplishments in life. But just as important as **n Ach** are the needs for power and affiliation, according to McClelland. Cross-cultural research also shows that societies vary in the intensity of their need for achievement, depending on their tendencies toward **individualism** or **collectivism**.

Psychologists have found that extrinsic rewards can destroy motivation for intrinsically rewarding tasks through **overjustification**. This is not always the case, however, but rather when rewards are given without regard for the quality of performance.

Great achievements usually come from people in a state of **flow**. Those in a flow state are intrinsically motivated by some problem or activity. The use of drugs or alcohol to achieve an artificial flow feeling is not usually effective.

10.2 How Are Our Motivational Priorities Determined?

CORE CONCEPT 10.2

A new theory combining Maslow's hierarchy with evolutionary psychology solves some long-standing problems by suggesting that functional, proximal, and developmental factors set our motivational priorities.

Psychology has no successful theory that accounts for all of human motivation. Psychologists have explained biologically based motivation in terms of **instinct theory,** **fixed-action patterns,** and **drive theory,** and **homeostasis.** Cognitive psychologists have emphasized **biological motives.** Freud called attention to **unconscious motivation** and taught that all our motives derive from unconscious sexual and aggressive desires. None of these approaches successfully explains the full range of human motivation, however.

With his influential **hierarchy of needs,** Maslow attempted to explain the priorities in which human motives appear. Critics have, however, pointed out many exceptions to his hierarchy. Recently, evolutionary psychologists have proposed a revision of Maslow's theory suggesting that our "default" motivational priorities can change, depending on developmental factors and on important (proximal) stimuli.

In trying to understand another person's motivation, a good place to start is with extrinsic incentives and threats. In addition, Alfred Adler taught that social motives explain many problem behaviors. Social psychologists combine these notions under the heading of the *power of the situation.*

10.3 Where Do Hunger and Sex Fit into the Motivational Hierarchy?

CORE CONCEPT 10.3

Although dissimilar in many respects, hunger and sex both have evolutionary origins, and each has an essential place in the motivational hierarchy.

Hunger is both a biological drive and a psychological motive, best understood by a multiple-systems approach. Americans receive mixed messages from the media, promoting both thinness and calorie-dense foods, which may play a role in disorders such as obesity, **anorexia nervosa,** and **bulimia nervosa.** None of these problems is completely understood, although both social and biological factors are thought to be involved. The problem of obesity has become an epidemic in America and is rapidly being exported throughout the world. Many people seek to control their appetite and body weight, although no weight-loss scheme is effective for most people over the long run.

Will power is a common term in everyday language, although psychologists avoid it because it suggests a separate faculty of the mind. They prefer *impulse control* or *self-control,* terms that can be explained in terms of brain mechanisms and environmental influences. Recently, researchers have found that impulse control takes a cognitive toll and is reflected in blood sugar levels.

Unlike hunger and weight control, the sex drive is not homeostatic, even though sexual motivation is heavily influenced by biology, but learning also plays a role, especially in humans. Particularly since Kinsey's surveys, the scientific study of sexuality has caused controversy in America, even though survey research shows that, over the last half century, Americans have become more liberal in their sexual practices. Masters and Johnson were the first to do extensive studies of sexual behavior in the laboratory, finding that the **sexual response cycles** of men and women are similar. More recently, Peplau has emphasized differences in male and female sexuality. Those adhering to the evolutionary perspective argue that differences in male and female sexuality arise from conflicting mating strategies and from the large biological investment women have in pregnancy—both of which encourage more promiscuity in men.

As Maslow's hierarchy did, the new evolution-based hierarchy generally gives hunger priority over sex, although the hierarchy is fluid.

The greatest puzzle about sexuality centers on the origins of **sexual orientation,** especially the factors leading to heterosexuality, homosexuality, and bisexuality. Transsexualism and transvestism are not predictive of sexual orientation. Most experts agree that sexual orientation involves a combination of biological, environmental, and social factors, although much of the research has focused on biology. Since the 1970s, homosexuality has not been viewed as a disorder by psychologists and psychiatrists.

10.4 How Do Our Emotions Motivate Us?

CORE CONCEPT 10.4

Emotions are a special class of motives that help us attend to and respond to important (usually external) situations and communicate our intentions to others.

Emotion is a process involving four main components: physiological arousal, cognitive interpretation, subjective feelings, and behavioral expression. Emotions can also act as motives. From an evolutionary standpoint, they help us approach or avoid recurring stimuli that are important for survival and reproduction. Socially, emotional expressions serve to communicate feelings and intentions, apparently aided by "mirror neurons."

Most experts posit a limited number of *basic emotions* that, in combination, produce a larger number of *secondary emotions.* At least seven basic facial expressions of emotion are universally understood across cultures, although these can be modified by culture-specific **display rules.** These universal emotions are probably biologically based.

Some emotional differences between males and females have biological roots. This is seen in differential rates of certain emotional disorders, as well as more frequent displays of anger in men. On the other hand, cultural differences demonstrate that some gender differences in emotion are learned. Specifically, different cultures teach men and women different display rules about controlling emotional expression. Despite the differences, neither sex can be said to be more emotional than the other.

10.5 What Processes Control Our Emotions?

CORE CONCEPT 10.5

Research has clarified the processes underlying both our conscious and unconscious emotional lives, shedding light on some old controversies.

Neuroscience has revealed two distinct emotion systems in the brain. One, a fast-response system, operates mainly at an unconscious level and relies on deep limbic structures, especially the amygdala. The other involves conscious processing in the cortex. The pathways intersect in the *ventromedial prefrontal cortex*. Emotions also involve visceral changes in response to messages transmitted by the autonomic nervous system and the hormone system. In addition to the two emotion pathways, the two hemispheres have a **lateralization of emotion** by which each specializes in processing a different class of emotion.

The inverted U theory describes the complex relationship between emotional arousal and performance: Increasing arousal improves performance—but only up to a certain optimum level of arousal, which depends on the complexity of the task. **Sensation seekers** seem to have an especially high need for arousal.

Understanding how the two emotion systems work has begun to resolve some long-standing controversies involving the roles of cognition and physical responses in emotion. The **James–Lange theory** argued that physical sensations and physical responses produce emotional feelings. The opposing **Cannon–Bard theory** stated that our cognitive appraisal produces both emotions and the accompanying physical response. Stanley Schachter's **two-factor theory** suggested that emotions are the result of cognitive appraisal of both our internal physical state and the external situation. The research shows that all three viewpoints have a share in the truth.

Emotional intelligence, the ability to keep one's emotions from getting out of control, is vital for maintaining good social relationships. It is distinct from the abilities measured by traditional IQ tests. Increased emotional control can be achieved by learning, as demonstrated in anger management programs. Tests of emotional intelligence show that those who score highly tend to succeed in social situations.

Under some circumstances, the expression of anger without aggression can have positive results. The public, however, generally holds the dangerous misconception that it is always best to "vent" one's anger and "get it out of the system." Studies show that such venting often leads to the increased likelihood of aggression later.

KEY TERMS

anorexia nervosa (p. 301)
bulimia nervosa (p. 301)
biological drive (p. 294)

Cannon–Bard theory
 (p. 319)
collectivism (p. 292)

developmental level of
 analysis (p. 297)
display rules (p. 312)
drive theory (p. 294)
emotion (p. 310)
emotional intelligence
 (p. 320)
extrinsic motivation (p. 290)
fixed action patterns (p. 294)
flow (p. 293)
functional level of analysis
 (p. 297)
hierarchy of needs (p. 296)
homeostasis (p. 295)
intrinsic motivation (p. 290)
instinct theory (p. 294)
individualism (p. 292)

inverted U function (p. 317)
James–Lange theory (p. 319)
lateralization of emotion
 (p. 316)
motivation (p. 289)
need for achievement (*n Ach*)
 (p. 290)
need (p. 294)
overjustification (p. 292)
proximal level of analysis
 (p. 297)
set point (p. 300)
sexual response cycle (p.305)
sexual orientation (p. 308)
sensation seekers (p. 317)
two-factor theory (p. 320)

CRITICAL THINKING APPLIED

Do Lie Detectors Really Detect Lies?

"Lie detectors" work on the assumption that people will show physical signs of arousal when lying. While polygraph examiners sometimes extract confessions when they convince suspects that the test can show them lying, the evidence does not indicate that the results are always reliable. Particularly troubling is that, under some circumstances, the polygraph test can identify more false positives than actual liars. Alternative approaches that use facial expressions or brain scans are being explored, but so far they have not been validated.

DISCOVERING PSYCHOLOGY VIEWING GUIDE

Watch the following video by logging into MyPsychLab (www. mypsychlab.com). After you have watched the video, answer the questions that follow.

PROGRAM 12: **MOTIVATION AND EMOTION**

Program Review

1. What is the general term for all the physical and psychological processes that start behavior, maintain it, and stop it?

   a. explanatory style   **b.** repression

   c. addiction   **d.** motivation

2. Phoebe has a phobia regarding cats. What is her motivation?

   a. environmental arousal

   b. overwhelming fear

   c. repressed sexual satisfaction

   d. a need for attachment to others

3. What is the role of the pleasure–pain principle in motivation?

   a. We repress our pleasure in others' pain.

   b. We seek pleasure and avoid pain.

   c. We persist in doing things even when they are painful.

   d. We are more intensely motivated by pain than by pleasure.

4. Which activity most clearly involves a "reframing" of the tension between desire and restraint?

   a. eating before you feel hungry

   b. seeking pleasurable physical contact with others

   c. working long hours for an eventual goal

   d. getting angry at someone who interferes with your plans

5. Sigmund Freud thought there were two primary motivations. One of these is

   a. expressing aggression.

   b. seeking transcendence.

   c. fulfilling creativity.

   d. feeling secure.

6. Compared with Freud's view of human motivation, that of Abraham Maslow could be characterized as being more

   a. negative.   **c.** optimistic.

   b. hormonally based.   **d.** pathologically based.

7. Behaviors, such as male peacocks displaying their feathers or male rams fighting, are related to which part of sexual reproduction?

   a. providing a safe place for mating

   b. focusing the male's attention on mating

   c. selecting a partner with good genes

   d. mating at the correct time of year

8. In Norman Adler's research on mating behavior in rats, what is the function of the ten or so mountings?

   a. to trigger hormone production and uterine contractions in the female

   b. to warn off rival males

   c. to cause fertilization

   d. to impress the female

9. What kinds of emotions tend to be involved in romantic love?

   a. mainly intense, positive emotions

   b. mainly intense, negative emotions

   c. a mixture of intense and weak emotions that are mainly positive

   d. a mixture of positive and negative emotions that are intense

10. Charles Darwin cited the similarity of certain expressions of emotions as evidence that

   a. all species learn emotions.

   b. emotions are innate.

   c. emotions promote survival of the fittest.

   d. genetic variability is advantageous.

11. Pictures of happy and sad American workers are shown to U.S. college students and to Italian workers. Based on your knowledge of Paul Ekman's research, what would you predict about how well the groups would identify the emotions?

   a. Both groups will identify the emotions correctly.

   b. Only the Americans will identify the emotions correctly.

   c. Only the Italians will identify the emotions correctly.

   d. Neither group will identify the emotions correctly.

12. Theodore has an explanatory style that emphasizes the external, the unstable, and the specific. He makes a mistake at work that causes his boss to become very angry. Which statement is Theodore most likely to make to himself?

   a. "I always make such stupid mistakes."

   b. "I was just distracted by the noise outside."

   c. "All my life, people have always gotten so mad at me."

   d. "If I were a better person, this wouldn't have happened."

13. Why does Martin Seligman believe that it might be appropriate to help children who develop a pessimistic explanatory style?

   a. These children are unpleasant to be around.

   b. These children lack contact with reality.

   c. These children are at risk for depression.

   d. Other children who live with these children are likely to develop the same style.

14. What other outcome will a pessimistic explanatory style likely affect, according to Seligman?

   a. health

   b. artistic ability

   c. reasoning skills

   d. language competence

15. All of the following are possible origins of a pessimistic explanatory style, *except*

    a. assessments by important adults in our lives.

    b. the reality of our first major negative life event.

    c. our mother's pessimism level.

    d. our level of introversion/extraversion.

16. Which theorist is best known for positing a hierarchy of needs that humans strive to meet?

    a. Freud

    b. Rogers

    c. Maslow

    d. Seligman

17. Although motivation can lead to unpleasant states (e.g., hunger, frustration), it seems to have evolved because of its benefits to

    a. survival.

    b. propagation of the species.

    c. health.

    d. all of the above.

18. What has Robert Plutchik argued about emotions?

    a. There are three basic types of emotions: happiness, sadness, and anger.

    b. There are eight basic emotions, consisting of four pairs of opposites.

    c. Love is not a universal emotion; some cultures do not show signs of having it.

    d. Emotional experience is determined by physiology alone.

19. Four people have been obese for as long as they can remember. Their doctors tell all of them that their obesity is putting them at risk for several illnesses. Who is most likely to join a gym, go on a diet, and get in shape?

    a. Al, whose explanatory style includes an internal locus of control

    b. Bob, who has a pessimistic explanatory style

    c. Chuck, whose explanatory style includes an unstable locus of control

    d. Dwayne, who is depressed about his obesity

20. Wolves and squirrels are most likely to show which of the following in their mating patterns?

    a. romantic love

    b. competition by females for males

    c. competition by males for females

    d. a preference for mating in the autumn so that the off-spring will be born during the winter

The Psychology of Self-Motivation

E. Scott Geller

Prologue

Exactly what is an external accountability intervention? In the work world, these motivational tools include time sheets, overtime compensation records, peer-to-peer behavioral observations, public posting of performance indicators, group and individual feedback meetings, and performance appraisals.

In schools it's all about grades, and teachers attempt to keep students motivated by emphasizing the relationship between the quality of their school-work and the all-important grade. Psychologists call these "extrinsic motivators," and managers and teachers use them to keep employees and students on track, respectively.

Sometimes it's possible for people to establish conditions that facilitate self-accountability and self-motivation. When people go beyond the call of duty to actively care for the welfare of others they are self-motivated to an extent. Achieving an actively-caring-for-people (AC4P) culture requires more people to be self-motivated at more times and in more situations. This chapter presents evidence-based ways to make this happen, as gleaned from research in the behavioral and social sciences. ■

Self-Motivation for AC4P[1]

Without safety regulations, policies, and external accountability systems, many more employees would get hurt or killed on the job and on the road, and more students would be victimized in schools. All of us, including employers, police officers, safety professionals, and school teachers need extrinsic controls to hold us accountable to perform safe and AC4P behavior, while avoiding risky and confrontational behavior. Why do we need such extrinsic controls?

The desired, safe, AC4P behaviors are relatively inconvenient, uncomfortable, and inefficient. The soon, certain, positive consequences (or intrinsic "natural" reinforcers) of at-risk and other undesirable behaviors often overpower one's self-motivation to be as safe or caring as possible.

Every driver knows it's risky to talk on a cell-phone or type a text message while driving, yet many drivers perform these behaviors regularly. Why? The immediate and naturally-reinforcing consequences take priority over the low likelihood of a crash. These risky drivers are not self-motivated to actively care for the safety of themselves and others on the road.

Here's the key question: What can we do to overcome the human nature implied by these profound quotations from B.F. Skinner: "Immediate consequences outweigh delayed consequences" and "Consequences for the individual usually outweigh consequences for others".[2]

In other words, AC4P behavior is seemingly not rewarded by soon, certain, and positive consequences for the individual. Therefore, we need techniques to overcome this natural tendency to avoid actively caring for others. Some practical solutions are derived from psychological science, especially research conducted by Edward Deci and Richard Ryan.[3]

Human Needs and Self-Motivation

We have three basic psychological needs, and when these needs are satisfied, we are self-motivated, according to Deci and Ryan. Specifically, self-motivation is supported by situational factors (e.g., environmental contexts and other people) that facilitate fulfillment of our needs for autonomy, relatedness, and competence. "Self-motivation, rather than external (or extrinsic) motivation, is at the heart of creativity, responsibility, healthy behavior, and lasting change."[4]

Autonomy

Autonomy is a matter of being self-governing or having personal control. I've described this condition as a person-state related to one's propensity to actively care for the safety and well-being of others.[5] Autonomous behavior is self-initiated, self-endorsed, and authentic. It reflects one's true values and intentions. Geller and Veazie[1] refer to this attribute as "choice," and plenty of research shows people are more self-motivated when they have opportunities to choose among action alternatives.[5]

Early Laboratory Research   More than 40 years ago when I was conducting research in cognitive science, I conducted a very simple experiment and obtained very simple results. The implications of the findings, however, are relevant to self-motivation in numerous situations.

Half of the 40 participants in this experiment were shown a list of five three-letter words (i.e., cat, hat, mat, rat, and bat) and asked to select one. Then, after a warning tone, the selected word was presented on a screen in front of the participant, and s/he pressed a micro-switch as fast as possible after seeing the word.

The latency in milliseconds between the presentation of the word and the participant's response was a measure of simple reaction time. This sequence of warning signal, word presentation, and participant reaction occurred for 25 trials. If a participant reacted before the stimulus word was presented, the reaction time was not counted, and the trial was repeated. The session took less than 15 minutes per subject.

The word selected by a particular participant was used as the presentation stimulus for the next participant. Thus, this participant did not have the opportunity to choose the stimulus word. As a result, the word choices of 20 participants were assigned to 20 other participants.

This simple experiment had two conditions—a *Choice* condition (in which participants chose a three-letter word for their stimulus) and an *Assigned* condition (in which participants were assigned the stimulus word selected by the previous participant). To my surprise, the mean reactions of participants in the *Choice* group were significantly faster than those of participants in the *Assigned* group.

Although these results were explained by presuming the opportunity to choose their stimulus word increased the motivation of the participants to perform in the reaction time experiment, the large group differences were unexpected. How could the simple choice of a three-letter word motivate faster responding in a simple reaction-time experiment? In fact, because I did not feel confident in the basic motivational explanation for these surprising results, I did not pursue publication of these data in a professional research journal. Only years later did I appreciate the real-world ramifications of these findings.[5]

From Laboratory to Classroom   About a year after the simple reaction-time study described above, I tested the theory of choice as a motivator in the college classroom. I was teaching two sections of Social Psychology; one at 8:00 A.M. Monday, Wednesday, and Friday, and the other at 11:00 A.M. on these same days. There were about 75 students in each class.

On the first day of class, I did not hand out a pre-prepared syllabus with weekly assignments, but distributed only a general outline of the course which introduced the textbook, the course objectives, and the basic criteria for assigning grades (i.e., a quiz on each textbook chapter and a comprehensive final exam on classroom lectures, discussions, and demonstrations).

In an open discussion and voting process, the 8:00 class was given the opportunity to choose the order in which the ten textbook chapters would be read for homework and discussed in class. They could also submit multiple-choice questions for me to consider using for the ten chapter quizzes, and they could hand in short-answer and discussion questions for possible application on the final exam.

The 11:00 class received the order of textbook chapters selected previously by the 8:00 class, and this class was not given an opportunity to submit quiz or exam questions.

Thus, I derived *Choice* and *Assigned* classroom conditions analogous to the two reaction-time groups I had studied one year earlier. Two of my undergraduate research assistants attended each of these classes, posing as regular students, and systematically counted the frequency of behaviors reflecting class participation. These observers did not know about my intentional *Choice* vs. *Assigned* manipulations.

From the day the students in my 8:00 class voted on the textbook assignments, this class seemed to be livelier than the later 11:00 class. My perception was verified by the participation records of the two classroom observers.

Furthermore, the ten quiz grades, final-exam scores, and my teaching-evaluation scores from standard forms distributed during the last class period were significantly higher in the *Choice* class than the *Assigned* class. (Although several students from the 8:00 class submitted potential quiz and final-exam questions, none were actually used. Each class received the same quizzes and final exam.)

I'm convinced the *Choice* versus *Assigned* manipulation was a critical factor. The initial opportunity to choose reading assignments increased students' motivation and class participation and this extra motivation and involvement led to more involvement, perceived choice, self-motivation and learning. The students' attitudes toward the class improved as a result of feeling more in control of the situation than controlled.

It's likely the "choice" opportunities in the 8:00 class were especially powerful because they were so different than the traditional top-down classroom atmosphere at the time, as typified by the organization of my 11:00 class. In other words, the contrast of the *Choice* class with the students' other courses made the "choice" opportunities in my 8:00 class especially salient, meaningful, and motivational.

A Corporate Safety Example

A decade after my laboratory and classroom research that showed the self-motivating impact of *choice;* I visited a chemical facility of 350 employees that exemplified the power of choice to impact occupational safety. The employees had initiated an AC4P and behavior-focused observation, feedback, and coaching process in 1992, and had reaped amazing safety benefits for their efforts. In 1994, for example, 98% of the workforce had participated in behavioral observation and feedback sessions, documenting a total of 3,350 coaching sessions for the year. A total of 51,408 behaviors were safe and 4,389 were at-risk.

Such comprehensive employee involvement in a behavioral observation and feedback process led to remarkable outcomes. At the start of their process in 1992, the plant safety record was quite good (i.e., 13 OSHA recordables for a TRIR of 4.11). They improved to 5 OSHA recordables in 1993 (TRIR = 1.60), and in 1994 they had the best safety performance among several plants in their company with only one OSHA recordable (TRIR = 0.35).

I've seen numerous companies improve their safety performance substantially with a process based on the principles of people-based safety (PBS),[6] but this plant holds the record for efficiency in getting everyone involved and obtaining exceptional results.

I'm convinced a key factor in this organization's outstanding success was the employees' choice in the development, implementation, and maintenance of the process. The employees owned their AC4P observation and feedback process from the start because they applied people-based techniques *their way.*

There is no best way to implement PBS. Rather, the principles and procedures from behavioral science need to be customized to fit the relevant work culture. The most efficient way to make this happen is to involve the target population in the customization process. At this facility, the entire workforce learned the AC4P principles by participating in ten, one-hour small-group sessions spaced over a six-month period.

These education/training sessions were facilitated by other employees who had received more intensive training in AC4P principles and PBS applications. At these group sessions, employees discussed specific strategies for implementing a plant-wide behavioral monitoring and coaching process, and they entertained ways to overcome barriers to total participation and sustain the process over the long term.

They designed an AC4P process which included employee choice at its very core. Although some specifics of the process have changed since its inception in 1992, the *choice* aspect has remained a constant.

From the start, employees scheduled regular AC4P observation and feedback sessions with two other employees (i.e., observers). That is, they selected the task, day and time for the coaching session. Additionally, they selected two individuals to observe their performance and give them immediate and specific feedback regarding incidences of safe and at-risk behaviors.

Employees chose their observers (and coaches) from *anyone* in the plant. At the start of their process the number of *volunteer* safety coaches was limited (including only 30% of the workforce), but today everyone in the workforce is a potential safety coach. Personal choice facilitated involvement, ownership, and trust in the process.

At first, some employees did not have complete trust in the process and resisted active participation. Some tried to "beat the system" by scheduling their observation and feedback sessions at inactive times when the probability of an at-risk behavior was minimal (i.e., while they watched a monitor or completed paperwork). And most employees were certainly "on their toes" when the observers arrived at the scheduled times.

At the same time, those observed were optimally receptive to constructive feedback and advice from the observers they had selected. Many people (whether observing or being observed) were surprised that numerous at-risk behaviors occurred in situations where employees knew the safe operating procedures and knew they were being observed for the occurrence of at-risk behaviors.

It wasn't long before most employees at this facility began scheduling their coaching sessions during active times when the probability of an at-risk behavior or injury was highest. Frequently, the observed individual pointed out an at-risk behavior necessitated by the particular work environment or procedure (e.g., a difficult-to-reach valve, a hose-checking procedure too cumbersome for one auditor, a walking surface made slippery by an equipment leak, a difficult-to-adjust machine guard).

Many employees chose to use their observation and feedback process to demonstrate that some at-risk behaviors are facilitated or necessitated by equipment design or maintenance, and/or by environmental conditions or operating procedures. This involvement often led to a beneficial change in environmental conditions or operations procedures.

Courtesy of George Vaughn Willis.

MAN, DO WE HAVE THIS
GUY CONTROLLED, EVERY TIME
WE PULL THE LEVER HE GIVES US
A FOOD PELLET.

We've All Been There   You need only reflect on your own life circumstances to realize how a perception of choice or personal control increases your self-motivation, involvement, and commitment. We are not always in control of the critical events of ongoing circumstances, and thus we've experienced the frustration, discomfort, and distress of being at the mercy of environmental circumstances or other people's decisions.

And we've certainly experienced the pleasure of having alternatives to choose from and feeling in control of those factors critical for successful performance. How much sweeter is the taste of success when we can attribute the achievement to our own choices?

Bottom Line: The message is clear. Whenever possible, give people opportunities to choose mission-relevant goals and the procedures to reach them; the result will be increased self-motivation, engagement, and ownership. This may require relinquishing some top-down control, abandoning a desire for a "quick fix," changing from focusing on outcomes to recognizing process achievements, and giving people opportunities to choose, evaluate, and refine their means to achieve the ends. The result: more people going beyond the call of duty on behalf of others when no one's watching.

Competence

Several researchers of human motivation have proposed that people naturally enjoy being able to solve problems and successfully complete worthwhile tasks[7]. In their view, people are self-motivated to learn, to explore possibilities, to understand what's going on, and to participate in achieving worthwhile

goals. The label for this fundamental human motive is *competence*. "All of us are striving for mastery, for affirmations of our own competence."[8]

Motivation researchers assume the desire for competence is self-initiating and self-rewarding. Behavior that increases feelings of competence is self-directed and does not need extrinsic or extra reinforcement to keep it going. Feeling competent to do worthwhile work motivates continued effort. When people feel more successful or competent their self-motivation increases. As one behavioral scientist put it, "People are not successful because they are motivated; they are motivated because they have been successful".[9]

The Power of Feedback   How do we know we are competent at something? How do we know this competence makes a valuable difference? You know the answer—feedback.

Feedback about our ongoing behavior tells us how we are doing and enables us to do better. That familiar slogan, "Practice makes perfect" is actually incorrect. Practice makes permanence, and without appropriate feedback well-practiced behavior can be wrong. We hone our skills through practice *and* behavior-focused feedback.

Some feedback comes naturally, like when we recognize our behavior has produced a desired result. But often behavioral feedback requires careful and systematic observation by another individual—a trainer or coach—who later communicates his or her findings to the performer. In each case, feedback enables development of perceived competence and self-motivation.

Feedback is essential to fulfill a basic human need—the need for competence. And helping people satisfy this need increases their self-motivation to perform the relevant behavior. But feedback regarding the *outcome* of a project or process does not reflect individual choices or competence, and thus can be ineffective. Only feedback that is behavior-focused and customized for the recipient can enhance an individual's perception of personal control and competence, and thus bolster self-motivation.

Is Feedback Reinforcing?   Technically, a reinforcer is a behavioral consequence that maintains or increases the frequency of the behavior it follows. So, if behavior does not continue or improve after feedback, the feedback was not a reinforcer. Likewise, praise, bonus pay, or frequent flyer points are not reinforcers when they don't increase the frequency of behavior they target; and they often don't. However, interpersonal, behavior-based rewards can increase our perception of competence.

Can well-delivered supportive or corrective feedback increase our perception of competence and self-motivation? Absolutely, but it's not a payoff for doing the right thing. Rather, its behavior-based information a person uses to feel more competent or to learn how to become more competent.

There is perhaps no other consequence with greater potential to improve competence, self-motivation, and individual performance than behavior-focused feedback. Behavioral feedback, delivered with an AC4P mindset, is usually a reinforcer because it maintains or increases a certain desired behavior.

A Paradigm Shift This discussion of feedback, competence, and self-motivation calls for a paradigm shift—a change in perspective about AC4P behavior. We should assume people are naturally self-motivated to help others, instead of calling on guilt or sacrifice to get people involved to improve the health, welfare, or safety of other people.

Simply put, we hate feeling incompetent or helpless. We want to learn, to discover, to become more proficient at worthwhile tasks. We seek opportunities to ask questions, to study pertinent material, to work with people who know more than we do, and to receive feedback that can increase our competence and subsequent self-motivation.

AC4P behavior is not a thankless job requiring self-sacrifice, obligation, or a special degree of altruism. Participation in an AC4P process provides opportunities to satisfy a basic human need—the need for personal competence.[7] Effective and frequent delivery of behavior-based feedback provides a mechanism for improving the quality of an AC4P process, as well as cultivating feelings of competence and self-motivation throughout a culture.

Relatedness

The innate need for *relatedness* reflects "the need to love and be loved, to care and be cared for ... to feel included, to feel related."[11] This is analogous to the state of belonging—a person-state influencing one's propensity to actively caring for the health, safety, and well-being of others. Geller and Veazie[1] use the term *community* to reflect this person-state because the concept of community is more encompassing than relatedness or belongingness.

A community perspective reflects systems thinking and interdependency beyond the confines of family, social groups, and work teams, as explicated by Peter Block[13] and M. Scott Peck.[14] Community is an AC4P mindset for human kind in general—an interconnectedness with others that transcends political differences and prejudices, and profoundly respects and appreciates diversity.

Systems Thinking and Interdependence Focus our efforts to optimize the system, W. Edwards Deming tells us in his best sellers on total quality management, *Out of The Crisis* and *The New Economics*.[15] Peter Senge stresses that systems thinking is *The Fifth Discipline*,[16] and key to continuous improvement. And Stephen Covey's discussion of interdependency, win-win contingencies, and synergy in his popular self-help book, *The Seven Habits of Highly Effective People*,[17] is founded on systems thinking and a community perspective.

SON, IT'S NOT WHETHER YOU WIN OR LOSE... UNLESS YOU WANT DADDY'S LOVE.

Courtesy of George Vaughn Willis.

Geller and Veazie propose and explicate in *The Courage Factor*[18] the amount of courage a person needs to intervene on behalf of another individual decreases as a function of the degree of connectedness between the two people.

Developing a community or interdependent spirit in an organization, a classroom, or a family unit leads to two primary human-performance payoffs: a) individuals become more self-motivated to do the right thing, and b) people are more likely to actively care for the well-being of others. In their reality-based narrative, Geller and Veazie[1] illustrate the do's and don'ts of building an interdependent community perspective.

More Paradigm Shifts A systems or community approach to improving people's welfare implicates a number of paradigm shifts from traditional management of an organization, a classroom, and yes, a family. We need to shift from trying to find one root cause of a problem (e.g., interpersonal bullying, sexual abuse, substance abuse, and occupational injuries) to considering a number of potential contributing factors from each of three domains–environment, behavior, and person.

Interdependent systems thinking requires a shift from down-stream outcome-based measures of individual or group performance (grades, injury rates, familial acceptance) to a more proactive and diagnostic evaluation of process variables within the environment, behavior, and person domains.

Systems thinking enables a useful perspective on basic principles of human motivation, attitude formation, and behavior change. Causation between antecedents (or activators) and consequences of behavior are thought to be linear, or so we believe. But systems-thinking implicates a circular or spiral perspective.

While an event preceding a behavior might direct it and a particular event following a behavior determines whether it will occur again, it's instructive to realize the consequence for one behavior can serve as the activator for the next behavior. With this perspective, behavior-based feedback can serve as a motivating consequence or a directive activator, depending on when and how it's presented.

Spiral causality and the consistency principle combine to explain how small changes in behavior can result in attitude change, followed by more behavior change and then more desired attitude change, leading eventually to personal commitment and total involvement in the process.[19] Similarly, the notion of spiral causality and the reciprocity principle explain why initial AC4P from a few individuals can result in more and more AC4P behavior from many individuals.

This *ripple effect* can eventually lead to families, work teams, and community groups actively caring regularly for the health, safety, and well-being of each other, with a win-win interdependent attitude and a proactive perspective. In the end we have AC4P synergy. It can all start with systems thinking and one intentional act of kindness from one person to another.

How to Increase Self-Motivation

The C-words of *Choice*, *Competence*, and *Community* are used by Geller and Veazie[1] in their narrative as labels for the three evidence-based person-states that determine self-motivation. Dispositional, interpersonal, and environmental conditions that enhance these states, presumed to be innate needs by some psychologists,[20] increase personal perceptions of self-motivation.

Researchers offer the following ten guidelines for increasing self-motivation by affecting one or more of the three person-states (or needs) defined above. Geller and Veazie[1] explain each of these with real-world examples from the workplace, schools, and families.

1. Explain Why

Rules and regulations should be accompanied with a meaningful explanation (i.e., why?) to provide a rationale for behavior that is not naturally reinforcing. Often, we tell people what (rules and regulations) to do without including the rationale— the why. At work, managers often quickly delegate without connecting the specific task to the organization's larger mission or vision—the "big picture." In educational institutions, policies regarding student admissions, staff-evaluation, and student grading, as well as changes in textbooks, are often announced without a reasonable rationale.

In the community, some people may choose to ignore residential speed laws (e.g., 20 mph zone) because they don't believe such a dramatic reduction in vehicle speed improves safety. In this case, it would help to know that pedestrians have an 85% chance of being killed when hit at 40 mph versus a 5% fatality rate when hit by a vehicle traveling 20 mph.[21]

If individuals were able to connect a speed restriction to saving a human life, as opposed to fear of a speeding ticket, there might be less speeding. Or at least those complying with the 20 mph speed limit would more likely perceive personal choice and more self-motivation regarding their decision to obey reduced mph mandates.

2. It's Not Easy

Acknowledge that "People might not want to do what they are being asked to do."[22] For example, admit certain behaviors (e.g., safety-related behaviors) are relatively inconvenient and uncomfortable, but given the reasonable rationale provided, the personal response cost is worthwhile.

And even though the value of AC4P coaching (i.e., giving a colleague interpersonal feedback to support right behavior and correct wrong behavior) is obvious, acknowledge it's natural to feel awkward in this situation, whether delivering or receiving the feedback. This justifies role-playing exercises to improve people's social skills at delivering and receiving behavior-based feedback.

3. Watch Your Language

Your language should suggest minimal external pressure. The common phrases "safety is a condition of employment," "all accidents are preventable," "bullying is a rite of passage," or "random acts of kindness" reduce one's sense of autonomy. The slogan, "AC4P is a value of our organization, school, or community" implies personal authenticity, interpersonal relatedness, and human interaction.

In the workplace, injuries are typically referred to as "accidents," implying limited personal choice or control and making it reasonable to think "when it's your time."

In schools, some teachers believe "students are just cruel at this age," or "bullying just happens." As a result they exercise limited personal interaction to prevent bullying behavior. The problem is "beyond their control".

The common phrase "random acts of kindness"[23] has a disadvantage when attempting to describe an AC4P behavior. Random implies the behavior happened by chance, which suggests it's beyond individual choice or control. The kind act may appear random to the recipient, but it was intentionally performed and usually self-motivated. Our preferred alternative: "intentional acts of kindness."

The language we use to prescribe or describe behavior influences our perceptions of its meaningfulness and its relevance to our lives. Language impacts culture, and vice versa.

4. Provide Opportunities for Choice

Participative management means employees have personal choice during the planning, execution, and evaluation of their jobs. People have a need for autonomy, regardless of dispositional and situational factors. In the workplace, managers often tell people what to do as opposed to involving them in the decision-making process.

In schools, students are often viewed as passive learners, because teachers plan, execute, and evaluate most aspects of the teaching/learning process. Students' perceptions of choice are limited. Yet cooperative teaching/learning—where students contribute to the selection and presentation of lesson material—has been shown to be most beneficial over the long term.[9]

5. Involve the Followers

Rules established by soliciting input from those affected by the regulation support autonomy.[11] Employees are more likely to comply with safety regulations they helped to define. Shouldn't they have significant influence in the development of policy they will be asked to follow? Those on the "front line" know best what actions should be avoided versus performed in order to optimize the safety and quality of their production system.

Similarly, before a rule or regulation is implemented in an educational system, those affected (i.e., faculty and/or students) should certainly be given opportunities to offer suggestions. In a family, as the children mature, certain rules should be open to discussion before being mandated. This takes more time, but the marked increase in effectiveness justifies the loss in efficiency.

6. Set SMARTS Goals

Customize process and outcome goals with individuals and work teams. The most effective goals are SMARTS: *Specific, Motivational, Achievable, Relevant, Trackable, and Shared.*[19]

Process goals reflect successive behavioral steps to achieve on route to accomplishing a significant outcome goal. A work team might set a process goal to complete a total of ten interpersonal observation-and-feedback sessions per week for one month, aiming to increase the percentage of safe behaviors recorded for their team. Of course, the long-term outcome goal is a reduction in personal injuries, but this can take substantial time to realize, especially if the group's injury rate is already low.

It's important to note and celebrate the periodic accomplishment of measurable process goals related to more remote and nebulous visions such as "culture improvement" and "injury free".

In educational settings, completing certain homework assignments and studying a certain number of hours per week serve as process goals, leading to the outcome of an improved exam grade, and eventually a desirable grade in a particular course. Achieving such process goals and obtaining

desirable grades leads to the more remote outcome goal of graduating with honors.

In family settings, goal-setting involving the participation of children may seem unreasonable, but at a certain point of their evolving maturity, full family involvement in defining the required individual and group behaviors (e.g., daily chores, school work, and budget management) to meet desired outcome goals (e.g., house and lawn maintenance, good school grades, and a family vacation) promotes mutual trust, perceived equity, and interdependent participation.

For optimal effectiveness, it's critical to apply the SMARTS acronym to the definition of a process goal. "S" for "specific" means the goal needs to be defined precisely with regard to the specific actions planned within a certain time period (e.g., perform ten coaching sessions per week for one month; complete a certain two-hour exercise routine three times a week for five consecutive months; recognize and reward five AC4P behaviors in a week).

Is Your Goal Motivating? "M" for "motivational" refers to the realization of the extrinsic and/or natural consequences acquired following goal attainment. For example, employees might look forward to a group pizza social (an extrinsic reward) after a month of averaging ten coaching sessions per week, and they might also anticipate improved communication skills and more AC4P relationships (an intrinsic reinforcer).

Similarly, an individual could plan for a weekend at the beach after completing the weekly exercise routine for five months (extrinsic reward), and anticipate fitting well in a new bathing suit (intrinsic reinforcer). Moreover, it naturally feels good to reward the AC4P behavior of others with an AC4P wristband, and such action contributes to cultivating an AC4P culture.

The "A" for "attainable" simply means the participants believe they can achieve the process goal, although it will not be easy. Fitting in ten coaching sessions a week for a month, for example, might be considered challenging but feasible. And, sticking to a specified exercise routine for five months will be difficult but doable. Recognizing and rewarding AC4P behavior is easier said than done, but it does get easier with practice.

The "R" for "relevant" refers to a clear, rational connection between achieving the process goal and obtaining an eventual outcome. Participants need to believe working toward accomplishing the process goal is consistent with their mission to obtain an eventual outcome goal. Interpersonal coaching is relevant to preventing injuries; regular exercise will lead to improved fitness, health, and well-being; and recognizing people regularly for their AC4P behavior is consistent with cultivating an AC4P culture of compassion.

The "T" for "trackable" reflects the need to track your progress toward attaining process goals. This implies, of course, goal-relevant behaviors can be counted successively as the participants get closer to realizing their goal. For example, interpersonal coaching sessions are tallied and posted on a chart for team members to observe; every two-hour exercise routine completed is marked on the calendar; and occurrences of AC4P behavior are indicated on a spread sheet that includes a space to specify the particular AC4P behavior rewarded.

Sharing Your Goal Finally, the "S" for "share" means it's useful to share your process goal with others. Public announcement of a group or individual goal increases commitment to work toward reaching that goal. And when others know your laudable goal and realize value in accomplishing that goal, they will likely help to motivate your progress.

For example, you might anticipate friends asking you about your goal-directed behavior, and such expected social accountability could enhance your self-motivation. In fact, just seeing those individuals who know about your goal can serve as a reminder to stay on course. You anticipate the question, "How's your goal progress these days," and you want to answer, "Very well, thank you".

So it's beneficial: a) for a work team to announce their coaching goals to other teams; b) to tell others of a fitness-routine goal, and c) for leaders of an AC4P movement to share their recognition goals with other advocates of an AC4P culture.

Observational learning is a positive side-effect of such goal sharing. When others interested in the mission implied by your goals learn about your goal setting and view your progress, they might consider setting similar goals for themselves or their team. Your shared goal setting and progress sets an impressive example for others to follow. This was a beneficial result of the following goal-setting story.

Joanne's AC4P Story Two years ago, my wife Joanne made a New Year's resolution to perform an AC4P behavior every day until her 60th Birthday on March 27th. She announced her goal to family and friends, including leaders of our campus AC4P Movement. She also described each of her AC4P behaviors on the website: ac4p.org. I hope it's obvious this was a SMARTS process goal. Joanne did accomplish this goal; but it wasn't easy.

Joanne knew she was setting a "stretch goal," but it was actually more challenging than she had expected. It took significant planning, preparation, and time to achieve daily AC4P behaviors, which varied widely from cooking meals and shoveling snow for neighbors to giving gift certificates to individuals she observed providing noteworthy community service.

Daily sharing of her AC4P actions sustained social support for her commitment, and set an impressive example many AC4P advocates have attempted to emulate on a smaller scale.

For example, each semester we initiate the "AC4P Challenge" among the 50 to 60 research students in our Center for Applied Behavior Systems. We evaluate whether students can attain the goal of performing five intentional AC4P acts in one week. "If Joanne can do 60 in 60," we say, "then surely you can accomplish five AC4P acts in seven days".

Most students willingly sign an "AC4P Commitment Card" for the "AC4P Challenge," but less than 50% report

meeting this seemingly easy goal. Actively caring on a daily basis is easier said than done when AC4P behavior is defined as going beyond the norm to benefit the health, safety, or well-being of another person.

7. Use Behavior-Based Feedback

Supervisors, teachers, and parents are more likely to notice and reprimand undesirable behavior, than discern and acknowledge desirable behavior. This is why the term "feedback" carries negative connotations.

What is one to think if asked, "Can I give you some feedback about your behavior last night"? Likewise, how do you feel after receiving an email from your supervisor that he wants you to come to his office at the end of the day for some feedback? Has your day been ruined? For many of us, the illustration below rings true.

It's unfortunate but true: Most people expect feedback to be more negative than positive. Of course, that perception can be changed if supervisors, teachers, and parents verbalized more *supportive* than corrective feedback.

Suppose that supervisor or teacher who asked to see you at the end of the day for a feedback session gives you only supportive feedback. She defines specific desirable behaviors she has observed you perform, and expresses genuine appreciation for the extra effort you consistently demonstrate to apply your notable skill sets on behalf of the organization's mission.

Courtesy of George Vaughn Willis.

How would that make you feel? Would "feedback" take on a more positive meaning, at least with this supervisor? Would you share this positive experience with others and likely enhance others' perception of "feedback" and this supervisor's leadership skills? That's the power of interpersonal recognition and approval in cultivating a self-motivated AC4P culture.

If-Then Rewards

Use *if-then incentive/reward contingencies* when individuals are not already self-motivated to perform the desired behavior or intrinsic reinforcers are not available. This does not mean the *if-then incentive/reward contingencies* are bad or undesirable, as some uninformed authors have claimed.[24] Extrinsic rewards influence many behaviors and this is not detrimental to self-motivation; they just might not increase it.

For example, I choose certain airlines and hotels in order to earn "points" that can translate to material rewards or improved services. My awareness of this "manipulation tactic" does not impact my disposition in any negative way. In fact, I'm pleased to be extrinsically rewarded for making certain choices. Indeed, my sense of choice to select the airline or hotel that offers the "if-then" rewards has a beneficial impact on my overall self-motivation.

In the same view, it is not detrimental to reward students for performing certain behaviors relevant to their education, as authors uneducated in psychological science have claimed.[24] The child who doesn't choose to read books, for example, cannot experience the inherent enjoyment (i.e., intrinsic reinforcement) of reading. In this case, an *if-then contingency* can be invaluable. The child is extrinsically rewarded for performing a behavior previously emitted only infrequently. Subsequently, the child may enjoy reading, especially after feeling competent at this worthwhile task. Then self-motivation takes control, and extrinsic incentives are no longer needed.

As I explained earlier, competence fuels self-motivation. People can help others feel competent by offering words of appreciation for behaviors that reflect their personal competence. Hence, genuine approval of a child's reading behavior from a parent increases the child's perception of competence and self-motivation.

Now-That Rewards

At times, special rewards of excellence are given to individuals and groups for excelling at performance in a given domain, from accomplishments in teaching and learning to winning an athletic competition. These extrinsic consequences are well received, often to the applause of an approving audience. Such acknowledgment does wonders to an individual's sense of personal competence, leading to more self-motivation to sustain or even enhance the relevant skill set.

It's noteworthy these latter examples of rewarding desirable behavior reflect a *now-that* contingency rather than *if-then*. These rewards do not include an incentive (i.e., the announcement of the availability of a reward if a designated behavior occurs). The behavior might be initiated for a variety of internal, intrinsic, or extrinsic reasons, but the unannounced *now-that* reward is given after the behavior occurs

in order to support its occurrence. In some cases, this rewarding consequence increases the probability the desirable behavior will recur. In most cases, a person's sense of competence increases following sincere *now-that* rewards, fueling self-motivation to continue the rewarded behavior.

Behavior-Based Recognition

In the workplace, managers should intermittently communicate one-on-one with employees to express sincere appreciation for their specific behaviors that contribute to the organization.

In school, teachers' interpersonal praise of their students' work are invaluable to boosting self-competence, confidence, and self-motivation to continuously improve. And every parent knows through personal experience the motivational benefits of demonstrating enthusiastic approval of a child's dedication to do well at a particular task.

Courtesy of George Vaughn Willis.

Words of approval, appreciation, and praise are relatively rare, especially when compared with the use of verbal reprimands, as experience has taught us. Mistakes or disruptive behaviors stick out and invite corrective action; but desirable behavior does not naturally attract attention and seemingly does not require intervention.

By now you certainly see the special advantages of supportive over-corrective feedback in enhancing self-motivation, right? Still, there are times when it's necessary to correct undesirable behavior. How should this be done?

8. Give Corrective Feedback Well

Make use of empathy and compassion to correct undesirable behavior. Be non-directive, actively-listen to excuses, and emphasize the positive over the negative. It can be uncomfortable to provide others with behavior-based corrective feedback, even when the recipient of your feedback is a family member or friend. Remind yourself and the feedback recipient that only with specific behavioral feedback can performance be improved. Remember, practice does not make perfect unless the performer receives supportive feedback for right behavior and corrective feedback for wrong behavior.

Incorrect or unsafe behavior is not an indictment of a person's attitude, values, or personality. Our unintentional mistakes do not reflect who we are. So it is critical to emphasize that your corrective feedback is only about behavior you have observed and not a judgment of the person.

Continuous improvement occurs when observers have the courage to give relevant behavior-based feedback, and when those observed have the humility to accept the feedback and make relevant behavioral adjustments. After all, we all want to improve behavior that's important to us, and this often requires behavioral feedback from others.

How should you approach someone to give corrective feedback? Your initial words are critical. If you come on too strong when directing a person to improve in a certain way, the "victim" may get defensive and offer excuses for a mistake. Or, if the observer has relevant authority over the victim, which is often the case, the victim might make the behavioral adjustments called for; but the change will not stick if the victim does not agree with and accept the behavioral advice.

How can you get buy-in for the behavioral feedback you have the courage to offer? Your opening words should be inquisitive rather than accusative. If the feedback targets a person's unsafe behavior, my good friend John Drebinger recommends beginning with a question like, "Could I look out for your safety?"[25] Who could say "No" to a request like this?

Then following a "Yes, of course," the observer mentions the behavior that needs adjustments for injury prevention. Often it's best if the observer can mention some desirable behavior first, and then suggest where there's room for improvement.

My partners at Safety Performance Solutions have been teaching behavioral coaching for occupational health and safety for almost two decades, and they've always emphasized the need to be empathic and nondirective when giving co-workers behavior-based feedback.[26] More specifically, an AC4P observer of a certain worker completes a critical behavior checklist (CBC) of safe vs. at-risk behavior, previously designed through interactive group discussions among line workers representative of the relevant workforce.[27] Workers give permission to be observed, and they know what behaviors are being observed. Even with this set up, at-risk behaviors are often observed and observers are challenged to offer corrective feedback to a co-worker.

How do they do this? From the start it's emphasized the observer (unlike a typical athletic coach) is not responsible for directing or motivating corrective action. The observer merely completes the CBC, and then shows the results to the person observed. The two workers might discuss environmental or system factors that discourage safe behavior and encourage at-risk behavior. And they might consider ways to remove barriers to safe behavior. The observer, referred to as an AC4P coach, might offer positive words of approval to recognize certain safe behavior, but gives no disapproving statements or directives related to any observed at-risk behavior.

An AC4P coach is nondirective when communicating corrective feedback. The coach provides specific behavior-based feedback for the person observed to consider. There is no pressure to change. The only accountability is self-accountability. Any adjustment in behavior is self-motivated, activated by the results of a nonintrusive and anticipated application of a CBC.

The perception of personal choice increases the likelihood this kind of corrective feedback will be accepted and lead to a self-motivated behavioral adjustment. Workers choose to be observed by an AC4P coach, and then choose to accept or reject the feedback provided by a CBC.

9. Celebrate to Increase a Sense Community

Celebrations, when done correctly, can motivate teamwork and build a sense of belongingness and community among groups of individuals, boosting their self-motivation. Of course the key words in the preceding sentence are "when done correctly". Let's consider seven guidelines for celebrating group accomplishments:

Reward the Right Behavior In the domain of occupational safety, it's common for organizations to give groups of employees a celebration dinner after a particular number of weeks or months pass with no recordable injury. This kind of achievement is certainly worth celebrating, but let's be sure the record was reached fairly. If people cheat to win by not reporting their injuries, the celebration won't mean much.

If a celebration for lower injuries is announced as an incentive, the motivation to cheat is increased. If employees are promised a reward when they work a certain number of days without an injury, it will be tempting to avoid reporting a personal injury if they can get away with it. This is, of course, peer pressure to cheat—a situation that reduces interpersonal trust and promotes a belief that improved levels of organizational safety cannot be reached fairly.

If the accomplishment of process activities is celebrated, then it's okay to establish an *if-then* behavior-consequence contingency, as discussed earlier. In this case, the behaviors needed from the group are specified in order to warrant a celebration. This is group goal setting. If the SMARTS principles discussed above are followed, teamwork for goal accomplishment will be motivated.

A group might decide to celebrate after everyone reports one observation of an AC4P behavior or when every group member performs an AC4P behavior, or after the total number of AC4P behaviors observed and performed by the group members reach a designated total. In these cases, a SMARTS group goal is set and progress is monitored. When the goal is reached, a celebration is warranted. It was earned for a successful journey, destined to eventually achieve an AC4P culture of compassion.

Focus on the Journey

Most of the corporate celebrations I've seen were for excellence in safety, and all of these gave far too little attention to the journey—the processes that contributed to reaching the milestone. Typically, the focus was on the end result, the outcome measure, like achieving zero injuries for a certain period of time.

There was scant discussion about *how* the outcome was achieved. It's natural to toast the bottom line, but there's more to be gained from taking the opportunity to diagnose and recognize process success.

When you pinpoint processes instrumental to reaching a particular milestone, you give valuable direction and motivation. Participants learn what to continue doing for an effective journey. Those responsible for the behaviors leading to the celebrated outcome receive a special boost in competence, personal control, and optimism. Plus, information is added to these individuals' internal recognition scripts which enhances their self-motivation.

Perhaps the most important reason to acknowledge journey activities leading to a noteworthy group outcome is that it gives credit where credit is due. Focusing on the process endorses the people and their actions that made the difference, fueling self-motivation. This leads to the next guideline.

Recipients Should Be Participants

Rarely do participants in a celebratory event discuss the processes they supported in order to reach the outcome. And so a valuable "teaching moment" is missed. Instead, speeches from top management often kick off a corporate celebration. Sometimes charts are displayed to compare the past with the improved present. Often a sincere request for continuous improvement is made, and a manager points out the amount of money saved or profits earned by the group's accomplishment. Sometimes promises for a bigger celebration are made following continued success.

Occasionally a motivational speaker or humorist gives everyone a lift and some laughs. Often special rewards are given to individuals or team captains, along with a handshake from a top-management official. Certificates and trinkets might be handed out, along with a steak dinner.

In the typical corporate celebration, management gives and the employees receive—certainly an impressive show of top-down support. But the ceremony would be more memorable and beneficial as both learning and motivational if employees were more participant than recipient.

Managers should listen more than speak, and employees should talk more about their experiences than listen to managers' pleasure with the bottom line.

Relive the Journey

Managers should facilitate discussion of the activities that led to the celebrated accomplishment. Relive the procedures that made the journey successful. This "reenactment" strengthens employees' internal scripts that direct and motivate their ongoing support of the effective process. Managers who listen to these discussions with genuine interest and concern are rewarding the participation that enabled the success and empowering employees to continue their journey toward higher-level achievement.

The best safety celebration I ever observed was planned by employees and featured a series of brief presentations by teams of hourly workers. Numerous safety ideas were shared. Some workers showed off new personal protective equipment, some displayed graphs of data obtained from environmental or behavioral audits, some discussed their procedures for encouraging reports of close calls and implementing corrective action, and one group presented its ergonomic analysis and redesign of a work station.

Even the after-dinner entertainment was employee-driven. A skit illustrated safety issues. A talent show had entrants from all levels of the organization, including top managers. There was no need to hire a band for live music—a number of talented musicians were found in the workforce of 600. Luckily, they didn't find a drummer, allowing me to sit in and relive my rock-n-roll gigging from the 1960s.

Discuss Successes and Failures

The work teams in this celebration discussed both successes and failures, displaying the positive results and recalling disappointments, dead ends, and frustrations. Pointing out the highs and lows made their presentations realistic, and underscored the amount of dedication needed to complete their projects and contribute to the celebrated reduction in injuries.

Presentations that point out hardships along the journey to success justify the celebration. The celebrated bottom line was not a matter of luck. It took hard work by many people going beyond the call of duty. The payoff: small-win contributions, pronounced interdependence, win-win collaboration, and synergy.

Make it Memorable

Goal attainment is meaningful and memorable when people discuss the difficulties in reaching a goal. When managers listen to these presentations with sincere interest and appreciation, the event becomes even more significant and credible. And when a tangible reward is distributed appropriately at such an occasion, a mechanism is established to sustain the memory of this occasion and promote its value.

Ideally, the memento should include words, perhaps a theme or slogan, that reflects the particular celebration. The tangible reward should be something readily displayable or usable at work—from coffee mugs, placards, and pencil holders to caps, shirts, and umbrellas, for example.

When delivering these keepsakes, it should be noted they were selected "to help you remember this special occasion and what it has meant to all of us. This small token of our appreciation will remind us how we got here."

One week after the safety celebration I described here, every participant received a framed group photograph of everyone who attended the event. That picture hangs in my office today, and every time I look at it, I'm reminded of the time several years ago when management did more listening than talking in a most memorable and educational group celebration.

Don't Neglect Your Leaders In every group project, some individuals take charge and champion the effort, while others sit back and "go with the flow". Some people exert less effort when working with a group than when working alone. Psychologists call this phenomenon "social loafing".[28]

Recognize the champions of a group effort one-on-one, and you let them know you realize the importance of their leadership in a team accomplishment. You appreciate their extra-effort contributions. This adds substantially to the self-motivation the person had already received from the earlier group celebration. As a result, you've increased the likelihood of continued leadership directed toward attaining further goals.

Solicit Ideas When I mentioned to my graduate students I was writing a book chapter on how to celebrate, one of them quickly responded, "That's easy, a $100 bottle of cognac, a $6 cigar, and a special friend". I had to tell him, of course, my focus was on a different kind of celebrating.

But it occurred to me that everyone has his or her own way of celebrating. And when it comes to group celebration, we often inadvertently impose our prejudices on others. We usually don't take the time to ask potential participants what kind of celebration party they would like.

When it comes to organizing a group accomplishment, many people don't know how to celebrate. Ask people what they want for their celebration, and the discussion likely focuses on tangible rewards. "What material commodity should we receive for our efforts?" This puts the celebration in a payoff-for-behavior mode and is not the real purpose of a group celebration. You want a meaningful and memorable event that increases a sense of belonging and community, and can serve as a stepping stone to even greater achievements.

10. Build Interpersonal Trust

To cultivate an AC4P culture, interpersonal trust is absolutely fundamental. Trust is the foundation for building a community of people who go beyond the call of duty to give each other behavior-based support and relevant corrective feedback.

Seven C-words capture the essence of building interpersonal trust and interdependence: communication, caring,

candor, consistency, commitment, consensus, and character. Let's consider how each of these C-words implicates interpersonal trust and community-building. The phrase associated with the following C-words summarizes the key definitions given in my American Heritage and New-Merriam-Webster dictionaries.[29]

"It's nice to get away, but I wish the boss trusted me more."

Courtesy of George Vaughn Willis.

Communication *exchange of information or opinion by speech, writing, or signals.* What people say and how they say it influences our trust in both their capability and their intentions.

I'm sure you've heard many times the way something is said, including intonation, pace, facial expressions, hand gestures, and overall posture, has greater impact than what was actually said. And, you've certainly experienced personal feelings of trust toward another person change as the result of how that individual communicated information.

Often we trust certain information because we respect the credentials of the communicator or we like the way the message is displayed. Personal opinion or "common sense" is relied on if the message sounds good to us and if the presentation is given well—with Clarity, Confidence, and Charisma.

Those three C-words suggest how we get others to trust our knowledge, skill, or ability. But what about trusting one's intentions? Do you know people who have impressive credentials and communicate elegantly, but something makes you suspicious about their intentions? You believe they know what to do, but you're not convinced they will do what they say. They have the right talk, but give the impression they don't walk it. This critical issue is reflected in each of the subsequent C-words for trust-building.

However, before moving on to the other C-words, let's consider the most powerful communication strategy for increasing trust in one's intentions—AC4P listening. There is probably no better way to earn someone's trust in your intentions than by listening attentively to that person's communication with an AC4P mindset. When you listen to others first before communicating your own perspective, you not only increase the chance they will reciprocate and listen to you, you also learn how to present your message for optimal understanding, appreciation, and buy-in.

Caring *showing concern or interest about what happens.* When people believe you sincerely care about them, they will care about what you tell them. They trust you will look out for them when applying your knowledge, skills, or abilities. They trust your intentions because they believe you care.

You communicate AC4P and build interpersonal trust when you ask questions. I'm referring to inquiry about a particular task or set of circumstances. Questions targeting a specific aspect of a person's job send the signal you care about him or her. This communication is more credible than the general, "How ya doing?" greeting.

Take the time to learn what others are doing. Listen and observe. Here I'm talking about "listening to the talk, and walking the walk". You want to "talk the walk" so people trust your intentions.

Candor *straightforwardness and frankness of expression; freedom from prejudice.* We trust people who are frank and open with us. People who don't beat around the bush.

When they don't know an answer to our questions, they tell us outright they don't know and they'll get back to us with an answer.

You have reason to mistrust individuals if their interactions with you reflect prejudice or the tendency to judge blindly. You question their ability to evaluate others and their intentions to treat people fairly.

When people give an opinion about others because of their race, religion, gender, or birthplace, you should doubt these individuals' ability to make people-related decisions. And, you should wonder whether their intentions to perform on behalf of another individual will be biased or tainted by a tendency to pre-judge people on the basis of overly simple and usually inaccurate stereotypes.

Consistency *agreement among successive acts, ideas, or events.* Consistency is a key determinant of interpersonal trust. Perhaps the *fastest* way to destroy interpersonal trust is to not follow through on an agreement. This is also the *easiest* way to stifle trust.

How often do we make a promise we don't keep? Most promises are *if-then* contingencies. We specify a certain consequence will follow a certain behavior. Whether the consequence is positive or negative, trust decreases when the behavior is not rewarded or punished as promised.

When my daughters were young, I frequently caught myself impulsively making promises (or policy statements) I didn't keep. For example, when they misbehaved while their mom and I were packing the car for a trip, it was not uncommon for one of us to say, "Stop doing that right now or we're not going". Often our daughters stopped the undesirable behavior. The "policy maker" was then reinforced for making the promise.

But what happened when my daughters didn't stop their misbehavior or resumed the undesirable behavior after a brief hiatus? Sure, we still made the trip. The punishment contingency might be shouted a few more times, but regardless, we eventually piled into our car and took off. What did these empty threats teach our daughters?

We would have been far better off promising a less severe negative consequence we could implement consistently, such as delaying the trip until the behavior stops. "We can't go until you stop fighting," would have been much better than a more severe *if-then* threat with inconsistent consequences.

Commitment *bound emotionally or intellectually to a course of action.* When you follow through on a promise or pledge to do something, you tell others they can count on you. You can be trusted to do what you say you will do.

The consistency principle reflects a spiral of causality and explains how behavior influences attitude, and vice verse. When we choose to do something, we experience internal pressure to maintain a personal belief system or attitude consistent with that behavior. And when we have a certain belief system or attitude toward something, we tend to behave in ways consistent with such beliefs or attitudes.

Commitment and total involvement result from a causal spiraling of action feeding attitude, then attitude feeding more action, which strengthens the attitude and leads to more behavior.

Researchers have found three ways to make an initial commitment to do something lead to the most causal spiraling and total involvement.[30] First, people live up to what they write down, so ask for a signed statement of a commitment. Second, the more public the commitment, the greater the relevant attitude and behavior change, presumably because social pressures are added to the personal pressure to be consistent in word and deed.

Third, and perhaps most importantly, for a public and written commitment to initiate causal spiraling of behavior supporting attitude (and vice versa), the commitment must be viewed as a personal choice. When people believe their commitment was their idea, the consistency principle is activated. But when people believe their commitment was unduly influenced by outside factors, they do not feel a need to live up to what they were coerced to write down.

Consensus *agreement in opinion, testimony, or belief.* Whenever the results of a group decision-making process come across as "win-lose," some mistrust is going to develop. A majority of the group might be pleased, but others will be discontented and might actively or passively resist involvement. And even the "winners" could feel lowered interpersonal trust. "We won this decision, but what about next time?" And without solid back-up support of the decision, the outcome will be less than desired. "Without everyone's buy-in, commitment and involvement, we can't trust the process to come off as expected."

How can group consensus be developed? How can the outcome of a heated debate be perceived as a win-win solution everyone supports? Consensus-building takes time and energy, and requires candid, consistent and caring communication among all members of a discussion or decision-making group. When people demonstrate the C-words discussed above for building trust in interpersonal dialogue, they also develop consensus and more interpersonal trust regarding a particular decision or action plan.

There's no quick fix to doing this. It requires plenty of interpersonal communication, including straightforward opinion sharing, intense discussion, emotional debate, active listening, careful evaluation, methodical organization, and systematic prioritizing. But on important matters, the outcome is well worth the investment. When you develop a solution or process every potential participant can get behind and champion, you have cultivated the degree of interpersonal trust needed for total involvement. Involvement in turn builds personal commitment, more interpersonal trust, and then more involvement.

Character *the combined moral or ethical structure of a person or group; integrity; fortitude.* Generally, a person with "character" is considered honest, ethical, and principled. People with character are credible or worthy of another person's trust because they display confidence and competence. They know

who they are; they know where they want to go; and they know how to get there.

All of the strategies discussed here for cultivating a trusting culture are practiced by a person with character. Individuals with character are willing to admit vulnerability. They are humble and realize they aren't perfect and need behavioral feedback from others. They know their strengths and weaknesses, and find exemplars to model.

By actively listening to others and observing their behaviors, individuals with character learn how to improve their own performance. And if they're building a high-performance team, they can readily find people with knowledge, skills, and abilities to complement their own competencies. They know how to make diversity work for them, their group, and the entire organization.

Courtesy of George Vaughn Willis.

Having the courage to admit your weaknesses means you're willing to apologize when you've made a mistake, and to ask for forgiveness. There is probably no better way to build trust between individuals than to own up to an error that might have affected another person.

Of course you should also indicate what you will do better next time or ask for specific advice on how to improve. This kind of vulnerability enables you to heed the powerful enrichment principle I learned from the late Frank Bird, "good better best, may we never rest until good is better and better is best".[31]

While admitting personal vulnerability is a powerful way to build interpersonal trust, the surest way to reduce interpersonal trust is to tell one person about the weakness of another. In this situation it's natural to think, "If he talks that way about her, I wonder what he says about me behind my back". It's obvious how criticizing or demeaning others in their absence can lead to interpersonal suspiciousness and mistrust.

Back-stabbing leads to more back-stabbing, and eventually you have a work culture of independent people doing their own thing, fearful of making an error, and unreceptive to any kind of behavior-based feedback. Key aspects of continuous performance improvement—team-building, interpersonal observation, and coaching—are extremely difficult or impossible to implement in such a culture. Under these circumstances it's necessary to first break down barriers to interpersonal trust before implementing a behavior-based observation and feedback process.

Start to build interpersonal trust by implementing a policy of no back-stabbing. People with character, as defined here, always talk about other people as if they can hear you. In other words, to replace interpersonal mistrust with trust, never talk about other individuals behind their backs unless you're willing to say the same thing directly to them.

A Summary

The seven C-words offer distinct directives for trust-building behavior. *Communicating* these guidelines to others in a *candid* and *caring* way opens up the kind of dialogue that starts people on a journey of interpersonal trust-building. Then people need to give each other *consistent* and *candid* feedback regarding those behaviors that reflect these trust-building principles.

With *character* and *commitment,* they need to recognize others for doing it right and offer corrective feedback when there's room for improvement. And of course it's critical for the recipient of such behavior-based feedback to accept it with *caring* appreciation and a *commitment* to improve.

Then, the feedback recipient needs to show the *character* to thank the observer for the feedback, even when the *communication* is not all positive and is not delivered well. S/he might offer feedback on how to make the behavior-based feedback more useful. Dialogue like this is necessary to build consensus and sustain a journey of continuous trust and community-building.

In Conclusion

An AC4P culture requires people to do the right thing on behalf of other people when no other person is holding them accountable. Such self-accountability to perform AC4P behavior usually requires self-motivation. This research-based chapter introduced a number of practical ways to facilitate the self-motivation needed to achieve and sustain an AC4P culture.

This book offers a number of real-world examples of the self-motivation principles and leadership lessons reviewed here, as well as practical ways to apply these principles and lessons for enhancing people's self-motivation to actively care for the health, safety, and well-being of others.

NOTES

1. Geller, E.S., & Veazie, R.A. (2010). *When no one's watching: Living and leading self motivation.* Newport, VA: Make-A-Difference, LLC.

2. Chance, P. (2007). The ultimate challenge: Prove B.F. Skinner wrong. *The Behavior Analyst, 30,* 153–160.

3. Deci, E.L. (1975). *Intrinsic motivation.* New York, NY: Plenum; Deci, E.L., & Flaste, R. (1995). *Why we do what we do: Understanding self-motivation.* New York, NY: Penguin Book; Deci, E.L., & Ryan, R.M. (1995). *Intrinsic motivation and self-determinism in human behavior.* New York, NY: Plenum; Ryan, R.M., & Deci, E.L. (2000). Self-determinism theory and the foundation of intrinsic motivation, social development, and well-being. *American Psychologist, 55,* 68–75.

4. Deci, E.L., & Flaste, R. (1995). *Why we do what we do: Understanding self-motivation.* New York, NY: Penguin Books, p.9.

5. Geller, E.S. (2001). *The psychology of safety handbook.* Boca Raton, FL: CRC Press; Ludwig, T.D., & Geller, E.S. (2001). *Intervening to improve the safety of occupational driving: A behavior-change model and review of empirical evidence.* New York, NY: The Haworth Press, Inc.; Monty, R.A., & Perlmuter, L.C. (1975). Persistence of the effect of choice on paired-associate learning. *Memory & Cognition, 3,* 183–187; Perlmuter, L.C., Monty, R.A., & Kimble, G.A. (1971). Effect of choice on paired-associate learning. *Journal of Experimental Psychology, 91,* 47–58; Steiner, I.D. (1970). Perceived freedom. In L. Berkowitz, L. (Ed.). *Advances in experimental social psychology,* Vol. 5, New York, NY: Academic Press.

6. Geller, E.S. (1994). Ten principles for achieving a Total Safety Culture. *Professional Safety, 39*(9), 18–25; Geller, E.S. (2001). *The psychology of safety handbook.* Boca Raton, FL: CRC Press; Geller, E.S. (2005). *People-based safety: The source.* Virginia Beach, VA: Coastal Training Technologies Corp.; Geller, E.S. (2008). *Leading people-based safety: Enriching your culture.* Virginia Beach, VA: Coastal Training Technologies Corp.

7. White, R.W. (1959). Motivation reconsidered: The concept of competence. *Psychological Review, 66,* 297–321.

8. Deci, E.L., & Flaste, R. (1995). *Why we do what we do: Understanding self-motivation.* New York, NY: Penguin Books, p.66.

9. Chance, P. (2008). *The teacher's craft: The 10 essential skills of effective teaching.* Long Grove, IL: Waveland Press, Inc.

10. Geller, E.S. (1996). *The psychology of safety: How to improve behaviors and attitudes on the job.* Radnor, PA: The Chilton Book Company; Geller, E.S. (1998). *Understanding behavior-based safety: Step-by-step methods to improve your workplace* (Second Edition). Neenah, WI: J.J. Keller & Associates, Inc; Geller, E.S. (2001). *The psychology of safety handbook.* Boca Raton, FL: CRC Press; Geller, E.S. (2005). *People-based safety: The source.* Virginia Beach, VA: Coastal Training and Technologies Corporation;

Geller, E.S., Perdue, S.R., & French, A. (2004) Behavior-based safety coaching: Ten guidelines for successful application. *Professional Safety*, 49(7), 42–49; Krause, T.R., Hidley, J.H., & Hodson, S.J. (1996). *The behavior-based safety process: Managing improvement for an injury-free culture* (Second Edition). New York, NY: Van Nostrand Reinhold; McSween, T.E. (2003). *The values-based safety process: Improving your safety culture with a behavioral approach* (Second Edition). New York, NY: Van Nostrand Reinhold; Weigand, D.M. (2007). Exploring the role of emotional intelligence in behavior-based safety coaching. *Journal of Safety Research*, 38, 391–398.

11. Deci, E.L., & Flaste, R. (1995). *Why we do what we do: Understanding self-motivation.* New York, NY: Penguin Books, p.88.

12. Geller, E.S. (1994). Ten principles for achieving a Total Safety Culture. *Professional Safety*, 39(9), 18–25; Geller, E.S. (2001). *The psychology of safety handbook.* Boca Raton, FL: CRC Press; Geller, E.S. (2005). *People-based safety: The source.* Virginia Beach, VA: Coastal Training Technologies Corp.

13. Block, P. (2008). *Community: The structure of belonging.* San Francisco, CA: Berrett-Koehler Publishers.

14. Peck, M.S. (1979). *The different drum: Community making and peace.* New York, NY: Simon & Schuster, Inc.

15. Deming, W.E. (1986). *Out of the crisis.* Cambridge, MA: Massachusetts Institute of Technology, Center for Advanced Engineering Study; Deming, W.E. (1993). *The new economics for industry, government, education.* Cambridge, MA: Massachusetts Institute of Technology, Center for Advanced Engineering Study.

16. Senge, P.M. (1990). *The fifth discipline: The art and practice of the learning organization.* New York, NY: Doubleday.

17. Covey, S.R. (1989). *The seven habits of highly effective people.* New York, NY: Simon and Schuster, Inc.

18. Geller, E.S., & Veazie, R.A. (2009). *The courage factor: Leading people-based culture change.* Virginia Beach, VA: Coastal Training and Technologies Corporation.

19. Geller, E.S. (2005). *People-based safety: The source.* Virginia Beach, VA: Coastal Training Technologies Corp., pp.95–98.

20. Deci, E.L. (1975). *Intrinsic motivation.* New York: Plenum; Deci, E.L., & Flaste, R. (1995). *Why we do what we do: Understanding self-motivation.* New York, NY: Penguin Book; Deci, E.L., &

Ryan, R.M. (1995). *Intrinsic motivation and self-determinism in human behavior.* New York, NY: Plenum; Ryan, R.M., & Deci, E.L. (2000). Self-determinism theory and the foundation of intrinsic motivation, social development, and well-being. *American Psychologist*, 55, 68–75.

21. United Kingdom Department of Transport (1987). *Killing speed and saving lives.* London, England: Department of Transport.

22. Deci, E.L., & Flaste, R. (1995). *Why we do what we do: Understanding self-motivation.* New York, NY: Penguin Books, p. 104.

23. Conari Press (1993). *Random acts of kindness.* Emeryville, CA.

24. Kohn, A. *Punished by rewards: The trouble with gold stars, incentive plans, A's, praise, and other bribes,* Boston, MA: Houghton Mifflin; Pink, D.H. (2009). *Drive: The surprising truth about what motivates us.* New York, NY: Penguin Group.

25. Drebinger, J.W. (2011). *Would you watch out for my safety? Helping others avoid personal injury.* Galt, CA: Wulamoc Publishing.

26. Geller, E.S. (2005). *People-based safety: The source.* Virginia Beach, VA: Coastal Training Technologies Corp., pp.95–98; Geller, E. S. (2008). *Leading people-based safety: Enriching your culture.* Virginia Beach, VA: Coastal Training Technologies Corp.; Geller, E. S., Perdue, S. R., & French, A. (2004). Behavior-based safety coaching: Ten guidelines for successful application. *Professional Safety*, 49(7), 42–49.

27. Geller, E.S. (1998). *Understanding behavior-based safety: Step-by-step methods to improve your workplace* (Revised Edition). Neenah, WI: J. J. Keller & Associates, Inc.; Geller, E.S. (2001). *The psychology of safety handbook.* Boca Raton, FL: CRC Press; Geller, E.S. (2001). *Working safe: How to help people actively care for health and safety* (Second Edition). Boca Raton, FL: CRC Press.

28. Latane, B., Williams, K., & Harkins, S. (1979). Many hands make light the work: The causes and consequences of social loafing. *Journal of Personality and Social Psychology*, 37, 822–832.

29. *The American Heritage Dictionary,* (1991). Boston, MA: Houghton Mifflin Company; New-Merriam-Webster Dictionary (1989). Springfield, MA: Merriam-Webster Publishers.

30. Cialdini, R.B. (2001). *Influence: Science and practice (4th Edition).* New York: Harper Collins College.

31. Bird, Jr., F.E., & Davies, R. J. (1996). *Safety and the bottom line.* Loganville, GA: Febco.

12

Therapies for Psychological Disorders

Taken from *Psychology: Core Concepts,* Seventh Edition, by Philip G. Zimbardo, Robert L. Johnson, and Vivian McCann

12.1 What Is Therapy?

Entering Therapy • The Therapeutic Alliance and the Goals of Therapy • Therapy in Historical and Cultural Context

CORE CONCEPTS Therapy for psychological disorders takes a variety of forms, but all involve a *therapeutic relationship* focused on improving a person's mental, behavioral, or social functioning.

PSYCHOLOGY MATTERS
Paraprofessionals Do Therapy Too

Some studies show that the therapist's level of training is not the main factor in therapeutic effectiveness.

12.2 How Do Psychologists Treat Psychological Disorders?

Insight Therapies • Behavior Therapies • Cognitive–Behavioral Therapy: A Synthesis • Evaluating the Psychological Therapies

CORE CONCEPTS Psychologists employ two main forms of treatment, the insight therapies (focused on developing understanding of the problem) and the behavior therapies (focused on changing behavior through conditioning).

PSYCHOLOGY MATTERS
Where Do Most People Get Help?

A lot of therapy is done by friends, hairdressers, and bartenders.

12.3 How Is the Biomedical Approach Used to Treat Psychological Disorders?

Drug Therapy • Other Medical Therapies for Psychological Disorders • Hospitalization and the Alternatives

CORE CONCEPTS Biomedical therapies seek to treat psychological disorders by changing the brain's chemistry with drugs, its circuitry with surgery, or its patterns of activity with pulses of electricity or powerful magnetic fields.

PSYCHOLOGY MATTERS
What Sort of Therapy Would You Recommend?

There is a wide range of therapeutic possibilities to discuss with a friend who asks for your recommendation.

12.4 How Do the Psychological Therapies and Biomedical Therapies Compare?

Depression and Anxiety Disorders: Psychological versus Medical Treatment • Schizophrenia: Psychological versus Medical Treatment • "The Worried Well" and Other Problems: Not Everyone Needs Drugs

CORE CONCEPTS While a combination of psychological and medical therapies is often better than either one alone for treating some (but not all) mental disorders, most people who have unspecified "problems in living" are best served by psychological treatment alone.

PSYCHOLOGY MATTERS
Using Psychology to Learn Psychology

Consider the ways in which therapy is like your college experience.

Chapter Problem

What is the best treatment for Derek's depression: psychological therapy, drug therapy, or both? More broadly, the problem is this: How do we decide among the available therapies for any of the mental disorders?

Critical Thinking Applied

Evidence-Based Practice

Off and on, Derek had felt tired and unhappy for months, and he knew it was affecting not only his work but also the relationship with his partner. Michele, a coworker and friend, tactfully suggested he seek professional help, but Derek was unsure where to turn. As many people do, he asked for a recommendation from another friend, who he knew had sought therapy three years ago. And that is how he ended up, somewhat apprehensively, at Dr. Sturm's office.

She was easy to talk to, it turned out, and it didn't take long for both of them to agree that Derek was depressed. After some conversation about the nature of depression, Dr. Sturm said, "We have several treatment alternatives." She added, "The one in which I am trained is cognitive-behavioral therapy, which approaches depression as a learned problem to be treated by changing the way a person thinks about life events and interpersonal relationships. If we take that route, we will explore what is happening at work and at home that might trigger depressive episodes. I would also give you 'homework' every week—assignments designed to help you build on your strengths, rather than focusing on your weaknesses. Just like school," she added with a little laugh.

"As a second option," she said, "I could refer you to a colleague who does psychodynamic therapy. If you choose that approach, you and Dr. Ewing would explore your past, looking for events that may have pushed you down the path to the feelings you are experiencing now. Essentially, it would be a treatment aimed at bringing some unpleasant parts of your unconscious mind into the light of day."

"The other thing I could do is to arrange to get you some medication that has been proven effective in treating depression. It would probably be one of those antidepressants, like Prozac, that you have seen advertised in magazines and on TV. The problem there is that it takes several weeks for them to have an effect. And, besides, I'm not sure they really treat the problems that keep making you feel depressed."

"Oh, yes," she added, "There are some additional medical options, such as electroconvulsive therapy—people often call it 'shock treatment,' but I don't think it is needed in your case."

"Just hearing that makes me feel better," Derek sighed. "So, the choice is between drugs and psychological therapy?"

"Or perhaps a combination of the two," replied Dr. Sturm.

"How do I decide?" Derek asked.

PROBLEM: What is the best treatment for Derek's depression: psychological therapy, drug therapy, or both? More broadly, the problem is this: How do we decide among the available therapies for any of the mental disorders?

Despite the diversity of approaches that Dr. Sturm and her colleagues bring to their work, the overwhelming majority of people who enter **therapy** receive significant help. Not everyone becomes a success case, of course. Some people wait too long, until their problems become intractable. Some do not end up with the right sort of therapy for their problems. And, unfortunately, many people who could benefit from therapy do not get it because of the cost. Still, the development of a wide range of effective therapies is one of the success stories in modern psychology.

As you read through this chapter, we hope you will weigh the advantages and disadvantages of each therapy we discuss. Keep in mind, too, that you may sometime be asked by a friend or relative to use what you, like Derek, have learned here to recommend an appropriate therapy. It's even possible that you may sometime need to select a therapist for yourself. ■

12.1 Key Question: What Is Therapy?

When you think of "therapy," chances are that a stereotype pops into mind, absorbed from countless cartoons and movies: a "neurotic" patient lying on a couch, with a bearded therapist sitting by the patient's head, scribbling notes and making interpretations. In fact, this is a scene from classic Freudian psychoanalysis, which is a rarity today, although it dominated the first half of the 20th century.

The reality of modern therapy differs from the old stereotype on several counts. First, most therapists don't have their patients (or *clients*) lie on a couch. Second, people now seek therapeutic help for a wide range of problems besides the serious *DSM-5* disorders: Counselors or therapists also provide help in making difficult choices, dealing with academic problems, and coping with losses or unhappy relationships. And a third way in which the popular image of therapy is mistaken: Some forms of therapy now involve as much *action* as they do talk and interpretation—as you will see shortly.

At first, the therapeutic menu may appear to offer a bewildering list of choices. But you will see that one constant threads through them all—as our Core Concept suggests:

CORE CONCEPT 12.1

Therapy for psychological disorders takes a variety of forms, but all involve a *therapeutic relationship* focused on improving a person's mental, behavioral, or social functioning.

Let's set the stage for our exploration of these many therapies by looking at the variety of people who enter treatment and the problems they bring with them to the therapeutic relationship.

---

therapy A general term for any treatment process; in psychology and psychiatry, therapy refers to a variety of psychological and biomedical techniques aimed at dealing with mental disorders or coping with problems of living.

Entering Therapy

Why would you go into therapy? Why would anyone? Most often, people enter therapy when they have a problem that they are unable to resolve by themselves. They may seek therapy on their own initiative, or they may be advised to do so by family, friends, a physician, or a coworker.

Obviously, you don't have to be declared "crazy" to enter therapy. But you may be called either a "patient" or a "client." Practitioners who take a biological or medical model approach to treatment commonly use the term *patient,* while the term *client* is usually used by professionals who think of psychological disorders not as mental *illnesses* but as *problems in living* (Rogers, 1951; Szasz, 1961).

Access to therapy depends on several factors. People who have money or adequate health insurance can get therapy easily. For the poor, especially poor ethnic minorities, economic obstacles block the doorway to professional mental health care (Bower, 1998d; Nemecek, 1999). Another problem can be lack of qualified therapists. In many communities, it is still much easier to get help for physical health problems than for psychological problems. Even the nature of a person's psychological problems can interfere with getting help. An individual with agoraphobia, for example, finds it hard, even impossible, to leave home to seek therapy. Similarly, persons with paranoia may not seek help because they don't trust mental health professionals. Obviously, many difficulties stand in the way of getting therapy to all those who need it.

[**CONNECTION**] The *medical model* assumes that mental disorders are similar to physical diseases.

The Therapeutic Alliance and the Goals of Therapy

Sometimes, you simply need to talk out a problem with a sympathetic friend or family member, perhaps just to "hear yourself think." But friends and family not only lack the training to deal with difficult mental problems; they also have needs and agendas of their own that can interfere with helping you. In fact, they may sometimes be part of the problem. For many reasons, then, it may be appropriate to seek the help of a professionally trained therapist. You might also want professional help if you wish to keep your problems and concerns confidential. In all these ways, a professional relationship with a therapist differs from friendship or kinship.

What Are the Components of Therapy?   In nearly all forms of therapy there is some sort of *relationship*, or **therapeutic alliance,** between the therapist and the client seeking assistance—as our Core Concept indicates. In fact, the

quality of the therapeutic alliance is the biggest single factor in the effectiveness of therapy (Wampold & Brown, 2005). (We must admit, however, that there are experimental computer-therapy programs, where the idea of a "relationship" is stretching the point.)

What makes for a good therapeutic alliance? You and your therapist must be able to work together as allies, on the same side and toward the same goals, joining forces to cope with and solve the problems that have brought you to therapy (Horvath & Luborsky, 1993). Accordingly, trust and empathy are two of the essential ingredients. And, as clinicians have become more aware of gender and ethnic diversity among their clientele, research has shown that the most effective therapists are those who can connect with people in the context of their own culture, experience, and native language (Griner & Smith, 2006).

In addition to the relationship between therapist and client, the therapy process typically involves the following steps:

1. *Identifying the problem.* This may mean merely agreeing on a simple description of circumstances or feelings to be changed, or, in the case of a *DSM-5* disorder, this step may lead to a formal diagnosis about what is wrong.

2. *Identifying the cause of the problem or the conditions that maintain the problem.* In some forms of therapy, this involves searching the past, especially childhood, for the source of the patient's or client's discomfort. Alternatively, other forms of therapy emphasize the present causes—that is, the conditions that are keeping the problem alive.

3. *Deciding on and carrying out some form of treatment.* This step requires selecting a specific type of therapy designed to minimize or eliminate the troublesome symptoms. The exact treatment will depend on the nature of the problem and on the therapist's orientation and training.

Who Does Therapy?   Although more people seek out therapy now than in the past, they usually turn to trained mental health professionals only when their psychological problems become severe or persist for extended periods. And when they do, they usually turn to one of seven main types of professional helpers: counseling psychologists, clinical psychologists, psychiatrists, psychoanalysts, psychiatric nurse practitioners, clinical (psychiatric) social workers, or pastoral counselors. The differences among these specialties are highlighted in TABLE 12•1. As you examine this table, note that each specialty has its own area of expertise. For example, in most states, the only therapists who are licensed to prescribe drugs are physicians (including psychiatrists) and psychiatric nurse practitioners.

Currently, through their professional organizations, clinical psychologists are seeking to obtain prescription privileges (Sternberg, 2003). In fact, New Mexico now grants prescription privileges to civilian psychologists who have

---

therapeutic alliance   The relationship between the therapist and the client, with both parties working together to help the client deal with mental or behavioral issues.

[TABLE 12·1] Types of Mental Health Care Professionals

Professional Title	Specialty and Common Work Settings	Credentials and Qualifications
Counseling psychologist	Provides help in dealing with the common problems of normal living, such as relationship problems, child rearing, occupational choice, and school problems. Typically counselors work in schools, clinics, or other institutions.	Depends on the state: typically at least a master's in counseling, but commonly private practice requires a PhD (Doctor of Philosophy), EdD (Doctor of Education), or PsyD (Doctor of Psychology).
Clinical psychologist	Trained primarily to work with those who have more severe disorders, but may also work with clients having less-severe problems; usually in private practice or employed by mental health agencies or by hospitals; not typically licensed to prescribe drugs.	Usually required to hold PhD or PsyD; often an internship and state certification are required.
Psychiatrist	A physician with a specialty in treating mental problems—most often by prescribing drugs; may be in private practice or employed by clinics or mental hospitals.	MD (Doctor of Medicine); may be required to be certified by medical specialty board.
Psychoanalyst	Practitioners of Freudian therapy; usually in private practice.	MD (some practitioners have doctorates in psychology, but most are psychiatrists who have taken additional training in psychoanalysis.)
Psychiatric nurse practitioner	A nursing specialty; licensed to prescribe drugs for mental disorders; may work in private practice or in clinics and hospitals.	Requires RN (Registered Nurse) credential, plus special training in treating mental disorders and prescribing drugs.
Clinical or psychiatric social worker	Social workers with a specialty in dealing with mental disorders, especially from the viewpoint of the social and environmental context of the problem.	MSW (Master of Social Work).
Pastoral counsellor	A member of a religious order or ministry who specializes in treatment of psychological disorders; combines spiritual guidance with practical counseling.	Varies.

completed a rigorous training program, including 850 hours of course work and a supervised internship (Dittmann, 2003). Similar legislation has been introduced in more than a dozen other states. Meanwhile, the U.S. military has embraced prescription privileges for psychologists (Dittmann, 2004). Nevertheless, the issue remains highly political, contested especially by the medical profession (Fox et al., 2009). Even some clinical psychologists oppose prescription privileges, fearing that psychology will "sell its soul" to serve a public that demands drug therapy. Said former APA President George Albee (2006):

> The current drive for people who are in practice to become drug prescribers is a matter of survival. Society has been sold the fallacy that mental/emotional disorders are all brain diseases that must be treated with drugs. The only way for psychology practitioners to survive is to embrace this invalid nonsense (p. 3).

Whether or not you agree with Albee, it appears that the era of prescription privileges for properly trained psychologists is coming. It remains to be seen how that will change the face of psychology.

Therapy in Historical and Cultural Context

How we treat mental disorder depends on how we *think* about mental disorder. If we believe, for example, that mental problems are *diseases,* we will treat them differently from those who believe that mental problems indicate a flaw in one's character or the influence of evil spirits. The way society has treated people with mental disorders has always depended on its prevailing beliefs.

History of Therapy People in medieval Europe interpreted mental disorder as the work of devils and demons. In that context, then, the job of the "therapist" was to perform an exorcism or to "beat the devil" out of the person with the disorder—to make the body an inhospitable place for a spirit or demon. In more modern times, however, reformers have urged that people with mental illness be placed in institutions called asylums, where they could be shielded from the stresses of the world—and from the brutal "therapies" that had been common in a less-enlightened era. Unfortunately, the ideal of the "insane asylums" was not often realized.

In this painting from the 1730s, we see the chaos of a cell in the London hospital, St. Mary of Bethlehem. Here, the upper classes have paid to see the horrors, the fiddler who entertains, and the mental patients chained, tortured, and dehumanized. The chaos of Bethlehem eventually became synonymous with the corruption of its name—Bedlam.

One of the most infamous of the asylums was also one of the first: Bethlehem Hospital in London, where, for a few pence, weekend sightseers could observe the inmates, who often put on a wild and noisy "show" for the curious audience. As a result, "Bedlam," the shortened term Londoners used for "Bethlehem," became a word used to describe any noisy, chaotic place.

In most asylums, inmates received, at best, only custodial care. At worst, they were neglected or put in cruel restraints, such as cages and chains. Some even received beatings, cold showers, and other forms of abuse. It's not hard to guess that such treatment rarely produced improvement in people suffering from psychological disorders.

Modern Approaches to Therapy Modern mental health professionals have abandoned the old demon model and frankly abusive treatments in favor of therapies based on psychological and biological theories of mind and behavior. Yet, as we will see, even modern professionals disagree on the exact causes and the most appropriate treatments—a state of the art that gives us a wide variety of therapies from which to choose. To help you get an overview of this cluttered therapeutic landscape, here is a preview of things to come.

The **psychological therapies** are often called simply *psychotherapy*.[1] They focus on changing disordered thoughts,

feelings, and behavior using psychological techniques (rather than biomedical interventions). And they come in two main forms. One, called *insight therapy*, focuses on helping people understand their problems and change their thoughts, motives, or feelings. The other, known as *behavior therapy*, focuses primarily on behavior change. In fact, many psychotherapists use a combination of the two, known as *cognitive–behavioral therapy*.

In contrast, the **biomedical therapies** focus on treating mental problems by changing the underlying biology of the brain, using a variety of drugs, including antidepressants, tranquilizers, and stimulants. Occasionally the brain may be treated directly with electromagnetic stimulation or even surgery. Sometimes therapists use a combination approach involving both drugs and psychotherapy.

Disorder and Therapy in a Cultural Context Ways of thinking about and treating mental disorder also vary widely across cultures (Matsumoto, 1996). People in individualistic Western cultures (that is, from Europe and North America) generally regard psychological disorders as the result of disease processes, abnormal genetics, distorted thinking, unhealthy environments, or stressors. But collectivist cultures often have quite different perspectives (Triandis, 1990; Zaman, 1992). Asian societies may regard mental disorder as a disconnect between the person and the group. Likewise, many Africans believe that mental disorder results when an individual becomes estranged from nature and from the community, including the community of ancestral spirits (Nobles, 1976; Sow, 1977).

In such cultures, treating mentally disturbed individuals by removing them from society is unthinkable. Instead, healing takes place in a social context, emphasizing a distressed person's beliefs, family, work, and life environment. An African use of group support in therapy has developed into a procedure called "network therapy," where a patient's entire network of relatives, coworkers, and friends becomes involved in the treatment (Lambo, 1978). Such treatments may also involve traditional shamans working alongside mental health professionals trained in modern psychology and psychiatry.

Had Derek been in such a culture, he would undoubtedly have received treatment from a sorcerer or *shaman* who was assumed to have special mystical powers. His therapy would have involved ceremonies and rituals that bring emotional intensity and meaning into the healing process. Combined with the use of symbols, these rituals connect the individual sufferer, the shaman, and the society to supernatural forces to be won over in the battle against madness (Devereux, 1981; Wallace, 1959).

---

psychological therapy Therapy based on psychological principles (rather than on the biomedical approach); often called "psychotherapy."

biomedical therapy Treatment that focuses on altering the brain, especially with drugs, psychosurgery, or electroconvulsive therapy.

psychology matters

Paraprofessionals Do Therapy, Too

Does the best therapy always require a highly trained (and expensive) professional? Or can **paraprofessionals**—persons who may have received on-the-job training in place of graduate training and certification—be effective therapists? If you are seeking treatment, these questions are important because hospitals, clinics, and agencies are increasingly turning to paraprofessionals as a cost-cutting measure: Those who lack full professional credentials can be hired at a fraction of the cost of those with professional degrees. They are often called "aides" or "counselors" (although many counselors do have professional credentials).

Surprisingly, a review of the literature has found no substantial differences in the effectiveness of the two groups across a wide spectrum of psychological problems (Christensen & Jacobson, 1994). This is good news in the sense that the need for mental health services is far greater than the number of professional therapists can possibly provide. And, because paraprofessional therapists can be effective, highly trained professionals may be freed for other roles, including prevention and community education programs, assessment of patients, training and supervision of paraprofessionals, and research. You should be cautioned about overinterpreting this finding, however. Professionals and paraprofessionals have been found to be equivalent only in the realm of the insight therapies, which we will discuss in a moment (Zilbergeld, 1986). Such differences have not yet been demonstrated in the areas of behavior therapies, which require extensive knowledge of operant and classical conditioning and of social learning theory.

CHECK YOUR UNDERSTANDING

✔️—Study and **Review** at **MyPsychLab**

1. **Recall:** People in individualistic cultures often view mental disorder as a problem originating in a person's mind. In contrast, people in collectivist cultures are more likely to see mental disorder as a symptom of a disconnect between the person and ————.

2. **Recall:** Identify three ways in which the relationship with a trained therapist would differ from that of a friendship.

3. **Application:** Which type of therapist would be most likely to treat depression by searching for the cause in the unconscious mind?

4. **Understanding the Core Concept:** In what respect are all therapies alike?
   a. All may be legally administered only by licensed, trained professionals.
   b. All make use of insight into a patient's problems.
   c. All involve the aim of altering the mind, behavior, or social relationships.
   d. All focus on discovering the underlying cause of the patient's problem, which is often hidden in the unconscious mind.

Answers: 1. the family or community **2.** Unlike a friend, a therapist is a professional who (a) is trained in therapeutic techniques, (b) will not bring his or her own needs into the therapeutic relationship, and (c) will maintain confidentiality. **3.** A psychodynamic therapist **4.** c

— — — — —

12.2 Key Question: How Do Psychologists Treat Psychological Disorders?

In the United States and most other Western nations, the sort of therapy Derek receives would depend on whether he had gone to a medical or psychological therapist. By choosing a psychologist like Dr. Sturm, he would almost certainly receive one of the two types of therapy described by the Core Concept for this section of the chapter:

CORE CONCEPT 12.2

Psychologists employ two main forms of treatment, the insight therapies (focused on developing understanding of the problem) and the behavior therapies (focused on changing behavior through conditioning).

The *insight therapies*, we shall see, were the first truly psychological treatments developed, and for a long time, they were the only psychological therapies available. In recent years, they have been joined by the *behavior therapies*, which are now among the most effective tools we have. But it is with the insight therapies that we begin.

Insight Therapies

The **insight therapies** attempt to change people on the *inside*—changing the way they think and feel. Sometimes called *talk therapies*, these methods share the assumption that distressed persons need to develop an understanding of the disordered thoughts, emotions, and motives that underlie their mental difficulties.

The insight therapies come in dozens of different "brands," but all aim at revealing and changing a patient's disturbed

---

paraprofessional Individual who has received on-the-job training (and, in some cases, undergraduate training) in mental health treatment in lieu of graduate education and full professional certification.

insight therapy Psychotherapy in which the therapist helps the patient/client understand (gain insight into) his or her problems.

mental processes through discussion and interpretation. Some therapies, like Freudian *psychoanalysis,* assume that problems lie hidden deep in the unconscious, so they employ elaborate and time-consuming techniques to draw them out. Others, like Carl Rogers's *client-centered therapy,* minimize the importance of the unconscious and look for problems in the ways people consciously think and interact with each other. We have space here to sample only a few of the most influential ones, beginning with the legendary methods developed by Sigmund Freud himself.

INSIGHT THERAPIES

- Freudian psychoanalysis
- Neo-Freudian therapies
- Humanistic therapies
- Cognitive therapies
- Group therapies

Freudian Psychoanalysis In the classic Freudian view, psychological problems arise from tension created in the unconscious mind by forbidden impulses and threatening memories. Therefore, Freudian therapy, known formally as **psychoanalysis,** probes the unconscious in an attempt to bring these issues into the "light of day"—that is, into consciousness, where they can be rendered harmless. The major goal of psychoanalysis, then, is to reveal and interpret the unconscious mind's contents.

To get at unconscious material, Freud sought ways to get around the defenses the ego has erected to protect itself. One ingenious method called for *free association,* by which the patient would relax and talk about whatever came to mind, while the therapist would listen, ever alert for veiled references to unconscious needs and conflicts. Another method involved *dream interpretation.*

With these and other techniques, the psychoanalyst gradually develops a clinical picture of the problem and proceeds to help the patient understand the unconscious causes for symptoms. To give you the flavor of this process, we offer Freud's

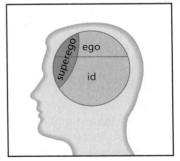

The psychodynamic therapies focus on the client's *motivation*—either conscious or unconscious.

_____

psychoanalysis   The form of psychodynamic therapy developed by Sigmund Freud. The goal of psychoanalysis is to release conflicts and memories from the unconscious.

Sigmund Freud's study, including the famous couch (right), is housed in London's Freud Museum. The 82-year-old Freud fled to London in 1938 upon the Nazi occupation of Austria and died there the following year.

interpretation of a fascinating case involving a 19-year-old girl diagnosed with "obsessional neurosis" (now listed in the *DSM-5* as *obsessive–compulsive disorder*). Please bear in mind that Freud's ideas no longer represent the mainstream of either psychology or psychiatry, but they remain important because many of his techniques have carried over into newer forms of therapy. Freud's ideas are also important because many of his concepts, such as *ego, repression, the unconscious, identification,* and *the Oedipus complex,* have become part of our everyday vocabulary. The following case, then—in which you may find Freud's interpretations shocking—will give you a sense of the way psychotherapy began about a century ago and is still practiced by a few orthodox psychoanalysts.

When Freud's patient entered treatment, she was causing her parents distress with a strange bedtime ritual that she performed each night. As part of this obsessional ritual, she first stopped the large clock in her room and removed other smaller clocks, including her wristwatch. Then, she placed all vases and flower pots together on her writing table, so—in her "neurotic" way of thinking—they could not fall and break during the night. Next, she assured that the door of her room would remain half open by placing various objects in the doorway. After these precautions, she turned her attention to the bed, where she was careful to assure that the bolster did not touch the headboard and a pillow must lie diagonally in the center of the bolster. Then, she shook the eiderdown in the quilt until all the feathers sank to the foot-end, after which she meticulously redistributed them evenly again. And, finally, she would crawl into bed and attempt to sleep with her head precisely in the center of the diagonal pillow.

To complicate matters, the girl was never sure that she had performed her ritual properly. She would do and then redo first one and then another aspect of the procedure—even though she acknowledged to Freud that all aspects of her nightly precautions were irrational. The result was that it took the girl about two hours to get ready for bed each night.

[CONNECTION] The *ego defense mechanisms* include repression, regression, projection, denial, rationalization, reaction formation, displacement, and sublimation.

Before you read Freud's interpretation, you might think about how you would make sense of such strange behaviors. Now then, in Freud's (1957/1920) own words, here is the psychoanalytic interpretation of the case:

> The patient gradually learnt to understand that she banished clocks and watches from her room at night because they were symbols of the female genitals. Clocks, which we know may have other symbolic meanings besides this, acquire this significance of a genital organ by their relation to periodical processes and regular intervals. A woman may be heard to boast that menstruation occurs in her as regularly as clockwork. Now this patient's special fear was that the ticking of the clocks would disturb her during sleep. The ticking of a clock is comparable to the throbbing of the clitoris in sexual excitation. This sensation, which was distressing to her, had actually on several occasions wakened her from sleep; now her fear of an erection of the clitoris expressed itself by the imposition of a rule to remove all going clocks and watches far away from her during the night. Flower-pots and vases are, like all receptacles, also symbols of the female genitals. Precautions to prevent them from falling and breaking during the night are therefore not lacking in meaning. . . . Her precautions against the vases breaking signified a rejection of the whole complex concerned with virginity . . .
>
> One day she divined the central idea of her ritual when she suddenly understood her rule not to let the bolster touch the back of the bed. The bolster had always seemed a woman to her, she said, and the upright back of the bedstead a man. She wished therefore, by a magic ceremony, as it were, to keep man and woman apart; that is to say, to separate the parents and prevent intercourse from occurring . . .
>
> If the bolster was a woman, then the shaking of the eiderdown till all the feathers were at the bottom, making a protuberance there, also had a meaning. It meant impregnating a woman; she did not neglect, though to obliterate the pregnancy again, for she had for years been terrified that intercourse between her parents might result in another child and present her with a rival. On the other hand, if the large bolster meant the mother then the small pillow could only represent the daughter. . . . The part of the man (the father) she thus played herself and replaced the male organ by her own head.
>
> Horrible thoughts, you will say, to run in the mind of a virgin girl. I admit that; but do not forget that I have not invented these ideas, only exposed them . . . (pp. 277–279).

This case shows how Freud used the patient's symptoms as symbolic signposts pointing to underlying and unconscious conflicts, desires, and memories. In the course of treatment, then, he would help the patient understand how her ego defense mechanisms had morphed her unconscious problems into her obsessive rituals. Thus, by the ego defense mechanism

of *displacement*, her fears about losing virginity became the ritual of protecting the vases in her bedroom. In this way, her ego was able to satisfy her unconscious needs. At the same time, it could keep the "real" problem blocked from consciousness by means of yet another defense mechanism called repression.

A psychoanalyst's main task, then, is to help a patient break through the barriers of repression and bring threatening thoughts to awareness. By doing so, the patient gains insight into the relationship between the current symptoms and the repressed conflicts. Freud argued that, when the patient comes to understand and accept these unconscious conflicts and desires, they will cease to cause trouble.

Ultimately, in the final stage of psychoanalysis, patients learn how the relationship they have established with the therapist reflects unresolved conflicts, especially problems they had with their parents. This projection of parental attributes onto the therapist is called *transference,* and so the final phase of therapy is known as the **analysis of transference.** According to psychoanalytic theory, this last step in recovery occurs when patients are finally released from the unconscious troubles established long ago in the relationship with their parents during early childhood (Munroe, 1955).

[**CONNECTION**] *Repression* is the Freudian ego defense mechanism that causes forgetting by blocking off threatening memories in the unconscious.

Neo-Freudian Psychodynamic Therapies Please pardon us for doing a bit of analysis on Freud: He obviously had a flair for the dramatic, and he also possessed a powerful, charismatic personality—or, as he himself might have said, a strong ego. Accordingly, Freud encouraged his disciples to debate the principles of psychoanalysis, but he would tolerate no fundamental changes in his doctrines. This inevitably led to conflicts with some of his equally strong-willed followers, such as Alfred Adler, Carl Jung, and Karen Horney, who eventually broke away from Freud to establish their own schools of therapy.

In general, the neo-Freudian renegades kept many of Freud's basic ideas and techniques while adding some and modifying others. In the true psychodynamic tradition, the **neo-Freudian psychodynamic therapies** have retained Freud's emphasis on motivation. Most now have abandoned the psychoanalyst's couch and treat patients face to face. Most also see patients once a week for a few months, rather than several times a week for several years, as in classical psychoanalysis.

So how do modern psychodynamic therapists get the job done in a shorter time? Most have shifted their emphasis to

---

analysis of transference   The Freudian technique of analyzing and interpreting the patient's relationship with the therapist, based on the assumption that this relationship mirrors unresolved conflicts in the patient's past.

neo-Freudian psychodynamic therapy   Therapy for a mental disorder that was developed by psychodynamic theorists who embraced some of Freud's ideas but disagreed with others.

conscious motivation—so they don't spend so much time probing for hidden conflicts and repressed memories. Most have also made a break with Freud by emphasizing one or more of the following points:

- The significance of the self or *ego* (rather than the *id*)
- The influence of experiences occurring throughout life (as opposed to Freud's emphasis on early-childhood experience)
- The role of social needs and interpersonal relationships (rather than sexual and aggressive desires)

Each of the neo-Freudians constructed a theory of disorder and therapy that had a different emphasis. We do not have space here to go into these approaches in greater detail, but let's briefly consider how a modern psychodynamic therapist might have approached the case of the obsessive girl that Freud described. Most likely, such a therapist would focus on the current relationship between the girl and her parents, perhaps on whether she has feelings of inadequacy for which she is compensating by becoming the center of her parents' attention for two hours each night. And, instead of working so intensively with the girl, the therapist might also work with the parents on changing the way they deal with the problem. And—to further illustrate the point—what about Derek, the depressed fellow whom we met at the beginning of the chapter? While an orthodox Freudian analyst would probe his early childhood memories for clues as to his depression, the modern psychodynamic therapist would be more likely to look for clues in his current relationships, assuming the cause to be social rather than sexual.

Humanistic Therapies
In contrast with the psychodynamic emphasis on conflicting motives, the *humanistic* therapists believe that mental problems arise from low self-esteem, misguided goals, and unfulfilling relationships. Indeed, the primary symptoms for which college students seek therapy would include feelings of alienation, failure to achieve all they feel they should, difficult relationships, and general dissatisfaction with their lives. Therapists often refer to these problems in everyday existence as *existential crises*, a term emphasizing how many human problems deal with

Humanistic therapist Carl Rogers (right center) facilitates a therapy group.

questions about the meaning and purpose of one's existence. The humanistic psychologists have developed therapies aimed specifically at such problems.

Again, in contrast with the psychodynamic view, humanistic therapists believe that people are generally motivated by *healthy* needs for growth and psychological well-being. They dispute Freud's assumption of a personality divided into conflicting parts, dominated by a selfish id, and driven by hedonistic instincts and repressed conflicts. Instead, the humanists emphasize the concept of a whole person engaged in a continual process of growth and change.

In the view of the humanistic psychologists, mental disorder occurs when conditions interfere with normal development and produce low self-esteem. **Humanistic therapies,** therefore, attempt to help clients confront their problems by recognizing their own freedom, enhancing their self-esteem, and realizing their fullest potential (Schneider & May, 1995). A humanistic therapist (if there had been one around a century ago) would probably have worked with Freud's patient to explore her self-concept and her feelings about her parents. As for Derek, a humanistic therapist might guess that his depression arose either from unsatisfying relationships or from a sense of personal inadequacy.

Client-centered therapy, perhaps the most widespread form of humanistic therapy, was developed by the legendary Carl Rogers (1951, 1977). His approach assumed that healthy development can be derailed by a conflict between one's desire for a positive self-image and criticism by self and others. This conflict creates anxiety and unhappiness. The task of Rogerian client-centered therapy, then, is to create a nurturing environment in which people can work through their concerns and finally achieve self-respect and self-actualization.

One of the main techniques used by Rogerian therapists involves **reflection of feeling** (also called *reflective listening*) to help clients understand their emotions. With this technique,

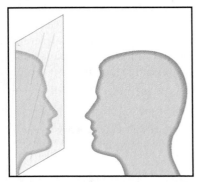

Humanistic therapists often help clients deal with low self-esteem, difficult relationships, and *existential crises*.

---

humanistic therapy Treatment technique based on the assumption that people have a tendency for positive growth and self-actualization, which may be blocked by an unhealthy environment that can include negative self-evaluation and criticism from others.

client-centered therapy A humanistic approach to treatment developed by Carl Rogers, emphasizing an individual's tendency for healthy psychological growth through self-actualization.

reflection of feeling Carl Rogers's technique of paraphrasing the clients' words, attempting to capture the emotional tone expressed.

therapists paraphrase their clients' words, acting as a sort of psychological "mirror" in which clients can see themselves. Notice how the therapist uses this technique to capture the emotional tone expressed by a young woman in the following excerpt from a therapy session (Rogers, 1951):

> **Client:** It probably goes all the way back into my childhood. . . . My mother told me that I was the pet of my father. Although I never realized it—I mean, they never treated me as a pet at all. And other people always seemed to think I was sort of a privileged one in the family. . . . And as far as I can see looking back on it now, it's just that the family let the other kids get away with more than they usually did me. And it seems for some reason to have held me to a more rigid standard than they did the other children.
>
> **Therapist:** You're not so sure you were a pet in any sense, but more that the family situation seemed to hold you to pretty high standards.
>
> **Client:** M-hm. That's just what has occurred to me; and that the other people could sorta make mistakes, or do things as children that were naughty . . . but Alice wasn't supposed to do those things.
>
> **Therapist:** M-hm. With somebody else it would be just—oh, be a little naughtiness; but as far as you were concerned, it shouldn't be done.
>
> **Client:** That's really the idea I've had. I think the whole business of my standards . . . is one that I need to think about rather carefully, since I've been doubting for a long time whether I even have any sincere ones.
>
> **Therapist:** M-hm. Not sure whether you really have any deep values which you are sure of.
>
> **Client:** M-hm. M-hm (p. 152).

Note how most of the therapist's statements in this example paraphrased, or "reflected," what the client has just said.

Is such an approach effective? In fact, client-centered therapy has abundant scientific support. An American Psychological Association task force, charged with finding science-based practices that contribute to the effectiveness of therapy, found that the common factor in therapies that work were precisely the Rogerian qualities of *empathy, positive regard, genuineness,* and *feedback* (Ackerman et al., 2001).

Cognitive Therapies

The insight therapies we have discussed so far focus primarily on people's emotions or motives (see **FIGURE 12•1**). **Cognitive therapy,** on the other hand, assumes that psychological problems arise from erroneous thinking and sees rational thinking as the key to positive therapeutic change (Butler et al., 2006). Cognitive therapy takes multiple forms, but we can give you some of its flavor with one example: Aaron Beck's cognitive therapy for depression.

---

cognitive therapy Emphasizes rational thinking (as opposed to subjective emotion, motivation, or repressed conflicts) as the key to treating mental disorder.

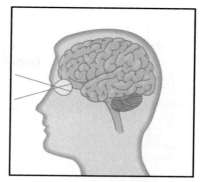

Cognitive therapies focus on changing the way clients *think* about themselves and their world.

Beck, who was originally trained in classical psychoanalysis, broke from the Freudian tradition when he began noticing that the dreams and free associations of his depressed patients were filled with negative thoughts (Beck, 1976; Bowles, 2004). Commonly they would make such self-deprecating statements as, "Nobody would like me if they really knew me" and "I'm not smart enough to make it in this competitive school." Gradually, Beck came to believe that depression occurs because of this negative self-talk. The therapist's job, then, is to help the client learn more positive ways of thinking.

Here's a sample of Beck's approach, taken from a therapy session with a college student of about Derek's age (Beck et al., 1979):

> **Client:** I get depressed when things go wrong. Like when I fail a test.
>
> **Therapist:** How can failing a test make you depressed?
>
> **Client:** Well, if I fail, I'll never get into law school.
>
> **Therapist:** Do you agree that the way you interpret the results of the test will affect you? You might feel depressed, you might have trouble sleeping, not feel like eating, and you might even wonder if you should drop out of the course.
>
> **Client:** I have been thinking that I wasn't going to make it. Yes, I agree.
>
> **Therapist:** Now what did failing mean?
>
> **Client:** (tearful) That I couldn't get into law school.
>
> **Therapist:** And what does that mean to you?
>
> **Client:** That I'm just not smart enough.
>
> **Therapist:** Anything else?
>
> **Client:** That I can never be happy.
>
> **Therapist:** And how do these thoughts make you feel?
>
> **Client:** Very unhappy.
>
> **Therapist:** So it is the meaning of failing a test that makes you very unhappy. In fact, believing that you can never be happy is a powerful factor in producing unhappiness. So, you get yourself into a trap—by definition, failure to get into law school equals "I can never be happy" (pp. 145–146).

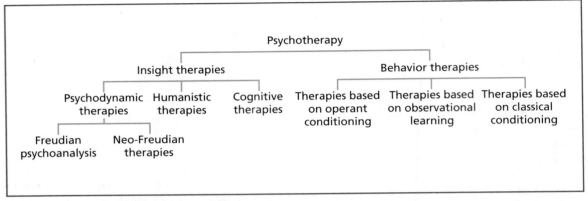

[**FIGURE 12•1**] **Types of Psychotherapy** Each of the two major branches of psychotherapy has many variations.

As you can see from this exchange, the cognitive therapist helps the individual confront the destructive thoughts that support depression. Studies have shown that Beck's approach can be at least as effective in the treatment of depression as is medication (Antonuccio, 1995; Beck, 2005).

In Derek's case, a cognitive therapist would undoubtedly probe for negative self-talk that might be feeding his depression. And how might a cognitive therapist have approached Freud's 19-year-old obsessive patient? The focus would have been on irrational beliefs, such as the idea that flowerpots and vases could, by themselves, fall down in the night and break. A cognitive therapist would also challenge the assumption that something catastrophic might happen (such as not being able to sleep!) if she didn't perform her nightly ritual. In both cases, the assumption would be that the symptoms would disappear as positive thoughts replaced negative ones.

Group Therapies The treatments we have discussed to this point usually involve one-to-one relationships between a patient or client and therapist. Most, however, can also be done with groups of two or more persons. Such **group therapy** offers real advantages over individual therapy, particularly in dealing with troubled interpersonal relationships. In fact, group therapy is often the preferred approach to therapy involving couples, families, or other groups of people who have similar problems, such as depression or drug addiction.

Therapy groups usually meet face to face once a week, although some groups are experimenting with sessions on the Internet (Davison et al., 2000). Most typically, the therapist employs a humanistic perspective, although psychodynamic and cognitive–behavioral groups are also common. Whatever the method, group therapy offers clients the opportunity to observe and imitate new social behaviors in a forgiving, supportive atmosphere. In the interest of brevity,

we will touch on only two representative types of group therapy below: *self-help groups* and *marital and family therapy.*

Self-Help Support Groups. Perhaps the most noteworthy development in group therapy has been the surge of interest in **self-help support groups.** Thousands of such groups exist. Many are free, especially those that are not directed by a paid health care professional. Such groups give people a chance to meet under nonthreatening conditions to exchange ideas with others having similar problems and who are surviving and sometimes even thriving (Schiff & Bargal, 2000).

One of the oldest support groups, Alcoholics Anonymous (AA) pioneered the self-help concept, beginning in the mid-1930s. Central to the original AA process is the concept of "12 Steps" to recovery from alcohol addiction. It is noteworthy that the 12 Steps are based not on psychological theory but on the trial-and-error experience of early AA members.

In the 1960s, the feminist consciousness-raising movement brought the self-help concept to a wider audience. As a result, self-help support groups now exist for an enormous range of problems, including:

- Managing life transition or other crises, such as divorce or death of a child.
- Coping with physical and mental disorders, such as depression or heart attack.
- Dealing with addictions and other uncontrolled behaviors, such as alcoholism, gambling, overeating, sexual excess, and drug dependency.
- Handling the stress felt by relatives or friends of those who are dealing with addictions.

Group therapy also makes valuable contributions to the treatment of terminally ill patients. The goals of such therapy are to help patients and their families live their lives as fully

---

group therapy Any form of psychotherapy done with more than one client/patient at a time. Group therapy is often done from a humanistic perspective.

self-help support groups Groups, such as Alcoholics Anonymous, that provide social support and an opportunity for sharing ideas about dealing with common problems. Such groups are typically organized and run by laypersons, rather than professional therapists.

In couples therapy, the therapist can help people work together to improve the communication patterns that have developed in their relationship.

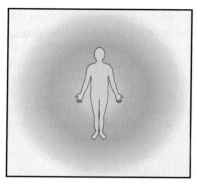

Behavior therapists focus on the person's environment and on problem *behaviors*, rather than on internal thoughts, motives, or feelings.

as possible, to cope realistically with impending death, and to adjust to the terminal illness. One general focus of such support groups for the terminally ill is to help them learn "how to live fully until you say goodbye" (Nungesser, 1990).

Couples and Family Therapy Perhaps the best setting in which to learn about relationships is in a group of people struggling with relationships. *Couples therapy* (or counseling), for example, may involve one or more couples who are learning to clarify their communication patterns and improve the quality of their interaction (Napier, 2000). By seeing couples together, a therapist can help the partners identify the verbal and nonverbal styles they use to dominate, control, or confuse each other (Gottman, 1994, 1999). The therapist then helps them to reinforce more desirable responses in the other and withdraw from conflicts. Couples are also taught *nondirective* listening skills that help clarify and express feelings and ideas without being confrontational (Jacobson et al., 2000; Wheeler et al., 2001).

In *family therapy,* the "client" is an entire family group, with each family member being treated as part of a *system of relationships* (Fishman, 1993). A family therapist helps troubled family members perceive the issues or patterns that are creating problems for them. The goal is to alter the interpersonal dynamics (interactions) among the participants (Foley, 1979; Schwebel & Fine, 1994). Family therapy not only helps reduce tensions within a family, but it can also improve the functioning of individual members by helping them recognize their roles in the group. It is also proved to be effective in the treatment of anorexia nervosa, depression, and other mood disorders, and even as a boon to families struggling with schizophrenia (Miklowitz, 2007).

Behavior Therapies

If the problem is overeating, bed wetting, shyness, antisocial behavior, or anything else that can be described in purely behavioral terms, the chances are good that it can be modified by one of the behavior therapies (also known as **behavior**

modification). Based on the assumption that these undesirable behaviors have been learned and therefore can be *unlearned*, **behavior therapy** relies on the principles of operant and classical conditioning. In addition to those difficulties listed above, behavior therapists report success in dealing with fears, compulsions, depression, addictions, aggression, and delinquent behaviors.

As the label suggests, behavior therapists focus on problem *behaviors* rather than inner thoughts, motives, or emotions. They seek to understand how unwanted behaviors might have been learned and, even more important, how they can be eliminated and replaced by more effective patterns. To see how this is done, we will look first at the behavior therapy techniques borrowed from *classical conditioning.*

BEHAVIOR THERAPIES

- Systematic desensitization
- Aversion therapy
- Contingency management
- Token economies
- Participant modeling

Classical Conditioning Therapies The first example of behavior therapy, reported by psychologist Mary Cover Jones (1924), treated a fearful little boy named Peter, who was afraid of furry objects. Jones was able to desensitize the boy's fear, over a period of weeks, by gradually bringing a rabbit closer and closer to the boy while he was eating. Eventually, Peter was able to allow the rabbit to sit on his lap while he petted it. (You may notice the similarity to John Watson's experiments on Little Albert. Indeed, Jones was an associate of Watson and knew of the Little Albert study. Unlike Albert, however, Peter came to treatment already possessing an intense fear of rabbits and other furry objects.)

[CONNECTION] In *classical conditioning,* a CS comes to produce essentially the same response as the UCS.

---

behavior modification   Another term for behavior therapy.

behavior therapy   Any form of psychotherapy based on the principles of behavioral learning, especially operant conditioning and classical conditioning.

Surprisingly, it was another 14 years before behavior therapy reappeared, this time as a treatment for bed wetting (Mowrer & Mowrer, 1938). The method involved a fluid-sensitive pad placed under the patient. When moisture set off an alarm, the patient would awaken. The treatment was effective in 75 percent of cases—an amazing success rate, in view of the dismal failure of psychodynamic therapy to prevent bed wetting by talking about the "meaning" of the symptom. And yet, it took yet another 20 years before behavior therapy entered the mainstream of psychological treatment.

Why the delay? The old Freudian idea—that every symptom has an underlying, unconscious cause that must be discovered and eradicated—was extremely well rooted in clinical lore. Therapists dared not attack symptoms (behaviors) directly for fear of *symptom substitution:* the idea that by eliminating one symptom, another, which could be much worse, could take its place. This concern was unfounded.

Systematic Desensitization. It took psychiatrist Joseph Wolpe to challenge the entrenched notion of symptom substitution. Wolpe reasoned that the development of irrational fear responses and other undesirable emotionally based behaviors might follow the classical conditioning model rather than the Freudian model. As you will recall, *classical conditioning* involves the association of a new stimulus with an unconditioned stimulus so that the person responds the same way to both. Thus, a fear response might be associated with, say, crowds or spiders or lightning. Wolpe also realized another simple truth: The nervous system cannot be relaxed and agitated at the same time because these two incompatible processes cannot be activated simultaneously. Putting these two ideas together formed the foundation for Wolpe's method, called **systematic desensitization** (Wolpe, 1958, 1973).

Systematic desensitization begins with a training program, teaching patients to relax their muscles and their minds (Rachman, 2000). With the patient in this deeply relaxed state, the therapist begins the process of *extinction* by having the patient imagine progressively more fearful situations. This is done in gradual steps, called an *anxiety hierarchy*, that move from remote associations to imagining an intensely feared situation.

To develop the anxiety hierarchy, the therapist and client first identify all the situations that provoke the patient's anxiety and then arrange them in levels, ranked from weakest to strongest (Shapiro, 1995). For example, a patient suffering from severe fear of public speaking constructed the hierarchy of unconditioned stimuli seen in TABLE 12•2.

Later, during desensitization, the relaxed client vividly imagines the weakest anxiety stimulus on the list. If it can be visualized without discomfort, the client goes on to the next stronger one. After a number of sessions, the client can imagine the most distressing situations on the list without anxiety (Lang & Lazovik, 1963)—hence the term *systematic* desensitization.

[TABLE 12•2] A Sample Anxiety Hierarchy

The following is typical of anxiety hierarchies that a therapist and a patient might develop to desensitize a fear of public speaking. The therapist guides the deeply relaxed patient in imagining the following situations:

1. Seeing a picture or a video recording of another person giving a speech
2. Watching another person give a speech
3. Preparing a speech that I will give to a small group of friends
4. Having to introduce myself to a large group
5. Waiting to be called on to speak in a meeting or in a large class
6. Being introduced as a speaker to a group
7. Walking to the podium to make a speech
8. Making an important speech to a large group

It turns out that Wolpe may have been too cautious about inducing anxiety in his clients. In a newer and more intense form of desensitization, known **exposure therapy,** the therapist may actually have the patient confront the feared object or situation, such as a spider or a snake, rather than just imagining it—and this seems to be even more effective than Wolpe's method (Barlow, 2010). You will recall that Sabra, went through a form of exposure therapy to overcome her fear of flying. The technique has been used successfully with a multitude of patients with phobias and anxiety disorders, including many whose fears of blood, injections, and germs stand in the way of getting needed medical or dental treatment (Dittmann, 2005b).

In the past few years, some behavioral therapists have added a high-tech twist to exposure therapy. By using computer-generated images of fearful situations, their clients can explore and extinguish fears and anxieties in a virtual-reality environment that they know is safe. To enter the virtual-reality environment, patients don a helmet containing a video screen, on which are projected images to which they will be desensitized: spiders, snakes, high places, closed-in spaces—all the common phobia-producing objects or images (Winerman, 2005e).

Aversion Therapy. So, desensitization and exposure therapy help clients deal with stimuli that they want to avoid. But what about the reverse? What can be done to help those who are attracted to stimuli that are harmful or illegal? Examples include drug addiction, certain sexual attractions, and tendencies to violence—all problems in which undesirable behavior is elicited by some specific stimulus. **Aversion therapy** tackles

---

systematic desensitization A behavioral therapy technique in which anxiety is extinguished by exposing the patient to an anxiety-provoking stimulus.

exposure therapy A form of desensitization therapy in which the patient directly confronts the anxiety-provoking stimulus (as opposed to imagining the stimulus).

aversion therapy As a classical conditioning procedure, aversive counterconditioning involves presenting the individual with an attractive stimulus paired with unpleasant (aversive) stimulation to condition a repulsive reaction.

In "virtual reality," phobic patients can confront their fears safely and conveniently in the behavior therapist's office. On a screen inside the headset, the patient sees computer-generated images of feared situations, such as seeing a snake, flying in an airplane, or looking down from the top of a tall building.

these problems with a conditioning procedure designed to make tempting stimuli repulsive by pairing them repeatedly with unpleasant (aversive) stimuli. For example, the therapist might use electric shocks or nausea-producing drugs, whose effects are highly unpleasant but not actually dangerous to the client. In time, the negative reactions (unconditioned responses) to the aversive stimuli come to be associated with the conditioned stimuli (such as an addictive drug), and so the client develops an aversion that replaces the desire.

To give another example, if you were to elect aversion therapy to help you quit smoking, you might be required to chain-smoke cigarettes while having a foul odor blown in your face—until you develop a strong association between smoking and nausea (see **FIGURE 12•2**). A similar conditioning effect occurs in alcoholics who drink while taking Antabuse, a drug often prescribed to encourage sobriety.

In some ways, aversion therapy resembles nothing so much as torture. So why would anyone submit voluntarily to it? Sometimes, the courts may assign a probationer to

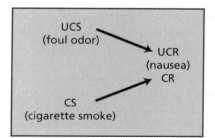

[FIGURE 12•2] Conditioning an Aversion for Cigarette Smoke Aversion therapy for smoking might simultaneously pair a foul odor with cigarette smoke blown in the smoker's face. The foul odor (such as rotten eggs) produces nausea. This response then becomes the conditioned response associated with cigarette smoke.

Source: Wolpe, J. (1991). *The practice of behavior therapy*, 4th ed. Boston, MA: Allyn & Bacon. Copyright © 1991 by Pearson Education. Reprinted by permission of the publisher.

aversion therapy. Usually, however, people submit to this type of treatment because they have a troublesome addiction that has resisted other treatments.

Operant Conditioning Therapies Four-year-old Tyler has a screaming fit when he goes to the grocery store with his parents and they refuse to buy him candy. He acquired this annoying behavior through operant conditioning, by being rewarded when his parents have given in to his demands. In fact, most behavior problems found in both children and adults have been shaped by rewards and punishments. Consider, for example, the similarities between Tyler's case and the employee who chronically arrives late for work or the student who waits until the last minute to study for a test. Changing such behaviors requires operant conditioning techniques. Let's look at two therapeutic variations on this operant theme.

[CONNECTION] In *operant conditioning*, behavior changes because of consequences, such as rewards and punishments.

Contingency Management. Tyler's parents may learn to extinguish his fits at the grocery store by simply withdrawing their attention—no easy task, by the way. In addition, the therapist may coach them to "catch Tyler being good" and give him all the attention he needs—but only for good behavior. Over time, the changing contingencies will work to extinguish the old, undesirable behaviors and help to keep the new ones in place. This approach is an example of **contingency management:** changing behavior by modifying its consequences. It has proved effective in treating behavior problems found in such diverse settings as families, schools, work, prisons, the military, and mental hospitals. The careful application of reward and punishment can also reduce the self-destructive behaviors in autistic children (Frith, 1997). And, if you would like to change some undesirable habit or acquire a new one, you can even apply contingency management techniques to yourself: See the accompanying box, *Do It Yourself! Behavior Self-Modification.*

Token Economies. A special form of therapy called a **token economy** is commonly used in group settings such as classrooms and institutions. Think of it as the behavioral version of group therapy (Ayllon & Azrin, 1968; Martin & Pear, 1999). The method takes its name from the plastic tokens sometimes awarded by therapists or teachers as immediate reinforcers for desirable behaviors.

In a classroom application, for example, a student might earn a token for sitting quietly for several minutes, participating in a class discussion, or turning in an assignment. Later,

contingency management An operant conditioning approach to changing behavior by altering the consequences, especially rewards and punishments, of behavior.

token economy An operant technique applied to groups, such as classrooms or mental hospital wards, involving the distribution of "tokens" or other indicators of reinforcement contingent on desired behaviors. The tokens can later be exchanged for privileges, food, or other reinforcers.

do it yourself!

Behavior Self-Modification   Is there a behavioral habit that you would like to acquire—studying, initiating conversations with others, exercising to keep fit? Write this activity in behavioral terms on the lines below. (Don't use mentalistic words such as "feeling" or "wanting." Behaviorists require that you keep things objective by specifying only an observable behavior.)

The desired new behavior: _____

_____

When or under what conditions would you like to engage in this new behavior? Below, write in the time or stimulus conditions when you want to initiate the behavior (for example: in class, when relaxing with friends, or at a certain time every morning).

The time or conditions for the new behavior: _____

_____

To increase your likelihood of producing the desired response, apply some positive reinforcement therapy to yourself. Choose an appropriate reward that you will give yourself when you have produced the desired behavior at the appropriate time. Write the reward that you will give yourself below.

Your reward: _____

_____

Give yourself feedback on your progress by keeping a daily record of the occurrence of your new behavior. This could be done, for example, on a calendar or a graph. In time, you will discover that the desired behavior has increased in frequency. You will also find that your new habit carries its own rewards, such as better grades or more satisfying social interactions (Kazdin, 1994).

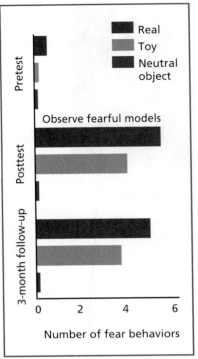

[**FIGURE 12·3**] **Fear Reactions in Monkeys** In a pretest, young monkeys raised in laboratories show little fear of snakes (top bars). But after observing other monkeys showing a strong fear of snakes, they are conditioned to fear both real snakes and toy snakes (middle bars). A follow-up test shows that the fear persists over a 3-month interval (bottom bars).

Source: Cook, M., Mineka, S., Wokenstein, B., & Laitsch, K. (1985). Observational conditioning of snake fear in unrelated rhesus monkeys. *Journal of Abnormal Psychology, 94,* pp. 591–610. Copyright © 1985 by American Psychological Association. Reprinted by permission of American Psychological Association.

recipients may redeem the tokens for food, merchandise, or privileges. Often, "points" or play money are used in place of tokens. The important thing is that the individual receives something as a reinforcer immediately after giving desired responses. With the appropriate modifications, the token economy also works well with children having developmental disabilities, with mental patients, and with correctional populations (Higgins et al., 2001).

Participant Modeling: An Observational-Learning Therapy

"Monkey see—monkey do," we say. And sure enough, monkeys learn fears by observation and imitation. One study showed that laboratory monkeys with no previous aversion to snakes could acquire a simian version of *ophidiophobia* by observing their parents reacting fearfully to real snakes and toy snakes. (You don't remember that phobia? Look back at Table 12.3 on pages 532–533.) The more disturbed the monkey parents were at the sight of the snakes, the greater the resulting fear in their offspring (Mineka et al., 1984).

A follow-up study showed that such fears were not just a family matter. When other monkeys that had previously shown no fear of snakes were given the opportunity to observe unrelated adults responding to snakes fearfully, they quickly acquired the same response, as you can see in **FIGURE 12·3** (Cook et al., 1985).

Like monkeys, people also learn fears by observing the behavior of others. But for therapeutic purposes, observational learning in the form of *participant modeling* can also encourage *healthy* behaviors. In **participant modeling,** then, the client, or *participant,* observes and imitates someone *modeling* desirable behaviors. Athletic coaches, of course, have used participant modeling for years. Similarly, a behavior therapist treating a snake phobia might model the desired behavior by first approaching a caged snake, then touching the snake, and so on. The client then imitates the modeled behavior—but at no time is forced to perform. If the therapist senses resistance, the client may return to a previously successful level. As you can see, the procedure is similar to systematic desensitization, with the

---

participant modeling   A social learning technique in which a therapist demonstrates and encourages a client to imitate a desired behavior.

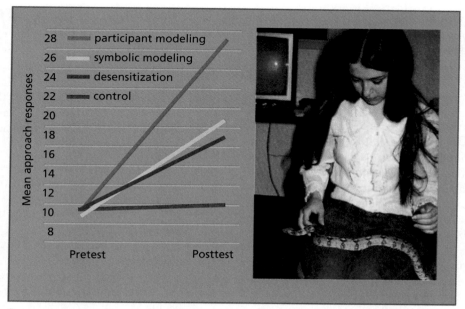

[FIGURE 12•4] **Participant Modeling Therapy** The client shown in the photo first watches a model make a graduated series of snake-approach responses and then repeats them herself. Eventually, she can pick up the snake and let it move about on her. The graph compares the number of approach responses clients made before and after receiving participant modeling therapy with the responses of those exposed to two other therapeutic techniques and a control group. The graph shows that participant modeling was far more effective in the posttest.

Source: Bandura, A. D. (1970). Modeling therapy. In W. S. Sahakian (Ed.), *Psychopathology today: Experimentation, theory, and research.* Itasca, IL: Peacock. Reprinted by permission of the author.

important addition of observational learning. In fact, participant modeling draws on concepts from both operant and classical conditioning.

The power of participant modeling in eliminating snake phobias can be seen in a study that compared the participant modeling technique with several other approaches: (1) *symbolic modeling,* a technique in which subjects receive indirect exposure by watching a film or video in which models deal with a feared situation; (2) desensitization therapy, which, as you will remember, involves exposure to an imagined fearful stimulus; and (3) no therapeutic intervention (the control condition). As you can see in **FIGURE 12•4**, participant modeling was the most successful. The snake phobia was virtually eliminated in 11 of the 12 subjects in the participant modeling group (Bandura, 1970).

Cognitive–Behavioral Therapy: A Synthesis

Suppose you are having difficulty controlling feelings of jealousy every time the person you love is friendly with someone else. Chances are that the problem originates in your cognitions about yourself and the others involved ("Marty is stealing Terry away from me!") These thoughts may also affect your behavior, making you act in ways that could drive Terry

away from you. A dose of therapy aimed at *both* your cognitions and your behaviors may be a better bet than either one alone.

In brief, **cognitive–behavioral therapy** (CBT) combines a cognitive emphasis on thoughts and attitudes with the behavioral strategies that we have just discussed. This dual approach assumes that an irrational self-statement often underlies maladaptive behavior. Accordingly, the therapist and client work together to modify irrational self-talk, set attainable behavioral goals, develop realistic strategies for attaining them, and evaluate the results. In this way, people change the way they approach problems and gradually develop new skills and a sense of self-efficacy (Bandura, 1986, 1992; DeAngelis, 2008b; Schwarzer, 1992). ◉

◉ **Watch** the **Video** Cognitive Behavioral Therapy at **MyPsychLab**

How well does cognitive–behavioral therapy work? Quite well, indeed, particularly for depression, anxiety disorders, alcoholism, bulimia nervosa, recurring nightmares, and post-traumatic stress disorder (Baker et al., 2008; Chamberlin,

cognitive–behavioral therapy A newer form of psychotherapy that combines the techniques of cognitive therapy with those of behavioral therapy.

2008). In fact, it is one of psychology's most prominent success stories. In all of these disorders, CBT can be at least as effective as medication—and sometimes *more* so. For certain other conditions, such as bipolar disorder and schizophrenia, a combination of CBT and medication is more effective than either one alone.

Rational–Emotive Behavior Therapy: Challenging the "Shoulds" and "Oughts"

One of the most famous forms of cognitive–behavioral therapy was developed by the colorful and notorious Albert Ellis (1987, 1990, 1996) to help people eliminate self-defeating thought patterns. Ellis dubbed his treatment **rational–emotive behavior therapy (REBT)**, a name derived from its method of challenging certain "irrational" beliefs and behaviors.

What are the irrational beliefs challenged in REBT, and how do they lead to maladaptive feelings and actions? According to Ellis, maladjusted individuals base their lives on a set of unrealistic values and unachievable goals. These "neurotic" goals and values lead people to hold unrealistic expectations that they should *always* succeed, that they should *always* receive approval, that they should *always* be treated fairly, and that their experiences should *always* be pleasant. (You can see the most common irrational beliefs in the accompanying box, *Do It Yourself! Examining Your Own Beliefs.*) For example, in your own daily life, you may frequently tell yourself that you "should" get an A in math or that you "ought to" spend an hour exercising every day. Further, he says, if you are unable to meet your goals and seldom question this neurotic self-talk, it may come to control your actions or even prevent you from choosing the life you want. If you were to enter REBT, your therapist would teach you to recognize such assumptions, question how rational they are, and replace faulty ideas with more valid ones. Don't "should" on yourself, warned Ellis.

So, how might a cognitive–behavioral therapist have dealt with Freud's obsessive patient? First, taking a cognitive approach, the therapist would challenge the girl's irrational beliefs, as we suggested earlier. Then, switching to a behavioral mode, the therapist might teach the girl relaxation techniques to use when she began to get ready for bed each evening. These techniques then would substitute for the obsessive ritual. It is also likely that the therapist would work with the parents, focusing on helping them learn not to reward the girl with attention for her ritual behavior.

[CONNECTION] Compare Ellis's "neurotic" goals with Karen Horney's neurotic trends.

Similarly, a cognitive–behavioral therapist would help depressed Derek by challenging the way he *thinks*—perhaps

---

rational–emotive behavior therapy (REBT) Albert Ellis's brand of cognitive therapy, based on the idea that irrational thoughts and behaviors are the cause of mental disorders.

do it yourself!

Examining Your Own Beliefs

It may be obvious that the following are not healthy beliefs, but Albert Ellis found that many people hold them. Do you? Be honest: Put a check mark beside each of the following statements that accurately describes how you feel about yourself.

1. _____ I must be loved and approved by everyone.
2. _____ I must be thoroughly competent, adequate, and achieving.
3. _____ It is catastrophic when things do not go the way I want them to go.
4. _____ Unhappiness results from forces over which I have no control.
5. _____ People must always treat each other fairly and justly; those who don't are nasty and terrible people.
6. _____ I must constantly be on my guard against dangers and things that could go wrong.
7. _____ Life is full of problems, and I must always find quick solutions to them.
8. _____ It is easier to evade my problems and responsibilities than to face them.
9. _____ Unpleasant experiences in my past have had a profound influence on me. Therefore, they must continue to influence my current feelings and actions.
10. _____ I can achieve happiness by just enjoying myself each day. The future will take care of itself.

In Ellis's view, all these statements were irrational beliefs that can cause mental problems. The more items you have checked, the more "irrational" your beliefs. His cognitive approach to therapy, known as rational–emotive behavior therapy, concentrates on helping people see that they can "drive themselves crazy" with such irrational beliefs. For example, a student who parties rather than studying for a test holds belief #8. A person who is depressed about not landing a certain job holds irrational belief #3. You can obtain more information on Ellis's system from his books.

blaming himself less and focusing more on constructive plans for doing better—can ultimately change how he feels and how he acts. Indeed, Peter Lewinsohn and his colleagues have found that they can treat many cases of depression effectively with such cognitive–behavioral techniques (Lewinsohn et al., 1980, 1990; Lewinsohn & Gottlib, 1995). Their approach intervenes at several points in the cycle of depression to teach people how to change their helpless thinking, to cope adaptively with unpleasant situations, and to build more rewards into their lives.

Positive Psychotherapy (PPT) Derek might also be a good candidate for a newer form of cognitive–behavioral treatment called **positive psychotherapy (PPT)**, developed by Martin Seligman. Like the humanists, Seligman and his fellow *positive psychologists* see their mission as balancing psychology's negative emphasis on mental disorders with their own positive emphasis on growth, health, and happiness. So it was a "natural" for Seligman to tackle the problem of depression by accentuating the positive (Seligman et al., 2006). Unlike the humanists, however, the PPT approach is largely cognitive–behavioral, with an emphasis on research.

In both PPT and Lewinsohn's therapy sessions, Derek might find himself treated more like a student than a patient. For example, the therapist might give him a "homework" assignment, such as the "three good things" exercise: "Before you go to sleep, write down three things that went well today and why they went well." Derek would also learn to focus on positive emotions, respond constructively to others, and otherwise to seek more pleasure in his work and home life. How well does PPT work? Seligman and his group have applied PPT to dozens of clients and report preliminary results showing that it relieved depression far more effectively than did conventional therapy or antidepressant medication (Seligman et al., 2006).

Changing the Brain by Changing the Mind Brain scans now show that cognitive–behavioral therapy not only helps people change their minds, but it can also change the brain itself (Dobbs, 2006b). In one study, patients who experienced compulsive obsessions, such as worrying that they had not turned off their stoves or locked their doors, were given cognitive behavior modification (Schwartz et al., 1996). When they felt an urge to run home and check on themselves, they were trained to relabel their experience as an obsession or compulsion—not a rational concern. They then focused on waiting out this "urge" rather than giving in to it, by distracting themselves with other activities for about 15 minutes. Positron emission tomography (PET) scans of the brains of subjects who were trained in this technique indicated that, over time, the part of the brain responsible for that nagging fear or urge gradually became less active.

As that study shows, psychology has come a long way since the days when we wondered whether thoughts and behavior were the product of nature *or* nurture. With cognitive–behavioral therapy, we now know that experience can change the biology behind behavior.

Evaluating the Psychological Therapies

Now that we have looked at a variety of psychological therapies (see FIGURE 12•5), let us step back and ask how effec-

---

positive psychotherapy (PPT)   A relatively new form of cognitive–behavioral treatment that seeks to emphasize growth, health, and happiness.

tive therapy is. Think about it: How could you tell objectively whether therapy really works? The answer to this question hasn't always been clear (Kopta et al., 1999; Shadish et al., 2000).

Lots of evidence says that most people who have undergone therapy *like* it. This was shown, for example, by surveying thousands of subscribers to *Consumer Reports* (1995). Respondents indicated how much their treatment helped, how satisfied they were with the therapist's treatment of their problems, how much their "overall emotional state" changed following therapy, as well as what kind of therapy they had undergone. Among the results: (a) Therapy works—that is, it was perceived to have helped clients diminish or eliminate their psychological problems; (b) long-term therapy is better than short-term therapy; and (c) all forms of therapy are about equally effective for improving clients' problems (see Jacobson & Christensen, 1996).

We can't give a thumbs-up to therapy, however, merely because people say they like it or that it helped them (Hollon, 1996). Testimonials don't make for good science—which is why psychologists now demand that therapy be judged by studies having a *comparison group* or *control group*. Let's turn, therefore, to the controlled studies of therapy's effectiveness, beginning with a report that nearly upset the therapeutic applecart.

[CONNECTION] A *control group* is treated exactly as the experimental group, except for the crucial independent variable.

Eysenck's Controversial Proclamation The issue of therapy's effectiveness came to a head in 1952, when British psychologist Hans Eysenck proclaimed that roughly two-thirds of all people who develop nonpsychotic mental disorders would recover within two years, *whether they get therapy or not*. Eysenck's evidence came from a review of several outcome studies of various kinds of insight therapy, all of which compared patients who received therapy to those who were on waiting lists, waiting their turn in treatment. What he noted was that just as many people on the waiting lists recovered as those in therapy. If taken at face value, this meant that psychotherapy was essentially worthless—no better than having no treatment at all! To say the least, this wasn't received happily by therapists. But Eysenck's challenge had an immensely productive result: It stimulated therapists to do a great deal of research on the effectiveness of their craft.

In Response to Eysenck Major reviews of the accumulating evidence on therapy began to be reported in 1970 (by Meltzoff & Kornreich), in 1975 (by Luborsky et al.), and in 1977 (by Smith and Glass). Overall, this literature—numbering some 375 studies—supported two major conclusions. First, therapy is, after all, more effective than no therapy—much to everyone's relief! And second, Eysenck

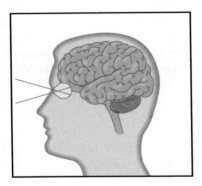

Behavior therapies
aim to change things *outside the individual*: rewards, punishments, and cues in the environment in order to change the person's external behaviors.

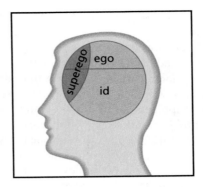

Psychodynamic therapies
aim to make changes *inside the person's mind*, especially the unconscious.

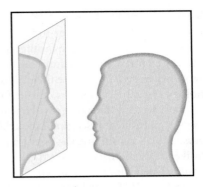

Humanistic therapies
aim to change the way people *see themselves and their relationships*.

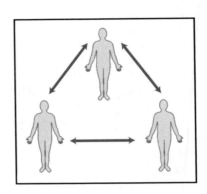

Cognitive therapies
aim to change the way people *think and perceive*.

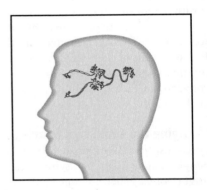

Group therapies
aim to change the way people *interact*.

Biomedical therapies
aim to change the structure or function of the brain.

[**FIGURE 12•5**] A Comparison of Different Types of Therapy

had apparently overestimated the improvement rate in no-therapy control groups.

Gradually, then, a scientific consensus supporting the value of psychotherapy emerged (Meredith, 1986; Vanden-Bos, 1986). In fact, for a broad range of disorders, psychotherapy has been demonstrated to have an effect comparable or superior to many established medical practices (Wampold, 2007). Moreover, research began to show that therapy was effective not only in Western industrialized countries (in the United States, Canada, and Europe) but also in a variety of cultural settings throughout the world (Beutler & Machado, 1992; Lipsey & Wilson, 1993).

New Questions But the new studies have raised new questions. Are some therapies better than others? Can we identify therapies that are best suited for treating specific disorders? The Smith and Glass (1977) survey hinted that the answers to those questions were "Yes" and "Yes." Smith and Glass found that the behavior therapies seemed to have an advantage over

insight therapies for the treatment of many anxiety disorders. And as we noted earlier, the use of cognitive–behavioral therapies for treating depression, anxiety disorders, bulimia nervosa, and a few other disorders now has solid empirical support. In addition, recent evaluations have found that insight therapies can also be used effectively to treat problems such as marital discord, depression, and even the tough-to-treat personality disorders (Shedler, 2010). Indeed, there is now a clear trend toward matching specific therapies to specific conditions.

Finally, we should note that, in judging the effectiveness of various psychotherapies, it is important to realize that success does not necessarily mean a "cure." Sometimes just making an improvement is all the success we can expect. In the treatment of schizophrenia, mental retardation, or autism, for example, psychological therapies may be deemed effective when people with these afflictions learn more adaptive behaviors and report leading happier lives (Hogarty et al., 1997).

psychology matters

Where Do Most People Get Help?

The effectiveness of psychotherapy for a variety of problems seems to be established beyond doubt. Having said that, we should again acknowledge that *most people experiencing mental distress do not turn to professional therapists for help.* Rather, they turn to "just people" in the community (Wills & DePaulo, 1991). Those suffering from mental problems often look to friends, clergy, hairdressers, bartenders, and others with whom they have a trusting relationship. In fact, for some types of problems—perhaps the most common problems of everyday living—a sympathetic friend may be just as effective as a trained professional therapist (Berman & Norton, 1985; Christensen & Jacobson, 1994).

To put the matter in a different way: Most mental problems are not the crippling disorders that took center stage. Rather, the psychological difficulties most of us face result from lost jobs, difficult marriages, misbehaving children, friendships gone sour, loved ones dying. . . . In brief, the most familiar problems involve chaos, confusion, choice, frustration, stress, and loss. People who find themselves in the throes of these adjustment difficulties may not need extensive psychotherapy, medication, or some other special treatment. They need someone to help them sort through the pieces of their problems. Usually, this means that they turn to someone like you.

So, what can you do when someone asks you for help? First, you should realize that some problems do indeed require immediate professional attention. These include a suicide threat or an indication of intent to harm others. You should not delay finding competent help for someone with such tendencies. Second, you should remember that most therapy methods require special training, especially those calling for cognitive–behavioral therapy techniques or psychodynamic interpretations. We urge you to learn as much as you can about these methods—but we strongly recommend that you leave them to the professionals. Some other techniques, however, are simply extensions of good human relationships, and they fall well within the layperson's abilities for mental "first aid." Briefly, we will consider three of these:

- **Listening.** You will rarely go wrong if you just listen. Sometimes listening is all the therapy a person in distress needs. It works by encouraging the speaker to organize a problem well enough to communicate it. Consequently, those who talk out their problems frequently arrive at their own solutions. As an **active listener,** you take the role a step farther by giving the speaker feedback: nodding, maintaining an expression that shows interest, paraphrasing, and asking for clarification when you don't understand. Active listening lets the speaker know that the listener is interested and *empathetic* (in tune with the other person's feelings). At the same time, you will do well to avoid the temptation of giving advice. Advice robs the recipient of the opportunity to work out his or her own solutions.

- **Acceptance.** Client-centered therapists call this a *nonjudgmental attitude.* It means accepting the person and the problem as they are. It also means suppressing shock, disgust, or condemnation that would create a hostile climate for problem solving.

- **Exploration of alternatives.** People under stress may see only one course of action, so you can help by identifying other potential choices and exploring the consequences of each. (You can point out that *doing nothing* is also a choice.) Remember that, in the end, the choice of action is not up to you but to the individual who owns the problem.

Beyond these basic helping techniques lies the territory of the trained therapist. Again, we strongly advise you against trying out the therapy techniques discussed in this chapter for any of the serious psychological disorders.

CHECK YOUR UNDERSTANDING

✓—[Study and Review at MyPsychLab

1. **Recall:** On what form of behavioral learning is the behavioral technique of *counterconditioning* based?

2. **Application:** You could use *contingency management* to change the behavior of a child who comes home late for dinner by
    a. pairing food with punishment.
    b. having the child observe someone else coming home on time and being rewarded.
    c. refusing to let the child have dinner when he comes home late.
    d. having the child relax and imagine being home on time for dinner.

3. **Recall:** What is the primary goal of psychoanalytic therapy? That is, what makes psychoanalytic therapy different from behavioral therapy or the cognitive therapies?

4. **Recall:** Carl Rogers invented a technique to help people see their own thinking more clearly. Using this technique, the therapist paraphrases the client's statements. Rogers called this _____.

5. **Recall:** Which form of therapy directly confronts a client's self-defeating and irrational thought patterns?

6. **Recall:** Eysenck caused a furor with his claim that people who receive psychotherapy _____.

---

active listener   A person who gives the speaker feedback in such forms as nodding, paraphrasing, maintaining an expression that shows interest, and asking questions for clarification.

7. **Understanding the Core Concept:** A phobia would be best treated by _____, while a problem of choosing a major would be better suited for _____.

 a. behavioral therapy/insight therapy
 b. cognitive therapy/psychoanalysis
 c. insight therapy/behavioral therapy
 d. humanistic therapy/behavioral therapy

Answers: 1. Classical conditioning **2.** c **3.** Psychoanalysis seeks to reveal and resolve problems in the patient's unconscious, particularly repressed traumatic memories, unfulfilled desires, and unconscious conflicts. **4.** reflection of feeling **5.** Rational–emotive behavior therapy **6.** improve no more often than people who receive no therapy at all **7.** a

– – – – –

12.3 Key Question: How Is the Biomedical Approach Used to Treat Psychological Disorders?

The mind exists in a delicate biological balance. It can be upset by irregularities in our genes, hormones, enzymes, and metabolism, as well as by damage from accidents and disease. When something goes wrong with the brain, we can see the consequences in abnormal patterns of behavior or peculiar cognitive and emotional reactions. The biomedical therapies, therefore, attempt to treat these mental disorders by intervening directly in the brain. Our Core Concept specifies the targets of these therapies:

CORE CONCEPT 12.3

Biomedical therapies seek to treat psychological disorders by changing the brain's chemistry with drugs, its circuitry with surgery, or its patterns of activity with pulses of electricity or powerful magnetic fields.

Each of the biomedical therapies emerges from the medical model of abnormal mental functioning, which assumes an organic basis for mental illnesses and treats them as diseases. We begin our examination of these biomedical therapies with medicine's arsenal of prescription psychoactive drugs. ✳

✳ **Explore** the **Concept** Drugs Commonly Used to Treat Psychiatric Disorders at **MyPsychLab**

Drug Therapy

In the history of the treatment of mental disorder, nothing has ever rivaled the revolution created by the discovery of drugs that could calm anxious patients, elevate the mood of depressed patients, and suppress hallucinations in psychotic patients. This brave new therapeutic era began in 1953 with the introduction of the first antipsychotic drugs (often called "tranquilizers"). As these drugs found wide application, many unruly, assaultive patients almost miraculously became cooperative, calm, and sociable. In addition, many thought-disordered patients, who had previously been absorbed in their delusions and hallucinations, began to respond to the physical and social environment around them.

The effectiveness of drug therapy had a pronounced effect on the census of the nation's mental hospitals. In 1955, more than half a million Americans were living in mental institutions, each staying an average of several years. Then, with the introduction of tranquilizers, the numbers began a steady decline. In just over ten years, fewer than half that number actually resided in mental hospitals, and those who did were usually kept for only a few months.

Drug therapy has long since steamrolled out of the mental hospital and into our everyday lives. Currently, millions of people take drugs for anxiety, stress, depression, hyperactivity, insomnia, fears and phobias, obsessions and compulsions, addictions, and numerous other problems. Clearly, a drug-induced revolution has occurred. But what are these miraculous drugs?

You have probably heard of Prozac and Valium, but those are just two of scores of psychoactive drugs that can alter your mood, your perceptions, your desires, and perhaps your basic personality. Here, we will consider four major categories of drugs used today: *antipsychotics, antidepressants and mood stabilizers, antianxiety drugs,* and *stimulants*.

DRUG THERAPIES

- Antipsychotic drugs
- Antidepressants and mood stabilizers
- Antianxiety drugs
- Stimulants

Antipsychotic Drugs As their name says, the **antipsychotics** treat the symptoms of psychosis: delusions, hallucinations, social withdrawal, and agitation (Dawkins et al., 1999). Most work by reducing the activity of the neurotransmitter dopamine in the brain—although the precise reason why this has an antipsychotic effect is not known. For example, *chlorpromazine* (sold under the brand name Thorazine) and *haloperidol* (brand name: Haldol) are known to block dopamine receptors in the synapse between nerve cells. A newer antipsychotic drug, *clozapine* (Clozaril), both decreases dopamine activity and increases the activity of another neurotransmitter, serotonin, which also inhibits the dopamine system (Javitt & Coyle, 2004; Sawa & Snyder, 2002). While these drugs reduce overall brain activity, they do not merely

---

antipsychotics Medicines that diminish psychotic symptoms, usually by effects on the dopamine pathways in the brain.

"tranquilize" the patient. Rather, they reduce schizophrenia's "positive" symptoms (hallucinations, delusions, emotional disturbances, and agitated behavior), although they do little for the "negative" symptoms of social distance, jumbled thoughts, and poor attention spans seen in many patients (Wickelgren, 1998a). Newer drugs have come online in recent years, but a recent study suggests that, for reducing psychotic symptoms, these "second generation" antipsychotic drugs may be no more effective than the older ones (Lieberman et al., 2005; Rosenheck et al., 2006).

Unfortunately, long-term administration of any antipsychotic drug can have unwanted side effects. Physical changes in the brain have been noted (Gur & Maany, 1998). But most worrisome is **tardive dyskinesia**, which produces an incurable disturbance of motor control, especially of the facial muscles. Although some of the newer drugs, like clozapine, have reduced motor side effects because of their more selective dopamine blocking, they also can cause serious problems. Are antipsychotic drugs worth the risk? There is no easy answer. The risks must be weighed against the severity of the patient's current suffering.

[CONNECTION] *Positive symptoms* of schizophrenia include active hallucinations, delusions, and extreme emotions; *negative symptoms* include withdrawal and "flat" emotions.

Antidepressants and Mood Stabilizers
The drug therapy arsenal also includes several compounds that have revolutionized the treatment of depression and bipolar disorder. As with other psychoactive drugs, neither the *antidepressants* nor *mood stabilizers* can provide a "cure." Their use, however, has made a big difference in the lives of many people suffering from depression and bipolar disorder.

Antidepressant Drugs. All three major classes of **antidepressants** work by "turning up the volume" on messages transmitted over certain brain pathways, especially those using norepinephrine and serotonin (Holmes, 2001). *Tricyclic* compounds such as Tofranil and Elavil reduce the neuron's reabsorption of neurotransmitters after they have been released in the synapse between brain cells—a process called *reuptake*. A second group includes the famous antidepressant Prozac (fluoxetine). These drugs, known as SSRIs (selective serotonin reuptake inhibitors), interfere with the reuptake of serotonin. As a result, the SSRIs keep serotonin available longer. For many people, this prolonged serotonin effect lifts depressed moods (Hirschfeld, 1999; Kramer, 1993). The third group of antidepressant drugs, the *monoamine oxidase (MAO) inhibitors,* limits the activity of the enzyme MAO, a

chemical that breaks down norepinephrine in the synapse. When MAO is inhibited, more norepinephrine is available to carry neural messages across the synapse.

Strangely, most patients report that it takes at least a couple of weeks before antidepressants begin to lift the veil of depression. And recent research seems to suggest why. In animal studies, antidepressants stimulate the growth of neurons in the brain's hippocampus. No one is sure why the hippocampus seems to be involved in depression, but the animal studies offer another tantalizing clue: Stress slows the growth of new neurons in this part of the brain—and depression is believed to be a stress response (Santarelli et al., 2003).

The possibility of suicide poses a special concern in the treatment of depression. And now, it seems that the very drugs used for treating depression may provoke or amplify suicidal thoughts, particularly during the first few weeks of therapy and especially in children (Bower, 2004b). One study revived hopes by showing that the increased short-term risk is small—less than 1 percent (Bridge et al., 2007). And another study shows that patients taking antidepressants have a somewhat *lower* risk of suicide over the long haul (Bower, 2007). Obviously, the picture is confusing at the moment, and the Food and Drug Administration is advising prescribers to use caution (Bower, 2006b; Jick et al., 2004).

[CONNECTION] *Reuptake* is a process by which neurotransmitters are taken intact from the synapse and cycled back into the terminal buttons of the axon. Reuptake, therefore, "tones down" the message being sent from one neuron to another.

Controversy Over SSRIs
In his book, *Listening to Prozac,* psychiatrist and Prozac advocate Peter Kramer (1993) encourages the use of the drug to deal not only with depression but also with general feelings of social unease and fear of rejection. Such claims have brought heated replies from therapists who fear that drugs may merely mask the psychological problems that people need to face and resolve. Some worry that the wide use of antidepressants may produce changes in the personality structure of a huge segment of our population—changes that could bring unanticipated social consequences (Breggin & Breggin, 1994; Sleek, 1994). In fact, more prescriptions are being written for antidepressants than there are people who have been diagnosed with clinical depression (Coyne, 2001). The problem seems to be especially acute on college and university campuses, where increasing numbers of students are taking antidepressants (Young, 2003). At present, no one knows what the potential dangers might be of altering the brain chemistry of large numbers of people over long periods.

Just as worrisome for the medical model, another report suggests that antidepressants may owe nearly as much to their hype as to their effects on the brain. According to data mined from the Food and Drug Administration files, studies showing positive results find their way into print far more

---

tardive dyskinesia An incurable disorder of motor control, especially involving muscles of the face and head, resulting from long-term use of antipsychotic drugs.

antidepressants Medicines that treat depression, usually by their effects on the serotonin and/or norepinephrine pathways in the brain.

often than do studies showing no effects for these medicines. While these drugs do better overall than placebos, reports of their effects seem to be exaggerated by selective publication of positive results (Turner et al., 2008).

Mood Stabilizers. A simple chemical, *lithium* (in the form of *lithium carbonate*), has proved highly effective as a mood stabilizer in the treatment of bipolar disorder (Paulus, 2007; Schou, 1997). Not just an antidepressant, lithium affects both ends of the emotional spectrum, dampening swings of mood that would otherwise range from uncontrollable periods of hyperexcitement to the lethargy and despair of depression. Unfortunately, lithium also has a serious drawback: In high concentrations, it is toxic. Physicians have learned that safe therapy requires that small doses be given to build up therapeutic concentrations in the blood over a period of a week or two. Then, as a precaution, patients must have periodic blood analyses to ensure that lithium concentrations have not risen to dangerous levels. In a welcome development, scientists have found a promising alternative to lithium for the treatment of bipolar disorder (Azar, 1994; Walden et al., 1998). *Divalproex sodium* (brand name: Depakote), originally developed to treat epilepsy, seems to be even more effective than lithium for most patients but with fewer dangerous side effects (Bowden et al., 2000).

Antianxiety Drugs
To reduce stress and suppress anxiety associated with everyday hassles, untold millions of Americans take **antianxiety drugs,** either *barbiturates* or *benzodiazepines.* Barbiturates act as central nervous system depressants, so they have a relaxing effect. But barbiturates can be dangerous if taken in excess or in combination with alcohol. By contrast, the benzodiazepines, such as Valium and Xanax, work by increasing the activity of the neurotransmitter GABA, thereby decreasing activity in brain regions more specifically involved in feelings of anxiety. The benzodiazepines are sometimes called "minor tranquilizers."

Many psychologists believe that these antianxiety drugs—like the antidepressants—are too often prescribed for problems that people should face rather than mask with chemicals. Nevertheless, antianxiety compounds can be useful in helping people deal with specific situations, such as anxiety prior to surgery. Here are some cautions to bear in mind about these compounds (Hecht, 1986):

- If used over long periods, barbiturates and benzodiazepines can be physically and psychologically addicting (Holmes, 2001; Schatzberg, 1991).
- Because of their powerful effects on the brain, these medicines should not be taken to relieve anxieties that are part of the ordinary stresses of everyday life.
- When used for extreme anxiety, antianxiety drugs should not normally be taken for more than a few days at a time.

antianxiety drugs A category of medicines that includes the barbiturates and benzodiazepines, drugs that diminish feelings of anxiety.

If used longer than this, their dosage should be gradually reduced by a physician. Abrupt cessation after prolonged use can lead to withdrawal symptoms, such as convulsions, tremors, and abdominal and muscle cramps.

- Because antianxiety drugs depress parts of the central nervous system, they can impair one's ability to drive, operate machinery, or perform other tasks that require alertness (such as studying or taking exams).
- In combination with alcohol (also a central nervous system depressant) or with sleeping pills, antianxiety drugs can lead to unconsciousness and even death.

Finally, we should mention that some antidepressant drugs have also been found useful for reducing the symptoms of certain anxiety disorders such as panic disorders, agoraphobia, as well as obsessive–compulsive disorder. (A modern psychiatrist might well have prescribed antidepressants for Freud's obsessive patient.) But because these problems may arise from low levels of serotonin, they may respond even better to drugs like Prozac that specifically affect serotonin function.

[**CONNECTION**] GABA is the major inhibitory neurotransmitter in the brain.

Stimulants
Ranging from caffeine to nicotine to amphetamines to cocaine, any drug that produces excitement or hyperactivity falls into the category of **stimulants.** We have seen that stimulants can be useful in the treatment of narcolepsy. They also have an accepted niche in treating *attention-deficit/hyperactivity disorder (ADHD).* While it may seem strange to prescribe stimulants (a common one is Ritalin) for hyperactive children, studies comparing stimulant therapy with behavior therapy and with placebos have shown a clear role for stimulants (American Academy of Pediatrics, 2001; Meyers, 2006). Although the exact mechanism is unknown, stimulants may work in hyperactive children by increasing the availability of dopamine, glutamate, and/or serotonin in their brains (Gainetdinov et al., 1999).

As you can imagine, the use of stimulants to treat ADHD has generated controversy (O'Connor, 2001). Some objections, of course, stem from ignorance of the well-established calming effect these drugs have in children with this condition. Other worries have more substance. For some patients, the drug will interfere with normal sleep patterns. Additionally, there is evidence that stimulant therapy can slow a child's growth (National Institute of Mental Health, 2004). Legitimate concerns also center on the potential for abuse that lurks in the temptation to see every child's behavior problem as a symptom of ADHD (Smith, 2002a). And finally, critics

stimulants Drugs that normally increase activity level by encouraging communication among neurons in the brain. Stimulants, however, have been found to suppress activity level in persons with attention-deficit/hyperactivity disorder.

suggest that the prescription of stimulants to children might encourage later drug abuse (Daw, 2001). Happily, recent studies have found cognitive–behavioral therapy (CBT) to be comparable to stimulants as a treatment for ADHD (Sinha, 2005). Even better, say many experts, is a *combination therapy* regimen that employs both CBT and stimulants.

Evaluating the Drug Therapies The drug therapies have caused a revolution in the treatment of severe mental disorders, starting in the 1950s, when virtually the only treatments available were talk therapies, hospitalization, restraints, "shock treatment," and lobotomies. Of course, none of the drugs discovered so far can "cure" any mental disorder. Yet, in many cases, they can alter the brain's chemistry to suppress symptoms.

But is all the enthusiasm warranted? According to neuroscientist Elliot Valenstein (1998), a close look behind the scenes of drug therapy raises important questions (Rolnick, 1998). Valenstein believes that much of the faith in drug therapy for mental disorders rests on hype. He credits the wide acceptance of drug therapy to the huge investment drug companies have made in marketing their products. Particularly distressing are concerns raised about the willingness of physicians to prescribe drugs for children—even though the safety and effectiveness of many drugs has not been established in young people (K. Brown, 2003a).

Few question that drugs are the proper first line of treatment for certain conditions, such as bipolar disorder and schizophrenia. In many other cases, however, the apparent advantages of drug therapy are quick results and low cost. Yet some research raises doubts about simplistic time-and-money assumptions. Studies show, for example, that treating depression, anxiety disorders, and eating disorders with cognitive–behavioral therapy—alone or in combination with drugs—may be both more effective and more economical in the long run than reliance on drugs alone (Clay, 2000).

[**CONNECTION**] Phineas Gage survived—with a changed personality—after a steel rod was blasted through his frontal lobe.

Other Medical Therapies for Psychological Disorders

Describing a modern-day counterpart to Phineas Gage, the headline in the *Los Angeles Times* read, ".22-Caliber Surgery Suicide Bid Cures Psychological Disorder" (February 23, 1988). The article revealed that a 19-year-old man suffering from severe obsessive–compulsive disorder had shot a 0.22 caliber bullet through the front of his brain in a suicide attempt. Remarkably, he survived, his pathological symptoms were gone, and his intellectual capacity was not affected.

We don't recommend this form of therapy, but the case does illustrate the potential effects of physical intervention in the brain. In this vein, we will look briefly at two medical alternatives

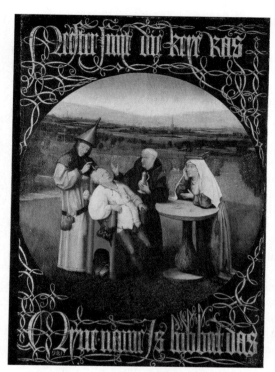

In medieval times, those suffering from madness might be treated by trephenation or making a hole in the skull. This painting portrays the operation as the removal of the "stone of folly."

to drug therapy that were conceived to alter the brain's structure and function, psychosurgery and direct stimulation of the brain.

Psychosurgery With scalpels in place of bullets, surgeons have long aspired to treat mental disorders by severing connections between parts of the brain or by removing small sections of brain. In modern times, **psychosurgery** is usually considered a method of last resort. Nevertheless, psychosurgery has a history dating back at least to medieval times, when surgeons might open the skull to remove "the stone of folly" from an unfortunate madman. (There is, of course, no such "stone"—and there was no anesthetic except alcohol for these procedures.)

In modern times, the best-known form of psychosurgery involved the now-discredited *prefrontal lobotomy*. This operation, developed by Portuguese psychiatrist Egas Moñiz,[2] severed certain nerve fibers connecting the frontal lobes with deep brain structures, especially those of the thalamus and hypothalamus—much as what happened accidentally to Phineas Gage. The original candidates for Moñiz's scalpel were agitated schizophrenic patients and patients who were compulsive and anxiety ridden. Surprisingly, this rather crude operation often produced a dramatic reduction in agitation and anxiety. On the down side, the operation

---

psychosurgery The general term for surgical intervention in the brain to treat psychological disorders.

permanently destroyed basic aspects of the patients' personalities. Frequently, they emerged from the procedure crippled by a loss of interest in their personal well-being and their surroundings. As experience with lobotomy accumulated, doctors saw that it destroyed patients' ability to plan ahead, made them indifferent to the opinions of others, rendered their behavior childlike, and gave them the intellectual and emotional flatness of a person without a coherent sense of self. Not surprisingly, when the antipsychotic drug therapies came on the scene in the 1950s, with a promise to control psychotic symptoms with no obvious risk of permanent brain damage, the era of lobotomy came to a close (Valenstein, 1980).

Psychosurgery is still occasionally done, but it is now much more limited to precise and proven procedures for very specific brain disorders. In the "split-brain" operation, for example, severing the fibers of the corpus callosum can reduce life-threatening seizures in certain cases of epilepsy, with relatively few side effects. Psychosurgery is also done on portions of the brain involved in pain perception in cases of otherwise intractable pain. Today, however, no *DSM-5* diagnoses are routinely treated with psychosurgery.

Brain-Stimulation Therapies

Electrical stimulation of the brain, also known as **electroconvulsive therapy (ECT)**, is still widely used, especially in patients with severe depression who have not responded to drugs or psychotherapy for depression. (You will recall that the therapist said that Derek was not a good candidate for ECT.) The treatment induces a convulsion by applying an electric current (75 to 100 volts) to a patient's temples briefly—from one-tenth to a full second. The convulsion usually runs its course in less than a minute. Patients are prepared for this traumatic intervention by putting them to "sleep" with a short-acting barbiturate, plus a muscle relaxant. This not only renders them unconscious but minimizes any violent physical spasms during the seizure (Abrams, 1992; Malitz & Sackheim, 1984). Within half an hour, the patient awakens but has no memory of the seizure or of the events preparatory to treatment.

Does it work? Crude as it may seem to send an electric current through a person's skull and brain, studies have shown ECT to be a useful tool in treating depression, especially those in whom suicidal tendencies demand an intervention that works far more quickly than medication or psychotherapy (Shorter & Healy, 2007). Typically, the symptoms of depression often abate in a three- or four-day course of treatment, in contrast with the one- to two-week period required for drug therapy.

Although most clinicians regard ECT, properly done, as safe and effective, some critics fear that it also could be abused to silence dissent or punish patients who are uncooperative

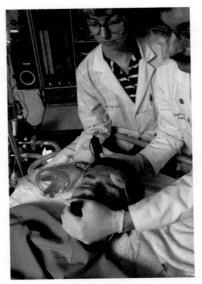

The sedated patient is about to receive electroconvulsive therapy. ECT involves a weak electrical current to a patient's temples, causing a convulsion. Some psychiatrists have found ECT successful in alleviating symptoms of severe depression, but it remains a treatment of last resort for most therapists.

(Butcher et al., 2008; Holmes, 2001). Other worries about ECT stem from the fact that its effects are not well understood. To date, no definitive theory explains why inducing a mild convulsion should alleviate disordered symptoms, although there are some hints that it may stimulate neuron growth in parts of the brain, particularly the hippocampus.

Most worrisome, perhaps, are the memory deficits sometimes caused by electroconvulsive therapy (Breggin, 1979, 1991). Proponents claim, however, that patients generally recover full memory functions within months of the treatment (Calev et al., 1991). In the face of such concerns, the National Institute of Mental Health investigated the use of ECT and, in 1985, gave it a cautious endorsement for treating a narrow range of disorders, especially severe depression. Then, in 1990, the American Psychiatric Association also proclaimed ECT to be a valid treatment option. To minimize even short-term side effects, however, ECT is usually administered "unilaterally"—only to the right temple—to reduce the possibility of speech impairment.

Another promising new therapeutic tool for stimulating the brain with magnetic fields may offer all the benefits of ECT without the risk of memory loss. Still in the experimental stages, **transcranial magnetic stimulation (TMS)** involves directing high-powered magnetic stimulation to specific parts of the brain. Studies indicate that TMS may be useful for treating not only depression but also schizophrenia and bipolar disorder (George, 2003). Because TMS therapy does

electroconvulsive therapy (ECT) A treatment used primarily for depression and involving the application of an electric current to the head, producing a generalized seizure; sometimes called "shock treatment."

transcranial magnetic stimulation (TMS) A treatment that involves magnetic stimulation of specific regions of the brain. Unlike ECT, TMS does not produce a seizure.

not require the induction of a seizure, researchers hope also that it offers a safer alternative to ECT.

Most recently, neurologist Helen Mayberg has reported using *deep brain stimulation,* which requires the surgical implantation of a microelectrode through a small hole in the skull and directly into the brain, where it delivers a continual trickle of electric current. Dr. Mayberg likens the treatment to a "pacemaker" for an area of cortex that seems to range out of control in depression (Gutman, 2006; Price, 2009). Although the treatment has been used on only a few patients, Mayberg reports highly encouraging outcomes (Mayberg et al., 2005). She views it not as an alternative to other therapies but as a promising last resort for severely depressed patients who have not responded to other approaches.

[CONNECTION] In most people, speech is controlled in the brain's left hemisphere.

Hospitalization and the Alternatives

We have seen that mental hospitals were originally conceived as places of refuge—"asylums"—where disturbed people could escape the pressures of normal living. In fact, they often worked very well (Maher & Maher, 1985). But by the 20th century, these hospitals had become overcrowded and, at best, little more than warehouses for the disturbed, with nowhere else to go. Rarely were people with money committed to these institutions; instead, they were given private care, including individual psychotherapy (Doyle, 2002a). 📖

▶ **Read** about The Therapeutic Community at **MyPsychLab**

The drugs that so profoundly altered treatment in mental hospitals did not appear until the 1950s, so prior to that time, institutionalized patients often found themselves controlled by straitjackets, locked rooms, and, sometimes, lobotomies. Meanwhile, in the large public mental hospitals, what passed for psychotherapy was a feeble form of "group therapy" performed on a whole ward—perhaps 50 patients—at a time. Too many patients, too few therapists, and too little time devoted to therapy meant that little, if any, real benefit accrued.

Deinstitutionalization and Community Mental Health
The advent of antipsychotic drugs ushered in huge changes. Thousands of patients who responded to the new drugs were sent home for outpatient treatment. The goal of **deinstitutionalization** was to return as many patients as possible to their communities, where they would (it was hoped) thrive in a familiar and supportive environment. The concept also gained popularity with politicians, who saw large sums of money being poured into mental hospitals (filled,

Deinstitutionalization put mental patients back in the community—but often without adequate resources for continued treatment.

incidentally, with nonvoting patients). Thus, by the 1970s, a consensus formed among politicians and mental health professionals that the major locus of treatment should shift from mental hospitals back to the community. There, both psychological and drug therapies would be dispensed from walk-in clinics, and recovering patients could live with their families, in foster homes, or in group homes. This vision became known as the **community mental health movement.**

Unfortunately, the reality did not match the vision (Doyle, 2002a; Torrey, 1996, 1997). Community mental health clinics—the centerpieces of the community mental health movement—rarely received the full funding they needed. Chronic patients were released from mental hospitals, but they often returned to communities that could offer them few therapeutic resources and to families ill equipped to cope with them (Smith et al., 1993). Then, as patients returned to the community and needed care, they entered psychiatric wards at local general hospitals—rather than mental hospitals. As a result, hospital care has continued to consume a large share of mental health expenditures in the United States (Kiesler, 1993; U.S. Department of Health and Human Services, 2002).

Despite the dark picture we have painted, community treatment has had some successes. After a review of ten studies in which mental patients were randomly assigned to hospital treatment or to various community treatment programs, Kiesler (1982) reported that patients more often improved in the community-based programs. Further, those given community-based treatment were less likely to be hospitalized at a later date. When these programs have adequate resources, they can be highly effective (McGuire, 2000).

Unfortunately, some 60 million Americans in rural areas have no easy access to mental health services. But, thanks to the Internet and the telephone, some of them now can get help through remote "telehealth" sessions (Stambor, 2006; Winerman, 2006c). Using the telehealth approach, psychologists and other professionals can quickly establish a link with their rural clients to answer questions, make referrals, and even provide therapy.

---

deinstitutionalization The policy of removing patients, whenever possible, from mental hospitals.

community mental health movement An effort to deinstitutionalize mental patients and to provide therapy from outpatient clinics. Proponents of community mental health envisioned that recovering patients could live with their families, in foster homes, or in group homes.

The "telehealth" approach to therapy brings mental health services to clients in rural areas, where help might not otherwise be available.

psychology matters

What Sort of Therapy Would You Recommend?

Now that we have looked at both the psychological and biomedical therapies, consider the following situation. A friend tells you about some personal problems he or she is having and requests your help in finding a therapist. Because you are studying psychology, your friend reasons, you might know what kind of treatment would be best. How do you respond?

First, you can lend a friendly ear, using the techniques of active listening, acceptance, and exploration of alternatives, which we discussed earlier in the chapter. In fact, this may be all that your troubled friend needs. But if your friend wants to see a therapist or if the situation looks in any way like one that requires professional assistance, you can use your knowledge of mental disorders and therapies to help your friend decide what sort of therapist might be most appropriate. To take some of the burden from your shoulders, both of you should understand that any competent therapist will always refer the client elsewhere if the required therapy lies outside the therapist's specialty.

A Therapy Checklist

Here, then, are some questions you will want to consider before you recommend a particular type of therapist:

- **Is medical treatment needed?** While you should not try to make a diagnosis, you should encourage your friend to see a medical specialist, such as a psychiatrist or nurse practitioner, if you suspect that the problem involves a major mental disorder such as psychosis, mania, or bipolar disorder. Medical evaluation is also indicated if you suspect narcolepsy, sleep apnea, epilepsy, Alzheimer's disease, or other problems recognized to have a biological basis. If your suspicion is confirmed, the treatment may include a combination of drug therapy and psychotherapy.

- **Is there a specific behavior problem?** For example, does your friend want to eliminate a fear of spiders or a fear of flying? Is the problem a rebellious child? A sexual problem? Is she or he depressed—but not psychotic? If so, behavior therapy or cognitive–behavioral therapy with a counseling or clinical psychologist is probably the best bet. (Most psychiatrists and other medical practitioners are not usually trained in these procedures.) You can call a prospective therapist's office and ask for information on specific areas of training and specialization.

- **Would group therapy be helpful?** Many people find valuable help and support in a group setting, where they can learn not only from the therapist but also from other group members. Groups can be especially effective in dealing with shyness, lack of assertiveness, and addictions, and with complex problems of interpersonal relationships. (As a bonus, group therapy is often less expensive than individual therapy.) Professionals with training in several disciplines, including psychology, psychiatry, and social work, run therapy groups. Again, your best bet is a therapist who has had special training in this method and about whom you have heard good things from former clients.

- **Is the problem one of stress, confusion, or choice?** Most troubled people don't fall neatly into one of the categories that we have discussed in the previous points. More typically, they need help sorting through the chaos of their lives, finding a pattern, and developing a plan to cope. This is the territory of the insight therapies.

Some Cautions

We now know enough about human biology, behavior, and mental processes to avoid certain treatments. Here are some particularly important examples:

- **Drug therapies to avoid.** The minor tranquilizers (antianxiety drugs) are too frequently prescribed for patients leading chronically stressful lives. As we have said, because of their addicting and sedating effects, these drugs should only be taken for short periods—if at all. Similarly, some physicians ignore the dangers of sleep-inducing medications for their patients who suffer from insomnia. While these drugs have legitimate uses, many such prescriptions carry the possibility of drug dependence and of interfering with the person's ability to alter the conditions that may have caused the original problem.

- **Advice and interpretations to avoid.** Although psychodynamic therapy can be helpful, patients should also be cautioned that some such therapists may give ill-advised counsel in problems of anger management. Traditionally, Freudians have believed that individuals who are prone to angry or violent outbursts harbor deep-seated aggression that needs to be vented. But, as we have seen, research shows that trying to empty one's aggressions through aggressive behavior, such as shouting or punching a pillow, may actually increase the likelihood of later aggressive behavior.

With these cautions in mind, then, your friend can contact several therapists to see which has the combination of skills and manner that offer the best fit for her problem and her personality.

CHECK YOUR UNDERSTANDING

✓—Study and Review at MyPsychLab

1. **Application:** Imagine that you are a psychiatrist. Which type of drug would you prescribe for a patient diagnosed with attention-deficit/hyperactivity disorder (ADHD)?

2. **Recall:** Which class of drugs blocks dopamine receptors in the brain? Which type magnifies the effects of serotonin?

3. **Recall:** Name three types of medical therapies for mental disorder, including one that has now been largely abandoned as ineffective and dangerous.

4. **Recall:** The community mental health movement followed a deliberate plan of _____ for mental patients.

5. **Understanding the Core Concept:** _____, _____, and _____ all are medical techniques for treating mental disorders by directly altering the function of the brain.

Answers: 1. a stimulant **2.** Antipsychotic drugs block dopamine receptors in the brain. Antidepressants, particularly the selective serotonin reuptake inhibitors (SSRIs), amplify the effects of serotonin. **3.** Electroconvulsive therapy, drug therapy, and prefrontal lobotomy; the latter is no longer done as a treatment for mental disorders. **4.** deinstitutionalization **5.** Any three of the following would be correct: drug therapies, psychosurgery, ECT, and transcranial magnetic stimulation.

- - - - - - -

12.4 Key Question: How Do the Psychological Therapies and Biomedical Therapies Compare?

Now that we have looked at both the psychological and medical therapies, can we say which approach is best? In this section, we will see that the answer to that question depends on the disorder. But before we look at the treatment choices for several major conditions, we should acknowledge some other influences that cloud the issue of medical versus psychological treatments.

We have seen that psychologists and psychiatrists have long been at odds over the best forms of treatment for mental disorders. In part, the dispute is over territory and money: Who gets to treat people with mental problems—and bill their insurance? The big pharmaceutical companies, with billions of dollars at stake, play a formidable role in this dispute, too. You can glimpse the sort of hardball game Big Pharma plays by noting the advertising for prescription drugs that is directed at the general public. Because of these conflicting interests and pressures, research on medical and psychological therapies has been done largely in parallel, with each side promoting its own approach and ignoring the other's. Unfortunately, this has meant that comparatively little research has focused on the effectiveness of **combination therapies,** involving both medication and psychotherapy used in concert.

That said, let's take a look at how we might weigh the options of medical and psychological treatment in some specific disorders with which you are now familiar. Here's the Core Concept:

CORE CONCEPT 12.4

While a combination of psychological and medical therapies is often better than either one alone for treating mental disorders, most people who have unspecified "problems in living" are best served by psychological treatment alone.

More specifically, what we will find is that a very large number of people with psychological problems do not have a *DSM-5* disorder but need psychological counseling or therapy to help them work through difficult periods in their lives. On the other hand, many of the well-known *DSM-5* disorders, including the depressive disorders and schizophrenia, are best treated by a combination of medical and psychological therapies. Let's begin with the latter.

Depression and Anxiety Disorders: Psychological versus Medical Treatment

Fluoxetine (Prozac) is the planet's most widely prescribed drug. Together with other SSRI medications, it represents a $10 billion, worldwide industry for the treatment of depression (Bower, 2006b). In addition, antidepressants are often used to treat panic disorder and other conditions marked by anxiety. These drugs may be worth every penny if they are effective in alleviating the suffering of these very common disorders. But just how effective

---

combination therapy   A therapeutic approach that involves both psychological and medical techniques—most often a drug therapy with a behavioral or cognitive–behavioral therapy.

Drug companies now do a hard sell on psychotropic drugs through advertisements like this one aimed at the general public. Here, the not-so-subtle message is that unhappy people can be treated with medication.

are they? And how effective are they in comparison with psychological therapies?

CBT versus Drugs Studies show that antidepressant drugs and cognitive–behavioral therapy (CBT)—the psychological treatment for which we have the most evidence of efficacy—are equally effective ways of treating depression and panic disorder, at least in the short run. Significantly, however, CBT holds an edge over drug therapy in the long–term—particularly in depression, where the rate of patient relapse for CTB is about *half* that of antidepressant medications (Baker et al., 2009; DeRubeis et al., 2005; Hollon et al., 2002).

But what happens if depressed patients get antidepressants *and* CBT? The research shows that they may do even better than with either treatment alone (DeAngelis, 2008a; Keller et al., 2000; Thase et al., 1997). Oddly, combination therapy seems *not* to offer an advantage for those with anxiety disorders.

Advances in understanding the brain now suggest why such a combination therapy approach seems to be effective for depression. Neuroscientist Helen Mayberg has shown that CBT and the antidepressants work their wonders by affecting different parts of the brain. Antidepressants apparently target the limbic system—which contains the brain's main emotion pathways. In contrast, CBT affects a part the frontal cortex associated with reasoning. The common factor in both approaches is an "alarm switch" that gets turned off, either by the effect of drugs on the "fast" emotion pathway in the limbic system or by the effect of CBT on the brain's "slow" emotional circuitry in the cortex (Goldapple et al., 2004). Thus, as research from the clinic and the lab come together, many clinicians have come to favor a *combination therapy* approach for depression, using both drugs and CBT. In fact, a combined approach would be a reasonable option for Derek's depression (described at the beginning of the chapter). A recent study also supports a combined drug-and-medicine approach for bipolar patients (Miklowitz et al., 2007).

ECT And what about electroconvulsive therapy (ECT)? Although clinicians commonly assert that ECT is the most effective treatment for psychotic depression (Hollon et al., 2002), only one study, done in Sweden, has compared ECT head-to-head with antidepressants. The principal finding: Suicide attempts were less common among those patients receiving ECT than among those taking antidepressants (Brådvik & Berglund, 2006). As for transcranial magnetic stimulation, it is too early to tell. As of this writing, no studies have reported a one-on-one comparison of TMS with other therapies for depression.

Schizophrenia: Psychological versus Medical Treatment

Ever since the discovery of antipsychotics more than 50 years ago, these drugs have represented the front line of treatment for schizophrenia. Supplemental treatment, in the form of family therapy, social skills training (often in community residential treatment centers), and occupational therapy (through sheltered workshops, such as Goodwill Industries), has brought schizophrenic patients back into contact with their communities. But until recently, conventional psychological treatments were little used. In the past few years, however, advocates of cognitive–behavioral therapy have been trying their hands at treating schizophrenia, with encouraging results, even with patients who have not responded to medication (McGurk et al., 2007; Rector & Beck, 2001).

"The Worried Well" and Other Problems: Not Everyone Needs Drugs

While a combination of psychological therapy and drugs may be best for some disorders, we have seen that drugs are *not* useful for treating specific phobias. Likewise, medication has little value as a therapy for most learning disabilities, psychogenic sexual dysfunctions, most personality disorders, and most developmental disorders (with the exception of ADHD). In addition, we should remember that many people who have psychological problems do not have a diagnosed mental disorder, such as depression, a phobia, or schizophrenia. Rather, they may have financial difficulties, marital problems, stress on the job, out-of-control children—or perhaps they just experience loneliness and feelings of inadequacy: These are the people that clinicians sometimes call "the worried well."

That's not to say that those whose problems don't qualify as an "official" disorder are not suffering. They struggle with what we might term generic "problems in living." The difficulty is that people with such issues too often persuade a physician to prescribe antidepressants or antianxiety medications. What they really need is a referral to a mental health professional who could help them sort through their problems and choices.

Early Intervention and Prevention Programs: A Modest Proposal
A recent federal report suggests that the United States could save as much as $247 billion a year by instituting tried-and-true programs that would nip mental health problems of children and adolescents in the bud (BCYF, 2009; O'Connell et al., 2010). "The effects of prevention are now quite well documented," says Irwin Sandler, director of the Prevention Research Center at Arizona State University (Clay, 2009, p. 42).

The report recommends identifying young people who are at risk for emotional and behavior disorders and getting early help for them. Such preventive programs include stress management sessions for youth at risk for depression, cognitive–behavioral therapy for children exhibiting excessive anxiety, and parenting skills classes and counseling services for families dealing with adversities, such as divorce or poverty. At present, such programs exist on only a small scale. What we need now is research on moving such interventions from the lab into the field, notes Sandler.

But prevention is not just for kids. For adults, it may mean practicing the stress-reduction and wellness techniques that we will discuss in the next chapter. Here, we will take special note of the new research showing the value of exercise. Everyone knows, of course, that exercise is a powerful tool in conquering obesity. Yet, clearly, the connection between exercise and mental health hasn't registered in the public mind. Nor is it widely understood among mental health professionals. Still, for more than 20 years, evidence has been accumulating that regular exercise works just as well as medication in combating depression, anxiety, and many of the problems-in-living we discussed earlier (Blumenthal et al., 2007; Novotney, 2008; Ströhle, 2009). A few studies even suggest that exercise may help sharpen the mind and fend off dementia (Azar, 2010). Clinical training programs are just starting to take notice of this valuable old tool with a newly discovered use.

psychology matters

Using Psychology to Learn Psychology

Consider the ways in which psychotherapy is like your educational experiences in college:

- Most therapists, like most professors, are professionals with special training in what they do.

- Most clients are like students in that they are seeking professional help to change their lives in some way.

- Much of what happens in therapy and in the classroom involves learning: new ideas, new behaviors, new insights, and new connections.

Learning as Therapy

It may help you learn psychology (and other subjects as well) to think of your college education in therapeutic terms. As we have seen, therapy seems to work best when therapist and client have a good working relationship and when the client believes in the value of the experience—and the same is almost certainly true for the student–professor relationship. You can take the initiative in establishing a personal-but-professional relationship with your psychology professor by doing the following two things: (a) asking questions or otherwise participating in class (at appropriate times and without dominating, of course) and (b) seeking your instructor's help on points you don't understand or on course-related topics you would like to pursue in more detail (doing so during regular office hours). The result will be learning more about psychology because you will be taking a more active part in the learning process. Incidentally, an active approach to the course will also help you stand out from the crowd in the professor's mind, which could be helpful if you later need a faculty recommendation for a scholarship or admission to an advanced program.

Now consider a parallel between group therapy and education. In group therapy, patients learn from each other as well as from the therapist. Much the same can occur in your psychology course if you consider other students as learning resources. As we noted earlier in this book, the most successful students often spend part of their study time sharing information in groups.

Change Behavior, Not Just Thinking

One other tip for learning psychology we borrow from cognitive–behavioral therapy: the importance of changing behavior as well as thinking. It is easy to "intellectualize" a fact or an idea passively when you read about it or hear about it in class. But you are likely to find that the idea makes little impact on you ("I know I *read* about it, but I can't *remember* it!") if you don't use it. The remedy is to do something with your new knowledge: Tell someone about it, come up with illustrations from your own experience, or try acting in a different way. For example, after reading about active listening in this chapter, try it the next time you talk to a friend. Educators sometimes speak of this as "active learning."

And, we suggest, it's one of those psychological therapies that works best without drugs!

CRITICAL THINKING APPLIED

Evidence-Based Practice

The field of therapy for mental disorders is awash in controversy. Psychologists and psychiatrists dispute the value of drugs versus psychological therapies. Arguments rage over the advantages and disadvantages of electroconvulsive therapy for treating depression. Debates still echo the issues Rosenhan raised more than three decades ago about the effectiveness of mental hospitals and the reliability of psychiatric diagnoses. But there is no dispute more acrimonious than the one over *evidence-based practice*, a dispute that is particularly bitter among clinical psychologists (Bower, 2005a).

What Is the Issue?

A decade ago, the American Psychological Association established a special task force charged with evaluating the effectiveness of various psychological therapies (Chambless et al., 1996). The thrust of their findings is that literally dozens of specific disorders can be treated successfully by therapies that have been validated in well-designed experiments (Barlow, 1996). Here are a few examples of therapies pronounced effective by the APA task force:

- Behavior therapy for specific phobias, enuresis (bed wetting), autism, and alcoholism
- Cognitive–behavioral therapy for chronic pain, anorexia, bulimia, agoraphobia, and depression
- Insight therapy for couples' relationship problems

More recently, a report by the Association for Psychological Science focused specifically on evidence-based treatments for depression (Hollon et al., 2002). That document asserts that several varieties of psychotherapy can be effective. These include cognitive–behavioral and family therapy. (The APS report also acknowledged that there is a legitimate role for both drug and electroconvulsive therapies in the treatment of depression.) As we have seen, some studies now suggest that, for depression, a combination of cognitive–behavioral therapy and drug therapy can have a greater effect than either treatment alone (Keller et al., 2000).

So, what's all the fuss about? At issue is whether counselors and therapists should be *limited* to the use of specific therapy methods known as **empirically supported treatments** (EST), that is, to treatments that have been validated by research evidence showing that they actually work (Kazdin, 2008; Westen et al., 2005). So how could anyone possibly object to that, you might ask?

Surprisingly, psychologists line up on both sides of this issue (Johnson, 2006). Those in opposition say that the devil is in the details: They say that they are not anti-science, but they believe "empirically supported treatments" is a fuzzy concept (Westen & Bradley, 2005). They also worry about an overly strict interpretation that might inhibit a practitioner's freedom to meet the needs of an individual client. Let's take a critical look at these details.

What Critical Thinking Questions Should We Ask?

No one doubts that the people on both sides of the evidence-based practice issue are decent and honorable and that among them are genuine experts on therapy. So we won't question their credibility. But it might be a good idea to ask: What biases does each side have that might make them weigh the options differently?

---

empirically supported treatment (EST) Treatment regimen that has been demonstrated to be effective through research. Also called empirically supported therapies.

The Evidence-Based Practice Movement Those pushing the idea of evidence-based practice point to a long history of misguided and even harmful therapies—from beatings to lobotomies—to which people with mental problems have been subjected. Even in modern times, some practitioners continue to advocate techniques that can potentially harm their clients (Lilienfeld, 2007). These include "scared straight" interventions for juvenile offenders, facilitated communication for autism, recovered-memory therapies, induction of "alter" personalities in cases diagnosed as dissociative identity disorder, DARE (antidrug education) programs in the schools, boot-camp programs for conduct disorder in prisoner populations, sexual reorientation for homosexuality, and catharsis ("get-it-out-of-your-system") treatment for anger disorders. An even longer list (based on a survey of clinical psychologists), ranging from the merely ineffective to the crackpot, would include: angel therapy, past lives therapy, treatments for PTSD caused by alien abduction, aromatherapy, therapeutic touch, neuro-linguistic programming, primal scream therapy, and handwriting analysis (Norcross et al., 2006).

In 2009, the Association for Psychological science issued a major report on the current status of clinical psychology (Baker et al., 2009; West, 2009). In that report, the APS blasted clinicians for their failure to use treatments grounded in science, noting that an "alarming number" of clinicians are unaware of empirically validated treatments. The report states:

> Research has shown that numerous psychological interventions are efficacious, effective, and cost-effective. However, these interventions are used infrequently with patients who would benefit from them . . . (p. 67)

An independent report by clinical researchers R. Kathryn McHugh and David Barlow (2010) concurs, emphasizing the difficulty of moving new treatment methods out of the laboratory and into clinical practice.

Those Favoring Caution While acknowledging that we have made great strides in developing highly effective treatments for a number of disorders, those urging caution point out that we are light-years from having the tools to treat all mental disorders—even with the use of drugs. Consequently, they fear that insurance companies and HMOs will be unwilling to pay for treatments not on the official list or for any deviations from "approved" treatments, no matter what the needs of the individual patient (Cynkar, 2007b). They also worry that the managed-care companies will force therapists into a one-size-fits-all approach that would ignore both the clinician's judgment and the client's complex needs (Shedler, 2006). Because therapy is such a time-consuming process, they also fear that nonmedical therapists will be squeezed out of the picture by drug prescribers who may take only a few minutes with each patient.

Those with reservations about evidence-based practice have several other, more subtle, concerns (Westen &

Bradley, 2005). For example, they point out that therapy is much more than the application of specific *techniques:* Researchers find that a common element in successful therapy is a caring, hopeful relationship and a new way of looking at oneself and the world (Wampold et al., 2007). This conclusion has been supported by studies that find the effectiveness of therapy to depend less on the *type of therapy* used and more on the *quality of the relationship* (also called the *therapeutic alliance*) between the therapist and client (Wampold & Brown, 2005). Therapy also involves a host of *individual client factors,* such as motivation, intelligence, and the nature of the problem itself. We can represent these three aspects of therapy graphically, as in FIGURE 12•6. For some problems (such as a relationship issue or a vocational choice problem—the "problems in living" that we discussed earlier), no specific ESTs exist. Moreover, the specific type of therapy used in such cases may be less important than a supportive therapeutic relationship (DeAngelis, 2005; Martin et al., 2000).

Finally, the critics of evidence-based practice also point out that everyday clinical practice is usually messier than the controlled conditions of research on therapy. For one thing, most clinical patients/clients present themselves with multiple problems, such as an anxiety disorder *and* a personality disorder. Yet, most ESTs have been validated on "pure" samples of people having only one specific diagnosis (DeAngelis, 2010; Kazdin, 2008). Rarely do researchers target the largest population in most clinical practices: individuals with multiple "problems in living," such as marital difficulties *and* financial woes *and* child-rearing issues *and* low self-esteem. Moreover, most research aimed at validating therapeutic techniques is severely restricted to just a few sessions—usually no more than a dozen—after which most patients still have some residual problems.

To end this discussion on a more encouraging note: A recent study of 200 practitioners found that they all tended to modify their approach to treatment to fit the needs of their clients as the situation unfolds during counseling or psychotherapy (Holloway, 2003b). That is, despite our emphasis in this chapter on conflicting methods for the treatment of psychological disorders, most practitioners are quite willing to adapt their methods to the individual client rather than holding rigidly to a particular theoretical orientation. And that is good news, indeed, coming from a field that has traditionally had strongly divided allegiances. It appears that the emphasis on science-based practice is finally breaking down the old therapeutic boundaries.

What Conclusions Can We Draw?

Both sides make good points (see TABLE 12•3). On the one hand, practitioners should favor empirically validated treatments when they are clearly appropriate and effective. And they certainly should eschew treatments that are ineffective or harmful. But who is going to make that determination: the individual practitioners, the insurance companies, legislators, or professional organizations? Your

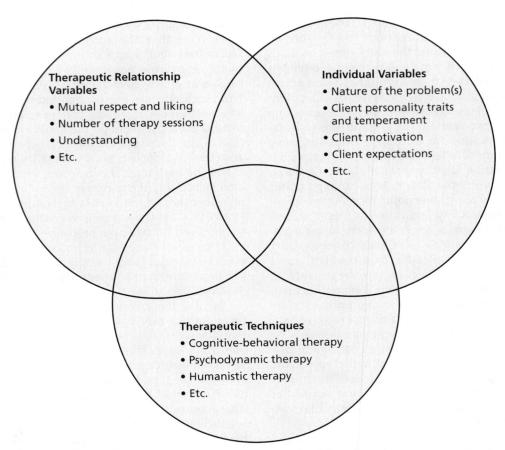

Therapeutic Relationship Variables
- Mutual respect and liking
- Number of therapy sessions
- Understanding
- Etc.

Individual Variables
- Nature of the problem(s)
- Client personality traits and temperament
- Client motivation
- Client expectations
- Etc.

Therapeutic Techniques
- Cognitive-behavioral therapy
- Psychodynamic therapy
- Humanistic therapy
- Etc.

[**FIGURE 13•6**] **Three Aspects of Therapy** Therapy is more than a set of techniques. It also involves a number of individual variables (including the nature of the problem) and the relationship between the client and therapist—the *therapeutic alliance*. All must come together for therapy to be successful.

authors think that the professional psychology associations, such as the APA, must take stands against putting the therapist into a straitjacket by limiting him or her to a cast-in-stone list of treatments and disorders for which those treatments may be applied.

In fact, the American Psychological Association has a proposed policy under consideration (APA Presidential Task Force, 2006). The policy would define *evidence-based practice in psychology* as "the integration of the best available research with clinical expertise in the context of patient characteristics, culture, and preferences." Who wouldn't agree with that? Many people, it turns out. In particular, the evidence-based practice advocates are concerned that "clinical expertise" could trump "research," with the result that clinicians could ignore the science and do as they please

(Stuart & Lilienfeld, 2007). It is a knotty issue that doesn't lend itself to easy answers.

Is there a solution in sight? A partial solution may lie in a proposal made by David Barlow (2004) who suggested that psychologists make a distinction between *psychological treatments* and what he calls "generic psychotherapy." The empirically validated therapies for specific *DSM-5* disorders would fall under the heading of *psychological treatments*, while reserving the term *psychotherapy* for work with the huge "Other Conditions" *DSM-5* category, including educational, occupational, and marital problems, sexual abuse, and antisocial personality disorder, which together make up a large proportion of the caseloads of many counselors and clinicians. Barlow's proposal would, at least, shrink the disputed territory.

[TABLE 12•3] Summary of the Evidence-Based Practice (EBP) Debate

Arguments Favoring EBP	Arguments Opposing EBP
• Some treatments are clearly harmful, and practitioners should not be allowed to use them. • Specific empirically supported therapies (ESTs) have been demonstrated to be effective in dealing with certain disorders. • Psychology is a science, and psychological practitioners should follow what the research shows to be best. • Giving clinical judgment equal weight with science would lead to anarchy, in which clinicians could ignore the evidence and do what they please.	• Empirically supported therapies (ESTs) is a poorly defined, even meaningless, concept. • EBP is a "one-size-fits-all" approach that would limit the flexibility of clinicians to deal with individual clients' problems, particularly those who have multiple problems or who do not fit a *DSM-5* category. • Insurance companies would not pay for therapy that was not on an approved list of empirically validated treatments. • EBP would prevent practitioners from trying new ideas and developing even more effective therapies. • Scientists have not yet validated treatments for many disorders, so under an EBP approach, many people might have to go without treatment. • Evidence suggests that certain common factors (e.g., the therapeutic alliance) are just as important as the specific type of treatment.

CHAPTER SUMMARY

PROBLEM: What is the best treatment for Derek's depression: psychological therapy, drug therapy, or both? More broadly, the problem is this: How do we decide among the available therapies for any of the mental disorders?

- The most basic choice is between one of the psychological therapies and a biological therapy—or a combination.
- Psychologists or other nonmedical practitioners opt for a psychological therapy when they believe the problem is learned or involves faulty cognitions, behaviors, or relationships.
- The psychological therapies can be further divided into the insight therapies and behavior therapies—or combined approaches known as cognitive-behavioral therapy and social learning. The specific therapy type depends primarily on the therapist's training and orientation.
- Biological therapies are delivered by psychiatrists and nurse practitioners when they believe the problem can best be treated by altering brain function through drugs or other biological interventions.

12.1 What Is Therapy?

CORE CONCEPT 12.1

Therapy for psychological disorders takes a variety of forms, but all involve a *therapeutic relationship* focused on improving a person's mental, behavioral, or social functioning.

People seek **therapy** for a variety of problems, including *DSM-5* disorders and problems of everyday living. Treatment comes in many forms, both psychological and biomedical, but most involve diagnosing the problem, finding the source of the problem, making a prognosis, and carrying out treatment. In earlier times, treatments for those with mental problems were usually harsh and dehumanizing, often based on the assumption of demonic possession. Only recently have people with emotional problems been treated as individuals with "illnesses," which has led to more humane treatment.

Currently in the United States, there are two main approaches to therapy: the **psychological therapy** and the **biomedical therapy** approaches. Other cultures often have different ways of understanding and treating mental disorders, often making use of the family and community. In the United States, there is a trend toward increasing use of **paraprofessionals** as mental health care providers, and the literature generally supports their effectiveness.

12.2 How Do Psychologists Treat Psychological Disorders?

CORE CONCEPT 12.2

Psychologists employ two main forms of treatment, the insight therapies (focused on developing an understanding of the problem) and the behavior therapies (focused on changing behavior through conditioning).

Psychoanalysis, the first of the *insight therapies,* grew out of Sigmund Freud's theory of personality. Using such techniques as *free association* and dream interpretation, its goal is to bring repressed material out of the unconscious into consciousness, where it can be interpreted and neutralized, particularly in the **analysis of transference.** Neo-Freudian **psychodynamic therapies** typically emphasize the patient's current social situation, interpersonal relationships, and self-concept.

Among other insight therapies, **humanistic therapy** focuses on individuals becoming more fully self-actualized. In one form, **client-centered therapy**, practitioners strive to be *nondirective* in helping their clients establish a positive self-image.

Another form of insight therapy, **cognitive therapy**, concentrates on changing negative or irrational thought patterns about oneself and one's social relationships. The client must learn more constructive thought patterns and learn to apply the new technique to other situations. This has been particularly effective for depression.

Group therapy can take many approaches. **Self-help support groups,** such as AA, serve millions, even though they are not usually run by professional therapists. *Family therapy* and *couples therapy* usually concentrate on situational difficulties and interpersonal dynamics as a total system in need of improvement rather than on internal motives.

The **behavior therapies** apply the principles of learning—especially operant and classical conditioning—to problem behaviors. Among the classical conditioning techniques, **systematic desensitization** and **exposure therapy** are commonly employed to treat fears. **Aversion therapy** may also be used for eliminating unwanted responses. Operant techniques include **contingency management,** which especially involves positive reinforcement and extinction strategies. And, on a larger scale, behavior therapy may be used to treat or manage groups in the form of a **token economy. Participant modeling,** based on research in observational learning, may make use of both classical and operant principles, involving the use of models and social skills training to help individuals practice and gain confidence about their abilities.

In recent years, a synthesis of cognitive and behavioral therapies has emerged, combining the techniques of insight therapy with methods based on behavioral learning theory. **Rational–emotive behavior therapy** helps clients recognize that their irrational beliefs about themselves interfere with life and helps them learn how to change those thought patterns. **Positive psychotherapy (PPT)** is a similar approach coming out of the positive psychology movement. Brain scans suggest that **cognitive–behavioral therapy** produces physical changes in brain functioning.

The effectiveness of therapy was challenged in the 1950s by Eysenck. Since that time, however, research has shown that psychotherapy can be effective for a variety of psychological problems. Often, it is more effective than drug therapy. As the research on mental disorders becomes more refined, we are learning to match specific psychotherapies to specific disorders.

Most people do not get psychological help from professionals. Rather, they get help from teachers, friends, clergy, and others in their community who seem sympathetic. Friends can often help through **active listening,** acceptance, and exploration of alternatives, but serious problems require professional assistance.

12.3   How Is the Biomedical Approach Used to Treat Psychological Disorders?

CORE CONCEPT 12.3

Biomedical therapies seek to treat psychological disorders by changing the brain's chemistry with drugs, its circuitry with surgery, or its patterns of activity with pulses of electricity or powerful magnetic fields.

Biomedical therapies concentrate on changing the physiological aspects of mental illness. Drug therapy includes **antipsychotic, antidepressant,** *mood stabilizing,* **antianxiety,** and **stimulant drugs.** Most affect the function of neurotransmitters. Such drugs have caused a revolution in the medical treatment of mental disorders such as schizophrenia, depression, bipolar disorder, anxiety disorders, and ADHD. Critics, however, warn of their abuse, particularly in treating the ordinary stress of daily living.

Psychosurgery is rarely done anymore because of its radical, irreversible side effects. **Electroconvulsive therapy,** however, is still widely used—primarily with depressed patients—although it, too, remains controversial. A new and potentially less-harmful alternative involves **transcranial magnetic stimulation** of specific brain areas. Meanwhile, hospitalization has been a mainstay of medical treatment, although the trend is away from mental hospitals to community-based treatment. The policy of **deinstitutionalization** was based on the best intentions, but many mental patients have been turned back into their communities with few resources and little treatment. When the resources are available, however, community treatment is often successful.

If someone asks your advice on finding a therapist, you can refer him or her to any competent mental health professional. While you should avoid trying to make a diagnosis or attempting therapy for mental disorders, you may use your knowledge of psychology to steer the person toward a medical specialist, a behavior therapist, group therapy, or some other psychological treatment that you believe might be appropriate. There are, however, some specific therapies and therapeutic techniques to avoid.

12.4   How Do the Psychological Therapies and Biomedical Therapies Compare?

CORE CONCEPT 12.4

While a combination of psychological and medical therapies is often better than either one alone for treating some (but not all) mental disorders, most people who have unspecified "problems in living" are best served by psychological treatment alone.

Both medical and biological therapies can point to their successes, but until recently, few studies have compared medical and psychological therapies directly. New studies show that for depression, a **combination therapy,** consisting of CBT and medication, is often best. Comparative data for ECT and the new transcranial magnetic stimulation are sparse. As for the anxiety disorders, some studies have shown a combination of drugs and CBT to be effective. A clear exception involves the specific phobias, for which behavioral therapy is superior to drug therapy—which may actually aggravate the problem. For schizophrenia, medications are the front line of treatment, although they do not cure the disorder. Until recently, conventional psychotherapies were not often used with schizophrenia, but new research suggests that combination therapy may be effective.

Medication is not useful for treating many psychological problems, such as learning disabilities, many sexual dysfunctions, most personality disorders, and most developmental disorders. In addition, most people who have psychological problems do not have a *DSM-5* disorder but rather suffer from "problems in living."

Education and psychotherapy have many points in common. In particular, both involve learning and the ultimate goal of changes in behavior. The authors suggest that both education and psychotherapy are more likely to be successful when the client takes an active role.

KEY TERMS

active listener *p. 369*

analysis of transference *p. 357*

antianxiety drugs *p. 372*

antidepressants *p. 371*

antipsychotics *p. 370*

aversion therapy *p. 362*

behavior modification *p. 361*

behavior therapy *p. 361*

biomedical therapy *p. 354*

client-centered therapy *p. 358*

cognitive therapy *p. 359*

cognitive–behavioral therapy *p. 365*

combination therapy *p. 377*

community mental health movement *p. 375*

contingency management *p. 363*

deinstitutionalization *p. 375*

electroconvulsive therapy (ECT) *p. 374*

empirically supported treatment (EST) *p. 380*

exposure therapy *p. 362*

group therapy *p. 360*

humanistic therapy *p. 358*

insight therapy *p. 355*

neo-Freudian psychodynamic therapy *p. 357*

paraprofessional *p. 355*

participant modeling *p. 364*

positive psychotherapy (PPT) *p. 367*

psychoanalysis *p. 356*

psychological therapy *p. 354*

psychosurgery *p. 373*

rational–emotive behavior therapy (REBT) *p. 366*

reflection of feeling *p. 358*

self-help support groups *p. 360*

stimulants *p. 372*

systematic desensitization *p. 362*

tardive dyskinesia *p. 371*

therapeutic alliance *p. 352*

therapy *p. 351*

token economy *p. 363*

transcranial magnetic stimulation (TMS) *p. 374*

CRITICAL THINKING APPLIED

Evidence-Based Practice

Psychological therapists are divided on the question of evidence based practice (EBP) and empirically supported treatments (ESTs). Opponents say that ESTs are not clearly defined, suppress innovative new treatments, offer no help in treating clients with multiple disorders, and deemphasize the importance of the therapeutic alliance. Proponents, however, counter that some treatments are clearly harmful and should be prohibited. They acknowledge that ESTs have not been found for all disorders. However, therapists as good scientists should be willing to practice those treatments for which science has found support.

DISCOVERING PSYCHOLOGY *VIEWING GUIDE*

Watch the following video by logging into MyPsychLab (www. mypsychlab.com). After you have watched the video, answer the questions that follow.

PROGRAM 22: **PSYCHOTHERAPY**

Program Review

1. What are the two main approaches to therapies for mental disorders?

    a. the Freudian and the behavioral

    b. the client-centered and the patient-centered

    c. the biomedical and the psychological

    d. the chemical and the psychosomatic

2. The prefrontal lobotomy is a form of psychosurgery. Although no longer widely used, it was at one time used in cases in which a patient

    a. was an agitated schizophrenic.

    b. had committed a violent crime.

    c. showed little emotional response.

    d. had a disease of the thalamus.

3. Leti had electroconvulsive shock therapy a number of years ago. She is now suffering a side effect of that therapy. What is she most likely to be suffering from?

    a. tardive dyskinesia

    b. the loss of her ability to plan ahead

    c. depression

    d. memory loss

4. Vinnie suffers from "manic-depressive" (bipolar) disorder, but his mood swings are kept under control because he takes the drug

   a. chlorpromazine.

   b. lithium.

   c. Valium.

   d. tetracycline.

5. The Silverman family is receiving genetic counseling because a particular kind of mental retardation runs in their family. What is the purpose of such counseling?

   a. to explain the probability of passing on defective genes

   b. to help eliminate the attitudes of biological biasing

   c. to repair specific chromosomes

   d. to prescribe drugs that will keep problems from developing

6. In psychodynamic theory, what is the source of mental disorders?

   a. biochemical imbalances in the brain

   b. unresolved conflicts in childhood experiences

   c. the learning and reinforcement of nonproductive behaviors

   d. unreasonable attitudes, false beliefs, and unrealistic expectations

7. Imagine you are observing a therapy session in which a patient is lying on a couch, talking. The therapist is listening and asking occasional questions. What is most likely to be the therapist's goal?

   a. to determine which drug the patient should be given

   b. to change the symptoms that cause distress

   c. to explain how to change false ideas

   d. to help the patient develop insight

8. Rinaldo is a patient in psychotherapy. The therapist asks him to free associate. What would Rinaldo do?

   a. describe a dream

   b. release his feelings

   c. talk about anything that comes to mind

   d. understand the origin of his present guilt feelings

9. According to Hans Strupp, in what major way have psychodynamic therapies changed?

   a. Less emphasis is now placed on the ego.

   b. Patients no longer need to develop a relationship with the therapist.

   c. Shorter courses of treatment can be used.

   d. The concept of aggression has become more important.

10. In the program, a therapist helped a girl learn to control her epileptic seizures. What use did the therapist make of the pen?

    a. to record data

    b. to signal the onset of an attack

    c. to reduce the girl's fear

    d. to reinforce the correct reaction

11. When Albert Ellis discusses with the young woman her fear of hurting others, what point is he making?

    a. It is the belief system that creates the "hurt."

    b. Every normal person strives to achieve fulfillment.

    c. Developing a fear-reduction strategy will reduce the problem.

    d. It is the use of self-fulfilling prophecies that cause others to be hurt.

12. What point does Enrico Jones make about investigating the effectiveness of different therapies in treating depression?

    a. All therapies are equally effective.

    b. It is impossible to assess how effective any one therapy is.

    c. The job is complicated by the different types of depression.

    d. The most important variable is individual versus group therapy.

13. What is the most powerful antidepressant available for patients who cannot tolerate drugs?

    a. genetic counseling

    b. electroconvulsive therapy

    c. psychoanalysis

    d. family therapy

14. All of the following appear to be true about the relation between depression and genetics, *except* that

    a. depression has been linked to a defect in chromosome #11.

    b. depression appears to cause genetic mutation.

    c. most people who show the genetic marker for depression do not exhibit depressive symptoms.

    d. genetic counseling allows families to plan and make choices based on their risk of mental illness.

15. For which class of mental illness would Chlorpromazine be prescribed?

    a. mood disorder

    b. psychosis

    c. personality disorder

    d. anxiety disorder

16. Which approach to psychotherapy emphasizes developing the ego?

    a. behavioral

    b. desensitization

    c. humanistic

    d. psychodynamic

17. In behavior modification therapies, the goal is to

    a. understand unconscious motivations.

    b. learn to love oneself unconditionally.

    c. change the symptoms of mental illness through reinforcement.

    d. modify the interpretations that one gives to life's events.

18. Which style of therapy has as its primary goal to make the client feel as fulfilled as possible?

    a. humanistic

    b. cognitive-behavioral

    c. Freudian

    d. social learning

19. Which psychologist introduced rational–emotive therapy?

    a. Carl Rogers

    b. Hans Strupp

    c. Albert Ellis

    d. Rollo May

20. Which type of client would be ideal for modern psychoanalytic therapy?

    a. someone who is smart, wealthy, and highly verbal

    b. someone who is reserved and violent

    c. someone who has a good sense of humor but takes herself seriously

    d. someone who grew up under stressful and economically deprived conditions

NOTES

1. No sharp distinction exists between counseling and psychotherapy, although in practice *counseling* usually refers to a shorter process, more likely to be focused on a specific problem, while *psychotherapy* generally involves a longer-term and wider-ranging exploration of issues.

2. In an ironic footnote to the history of psychosurgery, Moñiz was shot by one of this disgruntled patients, who apparently had not become as pacified as Moniz had expected. This fact, however, did not prevent Moñiz from receiving the Nobel Prize for Medicine in 1949.

13

From Stress to Health and Well-Being

Taken from *Psychology: Core Concepts*, Seventh Edition, by Philip G. Zimbardo, Robert L. Johnson, and Vivian McCann.

13.1 What Causes Distress?

Traumatic Stressors • Chronic Stressors

CORE CONCEPTS Traumatic events, chronic lifestyle conditions, major life changes, and even minor hassles can all cause a stress response.

PSYCHOLOGY MATTERS
Student Stress

College students face some unique stressors in addition to typical developmental stressors.

13.2 How Does Stress Affect Us Physically?

Physiological Responses to Stress • Stress and the Immune System

CORE CONCEPTS The physical stress response begins with arousal, which stimulates a series of physiological responses that in the short term are adaptive but that can turn harmful if prolonged.

PSYCHOLOGY MATTERS
Cognitive Appraisal of Ambiguous Threats

Threats to our well being are not always clear and obvious; thus how we identify and appraise them becomes vital for coping with them effectively.

13.3 Who Is Most Vulnerable to Stress?

Type A Personality and Hostility • Locus of Control • Hardiness • Optimism • Resilience

CORE CONCEPTS Personality characteristics affect our individual responses to stressful situations and, consequently, the degree to which we are distressed when exposed to stressors.

PSYCHOLOGY MATTERS
Using Psychology to Learn Psychology

Anyone—even people who don't think of themselves as "good writers"—can use writing as a valuable tool in the "coping strategies" toolbox.

13.4 How Can We Transform Negative Stress Into Positive Life Strategies?

Psychological Coping Strategies

Psychological Coping Strategies • Positive Lifestyle Choices: A "Two-for-One" Benefit to Your Health • Putting It All Together: Developing Happiness and Subjective Well-Being

CORE CONCEPTS Effective coping strategies reduce the negative impact of stress on our health, while positive lifestyle choices can enhance our mental and physical health as well as our overall well-being.

PSYCHOLOGY MATTERS
Behavioral Medicine and Health Psychology

These exciting new fields focus on how psychological and social factors influence health, and also on how these same factors can be applied to successful prevention of illness.

Chapter Problem

Were the reactions and experiences of the 9/11 firefighters and others at the World Trade Center attacks typical of people in other stressful situations? And what factors explain individual differences in our physical and psychological responses to stress?

Critical Thinking Applied

Is *Change* Really Hazardous to Your Health?

On September 11, 2001, at 8:46 A.M., retired firefighter Dennis Smith sat outside a New York clinic, waiting for his annual physical, when a nurse rushed in and announced that a plane had just crashed into the North tower of the World Trade Center in lower Manhattan (Smith, 2003b). The engine and ladder companies of New York's fire department (FDNY) were already responding to the alarms—trucks racing to the scene and firefighters running into the same buildings that hordes of people desperately sought to escape. Smith asked himself what conditions his coworkers were facing: the heat of the fire, the best access to the buildings, the stairwells' integrity. How many were already trapped inside and facing death?

One firefighter later described the chaos: "It looked like a movie scene, where the monster was coming . . . [W]e got showered with debris. . . . Things were hitting—bing, bang, boom—over your head" (Smith, 2003b, pp. 70–71). He had climbed high into the North Tower when the South Tower was hit, and "suddenly, there was this loud, loud noise overhead." He recalled huddling inside a stairwell, inventorying his resources: "I was thinking of my situation—what should I do, what can I do? What do I have that is positive? What tools do I have? . . . The main thing I had was my helmet. I remember thinking how important it was to have had that helmet" (p. 75).

But the critical need for the helmet was forgotten in one ironic moment by Smith's fellow firefighter, Father Mychael Judge. The FDNY chaplain was among the first to arrive and, after hearing that firefighters were trapped inside, rushed into the smoke. While performing last rites, he removed his helmet out of respectful habit—just as a shower of debris fell, killing him instantly (Downey, 2004).

In the weeks and months after the terrorist attacks, firefighters continued to search for bodies. They buried, memorialized, and mourned their brothers and sisters. Few of the 343 missing were ever recovered. Those who had made it—while others died just a few feet away—endured survivor's guilt, ambivalent and uncertain why they deserved to live, asking themselves, "Why me?" Some developed symptoms of posttraumatic stress disorder (PTSD), reliving the terrifying moments of the disaster again and again. And the aftereffects of that day weren't limited to those individuals personally involved: Millions of people around the world remained glued to their televisions for days, repeatedly watching the towers as they fell and hearing firsthand accounts from survivors.

The surviving firefighters continued to grieve. Many of them rejected false reverence or gloom in remembering their friends, preferring instead to laugh and joke about their fallen comrades' quirks and screw-ups. Manhattan's Engine 40/Ladder 35 lost 12 firefighters, more than any other firehouse and, like everyone else, wondered what really happened to the missing victims. Then, five months after 9/11, the members of 40/35 learned of a news tape that appeared to show their 12 lost partners entering the tower minutes before it collapsed on them. The video had been shot at a distance, but the moving figures gradually became recognizable. Staring intently at the screen, the surviving firefighters gazed once more on friends who had not returned. They played the video over and over again (Halberstam, 2002).

Firefighters are different from most other public servants because they spend much of their time in a shared communal house, their firehouse. Because fires and other emergencies are relatively rare, they spend lots of down time just hanging out with each other, playing cards and other games, as well as reading and watching TV. In most houses, a family sense evolves, with older guys becoming like dads and uncles or big brothers to the new guys. With this in mind, you can better appreciate the stressful impact on any of them from the sudden deaths of so many of their everyday families. In addition, each felt obligated to attend as many memorial services as possible, not only for their fallen house members but for all those they knew in recruit training or from other houses where they had served or had extended-family relatives working. For some, attending heart-wrenching church services was an enduring tribulation lasting more than a year—an unending source of secondary distress.

PROBLEM: Were the reactions and experiences of the 9/11 firefighters and others at the World Trade Center attacks typical of people in other stressful situations? And what factors explain individual differences in our physical and psychological responses to stress?

Of course, running into a falling building is not a typical human response; rather, it is a learned response of trained

How do differences in our environments and cultures create stress and affect our responses to stress?

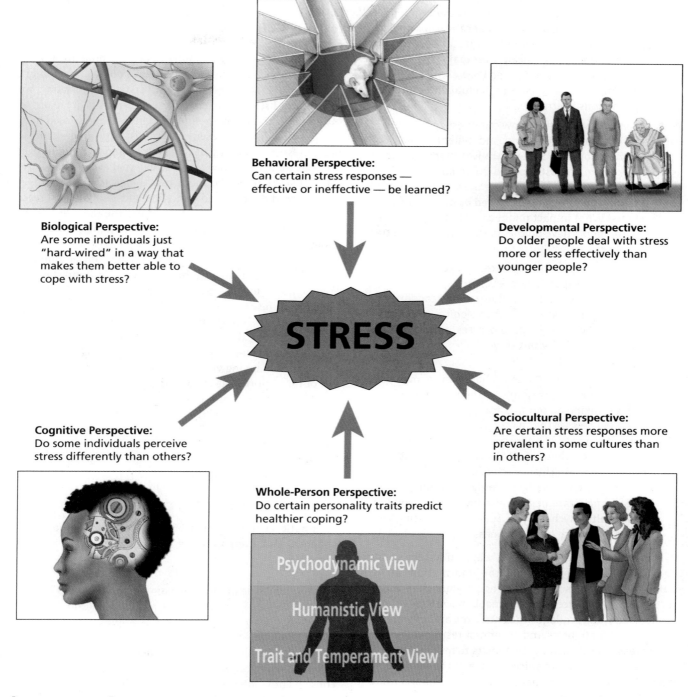

Behavioral Perspective:
Can certain stress responses —
effective or ineffective — be learned?

Biological Perspective:
Are some individuals just
"hard-wired" in a way that
makes them better able to
cope with stress?

Developmental Perspective:
Do older people deal with stress
more or less effectively than
younger people?

STRESS

Cognitive Perspective:
Do some individuals perceive
stress differently than others?

Sociocultural Perspective:
Are certain stress responses more
prevalent in some cultures than
in others?

Whole-Person Perspective:
Do certain personality traits predict
healthier coping?

Psychodynamic View

Humanistic View

Trait and Temperament View

[**FIGURE 13•1**] **The Multiple Perspectives Applied to Stress** This figure suggests just a few examples of the many ways
that multiple perspectives are necessary to understand the complex nature of stress.

rescue workers. But what about the survivor's guilt and
subsequent delayed stress reactions from repeated viewing of the disaster on websites and televisions around the
world—are these "normal" stress responses? What connections can we make between these reactions and our own

reactions to stress? In considering these questions, several
related issues emerge:

- Stress isn't limited to major tragedies, traumas, and
  disasters. All of us encounter potentially stressful
  situations in our everyday lives—at our jobs, in our

relationships, at school, in traffic, or as a result of illness. Have you ever noticed, though, that some people seem to get "stressed out" at even minor annoyances, while others appear calm, cool, and collected even in a crisis situation? In addition, some people bounce back quickly after major stress, while others have trouble regaining their equilibrium. How can we explain these individual differences in our reactions to stress?

- We must also consider how our stress responses have evolved over the years and millennia and how they functioned to aid our survival. Many cultures today live much faster-paced lives than those of previous generations. How are the stresses we face today different from those faced by our ancient ancestors? What impact might the differences in our environments have on the effectiveness of our stress response?

- Multiple perspectives are necessary to understand our human response to stress. What goes on in the body and the brain that influence our reactions to stress? And how are these physiological responses mediated by our thought processes, our prior learning, our personality, our stage in life, and our social context (see FIGURE 13•1)?

- Finally, to what extent do we have control over our own reactions to stress and to the potential toll stress is taking on our physical and mental health? The good news is that we are not "stuck" with our current stress level; there are specific changes we can make to help us meet the challenges of stress more effectively. Thus, we conclude this chapter on a more positive note by not only describing effective coping strategies but also introducing you to a new health psychology perspective promoting well-being, resilience, and happiness.

As we explore these questions, keep in mind the stresses you have faced and consider how this information can help you understand the sources of stress in your life—and improve the way you perceive and manage that stress. Although it would seem that college students' lives are less stressful than those of firefighters and other first responders, the recent increase in college students' visits to mental health facilities and higher rates of suicides forces us to examine, in a later section, where all this academic stress is coming from.

13.1 Key Question: What Causes Distress?

What images come to mind when you hear the word *stress?* Most people think of the pressures in their lives: difficult jobs, unhappy relationships, financial woes, health problems, and final exams. You may have some visceral associations with

stress too: a churning stomach, perspiration, headache, or tension in your neck or upper back. We use the word *stress* loosely in everyday conversation, referring to a situation that confronts us (Lazarus et al., 1985). For example, if your employer or professor has been giving you a difficult time, you may say that you are "under stress," as though you were being squashed by a heavy object. You may also say you are "feeling stress" as a result. Thus, in everyday conversation, we use the word **stress** to refer both to an external threat and to our physical and mental response we feel when exposed to it.

Psychologists, however, make a distinction between the outer pressure or event that causes stress and its inner impact on us as individuals. **Stressors** are external events that cause internal stress responses, both psychological and emotional ones, termed **distress,** and biological and physiological reactions (Krantz et al., 1985). We will use the term *distress* to refer to our personal reactions, both physiological and psychological, to experienced stressors.

Thus, a stressor is the sight of a police officer climbing out of her car after you ran through a stop sign while texting. Your response to that sight of the cop about to ticket you—your racing heart, shaky hands, and sudden perspiration—are signs of the biological changes induced by this stressor. Your psychological stress, or distress, is the complex mix of shame, sense of stupidity, and worry about losing your license for this third moving violation if you cannot plead your way out of this unfortunate situation.

What are the common stressors faced by humans today? We begin this chapter with a review of stressors found to have the most impact on us. These include everything from petty daily hassles to relationship problems with family, friends, and romantic partners to terrorist attacks, as noted in our Core Concept for this section:

CORE CONCEPT 13.1

Traumatic events, chronic lifestyle conditions, major life changes, and even minor hassles can all cause a stress response.

Before embarking on our discussion of stressors and how we respond to them, we should first recall the concept of *cognitive interpretation* from our study of emotion in Chapter 10. There, we learned that a key component in our emotional response to a situation is the interpretation we make of that situation. Stress is a type of emotional response—consequently, interpretation or **cognitive appraisal** plays an important role in the degree of stress we feel when faced with

---

stress The physical and mental response to a stressor.

stressor A stressful event or situation.

distress The psychological reaction created by external stressors, which can be an emotional, cognitive, or behavioral response. It is part of the stress response that also includes biological and physiological reactions to stressors.

cognitive appraisal Our interpretation of a stressor and our resources for dealing with it.

a stressor. We will see later in this chapter that cognitive appraisal accounts for some individual differences in how people respond to stressors as well as in how effectively we succeed in dealing with them. In the previous paragraph, for example, a person who had never before received a ticket may interpret that situation as less stressful (and thus feel less distress) than one who had several recent tickets and was at risk for losing his driver's license or paying higher insurance rates.

Traumatic Stressors

Catastrophic events, such as natural disasters and terrorist attacks, qualify as **traumatic stressors**—situations that threaten your own or others' physical safety, arousing feelings of fear, horror, or helplessness. On a more personal level, a sudden major life change, such as the loss of a loved one, constitutes a trauma as well—despite the fact that death and separation are likely to affect everyone at some time. We will examine traumatic stress by first considering natural and human-made catastrophes, then personal loss, and finally posttraumatic stress.

[CONNECTION] *Cognitive appraisal* is central to cognitive-behavioral therapy.

Catastrophe In May 2008, shortly before the Olympics in Beijing, a massive earthquake in China killed more than 67,000 people. Subsequent quakes in Haiti and Chile also had devastating consequences on the population for many months after—as did the 2011 earthquake, tsunami, and resulting breach of nuclear reactors in Japan. Natural disasters such as these, as well as man-made tragedies like terrorist attacks and warfare, comprise the category of traumatic stressors known as **catastrophic events.** These sudden, violent calamities are inevitably accompanied by extreme stress and loss of loved ones or possessions. Moreover, the psychological and biological consequences can last far longer than the original event, as in the weeks after 9/11 when firefighters and emergency workers sometimes found themselves reliving the events in nightmares and in daytime flashbacks.

Studies of catastrophe survivors provide some insight into the ways individuals respond to these ordeals (Asarnow et al., 1999; Sprang, 1999). It's worth noting here that research of this type is difficult: Obviously, ethical considerations prevent psychologists from creating even minor traumatic events to study their effects on volunteer subjects. Instead, field researchers must wait for a catastrophe to occur and then get to the scene immediately to hear the story and observe survivors in the immediate aftermath.

A Natural Laboratory for Disaster. One opportunity to understand disaster response presented itself in San Francisco in 1989, just as the baseball World Series was about to begin at Candlestick Park. Spectators were settling into their seats when the entire stadium began to shake violently. The lights went out, and the scoreboard turned black as a major earthquake struck. Elsewhere in the city, fires erupted, a bridge collapsed, highways were crushed—and people were dying.

One week after the quake, a team of research psychologists began a series of follow-up surveys with about 800 regional residents. Survey responses revealed a clear pattern: The lives of respondents who experienced the earthquake continued to revolve heavily around the disaster for about a month. After this period, they ceased obsessing, thinking, and talking about the quake, but simultaneously reported an increase in other stress-related symptoms including sleep disruption, relationship problems, and nightmares (Wood et al., 1992). Although most symptoms diminished gradually, one year later, as many as 20 percent of residents remained distressed (Pennebaker & Harber, 1991).

In contrast to natural disasters, human-made catastrophes such as crime and terrorism have an added dimension of threat because they are produced intentionally by other people. **Terrorism** has been defined as a type of disaster caused by "human malevolence" with the goal of disrupting society by creating fear and danger (Hall et al., 2002). Like survivors of natural disasters, terrorism survivors report elevated symptoms of distress that substantially subside after several months (Galea et al., 2003). What appears to be different about surviving a terror attack, however, is the long-term change in perception of threat. Studies of individuals affected—both directly and indirectly—by the 9/11 attacks in America or by the 2005 bombings at the underground train station in London found that 50 to 75 percent of the public continued to worry about the safety of themselves and their families for a year or more following the attack (Rubin et al., 2005; Torabi & Seo, 2004; Weissman et al., 2005).

The major recent earthquake in Japan, recorded as 9.0 on the Richter scale, triggered an enormous tsunami tidal wave of more than 33 feet that totally destroyed many towns in northern Japan, killing thousands of people. Consider the stresses it also created.

---

traumatic stressor A situation that threatens one's physical safety, arousing feelings of fear, horror, or helplessness.

catastrophic event A sudden, violent calamity, either natural or manmade, that causes trauma.

terrorism A type of disaster caused by human malevolence with the goal of disrupting society by creating fear and danger.

Psychological Response to Catastrophe. Psychological responses to natural and human-caused disasters have been theorized to occur in stages, as victims experience shock, feel intense emotion, and struggle to reorganize their lives (Beigel & Berren, 1985; Horowitz, 1997). Cohen and Ahearn (1980) identified five stages survivors typically pass through:

1. Immediately after the event, victims experience *psychic numbness,* including shock and confusion, and for moments to days cannot fully comprehend what has happened. Severe, sudden, and violent disasters violate our basic expectations about how the world is supposed to function. For some of us, the unimaginable becomes a stark reality.

2. During a phase of *automatic action,* victims have little awareness of their own experiences and later show poor recall for many details about what occurred.

3. In the *communal effort stage,* people pool resources and collaborate, proud of their accomplishments but also weary and aware they are using up precious energy reserves.

4. Next, survivors may experience a *letdown* as, depleted of energy, they comprehend and feel the tragedy's impact. Public interest and media attention fade, and survivors feel abandoned, although the state of emergency may continue.

5. An extended period of *recovery* follows as survivors adapt to changes created by the disaster. The fabric of the community changes as the natural and business environments are altered.

Keep in mind, however, that *stage theories* don't necessarily apply to the entire population but attempt to summarize commonalities among a range of individual experiences. In this instance, stage theories of stress response are useful for organizing individual accounts into aggregate summaries and also because they help us anticipate what future survivors may go through and what kinds of assistance they may need.

Research also indicates the importance of stories or **narratives** in working through catastrophic experiences. To learn from and make sense of catastrophic loss, we formulate accounts that describe what happened and why. We are especially likely to develop narratives when an event is surprising or unpleasant (Holtzworth-Munroe & Jacobson, 1985) or violates our basic expectations (Zimbardo, 1999). And, as we'll see later in this chapter, narratives help us find meaning in loss, which in turn facilitates healing.

[CONNECTION] *Stage theories* emphasize distinctive changes that occur as one develops or progresses through a life stage or event.

Catastrophic events merit extended news coverage, and in this Internet age, the sounds and images of others' pain are broadcast and viewed repeatedly. Viewers are not immune to such programs and may experience a sort of "secondhand" traumatization.

Trauma in the Media. Media news coverage expands the experience of catastrophe so all viewers can experience it. Students, like you, reported repeated viewing of the WTC towers collapsing on 9/11. Recall that, in our opening story, surviving members of the Manhattan firefighters' crew repeatedly viewed a videotape showing their now-dead comrades rushing into the World Trade Center just before the building collapsed. At last they knew for certain the fate of their friends. But was repeated viewing really therapeutic for them? Conventional wisdom suggests that identifying the figures on the tape as their friends might give them some closure, and their friends' heroism could help them find meaning in tragedy, but once that goal is achieved, how can repeated viewing be anything but stress enhancing?

Research clearly shows that revisiting and reliving catastrophe causes its own stress. **Vicarious traumatization** is severe stress caused when one is exposed to others' accounts of trauma and the observer becomes captivated by it (McCann & Pearlman, 1990). Whether it be plane crashes, riots in a far-off country, or natural disasters, what matters is the amount of exposure: Schuster and colleagues (2001) found that the more hours viewers spent watching television coverage of the 9/11 attacks, the more likely they were to report stress symptoms later. What's more, a whopping 90 percent of respondents all over the country—even those with no personal or job connection to New York—reported experiencing at least one symptom of stress in the aftermath of the attack. By reliving the disaster, heavy viewers of media coverage, including those who lived safely distant from the actual disaster site, nonetheless became engaged with the victims' suffering and experienced measurable stress as a result.

We will note later that one of the most widely mandated techniques for first responder stress reduction in police, fire, and military units is known as critical incident stress debriefing (CISD). Small groups of those affected by the disaster are essentially forced to share their horror stories, listening to others and telling their own tales of woe. Can you reflect on why such a process might backfire and *increase* rather than ameliorate distress? (Advance warning: It does not work, according to much solid research.)

[CONNECTION] One prominent theory of dreams asserts that dreams reflect current concerns.

Cultural Variations in Response to Catastrophes. The March 2011 disasters that befell Japan were the worst since its devastation in World War II from atomic bombing. It became a worst-case scenario of incredible proportions. Initially, the massive 9.0 earthquake that triggered a 33-foot tidal wave

---

narrative   A personal account of a stressful event that describes our interpretation of what happened and why.

vicarious traumatization   Severe stress caused by exposure to traumatic images or stories that cause the observer to become engaged with the stressful material.

wiped out entire villages, killing thousands and leaving many homeless and without food in the winter cold. Then, radiation exposure from the meltdown of nuclear power plants posed long-term threats of widespread cancer among Japanese residents. Yet, despite these catastrophic experiences, the general response by most Japanese was a communal sense of calm, civility, and moral courage. Veteran reporters on the scene expressed amazement at the way in which Japanese people showed decorum and fought chaos with orderliness. There was no evidence of looting, and no increase in crime. Indeed, in 10-hour-long traffic jams caused by wrecked highways, not a single instance of honking was reported.

The collectivistic cultural focus on politeness, group consensus, and concern for others led to sharing, without complaint, of meager food supplies with strangers. Experts on Japanese culture trace such behaviors to the spiritual strength found in critical, comforting rituals of their religion. Most Japanese are Buddhists or follow ancient Shinto beliefs. Fundamental to these belief systems is alleviating mental and physical suffering through practicing compassion and acceptance of death as the end part of the life process. Buddhism as now practiced is less about spirits of the natural world and more about rituals of society, family, and state, according to scholar of Japanese religion Duncan Williams (Grossman, 2011).

Personal Loss

Like many other species, humans are social creatures: We depend on each other for survival. The loss of a loved one is very distressing, even if it is anticipated (such as after a long illness). A sudden, unexpected loss is traumatic: In a rated listing of life changes at the end of this section, you will see "death of spouse" is the most stressful of all life changes (Holmes & Rahe, 1967; Scully et al., 2000). **Grief** is the emotional response to interpersonal loss, a painful complex of feelings including sadness, anger, helplessness, guilt, and despair (Raphael, 1984). Whether grieving the death of a loved one, the breakup of a romantic relationship, or the betrayal of a trusted friend, you experience the jolt of separation and loneliness and have difficult questions to ponder. Some of our core assumptions about life may be challenged, and we may be forced to adapt to a different reality (Parkes, 2001). As a result, our identities and future plans may be permanently altered (Davis et al., 1998; Janoff-Bulman, 1992).

Psychologists view grieving as a normal, healthy process of adapting to a major life change, with no "right" method or "normal" time period (Gilbert, 1996; Neimeyer, 1995, 1999). Some experts recommend achieving closure, a Gestalt term for perceiving an incomplete stimulus as complete. But grief psychologists oppose the goal of closing off the pain and memories of loss and instead recommend **integration**. To understand this, think for a moment about someone you have lost: Perhaps you have "gotten over it" and don't think about it much any more—yet it is still there in your memory, with images, emotions, and thoughts still vivid and accessible and still part of who you are (Harvey, 1996; Harvey et al., 1990). Thus, the final phase of grieving is more accurately thought of as an ongoing process of integration in which each life loss becomes a part of the self-narrative and part of your memory storehouse of meaningful events, both negative and positive (Murray, 2002).

The mourning process also requires you to interact socially at a time when you feel especially vulnerable and socially withdrawn. Ironically, friends offering help or sympathy sometimes add to the stress. Hollander (2004) writes of losing first her husband and then, a few months later, her mother. "Am I all right? Everyone seems to be asking me that. . . .Often I find I don't know how to respond to the question" (pp. 201–202). Her friends feel uncomfortable when she weeps openly, and they encourage her to cheer up, to be herself again. Hollander concludes that her pain cannot and must not be rushed: "Closure is not my goal. . . . I am all right exactly because I weep" (p. 204).

Humiliation as Loss. Which would be more stressful: losing your romantic partner when he or she dies, or having that person leave you for another lover? Both tragedies involve losing your partner, but in addition, being rejected involves not only grief but also humiliation and abandonment. One study interviewed thousands of adults, categorizing their experiences of loss and other life-event stressors and diagnosing their symptoms of major depression and anxiety. Results indicated that rejected respondents were more likely to develop depression than those whose partners had died (Kendler et al., 2003). In discussing their findings, researchers observed that the death of one's partner is a "pure loss event," which does not represent a potential failure or deficiency on the part of the grieving person. In contrast, being left by your spouse or romantic partner "raises issues . . . [such] as humiliation, which is usually seen as the loss of status, the loss of a sense of self-esteem and the loss of a sense of your own worth" (National Public Radio, 2003a).

In a different, more recent study, researchers examined how quickly people became depressed following different types of stress. Life events were categorized by whether they involved **targeted rejection,** defined as the "exclusive, active, and intentional social rejection of an individual by others." Results revealed that people who experienced a recent targeted rejection event became depressed three times faster than those who experienced other types of stress (Slavich et al., 2009). Interestingly, these effects were similar regardless of whether the targeted rejection occurred at work (for example, the person was fired) or in the context of a personal relationship (such as a breakup). In sum, then, stressors that involve humiliation or social rejection are more likely to cause depression than are other stressors and also appear to

---

grief The emotional response to loss, which includes sadness, anger, helplessness, guilt, and despair.

integration A final phase of grieving, in which the loss becomes incorporated into the self.

targeted rejection The exclusive, active, and intentional social rejection of an individual by others.

bring about depression more quickly (Slavich et al., 2009, 2010a).

Why do we feel so bad about humiliation and rejection? Animal studies reveal that in primate colonies, such as free-roaming baboon groups, individuals who lose status withdraw, lose their appetite, become more submissive, and show immediate huge increases in measurable biological stress (Sapolsky, 1998). In evolutionary terms, loss of social status threatens survival and has serious consequences. By taking action to prevent such losses, humans and other primates increase their chances of survival. Thus, perhaps rejection makes us feel bad because we *need* to feel bad; in other words, perhaps the depression or loss of self-esteem that accompanies rejection keeps us from entering into unwise or insecure partnerships, thus protecting us from further rejection or humiliation.

Disenfranchised Grief. Grief is also especially stressful when others minimize your loss and fail to sympathize. Experiences such as death, divorce, and trauma are recognized with formal condolences, such as funerals, hospital visits, sentimental greeting cards, and professional attention from undertakers, attorneys, and physicians (Lensing, 2001). But other painful losses with no official "status" may be ignored or dismissed by the community. For example, adults who grieve after a miscarriage, young adults who have lost friends, and children saddened by the death of a favorite TV or movie star may find themselves alone in their sorrow, getting little sympathy or understanding from others. Their **disenfranchised grief,** the emotion surrounding a loss others do not understand, cannot be mourned through public rituals like memorials or funerals. Fearing others' negative reactions, even behind your back, disenfranchised grievers may try to hide their sorrow—but continue to suffer (Doka, 1989, 1995; Rickgarn, 1996).

Confiding in others can help people cope with loss and trauma (Harvey, 1996; Pennebaker, 1990). During these times, keep in mind the role of professional counselors or psychotherapists, who might be counted on to take your grief seriously. Also, it is therapeutically worthwhile to "confide" in other ways, such as by keeping a written private journal of your feelings and what triggers them over time (see the *Psychology Matters* section later in this chapter).

Posttraumatic Stress Individuals who have undergone severe ordeals—rape, combat, beatings, or torture, for example—may experience a belated pattern of stress symptoms that can appear months or even years after their trauma. Those delayed reactions, however, can last a lifetime. In **posttraumatic stress disorder (PTSD),** the individual re-experiences mental and physical responses that accompanied the trauma. Nearly one adult in 12 in the United States will experience PTSD at some time in his or her life, with symptoms lasting more than ten years in more than one-third of cases. Traumas described by PTSD victims most frequently

include having witnessed another person being killed or badly injured, having lived through a natural disaster, and having survived a life-threatening accident. Men cite more experiences of physical attack, military combat, disaster or fire, or being held captive or hostage, whereas women cite more experiences of rape, sexual molestation, physical abuse, and neglect during childhood (Bower, 1995a). Women are more likely than men to develop symptoms of PTSD after experiencing a traumatic event (Tolin & Foa, 2006), and Hispanic Americans are more at risk than non-Hispanic Caucasian or Black Americans (Pole et al., 2005).

What Are the Symptoms of PTSD? Victims of posttraumatic stress disorder typically become distracted and disorganized and experience memory difficulties (Arnsten, 1998). They may feel emotionally numb and alienated from others and experience less pleasure from positive events. Problems sleeping, guilt about surviving, and an exaggerated "startle response" (wide-eyed, gasping, surprised behavior upon perceiving a sudden threat) are common symptoms as well. Rape survivors, for example, may experience a barrage of psychological aftereffects, including feelings of betrayal by people close to them, anger about having been attacked, and fear of being alone (Baron & Straus, 1985; Cann et al., 1981). 👁

👁 **Watch** the **Video** at **MyPsychLab**

Posttraumatic stress disorder can also have lasting biological consequences (Crowell, 2002; Sapolsky, 1998). The brain undergoes physical changes when stress is extreme in intensity or duration. Specifically, the brain's hormone-regulating system may develop hair-trigger responsiveness, making the victim of posttraumatic stress overreact to mild stressors.

PTSD in Combat Personnel. While the term *posttraumatic stress disorder* was coined fairly recently, historical accounts have noted similar symptoms, referred to as "combat fatigue," "shell-shock," or "soldier's heart," in soldiers for centuries. In the wake of the Vietnam War, where early estimates noted symptoms of PTSD in 30 percent of combat veterans, public attention on the disorder grew. Military psychologists now provide at least some minimal treatment for combat-related stress at deployment sites in Iraq, for instance, and a variety of educational programs aim to help soldiers and their families prepare more effectively for deployment and to cope better with the aftermath of war once the soldiers have returned home. And even though the military cultural norm has historically taught soldiers not to talk about combat experiences, which contributed to the stigma most veterans felt about

---

disenfranchised grief The emotion surrounding a loss that others do not support, share, or understand.

posttraumatic stress disorder (PTSD) A delayed stress reaction in which an individual involuntarily re-experiences emotional, cognitive, and behavioral aspects of past trauma.

asking for help with psychological symptoms, these new programs are helping participants slowly overcome that barrier to effective coping. A program entitled Battlemind, for example, was created to help soldiers develop realistic expectations of deployment prior to combat and also to help them readjust to life at home when they return from deployment. Initial research indicates that soldiers who participate in Battlemind report fewer symptoms of PTSD than their comrades who receive more traditional training (Munsey, 2007).

Increased scrutiny on PTSD in combat personnel has also unearthed a fascinating new finding about the brain's role in certain PTSD symptoms. Prompted by the groundbreaking research of neurologist Ibolja Cernak, U.S. military doctors now recognize that soldiers exposed to an explosion often develop cognitive symptoms such as memory loss, reduced ability to concentrate, slowed reaction time, and difficulty performing simple math tasks—even if the soldier wasn't hit by the blast. While researchers are still unsure exactly how the brain is affected by the blast, there is general agreement that the force of the explosion causes damage to brain functioning. Up to 20 percent of soldiers returning from Iraq and Afghanistan are estimated to experience some type of traumatic brain injury such as this, and researchers now think that neurological effects of blast exposure may account for the cognitive deficits seen in some veterans diagnosed with PTSD (Bhattacharjee, 2008).

Chronic Stressors

The stressors reviewed in the previous section—catastrophe, personal loss, and posttraumatic stress—involve events that, like the 9/11 attack, occur abruptly. In contrast, **chronic stressors** are relatively long lasting and may develop slowly over time. For example, they may involve ongoing financial problems, marital difficulties, or poor living conditions, such as one of the world's worse stress inducers—living in poverty. Here, we examine five different chronic stressors: societal stressors, burnout, compassion fatigue, major life changes, and daily hassles.

Societal Stressors   For most of us, stress comes not from sudden catastrophic events but from **societal stressors** or pressures in our social, cultural, and economic environment. These societal stressors often involve difficulties at home, work, or school that are chronic (recurring or continuing over time). Societal stressors also include unemployment, poverty, racism, and other conditions that handicap or oppress individuals because of their social group or status.

For example, a study of work stress and health revealed that unemployed men experience more depression, anxiety, and worries about health than comparable men with jobs. Almost miraculously, these symptoms usually disappeared when the unemployed individuals found work (Liem & Rayman, 1982). The startling results of a recent survey powerfully illustrate the prevalence of stress related to money concerns: 83 percent of Americans aged 20 to 45 viewed their

Societal stressors include unemployment, homelessness, and discrimination. Such conditions can exact a toll on both mental and physical health, especially among the poor and minorities.

current financial situation as "very or somewhat stressful." Only 14 percent reported they were not at all stressed out by their financial situation (American Express ZYNC survey, reported in *USA Today*, March 15, 2011).

Prejudice and discrimination can also be significant sources of stress (Contrada et al., 2000). How? For one, high blood pressure among African Americans—long thought to be primarily genetic—is correlated with chronic stress caused by the daily negative impact of having menial jobs, limited education, and low socioeconomic status (Klag et al., 1991). Also, people living in poverty have less access to good health care and are more likely to live in areas containing greater health hazards such as environmental pollutants, lead in their house paint, greater noise, and drug-dealing gangs. Such situational factors affect cognitive development in children and create a variety of adverse physical and emotional factors in adults (Evans et al., 1998; Staples, 1996).

Burnout   Having a job, however—even a high-paying one—does not inoculate one against stress. On the contrary, it can create stress of its own, both emotionally and physically. Continually stressful work can lead to **burnout,** a syndrome of overwhelming exhaustion, feelings of cynicism and detachment from the job, and a sense of ineffectiveness and lack of accomplishment (Maslach & Leiter, 1997). Christina Maslach (1998, 2003; Maslach et al., 2001), a leading researcher on this widespread problem, notes that burnout was first recognized in professions demanding high-intensity interpersonal contact, such as physicians with patients, teachers with students, and social workers with clients. We now know that burnout can occur anywhere—even among college students, stay-at-home parents, or volunteer workers. People experiencing

---

chronic stressor Long-lasting stressful condition.

societal stressor A chronic stressor resulting from pressure in one's social, cultural, or economic environment.

burnout A syndrome of emotional exhaustion, physical fatigue, and cognitive weariness, often related to work.

burnout report feelings of detachment, failure, and cynicism about coworkers and clients. They seek escape and avoid their work, leading to decreased personal accomplishment. Burnout has been found to correlate with many negative consequences: absenteeism, job turnover, impaired performance, poor coworker relations, family problems, and decreased personal health (Maslach & Leiter, 1997; Schaufeli & Enzmann, 1998). In some nations where citizens get extended sick leave based on their level of stress-related burnout, the cost can run into hundreds of millions in required benefits.

More recently, research has focused on the positive alternative to burnout, labeled **job engagement** (Schaufeli & Bakker, 2004). The practical significance of this burnout–engagement continuum is that engagement represents a desired goal for burnout interventions. This new framework leads people to consider what factors in the workplace are likely to enhance employees' energy, vigor, and resilience; promote their involvement and absorption with work tasks; and ensure their dedication and sense of efficacy and success on the job.

Although there is some evidence for individual risk factors for burnout, there is far more evidence for the importance of situational variables. In other words, the workplace carries far more of the predictive weight for burnout than does personality. More than two decades of research on burnout across many occupations in various countries have identified a plethora of organizational risk factors (Maslach, et al., 2001; Schaufeli & Enzmann, 1998). However, rather than posing an "either/or" question ("is it the person *or* the job?")—it may well be that an "and" question is the better way to frame the issue. That is, there are both personal *and* situational variables that determine burnout, and the key issue is how best to conceptualize the combination or interaction of them.

Early models in the field of industrial-organizational psychology (French et al., 1974) theorized that a better fit between the employee and the workplace would predict better adjustment and less stress. Building on those models, Maslach and Leiter (1997) formulated a burnout model that measures the degree of match or mismatch between the individual and key aspects of his or her organizational environment. The greater the gap, or mismatch, the greater the likelihood of burnout; conversely, the greater the match (or fit), the greater the likelihood of job engagement.

[**CONNECTION**] Industrial-organizational (I/O) psychologists focus on tailoring the work environment to maximize both productivity and morale.

What are these key aspects of the organizational environment? Six major areas of work life have been found relevant to employee/workplace fit: workload, control, reward, community, fairness, and values (Maslach & Leiter, 2005). *Workload* and *control* refer to the amount of work and the degree of autonomy enjoyed by the worker. *Reward* refers to

the relative match between the rewards offered by the job and those valued by the employee. The degree of social support and interpersonal conflict in the organization make up the fourth factor, which is *community*. *Fairness* is assessed by the match between the employee's sense of equity and social justice and that of the organization. The final factor, *values*, recognizes the cognitive and emotional power of job goals and expectations. Mismatches between the employee and the organization in these six key areas have been found to predict burnout, making researchers optimistic about the possibility of developing early-detection and intervention procedures to promote greater job engagement (Maslach & Leiter, 2008).

Thus, burnout is not a personal problem or a weakness in character, as was once thought. Effective burnout prevention requires both managers and workers to take responsibility for developing conditions that improve engagement with the job and create a better "fit" between employee and job and make decisions that focus on the long-term health of the employees and the organization (Berglas, 2001; Maslach & Goldberg, 1998).

Compassion Fatigue After the 9/11 attacks, New York Ladder Company 5's Lieutenant O'Neill joined others in day after day of fruitless rescue searches. One day, instead of going home, O'Neill checked into a hospital and asked for help with stress-related symptoms he was experiencing. He met with a doctor to whom he poured out the story of the horrors he had seen. Contrary to O'Neill's assumption that, as a doctor, "He . . . could handle this," the doctor himself went to the hospital psychologist after treating O'Neill. "[H]e kind of lost it," O'Neill learned. "He had become freaked out from the story I told him, because he lost a friend from the tragedy. . . . He didn't show up for work for a couple of days" (Smith, 2003b, p. 259). Even medical professionals and therapists, though trained to be objective, are at risk for the stress of vicarious traumatization (Sabin-Farrell & Turpin, 2003).

When medical professionals, caregivers, and therapists are overexposed to trauma and its victims, they are at risk for **compassion fatigue,** a state of psychological exhaustion that leaves caregivers feeling stressed, numb, or indifferent to those in need after extended contact with sufferers (Figley, 2002). Compassion fatigue is also called *secondary traumatic stress* because it afflicts the helpers, who "catch" the stress suffered by the victims. Consequences are similar to burnout in that it leaves people unhappy with their work and resistant to contact with people they are supposed to help. Dreading further stories of trauma, fatigued helpers may emotionally withdraw from their clients and overuse the

---

job engagement An employee's sense of being part of a meaningful work setting where her or his contribution is valued and equitably rewarded (the opposite of job burnout).

compassion fatigue A state of exhaustion experienced by medical and psychological professionals, as well as caregivers, which leaves the individual feeling stressed, numb, or indifferent.

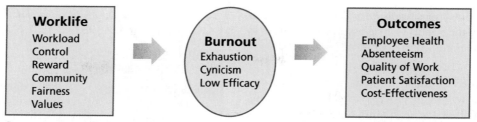

[FIGURE 13•2] Worklife and Burnout A schematic model of six input factors affecting burnout and four measurable outcomes.

"silencing response," distracting, minimizing, or redirecting what their clients are saying to reduce their own discomfort and pain (Baranowsky, 2002). When therapists or religious counselors feel unable to listen to their clients or parishioners, they can no longer function as effective healers. Compassion fatigue and burnout harm not only the providers and receivers of care and attention but entire professions as well. Fortunately, healers can learn the warning signs in time to take action—and researchers can suggest what kinds of action to take:

- First, caregivers must focus on their sense of **compassion satisfaction,** an appreciation of the work they do that drew them to their professions in the first place. Compassion satisfaction can be increased by creating and maintaining a sense of team spirit with coworkers. Whenever possible, caregivers and rescue workers should be able to see clients recover so they realize their work is effective (Collins & Long, 2003).

- While it is important to care for those one is helping, helpers must avoid becoming overinvolved, or their lack of control over most of their clients' experiences can lead to a sense of defeat (Keidel, 2002).

- Novice trauma counselors may simply distance themselves from stressful exchanges; more experienced workers are better able to cope directly with their own stress (Pinto, 2003).

- Caregivers should resist overvolunteering. Volunteers who worked with more than one agency or effort after 9/11 were at greater risk for compassion fatigue than those who volunteered with only one organization, such as the American Red Cross (Roberts et al., 2003).

- Finally, professional helpers and emergency workers should use humor—but use it carefully! While tasteless jokes and dark humor with fellow workers can relieve anxiety and establish a sense of camaraderie among coworkers, workers must be cautious with these types of humor. Because it is not publicly acceptable to laugh in the face of tragedy, humor should be expressed selectively, with sensitivity to the environment, so as not to offend or further hurt those already suffering (Moran, 2002).

Major Life Events The beginning or end of a relationship is always a time of adjustment, accompanied by emotional ups and downs, tension, and turmoil. Earlier in this section, we discussed the effects of sudden interpersonal loss. Other changes can cause stress too: a new job, starting or finishing college, or—ironically—even taking a vacation! Even events we welcome, such as the birth of a child, often require major changes in our routines and adaptations to new demands and lifestyles. Especially when the events are considered positive events (such as an exciting new job or getting married), we may not recognize their potential impact on our stress level. In general, any change can generate distress; the bigger the change in our lives, the bigger the impact.

What if a simple questionnaire existed that would assess your current stress level? Several decades ago, psychologists Thomas Holmes and Richard Rahe (pronounced *RAY*) developed just such a tool. They first identified a variety of common stressful events and had a large number of respondents rate the events in terms of how stressful each one was in their own lives. After analyzing all the results, they created the **Social Readjustment Rating Scale (SRRS),** which lists 43 life events—ranging from death of a spouse at the high end to pregnancy or a new job in the middle to getting a traffic ticket at the low end. Each life event is assigned a particular number of life-change units (LCUs), so anyone can calculate his or her current stress level by adding up the LCUs for each life change that was recently experienced.

Research has indeed found relationships between life changes and stress. The birth of a child, for example, is often associated with lower marital satisfaction (Cowan & Cowan, 1988). Since it was developed, the SRRS has been used in thousands of studies worldwide and has been found to apply cross-culturally. We must be cautious in interpreting our scores, though, in light of what we know about the role of cognitive appraisal in stress. We will examine the SRRS more closely at the end of this chapter. An undergraduate version

---

compassion satisfaction A sense of appreciation felt by a caregiver, medical or psychological professional, of the work he or she does.

Social Readjustment Rating Scale (SRRS) Psychological rating scale designed to measure stress levels by attaching numerical values to common life changes.

of the scale, developed specifically to reflect student stress reactions, gives you the opportunity to assess your own stress level in the *Do It Yourself!* feature (Crandall, et al., 1992).

Daily Hassles   After a difficult workday, you get stuck in a traffic jam on your way to the grocery store. Finally arriving, you find they don't have the very item or brand you wanted. After selecting a substitute, you proceed to the checkout, only to be snapped at by an impatient clerk when you don't have exact change. Taken individually, such minor irritations and frustrations, known as **hassles,** don't seem like much in comparison to a natural disaster. But psychologists confirm that hassles can accumulate, especially when they are frequent and involve interpersonal conflicts (Bolger et al., 1989).

In our fast-moving, highly technological society, a major life hassle is "waiting." Waiting for anything, instead of having it instantly available, has become a modern stressor: waiting for public transportation, waiting for service in a store or restaurant, waiting in traffic, waiting for your computer to boot up or download files.

Any annoying incident can be a hassle, but some of the most common hassles involve frustrations—the blocking of some desired goal—at home, work, or school. In a diary study, a group of men and women kept track of their daily hassles over a one-year period, also recording major life changes and physical symptoms. A clear relationship emerged between hassles and health problems: The more frequent and intense the hassles people reported, the poorer their health, both physical and mental (Lazarus, 1981, 1984, 1999). The opposite was also true: As daily hassles diminish, people's sense of well-being increases (Chamberlain & Zika, 1990). Thus, a life filled with hassles can exact as great a price as that of a single, more intense stressor (Weinberger et al., 1987).

Traffic can be a hassle and consequently contribute to your stress—if you choose to interpret it that way.

---

hassle Situation that causes minor irritation or frustration.

do it yourself!

The Undergraduate Stress Questionnaire: How Stressed Are You?

This scale, developed in 1992 specifically for undergraduates, initially contained an event about having problems with your typewriter—which we have removed for relevancy. For each of the following events, check off any item that describes a stressor that you have experienced in the past week. Tally up your check marks to compute your total (Crandell et al., 1992).

———— Lack of money

———— Someone broke a promise

———— Death (family member or friend)

———— Dealt with incompetence at the Registrar's office

———— Can't concentrate

———— Had a lot of tests

———— Thought about unfinished work

———— Someone did a "pet peeve" of yours

———— It's finals week

———— Living with boy-/girlfriend

———— No sleep

———— Applying to graduate school

———— Felt need for transportation

———— Sick, injury

———— Bad haircut today

———— Victim of a crime

———— Had a class presentation

———— Job requirements changed

———— Applying for a job

———— Assignments in all classes due the same day

———— Fought with boy-/girlfriend

———— No time to eat

———— Have a hard upcoming week

———— Felt some peer pressure

———— Lots of deadlines to meet

———— Went into test unprepared

———— Working while in school

———— Arguments, conflict of values with friends

———— Have a hangover

———— Problems with your computer

———— Lost something (especially wallet)

———— Death of a pet

———— Bothered by having no social support of family

———— Performed poorly at a task

———— Did worse than expected on test

———— Problem getting home from bar when drunk

———— Used a fake ID

———— Had an interview

———— Had projects, research papers due

———— Did badly on a test

———— Can't finish everything you needed to do

———— Heard bad news

———— No sex for a while

———— Someone cut ahead of you in line

———— Had confrontation with an authority figure

———— Maintaining a long-distance boy-/girlfriend

———— Crammed for a test

———— Parents getting divorce

———— Dependent on other people

———— Feel unorganized

———— Breaking up with boy-/girlfriend

———— Trying to decide on major

———— Feel isolated

———— Having roommate conflicts

———— Checkbook didn't balance

———— Visit from a relative and entertaining them

———— Decision to have sex is on your mind

———— Parents controlling with money

———— Couldn't find a parking space

———— Noise disturbed you while trying to study

———— Someone borrowed something without permission

———— Had to ask for money

———— Got a traffic ticket

———— Talked with a professor

———— Change of environment (new doctor, dentist, etc.)

———— Exposed to upsetting TV show, book, or movie

———— Got to class late

———— Erratic schedule

———— Found out boy-/girlfriend cheated on you

———— Can't understand your professor

———— Trying to get into your major or college

———— Missed your period and waiting

———— Coping with addictions

———— Registration for classes

———— Stayed up late writing a paper

———— Property stolen

———— Someone you expected to call did not

———— Holiday

———— Sat through a boring class

———— Favorite sporting team lost

———— Thoughts about future

———— TOTAL

How did you do? The following scale may be useful in providing you a general sense of how much stress you are experiencing as an undergraduate:

0–7: a very low level of stress

16–23: the amount of stress encountered by the average undergraduate

40+: a very high level of stress

You might want to compare your score at two different times, or with a friend.

Cognitive appraisal plays a role in the impact of hassles as well. If you interpret a frustrating situation as "too much" to deal with or as a major threat to well-being, it will affect you more than if you dismiss it as less important (Lazarus, 1984). Some people may be especially prone to see the world as hassle filled. One study showed that college students with a pessimistic outlook experienced both more hassles and poorer health (Dykema et al., 1995). This finding serves as a good reminder that correlation does not imply causation: In other words, we know a correlation exists between hassles and health but do not know what causes the link. On one hand, experiencing many hassles may have a negative impact on health—but on the other hand, having more health problems to begin with might increase a person's perception of minor annoyances as hassles. It is also possible that a third variable—something other than hassles or health—might be driving the correlation: For example, pessimists (as noted above) might be more likely to perceive minor annoyances as hassles and also more likely to have health problems.

One way to destress your life is to reconsider your own daily hassles. Look back on recent frustrations with a sense of humor, put problems in perspective, and consider just how unimportant such difficulties and delays really turned out to be. By reappraising everyday difficulties as minor, you enable yourself to remain good natured and productive and even to have a good laugh. Shake your head, put on the brakes, let the vending machine keep your dollar—and move along. Daily hassles are idiosyncratic: They are interpreted uniquely by each person experiencing them. What is a hassle or an annoyance to you may be unnoticed or even amusing to someone else. One person's agonizing traffic jam is another person's opportunity to listen to the radio, play a favorite CD, or engage in people watching. If your life seems hassle filled, some reappraisal of regularly irritating situations can save you psychological wear and tear. It almost always helps to connect with nature, take a walk in a park or on a beach, swim, hike, bike, even visit a local zoo. Later, we will see how cognitive reappraisal can play a central role in one's general strategies for coping with stress.

psychology matters

Student Stress

It's timely for you to be studying stress and well-being right now, because merely being a college student qualifies as a stressor. College freshmen in particular undergo major challenges in making the transition to college life. One study found that freshman stress unfolds in three phases. First, new students experience the shock and excitement of new roles, environments, and social relationships. Next comes a protracted period of disillusionment and struggle as students face both the serious work and mundane chores of academic life. Finally, as roles gel and mastery develops in at least some efforts, a sense of improved well-being and possibilities emerges (Rambo-Chroniak, 1999). But stress isn't limited to first-year students. All students experience a specific pattern of stress during the school year, with stress peaks at the beginning, middle, and end of each term (Bolger, 1997). Two points in time are particularly difficult, the "midwinter crash" and the final exam period, when studying competes with regular sleep and healthy

eating and when flu and cold viruses afflict those with low resistance.

Some causes of student stress are obvious, with academic pressure topping the list (Bolger, 1997). Also, new social interactions increase the possibility of problems in interpersonal relationships (Edwards et al., 2001). Romantic love, often a source of joy, can also be a source of stress and illness, especially among college women (Riessman et al., 1991). And when romance sours, breakup stress soars. An investigation of a large group of university students who had experienced a recent breakup of a romantic relationship was studied to determine its causes. Those who felt most distress from their breakup reported a *loss of intimacy* as the main cause for the breakup itself, leading to their failed romance; not as central were affiliation needs, sexuality, or autonomy reasons (Field et al., 2010).

Perhaps the essential source of stress for traditional-aged college students is freedom—specifically, the lack of structure in a college environment as contrasted with the structure of home and high school curriculum (*USA Today*, 1996). For students returning to college after years in the workforce or raising children, stress often involves the challenge of "retraining the brain" to process and retain massive amounts of new information—in quick time for exams.

And stress seems to be on the rise among college students. In a recent national survey, college freshmen and women reported record-low levels of emotional health: only 52 percent felt they had "good or above-average emotional health." This marks the lowest point since the survey first asked the question in 1985. The same survey also found that 76 percent rated their drive to achieve as "above average or in the highest 10 percent"—the highest point since 1985. More students than ever before admitted they frequently felt overwhelmed. Gender effects were also found: Only 46 percent of women reported their emotional health as "good" compared to a higher 59 percent of men. What do you think might account for this difference (Sieben, 2011)?

Solutions for student stress, fortunately, may be within arm's reach—the distance needed to reach for the phone and call a friend for support or the college health center, counseling office, or tutoring center for professional advice. Most students express a reluctance to seek help (Rambo-Chroniak, 1999); so simply overcoming this ambivalence—especially as an enlightened student of the many uses of psychology—can be a step toward feeling better. Young adults do better if they have positive attitudes about becoming independent individuals on a course of normal separation from their parents (Smith, 1995).

In terms of self-help, students report better results when taking specific action to resolve the problem rather than simply dwelling on their emotional response (Smith, 1995). Cultivating more hopeful attitudes and better self-esteem—for example, by setting and meeting realistic goals—also leads to lower stress and better adjustment. Students appear to be more adaptive if they report better social support and a greater sense of control in their lives (Rambo-Chroniak, 1999). Involvement in student organizations can offer both structure and social contact, but beware of the stress of excessive commitment (Bolger, 1997). Two qualities in particular characterize students who are most effective in preventing and coping with stress: *resilience*, based in part in self-acceptance, effective communication, and coping skills; and *cognitive hardiness*, an ability to interpret potential stressors as challenging rather than threatening (Nowack, 1983; Yeaman, 1995). We will examine these two characteristics in detail a little later in this chapter.

CHECK YOUR UNDERSTANDING

✓• **Study** and **Review** at **MyPsychLab**

1. **Recall:** External events or situations that cause stress are called ———, whereas the term ——— denotes the physical and mental changes that occur as a result.

2. **Application:** An example of a chronic societal stressor is ———.
   a. an earthquake
   b. vicarious trauma
   c. being stuck in traffic
   d. widespread unemployment

3. **Analysis:** Which of the following statements about daily hassles is true?
   a. Some of the most common hassles involve threats to survival.
   b. As daily hassles diminish, people's sense of well-being increases.
   c. More frequent and intense hassles are associated with better health.
   d. The effects of hassles do not accumulate: Many hassles are no worse than a few.

4. **Synthesis:** Your friend Rob recently lost his wife to cancer. Devon, another friend, recently found out his partner was cheating on him, and she left him for someone else. What difference would you predict between Rob and Devon in terms of the impact of these two different types of losses on their psychological well-being?

5. **Understanding the Core Concept:** Name four categories of common stressors, along with an example of each.

Answers: 1. stressors; stress 2. d 3. b 4. Both Rob and Devon have suffered a personal loss, which involves grief, stress, and mourning. Devon, however, is more at risk for depression due to the accompanying humiliation of being rejected, whereas Rob's loss is a "pure loss event." 5. Traumatic events, such as catastrophe and personal loss; chronic stressors, such as societal stressors, burnout, and compassion fatigue; major life events, such as a new job or the birth of a child; and daily hassles, such as traffic jams or computer crashes

13.2 Key Question: How Does Stress Affect Us Physically?

Since our earliest days on Earth, humans have survived by responding quickly and decisively to potentially lethal attacks by predators or hostile tribes. Our ancestors adapted to an enormous variety of environmental conditions worldwide, confronting climate extremes, scarce resources, and hostile neighbors. Faced with these challenges, quick action was necessary to obtain shelter and protection, to find food, and to defend themselves. The faster an individual was to feel fear or anger, appraise the situation accurately, and take appropriate action, the better his or her chances of success and survival. Those who responded most quickly and effectively to danger survived and passed those responsive genes to their offspring, whereas slower or less-clever individuals were less likely to survive and bear children in the course of human evolution.

Some of the serious stressors confronting our ancestors, such as catastrophe or combat, continue to face us today. Modern life, of course, adds some new dangers: demanding jobs, financial worries, and computer crashes. More often chronic in nature, these new threats aren't necessarily solved effectively with the same responses that suited our ancestors and their more immediate challenges. Yet, our stress response system remains the result of our ancestors' evolutionary legacy, because human physiology cannot evolve and change nearly as fast as our societies have. This ancient biological script is retained in our body's automatic responses to frightening or enraging conditions. If someone insults you, your face feels hot and your fists seem to clench by themselves, readying you for a physical contest. Or imagine a very different sort of "threat": Your instructor calls on you in a class discussion for which you are unprepared. Your heart races, your knees feel wobbly, and you feel the urge to run away.

These examples illustrate the two poles of the **fight-or-flight response,** a sequence of internal and behavioral processes triggered when a threat is perceived, preparing the organism for either struggle or escape. This response worked very well for our predecessors but doesn't always suit us as well today. After all, is running out of the classroom really an effective response to being called on in class? Our Core Concept summarizes this point:

CORE CONCEPT 13.2

The physical stress response begins with arousal, which stimulates a series of physiological responses that in the short term are adaptive but that can turn harmful if prolonged.

---

fight-or-flight response Sequence of internal responses preparing an organism for struggle or escape.

Amazingly, we deal with stress effectively most of the time, managing to be not only healthy but even happy. But, as you will see in this section, there can be serious consequences when we don't deal effectively with stress—no matter what its source. On the positive side, we should emphasize that the emotional arousal we call stress usually works to our advantage. It brings threatening events into focus and readies us to respond. On the negative side, extreme or prolonged emotional arousal threatens our health. The results can include physical conditions such as heart disease, stroke, high blood pressure, and ulcers. Our mental health can also suffer.

Some of us are prone to "worrying ourselves sick" by anticipating what might go wrong, from minor irritants to major traumas (Sapolsky, 1994). Depression, as well as PTSD and other anxiety disorders, has direct linkages to stress. We see these consequences not only in emergency response workers and air traffic controllers but also in public- and private-sector employees at all status levels and in people of all ages and all walks of life. Let's take a closer look at the physiology of our stress response, which will lay the foundation for a clear understanding of exactly how this adaptive response triggers negative health consequences when chronic stress strains the limits of our resources.

Physiological Responses to Stress

Firefighters usually report that they love their work, and for some the job is a family tradition. But their camaraderie and commitment cannot lessen the threat, the risk of injury and death—the stress they experience—when they answer the alarm and race into harm's way. How does the body of an experienced firefighter respond to the perception of that stressor? And what about your own physical responses to stress?

The Fight-or-Flight Response   When a stressful situation begins suddenly—as when a professional firefighter first hears the alarm—the stress response begins with an abrupt and

In cases of acute stress, such as this woman faces as a forest fire nears her village in Portugal and threatens her home, the stressor arises suddenly, and the stress response begins with abrupt and intense physiological arousal.

⌐ **CONNECTION** ⌐ *The autonomic nervous system (ANS) regulates our most basic vital functions.*

intense physiological arousal produced by the autonomic nervous system (ANS). Signs of this arousal include accelerated heart rate, quickened breathing, increased blood pressure, and profuse perspiration. This scenario illustrates a case of **acute stress,** a temporary pattern of stressor-activated arousal with a distinct onset and limited duration first described by physiologist Walter Cannon almost a century ago (Cannon, 1914).

Almost instantaneously, reactions in our nervous system, endocrine system, and muscles equip us to make an efficient and effective response—supplying, for example, extra strength if needed. **FIGURE 13•3** provides a detailed illustration of the many ways the body prepares for an emergency response.

The fight-or-flight response can be a lifesaver when you need to escape from a fire, confront a hostile rival, or swerve to avoid an oncoming car. When faced with a chronic stressor, though, it has a cost: Staying physiologically "on guard" against a threat eventually wears down the body's natural defenses. In this way, facing frequent stress—or frequently interpreting experiences as stressful—can create a serious health risk: An essentially healthy stress response can become a health hazard. In the next section, we will explore exactly how and why this occurs.

The General Adaptation Syndrome   Our understanding of how stress causes illness began in the mid-20th century with the work of Canadian endocrinologist Hans Selye (pronounced *SELL-yeh*). In brief, Selye discovered that different stressors trigger essentially the same systemic reaction, or general physical response, which mobilizes the body's resources to deal with the threat. Moreover, he found, all stressors provoke some attempt at adaptation or adjustment of the body to the stressor. Because the bodily response was a general rather than a specific adaptation effort, Selye dubbed it the **general adaptation syndrome (GAS)** (see **FIGURE 13•4**).

Normally, these responses are helpful, but under chronically stressful conditions, they can lead to heart disease, asthma, headache, gastric ulcers, arthritis, and a variety of other disorders (Carlson, 2007; Salovey et al., 2000). Selye's model of the GAS describes a three-phase response to any threat, consisting of an *alarm phase,* a *resistance phase,* and an *exhaustion phase* (Johnson, 1991; Selye, 1956, 1991).

The Alarm Phase.   In the first stage of stress, the body's warning system activates and begins to mobilize its resources against the stressor. Selye called this first stage the **alarm phase**—but it is similar to the pattern of reactions Cannon called the fight-or-flight response. The hypothalamus sets off two parallel emergency messages. One message signals the hormone system, especially the adrenal glands, through the

---

acute stress   A temporary state of arousal, caused by a stressor, with a distinct onset and limited duration.

general adaptation syndrome (GAS)   A three-phase pattern of physical responses to a chronic stressor.

alarm phase   First phase of the GAS, during which body resources are mobilized to cope with the stressor.

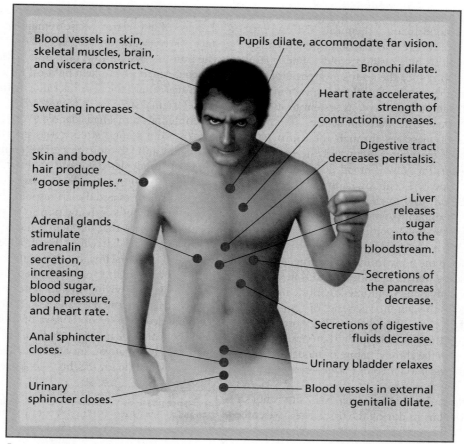

Blood vessels in skin, skeletal muscles, brain, and viscera constrict.

Sweating increases

Skin and body hair produce "goose pimples."

Adrenal glands stimulate adrenalin secretion, increasing blood sugar, blood pressure, and heart rate.

Anal sphincter closes.

Urinary sphincter closes.

Pupils dilate, accommodate far vision.

Bronchi dilate.

Heart rate accelerates, strength of contractions increases.

Digestive tract decreases peristalsis.

Liver releases sugar into the bloodstream.

Secretions of the pancreas decrease.

Secretions of digestive fluids decrease.

Urinary bladder relaxes

Blood vessels in external genitalia dilate.

[**FIGURE 13•3**] **Bodily Reactions to Stress** An amazing array of physiological reactions prepare us to fight or flee in acute stressful situations.

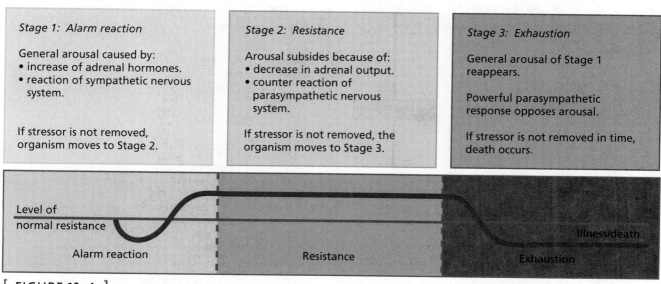

Stage 1: Alarm reaction

General arousal caused by:
• increase of adrenal hormones.
• reaction of sympathetic nervous system.

If stressor is not removed, organism moves to Stage 2.

Stage 2: Resistance

Arousal subsides because of:
• decrease in adrenal output.
• counter reaction of parasympathetic nervous system.

If stressor is not removed, the organism moves to Stage 3.

Stage 3: Exhaustion

General arousal of Stage 1 reappears.

Powerful parasympathetic response opposes arousal.

If stressor is not removed in time, death occurs.

Level of normal resistance

Alarm reaction

Resistance

Exhaustion

Illness/death

[**FIGURE 13•4**] **The General Adaptation Syndrome** In Stage 1, the body produces an emergency arousal response to a stressor. Then, in Stage 2, the body adapts to the continuous presence of the stressor. In Stage 3, if the stressor is not reduced, an arousal response begins again, although the body's defenses are depleted—with dangerous results.

pathway shown in FIGURE 13•5. The result is a flood of steroid hormones into the bloodstream—chemicals that support strength and endurance (the reason why some athletes might risk dangerous side effects by abusing steroids). Endorphins are also released, which reduce the body's awareness of pain signals. A concurrent message is relayed through the sympathetic division of the autonomic nervous system to internal organs and glands, arousing the body for action.

It's the cascade of messages through these two pathways—the sympathetic nervous system and the endocrine system—that readies us for action. Blood flow to the heart, brain, and muscles increases, enabling us to think and react better and faster. Blood flow to the digestive system, conversely, decreases—presumably so our bodies are not expending precious energy on nonessential functions during an emergency. Pupils dilate, enhancing peripheral vision, and perspiration helps keep the body from overheating. Available blood sugar increases as well, to provide an additional energy boost. All in all, our body is highly attuned to immediate danger. FIGURE 13•6 details this autonomic series of responses.

The function of the alarm phase is to enable the organism to fight or to flee from the threat, which usually didn't last very long for our ancestors. Given the chronic nature of modern stresses, though, we often progress into the second stage—resistance.

The Resistance Phase. If the stressor persists—but is not so strong that it overwhelms us during the first stage—we enter

the **resistance phase,** during which all the physiological changes of the alarm phase remain in effect. During this stage, the body attempts to fight off the effects of the stressor. The immune system is in high gear as well, and white blood cell count increases to help fight off infection.

Surprisingly, the resistance during this stage applies only to the original stressor. In his research, Selye found that if an experimental animal had adapted to one stressor (e.g., electric shock), but a second stressor was introduced (e.g., extreme cold), the animal soon died. The animal's resources were apparently so depleted it could not mobilize a defense against the new stressor. A tragic human example is found in a soldier who collapses and dies in response to the new stress of a prison camp after surviving months of stressful combat.

Thus, we see that our alarm and resistance defenses use physical energy. They reduce the resources available in case of additional stressors. Imagine this scenario, for example: You've just completed final exams; you've had minimal sleep, studying day and night, surviving on junk food and caffeine for a week. Now it's over. You can relax and rest at last. But the phone rings: It's the welcome voice of the love of your life, with an unwelcome note of some negative emotion. Before you can announce the good news that you survived your exams, the voice says, "I don't know how to say this, but—look, we have to talk . . ." This

---

resistance phase Second phase of the GAS, during which the body adapts to and maintains resources to cope with the stressor.

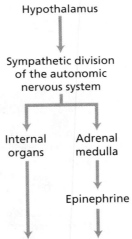

Hypothalamus

↓

Sympathetic division of the autonomic nervous system

Internal organs   Adrenal medulla

↓

Epinephrine

- Heart rate increases.
- Blood pressure increases.
- Blood sugar rises.
- Blood flow to gut decreases.
- Blood flow to heart, brain, and muscles increases.
- Perspiration increases.
- Pupils dilate.

[**FIGURE 13•5**] **Hormonal Response in the Alarm Phase** In the alarm phase of the GAS, the hormone system response shown here is one of the two parallel response pathways set off by the hypothalamus.

[**FIGURE 13•6**] **Sympathetic Nervous System Response in the Alarm Phase** This diagram shows the path of the sympathetic nervous system's response to acute stress, which occurs simultaneously with the parallel response of the hormone system.

Hypothalamus

Pituitary

Adrenal glands

Steroid hormones release

is probably not good news and may signal serious trouble, even a breakup—definitely a stressor. Already exhausted by the stresses of finals week, how will you handle this important conversation? You feel stricken, frightened, and even angry: Why this threat? Why now? Because your system is depleted, you may overreact and find yourself without the cognitive and emotional resources to handle the situation effectively.

The Exhaustion Phase. The resistance phase is the body's last-ditch effort to combat the stressor, and if the stressful situation is not ameliorated during that phase, the body can no longer keep up its intense physiological battle. In this third stage, the **exhaustion phase,** body functions drop back into normal range—and then fall below normal. At this point, the body requires rest and rejuvenation to bring our physiological functioning back up to acceptable levels. If it does not get that much-needed respite, as is often the case in today's world of chronic stressors, the very responses that were so adaptive in the first two phases put the body at risk for illness in the third phase.

Several processes may contribute to the physical and mental deterioration seen in the exhaustion phase. For example, increased blood pressure can cause headaches in the short term and, over an extended period of time, contribute to stroke and coronary heart disease (CHD)—two leading causes of death. Meanwhile, the compromised digestive system contributes to formation of certain types of ulcers and, over the long term, obesity. Chronic stress is also linked to increased fatty deposits in the bloodstream, which increases risk of stroke. Still other dangers lurk in the depleted immune system, making the stressed person a prime candidate for infections or other diseases. In addition, prolonged or repeated stress may produce long-term changes in the brain that provoke depression (Sapolsky, 1998; Schulkin, 1994). Stress hormones also act on the brain, interfering with its ability to regenerate neurons, especially in the hippocampus (Gould et al., 1998; Sapolsky, 1998). This helps explain why prolonged use of steroids—which are really stress hormones—is dangerous (except under certain

After responding to one stressor, such as finishing a difficult test, you may find your bodily resources somewhat depleted, leaving you less able to deal with another, unexpected stressor.

medical conditions): Long-term steroid use effectively sends the body into the final stage of the GAS, the stage of exhaustion, producing perilous deterioration.

So we see that Selye's GAS model offers a useful explanation of how stress can lead not only to the initial fight-or-flight reaction but also to chronic and debilitating conditions. And while new research is beginning to reveal that not all stresses produce exactly the same response from the endocrine system (Kemeny, 2003), the model remains widely accepted as the key to understanding the link between stress and illness. Before we look more closely at the details of the chronic stress response, let's first consider an intriguing alternative to fight-or-flight: nurturance. ✳

✳ **Explore** the **Concept** Selye's General Adaptation Syndrome at **MyPsychLab**

Tend and Befriend Psychologist Shelley Taylor noticed that the fight-or-flight model was developed by male theorists doing research with male subjects—male rats, mice, and humans. The fear and aggression so prominent in fight-or-flight may, noted Taylor, characterize the responses of males more than females (Taylor, 2003; Taylor et al., 2000b). A **tend-and-befriend** model may better explain the behavior of females in response to threats to themselves and their offspring. Taylor's theory argues that, because females are the primary caretakers of offspring, female biology assigns priority to protecting the survival of the young. From this perspective, fight-or-flight makes no sense. Aggression ("fight") can cause injury to oneself or one's children; escape ("flight") leaves children defenseless. Neither response promotes adaptation and survival from the female caretaker's point of view (Volpe, 2004).

This tend-and-befriend model proposes that females are biologically predisposed—through brain and hormonal activity—to respond to threat by nurturing and protecting their offspring. Seeking social support creates networks that increase an individual's ability to protect and nurture (Eisler & Levine, 2002; Taylor et al., 2000b). One study in support of the tend-and-befriend model examined men's and women's hormonal changes and self-reports prior to an important examination. While reported anxiety levels did not differ, men had significantly higher levels of **cortisol** production—an important steroid in the fight-or-flight response—than did women (Ennis et al., 2001). Additional research reveals that **oxytocin,** another stress hormone released on exposure to a stressor, may combine with estrogen in females to prompt affiliation-seeking behavior (Taylor, 2006). Higher oxytocin levels are also associated

exhaustion phase Third phase of the GAS, during which the body's resources become depleted.

tend-and-befriend Stress response model proposing that females are biologically predisposed to respond to threat by nurturing and protecting offspring and seeking social support.

cortisol A steroid produced by the fight-or-flight response.

oxytocin A hormone produced (by both women and men) in response to a stressor.

exhaustion phase Third phase of the GAS, during which the body's resources become depleted.

with greater calmness and decreased anxiety, which are important components of effective nurturing.

It might surprise you to know that both men and women seek social support as a stress response, although evidence at this point indicates women respond this way more frequently and consistently than men (Tamres et al., 2002). For women with early-stage breast cancer, for example, emotional support from their spouses buffered their daily stress (Gilmore et al., 2011). Importantly, however, the amount of support they needed from their spouses rose as their level of distress rose. Researchers urge spouses to understand the greater need and find ways to provide it rather than becoming disheartened and giving up. And doing so may benefit their own health; research indicates a lower mortality rate for older adults who give help and emotional support to friends, relatives, and neighbors (Brown et al., 2003).

The picture emerging from these complementary responses to stressful situations—fight-or-flight and tend-and-befriend—is of a more complex stress response than previously thought. We now see a response system that has evolved to enable both self-protection and reaching out to others in times of danger (Pitman, 2003). Tending and befriending powerfully complements the fight-or-flight pattern, together accounting for the survival not only of individuals but also of relationships and communities.

Stress and the Immune System

Earlier in this section, we noted that the immune system becomes compromised in the face of stress—specifically, when we enter the exhaustion phase of the GAS. Research has shown, for example, that individuals coping with the death of a spouse or the end of an important long-term relationship are frequently subject to both depression and **immunosuppression** (impairment in the function of the immune system), leaving them more vulnerable to disease (Cohen & Syme, 1985; Kiecolt-Glaser & Glaser, 1987, 2001).

Psycho-Neuroimmunology In recent years, advances in biotechnology have spurred the development of an exciting new field that seeks to understand how stress causes disease. **Psycho-neuroimmunology** pulls together psychologists with expertise in psychological factors of stress, such as cognition and emotion; neuroscientists, who study brain functioning; and immunologists, who have extensive knowledge of the immune system. While the field has an impressive multisyllabic title, interest in the mind–body connection is not new: In many ways, psycho-neuroimmunology is simply the rigorous study of questions pondered more than 2,000 years ago by ancient civilizations such as the Greeks and Chinese.

Bi-Directional Links between the Brain and Body A primary goal of psycho-neuroimmunology is to examine how

psychological and immunological processes influence each other and, in turn, how they are influenced by the external social world. Fundamental to this mission is the fact that the brain and periphery of the body communicate in a bidirectional fashion (Maier & Watkins, 1999). When a stressor is experienced, for example, the brain signals the adrenal glands to secrete cortisol, a major stress hormone. Cortisol then sends signals back to the brain to regulate its own production (Maier & Watkins, 2000). Psychological stress also activates the immune system. Among the chemical messengers shuttling between the brain and the immune system are proteins known as **cytokines.** One of the most interesting aspects of cytokines is that they signal the central nervous system to elicit behavioral changes that include fatigue, fever, and social-behavioral withdrawal. These changes are helpful because they help organisms recuperate and recover from illness or injury (DeAngelis, 2002a). If prolonged, however, these changes can increase risk for disorders, such as psychological depression. Again, we see the parallels with the functioning of the general adaptation syndrome, GAS.

In one of the first studies to examine how the brain regulates cytokine responses to stress, psychologist George Slavich asked participants to give an impromptu speech in front of an imposing panel of raters wearing white lab coats. As expected, people's cytokine levels increased significantly during the impromptu speech (Slavich et al., 2010b). Next, he scanned participants' brains while they played a virtual ball-tossing game in which they were suddenly excluded by two other players. When Slavich examined the cytokine and brain data together, he noticed that people who had greater brain-activity responses to being rejected had also exhibited more cytokine activity during the speech. What conclusions can we draw from these results? You'll recall that in addition to acting as "chemical messengers," cytokines can promote specific behaviors such as social-behavioral withdrawal. Consequently, the Slavich study helps explain how social stressors outside the body are translated into biological changes that can increase some individuals' risk for disorders like depression.

Stress Ages Cells. Psychological stress can also affect physical health by accelerating the rate at which cells age. One way to assess a cell's age is to measure the length of its **telomeres.** Telomeres are DNA protein complexes that cap the ends of chromosomes and protect against damage to DNA. In humans, telomeres shorten across the lifespan. Importantly, however, their length is associated with a number of diseases, including cancer, cardiovascular disease, and several neurodegenerative diseases (Fitzpatrick et al., 2007). Shorter telomeres are even associated with early death (Cawthon et al., 2003).

---

psycho-neuroimmunology Multidisciplinary field that studies the influence of mental states on the immune system.

immunosuppression Impairment in the function of the immune system.

cytokines Hormone-like chemicals that fight infection and facilitate communication between the brain and immune system.

telomeres DNA protein complexes that cap the ends of chromosomes and protect against damage to DNA.

In a landmark study examining the effects of stress on telomere length, psychologist Elissa Epel found that women who cared for a child with a serious illness had an accelerated rate of immune cell telomere shortening (Epel et al., 2004). In fact, women reporting high levels of stress had telomeres that were nine to 17 years "older." Subsequent research demonstrated that this effect may be explained in part by people's level of pessimism or their tendency to expect negative outcomes in the future (O'Donovan et al., 2009). Thus, those women with high levels of pessimistic tendencies were more likely, when stressed, to have developed older telomeres than peers with more optimistic outlooks. This is an important point because it shows that cognitive appraisals play a critical role in the stress–illness relationship. What are other reasons for why some people get ill when faced with stress while others do not? We devote the second half of this chapter to answering that very question.

psychology matters

Cognitive Appraisal of Ambiguous Threats

In the aftermath of 9/11, many of the first responders continued to work on site at the WTC for months after the explosive destruction of the twin towers. When authorities from the Environmental Protection Agency (EPA) and the mayor of New York City announced that the air was safe to breathe, many workers took off their safety masks, which were hot and impaired visibility. But was that "all clear" announcement really accurate? Dust an inch thick covered window frames as far as a mile from the smoldering debris on the "pile" at the WTC. Think about what must have been the fall-out from two airliners crashing into and demolishing two 110-story office buildings. What would you expect to find upon close inspection of that site? And what do you imagine was the psychological reason for the upbeat, positive public announcement by the EPA when on the ground conditions were so unhealthy?

Almost a decade later, the *New York Times* (2011) published this report on that "secondary tragedy"—the subsequent health damage to WTC first responders from having been encouraged by government officials that the air was safe to breathe when, in fact, it was lethal to do so.

Scientists have called the dust, smoke and ash unleashed by the destruction of the World Trade Center on Sept. 11, 2001, the greatest acute environmental disaster in New York City history. Fires burning at 1,000 degrees created a toxic plume that clouded lower Manhattan and spread to adjoining areas. The collapsing towers pulverized cement and everything the buildings contained, including some asbestos, while the tremendous pressure of the collapsing floors fused materials together in potentially dangerous combinations that scientists had not seen before.

Officials and medical experts estimate that in all, between 40,000 and 90,000 workers and volunteers spent time on the debris pile and may have been affected in some way by the dust. More than 9,000 workers at ground zero brought lawsuits against 90 government agencies and private companies related to illnesses and injuries they say stemmed from working at the site.

Were officials deliberately lying, then, when they made the announcement that the air was safe to breathe? Assuming they were fully cognizant of the dangers that were later discovered could be indicative of a judgment error known as the hindsight bias—similar to Monday-morning quarterbacks' analysis of what went wrong in the previous day's football game. While—with the benefit of hindsight—it may be easy to see the magnitude of the danger that workers faced, at the time, officials may have been overwhelmed by a variety of diverse predictions made in the face of a situation they had never before encountered. Similar processes may have been functioning in Japan's official optimistic announcements in the first few days following the 2011 quake, tsunami, and subsequent nuclear breach.

We must also acknowledge the power of cognitive appraisal. To make an effective cognitive appraisal of a situation, we must have a concrete understanding of the nature of the threat. For example, the victims of the 9/11 terrorist attacks indisputably experienced distress, recognizing the specific dangers in which they were immersed. But in the years following the attacks, airplane travelers also felt some distress when the government's color-coded warning system—created to assess terrorist threat level and keep the public informed—announced an increased terrorist

After the collapse of the twin towers on 9/11, many first responders continued to work on site for months without the protection of their safety masks.

[CONNECTION] Hindsight bias is the tendency, after an event, to assume that signs were evident and that the event could have been predicted.

threat level just before flying. Curiously, the advisory system created enough public confusion and distress—as well as public distrust about possible political motives for alerts imposed just prior to national elections (Zimbardo, 2004a)—that the system was scrapped in 2011. Here's the point: Uncertainty can add to the perceived stress of a situation. Thus, interpretation, or *cognitive appraisal,* can make the accumulated distress from a series of vague threats evoke essentially the same stress response as a single major traumatic incident.

In light of what you learned in the previous section about the stress response and about stress and our immune system, if you were a government official, what decisions and announcements would you make to the public about potential threats if the nature of the true threat was not yet known?

CHECK YOUR UNDERSTANDING

✓—Study and Review at MyPsychLab

1. **Recall:** The first stage in Selye's GAS is.

2. **Recall:** In George Slavich's research on social rejection as an external stressor that can lead to depression, what is the chemical messenger that mediates between the external event and the psychological state?
   a. cytokines
   b. telomeres
   c. oxytocin
   d. both a and b

3. **Synthesis:** According to researcher Shelley Taylor, how might the responses of a man and a woman differ in the face of the same stressor?

4. **Application:** Which of the following stressors would be the most likely to cause the immune system to malfunction and even cause harm?
   a. accidentally slipping and falling on an icy surface
   b. caring for a dying family member for a prolonged period
   c. being rejected by someone you are romantically interested in
   d. receiving a bad grade on an important test

5. **Understanding the Core Concept:** Describe how our stress response system is well suited to acute stress but less effective in the face of chronic stress.

Answers: 1. c 2. a 3. Taylor's tend-and-befriend model would predict that the woman would be more likely to seek social support, while the man would be more likely to respond with the aggression characteristic of the fight-or-flight response. 4. b 5. The short-lived alarm phase of the GAS sets off a host of physiological changes that help us combat stressors. We can maintain these high levels of "combat readiness" during the resistance phase, but if the stressor is chronic, the exhaustion phase kicks in, and our immune system suffers the effects of depleted resources.

13.3 Key Question: Who Is Most Vulnerable to Stress?

Why do some people bounce back after severely traumatic experiences such as 9/11 or the death of a loved one, while others are derailed by seemingly minor hassles? The stress we experience is determined not only by the quality and intensity of the stressful situation but also by how we interpret the stressor. In this section, we will focus our attention on the personality characteristics that influence our responses to stressors. A summary of what we will learn is captured in our Core Concept:

CORE CONCEPT 13.3

Personality characteristics affect our individual responses to stressful situations and, consequently, the degree to which we are distressed when exposed to potential stressors.

Before we delve into this fascinating field of study, we want to introduce to you a model of the stress–illness relationship that will serve as our guide for the remainder of this chapter.

FIGURE 13•7 gives you a visual picture of this model, showing how stressors can lead to stress, which in turn can cause physical and mental illness. Please take a close look at this figure before reading further. Note there are two opportunities for intervention: One lies between stressors and stress, and the other occurs between stress and illness. To put it another way, one set of factors can prevent stressors from causing us to feel stress; similarly, a second set of factors can prevent stress from escalating into physical or mental illness. The first set of factors—those that can intervene in the relationship between stressors and stress—we call **moderators** because they moderate or regulate the impact of stressors on our perceived level of stress. Most of them are variations on the concept of cognitive appraisal. In other words, these moderators influence the judgments and interpretations we make of the stressor. It is this set of possible interventions that we explore in this section, beginning with an example.

Consider this scenario: Demetria and Cory are newlyweds planning their life together. They want to buy a home as soon as possible and hope to start a family. They have recently begun to argue about these issues, however, as their outlooks toward their goals differ markedly. Demetria is optimistic they'll be able to afford the down payment on a home within a year and believes they can achieve this goal as long as they carefully manage their money. Cory is less positive. In his mind, it seems as though every time he gets close to reaching a goal, something gets in the way, and he's sure this will be no different. To him, "what's gonna happen will just happen," and he is afraid they risk disappointment if they get their hopes up about getting the house in a year.

---

moderator Factor that helps prevent stressors from causing stress.

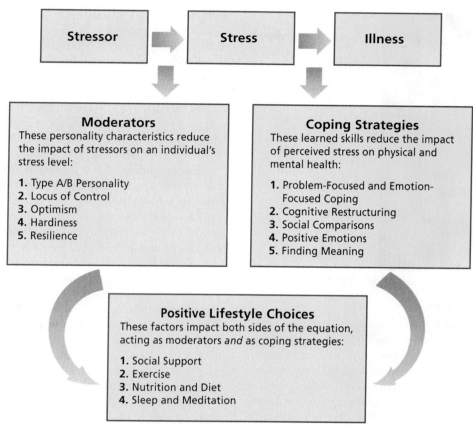

[FIGURE 13•7] **How Individual Factors Influence Our Stress Response**
Oftentimes, stressors cause stress, which in turn can cause illness. However, three categories of psychological responses can intervene in the stress–illness relationship. *Moderators* can help keep stressors from causing stress, *coping strategies* can help prevent stress from leading to illness, and *positive lifestyle choices* can intervene in both places.

[CONNECTION] *Personality* is the pattern of characteristics unique to an individual that persists over time and across situations.

Do you see yourself or someone you know in this example? If the different styles of approaching and perceiving events are long standing, consistent across situations, and similar to those of others, they could be called personality characteristics. Let's examine their impact on the stressor–stress relationship.

Type A Personality and Hostility

When cardiologists Meyer Friedman and Ray Rosenman (1974) hired an upholsterer to repair furnishings in their waiting room, the upholsterer noticed something the doctors had not: Most of the chairs showed an unusually high degree of wear on the front edges of the seats. When they became aware of this, the doctors wondered whether their patients' heart problems might be related to a certain style of coping with stress—it was as if they were always "on the edge of their

seats." The doctors began a series of studies to investigate their hypothesis, and interviews with patients revealed a striking pattern of common behaviors. Impatience, competitiveness, aggressiveness, and hostility—all stress-related responses—were noted again and again. Many also admitted they were notorious workaholics. Friedman and Rosenman ultimately found this collection of attitudes and behaviors not just correlated with heart disease but was actually predictive of it. They dubbed it the Type A pattern: Type A men and women were found to have twice as much risk of heart disease as the Type B individual, who takes a relaxed approach to life (Matthews, 1982).

Since the initial identification of the **Type A** personality, careful research has revealed that it is specifically the anger and hostility common in Type A people that increases risk of heart disease. Time urgency, perfectionism, and competitiveness, without the anger and hostility, are not risk factors. Hostile individuals are less trusting, quicker to anger, and

---

Type A Behavior pattern characterized by intense, angry, competitive, or hostile responses to challenging situations.

This basketball coach displays some Type A behaviors. What are they?

more antagonistic than their nonhostile counterparts. If you're noticing a connection to cognitive appraisal, you are right: Hostile people would be more likely than most to perceive threat in a situation. This interpersonal style makes it more difficult to maintain relationships, which in turn reduces availability of social support. Hostility is also associated with a variety of risky health behaviors—such as smoking, drinking alcohol, and overeating—that themselves increase risk of heart disease (Taylor, 2006).

From a physiological perspective, those high in hostility become aroused more quickly in the face of a potential stressor, exhibit greater levels of arousal, and take more time for their arousal level to return to normal once the stressor has passed (Fredrickson et al., 2000; Guyll & Contrada, 1998). Hostility is also associated with higher levels of cytokines, which can prolong the stress response (Niaura et al., 2002). Researchers aren't yet sure, though, whether these biological differences are entirely genetic in nature or partially a result of early childhood environment: Boys who grow up in families rife with conflict and low in acceptance and support are at greater risk to develop hostility (Matthews et al., 1996). At this time, both nature and nurture are thought to play roles in development of hostility and later heart disease. Clearly, though, there are multiple channels through which hostility promotes heart disease.

Let us reassure you that, while many people may sometimes feel angry, there are important differences between normal anger and a truly hostile personality style. We all feel angry at times in response to a negative situation—in these instances, anger can be healthy and even adaptive: It signals us that something is wrong and provides the energy to take measures to correct the situation. That type of normal anger stands in marked contrast to the hostile personality style, which reflects a long-term pattern of hostile behavior that manifests frequently across a variety of situations. The level of arousal is a distinguishing factor as well: It is reasonable to

feel irritated when a slow-moving vehicle blocks you in traffic, but feeling enraged is irrational and dangerous, especially if this becomes a common pattern in your life.

Besides cardiovascular diseases, other illnesses have been linked with Type A habits: allergies, head colds, headaches, stomach disorders, and mononucleosis (Suls & Marco, 1990; Suls & Sanders, 1988). Likewise, the perfectionism characteristic of Type A has been linked to anxiety (about reaching impossible goals) and to depression (from failing to reach them; Joiner & Schmidt, 1995).

Understanding the link between hostility and heart disease and between other Type A behaviors and their associated health risks can help in developing more effective disease prevention. Regular aerobic exercise, relaxation training, and even a program aimed at teaching hostile individuals to speak more slowly and quietly have proven effective at reducing risk of heart disease (Taylor, 2006). Comprehensive stress management training may offer some of the most promising benefits, however. One study in particular showed heart attack survivors given stress-management training had half as many heart attacks in the next three years as a control group who received no such training (Friedman & Ulmer, 1984). The researchers concluded: "No drug, food, or exercise program ever devised, not even a coronary bypass surgical program, could match the protection against recurrent heart attacks" afforded by learning to manage stress (p. 141). Thus, even though Type A behavior seems to show up early in life and persist into adulthood, well-designed interventions can be effective in helping Type As who are committed to change in their lifestyles.

Locus of Control

How confident are you that you can make your life turn out pretty much the way you want it to? In our example at the beginning of this section, newlyweds Cory and Demetria were struggling with their differences on this dimension of personality known as **locus of control** (from the Greek *loci,* meaning place). You probably remember our discussion of this concept in Chapter 10 on motivation, so you already understand it is a relatively stable pattern of expectations about our ability to influence the outcomes in our life. **Internals** (those with an internal locus of control) generally believe that if they take certain action, they are likely to gain the outcome they desire—diligent studying, for example, will result in good grades. **Externals,** on the other hand, see an unpredictable relationship between their efforts and their outcomes. They are more likely to believe that factors outside their control, such as the fairness of the test or how much the professor likes them, will have a decisive effect on

---

locus of control A relatively stable pattern of behavior that characterizes individual expectations about the ability to influence the outcomes in life.

internals People with an internal locus of control who believe they can do much to influence their life outcomes.

externals People with an external locus of control who believe they can do little to influence their life outcomes.

their grades—regardless of how much they study. In the face of a stressful event, internals are more likely to perceive the stressor as manageable than are externals, which leads to lower stress and, ultimately, to a variety of health benefits. And perception of control can, at least to some extent, be learned: Firefighters and other 9/11 personnel who were trained for such disasters experienced lower rates of PTSD in the years following the attacks (Perrin et al., 2007).

Locus of Control, Health, and Longevity

A landmark study illuminating the importance of perceived control on health took place in a Connecticut nursing home 30 years ago. Elderly residents on one floor were offered a variety of choices about their daily lives. For example, they were allowed to choose whether and when to watch available movies, how they wanted the furniture and personal items in their rooms arranged, and whether or not to have a plant in their room—which they were responsible for watering. In communications with this group, nursing home staff emphasized the residents' personal responsibility for their own satisfaction; the nursing home staff was happy to help in any way (for example, moving the furniture) on request of a resident. Residents on a different floor, matched on important characteristics such as health and age, acted as the control group. Here the staff took full charge of the residents' care, watering all the plants, assigning movie times, and arranging furniture as per administrative decisions.

[CONNECTION] Longevity is highly related to the time perspective future orientation of those who are highly conscientious.

The results? After 18 months, the "more responsible" residents were more active, more alert, and happier than the control group. What's more—in an entirely unexpected outcome—locus of control actually affected the residents' life spans. By the end of the study, the mortality rate of the control group was 67 percent higher than that of the group with increased personal responsibility (Rodin, 1986).

Locus of control impacts a wide range of health-related outcomes. In addition to being more likely to wear seat belts, exercise regularly, and pay attention to their diets—all of which have obvious health benefits—internals have better immune systems than do externals (Chen et al., 2003). They get sick less often and recover more quickly from illnesses and surgeries alike (Skinner, 1996). What's more, a strong sense of internal control actually dissolves the well-documented relationship between social class and health: Low-income individuals who have an internal locus of control are just as healthy as those with higher incomes (Lachman & Weaver, 1998).

Culture Affects Locus of Control

Cultural studies have identified an interesting distinction between perceptions of control in Western and Eastern cultures. **Primary control,** prevalent in the West, is the type of control discussed previously: taking action aimed at controlling external events. Eastern cultures are more likely to engage in **secondary control,** which emphasizes controlling one's reactions to events (Rothbaum et al., 1982). A culture's general value system, such as the individualist influences the type of control most highly prized and promoted in that culture. In Japan, for example, traditionally a collectivist culture, child-rearing practices encourage development of secondary control. Children are taught to adjust their reactions to a situation to help maintain social harmony. This stands in direct contrast to the individualistic approach to child rearing, which fosters efforts to control the situation itself. Research indicates that both strategies work well in the context of their respective cultures (Weisz et al., 1984). Furthermore, when efforts at primary control fail or are not possible for an individual, engaging in secondary control improves health—a topic we will explore a little later in this chapter.

[CONNECTION] *Individualistic cultures* value the individual over the group, whereas *collectivist cultures* prioritize group needs over individual needs.

Is Locus of Control Innate or Learned?

While locus of control does tend to appear early and run in families—factors that often indicate a genetic component—our experiences also impact our expectations. Individuals who repeatedly experience failure when they attempt to escape threatening conditions may simply stop trying, a concept called **learned helplessness.** Evidence of learned helplessness originally came from animal studies performed by Martin Seligman and his colleagues. Dogs receiving inescapable electric shocks soon gave up their attempts to avoid the punishment and passively resigned themselves to their fate (Seligman, 1975, 1991; Seligman & Maier, 1967). Later, when given the opportunity to escape the shocks, the dogs typically did nothing but whimper and accept them. In contrast, a control group of dogs that had not been subjected to previous punishment was quick to escape. Seligman concluded that the experimental group of animals had already learned that nothing they did mattered or altered the consequences, so they passively accepted their fate (Seligman & Maier, 1967).

An experiment by Donald Hiroto (1974) employed human participants in a variation of Seligman's dog research. One at a time, students were placed in a very noisy room; some found a way to turn off the noise, but for others, the noise controls did not work. When the students were sent to a new room and exposed to a different irritating noise, those who had successfully turned off the noise in the previous

---

primary control Efforts aimed at controlling external events.

---

secondary control Efforts aimed at controlling one's reactions to external events.

learned helplessness Pattern of failure to respond to threatening stimuli after an organism experiences a series of ineffective responses.

In hospitals and nursing homes, patients may learn to feel helpless because they are not given opportunities to make decisions or exert control over their own lives.

room quickly found the simple solution in the second room. In contrast, those who had failed in their efforts to shut off the noise earlier just sat in the new room, making no effort to stop the latest stressor. They had already learned to be helpless. Seligman and other scholars see symptoms of the same learned helplessness syndrome in a variety of human populations, including abused and discouraged children, battered wives, and prisoners of war (Overmier, 2002; Yee et al., 2003). Conversely, workers at all skill levels in a variety of professions report greater well-being when given some measure of control over their environment and working conditions (Faulkner, 2001; Zarit & Pearlin, 2003).

Thus, although we may be born with an individual predisposition to an internal or external locus of control, our experiences play a role as well. Research with 9/11 rescue personnel and regarding learned helplessness are just two areas in which this important fact has been illustrated.

Hardiness

One of the most effective stress moderators is **hardiness,** an outlook based on distinctive attitudes toward stress and how to manage it. In contrast with risky Type A behavior, hardiness is a personality pattern that promotes healthy coping. Hardiness first emerged in a large-scale study of managers working for Illinois Bell Telephone (IBT) in the 1970s and 1980s. Salvatore Maddi and a team of researchers from the University of Chicago gathered extensive data from the managers over a period of years, during which federal deregulation of public utilities resulted in massive layoffs and downsizing of IBT. Working conditions, positions, and expectations changed frequently, creating a highly stressful work environment. Two-thirds of the managers experienced negative health consequences, including heart attacks, strokes, depression, and anxiety disorders. The other third—exposed

to the same conditions—not only experienced no ill effects but actually appeared to thrive (Kobasa et al., 1979). The distinguishing factor, it turned out, came to be known as hardiness, a concept comprised of three specific characteristics:

- **Challenge.** Hardy people perceive change as a challenge to be overcome and an opportunity to learn and grow—rather than as a threat.
- **Commitment.** Hardy individuals become highly engaged in their lives, demonstrating a focused commitment to involvement in purposeful activity.
- **Control.** Hardy persons have an internal locus of control and are good at problem solving—that is, they have not become victims of learned helplessness.

Let's apply these three factors—known as "the three Cs" of hardiness—to the life of a college student. Suppose that on the day you must prepare for a major test, a friend confides in you about a terrible problem and begs for your help. These two stressors—an important test and a needy friend—could be overwhelming, especially if you are already stretching some of your resources to the limit. But a hardy individual would employ the "three Cs" to reduce the stress of the situation: commitment ("I'm committed to my friend and to preparing for this test; I'm not going to let either one down"); challenge ("Now I have two important things I need to do—what are my options for meeting both needs?"); and control ("I'll study all afternoon, talk to my friend over dinner—after all, I have to eat to keep my brain functioning—then review more before bed").

Hardiness has been shown to reduce the effects of stressful situations across a wide variety of populations: in businesspeople, children, couples, Olympic athletes, military, and law enforcement (Maddi, 2002). And—like locus of control—although some indications of a hardy personality show up early in life, hardiness can also be learned. Researchers have successfully developed hardiness training programs that help individuals learn more adaptive ways of reacting to stressors in their life (Beasley et al., 2003; Maddi, 1987).

Optimism

When you think about your future, do you generally expect good things to happen, or do you worry about all the things that could go wrong? Optimists see a future of bright possibilities; for them, "the glass is half full," whereas pessimists are far less positive, instead "seeing the glass as half-empty." And pessimism isn't simply a case of learned helplessness. "Life inflicts the same setbacks and tragedies on the optimist as on the pessimist," says psychologist Martin Seligman (1991), "but the optimist weathers them better." In general, optimistic people have fewer physical symptoms of illness, recover more quickly from certain disorders, are healthier, and live longer than pessimists do (Bennett & Elliott, 2002; Taylor

---

hardiness Attitude of resistance to stress, based on a sense of challenge (welcoming change), commitment (engagement), and control (maintaining an internal guide for action).

optimism An attitude that interprets stressors as external in origin, temporary, and specific in their effects.

et al., 2000a). What accounts for the differences? **Optimism** has a direct impact on health in that optimists feel more positive emotions, which in turn boosts their immune systems (Cohen et al., 2003). In addition, optimism aids in coping with stress via more active coping strategies, which we will discuss in the last section of this chapter.

A long-term research program by Seligman (2002) and associates indicates that an optimistic style of thinking makes three particular assumptions, or attributions, about negative events:

- They are the result of specific causes rather than global problems: *"I got a low grade on my last psychology test,"* instead of *"I'm doing badly in school."*

- They are situational rather than personal problems: *"It probably happened because I missed class the day before the exam when the professor gave a review session,"* rather than *"I'm not smart enough to do well."*

- They are temporary, rather than permanent: *"If I'm careful not to miss class anymore, I'll do better on the next test,"* rather than *"I won't be able to recover from this low score."*

Seligman, one of the founders of the International Positive Psychology Association, believes that an optimistic thinking style can be learned. One way to do so, he advises, is by talking to yourself in a particular way when feeling depressed or helpless. Positive self-talk, says Seligman, should concentrate on the meaning and causes of personal setbacks. For example, if a person on a diet splurges on a piece of dessert, instead of thinking, *"Because I've ruined my whole diet, I might as well eat the whole cake!"* she or he should think, *"Well, I enjoyed that, but I know I'm strong enough to stick to this diet most of the time."* In essence, Seligman argues that optimism is learned by adopting a constructive style of thinking, self-assessment, and behavioral planning.

In considering this, you might be reminded of the importance of cognitive appraisal in our stress response and of our Problem for this chapter concerning individual variations in the stress response. Learning to think more optimistically, or to respond with greater hardiness, changes our interpretation of a potential stressor and, thus, lowers our perceived stress. ◉

◉ |Watch the **Video** Optimism and
Resilience at **MyPsychLab**

Resilience

Actress Christina Applegate would seem to have a charmed life for her chosen profession. Born in Hollywood, California (1971), to an actress/singer mother and father who was a record producer, this beautiful, talented young woman went on to be the lead or supporting actress in dozens of films, television programs and Broadway stage shows. Winning numerous awards for her acting, with a popular fan base, she also hosted *Saturday Night Live* and was top of the list of the Most Beautiful People in 2009 of *People Magazine*.

A cancer-free Christina Applegate arrives at the "Stand Up To Cancer" event in 2010.

Beneath that public surface is a life filled with many sources of extreme stress. Her parents divorced soon after her birth. She divorced her first husband a few years after their marriage. Her close friend and former boyfriend died of an apparent drug overdose. The next month, Applegate discovered she had breast cancer that was treated with a double mastectomy operation. Early detection saved her now cancer-free life. How did she deal with the knowledge that she, like her mother before her, had developed cancer? She is reported to have said after her initial diagnosis: "I was just shaking and—and then also immediately, I had to go into 'take-care-of-business-mode.'" In an interview with *USMagazine.com* (2010), Applegate also said she has turned her life around in response to that life-threatening disease. "Right away, you kind of go gung-ho—you don't let any stress in your life, you don't eat any crap (food), you do a total 180 from where you were. You look at life a little bit differently." She has now dedicated herself to raising money for cancer research and treatment through her charitable foundation Right Action for Women.

Like cyclist star Lance Armstrong, whom we met in Chapter 9 on emotion and motivation, Christina Applegate's life has been filled with successes and setbacks. Is luck at work here? Instead, psychologists recognize in the decisions, attitudes, and behavior of both of these celebrities something more precious to well being than either talent or genius: **resilience.**

Resilience is the capacity to adapt and achieve well-being in spite of serious threats to children's development (Masten, 2001). In fact, the word *resilience* comes from a Latin root

---

resilience The capacity to adapt, achieve well-being, and cope with stress, in spite of serious threats to development.

meaning "buoyant"—literally bouncing amid waves. For more than two decades, most resilience research has focused on this quality in children and adolescents who have dealt with stressful life conditions, including parental neglect or abuse, parental mental illness, bereavement, and other serious risk factors. How could some at-risk children survive and even thrive when others became ill and failed *because* of the same types of risks?

Even at young ages, resilient children are distinguished by an assortment of qualities. They tend to have higher cognitive abilities, greater conscientiousness, better social skills, greater competence, and access to better caretaking or parenting resources (Masten, 2001; Riolli, 2002). Identifying resilient qualities so early in life supports the inference that one is either born resilient or not—it is an innate human quality. More recently, however, attention has been focused on the quality of resilience among adult populations and also on whether resilience can be learned.

One study of resilience among adults examined survivors of the 1999 conflict in Kosovo in the former Yugoslavia. Resilience was related to a combination of personality traits, including extraversion, conscientiousness, and optimism (Riolli, 2002). Of these, optimism in particular holds promise for helping people to become more resilient and less vulnerable or brittle. Also, you may have noticed that resilience seems to overlap somewhat with hardiness, and indeed the two concepts are related. While hardiness is focused on three specific characteristics, though, resilience encompasses a broader range of qualities. And, because hardiness can be developed with the help of specific training programs, perhaps the future will bring similar findings to resilience.

Psychologist George Bonanno of Columbia University is a pioneering figure in the field of bereavement and trauma. His extensive longitudinal and interview research on survivors of all sorts of extremely stressful experiences—from children to adults, in personal loss and major catastrophes—leads to the conclusion that "The ability to rebound remains the norm throughout adult life" (Bonanno, 2009). Based on his research, Bonanno finds that resilience and recovery are far more common than chronic dysfunction or delayed trauma. More detail about Bonanno's findings can be found in FIGURE 13•8.

Bonanno also coined the term *coping ugly* to refer to a variety of coping strategies that are helpful in stressful situations but might be inappropriate in normal circumstances. Among them are: self-enhancement biases, ego boosting, laughing and smiling, thought suppression, beliefs in personal mastery to survive no matter what, and others. His main point is that most of us survive anything and everything surprising well, and we do so using a range of personally invented strategies. It is a testimony to our human adaptiveness under almost all challenges. (Bonanno & Mancini, 2008).

Resilience: The ability of adults in otherwise normal circumstances who are exposed to an isolated and potentially highly disruptive event, such as the death of a close relative or a violent or life-threatening situation, to maintain relatively stable, healthy levels of psychological and physical functioning as well as the capacity for generative experiences and positive emotions.

Recovery: When normal functioning temporarily gives way to threshold or sub-threshold psychopathology (e.g., symptoms of depression or posttraumatic stress disorder [PTSD]), usually for a period of at least several months, and then gradually returns to pre-event levels.

Chronic Dysfunction: Prolonged suffering and inability to function, usually lasting several years or longer.

Delayed Grief or Trauma: When adjustment seems normal but then distress and symptoms increase months later. Researchers have not found evidence of delayed grief, but delayed trauma appears to be a genuine phenomenon.

[FIGURE 14•8] Bonanno's Trajectories of Psychological Functioning The first two trajectories, Resilience and Recovery, are common; the last two, Chronic Dysfunction and Delayed Grief or Trauma, are rare.

Source: Adapted from Bonanno, G. A. (2009). *The Other Side of Sadness: What the New Science of Bereavement Tells Us About Life After Loss.* New York: Basic Books; and Bonanno, G. A., & Mancini, A. D. (2008). The human capacity to thrive in the face of extreme adversity. *Pediatrics, 121,* 369–375.

The adjustments to crises revealed in the stories of Christina Applegate and Lance Armstrong are rather extraordinary, but their resilience need not be rare. In fact, many everyday heroes and "unknown celebrities" overcome terrible difficulties without our awareness. Their ability to deal with pain and challenge is actually the result not of extraordinary forces but of *ordinary magic*. It is the term that resilience researcher Ann Masten (2001) uses for normal adaptation processes, which, she argues, make people capable of greater outcomes than we might expect. By expecting more, perhaps we take a step toward greater optimism and resilience in our own lives.

psychology matters

Using Psychology to Learn Psychology

Imagine you have just suffered a loss: a friend picked a fight and insulted you, violating your sense of trust; the one you love doesn't return your feelings and has rejected you; or your family pet has died, leaving you grief stricken though friends insist you should "get over it." Whatever the stress, you aren't sure where to go or to whom you can talk—yet you feel a strong need to express your thoughts and feelings. What can you do? Here's a place to start: Write it out. In the process, you'll learn more about your own psychology.

Why write? Why not just rant and rave and get it out of your system? For one thing, aggressively venting emotions is not enough to relieve stress or support your health; on the contrary, it can even have aggravating or harmful effects (Gross & Psaki, 2004; Smythe, 1998). Conversely, writing about your fears and losses has therapeutic emotional effects (Pennebaker, 1990, 1997; Zimmerman, 2002), and writing about feelings and worries has been found to support the health of patients with immune disorders (Pennebaker, 1997). When you write out your thoughts and feelings, you talk only to and for yourself. With no audience to perform for and no patient listener to please, you can use frank language, tell all, and rest assured you don't have to explain anything. All you need is a place, a time, the materials you need, and commitment to maintain the habit. There are several ways to make the practice easier and more effective:

- Write in any medium that is efficient or comforting to you—it's OK to type at your keyboard, but you may not always have convenient access to your computer. Handwriting is more personally expressive, and you don't have to make it legible—it's for your eyes only. By using a pen and paper, you can not only write but draw or doodle, expressing yourself nonverbally. And a small notebook is inexpensive and easy to keep handy.

- Choose a topic or theme to get you started. If a loss or fear has prompted your writing exercise, start with that. If not, choose an "assignment" that prompts emotions and ideas about important challenges in your life. One professor asks students in a class on psychology of loss to develop a journal of loss, referring either to personal losses or to memorable events such as a terrorist attack or the death of a celebrity and what that has meant to the writer (Harvey & Hofmann, 2001).

- Write out your thoughts as well as your feelings. Focus on finding the meaning in difficult experiences. You may not know the answers (*"Why didn't our relationship last?"*), but you can reason and fantasize (*"Maybe this is a good time for me to be on my own anyway"*). An important purpose in therapeutic writing or talking is to achieve insight, growth, and change. It may also help to write out memories as if telling a story: with a beginning, middle, and end; descriptions of characters and events; and your own conclusions about the "moral of the story" and lessons you have learned (Harvey et al., 1990; Murray, 2002).

- Write in spare moments, setting a goal such as a few pages every week. Write as if you were a reporter, including whatever details seem important (DeSalvo, 2000). Experiment with various forms, such as writing love or hate letters. Identify blessings in disguise or categorize various things you do (e.g., things you do for others versus things you do for yourself; Zimmerman, 2002).

- Stick with it. Make writing a habit, not just a release for the bad times. One researcher found that writing only about trauma intensified the pain and left subjects less able to open up or work it through. So even at times when you don't "need" to write, write a few lines anyway—*because* you feel fine—so you can later remember that you have felt good and remind yourself how you got that way!

Your goal in writing is not to become a great writer (though it's possible!) but to work through your stress, learn about your responses and coping patterns, and heal. You set the goals, you make the rules. In doing so, you might consider how to incorporate some of what you have learned in this section about perceptions and hardiness. Perhaps, through writing, we can focus on improving our abilities to perceive stressors in an adaptive manner. In addition, remember our discussion in the first Core Concept of this chapter about the importance of narratives. But don't let it stress you out! Issue these writing "assignments" to yourself, so you can relax knowing there is no deadline pressure and no grade to worry about.

CHECK YOUR UNDERSTANDING

✓•[**Study** and **Review** at **MyPsychLab**

1. **Recall:** In terms of health, the riskiest component of Type A behavior is _____.

    a. hostility   **c.** competitiveness
    b. perfectionism   **d.** time urgency

2. **Analysis:** People who believe they can take action to affect their life outcomes have an _____ locus of control and are more likely to _____.

    a. internal; suffer more frequent frustrations
    b. external; suffer more frequent frustrations
    c. internal; live longer
    d. external; live longer

3. **Application:** Roz recently got a new assignment at work that she didn't really want. In responding to this change, she decided to see it as an opportunity for growth and to fully commit to doing whatever was necessary to do a good job with it. Which personality characteristic discussed in this section best describes Roz's response?

4. **Application:** Think of a recent negative event or situation in your own life. According to Martin Seligman, what three attributions should you make in perceiving the event/situation?

5. **Understanding the Core Concept:** Describe how personality characteristics fit into the stress–illness relationship.

Answers 1. a 2. c 3. Hardiness, as evidenced by Roz's high degree of commitment and challenge 4. Specific (rather than global), situational (rather than personal), and temporary (rather than permanent) 5. Personality characteristics moderate the relationship between stressors and stress by influencing the way we perceive and interpret stressors. People with more moderators feel less stressed when exposed to stressors and thus have greater resistance to stress.

13.4 Key Question: How Can We Transform Negative Stress Into Positive Life Strategies?

Is it possible to choose to live a long and healthy life? Or will your health be determined by factors out of your hands, such as your genetic background or your access to health care? After exposure to a traumatic stressor such as an earthquake or a chronic stressor such as the ones we have discussed in this chapter, is there something we can do to reduce its impact on our health?

By now, you've probably gathered that taking a hardy approach to these questions, with an internal locus of control and an optimistic attitude, will increase your odds of success! And there is more good news: Illness and mortality can also be affected by the coping strategies we employ and the lifestyle

President Obama made a positive lifestyle choice in early 2010 when he was finally able to quit smoking cigarettes.

choices we make (Elliott & Eisdorfer, 1982; Taylor, 2006). As you can see by "reading between the lines" in TABLE 13•1, many early deaths result from behaviors over which we have control. Stress, of course, is part of the lifestyle equation too. In this section of the chapter, we will explore effective ways of coping with stress, as well as lifestyle choices that can help us ward off the devastating effects of stress through better health. As our Core Concept puts it:

[TABLE 13•1] Number of Deaths for Twelve Leading Causes of Death

1.	Heart disease: 616,067
2.	Cancer: 562,875
3.	Stroke (cerebrovascular diseases): 135,952
4.	Chronic lower respiratory diseases: 127,924
5.	Accidents (unintentional injuries): 123,706
6.	Alzheimer's disease: 74,632
7.	Diabetes: 71,382
8.	Influenza and pneumonia: 52,717
9.	Nephritis, nephrotic syndrome, and nephrosis (kidneys): 46,448
10.	Septicemia: (bacterial infections): 34,828
11.	Intentional self-harm (suicide): 34,598
12.	Assault (homicide): 18,361

Note: In 2007, a total of 23,199 persons died of alcohol-induced causes in the United States. The age-adjusted death rate for alcohol-induced causes for males was 3.2 times the rate for females.

CORE CONCEPT 13.4

Effective coping strategies reduce the negative impact of stress on our health, while positive lifestyle choices can enhance our mental and physical health as well as our overall well-being.

Revisiting the model we introduced in the previous section (see FIGURE 13•7), **coping strategies** work by reducing the impact of stress—once we're feeling it—on our health. In other words, they decrease the effects of stress on our bodies. **Positive lifestyle choices** have the same power to help us cope effectively with stress and have an added benefit: They also act as stress moderators, diminishing the stress we perceive when exposed to stressors. That is, positive lifestyle choices increase our resistance to stress as well as our resistance to illness. We begin this section of the chapter by examining coping strategies that are most useful in combating stress. Then, we examine the lifestyle choices associated with stress reduction and disease prevention. Finally, we will look at the characteristics of people who say they have found happiness and a sense of well-being.

Psychological Coping Strategies

Earlier in the chapter, we saw how the Type A personality, pessimism, and learned helplessness can aggravate the stress response, just as hardiness, optimism, an internal locus of control, and resilience can moderate it. Certainly, we advise that for serious stressors and difficulties, you seek out professional advice and help. (If you don't know a psychotherapist or licensed counselor, ask a trusted instructor or health care provider for a referral.) What can you do on your own, however, to cope effectively with stress? And what exactly is meant by coping?

Defending versus Coping   There are two broad categories of stress management behaviors: defending and coping. **Defending** involves reducing the *symptoms* of stress or reducing one's awareness of them. For example, if you feel stress over an important psychology exam for which you feel unprepared, you might simply defend against that anxious feeling by distracting yourself with some activity that is fun—going to a party or visiting friends. Your defense won't make the problem go away—there will still be an exam, and now you'll be even less prepared for it! But for a brief period, you might feel less stress. Defending has the advantage of alleviating some symptoms like worry, discomfort, or pain; but it has the serious drawback of failing to deal with the stressor. Inevitably stress returns, only now it may be more difficult to alleviate.

In contrast with merely defending against stress, healthy **coping** involves taking action that reduces or eliminates the causes of stress, not merely its symptoms. To cope, you must confront the stress, identify the stressor, and develop a way of solving the problem or reducing the harm it causes you. This means not just feeling better but improving the entire stressful situation. To cope with stress over a looming psychology exam, you must (a) realize you feel unprepared for the exam, (b) identify effective strategies to study for the test, (c) implement the strategies in a timely manner, and (d) take the test. This way you will not only feel prepared, you will be prepared and feel less anxious. Of course, you may have to postpone having fun until after the exam, but you'll enjoy yourself more without the test anxiety. (Remember the Premack principle?)

[**CONNECTION**] The *Premack principle* notes the strategy of using a preferred activity as a reward for completing a less-preferred activity.

Problem-Focused and Emotion-Focused Coping   In general, there are two basic approaches to healthy coping: emotion-focused coping and problem-focused coping. **Problem-focused coping** involves clarifying the stressor and taking action to resolve it. This may involve some advance planning, such as when you are nervous about starting a new school. Problem-focused coping in that situation could involve a visit to the school to figure out where your classes are and to talk with an academic advisor to get some tips for success, thus reducing your anxiety about knowing your way around and about being able to do well. **Emotion-focused coping,** on the other hand, involves efforts to regulate your emotional response to the stressor by identifying your feelings, focusing on them, and working through them. Effective emotion-focused coping must be distinguished from **rumination,** which is dwelling on negative thoughts (rather than emotions); not surprisingly, rumination has been found to compromise our immune systems (Thomsen et al., 2004)—and it doesn't help us feel better either!

Both types of coping can be useful. In general, problem-focused coping is best when there is some concrete action that can be taken to reduce the stressor. In contrast, emotion-focused coping can help at times when you must simply accept a situation or when you need to work through your emotions before you can think clearly enough to act rationally (Folkman & Lazarus, 1980; Zakowski et al., 2001).

Sometimes, the two coping styles work best together. For example, if you get fired from your job, you might start

---

coping strategy   Action that reduces or eliminates the impact of stress.

positive lifestyle choices   Deliberate decisions about long-term behavior patterns that increase resistance to both stress and illness.

defending   Efforts taken to reduce the symptoms of stress or one's awareness of them.

coping   Taking action that reduces or eliminates the causes of stress, not merely its symptoms.

problem-focused coping   Action taken to clarify and resolve a stressor.

emotion-focused coping   Regulating one's emotional response to a stressor.

rumination   Dwelling on negative thoughts in response to stress, a behavior that compromises the immune system.

looking for another job (problem-focused) but find you can't focus on the task because you are too angry and confused about being fired. In that type of situation, try some emotion-focused coping to help yourself calm down and think more clearly. You might go for a run or to the gym, talk to a trusted friend, write in your journal, or engage in some other task that helps you work through your feelings. Alternatively, you might take a hot bath, get some rest, or eat something nourishing. Such emotion-focused coping is not merely a defense (as in distracting yourself completely from the problem). Rather, it focuses on processing your emotional responses before they career out of control and become hazardous to your health. Then, when you feel calm and prepared, you can concentrate on what it takes to address the stressor and solve the problem.

Cognitive Restructuring

Throughout this chapter, we have recognized the role of cognitive appraisal in the stress–illness relationship. And while the personality factors that make us less vulnerable to stress—such as hardiness and locus of control—are deeply ingrained in our general outlook, with a little conscious effort, we can apply their basic principles to our coping efforts (Kohn & Smith, 2003). **Cognitive restructuring** involves just that: cognitively reappraising stressors with the goal of seeing them from a less-stressful perspective (Meichenbaum & Cameron, 1974; Swets & Bjork, 1990). The approach involves recognizing the thoughts you have about the stressor that are causing anxiety, then challenging yourself to see the situation in a more balanced or realistic manner. Getting fired, for example, offers the opportunity to find a new job that is more enjoyable, offers better pay, or has more potential for advancement. Cognitive restructuring is especially suitable for people experiencing chronic stress. Indeed, it is one of the cornerstones of cognitive–behavioral therapy. This approach is more than just putting on a happy face; it puts people into a constructive problem-solving mode that facilitates effective action strategies.

Making **social comparisons** is a type of cognitive restructuring that specifically compares your own situation to others in similar situations. Health psychologist Shelley Taylor (1983) first noted the use of social comparison in a study of breast cancer patients. Some of them engaged in **downward social comparison,** in which they compared their own situations to those of women worse off than they were, which in turn helped them see their illness in a more positive light. (Please note that, in making these downward comparisons, no one is taking pleasure in others' pain; the strategy is simply noticing and acknowledging the existence of grimmer possibilities.) Others engaged in **upward social comparison** and used breast cancer patients who were doing better than they were as models and inspiration for improvement. Corroborating research has demonstrated that both types are effective coping strategies. In a sense, downward social comparisons represent a type of emotion-focused coping—in that the comparison ultimately makes you feel less worried—whereas upward comparisons are a type of problem-focused coping because the models serve as a guide for specific action (Wills, 1991).

Positive Emotions

If negative thinking and negative emotions such as hostility are stress inducing, then is the opposite true as well: Are positive emotions health inducing? Several areas of study indicate they may be.

One study investigated this question in a group of Catholic nuns who ranged in age from 75 to 95 years. Researchers gained access to autobiographies the nuns had written just prior to entering the convent (when most were in their early 20s) and measured the emotional content of the writings. Each one-page autobiography was rated for the number of positive, negative, and neutral emotional words used. Clear differences emerged: Nuns who used the most positive-emotion words lived an average of 9.4 years longer than those who expressed the fewest positive emotions! Moreover, expressing a wider variety of positive emotions in their autobiographies increased lifespan by an additional year (Danner et al., 2001).

Cultivating and expressing a sense of humor also buffers the effects of stress. The ability to find something to laugh about during exposure to a stressor not only improves mood but also decreases the physiological impact of the stressor (Dillard, 2007). Having a good sense of humor, as a personality characteristic, also appears to reduce an individual's cognitive appraisal of a stressor (Lefcourt, 2000; Kulper et al., 1993). These findings dovetail with work by Harvard psychologist George Vaillant, whose lifespan study of men noted joy in living as one of the key predictors of health and long life (Vaillant, 1990).

If you don't possess a naturally good sense of humor or don't characteristically experience a lot of positive emotions, you can still benefit from these tools in your coping efforts. Making a conscious effort to note positive moments in your

---

cognitive restructuring Reappraising a stressor with the goal of seeing it from a more positive perspective.

social comparison A type of cognitive restructuring involving comparisons between oneself and others in similar situations.

downward social comparison Comparison between one's own stressful situation and others in a similar situation who are worse off, with the goal of gaining a more positive perspective on one's own situation.

upward social comparison Comparison between one's own stressful situation and others in a similar situation who are coping more effectively, with the goal of learning from others' examples.

Feeling and expressing positive emotions can lengthen your lifespan.

life and to seek out situations in which you find humor and joy can and will improve your life, says positive psychology proponent Martin Seligman in his book *Authentic Happiness* (2002). A poignant expression of this was noted by an AIDS patient, who said this:

> Everyone dies sooner or later. I have been appreciating how beautiful the Earth is, flowers, and the things I like. I used to go around ignoring all those things. Now I stop to try and smell the roses more often, and just do pleasurable things (G. M. Reed, cited in Taylor, 1999).

Finding Meaning Viktor Frankl was a well-respected neurologist in Austria when Nazi forces deported him and his family to a concentration camp. They, along with thousands of other Jews, were subjected to various forms of deprivation, torture, and unspeakable atrocities, and many—including Frankl's wife and parents—died in the camps. Frankl, however, survived, and after the war ended, he made a significant contribution to the field of psychology with his work on the importance of finding meaning in seemingly inexplicable events such as what he had experienced in the camps. In his seminal work, *Man's Search for Meaning* (Frankl, 1959), he says, "When we are no longer able to change a situation—just think of an incurable disease such as inoperable cancer—we are challenged to change ourselves."

Frankl's hypothesis spawned research investigating the benefit of finding meaning in loss, which has identified two specific types of meaning, **sense making** and **benefit finding.** Following a significant negative life event, people try to make sense of the event in some way so it fits our perception of the world as predictable, controllable, and nonrandom (Tait & Silver, 1989; Tedeschi & Calhoun, 1996). For example, a death might be explained as inevitable if the person had been battling a long illness or if he or she had a history of heavy smoking. In the wake of Hurricane Katrina, discussions of long-standing problems with New Orleans' levees reflected a similar attempt for sense making. Individuals with strong religious beliefs may make sense of loss by attributing it to God's will. A second path to finding meaning lies in recognizing some benefit that ultimately came from the loss, such as a renewed sense of appreciation for life or other loved ones, or discovery of a new path in life.

Successful coping appears to involve both sense making and benefit finding, although at different times. Sense making is the first task people struggle with, but ultimately working through the loss and regaining momentum in life seems to hinge on resolving this first question and moving on to the second (Janoff-Bulman & Frantz, 1997). This may explain why people who have lost a child, individuals coping with an acci-

dental or violent death of a loved one, and others dealing with a loss that defies our perception of the natural order of life often have a harder time recovering from the loss (Davis et al., 1998).

Finding meaning in tragedy, then, is not an easy task. Is there anything that can help? Not surprisingly, perhaps, optimists have an easier time of it than do pessimists, especially with regard to benefit finding (Park et al., 1996). Strong religious beliefs appear to facilitate sense making, particularly with the loss of a child, as evidenced in a study of parents who had lost a child to sudden infant death syndrome (SIDS; McIntosh et al., 1993). And the benefits of social support—which we will explore shortly—are not limited to a particular personality type or to the religious but can play an important role in finding meaning of both types.

Psychological Debriefing: Help or Hindrance? On April 20, 1999, two heavily armed students at Columbine High School in Littleton, Colorado, carried out a planned massacre, fatally gunning down 12 students and a teacher before turning their guns on themselves. Those who survived needed help coping, but so did their horrified loved ones and the larger community. Although the vast majority of trauma survivors recover from early trauma without professional help, community leaders and mental health professionals may initiate counseling sessions—seeking out individuals or gathering groups in meeting spaces—in hopes of reducing posttraumatic stress. After the Columbine massacre, counselors visited all classes regardless of whether individual students had reported problems. Similarly, after the World Trade Center attacks, a program was funded to offer free counseling for New Yorkers—but only a fraction of the predicted number sought help, leaving $90 million in therapy funds unspent (Gittrich, 2003). Don't survivors want help—or isn't such help very effective?

This form of crisis intervention, called **psychological debriefing,** is a brief, immediate type of treatment focusing on venting emotions and discussing reactions to the trauma (McNally et al., 2003). This practice is based on the assumption that it is psychologically healthier to express negative feelings than to keep them inside. This belief, in turn, is based on the ancient concept of **catharsis,** which involves relieving emotional "pressure" by expressing feelings either directly (as by expressing them verbally or hitting a punching bag) or indirectly (as by watching a violent play or movie). Unfortunately, the theory of catharsis doesn't hold up to empirical scrutiny—rather than reducing arousal and feelings of distress, studies show it often prolongs them.

Critical Incident Stress Debriefing (CISD). Recently, a specific type of psychological debriefing known as **critical**

---

sense making One aspect of finding meaning in a stressful situation, which involves perceiving the stressor in a manner consistent with our expectations of the world as predictable, controllable, and nonrandom.

benefit finding The second phase of finding meaning in a stressful situation, which involves seeing some ultimate benefit from the stressor.

psychological debriefing Brief, immediate strategy focusing on venting emotions and discussing reactions to a trauma.

catharsis A theory suggesting that emotional pressure can be relieved by expressing feelings directly or indirectly.

critical incident stress debriefing (CISD) A specific type of psychological debriefing that follows a strict, step-by-step agenda.

incident stress debriefing (CISD) has emerged and taken center stage in the field of psychological debriefing. CISD programs typically offer group sessions to trauma survivors within 72 hours of the traumatic event; these sessions are two to three hours long and often mandated by organizations (such as by Columbine High School in the aftermath of the shooting and also in many police and fire departments). CISD programs follow a strict agenda that requires participants to first describe the facts of the traumatic event, then recount the immediate cognitive reactions they had to it, followed by their feelings and any symptoms of psychological distress they have begun to notice as a result. Next, program leaders offer information about frequently occurring symptoms and provide referrals for follow-up treatment. This is a commercial program that requires users to pay a fee to the CISD originators in order to employ these tactics.

Is CISD Effective? Does it really work as advertised? As we have learned, extraordinary claims require extraordinary evidence. Also, remember that we are biased when it comes to emotionally charged topics—our strong desire to find a "cure" can interfere with our ability to think critically about the evidence. In cases like this, it is all too easy to jump on the bandwagon of an exciting new treatment before it has been soundly tested. And while proponents of CISD argue for its effectiveness, very few studies have followed sound methodological procedures to accurately measure the outcomes (Devilly et al., 2006). On the contrary, some trauma experts are cautioning that the procedures of CISD can actually strengthen the memory of a traumatic experience—the opposite of helpful intervention. Moreover, the procedures involved in CISD run contrary to some long-established findings regarding the ineffectiveness of catharsis, which casts further doubt on the true efficacy of the program. The initial skepticism of your authors about this technique has been justified by several systematic evaluations, which have concluded that there is no value of such debriefing after psychological trauma work in helping trauma survivors (Beverley, et al., 1995; McNally et al., 2003).

One comprehensive survey of the effects of such techniques on first responders to the World Trade Center terrorist disaster concludes:

> Psychological debriefing—the most widely used method—has undergone increasing empirical scrutiny, and the results have been disappointing. Although the majority of debriefed survivors describe the experience as helpful, there is no convincing evidence that debriefing reduces the incidence of PTSD, and some controlled studies suggest that it may impede natural recovery from trauma (McNally et al., 2003, p. 45).

Cognitive and behavioral therapies that focus on cognitive reappraisal and use well-established procedures to reduce emotional arousal associated with the event may be more effective than CISD, especially when therapy is delivered not immediately but many weeks after the traumatic event (McNally et al., 2003).

These, then, are the coping strategies found to be effective in keeping stress from taking a toll on our health—problem-focused and emotion-focused coping, cognitive restructuring, upward and downward social comparisons, positive emotions, and finding meaning. Each of these factors offers an additional clue to help us understand individual differences in how stress affects us. As you consider your own use of these tools, please remember two things. First, people facing chronic stressors often rely on a combination of strategies. Second, there are also a number of lifestyle choices we can add to our "coping strategies toolbox" and gain the added benefit of moderating stress as well. We turn our attention next to a review of those factors.

[**CONNECTION**] Cognitive–behavioral therapies treat maladaptive behavior by helping to change both unwanted cognitions and unwanted behaviors.

Positive Lifestyle Choices: A "Two-for-One" Benefit to Your Health

If you are like most people, you like a bargain! We want the most for our money, the most for our time, and the most for our efforts. The positive lifestyle choices we will discuss in this section are bargains for your health, in that each investment you make in this category gives you not one but two benefits: They act both as moderators and as coping strategies (see **FIGURE 13•7**). The more of these you integrate into your life, the better health you will enjoy. Let's start with a little help from our friends.

Social Support One of the best antidotes for stress is **social support**: the psychological and physical resources others provide to help an individual cope with adversity. Research shows that people who encounter major life stresses, such as the loss of a spouse or job, experience fewer physical and psychological ailments if they have an effective network of friends or family for social support (Billings & Moos, 1985). They are less likely to contract colds and have less risk of depression or anxiety. Similarly, social support has demonstrable health benefits for those with physical disease (Davison et al., 2000; Kelley et al., 1997): Individuals diagnosed with conditions including heart disease, cancer, arthritis, and diabetes all recover more quickly with a good social support network (Taylor, 2006). By contrast, people with few close relationships die younger, on average, than people with good social support networks (Berkman & Syme, 1979; Pilisuk & Parks, 1986)—even when other factors known to affect lifespan, such as health and socioeconomic status, are controlled for. Remarkably, the lack of a reliable support network increases the risk of dying from disease, suicide, or

---

social support Resources others provide to help an individual cope with stress.

These women are doing two things to improve their health: spending time with friends and laughing.

accidents by about the same percentage as does smoking (House et al., 1988).

Benefits of Social Support.

What is it about social support that gives it such power to enhance our health? Research has revealed three specific benefits. *Emotional support* may be what immediately comes to mind when you think of social support, and this indeed is one of its benefits. Having trusted friends and loved ones we can count on during difficult times lends immeasurable relief. *Tangible assistance* comes in the form of specific, task-oriented help, such as rides to the doctor's office or hospital, help with housecleaning, or cooking meals. Finally, *informational support* aims to help an individual better understand the nature of the stressor as well as available resources to cope with it. In the aftermath of a serious auto accident, for example, someone with spinal cord injuries might benefit from information regarding a typical timeline and strategies for recovery but not be mobile enough to get to a computer to research it. A friend can help. And even though social support networks often consist of family and close friends, support groups or other community resources can provide these benefits as well.

Physiologically, social support reduces the intensity and the duration of the arousal associated with the fight-or-flight response. This finding has emerged from experimental studies that first expose participants to a stressor, then measure such responses as their heart rate, blood pressure, and levels of stress hormones either in the presence of social support or alone (Christenfeld et al., 1997). Social support in the form of a friend or loved one provides optimal benefits, but arousal is also reduced when the support comes from a stranger, a video (Thorsteinsson et al., 1998), or even a pet—although dogs somewhat outperform cats in this regard (Allen et al., 2002). And when social support is not present, simply thinking about loved ones even provides some benefit (Broadwell & Light, 1999).

Physical affection, such as hugs, hand holding, and touch, helps combat stress as well. Several studies note lower arousal in women exposed to a stressor when their partners held their hand or gave them a hug—and, recently, this effect was found in men as well (Coan et al., 2006; Light et al., 2005). For both sexes, as in animals, physical contact with a trusted partner raises oxytocin levels, which decreases anxiety and stress. These findings fit nicely with the tend-and-befriend model we introduced earlier in this chapter.

Supporters Reap What They Sow.

What impact does social support have on the supporter? People in need of social support sometimes worry they might raise their loved ones' stress levels by asking for help. And while this does sometimes occur—caregivers of Alzheimer's patients, for example, show greater risk of depression and disease—overall, support givers benefit from helping. In fact, one study of married couples measured amounts of support giving and receiving over a 5-year period and found that those who provided more support lived longer (Brown et al., 2003). It is important to note, however, that supporters need support as well.

Exercise For better or worse, our bodies are still better adapted to the strenuous, Stone Age demands of hunting and gathering than to sedentary life in a digital, urban world. Spending our days in relative inactivity at a desk or computer terminal is not a formula for physical or mental health. Unfortunately, while many of us may know this, few are taking it seriously—two-thirds of Americans aren't getting enough exercise, according to the Center for the Advancement of Health (2004).

Just 30 minutes of aerobic exercise per day lowers risk of heart disease, stroke, and breast cancer, among others (Taylor, 2006). It can increase muscle tone and eliminate fat—changes that produce a variety of health benefits. Most importantly, perhaps, it can prolong your life. A long-term study of 17,000 middle-aged men showed that those who were on an exercise regimen (the equivalent of walking 5 hours a week) had mortality rates that were almost one-third lower than their couch-potato counterparts (Paffenbarger et al., 1986). Even smokers who exercised reduced their death rate by about 30 percent.

Exercise is a good way to reduce stress and improve your general health.

Regular exercise has not only physical but psychological benefits, including stress reduction (McDonald, 1998) and mental health. For example, a regular aerobic exercise program improved the emotional health of female college students who were mildly depressed (McCann & Holmes, 1984). Another study found that a 20-week physical fitness course could produce measurably lower levels of anxiety in sedentary women (Popejoy, 1967). Exercise programs have also been shown to have a positive effect on self-concept (Folkins & Sime, 1981). And a study of people with depression found that compared to a group receiving antidepressant medication, those assigned to an exercise-only regimen had a similar decline in symptoms. Even better, the exercisers maintained their improvement longer and were less likely to become diagnosed again with depression than were nonexercisers (Babyak et al., 2000). 📖

📖● **Read** about Transformative Exercise at **MyPsychLab**

An exercise-for-health program has several big pluses. Exercise usually requires a change of environment, removing people from their daily hassles and other sources of stress. It also has a physical training effect by putting short-term physical stress on the body, which causes the body to rebound and become physically stronger. Third, when we exercise, we get a boost of endorphins and other pleasure chemicals such as serotonin, which improves our mood and makes us better able to respond effectively to potentially stressful situations. In this way, it moderates stress. The benefit of exercise as a coping strategy lies in its use as a healthy outlet for anger, as well as a facilitator of the cognitive functioning required for good problem solving. These benefits apply to all ages, from preschoolers to the elderly (Alpert et al., 1990).

Despite these advantages, most resolutions to increase exercise are short lived; people often find it difficult to maintain their motivation. Nevertheless, studies show that people can learn to make exercise a regular part of their lives (Myers & Roth, 1997). The keys are (a) finding an activity you like to do and (b) fitting exercise sessions into your schedule several times a week. Having an exercise partner often provides the extra social support people need to stick with their program.

Nutrition and Diet Good health and the ability to cope effectively with stress require a brain that has the nutrients it needs to function well. Fortunately, a balanced diet can provide all the nutrients necessary to accurately appraise potential stressors from a cognitive perspective. When we fuel ourselves with complex carbohydrates instead of simple sugars, for example, we metabolize the nutrients at a more stable pace, which may help keep us from overreacting. Many people, however, grab a fast-food meal or a candy bar instead of taking time for good nutrition. For example, a survey of students in 21 European countries revealed that only about half attempt to follow healthy eating practices. The same study found that women were more likely than men to be conscious of good nutrition (Wardle et al., 1997).

When chronic nutritional deficiencies occur in childhood—when the brain is growing fastest—development can be retarded (Stock & Smythe, 1963; Wurtman, 1982). Poor nutrition can have adverse affects on adults too. A diet high in saturated fat increases risk of heart disease and some types of cancer. Excessive salt intake increases risk of high blood pressure. Potassium deficiency can cause listlessness and exhaustion. One should be cautious, however, about going to the other extreme by ingesting large quantities of vitamins and minerals. Overdoses of certain vitamins (especially vitamin A) and minerals (such as iron) are easy to achieve and can cause problems that are even more severe than deficiencies.

What can you do to nurture your health through nutrition? The categories in TABLE 13•2 are good places to start. We suggest, also, you beware of nutritional fads, including dietary supplements that come with miraculous promises that seem almost too good to be true. Nutrition is a science in its infancy, and much remains to be discovered about its connections to physical and mental health.

Sleep and Meditation You learned about the benefits of good sleep. Sleep affects our health and stress in a variety of ways. First, given the link between REM sleep and cognitive functioning, we are reminded that to deal effectively with the cognitive demands of potential stressors, we must get enough sleep to enjoy the long REM periods that come only after about six hours of sleep. In addition to the increased risk of accidents chronic sleep deprivation has been linked to diabetes and heart disease, as well as decreased immune system functioning.

Meditation, which for many years was viewed with skepticism by Westerners, has earned increased consideration due to provocative new findings from a spate of studies. The ancient Buddhist practice of "mindful meditation" originated 2,500 years ago and, translated, means "to see with discernment" (Shapiro et al., 2005). Mindfulness-based stress reduction (MBSR), a modern variation on the Buddhist tradition, aims to increase awareness of one's reactions to stress, become at ease with them, and develop healthier responses. These goals are achieved in part through meditation that teaches the

[TABLE 13•2] Ten Steps to Personal Wellness

1. Exercise regularly.
2. Eat nutritious, balanced meals (high in vegetables, fruits, and grains, low in fat and cholesterol).
3. Maintain a sensible weight.
4. Sleep 7 to 8 hours nightly; rest/relax daily.
5. Wear seat belts and bike helmets.
6. Do not smoke or use drugs.
7. Use alcohol in moderation, if at all.
8. Engage only in protected, safe sex.
9. Get regular medical/dental check-ups; adhere to medical regimens.
10. Develop an optimistic perspective and supportive friendships.

20%   46%   27%   4%   2%   1%   0%

[**FIGURE 13•9**] **The Faces Scale** "Which face comes closest to expressing how you feel about your life as a whole?" Researchers often use this simple scale to obtain people's ratings of their level of well-being. As the percentages indicate, most people select one of the happy faces.

Source: Andrews, F. M., & Withey, S. B. (1976). The faces scale. *Social indicators of well-being: Americans' perception of life quality* (pp. 207, 306). New York: Plenum Publishers. Copyright © 1976 by Plenum Publishers. Reprinted by permission of Springer Science and Business Media.

participant first to focus on body sensations and cognitions involved in stress reactions and then to let them go by fully accepting (rather than judging or resisting) them. Research on MBSR indicates that participation in an eight-week training program reduces stress; decreases risk of anxiety, depression, and burnout; and increases immune system functioning (Carlson et al., 2007; Shapiro et al., 2005). This fascinating work is just one example of how, in the 21st century, the pursuit of health is relying increasingly on East–West collaborations.

Putting It All Together: Developing Happiness and Subjective Well-Being

Making changes to live a healthier life can lead to a feeling-good state that researchers call **subjective well-being (SWB),** a psychologically more precise term for what you might call "happiness." Do you usually have that feeling?

We cannot observe happiness directly. Instead, in SWB studies, researchers rely on respondents' own ratings of their experiences, answers to questions about what they find satisfying, and assessments of their well-being, mood, or success (Diener, 1984, 2000). To avoid confusion about what words like *well-being* mean, researchers also use nonverbal scales like the one in the smiley-faces in FIGURE 13•9 (Andrews & Withey, 1976).

Happiness, or SWB, is an increasingly popular subject of study with psychologists, evident in the emerging field of positive psychology. Accumulating research (Myers, 2000; Myers & Diener, 1995) shows that, despite many individual differences, SWB is defined by three central components:

1. *Satisfaction with present life.* People who are high in SWB like their work and are satisfied with their current personal relationships. They are sociable and outgoing, and they open up to others (Pavot et al., 1990). High-SWB people enjoy good health and high self-esteem (Baumeister et al., 2003; Janoff-Bulman, 1989, 1992).

2. *Relative presence of positive emotions.* High SWBs more frequently feel pleasant emotions, mainly because they

evaluate the world around them in a generally positive way. They are typically optimistic and expect success (Seligman, 1991). They have an internal locus of control and are able to enjoy the "flow" of engaging work (Crohan et al., 1989; Csikszentmihalyi, 1990).

3. *Relative absence of negative emotions.* Individuals with a strong sense of subjective well-being experience fewer and less-severe episodes of negative emotions such as anxiety, depression, and anger. Very happy people are not emotionally extreme. They are positive (but not ecstatic) most of the time, and they do report occasional negative moods (Diener & Seligman, 2002).

What underlies a healthy response on these dimensions? Twin studies show that feelings of well-being are influenced by genetics (Lykken & Tellegen, 1996), but biology is not destiny: Environmental effects are revealed in studies showing that people feel unhappy if they lack social support, are pressured to pursue goals set by others, and infrequently receive positive feedback on their achievements. Accordingly, experts in this field suggest that feelings of well-being require the satisfaction of (a) a need to feel competent, (b) a need for social connection or relatedness, and (c) a need for autonomy or a sense of self-control (Baumeister et al., 2003; Ryan & Deci, 2000).

So who are the happy people? What characteristics and experiences are linked with feelings of subjective well-being and happiness? Before reading further, take a moment to consider whether you think some groups of people are happier than others. If so, which ones? A review of the SWB evidence by Myers and Diener (1995) shows that:

- **Younger (or older, or middle-aged) people are not happier than other age groups.** SWB cannot be predicted from someone's age. Although the causes of their happiness may change with age (Inglehart, 1990), an individual's SWB tends to remain relatively stable over a lifetime.

- **Happiness has no "gender gap."** While women are more likely than men to experience anxiety and depression, and men are more at risk for alcoholism and certain personality disorders, approximately equal numbers of men and women report being fairly satisfied with life (Fujita et al., 1991; Inglehart, 1990).

---

subjective well-being (SWB) An individual's evaluative response to life, commonly called happiness, which includes cognitive and emotional reactions.

- **There are minimal racial differences in happiness.** African Americans and European Americans report nearly the same levels of happiness, with African Americans being slightly less vulnerable to depression (Diener et al., 1993). Despite racism and discrimination, members of disadvantaged minority groups generally seem to think optimistically—by making realistic self-comparisons and by attributing problems more to unfair circumstances than to themselves (Crocker & Major, 1989).

- **Money does not buy happiness.** It is true that people in wealthier societies report greater well-being. However, except for extremely poor nations like Bangladesh, once the necessities of food, shelter, and safety are provided, happiness is only weakly correlated with income. Poverty may be miserable, but wealth itself cannot guarantee happiness (Diener & Diener, 1996; Diener et al., 1993). The happiest people are not those who get what they want but rather those who want what they have (Myers & Diener, 1995).

- **Those who have a spiritual dimension in their lives most often report being happy (Myers & Diener, 1995).** This may result from many factors, including a healthier lifestyle, social support, and optimistic thinking. Whatever the reasons, spiritually involved people enjoy, on average, better mental and physical health (Seybold & Hill, 2001).

These findings tell us that life circumstances—one's age, sex, race, nationality, or income—do not predict happiness. The key factors in subjective well-being appear to be psychological traits and processes, many of which you have learned about in this chapter or elsewhere in this book. It is impressive to see how well people can adapt to major changes in their lives and still feel happy. For example, while the moods of victims of spinal cord injuries were extremely negative shortly after their accidents, several weeks later, they reported feeling even happier than they had been before sustaining their injuries (Silver, 1983).

It is possible to work at creating sustained happiness in your life, according to psychologist Sonja Lyubomirsky (2007), in the summary of her many years of scientific study of this elusive concept, *How of Happiness.* To do so involves a kind of social-emotional fitness training that encourages focusing on positive emotions, creating vibrant social support networks around yourself, goal setting, making and keeping commitments, working to stay healthy with an active life style, and being sociocentric, making others feel special. There is now a Happiness "app" you can buy for your mobile phone that gives daily exercises and activities that are fun and healthful.

Overall, studies of happiness and well-being show that people are exceedingly resilient. Those who undergo severe stress usually manage to adapt. Typically, they return to a mood and level of well-being similar to—or even better than—that prior to the traumatic event (Headey & Wearing,

1992). Using effective coping strategies and making smart lifestyle choices both increase the likelihood of positive outcomes. These, then, are the final components in our search to understand individual differences in the impact of stress on our health.

psychology matters

Behavioral Medicine and Health Psychology

Amazingly, 93 percent of patients don't follow the treatment plans prescribed by their doctors (Taylor, 1990). Obviously, this can have terrible consequences. Accordingly, the need to understand why people fail to take their medicine, get little exercise, eat too much fat, and cope poorly with stress has stimulated the development of two new fields: *behavioral medicine* and *health psychology.* **Behavioral medicine** is the medical field that links lifestyle and disease. **Health psychology** is the comparable psychological specialty. Practitioners in both fields are devoted to understanding the psychosocial factors influencing health and illness (Taylor, 1990, 2006). Among their many concerns are health promotion and maintenance; prevention and treatment of illness; causes and correlates of health, illness, and dysfunction; and improvement of the health care system and health policy (Matarazzo, 1980).

Both behavioral medicine and health psychology are actively involved in the prevention and treatment of trauma and disease that result from stressful or dangerous environments and from poor choices with regard to nutrition, exercise, and drug use. Both are emerging disciplines in countries all over the world (Holtzman, 1992). The two fields overlap, and the differences between them are ones of emphasis. Psychologists have brought increased awareness of emotions and cognitive factors into behavioral medicine, making it an interdisciplinary field rather than an exclusively medical specialty (Miller, 1983; Rodin & Salovey, 1989). Both fields also recognize the interaction of mind and body and place emphasis on preventing illness as well as on changing unhealthy lifestyles after illness strikes (Taylor, 1990, 2006).

But—as the saying goes—old habits die hard. To help patients change long-held habits that are harmful to their health, social psychologists have identified the specific persuasive strategies that are most effective (Zimbardo & Leippe, 1991). For example, research shows that people are more likely to comply with requests when they feel they

---

behavioral medicine Medical field specializing in the link between lifestyle and disease.

health psychology Field of psychology that studies psychosocial factors that contribute to promoting health and well being, and also those that influence illness, with the goal of educating the public about developing healthier life styles.

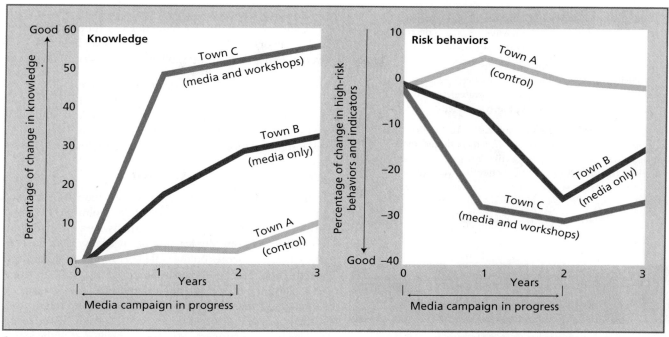

[**FIGURE 14•10**] **Response to Campaign for Healthy Change** Town A, whose residents received no mass media campaign for heart-healthy behavior, showed the least knowledge gain over two years. Town B residents, exposed to a media campaign, showed significant improvement. Knowledge gain was greatest for residents of Town C, whose residents participated in intense workshops and instruction sessions for several months prior to the media blitz. As knowledge increased, risk behaviors (bad health habits) and signs (indicators) decreased.

have freedom of choice. Therefore, instead of demanding that a patient strictly adhere to one course of treatment, a physician could offer the patient several options and ask him or her to choose one. Studies also suggest that patients are most likely to adhere to physicians' requests when they get active social support from friends and family (Gottlieb, 1987; Patterson, 1985). And one landmark study of heart disease prevention (see **FIGURE 13•10**) found that specific skills training, such as workshops designed to help participants implement positive changes to their health habits, was the key that resulted in greatest change (Maccoby et al., 1977).

Overall, the field of psychology has contributed numerous findings and strategies—based on solid scientific evidence—that can be applied to our efforts to improve our health, both physically and mentally. For example, behavioral principles can be combined with what we know about good thinking strategies and, indeed, often are combined in cognitive–behavioral therapy. Principles of emotion and motivation—the topics of Chapter 10—provide additional insight into factors affecting our emotional health and the behaviors that support our basic needs for food, social support, and other basic needs. You can apply many of these same principles on your own as you work toward maximizing your health and wellness—and we wish you well on your journey!

CHECK YOUR UNDERSTANDING

✓•⟦**Study** and **Review** at **MyPsychLab**

1. **Analysis:** Mai was recently in a car accident. In coping with the situation, she has focused on getting estimates for her car repair, seeking medical treatment, and working with her insurance agent to obtain compensation for the expenses of the car repair and her medical needs. What type of coping strategy is Mai employing?

2. **Recall:** In coping with a loss, efforts to make sense of what happened or to find some ultimate benefit from the loss are examples of _____, which is an _____ coping strategy.

    a. finding meaning; effective
    b. finding meaning; ineffective
    c. emotion-focused coping; effective
    d. emotion-focused coping; ineffective

3. **Application:** Think of a recent stressor in your own life. Now identify at least two ways that you can use cognitive restructuring to reduce the impact of the stressor on your health.

4. **Recall:** Name at least four lifestyle choices you can make that will reduce the impact of stress on your health.

5. **Understanding the Core Concept:** _____ reduce the effects of stress on our health, while _____ decrease our vulnerability to both stress and to stress-related illness.

   a. Stress moderators; coping strategies
   b. Positive lifestyle choices; stress moderators
   c. Positive lifestyle choices; coping strategies
   d. Coping strategies; positive lifestyle choices

Answers: 1. Problem-focused coping **2.** a **3.** You can compare your situation to those who are worse off, which should make you see your situation in a different perspective. You can also observe people in similar situation who are coping better than you are and can learn from their examples. **4.** You can seek social support, exercise regularly, eat a healthy diet, get adequate sleep, and meditate. **5.** d

---

CRITICAL THINKING APPLIED

Is *Change* Really Hazardous to Your Health?

The more we hear about the links between stress and illness, the more we might wonder if our own stress levels put us at risk. In this chapter, we have discussed a variety of factors that impact the stress–illness relationship. At least one issue, however, remains in question: To what extent do major life changes impact our vulnerability to illness?

Recall the Social Readjustment Rating Scale (SRRS) introduced in the first section of this chapter. Like many students, you probably calculated your own score in the *Do It Yourself!* box on page 610. But how should you interpret your score? If you scored high, does that mean you are at greater risk for illness?

What Are the Critical Issues?

Recall, first, that the SRRS lists 43 life events that purport to be stressful. Given what we've learned about the importance of cognitive appraisal in determining how stressful a situation is to an individual, we should probably take a close look at the list of events to see if each one really would qualify as a stressor in our own lives.

Does the reasoning avoid common fallacies? The SRRS can allegedly predict your risk of illness based on the events of the past year of your life. In other words, it presents a cause–effect hypothesis that the number of LCUs you have experienced in the last year will cause a particular risk of illness. Are the research findings in support of the LCU–illness relationship really causal, or are they merely correlational?

Extraordinary Claims Require Extraordinary Evidence. Second, if the claim that a quick and simple self-administered test can determine your risk for illness strikes you as extraordinary, you might be right. As we have learned, answers to questions psychological are rarely simple—humans are complex, and so are the explanations for our thoughts, feelings, and behaviors. At the very least, we might wonder if the SRRS oversimplifies the relationship between life events and illness.

Does the Issue Require Multiple Perspectives? Finally, we must acknowledge the many other factors involved in the link between stress and illness—such as those we have studied in this chapter—and ask what other perspectives might help explain the relationship between stress and illness.

What Conclusions Can We Draw?

In the first 15 years after it was published, the SRRS was used in more than 1,000 studies worldwide (Holmes, 1979), and research consistently found correlations between scores on the SRRS and both physical and behavioral symptoms. People with higher scores on the scale were more at risk for heart attacks, bone fractures, diabetes, multiple sclerosis, tuberculosis, complications of pregnancy and birth, decline in academic performance, employee absenteeism, and many other difficulties (Holmes & Masuda, 1974). High SRRS scores among federal prisoners were even associated with the length of their prison sentences. And the test was effective across cultural boundaries too: Both male and female respondents were found to rate events with similar scores (Holmes & Masuda, 1974), and ratings were also validated with Japanese, Latin American, European, and Malaysian samples.

However, the number of LCUs accumulated during the previous year is only a modest predictor of changes in a person's health (Johnson & Sarason, 1979; Rahe & Arthur, 1978). Many other factors—such as cognitive appraisal, stress moderators, and coping strategies—can intervene in the stress–illness relationship.

Moreover, the implication that stressful events cause illness is misleading (Dohrenwend & Shrout, 1985; Rabkin & Struening, 1976). The correlational data merely show a relationship between certain life changes and health; the research does not show that life changes are the cause of illness. The reverse could also be true: Illness can sometimes be the cause of life changes—someone who frequently gets colds or the flu is more likely to have problems at school, at work, and in relationships, for example. And remember the possibility of a third variable driving the relationship: Several other factors we've studied, such as economic status or Type-A hostility, could also be affecting both the frequency of life changes and the risk of illness.

The importance of multiple perspectives is critical to a thorough and accurate understanding of the stress–illness relationship. Let's review what we know about stress and health from the major perspectives we used to learn about psychology in this text:

- The *biological perspective* clearly plays a role in an individual's vulnerability to stress-related illness. We have seen that our hereditary makeup predisposes us to certain illnesses, such as heart disease, diabetes, obesity, and many forms of cancer. In addition, genetics probably gives some of us a better chance of being optimistic, hardy, or resilient—just as others of us are more at risk for hostility and other negative emotions.

- The *behavioral perspective* influences stress and illness in the health habits we learn as children growing up, in situations of learned helplessness, and in the coping strategies we see modeled by our parents and others in our immediate social environment. Likewise, the *socio-cultural context*—the culture in which we live—creates social norms that influence these learned habits and strategies. Currently, for example, in Western culture, we receive mixed messages about health. On one hand, we hear a lot about the importance of a healthy diet and regular exercise. On the other hand, however, the fast-paced nature of our culture—combined with a barrage of ads for fast food—encourages us to grab a burger and fries, then sit on the couch and watch television instead of working out and preparing a healthy meal.

- The *cognitive perspective* helps us understand why, in a particular culture, individual health habits and perspectives vary. Someone with an internal locus of control, for example, would be more likely than an external to pay attention to diet and exercise in pursuit of a healthy life. Likewise, an optimistic thinker or someone high in hardiness would be more likely to perceive certain life events as possibilities than as threats. In general, people's chances of incurring an illness may be more related to their interpretations and responses to life changes than to the changes themselves (Lazarus et al., 1985).

- The *developmental perspective* illuminates certain aspects of stress and health as well. College students, for example—who are primarily in early adulthood—are at change points in their lives and tend to get high scores; it is not clear, however, if they are more at risk for illness. Youth may offer some protection. Similarly, as our bodies age and our cells become less effective at regeneration, we develop greater susceptibility to illness in late adulthood. It is possible, though, that older adults who have mastered the challenges of generativity and integrity may offset their physical vulnerability with a better system of stress moderators and coping strategies. Much research remains to be done at the intersection of developmental and health psychology.

- The *whole-person perspective* explains many of the personal qualities that have an impact on an individual's vulnerability to stress. Locus of control, optimism, hardiness, resilience, and Type A behavior all originated in the study of personality psychology, and we have seen how these factors moderate an individual's response to stressors. Likewise, traits such as openness to experience and conscientiousness probably affect the degree to which individuals are willing to try new coping strategies or lifestyle habits, as well as their likelihood of sticking to the changes once they've made them.

Clearly, then, there is much more to the relationship between stress and illness than the particular life events you experience. A high score does not mean that illness is certain, nor does a low score guarantee health. People differ in their abilities to deal with change because of genetic differences, general physical condition, personality and outlook, lifestyles, and coping skills. The SRRS takes none of these factors into account, but it remains the most widely used measure of stress-related risk for illness.

Should you, then, pay attention to your SRRS score? We offer it as one source of information about your own possible vulnerability—and we trust that you will interpret your score with caution. Overall, we hope you will keep in mind the many tools you have accumulated that, together, can help you respond more effectively to potential stressors—and ultimately live a longer and healthier life.

CHAPTER SUMMARY

PROBLEM: **Were the reactions and experiences of the 9/11 firefighters and others at the World Trade Center attacks typical of people in other stressful situations? And what factors explain individual differences in our physical and psychological responses to stress?**

- Surviving firefighters had a variety of responses to their involvement in the WTC disaster, including physical, behavioral, cognitive, and emotional stress responses. Aside from physical injuries and memories peculiar to this particular event, their responses were typical of others who have experienced stressful situations.

- Despite a cluster of similar symptoms that occur regardless of the stressor, research is revealing some response differences that depend on whether the stressor involves personal loss, humiliation or rejection, experience of a catastrophe, and possibly other factors.

- Regardless of the cause, however, stress must be understood from multiple psychological perspectives, including the biological, behavioral, developmental, social-cultural, cognitive, and whole-person perspectives.

- There are also individual differences in our responses to stress. These depend on the intensity and duration of the stressor, culture background, coping strategies, social support, stress *moderators*, as well as other stressors present in our lives. Shelly Taylor has also suggested that women and men have different response styles in the face of stress.

13.1 What Causes Distress?

CORE CONCEPT 13.1

Traumatic events, chronic lifestyle conditions, major life changes, and even minor hassles can all cause a stress response.

Stressors are external events that cause internal stress responses, both psychological and emotional ones, termed **distress,** and biological and physiological reactions. And while **cognitive appraisal** influences our individual responses to stressors, there are several major categories of events that typically cause stress.

Traumatic stressors include natural disasters, acts of **terrorism,** or sudden personal loss such as the death of a loved one or an unforeseen breakup. All of these situations occur with little or no warning and almost always cause extreme stress in the immediate aftermath of the event. Research indicates that about 20 percent of survivors of natural disaster remain distressed after one year, while as many as 75 percent of those exposed to a terrorist attack report continued worry at the one-year mark. Repeated media coverage of the event often exacerbates and prolongs the effects and can also cause stress in people who were not directly exposed to the event in a phenomenon known as **vicarious traumatization. Grief** is a normal, healthy process in response to a personal loss, and the humiliation associated with rejection, such as that caused by **targeted rejection,** can put an individual at increased risk for depression.

Posttraumatic stress disorder (PTSD) can occur in individuals who have been exposed to severe circumstances such as combat, rape, or other violent attack. Symptoms of PTSD can be cognitive, behavioral, and emotional, as evidenced (for example) by difficulty concentrating, an exaggerated "startle response," and survivor's guilt. About 8 percent of Americans will experience PTSD at some time in their lives, with symptoms lasting more than ten years in more than one-third of the cases. Combat personnel may be especially at risk for PTSD, and military psychologists are working increasingly to develop and provide more effective education and treatment for combat veterans and their families.

Chronic stressors have a more gradual onset and are longer lasting than traumatic events. **Societal stressors** such as poverty and unemployment, as well as difficulties at home, school, or work, are one type of chronic stressor. Another is **burnout,** which is a syndrome of emotional exhaustion, physical fatigue, and cognitive weariness that results from demanding and unceasing pressures at work, at home, or in relationships. **Compassion fatigue** is found in medical and psychological professionals as well as caregivers and other individuals who spend a great deal of time caring for others. Research in this area offers at least five steps caregivers and service providers can take to reduce their risk of compassion fatigue.

Major life changes—whether positive or negative—can be a source of stress as well, in that they involve changes in our daily routines and adaptation to new situations and environments. Finally, minor **hassles** such as computer crashes or an incessantly barking dog can accumulate and cause stress that adds up over time.

13.2 How Does Stress Affect Us Physically?

CORE CONCEPT 13.2

The physical stress response begins with arousal, which stimulates a series of physiological responses that in the short term are adaptive but that can turn harmful if prolonged.

When faced with **acute stressors,** our bodies are equipped with amazing abilities to meet the challenges effectively. The **fight-or-flight response** is produced by the autonomic nervous system and includes such immediate changes as accelerated heart rate, increased respiration and blood pressure, perspiration, and pupil dilation. A more comprehensive explanation of our response to stress is offered by Hans Selye's **GAS.** A three-phase system, the GAS begins with the **alarm phase,** then progresses into the **resistance phase** and finally the **exhaustion phase** if the stressor is chronic in nature. Under such circumstances, the resources that so effectively helped us combat an acute stressor become depleted, resulting in a host of physical and emotional symptoms. Consequently, we become more vulnerable to illness. While the fight-or-flight response has been well documented in both animals and humans, psychologist Shelley Taylor notes an alternative pattern of response to stress. Her **tend-and-befriend** theory suggests that social support seeking can be a more effective response to stress when protection or survival of offspring is involved. These models complement each other rather than competing with each other in helping us understand the complex human stress response.

The field of **psycho-neuroimmunology** tries to understand how stress causes illness by studying brain–body relationships. Research in this area has revealed that the central nervous system and the immune system remain in constant communication with each other in response to stress. **Cytokines** are proteins that fight infection but, under prolonged stress, produce feelings of listlessness and depression. One way in which stress affects physical health is by accelerating the rate at which cells age, which can be measured by examining the length of **telomeres.** Shorter telomeres are associated with several diseases as well as with early death. On the positive side, cognitive appraisals affect cell aging and thus play an important role in the stress–illness relationship.

13.3 Who Is Most Vulnerable to Stress?

CORE CONCEPT 13.3

Personality characteristics affect our individual responses to stressful situations and, consequently, the degree to which we are distressed when exposed to stressors.

Stress moderators reduce the impact of stressors on our perceived level of stress. Most of them function as variations of cognitive appraisal (although often on a nonconscious level). Hostile individuals are more likely to perceive stress in the face of a stressful situation and consequently have twice the risk of heart disease. Fortunately, stress-management programs have proven effective at reducing these individuals' response to stress and their resulting health vulnerability.

Locus of control is a second personality characteristic that has an impact on the stressor–stress relationship. People with an **internal** locus of control have greater resistance to stress than do **externals,** probably as a result of their perceived capability to take some action to ameliorate it. Locus of control has been found to affect not only stress but also health and longevity. While locus of control may have some genetic underpinnings, our experiences also influence it, as evidenced by research on **learned helplessness.** From a cultural perspective, **secondary control** involves controlling one's reactions to events rather than controlling the events themselves and is more prevalent in Eastern cultures. Research has found both types of control to be effective in the cultures in which they operate.

Hardiness is an outlook based on three Cs—a perception of internal control, of change as a challenge rather than a threat, and of commitment to life activities rather than alienation or withdrawal. Individuals with a hardy attitude exhibit greater resistance to stress. Similarly, optimistic people feel less stressed in the face of stressful situations, as they are more likely to focus on the positives rather than the negatives of the situation. **Optimism** is also characterized by specific, situational, and temporary attributions about negative situations. Both hardiness and optimism, like locus of control, appear to have some biological underpinnings but can be improved with well-designed training programs. **Resilience** is the ability to rebound and adapt to challenging circumstances and is related to optimism and hardiness, as well as social skills, cognitive abilities, and resources such as caring parents or support providers.

13.4 How Can We Transform Negative Stress Into Positive Life Strategies?

CORE CONCEPT 13.4

Effective coping strategies reduce the negative impact of stress on our health, while positive lifestyle choices can enhance our mental and physical health as well as our overall well-being.

Coping involves taking action that reduces or eliminates the causes of stress rather than just the symptoms of stress. **Problem-focused coping** is accomplished by specific actions aimed at resolving a problem or stressor, whereas **emotion-focused coping** relies on efforts to regulate our emotional response to stress. Both types of coping can be useful and sometimes best work together. **Cognitive restructuring** is another type of effective **coping strategy** and involves modifying our perceptions of the stressor or our reactions to it. Cognitive restructuring can include **upward** and **downward social comparisons.**

Cultivating positive emotions, including humor, also helps reduce the effects of stress on our health, as can efforts to find meaning in the stressful situation. In finding meaning, making sense of the event appears to be the first step, but those who ultimately succeed in finding meaning in tragedy must also identify some benefit of the event or situation. **Psychological debriefing,** which in some cases takes the form of **critical incident stress debriefing (CISD),** has been found to be relatively ineffective in reducing the link between stress and illness.

A variety of **positive lifestyle choices** carry a two-for-one benefit to the stress–illness puzzle: They can increase our resistance to stress and also decrease our vulnerability to stress-related illness. **Social support** may be the most important of these lifestyle factors, as people with stronger social support live longer and healthier lives than those with little or no support. Social support is helpful in that it carries emotional, tangible, and informational benefits. Regular aerobic exercise has both physical and psychological benefits and has been found to reduce the impact of stress on our health. Similarly, a healthy diet, adequate sleep, and even meditation have been found to decrease our vulnerability to stress and illness.

Subjective well-being (SWB) includes satisfaction with life, prevalence of positive emotions, and absence of negative emotions. Like many of the concepts we have studied, an individual's SWB is influenced both by heredity and by environment. Neither age nor wealth predicts happiness—happy people can be found in the youngest and the oldest, the richest and the poorest, and even in victims of serious illness or life-changing injury.

KEY TERMS

acute stress *p. 404*

alarm phase *p. 404*

behavioral medicine *p. 426*

benefit finding *p. 421*

burnout *p. 397*

catastrophic event *p. 393*

catharsis *p. 421*

chronic stressor *p. 397*

cognitive appraisal *p. 392*

cognitive restructuring
  p. 420

pret the stressor, how we have learned to cope, the social support we can rely on, and other processes can alter that link of external stressor and personal health response.

DISCOVERING PSYCHOLOGY *VIEWING GUIDE*

Watch the following video by logging into MyPsychLab (www.mypsychlab.com). *After you have watched the video, answer the* questions *that follow.*

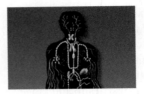

PROGRAM 23: **HEALTH, MIND, AND BEHAVIOR**

Program Review

1. How are the biopsychosocial model and the Navajo concept of *hozho* alike?
   a. Both are dualistic.
   b. Both assume individual responsibility for illness.
   c. Both represent holistic approaches to health.
   d. Both are several centuries old.

2. Dr. Wizanski told Thad that his illness was psychogenic. This means that
   a. Thad is not really sick.
   b. Thad's illness was caused by his psychological state.
   c. Thad has a psychological disorder, not a physical one.
   d. Thad's lifestyle puts him at risk.

3. Headaches, exhaustion, and weakness are
   a. not considered to be in the realm of health psychology.
   b. considered to be psychological factors that lead to unhealthful behaviors.
   c. usually unrelated to psychological factors.
   d. considered to be symptoms of underlying tension and personal problems.

4. When Judith Rodin talks about "wet" connections to the immune system, she is referring to connections with the
   a. individual nerve cells.
   b. endocrine system.
   c. sensory receptors.
   d. skin.

CRITICAL THINKING APPLIED

Is *Change* Really Hazardous to Your Health?

The relationship between life change events and illness, as indexed by the SRRS, is much more complex than originally thought. While extreme high and low scores offer some useful predictions of probabilities of future stress-related effects, they do not include all the many other factors outlined in this chapter. Illness can be caused by prolonged exposure to situational stressors, but that link is moderated by a host of cognitive, affective, social and cultural factors. How we inter-

5. What mind–body question is Judith Rodin investigating in her work with infertile couples?

   a. How do psychological factors affect fertility?

   b. Can infertility be cured by psychological counseling?

   c. What effect does infertility have on marital relationships?

   d. Can stress cause rejection of *in vitro* fertilization?

6. When Professor Zimbardo lowers his heart rate, he is demonstrating the process of

   a. mental relaxation.

   b. stress reduction.

   c. biofeedback.

   d. the general adaptation syndrome.

7. Psychologist Neal Miller uses the example of the blindfolded basketball player to explain

   a. the need for information to improve performance.

   b. how chance variations lead to evolutionary advantage.

   c. the correlation between life-changing events and illness.

   d. how successive approximations can shape behavior.

8. In which area of health psychology has the most research been done?

   a. the definition of health

   b. stress

   c. biofeedback

   d. changes in lifestyle

9. Imagine a family is moving to a new and larger home in a safer neighborhood with better schools. Will this situation be a source of stress for the family?

   a. No, because the change is a positive one.

   b. No, because moving is not really stressful.

   c. Yes, because any change requires adjustment.

   d. Yes, because it provokes guilt that the family does not really deserve this good fortune.

10. Which response shows the stages of the general adaptation syndrome in the correct order?

    a. alarm reaction, exhaustion, resistance

    b. resistance, alarm reaction, exhaustion

    c. exhaustion, resistance, alarm reaction

    d. alarm reaction, resistance, exhaustion

11. What important factor in stress did Hans Selye *not* consider?

    a. the role of hormones in mobilizing the body's defenses

    b. the subjective interpretation of a stressor

    c. the length of exposure to a stressor

    d. the body's vulnerability to new stressors during the resistance stage

12. Today, the major causes of death in the United States are

    a. accidents.

    b. infectious diseases.

    c. sexually transmitted diseases.

    d. diseases related to lifestyle.

13. When Thomas Coates and his colleagues, in their study of AIDS, conduct interview studies, they want to gain information that will help them

    a. design interventions at a variety of levels.

    b. determine how effective mass media advertisements are.

    c. motivate AIDS victims to take good care of themselves.

    d. stop people from using intravenous drugs.

14. The body's best external defense against illness is the skin, whereas its best internal defense is

    a. the stomach.

    b. the heart.

    c. T-cells.

    d. the spinal cord.

15. In which stage of the general adaptation syndrome are the pituitary and adrenals stimulated?

    a. exhaustion   c. reaction

    b. alarm   d. resistance

16. Which stage of the general adaptation syndrome is associated with the outcome of disease?

    a. alarm   c. exhaustion

    b. reaction   d. resistance

17. What claim is Richard Lazarus most closely associated with?

    a. The individual's cognitive appraisal of a stressor is critical.

    b. The biopsychosocial model is an oversimplified view.

    c. Peptic ulcers can be healed through biofeedback.

    d. The general adaptation syndrome can account for 80% of heart attacks in middle-aged men.

18. Thomas Coates and Neal Miller are similar in their desire to

    a. eradicate AIDS.

    b. outlaw intravenous drug use.

    c. institute stress management courses as part of standard insurance coverage.

    d. teach basic skills for protecting one's health.

19. How should an advertising campaign ideally be designed in order to get people to use condoms and avoid high-risk sexual activities?

    a. It should be friendly, optimistic, and completely nonthreatening.

    b. It should have enough threat to arouse emotion but not so much that viewers will go into denial.

    c. It should contain a lot of humor.

    d. It should feature an older, white, male doctor and a lot of scientific terminology.

20. Neal Miller is to biofeedback as Judith Rodin is to

    a. analgesics.

    b. meditation.

    c. a sense of control.

    d. social support.

14

Social Psychology: How We Affect Us

Dr. Chris S. Dula
—East Tennessee State
University
Dr. E. Scott Geller
—Virginia Tech

CHAPTER OUTLINE

Prologue

> "We human beings are social beings. We come into the world as the result of others' actions. We survive here in dependence on others. Whether we like it or not, there is hardly a moment of our lives when we do not benefit from others' activities. For this reason, it is hardly surprising that most of our happiness arises in the context of our relationships with others."
>
> —The 14th Dalai Lama

Section 1: We Are The World—The Essence

We're dependent on others, but few people truly understand and appreciate the powerful influences we have on one another. Why do we feel indebted to those who help us, even if we didn't ask for a favor? Why don't we always help others when they need us? Why are talented salespeople so good at getting us to buy things we don't need? Do others affect our attitudes and beliefs? Why is there so much hatred in the world? These are the kinds of questions addressed in this chapter. Though obviously we don't have all the answers, psychological science provides evidence-based insights to understand the social world and make it a better place.

Psychological Literacy—Why Psychology Matters

Social Psychology is important for understanding the human experience because we're all influenced by others and we all influence others. We all have valued relationships, including family, friends, co-workers, and even 'virtual' relationships on the Internet. We need to connect with others, and we do it in many ways. Some of our ties are informal, as with acquaintances, and some are formal, as with employment and marriages.

Psychological scientists have discovered that certain social influences are important to understanding health and safety. This includes such things as why some donate to charities, obey societal rules, persist in tasks after failures, and others abuse drugs, behave aggressively, and act in discriminatory ways toward others (Basic Behavioral Science Task Force, 1996). These are all important issues in the human experience, and the list is hardly exhaustive. Further, our science holds the potential to help us live in peace and prosperity as a global community. So, in this chapter we cover many of the social psychological processes that might mitigate problems and maximize benefits in mutual ways. The better you know these principles and their applications, the better off you'll be with regard to relationships with family, friends, and co-workers. And we'll all be better off if you teach these concepts to others.

Foundational Concepts—Getting Started

Learning Objectives At the end of this section, you'll be able to:

14.1.1 Explain the difference between Social Psychology and Sociology;

14.1.2 Discuss how others help us meet our needs.

Most institutions of higher education have a Psychology Department as well as a Sociology Department. If you take upper-level courses, you'll quickly see differences between these two complementary approaches to understanding human experience. But at an introductory level, the differences may not be readily apparent. Both disciplines look at human behavior, but from different perspectives.

The domain of Sociology is the *group*, comprised of two or more individuals with functional relationships (Sherif, Harvey, White, Hood, & Sherif, 1961). The domain of Psychology is the *individual*, with concepts such as perception, learning, memory, judgment, motivation, etc. Thus, Social Psychology examines effects of the group on the individual, and vice versa. So, while the two fields have different foci, they're really two sides of the same coin, and we can learn from both.

In a general sense, we all function within groups, both small and large. Sometimes we control or influence others and sometimes others control or influence us. Cultures, nations, political parties, religions and societal norms are a function of groups, and these influence us as individuals. We depend on others to help us meet our own needs and others profoundly affect the quality of our lives. Social forces affect such things as family, friendship, love, jobs, money, goods, and services, as well as with conflict we have with others. Groups and particular people partially define major aspects of our personal identities. And, our perceptions regarding others' behavior and/or their expectations, guide our own behavior within various situations. And, an important aspect of social psychology is our beliefs and their situational effects.

Section 2: Schema-Driven Perceptions—Situations & Interpretations

As children, others (e.g., parents, peers, preachers, teachers) provide us with the bulk of our knowledge. This knowledge forms a framework for understanding new experiences. Then we add our own experiences to these frames of reference known as **schemas**. But, once formed, our frames of reference often become fairly static and guide our perceptions and behavior in ways that can be beneficial or harmful. In fact, our schemas often cause us to have very pronounced perceptual and behavioral biases.

---

schemas Mental categories our brain uses to quickly make judgment about our surroundings in order to save processing power. At their most basic level schemas help us to assess our approach of stimuli, and more complex schemas can infer personality characteristics of people around us or how we should act.

social cognition The thoughts we have about the stimuli in our environment, which typically arise when a schema is activated.

Social Cognition, Attributions & Biases—Who Caused What, or What Caused Who

Learning Objectives At the end of this section, you'll be able to:

14.2.1 Explain how thoughts influence our perceptions of others;

14.2.2 Explain how social schemas develop;

14.2.3 Describe social biases and errors.

Social cognition reflects how we perceive others based on our schemas for different types of people, whether accurate or inaccurate. While schemas allow for quick reactions and communications, they can be flawed by incomplete or biased information and result in negative judgments about people based on the flimsiest of cues. We can help prevent errors in evaluating others if we realize how heavily we rely on schemas for perception, become conscious of the social bias, and take steps to ensure we are not jumping to unfair judgments.

Social schemas are often based upon attributes, or labels, we have for 'types' of people. Group schemas are based on many features, such as gender, race, ethnicity, nationality, religious association, political affiliation, socioeconomic status, and on and on. Once we believe someone is a member of a particular group, we use our schema-based attributes as a heuristic or shortcut for judging that person and this affects our perceptions of his/her behavior (BBSTF, 1996).

But individuals are more different from one another than they are alike. Think of your gender, race/ethnicity, religion, or political stance. Are you just like everyone else you know in these categories, or do you vary from other members of these groups? Our guess is you'd say something like, "Well I'm similar in some ways, but I'm also different in many ways." We don't want to be judged by simplistic labels, so why do we judge others with labels?

Schemas and much of social cognition, operate **implicitly**. In other words, our labels for others influence us without conscious awareness. When correct, schemas increase our efficiency in perceiving our world. For example, we recognize a 'chair' without conscious awareness, and we do it quickly. Although people are far more complicated, schema-based social cognition occurs just as automatically. However, the consequences of an error can be significant.

Social cognitive biases are tendencies to make assumptions about people and situations, based on our schemas. In other words, *bias* means our schemas affect our perception, such that we interpret data in a skewed manner, often unfairly judging others and/or their behavior. Even if we know we're biased, we're

---

social cognitive biases A reliance on schemas (which have solidified over time and become a bias) to make assumptions about social situations. They are often incomplete because they do not take into account numerous other influential factors.

unlikely to modify schemas or make fair-minded corrections to our judgments (McCaslin, Petty, & Wegener, 2010).

A judgment about why a person does something is called an **attribution**. We all want to understand the causes of behavior, and we often base explanations of behavior on the 'type' of person doing 'that kind' of behavior. Sometimes, we're correct, but such attributions are likely incomplete explanations at best; at worst our judgment is completely wrong.

The **fundamental attribution error** is the tendency to automatically attribute behaviors to a person's character, nature, personality traits or in one word—*disposition*. This process is called 'fundamental' because it's virtually universal. Because such judgments are frequently wrong, we make an 'error.' In other words, in explaining others' behavior, we usually overrate dispositional influences and underestimate situational influences.

For example, if a vehicle cuts in front of us on the road, we will likely make an automatic judgment of the driver. You may think "What a jerk!" We make this 'jerk' attribution because we think only a 'jerk' would cut us off. That is the 'type' of person who disregards others' safety. We make a dispositional attribution for the behavior. But, suppose we inadvertently cut somebody off. You probably don't think 'I'm a jerk!' We'd more than likely think something situational caused our behavior. After all, we're not the 'type' of people who intentionally cuts in front other drivers, right? Perhaps we were distracted or just forgot to check our blind spot. We wouldn't think we don't care about others' safety.

Self-serving bias is an attribution process reflecting a tendency to explain our behavior in a blameless or virtuous manner, despite evidence to the contrary (Mezulis, Abramson, Hyde, & Hankin, 2004). We maintain positive views of ourselves, by blaming bad outcomes on features of the situation, unless self-blame is unavoidable. Conversely, if things go well, we attribute the cause to our skills, abilities, and/or positive features of our personality, unless self-praise is not plausible. A self-serving bias in moderate doses is adaptive because it protects self-esteem and helps us overcome our failures. However, if we disregard the constraints of reasonably objective self-assessment, others may come to see us as excuse-makers and/or arrogant critics.

Thus, if someone else does something negative, we usually attribute it to a negative disposition (unless we know the person and know better); but if we do something negative, we tend to blame the *situation*. In FIGURE 14•1, a golfer's *self-serving bias* makes it easy for him to blame his subpar performance on situational factors, while an onlooker exhibits the *fundamental attribution error* by assuming a negative

Courtesy of George Vaughn Willis.

[**FIGURE 14•1**] Whose interpretation is correct?

disposition, that the man is characteristically a poor player. And even though we rarely get an entirely unbiased judgement from ourselves or others, what others think of us matters in a many ways.

Section 3: How Others Affect Us So Much—Living the Life of the Social Animal

Many powerful 'rewards' and 'punishers' come from our relationships with others. Social interactions bring us love, appreciation, and financial earnings. On the other hand, interactions with others sometimes lead to arguments, broken relationships, or the loss of a job. Exploring the science of how others affect us, and vice versa, holds promise for improving all our lives. For starters, we all belong to groups and these groups are powerful determinants of our behavior.

Group Membership & Affiliation— We Love to Love

Affiliation is one of the most powerful forces in the human experience. **Affiliation** is our connection to others with whom we identify in some way. Indeed, these connections define us in important ways. Once allied, we value people to whom we're connected. Being part of many groups seems perfectly natural, and we usually assume our groups are better than others.

---

attribution An assumption of why a person is acting the way they do.

fundamental attribution error Attributing a person's behavior to what we assume to be his or her personality rather than factors outside of that individual (e.g., the situation).

self-serving bias In order to maintain a positive view of ourselves we tend to take credit for our successes and blame failures on situational factors. In other words, we rely on the schema that we are generally skilled, capable, and good intentioned.

affiliation Connecting with others you identify with in some way (i.e., ethnicity, religiosity, political beliefs, or hobbies).

In & Out Groupings—We're Always the Best!
Learning Objectives At the end of this section, you'll be able to:

14.3.1. Explain how groups develop;

14.3.2. Define in-groups and out-groups;

14.3.3. Discuss group biases and attitudes.

Groups exist on many levels, from couples to nations. Category parameters include, but aren't limited to, such things as: families/friends, gender, age, race/ethnicity, socio-economic class, educational attainment, religious orientation, political stance, sexual orientation, and our geographical location. We are born into some categories (i.e., sex, race/ethnicity, family), some are learned early but could change (i.e., religion, politics), and some we develop ourselves (i.e., being a fan of particular artist or sports team). Each group has a sense of community and norms we observe and follow for genuine membership. But, each grouping sets itself at odds against other groups (i.e., this vs. that religion, this vs. that team's fans).

A group with which we identify is an **in-group. Out-groups** are those with which we do not identify. Group identification is a powerful factor in our lives, leading to **intergroup bias**, or the tendency to admire in-groups and to disparage out-groups. **In-group favoritism** results from seeing our group as being better than others. We tend to allocate more resources, praise, and rewards to members of our in-group. We value those in our in-groups, even if we're conflicted about them in some ways. For example, you may have issues with a particular family member and criticize him/her, but react negatively if someone outside your family criticizes this person. Loyal fans may complain about their team if they perform poorly, but they don't like criticism from rival fans.

Then we have **group-serving bias**, where we maintain positive evaluations of our in-group, in spite of contradictory evidence. For example, one study of intercollegiate athletes, found group-serving bias was stronger than self-serving bias in performance attributions, even after group failures (Taylor & Doria, 1981). Another showed athletes felt personal attributes (self-serving) and team attributes (group-serving) contributed more to wins than losses (Sherman & Kim, 2005). Such biases have repercussions.

For example, when employers have freedom to indulge personal preferences or beliefs, they may favor race/ethnicity or gender when hiring, when such factors should be inapplicable considerations (Kmec, 2006). One study concluded corporate

boards and CEOs compete to try and appoint directors more similar to themselves (Westphal & Zajac, 1995). Also, teachers of children should monitor their non-verbal behaviors (i.e., facial expressions, personal space) as they may unconsciously communicate favoritism toward students similar to them or rejection to dissimilar students (Richey & Richey, 1978).

Out-groups are often the target of disapproval, disdain, and/or disadvantage. This may take the form of stereotyping or prejudicial attitudes and behavior, which is affected by group size and relative power or status (Hewstone, Rubin, & Willis, 2002). The preeminent social psychologist Susan Fiske teaches her students that favoring people similar to ourselves is an unfortunate but natural and automatic human tendency. But, she reminds disillusioned students that though we've got a long way to go, we've come a long way toward improved intergroup acceptance and we now have evidence-based solutions to reduce group conflict (Hackney, 2005). These interventions are important because evidence shows it doesn't take much to create group identity, and sow seeds for conflict. See the **Beyond the Basics** (FEATURE 14•1) for more on that point. Of the types of people with whom we desire affiliation, one of the most desirable is those to whom we're attracted.

feature 14.1

Beyond the Basics: Minimal Groups Still Exert Maximal Power

The *minimal group paradigm* is a research technique that shows how easily group identity is formed and how we quickly value in-groups that are barely 'groups' in any formal sense. In one of these early studies, participants judgments of paintings were the only criteria for placing them in groups. Subsequently, participants reported liking their group members more than out-group participants (Tajfel, Billig, Bundy, & Flament, 1971). They also discriminated against out-group members in allocating rewards and penalties, though they got no advantage for themselves. In a later study, participants were *randomly assigned* to groups and " . . . as soon as the notion of 'group' was introduced into the situation, the subjects still discriminated against those assigned to another random category" (Billig & Tajfel, 1973, p.27). Given how easy it is for us to form essentially meaningless groups and develop affinity toward them and antagonism for others, we should pause and consider how such processes drive the endless conflict we see between more meaningful groups throughout history and the world.

in-group A group with which an individual is affiliated, that is, they identify with and believe they are part of that group.

out-group A group an individual believes he or she is a part of or affiliated in some way.

intergroup bias The tendency to favor in-groups (with which we identify) and undervalue out-groups (that we do not identify with).

in-group favoritism Believing our in-groups are better than out-groups and favoring those in-groups through actions or thoughts.

group-serving bias Accepting positive aspects of our in-group despite evidence contradicting these positive beliefs.

Social Effects of Attractiveness—The Clout of Cute

Learning Objectives At the end of this section, you'll be able to:

14.3.4. List different reasons we're attracted to others;

14.3.5. Describe the social aspects of attraction;

14.3.6. Discuss the impacts of social biases toward attraction.

We can be attracted to another person for many reasons, from personality, to physique, to ideology. **Attraction** is a powerful desire for affiliation and may lead to intimate relations (sexual or platonic), short or long-term, mild (e.g., liking an acquaintance), moderate (e.g., a half-hearted but long-standing friendship) or intense (e.g., a sexual relationship) (Sprecher & Felmlee, 2008). And, attraction often arises within groups with which we identify.

Here we'll consider how we're influenced by social dynamics of attraction. Most adults want some type of dating/mating relationship, and perhaps the most powerful determinant of this desire is physical attraction, or so it seems. Thousands of studies provide insight into the complexity of attractiveness.

Attractiveness isn't a universally objective quality; it's a socially-determined construct. It varies considerably across time and cultures and includes factors such as facial/body symmetry, body part/mass ratios, adherence to cultural practices, and perceived status (e.g., Dunn & Searle, 2010; Escasa, Gray, & Patton, 2010; Jones, Little, & Perrett, 2003; Silverstein, Peterson, & Perdue, 1986; Sorokowski, 2010; Swami & Tovée, 2007). Both sexes value attractiveness, but tend to view it somewhat differently.

Evolutionary mechanisms have been widely used to explain these differences, essentially arguing that people seek qualities promoting procreation. In a classic study of 37 cultures, Buss (1989) posited that ambition, industriousness, and resource acquisition were valued more by females, while males valued youth and physical attractiveness more. Yet evolutionary accounts have been challenged, notably from assessments of homosexual attraction. Howard, Blumstein and Schwartz (1987) found heterosexual and homosexual couples both valued many of the same partner qualities—yet procreation is not typically a top priority for homosexual couples. The two qualities with the highest levels of agreement were physical attractiveness and athleticism. It was concluded that while evolution may have some role in attraction, the " . . . richness of human mate preferences is better understood from a social perspective" (p. 200). But, attractiveness affects life circumstances beyond dating/mating preferences.

Johnson, Podratz, Dipboye, and Gibbons (2010) summarized some of the literature and noted physically attractive people were more likely to attain various types of success. Those who were rated as attractive: were perceived as more 'hireable,' received higher starting salaries, had higher performance evaluations, obtained better bargaining offers, were rated higher in academic program admissions, were regarded more favorably by voters when running for office, and received better judicial judgment. In a study of male defendants, more attractive convicts received lighter sentences and

were half as likely to be incarcerated as less attractive defendants (Stewart, 1980). Physically attractive people also tend to be more persuasive because they are typically perceived by others as being honest, intelligent, talented, kind and healthy (e.g., Joseph, 1982; van Leeuwen & Macrae, 2004). Doesn't really sound fair, does it?

This all speaks to the *'what is beautiful is good'* bias, which is a pervasive belief that attractive people have other positive characteristics (Berscheid & Reis, 1998). After analyzing over 900 studies, Langlois and colleagues (2000) concluded that " . . . attractiveness is a significant advantage for both children and adults in every domain of judgment, treatment, and behavior we examined" (p.404). In a study of job performance, attractive women were rated as being more responsible for good outcomes and less responsible for bad outcomes, while less attractive women received the opposite attributions (Seligman, Paschall, & Takata, 1974). Other studies have also shown a negative bias against people rated as unattractive (e.g., Griffin & Langlois, 2006; McKelvie & Coley, 1993). While, this isn't fair, it reflects a problem with all social-cognitive biases. But, there is a cost to being attractive.

Attractive women, for example, are more likely to be held to unrealistically high criteria, to be undermined by those who think beauty is the reason for their success, to be disliked by women who feel less attractive, and are less likely to be hired for masculine sex-typed jobs (e.g., Johnson, Podratz, Dipboye, & Gibbons, 2010; Loya, Cowan & Walters, 2006; Tseëlon, 1992). This line of research shows the power of biases cuts both ways. Perhaps being aware of such issues will help you make fair attributions and judgments about all kinds of people in your life, including yourself. To learn more about how perceived attractiveness is based on comparisons with others, check out **Beyond the Basics** (FEATURE 14•2). As with attractiveness, it seems proximity and similarity also play major roles in affiliation.

feature 14.2

Beyond the Basics

As it happens, we often create our own views of self by judging ourselves against others, a process called **social comparison** (e.g., Mussweiler, 2003). In the realm of attractiveness, the media tells us to revere beauty, thinness, and fitness, and as a result, it's easy to feel worse about ourselves (e.g., Fernandez & Pritchard, 2012; Micu & Coulter, 2012). While this issue is most often studied with females and the 'thin ideal,' males also have media-driven body image issues, especially with the 'muscular ideal' (e.g., Hargreaves & Tiggemann, 2009; Parent, 2013).

In recognition of this issue among females, the Unilever Company started the "Dove Real Beauty" advertising

---

attraction Feeling interested or drawn to another person. Attraction can manifest itself through an individual's characteristics (i.e., physical, intellectual, or emotional) or social standing (i.e., popularity, power, or affiliation).

social comparison Self-evaluation by comparison to others (i.e., "I'm smarter than they are" or "I'm more attractive than her/him").

campaign featuring female models of all ages, shapes, and sizes, rather than 'thin-ideal' models (Unilever, 2005; 2006). Why? Their survey study showed that of 3,000 women in 10 countries, only 2% saw themselves as beautiful and only 13% were satisfied with their bodies (Simmons, 2006). Thus, most of their potential customers did not identify with the 'thin ideal.' For a more evidence-based understanding, let's consider evaluations of many studies (i.e., meta-analyses). However, we'll also find such conclusions aren't always consistent.

Some meta-analyses concluded negative 'thin-ideal' media effects don't exist for most people, except for those with pre-existing body dissatisfaction (e.g., Ferguson, 2013; Holmstrom, 2004). In contrast, other meta-analyses found women's body dissatisfaction to be linked to an internalization of media-driven images (e.g., Cafri, Yamamiya, Brannick & Thompson, 2005; Grabe, Ward & Hyde, 2008). Bottom line: we're influenced by social concepts of attractiveness, particularly when we engage in social comparisons of ourselves to others and media imagery. We need to be conscious of such issues when we judge others and ourselves.

Proximity & Similarity–Loving Locality & Alikeness

Learning Objectives At the end of this section, you'll be able to:

14.3.7. Describe how proximity affects relationships;

14.3.8. Describe how distance can negatively and positively impact relationships;

14.3.9. Explain the benefit of getting to know people dissimilar to you.

Where do you find people to whom you may be attracted, either in terms of friendship or sexuality? It's certainly sensible those nearest to you are who you'll know and like. **Proximity** is how close someone is to you physically, and this is a major factor in relationship building. One study found freshmen being randomly seated near people significantly influenced later friendship development (Back, Schmukle & Egloff, 2008). But with the Internet, we now need to consider the impact of 'virtual' proximity.

Nowadays, you can have many important relationships online. Unsurprisingly, a number of studies have found Internet use to be a common 'mate selection strategy' (e.g., Cooper & Sportolari, 2003; Sautter, Tippett, & Morgan, 2010). In fact, Chris met his lovely wife, Denise, via Facebook. As it turned out, their initial online impressions of one another were confirmed when they met in person. However, some people strategically misrepresent themselves in Internet profiles (Hall, Park, Song, & Cody, 2010). Thus, it's difficult to have a completely objective impression of an online connection, though it seems we're not exactly objective when we first meet in person.

Early in the dating game, feelings are often intense and may lead to idealization, and even obsessive thinking about a partner. It seems distance may foster idealization. One study showed that while long-distance relationships had greater stability than short-distance relationships, the former were more likely to terminate upon moving closer (Stafford & Merolla, 2007). Another study of long-distance relationships found a third ended within three months of moving to the same location (Stafford, Merolla, & Castle, 2006).

Thus, prolonged interaction in physical proximity usually yields more realistic appraisals, and idealization fades with interpersonal conflict (Shulman, Mayes, Cohen, Swain, & Leckman, 2008). Sanderson and Cantor (1997) concluded, " . . . it is remarkable that individuals are able to experience satisfaction in their close relationships because it requires an intricate balance of the right person being in the right place at the right time" (p. 1431). And, finding 'the right person' also has something to do with the perceived similarity between people.

It's been known for some time that similarity in demographics and attitude predict higher levels of liking (e.g., Byrne, 1971; Newcomb, 1956). It seems similarity also has a relationship with proximity, as we tend to sit near people we think are similar to us, even after controlling for gender, race, and attractiveness (Mackinnon, Jordan, & Wilson, 2011). And, similarity-based liking starts early, with one study showing preferences for similar peers beginning at three years of age (Fawcett & Markson, 2010).

As Montoya and Horton (2013) concluded, the evidence is overwhelming: we affiliate with, and are attracted to, those similar to us. Given this, it might be worth your while to connect with people different from you, broadening your horizons. It's certainly beneficial to be aware of our biases based on the happenstance of proximity and similarity, and attempt to deal fairly with those unlike ourselves. Now let's flip the coin and consider factors that determine our dislike of others, and ways to avoid the negative consequences of such impressions.

Group Membership & Prejudice— We Love to Hate Us

We have all disliked someone at some time or another, and it may have been for good reason. Indeed, it seems disliking is as natural a process as liking. Hatred is an extreme form of dislike, and we'd like to think people reserve extreme dislike for people who truly deserve it. But, collectively speaking, we often harbor hatred for people we've never even met. And, many people have negative opinions about groups that lead them to have prejudicial attitudes toward members of those groups. This is so insidious and pervasive a problem in our world, as to deserve major attention in this chapter.

In vs. Out Groupings–We're Better Than You

Learning Objectives At the end of this section, you'll be able to:

14.3.10. Explain the homogeneity effect;

14.3.11. Differentiate between stereotypes, prejudice, and discrimination;

14.3.12. Describe ways of overcoming that stereotypes, prejudice, and discrimination.

'In-groups' and 'out-groups' is just another way of saying 'us' versus 'them.' When we look at other group members, we typically don't see a lot of diversity among individuals; rather, we perceive 'them' to be very similar. Interestingly, we realize members of our own group vary greatly (think how different you are from your family members). But when we look at members of other groups (even families), we see them as being highly similar to one another. This is called the **homogeneity effect**, and it's the basis of many stereotypes.

The automatic inclination to appraise in-group members more positively and out-group members more negatively, is not restricted to humans. This has been empirically demonstrated with monkeys, leading to the conclusion that tendencies to divide the world into 'us' and 'them' are shared across all primates (Mahajan et al., 2011). The researchers noted this may have been adaptive in our species' history by promoting coalitions that allowed for successful group efforts aimed at survival and navigation of intergroup rivalries. While this may have once been adaptive for our ancestors, this holdover now threatens collective harmony and prosperity. Plus, as noted in Beyond the Basics (Feature 14.1), in-groups form quickly and easily, and out-groups are just as quickly perceived negatively, leading to possible hostility.

So, how can we solve this pervasive problem? In the mid-20th century, Sherif and colleagues (1961) conducted a series of famous and informative experiments with children at a camp, in order to examine in-group/out-group tensions and explore ways to remedy the resulting conflict. Male children, around 11-years-old and from similar backgrounds (middle-class, White, Protestant, etc.) were assigned to particular groups. In their words, " . . . the subjects were normal, healthy, socially well-adjusted boys who came from families with the same or closely similar economic, ethnic, and religious backgrounds" (p. 210).

In their early experiments an initial stage allowed for spontaneous friendship choices between any of the children. After assignment to groups and time passed, researchers observed reversals of prior friendships as a function of in-group formation. In later experiments, children were kept in their own groups and apart from out-group members during Stage 1. To help build an in-group bond, they gave the children practical tasks and goals that required cooperation and reciprocity. Predictably, group members rapidly took on roles which led to status-based hierarchical structures and social group norms.

In Stage 2 the two groups competed for goals under conditions that fuelled frustration. These artificially formed groups quickly experienced enhanced in-group cohesion and developed disdain for the 'other' group. The findings confirmed that inter-group dislike was intense, inter-group competition was high, and inter-group cooperation was low. Each called 'other' group members bad names, rallied behind their own leaders,

and 'attacked' the other group members, including cabin raiding, a food fight, and a fist fight. Now that a problem had been created, what was the solution? In Stage 3 they introduced contrived situations that made the groups cooperate to accomplish shared goals, or what was termed **superordinate goals**.

Specifically, the two antagonistic groups had to come together to: 1) clear a blocked water line in order to obtain drinking water; 2) contribute money collectively in order to see a desired movie; 3) pull a seemingly broken down truck to get it running so the driver could get everyone food. These apparently 'naturally-occurring' experiences of inter-group cooperation radically shifted inter-group behaviors and attitudes, toward the positive. In fact, the " . . . change in behavior and patterns of interaction between the groups was striking to all observers" (p. 211).

As they shared resources and responsibilities, derogatory inter-group comments declined until they disappeared entirely. A series of socio-metric evaluations confirmed observed changes in group dynamics. The authors noted that achievement of a single superordinate goal was not sufficient to eliminate inter-group hostility, but that with a series of such goals, friction decreased and inter-group cooperation spontaneously widened into other activities.

The lesson is clear. Without cooperative interaction, hostility will develop and intensify between groups that view each other as competitors. Thus, carefully designed superordinate goal interventions should be developed to bring groups together for the mutual advantage of all involved. It is tempting to think this study (Sherif et al., 1961) can be dismissed because it involved groups of children, but the same dynamics hold true for all types of groups with members of all ages.

This study falls within the domain of Sociology, but its relevance to Psychology is the effect on the attitudes and behaviors of the individual members of the groups. Now, when you encounter in-group/out-group conflicts, you'll be able to help reduce conflict rather than make matters worse by falling into negative social-cognitive and behavioral traps, like subscribing to stereotypes, harboring prejudices, and engaging in unfair discrimination.

Stereotypes, Prejudice & Discrimination—Unfair Attitudes & Their Effects

Stereotypes are value-laden schemas, where we ascribe general characteristics, motives, and behaviors to entire groups of people (Aronson, 2004). Stereotypes serve as quick means to judge others. They affect the standards to which we hold others, the way we evaluate others, and how we behave toward them (Biernat, 2003). Stereotypes can be positive or negative. You could hold a negative stereotype about one perceived group characteristic (e.g., men are sexist, females are gossips), yet also hold a positive stereotype about another generalized quality (e.g., men are good at fixing things, females are caring and nurturing). Yet, no set of assumed

---

homogeneity effect The assumption that members of a particular out-group are "homogenous," or very similar to each other.

stereotypes Assumptions that members of a particular out-group share certain characteristics or behaviors.

characteristics would be applicable to all, or perhaps even most individuals in the target group.

Despite the common-sense popularity of stereotypes, empirical support is lacking for generalized characteristics of a particular group of people. Labelling a person as male or female, for example, doesn't tell you a whole lot about him or her as a human being. Some men may be sexist, but some are not. Some women are sexist, and some aren't. Some men may be good at fixing things, but not at all. Some women are good at fixing things, and some aren't. Stereotypes thus serve as general frames of reference to guide quick decisions about the people we encounter, but they are likely to be an inaccurate judgment of a particular person. However, we tend to deeply believe in the validity of schemas we acquire as children from personal or anecdotal experiences. FIGURE 14•2 shows a common male stereotype, namely that men don't ask for directions. Chris asked for directions a lot prior to GPS technology, but it didn't make him less of a 'man.'

Stereotypes are based on schemas we acquired growing up. The label 'hippie' may have positive connotations for some and for others it may have a negative meaning. If your stereotype is positive, then upon encountering a person who fits the 'hippie' schema, you might be inclined to think good things about the person (e.g., peaceful, artistic, liberal). But, if your stereotype is negative, you would be just as quickly inclined to infer bad things about the person (e.g., dirty, drug-user, liberal). Whether you feel being 'liberal' is a good or bad 'thing' would determine how you apply that stereotype to people you assume fit the category. If one person were a self-identified 'hippie,' that label might mean something very different to him/her than to another person who also identified as a hippie. Indeed, labels are oversimplifications because all sizeable groups are extremely diverse within themselves.

However, we can't objectively interview every person we meet, nor get a full life history to make fully informed judgments about these individuals, so we rely, however unfairly, upon schemas to help us process information. We need to realize this can be harmful to others (e.g., through unfair treatment) and to ourselves (e.g., missing opportunities or becoming the recipient of reciprocal negative actions). And, we need to realize we do this automatically.

The **halo effect** is the tendency to judge people holistically based on information about one aspect of their identity (Gilbert, 1998). For example, if we initially think someone has an 'honest look,' we'll then tend to assume they have other positive attributes, such as compassion, generosity, and ingenuity. Contrary to the implied meaning of 'halo,' this works in the reverse as well. Believing a person has a 'shady look' can lead to other negative assumptions.

When our negative attitudes toward certain people are based on stereotypes about a group to which they belong, we have **prejudice**. Prejudice is an *attitude* with emotional, cognitive and behavioral ramifications (e.g., Fiske, 1998). A prejudice is based on a number of assumed characteristics of an out-group, including race/ethnicity, sex, age, sexual orientation, socioeconomic status, politics, religion, and so on.

Early evidence that prejudice toward different groups were so highly correlated that eminent psychologist Gordon Allport concluded it " . . . constitutes a very strong argument for saying that prejudice is basically a trait of personality" (1954, p. 73). Yet he also said, "The bigot does not hate all out-groups equally" (p. 74). With the notion of *selective prejudice* he concluded prejudice couldn't be exclusively explained by personality. A more nuanced and evidence-based view is that prejudices are influenced by certain personality characteristics. See **Beyond the Basics** (FEATURE 14•3) for more information on personality types and prejudice.

feature 14.3

Beyond the Basics A robust finding from a meta-analytic review of the prejudice literature is that it's reliably associated with Right-Wing Authoritarianism (RWA) and a Social Dominance Orientation (SDO). The RWA personality type reflects a negative attitude toward those who don't adhere to dominant social norms of a culture or submit to established authorities, and SDO is a worldview favoring social hierarchy and fostering a lack of respect toward groups deemed 'inferior.' Prejudice is also correlated with the Big Five personality traits, especially lower levels of Openness to Experience and Agreeableness, and higher levels of Conscientiousness, whereby high levels denotes rigid conformity to rules/principles (Sibley & Duckitt, 2008).

---

halo effect The tendency to make assumptions about a person based on a single characteristic. This is best understood not in a religious sense (e.g., "good" or angelic) but in terms of light—a "halo" radiating from a single source of light, like the sun.

prejudice Negative *attitudes* stemming from stereotypes.

Courtesy of George Vaughn Willis.

[**FIGURE 14•2**] We now ask a GPS for directions.

A prejudice typically forms early and is modelled by adults in the child's environment. Examining 113 studies of ethnic, racial, and national prejudices among children, Raabe and Beelmann (2011) concluded many prejudices form as early as 2 to 4 years of age. They noted that while prejudice toward equal and lower-status out-groups increased from early to middle childhood, prejudice toward higher-status out-groups was not affected as much by age. This research reveals overt prejudice decreased between middle and late childhood, but implicit attitudes did not. In other words, older children learn to control outward expression of their prejudice, but don't change their internal negative views. On a positive note, contact with out-groups was associated with reduced levels of prejudice (Raabe & Beelmann, 2011).

This illustrates the **intergroup contact theory**, where the more members of an in-group associate with members of an out-group, the less prejudice the former will have toward the latter. An analysis of 41 studies found that while effects vary depending on the measures used to assess prejudice of heterosexuals (the in-group in this example) towards homosexuals (the out-group in this example), a consistent inverse relationship occurred between degree of prejudice and amount of contact with members of this out-group (Smith, Axelton & Saucier, 2009). Thus, the more people we actually know from an out-group, the less likely we will be prejudiced against them. Interestingly, simply having more knowledge about the out-group does not have as much effect on reducing prejudice as does interpersonal contact with out-group members (Pettigrew & Tropp, 2008).

Pettigrew and Tropp (2006) conducted a meta-analysis of over 500 studies of intergroup contact theory and concluded that interpersonal contact does indeed accomplish a reduction in prejudice and this impact tends to generalize to the entire out-group, beyond the members with whom one interacts. However, when groups dislike each other they tend not to interact with out-group members, unless compelled by circumstances to do so. Thus, creating *superordinate goals* or collaborative opportunities is critical, as pointed out earlier by Sherif and colleagues (1961). Bringing groups into positive contact with one another should decrease prejudice and conflict.

Indeed, prejudice predicts unfair discrimination over and above stereotypes themselves (Fiske, 1998). **Discrimination** is negative behavior directed toward individuals because of their membership in a group about which a person holds a prejudicial attitude. Having a prejudiced attitude doesn't guarantee a negative action, but prejudice often results in unjust discriminatory behavior. In real-world terms "discrimination" occurs when someone is negatively affected as a result of negative actions from someone in another group. Sometimes such behavior is obvious, yet nowadays it often

[**FIGURE 14·3**] Stereotypes lead to poor judgment.

Courtesy of George Vaughn Willis.

happens implicitly, without a person realizing s/he is acting on prejudice.

Prior to the Civil Rights movement, racial prejudice and discrimination against African-Americans was often openly advocated by many White people and legally maintained in many parts of the U.S. (Quillian, 2006). A 1945 national survey found 55% of White respondents felt Whites should have the first chance at any job. Since the 1960s, attitudes have changed. By 1972, only 3% of Whites felt this way. Yet in reviewing the literature, Quillian (2006) concluded while most Whites now support equal treatment regardless of race, many endorse stereotypical beliefs, and don't support government intervention to promote racial equality. Quillian also noted many studies of *implicit prejudice* show even egalitarian Whites hold racial stereotypes, such as illustrated in **FIGURE 14·3**. And, the effect is also present in other biases, like sexism. For a look at how discrimination operates in today's society, take a look at **Why We Care** (**FEATURE 14·4**). Let's look further at how social processes function to control our human experience, and specifically at how we're influenced directly by others.

feature 14.4

Why We Care: Racial Discrimination is Unfortunately Alive and Well

One finding that shows racial discrimination is still prevalent is that potential employers tend to prefer applications/resumes with White-sounding names over names that sound as if they belong to a minority group (e.g., Bertrand & Mullainathan, 2002). For example, one study compared ratings of multiple ethnicities and found *identical resumes* with White or Asian-sounding names were rated higher than Black and Hispanic-sounding names (King, Madera, Hebl, Knight, & Mendoza, 2006). The authors explained these results by invoking

---

intergroup contact theory A theory that states prejudice is based on a lack of information and more contact between groups will lead to greater understanding and less prejudice.

discrimination Negative *actions* stemming from stereotypes.

McConahay's (1986) *modern racism theory*. This theory says racism still exists, but that it's much more subtle currently because the social norm has changed such that most people no longer overtly support racism. Yet, many practice prejudiced discrimination implicitly (without conscious awareness), such as devaluing excellent credentials of minority applicants. This concept also applies to issues of ageism, disability status, religion (or lack thereof), sexism, sexual orientation, etc.

Section 4: Attitudes—How Do We Decide What We Believe?

Attitude—a little thing that makes a big difference! At least that's the prevailing lay wisdom. But, how much do our attitudes really predict our behavior? And, to what degree do we choose our own attitudes, rather than coming by them through happenstance in circumstances of birth, family, church, school, work, race, sex, age, socioeconomic status, etc.? As you may have inferred from much of this chapter, what seems simple to most, is actually quite complicated.

Affective, Behavioral & Cognitive Attributes of Attitudes—Simple as ABC

Learning Objectives At the end of this section, you'll be able to:

14.4.1. Explain the components of attitudes;

14.4.2. Describe the role of emotions and behaviors in attitudes;

Affect, behavior and cognition are familiar to you by now, and each may influence or be influenced by an 'attitude.' There's a cognitive (thinking) component, where your attitude about something calls to mind your views on any number of topics. You can state your positions and list related opinions, beliefs, and values, all of which influence cognitive aspects of an attitude. Think of your views on such things as abortion, religion, guns, drug use, and so on. You may have some very strong views on these and other important matters.

An attitude also connects to affect, sometimes very powerful ones. Thus, attitudes are linked to affect. You likely feel closer to those who feel similar to you on topics about which you care deeply. Likewise, you likely feel a touch of anger, frustration, or sadness toward those who feel your view is incorrect or who hold an opposite attitude. Of course, emotional connections can only be discerned by others when we engage in some behavior consistent with our thoughts and our emotions. We might calmly discuss an opinion or perspective, or get worked up into emotive expressions of our views. We might write posts on social networks, send letters to newspapers, organize meetings, attend protests, or a number of other things indicative of a certain attitude. So, some behaviors follow directly from attitudes.

On the other hand, would you argue with your boss about politics if your job were on the line? We're complex enough to sometimes explain away our lack of actions on tough issues, rather than always act on them. Of course, we might be persuaded to start acting on a particular attitude regardless of the consequences or to change our positions altogether. However, it's difficult to change a person's attitude.

Altering Attitudes—Come On, Change Your Mind Already

You've probably tried to persuade somebody to convert to your view on some topic. It may have been about politics, religion, views on workplace or school policies, or a number of other possibilities. And, you've likely encountered resistance. Can you imagine someone saying you're wrong to have a particular attitude, and ought to change it? Yet, we see this type of urging all the time. But, we tend to stay committed to our attitudes without challenging them and are more likely to challenge the competition.

It's common to see people ardently stating their views on social networks and seemingly unable to understand how others cannot grasp the obvious appeal of their position. We wind up 'preaching to the choir' for those in our in-group, and ignoring those in out-groups. We often see people insulting those not within their own ideological camp. We hope with an understanding of Social Psychology, you'll be able to generate empathy for those outside your ideological in-group. Yet, that doesn't mean you shouldn't try to persuade others of your convictions. Knowing various aspects of attitude formation and change can make you a more persuasive communicator.

Routes of Attitude Change—Taking the Scenic or Central Route?

Learning Objectives At the end of this section, you'll be able to:

14.4.3. Describe the peripheral route to changing attitudes;

14.4.4. Describe the central route to changing attitudes;

There are two 'routes' to changing someone's attitudes: peripheral and central (e.g., Petty, Wegener, & Fabrigar, 1997). The **peripheral route** of attitude change refers to attitudes we hold habitually, but not necessarily strongly, and where persuasive messages don't have to be particularly logical, clear or compelling to induce change. Many of our product preferences fall in this category. We may like a particular brand of food or cleaner, but creative marketing can change that. Promoting brand loyalty is the goal of any company, but breaking brand loyalty is the goal of the competitors' marketing team.

---

peripheral route One of two paths to changing an attitude; the peripheral route of attitude change attempts to intervene on beliefs that are not very strong.

To get a sense of the lengths to which manufacturers go to persuade you to buy their product, look at the toothpaste section of any large grocery store. There are dozens of choices, with all manner of 'pitches' to consumers as to why each one is desirable or superior, but all contain essentially the same active ingredients. Because brand preference is a *peripheral* issue, shiny packages, 'new and improved' labels, an 'extra' couple of ounces, a sale, or any number of other factors may convince people to try another brand. We're also swayed by attractive and/or famous people, which is why they're hired by advertisers.

The **central route** refers to the attitudes we hold central to how we see ourselves (our values), and thus messages must be logical, clear, and compelling. We don't change *central* attitudes without remarkable cause. However, convincing arguments are usually found on 'both' sides of any argument, or they wouldn't be arguments. What would it take to get you to change religion, political affiliation, or your stance on a hot-button topic? Probably, it would be hard for you to conceive of what it takes, but people do change, and messages motivate us to change must not only be compelling, but also delivered by people we feel are worthy of such serious attention. Thus, with attitude-change routes, 'who' conveys the message, and how, matters.

Source Factors of Attitude Change—Who Says?

Learning Objectives At the end of this section, you'll be able to:

14.4.5. Describe factors that impact the effectiveness of communicators;

14.4.6. Describe how communicator credibility affects willingness to listen to messages.

There are a number of factors that make a change agent more or less persuasive. One factor we've already talked about extensively is attractiveness. Attractive communicators are preferred by message recipients and they tend to be especially effective with peripheral route change. However, as you've likely guessed, communicator attractiveness is not sufficient to affect change via the central route, though it may hold someone's attention, at least initially.

A similar factor is fame. Name recognition, like attractiveness, may engage attention at first, and may be adequate to affect peripherally-processed attitudes. But to affect central route change, attention activated by attractiveness and/or fame, must be followed by meaningful and substantive message content. Thus, the credibility of the message deliverer is important.

Credibility refers to one's perception of a source's expertise or authority (e.g., Tormala, Briñol, & Petty, 2006). We place higher value on messages from credible sources. If we're

being asked to consider central route messages, we won't do so unless we believe (rightly or wrongly) the communicator is qualified to render opinions or convey facts worthy of our consideration. This is a problem for communicators believed to have hidden agendas which influence them to simply say what they think their listeners want to hear. If we feel a communicator doesn't have anything to gain by lying or twisting the truth, we'll be more likely to consider the message. Yet the manner in which the message is delivered also counts.

For example, one study showed that perceived credibility was influenced on the Internet by the mode of message transmission. Hu and Sundar (2010) outlined three categories of online source gatekeeping: unknown (Internet), individual (blogs, home pages, social networks), and collective (web sites, bulletin boards, wiki-based). They found people are more likely to change health behaviors when receiving messages from health bulletin boards and web sites, rather than blogs and personal web sites, even if those latter messages come from bona fide medical doctors. The authors also cited Sundar (1998) who noted people may use an "I-read-somewhere-that" approach to bolstering their views, without evaluating the credibility of the source. In an online world, the number of sources is staggering, so that the evaluation of those sources should be critical prior to adopting their messages as valid.

So, the most effective central route communications will come from attractive and/or famous sources who are credible authorities without ulterior motives, delivering messages in a manner that supports credibility. An effective central route communicator will be all the more effective with peripheral route attitudes. Yet, even with a high rating on each of these factors, a communicator cannot change the attitudes of those who aren't open to change.

Audience Factors of Attitude Change—You Talking to Me?

Learning Objectives At the end of this section, you'll be able to:

14.4.7. Describe how particular people or groups are targeted for attitudinal change;

14.4.8. Describe strategies used to maximize the effectiveness of a targeted message;

14.4.9. Explain real-world impact of social influence on an audience.

Advertising and political messages are usually targeted to a group with a specific 'demographic.' Relevant characteristics might be sex, age, socioeconomic status, political persuasion, etc. An ad for toothpaste may look very different from an ad for a political candidate, but the intention in both cases is similar: reach a target audience and persuade them to maintain a current attitude or adopt a new one. Typically, a communicator is trying to change the attitudes of individuals within a group, and wouldn't expect an entire group to change an attitude.

---

central route One of two paths to changing an attitude; the central route of attitude change attempts to intervene on core beliefs (e.g., personal values or other strongly held ideas).

When trying to convince an audience to maintain an attitude, the target group is like-minded people with regard to the communicator's message. However, when trying to change an attitude, the audience must be carefully assessed to maximize effectiveness. It simply wouldn't work for the leader of a political party to take the stage at an event sponsored by the opposite party and tell people they're all wrong and need to modify their attitudes. Regardless of the positive attributes of the speaker, the audience would be oppositional at the start. However, this speaker might be persuasive if the audience consisted of independent or undecided voters.

While persuading an individual to change views on an important issue may be difficult, it may be less difficult if others in his/her group go along with the message. As we'll see, the effects of social influence on our attitudes, behavior, and cognition can be profound.

Section 5: Six Social Influence Factors—How We Sway One Another

Cialdini (2001) described the following six influence tactics people use to get others to comply with their requests: 1) reciprocity, 2) consistency, 3) conformity (also called social proof), 4) authority 5) ingratiation (also called liking), and 6) scarcity. Let's consider how these forces influence us, oftentimes without our awareness. We'll show you how you are affected by these evidence-based social influence principles.

Reciprocity—One Good Turn Deserves Another

Learning Objectives At the end of this section, you'll be able to:

14.5.1. Define reciprocity;

14.5.2. Discuss how the concept of reciprocity may affect your daily life;

14.5.3. Describe the positive and negative implications of reciprocity.

Reciprocity reflects a feeling of obligation to respond 'in kind' when somebody does something for us. This powerful norm exists in virtually all cultures and facilitates mutual trust, social exchange, and a sense of interdependence (Cialdini & Trost, 1998; Gouldner, 1960). We reciprocate when we return a favor, and we expect others to do return favors we grant

---

reciprocity A feeling of obligation arising from the notion that we are in debt to someone when they do something for us.

them. This is reflected in the common saying "You owe me one!" We learn to say "thank you" as a minimal return gesture acknowledging our indebtedness.

Interestingly, a favor need not be desired by its recipient to create a perceived need to repay. You may have been offered a favor by someone you didn't like and turned it down because you didn't want to feel obligated. Why not just take a 'free' favor? Because there's no such thing as a 'free' favor.

It's such a powerful effect that a favor is sometimes 'returned' to someone other than the original giver, if that giver isn't available (e.g., Berkowitz & Daniels, 1964; Isen & Levin, 1972). However, the sense of obligation declines over time (Burger, Horita, Kinoshita, Roberts, & Vera 1997) and reciprocation is more likely in public versus private situations (Whatley, Webster, Smith, & Rhodes, 1999).

Salespeople and fundraisers frequently use this principle to get you to buy a product or contribute to a cause. For example, Chris was offered a 'reduced' price stay at a nice hotel and 'gifts' if he and his wife attended a sales meeting for a 'great deal' on a time-share arrangement. When Chris did not take the 'deal of a lifetime' offer, they attempted to make him feel guilty for taking up their time and accepting their gifts. Because he was aware of this reciprocity tactic, he didn't feel guilty. But these salespeople succeed in making many feel like they 'owe' them the 'favor' of taking their deal.

If you wait tables you may be interested to hear that most restaurant diners actually do tip (Speer, 1997), which is a form of reciprocity for service. Bill size and service quality are the biggest determinants of tip size, but factors which increase tip amounts by 20% or more include: servers introducing themselves; squatting by the table; smiling; touching the customers; writing 'Thank You!' or drawing a smiley face on the bill (Lynn, 1996). You'll notice these are all *social* factors. Yet, even simply including a piece of candy when presenting the bill reliably increases tip size, showing an enhanced reciprocity effect (e.g., Rind & Strohmetz, 1999; Strohmetz, Rind, Fisher, & Lynn, 2002).

Further, the principle works in destructive ways as well . . . when people repay an injury or an insult by doing something bad to the offender. Some call this 'negative reciprocity' and it's the essence of what motivates people who seek revenge. One possible dramatic result of negative reciprocity is road rage. A driver inadvertently cuts in front of another driver who then beeps his horn. Then the other driver honks his horn, and this is followed by a hand signal. Such negative reciprocity among drivers has on occasion resulted in fatalities. Another destructive effect of reciprocity is an insinuated 'obligation' that makes us feel uncomfortable, such as with the illustration in FIGURE 14•4. The idea that one is 'owed' sex or intimacy as a result of giving gifts is a particularly insidious and unfair attempt to take advantage of this principle. Thus, reciprocity can be both good and bad, and applies to both friends and enemies, but in general people are more likely to do favors for those they like, and this illustrates the 'liking' principle.

[FIGURE 14•4] Reciprocity can involve good or bad intentions.

Ingratiation/Liking—I'll Do It Because I Like You, or Want You to Like Me

Learning Objectives At the end of this section, you'll be able to:

14.5.4. Define impression management;

14.5.5. Describe the benefits of self-monitoring;

14.5.6. Discuss ways of managing your attitudes and behaviors to change the way others may perceive you.

If someone asked you for a favor, you'd be more likely to agree if you liked them, right? We've touched on many factors that increase affiliation and noted that people tend to like those similar to them. But, even the most inconsequential of perceived similarities results in increased compliance to requests (Burger, Messian, Patel, del Prado, & Anderson, 2003), so it seems this factor is worthy of further consideration.

We've already discussed that 'liked' (in-group) people are more likely to receive favorable treatment. But, can we 'make' people like us? It seems under certain circumstances, the answer is an unqualified 'yes.' **Ingratiation** is a conscious attempt to get others to like us so we'll later receive more favorable treatment. Jones and Jones (1964) defined ingratiation as a form of **impression management**, which is behaving intentionally to increase the amount one is liked by another.

Self-monitoring is the degree to which people pay attention to the impressions they are making and adjust their actions accordingly.

As you can imagine, people vary considerably in terms of their self-monitoring in various situations, and we all engage in impression management at times. One such situation is a first date, as illustrated in **FIGURE 14•5**, where the compliment is likely genuine, but also likely said at the outset to increase feelings of liking. Or, think of a job interview. Qualifications do count, but wouldn't you dress up, be on time, shake hands firmly, make eye contact, speak up, and attempt to be on your best behavior? We do this to make a good first impression, because we know we get one chance at a first impression. We also know a good first impression means we'll be liked and that being liked means we're more likely to get the job.

As it happens, people tend to have a greater liking for those who compliment them often (e.g., Drachman, DeCarufel, & Insko, 1978; Gordon, 1996). On the one hand, genuine praise, recognition, and rewarding feedback increase a recipient's sense of competence and self-efficacy (Allen, 1990; Daniels, 2000; Daniels & Larson, 2001; Geller, 1997). And, it makes sense to like and complement those who are responsible and competent. But on the other hand, even obviously inauthentic compliments can increase liking (Orpen, 1996).

For example, a study of 122 salespeople from 35 firms in 9 different industries showed " . . . supervisor-focused impression management was positively related to the supervisor's liking of the salesperson" (Vilela et al., 2007, p. 624). Ingratiation was accomplished mostly through showing admiration for supervisors, not work-focused impression management, and

---

ingratiation A conscious effort to get others to like us. This effort can take many forms, like complementing someone or taking acting more enthusiastic about their interests than you really are.

impression management Actively managing the way you believe others perceive you. (e.g., buying clothes you cannot afford to convey an appearance of wealth).

---

self-monitoring Actively monitoring *others*' reactions and adjusting *your* actions to change the way you believe they perceive you.

[**FIGURE 14•5**] A free compliment or hoping to earn interest?

success was reflected in better performance ratings by supervisors. In other words, 'kissing up' led to higher ratings, but hyping one's performance or importance did not. The authors speculated that direct self-promotion was ignored due to the obvious 'motive,' whereas superficial complements were more acceptable and desirable, and thus more effective.

We hope you'll always strive to be the best employee you can be, but be aware that a supervisor's 'liking' or 'disliking' of you may influence your performance appraisals. If you're a supervisor, we hope you'll always strive to value authentic merit and be fair to those who've not ingratiated themselves, but be aware that ingratiation will likely affect your judgment. Liking is indeed a powerful influence. We also tend to like people who are consistent in their words and deeds and consistency is another powerful social influence factor.

Consistency—I'll Do It Because I Said I Would

Learning Objectives At the end of this section, you'll be able to:

14.5.7. Define cognitive dissonance;

14.5.8. Explain how cognitive dissonance can be used to change attitudes and behaviors;

14.5.9. Describe the "foot-in-the-door" and "door-in-the-face" techniques.

When we develop attitudes, state intentions, or make choices, we encounter internal and external forces that pull us toward **consistency**. Like with reciprocity, this principle has roots in societies valuing stability in everyday life, and it serves as a heuristic to interpret situations and make decisions (Cialdini,

2001). Consistency is often assumed to be a central motive, serving as the basis for experiencing *cognitive dissonance* (Festinger, 1957) and *self-perception theory* (Bem, 1967). It explains, in part, why a change in behavior often leads to corresponding attitude change and vice versa (Aronson, 1999).

Cognitive dissonance occurs when one's attitude and behavior are inconsistent and this causes personal discomfort such that a person becomes motivated to adjust either their attitude or behavior so they match. This is critical to understanding why we sometimes do things that aren't exactly logical. A classic example is smoking. If we believe smoking is unhealthy, then smoking is inconsistent with that attitude. A smoker can't avoid the knowledge that it's unhealthy, so s/he should experience *cognitive dissonance*, which would be alleviated if s/he stopped smoking. But people still smoke, so something else must be going on; namely, attitude change. A smoker can also alleviate *cognitive dissonance* by downplaying the danger so it's in line with the behavior.

The following real example comes from a physician who tried to prompt a patient to quit smoking. The doctor asked her to evaluate pros and cons of smoking cessation. She readily listed several positive factors: improved health and lifespan, a decrease in allergy symptoms and sinus infections, no longer exposing family members to second-hand smoke, and financial savings (at that time $3/pack, this low-income patient realized she'd save over $1,000 per year). Those are very logical and compelling reasons to quit smoking. But, then the patient said, "Everyone has a bad habit, and smoking is better than

---

consistency The pressure we feel to behave in ways which are in concert with our attitudes and beliefs or to behave in ways we know others expect us to behave.

cognitive dissonance When an individual's attitudes and beliefs are not aligned.

drinking; besides, I could die in a car wreck tomorrow—when it's my time to go, I'll go." This attitude adjustment negated all the logic of quitting, and enabled the patient to engage in the otherwise dissonant behavior of smoking without being disturbed by its many realistic negative implications.

Cognitive dissonance was first explored by Festinger and Carlsmith (1959), who showed people unconsciously change their attitudes when induced into behaviors inconsistent with their self-view. They designed repetitive and very boring tasks about which the participant " . . . would have a somewhat negative opinion" (p.205). Participants were asked to put 12 spools on a tray, empty it, and refill it again, repeatedly, for half an hour. Next, they received a board with 24 pegs, and rotated each peg one quarter turn clockwise, continually, again for half an hour. They were told to use one hand and work at their own speed as a research assistant frequently took notes with a stop watch, to give an impression of scientific legitimacy.

Each participant had been randomly assigned to either a control group, a $1 group, or a $20 group. Those in the $1 and $20 group were told a bogus story that researchers employed a student to tell participants in a 'different condition' the tasks were enjoyable, interesting, and exciting, so researchers could see how these groups differed on performance. Participants were told the employee didn't come that day, and they were asked to serve as a paid substitute (either $1 or $20) to tell the next participant the tasks were enjoyable; or in other words, to lie.

Now in 1959, $1 was worth about $6 in 2012 dollars. However, $20 was worth about $155 in 2012 dollars (www .westegg.com/inflation; www.measuringworth.com). Thus, one group had a relatively small incentive to lie and the other had a very large incentive to lie. But, nobody likes to see themselves as a liar. The control group didn't lie to anyone, so their opinions served as a baseline for comparison with the two other groups. On average, the control group rated the tasks as neutral on enjoyment, felt they learned little, figured the experiment had only middling importance, and were somewhat unlikely to want to do something similar in the future.

After lying, the $20 group had virtually the same opinions of the study as the control group. But, the $1 group rated enjoyment significantly higher and said they would be somewhat likely to *want* to participate in a similar study later. Cognitive dissonance was thus assuaged one of two ways. Having lied for receiving a large amount of money amounted to sufficient personal justification. Who wouldn't tell a 'little white lie' for lots of money? Yet, receiving only a small amount for lying was insufficient for personal justification. These participants thus adjusted their attitude, so they didn't *feel* they were actually lying. And, they didn't seem to notice doing this.

Despite the pointless monotony, none of the groups rated the tasks as extremely negative, nor did they feel the study was worthless or without any value. Perhaps these attitudes were derived from the fact they spent an hour doing simple repetitive tasks, and to justify their effort they assumed there must be some value to the tasks. To what extent do we form our attitudes from observing our own behavior?

Darryl Bem (1967) derived the notion of **self-perception theory**, which says we actually infer some of our attitudes from interpreting our own behavior. An example might be having a second sandwich and saying to oneself, "I must have been hungrier than I thought." Now, how can *you* be hungrier than *you* thought? But, we make such cognitive adjustments to explain our own actions to ourselves. This may be the source of some of our more enduring and important attitudes. For example, if you grew up in a highly political (liberal or conservative) household, you may have found yourself in the midst of many political discussions, agreeing or disagreeing. Having been exposed to such activities much of your young life, on reaching adulthood you may infer your own attitude to be consistent with your behavior in those political discussions.

Psychologists have used *consistency* as a behavior change technique for years, for example, intervening to increase recycling behaviors by highlighting pro-environmental attitudes (e.g., DeLeon & Fuqua, 1995; Geller & Lehman, 1991; Werner et al., 1995) or using the method of motivational interviewing to get people to decrease health risks across a variety of domains (e.g., Lundahl et al., 2013). And it's useful in increasing sales and charitable contributions (Burger, 1999; Cialdini, 2001).

The '**foot-in-the-door**' method gets us to make a small commitment and then raises the stakes. We're more likely to agree to a larger request in order to feel consistent with our prior commitment. This drives the infamous 'low-balling' technique, where we agree to buy a product at a great price, going through formalities like signing paperwork, after which the salesperson 'finds out' from the manager' s/he wasn't authorized to offer the 'great' price. The price is raised, but the customer is *already* committed to buying and thus agrees to the higher price.

In fact, exceedingly small appeals are often very effective at getting much more than you might expect. This is variation is called *legitimizing paltry contributions*. Cialdini and Schroeder (1976) went door-to-door collecting for a charity, and said "Even a penny will help!" In this condition, a greater percentage of people contributed and more money was actually donated per person. Compared to just plain asking for donations, it garnered 60% more in contributions! Refusing a penny is hard to do because it is inconsistent with our self-view that we're caring people. But, giving just a penny seems almost shameful, as we also think we're generous; so we're inclined to give more. For another classic scientific demonstration of this consistency phenomenon, check out **Beyond the Basics** (FEATURE 14•5).

---

self-perception theory Observing our behavior and inferring what our attitudes are based on the way we've acted.

foot-in-the-door Obtaining a small commitment in order to later achieve a larger request.

[**FIGURE 14•6**] This approach may lead to a real door-in-the-face.

feature 14.5

Beyond the Basics Freedman and Fraser (1966) showed the inherent power of persuasion in the *foot-in-the-door* technique when they had a researcher pose as an activist asking people to sign a petition or display a very small sign, promoting either safe driving or keeping the environment beautiful. Two weeks later, a different researcher posing as an activist, asked the same people to install a very large sign saying 'Drive Carefully' in their front yard. They were shown a photograph of the supposed sign, which looked amateurish and concealed much of a home in the background. A control group was simply asked on first contact whether they would display the large sign. Thus, the dependent variable was agreement to displaying the sign.

Less than 20% in the control group agreed to display the large sign, showing it to be quite unpopular. No significant differences existed in the experimental groups regarding acceptance of the small first requests. Yet, of those people who agreed to a small request, an average of 55% agreed to display the large sign. For those where the first and second requests were dissimilar, average compliance was still 47%, more than double the control rate. However, when requests were similar (small and large 'Drive Carefully' signs), average compliance was 76%! Clearly, this technique is effective, so you're now less likely to become its victim. If using it on others, we hope you'll do so benevolently, perhaps promoting health, safety, or a charity.

The **'door-in-the-face'** technique also uses consistency, but takes the opposite tact: making an absurdly large request, virtually guaranteed to be refused, and following with a small request. This is illustrated in jest in **FIGURE 14•6**, where the man's first request is ridiculous, making the second seem 'reasonable' by contrast. More realistically, if asked "Would you please donate $500 to our charity?" you'd likely say, "I don't have that kind of money!" If then asked "Well, could you possibly donate as little as $5?" we'd likely perceive this 99% reduction as sensible in comparison and be more likely comply. The 'trivial' plea is what such requesters are after, and it often works. This approach is also associated with reciprocity, because when a requestor retreats, we feel a need to reciprocate by granting the next request. But, after refusing a large request, to reject a person again for a small request would be inconsistent with our self-view of being cooperative and caring. And, if asked in public, we'd also want to be seen by others as charitable. And, if others are doing similar things, we're more likely to go along.

Conformity—Everybody's Doing It

Learning Objectives At the end of this section, you'll be able to:

14.5.10. Describe Asch's Line Experiment;

14.5.11. Discuss how groups impact an individual;

14.5.12. Explain how social influence can impact attitudes, cognitions, and behaviors.

---

door-in-the-face Making a large, often irrational, request in order to make the smaller request that follows seem much more reasonable.

Some conformity is inevitable in life. We look to others to know what's acceptable, as well as what's 'in' and what's 'out' in society, and we get information from others' behavior. And, as we demonstrated above, we also feel an affinity to those 'similar' to us. In familiar situations, conformity may be motivated by a need for social approval; going along to get along, so to speak (Cialdini & Goldstein, 2004). Conformity is also why we don't have the freedom to yell 'fire!' in a crowded theater. It would take only a few panicked people to induce mass panic. As Solomon Asch (1907–1996) demonstrated, other peoples' behavior in an unfamiliar group situation can be a powerful influence on our own behavior.

Asch (1955) showed individuals would deny reality in order to conform to the obviously incorrect perceptions of strangers—with a study that's become known as 'the line experiment.' Groups of seven to nine male college students (confederates) acted like participants in an experiment. An actual participant was recruited at the last minute, and told that a 'visual discrimination experiment' was starting and another person was needed. A standard line was displayed on one card and three comparison lines were on another card (see FIGURE 14•7). While the supposed goal was to pick lines matching standards, the experiment really tested conformity.

Each person said, in turn, which of the three lines matched the first, and the real participant was always near last to report. Unbeknownst to the actual participants, the first confederate was instructed to pick wrong lines (covertly supplied by the experimenter) on 66% of the trials and all other confederates were then to confidently say the same wrong line matched the standard. A control group showed actual perceptual errors were unlikely, averaging near 100% correct in line matching. Lines ranged from 2 to 10 inches and prearranged errors ranged from moderate (¾ inch) to extreme (1¾ inch).

After everyone else said the wrong thing the actual participant was left either to state the obviously correct match, or bow to the pressure and agree with the group error. Most of us would probably think, "I'd never bow to pressure to say the wrong thing." But, actual participants had no idea what was going on and many fell victim to conformity. When unanimous confederates stated an error, 76% of 123 naive participants stated the same error; and while 24% never agreed, 27% agreed with most errors. On the whole, participants conformed to errors 37% of the time.

Thus, with no real penalty for stating the truth, participants often went along with these strangers, and some did almost every time. The power of conformity is even more pronounced when group size grows. Participants were less likely to agree with just one or two others, but the more confederates, the more likely the participant would agree with errors (see FIGURE 14•8).

There are many real life situations, such as behavior in bars, at parties, or in the workplace, where group pressures often influence us to take risks. There's even pressure in our legal system for jurors to conform to one another, despite any instructions to the contrary. For more on conformity in high-stakes legal outcomes, read **Psychological Literacy** (FEATURE 14•6).

The Standard Line   Line 1   Line 2   Line 3

[**FIGURE 14•7**] Example of Lines in Asch's experiment.

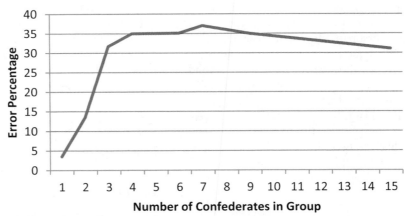

[**FIGURE 14•8**] Greater groups create greater pressure.

feature 14.6

| Psychological Literacy |

Perhaps the most important pillar of our legal system is the right to trial by a jury of our peers. And, we'd like to think juries are unbiased and objective in considering the evidence and rendering impartial verdicts. But, this isn't always the case. Consider that most juries are given many 'facts' and lawyers attempt to shape their views of those facts. Lots of legitimate questions might arise, but a jury is supposed to render a unanimous decision. Not doing so may ultimately result in a 'hung jury' where they 'fail' in their perceived civic responsibility to discern the truth. And, it certainly keeps jurors in the room or on the case longer if agreement isn't quick. A couple of jurors with strong personalities and convinced of their initial position, can likely sway others to go along with their certainty, making uncertain members feel they ought to go along.

One group of researchers concluded from a review of the literature that "a host of mock jury experiments have demonstrated that jury deliberations polarize already existing opinions (Peoples, Sigillo, Green & Miller, 2012, p. 179)." They showed distant versus close friendships among jurors modified conformity with the former increasing and latter decreasing conformity. They noted three factors influencing jury conformity: impression management, idiosyncrasy credits, and cognitive dissonance (Peoples et al., 2012).

You've read about the first and third factor in this chapter, but *idiosyncrasy credits* refer to building up enough positive social equity (credits) that disagreement doesn't overly strain a relationship. In close friendships, we don't work to 'look correct' or worry about 'offending' a buddy, and we're more confident saying what we feel and acting on those feelings. Conformity tends to increase when we are in unfamiliar stress-ridden social situations, like being on juries with strangers, in front of lawyers, a judge, and courtroom observers. When this happens, miscarriages of justice are possible.

In fact, even Supreme Court justices seem to fall prey to this phenomenon. Granberg and Bartels (2005) reviewed over 4,000 decisions from cases between 1953 and 2001, and found that unanimous decisions were the most common! These accounted for 35% of all decisions, with the more stereotypical 5 to 4 split occurring only 21% of the time. A lone nonconformist was present in only 10% of the cases, with the rest of cases falling within every other combination. So, we do influence each other, and that's not always a bad thing. But if it has the potential to alter lives, we recommend using extreme caution about being unduly influenced by the conformity factor.

If you sometimes long to be the lone voice of reason in group decision-making, you have reason to feel encouraged. Asch (1955) showed that by having just one confederate dissent and say the true match was correct, contradicting the confederates, actual participants were then more likely to also state the truth rather than conforming. Being a brave dissenter or a devil's advocate can be a very important role to play, though it tends to disrupt group harmony as we'll see when addressing *groupthink* below.

Staying true to you is more important in established groups, such as in the workplace where people often claim expertise in their judgments, as research shows conformity increases when the group members are seen as relatively experienced (Cialdini & Trost, 1998). Yet some group memberships are very brief, as with the line experiment, and behavior in contrived groups can influence an individual's compliance (e.g., Milgram, 1964, 1965a). Plus, as Stanley Milgram (1933-1984) established, nothing seems to generate extraordinary compliance more than seemingly legitimate authority.

Authority—I Was Just Following Orders

Learning Objectives At the end of this section, you'll be able to:

14.5.13. Describe Milgram's study of obedience and the Stanford Prison Study;

14.5.14. Discuss how perceived authority may influence your thoughts and behaviors;

14.5.15. Define psychological reactance.

For a society to run smoothly, obedience to certain types of authority are essential. Children obey parents, employees the boss, citizens the police, soldiers the commanders, etc. Benefits to such obedience include keeping order, deferring decisions to qualified experts, and carrying out difficult directives such as military action (e.g., Osofsky, Bandura, & Zimbardo, 2005). Yet, pro-social rule breaking or deviation is sometimes helpful (e.g., Morrison, 2006). For example, we benefit if an employee blows the whistle on a company polluting our environment, and it makes sense to ignore a 'no swimming' sign to save someone from drowning.

Milgram (1974) noted that we learn to obey and value legitimate authority in childhood. But on the other hand, his research provided chilling examples of the evil normal people may do in unusual situations where an authority figure demands compliance. Milgram got interested in the issue of obedience when noting the reaction of Nazi officers on trial at the Nuremberg Trials following the end of World War II. When questioned why they committed such atrocities, most denied responsibility, claiming they were 'only' obeying orders.

As Milgram duly noted (1963, p371), "It has been reliably established that from 1933–45 millions of innocent persons were systematically slaughtered on command. Gas chambers were built, death camps were guarded, daily quotas of corpses were produced with the same efficiency as the manufacture of appliances. These inhumane policies may have originated in the mind of a single person, but they could only be carried out on a massive scale if a very large number of persons obeyed orders." As this was so inhumane and shamelessly evil, Milgram wondered why Germans blindly followed such horrifying orders.

If Milgram could devise a means to measure dangerous obedience to authority, he reasoned he could establish relatively low levels in America, and go to Germany and find relatively high levels there. However, his findings showed that humans in general could be induced to perform terrible acts they would ordinarily never do on their own, simply by introducing what seemed to be a legitimate authority figure.

Among a series of experiments was Milgram's classic 1963 study of 40 men aged 20 to 50, from a wide range of jobs and educational backgrounds. Conducted at Yale University, they were surely thinking this was a high-quality research project. They were paid $4.50, about the equivalent of $35 these days (www.westegg.com/inflation; www.measuring-worth.com), and were told this was for " . . . simply coming to the laboratory, and that the money was theirs no matter what happened after they arrived" (p. 372).

Participants met a researcher in a lab coat, played by an actor with an 'impassive' and 'stern' demeanor. Then, they met a 'likable' and 'mild-mannered' participant, who was really a confederate actor. They were told the study was designed to understand how punishment affected learning, and how people learned from each other. One participant was to be a 'teacher' and the other a 'learner,' and the teacher would administer penalties to the learner so the researcher could see how it affected memory. A rigged drawing made the actual participant the teacher as both slips of paper said 'teacher.' When warranted, the teacher was to penalize the learner in another room, as both agreed to do. The penalty was an electric shock!

The learner was to learn word pairs from a list read by the teacher, and then recall the second word of each pair. If the learner got an item wrong, the teacher was to deliver a shock. Then, the learner was strapped into an 'electric chair' device in front of the teacher. The straps were said to prevent excessive movement, and an electrode was applied along with gel to 'avoid blisters and burns.' The electrode was said to be attached to a 'shock generator.' The teacher was then given a real shock of 45 volts to demonstrate what the learner would experience, thereby enhancing the notion this was a potentially painful situation for the learner. The teacher then went into the other room to read the words into an intercom.

The 'shock generator' was a detailed apparatus with 30 switches. Pressing a switch made a voltage meter needle swing, along with a flashing light and a loud buzzing noise, appearing to give a shock of the designated voltage. Switches started at 15 volts and increased in 15-volt increments up to 450 volts, with accompanying labels: 'Slight Shock,' 'Moderate Shock,' etc., up to 'Danger: Severe Shock' and finally, 'XXX,' which in those days denoted 'deadly.'

The teacher read word-pair lists to the learner, and after finishing the list started at the beginning with the first word of each pair, along with four other words. The learner was to

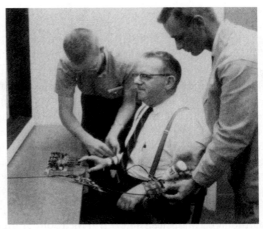

[**FIGURE 14·9**]   The learner in the Milgram's study being strapped to the shock plate by a research assistant.

From the film *Obedience*, © 1968 by Stanley Milgram; © renewed 1993 by Alexandra Milgram, and distributed by Alexander Street Press.

pick the word previously paired with the first, indicating his choice with a button that lit up one of four lights on the teacher's panel. The list was repeatedly read until the learner correctly recalled all pairs. The teacher was to give an incrementally higher level of shock for each error. If a teacher reached the end of the switches, delivering 450 potentially deadly volts, the researcher would then stop the experiment (Milgram, 1963).

Now Milgram didn't think participants would shock an innocent victim with 450 volts. He wasn't alone. He gave detailed descriptions of the experiment to 14 college seniors and asked them to predict what percentage of people they thought would go all the way to 450 volts in such a situation. Their answers were probably like what yours would be if you didn't know what was coming . . . they unanimously agreed only an 'insignificant minority' would persist. The estimates ranged from zero to 3%, with an average of 1.2%. Milgram also asked some colleagues and they indicated 'few, if any' would go beyond the Very Strong Shock label (Milgram, 1963). What happened was surprising to all: 65% of these regular folk shocked the learner with 450 volts!

Of course, no shocks were actually delivered, but the teachers thought it was real. The learner could be heard over an intercom, but the teacher heard standardized responses. First, the learner would verbally protest, then grunt in pain, then demand to quit the study and be let go, and eventually he gave no more answers and pounded on the wall. At 315 volts, he pounded and then was heard no more. A reasonable assumption would be that he was unconscious or dead.

If the teacher protested, he was met with standardized responses from the researcher, who said such things as 'please go on,' 'it is absolutely essential that you continue,' and the like. The researcher said he would 'accept responsibility' for the experiment, and "Although the shocks can be extremely painful, they cause no permanent tissue damage" (Milgram, 1963, p. 373). All continued to the 300-volt level, just before

'Extreme Intensity.' And, all who went as far as 390, went all the way. But, they didn't do it gleefully. Most were very upset, as Milgram described:

> "Subjects were observed to sweat, tremble, stutter, bite their lips, groan, and dig their fingernails into their flesh. These were characteristic rather than exceptional responses to the experiment. One sign of tension was the regular occurrence of nervous laughing fits. Fourteen of the 40 subjects showed definite signs of nervous laughter and smiling. The laughter seemed entirely out of place, even bizarre. Full-blown, uncontrollable seizures were observed for three subjects. On one occasion we observed a seizure so violently convulsive that it was necessary to call a halt to the experiment. The subject, a 46-year-old encyclopedia salesman, was seriously embarrassed by his untoward and uncontrollable behavior. In the post-experimental interviews, subjects took pains to point out that they were not sadistic types, and that the laughter did not mean they enjoyed shocking the victim (Milgram, 1963, p. 375)."

So, what 'made' these people theoretically injure or kill an innocent victim, despite their extreme discomfort and objections? Simply this: a supposed Yale scientist in a lab coat saying they should. There were no forces other than intangible institutional prestige, an experimenter's insistence, and a social pressure of consistency. For example, they'd already pressed each lever so why not the next? If one pressed 60, why not 75? If 300, why not 315? And, they did openly agree to do this, as did the learner. However, the teachers could have quit at any time.

If this was all it took to cause good U.S. citizens to do evil acts, then how much more 'evil' was a German soldier who obeyed a superior Nazi officer demanding compliance to kill others, knowing those who refused orders were killed, or their families would be tortured and/or killed in front of them? That's not to excuse Nazi atrocities, as there can be no excuse for such inhumanity. However, Milgram showed how regular people in extraordinary situations can be made to obey extremely unjust orders. For those controlled by dictators, obedience is commonly given to even the most illegitimate of authorities, under threat of force.

Milgram reported, "After the interview, procedures were taken to assure that the subject would leave the laboratory in a state of well-being. A friendly reconciliation was arranged between the subject and the victim and an effort was made to reduce any tensions that arose as a result of the experiment (p. 374)." However, if you watch the video made of this study, you see teachers were extremely uncomfortable and they had to reconcile themselves with the idea they theoretically injured or killed an innocent person because a stranger told them to do so. Talk about cognitive dissonance! This led to an outcry that such experiments were unethical and a demand for institutional oversight of research. We now have such oversight.

One may be tempted to think that was a different time, and people wouldn't obey so blindly today. However 45

years later, an ethical replication of this work showed people still obey this type of authority (Burger, 2009). While Milgram (1965b, 1974) found he could decrease obedience by modifying certain variables (e.g., putting the victim in the same room, downgrading the prestige of the institution or the researcher), others have shown that titles, uniforms, and other symbols of authority enhance obedience to authority (Bushman, 1988; Cialdini, 2001). The Stanford Prison Study was another extraordinary example of obedience to authority and it also raised major ethical concerns (Zimbardo, 1973, 1989, 2011).

In 1971, Phillip Zimbardo was chief researcher for a project funded by the U.S. Navy to study the effects of people in the roles of guard or prisoner. He had a simulated prison built in the basement of a building at Stanford University (hence the famous study nickname), complete with locked cells, a common room, and a warden's office. Zimbardo played the warden and enlisted the help of actual police and others who acted as legal counsel, parole board members, etc.

He advertised for participants to be paid $15 per day, which is roughly $85 in today's dollars (www.westegg.com/inflation; www.measuringworth.com), and obtained numerous applicants. They were subjected to psychological tests to rule out pre-existing mental health or behavioral problems. He then selected " . . . about two dozen normal, average, healthy American college males . . ." (1973, p. 244) and randomly assigned each to be either a guard or prisoner.

Guards on eight-hour shifts controlled the prison and were outfitted with uniforms and other symbols of power. In contrast, the prisoners were picked up by city police, handcuffed in front of neighbors, processed at the police station, and made to wear degrading sack-like outfits with numbers in place of names. They were taken to the 'Stanford Prison' where they were kept 24-hours per day as though they were real prisoners.

Almost immediately, abuse of prisoners began. It started with verbal taunting and some prisoners initially took this in stride. However, the abuse worsened as prisoners lost their dignity and sense of identity and began to take on passive, victim-like roles, becoming subservient to the guards. The guards eventually engaged in outrageous acts: withholding food, stripping some of the prisoners naked, making them engage in simulated sexual acts, having them clean toilet bowls with their bare hands, commanding them to do gruelling exercises, and so on.

Thus, normal college students randomly assigned to be guards took on serious authority roles, exerted power and then abused their power. Regular college students randomly assigned to be prisoners voluntarily had their freedom taken away by real and pretend authorities. Yet they obeyed these authorities and endured abuse. As all participants were essentially equal going into the experiment, an artificial situation created genuine power differences. Further, even though prisoners could have voluntarily withdrawn from the experiment, they didn't behave as though they were free to leave, any more than most participants in Milgram's study.

The first 'prisoner' released had an apparent nervous breakdown within 36 hours and the staff felt compelled to let him go. A few others went a similar route. But until it ended, the other prisoners accepted their degraded roles, and guards relished their power, with a few exceptions. It was only stopped when a graduate student informed Zimbardo she couldn't believe what he was allowing to happen. Zimbardo listened and stopped the study.

Here again, we see a simulated social situation inducing people to behave in ways they'd never predict prior to actually being in the situation. How much more then would an authentic situation influence people? For an answer we need look no further than the real-life Abu Ghraib scandal of the Iraq War, which you can read about in **Psychological Literacy** (**FEATURE 14•7**). Like Milgram, Zimbardo showed the power of intangible social psychological forces, providing information that has real-world implications. Yet such studies were ethically questionable and are now justifiably scarce. Interestingly, sometimes scarcity influences reactions to authority.

feature 14.7

Psychological Literacy

The Stanford Prison Study scenario is frequently found in the real world. An example was the Abu Ghraib scandal of 2003 and early 2004 of the Iraq War. Some American military guards at the Abu Ghraib prison were discovered to have abused prisoners under their watch. The official explanation was this was the work of a few 'bad apples.' But, did bad people or a bad situation cause the abuse?

Zimbardo (2011) was recruited by lawyers for guard Ivan 'Chip' Frederick, an Army Reservist who was court-martialled for abusing prisoners. The abuse was not in question, as many photos showed him and others degrading prisoners. However, his defense team knew of the Stanford Prison Study and wanted to show the situation induced their client, an otherwise decent, family-loving, duty-bound, decorated soldier, to act in ways counter to his personality. Frederick was a Staff Sergeant with nine medals and awards to his name; clearly, a patriotic and professional soldier before Abu Ghraib. So, what happened?

The situation at Abu Ghraib was challenging, to say the least. Like in most prisons, a few guards were responsible for maintaining order among many prisoners. But in this case they were literally in a war zone where U.S. soldiers were regularly killed, and attacks led by prisoners or their outside comrades were always possible. Plus, guards didn't speak the prisoners' language, so direct communication was impossible. They also worked 12-hour shifts, seven days a week, up to 40 days in a row. Zimbardo noted such duty is tediously dull, and invites abuse to relieve boredom. What usually starts out as mild abuse can only escalate. As with Zimbardo's study, the worst Abu Ghraib abuses occurred mainly at night, when intense supervision was lacking.

This doesn't *excuse* the bad behavior of these soldiers, but it certainly *explains* it better than simply blaming them for being bad people. It turns on its head the notion of the bad apples. Zimbardo suggests a better explanation is a bad barrel negatively affected otherwise good apples. Here an unethical real-world situation paralleled an unethical, yet important and unheeded study which was commissioned years earlier by the U.S. Navy to better understand these very issues.

Zimbardo questioned his own ethics after the Stanford Prison Study ended and the study changed how research was done. But, its findings and documented real-world situations ought to give us pause to consider how we might modify some of society's penal practices to create more humane systems for everyone involved; for prisoners and prison staff, whose own lives might be otherwise degraded by a bad situation. As it happened, Frederick was dishonorably discharged in 2004 and sentenced to 8 years in prison. He was released on parole in 2007.

Under authoritative orders, personal freedom is scarce, and some are motivated to disregard rules to reassert their sense of independence (e.g., Brehm & Brehm, 1981; Brehm, 1966; Brehm & Cole, 1966; Brehm, & Sensenig, 1966). **Psychological reactance** is when we passively aggressively undermine or disregard those in authority, in order to maintain our own self-views of being autonomous individuals. Unfortunately, whether at school, work or home, feeling controlled by others is not a scarce experience for many. A light-hearted look at this idea is found in **FIGURE 14•10**, where many have questioned why such signs are deemed as necessary and are always incomplete. And with that, let's look at scarcity itself, as a social factor that influences our behavior in some surprising ways.

Scarcity—I'll Do It Because I Might Not Get to Later

Learning Objectives At the end of this section, you'll be able to:

14.5.16. Define scarcity;

14.5.17. Describe how socially-constructed values may influence perceptions;

14.5.18. Discuss how social influence affects you.

In general, **scarcity** refers to the extent to which something is rare or difficult to acquire. In many cases, we value what is rare or hard to get and this serves as a heuristic in determining perceived values. For example, gold is a glittery metal,

---

psychological reactance A reaction to fight outside influences we believe are attempting to undermine the authority we have over our own thoughts and behaviors ("you can't tell me what to do/think!").

scarcity An attempt to influence people by conveying the notion that something is rare, valuable, or will not always be available.

[**FIGURE 14•10**] Some rule breaking results in cheeky behavior.

easy to shape, and resistant to corrosion. Aluminum is also shiny, malleable and resilient. But, gold is scarce and thus is valuable and we make soda cans from aluminum. Many people have been killed for gold, but nobody kills for aluminium. It's the same with diamonds versus quartz crystals.

An ordinary baseball card would only be worth the paper it's printed upon. But if it's a 1909 Honus Wagner card, it's a different story. Some people collect baseball cards and only 57 of those are known to still exist. The fact people want it and it's rare makes it valuable. Indeed, one was sold for $2.8 million! We didn't know who Honus Wagner was (see **FIGURE 14•11** for his photo), but we'd jump at a chance to get his card because they're scarce and demand is high. In fact, the law of supply and demand pivots upon scarcity. An unlimited supply can meet any demand. But, if there's a limited supply and high demand, value soars.

Scarcity prods people to seize what are perceived as rare opportunities (Cialdini, 2001). 'One-day only' sales and 'limited time' offers work because we desire freedom of choice, and scarcity makes freedom seem limited, prompting action (Cialdini & Trost, 1998). If something can only be had during a certain time frame, those who want it will be more motivated to obtain it during that time.

High cost also implies value because few people can afford it, even if actual materials or manufacturing processes aren't costly. For instance, many luxury items like shoes or handbags don't necessarily cost more to produce than those you might buy at a bargain/discount store, but they carry a certain status (e.g., Gucci, Prada, Lamborghini, Ferrari) and are sold at astronomical prices. Those who can't afford them often covet such items, because their exclusivity creates a perceived value. But, not everyone covets shoes, baseball cards,

Courtesy of Chicago History Museum/Getty Images, Inc.

[**FIGURE 14•11**] Honus Wagner—a face worth $2.8 million!

or even gold or diamonds. Nor is everyone equally influenced by any of the above social influence factors.

In the midst of social psychological material, the issue of individuality arises. To explore further, read **Why We Care (FEATURE 14•8)** and take our Social Influence Survey to graph your own influence susceptibility profile. Then discuss the results with your classmates. See how they feel about their scores for each social influence factor and note individual differences. As you've likely surmised, others' presence has a powerful effect on our behavior. So, let's look at some specifics of group dynamics.

feature 14.8

Why We Care: Determining Your Social Influence Susceptibility

Although a robust literature demonstrates the power of social influence techniques, individual responses vary in even the most powerful situations. In Zimbardo's prison, not all guards were severe abusers of prisoners, and not all prisoners did as they were told (Zimbardo, 1973, 1989). Milgram's (1963) experiment saw all participants deliver high levels of 'shocks' until the first disobedience occurred at 300 volts. Though most delivered 450-volts, 35% stopped earlier. Further, 24% of Asch's line experiment participants never conformed. Asch (1956) said people " . . . showed a marked tendency to be consistently independent, yielding, or intermediate in coping with the pressure of the majority (p. 70)." These various results suggest individual differences partially determine the impact of the social pressure.

There's also evidence of cross-cultural differences in propensity to be affected by conformity (Bond & Smith, 1996). Plus, when conformity and personality have been studied, some key individual-difference factors appear to be: locus of control (Larsen, Triplett, Brant, & Langenberg, 1979; Ryckman & Rodda, 1972), self-monitoring (Kurosawa, 1993; Santee

Social Influence Survey

Please read each question carefully and circle the number that indicates your level of agreement or disagreement with each statement: 1 = Strongly Disagree (SD), 2 = Disagree (D), 3 = Mildly Disagree (MD), 4 = Neutral (N), 5 = Mildly Agree (MA), 6 = Agree (A), 7 = Strongly Agree (SA)

	SD	D	MD	N	MA	A	SA
1. When someone does me a favor, I want to return the favor.	1	2	3	4	5	6	7
2. When I meet people with power over me, one of my main goals is to get them to like me.	1	2	3	4	5	6	7
3. I have a reputation for being true to my word.	1	2	3	4	5	6	7
4. I would put up with some discomfort to fit in with my group.	1	2	3	4	5	6	7
5. I always try to follow the rules.	1	2	3	4	5	6	7
6. I like buying one-of-a-kind items and/or collectables.	1	2	3	4	5	6	7
7. If a stranger helps me when I'm in need, I'm more likely to help another stranger in need.	1	2	3	4	5	6	7
8. I volunteer for jobs that will gain me the approval of others.	1	2	3	4	5	6	7
9. When I pledge to do something, it gets done.	1	2	3	4	5	6	7
10. I will change my beliefs to agree with other people I like.	1	2	3	4	5	6	7
11. It's more fun to break the rules.	1	2	3	4	5	6	7
12. I like being the only one with an item that everyone wants.	1	2	3	4	5	6	7
13. I treat others as I like to be treated.	1	2	3	4	5	6	7
14. I would do a job I disliked in order to gain respect or admiration from people who might be in a position to help me someday.	1	2	3	4	5	6	7
15. Being reliable is important to me.	1	2	3	4	5	6	7
16. It's hard for me to make up my mind about a TV show until I know what others think.	1	2	3	4	5	6	7
17. I believe in the statement, "Rules were made to be broken."	1	2	3	4	5	6	7
18. I try to pack as many fun things as possible into the last day of a vacation.	1	2	3	4	5	6	7
19. When people are nice to me, I'm more likely to be nice to them.	1	2	3	4	5	6	7
20. I do more than my fair share to impress others. 1	2	3	4	5	5	7	
21. My friends know they can count on me.	1	2	3	4	5	6	7
22. I would rather be myself than pretend to be someone I'm not to please others.	1	2	3	4	5	6	7
23. When I get "no" for an answer after I ask permission to do something, I do it anyway, if I can get away with it.	1	2	3	4	5	6	7
24. I don't mind paying more for something that is unique.	1	2	3	4	5	6	7

Determining Your Social Influence Survey Scores   Totals

Reciprocity:	Add	#1 (___)	+	#7 (___)	+	#13 (___)	+	#19 (___)	=
Liking / Ingratiation:	Add	#2 (___)	+	#8 (___)	+	#14 (___)	+	#20 (___)	=
Consistency:	Add	#3 (___)	+	#9 (___)	+	#15 (___)	+	#21 (___)	=
Conformity:	Add	#4 (___)	+	#10 (___)	+	#16 (___)	+	7 − (#22 ___) = ___	=
Authority:	Add	#5 (___)	+	7 − (#11 ___) = ___	+	7 − (#17 ___) = ___	+	7 − (#23 ___) = ___	=
Scarcity:	Add	#6 (___)	+	#12 (___)	+	#18 (___)	+	#24 (___)	=
Total Score:				Add All Totals					=

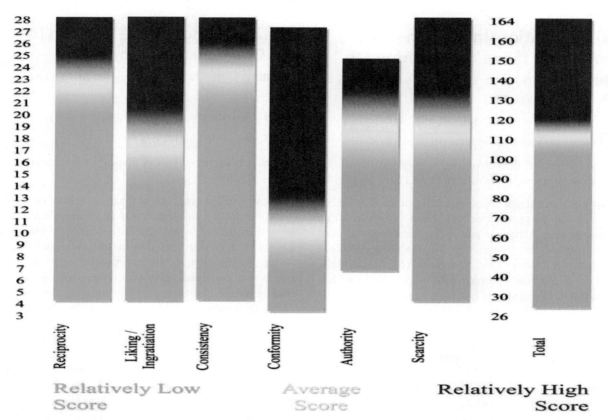

Social Influence Survey Scores, Averages, and Relative Interpretation The Normative/Comparison Group was comprised of college students at East Tennessee State University, circa 2007–2009. The total Number (*n*) = 1,121, with 756 females (67.4%) and 365 males (32.6%), averaging 21.3 years of age (Standard Deviation = 5.6; Range = 17 to 55) (Dula, 2014). Color code: Green = Relatively Low Score; Yellow = Average Range; Blue = Relatively High Score.

& Maslach, 1982), and self-esteem (Larsen, 1974; Stang, 1972). Yet individual differences and susceptibility to all six social influences have not been reported in the research literature.

We developed a Social Influence Survey (e.g., Lehman, Dula, Geller & Grandin, 2002) to teach these concepts. We've not yet published this measure in a peer-reviewed journal. But while it's not a rigorously-tested instrument, initial evaluations show it to have reliability and validity. For our purposes, it illustrates some rather intangible concepts in a more concrete way. So take the survey on the prior page as a fun and instructive demonstration, but don't take the results too seriously. Scoring your results should help you solidify your understanding of the six social influences covered in this section of the chapter.

Fill out the scale as honestly as possible, carefully score it, and then plot your scores in the table that allows you to compare it to one convenience sample. Scoring high or low on any scale does not indicate anything good or bad, just a possible tendency to be more or less swayed by a particular type of social influence. Keep in mind we all tend to answer surveys in ways we think are socially desirable! As you can see from the averages below, derived from one college sample, people rated themselves lowest on Conformity, and highest on Consistency. We feel those scores are 'consistent' with the social qualities deemed to be most and least socially desirable. Perhaps you can avoid this bias when you take the Social Influence Survey.

Section 6: Group Behavior— All Together Now!

Groups include individuals whose behaviors have collective effects. A group can exert pressure on an individual, and an individual can exert pressure on a group, if empowered. The interplay of group dynamics can have very interesting, influential, and sometimes unexpected results. Some effects are positive and some effects can even be dangerous. One initial social effect noticed was the effect of one person simply observing another's behavior.

Social Facilitation/Inhibition—I Do Better/Worse If You're Watching Me

Learning Objectives At the end of this section, you'll be able to:

14.6.1. Describe social facilitation and inhibition;

14.6.2. Discuss how arousal impacts performance;

14.6.3. Explain ways of bolstering your performance to account for the power of social influence.

When we get a boost out of productivity or an increase in performance quality simply due to others being present, this is **social facilitation**. When we perform worse simply because others are present, this is known as **social inhibition**. This is called the *Yerkes-Dodson Law of Arousal*, which essentially says that on many tasks, performance quality peaks with a moderate level of arousal, and quality suffers when arousal is either too low or too high (see **FIGURE 14•12**).

When we master a behavior, it can become sort of routine or automated, and isn't arousing. But, if we can do it well and people start watching, their presence increases arousal toward mid-level, and enhances performance. The arousal comes from our perceptions of their social evaluation, because we're aware they're judging us, for better or worse. People don't like being judged negatively, and arousal can boost performance, if we're good at the behavior. Whether a seasoned ball player in front of a crowd of cheering fans, or a senior sales clerk in front of a team of managers, well-learned behavior can reach peak quality levels.

On the other hand, when we're not very good at an activity, the arousal caused by others' observations and our concern about their potential negative evaluations is usually experienced as nervousness. This worry/anxiety/stress takes up our cognitive resources, making it harder for us to concentrate. Further, this state causes release of adrenaline in

a fight-or-flight physiological arousal (e.g., heart rate increase, butterflies in stomach) which if unchecked, can also distract us. Thus, performance quality is likely to be worse compared to doing the activity alone.

For example, if you've ever practiced a speech alone and then done it in front of a group, you may have noticed a difference in quality. If you're unconfident, an audience makes you self-conscious and performance will likely suffer. But if you're feeling confident, an audience will likely enhance your performance. So, depending on the task, having others around can be detrimental or helpful. At other times, the presence of others makes us just plain lazy.

Social Loafing—If We All Pitch In . . . We Don't Do as Much

Learning Objectives At the end of this section, you'll be able to:

14.6.4. Describe the diffusion of responsibility;

14.6.5. Define "social loafing";

14.6.6. Explain the impact of unclear social roles and responsibilities.

If you've worked on group projects, in school or on the job, you have noticed some do less than others. This is **diffusion of responsibility**, when the accountability for outcomes cannot be clearly connected to specific individuals. The more people, the less any one feels personally responsible. The result is that individual efforts decrease, which is called **social loafing**. While credit for a job well done is given to a group, rather than individuals, the same is true for blame. Often one person feels pressure to make sure the group does well and 'takes over' due to a need for control or achievement and this individual may wind up doing most of the work.

Diffusion of responsibility can be eliminated when the role of each group member is specified and each individual's performance is recognized as contributing to the overall outcome. When people are directly responsible for the quality of their own work, they usually work harder. We want people to think highly of us, and we don't want to be blamed for problems that occur. But we also often bow to the pressure of groups to avoid 'making waves' or being seen as an uncooperative team member.

Group Information Processing— Everyone Else Thinks That, Too!

A number of other interesting and useful concepts are relevant with regard to group behaviors and outcomes. Group dynamics produce some curious and sometimes problematic effects. But, many can be alleviated by becoming aware of them, at

---

social facilitation A performance boost stemming from the presence of other people—driven by feeling the need to perform well in front of others.

social inhibition A decrease in performance stemming from the presence of others; when an individual performs worse because of perceived social pressures.

diffusion of responsibility When responsibilities for a task within a group are unclear, and the success or failure of that group cannot be connected to any particular person's performance.

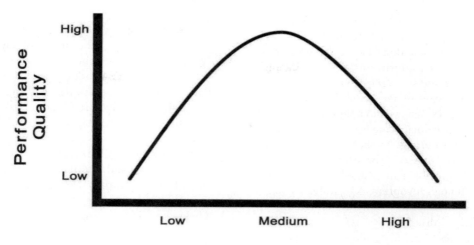

[**FIGURE 14•12**] The Yerkes-Dodson Law of Arousal

Courtesy of George Vaughn Willis.

[**FIGURE 14•13**] Don't rock the boat when your captain is speaking.

least to some degree. And if you teach the social dynamics of these problems to others, everyone benefits.

Groupthink, Polarization, & Risky Shifts—
Learning Objectives At the end of this section, you'll be able to:

14.6.7. Define "groupthink";

14.6.8. Discuss the dangers of groupthink;

14.6.9. Describe how individuals may be influenced by group attitudes.

Have you ever heard the expression, "a camel is a horse designed by committee"? The notion is that some committee (group) work leads to less than ideal outcomes which might have been better accomplished by an individual. Accommodating multiple opinions sometimes leads to awkward compromises and less than optimal solutions. Sometimes it's advantageous to have a leader who can enhance decisiveness, but at other times, inclusion of multiple viewpoints yields benefits which cannot be accomplished by individuals alone. In other words, the whole is often greater than the sum of its parts. Desirable outcomes of group decision-making can be achieved if certain typical pitfalls are avoided.

The first is **groupthink** (a compound word in Psychology), a tendency for groups to avoid dissention, thus increasing conformity. Typically, people don't like to disagree with 'the group.' When our views conform to those we like and respect, our sense of belonging is enhanced as are others' positive views of us, and we experience social validation of our own views and enhances. Yet, even in a tight work group, groupthink produces a disinclination to 'rock the boat' and a pressure to 'go along to get along.' In such cases, we're unlikely to challenge peers or colleagues for fear of losing status or friendship. And, this process is intensified when we consider other social psychological concepts like authority (e.g., the boss or teacher) and reciprocity (e.g., if we agree with others, they're less likely to disagree with us).

Besides social pressures to get along and maintain positive working relationships, organizational demands pull groups toward groupthink. A well-known and tragic example of a negative *groupthink* outcome was the case of the Space Shuttle Challenger disaster in 1986. The entire crew of seven died as a result of an explosion. At first it seemed a terrible accident, but the word 'accident' implies an outcome couldn't have been prevented. Later investigation revealed NASA managers had known of the potential of this very outcome since 1977. However, though this concern made its way through the NASA hierarchy, it didn't result in a launch delay. Why not? Key factors were groupthink and two additional social dynamics we address below. For more information on this particular disaster and the contributing human factors, read **Why We Care** (FEATURE 14•9).

It turns out the best decisions are made when all lines of inquiry are considered, and this requires people having the courage to ask difficult questions of the group, and to have patience to listen to all the discussion. Without a counterbalance to groupthink, groups are likely to engage in **polarization**—a tendency for group members to become more extreme in their commitment to an already dominant viewpoint. You can see how this concept applies to the Challenger disaster. Since everyone was aware that all prior launches were successful, conditions were ripe for the personnel to become more entrenched in the opinion that this launch would be no different. As a result, critical warnings were ignored as most team members seemed to be on the same page with regard to perceived safety.

Polarization can lead to a **risky shift**—the tendency for a group to make riskier decisions than any group member would make on his/her own. Diffusion of responsibility makes it easier for groups to make riskier decisions, because no particular member is actually designated as the 'one' responsible for outcomes. While the Challenger disaster is a

---

groupthink The tendency for group to agree, resulting in conformity from individuals within that group who may hold a different view.

polarization The tendency for group members to become more rigid in their views when faced with a countering view from other group members.

risky shift When groups make riskier decisions than any individual group member may make on their own, often resulting from diffusion of responsibility.

feature 14.9

Why We Care

The culture of any organization tends to pull for conformity and endorsement of common views. In the case of the Space Shuttle Challenger tragedy, the NASA group persuaded itself that the risk was not great enough to warrant a redesign of the system. The shuttle disintegrated 73 seconds into flight due to the failure of an O-ring seal on a solid rocket booster engine. This caused the engine and external fuel tank to separate and the shuttle to break apart. The O-ring failure was due in part to the outside temperature being around 28 degrees, just below freezing. Having known of this particular risk for a long time, why did they proceed?

Externally, the group felt some public pressure from having already engaged in a series of expensive and embarrassing delays, so they felt they needed to launch as soon as possible. And, all previous shuttles were successful, so it seemed a relatively unimportant concern that the outside temperature was far lower than desirable that fateful morning. Further, this was the first flight in which a civilian (a specially selected school teacher) was to accompany the crew, so media coverage was extensive, increasing pressure to launch.

Yet, review of a teleconference the night before between a primary engineering company and NASA revealed the temperature issue had been brought up by engineers concerned about danger. Nonetheless, pressures from outside and inside the organization combined to produce a groupthink-based decision to launch. Here we also see diffusion of responsibility in action. If each of the NASA personnel were clearly accountable for the ultimate safety of the mission, more people may have been inclined to question the decision. Knowing this type of thing is all too common in the realm of group dynamics, we hope you'll teach others to resist the urge to 'go along to get along' when serious outcomes are on the line.

---

dramatic example, this type of group information processing and decision making is quite common.

Imagine a neighborhood homeowners' association meeting to discuss beautification of the subdivision entrance. If a popular group member suggests planting bushes at the entrance, many would likely agree. Another member might think these bushes would grow and block a clear view of the main roadway and thus become dangerous. However, s/he may not feel very comfortable asserting the concern unless the group culture encourages expression of dissenting views. You can create that kind of open culture in your own organizations.

Your awareness of the dynamics of conformity, groupthink, polarization, and the risky shift can prepare you to educate your group members and discuss ways to ensure all possible views are considered, without making dissenters feel disowned or devalued. Temporary loss of a little group harmony may well save the group from later regrets. When members of groups are well known and visible, they're not likely to make decisions that identify them as an undesirable team member. But, what happens when group members and are not identifiable? Are the risks greater and the potential outcomes worse?

Deindividuation—You Can't See Me! You Can? Well, They Were Doing It Too!

Learning Objectives At the end of this section, you'll be able to:

14.6.10. Define deindividuation;

14.6.11. Describe how deindividuation may influence behavior;

14.6.12. Discuss social factors that can lead to risky behavior.

Deindividuation occurs when people feel they are anonymous and are thus more apt to engage in riskier or less socially acceptable behavior than they would if they could be identified. One example is riots. Riots aren't usually started by people who feel they can be identified. They usually get started in crowds where a few people incite others to vandalism and/or violence.

Trigger events are usually something about which many in the crowd are passionate, such as high-profile instances of perceived injustice or major outcomes for organizations in which most crowd members feel a personal connection (e.g., political affiliation, professional/college sports teams). Participants in a riot who are later identified don't usually attribute their behavior to their own disposition, but rather to the situation. They often sound mystified that they 'ended up' engaging in destructive behavior, claiming they were 'caught up in the moment,' 'beside myself,' and the inevitable 'everyone else was doing it.'

For instance, a Canadian beauty queen contestant who won the title "Miss Congeniality" (not a title awarded to an aggressive hooligan) participated in a riot. It was in Vancouver during the 2011 Stanley Cup, where over 100 were injured (including nine police officers) and over 100 were arrested after the home team, the Canucks, lost to the Boston Bruins. With around 100,000 packed into a small area set up by the city and monitored by police, people were incensed. A few who started the riotous behavior likely felt anonymous in the crowd. The contagion spread until chaos reigned and after it was over, a few individuals were held responsible. The beauty queen pled guilty as did others, but you won't hear much about the others. Due to a seeming paradox between the beauty queen's 'personality' and public behavior that night, she's received more than her share of negative repercussions.

You now know better than to be misled by dispositional attributions, when certain situational factors are prominent.

Other situations where hostile behavior is possible would be in cases of road rage, where people feel less identifiable within the confines of their vehicle. Also, wearing masks has been shown to increase lower inhibitions in children (e.g., Miller & Rowold, 1979). And, you know many criminals wear masks to hide their identity. A study of 500 violent attacks found that compared with unmasked assailants, the 206 disguised offenders assaulted a greater number of victims at crime scenes, caused more serious injuries, perpetrated more acts of vandalism, and were more likely to have intimidated victims after their crimes (Silke, 2003). In short, even though most of us aren't violent, anytime we feel we can't be identified, we're more likely to engage in uncharacteristic behavior. While riots in large crowds during emotional moments may seem predictable, aggression in other contexts may not be expected.

Section 7: Aggression & Altruism—Hurting and Helping Others

Aggression is behavior performed with intent to harm another person. Harm may be physical, as in cases of assault. Or it may be psychological as when someone uses name-calling or makes rude gestures, intending to hurt someone's feelings or offend them. Intention is the key factor. With friends, similar behavior may be perceived as just 'playing around' or 'having fun' and isn't deemed aggressive if harming another person isn't the intention (even if unintentionally harmful). If the intended outcome is to make another person suffer in some way, however mildly, the behavior may be deemed as aggressive.

Acts of Aggression—Social-Cognitive Sources of Conflict

Learning Objectives At the end of this section, you'll be able to:

14.7.1. Define the frustration-aggression hypothesis;

14.7.2. Describe how social-cognitive elements may influence aggressive behavior;

14.7.3. Discuss how hostile-attribution bias addresses individual and social factors.

By far the oldest theory with research support is the **frustration-aggression hypothesis** of Dollard and colleagues (1939). These authors felt aggressive behavior was always preceded by an emotional state of frustration. Of course propensity to experience frustration differs among individuals, and not everyone acts aggressively when frustrated. Later research showed a more complex picture exists and a number of

---

deindividuation A loss of individual identity within a group of people, which can lead to a disconnect with values and uncharacteristic behavior.

additional theories evolved. The emphases placed on attitudes, cognitive biases, and personality traits vary, but most modern theories tend to agree people's perception and interpretation of the situation is vital to predicting whether they will behave aggressively (e.g., Anderson & Bushman, 2002; Rudolph, Roesch, Greitemeyer, & Weiner, 2004).

Aggressive conduct can be understood to some degree in terms of cognitive schemas that help us organize and interpret information we encounter at any given moment, and a behavioral repertoire from which we choose our potential responses (e.g., Crick & Dodge, 1994; Crick & Dodge, 1996; Huesmann, Eron, & Yarmel, 1987). While many social-cognitive elements are relevant to aggression, a few you already read about in this chapter: the *fundamental attribution error* (i.e., assuming a person who does a negative action must have done so because s/he is a 'bad' person), *in-group/out-group biases* (i.e., assuming a person from an out-group is hostile or deserving of an aggressive response), *self-serving biases* (i.e., justifying one's aggression by blaming the victim, and then rationalizing, or minimizing the negative impact of aggressive behavior), *negative reciprocity* (i.e., trying to harm people we perceive as having tried to harm us), and *deindivduation.*

There are some 'trait-like' factors associated with aggressive behavior. For example, on average, males tend to be more physically and verbally aggressive than females and this is a robust finding. However, females also engage in high levels of aggression, but their aggression is more apt to be relationship-based, like withdrawing or refusing friendship, excluding a victim from social activities, spreading negative rumours, and the like. Females certainly engage in physical and verbal aggression, just not as much as males. Another 'trait-like' determinant of aggression is hostile-attribution bias.

Hostile-attribution bias is the tendency to interpret ambiguous or neutral behaviors of others, as intentionally antagonistic (Geen, 1998). This develops over time, when aggression is frequently part of a child's life. Children with aggressive behavior problems are more likely to have poorer social adjustment; and because they tend to be aggressive with others, fewer positive alternative behaviors are learned (Huesmann, Eron, & Yarmel, 1987). As aggressive schemas and **scripts** develop, the person is likely to perceive benign interpersonal situations as more hostile than do most other people.

These tendencies can carry over into adulthood, leading one to frequently misinterpret situations and respond with aggression (e.g., Crick & Dodge, 1994). Moreover, such individuals tend to view aggression as more acceptable and reasonable than do others (e.g., Driscoll, Jarman, & Yankeelov, 1994). Of course, there are other factors one should consider, such as the role of genetics, upbringing, and hormones; but in each case aggression occurs within a social situation. It's the interaction of the individual and the situation, combining

his/her perceptions and choices of behavior, which bring about or resolve aggressive situations. The opposite of aggressive behavior is helping behavior, or as it's often termed, altruism.

Acts of Altruism—Lending a Helping Hand

Learning Objectives At the end of this section, you'll be able to:

14.7.4. Define altruism;

14.7.5. Discuss how internal and external factors influence altruistic behavior;

Altruism means helping out somebody for no apparent reason, for no ulterior motive. Altruism is also known as 'helping behavior' and 'prosocial behavior' (e.g., Dovidio, Piliavin, & Schroeder, 2006; Eagly & Crowley, 1986). However, whether one *can* help another without also getting something in return is debatable. At the very least, when helping others we get a sense of well-being or gratification. That is, there are intrinsic or internal consequences to helping others. Sometimes we get extrinsic or external consequences, such as public awards or social approval. And positive consequences, whether internal or external (and they are often both) reinforce the helping behavior, meaning they increase the likelihood of helping again. But, if we count on an external reward, an expectation for reciprocation, helping behavior is not considered altruism.

We've all heard stories of people doing good things just because it was the right thing to do; for instance, turning in lost objects, giving a homeless person money, or even risking one's life to save another. This latter happens with some sparse regularity in large cities where people waiting for subways sometimes fall onto the tracks. In New York, dozens die that way annually. However, on occasion, they're saved by people like Wesley Autrey or Ramiro Ocasio.

What's interesting is that we could use the fundamental attribution error in the positive sense here and assume there's something in these people's character that drives them to act this way. But, such heroes often say things like "I don't feel like I did anything spectacular" or "I'm just an average Joe," as did Wesley and Ramiro, respectively. Yet, it seems there is something special about these individuals, because people don't seem wired to act so dramatically to help strangers. Yet, people do sometimes behave in amazingly positive, seemingly inexplicable ways. Let's try to untangle the mystery.

As noted, whether we benefit from seemingly selfless acts has long been questioned (e.g., Batson & Shaw, 1991; Cialdini, 1991; Köhler, 1977). Altruism could arise from: social norms and enhanced self-esteem from aligning with norms; engaging in behavior to reap future benefits due to reciprocity; or

---

scripts A specific type of schema that tells us how to behave in situations we've encountered before.

altruism Helping others without expecting a tangible (physical "thing"), social, or psychological reward.

an emotional need to reduce distress from perceiving another's suffering (Cialdini, 1991; Rachlin & Locey, 2011). Simpson and Willer (2008) differentiated between an egoist and altruist, where the former engages in prosocial behavior expecting something in return. This makes sense and we often figure when others do us favors, they are expecting something in return. That is the basis of reciprocity.

However, altruists don't anticipate getting something for their prosocial behavior. When people risk their lives to help strangers, they may have no time to consider whether they'll get rewards for their daring actions. In fact, if they took time to rationally consider the risks, they may not act. Keep in mind we're not talking here about those trained to act bravely in dangerous situations, like military personnel or emergency responders. In such cases, we expect those with such training to act heroically. For a few of the rest of us, the immediacy of a situation and an inner need to do the right thing may lead to unpredictable positive behavior.

Regardless of whether altruistic or helping behaviors are intrinsically or extrinsically motivated, it cannot be denied they're beneficial to society in general. Society encourages all manner of prosocial behavior from early ages and rewards it in various ways across the lifespan. We believe people usually care about others, even strangers, in terms of health and well-being, but we often don't have the courage to regularly act on our caring. Of course, many times we do act, but usually with those we love, like, and/or respect, or to whom we owe a debt of gratitude. When it comes to acting prosocially on the spur of the moment, situational factors often make us less likely to help.

Overcoming Barriers To Helping— Helping Heroes Emerge in Emergencies

Learning Objectives At the end of this section, you'll be able to:

14.7.6. Define the bystander effect;

14.7.7. Explain how social inhibition and diffusion of responsibility decrease altruism;

14.7.8. Describe ways of overcoming non-action in emergencies.

A story well-known in academia illustrates a phenomenon difficult to understand at the time. Late one night in 1964, a 28-year-old bar manager named Kitty Genovese was murdered in New York City by an assailant who attacked her for over half an hour. Oddly, around 38 people heard or saw glimpses of the assault. Actually, he was scared off a couple of times by people turning on lights or calling out from their homes. Yet, the police never came and he went back and raped her again, robbed, and finally killed her. The police weren't called until after he left.

This led to a news story that became huge over time and had many ridiculing those who lived in big cities as cold-hearted. While the initial article was somewhat misleading, it took hold in the public consciousness and led to the term *bystander apathy*, reflecting the perspective that city people didn't care and just stood around idly while a murder was committed.

For two psychologists, *apathy* didn't seem a plausible explanation for the lack of helping. John Darley and Bibb Latané investigated the **bystander effect**, demonstrating that the more people present at an emergency, the less likely any one person will help. This isn't to say people are uncaring, but rather they are reluctant to act in the presence of others. Two phenomena we discussed earlier in this chapter help explain the bystander effect, namely, *social inhibition* and *diffusion of responsibility*. When others are around in an emergency, we may be embarrassed to try and help, or assume somebody else is better qualified, or that someone else has already called for help. If we see others doing nothing, we assume doing nothing is the appropriate reaction.

Darley and Latané (1968) explored this with their intercom study, where participants were led to believe they'd be in a group discussion with others to talk about personal problems via intercom to preserve anonymity and reduce interpersonal awkwardness. The key independent variable was the number of people involved in the discussion, and the dependent variable was the amount of time taken to react to an emergency. During the discussion, one of the participants seemed to go into a serious seizure, as heard by those on the intercom. The experimental system was prompting participants to talk two minutes at a time, and others couldn't speak during this period. Thus, when the seizure was heard, participants knew the victim's microphone was on, but couldn't know if anyone else had reacted.

There were three conditions: a two-person group (participant and seizure victim), a three-person group, and a six-person group. The timer began when the 'victim' started speaking for the second time, said he was having a problem, asked for help, made choking sounds, and then went silent at about a minute and a half. The clearest signs of an emergency began after one minute, so one might expect anybody would be incited to help around 70 seconds. When a participant was the only other person to hear the victim, s/he took action 85% of the time, with an average response time of 52 seconds. However, when participants thought others were hearing the same thing, they helped only 31% of the time and took an average of almost 3 minutes to do so—a dramatic decrease in helping and a dramatic increase in delay of action.

Latané and Darley (1968) confirmed this phenomenon with their smoke-filled room study. Here, participants were filling out surveys in a room when a vent began to emit smoke. The independent variable was the number of confederates (presumed to be participants) in the room with the

---

bystander effect When a group of people are called to action a diffusion of responsibility occurs, and no one acts due to the belief that others will.

subject. In the single-participant condition, 75% percent reported the smoke with a median of 2 minutes to take action. However, when as few as two other people were present, the reporting rate dropped to 10%!

Latané and Darley realized inactive confederates inhibited actual participants and repeated the study with three actual participants. They inferred from single participant condition results (with 75% reacting), that of three actual participants (no confederates present), at least one would report the smoke at least 98% of the time. Yet smoke was reported in less than 40% of the groups. In fact, of 24 people in 8 groups, only 4 reported smoke and only one did so in less than 4 minutes . . . again, a dramatic decrease in helpful behavior and an increase in delay.

These researchers cited the Kitty Genovese case in both articles, reflecting its impact; and many more researchers have contributed to understanding this issue over the years. While many accuracy problems in the original and subsequent news stories led some to call it a 'parable,' it has also been noted that the case did much to promote later emergency behavioral research (Manning, Levine & Collins, 2007). Organizations teaching first aid and cardio-pulmonary resuscitation (CPR) use this information to improve their emergency responsiveness, which brings us to a summary of barriers to helping, and how to overcome them.

The first barrier is noticing something is happening, as you have to perceive it before anything else can happen. The second is to interpret it as an emergency. Many emergency situations are ambiguous, and we look to others to help us interpret situations when we're unsure what to make of them. When left to form our own interpretations we sometimes make incorrect assumptions—as in FIGURE 14•14, where the bystanders may have read one too many social psychology articles. The situation with Kitty Genovese showed that though some people saw glimpses of the attack or heard shouts, they didn't know whether this constituted an emergency. They may not have heard it clearly. Perhaps a lover's quarrel and they shouldn't get involved? Perhaps some intoxicated revellers? Looking around, they would have seen nobody helping, an indicator there's no emergency. The smoke-filled room study showed people watching others in an ambiguous situation did not seem to interpret the situation as an emergency.

So, good first aid/CPR training instructs students to check out ambiguous situations . . . to be aware at all times and take the lead to find out whether anything is wrong. Now that you know the first two steps, you can consider yourself ready for action! Be aware, and investigate any unusual situations. The next two steps are to take responsibility and to decide how to help, and training is very useful for the latter. However, even without training you can take helpful action. With the ubiquity of cell phones, almost anyone can call for help. But, the fact there are a lot of people around may lead us to believe someone has already called. You now know never to make such an assumption. Better 100 more calls than needed than one too few.

Also, if you have been trained in first aid/CPR, you'll know to assign roles to bystanders. If you determine a person may be having a heart attack, for example, you look at the first person and say clearly, "You call for help." Then look at another and say clearly, "You get the AED machine." Or, things like that, depending on the situation. Directing people

Courtesy of George Vaughn Willis.

[**FIGURE 14•14**] Assumptions in ambiguous situations can be dangerous.

to action resolves social inhibition and diffusion of responsibility. As you may be the only one on the scene with this information, be sure to use it. But, outside of emergencies, there are many ways you can step up and help out every day, and we'd like to encourage you to do so!

Actively Caring For People—Cultivating a Culture of Kindness

Learning Objectives At the end of this section, you'll be able to:

14.7.9. Describe Actively Caring;

14.7.10. Explain how Actively Caring can be applied across many domains;

14.7.11. Take part in the Actively Caring for People (AC4P) Movement.

Scott has been referring to altruistic behavior as 'Actively Caring' since 1991, and since early in his career his research has focused on prosocial behavior (e.g., Geller, 1991; Geller, Farris, & Post, 1973). Actively Caring has elements that relate to dispositional states, but also to situational variables and social norms. As noted above, some of situations and norms keep us from acting on our caring in some situations.

The prevailing norms often tell us not to get involved when we see problems, to mind our own business if we feel others might be in harm's way, to feel embarrassed to tell others we care about them, etc. But, if we apply our psychological knowledge, we can change norms and we can make the world a more prosocial place. In fact, Actively Caring can be applied to a wide range of settings. Such programs have been used to help promote industrial safety (e.g., Geller, Paterson, & Talbott, 1982; Geller, Roberts, & Gilmore, 1996), increase environmentally responsible behaviors (e.g., Geller, 1989; Allen & Ferrand, 1999), and to address school-based bullying (McCarty & Geller, 2011).

Actively Caring has dispositional components, such as self-esteem, self-efficacy, belongingness, optimism, and empowerment. While these are posited as traits by many, we feel they can be influenced from moment to moment by situational and social-cognitive factors, such that they're modifiable in the short-term, and with repeated activation, can be changed long-term. Social situations are co-constructed by all who participate in them, and if altruistic behavior were to occur and be reinforced more and more frequently, Actively Caring for People (AC4P) could become a social norm.

We encourage you to join the AC4P Movement and to acknowledge others whenever you see them go out of the way to help someone. If you're interested in connecting with others with a similar mission, please join us at www.facebook.com/activelycaring or www.ac4p.org/ And, if you want to go it on your own, just keep learning and applying the principles you find in this book and you'll be well on your way to cultivating a culture of compassion.

KEY TERMS

Affiliation *p. 438*
Altruism *p. 464*
Attraction *p. 440*
Attribution *p. 438*
Bystander Effect *p. 465*
Central Route *p. 446*
Cognitive Dissonance *p. 449*
Consistency *p. 449*
Deindividuation *p. 463*
Diffusion of Responsibility *p. 460*
Discrimination *p. 444*
Door-in-the-Face *p. 451*
Foot-in-the-Door *p. 450*
Fundamental Attribution Error *p. 438*
Group-Serving Bias *p. 439*
Groupthink *p. 462*
Halo Effect *p. 443*
Homogeneity Effect *p. 442*
Impression Management *p. 448*
In-Group *p. 439*
In-Group Favoritism *p. 439*

Ingratiation *p. 448*
Intergroup Bias *p. 439*
Intergroup Contact Theory *p. 444*
Out-Group *p. 439*
Peripheral Route *p. 445*
Polarization *p. 462*
Prejudice *p. 443*
Psychological Reactance *p. 456*
Reciprocity *p. 447*
Risky Shift *p. 462*
Scarcity *p. 456*
Schemas *p. 437*
Scripts *p. 464*
Self-Monitoring *p. 448*
Self-Perception Theory *p. 450*
Self-Serving Biases *p. 438*
Social Cognition *p. 437*
Social Cognitive Biases *p. 437*
Social Comparison *p. 440*
Social Facilitation *p. 460*
Social Inhibition *p. 460*
Stereotypes *p. 442*

ASSESSMENT ITEMS

1. Social psychology is the field of psychology that focuses on:

    a. The most effective forms of governance.

    b. How we affect and are affected by others.

    c. Choosing the best forms of recreational activity.

    d. Using group therapies to treat mental illness.

    e. The development of thought.

2. The process of analysing and interpreting the environment in relation to self, is called:

    a. Behavioral cognition.

    b. Social cognition.

    c. Psychoanalytic cognition.

    d. Observational interpretation.

    e. Attributional arousal.

3. When one thinks the cause of a behavior is due to the person performing it, it is called a(n) _____ attribution, while if it is due to the situation, it is called a (n) _____ **attribution.**

   a. communicator; recipient   b. message; medium

   c. internal; external   d. external; recipient

   e. internal; medium

4. Aside from physical characteristics, what similarity factor boosts attraction?

   a. Social class   b. Ethnicity

   c. Religion   d. Attitude

   e. All of the above

5. _____ is the tendency to make external attributions for one's own questionable behaviors, while _____ is the tendency to make internal attributions for others' behaviors.

   a. self-serving bias; actor-observer bias

   b. fundamental attribution error; self-serving bias

   c. actor-observer bias; fundamental attribution error

   d. actor-observer bias; self-serving bias

   e. self-serving bias; fundamental attribution error

6. A person who is unaware of his/her negative attitudes towards specific groups, may nonetheless act upon them, illustrating that these attitudes are:

   a. Explicit.   b. Implicit.

   c. Wrong.   d. Incentives.

   e. Social cognition.

7. Cognitive dissonance occurs when your _____ and your _____ are at odds.

   a. attitudes; behaviors   b. thoughts; emotions

   c. emotions; behaviors   d. behaviors; job

   e. friends; parents

8. Attitudes are

   a. fixed from early childhood.

   b. subject to change.

   c. impossible to change.

   d. only emotionally based.

   e. only cognitively based.

9. You are aware that smoking kills, but you smoke anyway. Thus, you say to yourself that smoking isn't that dangerous. Your attitude contradicts your knowledge because of your:

   a. Misunderstanding.   b. Cognitive dissonance.

   c. Self-deception.   d. Elaboration likelihood.

   e. Self-interest.

10. When a famous person tells an audience they should use a particular brand of toothpaste, this information is likely to travel through the:

    a. Peripheral route.   b. Central route.

    c. Temporal lobes.   d. Elaboration likelihood model.

    e. Incentive-based processing unit.

11. You are asked to consider switching from the political party you've been affiliated with for the last five years. The switch argument is likely to travel through the:

    a. Credibility sensor.   b. Peripheral route.

    c. Central route.   d. Incentive reception area.

    e. Elaboration likelihood model.

12. Joanie fell in love with Chachi who lived next door. This illustrates the principle of:

    a. Modeling.   b. Proximity.

    c. Attractiveness.   d. Adult attachment.

    e. Foot-in-the-door.

13. Chuck finds himself hanging out with people who think and act a lot like him, illustrating the principle of:

    a. Central processing.   b. Proximity.

    c. Attractiveness.   d. Similarity.

    e. Emotional logic.

14. Giving blood is a(n) _____ behavior.

    a. token   b. altruistic

    c. self-centered   d. conditioned

    e. primarily reinforced

15. Latane and Darley investigated why no one helped Kitty Genovese, who was killed in an attack witnessed by dozens of people over 30 minutes. What did they call this phenomenon?

    a. Witness fatigue   b. The apathetic society

    c. Rubbernecking   d. The bystander effect

    e. Problem blindness

16. What is likely to happen in an emergency if more than several strangers are the only witnesses?

    a. Diffusion of responsibility

    b. Cognitive dissonance

    c. Demotivation syndrome

    d. Social learning reversal

    e. The social loafing effect

17. When two people pull on a rope in tug-of-war, they are both likely to use all their strength. When more than two people are on either side, social loafing dictates that:

    a. All will pull together and try their hardest to win.

    b. Each person will pull less hard than if they pulled alone.

    c. Everyone will pull the same amount as if they pulled alone.

    d. People will tire quickly of the game and want to leave.

    e. The ones who win will make fun of those who lose.

18. The decision where all members of a group are seeking agreement rather than truly evaluating options, is called:

    a. Prejudice   b. Groupthink

    c. Obedience   d. Expedience

    e. Imitation

19. The tendency for people to shift opinions to extremes in group discussions is called:

    a. Conformity   b. Groupthink

    c. Group polarization d. Probability approximation

    e. Active stereotyping

20. After his team won the championship, everyone went crazy and Paul got swept up in the crowd, damaging property and setting fires. Later, Paul was caught on video doing these things, and couldn't explain why he did them. This is an example of:

    a. Conformity   b. Obedience

    c. Deindividuation   d. Insane cooperation

    e. Social influence

21. A(n) _____ is a fixed and overly simple idea about the characteristics of particular groups, while _____ is a behavior differentially targeted at a group member.

    a. stereotype; discrimination

    b. discrimination; prejudice

    c. outgroup; prejudice

    d. prejudice; stereotype

    e. discrimination; prejudice

22. Feeling that you are a member of a group makes that group a(n):

    a. In-group   b. Out-group

    c. Social category d. Peer group

    e. Good thing

23. When Milgram got people to "shock" people they thought were participants in the research, by simply wearing a lab coat and telling them sternly that they must continue, he was demonstrating the human tendency toward:

    a. Obedience

    b. Conformity

    c. Deindividuation

    d. Expressing biological impulses to aggress

    e. Social electrification

24. Asch got people to falsely say that a shorter line was the longest, when seven to nine confederates intentionally made the same assertion first. This is an example of:

    a. Groupthink   b. Deindividuation

    c. Social facilitation d. Conformity

    e. Social loafing

25. Danielle asked her mom for a new car. After being told "no," she then asked to use the family car that night and was told "yes." Danielle used the:

    a. Low-ball technique

    b. Foot-in-the-door technique

    c. Conformity technique

    d. Door-in-the-face technique

    e. Social influence technique

ANSWER KEY

1. b	2. b	3. c	4. e	5. e
6. b	7. a	8. b	9. b	10. a
11. c	12. b	13. d	14. b	15. d
16. a	17. b	18. b	19. c	20. c
21. a	22. a	23. a	24. d	25. d

REFERENCES

Allen, J. (1990). *I saw what you did & I know who you are: Bloopers, blunders and success stories on giving and receiving recognition.* Tucker, GA: Performance Management Publications.

Allen, J. B., & Ferrand, J. L. (1999). Environmental locus of control, sympathy, and proenvironmental behavior: A test of Geller's actively caring hypothesis. *Environment and Behavior, 31*(3), 338–353. doi:10.1177/00139169921972137

Allport, G. (1954). *The nature of prejudice.* Reading, MA: Addison-Wesley.

Anderson, C.A. & Bushman, B.J. (2002). *Human aggression*. Annual Reviews, Psychology, 53, 27–51.

Arkin, R. M., & Maruyama, G. M. (1979). Attribution, affect, and college exam performance. *Journal Of Educational Psychology, 71*(1), 85–93. doi:10.1037/0022-0663.71.1.85

Aronson, E. (1999). The power of self-persuasion. *American Psychologist, 54,* 875–834.

Aronson, E. (2004). *The social animal* (9th ed.). New York, NY US: Worth Publishers.

Asch, S. E. (1955). Opinions and social pressure. *Scientific American, 193,* 31–35.

Asch, S. E. (1956) Studies of independence and conformity: I. A minority of one against a unanimous majority. *Psychological Monographs, 70,* 70.

Back, M. D., Schmukle, S. C., & Egloff, B. (2008). Becoming friends by chance. *Psychological Science, 19*(5), 439–440. doi:10.1111/j.1467–9280.2008.02106.x

Basic Behavioral Science Task Force of the National Advisory Mental Health Council. (1996). Basic behavioral science research for mental health: Social influence and social cognition. *American Psychologist, 51*(5), 478–484. doi:10.1037/0003-066X.51.5.478

Batson, C. D., & Shaw, L. L. (1991). Evidence for altruism: Toward a pluralism of prosocial motives. *Psychological Inquiry, 2*(2), 107–122. doi:10.1207/s15327965pli0202_1

Bem, D. J. (1967). Self-perception: An alternative interpretation of cognitive dissonance phenomena. *Psychological Review, 74,* 183–200.

Burger, J. M. (2009). Replicating Milgram: Would people still obey today?. American Psychologist, 64(1), 1–11. doi:10.1037/a0010932

Berkowitz, L., & Daniels, L. R. (1964). Affecting the salience of the social responsibility norm: Effects of past help on the response to dependency relationships. *Journal of Abnormal and Social Psychology, 68,* 275–281.

Biernat, M. (2003). Toward a broader view of social stereotyping. *American Psychologist, 58*(12), 1019–1027. doi:10.1037/0003-066X.58.12.1019

Billig, M., & Tajfel, H. (1973). Social categorization and similarity in intergroup behaviour. *European Journal of Social Psychology, 3*(1), 27–52. doi:10.1002/ejsp.2420030103

Bukowski, W. M., & Moore, D. (1980). Winners' and losers' attributions for success and failure in a series of athletic events. *Journal Of Sport Psychology, 2*(3), 195–210.

Berscheid, E. & Reis, H. T. (1998). Attraction and close relationships. In Gilbert, D. T., Fiske, S. T., & Lindzey, G. (Eds.). *The Handbook of Social Psychology, Vol. 2* (4th ed.). (pp. 193–281). Boston, MA: Mcgraw-Hill.

Bertrand, M., & Mullainathan, S. (2002). Are Emily and Brandan more employable than Lakisha and Jamal? A field experiment on labor market discrimination. Retrieved from: http://www.chicagobooth.edu/pdf/bertrand.pdf

Bond, R., & Smith, P. B. (1996). Culture and conformity: A meta-analysis of studies using Asch's (1952, 1956) line judgment task. *Psychological Bulletin, 119,* 111–137.

Brehm, J. W. (1966). *A theory of psychological reactance.* New York: Academic Press.

Brehm, S. S., & Brehm, J. W. (1981). *Psychological reactance: a theory of freedom and control.* New York: Academic.

Brehm, J. W., & Cole, A. H. (1966). Effect of a favor which reduces freedom. *Journal of Personality and Social Psychology, 3,* 420–426.

Brehm, J. W., & Sensenig, J. (1966). Social influence as a function of attempted and implied usurpation of choice. *Journal of Personality and Social Psychology. 4,* 703–707.

Burger, J. M. (1999). The foot-in-the-door compliance procedure: A multiple-process analysis and review. *Personality and Social Psychology Review, 3,* 303–325.

Burger, J. M., Horita, M., Kinoshita, L., Roberts, K., & Vera, C. (1997). Effects of time on the norm of reciprocity. *Basic and Applied Social Psychology, 19,* 91–100.

Burger, J. M., Messian, N., Patel, S., del Prado A., & Anderson, C. (2003). What a coincidence! The effects of incidental similarity on compliance. *Personality and Social Psychology Bulletin, 30,* 35–43.

Bushman, B. J. (1988). The effects of apparel on compliance. *Personality and Social Psychology Bulletin, 14,* 459–467.

Buss, D. M. (1989). Sex differences in human mate preferences: Evolutionary hypotheses tested in 37 cultures. *Behavioral and Brain Sciences, 12*(1), 1–49. doi:10.1017/S0140525X00023992

Byrne, D. (1971). *The attraction paradigm.* New York: Academic Press.

Cafri, G., Yamamiya, Y., Brannick, M., & Thompson, J. (2005). The influence of sociocultural factors on body image: A meta-analysis. *Clinical Psychology: Science and Practice, 12*(4), 421–433. doi:10.1093/clipsy/bpi053

Cialdini, R. B. (2001). *Influence: Science and practice.* Boston: Allyn and Bacon.

Cialdini, R. B. (1991). Altruism or egoism? That is (still) the question. Psychological Inquiry, 2(2), 124–126. doi:10.1207/s15327965pli0202_3

Cialdini, R. B., & Goldstein, N. J. (2004). Social influence: Compliance and conformity. *Annual Review of Psychology, 55,* 591–621.

Cialdini, R. B., & Schroeder, D. A. (1976). Increasing compliance by legitimizing paltry contributions: When even a penny helps. *Journal of Personality and Social Psychology, 34*(4), 599–604. doi:10.1037/0022-3514.34.4.599

Cialdini, R. B. & Trost, M. R. (1998). Social influence: Social norms, conformity, and compliance. In Gilbert, D. T., Fiske, S. T., & Lindzey, G. (Eds.). *The Handbook of Social Psychology, Vol. 2* (4th ed.). (pp. 151–192). Boston, MA: Mcgraw-Hill.

Cooper, A., & Sportolari, L. (2003). Romance in cyberspace: Understanding online attraction. In, *Points & counterpoints: Controversial relationship and family issues in the 21st century (an anthology)* (pp. 4–9). Los Angeles, CA US: Roxbury Publishing Co.

Crick, N. R., & Dodge, K. A. (1994). A review and reformulation of social information-processing mechanisms in children's social adjustment. *Psychological Bulletin, 115*(1), 74–101. doi:10.1037/0033-2909.115.1.74

Crick, N. R., & Dodge, K. A. (1996). Social information-processing mechanisms on reactive and proactive aggression. *Child Development, 67*(3), 993–1002. doi:10.2307/1131875

Daniels, A. C. (2000). *Bringing out the best in people* (2ⁿᵈ ed.). New York: McGraw-Hill.

Daniels, J. A., & Larson, L. M. (2001). The impact of performance feedback on counseling self-efficacy and counselor anxiety. *Counselor Education and Supervision, 41*, 120–130.

Darley, J. M., & Latané, B. (1968). Bystander intervention in emergencies: Diffusion of responsibility. *Journal of Personality and Social Psychology, 8*(4, Pt.1), 377–383. doi:10.1037/h0025589

DeLeon, I. G., & Fuqua, R. W. (1995). The effects of public commitment and group feedback on curbside recycling. *Environment and Behavior, 27*, 233–250.

DeMichele, P. E., Gansneder, B., & Solomon, G. B. (1998). Success and failure attributions of wrestlers: Further evidence of the self-serving bias. *Journal Of Sport Behavior, 21*(3), 242–255.

Dollard, J., Miller, N. E., Doob, L. W., Mowrer, O. H., & Sears, R. R. (1939). *Frustration and aggression.* New Haven, CT US: Yale University Press. doi:10.1037/10022-000

Dovidio, J. F., Piliavin, J. A., & Schroeder, D. A. (2006). *The social psychology of prosocial behavior.* Mahwah, New Jersey: Lawrence Erlbaum Associates.

Drachman, D., DeCarufel, A., & Insko, C. A. (1978). The extra credit effect in interpersonal attraction. *Journal of Experimental Social Psychology, 14*, 458–465.

Driscoll, J. M., Jarman, B. J., & Yankeelov, P. A. (1994). Effects of a person's history of aggression on attributions of affect to aggressors. *Journal of Social Behavior & Personality, 9*(4), 685–700.

Dula, C.S. (2014). Social influence norms. Unpublished data.

Dunn, M. J., & Searle, R. (2010). Effect of manipulated prestige-car ownership on both sex attractiveness ratings. *British Journal of Psychology, 101*(1), 69–80. doi:10.1348/000712609X417319

Eagly, A. H., & Crowley, M. (1986). Gender and helping behavior: A meta-analytic review of the social psychological literature. *Psychological Bulletin, 100*(3), 283–308. doi:10.1037/0033-2909.100.3.283

Escasa, M., Gray, P. B., & Patton, J. Q. (2010). Male traits associated with attractiveness in Conambo, Ecuador. *Evolution and Human Behavior, 31*(3), 193–200. doi:10.1016/j.evolhumbehav.2009.09.008

Fawcett, C. A., & Markson, L. (2010). Similarity predicts liking in 3-year-old children. *Journal of Experimental Child Psychology, 105*(4), 345–358. doi:10.1016/j.jecp.2009.12.002

Ferguson, C. J. (2013). In the eye of the beholder: Thin-ideal media affects some, but not most, viewers in a meta-analytic review of body dissatisfaction in women and men. *Psychology of Popular Media Culture, 2*(1), 20–37. doi:10.1037/a0030766

Fernandez, S., & Pritchard, M. (2012). Relationships between self-esteem, media influence and drive for thinness. *Eating Behaviors, 13*(4), 321–325. doi:10.1016/j.eatbeh.2012.05.004

Festinger, L. (1957). *A theory of cognitive dissonance.* Stanford, CA: Stanford University Press.

Festinger, L. & Carlsmith, J. M. (1959). Cognitive consequences of forced compliance. *Journal of Abnormal and Social Psychology, 58*, 203–210.

Fiske, S. T. (1998). Stereotyping, prejudice, and discrimination. In D. T. Gilbert, S. T. Fiske, G. Lindzey (Eds.), *The handbook of social psychology, Vols. 1 and 2 (4th ed.)* (pp. 357–411). New York, NY US: McGraw-Hill.

Freedman, J. L., & Fraser, S. C. (1966). Compliance without pressure: The foot-in-the-door technique. *Journal of Personality and Social Psychology, 4*, 195–203.

Geen, R. G. (1998). Aggression and antisocial behavior. In Gilbert, D. T., Fiske, S. T., & Lindzey, G. (Eds.). The Handbook of Social Psychology, Vol. 2 (4th ed.). (pp. 317–356). Boston, MA: Mcgraw-Hill.

Geller, E. (1989). Applied behavior analysis and social marketing: An integration for environmental preservation. Journal of Social Issues, 45(1), 17–36. doi:10.1111/j.1540-4560.1989.tb01531.x

Geller, E. S. (1991). If only more would actively care. *Journal of Applied Behavior Analysis, 24*(4), 607–612. Retrieved from http://www.ncbi.nlm.nih.gov/pmc/articles/PMC1279613/pdf/jaba00022-0002.pdf

Geller, E. S. (1997). Key processes for continuous safety improvement: Behavior-based recognition and celebration. *Professional Safety, 42*, 40–44.

Geller, E., Farris, J., & Post, D. (1973). Prompting a consumer behavior for pollution control. *Journal of Applied Behavior Analysis, 6*(3), 367–376. doi:10.1901/jaba.1973.6-367

Geller, E. S., & Lehman, G. R. (1991). The buckle-up promise card: A versatile intervention for large-scale behavior change. *Journal of Applied Behavior Analysis, 24*, 91–94.

Geller, E., Paterson, L., & Talbott, E. (1982). A behavioral analysis of incentive prompts for motivating seat belt use. *Journal of Applied Behavior Analysis, 15*(3), 403–415. doi:10.1901/jaba. 1982. 15-403

Geller, E. S., Roberts, D. S., & Gilmore, M. R. (1996). Predicting propensity to actively care for occupational safety. *Journal of Safety Research, 27*(1), 1–8. doi:10.1016/0022-4375(95)00024-0

Gilbert, D. T. (1998). Ordinary personology. In D. T. Gilbert, S. T. Fiske, G. Lindzey (Eds.), *The handbook of social psychology, Vols. 1 and 2 (4th ed.)* (pp. 89–150). New York, NY US: McGraw-Hill.

Gioia, D. A., & Sims, H. P. (1985). Self-serving bias and actor–observer differences in organizations: An empirical analysis. *Journal Of Applied Social Psychology, 15*(6), 547–563. doi: 10.1111/j. 1559-1816.1985.tb00919.x

Gordon, R. A. (1996). Impact of ingratiation on judgments and evaluations: A meta-analytic investigation. *Journal of Personality and Social Psychology, 71*(1), 54–70. doi:10.1037/0022-3514.71.1.54

Gouldner, A. W. (1960). The norm of reciprocity: A preliminary statement. *American Sociological Review, 25*, 161–178.

Grabe, S., Ward, L., & Hyde, J. (2008). The role of the media in body image concerns among women: A meta-analysis of experimental and correlational studies. *Psychological Bulletin, 134*(3), 460–476. doi:10.1037/0033-2909.134.3.460

Granberg, D., & Bartels, B. (2005). On Being a Lone Dissenter. *Journal of Applied Social Psychology, 35*(9), 1849–1858. doi:10.1111/j. 1559-1816.2005.tb02198.x

Griffin, A. M., & Langlois, J. H. (2006). Stereotype directionality and attractiveness stereotyping: Is beauty good or is ugly bad? *Social Cognition, 24*(2), 187–206. doi:10.1521/soco.2006.24.2.187

Hackney, A. (2005). Teaching Students About Stereotypes, Prejudice, and Discrimination: An Interview With Susan Fiske. *Teaching of Psychology, 32*(3), 196–199. doi:10.1207/s15328023top3203_13

Hall, J. A., Park, N., Song, H., & Cody, M. J. (2010). Strategic misrepresentation in online dating: The effects of gender, self-monitoring, and personality traits. *Journal of Social and Personal Relationships, 27*(1), 117–135. doi:10.1177/0265407509349633

Hargreaves, D. A., & Tiggemann, M. (2009). Muscular ideal media images and men's body image: Social comparison processing and individual vulnerability. *Psychology of Men & Masculinity, 10*(2), 109–119. doi:10.1037/a0014691

Hewstone, M., Rubin, M., & Willis, H. (2002). Intergroup bias. *Annual Review of Psychology, 53*(1), 575–604. doi:10.1146/annurev. psych.53.100901.135109

Holmstrom, A. J. (2004). The effects of the media on body image: A meta-analysis. *Journal of Broadcasting & Electronic Media, 48*(2), 196–217. doi:10.1207/s15506878jobem4802_3

Howard, J. A., Blumstein, P., & Schwartz, P. (1987). Social or evolutionary theories? Some observations on preferences in human mate selection. *Journal of Personality and Social Psychology, 53*(1), 194–200. doi:10.1037/0022-3514.53.1.194

Hu, Y., & Sundar, S. (2010). Effects of online health sources on credibility and behavioral intentions. *Communication Research, 37*(1), 105–132. doi:10.1177/0093650209351512

Huesmann, L., Eron, L. D., & Yarmel, P. W. (1987). Intellectual functioning and aggression. *Journal of Personality and Social Psychology, 52*, 232–240. doi:10.1037/0022-3514.52.1.232

Isen, A. M. & Levin, P. F. (1972). The effect of feeling good on helping: Cookies and kindness. *Journal of Personality and Social Psychology, 21*, 384–388.

Izawa, M. R., French, M. D., & Hedge, A. (2011). Shining new light on the Hawthorne illumination experiments. *Human Factors, 53*(5), 528–547. doi:10.1177/0018720811417968

Johnson, S. K., Podratz, K. E., Dipboye, R. L., & Gibbons, E. (2010). Physical attractiveness biases in ratings of employment suitability: Tracking down the 'beauty is beastly' effect. *The Journal of Social Psychology, 150*(3), 301–318. doi:10.1080/00224540903365414

Jones, R. G., & Jones, E. E. (1964). Optimum conformity as an ingratiation tactic. *Journal of Personality, 32*(3), 436–458. doi:10.1111/ j.1467-6494.1964.tb01351.x

Jones, E. E., & Nisbett, R. E. (1971). The actor and the observer: Divergent perceptions of the causes of behavior. New York: General Learning Press.

Jones, B. C., Little, A. C., & Perrett, D. I. (2003). Why are symmetrical faces attractive?. In S. P. Shohov (Ed.), *Advances in psychology research, Vol. 19* (pp. 145–166). Hauppauge, NY US: Nova Science Publishers.

Joseph, W. (1982). The credibility of physically attractive communicators: A review. *Journal of Advertising, 11*(3), 15–24.

King, E. B., Madera, J. M., Hebl, M. R., Knight, J. L., & Mendoza, S. A. (2006). What's in a Name? A multiracial investigation of the role of occupational stereotypes in selection decisions. *Journal of Applied Social Psychology, 36*(5), 1145–1159. doi:10.1111/ j.0021-9029.2006.00035.x

Klein, K. M., Apple, K. J., & Kahn, A. S. (2011). Attributions of blame and responsibility in sexual harassment: Reexamining a psychological model. *Law And Human Behavior, 35*(2), 92–103. doi:10.1007/s10979-009-9216-6

Kmec, J. A. (2006). White hiring agents' organizational practices and out-group hiring. *Social Science Research, 35*(3), 668–701. doi:10.1016/j.ssresearch.2005.06.001

Köhler, B. (1977). Prosocial behavior: Research focuses and research themes. *Zeitschrift Für Sozialpsychologie, 8*(1), 23–49.

Kurosawa, K. (1993). Self-monitoring and conformity revisited: A case for a four-factor measurement model. *Japanese Psychological Research, 35*, 19–31.

Langlois, J. H., Kalakanis, L., Rubenstein, A. J., Larson, A., Hallam, M., & Smoot, M. (2000). Maxims or myths of beauty? A meta-analytic and theoretical review. *Psychological Bulletin, 126*(3), 390–423. doi:10.1037/0033-2909.126.3.390

Larsen, K. S. (1974). Conformity in the Asch experiment. *Journal of Social Psychology, 94*, 303–304.

Larsen, K. S., Triplett, J. S., Brant, W. D., & Langenberg, D. (1979). Collaborator status, subject characteristics, and conformity in the Asch paradigm. *Journal of Social Psychology, 108*, 259–263.

Larson, J. R. (1977). Evidence for a self-serving bias in the attribution of causality. *Journal Of Personality, 45*(3), 430–441. doi:10.1111/j.1467-6494.1977.tb00162.x

Larwood, L. (1978). Swine flu: A field study of self-serving biases. *Journal Of Applied Social Psychology, 8*(3), 283–289. doi:10.1111/ j.1559-1816.1978.tb00783.x

Latane, B., & Darley, J. M. (1968). Group inhibition of bystander intervention in emergencies. *Journal of Personality and Social Psychology, 10*(3), 215–221. doi:10.1037/h0026570

Lehman, P.K., Dula, C.S., Geller, E.S., & Grandin, D. (2002). Social influence profiles: Emerging patterns in student populations. Paper Presentation at the Annual Meeting of the Virginia Academy of Science.

Loya, B. N., Cowan, G., & Walters, C. (2006). The role of social comparison and body consciousness in women's hostility toward women. *Sex Roles, 54*(7–8), 575–583. doi:10.1007/s11199-006-9024-0

Lundahl, B., Moleni, T., Burke, B. L., Butters, R., Tollefson, D., Butler, C., & Rollnick, S. (2013). Motivational interviewing in medical care settings: A systematic review and meta-analysis of randomized controlled trials. *Patient Education and Counseling, 93*(2), 157–168. doi:10.1016/j.pec.2013.07.012

Mackinnon, S. P., Jordan, C. H., & Wilson, A. E. (2011). Birds of a feather sit together: Physical similarity predicts seating choice. *Personality and Social Psychology Bulletin, 37*(7), 879–892. doi:10.1177/0146167211402094

Mahajan, N., Martinez, M. A., Gutierrez, N. L., Diesendruck, G., Banaji, M. R., & Santos, L. R. (2011). The evolution of intergroup bias: Perceptions and attitudes in rhesus macaques. *Journal of Personality and Social Psychology, 100*(3), 387–405. doi:10.1037/ a0022459

Manning, R., Levine, M., & Collins, A. (2007). The Kitty Genovese murder and the social psychology of helping: The parable of the 38 witnesses. *American Psychologist, 62*(6), 555–562. doi:10.1037/ 0003-066X.62.6.555

McCarty, S., & Geller, E. (2011, Summer). Want to get rid of bullying? Then reward behavior that is incompatible with it. *Behavior Analysis Digest International, 23*(2), pp. 17.

McCaslin, M. J., Petty, R. E., & Wegener, D. T. (2010). Self-enhancement and theory-based correction processes. *Journal of Experimental Social Psychology, 46*(5), 830–835. doi:10.1016/j.jesp.2010.05.002

McConahay, J. B. (1986). Modern racism, ambivalence, and the Modern Racism Scale. In J. F. Dovidio & S. L. Gaertner (Eds.), *Prejudice, discrimination, and racism* (pp. 91–125). Orlando, FL: Academic Press.

McKelvie, S. J., & Coley, J. (1993). Effects of crime seriousness and offender facial attractiveness on recommended treatment. *Social Behavior and Personality, 21*(4), 265–277. doi:10.2224/sbp.1993.21.4.265

Mezulis, A. H., Abramson, L. Y., Hyde, J. S., & Hankin, B. L. (2004). Is There a Universal Positivity Bias in Attributions? A Meta-Analytic Review of Individual, Developmental, and Cultural Differences in the Self-Serving Attributional Bias. *Psychological Bulletin, 130*(5), 711–747. doi:10.1037/0033-2909.130.5.711

Micu, C. C., & Coulter, R. (2012). The effect of attractiveness in advertising and comparison motives on self-judgments and product evaluations: A cross-national perspective. *Journal of International Consumer Marketing, 24*(1-2), 79–99. doi:10.1080/08961530.2012.650140

Milgram, S. (1963). Behavioral study of obedience. *Journal of Abnormal and Social Psychology, 67*, 371–378.

Milgram, S. (1964). Group pressure and action against a person. *Journal of Abnormal and Social Psychology, 69*, 137–143.

Milgram, S. (1965a). Liberating effects of group pressure. *Journal of Personality and Social Psychology, 1*, 127–134.

Milgram, S. (1965b). Some conditions of obedience and disobedience to authority. *Human Relations, 18*, 57–76.

Milgram, S. (1974). *Obedience to authority: An experimental view.* New York: Harper & Row.

Milgram, S., Mann, L., & Harter, S. (1965). The lost-letter technique: A tool of social research. Public Opinion Quarterly, 29, 437–438.

Miller, F. G., & Rowold, K. L. (1979). Halloween masks and deindividuation. *Psychological Reports, 44*(2), doi:10.2466/pr0.1979.44.2.422

Montoya, R., & Horton, R. S. (2013). A meta-analytic investigation of the processes underlying the similarity-attraction effect. *Journal of Social and Personal Relationships, 30*(1), 64–94. doi:10.1177/0265407512452989

Morrison, E. W. (2006). Doing the job well: An investigation of prosocial rule breaking. *Journal of Management, 32*, 5–28.

Mussweiler, T. (2003). Comparison processes in social judgment: Mechanisms and consequences. *Psychological Review, 110*(3), 472–489. doi:10.1037/0033-295X.110.3.472

Newcomb, T. M. (1956). The prediction of interpersonal attraction. *American Psychologist, 11*(11), 575–586. doi:10.1037/h0046141

Orpen, C. (1996). Construct validation of a measure of ingratiatory behaviour in organizational settings. *Current Psychology: A Journal for Diverse Perspectives on Diverse Psychological Issues, 15*(1), 38–41. doi:10.1007/BF02686932

Osofsky, M. J., Bandura, A., & Zimbardo, P. G. (2005). The role of moral disengagement in the execution process. *Law and Human Behavior, 29*, 371–393.

Parent, M. C. (2013). Clinical considerations in etiology, assessment, and treatment of men's muscularity-focused body image distur-

bance. *Psychology of Men & Masculinity, 14*(1), 88–100. doi:10.1037/a0025644

Peoples, C. D., Sigillo, A. E., Green, M., & Miller, M. K. (2012). Friendship and conformity in group opinions: Juror verdict change in mock juries. *Sociological Spectrum, 32*(2), 178–193. doi:10.1080/02732173.2012.646163

Pettigrew, T. F. & Tropp, L. R. (2006). A meta-analytic test of intergroup contact theory. *Journal of Personality and Social Psychology, 90*(5), 751–783.

Pettigrew, T. F., & Tropp, L. R. (2008). How does intergroup contact reduce prejudice? Meta-analytic tests of three mediators. *European Journal of Social Psychology, 38*(6), 922–934. doi:10.1002/ejsp.504

Petty, R. E., Wegener, D. T., & Fabrigar, L. R. (1997). Attitudes and attitude change. *Annual Review of Psychology, 48*, 609–647. doi:10.1146/annurev.psych.48.1.609

Quillian, L. (2006). New Approaches to Understanding Racial Prejudice and Discrimination. *Annual Review of Sociology, 32*, 299–328. doi:10.1146/annurev.soc.32.061604.123132

Raabe, T., & Beelmann, A. (2011). Development of ethnic, racial, and national prejudice in childhood and adolescence: A multinational meta-analysis of age differences. *Child Development, 82*(6), 1715–1737. doi:10.1111/j.1467-8624.2011.01668.x

Rachlin, H., & Locey, M. (2011). A behavioral analysis of altruism. *Behavioral Process, 87*, 25–33. doi:10.1016/j.beproc.2010.12.004

Richey, H. W., & Richey, M. H. (1978). Nonverbal behavior in the classroom. *Psychology in the Schools, 15*(4), 571–576. doi:10.1002/1520-6807(197810)15:4<571::AID-PITS23101-50422>3.0.CO;2-U

Rind, B., & Strohmetz, D. (1999). Effect of restaurant tipping of a helpful message written on the back of customer's checks. *Journal of Applied Social Psychology, 29*, 139–144.

Ross, L. D. (2001). Getting down to fundamentals: Lay dispositionism and the attributions of psychologists. *Psychological Inquiry, 12*(1), 37–40.

Rudolph, U., Roesch, S. C., Greitemeyer, T., & Weiner, B. (2004). A meta-analytic review of help giving and aggression from an attributional perspective: Contributions to a general theory of motivation. *Cognition and Emotion, 18*(6), 815–848. doi:10.1080/02699930341000248

Ryckman, R. M., & Rodda, W. C. (1972). Conformity in college men and women as a function of locus of control and prior group support. *Journal of Social Psychology, 86*, 313–314.

Sanderson, C. A., & Cantor, N. (1997). Creating satisfaction in steady dating relationships: The role of personal goals and situational affordances. *Journal of Personality and Social Psychology, 73*(6), 1424–1433. doi:10.1037/0022-3514.73.6.1424

Santee, R. T., & Maslach, C. (1982). To agree or not to agree: Personal dissent amid social pressure to conform. *Journal of Personality and Social Psychology, 42*, 690–700.

Sautter, J. M., Tippett, R. M., & Morgan, S. (2010). The social demography of Internet dating in the United States. *Social Science Quarterly, 91*(2), 554–575. doi:10.1111/j.1540-6237.2010.00707.x

Seligman, C., Paschall, N., & Takata, G. (1974). Effects of physical attractiveness on attribution of responsibility. *Canadian Journal Of Behavioural Science/Revue Canadienne Des Sciences Du Comportement, 6*(3), 290–296. doi:10.1037/h0081875

Sherif, M., Harvey, O. J., White, B. J., Hood, W. R., & Sherif, C. W. (1961). *Intergroup conflict and cooperation: The Robbers Cave experiment*. Norman, OK: University Book Exchange.

Sherman, D. K., & Kim, H. S. (2005). Is There an 'I' in 'Team'? The Role of the Self in Group-Serving Judgments. *Journal of Personality and Social Psychology, 88*(1), 108–120. doi:10.1037/0022-3514.88.1.108

Shulman, S., Mayes, L. C., Cohen, T. H., Swain, J. E., & Leckman, J. F. (2008). Romantic attraction and conflict negotiation among late adolescent and early adult romantic couples. *Journal of Adolescence, 31*(6), 729–745. doi:10.1016/j.adolescence.2008.02.002

Sibley, C. G., & Duckitt, J. (2008). Personality and prejudice: A meta-analysis and theoretical review. *Personality and Social Psychology Review, 12*(3), 248–279. doi:10.1177/1088868308319226

Silverstein, B., Peterson, B., & Perdue, L. (1986). Some correlates of the thin standard of bodily attractiveness for women. *International Journal of Eating Disorders, 5*(5), 895–905. doi:10.1002/1098-108X(198607)5:5<895::AID-EAT2260050510>3.0.CO;2-W

Simmons, T. (2006). Real women, real results: A look at Dove's best of Silver Anvil-winning campaign. *The Public Relations Strategist, Summer Issue.*

Simpson, B., & Willer, R. (2008). Altruism and indirect reciprocity: The interaction of person and situation in prosocial behavior. *Social Psychology Quarterly, 71*(1), 37–52. doi:10.1177/019027250807100106

Smith, S. J., Axelton, A. M., & Saucier, D. A. (2009). The effects of contact on sexual prejudice: A meta-analysis. *Sex Roles, 61*(3–4), 178–191. doi:10.1007/s11199-009-9627-3

Sorokowski, P. (2010). Did Venus have long legs? Beauty standards from various historical periods reflected in works of art. *Perception, 39*(10), 1427–1430. doi:10.1068/p6621

Speer, T. L. (1997). The give and take of tipping. *American Demographics, 19*(2), 50–54.

Sprecher, S., & Felmlee, D. (2008). Insider perspectives on attraction. In S. Sprecher, A. Wenzel, J. Harvey (Eds.), *Handbook of relationship initiation* (pp. 297–313). New York, NY US: Psychology Press.

Stafford, L., & Merolla, A. J. (2007). Idealization, reunions, and stability in long-distance dating relationships. *Journal of Social and Personal Relationships, 24*(1), 37–54. doi:10.1177/0265407507072578

Stafford, L., Merolla, A. J., & Castle, J. D. (2006). When long-distance dating partners become geographically close. *Journal of Social and Personal Relationships, 23*(6), 901–919. doi:10.1177/026540-7506070472

Stang, D. J. (1972). Conformity, ability, and self-esteem. *Representative Research in Social Psychology, 3*, 97–103.

Stewart, J. E. (1980). Defendant's attractiveness as a factor in the outcome of criminal trials: An observational study. *Journal of Applied Social Psychology, 10*(4), 348–361. doi:10.1111/j.1559-1816.1980.tb00715.x

Strohmetz, D. B, Rind, B., Fisher, R., & Lynn, M. (2002). Sweetening the till: The use of candy to increase restaurant tipping. *Journal of Applied Social Psychology, 32*, 300–309.

Sundar, S. S. (1998). Effect of source attribution on perception of online news stories. *Journalism & Mass Communication Quarterly, 75*, 55–68.

Swami, V., & Tovée, M. J. (2007). The relative contribution of profile body shape and weight to judgements of women's physical attractiveness in Britain and Malaysia. *Body Image, 4*(4), 391–396. doi:10.1016/j.bodyim.2007.07.002

Tajfel, H., Billig, M. G., Bundy, R. P., & Flament, C. (1971). Social categorization and intergroup behaviour. *European Journal of Social Psychology, 1*(2), 149–178. doi:10.1002/ejsp.2420010202

Taylor, D. M., & Doria, J. R. (1981). Self-serving and group-serving bias in attribution. *The Journal of Social Psychology, 113*(2), 201–211. doi:10.1080/00224545.1981.9924371

Tormala, Z. L., Briñol, P., & Petty, R. E. (2006). When credibility attacks: The reverse impact of source credibility on persuasion. *Journal of Experimental Social Psychology, 42*(5), 684–691. doi:10.1016/j.jesp.2005.10.005

Tseëlon, E. (1992). What is beautiful is bad: Physical attractiveness as stigma. *Journal for the Theory of Social Behaviour, 22*(3), 295–309. doi:10.1111/j.1468-5914.1992.tb00221.x

Unilever. (2005). Unilever annual review and summary financial statement 2004. Retrieved from: http://www.unilever.com/images/2004%20Annual%20Review%20%20-%20English_tcm13-11991.pdf

Unilever. (2006). Unilever annual review and summary financial statement 2005. Retrieved from: www.unilever.com/images/ir_2005_Annual_Report_English%20amended_tcm13-35722.pdf

van Leeuwen, M. L., & Macrae, C. (2004). Is beautiful always good? Implicit benefits of facial attractiveness. *Social Cognition, 22*(6), 637–649. doi:10.1521/soco.22.6.637.54819

Vilela, B., González, J., Ferrín, P., & del Río Araújo, M. (2007). Impression management tactics and affective context: Influence on sales performance appraisal. *European Journal of Marketing, 41*(5–6), 624–639. doi:10.1108/03090560710737651

Werner, C. M., Turner, J., Shipman, K., Twitchel, F. S., Dickson, B. R., Bruschke, G. V., & von Bismark, W. B. (1995). Commitment, behavior and attitude change: An analysis of voluntary recycling. *Journal of Environmental Psychology, 15*, 197–208.

Westphal, J. D., & Zajac, E. J. (1995). Who shall govern? CEO/board power, demographic similarity, and new director selection. *Administrative Science Quarterly, 40*(1), 60–83.

Whatley, M. A., Webster, M. J., Smith, R. H., & Rhodes, A. (1999). The effect of a favor on public and private compliance: How internalized is the norm of reciprocity? *Basic and Applied Social Psychology, 21*, 251–259.

White, G. L. (1980). Physical attractiveness and courtship progress. Journal Of Personality And *Social Psychology, 39*(4), 660–668. doi:10.1037/0022-3514.39.4.660

Zimbardo, P. G. (1973). On the ethics of intervention in human psychological research: With special reference to the Stanford prison experiment. *Cognition, 2*(2), 243–256. doi:10.1016/0010-0277(72)90014-5

Zimbardo, P. (1989). *Quiet rage: The Stanford prison study video*. Stanford, CA: Stanford University.

Zimbardo, P. (2011, January). *A study of evil*. The Greater Good Science Center, University of California, Berkeley, CA. Retrieved from http://greatergood.berkeley.edu/gg_live/science_meaningful_life_videos/speaker/philip_zimbardo/a_study_of_evil/

Industrial a
Organizatic
Psychology

Taken from *Psychological Science: Modeling Scientific Literacy* by Mark Krause and Daniel Corts

15.1 Personnel Psychology: Hiring and Maintaining an Effective Workforce

Learning Objectives
After reading this module you should:

Know ...
- The key terminology of personnel psychology

Understand ...
- Interviews, testing, and assessment center methods of personnel selection
- Methods used in employee performance appraisals

Apply ...
- Your knowledge of personnel psychology to identify likely KSAOs for a given job

Analyze ...
- The relative value of structured versus unstructured interview selection techniques

The Apprentice began airing on network television in 2004, claiming to be the ultimate job interview. This game show pits a number of high-energy, high-ambition contestants against one another in a series of miniature business scenarios across each episode in the season. The winner gets to become an apprentice to real estate mogul Donald Trump. That is quite a way to win a job.

Why did this show become so popular? Perhaps it is because anyone who has been interviewed or tested for a job can relate to the tension it produces. There is the desire to say and do the right things, to impress the employer, and to win the job without selling yourself out. The popularity of *The Apprentice* has led networks around the world to create their own versions of the show with powerful business figures from all corners of the globe. Other job-interview shows have appeared on television, each trying to create bigger and more tension-producing scenarios: *Hell's Kitchen* is an attempt to find the best young chef, whereas *America's Next Top Model* tries to find a rising star in modeling. These shows stage contests and activities that are much too far-fetched to be part of the typical company's hiring procedures, and we should all be thankful for that. But even after all the effort and expense goes into producing one of these shows, there is little to guarantee that the best candidate has won the job. ■

FOCUS QUESTIONS

1. Which techniques ensure that employers hire the most suitable workers?

2. How can employers determine whether workers are doing their jobs well?

The typical American grows up in a household with one or two siblings. Young parents are often amazed and overwhelmed by the way two small children can wreak so much havoc in their lives. While many turn to self-help books for advice, another option might be to hire an efficiency expert to come to the home. Even better, you could become an efficiency expert and run the home with the scientific precision of an assembly line. In fact, this describes the home life of Frank and Lillian Gilbreth, pioneers in the field now known as *industrial and organizational (I/O) psychology*.

Frank was a high school graduate who had worked his way up from bricklayer to construction contractor; Lillian had a master's degree in literature (Purdue University Library, 2009). Although neither had formal scientific training, they learned about applying scientific methods to the workplace from a psychologist and began to systematically study their construction company's laborers. They eventually developed a new bricklaying technique that led to reduced physical strain and injuries, increased the speed of work, and produced a more satisfied and productive work team. Soon, the Gilbreths began studying the methods of all kinds of workers. Frank left construction for business consulting; Lillian earned a doctorate in psychology and joined the faculty of Purdue University.

Despite their busy careers, Lillian and Frank had 12 children together, so it should be no surprise that, as efficiency experts, the Gilbreths literally brought their work home with them. You might say that their household became a company: The parents were the chief executives who made the plans for the family, the older children were the middle managers who oversaw different chores, and the younger children provided hourly labor by doing the actual chores. This story may sound familiar to you: Their son Frank Jr. wrote the autobiographical novel, *Cheaper by the Dozen*, which was released as a film in 1950. Fifty years later, another film came out with the same title and the same large family, but without the efficiency experts involved.

The span of psychological science ranges from a laboratory-based discipline to a highly applied, practical one. We will use this chapter to apply psychology to the setting in which most adults spend the majority of their waking hours: the workplace. I/O psychology is the scientific study of behavior and thought in work settings. According to the Society of Industrial-Organizational Psychology (SIOP), the field serves three main goals: (1) to help employers deal with employees fairly; (2) to help make jobs more interesting and satisfying; and (3) to help workers be more productive.

The first hints of I/O psychology emerged in the late 1800s from a desire to develop management practices that would have the same degree of precision as engineering. In fact, much of the first scientific research on employee behavior was published in the major academic journal for mechanical engineers (van de Water, 1997). The merging of engineering and psychology into *industrial psychology* made sense at the time because the U.S. economy was based on manufacturing—mining raw materials and turning them into useful products. Industrial psychologists did the same thing with human labor—finding the raw strength and talent and turning it into a productive workforce. This work was largely focused on helping management hire people with potential and making sure they were adequately trained; managing and motivating employees; and evaluating performance. From this moment came a new type of profession: *personnel psychology*. Although the term "personnel psychology" is used less frequently today, this field has become one of the major components of I/O psychology. Psychologists working in this area focus on hiring people with potential, ensuring they are adequately trained, managing and motivating employees, and evaluating performance.

A number of societal forces helped I/O psychology gain a foothold. During the two World Wars, the military and its supporting industries gave I/O psychology a big boost by hiring hundreds of psychologists to work on personnel selection, training, and other related tasks (Katzell & Austin, 1992; van de Water, 1997). Later, in the 1960s, psychologists found more opportunities as the American economic structure began to shift from manufacturing to service industries (Katzell & Austin, 1992). More jobs moved into offices; a growing number of work teams began brainstorming and communicating together to solve problems rather than spreading out to individual stations along an assembly line. In addition, successful employees became very mobile, able to move from job to job based on the strength of their accomplishments. Thus psychology in the workplace began to include more *organizational psychology*, focusing on the culture and organizational qualities of work.

Job Analysis: Understanding the Requirements for the Job

Psychologists contribute to several aspects of hiring and evaluating employees. As you will read, this effort goes far beyond placing an ad in the paper and conducting interviews. For starters, psychologists take a scientific approach; I/O psychologists are systematic, provide operational definitions, collect data, and use many other basic principles adopted by laboratory psychologists. In addition, psychologists may work in all areas of the process, from creating a job description, to finding the right people to fill those positions, to training them, and finally to evaluating the quality of the work and the effectiveness of the personnel procedures.

One of the most important aspects of this process is the **job analysis**, *the process of writing a detailed description of a position in terms of the required knowledge, abilities, skills, and other characteristics required to succeed, as well as evaluating the value of the position for the overall organization* (Bobko

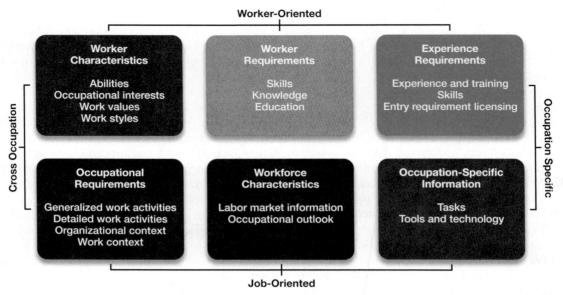

[**FIGURE 15•1**] The O*NET Concept Chart O*NET provides information about types of jobs and the requirements for workers that may fill them.

et al., 2008). As part of the job analysis, psychologists identify the **KSAOs**—*the knowledge, skills, abilities, and other traits required for a specific job*. Psychologists turn to a variety of sources for this task, such as *incumbents* (people who already hold the job), their supervisors, and *subject-matter experts* (people who have technical expertise related to the job). Interviewing multiple incumbents, supervisors, and subject-matter experts provides diverse perspectives on a job.

Job analysis might seem simple at first because it is relatively easy to find a collection of tasks and assign them to an individual. This might be the case for jobs that follow a set routine and include a fixed number of tasks—such as a custodial employee who vacuums and removes trash on a daily basis. However, the more complex and varied the task, the more difficult it is to pin down a job description (Dierdorff & Morgeson, 2008). Jobs also tend to change based on technology, the economy, and popular trends, so job analyses should be updated regularly, especially in high-tech positions (Bobko et al., 2008). Finally, incumbents often engage in a process called **job crafting**, *which means taking on or creating additional roles and tasks for a position over time*. Because these extra duties stem from the individual's unique KSAOs, they may distract newcomers from what the essential tasks of the job really are (Wrzesniewski & Dutton, 2001).

There are thousands of different occupations, and no individual psychologist could analyze them all. Fortunately, a substantial number of these jobs have already been thoroughly studied and the corresponding job analyses published on the Internet as part of a U.S. federal government project. This project is available to anyone in the general public—you just need to search for the *Occupational Information Network* or *O*NET* (Crouter et al., 2006; Occupational Information Network, 2009; http://online.onetcenter.org/). O*NET is a collection of databases that describe jobs from six domains (see **FIGURE 15•1**).

If you are interested in becoming a clinical psychologist, just go to O*NET, type in this job title, and start searching. There you will find the six categories of descriptors that will help you learn more about the job; if you are an employer, you will find which type of person you may want to hire.

Selection: Hiring the Right People

When the job analysis is complete, employers should have a list of KSAOs in hand and can turn their attention to hiring the best possible workers. The ideal worker would be someone whose KSAOs match those required for the job (see **TABLE 15•1**

QUICK QUIZ 15.1A

Job Analysis: Understanding the Requirements for the Job

KNOW...

1. Sometimes an employee expands her job to include new tasks and responsibilities over time. This departure from the original job description is known as:
   a. job crafting.   **c.** employee drifting.
   b. workplace expansion. **d.** job analysis.

2. If you are interested in finding out what is required for any given job, you should refer to _____ for important and accurate information.
   a. job net   **c.** O*NET
   b. job crafting   **d.** the occupational index

APPLY...

3. During job analysis, psychologists will identify the essential KSAOs. Which one of the following qualities is *not* a KSAO?
   a. Knowledge   **c.** Abilities
   b. Skills   **d.** Organizations

Answers can be found at the end of the chapter.

[**TABLE 15•1**] **KSAOs for a Job Analysis of Social Work**

Knowledge	Psychology, sociology, therapy and counseling, basic law
Skills	Listening, social perceptiveness, critical thinking, service orientation, judgment
Abilities	Oral communication, written communication, problem sensitivity (ability to anticipate problems)
Other traits	Concern for others, ability to control stress, persistence, integrity, dependability

for an example). Perhaps if you had Donald Trump's resources, you could stage a series of high-stakes competitions to examine how people would act in various challenging situations. Not surprisingly, though, the best methods in the real world only faintly resemble what you might see in entertainment (even if it is "reality" TV).

Interviewing Certainly the most familiar and most widely used employee selection method is the job interview. In the basic interviewing technique known as an **unstructured interview**, *an employer discusses a variety of job- and personality-related topics with a candidate with relatively few prepared questions to guide the conversation.* From this dialog, the employer can draw reasonably accurate conclusions about the applicant's personality (Blackman, 2002). However, the unstructured nature allows the interview to get off track, which raises several problems. For example, different candidates will experience different interviews, making comparisons less reliable.

Structured interviews remove some of the uncertainty by incorporating three main components (see TABLE 15•2). First, **structured interviews** *present the same set of questions to each job candidate with planned (rather than unstructured) follow-up questions.* Second, these questions are drawn directly from the job analysis to ensure that each is relevant to the position. Finally, the interviewer is trained to follow the same procedures in each interview, and uses a standardized form to ensure each interview session is consistent as possible (Campion et al., 1997).

Many structured interviews also include *situational interview* questions—questions about how the candidate would respond to a situation that is relevant to the job (Latham et al., 1980). These questions can actually be drawn from real situations that incumbents have faced in the past. When developing these questions, psychologists might ask low-quality and high-quality employees how they have responded to that situation in the past. By comparing a candidate's response to

the incumbents' responses, psychologists can get a sense of how well a candidate will perform on the job (see Table 15.2).

WORKING THE SCIENTIFIC LITERACY MODEL

Personality Selection Tests

Anyone who has interviewed for a job experiences concern over whether he or she is qualified or the "right" person for the position. Of course, employers are looking for just the right person, too, and many are turning to personality tests to help them in their search.

What do we know about personality selection measures?

One of the most significant aspects of job analysis is the identification of a list of KSAOs that can help employers make decisions about which type of person would be the best fit for a job. Therefore, one of the primary aspects of personnel selection is determining whether a person has the right knowledge, abilities, and other personality traits. One of the most popular means of assessing an individual's qualifications for a job is with a test, including testing of personality traits and cognition.

Before a personality test can be used by employers to select employees, I/O psychologists must first determine which personality traits are associated with success or failure in a specific position. This area of research is called **validation studies** *in which researchers administer tests to a large sample*

[**TABLE 15•2**] **Sample Situational Interview Question**

The following is an item from a situational interview for the position of sales associate at a jewelry store. The question would be presented and the candidate's response would be scored according to the scale below. The higher scores on the scale correspond to more desirable responses.

A customer comes into the store to pick up a watch he had left for repair. The repair was supposed to have been completed a week ago, but the watch is not back yet from the repair shop. The customer becomes very angry. How would you handle this situation?

1. Tell the customer the watch isn't back yet and ask him or her to check with you again later.
3. Apologize, tell the customer that you will check into the problem, and call him or her back later.
5. Put the customer at ease and call the repair shop while the customer waits.

Source: Weekley & Gier, 1987.

of incumbents and evaluate their performance to find correlations between job performance and personality traits or cognitive abilities (Sackett & Lievens, 2008; Van Iddekinge & Ployhart, 2008).

How can scientists study personality-based selection tests?

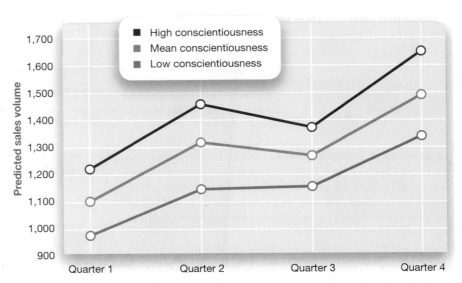

[**FIGURE 15•2**] **Conscientiousness Can Predict Job Performance** The red line shows that high conscientiousness is associated with better job performance than low conscientiousness scores (the green line) among pharmaceutical sales representatives. Performance was measured by the number of prescriptions written for a specific medication by physicians in his or her territory. Data were collected for each quarter during the first year the drug was available (Thoresen et al., 2004).

Tests of personality traits draw heavily from social-cognitive and trait theories. In fact, many of the self-report tests used in personality research are also used for personnel selection. Meta-analyses (which which combine the results of many earlier studies) as far back as 1991 have supported their use for this purpose (Barrick & Mount, 2005; Salgado, 1997; Tett et al., 1991). One of the more popular personality models is the Big Five (also known as the Five Factor Model; see TABLE 15•3), and the most popular self-report measure of the Big Five personality traits has been the NEO-PI.

For example, FIGURE 15•2 shows how conscientiousness predicts success among sales representatives for pharmaceutical companies (Thoresen et al., 2004). In each quarter of the year shown in the figure, those sales representatives who rate high in conscientiousness outperformed their peers with low levels of conscientiousness. Meanwhile, traits of agreeableness and openness did not predict success. Therefore, if we were consulting for a major drug company, we could recommend hiring applicants who score high in conscientiousness.

Can we critically evaluate this evidence?

To critique this research, we can begin with one of the most important concepts in psychological research: Correlational studies do not tell us about cause and effect. It is valuable to know that conscientious people are better

at some jobs, but is their success really due to their personality? This research is also limited in that it assumes personality is a relatively stable trait, but perhaps it is possible to create work environments that encourage specific trait-like behaviors. In other words, the right training program or incentives might help a person who is usually low in conscientious to be more conscientious while at work.

Why is this relevant?

Personality inventories measuring the Big Five can be useful across many different lines of work, as shown in TABLE 15•4.

Not only can personality tests be used to select specific individuals, but they can also be used to rule out individuals whose profiles suggest that they would be low-performers or disruptive employees across many different types of jobs (Salgado, 2002). For example, researchers studied a division of law enforcement using the California Personality Inventory and found distinguishing personality profiles among officers

[**TABLE 15•3**] The Big Five Personality Traits as Measured By the NEO-PI

Neuroticism (versus emotional stability)	Experiencing Negative Affect (anger, hostility, nervousness) and Being Emotionally Unsettled
Extraversion	Being sociable, affectionate, fun-loving
Openness	Showing imagination, seeking novelty and variety
Agreeableness	Being trusting, having the tendency to get along with others and to avoid conflict
Conscientiousness	Paying attention to procedures and details, following rules, being neat, organized, and timely

[**TABLE 15•4**] How the Big Five Can Predict Performance in a Wide Variety of Jobs

Type of Work	Traits Associated with High Performance	Citation
Pharmaceutical sales	Conscientiousness	Thoresen et al. (2004)
Fitness center managers and employees	A combination of extraversion and emotional stability	Judge & Erez (2007)
Factory production line workers	Emotional stability	Buttigieg (2006)
Entrepreneurs	Openness, Emotional Stability, and agreeableness	Zhao & Seibert (2006)
Camp counselors	Extraversion, agreeableness, conscientiousness	Loveland et al. (2005)

who were disciplined for inappropriate conduct (Sarchione et al., 1998). Another study investigated university employees and found that those who scored low on conscientiousness but high on extraversion were more likely to exhibit excessive absenteeism (Judge et al., 1997). I/O psychologists can apply similar methods to almost any imaginable career.

One issue you may have considered is that personality is not the *only* determining factor when selecting employees. Employers are also likely to want to know more about the various cognitive skills that applicants may bring.

Cognition-Based Selection Tests
As an alternative or supplement to personality tests, some psychologists utilize cognitive selection tests . For example, *situational judgment tests* put applicants in hypothetical situations, much like reality-show contestants find themselves in job-related scenarios (see **TABLE 15•5**). These tests, which are correlated with cognitive ability, predict job performance better than self-report personality tests (McDaniel et al., 2001). In fact, combining situation judgments with direct cognitive tests produces even better results (Clevenger et al., 2001). In meta-analyses across dozens of studies in a variety of fields, tests of cognitive ability have usually been shown to do a better job at predicting performance compared to personality tests (Salgado et al., 2003; Schmidt & Hunter, 1998; see **TABLE 15•6**).

Just like personality tests, cognitive tests must go through validation studies that serve to identify who should be selected and who should be turned away. Cognitive tests are far more difficult to fake than personality tests, but a new set of problems can arise from their use. Such instruments may be based on culturally specific skills or knowledge, and they may also induce *stereotype threat*, a phenomenon in which a person unintentionally conforms to a stereotype (Kirnan et al., 2009). For example, a well-qualified woman who applies for an engineering position may become aware of a stereotype implying that men are better at engineering and mathematics. If she then becomes anxious or preoccupied by this stereotype, she may perform below her normal level. More importantly, she may perform below the level of a male who has the same basic ability but does not face stereotype threat. Thus, due to stereotype threat, two individuals with different gender, ethnic, or cultural backgrounds may score very differently on the same test, despite having equal performance measures on the job. This possibility presents an ethical problem in that cognitive tests may discriminate based on ethnicity, gender, or culture rather than on candidates' actual potential.

The Assessment Center Personnel selection can be approached from a number of directions, as you can see, and it would seem that the best methods would involve a combination of techniques. **Assessment centers** *capitalize on multiple approaches to personnel selection by combining personality, cognitive, and sometimes physical ability tests.* Although this term suggests a physical location—perhaps an office complex where people come for day-long appointments—an assessment center actually refers to the process, not the location where it takes place.

Some of the unique aspects of assessment centers are the reliance on multiple raters, and the use of raters who have special training in assessment as well as the job that is being filled. This increases the validity of the process considerably (Hough & Oswald, 2000). Like the reality shows mentioned in the module-opening vignette, assessment centers regularly put candidates through **job simulations**—*role-playing activities that are very similar to situations encountered in the actual job.* A related activity is the *in-basket technique,* in which prospective employees sort through a set of incoming tasks and respond to them as if they were actual tasks.

[TABLE 15•5] A Sample Situational Judgment Test Item

A man on a very urgent mission during a battle finds he must cross a stream about 40 feet wide. A blizzard has been blowing and the stream has frozen over. However, because of the snow, he does not know how thick the ice is. He sees two planks about 10 feet long near the point where he wishes to cross. He also knows where there is a bridge about 2 miles downstream. Under the circumstances he should:

A. Walk to the bridge and cross it.
B. Run rapidly across on the ice.
C. Break a hole in the ice near the edge of the stream to see how deep the stream is.
D. Cross with the aid of the planks, pushing one ahead of the other and walking on them.
E. Creep slowly across the ice.

Source: Northrop, 1989, p. 190.

Perhaps the similarity of the judgments and games are what give assessment centers slightly higher validity than either situational judgment tests or cognitive instruments (Hermelin et al., 2007; Krause et al., 2006). Nevertheless, assessment centers are not without drawbacks. Given the number of tests and the complexity of the simulations involved, assessment centers can be time-consuming (they can last multiple days) and expensive (as much as $1,000 per day for a single candidate) to operate.

In summary, there will never be a perfect means of predicting which candidate will be the best possible person for the job. There are more techniques than we have described here, and even more are bound to be used in the future. Despite the inevitable change, several trends seem to be relatively fixed. Personnel selection tools will continue to match individuals with positions based on KSAOs, and the methods used to do so will be tested for validity. It is also likely that these methods will involve some combination of interviewing; tests of personality, cognitive ability, or physical ability; and some form of situational decision making.

PSYCH @
The Career Center

Most universities, colleges, and communities have career centers. These busy hubs of activity link employers to workers, with a focus on the job-hunter. They provide lists of internships and jobs, host career fairs for soon-to-be graduates, and aid students in crafting appealing résumés and personal statements to help them secure a spot in the workforce.

Career center personnel, even if they are not psychologists, often administer personality tests, interest inventories, and sometimes even skill or ability tests. These results are then matched with jobs that are likely to be available in the future, such as nurse or software engineer.

So what might a career center test look like? In a sense, it is the mirror image of a job analysis form on O*NET:

[TABLE 15•6] Cognition Predicts Training Success and Performance

Workers in a variety of careers completed tests of mental abilities and, for many careers, these scores correlated with performance during and after training.

Type of Work	Correlation With Training	Correlation With Performance
Apprentice	–	.26
Chemist	–	.28
Driver	.22	.26
Electrician	.28	.35
Information clerk	.31	.46
Engineer	.23	.28
Manager	.25	–
Mechanics	–	.21
Police	.12	.13
Sales	.34	–
Skilled worker	.28	.17
Typing	.23	.31

Source: Salgado et al., 2003.

Rather than identifying the KSAOs needed to perform a specific job, it asks which KSAOs you can provide—not to mention what your interests might be. Your KSAOs can then be matched against a list of job analyses to find the best match.

You can learn more about the most popular career interest tests at their websites, or visit your campus career center, as many offer these tests for free:

- Strong Interest Inventory: https://www.cpp.com/products/strong/index.aspx

- Jackson Vocational Interest Survey: http://www.jvis.com/

- The U.S. government's O*NET website offers consumer information on vocational testing: http://www.onetcenter. org/guides.html

Your campus career center may offer a number of valid and reliable tests of career interests and abilities.

QUICK QUIZ 15.1B

Selection: Hiring the Right People

KNOW…

1. An assessment center is:

   a. an office or meeting room that is used for structured interviews.
   b. a process of screening potential employees using a variety of tests and simulations.
   c. a method of evaluating how well a current employee is performing.
   d. a personality test.

UNDERSTAND…

2. A consultant measures 100 employees working in different branches at a government agency to determine whether their personality traits can be used to predict job performance. The consultant is most likely:

   a. running simulations for assessment centers.
   b. conducting a validation study.
   c. job crafting.
   d. doing structured interviews with each employee to get a sense of his or her personality type.

3. What is one of the unique aspects of assessment centers?

   a. Reliance on multiple assessment methods
   b. The size of the building
   c. Their physical location
   d. The reliance on a single type of assessment test

ANALYZE…

4 One advantage of structured interviews is that they:

   a. present the same questions to each candidate to ensure each interview is consistent.
   b. allow the conversation to drift from topic to topic depending on what is interesting.
   c. provide valid assessments of cognitive ability.
   d. remove any possibility of cultural bias and stereotype threat.

Answers can be found at the end of the chapter.

Performance Appraisal

Personnel selection may come first, but **performance appraisal—** *the evaluation of current employees*—is every bit as important (Kline & Sulsky, 2009). Evaluation ensures that employees are doing their jobs correctly; if not, then they may need additional training or incentives to bring their performance up to the desired level. When employees do their work well, they need to be recognized with awards, bonuses, or raises and, in some cases, they may be given more challenging tasks or additional responsibilities to keep them engaged. Unfortunately, when employees do not respond to feedback, evaluations can also result in termination. In short, without proper evaluation techniques, productivity suffers. Thus, even though employees often dread the scrutiny of an evaluation, the benefits to the company are typically well worth it.

What Needs to Be Evaluated? A good deal of employee evaluation is based on a supervisor's overall rating of an employee. An overall rating is often sufficient for evaluating work performance (Viswesvaran et al., 2005) however, employers often want to evaluate some more specific aspects of work performance (Rotundo & Sackett, 2002):

- *Task performance* describes how well an employee performs the assigned duties for his or her position in the organization.

- *Organizational citizenship behavior* (*OCB*) is the degree to which an employee contributes beyond what is expected (e.g., exceptional teamwork, leadership).

- *Counterproductive behavior* includes actions that interfere with one's own (and sometimes others') productivity, such as absenteeism, lateness, dishonesty, and inappropriate interpersonal behaviors.

Although overall ratings are often sufficient, collecting information from each of these three areas promotes balanced assessments that look at all the contributions an employee makes as well as anything that reduces productivity.

Who Conducts the Evaluation? The traditional approach to employee evaluation is for the immediate supervisor to review the employee's work over a period of time and provide one-on-one feedback. This makes sense because the supervisor knows which tasks have been assigned and how they were performed. However, the supervisor has only one perspective, which may be described as a *top-down* perspective. A clever employee may be substandard in many aspects of the job, yet have the ability to present a positive image to the boss. Therefore it is essential to include other points of view in the evaluation process.

Multisource assessment or **360-degree feedback** *provides evaluation information from many different perspectives within and beyond an organization.* The 360-degree analogy reminds us that the employee receives feedback from all angles (see **FIGURE 15•3**). In addition to the traditional supervisory evaluation, multisource assessments include information from an employee's co-workers, anyone whom he may supervise, and perhaps customers or clientele that he might serve. In many cases, the employee will even rate himself.

In theory, 360-degree feedback is a great method of employee evaluation because it covers all aspects of the job: The supervisor can look over workload and productivity, the peers and supervised employees can report on teamwork and leadership, and customers can report on professionalism and service. Indeed, research on 360-degree feedback generally has shown positive results with the approach (Conway et al., 2001; Facteau et al., 1998). However, problems can arise in this process. For example, power structures in an organization might appear to be threatened. Specifically, some managers do not seem to take subordinate feedback seriously. Also, managers appear to remember feedback from other management more so than feedback from subordinates, and some managers react cynically to subordinate feedback, especially if they believe that the procedure may be unfair (McCarthy & Garavan, 2007; Smither et al., 2005).

Preventing Bias in Evaluation If proper controls are lacking, a number of biases and errors have the potential to make the evaluation process more difficult. One such error is the **halo effect**, *in which a rater thinks highly about one aspect of an employee's job or personality and this leads him or her to provide similar ratings for other aspects of the employee's work.* Another error, called the **contrast effect**, *occurs when a rater evaluates one employee who is very strong in a number of dimensions such that, by comparison, the next employee is likely to appear weak, even if he is an average worker by other measures.* Think about these effects in the context of a sales office. One worker may be particularly good at making contacts with new clients, but only has moderate success actually completing the sale. We could see evidence of the halo effect if her manager rated her highly for both making contacts *and* completing sales. Now consider a moderately successful sales

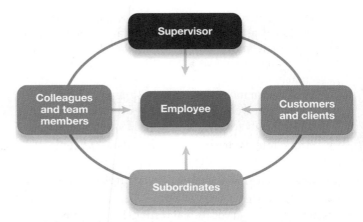

[**FIGURE 15•3**] **Employee Evaluation** The 360-degree feedback method provides evaluation information from all directions.

representative who is evaluated after the star performer. Despite his consistency, the contrast effect between him and the star salesperson may leave him with a lower rating than he deserves—unless an appropriate rating system is in place.

This module has merely scratched the surface of performance appraisals, but there are some clear messages to take home. First, appraisals are absolutely essential to successful businesses because they promote positive behaviors and create opportunities to correct negative behaviors. Because assessments occur infrequently, however, managers must rely on their memories to evaluate employees, which leaves a large opening for errors. Thus systematic methods should be used along with multiple points of view. With these in place, assessment should be a valuable tool for any employer.

QUICK QUIZ 15.1C
Performance Appraisal

KNOW...

1. If a psychologist completes a performance appraisal for a superstar employee, then the next employee may seem weak in comparison. This can lead to _____.
   a. the contrast effect   c. the downsizing effect
   b. the halo effect   d. stereotype threat

UNDERSTAND...

2. If a psychologist conducts a performance appraisal using feedback from supervisors, subordinates, peers, and clients, he is most likely using the _____ approach.
   a. telescoping   c. 360 degree feedback
   b. compass   d. task performance

3. A new start-up company has several employees who need to be evaluated. Which of the following would a personnel psychologist need to assess?
   a. Organizational citizenship behavior
   b. Counterproductive behavior
   c. Task performance
   d. All of these

Answers can be found at the end of the chapter.

Module Summary

Now that you have read this module you should:

KNOW ...

- **The key terminology of personnel psychology:**

360-degree feedback (p. 484)
assessment center (p. 481)
contrast effect (p. 484)
halo effect (p. 484)
job analysis (p. 477)
job crafting (p. 478)

job simulations (p. 481)
performance appraisal (p. 483)
structured interview (p. 479)
unstructured interview (p. 479)
validation studies (p. 479)

UNDERSTAND ...

- **Interviews, testing, and assessment center methods of personnel selection.** The two major types of interviews are structured and unstructured. Job candidates also may be tested to assess their personality type and cognitive ability. These results are used to determine whether a candidate is suited to a particular company and, if so, for which specific job she is most suited. Assessment centers often combine both personality and cognitive testing with simulations of actual work situations.

- **Methods used in employee performance appraisals.** 360-degree feedback (also known as multisource assessments) provide the most detailed information on employee performance. They typically involve evaluating task performance, organizational citizenship behavior, and counterproductive behavior.

APPLY ...

- **Your knowledge of personnel psychology to identify likely KSAOs for a given job.** To do so, complete TABLE 15•7 below and then check your answers by going to www.onetonline.org and searching for the job title.

ANALYZE ...

- **The relative value of structured versus unstructured interview selection techniques.** In an unstructured interview, an employer discusses a variety of job- and personality-related topics with a candidate, and asks a few prepared questions to guide the conversation. However, comparisons among employees can be difficult to make with this method, and potential sources of bias can creep into the interview. Structured interviews present the same set of questions drawn directly from the job analysis to ensure their relevance to the position. They provide for consistency across candidates and focus on job-related information rather than shared interests. Requiring interviewers to follow a specific set of questions reduces opportunities for bias.

((•——| **Listen** to the audio file of this module at **MyPsychLab**

15.2 Affect, Attitudes, and Behavior at Work

Learning Objectives

After reading this module you should:

Know ...
- The key terminology of employee affect and attitudes

Understand ...
- Job satisfaction, burnout, and the attitudes and affect that go along with them
- The risk factors for, and varieties of, workplace aggression

Apply ...
- Your knowledge of satisfaction and burnout to ensure you maintain high motivation for college courses and your career

Analyze ...
- Various methods for preventing burnout and encouraging job satisfaction

[TABLE 15•7] Identifying KSAOs

Pick an occupation. What do you think the KSAOs for this job might be? Try to come up with at least five qualities in each category and write them here or on a separate piece of paper. When you finish, compare your results with the O'NET description—just go to www.onetonline.org and type the occupation into the search bar.

Knowledge
Skills
Abilities
Other traits

Did you know that almost half of new teachers leave the profession within five years (Lambert, 2006)? This means more than half of all teachers spent about the same amount or more time in college than they did in their teaching careers! For Craig, a former teacher, the job seemed perfect because he liked reading and history, he interacted well with teens at the high school level, and he believed he could make positive changes in boys' lives on the wrestling and track teams. He knew that the pay would not be great, but he was so excited that he finished his education degree in four years and charged headlong into his first teaching job.

Craig does not know how it happened, but one day three years later, he looked around at the piles of papers and began to wonder if he should stay up all night grading or call in sick the next day. He would have finished the paperwork during his planning period earlier that day, except that he had to deal with overprotective parents who had no idea—and refused to believe—how poorly their son behaved at school. The apathy of many of his students began to sink in: If they could not bother to try harder on the assignments, then perhaps Craig should not put so much effort into planning classes and giving feedback on rough drafts. He began to feel emotionally and physically exhausted after each day's work, and felt resentment toward the principal who always sided with the parents and the superintendent. Faced with so many obstacles, he felt as if nothing he could do would matter in the long run. After his fourth year, Craig left teaching for good and took a job in sales.

This is an all-too-familiar scenario for educational professionals. What is interesting about this case is how motivated Craig was at the beginning of his career—he worked very hard for a modest salary, and even volunteered to do more than the typical teacher. But then frustration set in, and along with it came a range of negative physiological, psychological, and social effects.

FOCUS QUESTIONS

1. Which factors might lead someone to be highly engaged and satisfied with his or her work?

2. What can cause a highly motivated individual to become burned out?

Productivity and success at work are largely due to the behavior of the members who make up the workforce. This aspect of the workplace environment goes beyond the simple question of whether workers are doing their job or not. Indeed, the attitudes and emotional energy that people bring to work ultimately affect their overall productivity and job satisfaction. In this module, we will explore how emotions and behaviors in workplace can affect a company and its workers.

Employee Affect, Attitudes, and Job Satisfaction

I/O psychologists have become increasingly interested in researching *affect*—individuals' emotional responses—regarding their jobs and work in general (Thoresen et al., 2003). The work in this vein includes research on both **positive affect** (**PA**), *the tendency to experience positive emotions such as happiness, satisfaction, and enthusiasm,* and **negative affect** (**NA**), *the tendency to experience negative emotions, including frustration, anger, and distress.* Even if you have held only one job, chances are you have experienced both varieties of affect. However, some individuals tend to experience more of one type than another, a quality known as *trait affectivity*.

There are at least two important reasons for I/O psychologists' interest in affect, the first of which may be called the *happier is smarter hypothesis*: Employees who have PA traits seem to make better decisions and may also be more creative (Côté, 1999). In addition, a variety of research shows that PA is associated with teamwork, organizational citizenship,

Psychologists have found that employees who show positive affect perform better at work than employees with negative affect.

improved negotiating techniques, and general performance (Brief & Weiss, 2002). (Incidentally, the *happier is smarter hypothesis* has been found among college students as well—so remember to think positive about your psychology course.)

I/O psychologists also study affect because when positive or negative affect becomes so consistent that it is as reliable as personality traits, this attitude can influence job satisfaction or dissatisfaction (Connolly & Viswesvaran, 2000; Watson & Slack, 1993). Along these lines, PA employees are less likely to quit and, in general, show more organizational commitment (Côté, 1999).

BIOPSYCHOSOCIAL PERSPECTIVES

Affect as a Cultural Trait

You can likely identify positive and negative affect among your individual classmates and friends. As traits, these affective states can occur in spite of events that challenge them, so that a NA individual may feel glum, despite having achieved recent successes. These affective traits are actually quite similar to the Big Five dimensions (see Table 15.4 on page 481); negative affect is related to neuroticism while positive affect is related to extraversion (Judge et al., 2002; Watson & Clark, 1992). Biological psychologists have found that PA individuals experience more activity in the brain's reward circuitry, whereas NA individuals experience more activity in the circuits involved in fear and alert responses (Watson et al., 1999). Adoption and behavioral genetic studies even show a significant heritable component to trait affect (Tellegen et al., 1988).

Psychologist Edward Chang has also examined emotion traits across cultures. What do you think he has found? First consider whether the following statements are true or false:

1. Pessimism is more common among East Asians than among European Americans.

2. Asian Americans are more likely to ruminate (dwell on negative thoughts and experiences) than European Americans.

3. Pessimistic thinking is always a negative quality.

Across a wide variety of studies, Chang and his colleagues have found reliable cultural differences in some affective traits.

1. *True.* Pessimism does seem to be related to culture. East Asian cultures tend to score higher on measures of pessimism than European Americans (Chang et al., 2003).

2. *True.* Asian Americans are more likely to ruminate than their European American counterparts (Chang et al., 2010).

3. *False.* Pessimistic thinking can actually have benefits and lead to better performance on tasks than optimism (Norem & Chang, 2002).

Job Satisfaction Versus Burnout The balance between positive and negative emotions reflects how satisfied people are with their jobs. Positive or negative thoughts about work are expressed as *job attitudes*, a combination of affect and thoughts an employee holds about his or her job (Brief & Weiss, 2002). **Job satisfaction** *refers to the degree to which an employee is content with his or her work*, and is most likely to be achieved by people with positive job attitudes (see FIGURE 15•2). For many people, starting a new job can produce a sense of intense satisfaction, also known a *honeymoon period* (Boswell et al., 2009). Job satisfaction typically rises and falls throughout a career, however. The lower periods may include the experience of **burnout**, *a combination of persistent emotional and physical exhaustion, cynical attitudes about the job, and a sense that one's work has little meaning* (TABLE 15•8; Maslach, 2003).

PsychTutor
Click here in your eText for an interactive tutorial on Factors in Job Satisfaction

Professions such as teaching, law, and medicine require a conscious commitment and years of education, just as skilled labor and crafts (electricians, plumbers, artisans) require training, practice, and often an apprenticeship. It should not come as a surprise, then, that many people who make this type of commitment enter the workforce with a sense of satisfaction and engagement. But what keeps some people feeling satisfied? And what about those who experience job satisfaction despite taking a job they thought they would eventually dread?

The common-sense notion that enjoyable jobs, co-workers, and supervisors all contribute to job satisfaction does seem to be correct (Mossholder et al., 2005), but job satisfaction goes beyond these factors. For example, a teacher may be highly satisfied with the effect he could have on students, but only marginally satisfied with his income. Satisfaction also depends on the situation you find yourself in—you may be perfectly suited to design computer software but just because you have a job in this field does not guarantee satisfaction.

Satisfaction also reflects whether the job is what the employee expected (Wanous et al., 1992). Moreover, achieving job satisfaction and avoiding burnout depend on how employees are treated, promoted, and challenged. Research shows that it is actually good to challenge workers, particularly those high in

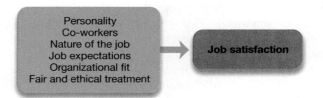

[**FIGURE 15•4**] **Sources of Job Satisfaction** Job satisfaction stems from multiple factors, including personal qualities and the work environment.

[**TABLE 15•8**] Job Satisfaction Versus Burnout

Job Satisfaction		Burnout
Energy	← *Physical and emotional experience* →	Exhaustion
Optimism	← *Attitudes about job* →	Cynicism
Accomplishment	← *Beliefs about self* →	Lack of accomplishment

cognitive ability, as long as the organization supports their extra efforts (Wallace et al., 2009). In fact, among teachers, more complex teaching strategies are equated with lower levels of burnout, even though they require more effort (Ben-Ari et al., 2003).

Individual differences in affective qualities lead to burnout for some people and job satisfaction for others, regardless of the job. For example, people who are extraverted and emotionally stable (the opposite of neuroticism) tend to be more satisfied with their job (Judge et al., 2002). Also, whether someone is satisfied or experiences burnout depends on his self-appraisals—his beliefs about ability, worth, and level of control (Judge & Bono, 2001). Thus job satisfaction is related to the following factors:

- *Self esteem*, which includes beliefs about one's value and worth as a human being.
- *Self-efficacy*, which involves beliefs about one's ability to accomplish certain goals or complete specific tasks.
- *Locus of control*, which is a set of beliefs about one's ability to control one's work environment and success.

As you can see, a certain degree of job satisfaction seems to be based on an individual's disposition, and this tends to make job satisfaction relatively stable as long as an individual holds a job (Dormann & Zapf, 2001).

The likelihood of experiencing job satisfaction versus burnout is also related to the interaction between the individual and his or her environment (Best et al., 2005; Maslach, 2003). When our skills, energy level, and aspirations match our job, then we are likely to be engaged. A mismatch—such as a teacher who is highly engaged and enthusiastic but works with students who are unmotivated and at a school with low administrative support—can be enough to lead an individual to change jobs (Staw et al., 1986).

Some people may become dissatisfied with a job simply because there is a lack of opportunity to express positive affectivity, or because they are not suited for the job in the first place. Our language is filled with phrases that illustrate this mismatch: *Another day, another dollar; it's a living; TGIF (thank God it's Friday)*. All of these phrases bring to mind a person who works out of necessity but does not find much fulfillment in the workplace. In contrast to these kinds of employed-but-uninspired workers, other people experience factors that actively drive satisfaction down; instead of boredom, they feel distress, dread, and perhaps even anger about their work.

Burnout is the overarching term describing feelings of low job satisfaction. It is characterized by three qualities: physical and emotional exhaustion; a cynical, pessimistic attitude about the organization; and a feeling that nothing of significance has been accomplished. The work environment can accelerate burnout through the nature of the tasks, insufficient resources, and unpleasant social situations (Spector, 2002). And if one employee gets burned out, beware: Burnout has even been shown to be contagious (Westman & Vinokur, 1998).

Exhaustion comes from the nature of the work: Dull, repetitive work can create stress by challenging a worker to maintain her attention despite severe boredom (Maslach, 2003). Similarly, piling on too much work can be stressful, even if the work would be interesting at a slower pace. *Cynicism* derives from a negative or ineffective interpersonal environment; it can be agonizing to walk into the office each morning if you are aware that you will have to face a boss who is out of touch and work on projects that seem to be pointless. Finally, *feelings of ineffectiveness* may arise from any situation in which the employee cannot access the necessary information or resources for the job. This can be a very stressful situation because the employee must constantly invent new ways to do her job or simply accept that she will not be able to perform up to her standards (Breaugh & Colihan, 1994; Hodge et al., 1994). Considerable stress may also be attributable to a lack of information and direction required to know which tasks need to be done, how work will be evaluated, or what purpose the work serves.

Burnout is characterized by physical and emotion exhaustion, cynicism, and a sense that the work has little importance.

Could the factors just described apply to our teacher's story from the beginning of the module? Certainly Craig felt the work piling up, and he believed that he lacked the resources to do his job well. Interpersonally, he felt the administrators did not support his work, and neither the students nor their parents offered much encouragement.

Absenteeism and Turnover As dissatisfaction and burnout increase, a number of undesirable behaviors may begin to surface. One of the first to appear is **absenteeism**—*regularly missing work for either legitimate or questionable reasons.* According to major surveys, 1.5% to 2.5% of the U.S. workforce is absent on any given workday (Commerce Clearing House, 2006). Although absence due to a major illness or crisis is completely excusable, burnout can lead people to lower their standards for what constitutes an emergency. In other words, a happy worker may miss one day with the flu whereas a burned-out worker might take three days off (Schaufeli et al, 2009; Ybema et al, 2010).

Many consider absenteeism to be the first step driving the problem of **turnover**, *the rate at which existing employees leave the organization* (Griffeth et al., 2000). Turnover is more than just a nuisance for managers who must hire and train new workers; it is also a major expense for organizations. The real cost of turnover includes searching for and hiring a new employee, training that employee, and the loss of productivity until the new worker becomes proficient.

Of course, having disgruntled workers on the job may not be any better than having them skip work. Dissatisfied employees are likely to engage in *counterproductive behaviors* that may reduce productivity for the rest of the organization (Berry et al., 2007). If the stress is social in nature, the disgruntled workers may engage in social forms of disruption aimed at other people. Examples include loud and incessant complaining, starting rumors, and even harassment. In other situations, workers who feel they have been treated unfairly may attempt to reward themselves through theft, or perhaps they may attack the company through vandalism.

Reducing the Effects of Burnout Given the major problems that burnout presents to both employers and employees, researchers have examined various ways to prevent or reduce burnout and its ill effects. Some key advice is that burnout interventions should occur at the organizational level, because qualities of the job, social environment, and availability of resources have the largest impact on burnout.

For example, physical exercise and cognitive-behavioral stress management skills may help employees manage their reactions to stress more effectively (Richardson & Rothstein, 2008). In addition, employers can offer raises in hopes of making the job more rewarding, although problems with the workload and social environment will not go away just because the paycheck is a little larger. As the phrase TGIF suggests, time away from work is beneficial, and even a single day off can help (Frankenhaeuser et al., 1989; Lounsbury & Hoopes, 1986). The effects of an extended break are even greater (as long as the worker enjoys the vacation) but, as shown in FIGURE 15·5,

the relief from burnout does not last much longer than the holiday itself (Fritz & Sonnentang, 2006; Kühnel & Sonnentang, 2011). After all, the employee who returns from vacation has to walk right back into the situation that led to burnout.

The real solution to employee dissatisfaction seems to be proactive—addressing the source of the problem before it gets out of control. A significant but limited amount of dissatisfaction seems to be related to personality, so a company can start by hiring people whose KSAOs fit the job and the organization—a selection process described in Previous Section. Once workers are hired, effective training is essential and mentoring can help make the transitions go smoothly (Payne & Huffman, 2005).

QUICK QUIZ 15.2A
Employee Affect, Attitudes, and Job Satisfaction

KNOW…

1. _____ is the rate at which existing employees leave the organization.

   a. Burnout   c. Turnover
   b. Negative affect   d. Job satisfaction

2. Absenteeism refers to:

   a. when an employee regularly misses work for illegitimate reasons.
   b. when an employee regularly misses work for any reason.
   c. the rate at which employees leave the company.
   d. the policy of allowing workers to accumulate sick leave and vacation time.

UNDERSTAND…

3. An employee who is enthusiastic about his job, even when times are tough, is expressing _____.

   a. positive affect   c. high self-efficacy
   b. negative affect   d. openness to experience

4. Which outcome would an employer not expect to find with employees who express negative affect?

   a. Diminished creativity   c. Ineffective teamwork
   b. Poorer decision making   d. High job satisfaction

APPLY…

5. You are a very capable employee who feels very positive about your work skills. However, layoffs are a constant threat and you play no part in deciding who stays and who goes at your company. Your job satisfaction may suffer because:

   a. you have low self-efficacy.
   b. you probably have low self-esteem about your job.
   c. you lack a sense of control over your work.
   d. the managers are verbally abusive.

ANALYZE…

6. How do exercise and stress-management skills work to reduce or prevent burnout?

   a. They provide a distraction from work.
   b. They make the job more rewarding.
   c. They help the employee reduce reactions to stress.
   d. Actually, they do very little to reduce or prevent burnout.

Answers can be found at the end of the chapter.

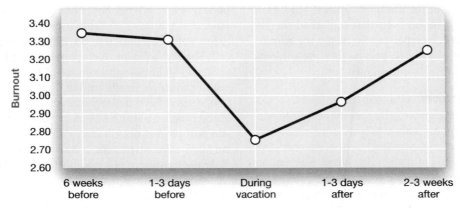

[**FIGURE 15•5**] **Vacation Temporarily Relieves Burnout** Burnout is measured here on a self-report scale ranging from 1 to 7, with 7 indicating the most burnout. As shown by the decline in the center of the graph, a week or more of vacation can greatly reduce burnout. However, burnout returns to nearly the same level in a matter of 3 weeks.

Workplace Aggression

On occasion, a frightening work-related story will dominate the news for a few days—a recently dismissed employee returns to his former workplace seeking violent revenge. The extreme nature of these nationally reported incidents tends to overshadow the vast majority of cases that present a real threat to workers and their businesses. In its more common forms, workplace aggression may involve verbal hostility, obstructionism (making someone's job more difficult), and overt aggression, such as assaults or vandalism (Baron et al., 1999). The victims of workplace aggression are likely to have lower satisfaction and may even quit their jobs, so psychologists have been trying to understand the causes of this undesirable behavior and its long-term effects on individuals and the organizations they work for (Lapierre et al., 2005).

episode of violence in the previous year (Bureau of Labor Statistics, 2006; see FIGURE 15•6). However, only 10% to 15% of these cases involved acts by current or recent employees; instead, the majority involved seemingly random criminal acts committed at certain organizations and against members of certain occupations (prison staff, caretakers for the mentally ill, and even teachers) and, in some cases, by clientele (LeBlanc & Barling, 2004).

An obvious response to this problem is to look for screening instruments that might be able to predict who is likely to become aggressive, and particularly those people who might become violent. Achieving this goal can be challenging, however. After all, potential employees probably do not intend to express aggressiveness when they begin their jobs and, even if they did, they would probably not disclose their planned aggression in an interview.

WORKING THE SCIENTIFIC LITERACY MODEL

Hostility in the Workplace

Common sense suggests that, to be productive and satisfied workers, people need to feel safe around their co-workers. However, not all workplaces meet this description. What leads some workers to create a hostile work environment?

What do we know about hostility in the workplace?

In a recent survey, more than 5% of businesses overall (and more than 50% of large establishments with 1,000-plus employees) reported an

How can scientists study hostility in the workplace?

A number of factors slightly increase a person's risk for being aggressive at work, such as fitting a highly competitive, achievement-oriented personality profile and having a history of aggressive behavior (LeBlanc & Barling, 2004). Research also suggests that males are more prone to aggression than females (Rutter & Hine, 2005). One particularly telling trait for aggression is alcohol abuse. Interestingly, alcohol use by itself does not predict aggression, though the combination of heavy alcohol use and perceived injustice or maltreatment is a very ominous pairing (Greenburg & Barling, 1999; Jockin et al., 2001). Some research has shown that organizational variables are better predictors of workplace aggression than personal traits. One such study looked at both personal and

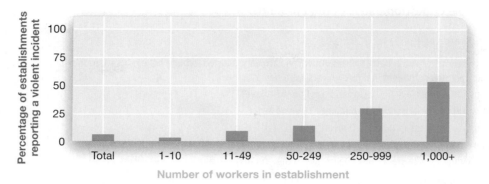

[**FIGURE 15•6**] **Prevalence of Workplace Violence** Percentage of establishments that have experienced an incident of workplace violence in the 12 months prior to the survey, by size of establishment.

situational variables and found that when organizational policies treated employees unfairly, or when supervisors were strict and abusive, the risk for aggression increased significantly (Inness et al., 2005).

Recently psychologists have turned to a new method of detecting aggressive tendencies: the conditional reasoning test. This method presents current or prospective employees with a series of word problems similar to the standardized reading comprehension tests you have probably completed in school (see TABLE 15•9 on p. 492; James et al., 2005; James & LeBreton, 2010). The word problems do not explicitly talk about aggression, yet this measure seems to be able to accurately identify potentially aggressive individuals. It appears to work because for each item in the test, one response choice seems reasonable only to the degree that an individual is willing to be aggressive. Can you detect which items in FIGURE 15•7 (p. 492) are associated with aggressive tendencies? It may not be as easy as you think.

Can we critically evaluate this evidence?

Although psychologists can identify risk factors, it is not clear exactly what actions managers should take when presented with this information. For example, being male is a risk factor—does that mean that companies should hire only females? To complicate matters, some risk factors for aggression—competitiveness and achievement motivation, for example—are also desirable qualities for certain positions.

Why is this relevant?

Despite these challenges, psychologists hope that a thorough understanding of workplace aggression will lead to methods of decreasing violence. In terms of selection, a predictive tool such as the conditional reasoning method may be able to distinguish between non-violent workers and those who present a

threat. Once these individuals are on the job, psychologists may eventually be able to monitor the work environment to identify situations that might interact with personalities to produce hostile situations. Thus preventive measures could be put in place before any overt acts of aggression occur.

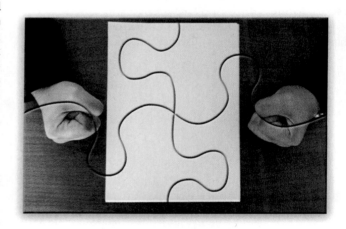

Sexual Harassment *Sexual harassment* is a well-known term in industrialized societies, so it might surprise you to learn that the term did not come into use until the 1970s. Despite its familiarity, the concept of sexual harassment can be difficult to define because sexuality is such a multi-faceted aspect of human behavior. The best way to distinguish harassment from other behavior is to emphasize the fact that harassment is *unwelcomed* sexual attention. In the United States, this understanding is clearly stated in the official legal definition of **sexual harassment** developed by the Equal Employment Opportunity Commission (EEOC, 2011): "*unwelcome sexual advances, requests for sexual favors, and other verbal or physical harassment of a sexual nature.*" Such harassment may come in various forms, such as *quid pro quo harassment* in which a supervisor promises raises or other benefits in return for sexual favors. A *hostile work environment* is a situation in which a worker feels threatened or

[**TABLE 15•9**] Sample Conditional Reasoning Problems

Illustrative Conditional Reasoning Problems

1. American cars have gotten better in the past 15 years. American carmakers started to build better cars when they began to lose business to the Japanese. Many American buyers thought that foreign cars were better made.
   Which of the following is the most logical conclusion based on the above?
   a. America was the world's largest producer of airplanes 15 years ago.
   b. Swedish carmakers lost business in America 15 years ago.
   c. The Japanese knew more than Americans about building good cars 15 years ago.
   d. American carmakers built cars to wear out 15 years ago so they could make a lot of money selling parts.

2. The old saying, "an eye for an eye," means that if someone hurts you, then you should hurt that person back. If you are hit, then you should hit back. If someone burns your house, then you should burn that person's house.
   Which of the following is the biggest problem with the "eye for an eye" plan?
   a. It tells people to "turn the other cheek."
   b. It offers no way to settle a conflict in a friendly manner.
   c. It can be used only at certain times of the year.
   d. People have to wait until they are attacked before they can strike.

Source: James et al., 2005.

demeaned by sexual advances, insults, or other comments of a sexual nature.

Over the past decade, the EEOC—the government agency that oversees formal charges of sexual harassment in the United

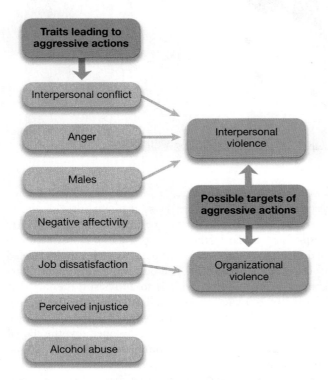

[**FIGURE 15•7**] **Qualities Leading to Workplace Violence** Each of these qualities is associated with increased risk of committing aggressive acts in the workplace. Traits with arrows are significantly more likely to contribute to one target than the other.

States—has received 12,000 to 15,000 complaints each year, with the vast majority (85% to 90%) being filed by women (EEOC, 2011). However, the number of complaints by males has been slowly increasing. Despite the large numbers, these incidents include only the legal complaints; many more cases likely go unreported because individuals are embarrassed or afraid to file complaints, they believe their case is not severe enough, or they do not have confidence in the formal procedures.

Aside from the sex differences in harassment, few demographic characteristics can be used to identify those individuals who are most likely to harass their fellow workers. Harassment seems to be equally likely to occur in all types of jobs and organizations, but is slightly more likely to occur when the harasser has higher educational levels and status in the organization (Pina et al., 2009). Personality researchers have found that the Big Five personality traits, which are so important to other I/O issues, have little or no relationship to sexual harassment. However, a few more specific traits are related to harassment, such as honesty-humility, which is negatively correlated with harassment (Lee et al., 2004), whereas authoritarianism is positively associated with harassment (Begany & Milburn, 2002).

Because of the gender differences and power issues inherent in the problem of sexual harassment, many psychologists have turned to the sociocultural perspective to explain why it occurs. Many social stereotypes depict men as the predominant breadwinners in the family and as leaders of organizations. For some men, the power ascribed to them by these stereotypes crosses over from home life and organizational roles into the realm of their sexual interests.

Other psychologists adopt a biological perspective, explaining that males and females have evolved differing motives for sex: Men seek quantity and diversity in sexual partners, whereas women look for partners with resources.

If this is true, then it might explain both the tendency for males to be the perpetrators of sexual harassment and the frequent power imbalances between males and females that exist in organizations (i.e., predominantly male supervisors) (Pina et al., 2009).

Both the sociocultural and biological views help explain why some men sexually harass, but they are not as successful in explaining why most men do not. Further, they do little to account for the cases in which women are the instigators.

Perhaps the most important aspect of sexual harassment is understanding exactly why it is such a serious problem. First and foremost is the obvious disrespect for an individual that harassment and other forms of aggression exhibit. Research also shows decreases in job satisfaction and commitment to the organization, as well as increases in physical and emotional illness, following sexual harassment (Willness et al., 2007).

MYTHS IN MIND

The Many Misunderstandings About Sexual Harassment

Psychologists investigating sexual aggression, including sexual harassment, have documented a number of pervasive myths. These myths are not just incorrect, but are actually dangerous. People who accept these myths are more likely to commit sexual harassment and other forms of sexual aggression. For the rest of the population, endorsing the myths makes it less likely that victims will receive the support they need. Here are some of the most widely-held myths about sexual harassment:

Myth: Modern work settings include more women and more protections, so harassment has not been a significant problem in recent years.

Reality: Sexual harassment is still a significant problem. Nearly half of all women report harassment at some point, and the EEOC receives as many as 15,000 complaints each year.

Myth: Sexual harassment must be sexual in nature.

Reality: Sexual harassment includes discrimination based on a person's sex, even if no sexual contact is suggested.

Myth: Sexual harassment requires the instigator to have bad intentions.

Reality: Sexual harassment is determined by its consequences, not the aggressor's intentions. If sexual advances are unwelcome but persist anyway, then they constitute harassment. This is true even if the instigator does not consciously mean any harm.

Myth: A person has to physically touch another person for the act to be considered harassment.

Reality: Sexual harassment is any unwanted sexual advance, including phone calls, emails, and notes.

Myth: Women secretly enjoy the sexual attention. Playing hard to get is just part of the game.

Reality: Sexual harassment by definition is unwelcomed and unwanted. Harassment is very different from consensual flirting and dating.

Myth: An individual could avoid being sexually harassed if he or she really wanted.

Reality: Some people suffer harassment quietly for fear of retaliation. The instigator may be physically intimidating or have control over raises and promotions at work.

QUICK QUIZ 15.2B

Workplace Aggression

KNOW...

1. Recent statistics indicate that more than _____ of businesses overall reported an episode of violence in the previous year.
   a. 2%   **c.** 10 %
   b. 5%   **d.** 20%

UNDERSTAND...

2. Which is likely to be the best predictor of aggression in the workplace?
   a. Presence of competitive employees
   b. Presence of males in the workplace
   c Policies in the workplace that treat employees unfairly
   d. Presence of females in the workplace

3. Which of the following is an accurate statement concerning sexual harassment?
   a. An individual could avoid being sexually harassed if he or she really wanted.
   b. Modern work settings include more women and more protections, so harassment has become much less of a problem in recent years.
   c. Sexual harassment is determined by its consequences, not by the aggressor's intentions.
   d. A person has to physically touch another person for the act to be considered harassment.

Answers can be found at the end of the chapter.

— — — — —

Module Summary

Now that you have read this module you should:

KNOW ...

• The key terminology of employee affect and attitudes:

absenteeism (p. 489)	positive affect (PA) (p. 486)
burnout (p. 487)	sexual harassment (p. 491)
job satisfaction (p. 487)	turnover (p. 489)
negative affect (NA) (p. 486)	

[**TABLE 15•10**] IThe Student Burnout Inventory

To complete the Student Burnout Inventory, circle the number that best describes you on the following scale. Simply add up the circled numbers in each section to find your scores.

	Never		Sometimes			Always	
I feel emotionally drained by my studies.	0	1	2	3	4	5	6
I feel used up at the end of a day at university.	0	1	2	3	4	5	6
I feel tired when I get up in the morning and I have to face another day at the university.	0	1	2	3	4	5	6
Studying or attending a class is really a strain for me.	0	1	2	3	4	5	6
I feel burned out from my studies.	0	1	2	3	4	5	6
Total Exhaustion Score =							
I have become less interested in my studies since my enrollment at the university.	0	1	2	3	4	5	6
I have become less enthusiastic about my studies.	0	1	2	3	4	5	6
I have become more cynical about the potential usefulness of my studies.	0	1	2	3	4	5	6
I doubt the significance of my studies.	0	1	2	3	4	5	6
Total Cynicism Score =							
I can effectively solve the problems that arise in my studies.	6	5	4	3	2	1	0
I believe that I make an effective contribution to the classes that I attend.	6	5	4	3	2	1	0
In my opinion, I am a good student.	6	5	4	3	2	1	0
I feel stimulated when I achieve my study goals.	6	5	4	3	2	1	0
I have learned many interesting things during the course of my studies.	6	5	4	3	2	1	0
During class I feel confident that I am effective in getting things done.	6	5	4	3	2	1	0
Total Professional Efficacy Score =							

Source: Schaufeli et al., 2002.

UNDERSTAND …

- *Job satisfaction, burnout, and the attitudes and affect that go along with them.* Job satisfaction seems to come from a combination of energy, optimism, and a sense of accomplishment, whereas burnout seems to derive from the opposite effects—exhaustion, cynicism, and feeling a lack of accomplishment. To maintain job satisfaction, it helps to have a challenging job with support from management. People with positive affectivity (PA) also tend to feel more satisfied.

- *The risk factors for, and varieties of, workplace aggression.* Aggression can take the form of physical acts, but also includes verbal aggression and some types of obstructionism. Many risk factors may potentially contribute to workplace aggression, such as having a competitive, achievement oriented personality or a history of aggression. In addition, substance abuse (e.g., alcohol), an abusive supervisor, and a sense that the individual has been treated unfairly increase the risk of workplace aggression.

APPLY …

- *Your knowledge of satisfaction and burnout to ensure you maintain high motivation for college courses and your career.* Psychologists have applied the concept of burnout to college students, who are prone to experiencing exhaustion, cynicism, and decreased efficacy, just as employees are. Complete the college student version of the Maslach Burnout Inventory in **TABLE 15•10** (Schaufeli et al., 2002) to see how you compare to others. In one study of 191 University of Georgia students, average scores for the three facets of burnout were 17.95 for exhaustion, 11.1 for cynicism, and 26.0 for personal effectiveness (Pisarek, 2009). If you score higher than that, you are at risk for being burned out!

ANALYZE …

- *Various methods for preventing burnout and encouraging job satisfaction.* The best techniques are probably preventive measures: Hiring people with the right skills and personality for the job reduces the chance for burnout while increasing chances for satisfaction. Stress management skills and time off from work are both helpful for existing employees. Although pay raises may seem like a good idea for boosting job satisfaction, they probably do little to address the actual causes of burnout.

((•—[**Listen** to the audio file of this module at **MyPsychLab**

"I don't handle losing very well ... I get physically ill," says Summitt, and she adds that the experience of losing is actually a chance to learn about how to improve your own performance. Fortunately for her, Coach Summitt does not lose very often; in fact, she is the winningest basketball coach of male or female teams in the National Collegiate Athletic Association (NCAA). In more than 30 years of coaching at UT, she has won 1,000 games, losing less than 10% of the time. Her teams have made it to the NCAA women's playoffs every year since the inception of the women's championship tournament in 1982. Summitt's teams have won 14 conference championships and a record 8 national titles.

Given that she is one of the most dominant coaches in college sports history, you might expect that Summitt thinks only of basketball. In reality, she perceives herself as a leader among women in other respects. "I can teach young women that there are no barriers... . you go for it. Whatever you want in life, you go for it," she explains. "Basketball is a great place to learn that." This leadership also accounts for the stellar graduation rate among her players—every single one has completed her coursework and made it to graduation. With such a track record, it is no wonder that Summitt is often invited to speak to community and business leaders.

FOCUS QUESTIONS

1. What are the qualities that make a person stand out as a leader?

2. Which factors lead teams to work together effectively?

It is difficult to imagine a work environment that does not benefit from high-quality leadership. Consider some of the benefits good leadership provides to an organization:

- A common set of objectives and goals

- A means of identifying, recognizing, and rewarding quality work

- Ethics, and acceptable practices for working toward those goals

- Guidelines for acceptable behavior at work, including how to treat colleagues and clients

Even a self-employed professional who works alone benefits from a clear understanding of these four areas. So if leadership is key, how can companies acquire good leadership? Do they simply need to find someone with all the right qualities? Or could anyone be a leader with the right training?

Finding and Producing Effective Leaders

Leadership emergence *is the degree to which individuals are viewed as leaders by others* (Judge et al., 2002). Leaders generally share a set of personal qualities that distinguish them

15.3 Leadership and Teamwork

Learning Objectives

After reading this module you should:

Know ...

- The key terminology associated with leadership and teamwork

Understand ...

- Which skills and personal qualities predict good leadership

- Why certain input and process qualities lead to more effective teams

Apply ...

- Your knowledge to identify types of leaders with whom you work or study

Analyze ...

- Whether leaders should focus more on inspiring good work or should stick to rewarding it

Every group of people has leaders: families, schools, nonprofit organizations, corporations—you name it. Some have formal roles, such as parents, principals, and managers; in other situations, leaders emerge through day-to-day activities, inspiring people to work or play harder. But even leaders have leaders, and at least one popular news magazine has attempted to sort out who are the best—the leaders among leaders—in the United States. Leafing through one year's issue (U.S. News, 2008), we came across a particularly impressive leader, and one whom we have had the privilege to watch in person: Patricia Head Summitt, who coaches the women's basketball team at the University of Tennessee.

from the rest of the workforce. When the opportunity arises, the individual who possesses these characteristics will naturally *emerge* from the group and the situation as a leader. In terms of personality, this means that researchers should be able to administer personality tests to members of a number of organizations and pick out the leaders simply by looking at the patterns in the test results (Foti & Hauenstein, 2007). In reality, identifying leaders is not so clear-cut, although relatively stable personality and cognitive traits do significantly predict who becomes a leader. From the Big Five personality dimensions (Table 15.3 on p. 480), high emotional stability, extraversion, openness, and conscientious are associated with leader emergence (Judge et al., 2002).

In addition to predicting leader emergence, it is important to predict which leaders will be most effective. The Big Five model has a fairly good track record of predicting who will be an effective leader, along with *self-monitoring*—the tendency to reflect on and regulate one's own behavior in response to social cues (Day & Schleicher, 2006). Individuals who score high on self-monitoring measures are likely to think about what makes an effective leader, and then monitor their own behavior to ensure they are exhibiting those traits. In doing so, a shy individual who knows that extraverts do well as leaders may try to develop habits to overcome his appearance of shyness. In contrast, a low self-monitoring individual is unlikely to notice that his introverted personality is preventing his emergence or effectiveness as a leader.

Despite the success of leaders such as Coach Pat Summitt, a commonly held stereotype says that men make better leaders than women. In fact, surveys suggest that in the United States, employees prefer to work for male bosses and women still face more difficulties in attaining leadership positions (Eagly, 2007). However, this stereotype does not stand up to investigation. On average, women show more desirable leadership styles and traits than men (Eagly, 2007), and both men and women attain the same levels of effectiveness (Eagly et al., 1995). Perhaps the survey results indicate that people expect leaders to be assertive—a characteristic that tends to be associated with masculinity.

Assertiveness *is the degree to which an individual will work to achieve or protect one's interests.* Television and films are filled with stereotypes of bosses ranging from meek pushovers to power-wielding bullies, and neither make for very good management in fiction or in real life. As **FIGURE 15•8** shows, leaders with the "right touch" can be assertive when it is called for, but not all the time (Ames, 2008).

To pull together the various traits and capabilities that produce effective leadership, researchers Hogan and Warrenfeltz (2003) developed the comprehensive model of leadership skills that is summarized in **TABLE 15•11** on page 479. As you read through the list of these skills, think about how they may apply to the people you know in leadership positions. Do these qualities capture what good leaders do? And are poor leaders lacking in

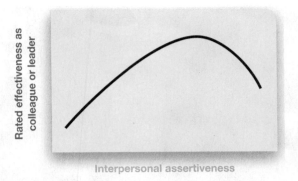

[FIGURE 15•8] **Assertiveness Predicts Leadership Effectiveness** The most effective leaders are neither the least assertive nor the most assertive—they have just the "right touch," as indicated by the peak in the middle of the graph (Ames, 2008).

one or more of these areas? Research confirms that this is the case, at least to a certain extent. Meta-analyses have found strong correlations between these four domains and performance (Ones et al., 1993; Vinchur et al., 1998).

Leadership Styles There are many ways to lead successfully, and psychologists have identified several different styles of leader (Bass, 1997). Typically, the most desirable style is **transformational leadership**, *which is a combination of charisma, intellectualization, and a focus on individuals within an organization.* Charisma blends together charm, attractiveness, and communication ability, which collectively produce an extremely influential personality. *Charismatic leaders* energize the organization by making a job seem to be extremely important and meaningful, thereby inspiring others through positive emotions (Shamir et al., 1993).

PsychTutor
Click here in your eText for an interactive tutorial on **Leadership**

Transformational leadership also involves *intellectual stimulation,* which encourages deliberate thought regarding work tasks and the job in general. Through intellectualization, the worker does not mindlessly perform tasks, but asks what the function of the task might be, and considers alternative and creative approaches to the task.

The transformational style is linked to a number of positive outcomes. For example, intellectualization and individual focus helps workers understand their tasks and roles more fully, which in turn leads to a greater sense of psychological well-being (Nielsen et al., 2008). In this environment, workers feel a heightened sense of commitment to their jobs and to others in the workplace. Ultimately, the transformational style leads to better productivity, thanks to the collective effects of motivated, thoughtful employees (Bass et al., 2003; Jung & Sosik, 2002). As such, it is often considered to be a preferred type of management.

[**TABLE 15•11**] **Skills and Abilities of Successful Leaders**

Domain	What it represents	Sample Capabilities
Intrapersonal	High standards of performance for oneself	Is able to control emotions Is willing to take a stand Has career ambition and perseverance Shows integrity, ethics Shows self-confidence
Interpersonal	Social skills and role-playing ability	Has talent for building relationships Is sensitive to office politics Exhibits listening and negotiating skills Shows good communication
Business	Abilities and technical knowledge needed to plan and coordinate efforts	Has intelligence and technical skill Shows experience and understanding how the organization functions Has decision-making ability Sets priorities and goals
Leadership	Influence and team-building skills	Supports and motivates workers Sets standards for others' behaviors Develops and communicates a vision for the organization Motivates others

Source: Adapted from Hogan & Warrenfeltz, 2003.

Whereas transformational leadership involves inspiration and vision, transactional leadership treats social exchanges like business transactions. Specifically, **transactional leadership** *encourages employee or team member behaviors through rewards and punishments.* An active approach to transactional leadership would involve a leader closely watching workers, rewarding those who follow instructions and meet expectations. Alternatively, transactional leaders can be passive, practicing *management by exception.* With this approach, leaders let workers go about their tasks and intervene only when an exception—some sort of problem—arises. Compared to transformation, transactions are much less inspiring; nevertheless, this style can be effective in certain situations, particularly those that require close attention to detail.

The final approach to leadership may not count as leadership at all. Translated from French, *laissez-faire* is roughly equivalent to the English phrase "leave it alone." Thus **laissez-faire leadership** *describes the style of someone who has been appointed to a position of leadership, but who does not engage in many (if any) leadership processes*—he or she simply leaves the workers alone.

In the end, both the transformational and transactional styles of leadership can be effective, and a great many managers use both. The important results to remember are the correlations with each leadership style: Transformational leadership has the strongest association with satisfied, motivated employees or team members, whereas a laissez-faire style does not (Lowe et al., 1996).

WORKING THE SCIENTIFIC LITERACY MODEL

Character and Leadership

Employees look to leaders to learn how to be productive and which tasks to take on. But leaders are also role models for what is acceptable and what is unacceptable. Since that is the case, should we look for leaders with character?

What do we know about character and leadership?

In the early 2000s, a number of highly publicized scandals erupted surrounding corporate executives, including events at major corporations such as Enron and Tyco. A few years later, the financial crisis in the United States began with the failure of many of the country's largest financial institutions. To many people, it appeared that we were experiencing a crisis in leadership (Riggio et al., 2010). This problem was not due to the inability to lead—in fact, many of the affected companies had very strong leaders—but rather to the moral and ethical qualities of the choices those leaders made. The response of many psychologists was to search for the virtues that we expect from our leaders. Another approach was to investigate character in leadership, with definitions of character centered on those individual qualities that guide a leader to make moral and ethical decisions (Thompson & Riggio, 2010).

How can scientists study character and leadership?

One approach to studying character in leadership is to consider the traits or virtues that separate a truly ethical leader from a person who simply leads. Ronald Riggio and his colleagues identified four primary virtues from philosophical and psychological works on leadership: prudence, fortitude, temperance, and justice. *Prudence* is a very practical type of wisdom that involves the ability to "make the appropriate decision that minimizes harm and maximizes good" (Riggio et al., 2010, p. 237). *Fortitude* is the courage to make difficult—even prudent—decisions. Virtuous leaders also display *temperance* in that they can exercise control over their emotional reactions and make reasonable decisions. Finally, the virtue of *justice* means that a leader should be able to follow rules, but also make decisions based on principles of fairness. The researchers administered a questionnaire to thousands of employees who rated various types of leaders on these virtues, and statistical analyses confirmed that these traits correspond with ethical leadership. Perhaps more importantly, these virtues correlate positively with desirable outcomes, such as a sense of empowerment among employees, and identification with the organization as a whole.

Can we critically evaluate this evidence?

We should be cautious in accepting the virtues of prudence, fortitude, temperance, and justice as the only ones that comprise character in leadership. The research techniques employed suggest that they are important, but other qualities may also play a role in ethical leadership. For example, some researchers have included personal integrity and forgiveness as important qualities (Grahek et al., 2010). In addition, researchers have asked about the nature and nurture of character. To what extent can these qualities be taught?

Why is this relevant?

One obvious application of this information is that leadership virtues can be applied to the study of leadership emergence, and it follows that psychological measures such as the Leadership Virtues Questionnaire might be used for screening potential leaders. Imagine you are in charge of hiring new managers for your organization: Would you like to know who possesses high levels of these four traits? Another application would be in the training of managers. Most definitions of character in leadership emphasize the idea that character comes

from experience; therefore it might be possible to train individuals who are strong in other aspects of leadership to also practice these virtues.

QUICK QUIZ 15.3A

Finding and Producing Effective Leaders

KNOW…

1. Assertiveness is best characterized by:

   a. how strict a person is.
   b. the degree to which a person protects his or her interests.
   c. how closely a leader monitors others.
   d. adherence to written policies.

UNDERSTAND…

2. Leaders with character exhibit which of the following traits?

   a. Frugality   c. Politeness
   b. Fortitude   d. Good looks

3. Which of the following best describes the laissez-faire approach to leadership?

   a. A team leader anticipates errors that people might potentially make and works to avoid them.
   b. A team leader controls worker behavior through rewards and punishments.
   c. A team leader strives to make rewards for good work equitable across all team members.
   d. A team leader spends little time offering direction or feedback on performance.

APPLY…

4. Lauren, your boss, encourages you to work hard by paying you extra when you succeed. What is her style of leadership?

   a. Transactional   c. Instinctive
   b. Transformational   d. Laissez-faire

ANALYZE…

5. Transactional leadership styles are most effective when:

   a. the leader is assertive.
   b. the leader manages by exception.
   c. the task requires close attention to detail.
   d. the employees are already highly motivated.

Answers can be found at the end of the chapter.

The intelligence, conflict resolution skills, and communication abilities of these workers will contribute to the success of their work team.

Working in Teams

Modern organizations almost always make use of teams—groups of individuals with shared goals and responsibilities. Most likely you are currently a member of several teams–perhaps a sports team, a group project for class, a drama or dance company, or, naturally, a team of co-workers. The past two decades have seen the rapid growth of **virtual teams**, *production or project teams that are physically separated but operate largely (or completely) by electronic communications*. New software tools facilitate collaboration and conferences over the Internet, so companies are able to save the time and expense of traveling while gaining greater access to experts around the world.

To understand how teams function, psychologists often divide teamwork into three parts: *input*, *process*, and *output*. These areas seem to apply to all teams, so what distinguishes a sports team from a software development project team is simply the specific types of inputs, processes, and outputs.

Inputs Team inputs include qualities such as the nature of the organization, management, the type of work the team is assigned, and the individuals who make up the team—basically, anything that is present before the process gets under way. For example, when members know that the team will be provided with motivation and rewards as a group, the outputs are usually more successful, and it is the responsibility of the organization's management to determine how rewards are allocated (Pritchard, 1995). Naturally, teams need members who have strong skills related to the assigned tasks, but did you know that teamwork itself is a skill? Research shows that intelligence, conflict resolution ability, and communication skills are all correlated with successful teams (Stevens & Campion, 1999). Not surprisingly, extraversion, agreeableness, and conscientiousness have also been associated with positive team outcomes (Barrick et al., 1998; Morgeson et al., Reider, & Campion, 2005).

Process: What the Team Does Team processes are essential to successful group performance (LePine et al., 2008). Obviously, communication will play an important role anytime multiple people are involved. Equally important, but perhaps less obvious, is the issue of *coordination*, meaning that individuals' tasks fit together in a timely and orderly fashion. Certainly Coach Summitt's basketball players need to be in the right place at the right time, or there will be errant passes, missed shots, and poor defense. The same concepts apply to work teams. Imagine a poorly coordinated assembly line where one group takes longer to complete its task than the next group down the line. Such a breakdown in coordination will leave one group idle and unproductive throughout portions of the shift.

Social loafing is particularly detrimental to group success: It occurs when some group members produce less effort on a team than they do alone. When social loafing occurs, the team does not realize the full benefit from its working members (Latané et al., 1979).

From a more cognitive perspective, group decision making can also be either an asset or a liability. In cases of *groupthink*, individuals within the team develop very strong convictions about an idea. As groupthink builds, all members begin to agree, and proposed actions tend to become riskier and maybe even too far-fetched to be feasible. Because the group seems to be approaching a unanimous decision, individuals become more and more certain about the correctness of their decision, and they maintain this belief until it is finalized. In some cases, this kind of agreement is helpful, but there are consequences when groupthink runs out of control: The decision can be wrong. One of the best-known examples led to the explosion of the space shuttle Challenger (Morehead et al., 1991). In this case, a small group of engineers had warned other workers about fuel tank seals freezing in cold weather. However, the team in charge of the launch convinced themselves that launching was a good idea, despite the risks linked to the seals. The Challenger launched, only to explode before it had been airborne for 2 minutes. Had team members employed correct team decision making, perhaps the disaster could have been avoided. Such an effort might have involved appointing a specific team member to question individual decisions, looking for outsiders to weigh in on the debate, or even breaking into smaller groups for discussions so that the social pressure would not be so great (Priem et al., 1995).

Output Perhaps the main reason to develop work teams is to increase efficiency. Certainly production teams are more efficient, as are well-coordinated project teams. When the goal is to innovate, teams—especially teams with diverse members—tend to outperform individuals (Axtell et al., 2006). Conversely, individuals are not subject to groupthink, so in many cases well-qualified people can make better decisions alone than with a group (Gigone & Hastie, 1997).

Outputs comprise more than just the products and services that result from teams; they also include benefits to the individual and the organization as a whole. Individuals may find increased job satisfaction thanks to positive experiences interacting with colleagues, a feeling of shared purpose, and the sense that they have achieved something bigger than they could have done by themselves (Cordery, 1996; West et al., 1998).

QUICK QUIZ 15.3B
Working in Teams

KNOW...

1. The design and layout of a work facility, along with the way in which bosses and employees are organized, is considered a(n) _____.

   a. input   c. process
   b. output   d. leadership style

UNDERSTAND...

2. _____ has occurred if an employee reduces the amount of work he completes because three fellow team members are assigned to collectively carry out a single task.

   a. Social loafing
   b. Charisma
   c. Self-monitoring
   d. Transactional leadership

3. The risk of groupthink can be reduced by all of the following except:

   a. appointing an individual to question decisions.
   b. breaking into smaller groups to reduce social pressure.
   c. asking for input from outsiders.
   d. encouraging group members to be very polite.

Answers can be found at the end of the chapter.

— — — — —

Module Summary

Now that you have read this module you should:

KNOW ...

- **The key terminology associated with leadership and teamwork:**

assertiveness (p. 496)
laissez-faire leadership (p. 497)
leadership emergence (p. 495)
transactional leadership (p. 497)

transformational leadership (p. 496)
virtual teams (p. 499)

UNDERSTAND ...

- ***Which skills and personal qualities predict good leadership.*** From a personality perspective, leaders tend to be emotionally stable, extraverted, open, and conscientious. Good leaders are able to monitor their own behavior. Transformational leaders—those who are charismatic and intellectual, and who focus on the individuals within an organization—are usually preferable.

- ***Why certain input and process qualities lead to more effective teams.*** Teams are usually most successful when the members share motivation and rewards. When individual members are intelligent, good communicators, and good problem solvers, the team will perform well.

APPLY ...

- ***Your knowledge to identify types of leaders with whom you work or study.*** Complete TABLE 15•12 (or create your own table on a separate piece of paper) for at least three leaders. Start by writing the definitions and qualities of each type of leader in the left column. Then, in the Instructor column, identify specific behaviors that demonstrate which type of leader your psychology instructor is. If you are employed, do the same for your supervisor. Finally, pick one additional leader, perhaps from your campus administration or from a campus group you belong to and do the same.

ANALYZE ...

- ***Whether leaders should focus more on inspiring good work or should stick to rewarding it.*** Research shows that leadership styles have their place. Transformational leadership—the more inspirational form—is probably better at fostering creativity, whereas transactional leadership may be better in situations that call for attention to detail.

((•—[**Listen** to the audio file of this module at **MyPsychLab**

[TABLE 15•12] Leadership Styles Activity

Define:	Psychology instructor	Supervisor	Other: _____
Transactional leader			
Transformational leader			
Laissez-faire leader			

CHAPTER IN FOCUS

15.1 :: Personnel Psychology: Hiring and Maintaining an Effective Workforce

FOCUS QUESTIONS:

1. **Which techniques ensure that employers hire the most suitable workers?** Television shows such as *The Apprentice* take the unstructured interview and simulation approaches to interviewing to unusual extremes. In the real world, structured interviews, personality tests, and cognitive tests are the norm. In some cases, the very in-depth method of the assessment center may even be used. Regardless of the method applied, I/O psychologists want to see evidence that this method is effective. Sound selection methods have gone through multiple validation studies to prove their effectiveness.

2. **How can employers determine whether workers are doing their jobs well?** A number of methods for evaluating an employee's performance have been developed. Perhaps the most thorough is the 360-degree feedback method. This approach gathers information on a worker's performance from all angles: supervisors, peers, subordinates, and even individuals outside the organization, such as clients or customers. In addition, employers should be concerned about measuring multiple aspects of a worker's performance, including task performance, organizational citizenship, and counterproductive behaviors.

15.2 :: Affect, Attitudes, and Behavior at Work

FOCUS QUESTIONS:

1. **Which factors might lead someone to be highly engaged and satisfied with his or her work?** People tend to be most satisfied with their work when they feel competent, in control, and challenged, regardless of the line of work. Satisfaction is most likely when an individual's expectations for a job are met by his or her actual experiences. However, not all people can be expected to feel the same; people high in positive affect are more likely to be satisfied than others.

2. **What can cause a highly motivated individual to become burned out?** Burnout includes a sense of emotional and physical exhaustion, cynicism, and a sense that the work has little meaning. Burnout can arise from multiple sources, including meaningless tasks, insufficient resources, and unpleasant interactions with co-workers and management.

15.3 :: Leadership, Teamwork, and the Organization

FOCUS QUESTIONS:

1. **What are the qualities that make a person stand out as a leader?** For Coach Summitt (described at the beginning of the module), it is her charisma and her ability to inspire and motivate that are especially notable. These are properties of a transformational leader, along with the personality traits of extraversion, openness, and conscientiousness. Other situations may call for different types of leadership, but clearly this style works for the competitive world of college sports. Interestingly, many people hold a stereotype that men make better leaders, although research shows that women are every bit as effective.

2. **Which factors lead teams to work together effectively?** Psychologists focus on inputs, processes, and outputs to determine what makes a team work effectively. Inputs associated with success include clear rewards for the group, skilled team members, and group members whose personality traits (e.g., extraversion and agreeableness) help them interact with others. Processes work best when they are well coordinated, such that individual tasks fit together in a timely and orderly fashion. These factors all contribute to the most desirable outputs: successfully completed projects and satisfied team members.

CHAPTER QUIZ

1. Which of the following is *not* one of the main goals of I/O psychology as defined by the Society of Industrial-Organizational Psychology (SIOP)?

   A To help employers deal with employees fairly

   B To help workers be more productive.

   C To help make jobs more interesting and satisfying

   D To help employers avoid lawsuits

2. As the United States evolved from a manufacturing economy to one based more on office work, I/O psychologists began to focus more on _____.

   A hiring

   B training

   C the culture and organizational qualities of work

   D managing employees

3. Which of the following statements is true regarding the use of personality-based selection tests for hiring?

   A Some personality traits can be useful predictors of performance at various jobs.

   B Personality traits can be useful predictors of which candidates will do poorly at a job, but do not predict which candidates are likely to succeed.

   C Conscientiousness is the only personality trait that correlates with performance across a wide range of jobs.

   D Personality-based selection tests are not a useful tool for predicting job performance.

4. An employee who always goes above and beyond what his or her employer asks is demonstrating good _____.

   A task performance

   B organizational citizenship behavior

   C situational judgment

   D counterproductive behavior

5. Joaquin's supervisor is always impressed at his ability to come up with creative solutions to problems at work. Because of this talent, the supervisor has a very good opinion of Joaquin as an overall employee, despite the fact that he is frequently late to work and sometimes has poor productivity. The supervisor's overall good opinion of Joaquin is likely the result of _____.

   A the contrast effect

   B the halo effect

   C the 360-degree bias

   D the mixed-performance bias

6. "Locus of control" refers to:

   A whether an individual feels more in control at home or at work.

   B a set of beliefs about the person's ability to control his or her work environment and success.

   C a person's beliefs about his or her value and worth as a human being.

   D the skills that a person can use to affect his or her work environment.

7. The "Conditional Reasoning Test" could theoretically be used by employers to detect _____ in employees.

   A mental illness

   B success potential

   C aggressive tendencies

   D high intelligence levels

8. Which of the following statements is true regarding male versus female leadership?

   A On average, women show more desirable leadership styles and traits than men.

   B On average, men show more desirable leadership styles and traits than women.

   C In the United States, employees prefer to work for female bosses.

   D Men are more effective leaders than women.

9. In general, the _____ style of leadership is considered the most desirable.

   A transactional

   B laissez-faire

   C passive

   D transformational

10. Which of the following would be an example of a virtual team?

   A A group of workers around the globe who coordinate their efforts through teleconferencing and email

   B A computer simulation of how employees might interact

   C A group of employees who have similar jobs, but who do not actually interact with one another

   D A group of employees in which one member does the majority of the work that is claimed by the team

ANSWERS

Quick Quiz 15.1a
1. A   2. C   3. D

Quick Quiz 15.1b
1. B   2. B   3. A   4. A

Quick Quiz 15.1c
1. A   2. C   3. D

Quick Quiz 15.2a
1. C   2. B   3. A   4. D   5. C   6. C

Quick Quiz 15.2b
1. B   2. C   3. C

Quick Quiz 15.3a
1. B   2. B   3. D   4. A   5. C

Quick Quiz 15.3b
1. A   2. A   3. D

Chapter Quiz
1. D   2. C   3. A   4. B   5. B
6. B   7. C   8. A   9. D   10. A

Work the Scientific Literacy Model ::
Understanding Employee Affect, Attitudes, and Behavior

What do we know about employee affect, attitudes, and behavior?

For most people, work occupies a significant portion their daily time and energy. Whether an individual enjoys his or her job depends on an interaction between personality characteristics and the job itself. Recall the discussion of positive affect and negative affect on page 486. Positive affect (PA) is the tendency to experience emotions such as optimism and enthusiasm, whereas negative affect (NA) is the tendency to experience emotions such as frustration and anger. If you tend to exhibit NA traits, then you will likely feel glum and unsatisfied even after a recent success, such as getting a B+ on an exam. Job satisfaction is directly related to negative or positive affect. Figure 15.4 on page 487 highlights several sources of job satisfaction, and its negative counterpart—job burnout—is profiled in Table 15.8 on page 488. Affect can even influence behavior at work, as employees are more likely to engage in counterproductive behavior, such as aggression and absenteeism, if they are unhappy with their job.

How can science help explain the importance of employee affect and attitudes?

Research shows that people with PA traits tend to outdo their NA co-workers when it comes to creativity, teamwork, and decision making. In fact, interesting research has revealed that people with negative and positive affect tendencies are simply wired differently. Reward centers in the brain are more active in PA individuals, whereas the brains of NA individuals have increased activity in fear and alert response circuitry. Studies show that feeling satisfied in your job is related to internal factors such as self-esteem, the belief in your ability to accomplish tasks (self-efficacy), and your belief about whether you control your own work environment and successes (locus of control). At the opposite end of the spectrum is burnout—a sense of mental and physical exhaustion, a cynical attitude, and the belief that one's work has little meaning. In addition, researchers have investigated the idea that intellectually challenging people with high cognitive ability contributes to a sense of job satisfaction. Even highly skilled people may burn out on their jobs, however. You can see the results of a study on burnout in Figure 15.5 on page 490, which suggested that vacation time can alleviate the negative feelings associated with burnout, at least temporarily.

Why is this relevant?

Watch the accompanying video excerpt on motivation. You can access the video at MyPsychLab or by clicking the play button in the center of your eText. If your instructor assigns this video as a homework activity, you will find additional content to help you in MyPsychLab. You can also view the video by using your smart phone and the QR code below, or you can go to the YouTube link provided.

Once you have read this chapter and watched the video, consider the following. Several aspects of the work environment have been found to increase job involvement, work motivation, and job satisfaction. Identify and describe these conditions. How is money related to work motivation?

Can we critically evaluate claims about reinforcement and punishment?

Should employees limit their hiring to people with sunny dispositions or positive affective traits? Keep in mind that some emotional traits are culturally influenced. The Biopsychosocial Perspectives feature on page 487 notes that negative traits such as pessimism seem to be related to culture, and that some measure of pessimistic thinking can actually lead to better performance on certain tasks than optimistic thinking. Burnout can happen to both positive and negative thinkers, and it can negatively influence individual performance, organizational morale, and even aggressive behavior.

Can employers buy their workers' loyalty? Does a big paycheck equal job satisfaction? While a raise might temporarily motivate a dissatisfied employee, it has the same effect as a vacation on a burned-out worker—a temporary one. The real solution seems to be taking a proactive approach. Organizations need to hire the right people for positions within the company, use training and mentoring to motivate them, and offer strategies and programs (such as gym memberships and other health benefits) to help their workers manage stress.

youtube.com/
scientificliteracy

MyPsychLab
Your turn to Work the Scientific Literacy Model: You can access the video at MyPsychLab or by clicking the play button in the center of your eText. If your instructor assigns this video as a homework activity, you will find additional content to help you at MyPsychLab. You can also view the video by using your smart phone and the QR code, or you can go to the YouTube link provided.

The Psychology of AC4P

E. Scott Geller

Prologue

The Large-Scale, Long-Term Health, safety, and welfare of people require us to routinely go beyond the call of duty on behalf of others. We call this Actively Caring for People or AC4P—the theme of this chapter. Usually AC4P involves *self-motivation*. Often AC4P behavior requires a certain amount of *courage*.

Research in social psychology,[1] applied behavior analysis,[2] and person-based psychology[3] provides principles and practical strategies for increasing the occurrence and improving the quality of AC4P behaviors throughout a culture. ▪

What is AC4P?

FIGURE 16•1 presents a simple flow chart summarizing a basic approach to culture change. We start a culture-change mission with a vision or ultimate purpose—for example, to achieve an AC4P culture of compassion. With group consensus supporting the vision, we develop procedures or action plans to accomplish our mission. These are reflected in process-oriented goals which denote goal-related behaviors.

The popular writings of Covey,[4] Peale,[5] Kohn,[6] and Deming[7] suggest behavior is activated and maintained by self-affirmations, internal motivation and personal principles or values. But, these authors as well as many motivational consultants miss a key component of human dynamics—the power of consequences.

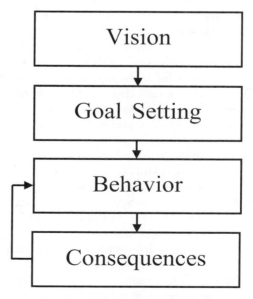

[**FIGURE 16•1**] An AC4P culture requires vision and behavior management.

Consequences are Critical

Appropriate goal setting, self-affirmations, and a positive attitude can indeed activate behaviors to achieve goals and visions. But we must not forget one of B.F. Skinner's most important legacies—*selection by consequences.*[8] As depicted in Figure 1, consequences follow behavior and are needed to support the right behaviors and correct wrong ones.

Without support for the "right stuff," good intentions and initial efforts fade away. How long does a weight-loss plan as a New Year's resolution (vision) last if one cannot see initial weight loss (consequence) after the first few weeks of exercise (behavior) in an effort to lose 15 pounds (an outcome goal)?

In *How to Win Friends and Influence People,* Dale Carnegie affirms, "Every act you have ever performed since the day you were born was performed because you wanted something".[9] Sometimes natural consequences are available to motivate desired behaviors, but often extrinsic consequences (or external accountabilities) need to be managed to motivate the behavior needed to achieve our goals.

For example, I presume my students often have visions of earning an "A" in my university classes, and they set relevant process goals to study regularly in order to achieve that ultimate "A" grade (an outcome goal). I hold them accountable to study the material by giving exams periodically throughout the semester.

When the days for exams are announced in the course syllabus, students typically adjust their study behavior according to this accountability scheme. They increase their frequency of studying successively as the day of the exam approaches, performing most of their studying behaviors the night before an exam.

But when my assessment protocol is changed from announced to unannounced exams, most students change their study behavior dramatically. Under this accountability system, students feel compelled to prepare for every class, anticipating a possible exam on any class day. Although students uniformly dislike this second approach, they are substantially more prepared for class when the occurrence of an exam cannot be predicted.

Some students study the course material consistently to reach their learning goals, regardless of the external accountability agenda set by their teacher. These individuals are self-motivated and implement their own self-management procedures to keep them on track. As well as ways to achieve this quality of personal responsibility.

Students' post-exam, course-related behaviors are usually affected by their test scores—the consequences of their test-taking behavior. But for a number of reasons, it's difficult to predict how a particular exam grade will influence an individual's goal-setting or study behavior.

A high grade does not always motivate a higher rate of course-related studying, as expected from the principle of positive reinforcement; and a low grade does not lead to less studying as could be predicted from punishment theory.

A sense of competence or confidence from a high grade could influence less study behavior; and fear of failure after receiving a low grade might surely affect more study behavior, including some self-management goal-setting and feedback strategies.

As you can see, the driving motivators are consequences. This is a key lesson to learn and use. The "pop psychology" notion that people can overcome their challenges and achieve whatever they want through positive thinking, self-affirmations, and relevant goal-setting before their behavior is just not true.

Without appropriate consequences to support the right behavior and correct the wrong behavior, goal-directed behavior will simply stop. People cannot reach their behavior-specific process goals unless they receive relevant feedback to keep them on track. I'm talking about behavior-based feedback to support desirable behavior and correct undesirable behavior.

Actively Caring is Critical

In FIGURE 16•2, a new box is added to the basic flow diagram in Figure 16.1. The point is simple but extremely important: Vision, goals and consequences are not sufficient for culture change. People need to *actively care* about the goals, action plans, and consequences. They need to believe in and own the vision.

They need to feel empowered and encouraged from peers to attain process goals that support the vision. And peers need to give them supportive and corrective feedback to increase the quantity and quality of behaviors consistent with vision-relevant goals.

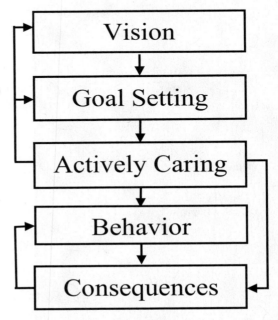

[**FIGURE 16•2**] Continuous improvement requires actively caring.

Corrective feedback is critical for individuals to improve their future behavior. Supportive feedback is a powerful consequence for the maintenance of behavior, because it tells individuals what they are doing right.

In most relationships, supportive feedback is rare, so special attention is needed to increase this important feedback process. Corrective feedback and supportive feedback are essential for continuous improvement and for achieving an AC4P culture of people contributing to the well-being of each other.

Three Ways to Actively Care

When individuals perform AC4P behaviors, they can improve environment factors, enhance person factors, or increase the frequency of others' AC4P behaviors. When people alter environmental conditions, or reorganize resources in an attempt to benefit others, they are AC4P from an environmental perspective. Examples of AC4P behaviors in this category include: attending to a housekeeping detail, posting a warning sign near an environmental hazard, shoveling snow from a neighbor's sidewalk, washing another person's vehicle, organizing a colleague's desk, helping a party host collect recyclables, and cleaning up a spill or removing a trip hazard.

Person-based AC4P occurs when people attempt to make others feel better. Often, it doesn't take much to improve an individual's emotions, attitudes, or mood states. Examples of person-based AC4P include: listening proactively to others, expressing concern for another person's difficulties, complimenting an individual's academic or work performance, sending a get-well card, and posting birthday wishes on a person's Facebook. These types of AC4P behavior will likely boost people's self-esteem, self-efficacy, personal control, optimism, or sense of belonging—increasing their propensity to actively care.

Also included here are *reactive* AC4P behaviors performed in crisis situations. For example, if you save someone from drowning, administer cardiopulmonary resuscitation (CPR), or give a drunk driver a ride home you're actively caring from a person-based perspective.

From a proactive perspective, behavior-focused AC4P is most beneficial, but is also the most challenging. This happens when people apply an instructive, supportive, or motivational intervention to improve another person's desirable behavior.

When we teach others how to promote AC4P behavior or provide supportive comments or possible improvements regarding observed behavior, we are actively caring from a behavioral focus. Teachers and athletic coaches do this when they help another person achieve a desired performance goal. Plus, recognizing the desirable AC4P behavior of others in a one-to-one conversation is also actively caring with a behavior focus.

Why Categorize AC4P Behaviors

Why go to the trouble of categorizing AC4P behaviors? Good question! Consider what these behaviors are trying to accomplish, and realize the relative difficulty in performing each of them. Environment-focused AC4P behavior might be the easiest approach for some people because it usually does not involve interpersonal interaction.

When people contribute financially to a charity, donate blood, or complete an organ donor card, they do not interact personally with the recipient of the contribution. These AC4P behaviors are certainly commendable and may represent significant commitment and effort, but the absence of personal encounters between giver and receiver is separate from other types of AC4P behavior.

Certain situations and dispositions might facilitate or inhibit one type of AC4P behavior and not the other. For example, communication skills are needed for actively caring on the personal or behavioral level. And different aspects of those communication skills usually come into play. Behavior-focused AC4P is more direct and usually more intrusive than person-focused actively caring.

It's more risky and potentially confrontational to intervene—to attempt to direct or motivate another person's behavior, in contrast to demonstrating concern, respect, or empathy for someone. Just consider the connotations of *intervention*. It's usually thought of as a form of confrontation, a negative interaction due to the frequent resistance of the person whose behavior is in question.

Helping someone in a crisis situation certainly takes effort and requires special skills, but there is rarely a possibility of rejection. On the other hand, attempting to step in to correct someone's behavior could lead to negative, even hostile, reaction. Effective behavior-based AC4P, as in interpersonal coaching, usually requires both interpersonal skills to gain the individual's trust, along with behavior-based skills to support desired behavior and/or correct undesired behavior.

Behavior-focused AC4P is actually expected from parents, teachers, supervisors, and coaches who are in charge of improving the behavior of certain individuals. Thus, some behavior-focused AC4P is part of one's job and is expected. But here the question is whether you apply the best AC4P methods (e.g., supportive and corrective feedback that improve both behavior and attitude).

Suppose you observe a stranger not using a vehicle safety belt or driving while talking on a cell phone. Would you say something to keep this person safe? Some people even hesitate to offer such proactive AC4P feedback for a friend, co-worker, or colleague.

Is it beyond the call of duty to look out for the well-being of a family member or friend? Most readers would say "No". But when AC4P becomes a social norm or the expected behavior in a culture, actively caring for a stranger will not stretch beyond one's normal routine.

As legislated in Australia, it's your "duty to care". AC4P behavior occurs whenever you look out for the well-being of another, but the degree of self-motivation and courage needed to actively care varies dramatically due to situational and dispositional factors.

A Hierarchy of Needs

Probably the most popular theory of human motivation is the hierarchy of needs proposed by humanist Abraham Maslow.[10] Categories of needs are arranged hierarchically, and it is presumed people don't attempt to satisfy needs at one stage or level until the needs at the lower stages are satisfied.

First, we are motivated to fulfill physiological needs. This includes basic survival requirements for food, water, shelter, and sleep. After these needs are under control, we are motivated by the desire to feel secure and safe from future dangers. When we prepare for future physiological needs, we are proactively working to satisfy our need for safety and security.

Next we have our social-acceptance needs—the need to have friends and to feel like we belong. When these needs are gratified, our concern focuses on self-esteem, the desire to develop self-respect, gain the approval of others, and achieve personal success.

When I ask audiences to tell me the highest level of Maslow's Hierarchy of Needs, several people usually shout "self-actualization". When I ask for the meaning of "self-actualization," however, I receive limited or no reaction. You see, the concept of being self-actualized is rather vague and ambiguous.

In general terms, we reach a level of self-actualization when we believe we have become the best we can be, taking the fullest advantage of our potential as human beings. We labor to reach this level when striving to be as productive and creative as possible. Once accomplished, we feel a sense of brotherhood and affection for all human beings. We desire to help humanity as members of a single family—the human race.[11] Perhaps it's fair to say these individuals are most ready to perform AC4P behavior.

Maslow's Hierarchy of Needs is illustrated in **FIGURE 16•3**. Note self-actualization is not at the top. Maslow[12] revised his renowned hierarchy shortly before his death in 1970, placing self-transcendence above self-actualization. Transcending the self means going beyond self-interest and is quite analogous to the AC4P concept.

According to Viktor Frankl,[13] self-transcendence includes giving ourselves to a cause or to another person and is the ultimate state of existence for the healthy individual. After satisfying our physiological needs, safety and security, acceptance, self-esteem, and self-actualization, people can be motivated to reach self-transcendence by reaching out to help others—to perform AC4P behavior.

It seems intuitive that various self-needs require satisfaction before self-transcendent or AC4P behavior is likely to occur. But scant research supports ranking needs in a hierarchy. It's possible to think of many examples where individuals

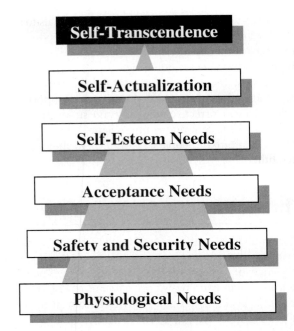

[**FIGURE 16•3**] The highest need in Maslow's revised hierarchy reflects AC4P.

perform many AC4P behaviors before satisfying all their own needs. Mahatma Gandhi is a prime example of a leader who put the concerns of others before his own. He suffered imprisonment, extensive fasts, and eventually assassination in his 50-year struggle to help his poor and downtrodden compatriots.

I'm sure you can think of individuals in your life, including yourself perhaps, who reached the top level of self-transcendence before satisfying needs in the lower stages. Later in this chapter I'll show that satisfying lower-level needs might not be *necessary* for AC4P behavior, but people are generally more willing to actively care after satisfying the lower need levels in Maslow's hierarchy.

Psychological Science and AC4P

Walking home on March 13, 1964, Catherine (Kitty) Genovese reached her apartment in Queens, New York, at 3:30 A.M. Suddenly, a man approached her with a knife, stabbing her repeatedly, and then raped her. Kitty screamed, "Oh my God, he stabbed me! Please help me!" into the early morning stillness. Lights went on and windows opened in nearby buildings. Seeing the lights, the attacker fled. When he saw no one come to the victim's aid, he returned to stab her eight more times and rape her again.

The murder and rape of Kitty Genovese lasted more than 30 minutes, and was witnessed by 38 neighbors. One couple pulled up chairs to their window and turned off the lights so they could get a better view. Only after the murderer and rapist departed for good did anyone phone the police. When the neighbors were questioned about their lack of intervention, they couldn't explain it.

The reporter who first publicized the Kitty Genovese story, and later made it the subject of a book,[14] assumed *bystander apathy* was caused by big-city life. People's indifference to their neighbors' troubles was a conditioned reflex in crowded cities like New York, he reasoned.

After this horrific incident, hundreds of experiments were conducted by social psychologists to determine causes of this so-called *bystander apathy*.[15] This research discredited the reporter's common-sense conclusion. Several factors other than big-city alienation contribute to bystander apathy.

Lessons from Research

Professors Bibb Latané, John Darley, and their colleagues studied bystander apathy by staging emergency events observed by varying numbers of individuals. Then they systematically recorded the speed at which one or more persons came to the victim's rescue. In the most controlled experiments, the observers sat in separate cubicles and could not be influenced by the body language of other subjects. In the first study of this type, the participants introduced themselves and discussed problems associated with living in an urban environment.

In each condition, the first individual introduced himself and then casually mentioned he had epilepsy and the pressures of city life made him prone to seizures. During the course of the discussion over the intercom, he became increasingly loud and incoherent, choking, gasping, and crying out before lapsing into silence. The experimenters measured how quickly the participants left their cubes to help him.

When participants believed they were the only witness, 85 percent left their cubicles within three minutes to intervene. But only 62 percent of the participants who believed one other witness was present left their cubicle to intervene,

Courtesy of George Vaughn Willis.

and only 31 percent of those who thought five other witnesses were available attempted to intervene. Within three to six minutes after the seizure began, 100 percent of the lone participants, 81 percent of the participants with one presumed witness, and 62 percent of the participants with five other bystanders left their cubes to intervene.

The hesitancy of observers of an emergency to intervene and help a victim when they believe other potential helpers are available has been termed the *bystander effect*. It has been replicated in several situations.[16] Some researchers suggest ways to prevent bystander apathy—a critical barrier to achieving an AC4P culture.

Keep in mind this research only studied reactions in crisis situations; behaviors we categorize as reactive, person-focused AC4P behavior. It seems intuitive, though, the findings are relevant for both environment-focused and behavior-focused AC4P behaviors in proactive situations.

Diffusion of Responsibility A key contributor to the bystander effect is the assumption that someone else should or could assume the responsibility. For example, many observers of the Kitty Genovese rape and murder assumed another witness would call the police, or attempt to scare away the assailant. Perhaps some observers waited for a witness more capable than they to rescue Kitty.

Does this factor contribute to lack of intervention when someone needs help? Do people ignore or deny opportunities to actively care for another person (i.e., a stranger) because they presume someone else will help? Perhaps some people assume, "If those who know the person seeking assistance don't care enough to help, why should I?"

Social psychology research suggests teaching people about the bystander effect can make them less likely to fall prey to it themselves.[17] Often, people have a "we-they" attitude or a territorial perspective ("I'm responsible for the people in this area; you're responsible for those in that area"). Eliminating this "we-they" perspective increases people's willingness to actively care for others.[18]

An AC4P Norm Many, if not most, U.S. citizens are raised to be independent rather than interdependent. However, intervening for the benefit of others, whether reactively in a crisis situation or proactively to prevent potential crises, requires a sincere commitment toward interdependence.

Social psychologists refer to a *social responsibility norm* as the belief people should help those who need help. Subjects who scored high on a measure of this norm, as a result of upbringing during childhood or special training sessions, were more likely to intervene in a bystander intervention situation, regardless of the number of other witnesses.[19]

Knowing What to Do When people know what to do in a crisis, they do not fear appearing foolish and do not wait for another, more skilled person to intervene. The bystander effect was eliminated when observers had certain competencies, such as training in first-aid treatment, which enabled them to take charge of the situation.[20] When observers believe they possess the appropriate tools to help, bystander apathy is decreased or eliminated.

Recognizing others for performing AC4P behaviors is critical for the development of an AC4P norm and an AC4P culture. But our field studies have shown this is easier said than done. Participants in these studies agreed with the mission to recognize others for their AC4P behaviors. Still, the percentage who delivered such recognition in prescribed ways was always much lower than expected and desired. These percentages increased dramatically following role playing to develop relevant interpersonal skills, accompanied by meetings of AC4P support groups.[21]

Most proactive AC4P action requires self-motivation and moral courage in addition to relevant interpersonal skills. Much of our AC4P research, some of which is reviewed in Chapter 19, addresses ways to facilitate the occurrence and improve the effectiveness of AC4P behaviors and remove barriers that hold us back from thanking people for their AC4P behavior.

It's Important to Belong Bystander apathy is reduced, according to research, when observers know one another and have developed a sense of belonging or mutual respect from prior interactions.[22] Most, if not all, of the witnesses to Kitty Genovese's murder did not know her personally. It's likely the neighbors did not feel a sense of community with one another. Situations and interactions that reduce a "we-they" or territorial perspective and increase feelings of relatedness or community will increase the likelihood people will actively care for each other.

Mood States Several social psychology studies have found people are more likely to offer help when they are in a good mood.[23] And the mood states that facilitated helping behavior were created very easily, for example, by arranging for potential helpers to find a dime in a phone booth, giving them a cookie, showing them a comedy film, or providing pleasant aromas. Are these findings relevant for cultivating an AC4P culture?

Daily events can elevate or depress our moods. Some events are controllable, while others are not. Clearly, the nature of our interactions with others can have a dramatic impact on the mood of everyone involved. The research on mood and its effects on helping behavior might motivate those of us who want to facilitate an AC4P culture to interject more positivity and optimism into our interpersonal conversations with others.

Beliefs and Expectancies Social psychologists have shown that certain dispositional characteristics or beliefs influence one's inclination to help a person in an emergency. Specifically, individuals who believe their world is fair and predictable, a place where good behavior is rewarded and bad behavior is punished, are more likely to help others in a crisis.[19] Also, people with a higher sense of social responsibility and the general expectancy that people control their own destinies showed a greater willingness to actively care.[24]

The beliefs and expectancies that influence AC4P behaviors are not developed overnight and obviously cannot be changed overnight. But a particular culture, including its policies, appraisal and recognition procedures, educational opportunities and approaches to discipline, can certainly increase or decrease perceptions or beliefs in a just world, social responsibility, and personal control, and in turn influence people's willingness to perform AC4P behavior.[25]

Deciding to Actively Care

As a result of their seminal research, Latané and Darley[26] proposed that an observer makes four sequential decisions before helping a victim. These four decisions (depicted in **FIGURE 16•4**) are influenced by the situation or environmental context in which an AC4P opportunity occurs, the nature of the crisis, the presence of other bystanders and their reactions, and relevant social norms and rules.

Although the model was developed to evaluate intervention in emergency situations—where there is need for direct, reactive, person-focused AC4P behavior—it's quite relevant for the other types of AC4P, as well.

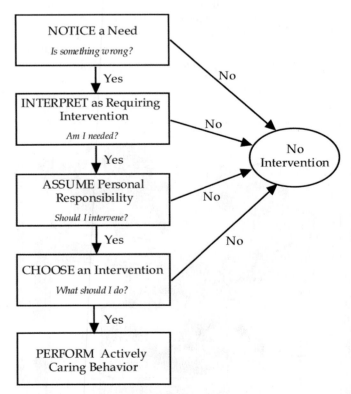

[**FIGURE 16•4**] AC4P behavior requires four sequential decisions.

Step 1: Is Something Wrong?
The first step in deciding whether to intervene is simply perceiving something is wrong. Some situations or events naturally attract more attention than others. Most emergencies are novel and upset the normal flow of life. However, as shown by Piliavin et al.,[27] the onset of an emergency, such as a person slipping on ice or falling down a flight of stairs, will attract more attention and helping behavior than the aftermath of an "injury," as when a victim is regaining consciousness or rubbing an ankle after a fall. Of course, we should expect much less attention to potential problems in daily, nonemergency situations at work, in school, and at home.

Similarly, in active and noisy work environments, people narrow their focus to what is personally relevant. We learn to tune out irrelevant stimuli. In these situations, environmental hazards are easy to overlook. Even less noticeable and attention-getting are the ongoing behaviors of people around us. Yet these behaviors need proactive AC4P support or correction.

But, even if the need for proactive participation is noticed, AC4P behavior will not necessarily occur. The observer must interpret the situation as requiring intervention. This leads us to the next question requiring a "Yes" answer for AC4P behavior to occur.

Step 2: Am I Needed?
Of course we can come up with a variety of excuses for not helping. Distress cues, such as cries for help, and the actions of other observers can clarify an event as an emergency. When we are confused, we look to other people for information and guidance. In other words, by watching what others are doing, we figure out how to interpret an ambiguous event and how to react accordingly. The behavior of others is especially important when stimulus cues are not present.[28]

In situations where the need for intervention or corrective action is not obvious, we usually seek information from others to understand what is going on and to receive direction. This is

Courtesy of George Vaughn Willis.

the typical state of affairs when it comes to noticing a need for AC4P behavior or recognizing another person's AC4P behavior. In fact, the need for *proactive* AC4P behavior is rarely obvious. When I ask my students to look for AC4P behavior around them and then recognize the person with an "AC4P Thank-You Card," I typically receive less than 10% compliance. The most frequent excuse for not recognizing AC4P behavior is, "I didn't see actively caring worthy of a thank-you card."

Step 3: Should I Intervene?
"Is it my responsibility to intervene?" The answer is clear if you are the only witness to a situation you perceive as an emergency. But you might not answer "Yes" to this question when you know other people are also observing the same emergency, or cry for help. You have reason to believe someone else will intervene, perhaps a person more capable than you. This perception relieves you of personal responsibility. But what happens when everyone believes the other guy will take care of it? This is likely what happened in the Kitty Genovese incident.

A breakdown at this stage of the decision model doesn't mean the observers don't care about the welfare of the victim. Actually, it's probably incorrect to call lack of intervention *bystander apathy*.[29] The bystanders might care very much about the victim, but defer responsibility to others because they believe other observers are more likely or better qualified to intervene. Similarly, employees might care a great deal about the safety and health of their co-workers, but feel relatively incapable of acting on their caring. People might resist taking personal responsibility to actively care because they don't believe they have the most effective tools to make a difference.

In addition to a "can do" attitude, people need to believe it's their personal responsibility to actively care for others. The challenge in achieving an AC4P culture is to convince everyone they have a responsibility to actively care for others. A social norm or expectancy needs to be established. All participants share equally in a daily assignment to keep everyone healthy and productive.

Plus, AC4P leaders need to accept the special responsibility of teaching others any techniques they learn at conferences or group meetings that could increase a person's perceived competence (or self-efficacy) to actively care more effectively. If we don't meet this challenge, many people are apt to decide AC4P is not for them.

Step 4: What Should I Do?
This last step of the Latane and Darley decision model pinpoints the importance of education and training. Education gives people the rationale and principles behind a particular intervention approach. It gives people information to design or refine intervention strategies, leading to a sense of ownership for the particular tools they help to develop. Through training, people learn how to translate principles and rules into specific behaviors or intervention strategies.

The bottom line: People who learn how to intervene effectively through relevant education and training are more likely to be successful agents of an AC4P intervention.

This decision logic suggests certain methods for increasing the likelihood people will actively care. Specifically, the model supports the need to teach people how to recognize a need for AC4P behavior at the environment, person, and behavior levels and then determine what intervention strategies are available and most effective in each case. Plus, people need to learn how to give supportive feedback and genuine recognition for those who emit AC4P behavior.

It's also imperative to promote AC4P as a core value of the particular culture. This means everyone assumes responsibility for the health, safety, and well-being of others in their culture and never waits for someone else to act.

Cultivating an AC4P Culture

Culture influences and sustains one's propensity to actively care. A work culture, for example, can incorporate an accountability system that encourages interpersonal helping. Plus, the daily interactions of people influence certain person-states that affect one's propensity to go beyond the call of duty for another person's well-being. The frequency of AC4P behavior varies *directly* with extrinsic-response contingencies and *indirectly* as a function of certain dispositional person-states.

The Direct Approach

For almost 30 years, I have promoted the use of a special "Actively-Caring Thank-You Card" at my University to recognize individuals for their AC4P behavior. The front of this brightly-colored card includes the mascot of our University and two University sponsors. The definition of AC4P behavior is given on the back of the card, along with specific examples of actively caring.

Several organizations have customized this thank-you card for their culture. I have seen this simple thank-you-card

cultivate a sense of interdependence and belongingness throughout a work group, as well as help people feel good about their own AC4P behavior.

In their book, *Measure of a Leader,* Aubrey and James Daniels describe a creative device they have used successfully for years to motivate discretionary behaviors throughout an organization. Specifically, managers hang a chart in a conspicuous location that lists the names of all employees in a certain work area. Then they give each person a sticker identifying that individual. Whenever a worker is helped by a colleague, that person puts his or her identifying sticker on the chart, next to the name of the person who performed the AC4P behavior.

The Daniels brothers report dramatic culture change. "Not only does it give recognition for those who help, but it is an antecedent for others to take the initiative in finding ways they can help other team members."[30]

In addition, for more than 20 years I've been promoting the use of a green wristband, embossed with the words "Actively Caring for People," to recognize people for their AC4P behavior. Over the years, I've distributed about 50,000 of these wristbands after my keynote addresses at conferences and organizations. Recently my students have used this recognition approach to reduce bullying by promoting and rewarding AC4P behavior in various educational settings.[31]

For these latter applications, the AC4P wristbands were redesigned to include a different identification number per wristband as well as the website (www.ac4p.org) where people can: a) share their AC4P stories (with the number of the wristband they gave or received), b) track worldwide where a particular AC4P wristband has been, and c) order more AC4P wristbands to reward others for actively caring.

To date, more than 1,500 AC4P stories have been shared on this website, and more than 30,000 AC4P wristbands have been purchased with proceeds going to the Actively Caring for People Foundation, Inc. We believe this particular

Courtesy of Center for Applied Behavior Systems.

accountability system for activating and rewarding AC4P behavior has great potential for spreading the AC4P paradigm worldwide and inspiring the development of AC4P cultures.

Genuine appreciation and recognition can have dramatic positive effects on a person's attitude, mindset, and disposition. A recognition system that directly acknowledges AC4P behavior can result in a spiraling cycle of favorable culture change. Positive regard for people's AC4P behaviors increases the frequency of the target behavior directly, while simultaneously feeding the five person-states that set the occasion for more AC4P behavior. These person-states are defined next, as well as ways to enhance them.

The Indirect Approach

Psychological science considers both the observable (outside) and non-observable (inside) aspects of individuals. Indeed, long-term behavior change requires people to change *inside* as well as outside. The promise of a positive consequence or the threat of a negative one can maintain desired behavior while the response-consequence contingencies are in place. But what happens when they are withdrawn? What happens when people are in situations, like at home, when no one is holding them accountable for their behavior?

If people do not *believe* in the AC4P way of doing something and do not *accept* AC4P as a value or a personal mission, they will not choose AC4P behavior when no one's watching. If people are not self-motivated to actively care, the frequency of AC4P behavior will be much less than desired.

FIGURE 16•5 illustrates how person factors interact with the basic activator-behavior-consequence model of behavior-focused psychology.[32] Activators direct behavior and consequences motivate behavior, but as shown in Figure 16.5, these events are first filtered through the person. Numerous internal and situational factors influence how we mentally process activators and consequences. If we see activators and consequences as schemes to control us, our attitude about the situation will be negative.

On the other hand, when we believe the external contingencies are genuine attempts to help us do the right thing, our attitude will be more positive. Personal or internal dynamics determine how we receive activator and consequence information. This can influence whether environmental events enhance or diminish what we do. Let's consider five states that influence one's propensity to perform AC4P behavior.

Self-Esteem (*"I am valuable"*). One's self-concept, or feeling of worth, is a central theme of most humanistic therapies.[33] According to Carl Rogers and his adherents, we possess both a real and an ideal self-concept. We have notions or aspirations of what we would like to be (our ideal self) and what we think we are (our real self). Our self-esteem decreases as the gap between our real and ideal self-concepts increases. The mission of many humanistic therapies is to help a client reduce this gap.

A healthy level of self-esteem and acting to help others raise their self-esteem has obvious benefits. Research shows people with high self-esteem report fewer negative emotions and less depression than people with low self-esteem.[34] Those with higher self-esteem also handle life's stresses better.[35]

Individuals who score higher on measures of self-esteem are: a) less susceptible to outside influences,[36] b) more confident of achieving personal goals,[37] and c) make more favorable

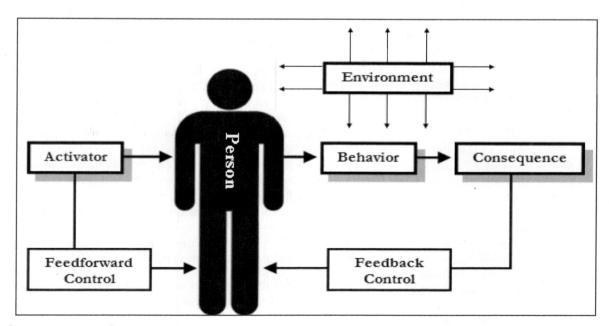

[**FIGURE 16•5**] Activators and consequences are filtered through the person.

" *Dear Diary,*
Sorry to bother you...."

impressions on others in social situations.[38] People with higher self-esteem also help others more frequently than those scoring lower on a self-esteem scale.[39]

Empowerment (*"I can make a difference"*). In management literature, empowerment typically refers to delegating authority or responsibility, or sharing decision-making.[40] In contrast, the AC4P perspective of empowerment focuses on *how a person reacts* after receiving more power or influence.

From a psychological perspective, empowerment is a matter of personal perception. Do you feel empowered or more responsible? Can you handle the additional assignment? This view of empowerment requires the personal belief that "I can make a difference".

Perceptions of personal control,[41] self-efficacy,[42] and optimism[43] strengthen the notion of empowerment. An empowered state is presumed to increase your motivation to "make a difference," perhaps by going beyond your normal routine on behalf of the well-being of another person. Empirical support exists for this intuitive hypothesis.[44] Let's look more closely at these three person states that affect our propensity to actively care.

Self-Efficacy In other words, *"I can do it"* (or, *"You can do it."*). I'm talking about your self-confidence. This is a key principle in social learning theory, determining whether a therapeutic intervention will succeed over the long term.[45] People who score relatively high on a measure of self-efficacy perform better at a wide range of tasks, and work harder to achieve a specific goal, according to dozens of studies. These "can do" believers also demonstrate greater ability and motivation to solve complex problems at work, have better health and safety habits, and are more successful at handling stressors.[46]

Self-efficacy contributes to self-esteem, and vice versa; but these constructs are different. Self-esteem refers to a general sense of self-worth; self-efficacy refers to feeling successful or effective at a particular task. Self-efficacy is more focused, and can vary markedly from one task to another. One's level of self-esteem remains relatively constant across situations.

Personal Control This is the sense that *"I am in control"*. J.B. Rotter[42] used the term *locus of control* to locate the forces controlling a person's life. People with an *internal* locus of control believe they usually have direct personal control over significant life events as a result of their inner knowledge, skill, and abilities. They believe they are captains of their life's ship. In contrast, persons with an *external* locus of control believe "outside" and random factors like chance, luck, or fate play important roles in their lives. Externals believe they are victims, or sometimes beneficiaries, of circumstances beyond their direct personal control.[47]

More than 2,000 studies have investigated the relationship between perceptions of personal control and other variables.[48] Internals are more achievement-oriented and health conscious than externals. They are less prone to distress, and more likely to seek medical treatment when they need it.[49] Having an internal locus of control helps reduce chronic pain, facilitates psychological and physical adjustment to illness and surgery, and hastens recovery from some diseases.[50] Internals perform better at jobs that allow them to set their own pace, whereas externals work better when a machine controls the pace.[51]

Optimism *"I expect the best"* sets the tone for optimism. It's the learned expectation that life events, including personal actions, will turn out well.[52] Optimism relates directly to achievement. Martin Seligman[53] reported, for example, that world-class swimmers who scored high on a measure of optimism recovered from defeat and swam even faster compared to those swimmers scoring low. Following defeat, the pessimistic swimmers swam slower.

Compared to pessimists, optimists maintain a sense of humor, perceive problems or challenges in a positive light, and plan for success. They focus on what they can *do* rather than on how they *feel*.[54] Optimists handle stressors constructively and experience positive stress more often than negative distress.[55] They essentially expect to succeed at whatever they do, and so they work harder than pessimists to reach their goals. Optimists are beneficiaries of the self-fulfilling prophecy.[56]

Fulfilling an optimistic prophecy can enhance our perceptions of personal control, self-efficacy, and even self-esteem. Realizing this should motivate us to do whatever we can to make interpersonal conversations positive and constructive. This will not only increase optimism in a certain culture, but also promote a sense of group cohesiveness or belonging–another person state that facilitates AC4P behavior.

Belonging (*"I am a team member"*). M. Scott Peck challenges us to experience a sense of true community with others in his best seller, *The Different Drum: Community making and peace*.[57] We need to develop feelings of belonging with one another regardless of our political preferences, cultural backgrounds, and religious beliefs. We need to transcend our

Courtesy of George Vaughn Willis.

frequency of our AC4P behaviors. Improvement in behavior requires interpersonal observation, feedback, and recognition. For this to happen, people need to adopt a collective win-win perspective instead of the individualistic win-lose orientation so common in many work and educational settings.

A sense of belonging and interdependency leads to interpersonal trust and caring—essential features of an AC4P culture. I explain how one's sense of community or relatedness to others affects self-motivation—a person's drive to do something without an external incentive or accountability system.

Someone at my group discussions with employees inevitably raises the point that a sense of belonging or community at their plant has decreased in recent years. Belongingness is a fading concept; "We used to be more like family around here" is a common theme.

For many companies, growth spurts, continuous turnover–particularly among managers—or "lean and mean" cutbacks have left many employees feeling less connected and trusting. People's need level on Maslow's hierarchy has regressed from satisfying social acceptance and belonging to concentrating on maintaining job security, in order to keep food on the table.

FIGURE 16•6 lists a number of special attributes prevalent in most families, where interpersonal trust and belonging are usually optimal. We are willing to actively care in special ways for the members of our immediate family. The result is

differences, overcome our defenses and prejudices, and develop a deep respect for diversity. Peck claims we must develop a sense of community or interconnectedness with one another if we are to accomplish our best and ensure our sustainability as human beings.

It's intuitive that building a sense of community or belonging among our friends and colleagues will increase the

---

- We use more rewards than penalties with *family* members.

- We don't pick on the mistakes of *family* members.

- We don't rank one *family* member against another.

- We brag about the accomplishments of *family* members.

- We respect the property and personal space of *family* members.

- We pick up after other *family* members.

- We correct the undesirable behavior of *family* members.

- We accept the corrective feedback of *family* members.

- We are interdependent with *family* members.

- We actively care because they're *family*.

[**FIGURE 16•6**]   A family perspective in an organization helps to cultivate an AC4P culture.

optimal trust, belonging, and AC4P behavior for the health, safety, and welfare of our family members.

To the extent we follow the guidelines in Figure 16.6 among members of our everyday peer group we will achieve an AC4P culture. Following the principles in Figure 16.6 will develop trust and belonging among people, and lead to the quantity and quality of AC4P behavior expected among family members—at home, at work, at school, and everywhere in between.

A Self-Supporting AC4P Cycle

The five person-states presented here as influencing people's willingness to actively care are shown in FIGURE 16·7 as an AC4P Model. Each of these person-states has a rich research history in psychology and some of this research relates directly to the AC4P Model. Research that tested relationships between these person-states and actual behavior has supported this model,[58] although much more research is needed in this domain.

A particularly important question is whether the AC4P person-states are both antecedents and consequences of an AC4P act. It seems intuitive that performing an act of kindness that is effective, accepted, and appreciated could

increase the helper's self-esteem, self-efficacy, personal control, optimism, and sense of belonging. This, in turn, should increase the probability of more AC4P behavior. In other words, one act of caring, properly appreciated, should lead to another and another. A self-supporting AC4P cycle is likely to occur.

Enhancing the AC4P Person-States

Sometimes participants at my workshops and seminars express concern the AC4P person-state model might not be practical. "The concepts are too soft or subjective," is a typical reaction. Teachers, parents, work supervisors, and individual employees accept the behavior-based approach to performance improvement because it's straight-forward, objective, and clearly applicable to educational, work, and family settings. But person-based concepts like self-esteem, personal control, optimism, and belonging appear ambiguous, "touchy-feely," and difficult to deal with. "The concepts sound good and certainly seem important, but how can we wrap our arms around these 'warm fuzzies' and use them to promote an AC4P culture?"

To be sure, person-states are more difficult to define, measure, and manage than behaviors. But we just can't ignore how

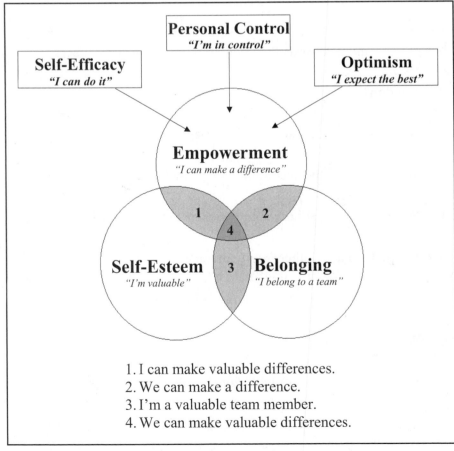

1. I can make valuable differences.
2. We can make a difference.
3. I'm a valuable team member.
4. We can make valuable differences.

[**FIGURE 16·7**]   Five person-states influence a person's willingness to actively care.

people *feel* about a behavior-improvement process. For people to accept a behavior-change process and sustain the target behaviors for the long term, we must confront internal person-states when designing and implementing an intervention.

After introducing the AC4P Model (Figure 16.7) at my workshops on AC4P, I often divide participants into discussion groups. I ask group members to define events, situations, or contingencies that decrease and increase the person-state assigned to their group. Then I ask the groups to derive simple and feasible action plans to increase their assigned dispositional state. This promotes personal and practical understanding of the concept.

The AC4P Model may be soft, but feedback from these workshops shows it's not too hard to grasp. Action plans have been practical and quite consistent with techniques used by researchers. Also, there has been substantial overlap of practical recommendations—workshop groups dealing with different person-states have come up with similar contributory factors and action plans. Let's take a look at what my workshop participants have proposed regarding factors and strategies related to each of these person-states.

Self-Esteem

Participants suggest a number of ways to build self-esteem, including: a) Provide opportunities for personal learning and peer mentoring; b) Increase recognition for desirable behaviors and individual accomplishments; and c) Solicit and follow up on a person's suggestions.

It's essential to give more positive (or supportive) than negative (or corrective) feedback. When offering corrective feedback, it's essential to focus on the act, not the actor. Emphasize an error only reflects behavior that can be corrected, not some deeper character flaw. Don't come off as a judge of character, implying a mistake suggests some subjective personal attribute like "carelessness," "apathy," "bad attitude," or "poor motivation".

Be a patient, active listener. Allow people to offer reasons for their error or poor judgement. Resist the temptation to argue about these. Giving a reason or excuse is just a way to protect one's self-esteem, and it's generally a healthy response. Remember, you already made your point by showing the error and suggesting ways to avoid the mistake in the future. Leave it at that.

If a person doesn't react constructively to corrective feedback, it might help to explore feelings. "How do you feel about this?" you might ask. Then listen empathically to assess whether self-esteem has taken a hit. You'll learn whether some additional communication is needed to place the focus squarely on what is external and objective, rather than subjective and internal.

Self-Efficacy

Self-efficacy is more situation-specific than self-esteem, so it fluctuates more readily. Job-specific feedback should be directed only at one's perception of what's needed to do a particular task successfully. It should not veer off in the nebulous direction of general self-worth.

Keep in mind that repeated negative feedback can have a cumulative effect, chipping away at an individual's perception of self-worth. Then it takes only one remark, perhaps one you would think is innocuous and job-specific, to "break the camel's back" and trigger what seems like an overreaction.

Our communication may not be received as intended. We might do our best to come across positively and constructively, but because of factors beyond our control, the communication might be misperceived. One's inner state can dramatically bias the impact of interpersonal feedback. Note that self-efficacy reflects a perception of competence.

Achievable Tasks What makes for a "can do" attitude? Personal perception is the key. A supervisor, parent, or teacher might believe s/he has provided everything needed to complete a task successfully. However, the employee, child, or student might not think so. It's important to ask, "Do you have what you need? We're checking for feelings of self-efficacy." This is easier said than done, because people often hesitate to admit their incompetence. Who wants to concede, "I can't do it?" Instead, we try to maintain the appearance of self-efficacy.

Ask open-ended questions when you give assignments to assess whether those on the receiving end are prepared to get the job done. In large groups, though, this probing for feelings of self-efficacy is impossible. As a result, in the classroom many students get left behind in the learning process (frequently because they skipped classes or an important reading assignment). As they get farther and farther behind in my class, their low self-efficacy is supported by the self-fulfilling prophecy and diminished optimism. Sometimes this leads to "raise-the-white-flag-behavior" and feelings of helplessness.[59]

All too often, these students withdraw from my class or resign themselves to receiving a low grade. In the workplace, employees who cannot keep pace with new procedures might withdraw into themselves or put up defensive resistance.

Personal Strategies Watson and Tharp[60] suggest the following five steps to increase perceptions of self-efficacy. First, select a task at which you expect to succeed, not one you expect to fail. Then, as your feelings of self-efficacy increase, you can tackle more challenging projects. A cigarette smoker who wants to stop smoking, for example, might focus on smoking 50 percent fewer cigarettes per week rather than attempting to quit "cold turkey". With early success at reducing the number of cigarettes smoked, the individual could make the criterion more stringent (like smoking no cigarettes on alternate days). Continued success leads to more self-efficacy.

Second, it's important to distinguish between the past and the present. Don't dwell on past failures. Past failures are history–today is the first day of the rest of your life. Focus on a renewed sense of self-confidence and self-efficacy.

Third, it's important to keep good records of your progress toward reaching your goal. Our cigarette smoker should record the number of cigarettes smoked each day, and note when the rate of smoking is 50 percent less for a week. This should be noted as an achievement, and then a new goal should be set. Focusing on your successes (rather than failures) represents the fourth step in building self-efficacy.

The fifth step: Develop a list of tasks or projects you'd like to accomplish and rank them from easiest to most difficult to accomplish. Whenever possible start with the easier tasks. The self-efficacy and self-confidence developed from accomplishing less demanding tasks will help you tackle the more challenging situations on your list.

Focus on the Positive Many of the strategies I've presented for improving person-states include a basic principle—focus on the positive. Whether attempting to build your own self-efficacy or that of others, success needs to be emphasized over failure. Thus, whenever you have the opportunity to teach others or give them feedback, you must look for small-win accomplishments and give genuine approval before commenting on ways to improve. Again, this approach is easier said than done.

Failures are easier to spot than successes. They stick out and interrupt the flow. That's why most teachers are quick to give negative attention to students who disrupt the classroom, while giving only limited positive attention to students who remain on task and go with the flow. Plus, many of us have been conditioned (unknowingly) to believe negative consequences (penalties) work better than positive consequences (rewards) to influence behavior change.[61]

Courtesy of George Vaughn Willis.

Personal Control

Employees at my seminars on AC4P have listed a number of ways to increase perceptions of personal control, including: a) set short-term goals and tracking progress toward long-term accomplishment; b) offer frequent rewarding and correcting feedback for process activities rather than only for outcomes;

c) provide opportunities to set personal goals, teach others, and chart "small wins";[62] d) teach employees basic behavior-change intervention strategies (especially feedback and recognition procedures); e) provide time and resources for people to develop, implement and evaluate intervention programs; f) show employees how to graph daily records of baseline, intervention, and follow-up data; and g) post response-feedback graphs of group performance.

The perception of personal control is analogous to perceptions of personal choice and autonomy. When people believe they are in control of a situation or challenge, they generally feel a sense of personal choice. "I choose to take charge of the mission which is within my domain of influence." Appreciate the similarity between these person-states.

Optimism

Optimism flows from thinking positively, avoiding negative thoughts, and expecting the best to happen. Anything that increases our self-efficacy should increase optimism. Also, when our personal control is strengthened, we perceive more influence over our consequences. This gives us more reason to expect the best. Again, we see how the person-states of self-efficacy, personal control and optimism are clearly intertwined. A change in one will likely influence the other two. Note also how these person-states relate to perceptions of choice and competence—determinants of self-motivation.

Belonging

Here are common proposals given by my seminar discussion groups to create and sustain an atmosphere of belonging among employees: a) decrease the frequency of top-down directives and "quick-fix" programs, b) increase team-building discussions, group goal-setting and feedback, and group celebrations for both process and outcome achievements, c) use self-managed or self-directed work teams.

Feelings of empowerment and belonging can be enhanced when groups are given control over important matters like developing a behavior-improvement observation and feedback process or a particular AC4P initiative. When resources, opportunities, and talents enable team members to assert, "We can make a difference," feelings of belonging occur naturally. This leads to synergy, with the group achieving more than could be possible from participants working independently.

In Conclusion

Continuous improvement in any endeavor involving human dynamics requires people to actively care for others as well as themselves. The research-based principles reviewed here are relevant to increasing the frequency and improving the quality of AC4P behavior throughout a particular culture. Some practical intervention procedures benefit AC4P behavior indirectly by enhancing the person-states that facilitate one's willingness to actively care. Other strategies target AC4P behaviors directly, but often have an indirect positive effect on the person-states that increase one's propensity to actively care.

Any procedure that increases a person's self-esteem, self-efficacy, personal control, and optimism, or sense of belonging or interdependence in a system will indirectly benefit AC4P behavior. A number of communication techniques enhance more than one of these states simultaneously, particularly actively listening to others for feelings and giving genuine praise for other people's accomplishments.

Reflect on your own life to appreciate the power of personal choice, and how the perception of personal control makes you more self-motivated, involved, and committed to a particular mission. The perception of choice activates and sustains AC4P behavior.

Perceptions of belonging are important, too. They increase when groups are given control over important decisions and receive genuine recognition for their accomplishments. Synergy is the ultimate outcome of belonging and win-win interpersonal involvement. It occurs when group interdependence produces more than what's possible from going it alone.

Courtesy of George Vaughn Willis.

AC4P behaviors are the building blocks of an AC4P culture. The more quality AC4P behaviors occurring among people in a given work, school, or family setting, the more likely will an AC4P culture evolve.

It usually takes self-motivation to initiate and sustain the kind of behavior needed for an AC4P culture because people are rarely held accountable for performing AC4P behavior. Chapter 11 explains how to increase perceptions of self-motivation, setting the stage for effective AC4P behavior. Do you see several direct connections between the person-states that increase one's propensity to actively care and those that enhance one's self-motivation.

NOTES

1. Cialdini, R.B. (2001). *Influence: Science and practice* (4th Edition). Needham Heights, MA: Allyn & Bacon; Schroeder, D.A., Penner, L.A., Dovidio, J.F., & Piliavin, J.A. (1995). *The psychology of helping and altruism.* New York: McGraw-Hill, Inc.

2. Geller, E.S. (1998). *Understanding behavior-based safety: Step-by-step methods to improve your workplace* (Revised Edition). Neenah, WI: J.J. Keller & Associates, Inc; Geller, E.S. (2001). *The psychology of safety handbook.* Boca Raton, FL: CRC Press; Geller, E.S. (2002). People-based safety: Seven social influence principles to fuel participation in occupational safety. *Professional Safety, 47*(10), 25–31; Geller, E.S., & Williams, J.H. (2001). *Keys to behavior-based safety.* Rockville, MD: ABS Consulting; McSween, T.E. (1995). *The values-based safety process: Improving your safety culture with a behavioral approach.* New York, NY: Van Nostrand Reinhold.

3. Geller, E.S. (1998). *Beyond safety accountability: How to increase personal responsibility.* Neenah, WI: J.J. Keller & Associates, Inc; Geller, E.S. (2001). Actively caring for occupational safety: Extending the performance management paradigm. In C.M. Johnson, W.K. Redmon, & T.C. Mawhinney (Eds.), *Organizational performance: Behavior analysis and management.* New York, NY: Springer.

4. Covey, S.R. (1989). *The seven habits of highly effective people.* New York, NY: Simon and Schuster; Covey, S.R. (1990). *Principle-centered leadership.* New York, NY: Simon & Schuster, Inc.

5. Peale, N.V. (1952). *The power of positive thinking.* New York, NY: Prentice-Hall.

6. Kohn, A. (1993). *Punished by rewards: The trouble with gold stars, incentive plans, A's, praise, and other bribes.* Boston, MA: Houghton Mifflin.

7. Deming, W.E. (1986). *Out of the crisis.* Cambridge, MA: Massachusetts Institute of Technology, Center for Advanced Engineering Study; Deming, W.E. (1993). *The new economics for industry, government, education.* Cambridge, MA: Massachusetts Institute of Technology, Center for Advanced Engineering Study.

8. Skinner, B.F. (1981). Selection by consequences. *Science, 213,* 502–504.

9. Carnegie, D. (1936). *How to win friends and influence people.* New York, NY: Simon & Schuster, Inc., p. 57.

10. Maslow, A.H. (1943). A theory of human motivation. *Psychological Review, 50,* 370–396; Maslow, A.H. (1954). *Motivation and personality.* New York, NY: Harper.

11. Schultz, D. (1977). *Growth psychology: Models of the healthy personality.* New York, NY: D. Van Nostrand.

12. Maslow, A.H. (1971). *The farther reaches of human nature.* New York. NY: Viking.

13. Frankl, V. (1962). *Man's search for meaning: An introduction to logotherapy.* Boston, MA: Beacon Press.

14. Rosenthal, A.M. (1964). *Thirty-eight witnesses*. New York, NY: McGraw-Hill.

15. Latané, B., & Darley, J.M. (1968). Group inhibition of bystander intervention. *Journal of Personality and Social Psychology*, *10*, 215–221; Latané, B., & Darley, J.M. (1970). *The unresponsible bystander: Why doesn't he help?* New York, NY: Appelton-Century-Crofts.

16. Latané, B., & Nida, S. (1981). Ten years of research on group size and helping. *Psychological Bulletin*, *89*, 308–324.

17. Beaman, A.I., Barnes, P.J., Klentz, B., & McQuirk, B. (1978). Increasing helping rates through informational dissemination: Teaching pays. *Personality and Social Psychology*, *37*, 1835–1846.

18. Hornstein, H.A. (1976). *Cruelty and kindness: A new look at aggression and altruism*. Englewood Cliffs, NJ: Prentice-Hall.

19. Shotland, R.L., & Heinold, W.D. (1985). Bystander response to arterial bleeding: Helping skills, the decision-making process, and differentiating the helping response. *Journal of Personality and Social Psychology*, *49*, 347–356.

20. McCarty, S.M., Teie, S., & Furrow, C.B. (2012). *Training students to observe and reward actively-caring behavior*. Technical Research Report, Center for Applied Behavior Systems, Department of Psychology, Virginia Tech, Blacksburg, VA.

21. Rutkowski, G.K., Gruder, C.L., & Romer, D. (1983). Group cohesiveness, social norms, and bystander intervention. *Journal of Personality and Social Psychology*, *44*, 545–552.

22. Carlson, M., Charlin, V., & Miller, N. (1988). Positive mood and helping behavior: A test of six hypotheses. *Journal of Personality and Social Psychology*, *55*, 211–229.

23. Bierhoff, H.W., Klein, R., & Kramp, P. (1991). Evidence for the altruistic personality from data on accident research. *Journal of Personality*, *59*, 263–280.

24. Schwartz, S.H., & Clausen, G.T. (1970). Responsibility, norms, and helping in an emergency. *Journal of Personality and Social Psychology*, *16*, 299–310; Staub, E. (1974). Helping a distressed person: Social, personality, and stimulus determinants. In L. Berkowitz (Ed.), *Advances in experimental social psychology*, Vol. 7. New York, NY: Academic Press.

25. Geller, E.S. (1998). *Beyond safety accountability: How to increase personal responsibility*. Neenah, WI: J.J. Keller & Associates, Inc; Geller, E.S. (2001). Actively caring for occupational safety: Extending the performance management paradigm. In C.M. Johnson, W.K. Redmon, & T.C. Mawhinney (Eds.), *Organizational performance: Behavior analysis and management*. New York, NY: Springer.

26. Latané, B., & Darley, J.M. (1970). *The unresponsible bystander: Why doesn't he help?* New York, NY: Appleton-Century-Crofts.

27. Piliavin, J.A., Piliavin, I.M., & Broll, L. (1976). Time of arousal at an emergency and likelihood of helping. *Personality and Social Psychology Bulletin*, *2*, 273–276.

28. Clark, R.D., III, & Word, L.E. (1972). Why don't bystanders help? Because of ambiguity? *Journal of Personality and Social Psychology*, *24*, 392–400.

29. Schroeder, D.A., Penner, L.A., Dovidio, J.F., & Piliavin, J.A. (1995). *The psychology of helping and altruism*. New York, NY: McGraw-Hill.

30. Daniels, A.C., & Daniels, J.E. (2005). *Measure of a Leader*. Atlanta, GA: Performance Management Publications, p. 158.

31. McCarty, S.M., & Geller, E.S. (2011, Summer). Want to get rid of bullying? Then reward behavior that is incompatible with it. *Behavior Analysis Digest International*, *23*(2), 1–7.

32. Kreitner, R. (1982). The feedforward and feedback control of job performance through organizational behavior management (OBM). *Journal of Organizational Behavior Management*, *4*(2), p. 3.

33. Rogers, C. (1957). The necessary and sufficient conditions of therapeutic personality change. *Journal of Consulting Psychology*, *21*, 95–103; Rogers, C. (1977). *Carl Rogers on personal power: Inner strength and its revolutionary impact*. New York, NY: Delacorte.

34. Straumann, T.J., & Higgins, E.G. (1988). Self-discrepancies as predictors of vulnerability to distinct syndromes of chronic emotional distress. *Journal of Personality*, *56*, 685–707.

35. Brown, J.D., & McGill, K.L. (1989). The cost of good fortune: When positive life events produce negative health consequences. *Journal of Personality and Social Psychology*, *57*, 1103–1110.

36. Wylie, R. (1974). *The self-concept* (Vol. 1). Lincoln, NE: University of Nebraska Press.

37. Wells, L.E., & Marwell, G. (1976). *Self-esteem*. Beverly Hills, CA: Sage.

38. Baron, R.A., & Byrne, D. (1994). *Social psychology: Understanding human interaction* (Seventh Edition). Boston, MA: Allyn and Bacon.

39. Batson, C.D., Bolen, M.H., Cross, J.A., & Neuringer-Benefiel, H.E. (1986). Where is altruism in the altruistic personality? *Journal of Personality and Social Psychology*, *1*, 212–220.

40. Conger, J.A., & Kanungo, R.N. (1988). The empowerment process: Integrating theory and practice. *Academy of Management Review*, *13*, 471–482.

41. Rotter, J.B. (1966). Generalized expectancies for internal versus external control of reinforcement. *Psychological Monographs*, *80*, No. 1.

42. Bandura, A. (1997). *Self efficacy: The exercise of control*. New York, NY: W.H. Freeman and Company

43. Scheier, M.F., & Carver, C.S. (1985). Optimism, coping and health: Assessment and implications of generalized outcome expectancies. *Health Psychology*, *4*, 219–247; Scheier, M.F., & Carver, C.S. (1993). On the power of positive thinking: The benefits of being optimistic. *Current Directions in Psychological Sciences*, *2*, 26–30; Seligman, M.E.P. (1991). *Learned optimism*. New York, NY: Alfred A. Knopf.

44. Bandura, A. (1986). *Social foundations of thought and action*. Englewood Cliffs, NJ: Prentice Hall; Barling, J., & Beattie, R. (1983). Self-efficacy beliefs and sales performance. *Journal of Organizational Behavior Management*, *5*, 41–51; Ozer, E. M., & Bandura, A. (1990). Mechanisms governing empowerment effects: A self-efficacy analysis. *Journal of Personality and Social Psychology*, *58*, 472–486; Phares, E.J. (1976). *Locus of control in personality*. Morristown, NJ: General Learning Press.

45. Bandura, A. (1990). Self-regulation of motivation through goal systems. In R.A. Dienstbier (Ed.), *Nebraska symposium on*

motivation, Vol. 38. Lincoln, NE: University of Nebraska Press; Bandura, A. (1994). Self-efficacy. In *Encyclopedia of human behavior*, Vol. 4. Orlando, FL: Academic Press; Bandura, A. (1997). *Self efficacy: The exercise of control*. New York, NY: W.H. Freeman and Company.

46. Bandura, A. (1982). Self-efficacy mechanism in human agency. *American Psychologist, 37*, 122–147; Betz, N.E., & Hackett, G. (1986). Applications of self-efficacy theory to understanding career choice behavior. *Journal of Social and Clinical Psychology, 4*, 279–289; Hackett, G., Betz, N.E., Casas, J.M., & Rocha-Singh, I.A. (1992). Gender, ethnicity, and social cognitive factors predicting the academic achievement of students in engineering. *Journal of Counseling Psychology, 39*, 527–538.

47. Rotter, J.B. (1966). Generalized expectancies for internal versus external control of reinforcement. *Psychological Monographs, 80*, No. 1; Rushton, J.P. (1984). The altruistic personality: Evidence from laboratory, naturalistic and self-report perspectives. In E. Staub, D. Bar-Tal, J. Karylowski, & J. Reykowski (Eds.), *Development and maintenance of prosocial behavior*. New York, NY: Plenum.

48. Hunt, M.M. (1993). *The story of psychology*. New York, NY: Doubleday.

49. Nowicki, S., & Strickland, B.R. (1973). A locus of control scale for children. *Journal of Consulting Psychology, 40*, 148–154; Stickland, B.R. (1989). Internal-external control expectancies: From contingency to creativity. *American Psychologist, 44*, 1–12.

50. Taylor, S.E. (1991). *Health psychology* (2nd Edition). New York, NY: McGraw-Hill.

51. Eskew, R.T., & Riche, C.V. (1982). Pacing and locus of control in quality control inspection. *Human Factors, 24*, 411–415; Phares, E.J. (1991). *Introduction to personality* (Third Edition). New York, NY: Harper Collins.

52. Peterson, C. (2000). The future of optimism. *American Psychologist, 55*(1), 44–55; Scheier, M.F., & Carver, C.S. (1985). Optimism, coping and health: Assessment and implications of generalized outcome expectancies. *Health Psychology, 4*, 219–247; Seligman, M.E.P. (1991). *Learned optimism*. New York, NY: Alfred A. Knopf.

53. Seligman, M.E.P. (1991). *Learned optimism*. New York, NY: Alfred A. Knopf.

54. Carver, C.S., Scheier, M.F., & Weintraub, J.K. (1989). Assessing coping strategies: A theoretically based approach. *Journal of Personality and Social Psychology, 56*, 267–283; Seligman, M.E.P. (2011). *Flourish: A visionary new understanding of happiness and well-being*. New York, NY: Simon & Schuster, Inc.; Peterson, C., & Barrett, L.C. (1987). Explanatory style and academic performance among university freshmen. *Journal of Personality and Social Psychology, 53*, 603–607.

55. Scheier, M.F., Weintraub, J.K., & Carver, C.S. (1986). Coping with stress: Divergent strategies of optimists and pessimists. *Journal of Personality and Social Psychology, 51*, 1257–1264.

56. Tavris, C., & Wade, C. (1995). *Psychology in perspective*. New York, NY: Harper Collins College Publishers.

57. Peck, M.S. (1979). *The different drum: Community making and peace*. New York, NY: Simon & Schuster, Inc.

58. Geller, E.S. (2001). Actively caring for occupational safety: Extending the performance management paradigm. In C.M. Johnson, W.K. Redmon, & T.C. Mawhinney (Eds.), *Organizational performance: Behavior analysis and management*. New York, NY: Springer; Geller, E.S. (2001). Sustaining participation in a safety improvement process: Ten relevant principles from behavioral science. *Professional Safety, 46*(9), 24–29.

59. Peterson, C., Maier, S.F., & Seligman, M.E.P. (1993). *Learned helplessness: A theory for the age of personal control*. New York, NY: Oxford University Press; Seligman, M.E.P. (1975). *Helplessness: On depression development and death*. San Francisco, CA: Freeman.

60. Watson, D.C., & Tharp, R.G. (1987). *Self-directed behavior: Self-modification for personal adjustment* (7th Edition). Pacific Grove, CA: Brooks/Cole Publishing Company.

61. Notz, W.W., Boschman, I., & Tax, S.S. (1987). Reinforcing punishment and extinguishing reward: On the folly of OBM with SPC. *Journal of Organizational Behavior Management, 9*(1), 33–46.

62. Weick, K.E. (1984). Small wins: Redefining the scale of social problems. *American Psychologist, 39*, 40–44.

Prologue

It's often not enough to know what to do in order to actively care effectively (i.e., competence) and to be motivated to perform AC4P behavior (i.e., commitment). The missing ingredient is *courage*. The same five person-states as determinants of AC4P behavior are discussed here as precursors to courage.

The simple AC4P strategies presented in this chapter are practical for large-scale application and evidence-based benefits. But, none have been adopted on a broad scale. Why not? Is it lack of compassion, courage, commitment, competence, self-motivation, or something else? Exploring answers to this question will help us determine the next steps in achieving an AC4P culture of compassion. ∎

Interpersonal Intervention and Courage

As with any program designed to improve behavior, people could claim they lack the resources and/or time to implement the intervention. They could doubt the effectiveness of the AC4P technique and wonder whether the time to implement the interpersonal intervention is worth the effort.

However, these excuses are irrelevant for the techniques described here. Why? Because they are straightforward and easy to accomplish with minimal effort. More importantly, empirical research (as cited below) has demonstrated the beneficial impact of these simple interpersonal approaches to promote human welfare and/or prevent harm to people.

Standard excuses for inaction cannot work here. So what is the barrier to large-scale implementation of simple-to-use interpersonal methods that clearly benefit everyone involved?

The key word is "interpersonal". Each effective intervention method requires personal interaction with other people. It is likely many people lack the courage to intervene as an agent of change. This chapter discusses the level of courage needed, and suggests ways to develop that courage in ourselves and others.

Bottom line: What does it take for more people to become interpersonal change agents on behalf of the welfare of others? Effortless evidenced-based techniques to help people prevent harm to themselves and others are available, but at this time too few people have the courage to use them.

What is Courage?

The American Heritage Dictionary[1] defines courage as "the state or quality of mind or spirit that enables one to face danger with self-possession, confidence, and resolution." This denotation is consistent with the two-page description of courage in *Wikipedia* (http://en. wikipedia.org/wiki/courage), except Wikipedia distinguishes between *physical courage*—when confronting physical pain, hardship, or threat of death, and *moral courage*—in the face of possible shame, embarrassment, or discouragement.[2]

Leaders certainly need competence and commitment to be effective change agents.[3] But, interpersonal intervention to prevent possible harm to a person (i.e., proactive AC4P behavior) takes *moral courage*. A person could have both competence and commitment in a particular situation, but not be courageous. Consider the following two authentic incidents related to AC4P, the first was dramatic and reactive while the other was temperate and proactive.

Responding to an Emergency

In the midst of a safety meeting, Joanne Dean, the safety director of a large construction firm in New Jersey is notified of a horrendous "accident." The operator of an industrial equipment truck with an attached auger was pulled into the auger by the weed mesh under the mulch on which he was standing. The worker chose not to stand on the safety platform provided for this task.

Joanne runs to help the bloody victim whose body is severed in half. She assists the on-site nurse with the AED (automated external defibrillator), covers the body parts with a blanket, and stays at the scene until the local EMS (emergency medical service) and coroner arrive.

It took commitment to step up and intervene in this horrible incident. It's likely Joanne's competence as an emergency-response instructor contributed to her propensity to actively care, but her AC4P behavior took more than commitment and competence.

Indeed, three key safety professionals of the company that hired the construction firm chose not to intervene. They stood at a distance and watched Joanne and the other responders. We can assume these experienced, professional bystanders possessed both the competence and commitment required for their leadership positions. But on this day they appeared to lack moral courage.

Responding to a Risky Situation

While waiting in the lobby of a Fortune-500 company, Bob Veazie, a safety consultant and former culture-change agent for a Fortune-100 company, observes an at-risk behavior. A maintenance worker has climbed to the top of an eight-foot step-ladder to change a light bulb. Because the ladder is not long enough for this job, the individual is standing with one foot on the top step of the ladder. A co-worker is looking up and talking to the man on the ladder, but he's not holding the ladder steady.

Imagining a serious injury from a fall to the hard marble floor of the lobby, Bob walks to the ladder and calls up to the at-risk worker. Holding the bottom of the ladder, he requests the man to come down because, "It doesn't seem safe to stand on the top of that ladder". Then he asks whether a longer ladder is available.

Bob Veazie showed moral courage by intervening with this at-risk stranger. Bob could have been publicly embarrassed, humiliated, or faced an unpleasant confrontation. Bob's competence and commitment as a safety trainer and consultant certainly contributed to his inclination to speak up. But competence and commitment were not sufficient for the courage he showed. In fact, Bob's training partner who has extensive competence and intense commitment for safety saw the same at-risk behavior, but she chose not say or do anything about it.

How Can Courage Be Encouraged?

Courage is a human characteristic distinct from competence and commitment. But these three qualities of leadership are interdependent to a degree. Individuals with greater competence and commitment in a given situation are more likely to demonstrate courage. One's propensity to demonstrate courage in certain circumstances is increased whenever relevant competence or commitment is augmented.

Developing Competence

Behavior-focused training increases one's competence at a particular task. This involves: a) describing and demonstrating a desirable behavior or skill-set, b) giving specific behavior-based feedback during a participant's role-playing of designated target behavior(s), c) practicing the desired behavior(s) with both corrective and supportive feedback, and d) implementing the new competency in real-world situations.[4]

When learners teach this skill-set to others, their perception of competence increases further, along with their personal commitment.[5] And as I commented above, greater feelings of competence and commitment are more likely to support acts of courage.

Developing Commitment

Motivation or commitment to do something is determined by the intrinsic and extrinsic consequences of a task, as well as one's personal interpretation of those consequences.[6] While many tasks are performed for expected soon, certain, and significant consequences, we use self-talk to avoid impulsive reactive behavior and work for long-term goals.[7] Self-talk is also a potential means of overcoming anxiety and reinforcing a commitment to step up and be courageous when called upon.

Cultivating Courage

The moral courage of Joanne and Bob was due to many factors. It suggests cultivating courage is more complex and less straightforward than developing competence and commitment. For example, both Joanne and Bob are extraverts. They gain energy from interacting with people. Both are naturally outgoing and inclined to communicate with others. They would be described as having excellent "people skills."

Another of the Big Five personality traits that facilitated the courage of Joanne and Bob is conscientiousness.[8] I know each of them very well and it's obvious they each carry an AC4P mindset with them at all times—both on and off the job.

Beyond personality *traits,* certain person-*states* increase one's propensity to show AC4P courage. These person-states—self-esteem, self-efficacy, personal control, optimism, and sense of belongingness—increase the probability an individual will perform AC4P behavior.

Culture and the Courage to Actively Care

Many of the factors that influence one's propensity to demonstrate AC4P courage can be filed under the general label—culture. Certain cultural factors related to the development and cultivation of courage are exhibited daily by people around us. Another real-life story not only illustrates physical courage, but also demonstrates some practical strategies for promoting the moral courage needed for the kind of interpersonal intervention needed to achieve an AC4P culture.

Physical Courage to Actively Care

On January 16, 2007, Dr. Kevin Brothers, executive director of the Somerset Hills Learning Institute, was wheeled into St. Barnabas' Renal Surgery Center. He was in top physical and mental health, and had never before "gone under the knife" and experienced surgery. He received a three-hour surgical procedure—not for himself but for someone else.

Dr. Brothers donated his kidney to his mentor and professional colleague—Dr. Patricia Krantz, Executive Director of the Princeton Child Development Institute. Seven months earlier Dr. Brothers had learned Dr. Krantz was in severe kidney failure. Without a transplant, she would require dialysis within a few months.

Dr. Krantz was not aware that Dr. Brothers and several other colleagues had agreed to donate one of their kidneys to her. Among all of Dr. Krantz's family, friends, and colleagues who received extensive blood work and tissue sampling, there was only one viable match—Kevin Brothers.

The difference between physical and moral courage is evident in the three real-world incidents I have described here. When we risk social embarrassment or interpersonal confrontation on behalf of another person's welfare, we show *moral* courage. In contrast, when we risk physical harm to ourselves when looking out for another person's well-being, we demonstrate *physical courage.*[2] While Joanne Dean and Bob Veazie demonstrated moral courage, Kevin Brothers' elective surgery exemplifies physical courage.

The AC4P courage of Dr. Brothers was extraordinary. Beyond a number of person factors, including Dr. Brothers'

self-esteem, self-efficacy, personal control, optimism and sense of belongingness, a number of cultural factors facilitated this display of courage. Let's consider these cultural factors as potential guidelines for promoting AC4P courage in your culture.

A Group Commitment Dr. Brothers' first courageous act was to pledge to give one of his kidneys to Dr. Krantz. When Kevin talked with me prior to his surgery, he admitted it was relatively easy to muster the courage to sign the donor pledge. The probability of him being the best antigen match was seemingly low. Surely one of Dr. Krantz's family members would be a better match.

Although surprised he was the best match, Dr. Brothers affirmed strong motivation to honor his commitment to the group of potential donors. He acknowledged the value of this two-part approach to motivate his AC4P behavior—first the promise and then the action. This two-step approach is applicable to many situations.

Suppose each member of a work team signed a group declaration to give each other corrective feedback wherever they saw behavior that could jeopardize the quality or the safety of their job. This commitment could be called a "Declaration of Interdependence." In fact this was the label on a large poster at a leadership seminar for supervisors, safety leaders, and maintenance personnel of Delta Airlines.[9] The commitment poster was signed by more than 100 Delta employees, and was prominently displayed in the maintenance workers' break room at the Hartsfield-Jackson International Airport in Atlanta, GA.

This group obligation, given voluntarily and publicly within a supportive social context, helps to sustain the moral courage required to give behavior-based feedback. Such courage increases the probability workers deliver AC4P coaching communications to their peers.

Group Support Both before and after his surgery, Dr. Brothers received substantial social support for his physical courage. This is often crucial in deciding to move forward in a courageous way. His wife Debbie, a registered nurse, and their four daughters totally supported Kevin's decision "to move ahead to give *our* kidney as soon as possible". Dr. Brothers said, "*Our* kidney, because this was a well-informed family decision made with the support of Debbie and our girls." Dr. Brothers' courage was also aided by the dedicated support group of friends and colleagues who pledged to donate a kidney.

Two weeks after a successful surgery, Kevin Brothers returned to work. "What an outpouring of support our family received from our school's parents and staff," reported Debbie Brothers. The parents and staff of the Princeton Child Development Institute were also extremely supportive, sending thank-you cards to Dr. Brothers for helping to prolong Dr. Krantz's life and enable her to continue her important work worldwide.

Substantial research reports verify the beneficial impact of social support on human performance, from enhancing motivation to engage in a challenging task to facilitating recovery from physical illness and injury[10]. This factor relates directly to the person-state of belongingness.

If you feel you belong to a social network or circle of friends or peers, this increases your inclination to actively care for another individual's health, safety, or general well-being. If that actively caring requires an act of courage, strong feelings of belonging create a sense of responsibility or obligation to not disappoint the group. Cultivating social support throughout a particular culture is extremely beneficial to increasing the courage factor and the frequency of AC4P behavior.

Various interpersonal activities can enhance social support and courage, including team goal setting, interpersonal coaching, collaborative work projects, and group celebrations. Relationship-building conversations are also critical.

A Trusting Culture When Kevin Brothers honored his pledge to give Patricia Krantz one of his kidneys, his courage was bolstered by his feeling that all of the others in his special donor group would follow through on their commitment if they had the best antigen match. He also trusted the expert medical staff at St. Barnabas Medical Center would give Dr. Krantz and him the very best healthcare. He expected a successful kidney transplant.

The topic of interpersonal trust, including the need to distinguish between trusting an individual's ability vs. his/her intentions, as well as in other publications.[11] I explained specific ways to increase interpersonal trust. In addition, you might consider asking colleagues or co-workers how specific events, policies, or communications impact their trust levels, and their courage to speak up about safety issues or risks.

Solicit ideas to eliminate barriers to interpersonal trust and nurture courage. Add policies and/or procedures that could enhance people's perception they can trust the intentions and abilities of their supervisors and co-workers. A number of practical action plans will likely result from this process. Still, just the process of soliciting ways to impact interpersonal trust will have a positive trust-building and courage-building effect.

A Common Worthwhile Purpose Dr. Brothers and his colleagues in the kidney-donor group admired and greatly appreciated the teaching and research of Dr. Patricia Krantz. Indeed, Dr. Krantz has pioneered the application of behavioral science for the treatment of autism, and she mentored Dr. Brothers while he was a research intern and Ph.D. student. In Dr. Brother's words, "Dr. Krantz gave me the opportunity to learn science, and her teachings continue to be the underpinnings of my career . . . (and) her guiding me into the field of autism treatment has given more children a chance for a better life".

The group that pledged to donate a kidney for Dr. Krantz had a common and commendable purpose. Likewise, advocates for an AC4P culture have a common and worthwhile mission. In fact, there is perhaps no more esteemed purpose than to actively care for another person's health, safety, and general welfare.

A Family Mindset

It certainly takes more courage to actively care for a stranger than a colleague. In fact, attending to the safety and/or welfare of a family member is usually not even considered courageous but rather an obligation. When members of a work team think of their co-workers as "family," actively caring for the well-being of these individuals becomes more an act of commitment than courage.

The probability of AC4P behavior is increased whenever interpersonal behavior supports a family mindset among friends, colleagues, or co-workers. FIGURE 17•1 illustrates this proposed relationship between the degree of courage needed for interpersonal AC4P behavior and the degree of relatedness or interpersonal connection between the person needing help and the observer.

It's unlikely many readers would undergo elective surgery to give a kidney to a stranger. Fortunately, actively caring for the welfare of others does not require the *physical courage* shown by Dr. Brothers.

Indeed, proactive AC4P behavior doesn't require any physical courage—only the *moral courage* to face possible embarrassment, rejection or conflict when giving feedback or advice to improve another person's behavior, or giving personal approval to reward the AC4P behavior of another person. A supportive *family* mindset among people removes the fear of

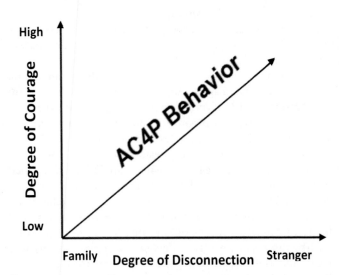

[**FIGURE 17•1**] The amount of courage needed to actively care increases directly with the degree of disconnection between the observer and the person in need of assistance.

negative consequences from such proactive and behavior-focused actively caring.

Actually, many AC4P actions do not require courage; they only present an inconvenience. If you saw a member of your immediate family get behind the steering wheel of a vehicle and neglect to buckle up, you would not hesitate to intervene. Courage would hardly enter the picture.

But what would you do if you got in a hotel shuttle van at the airport and noticed the driver and several passengers did not buckle up? Would you offer some proactive AC4P corrective feedback? Would you have the moral courage to intervene on behalf of these at-risk strangers?

You have several excuses for not speaking up, right? It's only a short trip to the hotel and the probability of a crash is miniscule. These folks are adults, and if they want to travel at-risk, that's their choice. Plus, if you say something about this, another occupant might be offended by your meddling and call you a "safety nerd".

So why actively care in this situation? Here's a thought: Consider that your moral courage sets a memorable leadership example. Such behavior could start a constructive AC4P conversation and initiate a ripple effect of actively caring.

Contemplating one's lack of moral courage can activate some disconcerting tension between what an individual thinks s/he would do in this and similar situations versus what the person knows s/he should do. The more one holds AC4P as a personal value, the greater the tension or cognitive dissonance.[12] Following through with moral courage relieves such tension and exemplifies AC4P leadership.

The following simple and convenient AC4P intervention strategies are straightforward and effortless, and they exemplify the kind of AC4P leadership needed to cultivate an AC4P culture.

Question: Do you have the moral courage to apply any of these, and encourage others to do the same? Implementing these on a large scale would move us one step closer to achieving our vision of an AC4P culture of compassion. And for the most part, they do not require a great amount of courage.

The Flash-for-Life

Developed initially in 1984 and replicated in several other situations, this rather intrusive but effective intervention merely involves the change agent holding up a card to request a certain safety-related behavior (i.e., vehicle safety-belt use); and if the target individual complies, the "flasher" flips the card over to reveal "Thank You". The front and back of this card is shown, which measures 11 × 14 inches and is brightly colored with bold lettering as depicted.

Here the courage factor is minimized by the physical distance between the actions taking place. In the first study, the "flasher" was positioned in the passenger seat of a vehicle stopped in the left lane at an intersection.[13] If the driver in the adjacent vehicle was unbuckled, the passenger held up the flashcard so the driver could see it. TABLE 17•1 depicts the impact of this simple activator intervention by specifying the

percentage of vehicle drivers who buckled up after viewing the card.

As shown in Table 17.1, seven different vehicle passengers of varying ages, ranging from 3.5 to 23 years of age, "flashed" a total of 787 unbuckled drivers in Blacksburg, VA, home of Virginia Tech; whereas only two of these passengers (i.e., Tim and Hollie) showed the Flash-for-Life card to 300 passengers in the adjacent rural town of Christiansburg, VA.

Some drivers did not turn their head to look at the sign, and therefore the compliance percentages are based on only those drivers who looked directly at the sign. It's noteworthy this prompting intervention was more successful in the university town than in Christiansburg (i.e., an average of 24.6 vs. 13.7 percent compliance, respectively). The age of the "flashers" did not have a reliable impact on the driver's compliance with the buckle-up prompt.

It's worth noting that this intervention did not result in any verbal or physical harassment. Although the "flasher" did get a few hand signals which didn't mean right or left turn. When my daughter asked, "What do they mean, Daddy," I told her they were signaling, "You're number one, they're just using the wrong finger." Incidentally, none of these one-finger hand signals came from females.

The first applications of the "Flash for Life" occurred before safety-belt use laws, when only about 20% of U.S. drivers buckled up. Twenty years later, with about 80% of U.S. drivers using their vehicle safety belts, my students and I compared the impact of a positive reminder ("Please Buckle Up I Care") with the more common negative-reinforcement

[**TABLE 17·1**] Summary of "Flash for Life" Results[13]

Flasher (Name & Age)	Number of Observations	Number Who looked	Number Who buckled	Percentage Who Looked	Percentage Who Buckled
Blacksburg, VA					
Karly age 3 1/2	179	154	37	86.0	24.0
David age 5	31	21	5	67.7	23.8
Abby age 7	68	47	16	69.1	34.0
Carrie age 7	64	48	9	75.0	18.8
Dane age 10	56	43	6	76.8	14.0
Hollie age 22	206	177	43	85.9	24.3
Tim age 23	183	148	41	80.3	27.6
Total	**787**	**634**	**157**	**80.9**	**24.6**
Christiansburg, VA					
Tim age 22	145	123	19	84.8	15.4
Hollie age 23	155	133	16	85.8	12.0
Total	**300**	**256**	**35**	**85.3**	**13.7**

[**TABLE 17·2**] Summary of Results from Positive vs. Negative Buckle-Up Prompting[15]

Intervention Sign	Percentage who Buckled-Up	Percentage of Positive Hand Gestures	Percentage of Negative Hand Gestures	Percentage of Positive Expressions	Percentage of Negative Expressions
Flash for Life n=895	33.6%	13.2%	.9%	25.0%	3.9%
Click it or Ticket n=927	25.6%	7.8%	2.6%	18.9%	9.2%

prompt (i.e., "Click it or Ticket") on both behavioral compliance and body language.[14]

TABLE 17·2 reveals the percentage of unbuckled drivers who buckled up after viewing one of the two types of cards. This table also shows the percentage of drivers giving positive vs. negative hand signals and facial expressions per type of prompt. It's noteworthy the positive "I Care" prompt was not only more effective at activating buckle-up behavior than the threatening reminder, it also prompted more positive and less negative body language than did the negative-reinforcement prompt (all *p's* < .05).

The AC4P-Behavior Promise Card

This nonintrusive and straightforward strategy is suitable for numerous circumstances and target behaviors.[15] It requires little in the way of courage. It has been used effectively to increase the occurrence of specific safety-related behavior (e.g., the use of safety glasses, gloves, and vehicle safety belts)[16] as well as to promote an interdependent AC4P paradigm or mindset.[17]

Based on the powerful social-influence principle of consistency,[18] this behavior-change tactic merely asks participants to sign an individual "promise card" or a "group pledge"

AC4P Promise Card

I promise to _____

_____

From _____ until _____

_____
signature   date

that declares an explicit commitment to regularly perform a particular AC4P behavior for a specified period of time.

For maximum behavioral impact, the pledge-card signing should be public and voluntary. A generic promise card is depicted below that can be used to increase the occurrence of a number of AC4P behaviors.

The AC4P Polite Light

Taking on the negative emotions of road-rage driving would seem to call for a greater degree of courage. But not so in this case. It involves the use of a vehicle light to signal a simple "Courtesy Code" under relevant conditions. Specifically, one flash means "Please," two flashes reflect "Thank You," and three flashes are used to signal "I am sorry". Vehicle emergency lights can be used to flash this "1-2-3 code," or a small green light as shown below can be affixed to the vehicle's rear window and operated with the convenient push of a button.

In a community-wide evaluation of this intervention strategy, the polite-driving code was promoted on radio stations and billboards throughout the town of Christiansburg, VA, and "polite lights" were distributed at various workshops. Results were encouraging, but the idea was not adopted.

The success of this intervention relied not on courage but on marketing and outreach, and then for people to use the Courtesy Driving Code. Marketing and the minor inconvenience of flashing the Courtesy Code were key barriers that prevented this AC4P behavior from large-scale use. So far, anyway.

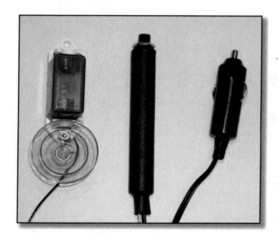

The "Airline Lifesaver"

Flying in an airplane requires courage for some people to the degree they need medication to reduce anxiety. Others never think of the risks involved in flying.

For this particular AC4P intervention, courage is needed for one-on-one interaction with a stranger. The 3 × 5 inches card depicted on the next page can be handed to the flight attendant when boarding an airplane. It requests the following announcement be made after landing: "Now that you have worn a seat belt for the safest part of your trip, the flight crew would like to remind you to buckle up during your ground transportation".

To intervene with busy flight attendants by handing them this card and requesting they add on an announcement at the flight's conclusion doesn't require much in the way of courage. Of course there is the fear of possible rejection. "No, I don't have the time." But what this exercise demonstrates is the more committed you are to AC4P, the more passionate you feel about it, the easier it is to risk rejection and go ahead with this simple and convenient intervention. It's also easier

if you have extroverted people skills, such as Joanne and Bob in the stories told earlier.

The first Lifesaver Card shown here is the first one I used, beginning in 1985. In 1994, I began using an incentive card that offered the flight attendants a prize if they read the announcement. The back of this card is depicted below, which specifies the *if-then reward contingency*. Later, I alternated the distribution of these two types of reminders to determine the impact of an incentive intervention.

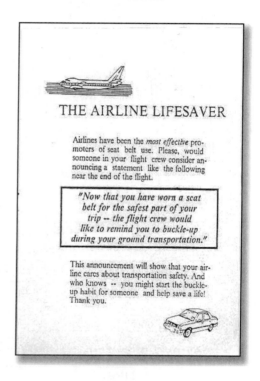

A 17-year study demonstrated substantial compliance with this Airline Lifesaver request,[19] but no current airline has adopted this simple safety-based intervention. And, I know of no individual using this technique consistently when boarding an airplane. When the request was made without an incentive (i.e., prompt only), 35.5% of 798 recipients read the message. However, when the flight attendant was offered a prize for delivering the buckle-up reminder, 53.3% of 245 recipients complied with the request.

Of course, showing that many flight attendants read the buckle-up reminder when asked to do so does not reveal behavior change directly related to people's welfare. Indeed, it is rare to see such direct benefits of proactive efforts to prevent personal injury. However, two behavior-change benefits of the Airline Lifesaver have been documented.[20] In one case, a passenger who heard the buckle-up reminder asked the driver of the airport commuter van to buckle up, claiming "If a flight attendant can request safety-belt use, so can I".

For a second testimony, I received a letter from a passenger who said he used the back-seat safety belt in a taxi cab because he had just heard the buckle-up reminder at the end of his flight. Traveling over 70 mph, the taxi hydroplaned on a wet road and struck the guardrail. Serious

injuries were prevented because this person had buckled up. The actual letter from this individual is printed in my first book on the psychology of safety.[21]

The Driver-Training Score Card

As mentioned earlier, it often requires less moral or physical courage to actively care for family members than for strangers, like in a class of workplace safety trainees. But here is an intervention that has proven successful in both applications.

More than 15 years ago, I documented an effective behavior-change intervention for driver training, which led to numerous adaptations in work settings.[21] Specifically, I worked with my 15-year-old daughter to develop a critical behavior checklist (CBC) for driving. As shown in FIGURE 17•2, this CBC lists a number of driving-related behaviors, along with columns to record whether each behavior is safe or at-risk, and a column to write comments relevant for a follow-up feedback session.

Critical Behavior Checklist for Driving

Driver:	Date:		Day:
Observer 1:	Origin:		Start Time:
Observer 2:	Destination:		End Time:
Weather:			
Road Conditions:			

Behavior	Safe	At-Risk	Comments
Safety Belt Use:			
Turn Signal Use:			
Left turn			
Right turn			
Lane change			
Intersection Stop:			
Stop sign			
Red light			
Yellow light			
No activator			
Speed Limits:			
25 mph and under			
25 mph- 35 mph			
35 mph- 45 mph			
45mph- 55 mph			
55mph- 65 mph			
Passing:			
Lane Use:			
Following Distance (2 sec):			
Totals:			

% Safe = $\frac{\text{Total Safe Observations}}{\text{Total Safe + At-Risk Obs.}}$ = _____ %

[**FIGURE 17•2**] The critical behavior checklist (CBC) for driving is a fundamental tool for behavior-based coaching.

While much research and even common sense indicates this process works to improve safety-related behaviors, I am unaware of a single adoption of this technique for driver education/training. However, this behavior-change technique is the foundation of behavior-based safety (BBS), and there is much empirical support for the BBS approach to increasing safety-related behaviors and preventing injuries.[22]

The Taxi-Cab Feedback Card

At keynote addresses to large audiences, I have proposed that safety leaders record the safety-related driving behaviors of cab, bus, and limo drivers on a simple observation-feedback card; and after the trip, show the results to the driver for valuable behavior-based feedback.[23]

A sample feedback card, applicable in numerous driving situations, is shown below. The top half of the card is given to the driver, while the bottom half has a return address and stamp on the back. This enables tracking of the driver behaviors observed by the passengers of public-transport vehicles.

This observation-and-feedback technique reflects another adaption of a basic process of BBS applied in industries worldwide with remarkable improvements in injury statistics. However, I know of no large-scale application of this evidence-based process for public transportation. It does take substantial moral courage to use this proactive AC4P strategy in taxi cabs, limos, and buses.

The AC4P Thank-You Card

For many years, I have promoted the use of a simple thank-you card for delivery to people following their performance of AC4P behavior.[24] In fact, "thank-you cards" have been

Please give this half to your driver.

Always remember to buckle up!

Your safe driving today:

You ☐ did ☐ did not use your safety belt.

During this trip, you used your turn signal correctly for _____ out of _____ turns you made.

You also made complete stops at _____ out of _____ intersections with red lights or stop signs.

For _____ out of _____ speed limit signs you passed, you were not speeding.*

*Please see the back of this card for a description of "speeding."

Your ticket to a safe ride!

Please return this half to C.A.B.S.

Safety Belt:	Yes	No
Turn Signal:		
Complete Stops:		
Speed:		

Date: _____ City: _____ Location: _____

Please remember to fill in the feedback card and give it to your driver, then return this half of the card to the address on the back.

customized for particular industrial sites and educational settings. For example, I have distributed the "Virginia Tech Thank-You Card" for more than 20 years (see Chapter 16).

Every semester I make these cards available for my students to use to acknowledge the AC4P behavior of others, but relatively few students take them. Student leaders in our Center for Applied Behavior Systems (CABS) have regularly used this recognition technique for more than two decades, because this recognition process has been institutionalized in our CABS culture. However, beyond applications in CABS, university use of a thank-you card is rare.

Given the power, generic applicability and relative convenience of one-to-one recognition, it's appropriate to end this chapter with evidence-based details about how to give and receive interpersonal recognition.

"Actively Caring Thank-You Cards" were introduced as a mechanism to cultivate a sense of connectedness and AC4P throughout an organization. I discussed interpersonal recognition within the context of supportive feedback to sustain and potentially increase the occurrence of AC4P behavior. Here I offer specific behavioral strategies for delivering and receiving recognition. First, it's critical to understand and believe in the importance of giving quality AC4P recognition.

In terms of the courage factor, it's worth noting many people are uncomfortable communicating rather intimately on a one-to-one, face-to-face basis. But the value of this sort of interaction makes it important to use whatever means you have at your disposal to overcome fears of interpersonal interaction. Ask for coaching on this critical skill-set. Observe others competent at up-close and personal interaction and model techniques that fit your style.

We Learn More from Success

"We can't learn unless we make mistakes." How many times have you heard this? This might make us feel better about the errors of our ways, and provide an excuse for focusing more on people's failures than on their successes, but in reality nothing could be further from the truth.

Behavioral scientists have shown convincingly that success—not failure—produces the most effective learning.[25] Edward Lee Thorndike, for example, studied intelligence at the start of the last century by putting chickens, cats, dogs, fish, monkeys, and humans in situations that called for problem-solving behavior. He then systematically observed how these organisms learned. He coined the "Law of Effect" to refer to the fact that learning depends upon behavioral consequences.

When a behavior is followed by a "satisfying state of affairs" the probability of that behavior occurring again is increased. But, if an "*annoying* state of affairs" follows a behavior, that behavior (considered an error) is less likely to recur.[26]

Which kind of consequence—positive or negative—leads to the most learning? Does an error have to occur in order to solve a problem? We can reflect on our own experiences to answer these questions. A pleasant consequence gives us direction and motivation to continue the behavior. We know what we did to receive the reward, and are thus motivated to earn another.

In contrast, a negative consequence following a mistake only tells us what not to do. It provides no specific direction for problem solution. An overemphasis on a mistake can be frustrating and discouraging, and de-motivate us to continue the learning process.

Errors are not necessary for learning to occur. In fact, when training results in no errors, made possible with certain presentation techniques, learning occurs most smoothly and is most enjoyable. Errors disrupt the teaching/learning process and can lead to a negative attitude, especially if negative social consequences accentuate the mistake. Even subtle reactions to an error—a disappointed face or verbal tone—can increase feelings of helplessness or despair and turn a person off to the entire learning process.

From the courage perspective, the less focus and talk of errors, the less courage is called for. Offering positive consequences (e.g., supportive feedback) requires substantially less courage, right?

The antidote to depressed learning from the negative consequences of incorrect behavior is to provide positive consequence for correct behavior. And the most powerful positive consequence to support a learning process is interpersonal recognition—the theme of this discussion. Below I offer seven guidelines for giving quality AC4P recognition.

Before leaving this topic of learning from success versus failure, it's noteworthy that Thorndike referred to the type of learning discovered in his problem-solving situations as "trial and accidental success."[26] Many textbook authors have used the term "trial-and-error learning" when describing Thorndike's research, even though Thorndike himself opposed the term because of its inaccurate implications. But let's not focus on this error; rather consider the need to support AC4P behavior with quality recognition.

1. Be Timely

In order for recognition to provide optimal direction and support, it needs to be associated directly with the desired behavior. This is not necessarily an act of courage, but recognition should be delivered promptly. People need to know what they did to earn the appreciation. Then they might be motivated to continue that behavior.

If it's necessary to delay the recognition, the conversation should relive the activity deserving recognition. Talk specifically about the behavior warranting special acknowledgement. Don't hesitate to ask the recipient to recall aspects of the situation and the commendable behavior. This enables direction and motivation to continue the desired behavior.

Courtesy of George Vaughn Willis.

2. Make It Personal

Recognition is most meaningful when it is perceived as personal. Recognition should not be generic, fit for any situation, as in "Nice job". Rather, it needs to be customized to fit a particular individual and circumstance. This happens naturally when the recognition is linked to designated behavior.

When you recognize someone you are expressing personal thanks. Sometimes, it's tempting to say "*we* appreciate" rather than "*I* appreciate," and to refer to company gratitude rather than *personal appreciation*. Speaking for the company can come across as impersonal and insincere. Of course, it's appropriate to reflect value to the organization when giving recognition, but the focus should be personal. "I saw what you did to support our AC4P process and I really appreciate it. Your example illustrates the kind of leadership we need around here to achieve an AC4P culture." This second statement illustrates the next guideline for quality recognition. Again, being positive and proactive shouldn't require that much courage, but some people are not at ease delivering interpersonal praise.

3. Take It to a Higher Level

Recognition is most memorable and inspirational when it reflects a higher-order quality. Adding a universal attitude like leadership, integrity, trustworthiness, or AC4P to your recognition statement makes the recognition more meaningful and thus rewarding. It's important to state the specific behavior first, and then make an obvious linkage between the behavior and the positive attribute it reflects.

Our attempts to get college students to recognize others for their AC4P behavior have been less successful than desired. Many claim they didn't observe AC4P behavior worthy of special recognition, whereas others admit lack of courage

to present a thank-you card or a Hershey PayDay candy bar (labeled "Pay-It-Forward") as a reward for AC4P behavior.

Some say, "It's unnatural or silly," while others resist because it could come across as manipulative. A sincere verbal "Thank You" is okay, they declare, "But giving someone a material reward could be seen as a ploy to control them."

One of my graduate students claimed he is more comfortable rewarding a stranger with a candy bar or a thank-you card than a friend because, "The embarrassment of using a behavior modification technique would be more personal and aversive among close friends than strangers."

My comeback is, "It's all in the delivery." My students hear this and review the seven steps given here for giving quality AC4P recognition, but the use of thank-you cards and candy bars to recognize AC4P behavior has not markedly increased. However, we have found less resistance to passing on an AC4P wristband when the wristband is viewed as more than a reward for behavior.

More specifically, when the wristband is presented as a symbol of AC4P leadership and worn to show membership in an elite group of individuals dedicated to cultivating an AC4P culture of compassion, my students show more interest and willingness to participate in such a recognition process. The AC4P wristband is given to not only reward AC4P behavior, but to signify membership in a Movement to cultivate an AC4P culture of compassion.

This connection brings the interpersonal recognition to a higher level, enabling positive impact on this recipient's self-esteem, competence, and sense of interdependency and belongingness. As mentioned earlier, courage should not be a significant issue here, but the depth of commitment and passion regarding AC4P can make a difference in "taking it to a higher level".

4. Deliver It Privately

Because quality recognition is personal and indicative of higher-order attributes, it needs to be delivered in private and one-on-one. This requires a certain degree of courage for those not comfortable in private, one-on-one conversations; especially with people they don't know well. But consider this: The recognition is special and only relevant to one person. So, it will mean more and seem more genuine if it's given from one individual to another.

It seems conventional to recognize individuals in front of a group. This approach is typified in athletic contests and reflected in the pop psychology slogan, "Praise publicly and reprimand privately". Many managers take the lead from this common-sense statement and give individuals recognition in group settings.

Indeed, isn't it maximally rewarding to be held up as an exemplar in front of one's peers? Not necessarily, because many people feel embarrassed when singled out in front of a group. Part of this embarrassment could be due to fear of subsequent harassment by peers. Some peers might call the recognized individual an "apple-polisher" or "brown-noser," or accuse him or her of "sucking up to management".

When I was in fifth grade, my teacher recognized me in front of the class for doing "an excellent job" on my homework. I was so embarrassed. Then after school, a gang of boys beat me up on the playground. Unfortunately, that teacher never found out the negative side-effect of her public recognition.

Courtesy of George Vaughn Willis.

In athletic events the participants' performance is measured fairly and the winners are objectively determined. However in educational and work settings it's usually impossible to assess everyone's relevant behaviors objectively and obtain a fair ranking for individual recognition.

Therefore, praising one individual in public may lead to perceptions of favoritism from individuals who feel they did equally well, but did not get praised. Plus, such ranking sets up a win-lose atmosphere—perhaps appropriate for sporting events but not in settings where interdependent teamwork is needed to achieve group goals.

It's beneficial, of course, to recognize teams of workers for their accomplishments, and this can be done in a group setting. Since individual responsibility is diffused or dispersed across the group, there is minimal risk of individual embarrassment or later peer harassment.

However, it's important to realize that group achievement is rarely the result of equal input from all team members. Some take the lead and work harder, while others "loaf" and count on the group effort to make them look good. Thus, it's important to deliver personal and private recognition to those individuals who went beyond the call of duty for the sake of their team.

5. Let It Sink In

In this fast-paced age of trying to do more with less, we try to communicate as much as possible when we finally get in touch with a busy person. After recognizing an individual's special AC4P effort, we are tempted to tag on a bunch of unrelated statements, even a request for additional behavior. This comes across as, "I appreciate what you've done, but I need more".

It does take a certain amount of courage, or "guts" to tell someone "I need more out of you". All the more reason to drop the request and let the praise sink in.

Resist the temptation to do more than praise the AC4P behavior you saw. If you have additional points to discuss, it's best to reconnect later, after the rewarding recognition has had a chance to sink in and become a part of the individual's self-talk for self-recognition and self-motivation.

By giving quality AC4P recognition, we give people a script they can use to reward their own behavior. In other words, our quality recognition strengthens the other person's self-reward system. And, positive self-talk (or self-recognition) is critical for long-term maintenance of AC4P behavior. Thus, by allowing our recognition communication to stand alone and soak in, we enable the internalization of rewarding words that can be used later for self-motivation of additional AC4P behavior.

6. Use Tangibles for Symbolic Value

Tangible rewards can detract from the self-motivation aspect of quality recognition. If the focus of an AC4P recognition process is placed on a material reward, the words of appreciation can seem less significant. In turn, the beneficial impact on one's self-motivation is lessened.

On the other hand, tangible rewards can add to the quality of interpersonal recognition if they are delivered as tokens of appreciation. Rewards that include a relevant AC4P slogan, as on the AC4P wristband, can help to promote the desired behavior. But how you deliver a tangible reward will determine whether it adds to or subtracts from the long-term benefit of your praise.

The benefit of interpersonal recognition is weakened if the tangible is viewed as a payoff for the AC4P behavior. However, if the reward is seen as symbolic of going beyond the call of duty for another person's well-being, it strengthens the praise. Have the courage to tell it like it is: The AC4P wristband or another tangible reward is a token of appreciation or a symbol of going beyond the call.

7. Consider Secondhand Recognition

Up to this point, I've been discussing one-on-one verbal communication in which one person recognizes another for a particular AC4P behavior. It's also possible to recognize a person's outstanding efforts indirectly, and such an approach can have special advantages. Suppose, for example, you overhear me talk to another person about your outstanding presentation about the AC4P Movement. How will this secondhand recognition affect you? Will you believe my words of praise were genuine?

Sometimes people are suspicious of the genuineness of praise when it's delivered face-to-face. Is there an ulterior motive? Perhaps a favor is expected in return. Or maybe the recognition is seen merely as an extension of a communication exercise and thus devalued as sincere appreciation. Secondhand recognition, however, is not as easily tainted with these potential biases. Therefore, its genuineness is less suspect.

Suppose I tell you someone else in your workgroup told me about the superb job you did leading a certain group meeting. What will be the impact of this type of secondhand recognition? Chances are you'll consider the recognition authentic because I was only reporting what someone else said. Because that person reported your success to me rather than you, there was no ulterior motive for the indirect praise.

Such secondhand recognition can build a sense of belongingness or group cohesion among individuals. When you learn someone was bragging about your behavior, your sense of friendship with that person will likely increase.

Gossip can be beneficial—*if it's positive*. When we talk about the achievement of others in behavior-specific terms, we begin a cycle of positive communication that can support desired behavior, as well as activate self-talk for self-recognition and self-motivation.

Have the courage to initiate this cycle of positivism. We also set an example for the kind of interpersonal communication that enhances self-esteem, self-efficacy, personal control, optimism, and group cohesion. These are the very person-states that increase the potential for AC4P behavior and the achievement of an interdependent culture of compassion.

A Summary

Referring to classic learning research, I made the case that success is more important than failure in developing and maintaining desired behaviors. This emphasis on success rather than corrective feedback should lessen the need for courage. It's usually more important to recognize people for their correct behaviors than to criticize them for their mistakes. But how we recognize people dramatically influences the impact of our interpersonal interaction. I offered seven basic guidelines to consider when planning to recognize others for their AC4P contributions.

This list of guidelines is not exhaustive, but it does cover the basics. Following these guidelines will increase the positive impact of interpersonal recognition. The most important point is that more recognition for AC4P behavior is needed, whether given firsthand or indirectly through positive gossip. It only takes a few seconds to deliver quality AC4P recognition.

Start giving AC4P recognition today—even for behaviors that occurred yesterday. Delayed recognition is better than no recognition. And, quality recognition does not need to occur face-to-face. Leaving a behavior-based and personal recognition message on phone-mail, e-mail, or in a written memo (formal or informal) can make a person's day. It shows you appreciate what you saw and helps to build that person's self-recognition script for later self-motivation. This behavior

takes minimal courage and can reap benefits far greater than the little inconvenience required.

Perhaps realizing the positive impact we can have on people's behaviors and attitudes with relatively little effort will be self-motivating enough for us to muster the courage, if that is what is needed, to do more recognizing. Even more important, however, are the social consequences we receive when attempting to give quality recognition.

The reaction of the people who are recognized can have a dramatic impact on whether AC4P recognition increases or decreases throughout a culture. We need to know how to respond to recognition in order to assure quality AC4P recognition continues. This is our next and final topic of this chapter.

Courtesy of George Vaughn Willis.

Accept Recognition Well

Most of us get so little recognition from others we are caught completely off guard when acknowledged for our commendable actions. We don't know how to accept recognition when it finally comes. Don't shy away when it does come; have the courage to embrace it.

Remember the basic behavioral-science principle consequences influence preceding behaviors. Thus, quality recognition increases the probability the behavior recognized will continue, and one's reaction to the recognition influences whether the behavior of recognizing someone will be attempted again. It's crucial to react appropriately when we receive recognition from others. Let's consider seven basic guidelines for receiving recognition.

1. Don't Deny or Disclaim

Often when I attempt to give quality AC4P recognition, I get a reaction that implies I'm wasting my time. I get disclaimer statements such as, "It really was nothing special," or, "Just doing my job." The most common reply: "No problem." This implies the commendable behavior is not special and should not have been recognized.

We need to accept recognition without denial and disclaimer statements, and without deflecting the credit to others. It's okay to show pride in our small-win accomplishments, even if others contributed to the successful outcome. After all, the vision of a compassionate AC4P culture includes everyone going beyond the call of duty for the well-being of others. In this context, numerous people deserve recognition daily.

Accept that recognition will be intermittent at best for everyone; and when your turn comes, accept the recognition for your most recent AC4P behavior and for the many prior AC4P behaviors you performed that went unnoticed. Keep in mind your genuine appreciation of the recognition will increase the chance that more recognition will be given by others.

2. Listen Actively

Listen actively to the person giving you recognition. You want to learn what you did, right? Plus, you can evaluate whether the recognition is given well. If the recognition does not pinpoint a particular behavior, you might ask the person, "What did I do to deserve this?" This will help to improve that person's method of giving recognition.

Of course, it's important not to seem critical but rather to show genuine appreciation for the special attention. Consider how difficult, yes how courageous, it is for many people to go out of their way to recognize others. So, revel in the fact you're receiving some recognition, even if its quality could be improved.

3. Use It Later for Self-Motivation

Most of your AC4P behaviors will go unnoticed. You perform many of these when no one else is around to observe you. Even when other people are available, they will likely be so preoccupied with their own routines they won't notice your extra effort. So when you finally do receive recognition for AC4P behavior, take it in as well-deserved.

Don't hesitate to relive this moment later by talking to yourself. Such self-recognition can motivate you to continue going beyond the call of duty on behalf of other people's well-being. As mentioned earlier, self-talk can help you muster the courage to perform more AC4P behavior.

4. Show Sincere Appreciation

You need to show sincere gratitude with a smile, a "Thank You," and perhaps special words like, "You've made my day." Your reaction to being recognized can determine whether similar recognition is apt to occur again. So be prepared to offer a sincere "Thank You" and words that reflect your pleasure in the memorable interaction. And consider the courage the other person might have needed to give you your recognition.

I find it natural to add "You've made my day" to the "Thank-You" because it's the truth. When people go out of their way to offer me quality recognition, they *have* made my day. I often relive such situations to improve a later day.

5. Reward the Recognition

When you accept recognition well, you reward the person for their appreciation. This can motivate that individual to do more recognizing. Especially if the person is more of an introvert and requires courage to step out and speak up to give recognition.

Sometimes, you can do even more to assure the occurrence of more quality recognition. Specifically, you can recognize the person for recognizing you. You might say, for example, "I really appreciate you noticing my AC4P behavior and calling me a leader of the AC4P Movement." Such rewarding feedback provides direction and motivation for those aspects of the AC4P recognition process that are especially worthwhile and need to become routine.

6. Embrace the Reciprocity Norm

Some people resist receiving recognition because they don't want to feel obligated to give recognition to others. This is the reciprocity norm at work. If we want to achieve an AC4P culture, we need to embrace this norm. When you are nice to others, as when providing them with special praise, you increase the likelihood they will reciprocate by showing similar behavior. You might not receive the returned favor, but someone will.[27]

It's important to realize your genuine acceptance of quality recognition will activate the reciprocity norm; and the more this norm is activated from positive interpersonal communication, the greater the frequency of interpersonal recognition and AC4P behavior.

So accept recognition well, and embrace the reciprocity norm. The result will be more interpersonal involvement consistent with the vision of an AC4P culture of compassion. Again, interpersonal involvement does not come easy to all of us. The quality of AC4P interactions can go a long way to easing one's resistance to involvement.

7. Ask for Recognition

If you feel you deserve recognition, why not ask for it? In terms of courage, yes, asking for praise is easier if you are an extrovert compared to an introvert.

Your request might result in recognition viewed as less genuine than if it were spontaneous, but the outcome from such a request can be quite beneficial. You might receive some words worth reliving later for self-motivation. Most importantly, you will remind the other individual in a nice way that s/he missed a prime opportunity to offer quality recognition. This could be a valuable learning experience for that person.

Consider the possible beneficial impact from your statement to another person that you are pleased with a certain result of your extra effort, including your performance of particular AC4P behavior. With the right tone and affect, such verbal behavior will not seem like bragging but rather a declaration of personal pride in a small-win accomplishment—something more people should feel and relive for self-motivation. The other person will support your personal praise with supportive testimony, and this will bolster your self-motivation. Plus, you will teach the other person how to support the AC4P behaviors of others.

Many years ago, I instituted a self-recognition process among my research students that increased our awareness of the value of receiving praise, even when it's self-initiated. I told my students during class or group meetings they could request a standing ovation at any time. All they had to do was specify the behavior they felt deserved recognition and then ask for a standing ovation. Obviously, such recognition is not private, personal, and one-to-one, and therefore it's not optimal. Plus, the public aspect of this process inhibited many personal requests for a standing ovation.

However, over the years a number of my students have requested a standing ovation, and the experience has always been positive for everyone. Each request has included a solid rationale. Some students express pride in an exemplary grade on a project; others acknowledge an acceptance letter from a graduate school, internship, or journal editor. The actual ovation is fun and feels good, whether on the giving or receiving end. Plus, we all learn the motivating process of behavior-based recognition, even when it doesn't follow all of the quality principles.

The Craving

William James, the first renowned American psychologist, wrote, "The deepest principle in human nature is the craving to be appreciated".[28] A little later John Dewey, the famous American educator who developed the field of school psychology, claimed, "The deepest urge in human nature is the desire to be important".[28] Then in 1936, Dale Carnegie advocated the key to winning friends and influencing people is to "always make the other person feel important".[28] How can we readily fulfill the human need to feel appreciated and important? The answer, of course, is to give and receive recognition well.

In Conclusion

Many excuses and barriers can be offered for the lack of large-scale application of effective AC4P interventions analogous to those discussed in this chapter. I explained three C-words reflecting the leadership qualities needed to achieve an AC4P culture of compassion: Competence, Commitment, and Courage. Many people are competent and committed regarding the achievement of an AC4P culture. In other words, they know what to do, and are motivated to do whatever it takes to increase the quantity and quality of AC4P behaviors in educational, work, and community settings.

However, I suggest the missing link is often *moral* courage, or the audacity to step up, take an *interpersonal risk* and go beyond one's predictable routine on behalf of the well-being of other people, especially complete strangers. Beyond

competence (or self-efficacy), four person-states that influence courage in this context (i.e., self-esteem, belongingness, personal control, and optimism), and guidelines for cultivating an AC4P culture have been entertained in chapters 16 and 17 of this book.

Test your *moral courage* as an AC4P leader by using these various intervention techniques. You can log on to ac4p.org and download airplane lifesaver cards, feedback cards, thank-you cards, and more.

NOTES

1. *The American Heritage Dictionary,* Second College Edition, 1991, New York, NY: Houghton Mifflin Company, p.333.

2. McCain, J., & Salter, M. (2004). *Why courage matters: The way to a braver life.* New York, NY: Random House, Inc.

3. Blanchard, K.P., Zigarmi, P., & Zigarmi, D. (1985). *Leadership and the one minute manager.* New York, NY: William Morrow and Company, Inc.

4. Geller, E.S. (1996). *The psychology of safety: How to improve behaviors and attitudes on the job.* Radnor, PA: Chilton Book Company; Geller, E.S. (1998). *Practical behavior-based safety: Step-by-step methods to improve your workplace.* Neenah, WI: J.J. Keller & Associates, Inc; Geller, E.S. (2001). *The psychology of safety handbook.* Boca Raton, FL: CRC Press.

5. Kouzes, J.M., & Posner, B.Z. (2006). *A leader's legacy.* San Francisco, CA: John Wiley & Sons, Inc.

6. Geller, E.S. (1996). *The psychology of safety: How to improve behaviors and attitudes on the job.* Radnor, PA: Chilton Book Company; Geller, E.S. (2001). *The psychology of safety handbook.* Boca Raton, FL: CRC Press; Geller, E.S. (2005). *People-based safety: The source.* Virginia Beach, VA: Coastal Training Technologies Corporation; Geller, E.S. (2006). Reinforcement, reward, & recognition: Critical distinctions and a reality check. *Industrial Safety & Hygiene News, 40(3),* pp. 12, 14; Geller, E.S. (2007). Why do people act that way? *Industrial Safety & Hygiene News, 41(10),* 21–22.

7. Mischel, W. (2004). Toward a integrative model for CBT: Encompassing behavior, cognition, affect, and process. *Behavior Therapy,* 35, 185–203.

8. Geller, E.S. (2008). *Leading people-based safety: Enriching your culture.* Virginia Beach, VA: Coastal Training Technologies Corporation; Geller, E.S., & Weigand, D.M. (2005). People-based safety: Exploring the role of personality in injury prevention. *Professional Safety, 50(12),* 28–36.

9. Geller, E.S. (2001). *The psychology of safety handbook.* Boca Raton, FL: CRC Press., p. 378.

10. Reif, C.D., & Singer, B. (2000). Interpersonal flourishing: A positive health agenda for the new millennium. *Personality & Social*

Psychology Review, 4, 30–44; Sarasson, B.R., Sarasson, I.G., & Gurung, R.A.R. (1997). Close personal relationships and health outcome: A key to the role of social support. In S. Duck (Ed.) *Handbook of personal relationships* (2ⁿᵈ Edition) (pp.547–573). New York, NY: Wiley; Sarasson, B.B., Sarasson, I.G., & Pierce, G.R. (1990). *Social support: An interactional view.* New York, NY: Wiley.

11. Geller, E.S. (1999). Interpersonal trust: Key to getting the best from behavior-based safety coaching. *Professional Safety, 44(4),* 16–19; Geller, E.S. (2002). *The participation factor: How to increase involvement in occupational safety.* Des Plaines, IL: American Society of Safety Engineers.

12. Festinger, L. (1957). *A theory of cognitive dissonance.* Stanford, CA: Stanford University Press.

13. Geller, E.S., Bruff, C.D., & Nimmer, J.G. (1985). The "Flash for Life": A community prompting strategy for safety-belt promotion. *Journal of Applied Behavior Analysis, 18,* 145–159.

14. Cox, M.G., & Geller, E.S. (2011). Community prompting of safety-belt use: Impact of positive versus negative reminders. *Journal of Applied Behavior Analysis, 43(2),* 321–325; Farrell, L.V., Cox, M.G., & Geller, E.S. (2007). Prompting safety-belt use in the context of a belt-use law: The "Flash-for Life" revisited. *Journal of Safety Research, 38,* 407–411.

15. Geller, E.S., & Lehman, G.R. (1991). The buckle-up promise card: A versatile intervention for large-scale behavior change. *Journal of Applied Behavior Analysis, 24,* 91–94.

16. Streff, F.M., Kalsher, M.S., & Geller, E.S. (1993). Developing efficient workplace safety programs: Observations of response covariation. *Journal of Organizational Behavior Management. 13(2),* 3–15.

17. Geller, E.S. (2001). *The psychology of safety handbook.* Boca Raton, FL: CRC Press.

18. Cialdini, R.B. (2001). *Influence: Science and practice* (4ᵗʰ Edition), New York, NY: Harper Collins College Publishers.

19. Geller, E.S., Hickman, J.S., & Pettinger, C.B. (2004). The Airline Lifesaver: A 17-year analysis of a technique to prompt safety-belt use. *Journal of Safety Research, 35,* 357–366.

20. Geller, E.S. (2005). *People-based safety: The source.* Virginia Beach, VA: Coastal Training Technologies Corporation.

21. Geller, E.S. (1996). *The psychology of safety: How to improve behaviors and attitudes on the job.* Radnor, PA: Chilton Book Company, p. 148.

22. Sulzer-Azaroff, B., & Austin, J. (2000). Does BBS work? Behavior-based safety and injury reduction: A survey of the evidence. *Professional Safety, 45(7),* 19–24.

23. Geller, E.S. (1998). *Practical behavior-based safety: Step-by-step methods to improve your workplace.* Neenah, WI: J.J. Keller & Associates, Inc.

24. Geller, E.S. (1998). *Practical behavior-based safety: Step-by-step methods to improve your workplace.* Neenah, WI: J.J. Keller & Associates, Inc; Geller, E.S. (2005). *People-based safety: The source.* Virginia Beach, VA: Coastal Training Technologies Corporation.

25. Chance, P. (1999). *Learning and behavior* (Fourth Edition). Belmont, CA: Wadsworth.

26. Thorndike, E.L. (1911). *Animal intelligence: Experimental studies.* New York, NY; Hafner, p. 174; Thorndike, E.L., (1931). *Human learning.* Cambridge, MA: MIT Press.

27. Cialdini, R.B. (2001). *Influence: Science and practice* (4th Edition). New York, NY: Harper Collins College Publishers; Gouldner, A.W. (1960). The norm of reciprocity: A preliminary statement. *American Sociology Review, 25,* 161–167.

28. Carnegie, D. (1936). *How to win friends and influence people* (1981 Edition). New York, NY: Simon & Schuster, p. 19.

Name Index

Photo Credits

Chapter 1

p. 1: Pablo Picasso, "Three Musicians," Fountainebleu, Summer 1921. Oil on canvas, 6'7" x 7'3 3/4". Mrs. Simon Guggenheim Fund (44.1949). Photograph © The Museum of Modern Art/Licensed by Scala/Art Resource, NY. © 2008 Estate of Pablo Picasso/Artists Rights Society (ARS) New York.; p. 2: AP Images/Steven Senne/; p. 3, top: Alfredo Estrella/AFP/Getty Images; p. 3, bottom: Corbis Royalty Free; p. 5: Michael J. Doolittle/The Image Works; p. 8, top: Waltraud Grubitzsch/epa/Corbis; p. 8, bottom: Kurt Scholz/SuperStock; p. 9: Mary Evans Picture Library/The Image Works; p. 12 & 13: National Library of Medicine; p. 15: Popperfoto/Getty Images; p. 17, top: Iain Masterton/Alamy; p. 17, bottom: National Library of Medicine; p. 19: The Ferdinand Hamburger, Jr. Archives of the Johns Hopkins University; p. 20, top: Archives of the History of American Psychology, The University of Akron; p. 20, bottom: Bettmann/Corbis; p. 21, top: Archives of the History of American Psychology, The University of Akron; p. 21, bottom: Archives of the History of American Psychology, The University of Akron; p. 23: McGill University, PR000387/McGill University Archives

Chapter 2

p. 26: Gilbert Mayers/SuperStock; p. 27: Peter Hvizdak/The Image Works; p. 29, top: Copyright © 2005 by the American Psychological Association. Reprinted with permission; p. 29, bottom: ©Charles Votaw; p. 30: Roy Morsch/Corbis; p. 31, left: Spencer Grant/PhotoEdit Inc.; p. 31, right: Michael Nichols/National Geographic Image Collection; p. 33 & 34: Courtesy of Neil Carlson; p. 40: Monkey Business Images/Shutterstock; p. 42: Anna Zuckerman-Vdovenko/PhotoEdit Inc.; p. 45: Jonathan Selig/Getty Images

Chapter 3

p. 55: Gilbert Mayers/SuperStock; p. 67: Allan Morgan/Peter Arnold, Inc.; p. 68: Jack Fields/Photo Researchers, Inc.; p. 70: Science Photo Library/Photo Researchers, Inc.; p. 60: Thomas Deerinck, NCMIR/Photo Researchers, Inc. p. 61 Eye of Science/Photo Researchers, Inc. p. 72: Courtesy of Neil Carlson; p. 73, top left: Casey McNamara/Photo library; p. 73, top right: Corbis/Superstock ; p. 74, top: Courtesy of VSM MedTech Ltd.

Chapter 4

p. 92: Gilbert Mayers/SuperStock; p. 94: Ben Schkade/Photodisc/Getty Images Royalty Free; p. 105: Gary Yeowell/Getty Images; p. 114: Michael Newman/PhotoEdit Inc.; p. 115: Omikron/Photo Researchers, Inc.

Chapter 5

p. 127: Gilbert Mayers/SuperStock; p. 129: Bob Mahoney/The Image Works; p. 137: Bill FoleyLandov; p. 135: SuperStock, Inc. © 2008 Salvador Dali, Gala-Salvador Dali Foundation/Artists Rights Society (ARS), New York p. 146 Wade Vaillancourt/Shutterstock.

Chapter 6

p. 154: Leslie Xuereb/SuperStock; p. 155: Andrew Holbrooke/Corbis; p. 157: Neil Harding/Getty Images; p. 162: Mark Richards/PhotoEdit Inc.; p. 163: The Copyright Group/SuperStock; p. 164: Steve Gordon/Dorling Kindersley; p. 168: Peter Hvizdak/The Image Works; p. 171: Clark Brennan/Alamy Royalty Free; p. 163: The Copyright Group/SuperStock; p. 175: Michael Newman/PhotoEdit Inc.; p. 177, top: Emilio Ereza/Alamy; p. 177. Bottom: Syracuse Newspapers/Gary Walts/The Image Works; p. 178: From "Brain Activation during Human Navigation: Gender-Different Neural Networks as Substrate of Performance" by Gron et. al, 2000, Nature Publishing Group, permission provided by Copyright Clearance Center/Rightslink.; p. 183: Cindy Charles/PhotoEdit Inc.; p. 186: Jeff Greenberg/PhotoEdit Inc.; p. 188: Nick Onken/Alamy; p. 189: Ariel Skelley/Corbis; p. 191: Brian Gavriloff/Edmonton Journal

Chapter 7

p. 195: M.L . Campbell/SuperStock; p. 196: ©Susan Van Etten; p. 199: Chad Ehlers/Getty Images; p. 202: Photodisc/Getty Images Royalty Free; p. 205: Kokyat Choong/The Image Works; p. 206: Karen D'Silva/Taxi/ Getty Images; p. 207, left: Mary Kate Denney/PhotoEdit Inc.; p. 207, right: Alin Dragulin/Glow Images; p. 210: First Image/The Image Works; p. 211, left: Syracuse Newspapers/Jennifer Grimes/The Image Works; p. 211, right: Ryan McVay/Getty Images; p. 213: From "What's new with the amnesic patient H.M.?" by Suzanne Corkin, 2/1/2002, Nature Reviews Neuroscience, Nature Publishing Group, permission provided by Copyright Clearance Center/Rightslink.; p. 217: Jeff Greenberg/The Image Works; p. 218, top: Chad Ehlers/Alamy; p. 218, middle: Visions of America, LLC/Alamy; p. 218, bottom: Dex Image/Alamy; p. 220: CBS Paramount Television ©1966 CBS Paramount Television. All Rights Reserved/Getty Images; p. 222: AP Images

Chapter 8

p. 227: Gilbert Mayers/SuperStock; p. 228, top: Tim Boyles/Getty Images; p. 228, bottom: Handout Courtesy of the Schiavo Family/Corbis; p. 219: S. Lousada/Petit Format/Photo Researchers, Inc.; p. 231: Photo courtesy of Cognitive Evolution Group, University of Louisiana at Lafayette; p. 234: Hiroko Masuike/Getty Images; p. 235: Blend Images/SuperStock Royalty Free; p. 245: Philippe Garo/Science Source; p. 251: Photodisc/ Getty Images Royalty Free

Chapter 10

p. 287: Courtesy of Steve Lipofsky/Corbis Images; p. 290: PhotosIndia.com LLC/Alamy; p. 291, top: Anthony Hatley/Alamy; p. 291, center: Antonio Scorza/AFP/Newscom; p. 291, bottom: Matt Rourke/AP Images; p. 292: Stephen Ford/Alamy; p. 295: Bobby Yip/Reuters/Landov; p. 301: Eightfish/Getty Images; p. 304: Radius Images/Alamy; p. 308: First Light/Alamy; p. 311: Larry Williams/CORBIS; p. 313, all: David Matsumoto; p. 319: 2happy/Shutterstock; p. 320, top: Randy Faris/Corbis;

p. 320, bottom: Robert L. Johnson; p. 322: Newhouse News Service/Landov; p. 323: Pearson; p. 324, left & right: Dacher Keltner, UC Berkley

Chapter 12

p. 349: Bebeto Matthews/AP Images; p. 354: Courtesy of the Trustees of Sir John Soane's Museum, London/The Bridgeman Art Library International; p. 356: Freud Museum, London; p. 358: Michael Rougier/Time & Life Pictures/Getty Images; p. 361: Nancy Sheehan/PhotoEdit, Inc.; p. 363: Bebeto Matthews/AP Images; p. 365: Philip G. Zimbardo, Inc.; p. 373: The Gallery Collection/Corbis; p. 374: Will & Deni McIntyre/Photo Researchers, Inc.; p. 375: David Grossman/Alamy; p. 376: Simon Price/Alamy; p. 378: The Advertising Archives

Chapter 13

p. 388: AF archive/Alamy; p. 390, top: Steve Welsh/Alamy; p. 390, bottom: imagebroker/Alamy; p. 393: The Yomiuri Shimbum, Miho Iketani/AP Images; p. 397: Denis Poroy/AP Images; p. 400: Tony Freeman/PhotoEdit Inc.; p. 404: Reuters/Jose Manuel Ribeiro; p. 407: Gary Conner/PhotoEdit, Inc.; p. 409: Anthony Correia/Shutterstock; p. 412: LM Otero/AP Images; p. 414: Mark Richards/PhotoEdit, Inc.; p. 415: Helga Esteb/Shutterstock; p. 418: Walter G Arce/Shutterstock; p. 420: Daniele La Monaca/Reuters/Landov; p. 423, top left: Jack Hollingsworth/Blend Images/Corbis; p. 423, bottom right: Jerry Wachter/Photo Researchers, Inc.